Alaska

written and researched by

Paul Whitfield

ROUGH GUIDES

NEW YORK • LONDON • DELHI

www.roughguides.com

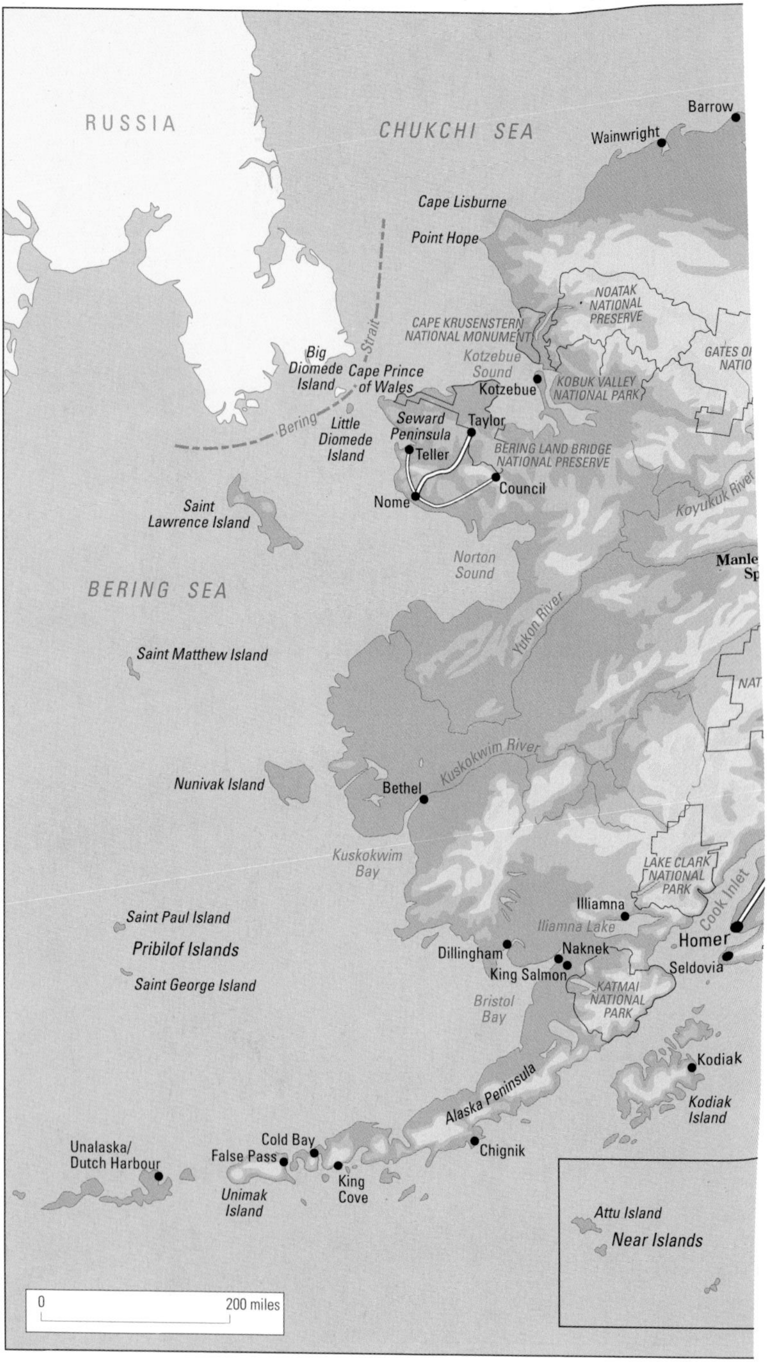
RUSSIA
CHUKCHI SEA
Barrow
Wainwright
Cape Lisburne
Point Hope
NOATAK NATIONAL PRESERVE
CAPE KRUSENSTERN NATIONAL MONUMENT
Bering Strait
Big Diomede Island
Cape Prince of Wales
Kotzebue Sound
Kotzebue
KOBUK VALLEY NATIONAL PARK
Little Diomede Island
Seward Peninsula
Taylor
Teller
BERING LAND BRIDGE NATIONAL PRESERVE
Council
Nome
Koyukuk River
Saint Lawrence Island
Norton Sound
BERING SEA
Yukon River
Saint Matthew Island
Kuskokwim River
Nunivak Island
Bethel
Kuskokwim Bay
LAKE CLARK NATIONAL PARK
Cook Inlet
Illiamna
Iliamna Lake
Saint Paul Island
Pribilof Islands
Homer
Dillingham
Naknek
Seldovia
King Salmon
Saint George Island
KATMAI NATIONAL PARK
Bristol Bay
Kodiak
Alaska Peninsula
Kodiak Island
Cold Bay
Chignik
Unalaska/ Dutch Harbour
False Pass
King Cove
Unimak Island
Attu Island
Near Islands
0
200 miles

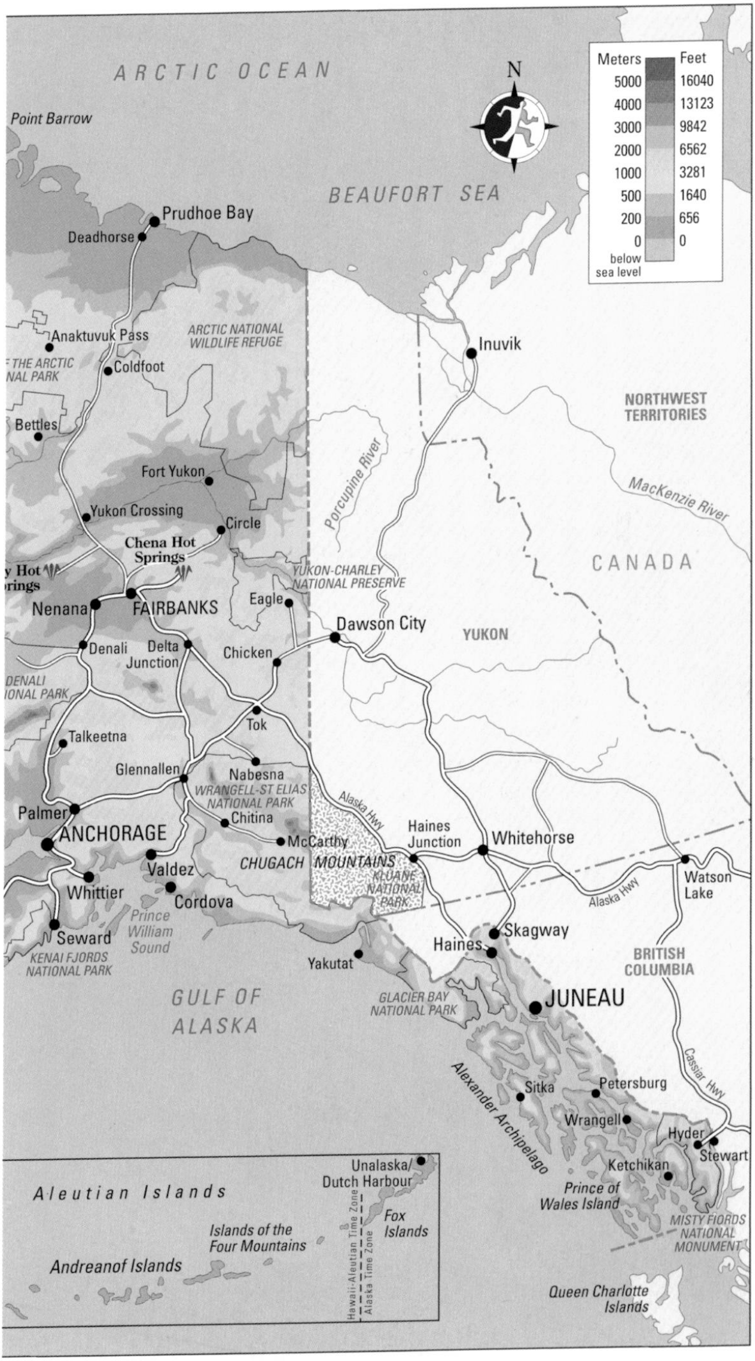
ARCTIC OCEAN
BEAUFORT SEA
N
Meters
5000
4000
3000
2000
1000
500
200
0
below sea level
Feet
16040
13123
9842
6562
3281
1640
656
0
Point Barrow
Prudhoe Bay
Deadhorse
Anaktuvuk Pass
ARCTIC NATIONAL WILDLIFE REFUGE
Coldfoot
Bettles
Fort Yukon
Yukon Crossing
Circle
Chena Hot Springs
Nenana
FAIRBANKS
Eagle
YUKON-CHARLEY NATIONAL PRESERVE
Dawson City
Denali
Delta Junction
Chicken
Tok
Talkeetna
Glennallen
Nabesna
WRANGELL-ST ELIAS NATIONAL PARK
Palmer
ANCHORAGE
Chitina
McCarthy
Valdez
Whittier
Cordova
CHUGACH MOUNTAINS
KLUANE NATIONAL PARK
Seward
Prince William Sound
KENAI FJORDS NATIONAL PARK
Yakutat
GULF OF ALASKA
Inuvik
NORTHWEST TERRITORIES
Porcupine River
MacKenzie River
CANADA
YUKON
Alaska Hwy
Haines Junction
Whitehorse
Watson Lake
Skagway
Haines
BRITISH COLUMBIA
GLACIER BAY NATIONAL PARK
JUNEAU
Cassiar Hwy
Alexander Archipelago
Sitka
Petersburg
Wrangell
Hyder
Stewart
Ketchikan
Prince of Wales Island
MISTY FIORDS NATIONAL MONUMENT
Queen Charlotte Islands
Aleutian Islands
Unalaska/ Dutch Harbour
Fox Islands
Islands of the Four Mountains
Andreanof Islands
Hawaii-Aleutian Time Zone
Alaska Time Zone

△ Independence Mine State Park

Introduction to

Alaska

Hardly anywhere in the world conjures up sharper images than Alaska; the name itself – a derivation of *Alyeska*, an Athabascan word meaning "great land of the west" – fires the imagination of many a traveler. Few who see this land of gargantuan ice fields, sweeping tundra, glacially excavated valleys, lush rainforests, deep fjords, and active volcanoes leave disappointed. Wildlife may be under threat elsewhere, but here it is abundant, with Kodiak bears reaching heights of eleven feet, moose stopping traffic in downtown Anchorage, wolves howling throughout the night, bald eagles soaring above the trees, and rivers solid with fifty-plus-pound salmon.

Alaska's sheer size alone is hard to comprehend – its vast expanse covers an area more than double that of Texas, and its coastline is almost as long as the rest of the US combined. All but three of the nation's twenty highest peaks are found within its boundaries, along with the two largest national parks, the two most extensive national forests, and more active glaciers than the rest of the inhabited world put together.

Not all the terrain is hospitable, though; only a little more than half a million people live in this huge state, of which forty-two percent live in Anchorage. Altogether, only a twentieth of one percent of the land area is developed, the rest remaining almost entirely untouched. In many ways it mirrors the American West of the nineteenth century, not surprising for a place often referred to as the **Last Frontier**: an endless space in which to stake a claim and set up anew without interference. Or at least that's how many Alaskans would like it to be. Throughout the twentieth century tens of thousands were lured by the promise of wealth, first by gold and then by fishing, logging, and, most recently, oil.

Alaska is the kind of place folks become obsessive about, and these obsessions fall into two camps. The majority love it, but treat it as a boundless treasure

Fact file

- Adrift from the rest of the United States, Alaska borders Canada's Yukon Territory, straddles the Arctic Circle, and separates the North Pacific and Arctic oceans. The western tip of the 1100-mile-long island necklace of the Aleutian Chain almost touches the Russian mainland and is on the same longitude as New Zealand.
- With 572,000 square miles, Alaska is the largest state in the union, over twice the size of Texas, a fifth the size of the entire Lower 48, and six times the size of Britain.
- With only 635,000 people, Alaska is one of the least populated states. Almost half the people congregate around the biggest city, Anchorage; Sitka, the fifth largest city, has fewer than ten thousand residents, and of the 348 locales listed in the 2000 census almost seventy percent have fewer than five hundred inhabitants.
- The state economy is heavily reliant on oil, which provides around eighty percent of general revenue. Current oil production is only half what it was in the late 1980s peak, however, and Alaska is struggling to make ends meet, particularly when world oil prices are low. With 38 percent of the US coastline, fishing is an important industry as well.
- Alaska's landscape is hugely varied, from acre upon acre of swampy, lake-pocked lowlands to the 20,320-foot summit of Mount McKinley, the loftiest point on the continent. Evergreen forests swathe much of the southern half of the state, thinning to the barren tundra of the north. Through it all run several mountain ranges, and altogether there are estimated to be 100,000 glaciers.

△ Snowshoes on cabin wall

Alaska is the kind of place folks become obsessive about

trove that is so far from Washington DC that anything is fair play. This state of grace has largely gone, but the myth persists and many Alaskans believe in their right to do whatever they want, and bitterly resent anyone who suggests they do otherwise.

A minority came to Alaska for its pristine qualities and want to keep it that way. With growing pressure from these green-minded activists and the federal government, **environmental issues** have increasingly made front-page news. Current controversies include the practice of clear-cutting in the national forests, the prospect of oil exploration in the Arctic National Wildlife Refuge, overfishing, and wolf culling which, according to animal-rights groups, is primarily to ensure that there are more caribou for hunters. Most infamously, there's been the unholy mess created by the *Exxon Valdez* oil tanker in 1989, although little visible evidence of the spill remains today.

Alaska's 86,000 Native people are largely marginalized from mainstream society. Most choose to live in remote communities, known as "Native villages," where services are often limited and earning a living can be entirely dependent on the number of salmon running that year. Very few live in the larger towns, and those that do often live in conditions that are harsh at best. Natives have largely been left behind by the state's periodic boom times, though a large land claim settlement in the 1970s paved the way for relatively wealthy Native corporations to provide much-needed income for their people.

One thing that is no myth in Alaska is the state's reputation for high prices; still, experiencing Alaska on a low **budget** is possible with a bit of planning. Traveling outside the peak summer season (see p.ix) will save you money on accommodation, which can be quite expensive. The exceptions are **camping**, which can be very cheap or free, and the thirty or so **hostels**, which are found mostly in the major towns, although a handful are sprinkled elsewhere throughout the state. Thanks to the long distances and high-priced rental cars, **transport** is far from cheap; and **eating and drinking** are, at best, about twenty percent more expensive than in the Lower 48.

Adventure Alaska

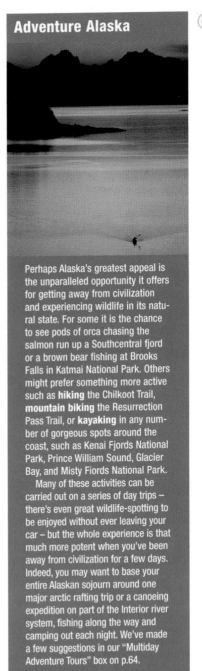

Perhaps Alaska's greatest appeal is the unparalleled opportunity it offers for getting away from civilization and experiencing wildlife in its natural state. For some it is the chance to see pods of orca chasing the salmon run up a Southcentral fjord or a brown bear fishing at Brooks Falls in Katmai National Park. Others might prefer something more active such as **hiking** the Chilkoot Trail, **mountain biking** the Resurrection Pass Trail, or **kayaking** in any number of gorgeous spots around the coast, such as Kenai Fjords National Park, Prince William Sound, Glacier Bay, and Misty Fiords National Park.

Many of these activities can be carried out on a series of day trips – there's even great wildlife-spotting to be enjoyed without ever leaving your car – but the whole experience is that much more potent when you've been away from civilization for a few days. Indeed, you may want to base your entire Alaskan sojourn around one major arctic rafting trip or a canoeing expedition on part of the Interior river system, fishing along the way and camping out each night. We've made a few suggestions in our "Multiday Adventure Tours" box on p.64.

Where to go

Traveling around the state demands a spirit of adventure, as well as patience. Unless you are flying to Alaska, there are only two **approaches**: the **Alaska Highway**, which cuts across British Columbia and the Yukon on its way to the Alaskan Interior and the Arctic North, and the **Marine Highway ferries**, which slip through the elegiac fjords, glaciers, and mountains bordering the Pacific linking Washington State with **Southeast Alaska**. From there a dozen small towns, including the capital, **Juneau**, are starting points for salmon-fishing, whale-watching, and glacier-viewing trips.

Flights from out of state almost all land in **Anchorage**, the largest city, and just as much an Alaskan experience as the great outdoors. From here,

Alaska's native people

Native Alaskans make up around fifteen percent of the state's population, and most have a semi-subsistence existence in small rural villages on the fringes of the mainstream economy. Many also receive annual dividends from **Native Corporations**, which have their fingers in tourism, forestry, fishing, oil, and more besides.

There are four broad groupings. The **Tlingit** traditionally occupied the lush forests of Southeast Alaska, making best use of the mild climate, rich plant life, and abundant fish and game, the bounty providing the time to develop a complex culture characterized by bright ceremonial costume, totem poles, and gorgeous buttoned blankets. The Interior is the preserve of **Athabascans**, close kin of the Navajo and Apache of the American Southwest. They had to learn to cope with a very short growing season and turned to fishing for salmon and tracking caribou and moose. The north and west of Alaska is the homeland of the Yup'ik and Iñupiat peoples, collectively known as **Eskimos** – a term not generally considered offensive in these parts. Aside from a few roots and berries gathered during the short, cool summer, the Eskimo mainly hunted sea mammals – seals, walruses, and small whales – taking to the water in skin-covered kayaks and larger umiaks. The final major grouping is the **Aleut**, who populate the Aleutian Islands and much of the Southwest. They became accomplished traders and raiders, paddling in their skin-covered canoes, or bidars, and relying on a constant supply of sea mammals.

▽ Margerie Glacier, Glacier Bay National Park

it's easy to get to the glacier-bound and wildlife-rich waters of **Prince William Sound** and the **Kenai Peninsula**, a kind of Alaska in miniature. Further west – and connected only by ferry – **Southwest Alaska** takes in **Kodiak** and a host of tiny communities en route to the **Aleutian Islands**. Also here is **Katmai National Park**, one of the best places to watch brown bears fishing for salmon.

North from Anchorage, the **Interior** is the most road-accessible part of the state with highways reaching the **Wrangell–St Elias National Park** and the enchanting twin settlements of **McCarthy** and **Kennicott**. Roads (and trains) also reach offbeat **Talkeetna** and **Denali National Park**, home to the nation's highest mountain, the 20,000-foot **Mount McKinley** (aka Denali). The train line ends at **Fairbanks**, Alaska's second-largest town and the gateway to the **Arctic North**, site of some unbelievably remote villages.

When to go

Alaska has a very short tourist season. For guaranteed long daylight hours and the greatest likelihood of fairly warm weather, you'll need to travel in the **peak season** from Memorial Day weekend (the last in May) until Labor Day weekend (the first in September). During this time, climates in Southeast Alaska, Anchorage, and the Kenai Peninsula are mild (45–65°F) and much more rain (in some towns 180-plus inches per year) falls than snow. Remarkably, the Interior in summer often gets as hot as 80°F.

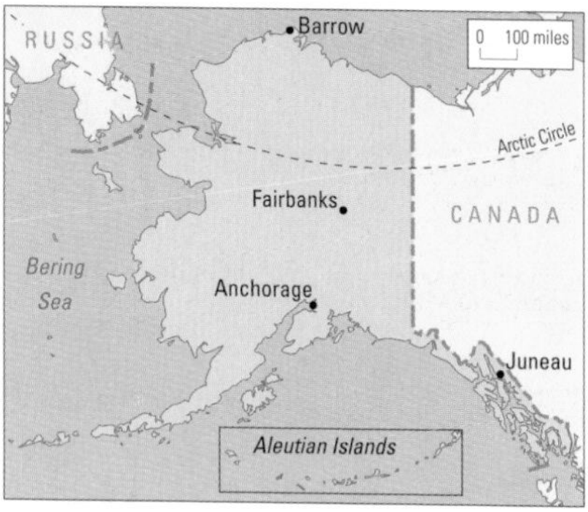

Everyone else has the same idea, so at this time hotel availability is at its tightest and prices go up accordingly. Being there with everyone else does have its advantages, though, since some of the smaller adventure trips require a minimum number of customers before they go. If you want to avoid the crowds and still find most tourism businesses operating, try the last two weeks in May and first two in September – Alaska's **shoulder seasons**. The weather at this time can be just as warm as midsummer, and you've got the added bonus of watching trees transform themselves from bare to full foliage in a matter of days, or experience the boreal forest in its autumnal plumage.

There is some regional variation, but in general anyone here before mid-May or after mid-September will find their options limited: there will be few glacier and whale-watching cruises; kayaking operations will have locked away their paddles; Denali shuttle buses will have stopped running; flightseeing trips will be grounded; and even whole towns (admittedly tiny ones like Chicken and McCarthy) will have shut up shop for the winter.

△ Denali National Park

Average rainfall and daily temperatures

	Jan	Feb	Mar	Apr	May	June	July	Aug	Sept	Oct	Nov	Dec	Tot
Anchorage													
rain (inches)	0.8	0.7	0.6	0.4	0.5	0.7	1.6	2.6	2.6	2.2	1.0	0.9	14.6
rain (mm)	20	18	15	10	13	18	41	66	66	56	25	23	371
Atka (Aleut.)													
rain (inches)	6.4	4.7	5.0	4.9	4.8	3.9	5.3	5.4	7.1	7.4	8.3	6.1	69.3
rain (mm)	163	119	127	125	122	99	135	137	180	188	211	155	1761
Barrow													
rain (inches)	0.2	0.1	0.1	0.1	0.1	0.3	0.9	0.8	0.5	0.5	0.3	0.2	4.2
rain (mm)	5	3	3	3	3	8	23	20	13	13	8	5	107
Fairbanks													
rain (inches)	0.9	0.5	0.7	0.3	0.6	1.3	1.9	2.1	1.3	0.8	0.7	0.6	11.7
rain (mm)	23	13	18	8	15	33	48	53	33	20	18	15	297
Juneau													
rain (inches)	3.5	3.7	3.3	3.2	3.3	2.7	4.1	4.8	6.1	7.2	4.8	4.6	51.6
rain (mm)	90	95	84	81	84	69	105	123	156	183	123	117	1310

	Jan	Feb	Mar	Apr	May	June	July	Aug	Sept	Oct	Nov	Dec	Avg.
Anchorage													
max °F	19	26	34	45	54	63	64	64	57	43	30	19	43
max °C	-7	-3	1	7	12	17	18	18	14	6	-1	-7	6
min °F	5	9	12	27	36	45	48	46	39	28	16	7	27
min °C	-15	-13	-11	-3	2	7	9	8	4	-2	-9	-14	-3
Atka (Aleut.)													
max °F	37	37	37	43	45	52	55	57	57	46	41	37	46
max °C	3	3	3	6	7	11	13	14	14	8	5	3	8
min °F	30	28	28	32	36	39	45	46	43	37	34	28	36
min °C	-1	-2	-2	0	2	4	7	8	6	3	1	-2	2
Barrow													
max °F	-9	-11	-8	7	25	39	46	45	34	21	7	-4	19
max °C	-23	-24	-22	-14	-4	4	8	7	1	-6	-14	-20	-7
min °F	-22	-26	-22	-8	12	28	34	34	27	12	-6	-17	3
min °C	-30	-32	-30	-22	-11	-2	1	1	-3	-11	-21	-27	-16
Fairbanks													
max °F	-2	10	41	43	59	72	72	66	54	36	12	1	39
max °C	-19	-12	5	6	15	22	22	19	12	2	-11	-17	4
min °F	-20	-9	-4	18	36	46	48	45	34	18	-6	-17	16
min °C	-29	-23	-20	-8	2	8	9	7	1	-8	-21	-27	-9
Juneau													
max °F	27	34	37	17	54	63	64	63	54	17	39	32	46
max °C	-3	1	3	8.5	12	17	18	17	12	8.5	4	0	8
min °F	16	21	25	31	37	46	48	46	45	36	28	21	4
min °C	-9	-6	-4	-0.5	3	8	9	8	7	2	-2	-6	1

The moderating effects of the ocean (and the more southerly latitude) mean that the season in **Southeast Alaska** is a little longer, with a few of the cruise-ship companies extending their seasons to include early May and

Alaskan gold

From a white American perspective, gold created Alaska, driving its transition from neglected territory towards eventual statehood. A sequence of gold strikes in progressively less accessible locales first brought steamers into the Interior along two thousand miles of the Yukon River, then precipitous railroads, and finally the overland all-weather roads that replaced the dog-sled routes. Initial gold strikes were wildly exaggerated on the Outside, precipitating a mass arrival of **argonauts** ill-equipped for the rigors of the North. A few fortunes were made, but most returned to the Lower 48 after a season or two penniless, having blown their earnings in the bars and brothels that sprang up in the towns alongside the diggings.

Lonely miners are still out there shoveling away at their "rocker" or using suction dredges to collect ore-bearing gravels from riverbeds. Wherever you go in rural Alaska, you'll find claims fiercely protected and meet prospectors happy to tell you just how much they're going to make next year.

Public claims dotted around the state allow visitors to try their hand. Most only do it for fun and a few flakes, but some stay all summer hoping to collect enough to forge their wedding ring.

late September. In **Anchorage**, the **Kenai Peninsula**, **Prince William Sound**, the **Interior**, and much of **Southwest Alaska** the mid-May to mid-September rule holds true, though in Anchorage, for example, the first serious snowfall probably won't come until mid-October, making this a good place to finish a late-season trip. In **Fairbanks and the Arctic North** your movements at the ends of the season may be more limited, particularly in the coastal towns of Nome, Kotzebue, and Barrow, where the sea ice may remain frozen until mid-June or later. It is often late May before the roads on the Seward Peninsula near Nome are plowed, so if you are planning to explore up here, go later.

Anyone here before mid-May or after mid-September will find their options limited

Hikers should avoid May and early June unless they like high-stepping through snow on the trail; late August and September are generally a much better bet.

Visitors traveling to Alaska in mid-September, particularly around Fairbanks, have a good chance of seeing the **aurora**

borealis, but keen watchers need to come in **winter**. Even the tourist promoters admit that for most visitors November, December, and January are just too cold and dark to enjoy. March and the first week in April are generally best for winter activities – from aurora watching to dog mushing – with a thick layer of snow on the ground, lengthening days, and temperatures that are just about bearable. The rest of April, early May and October are neither really winter nor summer and good for nothing: the snow isn't thick enough for winter pursuits, but it's too thick for summer activities.

What to take

In Alaska formal gear is out, but you need to be prepared for the physical demands of a trip to the state, and your comfort will largely be affected by **what you wear**. Multiple thin **layers** are warmer than a couple of thick ones and give you the freedom to strip a couple as the day heats up. In June, July, and August, you'll get by happily with normal clothing (including shorts and T-shirts), plus a fleece jacket, a waterproof coat, hat, gloves, and strong shoes. If you are heading to the north before the end of May or after the end of August, take thermal underwear and an extra warm layer. Winter visitors

Alaska beyond the myths

Mention you are off to Alaska and people react as though the whole state is snow and ice year-round. In fact, if you go in June, July, or August (as most visitors do), then about the only snow you'll see will be on the mountaintops and the only ice will be in glaciers. Landscapes of green trees, grass, wildflowers, and salmonberries are the typical visitor experience, and you'll often be in shorts and a T-shirt during the day.

Some arrive expecting to see **igloos**, and although it is true that Alaska's native Eskimos may have once used igloos as temporary shelters on hunting trips, with the advent of snowmachines they now just drive back to town. Some places in the far north do get visits from **polar bears** in winter, but you're not going to see any roaming through downtown Anchorage. That said, moose are pretty common in the city, and traffic sometimes has to stop for them.

Most people have figured out that the long winter nights equate to almost endless summer days, but many fail to realize that long hours of dusk make viewing the **northern lights** unlikely anytime from April to mid-September. Another enduring myth is that there are seven men for every woman in Alaska. This may still be true in small fishing and mining communities where the extreme male domination becomes really evident, but Alaska's population is now 48.3 percent women (against a national average of 50.9).

to Southeast Alaska need take no extra precautions, but in the Interior or Arctic, take down jackets, insulating pants, and specialist footwear, or buy once you arrive. Special considerations for **campers** are discussed on p.56.

Besides clothing, you'll want to bring a camera and binoculars and, rather more mundanely, bug spray – the **mosquito** is often referred to as the "Alaska State bird."

△ Creek Street, Ketchikan

25 things not to miss

It's not possible to see everything that Alaska has to offer in one trip – and we don't suggest you try. What follows is a selective and subjective taste of the state's highlights: unparalleled landscapes, rugged adventures, and curious celebrations among them. They're arranged in five color-coded categories to help you find the very best to see, do, and experience. All highlights have a page reference to take you straight into the guide, where you can find out more.

01 White Pass and Yukon Railway Page **182** • It's not cheap, but this thrilling ride past stupendous Southeast scenery is a must if you're anywhere near Skagway.

02 Sitka Page **122** • Set on an island-dotted bay, the old Russian colonial capital is the jewel of Southeast, with a striking Tlingit totem park and an onion-domed Russian cathedral.

03 Chicken Page **436** • A slice of the Alaska you've been looking for: rustic, rural, and just a little off the wall.

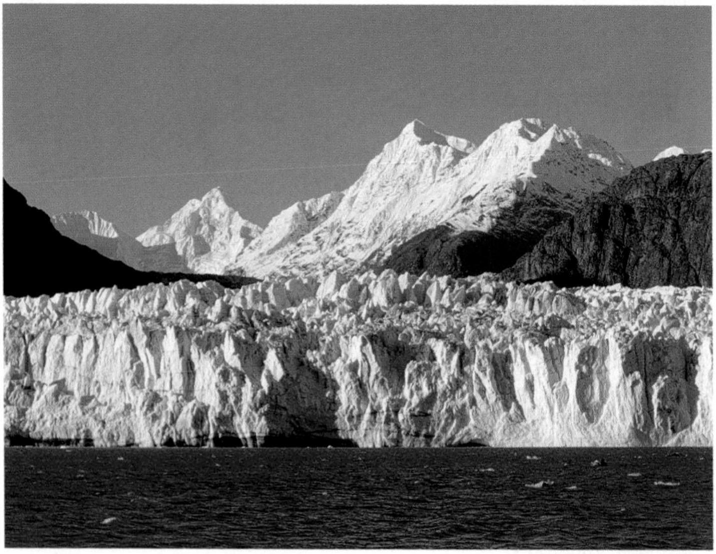

04 Glacier Bay National Park Page **159** • Alaska's most celebrated icy wonderland is one of the state's best places to witness hunks of glacier thundering into the sea.

05 Wildlife watching Chances are you'll spend a fair bit of your time in Alaska spotting wildlife (for suggestions and advice see Contexts, p.537), casually stopping beside the road to admire a couple of moose chomping on lake weed, or venturing out on a specialist day trip in Denali National Park, a whale-watching cruise in Prince William Sound, or even a bush-plane flight to view Kodiak bears.

▽ Humpback whale

△ Brown bear sow and cub

▽ Caribou

△ Bald eagle

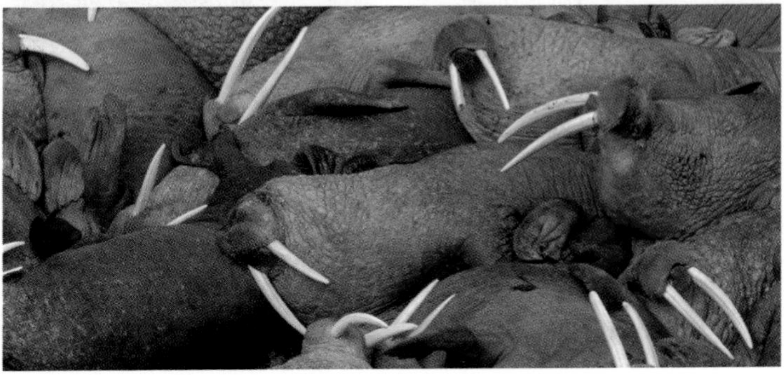
▽ Walruses

06 Drive (or cycle) the Denali Highway Page **399** • Fabulous scenery, ease of access, and no permits make the Denali Highway an excellent alternative to its namesake national park.

07 Halibut fishing Page **274** • You may never catch a big salmon, but go halibut fishing from Homer or one of numerous other Alaskan ports and you're almost guaranteed a thirty-pounder.

08 Stay in a fly-in cabin Page **49** • Fly in by float plane, then fish, kayak, and relax.

09 Aurora borealis Page **460** • Seeing the northern lights should be on everyone's lifetime tick list. Head for Fairbanks in mid-September or make a special winter visit.

10 Native crafts Page **92** • Pass on the tacky miniature totem poles in favor of finely crafted Iñupiat and Yup'ik spirit masks, Tlingit button blankets, and bentwood boxes from Southeast.

11 Independence Mine Page **362** • A wonderfully evocative collection of old mine buildings set high up in an alpine bowl, surrounded by snowy peaks.

12 Seldovia Page **276** • Soak in the secluded beauty of this delightful little community, with its boardwalks perched on stilts above the water, welcoming B&Bs, and views across the bay to snow-capped volcanoes.

13 Denali National Park Page **377** • Nowhere else in Alaska are you virtually assured of seeing brown and black bears, moose, caribou and even wolves in a single day's sightseeing. Add in views of ice-capped Mount McKinley and this will be a highlight of any trip.

14 Iditarod Trail Sled Dog Race Page **360** • Fancy hanging onto the back of a dozen mad sled dogs for a two-week, 1100-mile dash across the frozen Alaskan Interior? Neither do we, but each March almost a hundred people set off to do exactly that.

15 Moose Dropping Festival, Talkeetna Page **367** • Make time for this eccentric summer festival, where you can win prizes by tossing moose droppings, watch "mountain mothers" race around a wood-chopping and fly-casting course, or just revel in the revelry.

16 Salmon Page **51** • Sink your teeth into a lightly pan-fried steak of salmon freshly caught from an Alaskan stream, or try it air-dried Native-style on wooden fish racks.

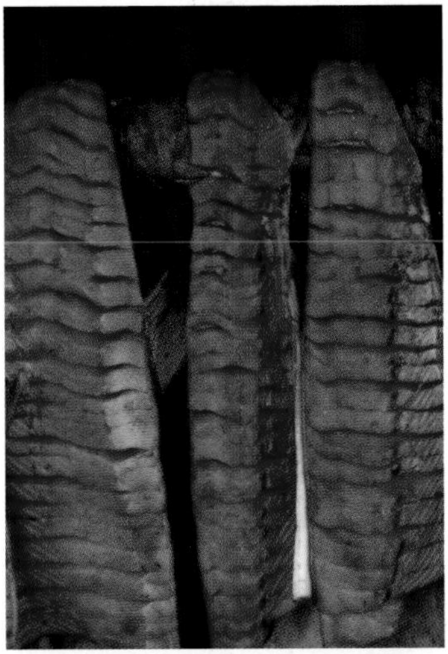

17 Sea kayaking Pages **242** & **290** • Don't miss the chance to see Alaska by kayak. It may be just a gentle paddle along the shore or near the face of a glacier, but even for beginners several days exploring Kenai Fjords National Park, Prince William Sound, or any of the Southeast's myriad waterways isn't a stretch.

18 Million Dollar Bridge Page **309** • Nearly swallowed by the Childs Glacier during construction and wrecked by the 1964 earthquake, the Million Dollar Bridge is a fitting finale to the Copper River Highway.

19 Eagle Page **439** • Launch an epic canoe adventure down the roiling Yukon River from this former fort town.

20 Combat fishing Page **65** • Try your luck in a salmon fishing derby, stand shoulder to shoulder with other anglers in what's known as "combat fishing," or just hire a guide to get you closer to the big catch.

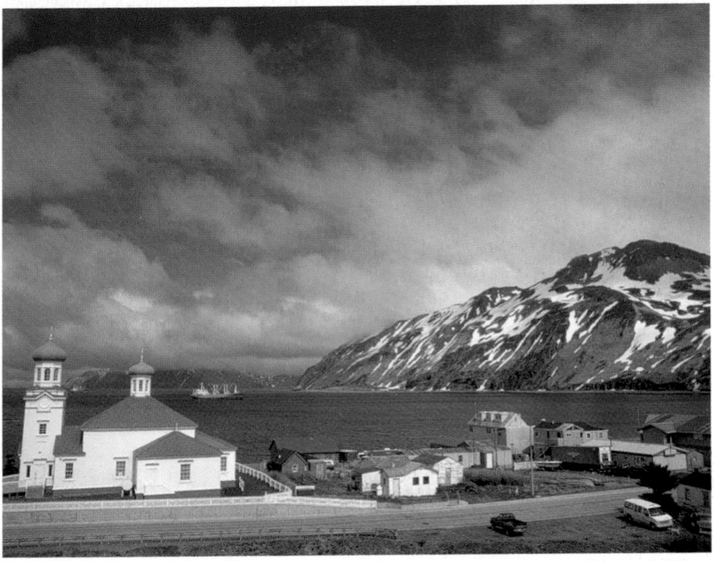

21 Aleutians ferry trip Page **335** • Ride the "Trusty Tusty" past the snow-capped volcanoes of the Alaska Peninsula, calling at isolated fishing ports and scanning the horizon for whales on a relaxing, three-day adventure on the cheap.

22 Hiking Page **58** • You can hardly expect to visit Alaska and not do some hiking; choice spots to hit include the Chugach Mountains, Denali (pictured), and the Chilkoot Trail, essentially a 33-mile gold-rush museum.

23 Katmai National Park Page **332** • Come to watch bears catching salmon at Brooks Falls, but leave time to explore the otherworldly Valley of 10,000 Smokes and canoe the 86-mile Savonoski Loop.

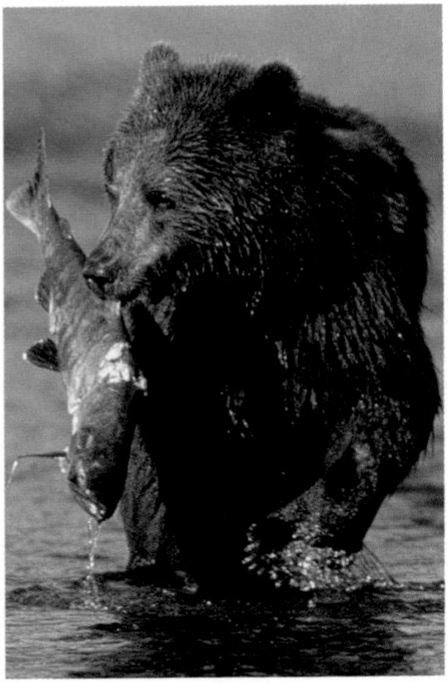

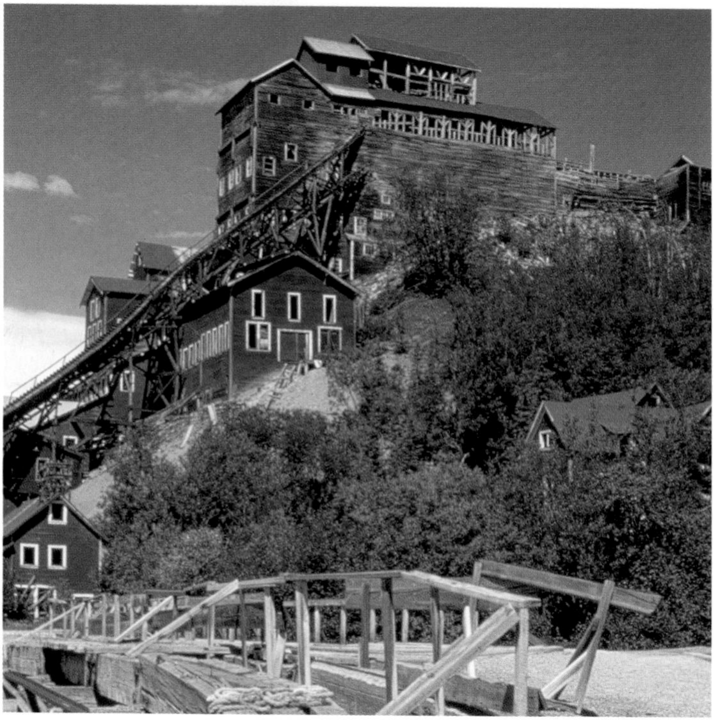

24 McCarthy and Kennicott Page **415** • Wrangell–St Elias National Park's enormous ice fields and dense cluster of lofty peaks are most easily accessed from quirky McCarthy and neighboring Kennicott, with its elegantly decaying copper-mill buildings.

25 Last Train to Nowhere Page **508** • These rusting steam locomotives once hauled gold, but they have now been left to sink slowly into the coastal plain just outside Nome.

Contents

Using this Rough Guide

We've tried to make this Rough Guide a good read and easy to use. The book is divided into five main sections, and you should be able to find whatever you want in one of them.

Color section

The front colour section offers a quick tour of Alaska. The **introduction** aims to give you a feel for the place, with suggestions on where to go. We also tell you what the weather is like and include a basic state fact file. Next, our author rounds up his favourite aspects of Alaska in the **things not to miss** section – whether it's a tiny fishing village, outdoor activity or local festival. Right after this comes a full **contents** list.

Basics

The Basics section covers all the **pre-departure** nitty-gritty to help you plan your trip. This is where to find out which airlines fly to your destination, what paperwork you'll need, what to do about money and insurance, about Internet access, food, car rental, national park access – in fact just about every piece of **general practical information** you might need.

Guide

This is the heart of the Rough Guide, divided into user-friendly chapters, each of which covers a specific region. Every chapter starts with a list of **highlights** and an **introduction** that helps you to decide where to go, depending on your time and budget. Likewise, introductions to the various towns and smaller regions within each chapter should help you plan your itinerary. We start most town accounts with information on arrival and accommodation, followed by a tour of the sights, and finally reviews of places to eat and drink, and details of nightlife. Longer accounts also have a directory of practical listings. Each chapter concludes with **public transportation** details for that region.

Contexts

Read Contexts to get a deeper understanding of what makes Alaska tick. We include a brief history, articles about **landscapes** and **wildlife**, and a detailed further reading section that reviews dozens of **books** relating to the state.

Index + small print

Apart from a **full index**, which includes maps as well as places, this section covers publishing information, credits and acknowledgments, and also has our contact details in case you want to send in updates and corrections to the book – or suggestions as to how we might improve it.

Map and chapter list

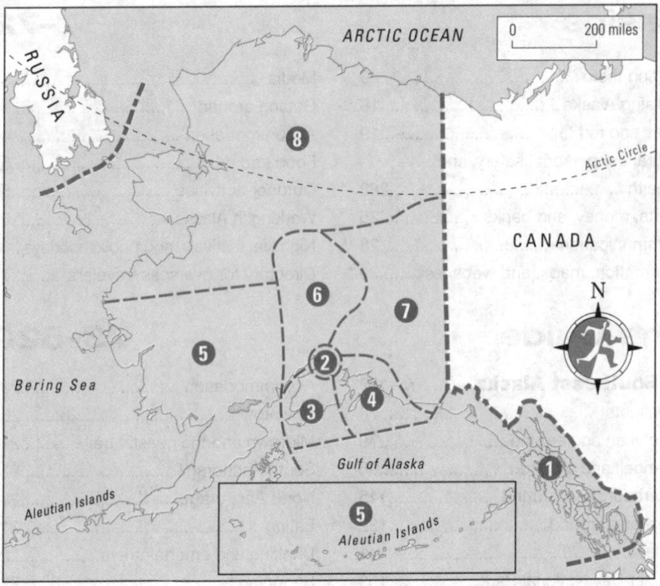

Contents

Color section i–xxiv

Basics 7–72

The Guide 73–520

Contexts 521–553

Index and small print 563–576

Basics

Basics

Getting there

Traveling to Alaska can be just as much of an adventure as being there. The quickest and easiest way is to fly, which not only leaves time for other holiday activities, but often turns out to be the cheapest way to reach Anchorage and the Interior. Most flights are from Seattle to Anchorage, though there are a number of direct flights from other parts of the world. All run throughout the year, but are most frequent during the main summer tourist season from late May to early September.

A more scenic approach is to join a cruise or take state-run ferries up through the sheltered and supremely scenic Inside Passage. Those after more adventure can drive (or even ride a series of buses) along the Alaska Highway right up through Canada's Yukon Territory and into Alaska. Better still, combine the sea and overland routes into one big loop.

Throughout the 1970s and 1980s Anchorage was a major refueling stop for transpolar flights between Europe and Asia, but with the advent of long-haul jets it has become something of a backwater.

Anchorage International Airport does receive some **international flights**, principally China Airlines from Taipei and Korean Airlines from Seoul, plus a number of direct flights from US cities – Chicago, Denver, and San Francisco with United; Salt Lake City with Delta; Minneapolis/St Paul with Northwest Airlines; and Las Vegas, Chicago, Phoenix, Los Angeles, San Francisco, and Portland, Oregon, with Alaska Airlines.

Fairbanks also has a few long-haul flights in summer, principally Northwest Airlines from Seattle and Minneapolis/St Paul, and Alaska Airlines from Chicago.

Almost everything else comes from **Seattle** either direct to Anchorage or via one or more of the Southeast towns such as Juneau or Sitka.

Airfares always depend on the **season**, with the highest being around June to August, when the weather is best; fares drop during the "shoulder" seasons – May and September – and you'll get the best prices during the low season, October to April (excluding Christmas and New Year's when prices are hiked up and seats are at a premium).

You can often cut costs by going through a **specialist flight agent** – either a consolidator, who buys up blocks of tickets from the airlines and sells them at a discount, or a discount agent, who in addition to dealing with discounted flights may also offer special student and youth fares and a range of other travel-related services, such as travel insurance, car rentals, tours and the like. Some agents specialize in charter flights, which may be cheaper than scheduled flights, but often have fixed departure dates and high cancellation penalties.

If Alaska is only one stop on a longer journey, you might be able to include it as part of an off-the-shelf Round-the-World (RTW) ticket, though with so few international flights this is unlikely unless you are very flexible.

Booking flights online

Many discount travel websites offer you the opportunity to book flight tickets and holiday packages online, cutting out the costs of agents and middlemen; these are worth going for, as long as you don't mind the inflexibility of non-refundable, non-changeable deals. There are some bargains to be had on auction sites, too, if you're prepared to bid keenly. Almost all airlines have their own websites, offering flight tickets that can sometimes be just as cheap, and are often more flexible.

Online booking agents and general travel sites

Ⓦ **www.cheapflights.co.uk** (in UK & Ireland), Ⓦ **www.cheapflights.com** (in US), Ⓦ **www.cheapflights.ca** (in Canada), Ⓦ **www.cheapflights.com.au** (in Australia and

NZ). Flight deals, travel agents, plus links to other travel sites.

Ⓦ **www.cheaptickets.com** Discount flight specialists (US only). Also at ⓣ 1-888/922-8849.

Ⓦ **www.ebookers.com** Efficient, easy-to-use flight finder, with competitive fares.

Ⓦ **www.etn.nl/discount.htm** A hub of consolidator and discount agent links, maintained by the nonprofit European Travel Network.

Ⓦ **www.expedia.co.uk** (in UK), Ⓦ **www.expedia.com** (in US), Ⓦ **www.expedia.ca** (in Canada). Discount airfares, all-airline search engine and daily deals.

Ⓦ **www.flyaow.com** "Airlines of the Web" – online air travel info and reservations.

Ⓦ **www.gaytravel.com** US gay travel agent, offering accommodation, cruises, tours and more. Also at ⓣ 1-800/GAY-TRAVEL.

Ⓦ **www.geocities.com/thavery2000** An extensive list of airline websites and US toll-free numbers.

Ⓦ **www.kelkoo.co.uk** Useful UK-only price-comparison site, checking several sources of low-cost flights (and other goods and services) according to specific criteria.

Ⓦ **www.lastminute.com** (in UK), Ⓦ **www.lastminute.com.au** (in Australia), Ⓦ **www.lastminute.co.nz** (in New Zealand). Good last-minute holiday package and flight-only deals.

Ⓦ **www.opodo.co.uk** Popular and reliable source of low UK airfares. Owned by, and run in conjunction with, nine major European airlines.

Ⓦ **www.priceline.co.uk** (in UK), Ⓦ **www.priceline.com** (in US). Name-your-own-price website that has deals at around forty percent off standard fares.

Ⓦ **www.skyauction.com** Bookings from the US only. Auctions tickets and travel packages to destinations worldwide.

Ⓦ **www.travelocity.co.uk** (in UK), Ⓦ **www.travelocity.com** (in US), Ⓦ **www.travelocity.ca** (in Canada), Ⓦ **www.zuji.com.au** (in Australia). Destination guides, hot fares and great deals for car rental, accommodation and lodging.

Ⓦ **www.travelshop.com.au** Australian site offering discounted flights, packages, insurance, and online bookings. Also on ⓣ 1800/108 108.

Ⓦ **travel.yahoo.com** Incorporates some Rough Guides material in its coverage of destination countries and cities across the world, with information about places to eat and sleep.

Flights from the US and Canada

Unless you live in the Pacific Northwest, you'll almost certainly find that the cheapest way to get to Alaska is to fly, and even from Seattle or Vancouver getting to Anchorage or Fairbanks is cheaper by air. Almost all the major American carriers fly to Alaska, primarily Anchorage (and to a lesser degree Fairbanks) from where Alaska Airlines and smaller carriers fan out to the rest of the state, often by propeller-driven "bush planes." The vast majority of flights reach Alaska via **Seattle**, which also acts as a hub for direct access to the Southeast towns of Ketchikan, Juneau, and Sitka with Alaska Airlines.

With fierce competition between the major carriers, it's always worth checking the Sunday newspapers for limited **special offers**, and if you are under 26 look for deals with student travel agents such as STA Travel (see opposite): Seattle to Anchorage round-trip for under $350 is a good deal. In the absence of special deals, the cheapest fares are with **APEX** (Advanced Purchase Excursion Fare) tickets, which have to be purchased between 7 and 21 days ahead of your departure date and require a Saturday night stay-over. Typically, the further in advance you buy, the cheaper the ticket will be, though the rules will be more restrictive. Prices vary, but those we've quoted below are for round-trip tickets throughout most of the summer, when you're likely to be going to Alaska; winter fares can be a little lower but not by a great deal. Flights to **Anchorage** are available from $350 from Seattle, $480 from Los Angeles, $520 from Chicago, $700 from Minneapolis/St Paul and $600 from New York. From Canada, prices are Can$800–850 from Toronto and Can$510 from Vancouver.

Many flights continue on from Anchorage to **Fairbanks**, often for only an extra $60, so you may want to make that your first stop and work south from there.

Many operators run **all-inclusive packages** that combine plane tickets and hotel accommodation with activities like whale watching, kayaking, hiking, or camping. Even if the "package" aspect isn't necessarily your thing, these deals can work out to be more convenient and sometimes more economical than arranging the same trip yourself, providing you don't mind losing a little flexibility. This is especially the case in

Alaska, where tour operators often have access to remote areas unknown to most visitors. With such a vast range of packages available, it's impossible to give a complete picture – but the accompanying list should get you on your way.

Airlines

Air Canada ⓣ1-888/247-2262, ⓦwww.aircanada.com.
Alaska Airlines ⓣ1-800/252-7522, ⓦwww.alaskaair.com.
America West Airlines ⓣ1-800/235-9292, ⓦwww.americawest.com.
American Airlines ⓣ1-800/433-7300, ⓦwww.aa.com.
Continental Airlines Domestic ⓣ1-800/523-FARE, International ⓣ1-800/231-0856, ⓦwww.continental.com.
Delta Domestic ⓣ1-800/221-1212, International ⓣ1-800/241-4141, ⓦwww.delta.com.
Northwest/KLM Domestic ⓣ1-800/225-2525, International ⓣ1-800/447-4747, ⓦwww.nwa.com, ⓦwww.klm.com.
United Airlines Domestic ⓣ1-800/241-6522, International ⓣ1-800/538-2929, ⓦwww.united.com.

Travel agents

Airtech ⓣ212/219-7000, ⓦwww.airtech.com. Standby seat broker; also deals in consolidator fares.
Flightcentre US ⓣ1-866/WORLD-51, ⓦwww.flightcentre.us, Canada ⓣ1-888/WORLD-55, ⓦwww.flightcentre.ca. Rock-bottom fares worldwide.
STA Travel US ⓣ1-800/329-9537, Canada ⓣ1-888/427-5639, ⓦwww.statravel.com. Worldwide specialists in independent travel; also student IDs, travel insurance, car rental, rail passes, and more.
Travel Alaska ⓣ1-888/522-5520, ⓦwww.travelalaska.net. One of the largest online reservation systems for all travel arrangements in Alaska, Yukon, and British Columbia.
Travel Cuts US ⓣ1-800/592-CUTS, Canada ⓣ1-888/246-9762, ⓦwww.travelcuts.com. Popular, long-established student-travel organization, with worldwide offers.
Travelers Advantage ⓣ1-877/259-2691, ⓦwww.travelersadvantage.com. Discount travel club, with cashback deals and discounted car rental. Membership required ($1 for a three-month trial).
Travelosophy US ⓣ1-800/332-2687, ⓦwww.travelosophy.com. Good range of discounted and student fares worldwide.

Tour operators

The following companies mostly handle "soft adventure" tours, but there are plenty of organizations running more intense adventure trips, the best of which are covered in the "Multiday adventure tours" box on p.64.
Adventures Abroad ⓣ1-800/665-3998, ⓦwww.adventures-abroad.com. "Soft adventure" specialists with trips through western Canada to Alaska.
Alaska Discovery ⓣ1-800/586-1911, ⓦwww.akdiscovery.com. Experienced Alaska tour provider offering kayaking, hiking, bear watching, whale watching, you name it.
Explore Tours ⓣ1-800/523-7405, ⓦwww.exploretours.com. A thorough, well-organized tour agent serving all of Alaska.

Overland from the US and Canada

The most adventurous way to approach Alaska is by road along the **Alaska Highway** (also known as the ALCAN Highway), two lanes of blacktop that stretch through remote, forested, and frequently mountainous scenery from Dawson Creek, on the BC/Alberta border, 1422 miles north to Delta Junction in Alaska. As daunting as that may sound, over a hundred thousand people in cars and RVs make the pilgrimage each summer braving limited and sporadic services, sometimes difficult weather, and a lot of frost heaves where repeated freezing causes the road to warp dramatically. Though road repairs through the summer can make the conditions unpleasant in parts, it is not a particularly difficult drive, and if you put your foot down it can be done in four or five days, though it is much more enjoyable to spread it over twice that, stopping to look at the scenery and relaxing in campgrounds along the way. The Alaska Highway and the sights and towns along the way to Alaska are covered in detail in *The Rough Guide to the Pacific Northwest* and *The Rough Guide to Canada*.

The highway remains **open all year**, with gas, food, and lodging every twenty to fifty miles in summer, though by early September places start closing down, frequently leaving hundred-mile gaps between services.

Consequently, you'll want to be certain your vehicle is in decent condition, though many people make the journey with no more problems than you might expect driving over two thousand miles of two-lane highway. When planning your travels, consider the **size of vehicle**: a couple of people, camping gear, spares, and a stack of food can soon overload a small car. Then again, something huge and gas-guzzling will soon drain your wallet at those expensive Canadian pumps. Make sure you have a jack and wheel brace suitable for installing your **spare tire**, preferably not one of the narrow space-saver variety which don't perform well in adverse conditions. Protection from bugs, dust, and rocks is important, so you'll need new windscreen wipers and plenty of washer detergent, and may want to fit headlight covers and even mats to protect the underside of the fuel tank – though neither is really necessary. Assorted spares – headlamp, hoses, and belts – and the tools to fit them are a good idea if you've got the mechanical knowledge; even if you haven't, it is wise to carry the parts, as local mechanics may not be able to get supplies quickly (and may charge the earth).

To find out about the latest **road conditions**, contact the State of Alaska Department of Transportation (ⓣ907/456-7623, ⓦwww.dot.state.ak.us), and Yukon Highways and Public Works (ⓣ867/456-7623 or 1-877/456-7623 toll-free in YT, ⓦwww.gov.yk.ca/roadreport/).

American citizens planning to drive their own cars into Canada should be certain to carry proper owner registration and proof of insurance coverage. The Canadian Non-Resident Inter-Provincial Motor Vehicle Liability Insurance Card, available from any US insurance company, is accepted as evidence of financial responsibility in Canada. See "Getting around" for car-rental agencies.

Rentals, driveaways, and shipping your rig

Most people who drive to Alaska take their own vehicle. Very few **rental** companies allow one-way drop-offs, and those that do charge astronomical prices. If you really want to drive up there and back and see something of Alaska, you'll need a month and will probably pay $60 a day for a compact, more like $110 for a 4WD.

With fortuitous timing, luck, and a degree of flexibility, you may be able to get a **driveaway**, thereby avoiding trashing your own rig on the road to Alaska. Look in the *Yellow Pages* under "Auto-transporters & Driveaway Companies," or contact Auto Driveaway (ⓣ1-800/346-2277, ⓦwww.driveaway.com), which lists regional offices and vehicles that currently need delivering on it's website.

Typically, there's no charge, but you'll be required to cover 300–400 miles a day and must pay for gas used. The same sort of deal applies with rental companies, who sometimes need cars and RVs delivered to Alaska at the beginning of the summer (especially in May), and back south in September and October; call around if you're interested.

Drivers who don't want to do the long haul in both directions can have their vehicle shipped between Anchorage and Seattle in about five days with Totem Ocean Trailer Express (in Seattle ⓣ1-800/426-0074, in Alaska ⓣ1-800/234-8683, ⓦwww.totemocean.com). In summer northbound rates are about double the southbound rates, which are around $790 for any passenger car or small truck, and $1000 for a camper or smallish RV.

The Alaska Highway by bus

Traveling by bus is the least appealing way to reach Alaska. There is none of the expedition feel of driving yourself, and you won't save much time over using the AMHS ferries. In fact, if you just want to get to Anchorage or Fairbanks, then it is usually as cheap to fly; but then you miss out on the scenery.

There is **no direct bus service** to Alaska. If you are **starting in Seattle**, Greyhound (ⓣ1-800/229-9424 or 402/330-8552, ⓦwww.greyhound.com) runs frequent buses (every 1 to 2hr) on the three-hour trip to Vancouver where you can transfer to Greyhound Canada (ⓣ1-800/661-8747, ⓦwww.greyhound.ca)

The AlaskaPass

Foot passengers planning on traveling up the Inside Passage to Anchorage, Denali, and Fairbanks may find considerable savings by purchasing the AlaskaPass, which allows unlimited ferry and train travel for a certain period. Currently, only the Alaska Marine Highway System ferries, the Alaska Railroad, and the White Pass & Yukon Railroad are members, but the situation changes almost annually, so it may be worth checking to see if other operators are on board. There are four passes: 15 consecutive days of travel ($779); 22 consecutive days ($1049); 8 travel days out of 12 ($649); and 12 days out of 21 ($799). Kids (2 to 11) travel half-price. You'll also have to factor in a $75 booking fee, which is charged per itinerary (not per person).

Buy your pass from AlaskaPass Inc, PO Box 351, Vashon, WA 98070 (☎206/463-6550 or 1-800/248-7598, ⓦwww.alaskapass.com).

for their service to Whitehorse, Yukon (mid-June to early Sept daily except Sat, early Sept to mid-June Tues, Thurs, Sun). It takes a grueling 45 hours to reach Whitehorse, with a three-hour break in Prince George and two hours in Dawson Creek. The standard through **fare** from Seattle to Whitehorse is US$155, though a seven-day non-refundable advance purchase costs only $89. This often works out cheaper than catching a Greyhound from Seattle to Vancouver (US$26) and then buying another ticket to Whitehorse. From Vancouver there is a walk-on fare of Can$350, which reduces to Can$160 if booked seven days in advance, and Can$135 if reserved 14 days ahead.

From Whitehorse there is a summertime service into Alaska with Alaska Direct (☎1-800/770-6652), which makes a daytime run to Anchorage (16hr; Can$165) and Fairbanks (13hr; Can$140) three days a week (Wed, Fri & Sun).

A completely different approach is to join the slightly countercultural **Green Tortoise** (☎1-800/867-8647 or 415/956-7500, ⓦwww.greentortoise.com), which runs one of their converted sleeper buses up to Alaska, with one 28-day trip (starting mid-June; $1700 + $290 for food kitty) starting in San Francisco and heading northbound to Anchorage via Prince Rupert, Ketchikan, Juneau, Haines, Fairbanks, Denali (for 5 days), Homer, and Seward. They also operate a couple of Anchorage-based 14-day loop trips within Alaska (starting mid-July & early Aug; $700 + $190 for food) visiting highlights of the Kenai Peninsula and Interior Alaska.

By train

There is **no direct rail connection** to Alaska from the rest of North America, although rail can be combined with sea travel to reach the 49th state, most easily done by catching Amtrak to Bellingham, WA, then taking the AMHS ferries (see p.36). In **Canada, Via Rail** (☎1-888/842-7245, ⓦwww.viarail.ca) runs right across Canada and serves Prince Rupert, which is an AMHS ferry port. Trains run from Jasper (on the trans-Canada route) three days a week (Wed, Fri & Sun) and a seven-day advance purchase will cost around Can$170, though you have to spend a night in Prince George along the way. In summer you should try to reserve a couple of months in advance, especially if you want the luxury of a sleeping compartment.

By sea from the US and Canada

Most towns in coastal Alaska are connected by the **Alaska Marine Highway System** (AMHS), state-funded vehicular ferries discussed in detail (along with prices) in "Getting around" (see p.36). If you travel by ferry, always **reserve** as far in advance as you can.

The ferries serve two ports outside Alaska, the most convenient for US visitors being **Bellingham**, in Washington State, 87 miles north of Seattle. A once-weekly service departs Friday at 6pm (plus additional sailings on Tuesday at 6pm in peak season) and skips all Canadian ports, making straight for the southernmost Alaskan port of Ketchikan (after 38hr), and going on to Wrangell (44hr), Petersburg (48hr), Juneau (59hr), Haines (65hr), and Skagway (66hr). Booking as early as April isn't unreasonable, particularly if you are taking a vehicle, and cabins on this route book out within four hours of going on sale, usually early in the previous December. To get to the Bellingham ferry dock, drivers should take exit 250 (the Fairhaven Parkway) off I-5, just south of downtown Bellingham and follow signs for the Fairhaven Transportation Center. Plan to arrive two hours before departure time. There are frequent buses and trains to Bellingham from Seattle and further afield: both types of service run on schedules well integrated with that of the ferries and drop you close to the ferry terminal.

One way of cutting costs on the journey to Alaska (particularly if you are taking a vehicle on the ferries) is to make your way overland to **Prince Rupert** in British Columbia and link up with Alaska's AMHS ferries there (typically 3–5 weekly; see p.38–39 for details of fares). The initial Bellingham to Prince Rupert section of the ferry journey is the least interesting, so traveling overland to Prince Rupert may save you both time and money without losing much in the way of scenic grandeur. Prince Rupert can be reached by car, train (see p.13), and by Greyhound Canada which, in summer, operates one or two buses a day on the twelve-hour run from Vancouver (Can$200, 14-day advance purchase Can$135).

By combining a couple of ferry systems it is also possible – though less convenient – to reach Alaska by sea directly from **Seattle**. Various possibilities exist, but the simplest sequence involves catching the vehicular *Victoria Clipper* (in summer 3 daily; 3hr; $77 one-way for foot passengers; ⓣ206/448-5000 or 1-800/888-2535, ⓦwww.victoriaclipper.com) from Pier 69 in downtown Seattle to Victoria on Vancouver Island. Once in Victoria, catch a Grayline of Victoria bus (daily at 8.30am; Can$94; ⓣ1-800/318-0818, ⓦwww.grayline.ca/victoria) to Port Hardy at the northern tip of the island. From Port Hardy, BC Ferries (ⓣ250/386-3431 or 1-888/223-3779 in BC, ⓦwww.bcferries.com) has a morning departure (7.30am; Can$102, small car Can$242, twenty percent savings outside peak season) every other day in summer, taking around fifteen hours to reach Prince Rupert, then returning the next day to Port Hardy. You'll need to spend the night in Port Hardy.

From the UK and Ireland

There are currently no direct flights from Britain or Ireland (or the rest of Europe for that matter) to Alaska, with all flights requiring at least one change of plane in the US, and sometimes as many as two or three. The main hub for flights to Alaska in the US is Seattle, though there are also a few connections through Minneapolis/St Paul, Portland, Oregon, and Chicago. Every flight from Britain or Ireland stops at one or the other.

The best selection of flights will be during the main June to August **tourist season**, although flights run all year for those ready to brave the winter cold to catch the aurora borealis, Iditarod, or winter ice-carving festivals. **Fares** are not particularly seasonal: there are sometimes winter bargains, but then the paucity of flights sometimes pushes winter prices higher.

Almost all Alaska-bound sequences from the British Isles leave from **Heathrow**, typically heading to Houston, Minneapolis/St Paul, or Chicago and then either to Seattle and Anchorage or direct to Anchorage. **Fares** tend to be cheapest in winter, a little more expensive in May and September and peak from June to August, though there is enormous variation depending on short-term demand and how far ahead you book. From **London** to Anchorage peak season fares are around £750, though you can often find something as low as £600, especially in the shoulder season.

There are flights direct to the US from Manchester (United Airlines) and Dublin (Aer Lingus/American Airlines and Continental), but prices are usually £150–300 higher than from Heathrow, so it makes sense to find your way to London and take it from there. Ryanair has flights from Ireland to London for as little as £40 return.

You should also consider the Alaska Airlines "Best of the West" **airpass** (see box p.35 for details), which may save you money by allowing you to get the cheapest flight to LA or Seattle then use the pass from there.

Booking your ticket through the airlines isn't necessarily the cheapest option. It is always worth checking out what **flight agents** have on offer (see below), especially if you are able to take advantage of their last-minute deals. The Internet also comes in handy as a useful resource for finding special deals.

Britain remains one of the best places in Europe to obtain flight **bargains**, though fares vary widely according to season, availability, and the current level of inter-airline competition. Shop around carefully for the best offers by checking the travel ads in the weekend papers, on the holiday pages of ITV's *Teletext*, and, in London, scouring *Time Out* and the *Evening Standard*. Giveaway magazines aimed at young travelers, like *TNT*, are also useful resources. If you are **under 26 or a student**, be sure to look into the student specialist flight agents such as STA Travel or USIT as they have a large range of special offers.

Airlines

Aer Lingus UK ⓣ0845/084 4444, Republic of Ireland ⓣ0818/365 000, ⓦwww.aerlingus.com.
American Airlines UK ⓣ0845/7789 789, Republic of Ireland ⓣ01/602 0550, ⓦwww.aa.com.
bmi UK ⓣ0870/607 0555, ⓦwww.flybmi.com.
British Airways UK ⓣ0870/850 9850, Republic of Ireland ⓣ1800/626 747, ⓦwww.ba.com.
Delta UK ⓣ0800/414 767, Republic of Ireland ⓣ1800/768 080 or 01/407 3165, ⓦwww.delta.com.
KLM/Northwest UK ⓣ0870/507 4074, ⓦwww.klm.com.
Ryanair UK ⓣ0871/246 0000, Republic of Ireland ⓣ0818/30 30 30, ⓦwww.ryanair.com.
SAS Scandinavian Airlines UK ⓣ0845/607 2772, Republic of Ireland ⓣ01/844 5440, ⓦwww.scandinavian.net.
United Airlines UK ⓣ0845/844 4777, ⓦwww.unitedairlines.co.uk.

Travel agents

Apex Travel Republic of Ireland ⓣ01/241 8000, ⓦwww.apextravel.ie. Specialists in flights to the US and consolidators for BA, American, and SAS Scandinavian.
Aran Travel First Choice Republic of Ireland ⓣ091/562 595. Good-value flights worldwide.
Bridge the World UK ⓣ0870/443 2399, ⓦwww.bridgetheworld.com. Specialists in long-haul travel, with good-value flight deals, round-the-world tickets, and tailor-made packages, all aimed at the backpacker market.
ebookers UK ⓣ0870/010 7000, ⓦwww.ebookers.com, Republic of Ireland ⓣ01/241 5689, ⓦwww.ebookers.ie. Low fares on an extensive selection of scheduled flights and package deals.
Flightcentre UK ⓣ0870/890 8099, ⓦwww.flightcentre.co.uk. Rock-bottom fares worldwide.
Flights4Less UK ⓣ0871/222 3423, ⓦwww.flights4less.co.uk. Good discount airfares. Part of Lastminute.com.
Flynow UK ⓣ0870/444 0045, ⓦwww.flynow.com. Large range of discounted tickets.
Holidays4Less UK ⓣ0871/222 3423, ⓦwww.holidays4less.co.uk. Discounted package deals worldwide. Part of Lastminute.com.
Joe Walsh Tours Republic of Ireland ⓣ01/676 0991, ⓦwww.joewalshtours.ie. Long-established general budget fares and holidays agent.
Lee Travel Republic of Ireland ⓣ021/427 7111, ⓦwww.leetravel.ie. Flights and holidays worldwide.
McCarthys Travel Republic of Ireland ⓣ021/427 0127, ⓦwww.mccarthystravel.ie. General flight agent.
North South Travel UK ⓣ01245/608 291, ⓦwww.northsouthtravel.co.uk. Friendly, competitive travel agency, offering discounted fares worldwide. Profits are used to support projects in the developing world, especially the promotion of sustainable tourism.
Premier Travel UK ⓣ028/7126 3333, ⓦwww.premiertravel.uk.com. Discount flight specialists.
Rosetta Travel UK ⓣ028/9064 4996, ⓦwww.rosettatravel.com. Flight and holiday agent, specializing in deals direct from Belfast.
STA Travel UK ⓣ0870/160 0599, ⓦwww.statravel.co.uk. Worldwide specialists in low-cost flights and holiday deals. Good discounts for students and under-26s.
Thomas Cook UK ⓣ0870/750 0512, ⓦwww.thomascook.co.uk. Long-established one-stop travel agency for package holidays, city breaks or flights, with bureau de change issuing Thomas Cook branded travelers' checks, plus travel insurance and car rental.
Top Deck UK ⓣ020/7244 8000, ⓦwww.topdecktravel.co.uk. Long-established agent dealing in discount flights and tours.

Trailfinders UK ⓣ020/7938 3939, ⓦwww.trailfinders.com, Republic of Ireland ⓣ01/677 7888, ⓦwww.trailfinders.ie. One of the best-informed and most efficient agents for independent travelers.
Travel Bag UK ⓣ0870/890 1456, ⓦwww.travelbag.co.uk. Discount deals worldwide.
USIT Northern Ireland ⓣ028/9032 7111, ⓦwww.usitnow.com, Republic of Ireland ⓣ0818/200 020, ⓦwww.usit.ie. Specialists in student, youth, and independent travel – flights, trains, study tours, visas, and more.
World Travel Centre Republic of Ireland ⓣ01/416 7007, ⓦwww.worldtravel.ie. Excellent fares to Europe and worldwide.

Tour operators

Abercrombie & Kent UK ⓣ0845/070 0610, ⓦwww.abercrombiekent.co.uk. Classy operator with a strong reputation organizing small-ship cruises in Alaska.
Arctic Experience UK ⓣ01737/214 214, ⓦwww.arctic-experience.co.uk. Well-established wildlife holiday specialist, with groups led by naturalists to Alaska, among other places. Part of the Discover The World group.
Bales Worldwide UK ⓣ0870/241 3208, ⓦwww.balesworldwide.com. Family-owned company offering high-quality escorted tours around the world, including to Alaska.
British Airways Holidays ⓣ0870/240 0747, ⓦwww.baholidays.co.uk. An exhaustive range of package and tailor-made holidays around the world, using British Airways and other quality international airlines.
Exodus UK ⓣ020/8675 5550, ⓦwww.exodus.co.uk. Adventure tour operators taking small groups on specialist programmes in countries around the world that take in walking, biking, overlanding, adventure and cultural trips. In Republic of Ireland, contact Worldwide Adventures ⓣ01/679 5700.
Maxwells Travel Republic of Ireland ⓣ01/679 3662. Agent for a wide array of deals from adventure operators worldwide.
MyTravel UK ⓣ0870/238 7788, ⓦwww.mytravel.com. Large, popular tour operator offering trips worldwide.
Trek America UK ⓣ01295/256 777, ⓦwww.trekamerica.com. Walking and soft adventure tours all over North America including Alaska.

From Australia and New Zealand

There are no direct flights from Australia or New Zealand to Alaska: all routes require at least one change of plane. The most popular route is across the Pacific to a West Coast city followed by either a connecting flight to Anchorage or a flight or ferry ride to one of the Southeast Alaskan towns. Savings can be made by skipping the Lower 48 entirely and flying to Anchorage via Asia, though there are far fewer flights, and you may have to spend a night, or the best part of a day, in the airline's home city.

Fares don't vary greatly with season, though you may find they jump up by around $200 or so in July. We've quoted fares below that can often be undercut by short-term specials and discounts offered through airline websites and travel agents, which generally offer the best deals and have the latest information on limited special offers, such as free stopovers and fly-drive-accommodation packages. Seat availability on most international flights out of Australia and New Zealand is limited, so it's best to book several weeks ahead.

Most people travel from Australia and New Zealand to Alaska **via LA**, which is typically reached on a twelve- to fourteen-hour nonstop flight, although some airlines allow stopovers in Honolulu and a number of the South Pacific Islands. Almost all the major US airlines, plus Qantas, Air New Zealand, Air Canada, and others have flights or code-share flights across the Pacific, usually with connections on to Anchorage. Traveling this route **from Australia**, fares to Alaska from eastern cities are roughly Aus$3000–3400, while from Perth you'll pay Aus$3600–4200. **From New Zealand** you'll pay NZ$3000–3400 from Auckland, or around NZ$3500–3700 from Christchurch.

Non-US residents are entitled to buy Alaska Airlines' **"Best of the West" airpass** (see box, p.35), which effectively allows you to buy a round-trip ticket from LA to Anchorage for US$340. It is worth looking into simply buying a flight to LA and then using the airpass from there.

Currently, the only flights from Australasia to Alaska that don't go through the Lower

48 are those **via Asia**. Korean Air have flights to Seoul with connections (after a twelve-hour layover) direct to Anchorage for around Aus$1800 (NZ$2050) from Sydney, Brisbane, or Auckland, Aus$1900 from Melbourne, and around Aus$3000 from Perth. Also check out Taiwan-based China Airlines, which offers similar deals with a stopover in Taipei.

Airlines

Air Canada Australia ⓣ1300/655 747 or 02/8248 5757, New Zealand ⓣ09/379 3371, ⓦwww.aircanada.com.
Air New Zealand Australia ⓣ13 24 76, ⓦwww.airnz.com.au, New Zealand ⓣ0800/737 000, ⓦwww.airnz.co.nz.
Air Pacific Australia ⓣ1800/230 150, New Zealand ⓣ0800/800 178, ⓦwww.airpacific.com.
American Airlines Australia ⓣ1300/130 757, New Zealand ⓣ0800/887 997, ⓦwww.aa.com.
Cathay Pacific Australia ⓣ13 17 47, New Zealand ⓣ0508/800 454 or 09/379 0861, ⓦwww.cathaypacific.com.
China Airlines Australia ⓣ02/9244 2121, New Zealand ⓣ09/308 3371, ⓦwww.china-airlines.com.
JAL Japan Airlines Australia ⓣ02/9272 1111, New Zealand ⓣ09/379 9906, ⓦwww.jal.com.
Korean Air Australia ⓣ02/9262 6000, ⓦwww.koreanair.com.au, New Zealand ⓣ09/914 2000, ⓦwww.koreanair.co.nz.
Qantas Australia ⓣ13 13 13, New Zealand ⓣ0800/808 767 or 09/357 8900, ⓦwww.qantas.com.
Singapore Airlines Australia ⓣ13 10 11, New Zealand ⓣ0800/808 909, ⓦwww.singaporeair.com.
United Airlines Australia ⓣ13 17 77, ⓦwww.united.com.

Travel agents

ecruising Australia ⓣ1300/369 848 or 02/9249 6060, ⓦwww.ecruising.com.au. Searchable fare database of cruises worldwide.
Flight Centre Australia ⓣ13 31 33, ⓦwww.flightcentre.com.au, New Zealand ⓣ0800 243 544, ⓦwww.flightcentre.co.nz. Rock-bottom fares worldwide.
Harvey World Travel Australia ⓣ13 27 57, ⓦwww.harveyworld.com.au, New Zealand ⓣ0800/427 839, ⓦwww.harveyworld.co.nz. Franchised organization with agencies all over Australasia.
Holiday Shoppe New Zealand ⓣ0800/808 480, ⓦwww.holidayshoppe.co.nz. Great deals on flights, hotels, and holidays.
OTC Australia ⓣ1300/855 118, ⓦwww.otctravel.com.au. Deals on flights, hotels, and holidays.
STA Travel Australia ⓣ1300/733 035, New Zealand ⓣ0508/782 872, ⓦwww.statravel.com. Worldwide specialists in low-cost flights, overlands, and holiday deals. Good discounts for students and under-26s.
Student Uni Travel Australia ⓣ02/9232 8444, ⓦwww.sut.com.au, New Zealand ⓣ09/379 4224, ⓦwww.sut.co.nz. Great deals for students.
Trailfinders Australia ⓣ02/9247 7666, ⓦwww.trailfinders.com.au. One of the best-informed and most efficient agents for independent travelers.
travel.com.au and **travel.co.nz** Australia ⓣ1300/130 482 or 02/9249 5444, ⓦwww.travel.com.au, New Zealand ⓣ0800/468 332, ⓦwww.travel.co.nz. Comprehensive online travel company, with discounted fares.

Tour operators

Abercrombie & Kent Australia ⓣ1300/851 800, New Zealand ⓣ0800/441 638, ⓦwww.abercrombiekent.com.au. Classy operator with a strong reputation organizing small-ship cruises in Alaska.
Adventure World Australia ⓣ02/8913 0755, ⓦwww.adventureworld.com.au, New Zealand ⓣ09/524 5118, ⓦwww.adventureworld.co.nz. Individual and small-group trips with small-boat cruises and packages combining train trips, and kayaking and wilderness experiences.
Canada & America Travel Specialists Australia ⓣ02/9922 4600, ⓦwww.canada-americatravel.com.au. North American specialists with Alaska expertise in accommodation, train travel, adventure sports, car and motorhome rentals, cruises, escorted tours, independent travel, and more.

Cruising Alaska

The most relaxed way to experience Alaska's stupendous scenery is undoubtedly on a cruise. With accommodation, transport, meals, and activities mostly taken care of, you can just lie back and take in the sights, or join in with all manner of on-shore fun. By opting for luxurious rooms in peak season with all the frills, it is possible to spend a small fortune. That said, the big cruise companies are fiercely competitive, and there are bargains to be had.

What you gain in ease of travel you lose in flexibility, with most cruises making a fairly similar circuit of the main Southeast and Southcentral ports, usually sailing overnight and then stopping to allow passengers to explore onshore during the day before gliding off again in the evening.

The **cruise season** is essentially late May to early September, though a few boats venture north a couple of weeks either side of the main rush.

Types of cruises

The majority of Alaska's visitors arrive on a **big-boat cruise**, sailing on some of the world's largest cruise ships, operated by Holland America, Royal Caribbean, and Celebrity Cruises. Fares may initially seem quite high, but they generally include all accommodation, 24-hour dining, nightly entertainment, and full use of the gyms, pools, and even onboard climbing walls. Several ships now carry 3000 passengers and over 1000 crew, and the emphasis is as much on the onboard facilities as it is on the place you're visiting. When one (or several) of these behemoths arrives in a tiny Southeast port the whole dynamic of the place changes, giving a somewhat distorted impression of what the place is about. Shore visits can be very packaged and perfunctory, though there's usually a huge array of activities on offer (for a fee) – from sled-dog rides on a nearby glacier to town tours in a horse-drawn carriage.

The alternative is a casual **small-ship cruise**, typically on a boat carrying 50 to 150 passengers. Obviously, the range of onboard facilities and distractions is going to be narrower than on the big boats, but comfort isn't sacrificed, and there's a welcome focus on the landscape and towns visited. Companies such as CruiseWest, Expedition Cruises, and Clipper tend to stop in more out-of-the-way places, giving a more intimate look at Alaska; they often chart narrower waterways and can get in closer to wildlife. Some even head around the coast up into Arctic waters or over to the Russian Far East. Activities are more likely to be naturalist-led trips ashore in small boats or even kayaks.

In practice, there are boats of almost every size, but the fundamental distinction holds true.

Schedules and fares

Arcane maritime laws and a desire among the larger cruise companies to employ cheap foreign labor means that most cruises start in Canada, specifically **Vancouver**.

There is an almost infinite variety of routes, but most are variations on the **standard cruise**, a seven-night run from Vancouver up the Inside Passage with stops in Ketchikan, Sitka, Juneau, and Skagway, and at one of the big tidewater glaciers, before finishing the run in Seward or Whittier. Nine- to twelve-day trips usually become **escorted cruise-tours** with a land component that includes a train journey to Anchorage and Denali National Park. Generally, you cruise in one direction and fly into or out of Anchorage for the other leg, though some cruises are circular.

Fares vary enormously. Shop around and you'll see newspaper and Internet offers for seven-night big-boat cruises for as little as $800. In practice, there are likely to be all sorts of hidden extras, though there are definitely good deals to be found. The standard fares offered by cruise lines for a **week-long trip** tend to start around $1800 twin-share in an interior cabin. For an ocean view room rates start at $2300, and for one of those suites with a balcony that feature on the covers of the brochures you'll be looking at a figure ranging from $3000 to $9000. There are usually **discounts** for early- and late-season sailings, and a saving of thirty percent or more can be had for **early bookings** made several months in advance.

Small-ship cruises are generally more expensive, though because of the size of ship all rooms usually have ocean views. One-week trips start around $3500, but there are three-night trips for $1100, and plenty of two-week expeditions with rates from around $5000.

Cruise companies

Celebrity Cruises ⓣ1-800/722-5941, ⓦwww.celebrity.com.
Clipper Cruise Line ⓣ1-800/325-0010 or 314/655-6700, ⓦwww.clippercruise.com.
CruiseWest ⓣ1-800/580-0072, ⓦwww.cruisewest.com.
Expedition Cruises ⓣ1-888/484-2244, ⓦwww.expeditioncruises.com.
Holland America ⓣ1-877/932-4259 or 206/281-3535, ⓦwww.hollandamerica.com.
Royal Caribbean ⓣ1-800/398-9819, ⓦwww.royalcaribbean.com.

Visas and red tape

US and Canadian citizens do not require passports to enter Alaska, but if you are crossing a national border you must carry some form of identification such as a birth certificate or naturalization papers: trying to cross the border with a driver's license or social security card is likely to see you turned back. Others must have a valid passport and required visas. Overland travelers shouldn't expect the rules to be relaxed by the Canadian border guards just because you need to pass through their country to get to Alaska, and it is worth keeping in mind that Canadian customs officials may also ask you to prove you have sufficient funds for the journey. Waving a credit card should see you through, but a wad of travelers' checks helps.

Visas

Under the **Visa Waiver Program** citizens of 27 countries – Andorra, Australia, Austria, Belgium, Brunei, Denmark, Finland, France, Germany, Iceland, Ireland, Italy, Japan, Liechtenstein, Luxembourg, Monaco, Netherlands, New Zealand, Norway, Portugal, San Marino, Singapore, Slovenia, Spain, Sweden, Switzerland, and the United Kingdom – need only a full passport and a **visa waiver form** to enter the United States for a period of less than ninety days.

Under the scheme, those arriving by air or sea need to show an onward or return ticket (at land borders this is not necessary) and must complete a visa waiver form provided either by your travel agency or by the airline (usually on the plane).

Note that passports generally need to be **machine-readable**: most issued in the past ten years will be, but it pays to check, especially if yours was issued at some minor embassy away from your home country.

If you intend to work, study, or stay in the country for more than ninety days, you must apply for a visa in advance. You should also apply for a visa in advance if you are a convicted felon, have a communicable disease – HIV/AIDS or TB in particular – or admit to being a communist or fascist.

Citizens of countries not covered by the Visa Waiver Program or people who don't fulfill the scheme's requirements need a **non-immigrant visa**. The tightening of national security since September 11 has made this a lengthy process often involving an interview and a wait of a month – plan ahead. Forms are available from your nearest embassy or consulate (see opposite), and can be downloaded from ⓦtravel.state.gov/visaforms. You'll need a passport valid until six months after your return date, a passport photo, and will be charged the equivalent of US$100.

Anyone approaching Alaska through Canada (either overland or on BC Ferries) will need to complete **Canadian formalities**: for full details check Citizenship and Immigration Canada (ⓦwww.cic.gc.ca). British citizens, as well as citizens of the European Union (EU), Norway, and most Commonwealth countries (including Australia and New Zealand) only need a valid passport. US citizens should carry a passport, their birth certificate or naturalization papers. If you are traveling on the Alaska Marine Highway System (AMHS) ferries from Bellingham, WA, your first stop will be in Ketchikan, Alaska, so although you will be traveling through Canadian waters, for immigration purposes you are not considered to be entering Canada. **Motorists** driving through Canada will be asked to show some proof of vehicle ownership and liability insurance cover.

Immigration control

The standard immigration regulations apply to all visitors, whether or not they are using the Visa Waiver Program. During the flight, you'll be handed an immigration form (and a customs declaration; see below), which must be given up at immigration control once you land. This I-94 form requires details of where you are staying on your first night (if you don't know, choose a likely place to stay from this book) and the date you intend to leave the US. You probably won't be asked unless you look disreputable in the eyes of the official on duty, but you should be able to prove that you have enough money to support yourself while in the US – $300–400 a week is usually considered sufficient – as anyone revealing the slightest intention of working while in the country is likely to be refused admission. You may also experience difficulties if you admit to being HIV-positive or having AIDS or TB. Part of the immigration form will be attached to your passport, where it must stay until you leave, when an immigration or airline official will detach it.

Customs

Foreign visitors flying to Alaska via another US airport will have to retrieve their bags and pass through customs at the first point of entry. Customs officers will relieve you of your customs declaration and check whether you are carrying any fresh foods. You'll be asked if you've visited a farm in the past month: if you have, you may well have your shoes (and possibly any camping gear) taken away for inspection. Unless you subsequently leave the US you will not need to complete customs or immigration procedures on arrival in Alaska.

The adult **duty-free allowance** is 200 cigarettes or 100 cigars (*not* Cuban), and 34 ounces (1 liter) of spirits, and goods up to a total of $800. Foodstuffs (particularly fresh fruit and vegetables, meats, and seeds) can be brought in but need to be declared and inspected. It is prohibited to carry into the country any articles from Afghanistan, Cuba, Iran, Iraq, Libya, Serbia or Sudan, obscene publications, drug paraphernalia, or pre-Columbian artifacts.

Anyone caught carrying drugs into the country will not only face prosecution, but be entered into the records as an undesirable and probably denied entry for all time. There is no limit to the amount of **cash** you can bring into the US, but amounts over $10,000 must be declared.

Exports are also restricted, particularly antiquities and anything made from endangered species (for more on this, see the box on p.224). **Hunters and anglers** wanting to take home their trophies or just a freezer-shelf-full of salmon, halibut, or moose steaks will usually find your guides can make the necessary arrangements.

Extensions and leaving

The date stamped on the I-94 form stapled into your passport is the latest you're legally allowed to stay. Leaving a few days later may not matter, especially if you're heading home, but more than a week or so can result in a protracted, rather unpleasant interrogation from officials, which may cause you to miss your flight and be denied entry to the US in the future. Your American hosts and/or employers could also face legal proceedings.

To get an **extension** before your time is up, apply to the Department of Homeland Security's Bureau of Citizenship and Immigration Service (BCIS: Ⓦwww.immigration.gov); the address will be under the Federal Government Offices listings at the front of the phone book. They will automatically assume that you're working illegally, and it's up to you to convince them otherwise. Do this by providing evidence of ample finances, and, if you can, bring along an upstanding American citizen to vouch for you. Start the process as early as possible, but at least 30 days before your visa expires. You'll also have to explain why you didn't plan for the extra time initially. If you have arrived via the Visa Waiver Program you may not be able to extend your stay, and if you suspect you may want to stay beyond the maximum ninety days it is usually better to obtain a suitable visa before leaving home.

Staying on

Anyone planning an extended legal stay in Alaska should apply for a special **working visa** at any American Embassy *before* setting off. Different types of visas are issued, depending on your skills and length of stay, but, unless you've got relatives (parents or children over 21) or a prospective employer to sponsor you, your chances are slim at best.

Illegal work is not as easy to find as it used to be, now that the government has introduced fines as high as $10,000 for companies caught employing anyone without a social security number (which effectively proves you're part of the legal workforce). Even in the traditionally more casual establishments like restaurants and bars, things have really tightened up, and if you do find work it's likely to be of the less visible, poorly paid kind – dishwasher rather than waiter (for more on this topic see "Working in Alaska," p.67). Making up a social security number, or borrowing one from somebody else, is of course completely illegal, as are **marriages of convenience**, usually inconvenient for all concerned and with a lower success rate than is claimed.

US embassies and consulates

In countries where there is consular representation in several cities, the embassy has been listed first. For links to other US embassies visit Ⓦusembassy.state.gov.

Australia

Canberra Moonah Place, Yarralumla, ACT 2600 Ⓣ02/6214 5600, Ⓦusembassy-australia.state.gov/embassy.

Melbourne 553 St Kilda Rd, VIC 3004 Ⓣ1902/941641, Ⓦusembassy-australia.state.gov/melbourne.

Perth 13th floor, 16 St George's Terrace, WA 6000 Ⓣ1902/941641, Ⓦusembassy-australia.state.gov/perth.

Sydney 59th floor, MLC Centre, 19–29 Martin Place, NSW 2000 Ⓣ1902/941641, Ⓦusembassy-australia.state.gov/sydney.

Canada

Ottawa 490 Sussex Drive, ON K1N 1G8 Ⓣ613/238-5335, Ⓦwww.usembassycanada.gov.

Denmark

Copenhagen Dag Hammerskjöld Allé 24, 2100 Ⓣ35 55 31 44, Ⓦdenmark.usembassy.gov.

Ireland

Dublin 42 Elgin Rd, Ballsbridge Ⓣ01/668 8777, Ⓦdublin.usembassy.gov.

Netherlands

The Hague Lange Voorhout 102, 2514 EJ Ⓣ070/310 9209, Ⓦthehague.usembassy.gov.

Amsterdam Museumplein 19, 1071 DJ Ⓣ020/575 5309, Ⓦwww.usemb.nl/consul.htm.

New Zealand

Wellington 29 Fitzherbert Terrace, Thorndon Ⓣ04/462 6000, Ⓦwellington.usembassy.gov.

Auckland 3rd floor, Citibank Center, 23 Customs St East ⓣ09/303 2724, ⓦusembassy.org.nz.

Norway

Oslo Drammensveien 18, 0244 ⓣ22/44 85 50, ⓦwww.usa.no.

South Africa

Pretoria 877 Pretorius St, Arcadia ⓣ12/342 1048, ⓦpretoria.usembassy.gov.
Cape Town Broadway Industries Center, Heerengracht, Foreshore ⓣ21/421 4280.
Durban Old Mutual Building, 31st floor, 303 West St ⓣ31/305 7600.
Johannesburg 1 River St, Killarney ⓣ11/644 8000.

Sweden

Stockholm Dag Hammarskjölds Väg 31, SE-115 89 ⓣ08/783 53 00, ⓦstockholm.usembassy.gov.

UK

London 24 Grosvenor Square, W1A 1AE ⓣ020/7499 9000, premium-rated visa hotline ⓣ0906/820 0280, ⓦwww.usembassy.org.uk.
Belfast Queen's House, 14 Queen St, BT1 6EQ ⓣ028/9032 8239.
Edinburgh 3 Regent Terrace, EH7 5BW ⓣ0131/556 8315.

Insurance, personal safety, and health

Alaska is a fairly safe place to visit. There is some physical danger from the sheer hostility of the environment, but nothing you can't learn to handle (or avoid altogether). In recent times there have been some fatal sightseeing accidents, and road conditions can pose a challenge, but on balance the risks are few. Things do go wrong, and when they do it is very comforting to know you are well covered with a good insurance policy.

Insurance

It is always advisable to take out an **insurance policy** before traveling to cover against theft, loss, and illness or injury. Before paying for a new policy, however, it's worth checking whether you are already covered: some all-risks home insurance policies may cover your possessions when overseas, and many private medical schemes include cover when abroad. In Canada provincial health plans usually provide partial cover for medical mishaps overseas, while holders of official student/teacher/youth cards in Canada and the US are entitled to meager accident coverage and hospital in-patient benefits. Students will often find that their student health coverage extends during the vacations and for one term beyond the date of last enrollment.

After exhausting the possibilities above, you might want to contact a specialist travel insurance company, or consider the travel insurance deal we offer (see box opposite). A typical travel insurance policy usually provides cover for the loss of baggage, tickets and – up to a certain limit – cash or checks, as well as cancellation or curtailment of your journey. Most of them exclude so-called dangerous sports unless an extra premium is paid for, say, whitewater rafting or skiing. Many policies can be chopped and changed to exclude coverage you don't need – for example, sickness and accident benefits can often be excluded or included at will. If you do take medical coverage, ascertain whether benefits will be paid as treatment proceeds or only after return home, and whether there is a 24-hour medical emergency number. When securing baggage cover, make sure that

Rough Guides Travel Insurance

Rough Guides Ltd offers a low-cost travel insurance policy, especially customized for our statistically low-risk readers by a leading British broker, provided by the American International Group (AIG) and registered with the British regulatory body, GISC (the General Insurance Standards Council).

There are five main Rough Guides insurance plans: **No Frills** for the bare minimum for secure travel; **Essential**, which provides decent all-round cover; **Premier** for comprehensive cover with a wide range of benefits; **Extended Stay** for cover lasting four months to a year; and **Annual Multi-Trip**, a cost-effective way of getting Premier cover if you travel more than once a year. Premier, Annual Multi-Trip and Extended Stay policies can be supplemented by a "Hazardous Pursuits Extension" if you plan to indulge in sports considered dangerous, such as scuba-diving or trekking. For a policy quote, call the Rough Guide Insurance Line: toll-free in the UK ⓣ0800/015 09 06 or ⓣ44 1392/314 665 from elsewhere. Alternatively, get an online quote at www.roughguides.com/insurance.

the per-article limit – typically $500–1000 – will cover your most valuable possession. If you need to make a claim, you should keep receipts for medicines and medical treatment, and in the event you have anything stolen you must obtain an official statement from the police.

Crime and the law

Alaska has recently earned itself a reputation for **violent crime**, with three times the level of sexual violence than the highest level of any other state, and a higher rate of homicides in Anchorage than the national average for a city of the same size. Still, much of this takes place behind closed doors or in places you are not going to visit, so as a visitor you are unlikely to be affected. You are more likely to be a victim of **theft**, though instances of bag snatching and personal assault are rare. Avoid carrying around and flaunting huge wads of cash, stash your valuables in the hotel safe (if there is one), and keep a photocopy of the important pages of your passport along with a record of the travelers' checks you haven't spent. Because of an increase in **theft from vehicles** at trailheads, especially those close to town, you should avoid leaving valuables in your car or truck. In practice, this is difficult to do, but at least store stuff out of sight.

Assuming you don't fall victim to any of this, you'll probably spend your entire time in Alaska without coming into contact with any of Alaska's various law enforcement agencies. Perhaps the easiest way to attract their attention is to fail to buy the appropriate hunting or **fishing license** or to infringe the bag-limit rules in some way. It is a complex business with rules that vary throughout the state, so always be sure to know what you are allowed to take. **Drugs** are, of course, totally illegal, though the Alaskan legal system has had a varied relationship with **marijuana**. It was illegal for years before being decriminalized in 1975 when a court declared that the state's constitutional right to privacy allowed people to smoke and possess – but not transport or sell – small quantities for personal use. For all practical purposes it was legal until a referendum in 1990 reversed the decision, and marijuana was again made illegal.

Prejudices

More than almost anywhere else in the US, Alaska seems to celebrate individuality, and those forging a different path from the mainstream may find that their individualism is unexpectedly celebrated. Nonetheless, prejudice exists, more so in rural areas where it's best to keep a low profile. Harassment will seldom be more than a little verbal abuse, but overtly homosexual behavior, for example, is liable to elicit a more vigorous response. **Gay** men and women will find support groups and even a small scene in Anchorage, Fairbanks, and Juneau (we've listed contacts throughout the book) but very little elsewhere.

Women should feel generally safe in Alaska, though you'll certainly encounter attitudes that may seem decades out of date. Alaska's famed paucity of women is more myth than reality these days, but there are still a lot of men living lonely lives in the bush, fishing at sea for weeks on end, or working on male-dominated oilfields, and women sitting in a bar are unlikely to avoid their attentions for long. Still, small-town familiarity, combined with long hours of summertime daylight, mean that personal safety is likely to be less of an issue than at home, though it's best to exercise the usual precautions.

Racism in Alaska is probably less prevalent than in large parts of the Lower 48, and what exists is likely to be directed at Native Alaskans. The vast majority of non-Natives are white, but with large military bases throughout Alaska black servicemen are a common enough sight to add some level of diversity. In the end, no matter what your race, you'll soon be recognized as a money-spending tourist, and whatever inherent prejudice there may be will soon evaporate.

Health and well-being

Travelers from Europe and Australasia do not require **inoculations** or special health certification to enter the US. Once in Alaska, if you have a serious **accident**, emergency medical services (dial ⓣ**911**) will get to you quickly and charge you later. Should you need to see a **doctor**, lists can be found in the *Yellow Pages* under "Clinics" or "Physicians and Surgeons," and there'll be a basic consultation fee of $50–100, payable in advance. Medication isn't cheap either – keep all your receipts for later claims on your insurance policy.

Many **minor ailments** can be remedied using the fabulous array of potions available in **drugstores**. Foreign visitors should bear in mind that many pills available over the counter at home need a prescription in the US – most codeine-based painkillers, for example. Local brand names can be confusing; ask for advice at the **pharmacy** in any drugstore.

Tap **water** is perfectly drinkable in Alaska, and many rural campsites have potable water from hand pumps. If you are drinking water from rivers or lakes, however, it should be boiled, filtered, or chemically treated (see p.57 for more).

At some time you'll probably find yourself on a ferry or day-cruise and will be glad that most boats travel in protected waters. Nonetheless those prone to **motion sickness** can improve their chances of feeling good by remaining close to the center of the ship, getting plenty of fresh air and avoiding reading or sitting in stuffy places. As a precaution, use one of the motion sickness patches or pills available over the counter at drugstores.

Cold, rain, wind, and sun

You are not likely to come down with any unpleasant diseases in Alaska, but dealing with the physical demands of the environment will be a day-to-day concern. **Hypothermia** can be a problem at any time in Alaska, but during the main May to September summer season, **cold temperatures** are likely to be less of a problem than you might expect. Still, you'll need to bring two or three warm layers (wool, polypropylene, and synthetic fleece are good materials; cotton is not), a hat, and some gloves, and always be prepared: a vehicle breakdown on a remote road in September could quickly turn into a nightmare if you are underdressed. Hypothermia isn't just about temperature, and protection from the **rain** may well be more of an issue, especially in Southeast Alaska where you are bound to encounter a downpour at some point. **Wind**, too, can be a problem in coastal areas (and on whale-watching cruises and the like), so a good waterproof and windproof coat is pretty much essential along with decent shoes and warm socks.

The sun also shines in Alaska, and with potentially twenty hours of sunshine a day through much of the summer **sunburn** is a real risk. Despite the low angle of the sun you should still slap on some sunscreen during the day, especially near snow and water where the reflection can catch you unawares; don't forget to cover the underside of your chin and nose. A peaked hat or baseball cap is a good idea, and be sure to wear glacier goggles or very dark sunglasses if spending time on or around glaciers.

Bugs, bears, and other nasties

In Alaska you don't need to worry about snakes, spiders, or poison oak, but bears and, particularly, mosquitoes can be troublesome. The size and number of **mosquitoes** is legendary and with good reason, though you also have to contend with **no-see-ums** (very small bitey things) and **white socks** (small black flies with white feet). They are seldom all around at the same time, but each has its few weeks of infamy in the summer, so always carry some bug dope of maximum potency. Anything with around 25 to 35 percent DEET is the optimum as higher levels don't increase effectiveness much. One application should last at least four hours, but DEET is pretty nasty stuff, so to reduce reliance on this wear long-sleeved shirts buttoned up to the neck, tuck your pants into your socks, and use citronella candles if you are sitting outside in the evening. Broad-brimmed hats with nets covering your face are only really necessary in extreme circumstances, usually on remote rafting, canoeing, and fishing trips.

Bears can be found all over Alaska – town centers excepted – though it is only brown (grizzly) and black bears that are widespread; polar bears are rarely seen apart from in Arctic towns such as Barrow and Kotzebue, and summer sightings are rare. Despite the number of grizzly stories you might hear, the risk of a bear attack is extremely low and, with a small amount of knowledge and some common sense, there is no need to let fear get the better of you. We've covered bear encounters in more detail in the box on p.56, but generally you just need to remember that bears don't like surprises and as long as you make noise whenever you are walking in forests or through scrub they are likely to move away before you know they are there. Some people advocate carrying a small bell, but talking, singing, or just clapping your hands is usually enough.

Alaska is full of smaller mammals, most of which won't bother you, though there is always a slim possibility you might get bitten, in which case you should definitely seek immediate medical treatment, and consider a series of **rabies** shots if you have any suspicion that the animal may be infected.

If you are a fan of shellfish, you need to be aware of **paralytic shellfish poisoning** (PSP), which attacks a handful of people each year and occasionally results in death. Shellfish sold commercially are routinely tested and are safe for consumption, but if you have collected your own, particularly from unmonitored beaches where there may be no warning signs, seek medical help if you sense tingling or numbness in the lips and tongue and loss of muscle coordination, dizziness, weakness, or drowsiness.

Costs, money, and banks

Alaska's astronomical prices have legendary status. The cost of transporting goods from the rest of the US has always made a big impact, but the reputation stems more from the pipeline construction years of the mid-1970s when bulging pay packets pushed prices to the stratosphere. There's no doubt that Alaska remains one of the most expensive states to visit, but in recent years prices have moderated to the point where Anchorage doesn't seem much more costly than any American city. Outlay really increases when you try to get out into the bush. Flights are always expensive and sometimes they are the only way to get to remote villages or to the headwaters of a pristine river for a float trip. Things should only improve, though, with increased infrastructure and tourism.

Alaska is a US state and you'll be using US currency; its proximity to Canada does not mean that Canadian dollars will be accepted – and if they are, the exchange rate won't be in your favor. **US currency** comes in **bills** of $1, $5, $10, $20, $50, and $100, plus various rarely seen larger denominations. Confusingly, they are all the same size and the same green color, though the new $20 has blue and peach tones to foil counterfeiters. Check each bill carefully and expect bartenders and shopkeepers to state the value of the bill you just gave them. The dollar is made up of 100 cents, with **coins** of 1 cent (known as a penny), 5 cents (a nickel), 10 cents (a dime), 25 cents (a quarter), and a newish gold-tinted dollar coin, which seems to have faded from view. For phones, vending machines, and buses it always pays to keep a stack of change handy, especially quarters.

Costs

There's no hiding from the fact that you are going to spend a fair bit of money on your travels here. If you are used to Lower 48 prices, you can safely assume that in the bigger towns you'll be paying 10 to 30 percent more for groceries and meals, and in remote communities anything up to double the usual cost. There is also a general trend for the towns of Southeast Alaska (which are closer to the supply entrepôt of Seattle) to be marginally cheaper than elsewhere.

The **minimum expenditure**, if you are camping, hitching or cycling, preparing most of your own food, and keeping a tight rein on tours and activities, would be in the region of $30 a day, rising to $40–60 if you stay in hostels, use buses, trains, and ferries, and indulge in the odd meal out. Couples staying in the cheaper motels, eating at unpretentious restaurants and not skimping on the main attractions and activities are looking at around $70–90 each per day; and if you rent a car for at least some of your stay, sleep in comfortable B&Bs, and eat well, you should reckon on at least $120 a day. All these figures can be ramped up dramatically if you start flying out to remote communities or staying at wilderness lodges, though this can be offset by abstemious days hiking and backcountry camping when you'll spend nothing.

Accommodation can be frighteningly expensive and is likely to be your biggest single expense, though off-season rates, especially in winter, can be half the summer rate; even May and September can offer savings. Camping in wilderness areas is often free, but if you want water and an outhouse expect to pay $6–10 per site; full-facility RV parks charge $18–25. Hostels vary from $12 to $25 per person (typically around $18), and some have a simple double room for two for as little as $45. You might occasionally find the odd roadhouse with poky rooms for $60, but generally there's a big step up from hostels to motels and B&Bs, both of which seldom cost less than $80. Resorts and hotels start around $120 in high season and go up from there. Remember that many communities add a **hotel tax** (usually 5 to 8 percent) to their quoted price.

As for **food**, the high price of groceries means you'll still need $15–20 a day for a basic life-support diet; anything perishable and imported – fruit, vegetables, and dairy products particularly – will command high prices. Eating in restaurants is likely to set you back at the very least $30 a day, more if you choose to splurge on dinner, and a considerable amount more if you add in a few drinks and a bit of socializing.

Given Alaska's size it should come as no surprise that **traveling costs** quickly mount up. A tour of Anchorage, the Kenai Peninsula, Denali, and Fairbanks can be done cheaply on buses and the train, but the public transport network is skeletal and at some stage you'll probably want to **rent a car**. For a compact car expect to pay $50–70 a day – perhaps more if your own vehicle insurance doesn't cover you – but this could be a good investment as it enables you to stay in cheaper out-of-town motels, or perhaps pull off the road and camp for nothing.

There's more good news. With few exceptions (mostly in Southeast), there is **no sales tax** on goods and services, so what you see is what you pay. **Tipping** is expected in restaurants, bars, and taxis, and a guide or tour host will welcome a similar appreciation; leave around fifteen percent of the bill.

Exchange rates

International exchange rates seem to fluctuate more wildly every year, but as we go to press one US dollar trades for Aus$1.40, Can$1.30, €0.86, £0.60, and NZ$1.60.

Kids get in to most things free if they're under 5 and will pay around half the adult fare if under 12 or so. There is often a small **discount** of around ten percent for military, seniors, and sometimes (though not often) students. Take some **student ID** if you've got one but it isn't worth making an effort to obtain one if you haven't. The **Hostelling International** membership card (see p.48) can also reap a few discounts.

Credit cards, travelers' checks, and banks

If you don't already have a **credit card** you should seriously think about getting one before traveling to Alaska; it'll make your life a lot easier when renting a car, bike, or whatever, as they won't feel obliged to extract a huge deposit. Even checking into a hotel you may be asked for an imprint to establish your creditworthiness. Besides, paying by plastic is accepted almost everywhere and 24-hour **ATMs** are now so common (even in tiny, remote communities) that you can always get a **cash advance** when you need it. Visa and MasterCard (known elsewhere as Access), and to a lesser extent American Express, Discover, and Diners Club, are all widely accepted. You should also carry a **cash machine card** that works on either Cirrus or Plus, international systems widely established in Alaska that enable you to obtain money from your home account.

It is always worth checking with your home bank, but accessing your own account or obtaining a credit-card cash advance can often work out cheaper than buying travelers' checks. Nonetheless, **US dollar travelers' checks** are still the safest way to carry money for both American and foreign visitors. They offer the security of being replaced if stolen (always keep a record of the numbers separately from your checks) and can be used as cash in restaurants and shops; just hand over the signed check and you'll get your change in cash. Don't be put off by "no checks" signs in the window: that only refers to personal checks. With the exception of Canadian currency, exchanging **foreign travelers' checks** and bills is almost impossible; you should be okay in Anchorage, Juneau, and Fairbanks but chances are slim elsewhere. Wells Fargo banks are your best bet.

Bearing in mind all the above, you'll probably have little cause to visit the inside of **banks**, which are generally open Monday to Friday from 10am to 4.30pm.

Wiring money

If things go horribly wrong, or you unexpectedly decide to do that ten-day float trip down some Arctic river and suddenly need $3000, the best way to get money sent out is to get in touch with your bank at home and have them **wire money** to the nearest bank. Depending on how much you're prepared to pay for a fast buck, this takes anything from a few minutes to a week and prices vary depending on where you are sending from, how much, and even whether you do it via the website or by phone. Thomas Cook (Ⓦwww.us.thomascook.com) and American Express (Ⓦwww.americanexpress.com) both operate such services, but generally the most convenient is Western Union (Ⓦwww.westernunion.com), with near-instantaneous transfers to a local agent (maybe a post office, bank, car-rental agency, or even a kiosk in a supermarket) and the facility for the sender to phone the transfer through using their credit card.

Communications

In most parts of Alaska you're not going to have any trouble keeping in touch. Even remote villages have efficient telephone communications and daily mail deliveries. Internet access is everywhere, even tiny communities having wired public libraries with free access.

Telephones

It is almost always cheaper to call from a private phone, but in most cases you'll find yourself having to use **public telephones** (mostly run by AT&T Alascom). These almost always work and are plentiful but are seldom found on street corners; in most parts of Alaska, winter conditions dictate that phones be located in shopping malls, convenience stores, and even in the entrance to fast-food outlets. They take 5¢, 10¢, and 25¢ coins and charge either 25¢ or 50¢ for a **local call** of unlimited duration. Since the whole of Alaska has the same **☎907 area code** (with the sole exception of Hyder in the very southeast corner, area code ☎604), this is no indication of what constitutes a long-distance call. As a guide, anywhere in the town you're in and its immediate surroundings will be a local call (just dial the number) and anywhere outside that will be non-local or **long distance** (dial ☎1-907 and the number): a disembodied voice will come on the line telling you how much to pay for the call. **Call rates** for non-local and long-distance calls are much lower on weekends and between 6pm and 8am. Calls from motel and **hotel rooms** are usually much more expensive, though local calls are usually free.

Many government agencies, car-rental firms and just about everyone with something to sell have **toll-free numbers**, which always have the prefix ☎1-800, ☎1-866, ☎1-877, or ☎1-888. Within the US you can dial such numbers free of charge, though some numbers only operate within Alaska: it isn't apparent until you try. Numbers with the prefix ☎1-900 are premium-rated lines, generally quite expensive and frequently salacious. You'll also come across companies using the mnemonic device of including letters in their number. The letters are on the buttons, thus for example ☎1-800/BLUE CAB becomes ☎1-800/258-3222.

Occasionally, you'll need to talk to folk who can only be contacted on **mobile phones**, which have numbers indistinguishable from land lines, but cost more to dial.

Phone and charge cards

If you are making a lot of long-distance calls, it works out much cheaper if you buy a **phone card**, usually available in denominations of $5, $10, $20, and $50 from convenience stores, supermarkets, post offices, and motel front desks. The card is not inserted in the phone, but has a number printed on it giving access to an account with the issuing company. Simply dial the toll-free number on the card, and you'll be prompted to punch in your account number followed by the phone number you are after. A card normally gives you a fixed number of minutes of talk time irrespective of where in the US and Canada you call, or what time of day. Rates are now as low as 5¢ a minute, though there is sometimes a connection fee (around 50¢) charged per call, and cards often have an additional 50¢ charge for using a pay phone.

Interstate and international calls

To **call Alaska** from the rest of the United States or Canada, dial ☎1 followed by the state's code (☎907) then the number listed. When calling **from outside the US or Canada**, dial the international access code (☎00 from Ireland, Netherlands, New Zealand, and the UK, ☎0011 from Australia), followed by ☎1-907, and then the number.

To make **international calls** from Alaska, it's ☎011 followed by the country code (see

Useful phone numbers

Emergencies ⓣ911; ask for the appropriate emergency service: fire, police or ambulance.
Directory assistance ⓣ411 (press 1 after the listed number to be connected)
Directory assistance for 800 numbers out of state ⓣ1-800/555-1212
Long-distance directory assistance within Alaska ⓣ1-907/555-1212, outside Alaska ⓣ1-(area code)/555-1212
Operator ⓣ0

below), then the area code (without the initial zero if there is one) and the number. International calls can be dialed direct from private or (more expensively) public phones. You can get assistance from the **international operator** (ⓣ00), who may interrupt every three minutes asking for more money, and call you back for any money still owed immediately after you hang up. Remember that there will be a considerable time difference between your country and Alaska.

Country codes

Australia 61
Canada not considered an international call
Ireland 353
Netherlands 31
New Zealand 64
UK 44

Internet access

The cheapest and often the most convenient way to keep in touch is by **email**. If you are patient, it is usually possible to get **free Internet access** at the local library, but high summer demand (especially in popular tourist areas) means you sometimes have to wait hours to get on. For more immediate needs there is almost always a shop (or café) nearby offering Internet access, and in some cases it won't cost you more than the price of your coffee. More often you'll have to pay around $2.50 for fifteen minutes, though some places impose a half-hour minimum ($5–6). Fear of viruses means some places ban the use of your own disks, though for those traveling with laptops, they often have dataports allowing you to plug in directly. Commercial photocopying and printing shops such as Kinko's are also a good bet, the high prices justified by fast machines hooked up to top-quality printers and scanners. Most mid- to upper-end hotels and motels now also have dataports in all rooms.

Unless you can somehow hook into your home account, the easiest way to collect and send email on the road is to sign up with one of the dozen-or-so web-based **free email accounts** such as ⓦwww.hotmail.com, or ⓦwww.yahoo.com: just go to their webpage, fill in the form, and you're done. Emails are kept indefinitely, but you are typically limited to a total of 2Mb of disk space (discourage friends from sending you clever, space-guzzling attachments) and, depending on the service supplier, if you fail to use the account for a month or so you may be closed down.

Mail

With the sophistication of the US phone network and the ease of sending emails you may want to bypass the US Postal Service altogether. Compared with the mail in Britain and Australasia, it is both slow and careless, though things tend to turn up eventually. Alaskan **post offices** are usually open Monday to Friday from 9am to 5pm, and Saturday from 9am to noon. **Stamps** can also be bought from automatic vending machines, the lobbies of larger hotels, and many retail outlets and newsstands. Blue **mail boxes** stand on city street corners but are less common in rural areas.

Ordinary **mail** costs 37¢ for a letter (weighing not more than one ounce) sent within the US; postcards are 23¢. The international rate for letters weighing up to half an ounce (a single sheet) is 60¢ to Canada, 60¢ to Mexico, and 80¢ elsewhere. Postcards are 50¢, 50¢, and 70¢ respectively, and aerogrammes to all destinations are 70¢.

Letters can be sent c/o **General Delivery** (what's known elsewhere as **poste restante**) to the main post office in each town and must be addressed using AK, for the state of Alaska, followed by the five-digit **zip code**: we've included zip codes of larger towns in "Listings" at the end of their section. Mail will usually be held for thirty days before being returned to sender – so make sure there is a return address on the envelope. If you are receiving mail at someone else's address, it should include "c/o" and the regular occupant's name, otherwise it is likely to be returned. This is especially true in small towns where the postie is likely to know people by name. Mail will also be held at hotels if labeled "Guest Mail, Hold for Arrival" along with a collection date.

Information, maps, and websites

Alaska does relatively little to promote itself, preferring to let individual businesses and local tourism organizations conduct their own promotions. Nonetheless, for advance information a good starting point is the Alaska State Division of Tourism, which publishes the annual *North! To Alaska* booklet (Ⓦ www.northtoalaska.com), which is mostly glossy tourism promotion material on Alaska and the Yukon. Of course, the Internet is a great source for up-to-date information, and we've listed some of the most useful (and fun) websites to help you get started.

You can also obtain the hefty and useful *Alaska Vacation Planner* by either calling the Alaska Travel Industry Association or visiting their website, though if you live outside the US and Canada you'll have to pay $10 (US dollar check, money order, or credit card).

Visitor centers

Once in Alaska you'll soon be weighed down with leaflets and brochures, most easily available through **visitor centers** (the term we've used throughout the book), which also go by such names as visitor information center, Chamber of Commerce, and Conventions and Visitors Bureau (CVB). At best they're well-stocked places laden with bumf on just about everything in the state and staffed by enthusiastic and knowledgeable personnel, but they can be just a small office with a handful of leaflets, or even a simple rack of advertising in the corner of the village store. Hours are equally varied, with some opening whenever they've got a volunteer available, but most staying open daily in summer from 9am or 10am to 5pm or later. In general, they don't make bookings for tours or accommodation, but will often have a phone you can use.

In small towns the visitor center is likely to be your first contact for information about local hikes and cabins, though occasionally there is a separate visitor center run by the US Forest Service. National parks also have visitor centers, but by far the best sources of information about the outdoors are the four interagency **Alaska Public Lands Information Centers** (APLIC) – in Anchorage, Fairbanks, Ketchikan, and Tok – run jointly by the authorities responsible for national parks, state parks, national forests, and national wildlife refuges, along with the Bureau of Land Management (BLM). They will provide just about everything you need to plan hiking, camping, canoeing, fishing, or wildlife-viewing trips.

Trip-planning resources

Alaska Department of Fish and Game PO Box 25526, Juneau, AK 99802-5526 Ⓣ 907/465-4100, Ⓦ www.adfg.state.ak.us.

Alaska Marine Highway System 6858 Glacier Hwy, Juneau, AK 99801-7909 ⓣ907/465-3941 or 1-800/642-0066 in US, ⓦwww.alaska.gov/ferry.
Alaska Public Lands Information Centers ⓦwww.nps.gov/aplic. Anchorage: 605 W 4th Ave, #105, AK 99501-5162 ⓣ907/271-2737; Fairbanks: 250 Cushman St, #1a, AK 99701-4640 ⓣ907/456-0527; Ketchikan: Southeast Alaska Discovery Center, 50 Main St, AK 99901 ⓣ907/228-6234; Tok: PO Box 359, AK 99780 ⓣ907/883-5667.
Alaska State Division of Tourism PO Box 110801, Juneau, AK 99811-0809 ⓣ907/465-2017, ⓕ 907/465-3767, ⓦwww.dced.state.ak.us/tourism.
Alaska Tourism Industry Association 2600 Cordova St, Suite 201, Anchorage, AK 99503 ⓦwww.travelalaska.com.
Alaska Wilderness Recreation and Tourism Association 2207 Spenard Rd, Suite 201, Anchorage, AK 99503 ⓣ907/258-3171, ⓦwww.awrta.org.

Maps

Specialist travel booksellers should have general maps of Alaska. Once there you'll find that gas stations sell tolerably useful and cheap state maps, the best of which is the one by Rand McNally ($4), which at an inch to 75 miles gives only a broad sweep but does have handy enlargements of most of the areas where you are likely to spend time. Map enthusiasts won't be able to resist the weighty *DeLorme Alaska Atlas and Gazetteer* ($20), which covers most of the state at an inch to five miles, marks all hikes, huts, peaks, landing strips, and comes complete with contour lines and GPS grids. There's little worthwhile in between these two extremes, though there are regional maps available in each area.

If you are planning to do some serious hiking, you'll need a topographic map. These are sold by visitor centers in popular hiking areas, such as Denali National Park, at the Alaska Public Lands Information Centers, and by mail order through the US Geological Survey (12201 Sunrise Valley Drive, Reston, VA 20192 ⓣ1-888/275-8747, ⓦask.usgs.gov). An order form can be downloaded from their website and, on top of the price of the maps, you can expect to pay $5 handling.

Map outlets

North America

Adventurous Traveler.com US ⓣ1-800/282-3963, ⓦadventuroustraveler.com.
Book Passage 51 Tamal Vista Blvd, Corte Madera, CA 94925 ⓣ1-800/999-7909, ⓦwww.bookpassage.com.
Distant Lands 56 S Raymond Ave, Pasadena, CA 91105 ⓣ1-800/310-3220, ⓦwww.distantlands.com.
Elliot Bay Book Company 101 S Main St, Seattle, WA 98104 ⓣ1-800/962-5311, ⓦwww.elliotbaybook.com.
Globe Corner Bookstore 28 Church St, Cambridge, MA 02138 ⓣ1-800/358-6013, ⓦwww.globecorner.com.
Map Link 30 S La Patera Lane, Unit 5, Santa Barbara, CA 93117 ⓣ1-800/962-1394, ⓦwww.maplink.com.
Rand McNally US ⓣ1-800/275-7263, ⓦwww.randmcnally.com. Stores across the US; call or check the website for the nearest location.
The Travel Bug 3065 W Broadway, Vancouver V6K 2G9 ⓣ604/737-1122, ⓦwww.travelbugbooks.ca.
World of Maps 1235 Wellington St, Ottawa, ON K1Y 3A3 ⓣ1-800/214-8524, ⓦwww.worldofmaps.com.

UK and Ireland

Blackwell's Map and Travel Shop 50 Broad St, Oxford OX1 3BQ ⓣ01865/793 550, ⓦmaps.blackwell.co.uk.
Easons Bookshop 40 Lower O'Connell St, Dublin 1 ⓣ01/858 3881, ⓦwww.eason.ie.
Heffers Map and Travel 28b The Grafton Centre, Cambridge CB1 1PS ⓣ01223/568573, ⓦwww.heffers.co.uk.
Hodges Figgis Bookshop 57 Dawson St, Dublin 2 ⓣ01/677 4754.
The Map Shop 30a Belvoir St, Leicester LE1 6QH ⓣ0116/247 1400, ⓦwww.mapshopleicester.co.uk.
National Map Centre 22–24 Caxton St, London SW1H 0QU ⓣ020/7222 2466, ⓦwww.mapsnmc.co.uk, ⓔinfo@mapsnmc.co.uk.
Newcastle Map Centre 55 Grey St, Newcastle-upon-Tyne NE1 6EF ⓣ0191/261 5622.
Ordnance Survey Ireland Phoenix Park, Dublin 8 ⓣ01/802 5300, ⓦwww.osi.ie.
Ordnance Survey of Northern Ireland Colby House, Stranmillis Ct, Belfast BT9 5BJ ⓣ028/9025 5755, ⓦwww.osni.gov.uk.

Stanfords 12–14 Long Acre, London WC2E 9LP ⓣ020/7836 1321, ⓦwww.stanfords.co.uk, ⓔcustomer.services@stanfords.co.uk.
The Travel Bookshop 13–15 Blenheim Crescent, London W11 2EE ⓣ020/7229 5260, ⓦwww.thetravelbookshop.co.uk.

Australia and New Zealand

The Map Shop 6–10 Peel St, Adelaide, SA 5000 ⓣ08/8231 2033, ⓦwww.mapshop.net.au.
Mapland 372 Little Bourke St, Melbourne, VIC 3000 ⓣ03/9670 4383, ⓦwww.mapland.com.au.
MapWorld 173 Gloucester St, Christchurch ⓣ0800/627 967 or 03/374 5399, ⓦwww.mapworld.co.nz.
Perth Map Centre 884 Hay St, Perth, WA 6000 ⓣ08/9322 5733.
Specialty Maps 46 Albert St, Auckland 1001 ⓣ09/307 2217, ⓦwww.specialtymaps.co.nz.

Websites

The remote nature of Alaska encouraged the people of the last frontier to adopt the Internet early and wholeheartedly, a trend that has continued. We've included **web addresses** throughout the guide and brought together a few more sites of general interest below.

Travel and tourism sites

Alaska Marine Highway System ferries ⓦwww.alaska.gov/ferry. Alaska Marine Highway System homepage for downloadable ferry schedules, reservations, fares, and the lowdown on vessels and ports.
Alaska Railroad ⓦwww.akrr.com. Alaska railroad timetables and reservations.
Division of Tourism ⓦwww.dced.state.ak.us/tourism. Official state tourism site and a good starting point for information on national and state parks, CVB addresses, local weather, online maps, and more.

Outdoor sites

Gorp ⓦwww.gorp.com. General outdoor activities site that's great for adventure-trip listings and has wide Alaska coverage.
Mountain Biking ⓦwww.dirtworld.com. Links to a brief listing of bike trails in Alaska.
National Parks ⓦwww.nps.gov. General access page for US national parks, preserves, and monuments, with links to those in Alaska.
US Fish and Wildlife ⓦwww.r7.fws.gov. The US Fish and Wildlife service, the first stop for information on national wildlife refuges, bird populations, and general wildlife management.

General sites

Alaska Native Resources ⓦwww.alaskanativeresources.com. Alaska Native issues and plenty of links to similar topics.
Alaskan.com ⓦwww.alaskan.com. Rambling commercial site with extensive Alaskan links.
Anchorage Daily News ⓦwww.adn.com. Alaska's biggest and most influential newspaper.
Northern Alaska Environment Center ⓦnorthern.org. Grassroots organization campaigning for the preservation of the Arctic National Wildlife Refuge and boreal forests. Extensive links to like-minded sites.
Northern Lights ⓦwww.pfrr.alaska.edu/~pfrr/aurora. Aurora videos, forecasts, and much more.
Sierra Club ⓦwww.sierraclub.org/ak. The Alaska section of the environmental group's site, full of info on current issues.

Media

The standard of media coverage in Alaska is much as you'd expect elsewhere in the United States but on a smaller scale. There are fewer TV and radio stations than in the Lower 48, though some towns have such poor reception that almost everyone has cable (or satellite), with the usual fifty-plus channels. Mostly it is the standard diet, with inserts for local news, weather, and current affairs, but other locally produced shows are rare. In villages you may come across the Rural Alaska Communications Service, which serves almost 250 rural communities with commercial content from Anchorage stations, material from the Alaska Public Broadcasting Service (PBS), and some local or regional programming.

Radio varies greatly throughout the state with only the serious, publicly funded Alaska Public Radio Network (FM frequencies 87–92MHz) having wide coverage; much of its content is straight from **National Public Radio**. The bigger towns have a selection of niche stations (alternative rock, classic rock, Seventies, country, etc), but smaller places might have just one, and it is on these that you should listen out for "bushlines," a kind of radio bulletin board for people who don't have phones. The whole town, and particularly those in cabins out in the bush, will listen to the messages, usually prosaic instructions for someone to meet somewhere, or sending thanks for the side of moose delivered Tuesday. Between towns there may be nothing at all: get a rental with a cassette or CD player for those long hauls.

The widest circulation **newspaper** is the *Anchorage Daily News* (Ⓦwww.adn.com), which provides Alaska's most comprehensive coverage of local and world events. It is pretty much the de facto state newspaper, much to the chagrin of a good portion of the state's residents, not just because they resent Anchorage's dominance, but because of its left-leaning, liberal politics (at least by Alaskan standards). Some years back it absorbed the city's afternoon paper, the *Anchorage Times*, and as a sop to its former readers and "in the interests of preserving a diversity of viewpoints in the community," the *Anchorage Daily News* prints the "Voice of the Times," a daily half-page of right-wing Libertarian views. Anchorage also has the excellent *Press*, an alternative views and listings weekly.

The *Fairbanks Daily News-Miner* (Ⓦwww.news-miner.com) and *Juneau Empire* (Ⓦwww.juneauempire.com) are the two other papers with a large regional following, the former covering much of the Interior and the North, the latter found all over Southeast. None is likely to win you over with outstanding standards of journalism, but they're quite adequate, and the weekend magazine sections offer interesting insights into aspects of the state you may not otherwise come across. In addition, each sizeable town produces its own local-interest rag – the *Arctic Sounder*, the *Tundra Drums*, the *Nome Nugget*, and a dozen more around the state – though the content often fails to live up to the promise of the title.

Supermarket magazine stands in the bigger towns might stock the major dailies from the Lower 48, but most likely you'll be reduced to *Time* and *Newsweek* for wider coverage.

Alaska-specific **magazines** are rare, though you might look for the monthly *Alaska* (Ⓦwww.alaskamagazine.com), which tries for a wide coverage of outdoor issues but fails to disguise its hunting and fishing heritage. Women looking to spend a lot more time in Alaska should seek out *AlaskaMen* (Ⓦwww.alaskamen-online.com), a matchmaking magazine which claims to feature "interesting and exciting men whose individualism, spirit and vitality make them unique among men of the world."

Getting around

Traveling around Alaska it is not unusual to ride ferries, buses, and trains, drive a rental car, cycle, fly out to bush communities, or hike. Come in winter and you may well ski, ride a snowmachine, and drive a dog team. In any case, getting around is liable to take up a fair bit of your time and money, but don't treat it as a hardship – often the journey is as enjoyable as the destination. The scenery is wonderful whether viewed from a bus headed up towards the Arctic Ocean, on the train headed for Denali, chugging through the Inside Passage on a ferry, or stopped beside the road gazing across the tundra. Better still, wildlife is often less disturbed by people encased in their metal cocoon, and, if you are flying, the extra height you have for peering over trees affords some of your best animal spotting.

All the mountain ranges, glaciers, and vast stretches of boggy wilderness put up significant barriers to ground transportation – only surmounted by taking to the air or water. Consequently, Alaskans **fly** more than anyone else in the nation, and you should follow suit to reach remote villages or even just to do some flightseeing. Although much of Alaska is inaccessible to road traffic, the Kenai Peninsula, the Interior, and the region around Fairbanks all have a fair **highway** network that you could spend weeks exploring, though a couple of sections are best viewed from the wonderfully scenic **train** line. For many, the highlight is making full use of the **ferry system**, which links over thirty ports, mostly in the Southeast "panhandle," but also around Prince William Sound, the Kenai Peninsula, and west beyond Kodiak Island to the Aleutian Islands. Thoroughly relaxing, they leisurely thread their way through unbelievably narrow channels and across deep sounds where whales and dolphins make regular appearances.

If you stick to the roads and ferry routes, **transportation costs** aren't especially high, and, considering the distances involved, ferries and buses are quite cheap. You can see a lot of what the state has to offer this way, but start flying out to remote bush communities and you'll soon start racking up the bills. **Savings** can be made on transport by investing in an **AlaskaPass** (for details see box, p.13,) which combines Alaska Marine Highway System (AMHS) ferries and the Alaska Railroad; and Alaska Airlines' **airpass** (see box, opposite), the latter only available to foreign visitors.

Domestic flights

Alaskans make more than twice the average number of commercial flights taken by US citizens, and the statistics for small planes are even more astounding. Roughly one in every sixty Alaskans is a certified pilot, and almost all of them own their own plane. That is something like sixteen times the number of planes per capita as the rest of the United States.

Clearly, flying is the quickest way to get around – and sometimes the only way – especially as surface travel is hampered by long distances, impassable mountain ranges, and inconveniently sited bodies of water. Short **scheduled flights** can save you a lot of time, and sometimes money. If you need to get from Juneau to Anchorage you can wait for the twice-monthly ferry to Valdez, continue by ferry to Whittier and then catch the train (taking two days in all), or fly for less money in ninety minutes. Services between the larger towns are mostly run by the state carrier Alaska Airlines, though in some areas flights are contracted out to partner airlines, such as ERA and PenAir. If any of these fly to your destination, this will almost certainly be the cheapest way to go, especially if you are an overseas visitor and have pre-purchased an Alaska Airlines **airpass** (see box opposite). Otherwise it is difficult to pin down exact **fares**, which vary enormously depending on demand and how far in advance you can reserve. In general, the most expensive fares are those bought less than two weeks in advance: a fourteen-day advance purchase will save perhaps thirty percent. On some routes buying a ticket 21 days in advance will cut almost forty percent off the walk-up rate. **One-way tickets** are generally half the round-trip fare, and it is always worth checking for specials on the Alaska Airlines website.

As an example, a round-trip flight from Anchorage to Juneau could range from $250, if bought well in advance, to $540 for a walk-up. Other routes tend to vary less: Anchorage–Fairbanks round-trip costs $260–320, and Juneau–Ketchikan $240–340.

Anchorage is very much the hub of operations and, if you stick with Alaska Airlines, you'll be continually shuttling back to the big city. Smaller airlines sometimes work out more convenient. For example, if you want to get from Kotzebue to Barrow, you could do it with Alaska Airlines via Anchorage or do it more directly taking local bush flights linking tiny communities.

Scheduled services from Anchorage and Fairbanks to the larger remote communities, such as Nome, Barrow, and Dutch Harbor, carry mail, newspapers, and essential supplies. These places rely so heavily on air deliveries that you may well find yourself on a 737 almost entirely given over to freight, with only two dozen seats left for passengers.

Main scheduled airlines

Alaska Airlines/Horizon Air ⓣ1-800/252-7522, ⓦwww.alaskaair.com. The main intrastate and international airline with flights to all major towns in Alaska and frequent out-of-state flights to Seattle, San Francisco, Los Angeles, Chicago, Detroit, Puerto Vallarta (Mexico), and more, plus an extensive Pacific Northwest schedule through Horizon Air.

ERA Aviation ⓣ1-800/866-8394, ⓦwww.flyera.com. Alaska Airlines partner with flights from Anchorage to Cordova, Homer, Kenai, Iliamna (summer only), Kodiak, and Valdez.

PenAir ⓣ1-800/448-4226 or 907/243-2323, ⓦwww.penair.com. Works in partnership with Alaska Airlines covering the Southwest and Aleutians with flights from Anchorage to Dutch Harbor, King Salmon, Dillingham, the Pribilof Islands, Unalakleet, and others.

Bush planes

Scheduled flights are fine for getting around, but you cannot truly appreciate Alaska without spending at least some time in those workhorses of Alaskan aviation, the **bush planes** – typically small Cessnas, Beavers, and Piper Navajos. It sometimes seems that there isn't a place in the state that they

Alaska Airlines' "Best of the West" airpass

Big savings can be made on internal and out-of-state flights with Alaska Airlines provided you're not a US citizen (or are a US citizen but currently reside in some other country) and are starting your travels outside the US. The airline's "Best of the West" **airpass** requires you to buy between two and ten coupons (called sectors), each valid for one one-way Alaska Airlines flight. Coupons for flights beginning and ending within the state cost $109, which for short flights is no saving, but you'll cut costs enormously on trips to places such as Barrow, Nome, and Dutch Harbor. Flights such as one from Anchorage to Ketchikan that stops twice but retains the same code number can still be bought for just one $109 coupon.

Coupons for flights beginning or ending outside the state go for $169, and two of these can often work out cheaper than a round-trip ticket from LA to Anchorage.

The airpass (which cannot be bought in the US) does not have to be bought in conjunction with any international flights, but all coupons must be used within 60 days of using your first one, and all flights must be taken within 120 days of arrival in the US.

won't land, and hair-raising stories of pioneering touchdowns on postage-stamp lakes and crevasse-riddled glaciers are legion. Talk of narrow escapes from horrendous crashes gets similarly lurid coverage, but that shouldn't deter you: **bush pilots** probably negotiate more tricky maneuvers in a week than pilots elsewhere do in a lifetime of flying. Besides, most are very good at distracting you with endless tales of derring-do on the Last Frontier.

Many bush flights run on regular schedules using the larger towns as hubs for services to tiny villages. Services are run to a less rigid but still frequent timetable, and **fares** tend to be more stable than on the intercity routes. You'll also come across dedicated mail flights that briefly visit three or four communities and often have a few seats for passengers. Take the whole tour, or just use one leg to reach a particular village.

Apart from regular services, **chartered bush planes** are the only way to get to some of the real gems of the great Alaskan outdoors. Nowhere is too tough: some planes come equipped with floats for lake and river landings, while others have skis for snow and glaciers, though these can often be swapped for ordinary wheels to land on gravel airstrips or bulbous tundra tires for rough-field and gravel-bar touchdowns. Even international airports like Fairbanks are designed to cope with all types of landing gear: the tarmac runway is flanked by a gravel strip and a float pond.

Arranging a flight is usually no problem. Reserving in advance is always a good idea, but in summer pilots work long hours and can usually tack an extra flight onto the end of their schedule to get you out to your river bar. The price is usually for the plane and pilot, with little or no extra cost for additional passengers. Consequently, it is a good idea to join up with others to make up a full load. If you are going somewhere popular, the bush plane company may well do this for you, but the more exotic the destination, the more you'll have to organize this yourself. Remember that unless they have found a return fare, you are paying for the plane until it gets back to base, though when flying to USFS cabins – which are often continuously booked throughout the summer – you can almost always share the cost with the previous occupants flying out. A five-seater bush plane will typically cost around $300–350 an hour.

There are a number of **precautions** to consider when arranging **pickups**. Firstly make sure you can get to the designated spot. Hiking across tundra is slow going and apparently benign rivers can turn out to be impassable. Weather can make it impossible for your pilot to pick you up at the arranged time and, with supplies running low, it is comforting to know when subsequent attempts will be made. Your pilot will probably return to the designated spot later on (or the next day), but it is essential to have a clear **contingency plan** understood by all parties. With this in mind, make sure you don't have any pressing engagements (like international flights) immediately after bush trips.

Pilots know their patch very well and will only arrange to pick you up somewhere they know they can land, but it always pays to check. Spring break-up (mid-April to late May) severely limits water landings in the Interior, and around the coast you should consider the **tides** to ensure the pilot can get close in to the shore.

Ferries

If you are heading north through Southeast Alaska, you'll almost certainly be making extensive use of the **Alaska Marine Highway System** (for contact info see p.39), also known as the state ferry or even the "blue canoe." This state-run network of nine vehicular passenger ferries provides the principal means of transport between 34 ports in Southeast and Southcentral Alaska. Our chapter maps (p.78, p.232, 386, and p.314) show the routes and ports of call made by ferries, which are each named after an Alaskan glacier, in line with some arcane state law. In general, the ferry system has daily departures from major ports and perhaps one or two a week in each direction from smaller places. The main problem with the ferry system is that it comes in two separate sections: Southeast, which extends from Bellingham in Washington State to Haines and Skagway, and Southcentral/

For details of ferry connections from Bellingham, WA, and through British Columbia, see pp.13–14.

Southwest, which covers Prince William Sound, the Kenai Peninsula, Kodiak Island, and the Aleutian chain. One ferry does make **"cross-gulf" trips** between Juneau and Valdez, but only twice a month in each direction in June, July, and August, and once in September. If you don't catch these, you'll have to fly or go by road through Canada to make the link.

Ferries tend to be in port for only a short time (1–3hr) and many of the Southeast ferry docks are inconveniently sited several miles from the heart of town making it difficult (if not impossible) to get a feel for the place without making **stopovers**. These should be planned in advance: you need to buy a series of journeys between your chosen ports of call rather than buying, say, Bellingham to Juneau and expecting to stop off where you feel like. If you have bought such a ticket and then decide to make extra stopovers, alterations can be made for a fee, which varies according to the changes. This will also affect your reservations, an important consideration in the busy summer months.

New and fast ferries

In 2004, AMHS began a modernization program through which it is gradually phasing in new catamaran-style **fast ferries**, which still carry vehicles but travel at roughly twice the speed of the vessels they replace. Towns previously limited to a sporadic and infrequent service will get regular contact with their neighbors, and visitors will gain flexibility when touring Southeast Alaska.

The first to be put into service is the *Fairweather* running between Juneau, Haines and Skagway with twice-weekly runs to Sitka. This will be joined in 2005 by its sister, the *Chenega*, making a regular circuit of Whittier, Valdez and Cordova. A year later, more new fast ferries are planned to be based in Juneau and Ketchikan.

The long-standing AMHS monopoly on ferries is also being broken. Prince of Wales Island now runs its own ferry service from Ketchikan (see p.79), operated by the island's own Inter-Island Ferry Authority.

Onboard facilities

Facilities on board depend on the vessel in question, though all carry vehicles and passengers. The new fast ferries have airline-style reclining seats, an external solarium, work/study areas, and a snack bar, but no cabins. After all, journeys are now much shorter.

The older ferries are more oriented towards leisurely cruising, all having coin-operated lockers for your valuables and somewhere to lay down a sleeping roll. All except the *LeConte* and *Aurora* have **cabins**, mostly with private bathrooms. If you can't afford a cabin on the longer journeys, obtaining a good place to sleep becomes critical, to the point that in Bellingham it can be a mad dash for the top-deck **solarium**, widely regarded as a prime spot for its fresh air, good views, and nighttime peace. Some people even erect their tent on the upper deck, making sure to secure it firmly against the stiff breeze when under way.

Lounges have reclining seats you can sleep in, and pillows and blankets can be rented for a modest fee on most sailings. Ferries have hot **showers** (either free or coin-operated), and some boats even have a **laundry** room. In addition, there are usually free educational programs run by interpreters from the Tongass National Forest, as well as films and Alaska videos.

The **meals** available in the ship's buffet-style restaurant are not gourmet affairs but are pretty good and reasonably priced by Alaskan standards. The larger boats also have a bar. You are welcome to lug aboard your own supplies to prepare snacks (they even provide free hot water – good for tea, coffee, and packet soups) but use of backpacking stoves is strictly prohibited.

Except for brief visits to attend to **pets**, passengers are not allowed on the vehicle deck when sailing, so sleeping in your RV is not on.

Timetables, reservations, and fares

When it comes to planning your travels it is imperative to get hold of up-to-date

Ferry fares

			Kodiak	Seldovia	Homer
			247	300	295
Ketchikan	201	50		67	63
Metlakatla	206	54	21		27
Wrangell	219	72	32	39	
Petersburg	235	82	50	54	27
Sitka	254	108	70	74	50
Juneau	275	132	90	99	72
Haines	297	150	113	121	90
Skagway	306	159	123	127	102
Tenakee	275	132	90	99	72
	Bellingham	**Pr. Rupert**	**Ketchikan**	**Metlakatla**	**Wrangell**

timetables, which change each year in line with predicted tidal variations. An official schedule for the May to September summer season is published early in the year: pick up a free brochure locally or download it from the AMHS website.

Foot passengers can almost always find a space on board, but during the summer months vehicle space and cabins can be fully booked. If you are traveling at this time, it is wise to make **reservations** as far in advance as possible. The AMHS website allows online booking, though if you have a complex itinerary it may work out quicker calling on the toll-free number, or sending in your requirements by fax or mail.

The website has a reservation form you can print out; or simply list the relevant details: the journeys required; number, names, and ages (if under 12) of those in the party; width, height, and overall length of any vehicles; a mailing address and phone number; alternate travel dates; and the date you plan to leave home. If full, ask to be put on a waitlist. Cabin waitlists exist for trips north from Bellingham, Juneau to Valdez, and west to the Aleutians; vehicles can only be waitlisted on the latter two. **Payment** is expected soon after your booking is confirmed and can be made using a major credit card, a certified or cashier's check, or a money order in US dollars.

In practice, foot passengers can often wend their way through Southeast without making any reservations by putting themselves on **standby** and paying for their ticket at the terminal. Once in Southeast you will find that mechanical breakdowns, tides, logistics, and, occasionally, industrial action can play havoc with the schedule. It always pays to **double-check departure times** with the nearest office to your port of call.

We've included 2004 passenger **fares** on the accompanying chart, but prices go up – check the AMHS website (see box, opposite) for the latest info. The total fee is arrived at by adding together the various components – passenger fares, cabins, vehicles, and so forth. **Round-trip** fares are double the single journey fare; **kids'** fares (2–11 inclusive) are half of the adult fare; and kids under 2 travel free. **Cabins** start with a two-berth cabin (0.8 times the adult fare) and range up to a large four-berth affair (1.4–1.7 times the adult fare). A small **car** (up to fifteen feet long) will cost twice the adult fare, something up to 21 feet will be three times, and a **bicycle** travels for one-sixth of the adult fare.

On cross-gulf trips, adult passengers travel from Juneau to Valdez for $114

Trains

Mention that you are traveling on the **Alaska Railroad** and Alaskans will usually mumble something about never having gotten around to riding it. This is largely because train travel in Alaska is something of a luxury, unless you're one of the few hundred people who live in the bush close to tracks and rely on the train for your access to town. Nonetheless, it is an experience cherished by the state's summer visitors, who make up the vast majority of the passengers, paying around twice the comparable bus fare.

There is just one passenger line, a 470-mile

Seward	Whittier	Valdez	Cordova	
303	383	355	355	**Unalaska**
70	148	123	123	**Kodiak**
125	204	174	174	**Seldovia**
121	199	170	170	**Homer**
		74	74	**Seward**
37		74	74	**Whittier**
55	37		41	**Valdez**
75	55	32		
84	65	42	26	
55	30	30	50	60
Petersburg	**Sitka**	**Juneau**	**Haines**	**Skagway**

run from the ice-free port of Seward to Fairbanks in the heart of the Interior, traversing two major mountain ranges, spanning deep chasms, and crossing mile after mile of spruce forests threaded by braided rivers and beaver-dammed streams. With steep mountain passes, discontinuous permafrost, ice floes during spring break-up, and the sheer remoteness of it all, construction difficulties seemed insurmountable, but by 1923 President Warren Harding was able to visit Alaska in time to drive the golden spike near Nenana.

Services along the line are both infrequent and slow, pretty much precluding their use as practical transport, but the stately pace and matchless scenery make the Alaska Railroad the most pleasurable way to get to the few places it does reach. Note though that fuel and **camping stoves** cannot be taken on trains, virtually ruling out train use for campers.

With so much of Alaska's tourist industry tied in to the major cruise and package companies it comes as no surprise to find that most trains are largely made up of luxurious, dedicated Princess and Holland America carriages. Independent travelers will find themselves getting jounced along in less salubrious cars; they're still very spacious, air-conditioned, and comfortable, but with high-back seats set so low you find yourself standing up to get a good view of the scenery. Of course, you can amble along to the upper-deck **observation car**, or hang out in the **dining car**, which sells good food at reasonable prices. Get there before the lunchtime rush, wait it out until much later, or bring your own tucker. The journey is accompanied by a running commentary complemented by a free route map.

Tickets can be bought in advance by mail, by phone, or online from Alaska Railroad Corporation, PO Box 107500, Anchorage, AK 99510-7500 (Ⓣ265-2494 or 1-800/544-

AMHS ferry contact numbers

When planning and reserving your ferry travel contact the Alaska Marine Highway System, 6858 Glacier Hwy, Juneau, AK 99801-7909 (Ⓣ907/465-3941 or 1-800/642-0066, Ⓕ 907/277-4829), or consult their website Ⓦwww.alaska.gov/ferry, which has schedule and fare information along with details of how to make reservations. Locally, call the numbers listed below:

Anchorage	Ⓣ272-7116
Bellingham, WA	Ⓣ360/676-8445
Cordova	Ⓣ424-7333
Haines	Ⓣ766-2113
Homer	Ⓣ235-8449
Juneau	Ⓣ465-3940
Ketchikan	Ⓣ225-6181
Kodiak	Ⓣ486-3800
Petersburg	Ⓣ772-3855
Prince Rupert, BC	Ⓣ250/627-1744
Seldovia	Ⓣ234-7868
Seward	Ⓣ224-5485
Sitka	Ⓣ747-3300
Skagway	Ⓣ983-2229
Valdez	Ⓣ835-4436
Wrangell	Ⓣ874-3711

0552; Ⓦ www.alaskarailroad.com), but seats are not allocated until just before you travel; arrive at the station half an hour early.

Alaska's only other train service is the **White Pass & Yukon Route** railway, an almost exclusively tourist-oriented service, which climbs the mountains behind Skagway as it follows a route used by Klondike gold seekers. It is covered in detail on p.182.

Anchorage to Denali and Fairbanks

North of Anchorage the train gradually shakes off the city and the towns of the Mat-Su Valley as it threads through spruce forests, which occasionally draw back to reveal grand vistas of the Alaska Range and Denali. Passengers are always spotting wildlife, and you'll probably see bears, moose, eagles, or at least the evidence of industrious beavers. North of Talkeetna, Denali appears increasingly monstrous, and as you climb towards the Alaska Range the trees thin out providing ever-longer views. You see almost nothing of Denali National Park itself from the train, but since almost everyone gets off here that's of little consequence.

Between Anchorage and Fairbanks the main train is the **Denali Star** (daily from mid-May to mid-Sept), which departs Anchorage at 8.15am, stopping at Wasilla (9.45am), Talkeetna (11.25am), and Denali Park (3.45pm), and arriving in Fairbanks at 8.15pm. In the opposite direction the daily service leaves Fairbanks at 8.15am and calls at Denali Park (noon), Talkeetna (4.40pm), Wasilla (6.05pm), and Anchorage (8.15pm). In addition, there is the **Local "Flagstop" Service** (mid-May to mid-Sept Thurs–Sun only), which only runs from Talkeetna (departing 12.15pm) 55 miles north to Hurricane and back (arriving 5.45pm). Designed around the needs of bush dwellers, who pull up in their canoes or off-road buggies next to the track and hang out a white sheet to get the train to stop, this is claimed to be the only such service left in the US. It mostly runs through pretty swampy country and so is of little use to hikers, though anglers benefit, and you could just go for the ride to get a taste of bush life. Two services run **in winter**. From Anchorage there's the **Aurora** (mid-Sept to mid-May), a flag-stop train – usually just two carriages and a luggage car with a very limited buffet service – running to Fairbanks on Saturday, returning to Anchorage on the Sunday. In addition, there's the **Hurricane** (Oct to early May first Thurs of the month only), which runs north from Anchorage to Hurricane then returns the same day. There are no other weekday trains.

Fares are one-way and depend on whether you travel during the peak season (early June to Aug) or the value season (mid-May to early June and the first two weeks in Sept). From Anchorage to Fairbanks the fares are $175 peak, $140 value. There are also section fares: Anchorage–Talkeetna ($78, $63); Anchorage–Denali ($125, $100); Talkeetna–Denali ($73, $59); Talkeetna–Fairbanks ($100, $80); and Denali–Fairbanks ($50, $40). Bikes, canoes, and kayaks can be carried on the train at a cost of $20 per trip. If these prices seem too steep, and the bus is beckoning, consider making the run from Talkeetna to Denali, the most spectacular section.

Anchorage to Seward

South from Anchorage, the line heads past the wildlife-viewing area of Potter Marsh along Turnagain Arm to Portage Junction, from where the Whittier Spur runs through a couple of tunnels to Whittier. The main line then continues through the Placer River valley into the Kenai Mountains, all plunging gorges overhung by massive glaciers – the Spencer, Bartlett, and Trail glaciers all come within a few hundred yards of the track – before following the broad Resurrection Valley to Seward.

The **Coastal Classic** (mid-May to mid-Sept daily) runs south from Anchorage leaving at 6.45am and arriving in Seward at 11.05am. The return service leaves Seward at 6pm arriving back in Anchorage at 10.25pm, giving day-trippers almost seven hours in Seward; the one-way **fare** is $59 (round-trip $98), and bikes cost $5.

A separate service, the **Glacier Discovery** (mid-May to early Sept daily), leaves Anchorage at 10am for Whittier arriving at

12.20am. The return service leaves Whittier at 6.45pm and gets into Anchorage at 9.15pm. The fare is $49 one-way, $59 round-trip, and $5 for bikes. There are no services south of Anchorage in winter.

Buses

There are **no winter buses**, but from early May to mid-September most of the blacktop roads in Southcentral and Interior Alaska have scheduled **bus services**. In most cases there is only one bus a day in each direction (if that), making bus travel possible but not very flexible. The main exception is the 360-mile run from Anchorage to Denali National Park, which is plied by several buses each day. Companies have been notoriously short-lived, but even with the increased stability in recent years it still pays to check who is operating and pick up the relevant timetables from visitor centers when you reach Alaska. Detailed coverage of routes, frequency, and journey times is given in **"travel details"** at the end of each chapter. Bus stops (usually visitor centers, major hotels, and hostels) are noted in town accounts.

Almost all companies run minibuses seating 20–30 passengers. Along the Anchorage–Denali–Fairbanks route competition keeps fares low, with companies more or less in line with one another. Nonetheless, it is worth shopping around as there are bargains to be had, and some companies' timetables will be more suitable than others. **Expect to pay** $80 between Anchorage and Fairbanks, $40 from Fairbanks to Denali, $50 from Anchorage to Denali, $90 from Fairbanks to Valdez, $155 from Fairbanks to Dawson City, Yukon, $40 from Anchorage to Seward, and $50 from Anchorage to Homer. **Round-trip** rates are usually twice the one-way fare, though there are sometimes small savings to be made.

Bus companies and their routes

Alaska Direct Bus Line ⓣ1-800/770-6652, in Anchorage ⓣ277-6652, ⓦwww.tokalaska.com/dirctbus.shtml, ⓔakdirectbus@msn.com. One service (mid-May to Sept, 3 days a week) from Anchorage to Whitehorse via Palmer, Glennallen, and Tok. At Haines Junction you can transfer onto a bus to Haines. There is a service from Fairbanks that meets the Whitehorse-bound bus at Tok, and a further bus that connects Whitehorse to Skagway.

Alaska Park Connection ⓣ245-0200 or 1-800/266-8625, ⓦwww.alaskacoach.com. A daily run in each direction (mid-May to mid-Sept) connecting Seward, Anchorage, Talkeetna township, and Denali; a daily run from Anchorage to Seward and back (mid-May to mid-Sept); and an express run from Anchorage to Denali and back (June to early Sept).

Alaska Trails & Tours ⓣ1-888/600-6001, ⓦwww.alaskashuttle.com. Fairbanks-based service with daily runs along the Parks Highway between Fairbanks and Anchorage (mid-May to late Sept); a daily extension south from Anchorage to Seward (late May to mid-Sept); and a thrice-weekly service between Fairbanks and Dawson City, Yukon, via Tok and Chicken (Wed, Fri & Sun westbound; Tues, Thurs & Sat eastbound). There is also a reservation-only service from Fairbanks through Delta Junction and Glennallen to Valdez.

Homer Stage Line Anchorage ⓣ868-3914, Homer ⓣ235-2252, Soldotna ⓣ262-4584, ⓦwww.homerstageline.com. Homer to Anchorage in the morning and back again that afternoon (June–Aug daily, May & Sept Mon, Wed & Fri, Oct–April Mon & Thurs to Anchorage, Tues & Fri to Homer); plus Homer to Seward and back again in the afternoon (mid-May to mid-Sept Mon–Fri).

The Magic Bus ⓣ441-8420, ⓦwww.themagicbus.com. A daily run to Girdwood leaving the visitor center at 4.30pm.

Seward Bus Line Seward ⓣ224-3608, Anchorage ⓣ563-0800, ⓦwww.sewardbuslines.com. One daily run from Seward to Anchorage, returning the same afternoon.

Talkeetna Shuttle Service ⓣ733-1725 or 1-888/288-6008. Door-to-door service between Anchorage and Talkeetna, once daily in summer and more frequently during the mid-April to mid-June mountaineering season.

Driving

Whether you make the epic journey up the Alaska Highway, or simply rent a vehicle on arrival, **driving** is the best way to explore Southcentral, the Interior and parts of the North. You can get to places well beyond the reach of public transport, set your own timetable, and access points of interest in the larger towns much more easily. Anchorage and Fairbanks, in particular, have grown up since the invention of the car and are based on the understanding that everyone has one. With the exception of Denali, national and state parks are very poorly served by public transport. What's more, two or more people traveling together and renting a car can save a fair bit of money by staying in cheaper but less central accommodation, or camping out pretty much anywhere.

Road conditions (ⓣ456-7623 or ⓦwww.dot.state.ak.us) vary enormously, from six-lane freeways in Anchorage and Fairbanks to remote gravel roads with a hundred miles between settlements. If you come in summer and stick to the paved highways, you'll encounter no more difficulty than driving at home. Stray onto dirt roads and you need to slow down and take some precautions. **Snow** is possible in any month of the year, especially on a couple of high passes, and winter really starts showing its face by the end of September. If in doubt, don't travel. If you must, then take it slow and be sure you have survival gear in case of an accident or breakdown. In winter many of the gravel highways are impassable, but the asphalt roads are kept open year-round.

Though distances are great, **gas** is still relatively cheap. It is about the same as in the Lower 48 and way cheaper than in Europe. Basic unleaded (fine for most rental vehicles) is currently around $1.70 a US gallon (which is equivalent to 3.8 liters) in Anchorage and Fairbanks, $2 further out, and over $2.50 in remote spots. At most gas stations you can use your credit card to pay at the pump, even if it is unattended.

Renting a car

Renting a car in Alaska is not cheap, but for two or more people traveling together it can work out to be good value, particularly if you rent in Anchorage where competition keeps rates down. That said, you can rent a car in almost any small town; this can be handy if you are normally using public transport but need to get somewhere otherwise inaccessible – the hot springs around Fairbanks, for example.

Through most of the summer it is important to **reserve well in advance**: a month

Tips for foreign drivers

In most cases, a **driver's license** from your home country is valid in the United States: check with a national motoring organization if you have any doubt. Road rules are similar to those in the UK or Australasia except that you drive on the right; if you've just come off a long flight, consider waiting a day or so before driving. **Seatbelts** are compulsory for all passengers. In urban areas the **speed limit** is usually 35–45mph; on the open road 55mph is common and sections of the George Parks Highway from Anchorage to Fairbanks, and the Seward Highway south of Anchorage, allow you to belt along at 65mph. If the **police** flag you down, don't get out of the car or start searching for your license; simply sit with your hands on the wheel; when questioned, be polite and don't attempt to make jokes. Of course, **driving while intoxicated** (DWI) is a very serious offense, and if you are carrying any alcohol it should be kept unopened in the trunk.

A couple of things may be new to you. At intersections you can turn **right on red** lights, provided there is no traffic coming from the left and only after coming to a stop. Stopping is also compulsory, in both directions, when you come upon a **school bus** with its lights flashing, disgorging passengers. Driving with **headlights on** during daytime is only required along the Seward Highway between Anchorage and Seward, but because reflections off water and the long shadows cast by the eternal low sun make vehicles less visible, many people now light up as a matter of course once out of town.

Foreign drivers who are members of motoring organizations may find they can get reciprocal membership at the **American Automobile Association** (AAA; main AK office: 9191 Old Seward Highway #20, Anchorage 99515; ⓣ344-4310 or 1-888/391-4222, ⓦwww.aaa-mountainwest.com), which offers maps and guides to international affiliate members who present their valid membership card.

should be enough. Arrive in June without a reservation and you'll be lucky to find anything, and even if you find a vehicle most agencies charge more for walk-ins. Plan to drop off your rental where you picked it up: few places allow one-way rentals, and those that do charge high **relocation fees** amounting to around $200 between Anchorage and Fairbanks, and more like $400 between Anchorage and either Haines or Skagway. Some companies don't allow you to go into **Canada**, so make sure you are clear on this point when you make your reservation. Note that Canadians are not allowed to drive a US rental car into Canada.

The other major consideration is whether you will want to drive on **gravel roads**. Most agencies refuse to insure or provide logistical back-up once you stray from the paved highways, and yet seeing many of Alaska's finest features requires travel along just such roads: the road to McCarthy in the Wrangell-St Elias National Park, the Taylor Highway to Chicken and Eagle, the Elliott Highway to Manley Hot Springs, and the Denali Highway along the southern side of the Alaska Range.

There are a number of ways around this, and the best is to rent a car from Affordable Rentals (listed in our Anchorage and Fairbanks accounts) or a camper from GoNorth in Fairbanks (see p.468), which rent almost-new cars at affordable prices and allow them to be used (and insured) on all roads except the Dalton Highway north of the Yukon River and the Top of the World Highway from Chicken to Dawson City in the Canadian Yukon. A second alternative is to simply ignore the rental company's rules. This is a common enough practice, but remember that even if you have insurance independent of the rental agency, the fact that you are breaking the rental agreement by driving off the paved highways is likely to invalidate your insurance. Consider, too, that no one is going to organize a mechanic for you, so if you get in trouble you may have to stump up for large towing bills. The last option is to **rent a 4WD**, some of which can be insured for gravel roads. The downside here is that you'll be paying at least twice the daily rate of an ordinary compact (say, $100–130 a day).

Car-rental agencies fall into two main groups. The **majors** – Avis, Budget, Dollar, Hertz, National, Payless and Thrifty – all rent new compacts for around $55–65 a day in summer with unlimited mileage. **Local companies** are usually about $5–10 a day cheaper in return for slightly (sometimes substantially) older vehicles and a poorer back-up network. We've listed the best of these at the end of major town accounts (especially Anchorage on p.226 and Fairbanks on p.474), and you'll find more in the local *Yellow Pages*. Many companies offer **weekly rates**, though in peak season the savings are small. Rental companies advertise prices exclusive of **local taxes**, which have risen considerably recently. Expect to have 10–20 percent added to listed prices (29 percent at Anchorage airport).

Insurance may raise your car rental fees further. If you have your own vehicle insurance at home, it is worth checking if it provides any coverage for rentals (either with or without some extension fee). There are no hard-and-fast rules, but most US policies will cover you in Alaska. It's also worth checking to see if your credit card provides any cover. Quite likely you will find yourself faced with a collision damage waiver (CDW, sometimes called Liability Damage Waiver), a form of insurance that's well worth considering as it covers you for damage to the vehicle you are driving. It may cost you $12–30 a day (normally around $16) but otherwise you are liable for every scratch to the car – even those that aren't your fault. Often CDW comes with several levels of cover, the cheaper ones leaving you liable for, say, the first $1000–2000 of any claim, while the more expensive policies cover you for everything. Always make sure you understand the fine print.

You'll need to be 20 or over to rent a vehicle, and many places won't rent you a vehicle if you're under 25. Even if they do, you will have to pay an additional $5–10 a day.

Car-rental companies

Alamo ⓣ1-800/462-5266, ⓦwww.alamo.com.
Avis ⓣ1-800/230-4898, ⓦwww.avis.com.
Budget ⓣ1-800/527-0700, ⓦwww.budgetrentacar.com.
Dollar ⓣ1-800/800-4000, ⓦwww.dollar.com.
Enterprise ⓣ1-800/736-8222, ⓦwww.enterprise.com.

Hertz ⓣ1-800/654-3131, ⓦwww.hertz.com.
National ⓣ1-800/227-7368, ⓦwww.nationalcar.com.
Payless ⓣ1-800/729-5377, ⓦwww.paylesscarrental.com.
Rent-A-Wreck ⓣ1-800/944-7501, ⓦwww.rent-a-wreck.com.
Thrifty ⓣ1-800/367-2277, ⓦwww.thrifty.com.

Renting an RV

In summer Alaskan roads and campgrounds are thick with **RVs** (recreational vehicles or motorhomes). Most have been driven up the Alaska Highway or transported by ferry up the Inside Passage, but many more are rented in Alaska (principally Anchorage) from one of around a dozen agencies. Deciding to rent an RV isn't something to be undertaken lightly: summer rental rates (based on a minimum one-week rental period) start at around $130 a day for a model that's comfortable for two – and on top of that you may have mileage charges, insurance, and a lot of gas (some RVs achieve under ten miles per gallon). Unless you've lugged half your kitchen with you then there may also be a fee for a "housekeeping" kit of pans, plates, bedding, and towels.

All this is offset, of course, by the reduction in accommodation costs. Instead of $70–100 a night in a motel you can get away with $20–30 a night for a full hookup in a campground, or nothing at all parked by the side of the road. Some RV-rental companies even offer a free pass for camping in state parks and selected commercial campgrounds around Alaska.

Motorhomes come in several sizes, some lumbering behemoths that are the curse of everyone else on the road, others relatively nimble though obviously less spacious. Generally, the smallest offered is the camperhome (roughly $130–180), essentially an eighteen-foot flat-deck truck with a camper strapped onto the back. These sleep two reasonably comfortably (and perhaps one child) and have a toilet and cooking stove but not much room to move. A compact ($140–200) measures around 21 feet and sleeps two adults and two kids in some comfort. The 23-foot **standard models** ($150–215) are more spacious, with a higher level of fittings and appliances. Two (or even three) couples traveling together might prefer a 26-foot intermediate ($180–230) or 30-foot large ($200–240) model. The prices quoted above are for summer high season; rates drop by twenty to thirty percent in May and September, and are reduced a little further in winter. You'll pay around ten percent more if your rental is for less than a week. AAA and AARP members (American Association of Retired People; ⓦwww.aarp.org) typically get a five percent discount.

Some companies charge premium all-in rates, while others cut corners on their basic rates but add assorted extra charges – it is always worth asking. You might find you get fifty or a hundred **free miles** (especially during shoulder season) but most likely you'll pay 15–20¢ a mile. **Insurance** is often included, but there may be a $1500 deductible on accidents; a collision damage waiver ($12–15 a day) will reduce this to a couple of hundred dollars or less. A housekeeping kit might be a few dollars a day or just a $100 flat fee; TVs, deck chairs, fishing rods, and bike racks may be included or extra; and 24-hour roadside assistance may be included.

As with cars, you'll need to make **reservations** early (three months ahead isn't ridiculous at peak times), but once you've got your RV you've usually got access to most highways, including trips into Canada. **One-way rentals** are not usually worthwhile, though some companies will let you pick up or drop off a vehicle in Fairbanks for a $750 fee, or Skagway for $1200. If you are headed north in May, it is worth calling around for a delivery run (try ABC to start with); you may be able to drive a new RV from the Lower 48 at around seventy percent of the normal rate. The **minimum age** for drivers varies from 21 to 25.

If you are bringing your own RV to Alaska but don't want to drive both ways, consider shipping your rig (see p.12).

Most of the companies listed below are based in Anchorage, and all offer airport transfer.

RV rental companies

ABC Motorhome & Car Rentals 3875 W Old International Airport Rd ⓣ279-2000 or 1-800/421-7456, ⓦwww.abcmotorhome.com. Large company renting late-model RVs with everything included except your gas. Rates start at $180 a day for an upscale camper with shower and toilet and range to $200 for a compact, $215 for a standard, and $230 for an intermediate model.

Alaska Motorhome Rentals ⓣ1-800/254-9929, ⓦwww.alaskarv.com. Smaller company offering compact models for $165, intermediate RVs for $185, and one-way Skagway drop-offs.

Alaska Panorama RV Rentals 712 W Potter Drive ⓣ562-1401 or 1-800/478-1401, ⓦwww.alaskapanorama.com. Family-run RV-rental business, which along with late-model rentals has slightly older models: compacts for $120 a day plus 10¢ a mile, standards at $135, intermediate models costing $145, and large motorhomes for $155–180 a day.

Alexander's RV Rental 212 E 51st Ave ⓣ563-5115 or 1-888/660-5115, ⓦwww.anc-biz.com/alexandersrv. Smallish company offering new motorhomes with good shoulder-season discounts. Standard models from $130, intermediate $140, and huge 34-foot beasts for $170 a day. All charged at an additional 17¢ a mile.

Cruise America 8850 Runamuck Pl ⓣ349-0499 or 1-800/RV4RENT, ⓦwww.cruiseamerica.com. One of the biggest operators in the business with a huge range of vehicles at relatively high prices.

Great Alaskan Holidays 3901 W International Airport Rd ⓣ248-7777 or 1-888/225-2752, ⓦwww.greatalaskanholidays.com. Major player offering rigs with all the extras included. Rates can be unlimited mileage (compact $185, large $210) or charged at 17¢ a mile ($155/$185).

Cycle touring

We've covered recreational mountain biking elsewhere in this book (see p.60), but it is also feasible to get around Alaska by **bicycle**. It can be a wonderful experience, with plenty of time to savor the stunning scenery, long summer days, and relatively cool temperatures. It can also be a major slog, but this largely depends on where you go and how ambitious your plans are. Southeast Alaska is especially well suited for touring since you can take your bicycle on the **ferries** and then more easily explore the few miles of road around each port of call. You have to be a bit more dedicated to cycle in the Interior where distances between points of interest are great and (once you get off the main highways) the surfaces can be rough. In compensation, major road construction projects must include **bike paths**, so increasingly long sections exist beside main highways.

Where public transport exists, you can usually take your bike on the **bus** (around $10 per trip) or **train** ($5–20 per journey), which means you don't need to pedal every mile just to get to the good bits. With so many gravel roads, fat-tired mountain bikes are the machines of choice. You may never go off-road, but you'll appreciate good suspension and a forgiving geometry on prime cycle touring routes like those listed in our favorites box (see p.46) and on long gravel highways, such as the Steese and Elliott highways around Fairbanks, the Taylor Highway up to Eagle on the Yukon River and even the Dalton Highway to Prudhoe Bay – lengthy and esoteric but possible.

If you are sticking entirely to **paved roads**, you'll do better either on a touring bike or with narrower tires fitted to your ATB. Of the paved road routes, the Kenai Peninsula is probably the most rewarding, with wonderful scenery, challenging terrain, and relatively short distances between towns. For something longer, try the route from Anchorage to Valdez (with a possible side trip to McCarthy) followed by a ferry to Whittier, Seward, or Homer and some time on the Kenai. The George Parks Highway from Anchorage to Fairbanks is perhaps the busiest and least appealing of the main routes, though you can skip sections by riding a bus or train.

Bikes can be rented in larger towns ($20–30 a day) but for touring it is better to bring your own bike. Most international airlines will carry bicycles either free or for a small charge. Some companies will only ask you to remove the pedals, deflate the tires, lower the saddle and turn the handlebars ninety degrees; others will demand you break it down to fit into a cardboard bike delivery box (usually available free from your friendly local bike dealer); ask before you fly. If planning numerous flights around Alaska with your bike it is worth considering that Alaska Airlines is not bike-friendly, insisting on the box approach and charging US$50 per bike for each day you fly.

To be fully prepared you should be kitted out for rain in the coastal areas, cold in the Interior and bugs whenever you stop. **Spare**

Rough Guide favorites: cycle touring routes

- Copper River Highway p.309
- Denali Highway p.399
- Denali Park Road p.382
- Hatcher Pass p.364
- McCarthy Road p.414
- Prince of Wales Island p.98
- Top of the World Highway p.437

parts are thin on the ground outside Anchorage and Fairbanks, so be sure to carry anything you might reasonably need – tubes, cables, spokes, and the like. One thing you probably won't need if you are here in the middle of summer is lights; it barely ever gets dark.

For more detailed information consult the *Alaska Bicycle Touring Guide* by Pete Praetorius and Alys Culhane (Denali Press) and Richard Larson's *Mountain Bike Alaska* (Glacier House).

Hitching

Among hitchhikers Alaska enjoys a reputation for relative safety that seems completely out of step with the scaremongering in the rest of the US. **Don't hitch** remains the official advice, but with Alaska's skeletal public transport network many choose to do so anyway, if only to get back to their car at the end of a long hike. While Alaskan drivers are generally well disposed to picking up hitchers, there aren't many of them, and along gravel roads (where hitching is more common) you could wait hours without seeing anyone. In high summer, though, prospects are decidedly more rosy.

Sadly, Alaska has its share of unpleasant individuals, so always travel in pairs (no guarantee of avoiding trouble but safer than going solo). **Women**, especially, should trust their instincts. It is better to refuse a lift than regret it later; there will always be another vehicle at some point. Always ask the driver where they are going, rather than telling them where you are headed, and keep your gear with you so you can make a quick getaway if it becomes necessary. Remember, too, that even the most helpful driver may drop you in the middle of nowhere with the weather deteriorating. You should really be fully equipped for a night out by the roadside or make sure you can be dropped somewhere you can seek food and shelter.

Finding a good **hitching spot** is usually just a matter of walking towards the edge of town and using your common sense: pick a spot where you can be clearly seen and drivers can stop safely. If you don't mind advertising where you are bound, then making a destination sign can be a good idea, but with so few roads it is usually pretty obvious where you are going.

Accommodation

At its best accommodation in Alaska is warm, welcoming, and comes with a superb view and maybe even a moose or bear strolling past your bedroom window. Unfortunately, it is usually expensive for what you get, and high demand, especially in July and August, allows hotels to ratchet the rates up even higher. If money is tight, the cost can be offset to some degree by nights spent in one of the increasing number of hostels or a US Forest Service cabin. Camping, too, is a big money saver, and nowhere near as cold as you might expect, especially in the middle of summer when you've got close to 24-hour daylight.

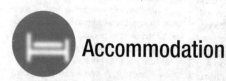

Roadhouses, hotels, and motels

The backbone of Alaska's accommodation was traditionally made up of **roadhouses** – all-in-one hotel, bar, restaurant, and stable establishments, which cropped up a day's hike (or sled ride) apart along the trails. Most have gone the way of the miners and mail carriers who frequented them, but a few still fly the flag in rural areas, typically offering warped floors, shaky beds, thin walls, a bathroom down the hall, and bags of character. Several have been taken over by proprietors who really care about the tradition and go to some lengths to provide good hearty food and a convivial lounge centered on a wood-burning stove. After campgrounds and hostels, these are often the cheapest places to stay, at around $70–90 per room.

As communities consolidated in the fledgling territory, the roadhouses were replaced by **hotels**. A few originals exist in the larger towns, but these days the market is dominated by faceless corporate chains aimed squarely at businesspeople and package tourists. Standards are as high as you would expect, but the prices are higher, at least in the peak summer months when you won't get a room in a top-line hotel in Anchorage for under $200, sometimes $250. Off-season, and especially on winter weekends, such places are almost empty and prices drop dramatically: haggle a bit, and you might find yourself with a tremendous bargain.

Almost invariably, though, you are better off in a **motel**. These tend to string out along approach roads into urban areas, but since most towns are pretty small this isn't much of an inconvenience. A few belong to nationwide chains, but, most are independently run places, and standards vary little. All offer private bathrooms, cable TV, and phone (often with free local calls, the more upmarket places having phone jacks for Internet connection) for $70–110 a room. A coffee pot and in-room microwave are common, and many motels have at least some rooms with a kitchenette. Pay a little more, and everything will be newer, larger, and you may possibly have a hot tub, but if you've got this sort of money then there is usually somewhere nicer to stay.

B&Bs

The **bed and breakfast** (B&B) phenomenon is a relative newcomer to Alaska, but it has quickly established a foothold. All over the state homeowners are throwing open a couple of rooms to guests throughout the summer, while others are following the Californian tradition and fashioning their places as boutique inns with every imaginable luxury. Some, recognizing a desire for privacy, offer a separate entrance so you don't feel like you're invading the family home.

If a tent or a hostel bunk is not for you, B&Bs may be the best bet, as they're usually cheaper than a hotel or motel and come with a high degree of personal attention. The host may well be your best introduction to the

Accommodation price codes

Accommodation listed in this book has been price-coded using the symbols below. The rates quoted represent the **cheapest** double or twin **room** in high season. Single rooms generally cost only 10 to 20 percent less. Fees for **tent sites** and cabins are quoted and are for the site or cabin unless otherwise stated. **Hostel** bed prices are also quoted. Most towns in Alaska impose some kind of local or bed tax, usually between 4 and 12 percent. We've included these taxes in our calculation of the price codes, but it is worth remembering that locally quoted prices will be exclusive of these taxes.

In **winter** you can generally expect prices to drop by one (or possibly two) price codes except for hostels and campgrounds, which generally don't vary.

❶ up to $50
❷ $50–65
❸ $65–80
❹ $80–100
❺ $100–130
❻ $130–160
❼ $160–200
❽ $200–250
❾ $250 and over

region, either helping plan your travels or just clueing you in to more about the state and its strange ways. What's more, there's always a substantial breakfast that may well keep you going past lunchtime. Summer room **rates** start around $80 (with genuinely swanky places charging perhaps $120–150), although there is occasionally a small supplement for stays of only one night. In winter many places close, but those that stay open might drop their rates by around thirty percent.

As ever, it is usually advisable to **book a few days ahead** (weeks if you want one particular B&B), though if you'd rather remain flexible you can get help from visitor centers, which often call around the local area on the day and know what's available.

Throughout the Guide section of this book, we've selected some of the best B&Bs across a range of prices. In larger towns there are dozens of others, however, and if you are planning ahead, it is worth spending a little time browsing some of the B&B websites, which usually have links to the homepages of various establishments and a provision for making reservations. Good starting points are ⓦwww.bbonline.com/ak, ⓦwww.bedandbreakfast.com/USA/Alaska, and ⓦwww.innsite.com/browse-AK.html.

Hostels

For a roof over your head at minimal cost, **hostels** are your only viable option. With dorm beds starting at as little as $10 ($18–22 is more normal) and some establishments offering basic double rooms for under $50, you can't go wrong. The trouble is hostels are thin on the ground: although Anchorage and Fairbanks are reasonably well supplied and several smaller towns have a hostel, in many regions you can go for hundreds of miles without finding one.

Basically, Alaskan hostels come in two flavors. The only established network is the nationwide **HI-USA** (abbreviated to HI in listings: 8401 Colesville Rd, Suite 600, Silver Spring MD 20910 ⓣ301/495-1240, ⓕ495-6697, ⓦwww.hiusa.org) which has international affiliation in most countries. There are currently four HI hostels around the state – Anchorage, Ketchikan, Ninilchik (on the Kenai Peninsula), and Sitka. Most are very simple and each has its own distinct character and rules. Most Alaskan hostels are still closed during the day (usually 10am to 5pm), maintain a curfew (typically 11pm), have separate men's and women's dorms, and expect you to do a small morning chore. You'll usually be allowed to use your own sleeping bag, though a few places insist on **sheets**, which can be rented at the hostel. No Alaskan hostels currently offer meals, but all provide **cooking facilities**. Alcohol, smoking, and, of course, drugs are banned.

Non-members can stay at hostels by paying $3 per night over the normal rate, but you can often save money by becoming a member. US residents can get **membership** (free to those 17 and under, $28 for adults and $18 for those 55 and over) at any hostel, through their website, or by calling, faxing, or mailing the national office (see above). There's a downloadable form on the website. International visitors should join in their home country (visit ⓦwww.hihostels.com for contact details).

If you are traveling in the high season, it pays to **reserve ahead** directly with the hostel concerned. The credit-card reservation service in place at some other US hostels is not currently used in Alaska, and remember that most hostels are small operations, so you'll probably have to pay in cash. The annual *Discover America* hostel directory lists over 100 hostels and is free to members or available ($3) direct from the national office or through the website.

The number of **independent hostels** is increasing by the year, as people start turning part of their homes into dormitory accommodation. The very short tourist season all but rules out dedicated hostels, so their character and quality is more dependent on the owner (it can go either way), and the restrictions are often looser with similarly varied effects. In general, though, the standard is high. They're mostly run along the same lines as HI places, but sleeping bags are more likely to be acceptable, some places provide sheets as a matter of course, and others are closely associated with local tour and activity companies, which often offer discounts to guests. No membership is required at independent hostels, just front up (reserving by phoning ahead at busy times) and sign in.

Campgrounds

It is quite possible to see most of Alaska without ever going near a campground, but spending nights out of doors is so much part of the Alaskan experience that it seems unsporting to spend every night in comfort. Although you may plan on sticking to more rigid forms of shelter, it is still worth bringing a tent: it's the only way you can begin to feel in tune with all that wilderness, and besides, the high price of everything else might just force your hand.

All you need to know for **backcountry camping** – including tent selection – is covered in our "Outdoor activities" section (see p.55). Even if you're not about to go trudging off across the tundra, you can still spend time in some wonderful campgrounds strung along the highway system. At its most basic, camping involves wandering off the roadside and setting up camp: no one is likely to bother you if you stay just one night. In practice, this isn't as easy as it sounds, with much of the accessible landscape being unsuitable, either too heavily wooded, or too boggy. You'll occasionally come across free campgrounds, with a pit toilet and nearby river water (which needs to be treated), but most campgrounds cost between $6 and $12 per site and comprise a spacious area divided into campsites often separated by trees, picnic tables, fire rings, a hand pump for drawing water, and an outhouse. This isn't usually the traditional wooden shack over a hole, but a concrete structure cleverly designed to minimize odors. You'll soon get used to them – you'll have to.

A few campgrounds have peaceful **walk-in sites**, where you must leave your vehicle a few yards away. Most places, however, have car parking next to the site. During the three months of summer, many of the more popular places have a campground host, who will come round and check you've paid your fees – though sometimes you just drop the money in an "iron ranger," a metal post with a slot in it. The fee is usually per site, typically allowing up to two vehicles and as many as ten or a dozen people, but sometimes (and we've indicated where throughout the book) the price is per vehicle.

The more spacious campgrounds have sites capacious enough to cope with all but the largest **RVs** and offer "dry parking," just a place to park with water and toilets accessible nearby. From there you step up to private campgrounds with proper shower and toilet blocks and varying degrees of connectedness: electrical hookup, then piped water, and finally full hookup with wastewater pipe and even cable TV and a modem jack. Tenters will normally pay $15–18 in such places, with full hookup going for $25–30.

Cabins

A tent undoubtedly gives you maximum flexibility in the wilderness, but sometimes you can spare yourself lugging the thing around by staying in **public-use cabins**. They're not intended to be used for a sequence of overnight stops, but rather as a short-term base, with users flying or boating in, then exploring the area on foot or by canoe, with an arrangement to be picked up several days later: a true wilderness experience without much struggle.

Several land-management authorities operate cabins, but the **US Forest Service** (USFS) leads the pack, maintaining over 200 throughout the Southeastern panhandle (in the Tongass National Forest) and Southcentral Alaska (in the Chugach National Forest). Usually, the cabins are in scenic or remote spots, sometimes beside a trail, but frequently only accessible by float plane or boat. Ketchikan, Petersburg, Sitka, Juneau, Cordova, and Seward are the closest access points to the majority of cabins, several of which are listed in the text. A full rundown of cabins, their features, access, and availability can be found on the Internet (see box, p.50) or through the various USFS ranger district offices, which we've listed in the text for each town.

Cabins ($25–45 per night) tend to be clean but fairly primitive, typically sleeping four to six on wooden bunks and coming equipped with a wood-burning stove for heating. There'll be an outhouse, water nearby that needs treating, and possibly a canoe or rowboat. You need to bring everything you'd need for camping except a tent. The cabins are very popular with Alaskans, and many are in great demand during hunting and fishing seasons. Nonetheless, with some flexibility and a willingness to visit the less popular areas, you can usually find something pretty amazing, especially midweek.

Wilderness lodges

Throughout this book you'll often read of incomprehensibly large pieces of wilderness without so much as a managed trail. It is all true except for the presence of dozens of **wilderness lodges** built on the dream of a charmed life in the Alaskan backcountry. The great majority cater to the rod-and-gun set, who hunt and fish in barely charted territory but stay in beautifully sited lodges or in cabins around a central lodge where gourmet meals and wines are served. Access is usually by float plane, and you might typically expect to stay 3–7 days, often on a package with everything thrown in, including fishing guides and daily flights to remote rivers. Of course, all this pampering comes at a price, which can be anywhere from $200 to $800 per person per day, with many places offering three-day packages in the $1200–2500

Reserving campsites and cabins on public land

With so many authorities managing public lands in Alaska, booking cabins and campsites can be a confusing business. To simplify the task, we've listed the main players below. All agencies that manage cabins on public lands throughout the state can be accessed from the APLIC website at Ⓦwww.nps.gov/aplic/cabins.

Campgrounds

Bureau of Land Management All campgrounds on BLM land are first-come, first-served; there is no booking system.

Denali National Park See "Reserving in advance" box on p.381.

National Forests There are a handful of campgrounds in the Chugach and Tongass national forests that can be booked through the National Recreation Reservation Service (see cabins information below).

State Parks and **State Recreation Areas** There is no reservation system for campgrounds in state parks; all are first-come, first-served.

Cabins

Bureau of Land Management The BLM's ten public cabins ($25 per night on weekends, $20 during the week) in the White Mountains north of Fairbanks can be booked up to 30 days in advance by phone (Ⓣ472-2251 or 1-800/437-7021); credit cards are accepted. Alternatively, write or turn up in person at BLM Public Room, 1150 University Ave, Fairbanks, AK 99709. Stays are limited to three consecutive nights. Information about the cabins can be found at the White Mountains website (Ⓦwww.aurora.ak.blm.gov/WhiteMtns).

National Forests Chugach and Tongass. Roughly 200 cabins ($25–45 a night, mostly $35 in summer, $25 in the off-season) can be booked using a credit card up to 180 days in advance through the National Recreation Reservation Service by phone on Ⓣ1-877/444-6777 or 518/885-3639 (daily: April–Aug 8am–midnight, Sept–March 10am–7pm EST) and on the Net at Ⓦwww.ReserveUSA.com. The website also has some details about the cabins.

State Parks and **State Recreation Areas** Around forty recreational cabins all over the state, sleeping three to eight people and charged at $25–65 a night (mostly $35) plus a $5 reservation fee. The state parks website (Ⓦwww.alaskastateparks.org) has stacks of information on location, facilities, and cost, though you can't make reservations. There are no phone reservations either, so to make a booking (up to 180 days in advance) go in person or write to one of the Department of Natural Resources offices, such as DNR, 550 W 7th Ave, Suite 1260, Anchorage, AK 99501-3557 (Ⓣ269-8400). Booking forms can be printed out from the website, payment should be by money order made out to "State of Alaska," and there's a maximum stay of between three and seven days.

range, and seven-day packages for around twice that. We've listed a few in the appropriate sections of the Guide, but if you are especially interested in this kind of experience then get on the Internet and look at sites such as ⓦwww.theoutpostmall.com/alaska.htm and ⓦwww.alaskafishing.com, which have links to dozens of such places.

A few lodges wear the **ecotourism** badge, though many of these turn out to be fishing lodges by another name. For guidance here, seek out the assistance of the Alaska Wilderness Recreation and Tourism Association, 2207 Spenard Rd, Suite 201, Anchorage, AK 99503 (ⓣ258-3171, ⓦwww.awrta.org).

Food and drink

Salmon, halibut, and king crab, lightly cooked, simply dressed, and served within hours of being hauled from cold Alaskan waters is a culinary highlight worth traveling for. Catch it yourself, and the pleasure is doubled. After that things go downhill pretty rapidly, and in many parts of Alaska it seems like there is only one menu endlessly recycled, with the prices getting higher the further away you get from the transport lines. You'd better like burgers, sandwiches, pizza, and clam chowder.

There is no hiding it: food in Alaska is expensive. The growing season is short but intense, and despite the high latitude people do manage to grow **huge vegetables**. The trouble is, few can grow things reliably enough to suit the wholesalers, so most of what you (and the restaurants) buy comes direct from Seattle either by barge up the Inside Passage, or by air freight. This adds to **costs** that are already inflated because of high wages. Additionally, the range is often limited; most Alaskan communities are small – even large dots on the map might only represent a thousand people – and can't support establishments that cater to anything other than the mainstream demands. Still, for short visits the selection is varied enough, and at its best the quality can be outstanding.

Alaskan specialties

Alaska doesn't have a distinctive cooking style, but its cuisine stands apart in its use of local ingredients. The treat is tucking into an abundance of **fresh seafood** plucked from the waters around the coast or hauled out of the super-rich rivers inland. Mention Alaska and thoughts quickly turn to **salmon**. The five species of Pacific salmon (see p.543 in Contexts for further discussion of salmon) have been canned around the Alaskan coast in vast quantities for over a century and shipped all around the world. As salmon stocks have declined, so has the number of canneries, though a few still exist at remote locations. Most salmon is now vacuum-packed for export or frozen ready for delivery to restaurants, the main exception being the **Copper River kings**, the early-season catch (at the beginning of June) being whisked off to Seattle restaurants where they're on a plate within hours of being caught. The better restaurants around the state serve salmon fresh, usually simply prepared, perhaps grilled over alder. It is listed on the menu along with the species – typically **king (chinook)**, **red (sockeye)**, **or silver (coho)** – and sometimes the river where the fish was caught. Freezing robs the fish of some of its delicacy, but if you are sticking to cheaper places and diners, that's what you're likely to get, often stuffed in a burger or even as salmon balls, batter-dipped and deep-fried.

Of equal importance on every Alaskan menu is **halibut**, a white-meat flat fish that grows to enormous proportions (over 400 pounds is possible), though it is meat from the twenty- to forty-pound specimens (known as "chicken halibut" for its tender flesh) that ends up on dinner plates, typically as a char-grilled fillet or wedged into a sandwich. Either way, the delicate flesh is superb. You'll also find more exotic fruits of the sea, such as clams, most commonly in a chowder, and crab, sometimes king or, more likely, Dungeness.

Most Alaskans spend at least some of the year dining on their **hunting** acquisitions, principally moose, caribou, and, to a much lesser degree, bear. Though largely absent from restaurant menus, you may taste them at a private barbecue and can often try caribou stew or moose steak at a salmon bake, or one of the tourist-oriented dinner shows, where the gold-rush stage entertainment is accompanied by tasty morsels designed to mimic the pioneer diet.

Gold prospectors and early trappers aimed to lighten their hard and tasteless bread by using a **sourdough culture**, a yeasty concoction passed from one generation to the next. There are people in the state who claim their sourdough is a distant relative of one that some ancestor carried over the Chilkoot Pass or Valdez Glacier. Sourdough bread remains popular and can be wonderful dunked into a steaming pot of clam chowder. Almost any diner will give you the option of sourdough bread for your sandwich and will also have sourdough pancakes served up for breakfast. One local delicacy to look out for in May is the fiddlehead, the still-unopened head of a fern that is used in salads and even as a pizza topping in some of the more adventurous restaurants.

You are more likely to hear about **Eskimo delicacies** than taste them. Unlike most Alaskans, Natives are permitted a subsistence harvest of sea mammals, such as seals and whales. If you are in a northern coastal town like Barrow or Kotzebue during the spring and fall hunting season, you may be around for a kill. Once a whale has been butchered, it is brought in from the sea ice, and some of the blubber, or muktuk, is distributed in the community, and sometimes to visitors. Seal oil was once a staple in the north and still gets used in Native villages, sometimes for Eskimo ice cream, or akutug, a confection in which it is combined with caribou or reindeer fat, sugar, and water, fluffed up into a sorbet and served in a sea of ice and berries – something of an acquired taste.

Restaurants

Found everywhere on the Alaskan culinary scene is the **diner**. This is where you'll come for **breakfast** ($4–8), the most filling and often the best-value meal of the day. The staple is eggs cooked any way you like – scrambled, sunny-side-up, over easy, and so on – perhaps with hash browns and bacon, or worked into an omelet with onions, mushrooms, cheese, bell pepper, or sliced sausage. Pancakes are another favorite: either the full stack of three or a "short stack" of two, ample for most appetites. Have them with maple syrup, or order sourdough or blueberry variations. More upmarket joints may also offer French toast, eggs Benedict or huevos rancheros, and all of this comes washed down with as much weak **filter coffee** as you can stomach.

Breakfast is sometimes available all day, but often stops at 11am when the **lunch** menu takes over. Staples here are soups – usually clam chowder plus one other – sandwiches and burgers, in a variety of guises. **Sandwiches** are often served with a packet of chips (not fries), though of course fries are always available. Most diners offer a soup and sandwich combo ($7–9) or the more manageable soup and half-sandwich ($5–7). Other favorites include BLTs, tuna melts, and the French dip – a chunk of toasted French bread with meat *au jus*.

In larger towns diners often close around 4pm or 5pm, but in small communities the diner is the social center and stays open much later, serving plates of steak, salmon, and halibut ($16–25), usually with potatoes and vegetables. The entrée (American for the main course) is typically preceded by salad topped with a choice of dressings – blue cheese, Italian, ranch, and thousand island being the most common. If you see something described as a **dinner**, you'll get soup as well as the entrée. There will probably also be Caesar salad ($8–10), pasta dishes ($12–17), and pizza ($10–16) with a huge variety of toppings. **Dessert** is typically fruit pie ($3), sometimes homemade, with a fabulous range of fillings – cherry, blueberry, chocolate, lemon meringue – served either on its own or à la mode (with ice cream; $4). The only significant difference between a diner and an Alaskan restaurant is that the latter are licensed, though sometimes just for sales of beer and wine (about $4 a glass and up).

Meals are usually delivered in huge portions, but at least everyone is happy to "box up" what you leave for later.

Relief from diner boredom can be found at a **salmon bake**, sometimes just a restaurant with a menu heavy with salmon and halibut dishes, but more likely an outdoor venue, or well-ventilated but bug-proof enclosure, where they dish up an all-you-can-eat salmon and halibut feast which extends to ribs, caribou stew, baked potatoes, and a salad bar, usually for $15–20. These are most common in the tourist haunts of Southeast, though Anchorage, Fairbanks, and a few other places get in on the act.

Relatively small numbers of **ethnic restaurants** are scattered around the state, many of them very authentic and run by native Mexicans, Chinese, Thai, and Vietnamese. In smaller towns they may well feel compelled to augment their menu with burgers, pizza, and pasta dishes, and sometimes lose their focus entirely. Chinese and some Thai places can be especially good value with heaped plates for $8–10, and all-you-can-eat lunchtime buffets for much the same price.

Fast-food culture is now fairly well established in Alaska, and towns of any size all have at least one of the major chains represented; Anchorage and Fairbanks have most of the familiar names.

If you just want to cut down on red meat, the Alaskan diet is ideal, but **vegetarians** are less well catered for. Still, diner breakfasts are varied, meat-free pizza is almost always available, and you can survive for ages on salads and pasta dishes. **Vegans** will find things much harder and may want to spend at least some of their time self-catering.

Self-catering

The lure of money-sucking whale-watching trips and flightseeing around Denali may fuel your desire to **economize** on food expenses. If you are camping, driving an RV, staying in hostels, or seeking out motels with kitchens, you can cut costs (and avoid an overly fatty or meat-laden diet) by cooking your own meals. You might even gather your own ingredients; it is easy enough to **catch your own fish** (salmon and halibut are the prize species), or even gather a bucket of razor clams. Berries – salmonberries, blueberries, wild strawberries, high- and low-bush cranberries – are also good from midsummer to fall and, if you know what you are looking for, there are mushrooms and fiddlehead ferns to be found.

For the less adventurous there are always **supermarkets** – Carr's, Safeway, and IGA are the major names. Every town has one (often at the expense of older grocery stores). In smaller towns they don't just sell groceries, but also act as the video rental outlet, Western Union counter, and liquor store. Larger places may also have an extensive deli, in-shop bakery, fresh-fish counter, and useful buy-as-much-as-you-need bulk food bins; in remote communities the supermarket may have fast-food outlets and sell everything from Carhartt clothing to snowmachines. Near popular hiking areas you may also find **freeze-dried meals**, though you can often prepare something tastier for less money.

Prices depend mostly on location. In Anchorage non-perishable items are only ten or twenty percent more expensive than in the Lower 48, though stuff like **milk**, **fresh vegetables**, and **fruit** might be fifty percent more, or even twice what you'd expect. Stores in main towns on the highway system and the larger ports of Southeast will charge a little more, again with perishable products the worst affected. Visit places such as Dutch Harbor, Kotzebue, and Barrow, and you'll find prices get seriously inflated: $4 for a half-gallon of milk isn't unheard of and the range of fresh vegetables may be seriously depleted. Lastly, don't expect grocery store seafood to come cheaply. It may be plentiful, but local wages are high and the prices correspondingly so.

Drinking

Nights spent chatting in historic roadhouses or spit-and-sawdust wayside bars are likely to be some of the most enjoyable (though poorly remembered) times you'll have in Alaska. At their best, these are dimly lit convivial places where the owner feels compelled to string up as many moose racks, stuffed salmon, ancient snowshoes, and fly-fishing rods as possible. As often as not you'll find a line of beards in baseball caps deep in conversation about hunting and fishing. In the towns it is a bit more cosmopolitan, with Anchorage even boasting a couple of sleek and fashionable cocktail bars, and a slew of excellent microbreweries. But, on the whole, consumption prevails over style. Something to look out for is **the bell** all too prominently displayed above the bar in some establishments: ring it and you're signaling your intention to buy a drink for everyone in the bar.

Sadly, Alaska has one of the highest rates of alcoholism in the US, a figure boosted by frighteningly high rates among Alaskan Natives. In an attempt to combat this problem, many rural communities **ban alcohol** sales (see box, p.519) and in some cases forbid the transportation of any booze to that town. Elsewhere the **drinking age** is 21, and anyone who could conceivably be thought to be underage (however remotely) may be asked to produce picture ID on entry to a bar. Ordinances also prevent supermarkets from selling alcohol, though there is almost always a liquor store next door (or even as part of the supermarket with a separate checkout system). **Bar hours** are more lenient and vary depending on who is in that night; only the most inveterate late-night drinker will have trouble finding a bar to lean on. It is a different story in public places, where drinking is generally proscribed. Sipping a glass of wine or beer in a park or on a beach isn't allowed, and America's puritanical attitudes towards alcohol prevail even at outdoor festivals, where drinkers will find themselves imprisoned in a kind of corral and certainly not strolling about beer in hand.

American beers fall into two camps: wonderful and tasteless. You may be familiar with the latter, which are found throughout Alaska: light, fizzy brands such as Budweiser, Miller, Michelob, and Rainier, costing around $3–4 a pint. The alternative is a fabulous range of microbrewed beers, some arriving in bottles from California and the Pacific Northwest, with others being more local concoctions. Juneau's Alaskan Brewing Co is the major regional brewer, and its golden, medium-weight Amber Ale is an excellent starting point. Look out, too, for beers from Silver Gulch Brewing & Bottling Co near Fairbanks (claimed as the world's northernmost brewery), whose brews even have the Anchorage beer cognoscenti taking notice.

Increasingly, Alaskan brewers are setting up shop in their home towns, brewing their own beer, and selling it through **brewpubs**, where you'll find handcrafted beers such as crisp pilsners, wheat beers, and stouts on tap, at prices only marginally above those of the national brews (say, $4–5 a pint). Anchorage is especially well catered for in this regard, though anywhere with the population to support it will have somewhere with some stainless-steel tanks in the corner. Most bars also stock a fair range of **foreign brews**, particularly European and Canadian beers, and Mexican beers such as Corona, Dos Equis, and the excellent Bohemia.

Beer is usually sold by the glass or pint (four-fifths the size of a British pint), though in all but the most pretentious places, a group can save money by buying a "pitcher" for $10–13. Margaritas and daiquiris come by the pitcher too, though at higher prices.

No one has yet managed to successfully grow commercial quantities of grapes in Alaska, so there is no indigenous **wine industry** except for a couple of places making fruit wines. Wine drinking is largely confined to restaurants, where menus are dominated by Californian varietals at fairly high prices. **Cocktails** are always popular, though if you are expecting the half-price happy-hour drinks common in the Lower 48 you'll be disappointed: Alaskan law forbids drink specials, though there is occasionally free food.

Many bars also have some form of **entertainment**, particularly on weekends. Typically, this will involve a band in the corner cranking out blues, rock, or country tunes with the emphasis on getting everyone up dancing. A **cover charge** is rare, though you might be asked for a couple of dollars for the better-known local acts.

Coffee and tea

An increasing social alternative to drinking dens is the **coffeeshop**. With Alaska's long-standing economic and cultural ties to the Pacific Northwest, coffee culture has become almost as highly developed here as it is in Seattle. The terms espresso, cappuccino, and latte have nearly become meaningless in themselves, requiring half a dozen qualifiers before you'll get served anything: size, strength, regular or decaf, type of milk, amount of froth, additional syrup flavors, to go or stay, and so forth. It can all seem baffling at first, but most baristas are happy to explain, and the coffee is almost always excellent. (Proper cups are rare, however, with paper the norm.) The good stuff can also be found in bookshop cafés, drive-in kiosks beside city streets, and in cybercafés, where the purchase of a coffee (or any of the snacks and specialty teas on offer) may get you half an hour's free surfing.

Diner **coffee** is filtered, almost tasteless and keeps coming as long as you sit there. For those who don't like it black there is usually a basket of whiteners on the table ranging from non-dairy powders to half-and-half, a thick liquid halfway between milk and cream.

Restaurants also serve **tea**, though visitors from countries where tea drinking is more a religion than a way of quenching thirst will undoubtedly find what's on offer an insipid brew and may be induced to head straight for a coffeeshop selling specialist teas, or try one of the herbal infusions also widely available. No matter what you go for it is likely to be inelegantly served by dropping a teabag into a mug of hot water: fish it out when it has reached the required strength.

Corporate America is well and truly entrenched in Alaska, so you'll find all your favorite brands of **soft drink**, though the choice diminishes rapidly as you move away from the bigger towns.

Outdoor activities

Alaska has more outdoors than just about anywhere else, and a large portion of your time in the state is likely to be spent in it. This might be something as gentle as whale watching in Prince William Sound or wandering along a paved path to the face of a glacier, but could equally involve a ten-day rafting trip in the Arctic or hiking the famed Chilkoot Trail.

With such a vast expanse of territory and a limited transportation infrastructure, access to the wilderness can be an issue, especially if you haven't the money for frequent bush-plane flights or water taxis to remote bays. If you're going out into the bush, it is important to try not to do too much, deciding instead on a couple of areas you most want to visit and concentrating your energies (and resources) on those.

Much of the outdoors is classed as public land, managed by state and federal authorities. Though there are **charges** for camping, access is usually free, with the exception of Denali National Park and Exit Glacier near Seward (both $5 for 7 days), which are run by the National Park Service. The NPS offers the Golden Eagle Passport ($50 for one year from date of purchase), which gives free entry into almost all national parks, preserves, monuments, historic sites, and wildlife refuges in the United States, though this will only be a saving if Alaska forms part of a wider US exploration. US citizens and

Backcountry dangers and considerations

For a discussion of keeping warm and dry as well as avoiding mosquitoes and other annoyances, read our more general "Health and well-being" section (p.24); what follows covers dangers specific to backcountry hikers and campers.

Bears

Alaska's brown (grizzly) and black bears don't think of us as food and are seldom a problem, though they're inquisitive animals and in some cases have learned that humans often have snacks stashed away in tents. They don't like surprises, so **avoid bear encounters** by making plenty of noise by whistling, clapping, singing, or strapping a **bear bell** onto your pack. In open country try to walk with the wind at your back – a bear's sense of smell is better than its sight or hearing. **If you see a bear** and it hasn't seen you, move away, keeping downwind if possible – and never get between a mother and a cub. If the bear has seen you, **don't run** – as this tells the bear that you are worth chasing – but stand still, gently waving your arms while talking firmly but calmly and avoiding any aggressive behavior such as staring at the bear. If you look slightly away and move slowly backwards the bear will probably move off, but if it follows, hold your ground. Very rarely, they will charge: if they do, it is usually a bluff and if you stand firm (or as firm as you can manage), the bear will probably veer away at the last moment.

Advice varies about what you should do if a bear gets so close it can touch you, and much of what is offered depends on you being able to tell a brown from a black (which doesn't have a shoulder hump; see p.540 for more on bear identification) in a very stressful situation.

The best advice is to try to determine the bear's motivation. If the bear is mostly interested in feeding or protecting its young, it may see you as a threat and you should "play dead," lying on your front with your pack on, your hands behind your neck and your legs splayed to prevent the bear rolling you over. If the bear seems to be hunting, you then fight back with bear spray, sticks, rocks or whatever: the bear will probably (hopefully) be so surprised it will back off.

Don't **camp** beside salmon streams or near paths worn by bears, usually identifiable by their tracks and scat. Learn to recognize droppings, which are always large but vary in content: grass in spring, animal hair and bones any time, and berries in fall. You should also be sure to prevent bears getting at your food. Once bears get the idea that humans equal free food they become a problem and are sometimes shot: as they say up here "A Fed Bear is a Dead Bear."

Where they've been provided, use bear poles to hang your food or lockers to store it. Otherwise hang your food fifteen feet up a tree (carry rope). Any **smelly items**, such as sunscreen, toothpaste, and mosquito repellent, should stay with the food, and you're better off doing without soap and deodorant for a couple of days.

In open areas with no substantial trees, follow the **triangle principle** in which your tent, cooking spot and food storage area are at the points of an equal-sided triangle with sides at least a hundred yards (preferably 200yds) long. Your tent should be the most upwind of the three spots, so a bear that does seek out your kitchen or pantry won't go past your tent to get to it. Choose **low-odor food** (not tuna, sardines, or bacon) and keep it stored in airtight containers or Ziploc-style bags. In areas with high bear concentrations you should use a **bear-resistant food canister**, a hard plastic cylinder that holds enough food for about four days. These can be bought for around $80 from sports and outdoor stores or rented locally for $4 a day. In Denali and Wrangell–St Elias the National Park Service will provide them free. Take all your **garbage** with you.

Many Alaskans carry a **gun** for bear protection, though unless you have specifically come to hunt you probably won't have a gun and can survive just as well with the kind of good bushcraft described above. A compromise is to carry a handheld can of **pepper spray** or mace, which can be effective though you need to be careful not to use it directly upwind of yourself, and the range is only around six yards (rather closer than you really want to be). A can costs around $40, has a limited shelf life, and won't be allowed on scheduled flights, so you may feel that you can manage without.

In Arctic Alaska you are no longer at the top of the food chain. **Polar bears** have been known to stalk humans over several miles, so in their territory you want to be in a very strong vehicle or equipped with a powerful rifle and the ability to shoot straight under pressure. Fortunately, unexpected encounters are rare, and polar bears only really come onshore in the very far north – Kotzebue, Barrow, and Prudhoe Bay for example – when the pack ice is solid, anywhere from October through to May.

River crossings

When hiking away from formed trails you may well find yourself needing to cross a river, something which causes more hiker deaths each year than bear attacks do. Most rivers in Alaska are **glacial rivers**, which are very cold, contain silt which makes it hard to pick your route across, and exhibit rising water levels as the sun increases meltwater late in the day – early morning is the best time to cross and you should plan your trip accordingly. If in doubt, wait a few hours (or overnight) and try again, or go back. Pick the widest section of river you can find (it is likely to be the shallowest) and shuffle across facing the opposite shore keeping your feet apart to provide a secure brace. Groups should link up (with arms around waists or shoulders) to form a line parallel to the current with the strongest person upstream; lone hikers should find a stout stick to use as a "third leg," which allows you to always keep two points of contact. If you do get swept off your feet, don't panic, rid yourself of your pack (some recommend wearing the pack loosely with the waist belt unbuckled) then float on your back with your feet pointing downstream and swim across the current to the bank. Don't put your feet down; ankles can get trapped.

Hypothermia

Hikers are usually aware of the possibility of hypothermia, though most cases occur under relatively benign conditions (say, 30–50°F) when people are least prepared. Always dress in layers: synthetic materials – polypropylene and fleeces – are best as they are warm, lightweight, and dry quickly. Avoid cotton (including jeans) as it provides little warmth, and none when wet. A windproof and waterproof layer (preferably breathable) is also essential, and you should beware of wet clothing – change after a river crossing and keep your wet gear to use for the next one. It is also a good idea to keep feeding yourself warm food and drinks, so a portable stove is quite important.

If anyone in your party exhibits symptoms such as lethargy, irrational behavior, muscle cramps, and even taking off clothing claiming they are hot, then you should treat them for hypothermia. Keep them out of wind and rain, ensure they are wearing dry clothing, and feed them high-energy foods and hot drinks. A sleeping bag and human warmth are the next stage. In extreme conditions, send for medical assistance.

Water purification

Water from a spigot or pump in a campground should always be safe to drink, but any water gathered from streams and lakes (no matter how clean it looks or how remote the area) should always be purified to kill the parasites that cause giardia. Many people carry a **water filter**, which must be rated down to five microns. Though convenient, filters are just one more thing to carry and easily clog up in silt-laden glacial waters. You should let any silty water settle overnight before filtering. **Iodine** tablets and solutions are just as effective, if properly used, and weigh next to nothing. (With very cold water you may need to leave it for twenty minutes before drinking.)

permanent residents who are 62 or older are eligible for a Golden Age Passport ($10), which is valid for life and also gives free entry to federal areas as well as a fifty percent reduction on camping fees.

Hiking

Hiking in Alaska is no walk in the park, but it is the easiest and least expensive way of getting out into the wilderness. For many it is the main justification for the expense of getting to Alaska, and with good reason. There are few spots on earth where it is so easy to get to places where you can walk for days without seeing a soul, and fewer still with such wonderful wildlife. The range of hikes varies enormously from short strolls along a hard-packed trail to see a glacier to multiday fly-in epics. Many people come to Alaska and stick to the former, and even if you think you are in this category, it is worth trying something slightly harder. You may find yourself captivated by stunning vistas of snow-capped mountains, dense dripping forests, or vast stretches of tundra rolling away to the horizon.

Most of your hiking is likely to be along formed trails, but in theory you can stop almost anywhere – take a compass and set off for days across ranges of hills, fording rivers when necessary and camping when you get tired. The reality can be considerably different, however. In Southeast dense forest restricts your passage, and in the boggy terrain of the Interior and North, it is all too obvious why Native Alaskans and early pioneers traveled in winter when the rivers were frozen and skis, snowshoes, and dog teams could be put to good use. Off-trail hiking can be an arduous task, watching every step to avoid bog-filled holes, high-stepping onto spongy mounds and then wrestling with low willow and blueberry bushes. For more on hiking in tundra see the Denali practicalities on p.394.

With a short summer **hiking season**, picking your time can have the biggest impact on your wilderness enjoyment. Except for the odd lowland walk, don't even think about hiking in May, when large sections of the trails will still be covered in snow. Similar conditions persist well into June in some areas – strong waterproof boots and gaiters are essential at this time. By July most hikes will be free of snow and starting to dry out, but bugs can be at their worst. Generally, the best time for hiking is late summer (mid-Aug to Sept), when days are still long, the ground is as dry as it is going to get, and nights aren't that cold. In the North you might even see the aurora at this time.

Most land in Alaska (and almost all the territory covered by hikes in this book) is **public land**, owned by either the federal or state government and managed through a confusing array of bodies – national parks, national forests, state parks, and reserves of various kinds. With the exception of Denali's complex rules and the Chilkoot Trail's booking system, there is **no reservation system** for trails in Alaska, though restrictions exist for campsites and cabins (see "Accommodation," p.50).

No matter where you are going, you should always leave a reasonably detailed **trip plan** with someone responsible and be sure to check in when you return. Besides a few short walks close to town, most of the hikes in this book may be more of a wilderness experience than you are used to. Conditions could be harsh, you may not see anybody for days, cell phones will be out of range, and no one is going to come and help until after you are due back, which may be a couple of days away. Since you will need to be entirely self-sufficient, we've given a few helpful pointers below, but they are no substitute for discussing your plans with local park and forest service rangers, making sure your map-reading skills are well honed, and using a good deal of common sense.

Rough Guide favorites: hikes

Raven's Roost Trail p.123
Mount Edgecumbe Trail p.135
West Glacier Trail p.153
Chilkoot Trail p.186
Tony Knowles Coastal Trail p.212
Flattop Mountain p.215
Harding Icefield Trail p.247
Resurrection Pass Trail p.255
The Valley of 10,000 Smokes p.333
Granite Tors Trail p.477
Pinnell Mountain Trail p.482

Equipment

Alaska's backcountry cabins are seldom sited along hiking trails, so to spend any time hiking in the backcountry you'll need to bring a fair amount of equipment. If you live outside the US, it is worth considering buying gear once you arrive. Anchorage has a good stock of outdoor stores selling competitively priced gear (particularly American manufactured goods) and there is no sales tax.

Put some thought into your choice of **tent**. A freestanding dome-style tent (or some variation on that theme) allows you to avoid trying to drive pegs into rocky Alaskan campgrounds or make them stay put in boggy tundra and the loose gravel of river bars. Something rated for three seasons is a minimum requirement, because high winds and driving rain strike at any time of year; a four-season model is better still. Remember that it can snow in any month in Denali, and that tents injudiciously pitched in river valleys are frequently blown inside out throughout the summer. If you want to get any sleep at all, make sure it is also completely mosquito-proof with an ample expanse of fine-mesh netting.

As many areas do not permit campfires and the few huts and shelters you'll come across have only a heating stove unsuitable for cooking, you'll need to carry a **cooking stove** and fuel. Something burning efficient, widely available, and cheap white gas (also known as Coleman fuel; around $5.50 a gallon) is the best bet. Canisters for propane and butane stoves – such as Camping Gas, Primus, MSR, and Snowpeak – are only sporadically available. EPIgas canisters appear to be even harder to come by. It is also worth noting that owners of Trangia stoves will have difficulty obtaining methylated spirits (denatured alcohol in US parlance): it can be found at REI in Anchorage and in some hardware stores but costs roughly four times the price of Coleman fuel. You'll also go through it quicker – a serious consideration if you're spending a few nights in the backcountry. If you have any of this kit, then traveling by train is off-limits; you'll need to have a car or travel by bus.

A further issue is that airlines will not carry fuel (or even a bottle smelling of fuel) on scheduled flights. If you a charter a bush plane, some provisions will be made for flying fuel in, but if you are on a scheduled service to a bush town, you want to be sure you can buy fuel when you get there. The best bet is to carry a stove that will burn standard unleaded gasoline (petrol). MSR and several other manufacturers make compact models that burn both Coleman fuel and unleaded gasoline without modification.

You'll also want to bring along some form of insulated sleeping mat, a warm sleeping bag, some reliable method of purifying water (see box, p.57), a detailed map, compass, insect repellent, and an insect-proof head net (not stylish but you won't care). Extras might include waterproof matches and a lighter, a first-aid kit, a signaling device such as a whistle, light or flare, and strong plastic bags for keeping clothes and sleeping bag dry.

Minimum-impact hiking and camping

Wherever you go you should always practice **minimum-impact** hiking and camping, but nowhere more so than in Alaska. Like all Arctic and sub-Arctic regions, the Alaskan landscape is very fragile and a small amount of damage can take a long time to recover: tundra plants grow so slowly that vehicle tracks can take decades to disappear, and ten-foot-high trees only a few inches in diameter might be a hundred years old.

How you go about minimizing your impact depends on where you are hiking. On well-formed trails you'll probably be following familiar rules: stick to the trail, walk in single file, don't cut switchbacks, and only camp at designated sites where others have camped. When hiking in Denali or anywhere away from managed trails, you do the exact opposite, the idea being that in trackless areas you should do what you can to avoid creating tracks. We've discussed this in more detail in our Denali account (p.394), but essentially you walk in small groups fanned out across the landscape each finding your own route, then camp where there is no evidence of previous campers, being sure to move on every day or so. Ensure you leave nothing behind, avoid lighting fires, and where possible camp on **river bars** where the evidence is washed away in spring floods. The breeze on river bars often keeps the bugs down as well, but you need to be prepared to move if rains cause the river to rise. Some people even carry light comfortable shoes to minimize the impact around the campsite.

Maintaining your personal hygiene can adversely affect the fragile environment. Bury **human waste** and ashes from your burnt toilet paper in a shallow hole at least a hundred feet away from a watercourse. If you bury it too deep, the permanently cold ground won't support decomposition. **Soap** should be used sparingly if at all – even biodegradable soaps take a long time to decompose up here and hikers downstream may be using the river for drinking water. Pots can be cleaned with river sand and hot water; any sudsy water you do create should be discarded well away from streams and standing water.

Mountain biking

Many of the trails listed as hiking trails are equally (if not more) suited to **mountain biking**, offering long stretches with relatively easy gradients and only short technical sections. Most of the best riding is relatively distant from places you can rent bikes, so unless you are prepared to stump up for fairly expensive long-term rental it definitely pays to have your own machine: if you're driving up here, consider strapping your bike on.

Throughout the Guide we've indicated which trails are most suited to biking, but there are numerous gravel roads that can be fun – the longer ones are listed under "Cycle touring" on p.45. Except on trails where bikes are banned, there are no special rules, but common courtesy demands you ride within your ability and pull over for hikers.

Rough Guide favorites: mountain biking

Prince of Wales Island forest trails p.98
Resurrection Pass Trail p.255
Crescent Creek Trail p.254
Eklutna Lakeside Trail p.351
Gold Mint Trail p.354

You should also be aware of **bears**. They tend to move away from approaching hikers, but bikers travel faster and often more quietly, so be especially wary when rounding blind corners.

Rafting, canoeing, and kayaking

Most people shy away from immersing themselves in Alaskan waters, but that doesn't rule out rafting, canoeing, and kayaking. Visitors enjoying these activities seldom get very wet – except on commercial whitewater-rafting trips – as the emphasis is mostly on gentle appreciation of the surroundings, and maybe a bit of fishing. People do go kayaking on the inland rivers, but by far the majority of people kayaking in Alaska restrict themselves to coastal regions, where you can paddle among whales in sight of huge tidewater glaciers.

Rafting

Rafting trips in Alaska fall into two broad categories: float trips, usually on gentle water where you'll spend your time admiring the scenery and spotting wildlife; and whitewater trips, where the focus is on getting wet, though the scenery is usually spectacular as well. We've listed some of our favorites in both categories in the accompanying box, opposite.

In a few places along the highway system, and even in Southeast, you'll find short **float trips** only a couple of hours long, perhaps finishing off with a barbecue beside the river. Many more, however, are specialist multiday affairs through genuinely remote wilderness areas, such as in the Gates of the Arctic National Park, the Noatak National Preserve, or the Arctic National Wildlife Refuge. Some trips even run up to two weeks long and may make up your entire vacation. Your options are wide open.

Whitewater-rafting trips exist mostly in a few road-accessible areas in the Interior and on the Kenai Peninsula. If you have been whitewater rafting outside the US, you may be used to small rafts entirely controlled by paddle-wielding customers. Here, larger rafts are the norm, with the guide maneuvering the raft using oars, leaving the customers

Rough Guide favorites: river trips

Sixmile Creek p.240
Savonoski Loop p.333
Delta River p.403
Lion Head on the Matanuska River p.422
Yukon River from Eagle to Circle p.442
Chena River p.476
North Fork of the Koyukuk River p.498

pretty much as passengers. On wilder trips, customers are armed with paddles, though the guide still has ultimate control. Pure paddle rafting is a rarity here, and although this is undoubtedly a very safe way of running rafting trips, it does take the edge off the excitement of pulling together as a team to get through the rapids. The main rivers for short trips are Sixmile River near Hope, the Matanuska River near Chickaloon, and the Nenana River by Denali National Park. There are also multiday trips, usually combining whitewater rafting, wildlife viewing, and a complete wilderness experience: the pick of these are the Talkeetna River near Talkeetna and the Alsek and Tatshenshini rivers, which are rafted from Haines.

If you can get a group together and have some backcountry experience, you might want to **rent a raft**, then charter a plane to fly you into the headwaters of some remote river and float down to some prearranged meeting point. Multiday trips usually involve a lot of drifting and occasional stretches of whitewater, which you can often portage, by carrying the raft around the worst of the rapids. It can be a heavy and tiring job, so it is good to learn how to **line** your vessel, allowing the raft to follow the river while you walk the bank holding on by a rope.

Companies running such trips are listed in the relevant sections of the Guide. There's also a good listing of Alaska river-rafting guides at Ⓦalaskan.com/outdoors/rafting.htm.

Canoeing and river kayaking

Alaska has over a hundred rivers suitable for canoeing and kayaking, ranging in difficulty from flat water to some of the wildest water anywhere (see box, p.63, for river grading). Some of these rivers are road-accessible, but there are often long distances between put-in and take-out, and access can still be difficult since car-rental agencies don't like renters putting racks on their cars and often don't allow driving on gravel roads. Consequently, keen river paddlers are better off driving up from the Lower 48 or Canada and bringing their own gear. Rental kayaks and canoes are available but most companies have strict rules as to what rivers you put them in.

Some of Alaska's finest inland paddling is on **lakes**, particularly sequences of several lakes and easy rivers that can be combined into overnight or week-long trips. Much of the best lake paddling is not accessible by road, requiring bush flights to the access points. Rigid shell canoes and kayaks don't lend themselves to easy transport and those pilots who do fly them in – usually strapped to the floats of a float plane – will often insist on a separate passenger-free flight for the boats, thereby adding to the overall cost of the trip. To get around this, many people opt for a **folding kayak** (sometimes known as a Klepper, one of the most common brand names), typically a slot-together aluminum frame with an outer coating of plasticized canvas. These can be surprisingly rigid and hold enough gear for a two-week trip or longer. Rentals are sometimes available, but if you are doing an extended trip it often works out better to buy one and make sure it is comfortable and equipped to your specifications.

No matter where you are going, you'll need to do a little **advance planning**, best done by reading the river guidebooks listed in the Contexts section of this book (see p.549) and contacting one of the Public Lands Information Centers (see p.31), where you can also obtain their free *Planning a River Trip in Alaska* leaflet. You must also keep in mind the potential **dangers**, and remember that you'll need to be totally self-reliant; it may be days before anyone comes looking for you. Most Alaskan rivers are fed by snowmelt and are incredibly cold. You should never underestimate how quickly a dunking can turn into a serious situation. To reduce the chances of a swim you should lower your estimate of your abilities, so if you normally paddle Class III, then you shouldn't be looking at anything harder than Class II in Alaska. There's no substitute for getting sound advance information about the river, but you should also **scout ahead**, even if you think you can cope with upcoming obstacles. Remember that damaging a boat or losing a paddle can mean a very long, arduous, and possibly life-threatening walk out. Keep in mind that rapids aren't the only problem: rivers often meander through forested river valleys, cutting away at the outside banks until trees along the river fall in and create perhaps the biggest threat of all, **sweepers** (also known as strainers). Sweepers drag their branches in the water: you don't get washed around them like you would a rock, but get sucked under into an impenetrable tangle of branches. If anything, they are more common on easier-class rivers, posing a particular challenge to the inexperienced. Always steer well clear. Where there are log-jams or harder rapids than you are prepared to tackle, you'll have to portage around the obstacle or line your boat through (see "Rafting," p.61, for explanations of both terms).

Sea kayaking

For most visitors the majority of Alaska's stupendously scenic coastline – longer than that of the rest of the US put together – remains inaccessible. You can ride the ferries and take a wildlife-viewing cruise, but to see everything at your own pace the solution is sea kayaking (sometimes known here as **blue-water paddling**). Huge expanses of water sheltered from ocean swells by protective islands make Alaska a perfect sea-kayaking destination, and enthusiasts turn up with their own gear to spend weeks paddling along the coast, particularly around Misty Fiords National Park, Sitka, Glacier Bay, Prince William Sound, Resurrection Bay, Kachemak Bay, and Kodiak Island. For **beginners**, it needn't be as daunting as it might at first sound, and every summer hundreds of people with no paddling experience join guided trips ranging from a few hours to several days.

Rough Guide favorites: sea-kayaking areas

At their most basic, commercial trips might depart the harbor of a Southeast port and paddle around the wharves and along the nearby coastline, but it is only a small step up to transport a kayak to the face of some nearby glacier and paddle around. Longer trips may extend to several days, camping out each night and spending the next day moving on to the next campsite: kind of like hiking without a pack.

If you already have some experience you may want to **go it alone**, either with your own equipment or gear rented locally. A double kayak always works out much cheaper than two singles, and it allows you to move more quickly. You'll need to show the rental agency some evidence of your abilities and should also have a solid knowledge of **winds and tides**, both of which can be treacherous, even during the main mid-May to August paddling season. Be prepared for all eventualities no matter how benign the conditions are when you set out, and always carry a couple of days' extra food and fuel in case you are delayed. Almost the entire Alaskan coastline experiences a wide tidal range, so you should always leave your boat well above the high-water mark.

For kayak camping trips you'll need to put everything in small waterproof bags that will fit in the kayak; if you get wet and cold, the last thing you need is a sodden sleeping bag. Always file a **trip plan** with friends or the agency managing the area, try to stick to it whenever possible, and let them know when you get back. Lastly, if you've arranged for a boat or plane to pick you up at a particular time, be sure to have a contingency plan in case something turns against you.

Fishing

In some circles Alaska is synonymous with fishing, and many people base their whole

River grading

Both rivers and rapids are graded according to the six-level system below. The river class is dictated by the most demanding rapid. This lends itself to some creative marketing, since a river hyped as Class V might be almost entirely Class III with one Class V rapid. For those looking for an adventure, the expression to look out for when browsing brochures is "Continuous Class IV." Float trips, where the emphasis is more on the scenery and wilderness experience, tend to be on Class I and II rivers.

I Fast water and a few small waves.

II Choppier wave patterns and easily avoided rocks increase the dunking potential for inexperienced kayakers, though it is no problem in a raft.

III Bigger but still easily ridden waves make this class bouncy and fun, though there may be more technical sections. Good proving ground for first-time rafters.

IV Huge, bouncier, and less predictable waves churned up by rocks midstream demand much greater boat control and teamwork. This makes for excellent fun but dramatically increases the chance of a swim.

V Serious stuff with chaotic standing waves, churning narrow channels and huge holes ready to swallow you up. Best avoided by first-time rafters but thrilling for the experienced.

VI Dicing with death. Grade V taken to new heights; commercially unraftable and only tackled by the most experienced of paddlers.

vacation around the pursuit of the fighting **salmon** and **trout** (see the Contexts section of this book for a discussion of fish species) in the rivers of Southcentral and the Interior. Armed with a license and suitable tackle, you won't have much trouble finding a place to fish – and there are a lot of fish out there waiting to be caught. But fishing is popular, and there's a good deal of competition beside the more accessible rivers. Keen anglers can improve their chance of a full catch bag by hiring **fishing guides** (costing perhaps $120–170 for half a day) or staying in isolated **fishing lodges**, where the remote locations have kept the fish-per-angler quotient high. You can still catch fish without going the big-money route simply by fishing in rivers you pass on your travels, such as when you are out hiking or on a backcountry trip. If you've got a lightweight rod at home, bring it along, or purchase one of the compact models that you can keep in your day-pack. Your chances of catching trophy-size fish are slim, but if you are just after something for your evening meal then a quiet hour or two by the riverside could hardly be better spent.

Even visitors who would never consider lugging fishing tackle around the state find themselves on **halibut-fishing** trips, hoping to land a fifty-pound fish that will keep them in fillets for the rest of their trip. Some end up landing a monster four or five times that size and have to give most of it away.

Winter visitors might try their hand at **ice fishing**, generally from early December to late March. It's a slightly bizarre pastime, usually involving sitting huddled in a hut out on some frozen lake dangling a line through a hole in the ice hoping to land king salmon, rainbow trout, Dolly Varden, Arctic char and Arctic grayling.

Regulations

The **regulations** about where and when you can fish, bag limits, and so forth are complex. For the latest information you should consult the Alaska Department of Fish and Game, PO Box 25526, Juneau, AK 99802-5526 (☎465-4100, Ⓦwww.adfg.state.ak.us), which has a very informative website with all the rules, links to handy publications, and the latest fishing news and feature stories.

First up, you'll need to get an Alaska State **sportfishing license** for non-residents, which costs $10 for one day, $20 for three days, $30 for a week, $50 for two weeks, and $100 for

Multiday adventure tours

Alaska is a place that encourages the grand gesture. Elsewhere you might spend the afternoon rafting or devote a couple of hours to paddling around some shoreline, but in Alaska you're as likely to build your entire vacation around a single float trip down some Arctic river or spend a week exploring Prince William Sound by sea kayak. Below, we have brought together some of the best full-commitment adventure trips available.

As well as the activity-specific sites listed below, it is worth considering getting on trips run by the Sierra Club (Ⓣ415/977-5522, Ⓦwww.sierraclub.org), which organizes around two dozen trips a year, ranging from winter dog mushing (7 days; $2175) to backpacking in the Arctic National Wildlife Refuge (12 days; $3000) to yachting around Glacier Bay (7 days; $3500).

Many of the trips detailed here only run a few times a year (sometimes only once), and numbers are limited, so plan as far in advance as possible.

Sea kayaking

Anadyr Adventures Ⓣ835-2814 or 1-800/865-2925, Ⓦwww.anadyradventures.com. Valdez-based company (see p.301) running assorted multiday kayaking excursions in Prince William Sound (7 days; $1600), other trips where you're based at a comfortable remote lodge (3 days; $900), and "mothership" adventures involving kayaking during the day but spending the night on a comfortable motor yacht (6 days; $2700).

Pangaea Ⓣ835-8442 or 1-800/660-9637, Ⓦwww.alaskasummer.com. Valdez-based Prince William Sound tours, including guided camping excursions ranging from two days around Shoup Glacier ($410) to an eight-day exploration of Prince William Sound's highlights ($1895) and "mothership" trips using either a sailboat (6 days; $2100) or motor yacht (4 days; $1800).

Southeast Sea Kayaks Ⓣ225-1258 or 1-800/287-1607, Ⓦwww.kayakketchikan.com. Inclusive guided kayaking trips into Misty Fiords National Park from Ketchikan (4 days; $900), plus plenty of advice if you'd rather go alone.

Rafting and canoeing

Chilkat Guides Ⓣ766-2491, Ⓦwww.raftalaska.com. Haines-based company running on two supremely scenic, remote rivers on the US/Canada border: the Alsek (13 days; $2795) and the Tatshenshini (10 days; $2295). They also run the Kongakut (8 days; $3595) in the Arctic National Wildlife Refuge.

GoNorth Ⓣ479-7272 or 1-866/236-7272, Ⓦwww.gonorthalaska.com. Fairbanks-based operation organizing all manner of trips throughout the north. Particularly good for rafting and canoe trips in the Brooks Range – North Fork of the Koyukuk (10 days; $2000); John River (10 days; $2200); Yukon River (8 days; $1500); rivers in the Arctic National Wildlife Refuge (9 days; around $3000).

the full year. If you are planning to fish for chinooks (and you are over 16), you'll also need a **king salmon stamp** (same prices as above), which should be attached to your fishing license. If you are only fishing for kings, this will effectively double your license cost. One way to cut costs is to buy a two-week general license, with a daily king salmon stamp for the days you're fishing for that species.

Licenses can be bought all over the state, primarily from tackle shops but also from general stores and even campgrounds. Ask just about anyone, and you'll be directed to the nearest spot. Licenses can also be bought online at Ⓦwww.admin.adfg.state.ak.us/license.

For **recorded fishing info** call Ⓣ267-2510 in Anchorage.

Fishing derbies

Just about every coastal town has a **fishing derby** throughout the summer months, or sometimes just for the few weeks a particular

Sourdough Outfitters ⓣ692-5252, ⓦwww.sourdough.com. Bettles-based five- to ten-day rafting trips on the rivers of the southern Brooks Range – including the Noatak, John, and the North Fork of the Koyukuk – costing $1800–2900.

Too-loó-uk River Guides ⓣ683-1542, ⓦwww.akrivers.com. Extended wilderness raft trips from this Denali-based company include the likes of the gentle Kongakut River through the Arctic National Wildlife Refuge (10 days; $3200), the Class III–IV Tana/Copper rivers (12 days; $2400), and the continuous Class III–IV Talkeetna (5 days; $1200).

Dog sledding

Denali Dog Sled Expeditions ⓣ683-2863, ⓦwww.earthsonglodge.com. Get deep into the heart of Denali National Park on tours run by former park ranger Jon Nierenberg in the November to January sledding season. Usually with just two or three customers, these range from basic day trips ($75–200 per person) and overnight jaunts ($400–500 per person per day) staying in cabins and heated tents to multiday epics along the Stampede Trail (5 days; $2500) and a Grand Tour to Wonder Lake (10 days; $5000).

Sourdough Outfitters (see above). Winter dog-sledding trips in the Brooks Range (7 days; $2600), around Arrigetch Peaks (11 days; $4000), and on the North Slope (April only; 7 days; $3000).

Cycling

Alaska Backcountry Bike Tours ⓣ746-5018 or 1-866/354-2453. ⓦwww.mountainbikealaska.com. Single-track adventures in the Chugach National Forest near Anchorage – two days for $295, four days for $595, and six days for $995.

Alaska Cycling Adventures ⓣ245-2175, ⓦwww.alaskabike.com. Anchorage-based outfit mainly offering bike trips through the Interior, averaging 65 miles a day and staying in lodges and cabins with all meals provided (8 days; $2695).

Backroads ⓣ1-800/462-2848 or 510/527-1555, ⓦwww.backroads.com. Cycling, hiking, and multisport tours to Alaska (mid-June to Sept).

Multisport

Mountain Travel-Sobek ⓣ1-888/687-6235, ⓦwww.mtsobek.com. Kayaking, rafting and multisport adventure tours to Alaska.

Sockeye Cycle Co ⓣ983-2851, ⓦwww.cyclealaska.com. This Haines-based company works with other local operators to offer a "Best of Southeast Alaska" trip, combining hiking, mountain biking, sea kayaking, rafting, and glacier trekking (6 days; $1920).

salmon species makes its run for the breeding grounds. Usually, there are daily prizes for the biggest fish, a prize for the biggest caught during the entire derby, and one or more tagged fish, often with prizes of $100,000 or more on their head (though this may not be claimed if said fish isn't caught). Most derby tickets only cost about $10 to enter for the few days you're likely to be in town, and if you don't join in, you may just live to rue the day you could have caught the big one. Even if you aren't participating, it is fun to wander down to the dockside in the late afternoon for the daily weigh-in.

We've mentioned several such derbies throughout the text; there are more detailed listings at ⓦalaskaoutdoorjournal.com/Derbies/derbies.html and under the fishing section of ⓦwww.alaska.com.

Combat fishing

Alaska may be huge and have miles of productive salmon streams, but most of the people are concentrated fairly close to Anchorage and only have access to rivers along the limited road system. The result is combat fishing, with anglers standing shoulder to shoulder trying to avoid snagging their neighbor with each cast. If this is what you're after (or you just want to see this freak show in action), head down to **Ship Creek**, right in the heart of Anchorage, or to **Bird Creek**, along the Seward Highway 25 miles to the south. Be sure to follow the lead of those around to avoid tangled lines: cast slightly upstream and synchronize with your neighbors so that the lines drift downstream together. When someone else has a "fish-on", reel in your line so that the other fisher has a fair chance of landing the fish.

Winter sports

The vast majority of visitors come to Alaska between late May and early September, which virtually rules out winter sports. Early-summer visitors might get in a few days of downhill skiing near Anchorage or could fit in some fly-in snowmachining or cross-country skiing. Later in the summer helicopters can whisk you up to do some dog sledding on glaciers above Seward, Skagway, and Juneau. But, in general, anyone wanting to undertake winter activities has to come from **November to March**. Arguably the best time is late February and March, when the days are reasonably long and yet there is enough darkness to coax out the aurora borealis. At this time, temperatures aren't that bad, but it's still cold enough for you to appreciate retiring to the huge fire in the lodge at the end of the day.

Skiing

Although Alaska has plenty of mountains and snow, its lack of population and convenient, suitable sites means there are very few places dedicated to **downhill skiing**. The only real resort is Alyeska Resort at Girdwood (see p.236), forty miles southeast of Anchorage. After that you're down to tiny fields such as Alpenglow (ⓦwww.skialpenglow.com) and Hilltop (ⓦwww.hilltopskiarea.org), both in Anchorage; Cleary Summit, twenty miles north of Fairbanks; Eaglecrest in Juneau (ⓦwww.juneau.org/ecrestftp); and the Mount Eyak Ski Area in Cordova (see p.306).

Skiing in Alaska is all about **cross-country skiing**, and there is virtually no limit to where you can go. The boggy lakeland that fills much of the Interior is virtually impenetrable in summer, but it's fair game when frozen and snow-covered. Although you can ski beside the sea and follow mountain valleys back to hidden glaciers, in practice most people head for recognized cross-country ski areas around Anchorage, on the Kenai Peninsula, throughout the Interior, and north of Fairbanks. Good places to kick off are Anchorage's Kincaid Park, site of the 1994 Olympic Trials, the area around Chena Hot Springs outside Fairbanks, and the Hatcher Pass Recreation Area near Palmer.

Dog mushing and ski-joring

Dog mushing is the official sport of Alaska, so it is appropriate that the one event for which Alaska is known worldwide is the **Iditarod** (see box, p.360), an 1100-mile dog-sled race across the state's frozen Interior. This is just the highest-profile of a slew of such races (most of which are shorter, although still frequently several hundred miles long) that take place during the winter. Throughout much of the state, you'll come across riotous compounds where dogs are chained to their kennels impatiently waiting their turn "in the traces" of a sled. A few dog mushers offer summertime rides behind a wheeled sled, and there are expensive trips on glaciers in the peak visiting season, but both are pale substitutes for the real thing, a hell-for-leather charge through forested trails behind a team of spirited huskies and cross-breeds. Kennels offer widely differing experiences, but a good place to start is Alaskan Sled Dog Kennel (ⓣ495-RIDE or 1-877/495-RIDE, ⓦwww.alaskansleddogs.co). Based at Willow, ninety miles north of Anchorage, it offers a taster with a chance to drive a team (4–5hr; $225), a two-day trip with a night in a lodge ($500), and wilderness adventures (3–5 days; $700–1200).

Alaskans love their dogs so much they even want to take them skiing, or the other way round to be precise. Put on your cross-country skis, strap your dog into a harness, hang on, and you are **ski-joring**. It certainly makes those uphill sections a good deal easier. There are only limited possibilities for experiencing this, unless you bring all your own equipment (including dog), but you may be able to hook up with people who will show you the ropes through the Alaska Skijoring & Pulk Association (Ⓣ457-5456 in Anchorage, Ⓦwww.sleddog.org/skijor).

Snowmachining

Snowmachines are almost as popular as dogs, and it sometimes seems that everyone has one hidden under a blue tarp for the summer awaiting the return of deep powder. They're not just for fun either, as anyone living away from the road system relies on them for getting around in winter.

There are spots all over the state where you'll see machines in action: generally, areas for mechanized shenanigans of this sort are separate from those designated for quieter pursuit so there is minimal conflict.

In the popular areas you can often rent machines (from around $170 a day for a 550cc model), though unless you know what you're doing it is far better to join a guided tour. Try Anchorage-based Alaska Snow Safaris (Ⓣ868-7669 or 1-888/414-7669, Ⓦwww.snowmobile-alaska.com), which does rentals as well as introductory trips (3hr; $130), backcountry runs (5hr; $190), and full-day tours (from $270). There are numerous other companies offering similar deals: look for advertisements during the snowy months.

Working in Alaska

Stories of astonishing wages in Alaska still hang wilting on the travelers' grapevine, but the reality is that you are unlikely to earn a bundle. Some people do get rich quick, though more frequently they spend the summer up here working hard in unpleasant conditions and going home with little more than what they came with, having spent their meager earnings quickly. Nonetheless, it is one way of spending time in Alaska without blowing your savings, and you may end up with an experience you'll cherish for a lifetime.

Most high-earning legends stem from the late 1970s construction of the Alaska Pipeline, or from good fishing seasons when fishermen returned with a share of the profits that amounted to a small fortune. Such hauls are rare these days, and your chances of getting a good slice of the action are slim. Alaskan unemployment is some of the highest in the US, and there are plenty of experienced old-hands who will always get first pick over first-timers with no proven track record.

This kind of hierarchy can work in your favor if you are prepared to work more than one season up here; those who make it through the summer are almost guaranteed work the following year, often in a better position with a greater earning potential. You can also improve your chances of getting something worthwhile by **planning ahead**. Most employers want their new employees to work the full season from May to sometime in September, and they recruit between December of the previous year and February. You can get work by just turning up and asking around in May, but many positions will already be taken, and you'll be hoping to fill in for no-shows and early sackings.

Securing a position in advance also opens up the possibility that your employer may pay for, or subsidize, your travel to Alaska, though this is more usual if you've worked for that employer before. More frequently, you'll get free or cheap accommodation, and maybe meals, especially if you are working away from town.

No matter where you hope to work, be sure to **ask questions** about rates of pay, work and living conditions, expected duties, hours of work, potential overtime, tips, taxes, location of the work, time off, and anything else you can think of to get the lay of the land; and get as much of it as you can down in writing. You always hear of unscrupulous employers exploiting their hired help, demanding they work long hours for limited pay, then extracting all manner of deductions from the wage packet for transportation, lodging, laundry, or whatever.

US citizens have no legal difficulties working in Alaska, but if you are **not a US citizen** you will need a work visa to legally work in the country. These can be obtained from the US embassy before you leave home (see box, p.21), though in practice, it is almost impossible to get one for the sort of seasonal work typically on offer in Alaska. Most visas go to foreigners working in summer camps in the Lower 48, and to those sponsored by an employer, who needs to prove that there is no US citizen available to take the job. Some people choose to work illegally, though with employers facing stiff fines if caught they are often reluctant to involve themselves, and if caught you may find yourself fined, deported, and unwelcome in the future. If you are still keen, the best bets are usually with the smaller restaurants and tourism operators who are prepared to pay cash-in-hand.

Jobs

The major considerations are the type of job you're after and the location; there's not much point landing a job on a fish-processing ship in the Bering Sea if you are interested in exploring Alaska in your free time.

Many of the jobs on offer are in coastal regions, particularly in **salmon canneries** and other fish-processing plants which hire staff, usually offering around $7–9 an hour for standing beside a noisy and wet canning line gutting or filleting fish. If you can hack the arduous and boring work, it is possible to earn a packet doing long shifts with plenty of overtime, and keeping living costs down by bringing a tent or staying in cannery-owned bunkhouses. The season in each place is often short and the catch uncertain, so you'll need to be flexible enough to cope with early lay-offs and may have to move towns several times during the summer. You can sometimes land jobs by turning up at canneries early in the morning – Ketchikan, Petersburg, Pelican, Cordova, and Kodiak are all worth trying – but it is far better to contact companies well in advance. Many of the companies are based in Seattle, so consult the Seattle *Yellow Pages* (or surf the Net) and phone, preferably in January or February, though there may be fill-in places as late as May and June.

Working offshore on **fish-processing ships** is more of a lottery. In a good season rewards can be higher than for onshore workers (around $14 an hour or a percentage of the catch), but it is dirty, miserable, and dangerous work with no relief from the pitching seas; boats often stay at sea for weeks at a time.

On the whole, there's more fun and profit working with the **tourism industry**, often in the most beautiful parts of Alaska where tourists like to be. Jobs might include driving buses (either between towns or on city tours), hotel reception, expediting, tour narrator, or hotel work. Rates around $7 an hour are normal in jobs where tips are common, more like $8–12 an hour where no tips are likely. If you've got specialist skills, you might even get a position as a rafting guide or leading mountain-bike trips, though these are seldom offered to first-time Alaska workers. The biggest operators are Gray Line of Alaska, 300 Elliott Ave W, Seattle, WA 98119 (Ⓣ1-800/544-2206, Ⓦwww.graylinealaska.com), and Princess Tours, who accept online applications at Ⓦwww.princessjobs.com. You might want to try smaller companies we've listed throughout the Guide, or approach the bigger hotels directly.

There is also the possibility of working for the **federal government** through one of their land management agencies – the National Park Service (Ⓦwww.nps.gov/personnel), the Forest Service (Ⓦwww.fs.fed.us/fsjobs), the Fish and Wildlife Service, or the Bureau of Land Management (Ⓦwww.ak.blm.gov). You can log on to each organization's website, but eventually they all lead to the federal government's Office of Personnel Management site (Ⓦwww.usajobs.opm.gov), which handles most positions.

For a wide listing of jobs available throughout the state, surf to the Department of Labor's Alaska Jobs Bank at Ⓦwww.labor.state.ak.us/esjobs/jobs.

Volunteer work

For those not legally allowed to work in the US, the only chance of working for the federal government is as a **volunteer**, and even US citizens might want to take this approach as it is much easier to land a volunteer position than a paid job. Though you will probably get free accommodation and food, and may even have some of your transport costs taken care of, you won't get paid. In return for this poor remuneration, you may get to work in fabulous places learning valuable skills working alongside professionals conducting wildlife surveys or helping restore salmon breeding areas. Then again, you may end up doing fairly dull work, such as cleaning up campgrounds, or find yourself working in rugged conditions doing something physically demanding; always make sure you know what you are letting yourself in for. The websites of the federal agencies listed above will take you to information on their volunteer programs, the most active being that run by the Forest Service.

Nightlife, festivals, and public holidays

Few places are as seasonal as Alaska, and most of the businesses you are likely to come into contact with are well attuned to making money while tourists are around. Consequently, you'll find shops, cruises, tour offices, and restaurants have long opening hours every day of the summer, the only exceptions being public holidays – such as Memorial Day, Independence Day, and Labor Day – when some businesses may close. Museums are mostly open 10am–5pm throughout the week, with visitor centers usually staying open a little longer.

During the winter months most tourist-related businesses shut down altogether or operate with vastly reduced hours; you should always call ahead to check opening hours and off-season schedules.

Holidays and festivals

Many of the festivals listed below are covered in more detail in the relevant section of the Guide.

January

New Year's Day (Jan 1).
Russian Orthodox Christmas (Jan 7). Solemn services held in Kodiak, Sitka, and elsewhere.
Martin Luther King Day (third Mon).

February

Yukon Quest International Sled Dog Race (second week). Starts or finishes in Fairbanks. Ⓦwww.yukonquest.org.
Ice Climbing Festival near Valdez (middle week). Competitive ice climbing in Keystone Canyon.
Iceworm Festival in Cordova (middle weekend). Giant model iceworm paraded through the streets and general carousing.
President's Day (third Mon).
Fur Rendezvous in Anchorage (second to third weekend). Ten-day citywide "Fur Rondy," packed with uniquely Alaskan activities and events. Ⓦwww.furrondy.net.

March

Ice Carving Competition in Anchorage (first week).
World Ice Art Championships in Fairbanks (first two weeks). Major competition with larger-than-life sculptures. ⓦwww.icealaska.com.
Nenana Ice Classic tripod raising (first weekend).
Iditarod Trail Sled Dog Race from Anchorage to Nome (for 12 days from first Sat).
Miners & Mushers Ball in Nome (second Sat). A black-tie ball coinciding with the Iditarod.
Bering Sea Ice Golf Classic in Nome (third Sat). Fund-raising 6-hole golf on ice.
Seward's Day (last Mon). Commemorates the signing (on March 30, 1867) of the treaty by which the United States bought Alaska from Russia.
Pillar Mountain Golf Classic (last weekend, or first in April). One-hole par 70 cross-country golf. See p.322.

April

Good Friday and Easter Monday (late March or early April).
Mountain Master Extreme Snowboard Competition in Valdez (first two weeks).
Alaska Folk Festival in Juneau (second week). ⓣ754-3316, ⓦwww.juneau.com/aff.
Garnet Festival in Wrangell (third week).

May

Shorebird and Wooden Boat festivals in Homer (first or second weekend). All sorts of shorebird events. Some info on ⓦbirdinghomeralaska.org.
Copper River Delta Shorebird Festival in Cordova (first weekend). Serious bird-watching and associated events.
Little Norway Festival in Petersburg (third full weekend).
Memorial Day (last Mon). Signals the beginning of the summer season.
Hunter Creek "Kickoff" at the Alaska State Fairgrounds in Palmer (Memorial Day weekend). Three-day acoustic music festival with camping on site (around $40 for the weekend). ⓦwww.americanbluegrass.com.
Kodiak Crab Festival (Memorial Day weekend). See p.322.

June

Blues on the Green in Anchorage (first or second Sat). Alaska's premier blues festival (along with soul and bluegrass) held in Anchorage's Kincaid Park. Around $35. ⓦwww.bluescentral.net.
Colony Days in Palmer (second weekend Fri–Sun).
Sitka Summer Music Festival (first or last three weeks). See p.137.
Summer Solstice Celebrations in Fairbanks (weekend nearest to June 21). Fun run, midnight basketball, and other like-minded events.
Seldovia Summer Solstice Music Festival (solstice weekend). See p.277.
Midnight Sun Festival in Nome (weekend nearest to June 21). Complete with Polar Bear Swim. ⓣ443-6624, ⓦwww.nomealaska.org.
Nalukataq in Barrow (mid- to late June). Celebration of the end of the spring whale hunt.
Last Frontier Theatre Conference in Valdez (third or last week). See p.301.
Great Alaska Craftbeer & Homebrew Festival in Haines (fourth weekend). Tasting, jazz, blues, and a $40 Saturday-night banquet.

July

Independence Day (July 4). Street fair and fireworks in just about every town in the state.
Alaska Women's Festival in Anchorage (July 4 weekend). Women-only three-day music festival held at the Alpenglow ski area, with an entry fee of around $75. ⓦwww.akwomensfest.com.
Mount Marathon Race in Seward (July 4). See p.247.
Girdwood Forest Fair (July 4th weekend). See p.237.
Moose Dropping Festival in Talkeetna (second weekend). See p.367.
World Eskimo-Indian Olympics in Fairbanks (second week).
Golden Days in Fairbanks (second two weeks).
Kodiak Bear Country Music Festival in Kodiak (middle weekend). See p.323.
Anderson Bluegrass Country Music Festival Mile 283 Parks Hwy (last weekend). See p.397.

August

Talkeetna Bluegrass Festival at Mile 102 Parks Hwy (first weekend). See p.367.
Tanana Valley State Fair in Fairbanks (second week). ⓣ452-3750, ⓦwww.tananavalleyfair.org.
Blueberry Arts Festival in Ketchikan (second week). ⓣ225-2211.
Alaska State Fair in Palmer (late Aug to early Sept). Ten days over two weekends. See p.353.

September

Labor Day (first Mon). Signals the end of the summer season.
Rubber Duck Race in Nome (Labor Day). Sub-Arctic pooh-sticks. ⓣ443-2798.
Bathtub Race in Nome (Labor Day). A wheeled bathtub push. ⓣ443-2798.
Blueberry Festival in Seldovia (Labor Day weekend).
Equinox Marathon in Fairbanks (nearest Sat to Sept 21). ⓦwww.equinoxmarathon.org.

October

Oktoberfest in Kodiak (first Sat). German music and food. ⓣ486-5557.
Columbus Day (second Mon).
Alaska Day (Oct 18). Anniversary of the formal transfer of the territory from Russia and the raising of the US flag at Sitka in 1867.
Alaska Day Festival in Sitka (Oct 18).

November

Veteran's Day (Nov 11).
Thanksgiving (last Thurs).

December

Bachelor Society Ball and Wilderness Woman Contest in Talkeetna (first weekend). See p.367.
Christmas Day (Dec 25).

Nightlife

With those **long Alaskan evenings** the tourist day doesn't need to stop at 6pm. Strolling along a Southeast boardwalk after dinner, or along a sub-Arctic beach at midnight with the sun still in the sky can be one of your trip's highlights. In small towns and anywhere off the beaten path the sun may be your only evening entertainment, though there will always be a local bar or movie theater around. If you are lucky, you might find a **band** playing, though your chances are greater in the bigger towns where a few well-known names have a loyal following. The music is seldom edgy and is more likely to be a solid rock or blues band churning out reliable danceable tunes. You may also come across acoustic sets by Alaska's coterie of singer-songwriters. Out-of-state bands occasionally make it up here to play big venues in Anchorage and Fairbanks, and perhaps one of the summer festivals (see opposite).

In some of the most popular destinations you'll find events laid on especially for tourists. In areas with significant Native populations – particularly in coastal areas – groups perform **traditional dance**, usually in full costume and often in a replica of a traditional house. In the Interior and parts of Southeast it is the gold-mining heritage that holds sway, and mock-up saloons play host to music hall shows, typically with performers in period costume who sometimes stay in character while waiting tables.

Directory for overseas travelers

Addresses and mileposts Larger Alaskan towns follow the straightforward grid system used elsewhere in the country, whereby the Anchorage address 3901 Old Seward Highway will be at the intersection of Old Seward Highway and 39th Ave. In rural areas every Alaskan highway – Alaska, Richardson, Glenn, George Parks, Taylor, and so on – is demarcated by mileposts marking the distance from the town regarded as the beginning of that highway. Addresses along that highway are simply given as the milepost reading to the nearest tenth of a mile.

Cigarettes and smoking The legal age for smoking in Alaska is 19. Vendors are required to keep cigarettes and cigars out of reach and not on display. Smoking is widely considered anti-social and, as in many other states, it is banned in most public areas and restaurants must provide a non-smoking section.

Departure tax There is no Alaska-specific departure tax. US departure tax is included in the price of your air ticket.

Electricity Alaska uses the same power supply as the rest of the US: 110 volts at 60Hz. North Americans can use appliances with no modification; pretty much everyone else will need a plug adapter and some form of transformer.

Floors In the US, what would be the ground floor in Britain is the first floor, the first floor the second floor and so on.

Laundries and showers Many rural Alaskans live in cabins without running hot water, and laundromats almost always have showers to cater to them and campers. Showers cost $3–4 plus 50¢ for a towel.

Measurements and sizes The US has yet to go metric, so measurements are in inches, feet, yards, and miles; weight in ounces, pounds, and tons. American pints and gallons are four-fifths of Imperial ones. Clothing sizes are always two figures less than they would be in Britain – a British woman's size 12 is a US size 10 – while British shoe sizes are half a size below American ones for women, and one size below for men.

Photography and film Photography in Alaska has special demands, requiring a lens as wide as 28mm to really capture the magnificent scenery, but something as long as 300mm (and consequently a tripod) if you don't want to have to explain that the distant brown smudge is a bear. Most point-and-shoot cameras will not return decent wildlife shots. Remember, too, that the best time for seeing animals is at the end of the day when light levels are low and shadows are long. Low light levels increase the need for faster films, usually 400ASA or better. Film and camera equipment is widely available in the larger towns, though in the more remote areas you'll be limited to the most popular film types. Prices are tolerable, though you may want to stock up before leaving home.

Shoes To avoid traipsing mud everywhere many Alaskans (B&B hosts included) ask you to remove your outdoor footwear.

Souvenirs Craft items bearing the Silver Hand logo are supposed to be authentic Native Alaskan handiwork; those marked with a polar bear symbol claim to be non-Native but Alaskan-made goods. For more on Native craft purchases, see the box on p.224.

Taxes Despite recent efforts to initiate new taxes to balance the budget, there is no state sales tax. Some communities (particularly in Southeast) impose their own sales tax (typically 2–7 percent), and many cities charge an additional bed tax of 2–7 percent.

Time zone Alaska Standard Time is observed throughout the whole state (except for a few far western Aleutian Islands not covered in this book) and daylight saving is observed from the first Sunday in April to the last Sunday in October – the same as in most of the rest of the US and Canada. In summer when it is noon in Anchorage it is 1pm in Vancouver, 1pm in Seattle, 4pm in New York, 9pm in London, 6am (the next day) in Sydney, and 8am (the next day) in Wellington.

Tipping You should always tip the waiting staff in a bar or restaurant at least fifteen percent, though something less will do if you are sitting at the bar. A similar percentage should be added to taxi fares. A hotel porter should get roughly $1 for each bag carried to your room. When paying by credit card you are expected to add the tip to the total bill before filling in the total and signing.

Video Like the rest of North America, Alaska uses the NTSC TV and video standard which is incompatible with the PAL system used in most of the rest of the world. If you buy a video, make sure it is in the right format or be prepared for an expensive conversion (though modern VCRs are often configured to play both formats).

Guide

Guide

1

Southeast Alaska

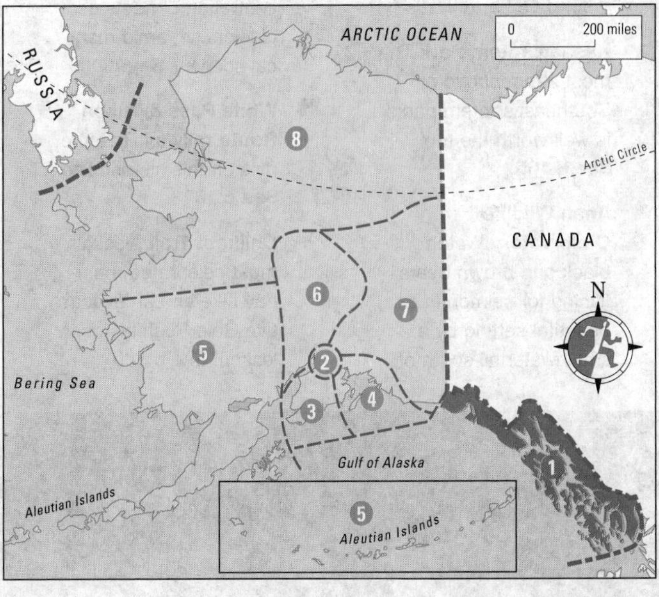

CHAPTER 1

Highlights

* **Blue-water kayaking** Explore the region by kayak for fabulous scenery and the chance to see marine mammals up close: Misty Fiords National Monument, Tracy Arm Fjord; and Glacier Bay National Park are three of many worthy candidates. See p.95, p.157 and p.164
* **Kasaan Totem Park** The most atmospheric of Southeast's totem parks is well worth the trip. See p.105
* **Anan Wildlife Observatory** Watch black and brown bears fishing for salmon in a beautiful setting by a small waterfall south of Petersburg. See p.113
* **Sitka** This immensely appealing town has a sublime island-studded coastal setting, superb totem poles, and a fascinating Russian heritage. See p.122
* **Glacier Bay National Park** An impressive concentration of tidewater glaciers set amid magical scenery. See p.159
* **White Pass & Yukon Route railway** Ride the rails on this historic line. See p.182
* **Chilkoot Trail** Alaska's most celebrated multi-day hike and an evocative Gold Rush history lesson. See p.186

△ Tlinigit mural

1

Southeast Alaska

Visitors arriving in **SOUTHEAST ALASKA** have a treat in store, a landscape writ on a grand scale, stretching four hundred miles along the coast. This is the Alaskan Panhandle, flanked by impenetrable snow-capped coastal mountains and incised by hairline fjords that create an interlocking archipelago of densely forested islands. Along its length runs the continuous thread of calm waterways known as the Inside Passage. So narrow are some of the glacier-carved channels that on larger boats you feel you could reach out and touch the steeply shelving rocks. Sheltered beaches are rare, and out of necessity towns are crammed onto whatever flat land can be found, often spilling out over the sea on a network of boardwalks: shops, streets, and even whole salmon canneries are perched picturesquely along the waterside on spruce poles.

Like much of Alaska, Southeast is defined by its weather, though here the moderator is rain rather than cold. With a maritime climate and a latitude similar to Scotland, Southeast seldom gets really cold in the winter, and summer highs are tempered by incessant low cloud and heavy rainfall, which can top 200 inches a year in places; it is quite feasible to visit Southeast at any time, even for late-season events like Sitka's Alaska Day in October. The mountains still get covered with snow, though, and this lingers well into late June, making late summer and fall the best times for hiking.

The dripping leaves, sodden mosses, and wispy mist seem to suit ravens and bald eagles, which are everywhere, and it comes as no surprise that they became the prime crest symbols of the native **Tlingit** people. The Tlingit (*thling-get*), along with the Haida (*HI-da*) and Tsimshian (*SIM-shee-an*), have left an enduring legacy: **totem poles**, typically found clustered around replicas of the clan houses in which they once lived. Their original village sites were located to exploit the abundance of plunderable sealife: as they say here, "when the tide's out, dinner's in." The early Russian fur traders and American gold seekers didn't disrupt the social fabric too much, but with the arrival of the missionaries the Tlingit abandoned their villages in favor of the schools and churches of the white towns that sprang up around gold mines, forts, canneries, and fishing ports. Suddenly, the motto changed to "we eat what we can, and can what we can't."

The importance of canneries gradually declined with the rise of logging in the 1960s. Almost the entirety of Southeast falls within the immense **Tongass National Forest**, and for decades cutting rights ensured the profitability of pulp and saw mills and guaranteed extensive clear-cutting of old-growth spruce and hemlock forests. In the past decade, however, logging has rapidly declined. Some concede that the market has changed, but the families of most

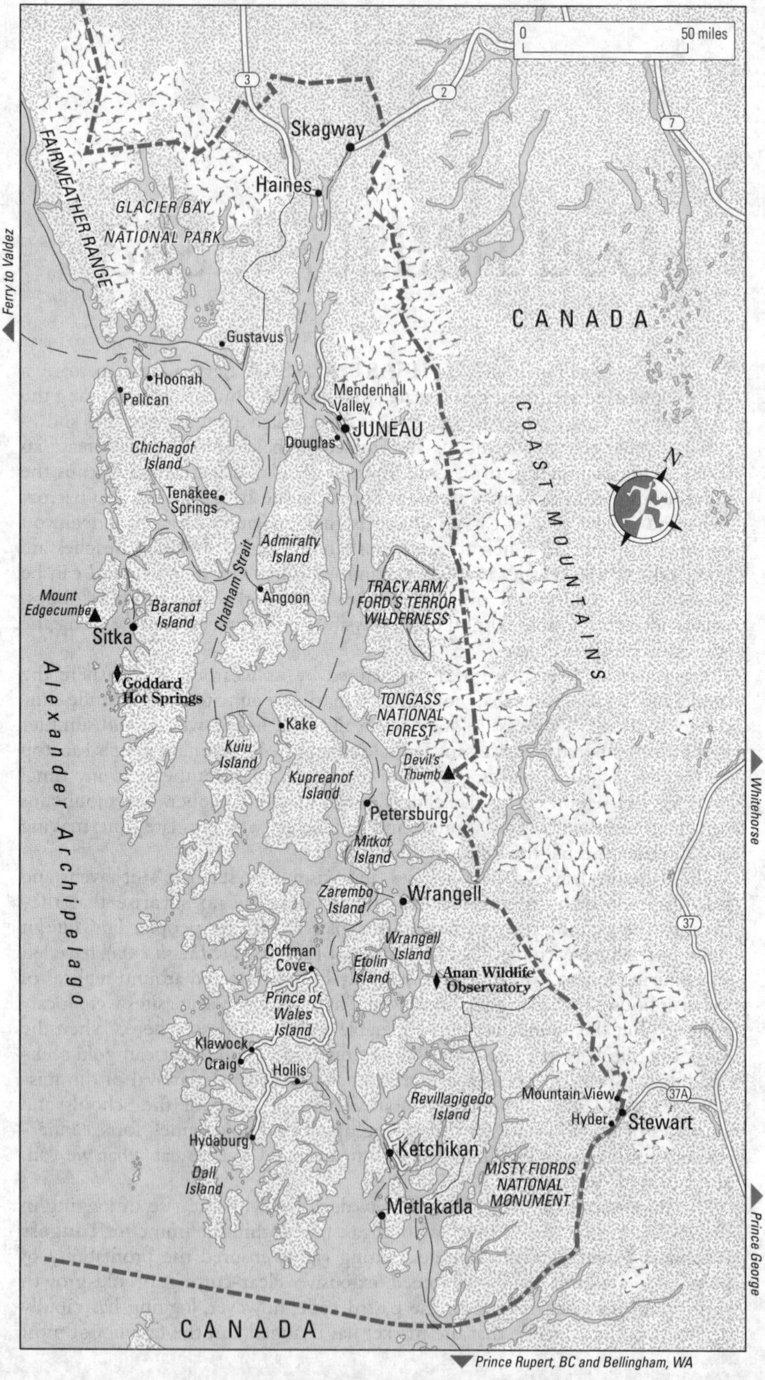
0
50 miles
3
2
7
Skagway
Haines
FAIRWEATHER RANGE
GLACIER BAY NATIONAL PARK
Ferry to Valdez
CANADA
Gustavus
Hoonah
Pelican
Mendenhall Valley
JUNEAU
Douglas
COAST MOUNTAINS
N
Chichagof Island
Tenakee Springs
Admiralty Island
Chatham Strait
Angoon
TRACY ARM/ FORD'S TERROR WILDERNESS
Mount Edgecumbe
Baranof Island
Sitka
Goddard Hot Springs
Alexander Archipelago
TONGASS NATIONAL FOREST
Kake
Kuiu Island
Kupreanof Island
Devil's Thumb
Petersburg
Whitehorse
Mitkof Island
Zarembo Island
Wrangell
Wrangell Island
37
Coffman Cove
Etolin Island
Anan Wildlife Observatory
Prince of Wales Island
Klawock
Craig
Hollis
Revillagigedo Island
Mountain View
37A
Hyder
Stewart
Hydaburg
Ketchikan
Dall Island
MISTY FIORDS NATIONAL MONUMENT
Metlakatla
Prince George
CANADA
Prince Rupert, BC and Bellingham, WA

Ferry fares

The price of AMHS ferry journeys is given in the chart in Basics, pp.38–39.

unemployed loggers and mill workers blame eight years of Clinton government. The shifting political climate under Bush has given some hope, though there are few signs of buoyancy in the industry.

With mills closing or downsizing, small communities feel under siege and are turning to tourism as their savior. They hope to tap into the rich vein of the **cruise-ship industry**, which conditions almost every element of tourist life in Southeast. When a boat ties up (and most towns have at least one per day, sometimes four or five), it feels as if the circus is in town. Tour buses line the dock, helicopters and planes buzz the skies, and the gift shops and restaurants brace themselves for the onslaught of visitors who bring much needed cash but swamp towns like Ketchikan, Juneau, and Skagway.

Yet even in the most popular ports of call, a little imagination and judicious timing can leave you in pristine environments without a soul in sight. **Ketchikan** is rightly celebrated for its wonderful examples of native culture, but if you find its totem parks too busy, head for Prince of Wales Island, where similar sites are well off the tourist trail. Kayaking is a superb way of seeking a little solitude, and the glacial granite masterpiece of **Misty Fiords National Monument** is a prime destination for a paddling expedition, although it's more commonly visited on a day trip. Up the coast the beachside petroglyphs of Wrangell can be visited on a short stopover, though the town's totem parks and fine hikes take a little longer. The constricting Wrangell Narrows are just wide enough for ferries to reach the lively Norwegian fishing town of Petersburg, a base for visiting the LeConte Glacier, the southernmost of the dozens of glaciers that regularly calve into the waters of the Inside Passage. The jewel in Southeast's crown is **Sitka**, where Native and Russian culture come together in beautiful surroundings. The state capital, **Juneau**, puts up a good fight for your attention with its cosmopolitan edge, a fascinating gold-mining history, and unparalleled access to the marvelous **Glacier Bay National Park**. From here, Lynn Canal runs north to two towns: Haines, with its unusual wintertime congregation of bald eagles and low-key charms, and the gold-rush town of Skagway, the start of the **White Pass & Yukon Route railway** as well as the challenging **Chilkoot Trail**.

Throughout the Southeast you'll find boat captains eager to take you out fishing, sightseeing, or, most of all, **whale watching**, in the hopes of catching a breaching humpback or the prominent dorsal fin of an orca.

Ketchikan and around

KETCHIKAN, almost seven hundred miles north of Seattle, likes to bill itself as Alaska's "first city," the initial Alaskan port of call for northbound AMHS ferries and cruise ships. With over fifteen thousand people it ranks as Alaska's fourth largest city, and yet on arrival you are struck not so much by the town itself but by its insignificance after the miles of dense forest you've just sailed past or flown over. On most summer days downtown Ketchikan disappears behind a white wall of cruise ships which feed up to five thousand tourists into the compact town center, affecting almost every activity you take part in and quite possibly souring your opinion of this otherwise likeable community.

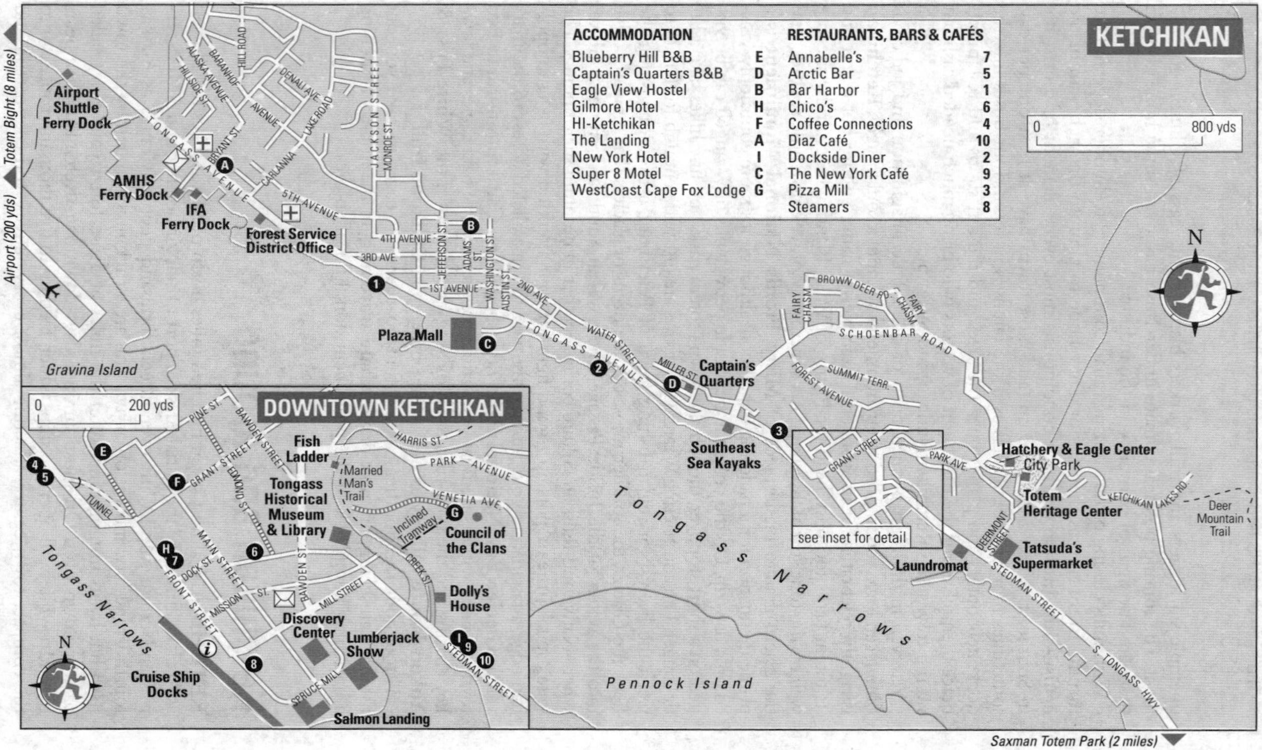
KETCHIKAN
ACCOMMODATION
Blueberry Hill B&B E
Captain's Quarters B&B D
Eagle View Hostel B
Gilmore Hotel H
HI-Ketchikan F
The Landing A
New York Hotel I
Super 8 Motel C
WestCoast Cape Fox Lodge G
RESTAURANTS, BARS & CAFÉS
Annabelle's 7
Arctic Bar 5
Bar Harbor 1
Chico's 6
Coffee Connections 4
Diaz Café 10
Dockside Diner 2
The New York Café 9
Pizza Mill 3
Steamers 8
0 800 yds
N
Totem Bight (8 miles)
Airport (200 yds)
Airport Shuttle Ferry Dock
AMHS Ferry Dock
IFA Ferry Dock
Forest Service District Office
Plaza Mall
Gravina Island
Captain's Quarters
Southeast Sea Kayaks
Tongass Narrows
Pennock Island
see inset for detail
Hatchery & Eagle Center
City Park
Totem Heritage Center
Tatsuda's Supermarket
Laundromat
Deer Mountain Trail
Saxman Totem Park (2 miles)
TONGASS AVENUE
WATER STREET
SCHOENBAR ROAD
BROWN DEER RD.
FAIRY CHASM
SUMMIT TERR.
FOREST AVENUE
MILLER ST.
GRANT STREET
PARK AVE.
KETCHIKAN LAKES RD
DEERMONT STREET
STEDMAN STREET
S. TONGASS HWY
HILLSIDE ST.
ALASKA AVENUE
BARANHOF AVENUE
HILL ROAD
DENALI AVE.
LAKE ROAD
CARLANNA
BRYANT ST.
5TH AVENUE
JACKSON STREET
MONROE ST.
4TH AVENUE
3RD AVE.
JEFFERSON ST.
ADAMS ST.
WASHINGTON ST.
AUSTIN ST.
1ST AVENUE
2ND AVE.
DOWNTOWN KETCHIKAN
0 200 yds
Fish Ladder
Married Man's Trail
Tongass Historical Museum & Library
Inclined Tramway
Council of the Clans
Dolly's House
Discovery Center
Lumberjack Show
Cruise Ship Docks
Salmon Landing
PINE ST.
BAWDEN STREET
HARRIS ST.
PARK AVENUE
VENETIA AVE.
GRANT STREET
EDMOND ST.
TUNNEL
MAIN STREET
DOCK ST.
FRONT STREET
MISSION ST.
BAWDEN ST.
MILL STREET
CREEK ST.
SPRUCE MILL
STEDMAN STREET

Shoehorned onto the southwestern edge of **Revillagigedo Island** (correctly, Ruh-vee-uh-hih-HAY-do, but usually just "Revilla"), Ketchikan is – like most Southeast towns – squeezed tightly between forested hills and the plunging depths of the Inside Passage, in this case the waters of Tongass Narrows. Land is in such demand that precipitous hillsides have been put to residential use, the houses linked by long staircases that are significant enough to have street names. Some lack vehicular access to their residences, while others drive home on streets that are really just wide boardwalks. Climb up to the wooden Warren, G, and Harding streets – jointly named for the 29th president who visited in 1923 – from where it is apparent just how much of the waterfront is on stilts. The other side of Ketchikan is the historic downtown core, now overdeveloped with flashy diamond and fur shops, cheek by jowl with tacky souvenir emporia.

Nonetheless, Ketchikan remains one of Southeast's more interesting towns. Nowhere else can you get such a broad sweep of Southeast Native culture, starting with one of the world's finest collections of authentic nineteenth-century totem poles in the **Totem Heritage Center**. A few miles along Ketchikan's limited road system, the Totem Bight State Historic Park and Saxman Totem Park both exhibit fine replicas in a more natural, outdoor setting; the latter runs a carving center where you can watch new totem poles being carved. There's also the celebrated boardwalks of **Creek Street**, now somewhat sanitized from their red-light past but still a good place to stroll while checking out the craft and book shops, and the salmon in the waters below.

To escape the pressures of mass tourism make use of some of the area's hiking trails, though bear in mind Ketchikan is a strong contender to be the nation's wettest town – annual precipitation averages over 160 inches (and has topped 200 inches).

Although you may only want to spend a day or two in Ketchikan itself, there's no shortage of intriguing destinations a short flight or ferry trip from the city. Flightseeing and boat-charter companies are eager to take you into the granite wonderland of **Misty Fiords National Monument**, a trip that can be extended by staying in Forest Service cabins, or camping out beside your kayak.

For a less intense approach to the grandeur of Southeast Alaska, spend a few days on **Prince of Wales Island** (see p.58), or pay a visit to the Tsimshian community of **Metlakatla**, the only Native reservation in the state. If it's **bears** you want to see, you've got a fair chance of spotting one just driving around Prince of Wales Island, but there's more structured viewing at Anan Creek (see "Wrangell," on p.106, although it's accessible from Ketchikan) and at **Hyder** (see box, p.97), a tiny piece of Alaska that feels a lot more like Canada.

Arrival and information

Near-daily AMHS **ferries** (Ⓣ225-6182) and twice-daily Inter-Island Ferry Authority ferries from Prince of Wales Island (Ⓣ826-4848 or 1-866/308-4848, Ⓦwww.interislandferry.com) pull in at separate docks two miles north of downtown on N Tongass Highway; city buses (see below) stop outside. Ketchikan's **airport** (with frequent Alaska Airlines flights from Seattle and Juneau, and occasional links to the smaller Southeast towns; Ⓣ225-6800) is on Gravina Island, separated from the town by the two-hundred-yard channel of Tongass Narrows. A vehicular **shuttle ferry** (every 15min to 9.30pm; $4 round-trip, vehicles $6 each way) plies the gap and drops you two miles north of downtown (close to the AMHS ferry terminal) where you can catch a bus (see below) into town. Alternatively, hop aboard the frequent Airporter (Ⓣ225-5429) right outside the airport terminal for a combined ferry ride and drive into town for $18. The Airporter meets all planes and picks up and drops off at hotels around town.

Stacks of leaflets and information on the town are available at the **visitor center**, 131 Front St (May–Sept daily 6am–6pm, hours extended when cruise ships stay later; Oct–April Mon–Fri 8am–5pm; ⓣ225-6166 or 1-800/770-3300, ⓦwww.visit-ketchikan.com). For anything related to the outdoors, you're better off at the Southeast Alaska Discovery Center, 50 Main St (early May–Sept daily 8am–5pm; Oct–early May Tues–Sat 10am–4.30pm; ⓣ228-6220, ⓦwww.fs.fed.us/r10/tongass), where there's an unstaffed area with plenty of brochures on trails, camping, and kayaking, and a computer for reserving Forest Service cabins. For something more specific, call at the Forest Service's District Office, 3031 N Tongass Hwy (Mon–Fri 8am–4.30pm; ⓣ225-2148), out near the ferry dock.

Getting around and tours

Getting around the downtown area is very easy on foot, though to get to the ferry terminal and airport (and perhaps to your accommodation) you might need the **bus** services provided by "the Bus" (Mon–Sat 5.15am–9.45pm every 30min, Sun 8.45am–3.45pm every hour; ⓣ225-8726, ⓦborough.ketchikan.ak.us). The most useful of the two routes is the Blue Line ($1.50) which makes an hour-long loop from the airport ferry dock, past the AMHS ferry dock, into town and south to Saxman (though it's rumored that the Saxman leg may be dropped in future). The Green Line ($2.25) replaces the Saxman leg with a loop through the suburbs but also calls at the airport, ferry dock, and town center. These options are satisfactory if you plan ahead, but for more impulsive moves or to visit the totem parks you may want to **rent a car** (good value for two or more), rent a **bike**, or grab a **taxi** (see "Listings," p.94).

Ketchikan has at least a dozen land-based **tours**, most of them geared up to deal with the waves of passengers piling off the cruise ships each day. In fact, many of the tours are only sold on the ships and independent travelers are either ignored or vastly outnumbered by ship passengers. Horse-drawn buggy circuits, double-decker-bus tours, self-drive Jeep adventures, Tlingit canoe paddles and many more are all available: call at the tour reservation area of the visitor center if you are interested.

The difficulty of viewing both Saxman and Totem Bight without your own transport may induce you to join Rainbird Deluxe Tours (ⓣ1-888/505-8810), who do a tour through the sights of town and visit Saxman (2hr; $30). Northern Tours of Alaska (ⓣ247-6457, ⓦwww.northerntoursofalaska.com) do a similar tour and sometimes have an extended tour (3hr; $40), which also visits Totem Bight. For something a little different look out for the enthusiastic Lois Munch, who runs Classic Tours (ⓣ225-3091, ⓦwww.classictours.com), using a restored 1955 Chevy to visit Saxman (2hr; $70) or, additionally, a forest, which includes looking at an eagle's nest (3hr; $90).

Accommodation

Ketchikan's modest range of accommodation sets the pattern for what you'll find all the way up the coast; downtown hotels and B&Bs, a couple of motels, a hostel or two and some wooded campgrounds out of town. There are few genuinely luxurious places, but in general standards are high and prices tolerable. Most of the hotels are downtown, with B&Bs scattered along the road system.

The closest **campgrounds** to town are in the attractive Ward Lake Recreation Area, five miles northwest of the ferry terminal. Although these spots accept RVs, there are no hookups, and motorhome drivers wanting power and cable TV will have to stay fourteen miles north of downtown.

You should book directly with the establishments as far in advance as you can manage in summer, but if you're in real difficulty contact the visitor center, or Ketchikan Reservation Service (ⓣ247-5337 or 1-800/987-5337, ⓦwww.ketchikan-lodging.com), who can arrange accommodation.

There are also dozens of Forest Service **cabins** around Ketchikan, some of which we've listed in the boxes on pp.90 and 94. If you're geared up for camping, then you've everything you need for staying in a cabin – those less well equipped can rent everything they need from Alaska Wilderness Outfitting, 3857 Fairview Ave (ⓣ225-7335, ⓦwww.latitude56.com/camping), including a complete cooking kit for $22 a day.

Hotels, motels, and B&Bs

Blueberry Hill B&B 500 Front St ⓣ247-2583 or 1-877/449-2583, ⓦwww.blueberryhillbb.com. Lovely B&B in a historic home a five-minute walk from downtown, with tastefully decorated guest rooms all featuring Alaskan artworks, colorful quilts, and private bathroom. Most have a partial or full sea view. ❺

Captain's Quarters B&B 325 Lund St ⓣ225-4912, ⓦwww.ptialaska.net/~captbnb. Three spacious rooms separate from the owner's house, all with queen beds and cable TV – and one with a kitchen – in a nautically themed hillside house with some great views over the town. Continental breakfast included. ❹

Gilmore Hotel 326 Front St ⓣ225-9423 or 1-800/275-9423, ⓦwww.gilmorehotel.com. Despite recent remodeling this 1927 establishment retains the tenor of an old-style hotel, with a range of rooms from poky doubles without a view, to larger water-view rooms and much more spacious queen suites with a tub in the bathroom. Suites ❻, water view ❺, standard rooms ❹

The Landing 3434 Tongass Ave ⓣ225-5166 or 1-800/428-8304, ⓔ bcokelanding@kpunet.net. Comfortable, well-appointed Best Western hotel two miles north of downtown, right opposite the AMHS ferry terminal and within walking distance of the airport ferry. There's cable TV, a fitness center, a restaurant and bar, a courtesy van into town, and some spacious suites for not much more than the room rate. Reserve well in advance. Suites & rooms ❼

New York Hotel 207 Stedman St ⓣ225-0246, ⓦwww.thenewyorkhotel.com. Excellent-value older hotel that's tastefully refurbished with black-and-white-tiled bathrooms and an antique vanity or armoire in each room. Most rooms are fairly small, but if you reserve in time you may be able to get the large harbor-view rooms at the front. Alternatively, step up to the attractive suites in a separate building around the corner on Creek St, each with a small sunny balcony and full kitchen with everything you need but food. Suites ❼, rooms ❺

Super 8 Motel 2151 Sea Level Drive ⓣ225-9088 or 1-800/800-8000, ⓦwww.super8.com. The cheapest motel in town, fairly uninspiring but decent enough, with all the facilities you'd expect. Large rooms. Suites ❺, rooms ❹

WestCoast Cape Fox Lodge 800 Venetia Way ⓣ225-8001 or 1-800/325-4000, ⓦwww.westcoasthotels.com. The top hotel in town, attractively sited on the hill behind the downtown area, featuring international-standard rooms, many with water views glimpsed through the spruce and hemlocks. Suites just ❾, rooms ❼

Hostels and campgrounds

Clover Pass Resort at Knudson Cove, 14 miles north along Tongass Hwy ⓣ247-2234 or 1-800/410-2234, ⓦwww.cloverpassresort.com. The only RV site around Ketchikan with hookups. No tent sites. They also rent skiffs from $65 a day. $28.

Eagle View Hostel 2305 5th Ave ⓣ225-5461, ⓦwww.eagleviewhostel.com. Great views of the Narrows from this converted suburban house, which has one double, a male dorm sleeping five, and a women's room for three with its own bathroom. The $28 rate includes tax, bed linens, and towel as well as use of the kitchen, barbecue, and sauna. No lockout or curfew. Owner Dale also runs occasional kayak and sightseeing trips – and won't let you get bored even on the wettest days. Follow Jefferson off Tongass Hwy, then turn right onto 5th. Open April–Oct and by reservation. ❶

HI-Ketchikan 400 Main St at Grant St ⓣ225-3319, ⓔktnyh@eagle.ptialaska.net. Very basic and rigidly managed hostel in the United Methodist Church with simple dorm beds for $12 (non-members $15), reasonable kitchen and often some free baked goods in the evening. Bring a sleeping bag and expect a daytime lockout (9am–6pm), an 11pm curfew, and a chore requirement. For advance bookings send a money order for the first night's fee (and an SAE if you want confirmation) to PO Box 8515, Ketchikan, AK 99901. Open June–Aug. ❶

Totem poles

Despite the teachings of early missionaries, **totem poles** – the enduring image of the Alaskan (and whole Pacific Northwest) coast – were never intended as objects of worship or religious veneration but stood as cultural symbols recording the lineage, legends, history, and lore of a people: silent storytellers in a land with no written language. Equally, they were visual statements of a clan's wealth: the cost of employing highly esteemed carvers added greatly to the commissioner's prestige. The raising of a pole was always accompanied by a **potlatch**, a kind of feast where the clan could give away a vast portion of their property. In contrast to modern values, status was determined by how much a person gave away rather than how much they accumulated.

Totem poles exist from Puget Sound in Washington State right through the Alaskan Panhandle, exactly the range of the western red cedar, whose timber is preferred for its easy-to-work straight grain and unusual rotting characteristics. It decomposes from the inside out, thus lasting longer in the eternally damp climate, though still only sixty to seventy years.

Every element in the preparation of a pole – selecting and felling the tree, the carving, the painting, and finally the raising – was marked by ceremony, culminating with the singing, dancing, and drumming of the final potlatch given by the patron's clan. The assembled throng would be put to work digging a six-foot hole, and then raising the pole by means of a scaffold and ropes. Simultaneously, the head of the clan would recite the history represented on the pole to publicly validate their right to use the crests and associated songs and dances. Once erected the poles were not changed or repaired but allowed to decay until they finally fell over and rotted into the undergrowth.

The raising of totem poles reached its "**golden age**" in the latter half of the nineteenth century, peaking around 1860. Wealth increased by the fur trade and a thriving culture unleashed a great burst of creativity, enhanced by access to abundant iron for carving and newly available artificial pigments. Hundreds of poles sprouted up along the coast, and photos of the era show whole forests of poles clustered around traditional clan houses.

This era ended with the arrival of missionaries who discouraged pole raising, built schools and churches, and encouraged the Natives to abandon many of the old traditions. Meanwhile, late nineteenth-century tourists were fascinated with totem poles as an art form, and many poles were relocated to sites closer to the steamer routes, breaking the tradition of leaving them in situ. From around 1875 onwards, private and museum collectors began removing them from abandoned villages. With the exception of the replicas described below there were very few poles carved between the late 1880s and the 1970s.

A brief resurgence of interest came in the late 1930s when the Civilian Conservation Corps (CCC) undertook an unemployment relief program to salvage poles and employ skilled carvers to create replicas. Honoring tradition, handmade tools as close as possible in design to pre-European models were utilized, and color matching, where necessary, was done by combining natural pigments with chewed, dry salmon eggs.

The skills retained by older carvers were passed on to a younger generation of artisans who still carve poles, often replicating older designs. Without these efforts the tradition of raising totem poles might not have survived into the twenty-first century. Nonetheless, there are still factions that believe the CCC project wrongly broke the tradition of leaving poles to rot where they stood, free from the well-meaning preserve-and-protect instincts of whites. The replica totems have survived well and can be seen in totem parks on Prince of Wales Island, Saxman and Totem Bight in Ketchikan, Shakes Island in Wrangell, and in Sitka. In most cases the originals were discarded.

The real renaissance in totem pole carving didn't come until after the **Pole Survey and Retrieval Project**, which in the late 1960s set out to collect the last remaining original poles from abandoned villages. Only 44 were found. These formed the basis of Ketchikan's Totem Heritage Center collection and encouraged the development of a modern carving tradition both here and at the Carving Center at nearby Saxman. Reproductions and adherence to traditional forms and color schemes remains strong but, fostered by a renewed sense of cultural identity and tribal pride, brighter paints and modern elements have been increasingly incorporated. Today, replica and original poles are still raised in the traditional manner, but steel tools have replaced those of stone, bone, and sinew.

Pole types

Totem poles fall into five main categories. Perhaps the best known, and the style seen reproduced all over the place, are **heraldic poles**, also known as crest poles or story poles for the complex series of designs showing the matrilineal genealogy and aspects of the history of the clan or family who commissioned it. Some of the same elements – particularly the family histories – are incorporated into **house posts**, which support the roof beams in clan houses, and the entrance poles designed into Haida clan houses.

Mortuary poles were designed to honor the dead and are usually topped with the crest symbol of that person. Many originally had a recess in the back where the ashes could be placed, but missionaries strongly discouraged cremation and this practice died away, the mortuary pole being replaced by the **memorial pole.** These often only had a couple of crest figures in a simple design, and were usually placed adjacent to the village or around the house of the deceased.

Finally, there are **shame poles** or ridicule poles, the least common type but usually prominently placed where they could poke the most fun. Erected to discredit someone who had failed to clear a debt, behaved dishonorably or broken their word, these would be cut down when amends were made.

Another feature to look out for are watchmen crouched on top of some Haida totems to protect the inhabitants with their supernatural powers. Their high status is often marked by a potlatch hat (thus these are sometimes referred to as potlatch poles), which is otherwise reserved for memorial poles, with the number of rings around the hat denoting the number of potlatches the person threw.

Interpretation

Totem poles often come without any explanation of their meaning, partly because the story associated with the pole belongs to the clan concerned. Nonetheless, something can be gleaned from the design elements, which are based on interlinking ovoids – rounded rectangles – depicting anything from a whole head or torso down to teeth. Typically, ovoids exist within ovoids building a pattern one within another, interlinked by incomplete ovoids distorted to create U- and S-shapes which tie the whole together. All this encourages a high degree of stylization which can make detecting which creatures are represented difficult at first, though it gets easier with a few clues. First, animals always have ears on top, while humans have theirs on the side. The most common representations are of Eagle and Raven, which are easily confused, though the Eagle always has a hooked beak-tip. Bear and Wolf both have a rounder shape to their mouths, the latter sporting sharper teeth and a more slender snout. Whales crop up fairly often, particularly Killer Whale with his straight dorsal fin, sometimes created by adding a plank to the totem pole rather than carving it into the main body of the pole. Beaver always has two prominent front teeth and usually a flat, cross-hatched tail.

Settlers Cove State Recreation Site Mile 18.2 N Tongass Hwy. First-come, first-served campground and picnic area overlooking Clover Passage that is probably the nicest, least crowded, and most inconveniently sited spot around Ketchikan. No hookups, but there's a beach and a mile-long loop trail to Upper Lunch Creek Falls. $10.

Ward Lake Recreation Area ⓣ1-877/444-6777, ⓦwww.reserveUSA.com. Two Forest Service campgrounds in the temperate rainforest with easy access to scenic lakes and gentle trails. They are all located on (or just off) Revilla Rd, which cuts inland six miles north of Ketchikan. Ward Lake Rd leads off Revilla Rd at Mile 1.4 and runs to *Signal Creek Campground* (May to late Sept), with lots for small RVs. Go 2.3 miles along Revilla Rd to get to *Last Chance Campground* (late May to mid-Sept), amid old-growth forest with designated RV lots. Both cost $10.

The town and totem parks

Ketchikan's popularity as a tourist destination is due in part to its concentrated collection of sites around a central core of **historic streets**, notably Creek Street, now cleaned up from its seedy origins. It's an appealing spot for a stroll along the boardwalks, stopping to peek into one of the galleries or gaze over the bridge to watch the salmon make their way to the Deer Mountain Tribal Hatchery. Perhaps Ketchikan's most compelling claim to greatness is its unmatched expression of Southeast Native culture through the superb **Totem Heritage Center**, assorted totem poles around town, and the two **totem parks** just outside town: the Totem Bight State Historic Park of replica poles and clan house, and the Saxman Totem Park at the Native village of Saxman.

Downtown Ketchikan

If Ketchikan is your introduction to Alaska, your first stop should be the **Southeast Alaska Discovery Center**, 50 Main St (May–Sept Mon, Tues, Fri & Sat 8am–5pm, Wed & Thurs 8am–6.30pm, Sun 8am–4pm; $5; Oct–April Tues–Sat 8.30am–4.30pm; free), a striking cedar-framed building with absorbing displays on the region's natural ecosystems, resources, and Native culture. (In 2005 these will be joined by a re-creation of some of the limestone caves on Prince of Wales Island.) Those who have already spent time in the state may find it a little simplistic, even promotional. It can be all too obvious that the Forest Service has provided much of the funding here; you might wonder why they've bothered replicating a temperate rainforest when there are seventeen million acres of it right outside the door. It also operates as an outdoor information center (see "Arrival and information," p.82).

For local flavor visit the small and well-laid-out **Tongass Historical Museum**, 629 Dock St (mid-May to Sept daily 8am–5pm; Oct to mid-May Wed–Fri 10am–5pm, Sat & Sun 1–4pm; $2), which is full of fascinating old photos of the town and its happenings, mining paraphernalia, and a great corner filled with Native artifacts: a carved bowl from the 1880s and large, carved bentwood boxes, watertight storage vessels, the sides of which are formed from a single piece of wood that was shaped by steaming and bending. There are also old "coppers" – essentially large sheets of copper that, in the early years of trade with Europeans, gave their owners great status and were accordingly the ultimate item to give away at potlatches (see box on pp.84–85).

The bulk of the town's packaged heritage lies along **Creek Street**, a rickety-looking boardwalk perched high above the tidal waters of Ketchikan Creek. This was Ketchikan's red-light district from 1903 until 1954 when the brothels were closed down. Its notoriety was enhanced during prohibition when boats laden with illicit liquor were floated up at high tide, the contraband being fed up through trapdoors in the floors of the houses. Today the former houses of ill repute have been smartened up, painted in bright colors and mostly set up as gift shops, though there are a few higher-quality galleries and an excellent bookshop (see "Listings," p.93). The main destination for those fancying a glimpse of the old days is **Dolly's House**, 24 Creek St (generally daily 8am–5pm though dependent on cruise ships; $4), once the home and workplace of Dolly Arthur, the town's most famous prostitute, and now a small museum with original decor and saucy memorabilia. Ignoring the fact that Dolly ceased her trade here only half a century back, the guides have gone for the Victorian look, and "ladies" dressed in puffy gold-rush dresses will usher you in for a tour and headful of anecdotes from Dolly's intriguing life.

A short **inclined tramway** ($2) climbs the bluff behind Creek Street to the lobby of the *WestCoast Cape Fox Lodge* (see pp.83 and 92), which has a small display of quality Native crafts and commands a great view of the town and Tongass Narrows. In front of the hotel stands the "Council of the Clans" ring of short totem poles commissioned by the Cape Fox Native Corporation which owns the hotel. From here, Venetia Avenue leads down to Park Avenue and City Park.

An alternative route to City Park is known as the **Married Man's Trail** for the secretive escape route it provides from Creek Street. It follows a narrow boardwalk upstream past some small rapids and beside a fish ladder where throughout the summer you'll see salmon fighting the current. This brings you to Park Avenue which runs inland to **City Park**, a small but attractive area of grass, small streams and a riot of summer blooms. Tall cages on the west side of the park mark the **Deer Mountain Tribal Hatchery and Eagle Center** (May to Sept daily 8.30am–4.30pm; $8, combo ticket with Totem Heritage Center $11), where a couple of injured bald eagles are kept to educate the public about these majestic birds. You may be more interested in the hatchery, concrete tanks with fish at different stages in their development. Either follow the guided tour or make your own way around, learning about the king and coho salmon that find their way up Ketchikan Creek to breed here. Outside, a footbridge over Ketchikan Creek leads to the Totem Heritage Center (see below).

For something a little less serious, return to the waterfront behind the Discovery Center where you'll find the **Great Alaskan Lumberjack Show** (usually three shows daily, call for times ⓣ225-9050; $29), a ninety-minute extravaganza coaxed along by an MC whipping the audience into a light-hearted frenzy of US–Canadian rivalry as "frontier woodsmen" are put through their paces chopping and sawing wood, log rolling, tree felling, and speed climbing with spiked shoes. It has the tenor of a circus sideshow and, when it opened in 2000, put a few noses out of joint. The local pulp mill had only recently closed, and unemployed loggers – they don't even call themselves lumberjacks around here – were understandably put out by the tourist industry appearing to cash in on a dying industry.

Bear viewing

Several spots around Ketchikan are known for their exemplary bear viewing. Anan Wildlife Observatory (see "Around Wrangell," p.113) and Fish Creek Wildlife Viewing Area (see "Hyder," p.97) are both possibilities, but the most accessible is **Traitors Cove**, a twenty-minute float-plane flight from Ketchikan. Here, black bears actively fish from late July until September. Taquan Air (see p.93) runs the Traitors Cove Bear Adventure (2hr 30min; $249), a tour that involves a flight, a short van ride, and a quarter-mile walk to a viewing platform beside a waterfall.

Totem Heritage Center

The wonderful **Totem Heritage Center**, 601 Deermount St (May–Sept daily 8am–5pm; Oct–April Mon–Fri 1–5pm; $5, combo ticket with hatchery $11), was set up in 1976 to preserve and exhibit the largest collection of original totem poles in the US, 33 in all. Most of the poles you'll see around town and elsewhere in Southeast are replicas (see box, pp.84–85), many of them based on the poles, house posts, and fragments gathered here. For much of the twentieth century it had been recognized that unless something was done the nation's rapidly dwindling stock of original nineteenth-century totem poles would rot away and be lost forever. So, in 1973, the Totem Pole Survey and Retrieval Project was established to collect the remaining poles from abandoned Tlingit and Haida villages within fifty miles of Ketchikan. Of the hundreds noted and photographed previously by explorers and early steamship tourists, only 44 remained, eleven of which were unsalvageable.

Before entering, pause a moment to see how modern themes and techniques have been incorporated into the vibrantly painted "Honoring Those Who Give" pole, raised in 1999 to recognize those who helped fund the center. It was created by renowned carver **Nathan Jackson**, whose first pole "Raven-Frog Woman," carved in 1978, stands nearby. There's yet more of his work at Totem Bight State Park and in public places all over town.

Inside the center you are confronted with five magnificent poles from the "golden age" of totem-pole carving – two memorial, one heraldic, one potlatch, and one mortuary – all over a century old. Greatly weathered and often missing parts of various appendages, they are mostly free of any coloring, although under the beaver's chin on the Haida potlatch pole you can still see a hint of green, made from copper oxide mixed with crushed salmon eggs. For all their crumbling fragility, they still retain a menacing power, something robbed from the remaining poles and house posts that are too delicate to display upright. Almost a dozen such poles occupy an adjacent room, many of them broken and laid down in cradles, but still impressive. Panels around the walls have photos of how the poles appeared in their original locations and explain almost all you ever wanted to know about this art form. Museum staff is on hand to fill in the gaps and conduct ad hoc tours.

The poles provide inspiration for the off-season **Native Arts Studies Program**, a series of non-residential courses covering anything from cedar-bark weaving, regalia-making, and introductory carving to more advanced techniques such as bentwood-box manufacture and drum making. Courses run from mid-September to April, and start at $55 for a two-day workshop, going up to $150–250 for one- and two-week courses. For details, click to the museums website from Ⓦwww.city.ketchikan.ak.us/ds/tonghert.

North of town: Totem Bight State Historic Park

Following the Tongass Highway north of the AMHS and airport-ferry docks, Ketchikan begins to thin out. The road hugs the coast to Ward Cove, an unsightly industrial wasteland occupied until 1997 by the Ketchikan Pulp Mill and now the site of a much smaller saw mill and veneer plant. A road heads inland from here to the **Ward Lake Recreation Area**, a wooded site of attractive picnic areas, two campgrounds, and several good local hikes (see box, p.90).

A couple of miles on, **Totem Bight State Historic Park** (unrestricted access) comprises a replica Native village breathtakingly set on a forested strip of coast overlooking the Narrows, ten miles north of town. Here, fourteen of the finest replica totem poles and a recreated tribal house look majestically out over the water, making this about the best place to easily get a sense of what a

Tlingit village looked like a hundred or more years back. Although it is unlikely that the site was ever permanently settled – it was originally a summer fish camp – in the late 1930s the Civilian Conservation Corps (see box, pp.84–85) decided to reconstruct an entire Native village here. Lack of money and manpower during World War II stunted initial ambition, but the result still includes a very fine **clan house**. The front is strikingly painted in a Raven design flanked by squat figures wearing potlatch hats and centered on the large "Raven Stealing the Sun" entrance pole. The hole in this pole would have been the sole way to get into the house, an important security feature. Up to fifty people could live inside, with separate family areas on the raised platforms around the central fire pit and belongings stored underneath the planks.

Eleven of the totem poles are clustered in a couple of semicircles beside the clan house, almost all of them executed in the late 1930s, though a couple have had to be replicated again. (This third generation was completed in the 1990s, mostly by Nathan Jackson.) There's a great variety: Tlingit and Haida – despite this being a traditionally Tlingit area – mortuary poles, grave markers, heraldic poles, and the lovely "Sea Monster" pole, topped by a human figure representing the village watchman.

On arrival, call at the Alaska Natural History Association bookstore (Tues–Sat 9am–4.45pm, Mon & Sun 9am–2pm), which stocks an excellent leaflet ($1 donation requested) explaining what the poles depict and has an original section of a pole wedged into one corner. By going in the evening you'll miss the bulk of the bus tours, but may not be able to see inside the clan house.

The Tongass Highway continues for another eight miles past Knudson Cove marina to *Settlers Cove Campground* on the shores of Clover Passage.

South of town: Saxman Native Village

Just under three miles along S Tongass Highway from downtown Ketchikan, the Tlingit village of **SAXMAN** centers on the **Saxman Totem Park** (unrestricted access), which encompasses the world's largest collection of replica totem poles, a replica clan house, and an active carving center. Most people visit on a tour (see below) but it is possible to drive, cycle or catch "the Bus" there and simply wander round the poles by yourself, listening to the spiel of assorted tour guides and perhaps buying the walking tour map ($4) from the Village Store. The store is at the end of the approach avenue where a dozen Tlingit poles lead up to the main arc of poles. Look out for the famous Abraham Lincoln pole surmounted by an image of Honest Abe, who has been carved with stunted legs, apparently because the only image the carvers had of him was in a photo which cut him off at the knees. There's also a shame pole to William Seward, who during a visit to Alaska attended four potlatches without ever throwing one in return, a dishonorable omission that earned him the distinctive red ears, nose, and lips on his pole.

Unless you are on a tour, you won't get to see inside the cedar-scented **Beaver Clan House** where the **Cape Fox Dancers** put on a diverting performance during which you'll learn a little Tlingit and can join in one of the dances alongside the troupe made up of adults, kids, and even babes in arms, many wearing superb blankets and robes.

Possibly the most interesting bit of all is the nearby **Carving Center** (officially only open to those on tours, though it is easy enough to wander in) where highly respected Haida and Tlingit craftsmen (Nathan Jackson among them) can be seen at work on large poles, commissioned by institutions and individuals from all over the US. The carvers are usually happy to chat as they work on poles which proceed at a rate of around one foot per week. Don't set your hopes on possessing one anytime soon; they cost tens of thousands of dollars depending on size of pole, intricacy of design, and reputation of carver, and they're backordered for over a year.

Several tours visit the village on their circuit of Ketchikan, but to get the full Saxman experience, including a short video, interpretation and a visit to the clan house and dancers, you'll need to join the **Saxman Native Village Tour** (May–Sept daily; 1hr; $35) run by the local Native corporation's Cape Fox Tours (Ⓦwww.capefoxtours.com, Ⓔinfo@capefoxtours.com). You'll need to email them in advance, then get yourself to Saxman in time to meet one of the tours from the cruise ships.

South Tongass Highway continues a further ten miles past the site of a planned new **Tongass Coast Aquarium**, due to open in the summer of 2006. The road ends at the former Libby, McNeill, and Libby cannery, now

Ketchikan hikes

Extremely high rainfall and what can sometimes seem like constant clouds and drizzle may put some people off hiking around Ketchikan, but if you strike it lucky – or are feeling especially hardy – it can be very rewarding. Four local trails are particularly worthwhile. Only Deer Mountain Trail is readily accessible from town, but it is best hiked from late June to September as snow cover limits access to the alpine sections during the rest of the year. The remaining three can be hiked in any season, but you'll need to get out to Ward Cove and hike inland from there to the trailheads. All hikes are marked on the "Around Ketchikan" map (see opposite). Pick up the useful and free "Ketchikan Area Hiking Guide" from the Discovery Center.

Connell Lake Trail (4.5 miles round-trip; 2–3hr; 100ft ascent). Easy trail mostly beside Connell Lake and running to Talbot Lake with good birding, excellent berries in summer and fall, and fishing access to both lakes. The trail starts on dammed Connell Lake Road, which spurs off Revilla Road just past the entrance to *Last Chance Campground*.

Deer Mountain Trail (10 miles one-way; 2 days; 3350ft ascent). Easily accessible trail that makes a perfect escape from the daytime crowds for a couple of hours, switchbacking up across the face of Deer Mountain through old-growth Sitka spruce, hemlock, and red cedar. It takes an hour or so to reach a wooded overlook (1500ft) with a wonderful view over the city, Pennock, Gravina, Annette, and Prince of Wales islands; and close to three hours to reach the 3000-foot alpine summit of Deer Mountain. Deer Mountain Trail can be extended as an overnight one-way trek to the Beaver Falls Powerhouse on George Inlet – either camp beside Blue Lake or stay in the four-bunk Forest Service cabin (Ⓣ1-877/444-6777; $25; reserve in advance) on the upper flank of Deer Mountain. This alpine section of the hike is exposed to bad weather and is steep in places, remaining high for several hours before a final steep descent past Silvia Lakes. The trail starts on Ketchikan Lakes Road, which begins near a trailer park half a mile along Deermount Street near the junction of Fair Street (see "Ketchikan" map) and finishes fourteen miles out along S Tongass Highway. There is very little traffic out this way, so it is best to arrange a ride back to town before you start – or do the whole thing in reverse and finish in town.

Perseverance Trail (4.5 miles round-trip; 2–3hr; 450ft ascent). An easy but enjoyable (partly boardwalk) trail up to Perseverance Lake through temperate rainforest and muskeg. It starts on Ward Lake Road, 2.5 miles off the N Tongass Highway at Ward Cove.

Ward Lake Nature Trail (1.3-mile loop; 1hr; negligible ascent). Gentle stroll round Ward Lake on an easy gravel path, past panels on the region's flora and fauna. The trailhead is seven miles along N Tongass Highway to Ward Cove, then 2.5 miles inland along Ward Lake Road.

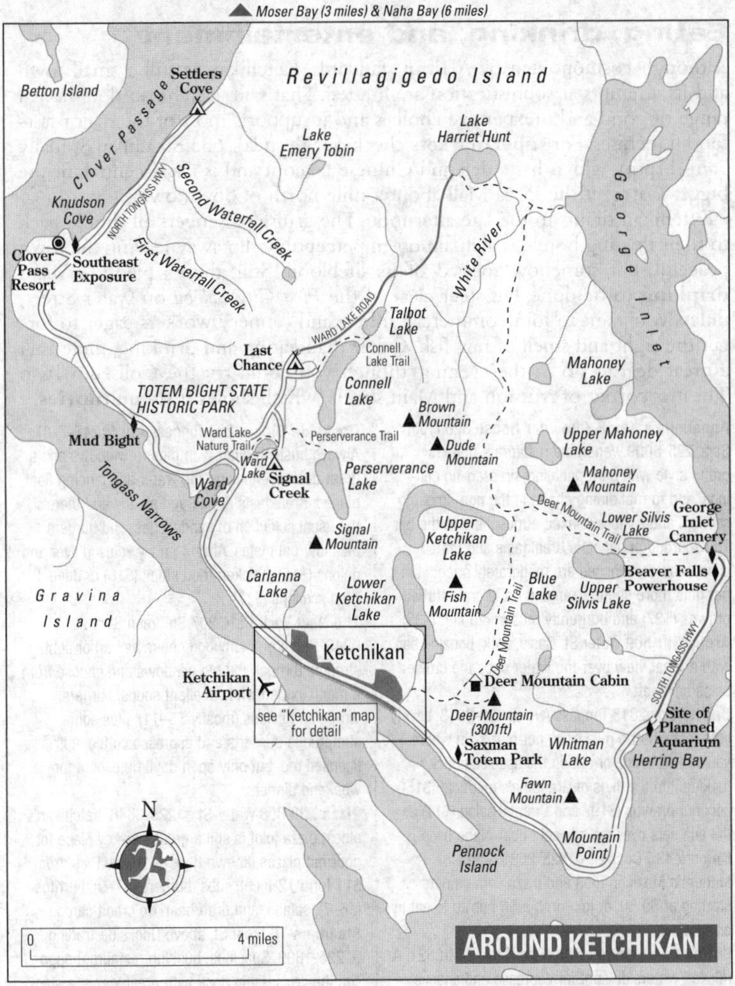

known as the **George Inlet Cannery**, which stands majestically on poles over the tide of George Inlet where, from 1913 until 1958, it processed salmon caught in fish traps. When Alaska became a state, fish traps were banned and the cannery was forced to close its doors, but proximity to Ketchikan has saved it from complete abandonment. Commercial fishermen still use the lockers here, and it has now been set up for tours which start with an excellent video covering a potted history of commercial salmon fishing. Material on the lifecycles of salmon and halibut is followed by a demonstration on fishing-boat winches, a mock-up of a worker's shack on a fish trap, and a good deal of role playing. Unfortunately, most of the canning line has been removed, but there's enough left to evoke something of the old days. Cape Fox's cruise-ship-oriented Historic Ketchikan Tour (2hr; $20) visits the cannery, but you'll need to contact them in advance and meet a tour at the cannery.

Eating, drinking, and entertainment

Although cosmopolitan by Alaskan standards, Ketchikan is still a small town and its attempts at sophistication are limited. That said, Ketchikan does have a range of good and inexpensive choices and it supports most of the major fast-food franchises. For **supermarkets** check out Tatsuda's, 633 Steadman St (daily 7am–11pm), which has a deli and Chinese takeout and is fairly central, or the bigger Carr's, at the Plaza Mall about a mile north of downtown.

Ketchikan drains in the late afternoon. The cruise passengers all shuffle back to their floating hotels, which almost imperceptibly slip away, leaving the town peaceful, but somehow robbed of its lifeblood. Still, there's plenty of hard **drinking** to be done, but steer clear of the *First City Saloon* on Water Street, unless you want to join commercial fishers and cannery workers eager to forget the sight and smell of raw fish. Other than eating and drinking, there isn't a great deal to do in the evening, though you could try the Coliseum Twin Theatre, corner of Mission and Main streets, which shows first-run **movies**.

Annabelle's Keg & Chowder House 326 Front St ☎225-6009. Venerable restaurant done in grand style with dark paneling, pressed-tin ceilings, and formal dining chairs in the non-smoking section, and a more relaxed atmosphere in the bar. The sourdough pancake breakfasts and famed clam chowder lunches are moderately priced; dinner gets more spendy, ranging up to crab-stuffed prawns ($27) and burgundy mushroom filet ($33).

Arctic Bar 509 Water St. Basic, dark, boozing bar with a great view over the water once the cruise ships have left.

Bar Harbor 2813 Tongass Ave ☎225-2813. Lovely little restaurant a mile or so north of town where you can sit inside or out on the spacious deck tucking into the likes of Grandma's meatloaf ($15), coconut prawns ($19), and Oriental salad ($11) as the sun sets over the adjacent float-plane base.

Chico's 435 Dock St ☎225-2833. Bargain authentic Mexican food and pizza with dinners starting at $9.50, or just grab a $6 burrito to eat in or take out.

Coffee Connections 521 Water St ☎247-0521. A relaxed waterside spot for espresso and snacks with a few sunny seats and a deck that's ideal for browsing newspapers and magazines. If the view is often blocked by cruise ships (as it often is) get your coffee to go and sit in the adjacent Harborview Park.

Diaz Café 335 Stedman St ☎225-2257. Some of the finest inexpensive food in town with widely acclaimed burgers and fries rounding out a menu specializing in Chinese and tasty Filipino dishes: fried rice for $8, chow mein and chicken adobo for around $12. Closed Mon.

Dockside Diner 1287 Tongass Ave ☎247-7787. Always bustling diner with picture windows and a great deck overlooking the water and landing float planes. Breakfasts are served all day and there's the usual selection of sandwiches, and burgers plus low-cal plates. After 4pm try venison liver and onions ($15), chicken fried steak ($16) or deep fried scallops ($17).

The New York Café 207 Stedman St ☎225-0246. Perch on bentwood chairs as harbor light streams through the big windows and choose from a menu loaded with excellent soups, burgers, wraps and salads (mostly $8–11), plus some sumptuous desserts and espresso coffee. It is licensed too, but only open daytime except for weekend dinners.

Pizza Mill 808 Water St ☎225-6646. Ketchikan's oldest pizza joint is still a great low-key place for gourmet pizzas (known here as Yuppie Pies; from $11 for a 12-inch), subs, burgers ($7–9), burritos ($6–7), salads, and draft beer. No credit cards.

Steamers 76 Front St, above Dockside Trading ☎225-1600. Spacious, bustling restaurant opposite the cruise-ship dock with great views, a stack of microbrews on tap, and occasional live music. The food's good too – try the $26 hazelnut halibut with Frangelico cream sauce.

WestCoast Cape Fox Lodge 800 Venetia Way ☎225-8001. Fairly upmarket dining in the town's best hotel with great views over town. Lunch is fairly casual with manageable prices for sandwiches ($8–11) or the excellent halibut and chips ($11). Dinner is more formal, with dishes ranging from a chicken fettuccini ($18) to baked salmon ($24) and king crab.

Listings

Arts and crafts Ketchikan prides itself on its nationwide reputation for indigenous and non-Native crafts. Locally renowned artists display their work, but some of the most striking material is that produced by Alaska Natives, which here reaches its highest expression. Wandering around town you'll see a lot of cheap stuff, but the more discerning galleries are full of good stuff, much of it correspondingly expensive. Check out the Native-owned Carver at the Creek, 28 Creek St (ⓣ225-3018), where Norman Jackson can be seen executing fine carving amid work by other Native craftspeople – lovely Tlingit blankets ($2000–4000), wooden masks from around $800, cedar-bark hats, silverwork, and fine prints, some excellent ones for under $100. Also check out Soho Coho, 5 Creek St (ⓣ225-5954, ⓦwww.trollart.com), which is particularly good for prints, paintings, and original work by local artists, and Eagle Spirit Gallery, 310 Mission St (ⓣ225-6626 or 1-866/867-0976, ⓦwww.eaglespiritalaska.com), with quality merchandise including bentwood boxes. For more information, pick up the free *Ketchikan Arts Guide*, available all over town.

Banks Several downtown, all with ATMs, including First Bank, 331 Dock St.

Bike rental Downtown at the Lumberjack Show (see p.87) for $8 an hour or $25 a half-day, or from Southeast Exposure ($12 for half-day, $22 a day; ⓣ225-8829), which has inconveniently moved their operations fourteen miles north of town, though they may still offer bikes in the downtown area. Ask around.

Boat charters There are dozens of boat-charter operators keen to take you out fishing, sightseeing in Misty Fiords National Monument, or who will drop you off at some remote cabin. With a group of four or five, this option can work out to be a flexible and cost-effective alternative to the cruise boats. Northern Lights Charters (ⓣ247-8488 or 1-888/550-8488, ⓦktn.net/nlck), which has a booth at the visitor center, is particularly good and runs fishing trips from $95 for 3hr.

Bookshop Parnassus Books, upstairs at 5 Creek St (ⓣ225-7690), is easily the best bookstore in town with a matchless selection of Alaskana, alternative topics, as well as more mainstream titles.

Car rental Alaska Car Rental, 2828 Tongass Ave (ⓣ225-5000 or 1-800/662-0007, ⓦwww.akcarrental.com), and Budget, 4950 N Tongass Hwy (ⓣ225-8383 or 1-800/478-2438, ⓔlewis-chev@kpunet.net), both have desks at the airport and offer similar rates of around $50 a day.

Flightseeing and air-charter companies Island Wings, 1935 Tongass Ave (ⓣ225-2444 or 1-888/845-2444, ⓦwww.islandwings.com), does Misty Fiords flightseeing tours from $189. Pacific Airways (ⓣ225-3500 or 1-877/360-3500, ⓦwww.flypacificairways.com) operates good-value flightseeing trips to Misty Fiords ($179, min 4), and runs scheduled flights to Prince of Wales Island, including Craig (3 daily; $85), Thorne Bay (3 daily; $70), and Hollis (3 daily; $70). Promech Air, 1515 Tongass Ave (ⓣ225-3845 or 1-800/860-3845, ⓦwww.promechair.com), also flies float planes to Misty Fiords, Metlakatla, and various points on the coast of Prince of Wales Island. Taquan Air, 1007 Water St (ⓣ225-8800 or 1-800/770-8800, ⓦwww.taquanair.com), has scheduled departures for Hyder and Prince of Wales Island – Coffman Cove ($106 one-way), Craig/Klawock ($65), Hyder ($135), Metlakatla ($25), and Thorne Bay ($70) – but also does a number of worthwhile flightseeing trips, including Misty Fiords (1hr 30min; $179). Consider taking one of their Alaska Bush Pilot tours (1–2hr; $119–159), which follow a different route each day depending on what their schedule is – if the weather is good, don't miss the chance to go on their mail run and freight flight (Mon & Thurs; $159) from Ketchikan to Hyder (see p.97), a trip which overflies Misty Fiords. Although not as good as a dedicated Misty flightseeing trip, it's just about the cheapest way to see the park. They'll also fly you to Anan Wildlife Observatory (see p.113) and to see the bears at Traitors Cove (see p.87).

Internet access Seaport CyberStation, upstairs inside Salmon Landing, has the best rates for fast machines. Surf City, in the Sockeye Sam's building by the tunnel, is more expensive. The library (see below) has free use for members. Membership is available for a $5 fee plus a $20 deposit refundable when you leave town – worthwhile for stays of a few days.

Laundry and showers The Mat, 989 Stedman (daily 6am–11pm; ⓣ225-0628), is half a mile south of downtown.

Left luggage Nowhere currently holds bags – a real pain if you've got a late ferry.

Library Ketchikan Public Library, 629 Dock St (Mon–Wed 10am–8pm, Thurs–Sat 10am–6pm, Sun 1–5pm; ⓣ225-3331).

Medical assistance Ketchikan General Hospital, 3100 N Tongass Ave, near the AMHS ferry dock (ⓣ225-5171), has daytime clinics and 24hr ER.

Pharmacy Downtown Drugstore, 300 Front St ⓣ225-3144.

Photographic supplies Schallerer's, 212 Front St (ⓣ225-4210, ⓦwww.schallerers.com), is the best around.

Post office The main post office, 3609 Tongass Ave (ⓣ225-9601), is a few yards north of the AMHS ferry dock (Mon–Fri 8.30am–5pm) and has **General Delivery** (zip code 99901). There's a more convenient suboffice at 422 Mission St (Mon–Sat 9am–5.30pm).

Kayaking around Revillagigedo Island and Misty Fiords

Wherever you are in Southeast Alaska, the range of places you can go paddling is only limited by your imagination and your budget. Dozens of possibilities present themselves, but from Ketchikan the most common destinations are relatively short paddles close to town and trips into Misty Fiords National Monument, which can take on the feeling of an expedition without requiring really long periods away from civilization.

The simplest approach is to hook up with one of the two **kayaking companies** in Ketchikan. Southeast Sea Kayaks, 1007 Water St (Ⓣ225-1258 or 1-800/287-1607, Ⓦwww.kayakketchikan.com), tends to be slightly the more expensive of the two but it's fully geared toward independent visitors, offering more personal treatment, small groups and no minimum numbers. Southeast Exposure, 37 Potter Rd, 14 miles north of town near Knudson Cove (Ⓣ225-8829, Ⓦwww.southeastexposure.com), is more closely linked-in with the cruise ships, the larger numbers resulting in lower prices. They still cater to independents, but you'll need a $25 taxi ride to get out there.

For a taster, try Southeast Sea Kayaks' Pennock Paddling (2hr 30min; $76) in the channel in front of Ketchikan; for a good deal more peace and quiet step up to the Orcas Cove trip (4hr; $139), which starts with a short boat ride and then takes you kayaking along the shore with fabulous wildlife viewing and gorgeous scenery. Custom full-day trips cost $189 including lunch. Southeast Exposure concentrates on trips close to their base: the Guide's choice ($129, including transport from town) involves almost four hours exploring the narrow waterways and islands of Clover Passage. Both companies offer guided multiday trips to **Misty Fiords National Monument** (4–6 days; $700–1000) with access by tour boat and nights spent camping beside the fjord.

Going it alone

The two guided kayaking companies rent kayaks at similar rates (which reduce for longer rental periods) and will drop you along the road system for a small fee: expect to pay $50–60 a day for a double fiberglass sea kayak, $40–45 for a fiberglass single and $30–40 for a plastic single. You don't need much prior experience to be let loose around the Ketchikan waterfront, but for longer journeys you'll have to be a moderately competent paddler and have some knowledge of tides and backcountry camping. Don't be put off, though – the generally sheltered waters in these parts can be tackled by people of quite modest ability (see below for suggested trips). Wherever you go, get the latest information (maps, tide tables, and so forth) from the rental company, pick up the "Ketchikan Area Kayak Guide" from the Discovery Center, and be sure you leave the company an itinerary of your likely movements.

George Inlet (1–2 days). Pretty coves, loads of small islands and the old George Inlet cannery add to this trip to the south and west of Ketchikan. Either paddle from

Taxes City sales tax is 5.5 percent. Hotel rooms incur a whopping 11.5 percent tax, which is included in our price codes.

Taxis Sourdough (Ⓣ225-5544) and Yellow Cab (Ⓣ225-6800) are both fine.

Misty Fiords National Monument

The essential excursion from Ketchikan is to the Connecticut-sized **MISTY FIORDS NATIONAL MONUMENT**, an awe-inspiring tranche of narrow fjords flanked by sheer 3000-foot glacially scoured granite walls strung by gossamer waterfalls and surrounded by dense rainforest. Located between twenty and sixty miles east of Ketchikan, Misty Fiords drapes partly over the eastern side of Revillagigedo Island but is primarily defined by the mountainous terrain between two fjords, the 117-mile Behm Canal and the 72-mile hairline thread of Portland Canal, which marks the US–Canada border.

downtown or get a ride out to the Hole-in-the-Wall marina (7.5 miles south on Tongass Highway).

Gravina Island Circumnavigation (3–4 days). Sixty miles of rocky shoreline with abundant wildlife, all easily accessible from Ketchikan. Note that one ten-mile section offers almost no protection from the weather.

Moser Bay (1 day). Just four miles from the northern end of Tongass Highway, Moser Bay is a pretty spot to hang out, but is also the trailhead for Wolf Lake Trail, which runs through 2.5 miles of forest and muskeg to a poorly maintained three-sided shelter (first-come, first-served; free).

Naha Bay (2–4 days). With great scenery, plenty of wildlife, and excellent salmon and trout fishing along the Naha River, this excursion provides a wonderful opportunity to get a real wilderness feel without straying too far from Ketchikan. The trip can also work out to be pretty inexpensive, as you can start your paddle right from town and camp out every night. If you'd like to save time, catch a ride out to Knudson Cove marina (14.5 miles north of town) for around $30 per person. Aside from the pleasures of gentle paddling, you can hike the Wolf Lake Trail from Moser Bay (see above) and the 5.4-mile Naha River National Recreation Trail, which leads from Naha Bay past Jordan Lake to Heckman Lake. Both lakes have Forest Service cabins ($35). You don't need to paddle into the nearby Roosevelt Lagoon to access the trail, but if you do want to paddle in the lagoon be warned that racing tides make its entrance very dangerous – use the old tramway to transport your kayak. There is also a lot of black bear activity during the salmon runs: good for viewing as long as you are careful.

Tatoosh Islands (1–4 days). Easily accessible islands just north of Ketchikan, with beautiful beaches where seals haul out on the rocks to rest and plenty of opportunity for camping and exploring.

Misty Fiords

The most ambitious kayaking destination is **Misty Fiords National Monument**, for which Southeast Sea Kayaks sells a superb trip-planning kit ($18) complete with topographic maps, tide tables, and plenty of itinerary suggestions. It can be reached directly by kayak from Ketchikan, though it is at least two days' paddle each way and requires open-water kayaking skills. Most paddlers get a ride with Alaska Cruises (see p.96), which charges $200 for combined drop-off and pickup, depending on location. Once there, the scope is enormous, with some people happily spending three or four weeks in the monument. The main northern arm of Behm Canal is a little exposed for most paddlers, who aim for narrow corners such as Rudyerd Bay, Punchbowl Cove, and Walker Cove, typically camping or making use of a Forest Service cabin or shelter (see p.96).

At its most atmospheric when wreathed in low-lying cloud, Misty, as it is often known, was created by presidential proclamation in 1978 and remains almost entirely undeveloped. No roads lead here. There aren't even any airstrips, so access is by cruise boat, float plane, or kayak. As with so many vast areas of wilderness, most people visit roughly the same area, though it is quite possible to get air-charter companies to fly you anywhere you want. Day cruises and scheduled flightseeing trips tend to concentrate on the area around **Rudyerd Bay**, off Behm Canal some twenty minutes by plane or fifty sea miles from Ketchikan. Here the cliffs plunge as far below the surface as they soar above it, notably in **Punchbowl Cove**, widely regarded as the highlight of the monument and an obligatory stop on every boat trip. Along the way you pass the volcanic plug of **New Eddystone Rock**, a 237-foot pillar of rock rising from the middle of Behm Canal, which Captain Vancouver, exploring here in 1793, obviously thought was reminiscent of the lighthouse-topped namesake off the southern English coast. The trees around its base are almost swamped at high tide, but there is just enough room for kayakers to pitch a tent, provided the waves aren't too high.

Wildlife-spotting opportunities are plentiful, with seals, porpoises, and orca in the fjords, and bears, deer, mountain goats and more on land, all watched over by bald eagles.

Cruises, flights, and cabins

The most convenient way to see something of Misty Fiords is with Alaska Cruises (ⓣ225-6044 or 1-800/228-1905, ⓦwww.goldbelttours.com), which runs six-hour **cruises** (early May–Sept; $150) and four-hour cruise and flight packages ($240). Trips are geared around the combo packages, so if you can afford the extra cash, go for the cruise/fly option (preferably in that order), not only to take in the excellent airborne views, but to avoid the identical itinerary and commentary on the return journey.

If time is limited you can **fly** both ways; several flightseeing companies have good deals (see p.93). These same companies will also fly you and your supplies to one of the fourteen rustic **cabins** rented out by the Forest Service (ⓣ1-877/444-6777; $25–45), two of which are beside salt water, with the remaining twelve on freshwater lakes, often linked to the fjord by a short trail. Alternatively, you can kayak here (see box, pp.94–95) and gain access to some cabins and shelters that way. Shelters are first-come, first-served and free. Possibilities include: Alava Bay Cabin; following the mile-long trail at the back of Punchbowl Bay up the face of a solidified lava flow to Punchbowl Lake and the three-sided Punchbowl Lake Shelter; hiking a mile from Rudyerd Bay to Nooya Lake Shelter; hiking the 2.3-mile Winstanley Lake Trail to Winstanley Lake Shelter; Winstanley Island Cabin; Manzanita Bay Shelter; and Manzanita Lake Cabin, reached by the 3.5-mile Manzanita Lake Trail from near the shelter. See the Southern Inside Passage map (pp. 102–103) for cabin and shelter locations.

Metlakatla

If you arrive by float plane at the small Native village of **METLAKATLA**, twelve miles southeast of Ketchikan on the western shore of Annette Island, you'll set foot on the very spot where Anglican missionary **William Duncan** landed in 1887 along with 823 followers, all Tsimshian Natives. They were on the run from the authorities in British Columbia, where Tsimshian land claims weren't respected, and from the more threatening Canadian bishops of the Church Missionary Society (CMS), with whom Duncan had fallen out. Fortunately, he had friends in high places in New York – Henry Wellcome and Thomas Edison among them – who pulled strings for him in Washington and coaxed the US government to grant the community Annette Island, site of a largely abandoned Tlingit settlement. Many Alaskan Natives live in remote villages largely populated by their own people, but Annette Island became the only Native reservation in Alaska.

Under the leadership of Father Duncan, Alaska's sole Tsimshian settlement grew into one of the most successful CMS missions, a model of religious, social, and economic independence that became a template for similar communities elsewhere. Duncan had already spent thirty years working with the Tsimshian in BC and continued his efforts to get rid of intertribal slavery, while keeping the church in control of secular as well as religious activities. He also became something of a patriarch, allegedly siring dozens of children to Native women.

Hyder

The remote outpost of **HYDER** (pop. 130) is so entirely isolated from the rest of Alaska that it might as well be part of Canada. Indeed, it is far more closely linked with its immediate British Columbian neighbor, Stewart, with which it shares a Canadian phone code (ⓣ250), time zone, Canadian currency (though greenbacks are also accepted), and Canadian national holidays. Even the police are of the Mountie variety.

This easternmost of Alaskan towns is a ramshackle place that has traditionally only attracted people visiting Stewart, just two miles away by road, who come here so that they can say they've been to Alaska. But in recent years the biggest draw has become **bears**, which congregate at the Forest Service's **Fish Creek Wildlife Viewing Area** (daily 6am–10pm; free), three miles east of Hyder along Salmon Glacier Road. Throughout July, August, and September, both black and brown bears come down to the stream to feast on spawning chum and pink salmon, occasionally observed by bald eagles, which also fancy an easy fish snack. Come early in the morning or towards dusk for the best viewing, though you'll still have to compete for the best spots with professional photographers and a stack of other tourists.

At some point during your visit, you'll probably find yourself in one of Hyder's two bars, where if you toss back a shot of overproof liquor you'll receive an "I've Been Hyderized" card. At the *Glacier Inn* an additional tradition is to pin a dollar to the wall in case you return broke and need a drink. Although it's a fairly common tradition in northern bars, the effect here is particularly spectacular, with many thousands of dollars creating the "world's most expensive wallpaper."

It sounds a bit of a tourist carry-on, but if you arrive out of season there's a genuine warmth about the place that warrants its claims to be the "Friendliest Ghost Town in Alaska."

If you plan on staying over, Hyder has a handful of **motels and B&Bs**, as well as a couple of RV parks with tent space and full hookups. Try the budget *Sealaska Inn*, Premier Avenue (ⓣ250/636-2486; ❶), or the preferable *Grand View Inn* (ⓣ250/636-9174, ⓔgrandviewhyder@yahoo.com; ❷), with nicely kept units, all with microwave and fridge, plus some with full kitchen for which there is an additional $10 one-time charge. There's more accommodation across the border in Stewart, mostly more expensive, and some very appealing.

After a hard morning's bear viewing, follow the **breakfast** crowds to the excellent *Wildflour Coffee Shop* (ⓣ250/636-2875), which also does tasty baked goods. Later in the day you'll have to make do with the limited offerings at the *Sealaska Inn* or head across to Stewart.

The only direct **access to Hyder** from the rest of Alaska is by air, although you can drive through Canada along the especially beautiful Glacier Highway, which is strung with hanging glaciers that appear about to calve right onto the road at the slightest provocation. (Until the service was axed in the late 1990s, there used to be an AMHS ferry from Ketchikan – but even that docked in Stewart.) Taquan Air (ⓣ225-8800 or 1-800/770-8800, ⓦwww.taquanair.com) flies here for $135 each way; alternatively, you can get a quick sense of the place on one of their twice-weekly mail-runs (Mon & Thurs; $159), which won't give you any time to explore but will give you superb views of Misty Fiords National Monument.

The group's landing point proved highly suitable, with a waterfall (close to the modern ferry dock) that could be harnessed for power and water, a sloping beach which made an ideal site for a cannery, and enough timber to start a sawmill, build frame houses and the church. What is known as the **Duncan Memorial Church**, on 4th Avenue, is a replica of the original that burned down in 1948 and is guarded by Duncan's grave. Although Duncan is well remembered, his religion has failed to flower. None of Metlakatla's nine churches is now Anglican.

There's more to be seen in the single-story wooden-frame **Duncan Cottage Museum**, Jail Street, close to the small boat harbor (June–Aug Mon–Fri 8.30am–12.30pm and during scheduled tours, or appointment on ⓣ886-8687; $2), in the house where Duncan lived from 1894 until his death in 1914. It contains plenty of photos and material on the life and times of Duncan and the people of Metlakatla along with the Bible Duncan brought with him from England, a very early Edison phonograph, a prominent portrait of Queen Victoria, and Duncan's bedroom complete with his personal effects and a couple of large safes. There's also discussion of World War II, when Annette Island became an important military base.

Once you've seen the museum, there's not a great deal to do. Entry to the tribal longhouse and Native dancing are only for those visiting with Metlakatla Tours (see below), and an hour or two is enough to wander the waterfront with its cannery, the mothballed sawmill, and the only **fish traps** left in the state. With time on your hands, stroll half a mile out along Western Avenue until you reach Pioneer Park, a small nub of land threaded by rough boardwalks with great sea views. Alternatively, hike a mile and a half out along Airport Road to the sandstone outcrop of **Yellow Hill**, which affords a great view over the town and Prince of Wales Island. **Cyclists** have the run of the island's fairly extensive road system, giving access to more hiking along the **Purple Lake Trail**, four miles south of town, and to the appropriately named **Sand Dollar Beach**.

Practicalities

Traditionally, most visitors have come to Metlakatla on the one day a week when the *Aurora* made two sailings, allowing at least eight hours sightseeing without requiring an overnight stay. This should all change from spring 2004 when the new **Metlakatla Shuttle** is expected to provide frequent sailings between Ketchikan and the Metlakatla ferry dock a mile from town.

You may find it more convenient to arrive by float plane with Promech Air (ⓣ1-800/860-3845, ⓦwww.promechair.com), which flies several times daily and charges $66 per round-trip (twice as much as the ferry), or join the four-hour Metlakatla Tours (May–Sept Wed & Fri; $40; reservations essential ⓣ886-8687, ⓦtours.metlakatla.net), which include a salmon bake, tribal dance in full regalia, and a tour of the town's fish-processing facility; flights are extra. The dance presentation alone (same days) costs $10.

You probably won't want to stay, but there are **rooms** with shared or private bath at *Tuck 'em Inn*, corner of Hillcrest and Calvin (ⓣ886-6611 or 886-7853, ⓦwww.alaskanow.com/tuckem-inn/; ④), and *Metlakatla Hotel and Suites* (ⓣ886-3456; ④). There are no formal campgrounds and **camping** isn't encouraged, though if you walk far enough out of town you can pitch a tent pretty much anywhere for a night or two: try along Western Road beyond the cemetery.

The *Metlakatla Hotel* has about the only real **restaurant** in town, with sandwiches and burgers at reasonable prices, though you might just want to grab a burger, donut, or espresso at the Laesk Mini-Mart on Milton Street, which is your best bet for **groceries**. Note that this is a dry community, so **no alcohol** is allowed.

Prince of Wales Island

Prince of Wales Island is the third largest in the US (after Kodiak and Hawaii's Big Island), over 135 miles long and threaded by more miles of road than the rest of Southeast put together – over 1500 in total, though only fifty-odd are paved. Many are dead-end logging roads, but they provide unparalleled access to this mountainous landscape shaped by ancient glaciers and subsequently flooded to create a deeply indented coastline pocked by small bays and rocky coves. **Wildlife** is abundant, and everywhere you go there are streams thick with salmon – indeed, the **fishing** is legendary, and many of the island's visitors are here to haul in prize specimens while staying in the exclusive fishing lodges that line the coast. Below ground, the underlying limestone has been eroded to form Alaska's only sizeable **cave system**.

The spruce and hemlock forests that cloaked the steep island's hillsides for millennia have, in recent decades, become the most savagely logged area of the Tongass National Forest. Forestry has downsized drastically in recent years, but scars left by clear-cuts can appear unsightly for thirty years or more after cutting. Still, the forest seems to recover quickly and without trees crowding in on all sides the long views are excellent. What's more, the logging legacy makes this a wonderful place to explore by 4WD, by mountain bike, or more carefully in an ordinary car.

With the exception of the limestone caves in the north of the island and several excellent collections of recarved totem poles, there are few sights, but POW (as it is often known) is a great place to unwind for a few days. It's not the sort of place that rewards a quick visit – you really need time to explore and slip into the pace of the place: resting up in one of the more than twenty Forest Service cabins (many of which have lake access and good fishing), spending a few days paddling one of the canoe routes, or just strolling the driftwood-strewn beaches. The island is also a big hunting destination and, in late April and May, **bear hunters** hog the roads and rental cars can be hard to get.

Hiking and paddling on Prince of Wales Island

Although Prince of Wales Island has a couple of well-known short trails, it isn't especially noted for its hiking; serious outdoors fans might be better off considering the two excellent **canoe routes,** best tackled from May to September. The coastline lends itself superbly to **kayaking**. Although no formal routes have been mapped out, there's scope for anything from a paddle of a couple of hours to a several-week circumnavigation. The best source for suggestions and boats is Alaska Kustom Kayaks in Klawock (see p.101).

One Duck Trail (2.5 miles round-trip; 2hr; 1200ft ascent). Moderately steep but rewarding hike with magnificent views from the small shelter and open muskeg at the top. Starts on Hydaburg Road, two miles south of the Craig–Hollis Highway.

Soda Lake Trail (5 miles round-trip; 3hr; negligible ascent). Fairly easy walking across muskeg and through forest, ending at Soda Lake and some bubbling mineral springs with good bird and wildlife spotting. Starts on Hydaburg Road, twelve miles south of the Craig–Hollis Highway.

Honker Divide Canoe Route (30 miles; 3–4 days; 150ft elevation gain). A rugged and strenuous route formerly used by early trappers and requiring good canoeing and backcountry camping skills. Long sections may need lining unless there has been recent rain, and waterfalls and rapids need to be portaged. There will also be sweepers to avoid. It is a rewarding experience, though, and the Forest Service's *Honker Lake Cabin* (only accessible through this route; $25) may be available for the first or second night.

Sarkar Lake Canoe Route (15-mile loop; 6–8hr; negligible ascent). Easy route through a roadless area linking six lakes by means of stream and short boardwalk portages, often spread over two to three days. Good fishing and wildlife viewing. There's a Forest Service cabin beside Sarkar Lake, two miles from the put-in.

Traditionally, Prince of Wales Island was Tlingit territory, but around three hundred years ago – and a hundred years before European contact – Haida from Canada's Queen Charlotte Islands got a toehold and gradually occupied much of the island. They continued to trade with their kin on the Nass River in what is now British Columbia and, during the fur-trade years under Russian rule, amassed great wealth. At this time the potlatch reached its peak and totem-pole raising was at its height, a tradition remembered in the **totem parks** at Hydaburg, Klawock and, most notably, Kasaan.

By the late nineteenth century, Presbyterian missionaries and fishing interests were well entrenched here, the former suppressing Native traditions and the latter bringing disease and altering the economic dynamic. Haida numbers dropped from an estimated 10,000 to around 800 as canneries were set up around the coast. The importance of these gradually gave way to logging, which for the second half of the twentieth century was the mainstay of the local economy. With the 1999 closure of a large mill in Ketchikan, logging has declined drastically leading to high unemployment in some areas. Poor world prices for timber products undoubtedly contributed, but in these parts the Clinton administration's policies received a lot of flak. Environmentalist is a dirty word around here, and many hope George W Bush will be their savior.

Planning, arrival, and getting around

Before you head out to Prince of Wales Island, contact the island's Chamber of Commerce (see opposite), which puts out the comprehensive and widely available *Prince of Wales Island Guide* (free). You should also find it at Ketchikan's Discovery Center – a good starting point for detailed information on campgrounds, canoe routes, hikes, and Forest Service cabins – which also stocks the worthwhile (though a little dated) *Prince of Wales Island Forest Service Road Guide* ($4).

The vehicle-carrying *Prince of Wales* **ferry**, operated by the Island Ferry Authority (ⓣ826-4848 or 1-866/308-4848, ⓦwww.interislandferry.com), makes the three-hour run between Ketchikan and Hollis year-round, with twice-daily sailings in summer (June–Aug; adult one-way $29, bikes $12, kayaks $22, vehicles $57–68 for most normal sizes) and one trip at reduced rates during the rest of the year. The ferry drops you at the Clark Bay terminal in **Hollis**, Craig–Hollis Hwy Mile 31, where there's nothing more than a booking office and public phone. Ferries are met by My Cab (ⓣ826-3077), which will run you into Klawock or Craig for $13.50. Plans are well advanced for a second ferry, the *Stikine*, to begin operation in 2006 and run between Coffman Cove, in the north of the island, Wrangell and Petersburg – thereby creating the opportunity to use Prince of Wales Island as a through route between Ketchikan and Southeast's more northerly ports.

Alternatively, catch a **float plane** from Ketchikan to Craig or Klawock, where you can pick up a rental car without the delivery fee. Pacific Airways (ⓣ225-3500 or 1-877/360-3500, ⓦwww.flypacificairways.com) flies to Craig or Klawock for $95 each way; Promech Air (ⓣ225-3845 or 1-800/860-3843, ⓦwww.promechair.com) flies three to four times daily to Craig for $99.

To **get around** you really need a car. For long stays it may be worth bringing one over from Ketchikan, but **rental vehicles** can be had on the island. Most are SUVs or trucks designed for the more rugged island roads and costing close to $100 a day; call early to get smaller, cheaper vehicles. For the best selection of vehicles try Klawock-based Wilderness Rent-a-Car (ⓣ826-5200 or 1-800/949-2205, ⓦwww.wildernesscarrental.com), which offers compact

4WDs starting at $69 a day and 4WD Ford Explorers from $89 (both plus 30¢ a mile after the first hundred). It's an extra $50 to pick up and drop off the vehicle at the ferry. A second option is to call Craig-based Alaska Rentals (Ⓣ826-3468 or 1-800/720-3468, Ⓦwww.alaskarentals.com), which has similar prices. Remember to fill up where you can: **gas** is only available at Craig, Klawock, Thorne Bay, Coffman Cove, and Naukati. Distances are large enough that **renting a bike** makes little sense as transport; however, you may want one to explore the forest roads. If you're looking to get out on the water, almost everywhere you go on Prince of Wales Island you'll find someone keen to rent you a boat or take you fishing.

Once out of town you can **camp** on any Forest Service land: the map in the *Prince of Wales Island Guide* shows where private land is located and also pinpoints several popular "dispersed" camping sites. On the other end of the price scale, exclusive **fly-in lodges** dot the coast, some in abandoned canneries and most charging four-figure sums for the privilege of spending two or three days there: the visitor center in Craig can point you in the right direction.

Hydaburg and Klawock

From the dock at Hollis (Mile 31) the road runs ten miles west to the Harris River junction. Turning south, Hydaburg Road heads for twenty miles past the trailhead for One Duck Trail (Mile 2), the Cable Creek Fish Pass (Mile 8), and the trailhead for Soda Lake Trail (Mile 12) to **HYDABURG**. This small waterside Haida town, established in 1911 when three local villages combined, is devoted to preserving its culture and isn't particularly interested in visitors, although you might call in to inspect the Civilian Conservation Corps totem park constructed in the late 1930s.

Instead, most head north at the Harris River intersection from where it is smooth asphalt all the way to Klawock and beyond. At Mile 19.7 there's the first-come, first-served *Harris River Campground* ($8 per vehicle), an attractive and organized site with toilets, pump water, and pleasant walks through the forest. Ten miles on, you can stop to see the workings of the community-run Prince of Wales Hatchery (daily 8am–5pm; Ⓣ755–2231), where you are welcome to wander around the tanks and fish ladder outside, or stick around for one of the guided tours (Mon–Sat 1–6pm and by arrangement; donations appreciated).

It is a mile on to **KLAWOCK**, which serves as the island's main intersection where Boundary Road heads north. The junction is marked by a modern Bell Tower mall with a post office, liquor store, supermarket, and the island's Chamber of Commerce visitor center (Tues–Fri 9am–3pm; Ⓣ755-2626, Ⓦwww.princeofwalescoc.com).

Nearby on Big Salt Lake Road, Alaska Kustom Kayaks (Ⓣ755-2800) rents bikes ($12 for 8hr, $20 for 24hr) and top-quality fiberglass kayaks (singles $30 a half-day and $40 a day, doubles $35/$45). They also have plastic canoes ($15/$25) and will advise on the best places to suit your needs. Camping gear may also be available to rent, and they'll run guided trips to order.

There's accommodation nearby at *Log Cabin Resort & RV Park*, Big Salt Lake Road (Ⓣ755-2205 or 1-800/544-2205, Ⓦwww.logcabinresortandrvpark; ❶), with two-berth cabins for $55, campsites ($7 per person), and assorted canoe and boat rentals and fishing charters. For something more luxurious, try the fishing-oriented *Fireweed Lodge*, Hollis–Craig Highway (Ⓣ755-2930, Ⓦwww.fireweedlodge.com), where you'll pay around $160 each per night for room, hot tub, meals, and guided fishing. Eat at *Dave's Diner* (Ⓣ755-2986) near the start of Big Salt Lake Road.

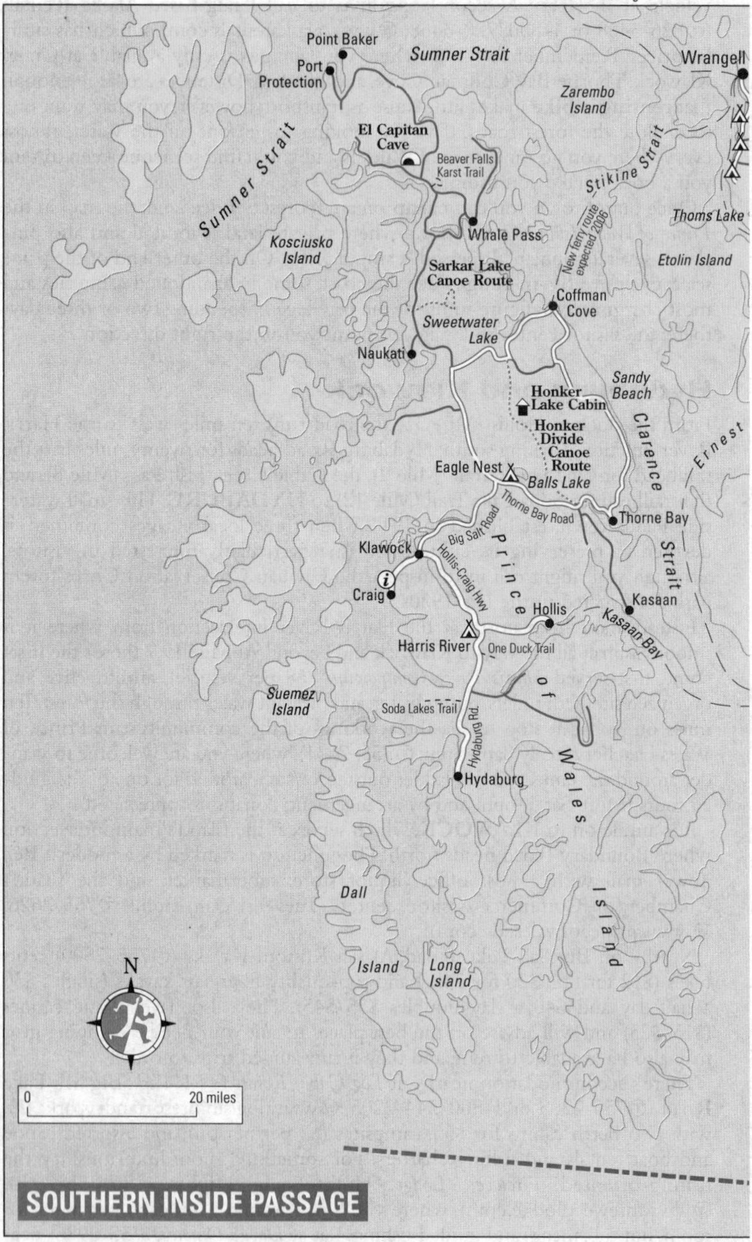
Petersburg
Point Baker
Port Protection
Sumner Strait
Wrangell
Zarembo Island
El Capitan Cave
Beaver Falls Karst Trail
Sumner Strait
Stikine Strait
Thoms Lake
Whale Pass
New ferry route expected 2006
Kosciusko Island
Etolin Island
Sarkar Lake Canoe Route
Coffman Cove
Sweetwater Lake
Naukati
Sandy Beach
Honker Lake Cabin
Honker Divide Canoe Route
Clarence
Ernest
Eagle Nest
Balls Lake
Thorne Bay Road
Thorne Bay
Big Salt Road
Prince
Strait
Klawock
Hollis-Craig Hwy
Craig
Kasaan
Hollis
Kasaan Bay
Harris River
One Duck Trail
of
Suemez Island
Soda Lakes Trail
Hydaburg Rd.
Wales
Hydaburg
Dall
Island
Island
Long Island
N
0
20 miles
SOUTHERN INSIDE PASSAGE

Garnet Ledge
Rainbow Falls &
Institute Creek Trails
BRITISH
COLUMBIA
Long Lake
Trail
Long Lake
Wrangell
Island
Anan Wildlife
Observatory
Sound
Behm Canal
MISTY FIORDS
NATIONAL
MONUMENT
Hyder
Stewart
Cleveland
Peninsula
Behm Canal
Revillagigedo
Island
Manzanita
Lake Cabin
Walker Cove
Tatoosh
Islands
Naha Bay
Manzanita
Bay Shelter
Rudyerd Bay
see "Around Ketchikan"
map
Manzanita
Lake
Nooya Lake Shelter
Punchbowl Cove
New
Eddystone
Rock
Punchbowl Lake Shelter
Punchbowl Lake
Ella Lake
Portland Canal
Winstanley Island
Upper Checats Lake
Ketchikan
Winstanley
Island Cabin
Winstanley Lake
Winstanley
Shelter
Gravina
Island
Smeaton
Island
Alava Bay
Cabin
Alava Bay
Point
Alava
Metlakatla
Annette
Island
Smeaton
Bay
Boca de Quadra
Revillagigedo Channel
UNITED STATES
CANADA
BRITISH
COLUMBIA
Prince Rupert & Bellingham

Across the highway from the Bell Tower mall, look out for Tlingit carver John Rowan, working on totem poles in The Carving Shed. He is usually around weekdays until 2pm and, if not too busy, he's often happy to chat about his work. Most of his recent poles have been recarvings of poles from the Tlingit Native village of Klawock, a mile or so to the west. This was a very important place in the early years of American Alaska; the first cannery in Alaska was set up here in 1878, and two of Alaska's first three sawmills were constructed nearby. Now it is chiefly known for the collection of fifteen totem poles erected under the auspices of the CCC and displayed on a sloping hill beside a couple of roads. New poles have been added in the past few years, underscoring the continued importance of totem carving in Tlingit community life.

Craig

South of Klawock, the highway runs seven miles to **CRAIG**, the island's largest town, although it has fewer than 1500 residents. In the early 1990s it was one of the fastest-growing communities in the state, but the downturn in logging and reduction in fishing receipts has caused a net population loss in the past few years. With a couple of fish-processing plants, boats bobbing in the harbor and the hard-bitten tenor of a real working town, it is a likeable place and is pretty enough to wander round on a sunny afternoon. There are no real sights, however, and apart from making use of the island's densest concentration of hotels, restaurants, and bars, you'll soon find yourself wanting to move on. Before you do, call in at Stone Arts of Alaska, 118 JT Brown St (Tues–Sun 10am–6pm; Ⓣ826-3571, Ⓦwww.stoneartsofalaska.com), where Gary McWilliams produces some beautiful **stone carvings**, mostly using local rock.

For outdoor activities, get along to Log Cabin Sporting Goods, 1 Easy St (Ⓣ826-2205 or 1-888/265-0375, Ⓦwww.seatoursalaska.com), which rents out canoes for $25 a day and kayaks at $40 a day (doubles $50) and stocks lots of fishing and outdoor gear.

Although you'd barely know it, Craig occupies Craig Island, linked by a short bridge to Prince of Wales Island. As you approach over the bridge from Prince of Wales Island you find yourself on Water Street passing the town's cluster of mini-malls, where you'll find a supermarket, the post office, a bank (with ATM), *Papa's Pizza*, and Voyageur Bookstore (Mon–Sat 9am–7pm, Sun 9am–5pm; Ⓣ826-2333), the best place on the island to relax over an espresso and muffin or check your email. The older commercial heart of Craig is half a mile straight on beside the picturesque remains of an old cannery.

Craig has easily the largest range of **accommodation** on the island, much of it booked up with fishing parties. The cheapest rooms are the simply furnished, but perfectly acceptable, ones above the *TLC Laundry & Rooms*, Cold Storage Road near the mini-malls (Ⓣ826-2966; ❶). If you can, step up to *Dreamcatcher*, 1405 Hamilton Drive (Ⓣ826-2238, Ⓦwww.alaskaone.com/dreammbb; ❹), a lovely three-room B&B in a wooded setting close to town that has great sea views. All rooms have private bath, and a continental breakfast is included. For hotel rooms, try *Ruth Anne's Hotel* on Water Street (Ⓣ826-3878, Ⓔruthanns@aptalaska.net; suites ❻, rooms ❹), with spacious modern rooms equipped with TV, microwave, refrigerator, and coffeepot, plus older and smaller rooms that have a bit more character.

For **eating**, the *Bait Box*, 510 Water St (Ⓣ826-2303; closed Sun), does wraps, subs, and burgers to go, but the locals' favorite is *Ruth Anne's* with a bar and restaurant built on pilings over the water by the dock. The adjacent *Hill Bar* is always animated and has **live music** whenever they can coax a band over here.

Kasaan

Until recently, the roads north of Klawock were all unpaved, but the prospect of a new ferry terminal at Coffman Cove has set construction wheels in motion. Miles of smooth, broad asphalt have already been laid and both eastern and western routes to Coffman Cove should be completed by the spring of 2006. The rest of the northern roads are single-lane and often potholed: take things steady and be sure to have a good spare tire.

Leaving Klawock, the road heads north past Klawock airport through some open hill country sixteen miles to a road junction: turn left to Coffman Cove and the caves, or right to Kasaan and Thorne Bay. A couple of miles along the Klawock–Thorne Bay road you reach the lovely first-come, first-served *Eagle Nest Campground* ($8 per vehicle), with well-spaced sites, some of which are walk-in platforms with lake views. Take a few minutes to stroll along the half-mile boardwalk around **Balls Lake**.

Beyond the campground a bone-shaking seventeen-mile road cuts southeast to the tiny waterside Haida village of **KASAAN**, one of Southeast's best (if least convenient) places to see totem poles. It was originally founded a century back when the lure of mining and fishing jobs attracted Haida here from the now-abandoned village of Old Kasaan. The only reason to come here is to visit the abandoned **totem park**, a mile west of the village. Park by the Community Hall and walk back towards the beach, taking the last track on the right. Follow this for twenty minutes or so through beachside woods to the next bay, where you'll find what is perhaps the finest setting of any Alaskan totem park. The poles and clan house are the work of the CCC in the late 1930s, but its neglected state, the authentic feeling of its location, and the lack of any commercial trappings make it a wonderful spot. If you're here alone, especially in the early morning or at dusk, it is particularly affecting.

The beach is backed by the clan house, with its platforms around the sunken fire pit and powerfully carved roof supports now only partly achieving their intended purpose, as the forest gradually reclaims its own. In front, a superb pole faces out to sea, 4ft thick at its base and over 50ft tall, with bulbous eyes set in four-foot-high faces. Nearby, several other poles lurk in the woods, four of them in a ring almost swallowed by the undergrowth.

Thorne Bay and Coffman Cove

Thorne Bay Road runs, not surprisingly, to **THORNE BAY**, which from 1962 to 2001 was the site of the Ketchikan Pulp Company's main log-sorting yard. Once described as the world's largest logging camp, it is now mostly of interest to anglers. The *Welcome Inn B&B* (Ⓣ828-3950 or 1-888/828-3940, Ⓦwww.aptalaska.net/~welcome; ❸) offers shared-bath rooms; **campers** should stock up at the Thorne Bay Market before making for the bays to the north.

North of Thorne Bay, the road hugs the coast for ten miles, passing some beautiful little bays with numerous camping possibilities, none of which is formal. **Sandy Beach**, six miles out, is the most popular spot, with picnic table, toilets, and fire rings.

Occupying an idyllic bay around thirty miles north of Thorne Bay, **COFFMAN COVE** is the former site of a Tlingit village and a 1950s logging camp. Again there's little to do but beachcomb and fish, perhaps best done while **staying** at *Oceanview RV Park and Campground* (Ⓣ329-2015, Ⓦwww.coffmancove.org/rvpark), which has camping for $15, full hookup for $25, doubles and twins with shared bath ($30 per person), and a basic trailer sleeping two ($35) to four ($55). It is nicely set by the sea, but is simple.

Another option is *Rain Country B&B*, located just as you enter town on the road from the south (Ⓣ329-2274, Ⓦwww.coffmancove.org/rcbandb.html; ④), where plain rooms share a wonderful deck with great views across to Etolin Island and an outdoor barbecue to grill your catch. Skiff rentals are available at $75 a day. If you don't plan on fishing for your meals, you'll want to avail yourself of lunch and dinner for $15 a day extra as there are no restaurants for miles.

Beaver Falls and the El Capitan Cave

Much of the north of the island is karst landscape, underlain by limestone riddled with dozens of caves, most of them barely explored. A sense of what lies below can be gleaned on the new, accessible Beaver Falls Karst Trail, an interpretive network of boardwalks located 31 miles north of the Coffman Cove road junction. Set aside at least half an hour to wander across muskeg and into dripping forest to depressions in the forest floor marking sinkholes, some of which swallow small streams.

As appealing as the boardwalk is, the prize exhibit around here is **El Capitan Cave**, used by Native peoples as early as 3400 years ago judging by charcoal left from torches. Modern speleologists only started extensively mapping the caves in the late 1980s and have since discovered the El Cap Pit, which is the deepest known natural pit in the US, with an initial drop of almost 600ft. The Forest Service runs **guided tours** (late May to early Sept Thurs–Sun; free; Ⓣ828-3304) several times throughout the day – as they are becoming popular and groups are limited to six, book a few days in advance. Taking about an hour and a half and penetrating some 600ft into the cave, the tours take in the usual limestone formations along with hollows where otters hibernate, crevices where bats roost and even spots where bears once spent the winter. Bring along a flashlight, warm clothing to combat the cave's constant 40°F temperatures, and some reasonably sturdy footwear. Note that you'll have to make your own way to the site, which is almost a hundred miles from the Hollis ferry dock and a three- to four-hour drive.

Freelance exploration is prevented by a locked gate fifty yards in, but you are welcome to explore the entrance area after negotiating the gorgeous fifteen-minute forest access trail and its 370 steps.

Wrangell and around

Eighty miles north of Ketchikan, the small fishing town of **WRANGELL** occupies a strategically significant spot on the northern tip of Wrangell Island, just seven miles south of the mouth of the **Stikine River**, the only passable break in the Coastal Range between Prince Rupert and Skagway. The area became a major conduit for prospectors bound for the early gold rushes, first during the stampede to central British Columbia in the early 1860s and later during the Yukon rush in 1897, when the Stikine became the so-called backdoor route to the Klondike.

Although for many visitors Wrangell is just a forty-minute ferry stop on the run from Ketchikan, the town, altogether quieter and more old-fashioned than its bustling rival, is not without appeal. There are just a few relatively minor sights all easily accessible on foot. **Chief Shakes Island**, right in the busy harbor and accessible by a short boardwalk, holds an excellent collection of totem poles and a replica tribal house filled with Tlingit blankets, and about a mile to

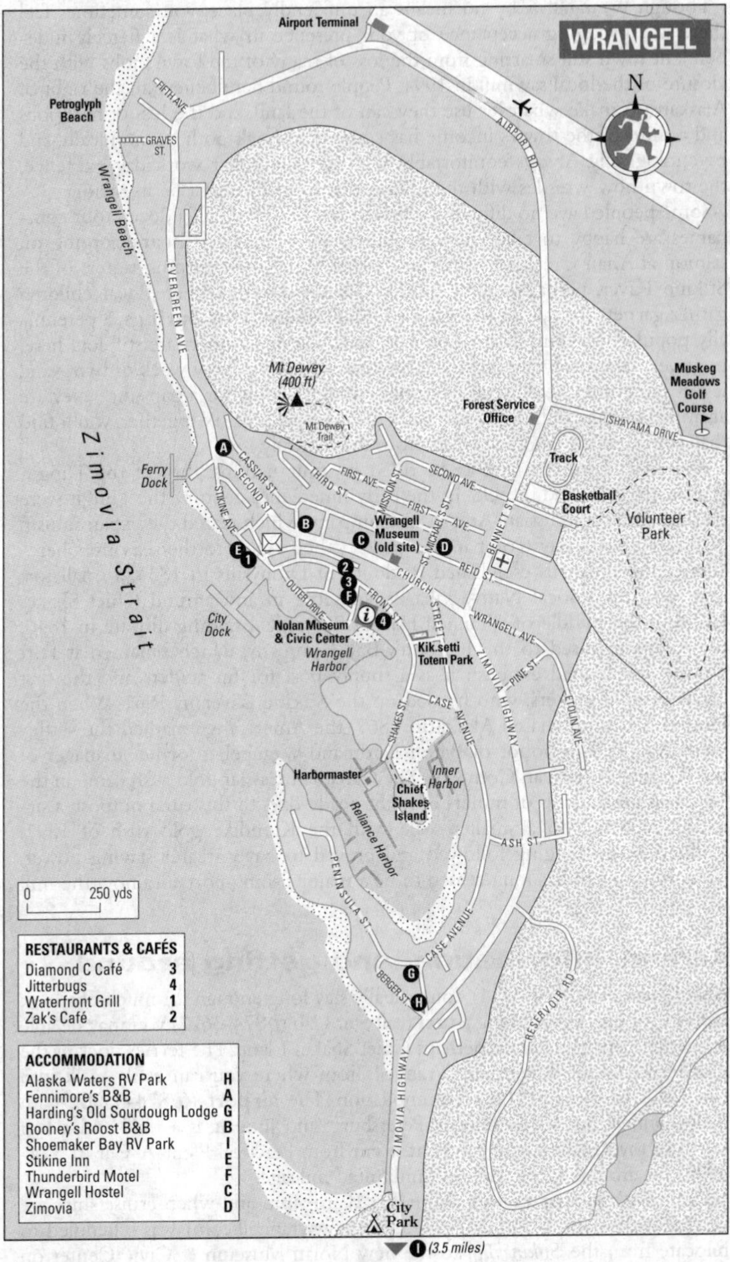
WRANGELL
N
Airport Terminal
Airport Rd
Fifth Ave
Petroglyph Beach
Graves St
Wrangell Beach
Evergreen Ave
Mt Dewey (400 ft)
Mt Dewey Trail
Forest Service Office
Muskeg Meadows Golf Course
Ishayama Drive
Track
Basketball Court
Volunteer Park
Zimovia Strait
Ferry Dock
Cassiar St
Second St
Third St
First Ave
Second Ave
Mission St
St Michael's St
Bennett St
Stikine Ave
Wrangell Museum (old site)
Church St
Reid St
Front St
Outer Drive
City Dock
Nolan Museum & Civic Center
Wrangell Harbor
Kik.setti Totem Park
Church Street
Wrangell Ave
Zimovia Highway
Pine St
Etolin Ave
Case Avenue
Shakes St
Inner Harbor
Harbormaster
Chief Shakes Island
Reliance Harbor
Ash St
Peninsula St
Berger St
Reservoir Rd
City Park
(3.5 miles)
0 250 yds
RESTAURANTS & CAFÉS
Diamond C Café 3
Jitterbugs 4
Waterfront Grill 1
Zak's Café 2
ACCOMMODATION
Alaska Waters RV Park H
Fennimore's B&B A
Harding's Old Sourdough Lodge G
Rooney's Roost B&B B
Shoemaker Bay RV Park I
Stikine Inn E
Thunderbird Motel F
Wrangell Hostel C
Zimovia D

the north lies **Petroglyph Beach**, where ancient rock carvings defy explanation and have proven difficult to date.

Though Wrangell is by no means an unfriendly place, you sometimes feel there is a grudging acceptance of your presence in what is a fiercely independent town still smarting from the loss of many of the town's jobs with the closure of the local sawmill in 1994. People round here believe in the right of Alaskans to make whatever use they can of the land, and the loss of both jobs and a third of the town's income has come as a shock both economically and psychologically. Always comfortable with its blue-collar workaday existence, the town now wrestles with the notion that tourism might be its savior.

Some people have no difficulty with the concept, and half a dozen tour companies are happy to take you out, either south to watch **bears** gorging on salmon at Anan Creek, or north and inland along the churning waters of the Stikine River, perhaps calling at the **Garnet Ledge**, where local children gather garnets for sale to tourists, or **Chief Shakes Hot Springs**, a perennially popular weekend destination for locals. Visitor numbers are still low here, however – they only get one medium-size cruise ship every week or two – and it can sometimes be difficult to gather enough people for a trip since they are arranged by demand. If you can get a group of four or six together, you'll find that your options (and prices) improve dramatically.

Wrangell claims to have been ruled by four nations: that of the Tlingit, Russia, the UK, and the US. In the early nineteenth century, the Tlingit were trading with the Russian-American Company, which feared the expansionism of the Hudson's Bay Company. To protect their rights to the sea otters hereabouts, the Russians established Redoubt St Dionysius in 1834, a small fort that soon drew local Native villagers to settle in and around Chief Shakes Island in the middle of Wrangell Harbor. To settle a trading dispute in 1840, the fort was leased to the Hudson's Bay Company, which renamed it Fort Stikine and helped establish it as a supply post for fur traders and the first batch of gold seekers, who headed up the Stikine River in 1861. When the United States purchased Alaska in 1867, the Americans renamed the settlement Wrangell in honor of Baron Ferdinand Wrangel, a former manager of the Russian-American Company. The Canadian Cassiar gold rush came in the 1870s and thousands of miners brought heady days to this rural outpost, a situation repeated on a smaller scale with the Klondike gold rush of 1897. Canneries and logging followed and proved to have greater staying power, though Wrangell has long ceased to be a major fishing port, and now the mill has gone.

Arrival, information, and getting around

AMHS ferries (Ⓣ874-3711) don't usually stay long enough for much of a look around, though by grabbing a **taxi** (call Star Cab Ⓣ874-3622) you may be able to see the petroglyphs and perhaps Chief Shakes Island. The ferries dock at the northern edge of downtown Wrangell, from where you can easily walk into town and to most of the accommodation. The **airport** (Ⓣ874-3308), with daily connections to Ketchikan, Petersburg, and Juneau, is a mile and a half north of town, where you can **rent a car** from Practical Rent-A-Car (Ⓣ874-3975) for around $55 a day with unlimited mileage.

The town's **visitor center** (Mon–Fri 10am–4pm and when cruise ships are in; Ⓣ874-3901 or 1-800/367-9745, Ⓦwww.wrangell.com) was scheduled to relocate from the *Stikine Inn* to the new Nolan Museum & Civic Center on Outer Drive in early 2004. If it's closed, pick up a free *Wrangell Guide* from the ferry terminal. For information on hikes, cabins, and anything else in the surrounding Tongass National Forest, visit the Wrangell Ranger District **Forest Service Office**, 525 Bennett St (Mon–Fri 8am–4.30pm; ⓣ874-2323).

Though it is easy enough to wander around the main sights in Wrangell, you might want to **rent a bike** from Solo Cat Sports (ⓣ874-2920 or 1-877/874-2923), which charges $27 a half-day and $45 a day.

Rain Walker Expeditions (ⓣ874-2549, ⓦwww.rainwalkerexpeditions.com) runs a series of naturalist-guided walking and van **tours**, among them a visit to Petroglyph Beach (1hr 30min; $15), a tour of historic downtown (1hr 30min; $12) and Chief Shakes Island, and a half-day island exploration ($89).

Accommodation

For such a tiny place, Wrangell is fairly well supplied with accommodation, including a simple hostel, a couple of motels and several B&Bs. Camping is good, too, with half a dozen designated places to camp along the road system. In addition to the **campgrounds** and RV parks listed below, there are several more free sites further along Zimovia Highway at Mile 11, Mile 14, Mile 17, Mile 23, and Mile 28.

Alaska Waters RV Park 241 Berger St ⓣ874-2378. Small and not especially attractive lot with just seven power and water hookup sites for $19. The city dump station is at the corner of Front St and Case Ave.

City Park 1.5 miles south on Zimovia Highway. The nearest campground to town, well sited in woods beside the channel, with first-come, first-served sites available for a one-night maximum stay. There are shelters to cook under and marginal toilets but no showers. Free.

Fennimore's B&B 312 Evergreen Ave ⓣ874-3012, ⓔ wrgbbb@aptalaska.net. Comfy and friendly B&B conveniently located by the ferry dock. Two upstairs rooms with shared bath and three downstairs rooms with private entrances and their own bathrooms, all of which are pleasantly furnished, have cable TV, and include a continental breakfast supplied in your room. ④

Harding's Old Sourdough Lodge 1104 Peninsula St ⓣ874-3613 or 1-800/874-3613, ⓦwww.akgetaway.com. Large cedar log building at the southern edge of town with high-standard rooms in various sizes to suit individuals and small groups. The best deals are the wilderness and adventure packages, such as two nights with one day spent on the Stikine River, viewing bald eagles, whale watching, or visiting the Anan Wildlife Observatory ($363 per person); two nights with car rental and green fees for Wrangell's nine-hole golf course ($298); and six nights, with five days spent kayaking the Stikine and flightseeing the LeConte Glacier ($1350). Home-style meals for guests only (breakfast and lunch $10, dinner $20). Six-person suite ⑧, sauna room sleeping three ⑦, standard rooms ④

Rooney's Roost B&B 206 McKinnon St ⓣ874-2026, ⓦwww.rooneysroost.com. Attractive B&B, close to town, with modernized rooms, phones, TV, antique furniture, clawfoot baths in the rooms with bathrooms, a large lounge and a full sit-down breakfast. Private bath ④, shared bath ③

Shoemaker Bay RV Park 4.5 miles south on Zimovia Highway. First-come, first-served RV and tent campground with 26 spaces, toilets, picnic tables, and shelters, plus beach fishing. Electrical hookup sites are $10, dry sites $6. Handy for the Rainbow Falls Trail.

Stikine Inn 107 Stikine Ave ⓣ874-3388 or 1-888/874-3388, ⓦwww.stikine.com. Wrangell's largest hotel, a little dated but right on the waterfront, with spacious rooms all with cable TV and coffeemakers. The waterside rooms are worth the extra $10. Suites ⑥, rooms ⑤

Thunderbird Motel 223 Front St ⓣ874-3322. Budget motel with fairly spacious phone- and shower-equipped rooms (ask for one with an external window), each with cable TV and some with refrigerator. ③

Wrangell Hostel 220 Church St ⓣ874-3534, ⓔpresby@aptalaska.net. Eighteen dollars seems like a lot for an inflatable mattress on the floor of a room in the First Presbyterian Church, but if you want a cheap roof over your head here it is. It is clean and central, though, with a good kitchen and no daytime lockout. There is an 11pm curfew, but this is flexible. Open mid-June to early Sept. ①

Zimovia 319 Webber St ⓣ874-2626, ⓦwww.zimoviabnb.com. Excellent-value, comfortable, and convenient B&B offering pleasant rooms with kitchenette, access to a sauna, and continental breakfast. ②

The Town

Young garnet sellers clustered on the docks usually greet arriving ferry passengers with their red jewels from the Garnet Ledge (see p.114). Although many visitors get no further, if you're determined (and fast) you can see a little of what Wrangell has to offer – either Petroglyph Beach or the Kik.setti Totem Park – in the forty minutes or so before the ferry leaves. You'll need more time to view the museum, Chief Shakes Tribal House or explore the town's hiking trails.

Petroglyph Beach and the Wrangell Museum

By grabbing a taxi (or walking very quickly) it is possible to blitz **Petroglyph Beach**, just over half a mile north of the ferry dock off Evergreen Avenue at Graves Street. Of course, it is better to stay overnight and give yourself more time to explore the extensive boardwalk, which guides you down to the beach where Southeast's most concentrated array of ancient petroglyphs are etched onto the rocks. Little is known about the purpose of these forty-odd shapes – spirals, birds, orca, faces, and masks – and even the age is uncertain, with numbers ranging from a thousand to ten thousand years bandied about. The range of designs – from simple human forms to more detailed images resembling modern Tlingit iconography – indicate that the petroglyphs were produced in several eras, many predating the relatively modern Tlingit culture. Since they are located on an active beach, stratification studies to determine age are impossible.

It sometimes takes a few minutes to spy your first image, but then you seem to see them everywhere. The most concentrated batch is found around the high-tide line thirty to fifty yards to the right (north) of the boardwalk steps; don't miss the orca and owl forms close to the grass. The best time is usually as the high tide is receding and the glyphs are shiny and more visible (and photogenic). The low light of morning and evening is also helpful. Taking rubbings from the originals is strongly discouraged, and some replicas have been installed on the boardwalk for this purpose.

Some of the more portable glyphs have been removed for safekeeping to the **Wrangell Museum** (May–Sept Tues–Sat 10am–5pm, Sun and Mon whenever cruise ships are in port; $3), which is slated to move from 122 2nd St to its new waterside Nolan Museum & Civic Center location on Outer Drive in time for summer 2004. Modernization is planned with the relocation, but it is currently an eclectic community museum that's surprisingly extensive for such a small town. The prize exhibit is a set of four very fine house posts that are thought to be the oldest Tlingit house posts in existence, having probably been carved between 1775 and 1790 (and possibly as early as 1740). They're less stylized and more naturalistic in execution than many of the later models seen throughout Southeast; they're also heavily weathered from the years they spent outdoors before being incorporated into the Chief Shakes Tribal House (see opposite). There's also a slab of rock from the Garnet Ledge with the garnets firmly embedded, as well as extensive coverage of the 1899 Harriman Expedition (see p.287), in which railroad magnate Edward H Harriman rented a steamer and led a two-month-long combined family vacation and scientific expedition along the Alaskan coast with John Muir in tow.

The Totem Park and Tribal House

Right downtown, at the corner of Front and Episcopal streets, you'll pass the **Kik.setti Totem Park**, a tiny grassed area created in 1987 on the original site of a long-lost pole known as Kik.setti. Noted carvers Steve Brown and Wayne Price used only traditional hand tools to recreate the Kik.setti totem – depicting the symbols of the Kik.setti people who settled Wrangell Island – which now stands in pride of place, backed by three other replicas of highly regarded poles. Among them is the **Raven totem**, with the Raven creator at the top, just above what is known as the chief's box, which is said to have spiritual powers. Below that a young Raven clasps a man between its wings signifying how Raven could change into a man at will. The lowest figure is Ha-ya-shon-a-gu, described as the "Native American Atlas" holding up the Earth.

Front Street continues south as Shakes Street to **Chief Shakes Island**, a small grass plot and the heart of the inner harbor, linked to the docks by a short boardwalk. Dominated by the Chief Shakes **Tribal House** ($2.50 when cruise ships are in port, and by appointment on ⓣ874-2023 when it is $25 for the party) and ringed by a forest of **totem poles**, it makes a wonderfully peaceful place to while away an hour or two. The replica high-caste clan house was rebuilt as part of the Civilian Conservation Corps project (see box, p.84) on the site of an ancient house and dedicated in 1940 at one of the largest gatherings of Native people seen for many years. With the decline in traditional Tlingit ways in the early part of the twentieth century, there hadn't been a Chief Shakes (overall chief hereabouts) since 1916, and the potlatch – attended by the territorial governor – was seen as an opportunity to inaugurate the nephew of the last chief as Chief Shakes VII. Some 1500 people and several war canoes arrived from all over Southeast for what is generally regarded as the last great potlatch of the Tlingit people. Ancient house posts were incorporated into the building and only removed to the Wrangell Museum in 1982 when replicas were carved to replace them. If the house is open, nose around the

Hikes from Wrangell

Although a couple of easy walks are close at hand, the more challenging hikes require some means of getting out along the road system: either rent a vehicle or try hitching out to the relatively accessible hikes off Zimovia Highway. Listed below is a taste of what's on offer in the area; for more information seek out the free *Wrangell Guide,* which lists the more popular trails and is available from the ferry terminal. The Forest Service is also helpful with suggestions and sells topographic maps for $4. If they're closed, try Alaska Vistas, at the foot of the City Dock.

Long Lake Trail (1.2 miles round-trip; 30–40min; negligible ascent). Easy boardwalk to a lake where there's a shelter and a skiff with oars that's perfect for a little trout fishing. The trailhead is 27 miles southeast of Wrangell in the center of the island on Forest Road 6270.

Mount Dewey Trail (1-mile round-trip; 30–40min; 300ft ascent). Pleasant, at times steep, hike through woods to the top of the hill that rises behind downtown Wrangell. There's a good observation point overlooking the town, undoubtedly also used by John Muir when he made the ascent in 1879. The trail starts on Third Street.

Rainbow Falls Trail (2 miles round-trip; 1hr; 300ft ascent). Moderate and sometimes boggy trail through the rainforest to the top of a waterfall. From here, keen and fit hikers can continue up what's known as **Institute Creek Trail** (4.5 miles round-trip; 2–4hr; 1200ft ascent) to the three-sided Shoemaker Bay Overlook Shelter atop a high ridge with long views. The trailhead is almost five miles south along Zimovia Highway, opposite the Shoemaker Bay Recreation Site.

Volunteer Park Trail (800-yard loop; 20min; flat). Easy nature walk along the edge of a spruce forest, with interpretive panels along the way. Starts near the basketball courts opposite the Forest Service office.

adze-beamed interior as the guide explains traditional life inside a clan house. Otherwise you'll have to make do with the intricately carved exterior and half a dozen poles, including the **Three Frogs totem**, a shame totem erected to mock the Frog clan who married slaves decades ago. The Frog clan was distinctly put out by its controversial raising in 2000.

Outdoor activities

Wrangell has plenty of good hiking (see box, p.111) and serves as a base for some excellent **kayaking**. (For bear viewing, jetboat trips, and visits to the Garnet Ledge, see "Around Wrangell," opposite). Half a day spent bobbing around the harbor and along the coast to Petroglyph Beach can be satisfying, but a multiday trip along the sheltered Eastern Passage to Anan Wildlife Observatory is also worth considering. Despite the current, you can also kayak up the mighty Stikine River as far as the Canadian border by utilizing eddies and the slack-water sloughs marked on the Forest Service's schematic *Stikine River Canoe/Kayak Route Map* ($4), which also marks tent sites, cabins, and log jams. You can even pay to be transported upriver and paddle gently back down over several days (for more on the river, see "Around Wrangell," opposite).

Alaska Vistas (Ⓣ874-3006, Ⓦwww.alaskavistas.com) runs **guided trips** for around $150 a day and multiday excursions such as a six-day paddle to LeConte Glacier ($1300). **Going it alone**, you can rent kayaks from Alaska Vistas, which offers singles ($45 a day) and doubles ($55) and does drop-offs at good starting points.

Eating and drinking

There's nothing special about **eating** in Wrangell, but you won't go hungry and there's enough variety for the night or two you'll be here. Bob's IGA supermarket on Outer Drive is reasonably well stocked and has an in-store bakery.

Diamond C Café 223 Front St Ⓣ874-3677. Standard diner that's popular with locals for its good-quality food at fair prices.
Jitterbugs 309 Front St Ⓣ874-3350. Espresso to go.
Waterfront Grill inside the *Stikine Inn* Ⓣ874-2353. About the best restaurant in town with good sea views, serving the usual menu of burgers, sandwiches, and Caesar salads. Dinner ($14–21) ranges from pasta with mushrooms in a garlic and white-wine sauce to New York pepper steak.
Zak's Café 316 Front St Ⓣ874-3355. The fairly antiseptic interior seems about right for a place that tries for a wide-ranging menu but only achieves tolerable quality. It is fairly cheap, though, with entrées at $7–13.

Listings

Banks Wells Fargo, 115 Front St, has an ATM.
Festivals The Garnet Festival, 3rd week in April, celebrates the coming of spring and the gathering of bald eagles on the Stikine River with special boat trips and various events that have nothing to do with garnets; there's a king salmon derby from mid-May to mid-June; and a 4th of July celebration with the usual fireworks and parade, plus a log-rolling competition in the harbor.
Internet access Free at the library.
Laundry and showers The Thunderbird Laundromat is at 225 Front St. The Community Center, next to the High School on 2nd St (Ⓣ874-2444; closed Sun), has a pool, weight room, and showers ($3).
Library Irene Ingle Public Library on 2nd St (Mon & Fri 10am–noon & 1–5pm, Tues–Thurs 1–5pm & 7–9pm, Sat 9am–5pm).
Medical assistance Wrangell Medical Center, 310 Bennett St Ⓣ874-7000, Ⓦwww.wrangellmedicalcenter.com.
Post office On Federal St. The **General Delivery** zip code is 99929.
Taxes There's a seven percent city sales tax, plus a $4 bed tax, all included within our price codes.

Around Wrangell

Wrangell is well positioned to make the best of the local scenery and wildlife. Bear viewing is usually near the top of most people's list, and there are few places in Alaska you can get close as cheaply as at the **Anan Wildlife Observatory**, little more than a hide and viewing platform but nonetheless a wonderful spot to commune with these fearsome beasts.

Wrangell sits seven miles south of the mouth of the **Stikine River** ("the Great River"), which is said to be the fastest navigable river in North America, with peak flows around six miles per hour. Riverboats that started during the gold rushes continued to run regularly on the river until 1969, a tradition now continued by jetboats that whisk tourists as far upstream as Telegraph Creek in British Columbia. Several companies in Wrangell run trips on the Stikine and to Anan; *Harding's Old Sourdough Lodge* offers competitive packages (see "Accommodation," p.109).

Jetboats also run from Wrangell to the **LeConte Glacier** (see p.122), typically taking five to eight hours and costing $135–150.

Anan Wildlife Observatory

Easily one of the most rewarding outings from Wrangell is to see the **bears feeding** at the Anan Wildlife Observatory, located on the mainland some thirty miles south of town and only accessible by boat or plane. Here, a waterfall a few hundred yards inland from the gorgeous Anan Lagoon slows the progress of one of the state's largest runs of "humpies" or pink salmon, and black bears (and a few browns) come to dine on the floundering fish. To provide more comfortable viewing conditions and limit the risk of bear–human contact, the Forest Service has constructed an open-sided observation platform reached by a half-mile-long trail from the beach. Photographers will want to sign up for half an hour in the viewing hide (free), where being close to the stream gives you a better angle on the bears feeding.

Such is the rise in Anan's popularity in recent years that 2004 sees the introduction of a **quota system** for visiting the observatory. From July 5 to August 25, only sixty people a day will be allowed to visit the observatory. Of these slots, half will be available to tour operators, with the other half open to private individuals from March 1. For the benefit of the non-planners among you, twelve places will only come available three days in advance. For reservations contact the Wrangell Ranger District Office ($10; ⓣ874-2323). There are no limitations outside the quota period, but bear numbers during this period are likely to be low.

Head half a mile in the other direction and you'll reach the Forest Service's *Anan Bay Cabin* ($35; book months in advance on ⓣ1-877/444-6777, ⓦwww.reserveUSA.com), which is perfect if you want to stay a few days, perhaps watching bald eagles or harbor seals out in the lagoon. Up to four people can stay in the cabin, effectively bypassing the quota system and getting free entry during their stay.

Access is by fifteen-minute flight, one-hour boat journey or at least two days by kayak. Unless you are experienced in dealing with bears (or avoiding having to), it is much safer to visit on a guided trip on which the guide stays with you the whole time (and usually has bear spray and a gun). The cheapest of these is Alaska Waters (ⓣ874-2378 or 1-800/347-4462, ⓦwww.alaskawaters.com), which gives you two to three hours at Anan for $180. Stikine Wilderness Adventures (ⓣ874-2085 or 1-800/874-2085, ⓦwww.akgetaway.com) makes it a full-day trip ($200) with up to six hours at the observatory and a little more personal attention. Breakaway Adventures (ⓣ874-2488 or 1-888/385-2488,

Ⓦwww.breakawayadventures.com) also runs a full-day trip by boat, spending three to six hours at Anan for $200.

Good-value flights can be had with Sunrise Aviation (Ⓣ874-2319 or 1-800/874-2311, Ⓦwww.sunriseflights.com), which charges $500 per round-trip for up to four people, with as much time as you want at Anan, though you won't get a guide.

Garnet Ledge

Wrangell's dockside garnet-selling industry is one of Southeast's more curious tales. In the 1860s garnets were found on the mainland, seven miles northeast of Wrangell, alongside a creek in an area that has become known as the **Garnet Ledge**. From 1907 to 1923, the Alaska Garnet Mining and Manufacturing Company – said to be the world's first corporation entirely run by women – was commercially mining the gems from the soft mica schist and making hat pins, watch fobs and the like.

By the 1930s, deft political maneuvering had left ownership in the hands of Wrangell mayor Fred Hanford, who subsequently (in 1962) deeded the Garnet Ledge to the local Boy Scouts, with local children having the right to take garnets "in reasonable quantities." They decreed that children under 16 had the sole right to gather and sell the sub-jewelry-quality garnets. When "mining" they must be accompanied by an adult, and enthusiastic parents often take their kids over to the Ledge in their skiff and let them fossick around, mining by hand. After all, a good session of selling to cruise-ship and ferry passengers can easily net $200.

You can join the fun provided that you pay $10 and commit ten percent of your find to the Scouts. Visitors are not allowed to sell their finds, however. Most of the boat operators running trips up the Stikine River, which passes by Garnet Ledge, can drop you off and will be happy to relieve you of your money. An hour will be enough for most people, but you can **stay** at the Forest Service's *Garnet Ledge Cabin* ($25; Ⓣ1-877/444-6777) should you wish to stay longer.

Exploring the Stikine River

From the mountains of British Columbia, the Stikine River threads its way almost four hundred miles to the sea, with only the last thirty miles running through the Stikine–LeConte Wilderness in Alaska. It is a spectacular journey, with dramatic mountains, canyons, glaciers, forests, and matchless wildlife, all able to be seen on jetboat trips or fly-in rafting, canoeing, and kayaking expeditions.

The river reaches tidewater at the **Stikine Flats**, a broad and shallow delta full of small islands sprouting willows and cottonwoods. The surrounding mudflats are covered in spring and fall with **birds** – ducks, geese, sandhill cranes – resting along their migration route (known as the Pacific Flyway). The area around Mallard Slough, and the *Mallard Slough Cabin* ($35; Ⓣ1-877/444-6777), is particularly good in late April and early May for spotting shorebirds, including huge flocks of western sandpipers. From late March to early May, small oily fish called eulachon (usually bowdlerized to "hooligan") flood up the river, chased by the state's second largest concentration of **bald eagles** (after Haines), often numbering well over a thousand.

The delta is a popular destination in summer when it can seem as though half of Wrangell is out here fishing, sightseeing, visiting the Garnet Ledge or making for **Chief Shakes Hot Springs**, 28 miles by boat from Wrangell, for a soak in one of the redwood tubs (one of which is enclosed).

The river is navigable for 160 miles upstream from the hot springs, to the small British Columbian Native town of **Telegraph Creek**, cutting through some wonderful scenery, which John Muir favorably compared to his beloved Yosemite. Jetboat trips either stick to the delta and lower river or head right up to Telegraph Creek. Most operators are prepared to take you and your kayaks, canoes, or rafts up there and leave you to float back down to Wrangell. Breakaway Adventures runs a slew of trips, including one around the delta that visits the Garnet Ledge, hot springs, and glaciers (7hr; $135), and multiday trips upstream, charged at $600 a day for a six-person boat. Alaska Waters has a comparable local trip (6hr; $145) and takes three days for their trip up to Telegraph Creek and back ($726), with two nights at a lodge in Telegraph Creek.

If you're planning to enter Canada, you'll need to call **Canadian customs** (Ⓣ250/627-3003 in Prince Rupert) to give them the details of your party, and also to contact US customs (Ⓣ874-3415) as soon as possible after your re-entry into Alaska.

Petersburg and around

One of the highlights of riding the Inside Passage ferries from Wrangell is sitting up front to watch the boat negotiate the 46 slalom-course turns of the 22-mile-long **Wrangell Narrows** between Mitkof and Kupreanof islands. It's a beautiful run by day, when it feels like you can reach out and touch the steep-walled shore and crumbling wooden piers, and doubly so at night, when it is baffling how the captain can pilot a course through the maze of lights from the marker buoys.

As the passage broadens, the starboard shore sprouts a straggle of jetties and wharves that run for a mile along the waterfront of **PETERSBURG**, with its canneries perched above the water on forests of poles on the northern tip of Mitkof Island. No prizes for guessing that Petersburg is primarily a fishing port. The citizens are more interested in salmon, halibut, black cod, shrimp, crab, and herring than they are in tourists, which is a good part of the appeal. The larger cruise ships can't negotiate the Narrows, thus saving Petersburg from their hit-and-run attentions; no one is out to sell you anything, and it is refreshing to just saunter around the docks and gaze across Frederick Sound at the summit of **Devil's Thumb** on the US–Canada border.

Petersburg gets its name from Peter Buschmann, the Norwegian fisherman who, in 1897, decided that the abundant fish, free ice from the nearby LeConte Glacier and relative proximity to markets made this a good place to found a fishing port. He proved to be very right, and many of his countryfolk followed his lead, giving some credence to Petersburg's claim to be "Alaska's Little Norway." Unless you are here on the third full weekend in May (nearest Norwegian Independence Day on May 17) for the **Little Norway Festival,** when a model Viking longboat is trundled down the street, evidence is fairly scant, though several buildings have the Norwegian-style scrolled detailing around their windows known as "rosmaling", and the general store on Main Street does a nice line in Norwegian sweaters and knick-knacks. Otherwise it's just a busy Alaskan fishing port, where the streets are often filled with the thousand or so temporary cannery workers, who significantly swell the ranks of this town of three thousand in summer.

Sights are fairly thin on the ground, though anyone with a taste for the work of ancient civilizations shouldn't miss the easily accessible **fish traps** and

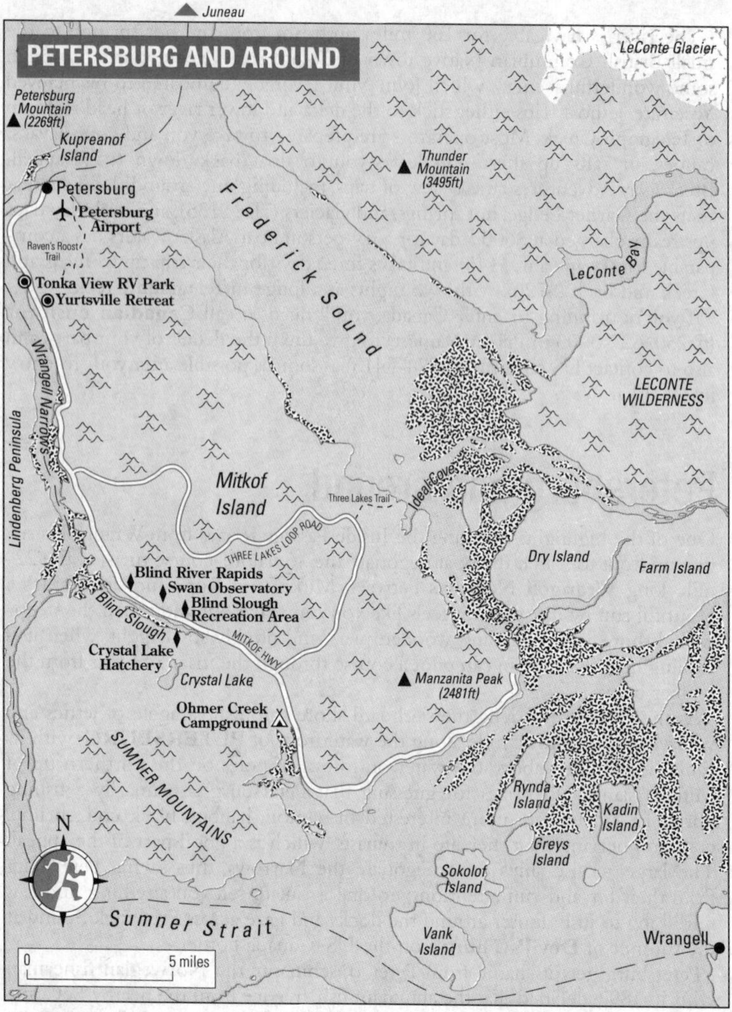

petroglyphs at Sandy Beach. Further exploration requires transport: along the road system to some gentle hikes; across Wrangell Narrows to the small settlement of Kupreanof from where more serious hikes begin; or by boat across the **whale-rich waters** of Frederick Sound to the **LeConte Glacier**.

Arrival, information, and getting around

Roughly daily AMHS **ferries** (Ⓣ772-3855) from Sitka and Wrangell arrive a mile west of downtown Petersburg on S Nordic Drive, an easy walk from town, though you could catch one of the waiting taxis, or call Maine Cabs (Ⓣ772-6969). Petersburg is on Alaska Airlines' Juneau–Petersburg–Wrangell–Ketchikan–Seattle run, and one southbound and one northbound flight per day lands at Petersburg **airport** (ⓣ772-4255), a mile east of town on Haugen Drive. Again, you can walk or catch a cab. LAB (ⓣ772-4300, ⓦwww.labflying.com) does short-haul flights from Kake ($65 one-way) and Juneau ($160 one-way).

The **visitor center**, 17 Fram St at 1st St (May–Sept Mon–Sat 9am–5pm, Sun noon–4pm; Oct–April Mon–Thurs 10am–2pm; ⓣ772-4636 or 1-866/484-4700, ⓦwww.petersburg.org), which also acts as the public face of the **Forest Service** (ⓦwww.fs.fed.us/r10/tongass), has all the info you need and free copies of the *Viking Visitor Guide*.

There are no city buses, and no **car rental** desks at the airport, though you can arrange for a vehicle through Allstar Car Rentals at *Scandia House* ($52 a day with unlimited mileage; see below), or from Avis at *Tides Inn* ($65 a day with unlimited mileage; see below). No one is currently doing bike rental.

If you fancy an **educational walk** in the rainforest south of town, go with See Alaska Tours (3hr; $39; ⓣ772-4656, ⓔhendyhut@alaska.net), which links in with the occasional small cruise ship; call for a schedule.

Accommodation

Petersburg is small so the range of accommodation isn't that broad, but there's one hostel and plenty of places very prettily set beside the water. **Camping** in town isn't appealing, and although you can camp for free on public land, city limits stretch out seventeen miles, so you'll need a vehicle to drive "out the highway". With only one small RV park in town and limited parking, the needs of RV drivers have been addressed by providing a downtown **staging area**, corner 2nd Street and Haugen Drive ($1 per hour), where you can park for up to twelve hours while waiting for your ferry.

Broom Hus 411 S Nordic Drive ⓣ772-3459, ⓦwww.aptalaska.net/~broomhus. Well-equipped apartment (sleeping up to six) in the half-basement of an original 1920s house (with a separate entrance). Continental breakfast is provided, and there's a lovely flower-filled deck out back for those occasional sunny afternoons. ❸

LeConte RV Park cnr Haugen Drive and 4th St ⓣ772-4680. A cramped and scruffy gravel lot large enough for half a dozen RVs; there's also a tiny, semi-grassy patch for tents. Some traffic noise, and showers are $1.25 extra, but facilities are clean and it is central. Water and electricity $15, dry RV $10, tents $7.

Nordic House B&B 806 S Nordic Drive ⓣ772-3620, ⓦwww.nordichouse.net. Appealing B&B superbly sited close to the ferry dock with six comfortable rooms with shared bath. There's free use of the kitchen and large lounge, which hangs right over the water, as well as buffet breakfast and free local calls and Internet access for guests. If you catch any fish, they'll handle it for you – or you can just grill it on the sunny deck. Courtesy van from the airport or ferry, plus bargain bikes for rent. ❹

Ohmer Creek Campground Mile 22 Mitkof Hwy. Picturesque and very appealing Forest Service site on the southern shores of Mitkof Island with fire rings, a canopy of trees, stream water, and space for RVs and tents. First come, first served. May–Sept $6, Oct–April free.

Petersburg Bunk and Breakfast Hostel 805 Gjoa St ⓣ772-3632, ⓦwww.bunkandbreakfast.com. Welcoming hostel handily located between downtown and the airport, with three four-bunk rooms, each bunk being supplied with bedding, lockers, and a private reading light. A freshly made continental breakfast is included in the $25 per person cost. There's free Internet access, stacks of info on the local area, and plenty of games and books to entertain you on wet evenings. Reservations recommended in summer (mid-May to mid-Sept) and essential in winter. Call 8–10am or 5–8pm. ❶

Scandia House 110 N Nordic Drive ⓣ772-4281 or 1-800/722-5006, ⓦwww.scandiahousehotel.com. The best hotel in town, with clean, modern rooms, all with cable TV, phone, and coffeemaker, plus there's a light continental breakfast. Some rooms come with water views, others have kitchenettes, or are suites with jacuzzis. There's also a courtesy van. Suites ❽, kitchen rooms and standard rooms ❺

Tides Inn cnr Dolphin and 1st sts ⓣ772-4288 or 1-800/665-8433, ⓦwww.tidesinnalaska.com. Ordinary motel made more appealing if you can get a room with a view. All rooms come with bathtubs, cable TV and dataports. Free Internet access for guests. ❹

Tonka View RV Park 126 Scow Bay Loop Rd, 3 miles south of town ☎772-4814. Look away from the container terminal and you've great views of Wrangell Narrows from this gravel lot where electricity and water hookups cost $20.

Yurtsville Retreat 415 Mitkof Hwy, 4 miles south of town ☎772-2921, Ⓦwww.alaska.net/~yurts. New yurts with propane fireplace, refrigerator, range, comfortable queen beds and fold-out sofa, set amid 22 acres of woods around four miles south of town. ❷

The Town

If the weather behaves, there's nothing better to do in Petersburg than just wander the waterfront boardwalks as the fishing boats come and go and the ferry glides silently through the Wrangell Narrows. From the aptly named **Eagle's Roost Park**, north of downtown, it's all canneries and wharves through the center of town down to the single most striking section, **Sing Lee Alley**, a boardwalk built entirely over the water and named for a Chinese merchant who had his premises here in the early days. The boardwalk is lined by shops and a couple of cafés on one side, and on the other by the town's only real bookshop and the large white clapboard **Sons of Norway Hall**, built in 1912 as a meeting place for this fraternal organization. With its double-pitched roof design and subtle use of "rosmaling" around the windows, it is easily the most distinctly Norwegian building in town. As though to further underline the connection, the adjacent parking lot is home to a model Viking longboat, which is used in the annual Little Norway Festival, held every third full weekend in May. Nearby, the ten-foot-tall bronze Bojer Wikan Fisherman's Memorial is the centerpiece of a small boardwalk "park" and was commissioned according to the will of one Bojer Wikan, a local fisherman deeply involved with the Sons of Norway. Both hall and "park" stand on poles above **Hammer Slough**, a narrow estuary lined by brightly painted houses that seem to glow in the evening light.

Although there are two major canneries on and over the waterfront, if you'd like a peek inside the industry, you'll have to settle for the hour-long tour around the specialist **Tonka Seafoods** on Sing Lee Alley (Mon–Fri and some weekends 1.30pm; $5; and by appointment on ☎772-3662 with a minimum $30 fee). Not exclusively a cannery, they also smoke and dry fish in what is really just two small rooms. The equipment isn't especially interesting to look at, but the tours are personal enough that you can direct the discussion to whatever interests you most, be it the life cycle of the fish, means of catching, fishery management, boat type, or processing. Of course, there are free samples of the product and the opportunity to buy what you like.

Moving away from the waterfront, call in at the **Clausen Memorial Museum**, 203 Fram St at 2nd St (May to early Sept Mon–Fri 10am–5pm, Sat 10am–4.30pm; $2), marked by the distinctive steel sculpture of salmon, halibut, and herring entitled *Fisk* – Norwegian for fish. There's not a great deal inside, but the staff are usually eager to help you interpret the small collection of Tlingit artifacts (particularly a large bentwood storage box), some great old photos of early Petersburg life, and what is reputed to be the largest salmon ever caught, though no one thought to weigh it before it was gutted (estimates put it at 126 pounds).

Sandy Beach fish traps and petroglyphs

If you don't fancy tackling one of the more robust walks (see box, p.123), consider strolling north along the roads past Hungry Point to **Sandy Beach**, a pleasant little park-backed cove that's best visited at low tide when it is

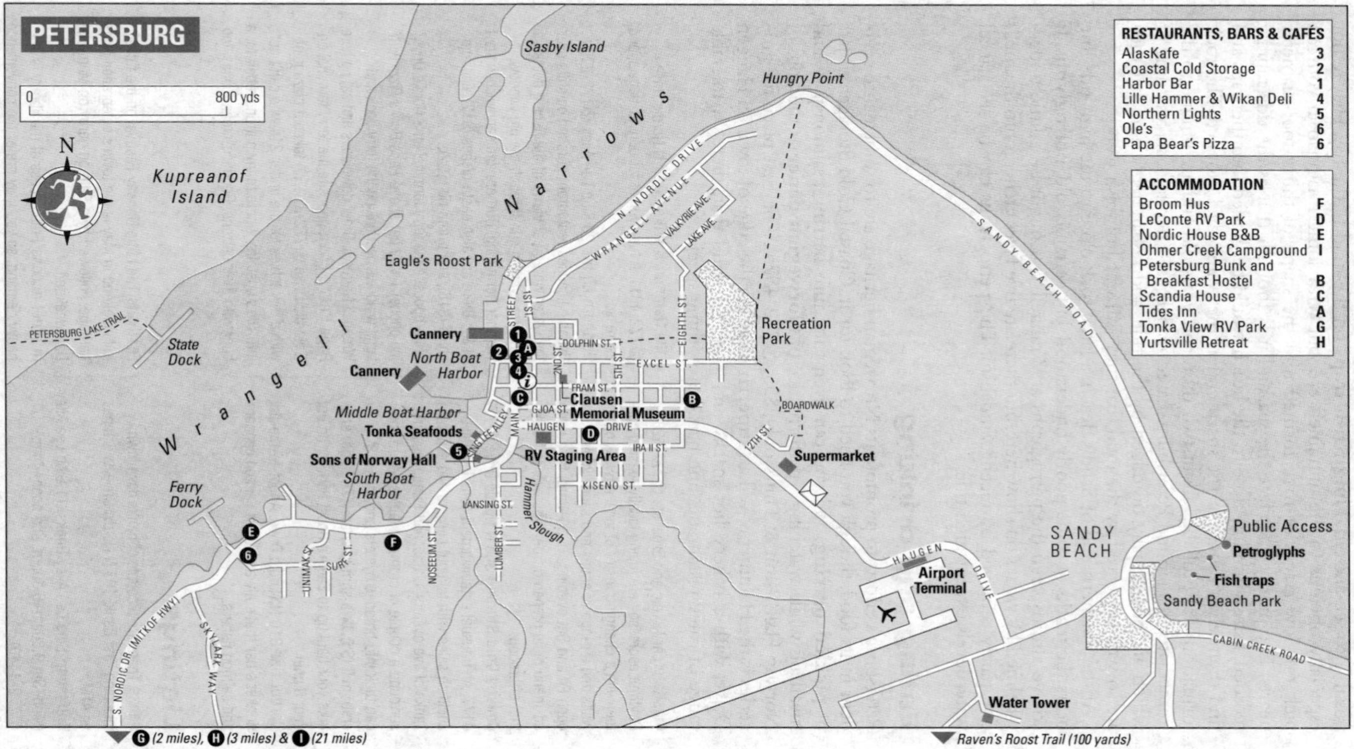
PETERSBURG
0 800 yds
N
Kupreanof Island
Sasby Island
Wrangell Narrows
Hungry Point
Eagle's Roost Park
State Dock
Ferry Dock
PETERSBURG LAKE TRAIL
Cannery
Cannery
North Boat Harbor
Middle Boat Harbor
South Boat Harbor
Tonka Seafoods
Sons of Norway Hall
Clausen Memorial Museum
RV Staging Area
Recreation Park
Supermarket
Airport Terminal
Water Tower
SANDY BEACH
Public Access
Petroglyphs
Fish traps
Sandy Beach Park
N. NORDIC DRIVE
WRANGELL AVENUE
VALKYRIE AVE
LAKE AVE
SANDY BEACH ROAD
CABIN CREEK ROAD
HAUGEN DRIVE
S. NORDIC DR. (MITKOF HWY)
SKYLARK WAY
MAIN STREET
1ST ST.
2ND ST.
5TH ST.
EIGHTH ST.
12TH ST.
DOLPHIN ST.
EXCEL ST.
FRAM ST.
GJOA ST.
IRA II ST.
KISENO ST.
LANSING ST.
LUMBER ST.
NOSEEUM ST.
SURF ST.
UNIMAK ST.
SING LEE ALLEY
BOARDWALK
Hammer Slough
RESTAURANTS, BARS & CAFÉS
AlasKafe 3
Coastal Cold Storage 2
Harbor Bar 1
Lille Hammer & Wikan Deli 4
Northern Lights 5
Ole's 6
Papa Bear's Pizza 6
ACCOMMODATION
Broom Hus F
LeConte RV Park D
Nordic House B&B E
Ohmer Creek Campground I
Petersburg Bunk and Breakfast Hostel B
Scandia House C
Tides Inn A
Tonka View RV Park G
Yurtsville Retreat H
G (2 miles), H (3 miles) & I (21 miles)
Raven's Roost Trail (100 yards)

possible to see ancient **Tlingit fish traps** on the mud of the bay. They're not especially obvious to the untrained eye, but with some imagination you can pick out low ridges of rock formed into the shape of thirty-foot-diameter hearts. The pointy ends face the sea, and it is thought that as the tide rapidly receded, fish swimming close to the beach would be guided into the traps and find themselves caught at the sharp end as the water level dropped. The rock formations are probably about two thousand years old and are unique to the immediate area around Petersburg. Later models used hemlock stakes, some of which are occasionally dislodged by the tide, and researchers claim that they are so well preserved by the mud that they still smell of fresh wood.

At the northern end of Sandy Beach, a large rock close to the high-tide line bears the marks of some poorly understood, but certainly old, **petroglyphs**. If you've already seen the petroglyphs at Wrangell you might be a little underwhelmed by what's on show here, but there are five faces etched onto the rock, one partly removed by recent vandalism. The petroglyphs can be seen at all water levels except high tide.

Eating and drinking

Petersburg's efforts to promote its Norwegian heritage are to some degree evident in its food, though you need to look for it. Coastal Cold Storage sell jars of **pickled herring**, and you can even tuck into herrings, salmon pâté, and meatballs while watching a performance of **Norwegian dance** at the Sons of Norway Hall (Mon & Thurs only; $35; ⓣ772-4575). The best place for groceries is the Hammer & Wikan **supermarket**, on the edge of town on Haugen Drive, with a bakery, hot snacks, and a deli. Beyond that, there's a tolerable range of cafés, restaurants, and bars, but nothing special.

AlasKafe cnr Nordic and Excel sts ⓣ772-5282. Daytime espresso café (using locally roasted coffee) with a changing roster of local artwork on the walls and a range of soups and sandwiches. Also open Fri and Sat evenings (5.30–8pm) for a limited-menu meal prepared from whatever is fresh that afternoon.

Coastal Cold Storage 306 N Nordic Drive ⓣ772-4177. An unusual establishment combining live-shellfish sales with takeout burgers and espresso. Tanks of live oysters, clams, and Dungeness crabs surround a couple of cramped tables where you can tuck into breaded oysters and fries ($8), a crab melt ($6), or a shrimp wrap ($7). Better still, take your haul up to Eagle's Roost Park for an outdoor dinner.

Harbor Bar 310 N Nordic Drive. A foot-to-the-floor drinker's bar that's always full of salmon canners and salmon fishers.

Lille Hammer & Wikan Deli N Nordic Drive ⓣ772-4811. A handy spot for donuts, bagels, and espresso.

Northern Lights 28 Sing Lee Alley ⓣ772-2900. Reliable licensed restaurant perched on stilts over the water with great views of the fishing boats and dazzling evening sun through the big window, weather permitting. Burgers and sandwiches start at $7; there are also pasta dishes ($12), fish and chips ($18), and prime rib ($22).

Ole's opposite the ferry terminal on S Nordic Drive (no phone). Lively bar above *Papa Bear's Pizza* with large windows overlooking the ferry dock and Wrangell Narrows. Order downstairs and eat up here.

Papa Bear's Pizza opposite the ferry terminal on S Nordic Drive ⓣ772-3727. A takeout pizza joint with a few tables for the under-21s who can't get into *Ole's* upstairs, where many patrons repair for a beer with their calzone. Good ice-cream cones, too.

Listings

Banks There are a couple of banks downtown, including First Bank, 103 N Nordic Drive, which has an ATM.

Bookshop Sing Lee Alley Books, 11 Sing Lee Alley (Mon–Sat 9.30am–5.30pm, Sun noon–4pm; ⓣ772-4440).

Festivals The Little Norway Festival on the third full weekend in May is the town's celebration of its heritage. Followed by a Salmon derby on Memorial Day weekend.

Internet access Free access at the library is in heavy demand, so you may prefer the convenience of the pricey machines at Mitkof.net, 110 Harbor Way (Mon–Fri 8am–5pm; ⓣ772-2343).

Laundry and showers Take a swim and shower ($3) at the Melvin Roundtree Pool (ⓣ772-3304); laundry is best done at Glacier Laundry, 313 N Nordic Drive (daily 6am–10pm; ⓣ772-4144), where they also have showers ($2).

Library Petersburg Public Library, 12 S Nordic Drive (Mon–Thurs noon–9pm, Fri & Sat noon–4pm; ⓣ772-3349).

Medical assistance Petersburg Medical Center, 2nd & Fram sts (Mon–Fri 9am–5pm and 24hr ER; ⓣ772-4291).

Post office 1400 Haugen Drive. The **General Delivery** zip code is 99833.

Taxes Petersburg imposes a six percent sales tax plus a four percent bed tax, all included in our accommodation price codes.

Travel agency Viking Travel, 101 N Nordic Drive ⓣ772-3818.

Around Petersburg

The simplest way to get out of town is to rent a car and drive out along **Mitkof Highway**, seventeen miles of paved two-lane road from which a couple of roads fan out across the island. Fishing streams, easy boardwalk trails, picnic sites, a hatchery, and a seasonal swan-viewing area are the main draws here, along with more serious hikes (see box, p.123).

Getting off the island typically involves getting on some kind of tour, either **kayaking**, **whale watching**, visiting the **LeConte Glacier** or fishing. As tourists are few, it can be difficult getting the numbers to make trips viable: befriending like-minded travelers on your way here and fronting up as a ready-to-go group of four or more can be a big advantage. Conversely, when the occasional small cruise ship is in town you may find it hard to get a place on trips pre-booked by the ship. Many tours can be booked through Viking Travel at 101 N Nordic Drive (ⓣ772-3818): a quick visit here can save you a lot of phoning around. They're particularly helpful for hooking you up with one of the many fishing charters run from town.

Along the road system

Petersburg has a reasonably extensive road system, and if you rent a car there's a fair bit to keep you entertained, though nothing that's essential viewing. Almost everything is along, or just off, the mostly paved Mitkof Highway, which follows Wrangell Narrows for around fourteen miles then cuts inland to finish on the southern shores of Mitkof Island.

There are no specific sights until you reach **Blind River Rapids**, Mile 14, where there's a quarter-mile-long boardwalk to a tidal stream where salmon come in to spawn and work their way up the gentle rapids. Beyond here, the highway cuts inland along Blind Slough to the **Swan Observatory**, Mile 16, where a kind of primitive hide beside the highway aids in viewing trumpeter swans, which call here on their way south from mid-October to December, a few dozen overwintering until around April. In summer salmon can be seen in the stream. At Mile 18 you can wander around Crystal Lake Hatchery (Mon–Fri 8am–4pm, Sat & Sun 8am–2pm; free) and learn a little of what's going on from the staff on hand. The adjacent **Blind Slough Recreation Area** is good for picnics and swimming (for the brave). Beyond the hatchery you're on gravel. At Mile 20, Man-Made Hole Lake offers a pleasant boardwalk around a small pond that looks far from man-made; if you want to camp, push on to *Ohmer Creek Campground* (see p.117), Mile 22, which acts as the trailhead for a mile-long path along a good trout and salmon fishing stream with some interpretive panels.

Though the road continues an uneventful eleven miles along the island's south coast, you're better off backtracking a mile and heading northeast on Three Lakes Loop Road (Road 6235) which, after 21 miles, rejoins Mitkof

Highway at Mile 11. Roughly midway around the loop, you come to a series of three trailheads all interlinked as the **Three Lakes Loop Trail** (30min–3hr), where any number of boardwalk variations allow you to visit one or more of Crane, Hill, and Sand lakes, and access the sea along Ideal Cove Trail. A mile or so north of here, the road passes the **LeConte Overlook**, the only place on the island where you can get a direct view across Frederick Sound to the face of the LeConte Glacier.

Kayaking, whale watching, and the LeConte Glacier

At some point during their stay, most people want to get out on the water. One prime destination is the **LeConte Glacier**, which peals off the Stikine Icefield, fifteen miles east across Frederick Sound. It is the southernmost tidewater glacier in the northern hemisphere, and Frederick Sound is usually dotted with small icebergs (especially in spring) that get bigger the closer you are to the glacier, some with seals on them idling their day away. Often LeConte Bay is so packed with ice that you can't even penetrate far enough to see the face of the glacier, which means that you probably won't be able to see calving. Extended trips also continue a few miles south and visit the delta of the Stikine River (see "Wrangell," p.106). Wherever you go, there is a chance of seeing whales, particularly the humpback whales that usually pass through Frederick Sound from late June to early September.

About the most peaceful way to get on the water is by **kayak** with Tongass Kayak Adventures (Ⓣ772-3818, Ⓦwww.tongasskayak.com), which runs four-hour trips ($70) around the Petersburg waterfront and across the Narrows to Petersburg Creek. Though very enjoyable, these half-day trips are really just a taster for their multiday whale-watching trips – relatively gentle affairs involving three to five hours paddling a day that need to be booked well in advance. Their Base Camp trips (3 nights for $790, 8 nights for $1800) fly you to base camps beside Frederick Sound and near the LeConte Glacier from where you explore by day; the eight-night Explorer Tours ($1400–1700) tend to move on to a new camp each day. The company also rents single ($45 a day) and double ($55) kayaks with a three-day minimum.

If you'd rather someone else did the work, join marine biologist Barry Bracken of Kaleidoscope Cruises (Ⓣ772–3736 or 1-800/868-4373, Ⓦwww.alaska.net/~bbsea), which runs entertaining half-day trips to LeConte Glacier in a comfortable 28-foot boat ($130) and full-day **whale-watching** trips ($180), which include listening to the whales through a hydrophone.

The visitor center has information about several other operators who do similar trips; alternatively, go your own way with a skiff and forty-horse motor from *Scandia Hotel* (guests $135 a day, non-guests $160 a day).

Sitka and around

Perched on the seaward edge of the Inside Passage, **SITKA** ranks as one of Alaska's prettiest and most historic towns, with a bay chock-full of tiny islands plumed with hemlock and spruce, and the looming presence of the near-conical **Mount Edgecumbe** volcano rising menacingly across Sitka Sound.

The appeal of the outdoors – hiking and kayaking in particular – is hard to pass up, but Sitka also revels in its sixty-year reign as the political and cultural hub of Russian America. This is where Imperial Russian colonists established their capital, Novo Arkhangel'sk (New Archangel) in 1808, and their legacy is

Hikes in and around Petersburg

There are a dozen or more good hikes around Petersburg, but few are especially convenient unless you've got transport. Although drivers and cyclists can get the best from several short trails out along Mitkof Highway (see p.121), serious hikers should think about two excellent trails a few hundred yards across Wrangell Narrows on Kupreanof Island. People have traditionally tried to hitch a ride across the water, but as local hospitality has been strained over the years you should arrange transport over and back before you head out – or risk being stranded over there. Rent a skiff from the *Scandia Hotel*, contact Craig Curtis (☎772-2425), who charges $25 there and back, or ask the staff at the visitor center who will help you call likely boat-charter companies. Remember that there is no camping on the immediate Kupreanof side of the Narrows as it's private property, but Forest Service cabins can be booked on ☎1-877/444-6777.

Petersburg Lake Trail (10.5 miles one-way; 4hr; 200ft ascent). Moderately difficult trail on Kupreanof Island leading left (west) over a low saddle, then gradually ascending to Petersburg Lake and the *Petersburg Lake Cabin* ($35), which is a good base for salmon and trout fishing and bear viewing in fall. If you use the upper trailhead, which is only accessible at high tides greater than 14ft, you can shorten the hike by four miles. Keen adventurers can continue beyond Portage Lake to a couple more cabins, though it is tough going and you'll need the latest information from the visitor center.

Petersburg Mountain Trail (7 miles round-trip; 4–6hr; 2750ft ascent). Challenging trail on Kupreanof Island leading right (east) from the dock opposite Petersburg to the summit of Petersburg Mountain, from where there are long, long views down the Wrangell Narrows and across Frederick Sound to the coastal mountains and glaciers. The final section is a bit of a scramble.

Raven's Roost Trail (8 miles round-trip; 5–6hr; 2000ft ascent). An initial boardwalk leads to an at times steep trail, climbing up to alpine country and eventually to the Forest Service's four-berth *Raven's Roost Cabin* ($35), which has lovely views. Best done from mid-July to September when the likelihood of snow cover is least, though lack of water at the cabin means it is good to have some snow around. The trailhead is by the orange-and-white water towers just south of the airport.

Town Loop (30min–1hr 30min). A number of possibilities exist using the short boardwalks and the gravel path to Hungry Point (see map, p.116). A loop out past the airport to Sandy Beach and back past Hungry Point takes around 90 minutes.

a major draw. When the United States bought Alaska, New Archangel became Sitka (a contraction of the Tlingit Shee Atiká), and development since then has been relatively benign, with the skyline still dominated by **St Michael's Cathedral**, just as it was when General Jefferson Davis came here to formally receive the territory on Castle Hill in 1867.

Although it's the third largest town in Southeast, Sitka is small enough to retain a compact and walkable core as well as a relaxed and friendly ambience. Better still, it isn't as crowded as you'd expect, being off the main Inside Passage cruise-ship lanes and lacking a dock deep enough for the bigger vessels (passengers have to come ashore in lifeboats). Large ships still visit most days in summer, though, ensuring steady interest in the tacky "Russiocana" – you'll find more nesting dolls here than in the rest of the US put together.

Ambling around is half the pleasure in Sitka, but focus is provided by the historic **Russian Bishop's House**, the densely packed **Sheldon Jackson Museum**, a magnificent array of totem poles in the **Totem Park**, and the popular **Raptor Center**, with its bald eagles.

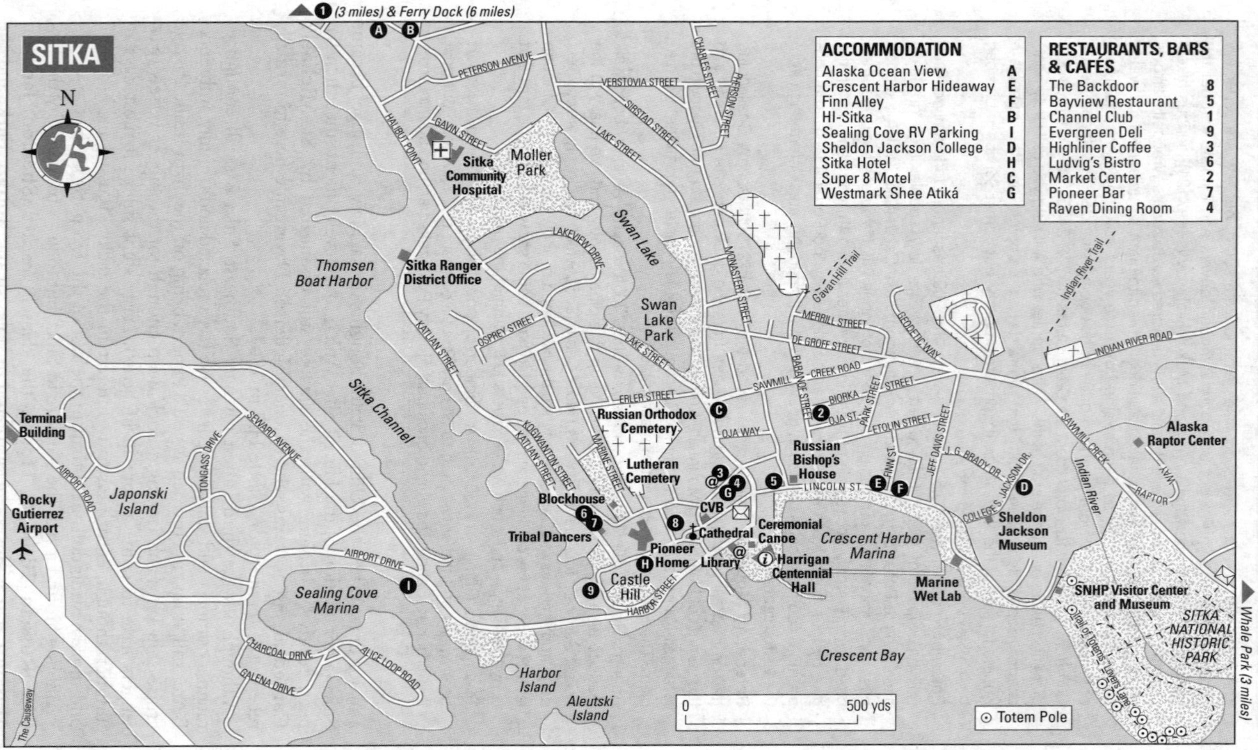
SITKA
N
(3 miles) & Ferry Dock (6 miles)
Whale Park (3 miles)
ACCOMMODATION
Alaska Ocean View A
Crescent Harbor Hideaway E
Finn Alley F
HI-Sitka B
Sealing Cove RV Parking I
Sheldon Jackson College D
Sitka Hotel H
Super 8 Motel C
Westmark Shee Atiká G
RESTAURANTS, BARS & CAFÉS
The Backdoor 8
Bayview Restaurant 5
Channel Club 1
Evergreen Deli 9
Highliner Coffee 3
Ludvig's Bistro 6
Market Center 2
Pioneer Bar 7
Raven Dining Room 4
PETERSON AVENUE
VERSTOVIA STREET
CHARLES STREET
PHERSON STREET
SIRSTAD STREET
LAKE STREET
HALIBUT POINT
GAVIN STREET
Sitka Community Hospital
Moller Park
Swan Lake
LAKEVIEW DRIVE
Thomsen Boat Harbor
Sitka Ranger District Office
Swan Lake Park
MONASTERY STREET
Gavan Hill Trail
Indian River Trail
MERRILL STREET
DE GROFF STREET
GEODETIC WAY
INDIAN RIVER ROAD
OSPREY STREET
KATLIAN STREET
SAWMILL CREEK ROAD
BARANOF STREET
BIORKA STREET
PARK STREET
OJA ST.
ETOLIN STREET
JEFF DAVIS STREET
ERLER STREET
OJA WAY
Sitka Channel
Russian Orthodox Cemetery
Lutheran Cemetery
MARINE STREET
KOGWANTON STREET
Russian Bishop's House
LINCOLN ST
FINN ST.
J. G. BRADY DR.
S. JACKSON DR.
COLLEGE
Sheldon Jackson Museum
SAWMILL CREEK
Indian River
RAPTOR WAY
Alaska Raptor Center
Terminal Building
SEWARD AVENUE
TONGASS DRIVE
AIRPORT ROAD
Japonski Island
Rocky Gutierrez Airport
Blockhouse
Tribal Dancers
CVB
Cathedral
Ceremonial Canoe
Crescent Harbor Marina
Pioneer Home
Library
Harrigan Centennial Hall
Marine Wet Lab
SNHP Visitor Center and Museum
SITKA NATIONAL HISTORIC PARK
Trail of Totems "Lovers Lane"
AIRPORT DRIVE
Sealing Cove Marina
Castle Hill
HARBOR STREET
Crescent Bay
CHARCOAL DRIVE
ALICE LOOP ROAD
GALENA DRIVE
Harbor Island
Aleutski Island
0 500 yds
Totem Pole
The Causeway

Some history

Sitka's Kiks.ádi Tlingit clan have probably lived for 9000 years at their settlement Shee Atiká, meaning village on the outside of Shee – their name for Baranof Island. In 1799 the Russian-American Company came to pursue fur trading and established the first European settlement in Southeast Alaska, seven miles west of Sitka just beyond the AMHS ferry dock. They continued to trade in sea otter pelts until the Kiks.ádi, living on the site of modern Sitka, got tired of their presence and stormed their fort, killing nearly all the Russians. Alexander Baranov, the chief manager of the Russian-American Company in Kodiak got wind of this and, in 1804, returned with four ships and several *baidarkas*. The Kiks.ádi, under their leader Katlian, had established a fort at what is now the Totem Park, and the Russians sent a landing party of 150 to conduct the **Siege of Shiskeenu**. Tsarist ships pounded the stockade for six days. On the sixth night the Russians heard strange chanting and, on the next day, discovered ravens hovering over the fort. Though there were ample provisions, suggesting that the Tlingit could have held out for a while, the fort was empty except for the bodies of dead children – allegedly murdered so the Tlingit could retreat in complete silence. The Russians burnt the fort, looted and burned the Tlingit community of Shee Atiká and on the ashes of the village built the stockaded settlement of New Archangel. The Tlingit didn't return for twenty years but eventually settled outside the palisades in a strained but workable relationship with the Russians.

In 1808 Novo Arkhangel'sk became the colonial capital, with food imported from Fort Ross in California and a social scene of dress balls and grand receptions. Still, those who described it as the "Paris of the Pacific" had obviously never been to Paris.

Sitka's status survived the transfer of ownership to the United States, with the town continuing as the capital of the territory of Alaska. As soon as America got hold of Alaska, adventurers flocked north, but gold drew people elsewhere. Capital status passed to Juneau in 1906, and Sitka was left to grow steadily on its fishing, and later logging. As fishing receipts ebb and flow, and logging returns are greatly diminished since the closure of the pulp mill here in 1993, tourism is increasingly filling the gaps.

Arrival, information, and getting around

To reach Sitka, AMHS **ferries** must pass through Segius Narrows and Peril Strait, narrow twisting watercourses that need to be negotiated at slack tide. Ferries often have to wait for three or more hours at the dock, seven miles northwest of town, for the tide to turn. Call the Sitka terminal (☎747-8737) for details of particular sailings and see the box overleaf for possible diversions during a brief stay.

As of 2004 some or all of the traditional ferry sailings to Sitka will be replaced by the new passenger and vehicle-carrying *Fairweather* fast ferry between Sitka and Juneau. It is expected that there will be a run from Juneau to Sitka and back on Wednesdays and Sundays.

Shuttle buses operated by Sitka Tours (☎747-8443) meet arriving ferries and run downtown as well as to your accommodation ($5 one-way, $7 round-trip). They also conduct short **tours** (see box overleaf).

The **airport**, on Japonski Island a mile or so from downtown, sees Alaska Airlines (☎966-2926) jets direct from Juneau, Ketchikan, and Seattle. Sitka Tours also meets planes and runs into town ($5 one-way, $7 round-trip); a ferry–downtown–airport sequence or vice versa is $7.

Just an hour or two in Sitka?

The vagaries of the ferry timetable mean you're quite likely to have a couple of hours to spare at the Sitka dock, seven miles northwest of town. Most people who come ashore join one of the Sitka Tours buses that do a one- to two-hour circuit of the town's main sights for $12. If this is your only visit to Sitka, it's an opportunity that's hard to pass up. On a fine day, however, you might prefer to stroll fifteen minutes west from the dock to the Starrigavan area, where you'll find a network of easy walks (see box, p.134) – through wetlands and muskeg and along the shoreline – along which there are several well-placed benches with panoramic views.

There's a visitor **information desk** (summer daily 8am–5pm; ⓣ747-5940, ⓦwww.sitka.org) inside the Harrigan Centennial Hall on Harbor Drive. It is generally only staffed when large cruise ships hit town, but loads of free literature on the town is always available. For anything more complicated, call at the Convention & Visitors Bureau (Mon–Fri 9am–5pm) upstairs at 303 Lincoln St. For information on the surrounding Tongass National Forest, contact the Sitka Ranger District Office, 204 Siganaka Way (Mon–Fri 8am–4.30pm; ⓣ747-6671, ⓦwww.fs.fed.us/r10/tongass).

Once in town, **getting around** is easy. You can walk just about anywhere you're likely to want to go, plus there's a visitor transit bus (late May to early Sept Mon–Fri only; $7 all-day pass) that runs a loop through town every half-hour. The bus is perhaps most useful for the run out to the Raptor Center, for which there is a $5 one-way ticket encouraging you to walk back through the Totem Park. Alternatively, rent a bike (see "Listings," p.137), or call a cab, such as Sitka Taxi (ⓣ747-5001), which charges around $15 to the ferry terminal and $5 to the airport. Rental cars are available for about $65 a day from North Star Rent-A-Car at the airport (ⓣ966-2552 or 1-800/722-6927), with your mileage only limited by the extent of the road system.

Accommodation

Sitka has a good range of accommodation, with a fine hotel, two dorm-style lodgings, and several B&Bs. If you're looking for something a bit different, there are a few cabins for short-term rent on islands in Sitka Sound that make a great hideaway for a few days: either get there by water taxi or rent a kayak for a few days and explore.

There's also a variety of **campgrounds** hereabouts as well as a solid selection of Forest Service **cabins**. Although none of the cabins is walk-in, almost two dozen can be accessed by kayak or water taxi. Some of the more convenient are listed below (for bookings contact ⓣ1-877/444-6777 or ⓦwww.ReserveUSA.com).

Hotels, motels, and B&Bs

Alaska Ocean View B&B Inn 1101 Edgecumbe Drive ⓣ747-8310, ⓦwww.sitka-alaska-lodging.com. Very high-standard B&B with all rooms featuring cable TV and VCR, CD stereo, dataport, bath robes, and slippers. Guests also have the use of a patio spa pool and espresso machine, and there are facilities for business travelers. Beds are large and comfortable, the breakfasts generous, and the atmosphere's cheerful. ❺

Crescent Harbor Hideaway 709 Lincoln St ⓣ & ⓕ 747-4900, ⓦwww.ptialaska.net/~bareis/b&b.htm. Handily sited B&B with good water views from the common room, and very comfortable cable TV-equipped rooms and apartment. ❺

Finn Alley Inn B&B 711 Lincoln St ⓣ747-3655, ⓦwww.ptialaska.net/~seakdist/finn.htm. Well-located and large half-basement apartment with private entrance, full kitchen, and a continental breakfast delivered to the room. ❺

Sitka Hotel 118 Lincoln St ⓣ747-3288, ⓦwww.sitkahotel.com. Renovated historic hotel, offering good-value rooms with and without bathrooms and a touch of old-fashioned style, in the town center. Very few rooms have views and fewer still have tubs. Suites with kitchenette ❺, rooms with private bathroom ❹, shared bath ❷

Super 8 Motel 404 Sawmill Creek Rd ⓣ747-8804 or 1-800/800-8000, ⓦwww.super8.com. Spacious rooms, large TVs, free local calls, breakfasts of toast, donuts and coffee as well as the use of a big jacuzzi make this motel good value. ❺

Westmark Shee Atiká 330 Seward St ⓣ747-6241 or 1-800/544-0970, ⓦwww.westmarkhotels.com. Sitka's best hotel, with international-standard rooms made a little more interesting with Native paintings and trimmings. Harbor-view rooms are only slightly more expensive. ❻–❼

Hostels and campgrounds

HI-Sitka 303 Kimsham St ⓣ747-8661. Unusual hostel with camp beds in the basement of a Methodist church, but it actually works quite well, with good cooking facilities, a spacious common area, and free bikes. Phone reservations are accepted, although you probably won't be turned away even if they are full. They impose an 11pm curfew, and there's a daytime lockout from 10am to 6pm – though this is flexible if there are ferry arrivals. Bedding can be rented. June–Aug. Members $13, non-members $16.

Sawmill Creek Campground Blue Lake Rd. Wooded Forest Service site seven miles east of Sitka and at the start of the Beaver Lake Trail. There's only creek water (treat it), pit toilets, and fire rings – and no sea views – but it's free. April–Nov.

Sealing Cove RV Parking Airport Rd, Japonski Island ⓣ747-3439. Asphalt parking lot a ten-minute walk from downtown beside a fishing boat harbor, with water and electrical hookups and a dump station for $21. April–Sept.

Sheldon Jackson College Sheldon Jackson Drive ⓣ747-2518. These simple college rooms with two single beds (including bedding) and shared bathroom are a steal for around $55 a night. Mid-June to Aug. ❶

Sitka Sportsman's Association RV Park Halibut Point Rd ⓣ747-6033. Parking lot next to the ferry dock with electrical and water hookups for $18. All year.

Starrigavan Campground Halibut Point Rd. Gorgeous Forest Service campground 0.7 miles north of the ferry dock, with secluded sites, shore fishing, easy hiking trails, water, and pit toilets. There's a range of walk-in (and kayak-in) tent sites, plus plenty of RV- and car-accessible spots. Some of all site types are first-come, first-served, while others are reservable. Prices start at $12 per site but the prime waterside locations are $16. Late May to early Sept.

Boat-access accommodation

Allan Point Cabin Nakwasina Passage, 14 miles north of Sitka. Large two-story Forest Service cabin sleeping up to fifteen, located on a sheltered shore in an area with plenty of deer and brown bears. Take fuel oil for heating. $45.

Camp Coogan Bay Hideaway 6 miles southeast of Sitka ⓣ747-6375. A secluded and private 72-foot float house sleeping up to ten ($170) and supplied with a kitchen, propane stove, living room with wood stove, bunks, futons and cots, an outhouse, sauna, and a double kayak for guest use (as well as others available for rent). ❼

Fred's Creek Cabin southeast shore of Kruzof Island, ten miles west of Sitka. Brand-new Forest Service cabin at the base of Mount Edgecumbe. A good base for the summit hike. $35.

Kanga Bay Cabin 12 miles south of Sitka. This chalet-style Forest Service cabin, equipped with a wood-burning stove, rests beside a beautiful cove and makes a good stopping point on the way to Goddard Hot Springs. Day trips to the springs are possible from here, although you may prefer to continue three miles beyond the springs and stay at the Forest Service's Seven Fathoms cabin. $35.

Middle Island Recreation Cabin Middle Island, 5 miles southwest of Sitka ⓣ747-5169, ⓦwww.ptialaska.net/~jehly. Cabin sleeping eight ($65 for two, plus $10 per extra person) on a small island, with everything provided except food, stove fuel, and sleeping bags. A water taxi costs around $60 each way. ❷

Samsing Cove Cabin 6 miles south of Sitka. Easily accessible, rustic, two-story Forest Service cabin set by a sandy gravel beach. Take fuel oil for heating. $45.

Shelikof Cabin Kruzof Island. A-frame Forest Service cabin located at Kruzof Island's gorgeous Shelikof Bay, an outside beach most easily accessed by a six-mile hike across the island from sheltered Mud Bay. Equipped with a wood-burning stove. $35.

The town and around

Nowhere in Southeast Alaska has as many diverting cultural and historic sights as Sitka. What's more, the attractions are easily accessible on foot and located conveniently along the waterfront. At Sitka's western end, the downtown area is overlooked by the rebuilt onion-domed St Michael's Cathedral, which, along with the immaculately restored Russian Bishop's House nearby, captures something of the spirit of Russian Alaska. Further east along the waterfront, the Sheldon Jackson Museum brings together a wonderful collection of Native crafts from around the state and leads directly to the Totem Park, which forms the major component of the Sitka National Historic Park. Save time, too, for the Raptor Center, one of your few chances to get close and personal with a bald eagle, and some of Sitka's scenic hikes.

Downtown Sitka

Sitka's Russian past is immediately accessible, and the best place to start is from the vantage point of **Castle Hill**, a rocky knob that was the original site of Tlingit Shee Atiká. It subsequently became the site of Baranov's Castle, not a castle at all but a large wooden residence that was the nerve center of the Russian town and the place where US official Jefferson Davis came for the formal transfer of ownership of Alaska from Russia to the US on October 18, 1867. Baranov's Castle burnt down in 1894, but a plaque marks the spot, and the US, Alaskan, and Russian-American Company flags flutter above.

Vying with Castle Hill for dominance on the city skyline is **St Michael's Cathedral**, Lincoln Street (May–Sept Mon–Fri 9am–4pm, when ships are in port, and by appointment on ⓣ747-3560; $2), with its teardrop spire bearing a gold triple-bar cross. This fine piece of Russian architecture was built for Bishop Innocent, whose watchmaking skills were put to good use in the design of the church clock. It is, in fact, a faithful replica of the 1848 original, which burned down on January 2, 1966 when a fire spread from a neighboring building to the cathedral tower. In the spirit of co-operation, the townspeople rallied to form a rescue line along which almost all the church's icons and religious treasures were passed in twenty minutes, although the irreplaceable library of books in Russian, Tlingit, and Aleut was lost. They did save the chandelier, however, and eventually even the melted heap of bronze from the church bells was gathered up and recast as new bells. Inside is a priceless collection of icons, thought to be the best in the US, all of which are touched upon on the short tour. You are welcome to attend services (Sat 6.30pm, Sun 10am), which are held in English with elements of Tlingit and Old Slavonic.

Continue your explorations of the old Russian town by calling at the replica blockhouse (not open to the public), a two-story octagonal fort of thick logs on the site of one of the three that guarded the palisades which kept the Russians safe. They feared the Kiks.ádi, whose land they'd stolen but who lived in an uneasy peace in the *ranche*, an area outside the stockade from where they would trade furs and food and accepted the benefits of education and religion. On the hill behind, the **Lutheran Cemetery** reveals a few triple-bar crosses and the grave of Princess Maksoutoff, the daughter of the last Russian governor of Alaska.

Easily the most significant non-Russian building in town, the 1934 **Pioneer Home**, on Lincoln Street, gives Sitka the architectural solidity that is lacking from so many Alaskan towns. It is really just an old folks' home, and you'll see sourdoughs of both sexes sunning themselves on the porch. Outside, a bronze statue of *The Prospector* stands resolute with staff, gun, pick, shovel, and the obligatory passage of Robert Service poetry (see box, p.189).

Walk back past the cathedral to get to the Harrigan Centennial Hall, which contains the visitor center and the **Isabel Miller Museum**, 300 Harbor Drive (May–Sept Mon–Fri and some weekends 8am–5pm; Oct–April Tues–Sat

Russian Alaska and the US purchase

With a post–Cold War mindset it is easy to forget that Alaska – firmly part of the US in the American psyche – was once part of the Czarist Russian Empire. For well over a hundred years, from 1741 to 1867, Russia was the dominant power in the North Pacific, as it oversaw the near extinction of sea otters for their valuable pelts. The impetus for the colonizing drive was not territorial expansionism, but rather a desire to top up the ever-draining coffers of the Imperial court. Though the Russian government enlisted Danish captain Vitus Bering to explore whatever was east of the Kamchatka Peninsula, they didn't subsequently run the show, leaving it up to *promyshleniki* – private fur traders – to reap huge profits under license. The Russian-American Company had already secured control of the entire coast from the Aleutians to Southcentral Alaska when, in 1799, Czar Paul granted them exclusive rights to Alaska and effectively gave them permission to subjugate the Aleut people.

About the only limitation put on the Russian-American Company was that they assist the Russian Orthodox Church in its proselytizing. And so began a symbiotic relationship between the two, with the company providing logistical support and housing for the Church and the priests educating and converting the Natives – thereby keeping them subservient and providing an underclass of semi-skilled workers. From 1790 to 1818 Chief Manager **Alexander Baranov** (1747–1819) oversaw the region, with the failed Siberian fur businessman arriving in Pavlovsk (Kodiak) ready to put his aggressive political skills to work. With extremely long supply routes and no military backing from St Petersburg, Baranov was forced to cultivate cordial relations with British and American captains trading in the area. Nonetheless, in short order he expanded the company's domain along the coast. When the profitability of the fur trade declined around Kodiak in the early nineteenth century, he decamped to fresh killing fields around Novo Arkhangel'sk, now Sitka. With untold riches at his behest, he turned Sitka into the envy of the North Pacific. In his early seventies he retired, but never made it back to Russia, dying of fever on the ship home.

Under the second chief manager, **Ferdinand Wrangel**, and others, the sea otter and seal populations continued to decline. Meanwhile, with the government distracted by the Crimean War, Russia began to look less favorably on its North American possessions. With the British-owned Hudson's Bay Company encroaching on their territory from the east and American traders sailing out of the new settlements on the West Coast, it became increasingly obvious that Russia wouldn't be able to hold on much longer. They found a willing buyer in the United States, still a relatively minor country politically and one just recovering from the horrors of the Civil War. Many Americans thought that the $7.2 million the US paid was too much for this unexplored wasteland and dubbed it **"Seward's Folly,"** after the secretary of state, William Seward.

The sale of land didn't cover private dwellings, warehouses, businesses, and the property of the Orthodox Church – including St Michael's Cathedral and the Bishop's House in Sitka – which kept its clergy in Alaska and continued to fund them from Russia until the Marxist Revolution in 1917. Russian residents were offered US citizenship but most left, taking their chattels with them and only leaving behind the racially mixed children with their Native mothers.

With around fifteen thousand believers, Russian Orthodoxy has turned out to be the most durable legacy of the Russian past. Apart from a couple of museums in Sitka and Kodiak, however, the only significant reminders of Russia's century-long presence here are the onion-domed churches, filled with exquisite icons and topped with triple-bar gold crosses.

10am–noon & 1.15–4pm; donations welcome), full of a little bit of everything, including a model of Sitka as it was at the time of the transfer, and lots of personal tales of early life in the town, which quickly draw you in once you get reading. Outside, the fifty-foot-long Tlingit ceremonial canoe, with an Eagle at one end and a Raven at the other, was carved in 1967 as part of the centennial of the transfer.

The Russian Bishop's House

With the loss of Sitka's original cathedral, there are now just four buildings left in America from the Russian past: the Log Cache gift shop at 206 Lincoln St in Sitka, the museum in Kodiak, one building at Fort Ross in California, and the large mustard-colored **Russian Bishop's House** on Lincoln Street (May–Sept daily 9am–5pm; rest of year by appointment on ⓣ747-0110). Now part of Sitka National Historic Park (see p.132), the house was completed in 1843 from Sitka spruce logs by Finnish shipwrights (who were then subjects of the Russian Czar) in a style and color scheme aimed to create a little piece of St Petersburg in the North Pacific. The Russian Orthodox Church maintained a bishop here until 1969, but after the building had nearly collapsed from the rot induced by ninety inches of rain a year, it was sold to the National Park Service in 1972. The NPS then began a sixteen-year restoration to recapture the atmosphere of Russian nobility in which the incumbent bishop lived. Reproduction wallpaper and sleigh beds as well as original pieces of furniture, including a sofa that could be dismantled to travel flat, give a sense of the comforts of home.

The house's first occupant, Ivan Veniaminov, who became Bishop Innocent of the Kamchatka Peninsula and the Russian-American Company's holdings on the Pacific Coast, rarely experienced such luxuries. He would often travel for months on end, spreading the word while learning Aleut and Tlingit. Back home in Sitka he wrote a Russian–Aleut dictionary, recorded weather patterns, and became a skilled mason, blacksmith, and carpenter.

You can wander freely around the lower level of the house, which was used at various times as a grade school, seminary, orphanage, and apartment, and now contains a model of New Archangel as it was in 1845 as well as several cases of artifacts and icons. Note the sections of the actual wall and floor that have been cut away to reveal the ingenious insulation – sawdust in the walls and draft-preventive joints. Guided tours (usually every 30min; $3) lead you upstairs to the bishop's private apartments, a small library of original books, and the ornate one-room **chapel** that is still consecrated and is used occasionally.

The Sheldon Jackson Museum

Half a mile east along Lincoln Street, the octagonal **Sheldon Jackson Museum**, 104 College Drive (mid-May to mid-Sept daily 9am–5pm; mid-Sept to mid-May Tues–Sat 10am–4pm; $4; ⓣ747-8981, ⓦwww.museums.state.ak.us), contains a compact but fascinating collection of Native artifacts. It was put together by the Reverend Dr Sheldon Jackson, a Presbyterian missionary who was Alaska's first general agent for education – although he turned out to be much more. As Orthodoxy had never gained any widespread acceptance under the Russians, Jackson, on his wide-ranging travels throughout Alaska, took it upon himself to divide the state up into a dozen broadly equivalent sections and encourage any religion he could interest to accept a kind of ecclesiastical monopoly within that region. The Presbyterians took the Arctic north and much of Southeast, Philadelphia Quakers got Kotzebue and a patch near Juneau, Methodists took the Aleutian Islands and so on, and for a long time these divisions remained.

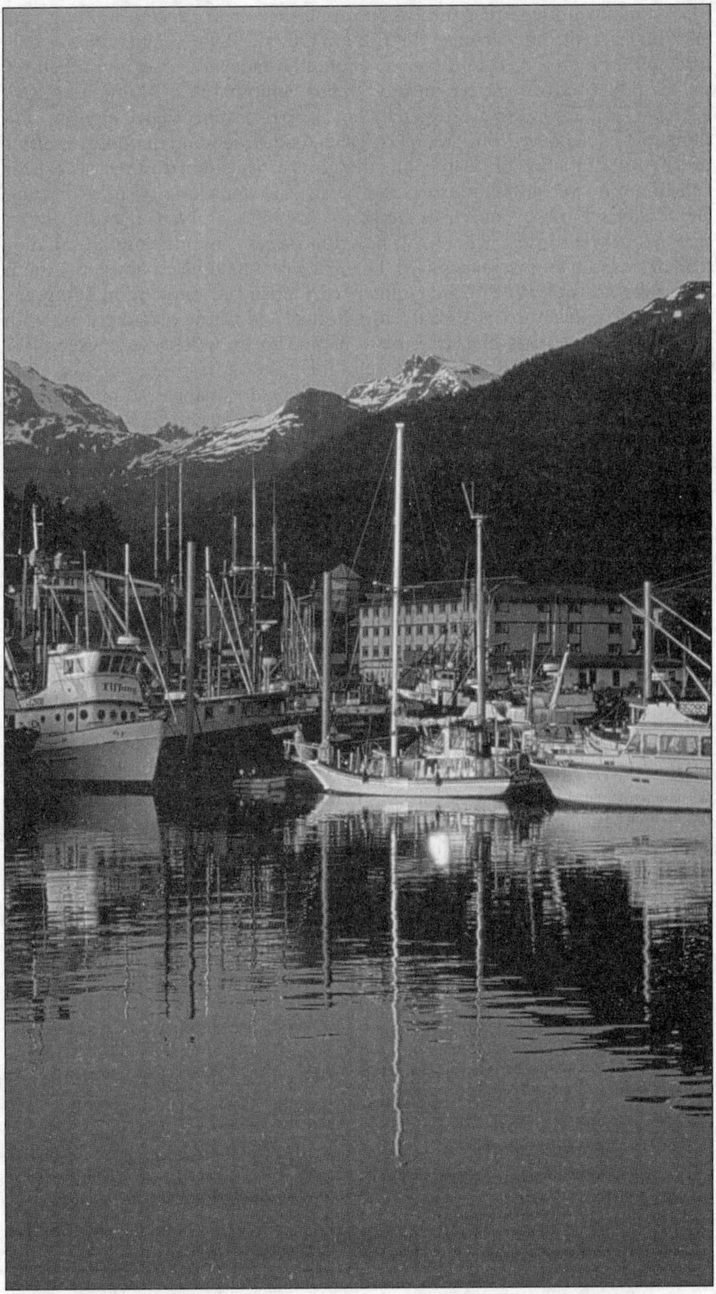

△ Sitka harborfront

Jackson also noticed that the European presence had affected hunting patterns and significantly changed the Eskimo lifestyle. Believing that Native culture could be preserved by fostering economic independence, he pushed for the introduction of reindeer on the Seward Peninsula near Nome. The government initially wasn't interested, but Jackson went ahead anyway and shipped 171 reindeer from Siberia in 1892. Acknowledging the positive effect of Jackson's initiative on Native life, the government joined in ten years later and brought over an additional 1280 beasts. Jackson, along with his friends, also collected more than five thousand examples of Native work, always meticulously recording where and how the pieces – be they useful, ceremonial, or decorative – were acquired. The first shack he built to house the items soon filled up and, in 1897, he constructed the current museum building, the first concrete structure in Alaska. Though small and a little old-fashioned with its ranks of glass cases, the museum is packed to the rafters with exemplary works from throughout the state. Totems form the centerpiece, but all around are Tlingit items such as feast bowls made from alder, maple, and birch in bird and bear designs with decorative pieces picked out in bone. The wood-and-fur **Raven battle helmet** worn by the Kiks.ádi leader, Katlian, in the 1804 conflict with the Russians vies for pride of place with armor made from leather and wooden slats, an Athabascan birch-bark canoe, an Eskimo reindeer sled, and drawers full of smaller and more delicate items that could keep you occupied for hours.

Across Lincoln Street from the museum, don't miss the college's **Marine Wet Lab & Aquarium** (Mon–Fri 9am–3pm; $3), effectively a biology classroom with a handful of small tanks containing specimens collected locally and three wet tables filled with weird and beautiful creatures you can touch, pick up or simply watch as they go about their business. Mussel beds, clams, anemones, tube worms, and sea cucumbers all pale next to the wonderfully colorful starfish.

The Totem Park and the Raptor Center

At the end of Lincoln Street, in a verdant copse between ocean and creek, you'll find the main section of the **Sitka National Historic Park**, known locally as the "Totem Park." This wooded area bordered by totem poles occupies a small peninsula where the Kiks.ádi Tlingits established a fort shortly after driving off early Russian settlers in their 1802 attack. Returning two years later, the Russians destroyed the fort, and today all that's left is a grassy patch around a particularly striking totem pole. Somehow this area seems a little out of character with the rest of the park, all brooding spruce and hemlocks swathed in almost incessant mist, out of which loom the poles gazing balefully out to sea. As elsewhere in Southeast, most are replicas of nineteenth-century totems.

Set aside in 1890 by President Benjamin Harrison, the park was later developed by Alaska Governor John Brady, who chose the area as the resting place for poles rounded up around Southeast for the Louisiana Purchase Exposition of 1904. None had actually come from here (most were from Haida villages on Prince of Wales Island), but with land already set aside this seemed the most sensible place for them. As the poles continued to rot, the Civilian Conservation Corps began a program to replicate the originals, accounting for most of the thirteen poles now present. A couple are more recent creations, however, notably the colorful pole nearest the visitor center, which was ceremoniously raised in 1996 after considerable debate within the Tlingit community about Raven and Eagle appearing on the same pole.

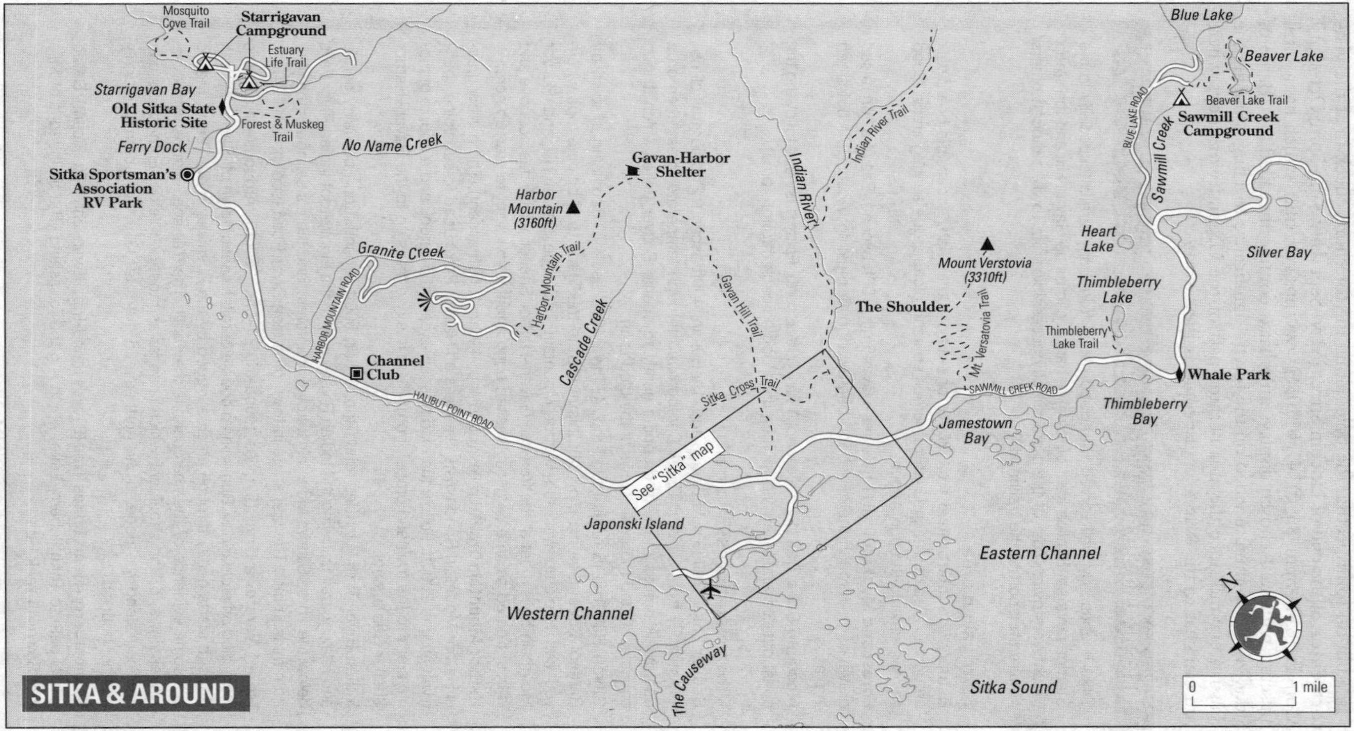
SITKA & AROUND
Mosquito Cove Trail
Starrigavan Campground
Estuary Life Trail
Starrigavan Bay
Old Sitka State Historic Site
Forest & Muskeg Trail
Ferry Dock
Sitka Sportsman's Association RV Park
No Name Creek
Gavan-Harbor Shelter
Harbor Mountain (3160ft)
Granite Creek
Harbor Mountain Trail
Harbor Mountain Road
Channel Club
Cascade Creek
Halibut Point Road
Gavan Hill Trail
Indian River
Indian River Trail
Sitka Cross Trail
See "Sitka" map
Japonski Island
Western Channel
The Causeway
The Shoulder
Mount Verstovia (3310ft)
Mt. Versatovia Trail
Sawmill Creek Road
Jamestown Bay
Eastern Channel
Sitka Sound
Heart Lake
Thimbleberry Lake
Thimbleberry Lake Trail
Thimbleberry Bay
Whale Park
Silver Bay
Blue Lake
Blue Lake Road
Sawmill Creek
Sawmill Creek Campground
Beaver Lake Trail
Beaver Lake
N
0
1 mile

In addition to inspecting the poles along the foreshore, check in at the **visitor center**, at the end of Lincoln Street (May–Sept daily 8am–5pm; Oct–April Mon–Fri 8am–5pm; $3; ⓣ747-0110, ⓦwww.nps.gov/sitk), which has a small museum with well-chosen displays on what is commonly called the "Battle of Sitka," a twelve-minute video on the town's significance to Tlingits during the Russian era and since the area became part of the US, and workshops where you can chat to the Native craftspeople as they work.

Hikes around Sitka

Sitka is unusually well served with good hikes, from easy strolls (especially in the Starrigavan area, 8 miles west of town) to harder climbs up Gavan Hill and the steep Mount Verstovia. Most of them are directly accessible from town, although others require transport to the trailhead.

Starrigavan area

Estuary Life Interpretive Trail (200yd one-way; 10min; flat). Accessible boardwalk around an area of wetland with numerous spurs to picturesque seating areas. Good salmon viewing through August.

Forest and Muskeg Trail (1 mile one-way; 45min; 100ft ascent). Easy trail on raised gravel paths through the forest and boardwalk over muskeg. Accessible but steep in places.

Mosquito Cove Trail (1.2-mile loop; 1 hr; 100ft ascent). Fairly easy trail following the coast past several lovely viewpoints, then looping back through forest.

Other road-accessible trails

Beaver Lake Trail (3 miles round-trip; 1hr 30min; 400ft ascent). Popular trail climbing steadily from *Sawmill Creek Campground* through temperate forest, then on a boardwalk across muskeg, dropping gently to scenic Beaver Lake, which it then encircles. Good mountain views, if the clouds lift.

Gavan Hill Trail (6 miles round-trip; 4–7hr; 2400ft ascent). Beginning in town off Baranof Street (see map, p.124), this moderate trail leads to subalpine tops where you can hook up with the Harbor Mountain Trail. The Gavan Hill and Harbor Mountain trails meet at the free-use Gavan–Harbor Shelter, which has no stove and is best treated as an emergency shelter: bring a tent if you want to stay up here.

Harbor Mountain Trail (8 miles round-trip; 4–6hr; 1500ft ascent). The narrow gravel Harbor Mountain Road twists five miles off Halibut Point Road to subalpine country at around 2000ft. Follow the road past an excellent overlook and a couple of picnic areas to the trailhead proper, from where it is two miles up to the Gavan–Harbor Shelter (see above).

Indian River Trail (11 miles round-trip; 6–8hr; 500ft ascent). Long but fairly gentle and relaxing trail following the Indian River valley to the eighty-foot Indian River Falls below the Three Sisters Mountains. Lovely rainforest, and there's salmon in the river from midsummer. The trail starts in town off Indian River Road (see map, p.124).

Mount Verstovia Trail (5 miles round-trip; 4–5hr; 2500ft). Arduous hike that's rewarding on a clear day. Beginning a couple of miles east of town off Sawmill Creek Road, it starts gently through an area logged by the Russians in the 1860s; there's still some evidence of the charcoal pits they built. The trail soon climbs with ever-longer views to "the shoulder," which is as far as most people go. Enthusiasts can continue along the ridge to the northeast to the true 3310-foot summit, roughly another hour on.

Thimbleberry–Heart Lakes Trail (2 miles round-trip; 30min–2hr; 50ft ascent). Broad gravel path to Thimbleberry Lake, which is good for fishing. The trailhead is at Mile 4 of Sawmill Creek Road.

Hiking Mount Edgecumbe

The near-conical **Mount Edgecumbe**, at the southern end of Kruzof Island, is temptingly visible on Sitka's western horizon, separated only by seventeen miles of Sitka Sound. Part with round-trip water taxi fees of around $140 for up to six people and you've got the place to explore, notably the **Mount Edgecumbe Trail** (13.5 miles round-trip; 7–10hr; 3200ft ascent). This climbs the peak from the Forest Service's *Fred's Creek Cabin* (Ⓣ1-877/444-6777; $35), a new shoreline affair where the water taxis drop off. The trail crosses muskeg rising gently for four miles, arriving at a three-sided emergency shelter. From there the path steepens to the tree line at 2000ft, then follows a line of poles, though if the weather is clear you're encouraged to make your own route to avoid wearing a path. If there is low cloud, follow the poles to get down.

Before returning to town consider a visit to the wooded, streamside confines of the nonprofit **Alaska Raptor Center**, 1000 Raptor Way (May–Sept Mon–Fri & Sun 8am–4pm; $12; Ⓣ747-8662, Ⓦwww.alaskaraptor.org). Here, wounded raptors – owls, hawks, peregrine falcons, and bald eagles – are cared for and released back into the wild, except for those that are unable to fly or hunt, which are kept as "raptors in residence." The birds stay in large and thoughtfully constructed compounds and are introduced by the enthusiastic and well-informed staff members, who guide you around the compound and the new flight-training center where soon-to-be-released birds are put through their paces. When groups turn up (it pays to come on a day when there's a cruise ship in town) they'll even bring one of the bald eagles out, perhaps your only chance to come face to beak with one of these regal birds.

Along the road system

Unless you are camping or trying to reach distant trailheads, there is little point in renting a car in Sitka: there are only about seven or eight miles of road in each direction from town, and not a great deal along them. Heading east along Sawmill Creek Road, you pass the trailhead for Mount Verstovia Trail at Jamestown Bay about three miles out; a mile further is **Whale Park**, three covered observation platforms linked by boardwalks. Another mile or so further west, the site of the pulp mill, which closed in 1993, marks Blue Lake Road, which leads to *Sawmill Creek Campground* and Beaver Lake Trail. Cars are banned beyond the end of the paved road, but **bikers** can continue a further six miles past the Medvejie Hatchery to the dammed Green Lake, which provides power and water for Sitka.

Four miles west along Halibut Point Road you hit Halibut Point State Recreation Site, where there are some picnic tables as well as some short trails. More robust hikes can be found at the top of Harbor Mountain Road, which heads inland almost opposite. From here, Halibut Point Road continues to the AMHS ferry dock and, half a mile beyond, the **Old Sitka State Historic Site**, where barely discernable remains mark the original site of the Russian presence in 1799. Cross Starrigavan Creek to reach the *Starrigavan Campground*, a very pleasant area open for day-use and with a selection of easy trails threading along boardwalks and raised gravel paths through the forest. Strategically sited seats make great spots for watching waterbirds wading or salmon jumping.

Cruises and kayaking

Sitka's setting, open to the ocean and yet hemmed in by myriad islands, is so beguiling that almost all your time on land is spent wishing you were on the water. That's easily rectified with Sitka Wildlife Quest (late May to early Sept; ⓣ747-8100 or 1-888/747-8101, ⓦwww.allenmarinetours.com), which runs educational and entertaining two-hour **wildlife tours** (Tues & Thurs 6pm, Sat & Sun 9am; $49) out on Sitka Sound, with every chance of seeing humpback whales (especially in late summer), sea otters, seals, and bears and deer along the banks of numerous islands. Weather permitting, the trips go out to the sheer volcanic **St Lazaria Island**, a federal wildlife refuge at the mouth of Sitka Sound with cliffs that, during the summer months, are black with seabirds, notably comical puffins, murres, and petrels. The cliffs plunge so steeply into the sea that you can get within a few feet of the creatures. Trips leave from Crescent Harbor Marina.

Sitka has some of the best **sea kayaking** in Southeast, with mile upon mile of sheltered waterways, narrow channels, gorgeous coves, and tide pools. Paddle beyond the swanky homes that dot the islands near Sitka, and you can camp anywhere, or stay in one of the couple of dozen saltwater-accessible cabins (see "Accommodation," p.127). In as little as a few hours you can explore **the Causeway**, a series of small islands south of the airport which were linked up during World War II to provide access to gun emplacements. Remnants of the emplacements are still visible, but as they can be hard to find it pays to ask whoever is renting you a kayak before you set out.

One popular destination is **Goddard Hot Springs**, seventeen miles to the south, where two covered hot tubs face out to sea. Don't expect to have the place to yourselves as it is a popular rest spot for commercial fishermen, but it makes an excellent destination for a kayak expedition (3–4 days round-trip from Sitka). *Kanga Bay Cabin* is on the way, but there is no cabin right at the springs. You can camp if you don't mind the mosquitoes – at their midsummer peak it is better to find spots on offshore islands.

Probably the best of the **kayak rental and tour** businesses is Baidarka Boats, 320 Seward St (ⓣ747-8996, ⓦwww.kayaksite.com), which rents top-quality kayaks from $60 a day (doubles $85), a price that drops to $25/35 for five- to nine-day rentals. They also have folding kayaks ($95 a day; $80 a day for over 5), which are ideal if you want to do a one-way paddle and fly back. Boats come with everything you'll need, including VHF radio. Costs for guided trips depend on numbers: for example, four people in two double kayaks runs $125 per person for a full day out with lunch.

Sitka Sound Ocean Adventures (ⓣ747-6375, ⓦwww.ssoceanadventures.com) also rents kayaks (half-day rate $30 single, $40 double; full-day $50/$65; multiday roughly $40/$55) and conducts guided kayak tours, with two-hour paddles around the Totem Park shoreline and out to the closer islands ($55), full-day trips ($125) and multiday affairs ($150 per day). They work out of a bus parked by Harrigan Centennial Hall.

Eating, drinking, and entertainment

With one exception, Sitka's **restaurants** aren't exactly going to set gourmet tongues wagging, though you can eat well enough for a few days. **Groceries** are most conveniently bought at Market Center (see below). For evening drinks, join the crowds in the *Westmark Shee Atiká* hotel's bar or head along to the more colorful **bars** on Katlian Street.

Daytime **entertainment** is more varied, with a couple of local **dance troupes** vying for your attention. The choice venue would have to be the Community House, 200 Katlian St, where the Sheet'ka Kwaan Naa Kahidi Dancers (May–Sept; $6; ⓣ747-7290 or 1-888/270-8687, ⓦwww.sitkatribal.com) perform for half an hour in traditional costume, complete with a narration of local legends. Performance times (which are dependent on cruise-ship sailings) are posted outside the 1997 replica clan house, beside the stridently painted Eagle and Raven design screen. The alternative is the New Archangel Dancers, Harrigan Centennial Hall ($7; ⓣ747-5516), who also do a half-hour show scheduled around the cruise ships, but concentrate on authentic Russian folk dances performed by local women.

Fans of chamber **music** will want to time their visit to coincide with the Sitka Summer Music Festival (ⓣ747-6774, ⓦwww.sitkamusicfestival.org), which takes place throughout most of June. The festival includes around eight evening concerts, mostly in Harrigan Centennial Hall, and features up to twenty artists of international renown. Call for tickets or drop by Old Harbor Books, 201 Lincoln St (ⓣ747-8808); book in advance or you'll have to be content with sitting in on rehearsals, which are free.

The Backdoor 104 Barracks St ⓣ747-8856. Daytime café with great coffee, plus tasty sandwiches, pastries, and light lunches. Access through Old Harbor Books.

Bayview Restaurant upstairs at 407 Lincoln St ⓣ747-7177. Good restaurant with great sea views and a standard, but well prepared, range of burgers, salads, and sandwiches, plus the likes of chicken quesedilla ($9).

Channel Club 2906 Halibut Point Rd, 4 miles west of town ⓣ747-9916. If you've an appetite for steak, this is the only place to consider. An enduring favorite with Sitka residents, with full-service bar and a free shuttle from downtown. Call for reservations and hotel pickup.

Evergreen Deli 2a Lincoln St ⓣ747-6944. Good deli selling great salmon chowder and freshly made sandwiches on home-baked bread (only open weekdays until around 4pm), in a building also housing the Evergreen Natural Foods store.

Highliner Coffee Seward Square Mall, Seward St ⓣ747-4924. Daytime coffeeshop with relaxing sofas, espresso coffee, good cakes, bagels, and Internet access at commercial rates.

Ludvig's Bistro 256 Katlian St ⓣ966-3663. If it wasn't for the 10pm sunset outside and the fish canneries down the street, you could easily imagine yourself in a tiny Mediterranean bistro dining on a smoked black cod ensalada appetizer ($12.50) or Alaskan paella ($25). Everything on the mostly Spanish, French and Italian menu is cooked to perfection, and the Old World wines, ports, and sherries served are all available by the glass. It's not cheap, but be sure to make it part of your Sitka plans and reserve ahead.

Market Center 210 Baranof St ⓣ747-6686. Central grocery store with good line in prepared sandwiches and salads, plus espresso. Open until midnight in summer.

Pioneer Bar 212 Katlian St ⓣ747-3456. Down-to-earth spot with boozing at the bar or in booths surrounded by hundreds of black-and-white photographs of fishing boats.

Raven Dining Room and Kadataan Lounge 330 Seward St ⓣ747-0979. Smart restaurant and bar inside the *Westmark Shee Atiká* hotel with good views of the water. The lounge serves the usual range of burgers, sandwiches, and salads ($9–12), while the dining room dishes up the likes of seafood fettuccini ($22) and barbecue pork ribs ($17 a half-rack).

Sheldon Jackson College Dining Room David Sweetland Hall. The best bargain in town for diners on a budget. A simple cafeteria-style place with all-you-can-eat breakfast (6.30–8am; $5), lunch (11.30am–1pm; $7), and dinner (4.45–6pm; $10). On Sunday breakfast and lunch become brunch (11.30am–1pm; $10). Follow the road opposite the entrance to the Sheldon Jackson Museum.

Listings

Banks The First National Bank at 318 Lincoln St has an ATM.

Bicycle rental and repair The handiest spot is Yellow Jersey Cycle Shop, 329 Harbor Drive (ⓣ747-6317), which rents bikes at $25 a day ($30 for 24hr).

Bookshop Old Harbor Books, 201 Lincoln St ⓣ747-8808, ⓔoldharbr@ptialaska.net.

Car rental North Star Rent-a-Car, at the airport (ⓣ966-2552 or 1-800/722-6927, ⓦwww.allstarsitka.com).

Festivals Apart from the Summer Music Festival (see above), there's a salmon derby on the last weekend of May and first weekend in June; a lively Fourth of July parade and fireworks; a period-costume ball, parade, and dinners to celebrate the lead-up to Alaska Day and the anniversary of the transfer on Oct 18; and a celebration of all things cetacean in the Sitka WhaleFest (Ⓦ www.sitkawhalefest.org) in the first week of Nov. It is also worth noting that the Russian Orthodox Church follows the Julian (rather than the standard Gregorian calendar), so religious festivals – Christmas and Easter in particular – are celebrated twice here, roughly twelve days apart.

Internet access In-demand free access by the hour at the library (reserve in advance). For more immediate needs try Alaska Computer Center, 205 Harbor Drive (Mon–Sat 10am–5pm; Ⓣ747-0600), or Highliner Coffee (see p.137).

Laundry and showers The Hames PE Center at Sheldon Jackson College (early May to early Sept Mon–Fri 6am–9pm, Sat noon–8pm, Sun noon–6pm; Ⓣ747-5231) has a pool, racquetball courts, and showers for $4. Super 8 Laundromat, 404 Sawmill Creek Rd (Ⓣ747-8804), is the handiest for laundry.

Library The Kettleson Memorial Library, Harbor Drive (Mon–Thurs 10am–9pm, Fri 10am–6pm, Sat & Sun 1–5pm) makes a perfect place to while away a rainy day, with plenty to read, Internet access and superb picture windows with views of the bay.

Medical assistance Sitka Community Hospital, 209 Moeller Drive (Ⓣ747-3241), has emergency medical services and outpatient clinics.

Pharmacy White's Pharmacy, 705 Halibut Point Rd Ⓣ747-5755.

Post office There's a sub-post office downtown at 338 Lincoln St (Mon–Sat 8.30am–5.30pm) and the main on Sawmill Creek Rd out by the Raptor Center. The **General Delivery** zip code is 99835.

Taxes There's a 5 percent sales tax and an additional 6 percent bed tax, all included within our price codes.

Travel agency Totem Travel, 903 Halibut Point Rd Ⓣ747-3251 or 1-800/478-3252, Ⓔtotemtvl@ptialaska.net.

Water taxis Sitka Water Taxi (Ⓣ747-5970, Ⓦhome.gci.net/~snewell/) charges around $75 per hour for their services. Ester G Sea Taxi (Ⓣ747-6481, Ⓦwww.puffinsandwhales.com) charges about $90 an hour for up to four people in a faster boat.

Minor ports

All over Southeast Alaska there are small settlements of a few hundred people, some of which are Native villages that have survived intact, some former logging camps or canneries that have developed enough momentum to exist beyond the death of the industry that spawned them. Many of these places are off the main sea lanes plied by the AMHS ferries, while others get regular (though not especially frequent) visits; it is the latter we have covered here. None really warrants a special visit, and in most cases the hour you'll spend at the ferry dock is ample. Kayakers, however, may want to paddle to one of these ports, and then catch the ferry back to their starting point. Trips to consider include Petersburg to Kake and Sitka to Tenakee Springs.

Wherever you plan to stop, be sure to study the ferry schedule carefully to ensure you don't end up spending five nights in a place you only intended to spend two.

Kake

Roughly two southbound and two northbound AMHS ferries call in each week at **KAKE**, an eight-hundred-strong Tlingit village on the northwest coast of Kupreanof Island, between Petersburg and Sitka. Fishing and subsistence hunting keep the town afloat, with the occasional visitor using the town as a springboard for kayak trips to Kuiu Island, or as a destination for a paddling expedition from Petersburg. Ferries dock a mile and a half from town, so you probably won't have long enough to closely inspect the town's 132-foot **totem pole**, carved for the 1970 World's Fair in Japan and said to be the tallest in the world. You can **stay** at the *Waterfront Lodge* (Ⓣ785-3472, Ⓦwaterfrontlodgekake.com; ④), **eat** at the *Nugget Inn* (Ⓣ785-6469), and buy groceries from several stores.

Angoon

The Tlingit village of **ANGOON**, sixty miles southeast of Juneau, is the only significant settlement on Admiralty Island and occupies one of Southeast's warmest and driest locations on the island's western coast, facing Chatham Strait. Its seven hundred residents survive on fishing and subsistence hunting and do nothing to encourage tourism, which only touches their lives when the AMHS ferries arrive every few days; and since the ferry dock is three miles from town the impact is very slight. About the only reason to stop is to do a little kayaking using *Favorite Bay Inn* (Ⓣ788-3123 or 1-800/423-3123, Ⓦwww.favoritebayinn.com; ❻) as your base.

Tenakee Springs

The ferry schedule occasionally allows visitors enough time to wallow in the soothing no-clothes **hot pool** (men daily 2–6pm & 10pm–9am, women at all other times) at **TENAKEE SPRINGS**, sixty miles southeast of Juneau on the eastern side of Chichagof Island. The stark concrete bathhouse containing the pool is at the base of the ferry dock just 50yd from the boat, but the pressure of the soon departing boat makes it less than relaxing and you may not find yourself warmly welcomed by the locals. They're far from hostile; it's just that most of the hundred residents came here for a quiet life and can be easily overwhelmed by the masses. A case in point was the 1997 visit of a cruise ship, the *World Discoverer*, that disgorged a hundred-plus passengers onto the single car-free dirt path that serves as the town's main street. The people shut up shop and effectively hid until the ship went away promising never to return.

Individuals will feel much more welcome, yet there's not a great deal to do except fall into the pattern of daily baths, perhaps do a little fishing, or hike eight miles east along the single road to the site of the old cannery, whose workers initially popularized the springs in the late nineteenth century.

If you want to stay, you can **camp** for nothing at the undeveloped site a mile east of the ferry dock at the mouth of the Indian River. There are a few $50 cabins and limited groceries at *Snyder Mercantile* (Ⓣ736-2205; ❶), at the foot of the dock opposite the hot pool. It pays to bring some food and be prepared to self-cater.

Hoonah

Several ferries a week on the Sitka–Juneau run make the slight detour to **HOONAH**, a beachside Huna Tlingit fishing village on the northeast side of Chichagof Island, forty miles west of Juneau.

With around nine hundred residents Hoonah is the largest Native village in Southeast and has until recently survived on fishing and on logging, as the surrounding denuded hillsides attest. Now both industries are almost defunct and in desperation the local community has turned to tourism. From 2004 cruise ships will be pulling in to view the partially restored remains of the Hoonah Packing Company **cannery**, which sits picturesquely on the shore around a mile north of town. One of the few intact canneries left in Alaska, it still has some of the old canning lines, but in the tradition of Southeast cruise-ship tourism space will be made for retail outlets. It remains to be seen if any of this will open for casual visitors, though you should still be able to visit the Hoonah Indian Association **Cultural Center and Museum** (Mon–Fri 8am–4.30pm; free), on the hill behind the town, which has displays of local history and Native culture, including some interesting totem poles.

Pelican

The cheapest way to visit **PELICAN**, seventy miles west of Juneau, deep within Lisianski Inlet on the northeast corner of Chichagof Island, is to come from the capital on the AMHS ferry, which makes its run about every two weeks in summer, always on a Sunday ($74 round-trip). A stroll along the town's three-quarter-mile boardwalk during the two-hour stopover here is enough to give you a flavor of the place. The real appeal of the trip, however, is the five-hour ferry journey (each way), which passes close to Glacier Bay, through Icy Strait, and around **Point Adolphus**, regarded as one of the world's best places for **watching humpback whales**. This can be the cheapest whale-watching trip you are likely to get.

This tiny fishing village on the shores of Lisianski Inlet takes its name from the boat belonging to Finnish immigrant fisherman Charlie Raatikianen, who, with a few mates, established the town in 1938 to more conveniently process his catch. The setting proved favorable and the settlement added a post office in 1939, a cannery by 1943, and subsequently a school, a small sawmill, and a hotel. Most of the ramshackle buildings stand on piles over the water, linked by boardwalks, with only a couple of miles of roads.

If the ferry schedule doesn't suit, you can fly here daily from Juneau with Alaska Seaplane Service (Ⓣ789-3331 or 1-800/478-3360, Ⓦwww.akseaplanes.com) for around $120. There are a few places to **eat and drink**, but most visitors seem to gravitate towards *Rosie's Bar and Grill*, on the boardwalk (Ⓣ735-2265), which has rooms (❸) and a bar that's usually full of commercial fishermen.

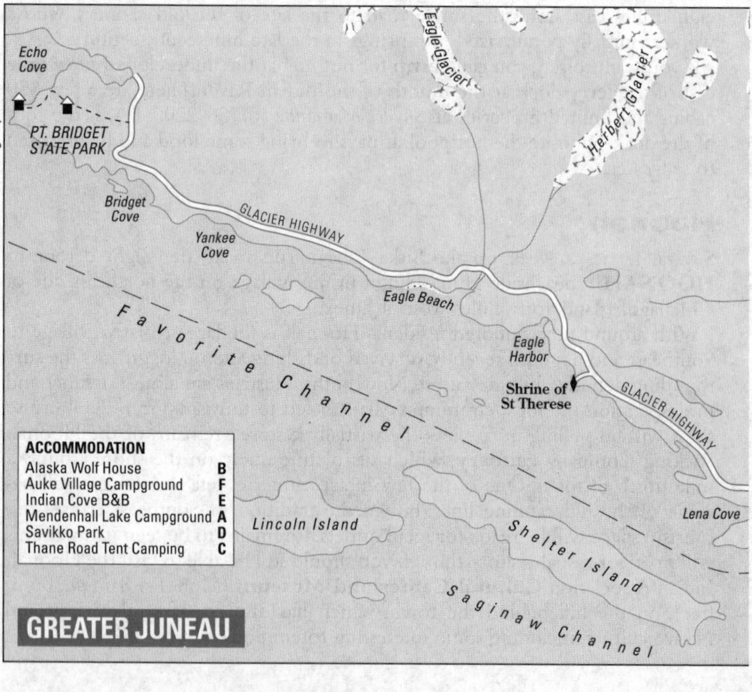

Juneau and around

The sophisticated and vibrant city of **JUNEAU** (JUNE-oh) is unlike any other state capital in the nation. Accessible only by sea or air, it is exceptionally picturesque, hard against the **Gastineau Channel**, with steep, narrow roads clawing up into the rainforested hills behind. With no flat land to speak of and a giant ice field blocking off any chance of direct land access to the interior, it would be hard to think of a less practical site for a state capital, but the vagaries of history and man's lust for gold tipped the balance.

Waste rock from the town's gold mines was dumped into the channel to create the flat downtown area, where a ragged gold-rush town sprang up in the 1880s with the usual complement of bars, churches, and brothels. Juneau had the good fortune to avoid a major fire – a common occurrence in northern towns built entirely of timber where wood-burning stoves raged many months of the year – and most of the older buildings remain, leaving a viable sense of history and creating a harmonious focus for what has to be one of the most physically beguiling town centers in Alaska.

The trouble is, much of the beauty is often obscured by the weather. It is not so much the annual ninety-plus inches of rain, but the consistency with which it comes – two out of every three days on average. Even when it is not raining, it is often cloudy. That hasn't stopped Juneau from becoming one of the busiest cruise-ship ports in Alaska, and the result is a frenetic atmosphere in which huge floating hotels loom over narrow central streets where diamond and emerald jewelry, handmade Swiss watches, and immaculately cut fur coats

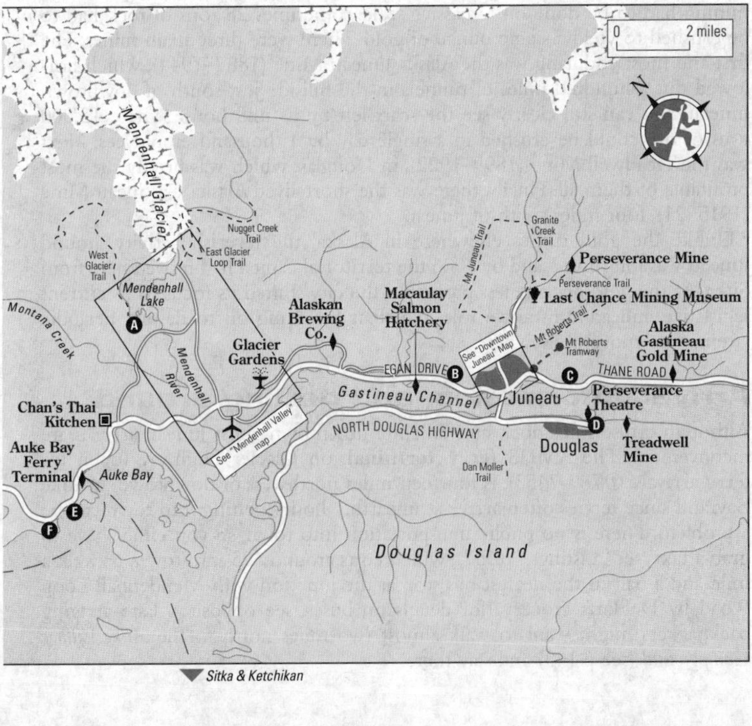

vie for shelf space with tasteless trinkets and mini totem poles. Still, it keeps the place lively and makes for a dramatic contrast on those languid evenings when the ships glide away, the streets empty out, and the buildings take on a glossy sheen as the low sun casts its last rays under the blanket of cloud.

A couple of excellent **museums**, a pretty Russian Orthodox church and a tramway ride to some easy subalpine hikes provide the bulk of the interest downtown, though there's interest around about in visiting some old gold mines. Further out, there's an educational salmon hatchery visit, tasting at one of Alaska's premiere breweries and close-up viewing of the majestic **Mendenhall Glacier**.

Some history

Juneau was founded on gold. No one took much notice of the Auk Tlingit fishing village on Gastineau Channel until 1880, when George Pilz, a mining engineer from Sitka, dispatched Joe Juneau and Dick Harris there with Auk chief Kowee. Kowee had responded to Pilz's offer of a reward for divulging the whereabouts of gold, but these hapless, drunken prospectors were unable to find much. The chief insisted there was ore to be found and, on the second attempt, they unearthed "little lumps as large as peas and beans" at the head of Gold Creek. In no time Alaska had its first gold rush, and Harrisberg became the first American-established town in the new territory. Miners became disenchanted with Harris' dubious claim-staking practices and briefly switched the name to Rockwell before settling on Juneau in 1881.

Gold in the streams quickly ran out, but reef gold – locked in the hard rock below ground – was abundant. Early efforts at extraction from the Perseverance Mine (1885–1921) soon exhausted the best-grade ore, and throughout most of Juneau's sixty-year gold-mining era, the town's massive mines and crushing mills had to content themselves with low-grade ore. In order to be profitable, mining had to be done on a massive scale: sometimes 28 tons of rock had to be crushed to yield a single ounce of gold. There were three main mines. The first and most enduring was the Alaska Juneau Mine (1887–1944), which hollowed out a hundred miles of tunnels in the hillside just south of downtown Juneau. You can still clearly see the scars left by its mill house where 12,000 tons of ore could be crushed in a single day by a thousand employees. Next was the Treadwell Mine (1899–1922), in Douglas, which was briefly the most profitable of them all. Finally, there was the short-lived Alaska Gastineau Mine (1915–21), four miles south of Juneau.

Unlike the gold rushes elsewhere in Alaska, the feverish activity around Juneau was long-lived, and by 1906 the territorial capital had moved here from Sitka. As the gold became less profitable, the city shifted its focus to its current legislative and administrative role, which it has hung on to despite periodic attempts to move it elsewhere.

Arrival, information, and getting around

Although cruise ships dock conveniently downtown, most Juneau arrivals are inconvenient. The AMHS **ferry terminal**, on Glacier Highway (open for ferry arrivals; ☎789-7453), is fourteen miles northwest of downtown at Auke Bay, and since ferries often arrive at unearthly hours, getting into town can be a problem. There is no public transportation into town, so you either have to grab a taxi (see "Listings," p.157), which costs around $25 into town, or walk a mile and a half to the nearest bus stop at the junction with Mendenhall Loop Road by DeHarts grocery (for details on buses, see opposite). Late-arriving backpackers might want to walk almost two miles north to the *Auke Village Campground* (see p.145) and stay there.

Juneau **airport**, nine miles northwest of downtown (Ⓣ789-7821), is the main hub for flights around Southeast, with numerous Alaska Airlines arrivals and several from smaller local carriers. You'll find taxis outside ($15–20 downtown) and a small **visitor kiosk** that is sometimes staffed for arrivals and always has brochures, free phones to various businesses and directions to the nearest bus stop. You'll need to walk about a quarter of a mile to the stop on Mallard Street, just behind the Nugget Mall.

Information

The **visitor center**, 101 Egan Drive (May–Sept Mon–Fri 8.30am–5pm, Sat & Sun 9am–5pm; Oct–April Mon–Fri 9am–5pm; Ⓣ586-2201 or 1-888/581-2201, Ⓦwww.traveljuneau.com), is inside Centennial Hall, a space it shares with an AMHS ferry booking desk and an unstaffed desk devoted to brochures about the Tongass National Forest, including material on Glacier Bay, Tracy Arm fjord, and the trails and cabins in Juneau's wooded surroundings. For more details, call at the Tongass National Forest District **Ranger Office**, 8465 Old Dairy Rd (Mon–Fri 8am–5pm; Ⓣ586-8800, Ⓦwww.fs.fed.us/r10/tongass). You'll find additional daytime **information booths** at Marine Park on the waterfront and by the cruise-ship dock.

For entertainment listings check out the *Juneau Empire* newspaper as well as its widely available annual *Juneau Guide* (free), which also has general city information on its useful website (Ⓦwww.juneaualaska.com).

Getting around

Juneau's main points of interest (with the exception of the ferry terminal) can all be reached using city **buses**, operated by Capital Transit (Ⓣ789-6901), which has four services, all costing $1.50, exact fare. Buses run every thirty to sixty minutes, depending on time of day. The main routes – #3 and #4 (Mon–Sat 7.20am–10.50pm, Sun 9.20am–5.20pm) – travel from downtown along the waterfront past Lemon Creek to the airport and then loop through the Mendenhall Valley. Capital Transit also operates a service (Mon–Sat 7am–10.30pm, Sun 9.30am–6pm) from downtown over the bridge to Douglas: change for this line at the Federal Building stop (transfers free). There's also an hourly **express service** (Mon–Fri 7.30am–6pm) between downtown and the university, about two miles short of the Auke Bay ferry terminal. The timetable is reasonably clear, and the *Understanding the Public Bus System* leaflet, available free from the visitor center, has detailed descriptions of how to get to various sights. Bikes travel free on the buses.

Also useful as a means of getting around, MGT (Ⓣ789-5460, Ⓦwww.mightygreattrips.com) offers a couple of **bus tours** that are cheap enough to regard as transportation. Check out their Glacier Express ($5 each way), which is effectively a bus service between the cruise-ship dock downtown and the Mendenhall Glacier visitor center. They also do a City & Hatchery tour ($10), taking you past the downtown sights and out to the Macaulay Salmon Hatchery (see p.149), with the option of staying at the hatchery and picking up a later bus. Last Frontier Tours (Ⓣ321-8687, Ⓦwww.lastfrontiertours.com) does a similar Mendenhall Glacier trip ($5 each way), with optional stops at the hatchery and at Glacier Gardens (see p.151).

The bus system is infrequent enough and the road system extensive enough that it makes sense to **rent a car** (see "Listings," p.156) for at least part of your stay. **Cycling** can also work well, with a number of dedicated bike routes that hit all the main destinations. Pick up the free *Biking in Juneau* leaflet from the visitor center and rent bikes for around $25 a day from *Driftwood Lodge* (see overleaf).

City, glacier, and gold-mine tours

Being a major cruise-ship destination, Juneau offers dozens of city tours primarily geared towards giving cruise passengers a quick look at the main sights and delivering them back in time for their sailing. If you have the time you probably won't bother with a tour, but if you're in a rush MGT's two-hour-plus Mendenhall Glacier and Juneau City Tour (early May to late Sept; $20; ⓣ789-5460), provides low-cost access to the Mendenhall Glacier, allowing forty minutes at the glacier visitor center. With prior notice (and suitable interest) they'll also take in the salmon hatchery ($25 total).

One sight you can't see on your own is the Alaska Gastineau gold mine, four miles south of Juneau. Access is only on the pricey three-hour Alaska Gastineau Mill & Gold Mine Tour ($60; ⓣ1-800/820-2628), where staggering facts about the size of the mine and anecdotes about the people who worked there keep you entertained as you walk underground along a 360-foot flat tunnel, troop around the old buildings and drive up the mountainside to a small mining museum.

Accommodation

Juneau has the widest range of accommodation in Southeast, from beautiful campgrounds and a conveniently sited hostel to luxurious B&Bs. Unless you have your own transport, it makes sense to stay downtown, though you might want to stay in Mendenhall Valley for proximity to the airport, access to hiking trails, or just to avoid the bustle of the center of town.

As well as the developed sites listed here, tent **campers** are also free to use an undeveloped area forty miles north of downtown at the end of Glacier Highway. **RV drivers** who just need a place to park up overnight can currently stay near the airport in the parking lots of the now-closed K-Mart at 6525 Glacier Hwy. Pick up the free and very useful *Tent Camping & RV Facilities and Services* leaflet from the visitor center.

Hotels and motels

Alaskan Hotel 167 S Franklin St, downtown ⓣ586-1000 or 1-800/327-9374, ⓦwww.ptialaska.net/~akhotel. Juneau's oldest hotel dates to 1913 and, with the cheapest rooms in town, makes good on its claim, "Styles & Rates of a bygone era." Rooms all have antique furniture of some sort, and around half of them have private bathrooms. TVs and kitchenettes are more randomly scattered, and some rooms are pretty small. Avoid the second-floor rooms above the bar, if you fancy an early night. Suites and private bath ❹, shared ❷

Aspen Hotel 1800 Shell Simmons Drive, Mendenhall ⓣ790-6435 or 1-866/483-7848, ⓦwww.aspenhotelsak.com/juneau.html. Modern hotel opposite the airport made up entirely of two-room suites with all the expected in-room facilities, plus pool, spa, exercise room, and downtown shuttle. ❻

Baranof Hotel 127 N Franklin St, downtown ⓣ586-2660 or 1-800/544-0970, ⓦwww.westmarkhotels.com. Now over sixty years old, this is Juneau's grandest hotel, though the rooms have become somewhat sanitized now that it's part of the statewide Westmark chain. All rooms are slightly different so ask to look at a few. Suites ❽, rooms ❼

Driftwood Lodge 435 Willoughby Ave, downtown ⓣ586-2280 or 1-800/544-2239, ⓦwww.driftwoodalaska.com. Three-story motel one block from the waterfront, with large rooms that include kitchenettes and some one-bedroom and two-bedroom apartments. Courtesy bus to airport and ferry, and bikes available for rent at $15 per half-day, $25 per day. Suites ❺, rooms ❹

Prospector Hotel 375 Whittier St, downtown ⓣ586-3737 or 1-800/331-2711, ⓦwww.prospectorhotel.com. Probably the nicest business hotel in town, featuring recently remodeled suites and rooms – many with water views – with cable TV (including HBO). Prices are reasonable for its central location. Suites ❼, rooms ❻

Silverbow Inn 120 2nd St, downtown ⓣ586-4146 or 1-800/586-4146, ⓦwww.silverbowinn.com. Attractive, small hotel linked to the restaurant and bakery of the same name, with smallish but nicely furnished and tastefully decorated rooms, each with TV and phone, and with a good continental breakfast included. Reasonable off-season rates. ⑥

Super 8 Motel 2295 Trout St, Mendenhall ⓣ789-4858 or 1-800/800-8000, ⓦwww.super8.com. The cheapest option near the airport – they run a free shuttle, though it is only about five hundred yards away. Rooms are unexciting but well equipped and were upgraded fairly recently. ③

B&Bs

Alaska Wolf House 1900 Wickersham St, downtown ⓣ586-2422 or 1-888/586-9053, ⓦwww.alaskawolfhouse.com. Spacious and very comfortable B&B in a large, cedar-log house with views of Gastineau Channel. The hosts excel at helping their guests explore Juneau, inviting them onto their 32-foot wooden boat for a day-long cruise ($150) viewing glaciers, shipwreck sites, and wildlife. Back at the B&B there's a range of individually styled suites and tastefully decorated rooms, two with shared bath, and all with plenty of good books. Breakfasts are delicious. Suites ⑥, rooms ⑤, shared bath ④

Alaska's Capital Inn 113 W 5th St, downtown ⓣ586-6507 or 1-888/588-6507, ⓦwww.alaskacapitalinn.com. Elegantly restored 1906 mansion hosts one of Juneau's more luxurious B&Bs, with a range of mostly large rooms, all with original features and beautiful fittings, and some with great views. The attic Governor's suite is superb. There's also an outdoor hot tub and a five-course sit-down breakfast. Governor's suite ⑧, rooms ⑥

Cashen Quarters 315 Gold St, downtown ⓣ586-9863, ⓦwww.cashenquarters.com. Quiet B&B with five comfortable rooms (one of them a spacious suite) in a centrally located two-story house. The owners, who live next door, deliver abundant ingredients for a self-made continental breakfast to your room. Open all year. Suite ⑦, rooms ④

Indian Cove B&B Glacier Hwy, a mile north of Auke Bay ⓣ789-2726, ⓦwww.indiancovebb.com. The main attraction at this pleasant, waterside B&B with good views is its proximity to the ferry dock. Continental breakfast. ⑥

Pearson's Pond Luxury Inn 4541 Sawa Circle, Mendenhall ⓣ789-3772 or 1-888/658-6328, ⓦwww.pearsonspond.com. Very comfortable rooms in a spacious, modern house a mile from Mendenhall Glacier, with CD and VCR, personal gyms, Internet access, kitchenettes with self-serve breakfasts, hot tubs, boating, bikes, in fact just about every amenity you can think of. Each room has a water or garden view and leads out to two communal hot tubs. Prices start at $280 a double. ⑨

Hostels and camping

Auke Village Campground Mile 15 Glacier Hwy. First-come, first-served Forest Service campground almost two miles north of the Auke Bay ferry terminal and close to a scenic beach. RVs and tent sites have pit toilets and water and cost $8. May–Sept.

Juneau Hostel 614 Harris St, AK 99801 ⓣ586-9559, ⓦwww.juneauhostel.org. At $10 a bunk this is an Alaskan bargain, but in return you have to put up with a daytime lockout (9am–5pm), an evening curfew (midnight), and limited office hours (7–9am & 5pm–midnight). Still, it is a comfortable, relaxed, and central place set in an old Juneau home with separate floors for men and women, a spacious kitchen and lounge, a family room, free Internet access and laundry facilities. Reservations (necessary at least June–Aug) can only be made by mail and should include the first night's fee for each person. They'll reply by SAE or email. ①

Mendenhall Lake Campground Montana Creek Rd, off Mendenhall Loop Rd, 13 miles from downtown. The place to camp if you have transport. A gorgeous first-come, first-served Forest Service campground within sight of the Mendenhall Glacier and with space for RVs (full hookup $26, water and electricity $24, dry $10) and some lovely lakeside walk-in tent sites ($10). Mid-May to mid-Sept.

Savikko Park Savikko Rd, Douglas. Free space for four RVs to park with water and toilets nearby, located in Douglas, two miles south of the Douglas Bridge. Call for a free permit at the Harbormaster's office, 1600 Harbor Way (ⓣ586-5255), on the waterside of Egan Expressway in Juneau. Maximum three-day stay.

Thane Road Tent Camping Mile 1 Thane Rd. Small, primitive site with chemical toilets and stream water located just fifteen minutes' walk south of downtown. First-come, first-served sites are only $5, but you'll have to put up with the all-night clatter from the docks nearby. May–Sept.

The City

Despite its relative sophistication and undoubted scenic qualities, **downtown Juneau** is a faintly disturbing place, torn between the demands of herd tourism and the more prosaic needs of long-standing residents. Though largely populated by elderly cruise-ship passengers window-shopping and poking around,

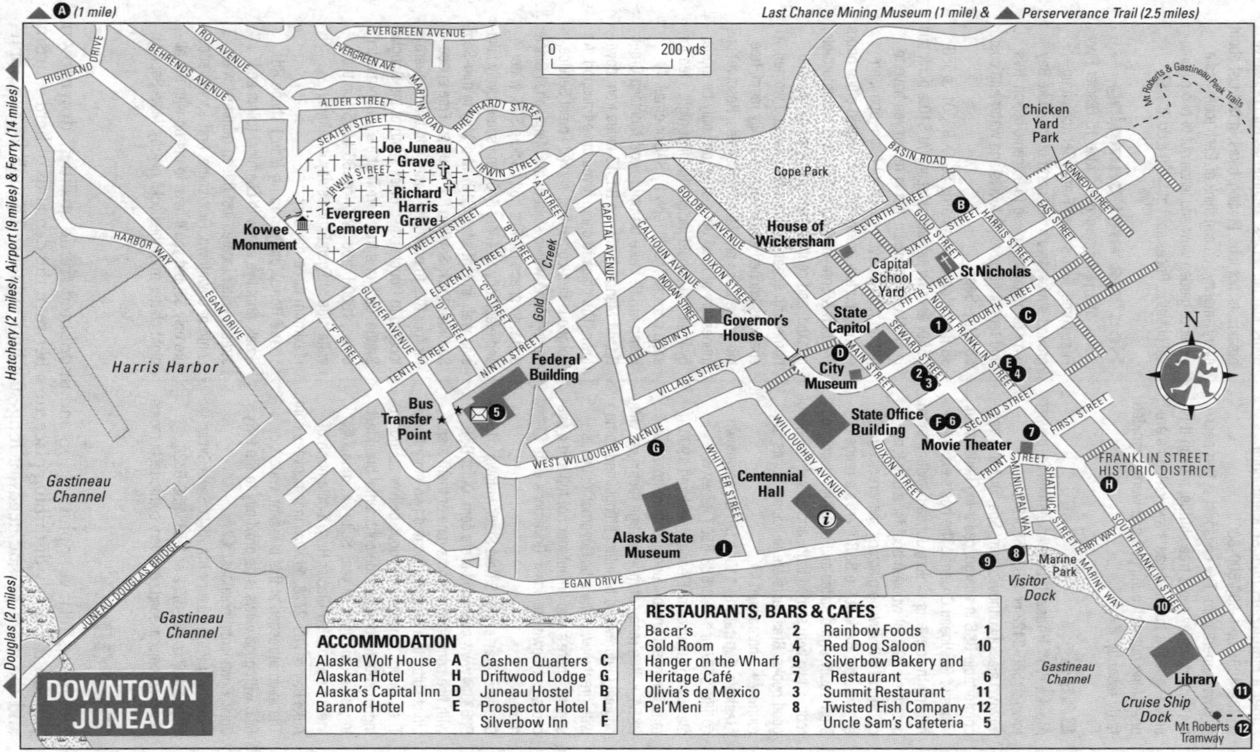

DOWNTOWN JUNEAU
A (1 mile)
Last Chance Mining Museum (1 mile) & Perserverance Trail (2.5 miles)
Hatchery (2 miles), Airport (9 miles) & Ferry (14 miles)
Douglas (2 miles)
0 200 yds
N
Mt Roberts & Gastineau Peak Trails
Chicken Yard Park
Cope Park
House of Wickersham
Capital School Yard
St Nicholas
State Capitol
Governor's House
City Museum
State Office Building
Movie Theater
Franklin Street Historic District
Centennial Hall
Alaska State Museum
Federal Building
Bus Transfer Point
Joe Juneau Grave
Richard Harris Grave
Evergreen Cemetery
Kowee Monument
Harris Harbor
Gastineau Channel
Marine Park
Visitor Dock
Library
Cruise Ship Dock
Mt Roberts Tramway
Gold Creek
Evergreen Avenue
Evergreen Ave
Troy Avenue
Behrends Avenue
Highland Drive
Alder Street
Martin Road
Rheinhardt Street
Seater Street
Irwin Street
Harbor Way
Egan Drive
Juneau-Douglas Bridge
Twelfth Street
Eleventh Street
Tenth Street
Ninth Street
Glacier Avenue
'A' Street
'B' Street
'C' Street
'D' Street
'F' Street
Capital Avenue
Calhoun Avenue
Goldbelt Avenue
Dixon Street
Indian Street
Distin St.
Village Street
West Willoughby Avenue
Willoughby Avenue
Whittier Street
Basin Road
Kennedy Street
East Street
Harris Street
Seventh Street
Gold Street
Sixth Street
Fifth Street
Fourth Street
North Franklin Street
Seward Street
Main Street
Second Street
First Street
Front Street
Municipal Way
Shattuck Street
Ferry Way
South Franklin Street
Marine Way
ACCOMMODATION
Alaska Wolf House A
Alaskan Hotel H
Alaska's Capital Inn D
Baranof Hotel E
Cashen Quarters C
Driftwood Lodge G
Juneau Hostel B
Prospector Hotel I
Silverbow Inn F
RESTAURANTS, BARS & CAFÉS
Bacar's 2
Gold Room 4
Hanger on the Wharf 9
Heritage Café 7
Olivia's de Mexico 3
Pel'Meni 8
Rainbow Foods 1
Red Dog Saloon 10
Silverbow Bakery and Restaurant 6
Summit Restaurant 11
Twisted Fish Company 12
Uncle Sam's Cafeteria 5

the tiny downtown core is also where you're likely to spend most of your time, especially on wet days when a couple of excellent museums, the State Capitol, and the Russian Orthodox church provide suitably protected distraction. On better days the Mount Roberts Tramway gives instant access to the high country above town, and it is easy to while away an afternoon wandering the precipitous streets and perhaps strolling out to the Last Chance Mining Museum.

Much of Juneau's real commercial life has moved nine miles northwest to **Mendenhall Valley**, the largest piece of flat land around, left behind by the shrinking Mendenhall Glacier; you may well arrive here at the airport, and will likely return to visit the glacier and go hiking. Glacier Highway and the roughly parallel Egan Drive freeway link downtown Juneau with Mendenhall, passing the fascinating salmon hatchery, and Alaska's largest and most exalted brewery.

You'll have to cross Gastineau Channel by the Juneau–Douglas Bridge to reach the ruins of the **Treadwell Mine**, the most accessible of all Juneau's gold-mining remains.

Downtown: the historic district

By avoiding fires, which plagued neighboring communities, Juneau has retained much of its original architecture, particularly in the **South Franklin Street Historic District**, where the ageing upper frontages are in marked contrast to the glitz below. You could follow the self-guided walking tour outline in the *Historic Downtown Juneau* leaflet (available free from the visitor center), but a quick whip around the highlights should satisfy most people.

The town's two museums (see overleaf) are both well worth visiting, but they're perhaps best saved for a wet day. In better conditions direct your wandering to the marble porticoed entrance of the **State Capitol**, corner of Main and 4th streets (early June to late Aug Mon–Fri 9am–4.30pm, Sat 12.30–4.30pm), a six-story brick monster built in 1931 as the Territorial Capitol. Follow a self-guided tour (leaflet from reception) or join the free, guided tour (30min) around the corridors of power. You'd have to have a deep interest in Alaskan politics to appreciate seeing the Finance Committee Room where they passed legislation establishing the Permanent Fund Dividend, or the chamber where, in 1945, Natives were given the right to sit in restaurants with whites, but it is made all the more interesting by a superb collection of Alaskan photos lining the walls. Outside, there's a replica Liberty Bell which, at statehood, was struck seven times by seven people to denote the creation of the 49th state.

Follow Fifth Street inland from the State Capitol to reach the octagonal, onion-domed **St Nicholas** Russian Orthodox Church, 326 5th St at Gold St (mid-May to Sept Mon–Sat 9am–6pm; $2 donation), perhaps the most striking building in the city. Originally built in 1894, it was mainly used by Slavic immigrants and by Tlingits who, when virtually forced to accept Christianity, chose the only one with services in Tlingit. It was restored in the 1970s and continues in use today with Divine Liturgy sung in English, Tlingit, and Slavonic (Sat 6pm & Sun 9am). At other times guides will explain the significance of the assorted icons and religious treasures.

Up the hill the **House of Wickersham** State Historical Site, 213 7th St (May–Sept daily except Wed 10am–noon & 1–5pm; $2 suggested donation; Ⓣ586-9001, Ⓦwww.dnr.state.ak.us), is the historic home of Alaska's pioneering judge, statehood advocate, and general polymath. The enthusiastic and well-informed guide leads you around the house (kept much as it was when Wickersham purchased it in 1928), giving a flavor of the man and the times in which he lived.

Weave down Dixon Street, off Goldbelt Avenue, and you could ring Frank and Nancy Murkowski's doorbell at the 1912 **Governor's House**, 716 Calhoun Ave, a Greek Revival style antebellum affair that's easily the grandest house on the downtown skyline.

While you're up this way, head over to **Evergreen Cemetery**, which contains a monument to Chief Kowee (next to Glacier Ave) and the graves of Joe Juneau and Richard Harris (opposite each other near Irwin St). Following Glacier Highway back to town you pass the Federal Building, 709 W 9th St, which contains the main post office, the bargain *Uncle Sam's Cafeteria*, a tiny and uninteresting museum, and a small room set aside as a time capsule. You can peer inside, but since it was only encapsulated in 1994 there's little that is surprising.

Downtown: the museums

One of Juneau's essential sights is the **Alaska State Museum**, 395 Whittier St (mid-May to mid-Sept daily 8.30am–5.30pm; mid-Sept to mid-May Tues–Sat 10am–4pm; summer $5, winter $3; Ⓦ www.museum.state.ak.us), which rivals the main museums in Anchorage and Fairbanks for its broad coverage of Alaska's culture and history. Much of the content is similar to what you'll see in museums all over Alaska, but nowhere is it better displayed, or interpreted, often with conceptualizing text alongside. The Russian era is especially well covered, balanced between the historical perspective – they have the logbook in which Bering reported his first sighting of Alaska – and the domestic, with samovars, period furniture, and some luminous icons. Panels explaining the circumpolar distribution of Eskimos (as far east as Greenland) stand beside a hunter seated in his kayak decked out in a seal-gut parka. The Eskimo carvings, very expressive in their simplicity, are especially beautiful. Elsewhere, the powerfully carved Frog House replicates one from Klukwan, the last Chilkat village, with the meaning of each element in the design clearly explained. To reach the museum's upper level you follow a ramp that curls around a tree with an eagle's nest. The birds are stuffed, but this is likely to be your best chance to appreciate the immense size of an eagle's nest. None of this is overwhelming, but you might want to take the kids to the hands-on Discovery Room.

Outside stands *Nimbus*, a modern sheet-metal sculpture in an off shade of green. Originally located near the corner of 4th and Main streets, it was so reviled that the citizens eventually had it removed and replaced with *Windfall Fisherman*, a bronze sculpture of that Alaskan archetype, the bear fishing for salmon.

You can see the bear on your way up to the **Juneau–Douglas City Museum**, corner of Main and 4th streets (mid-May to Sept Mon–Fri 9am–5pm, Sat & Sun 10am–5pm; Oct to mid-May Fri & Sat noon–4pm; summer $3, winter $2), which gives a vivid picture of how Juneau's past fits into the broader statewide picture. Drills, crucibles, ore samples, carbide lamps, assay scales, and a scale model of the fourteen underground levels of the Perseverance Mine reflect the institution's origins as a mining museum, an impression reinforced by the excellent "Juneau: City Built on Gold" documentary detailing the early history of Juneau, with a particular focus on the hard-rock gold mining. But this is more than a mining museum. In addition to major temporary exhibitions and displays of local artwork, there's also a wonderfully accurate relief model of how Juneau was in 1967 (witness the extent of the Mendenhall Glacier just thirty-some years ago) and plenty on the city's maritime past. Be sure to look for the photo of the *Princess May,* which was wrecked on nearby Sentinel Island at high tide. When the water level dropped the hull was left stranded high and dry, 30ft above the water. Notice the retouching where the anchor chain should have been.

If all the mining history has ignited a spark, consider buying the useful leaflets covering the Perseverance Trail and the Treadwell Mine.

The Tramway and Last Chance Mining Museum

For a bird's-eye view of downtown, and much more, take the **Mount Roberts Tramway**, 490 S Franklin St (early May to late Sept daily 9am–9pm; $22; Ⓦwww.goldbelttours.com), which deposits you on a relatively level area 1800ft up Mount Roberts. Here, several gentle and moderate walks fan out from a restaurant and nature center where an 18-minute-long video, *Seeing Daylight*, focuses on Tlingit culture – the tramway is run by Goldbelt, the local Native Corporation. Your ticket is valid for as many rides as you want all day, but you still might prefer to hike up (see box, p.152), then pay just $5 to ride down (or make $5 worth of purchases at the tram-top restaurant).

You'll have to go a couple of miles inland to see the **Last Chance Mining Museum** (mid-May to late Sept daily 9.30am–12.30pm & 3.30–6.30pm; $4), around forty minutes' walk from downtown at the end of Basin Road. The hands-on museum features tools, machines, and infrastructure from what was once the world's largest and most advanced hard-rock gold mine. Buildings that once held the assay office, blacksmith shops, and locomotive repair shops now contain displays, antiques, minerals, and the 3-D glass map of the mine tunnels and massive "glory holes" inside the mountain.

Towards Mendenhall Valley and the Mendenhall Glacier

Three miles north of downtown, Egan Drive charges past the **Macaulay Salmon Hatchery**, 2697 Channel Drive (May–Sept Mon–Fri 10am–6pm, Sat & Sun 10am–5pm; $3; Ⓣ1-877/463-2486, Ⓦwww.dipac.net), one of the best places in the state to learn the intricacies of artificially rearing salmon. Although it is very much a working hatchery, responsible for stocking streams throughout the region, the site was partly designed with visitors in mind.

The salmon return, but not the profits

Returns are not what they were in the salmon industry. Every year swarms of salmon from all five Pacific species struggle from the ocean to their birthplace in the headwaters of northern rivers to spawn, and dozens of Alaskan communities rely on the annual bounty. Some years the numbers are low, and whenever small returns occur in consecutive years the newspapers are full of hand-wringing articles about the demise of the wild salmon fishery. These years always seem to be followed by a bumper harvest the next season and the trawlers are back in business.

But recently everyone has been hurting, no matter how abundant the fish. Diminished sales to the once-lucrative but now depressed Japanese market don't help, but prices are down across the board. And the blame is laid squarely on the salmon-farming industry, now thriving in Chile and Canada. Throughout Alaska, bumper stickers urge "Don't let friends eat farmed salmon," as concerned citizens try to stem the seemingly inevitable switch to the farmed product. Wild salmon is pure, natural, tastes great, and doesn't have to be fed dye-laden food to make the flesh pink. But its farmed cousin is available fresh throughout the year, always looks and tastes the same (even if it isn't quite as succulent and firm), and most of all is cheap. And that suits the restaurant and supermarket trade just fine thank you very much.

Salmon farming has been banned in Alaska since 1990, so even if aquaculturists hold all the cards in your neighborhood, the least you can do when in Alaska is support the small fishing communities and eat plenty of local wild salmon.

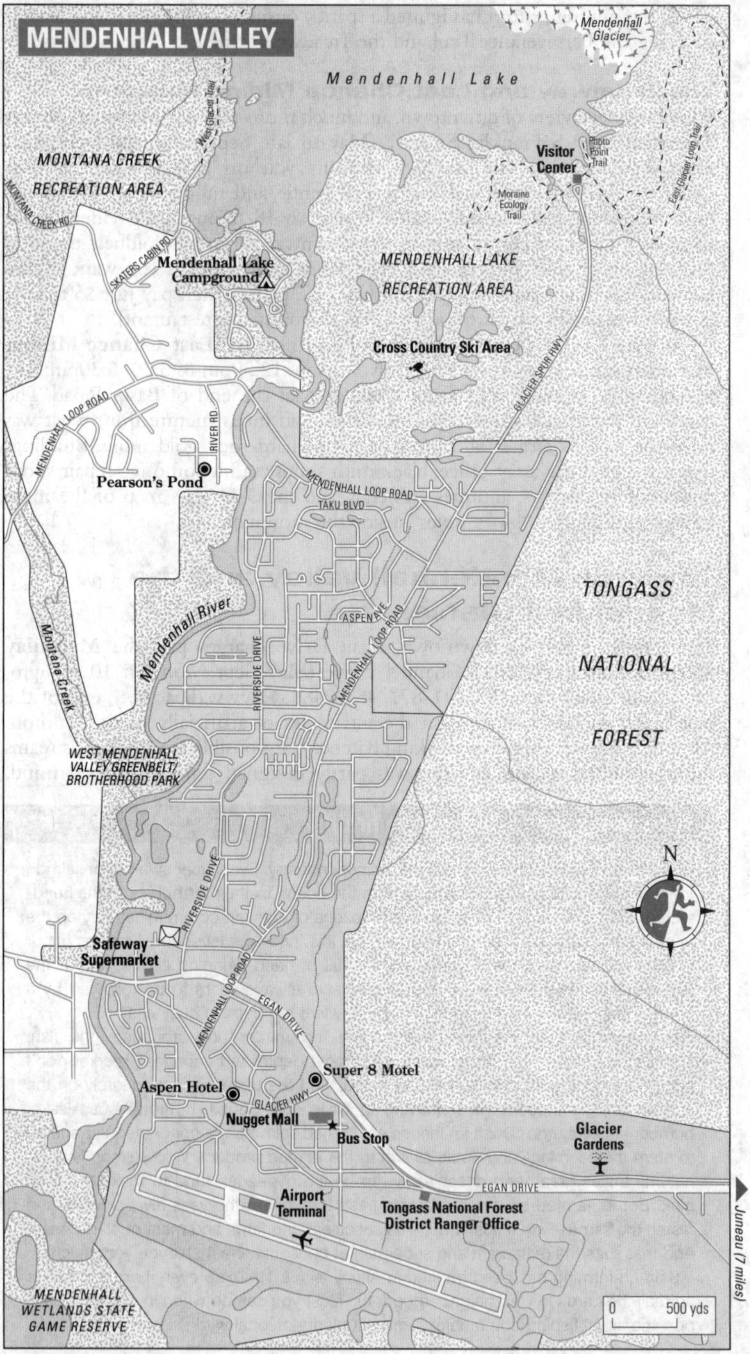
MENDENHALL VALLEY
Mendenhall Glacier
Mendenhall Lake
West Glacier Trail
MONTANA CREEK
RECREATION AREA
MONTANA CREEK RD
Visitor Center
Photo Point Trail
Moraine Ecology Trail
East Glacier Loop Trail
SKATERS CABIN RD
Mendenhall Lake Campground
MENDENHALL LAKE
RECREATION AREA
Cross Country Ski Area
GLACIER SPUR HWY
MENDENHALL LOOP ROAD
RIVER RD.
Pearson's Pond
TAKU BLVD
TONGASS
NATIONAL
FOREST
Mendenhall River
ASPEN AVE
RIVERSIDE DRIVE
Montana Creek
WEST MENDENHALL
VALLEY GREENBELT/
BROTHERHOOD PARK
N
Safeway
Supermarket
EGAN DRIVE
Super 8 Motel
Aspen Hotel
GLACIER HWY
Nugget Mall
Bus Stop
Glacier
Gardens
Airport
Terminal
Tongass National Forest
District Ranger Office
Juneau (7 miles)
MENDENHALL
WETLANDS STATE
GAME RESERVE
0
500 yds

Inside, large saltwater aquariums are filled with local sea creatures in something akin to their natural environment, while outside you can follow walkways overlooking the entire hatchery process from pink and chum salmon struggling up the 450-foot-long fish ladder (the longest in the state), through various stages of development up to ready for release. The fish only run from late June to October, so in the early part of the season you are shown the incubation room instead. Anglers with the appropriate state license ($10 for one day, $15 for three) can dip a line in the water (rentals $5 an hour, $26 a day) with a fair chance of bagging their limit in double-quick time. If you're arriving by bus, ask the driver the best spot to get off and reboard.

City buses also pass through the suburb of Lemon Creek, five miles north of downtown, where you'll find the **Alaskan Brewing Co**, 5429 Shaune Drive (May–Sept daily 11am–5pm; Oct–April Thurs–Sat 11am–4.30pm; free; Ⓣ780-5866, Ⓦwww.alaskanbeer.com), which was one of the first microbreweries in the United States (it was founded in 1986) and is now Alaska's largest brewer. The twenty-minute tour mostly involves looking at half a dozen stainless-steel tanks while they explain the process, but it does entitle you to a free tasting of their award-winning brews.

A couple of miles further out, adversity has been channeled to good effect at **Glacier Gardens**, 7600 Glacier Way (May–Sept daily 9am–6pm; $18; Ⓣ790-3377, Ⓦwww.glaciergardens.com), the site of a devastating mudslide in 1984 and now a landscaped woodland garden. It costs nothing to see their signature display of upturned tree trunks (salvaged from the mudslide) festooned with brightly colored begonias, petunias, and fuchsias in hanging baskets, a curiously arresting sight. But the entry price seems high to see the rest of the garden, a hillside of spruce and hemlocks mostly visited on a golf-cart tour through the woods up to a good viewpoint high above Gastineau Channel.

There are certainly bigger and more spectacular glaciers in Alaska, but the twelve-mile-long, one-and-a-half-mile-wide **Mendenhall Glacier**, thirteen miles north of downtown, is one of the most accessible. You can drive within a mile of the face and gaze across Mendenhall Lake at the huge sheet of white creeping down from the immense Juneau Icefield. When John Muir saw the glacier in 1879, it ended halfway down the valley where the suburb of Mendenhall now lies, but like most glaciers in Alaska it has been retreating rapidly, leaving behind all sorts of geological evidence of its passage. Should your knowledge of cirques and striations be a little rusty, there's detailed explanation, along with a wonderful relief map of the Juneau Icefield and an entertaining ten-minute video, inside the Forest Service's Mendenhall Glacier Visitor Center (May–Sept daily 8am–6.30pm, $3; Oct–April Thurs & Fri 10am–4pm, Sat & Sun 9am–4pm, free; Ⓣ789-0097), located on a point occupied by the glacier as recently as 1940. If this inspires, consider joining one of the Forest Service's hour-plus **nature hikes** (late May to early Sept daily 10am & 2pm; free). The morning one is the better of the two and follows the educational Moraine Ecology Trail (1.5-mile loop; 40min–1hr; negligible ascent). This trail and the handicap-accessible Photo Point Trail (0.6 miles round-trip; 20min; negligible ascent) are the shortest of the local walks and therefore the most popular. Three longer trails are listed in the box overleaf.

Getting to the glacier without your own transport isn't too difficult: Capital Transit buses leave hourly from downtown and pass Glacier Spur Road, where you need to get off and walk the final mile or so. A visit to Mendenhall Glacier is also pretty much *de rigueur* on any of the Juneau city tours (see p.143): about the cheapest is with MGT (Ⓣ789-5460), which offers a two-hour city tour for $20 and also provides a $5 (each way) shuttle service from downtown.

Glacier Highway

Beyond the suburb of Mendenhall Valley and the airport, Glacier Highway continues past Auke Lake and the University of Alaska Juneau campus, and then passes the AMHS ferry dock at Auke Bay. The road ends forty miles north of Juneau, though there is perennial talk of creating a ninety-mile road link to Skagway and the outside world. With Governor Frank Murkowski firmly behind the idea, the project looks more likely to go ahead than ever before – though boosters still have to contend with a groundswell of opposition in Juneau to any outside road connection.

Glacier Highway is only worth exploring if you've got your own transport, in which case you could call in at the **Shrine of St Therese**, Mile 23 (generally open daily 8.30am–10pm in summer; donations appreciated), an attractive little church on a promontory accessed by a five-minute walk along a narrow spit. Built from beach stones in the 1930s and surrounded by the Stations of the Cross, the church is now very popular for weddings, and the spit is a favored spot for anglers keen to bag kings, silvers, and pinks from the shore.

The highway ends close to **Point Bridget State Park**, Mile 39, a forested area overlooking Lynn Canal, with three short trails and a couple of rental cabins ($35; ⓣ465-4563). Push on a mile to very end of the road and you can

Hikes around Juneau

Juneau is unmatched in Southeast for the number of top-quality trails accessible from the road system, many of which are easily approached either from downtown or by the city bus out to the Mendenhall Valley. Glaciers, forests, alpine high country, the remains of gold mines, and abundant wildlife make for a varied selection of trails, some easy and some fairly demanding.

If you are planning to spend a few days hiking in the area, it is definitely worth purchasing the plasticized inch-to-a-mile *Juneau Area Trails Guide* ($10); otherwise make do with the free leaflets from the Forest Service visitor center.

Only one of the hikes listed below passes a Forest Service cabin, but there are loads of them in the area. The more accessible cabins – whether you're arriving on foot, on skis, by float plane, or by boat – are all frequently used by Juneau residents. Getting one at short notice should be possible during the week, but weekends will be more difficult. The Forest Service desk at the main visitor center (see p.143) has good information about the location of cabins, but for availability and reservations contact ReserveUSA (ⓣ1-877/444-6777, ⓦwww.ReserveUSA.com).

From Downtown Juneau

Perseverance Trail, **Granite Creek Trail**, and **Mount Juneau Trail** (1–10hr). The most popular and easily accessed system of trails in Juneau, suitable for a couple of hours of easy valley strolling or an overnight hike along a rugged alpine ridge with stupendous views. The Perseverance Trail (3 miles round-trip; 2–4hr; 700ft ascent; $1 historic trail guide from the City Museum) follows Perseverance Creek to Silverbow Basin, where the Perseverance Mine operated intermittently from 1885 to 1921. Be very careful when exploring the old mine workings. The Granite Creek Trail and Mount Juneau Trail both spur off the Perseverance Trail and can be linked up using the Mount Juneau Ridge Route, creating a ten-hour expedition. There are no cabins along the way, but Granite Creek has a couple of lovely places to camp. The trailhead is 2.5 miles from downtown at the end of Basin Road. There's no public transport but you could grab a taxi or just walk from town.

Mount Roberts Trail (9 miles round-trip; 5–6hr; 3800ft ascent). A moderately difficult trail to the summit of Mount Roberts, switchbacking and climbing all the way, with increasingly good views and plenty of wildlife. You don't have to do the whole

camp free for as long as you wish at **Echo Cove**. There are no facilities, so bring everything you need.

Douglas and the Treadwell Mine

Downtown Juneau is connected by a road bridge to **Douglas Island**, a mountainous, forest-clad place that partly acts as a dormitory suburb for Juneau. There was a brief time around 1910 when the city of **DOUGLAS** was the largest in Southeast Alaska because of the employment opportunities at the Treadwell Mine. Like all of Juneau's mines, the Treadwell relied on economies of scale to turn a profit, processing huge quantities of low-grade ore to extract the valuable metal – $67 million worth between 1882 and 1922. At one stage it was the most extensive gold-mining operation in the world, supporting a town of 15,000 people and burrowing 2800ft below Gastineau Channel. In 1917 a serious cave-in and the subsequent flooding closed all but one shaft, and work ceased entirely by 1922, just four years before the whole place burned to the ground. Today most of the mine buildings have been enveloped by the regenerating alder and spruce forest, with saplings sprouting from the moldering concrete shells of buildings, hulks of old machinery rusting quietly, and

thing, since the trail passes the upper station for the Mount Roberts Tramway (2 miles one-way; 1hr to 1hr 30min; 1800ft ascent), where there's a nature center and a possible ride down in the tram for $5 (or $5 worth of purchases at the tram-top restaurant). Continue a little further on and you come to a wooden cross, a replica of one erected up here in 1908 by a local Jesuit priest, Father Brown. The trail starts downtown from the top of 6th Street.

From Mendenhall Valley

East Glacier Loop Trail (3.5-mile loop; 2–3hr; 400ft ascent). Moderate trail from the Mendenhall Glacier visitor center around the east of Mendenhall Lake, with good views of the glacier, though more distant than those from the West Glacier Trail. The upper portion of the trail passes the remains of an old wooden flume and rail tram left over from a Nugget Creek hydropower project that was designed to provide energy to the Treadwell Mill in 1911. A 600-foot tunnel drilled for the project (which was taken over by the Alaska-Juneau Mine) spews the water that creates the A-J waterfall, visible from the trail. Midway round the **Nugget Creek Trail** (add 5 miles round-trip; 3hr; 300ft ascent) spurs up Nugget Creek to the free-use Vista Creek Shelter.

West Glacier Trail (7 miles round-trip; 4–6hr; 1300ft ascent). Excellent and fairly tough hike that skirts the northwestern side of Mendenhall Lake before climbing through alder and willow to a scenic overlook. There are great views of icefalls and even access to ice caves on the glacier (don't explore unless you know what you're doing and have the proper equipment). The trail is generally in good condition but deteriorates into a series of rock cairns near the end. You can continue for another couple of miles to the summit of Mount McGinnis, making it a full-day outing. The trailhead is on Skaters Cabin Road, about a mile from the Capital Transit bus stop at the junction of Montana Creek Road and Mendenhall Loop Road.

On Douglas Island

Dan Moller Trail (6.5 miles round-trip; 3–5hr; 1800ft ascent). A moderate trail ending high in an alpine cirque where there is a Forest Service cabin ($35; ⓣ1-877/444-6777). The trail starts close to the junction of Cordova and Foster streets (bus stop): follow Pioneer Street and the trailhead is by the fifth house.

several rows of pilings from long-gone wharves running out into the channel. The remains are threaded by the **Treadwell Mine Historic Trail**, a network of paths and numbered markers, which are meaningless without the *Treadwell Mine Historic Trail* explanatory leaflet (50¢) available from the City Museum.

Capital Transit's Douglas **bus** runs every half-hour to downtown Douglas, from where you can wander past the Douglas boat harbor to **Sandy Beach Park**, a small strand created from the tailings from the mine. The Treadwell Mine Historic Trail starts at the southern end of the park. There are a couple of cafés in Douglas, if you can't wait until you get back to town, but the only real reason to stick around is to attend a performance at the Perseverance Theatre (see p.156).

Flightseeing, rafting, and kayaking

A visit to the Mendenhall Glacier only gives you a tiny sense of what lies behind the immense 1500-square-mile Juneau Icefield, which feeds close to forty glaciers, some creaking down the hills behind Juneau, others flowing the other way into Canada. The easiest and cheapest way to see all this is on a scenic plane flight with Wings of Alaska (Ⓣ789-0790, Ⓦwww.wingsofalaska.com), which charges $145 for a 45-minute flight. **Helicopter flights** are an increasingly popular way to tour the area. Temsco (Ⓣ789-9501 or 1-877/789-9501, Ⓦwww.temscoair.com) offers a 55-minute Mendenhall Glacier Tour ($190), including a 25-minute glacier landing, and a ninety-minute variation ($290) with two glacier landings. Coastal Helicopters (Ⓣ789-5600 or 1-800/789-5610, Ⓦwww.coastalhelicopters.com) does one-hour overflights ($173) and ninety-minute trips with glacier landing ($290) and also offers Dog Sled Tours ($365) involving two scenic flights sandwiching a spin across the glacier on a sled towed by six dogs. North Star Trekking (Ⓣ790-4530, Ⓦwww.glaciertrekking.com) offers a helicopter flight with time spent hiking across a glacier decked out in crampons and trekking poles. The gentle Walkabout ($249) gives about an hour on the ice, though you can double this on the slightly more strenuous Trek ($319) or opt for up to four hours on the X-Trek ($439), which includes some roped ice climbing.

If you're heading to Skagway and fancy some tremendous **flightseeing** over Glacier Bay National Park (see p.159), go with Skagway Air Service (Ⓣ789-2006, Ⓦwww.skagwayair.com), which will include a diversion over Glacier Bay on their scheduled flight between Juneau and Skagway ($160).

Staying closer to Juneau, the Mendenhall River offers the only **rafting** in these parts, with a little low-grade whitewater and a good deal of even gentler stuff with guides explaining the local natural history. Auk Ta Shaa ($100; Ⓣ586-8687 or 1-800/820-2628) and Alaska Travel Adventures ($95; Ⓣ789-0052 or 1-800/478-0052, Ⓦwww.alaskaadventures.com) both run trips spending a couple of hours on the water.

Out on the Inside Passage, several opportunities exist for **kayaking**, either on guided tours or on your own, just paddling around the islands in Auke Bay with kayaks rented locally (see p.156). Alaska Travel Adventures runs gentle three-and-a-half-hour trips around the bay (May–Sept; $76), mainly geared to cruise-ship passengers, while Auk Ta Shaa organizes six-hour trips ranging slightly further for $79. For more dedicated kayaking, go with Alaska Discovery (Ⓣ780-6226 or 1-800/586-1911), which has a good selection of multiday trips to Tracy Arm and Pack Creek (see "Around Juneau," p.157).

Eating, drinking, and entertainment

As the largest town in Southeast Alaska, not to mention the state capital, you'd expect a decent range of restaurants and bars, but this is still only a town of

30,000 and your choices are fairly limited. Most of the worthwhile places are downtown, and there's little reason to go elsewhere, except perhaps to Douglas for the Perseverance Theatre. That said, there are enough **restaurants** to keep you well fed for a few days. South Franklin and Front streets have so far resisted the downtown gentrification and retain a number of dark **bars** where back-slapping camaraderie prevails. Of these, you may find the places we've listed more convivial than most.

For **entertainment listings**, the best source is the "Preview" section of Thursday afternoon's *Juneau Empire*. One regular piece of entertainment is the free **organ recital** on Fridays at noon in the State Office Building, 333 Willoughby Ave, home to numerous Alaskan government departments and always referred to as the SOB (which locals seem to think is amusing, if not a little risqué).

Cafés and restaurants

Bacar's 230 Seward St ⓣ463-5091. Quirky little restaurant that's not much to look at, but is worth seeking out for all-day breakfast ($6–9), and clam chowder and burger lunches ($8–11). Daily 6am–3pm.

Chan's Thai Kitchen 11280 Glacier Hwy ⓣ789-9777. No-frills eatery dishing out excellent Thai dishes for under $10. Reasonably handy for the ferry terminal, a mile to the west. Closed Sun & Mon.

Gold Room 127 N Franklin St ⓣ586-2660. One of Juneau's finest restaurants in a subdued sky-lit room in the heart of the *Baranof Hotel*, all white linen tablecloths and refined atmosphere. Start with grilled rock shrimp skewers ($9) and follow with a seafood sample platter ($19) or pan-seared game hen with caramelized pears and onions ($19).

The Hanger on the Wharf Merchants Wharf ⓣ586-5018. Although mostly a place to drink (see overleaf), the *Hanger* serves wraps and burgers at lunch and the likes of jambalaya and halibut tacos ($9–12) at dinner.

Heritage Café Emporium Mall, 174 S Franklin St ⓣ586-1087. About the best café in Juneau, with good espresso, lunch specials, soups, and sandwiches.

Olivia's de Mexico 222 Seward St ⓣ586-6870. Juneau's most authentic Mexican may be tucked away in a basement, but it produces excellent mole and fajitas along with the expected staples. Closed Sun.

Pel'Meni 2 Marine Way ⓣ463-2630. Dave keeps threatening to expand his repertoire, but he currently serves just one item, a $5 helping of the Russian dish that gives this restaurant its name. These mini-dumplings are made from spicy ground sirloin wrapped in fresh pasta dough, which is boiled and topped with hot sauce, curry powder, and cilantro – they're good anytime but especially after a drinking session at one of the Front St bars. The varied clientele also hangs out, selecting something from the eclectic collection of vinyl.

Rainbow Foods 224 4th St ⓣ586-6476. Wholefood and organic grocery that also has sandwich lunches and an extensive notice board full of holistic classes and massage workshops.

Silverbow Bakery and Restaurant 120 2nd St ⓣ586-4146. Out front there's a wonderfully relaxed eat-in bakery and coffee bar with big windows that on a good day catch the morning sun. Bagels and superb pastries bolster a menu of homemade breads used in hot and cold deli sandwiches ($6–11). The *Back Room* restaurant has one of the most varied and imaginative menus in town, with everything from salads and soups ($6–9) to kielbasa and pirogies ($12), Indonesian peanut pasta with either tofu or chicken ($13) and vegetarian burgers ($9). The restaurant is only open on Sat, when there's a movie or gig on (see overleaf).

Summit Restaurant 455 S Franklin St ⓣ586-2050. White linen tablecloths and crystal stemware set the tone for this small restaurant, which serves the likes of vodka-cured lox and crème fraiche ($11), pecan-crusted halibut with yam puree ($23), and lime tart with blueberry coulis ($6). Reservations essential.

Twisted Fish Company 550 S Franklin St ⓣ463-5033. Bustling waterfront restaurant with a cosmopolitan feel, an extensive wine list, and a wide-ranging menu centered on fish and gourmet pizzas. Naturally salmon and halibut get a high billing, whether eating inside or out at the salmon bake on the dockside. Personal pizzas and appetizers around $12, main courses $18–25.

Uncle Sam's Cafeteria 2nd floor, 709 W 9th St ⓣ586-3430. Low-cost dining with a view, inside the Federal Building. Open for breakfast ($4) from 7am, then lunches including daily specials ($6) such as taco salad or chicken fried steak. Closes 4pm.

Bars

Alaskan Hotel Bar 167 S Franklin St. Ancient bar dating back to 1913 and still exuding a raucous atmosphere, with live music most nights (especially weekends) which might be anything from funk to bluegrass, an open-mic night on Thursday and plenty of bar propping anytime.

The Hanger on the Wharf (see p.155). Renovated, historic float-plane hanger right on the wharf, with one glass wall that gives a tremendous view of the waterfront. There are over twenty beers on tap, pool tables on the mezzanine, and a lively atmosphere, especially on weekends when there's live rock or jazz.

Red Dog Saloon 278 S Franklin St ⓣ463-3777. Straightforward, sawdust-on-the-floor tourist trap and merchandizing empire masquerading as a raucous, historic bar. Musicians get the cruise-ship crowd going from around 2pm. Pretty quiet once the boats leave.

Theaters and shows

20th Century Theater 222 Front St ⓣ586-4055. Shows first-run movies nightly.

Back Room Cinema 120 2nd St ⓣ586-4146 or 1-800/586-4146. Part of the *Silverbow* hotel and bakery complex, this restaurant and movie theater in one shows cult, classic, and recent independent releases on Saturday nights. Best of all it's only $4, plus a minimum $5 food or drink order, though there are also full meals available while you view.

Perseverance Theatre 914 3rd St, Douglas ⓣ364-2421, ⓦwww.perseverancetheatre.org. Alaska's largest professional theater and one of the nation's foremost regional houses, presenting revisions of classic texts, cutting-edge works, and new plays by Alaskan playwrights. Paula Vogel's Pulitzer Prize-winning *The Mineola Twins* premiered here in 1996. Sadly, summer is usually a quiet time for the theater.

Listings

Banks Several with 24hr ATMs in the downtown area, including Wells Fargo, 123 Seward St (ⓣ586-3324). There is nowhere to exchange foreign currency.

Bookshops The most extensive selection is at Hearthside Books, either downtown at 254 Front St (ⓣ586-1725, ⓦwww.hearthsidebooks.com) or in the Nugget Mall close to the airport (ⓣ789-2750), the latter good for whiling away an hour between flights. Rainy Day Books, 113 Seward St (ⓣ463-2665), is good for new and used books.

Car rental Almost all the rental agencies are located at the airport, but most will drop off downtown. Evergreen Ford (ⓣ789-9386 or 1-888/267-9300 in Southeast), Avis (ⓣ789-9450), and Budget (ⓣ790-1086) all cost roughly $50 per day. If you're looking to save, call Rent-A-Wreck (ⓣ789-4111), which is around $40 a day plus 30¢ a mile after the first hundred, or Mendenhall Auto Center (ⓣ789-1386 or 1-800/478-1386), which has similar prices.

Climbing wall Looking for a wet-day diversion? Try the Rock Dump, 1310 Eastaugh Way (ⓣ586-4982, ⓦwww.rockdump.com), Alaska's largest climbing gym, which charges $10 all day until 10pm and rents gear at bargain prices. About a mile south of town along S Franklin St.

Ferries The AMHS's main ticket office is at 6858 Glacier Hwy (Mon–Fri 8am–5pm; reservations ⓣ465-3941, schedule info ⓣ465-3940).

Festivals The Alaska Folk Festival (ⓣ364-3316) in mid-April involves a week of performances, workshops, jams, and dances, mostly in Centennial Hall; the Juneau Jazz and Classics Festival (ⓣ463-3378) takes place during the third week of May. On July 3 Juneau sets off its fireworks to celebrate the arrival of July 4 and the ensuing parade and carnival.

Internet access The library (see below) has free use and 15min express machines if you can't be bothered signing up in advance. For more immediate needs try Great NETspectations, 211 Front St (ⓣ586-5888), or Seaport Cyber Station, 175 S Franklin St (ⓣ586-8676).

Kayak rentals Auke Bay–based Juneau Outdoor Center (ⓣ586-8220, ⓦwww.juneaukayak.com) rents out top-quality kayaks (single $45 a day, double $60) and skiffs with a 40-horse outboard: either paddle direct from Auke Bay or have them deliver ($40–60).

Laundry and showers Harbor Washboard, 1114 F St, downtown (Mon–Fri 7.30am–9pm, Sat 9am–9pm, Sun 8am–6pm; ⓣ586-1133), has a laundry facility and showers ($2). You can also shower at the *Alaskan Hotel* for $3.50 and the Augustus Brown Swimming Pool, 1619 Glacier Ave, near the north end of Douglas Bridge (ⓣ586-5325), which has showers and sauna for $3.75.

Left luggage No lockers downtown or at the Auke Bay AMHS terminal, but the *Juneau Hostel*, 614 Harris St (ⓣ586-9559), will store bags.

Library The Juneau Public Library, 292 Marine Way (Mon–Thurs 11am–9pm, Fri–Sun noon–5pm; ⓣ586-5249), has an extensive range of books and newspapers, Internet access and a great view of Gastineau Channel.

Medical assistance Bartlett Regional Hospital,

3260 Hospital Drive, 3 miles north of downtown (Ⓣ796-8900).
Outdoor equipment Foggy Mountain Sports, 134 N Franklin St (Ⓣ586-6760), stocks top-brand gear and loads of it at slightly inflated prices.
Pharmacy Juneau Drug Co, cnr Front and Seward sts (Mon–Fri 9am–9pm, Sat & Sun 9am–6pm).
Photographic supplies Front Street Photo, 220 Front St (Mon–Fri 8am–7pm, Sat & Sun 10am–5pm; Ⓣ586-FILM), has the best supply of specialist photographic gear and film.
Post office Inside the Federal Building, 709 W 9th St (Mon–Fri 9am–5pm). The **General Delivery** zip code is 99801.
Taxes Juneau has a six percent sales tax; the bed tax is twelve percent and has been included in our price codes.
Taxis Juneau Taxi & Tours Ⓣ790-4511; Capital Cab Ⓣ586-2772.
Travel agency US Travel, 111 S Seward St Ⓣ463-5446 or 1-800/478-2423, Ⓦwww.ustravelak.com.

Around Juneau

Though two or three days might suffice for seeing Juneau, you could easily use it as a base from which to make frequent forays into its hinterland by boat and plane. Day cruises head south to the hairline fjord of **Tracy Arm**, a vast granite and ice wonderland that also lends itself to extended exploration by kayak. When the salmon are running, brown bears find themselves sharing **Pack Creek** with humans eager to watch them gnawing on fish and fattening up for winter. Either drop in for a few hours during the day, or visit by kayak and spend a couple of days in the area camping nearby.

For extended trips away from Juneau, the prime destination is **Glacier Bay National Park**, often the place around which people build their entire Alaskan vacation. We cover it, along with the humpback-whale-watching territory of **Point Adolphus**, in the section beginning on p.159.

Tracy Arm fjord

If you would like to visit Glacier Bay but don't really have the time or money, consider the cost-effective eight-hour trip to Tracy Arm fjord, which cuts deeply into the Coast Mountains 45 miles south of Juneau. The glaciers may not be quite as spectacular, but the scenery is definitely on a par with its more exalted neighbor. There's never more than a mile between the sheer waterfall-fringed cliffs that frame your approach to the head of the thirty-mile-long fjord and the North Sawyer and South Sawyer glaciers. At any time these may be calving, but even if they're not there are always seals basking on the ice floes, mountain goats high up on the almost barren hills, and possibly dolphins and whales frolicking in the channels. John Muir was impressed when he visited in 1879; he said it reminded him of his beloved Yosemite, but then much of Southeast had the same effect on him.

The most popular way to visit is on the Tracy Arm Fjord Glacier Day Cruise (mid-May to early Sept Tues, Thurs & Sat at 8.45am; $119; Ⓣ586-8687 or 1-800/820-2628, Ⓦwww.goldbelttours.com), a fast catamaran which departs from beside the cruise-ship dock downtown, returning eight hours later. For a slightly more personal touch, go with Adventure Bound Alaska (Ⓣ463-2509 or 1-800/228-3875; $105), which runs a smaller, single-hulled boat from the north end of Marine Park. Being smaller, the boat can get in a little closer through the densely packed icebergs, but the single hull means they go slower, extending the day from 8.15am to 6pm.

The fjord is also a popular destination for kayakers. Alaska Discovery (see Basics, p.11) runs a fairly adventurous seven-day paddling and camping trip here for $2200, including a charter-boat drop-off and pickup. You can also go it alone using rental kayaks (see "Listings," p.156), getting dropped off and picked up by water taxi (around $120 each).

Bear viewing at Pack Creek

Douglas Island separates Juneau from the northern tip of Admiralty Island, a hundred-mile-long landmass of rugged 4000-foot-high mountains cloaked in temperate forests known to the Tlingit as Kootznoowoo or "fortress of the bears." There is said to be a greater concentration of brown bears here than anywhere else in the world, and despite the town of Angoon sharing the island, the bears outnumber people. That's not to say you fall over them wherever you go – there is still only one per square mile – so in an effort to guarantee a sighting, most people head straight to the **Stan Price State Wildlife Sanctuary** at Pack Creek, on the east side of the island. From June to mid-September the

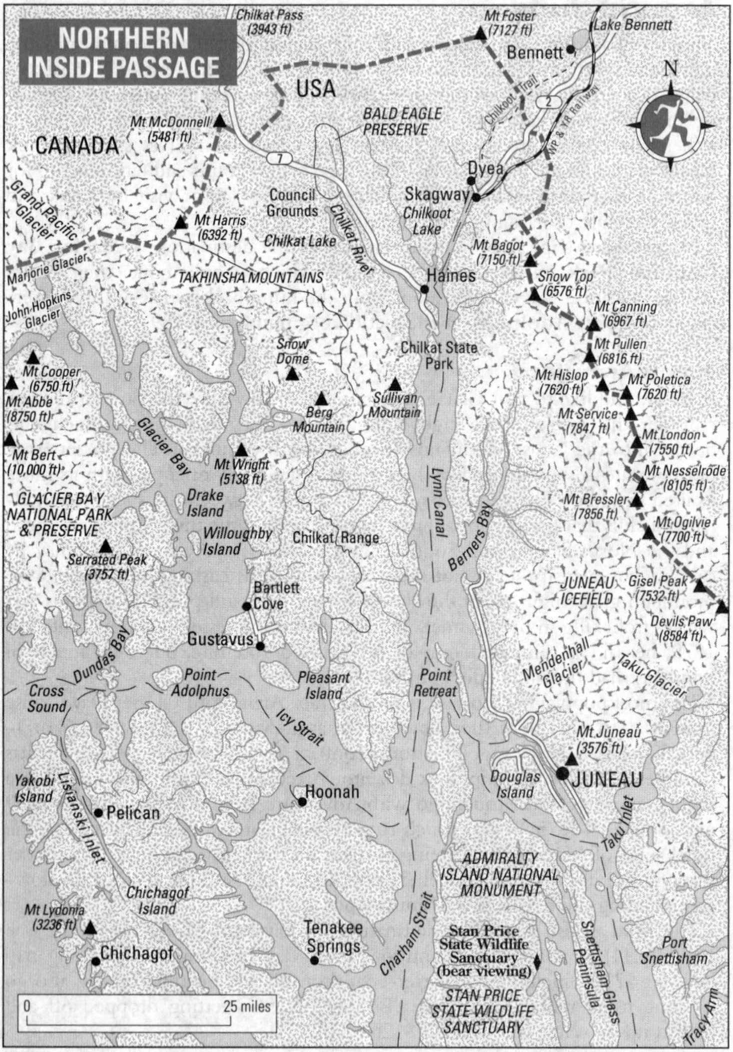

pink and chum salmon are running and bears flock to the tidal flats around the Seymore Canal and to Pack Creek itself. Hunting was banned here back in the 1930s and brown bears have become used to having people watching them fish in what is considered a textbook case of low-stress habituation. The number of float planes landing each day does drive away some of the bears, but you can still expect to see three or four on an average day.

To help preserve this benign situation, the area has been designated for day-use only, so most people visit from Juneau on a day trip. During the bear season (June–Sept 10) you'll need a viewing **permit** (June 1–July 5 & Aug 26–Sept 10 $20 a day; July 6–Aug 25 $50 a day) from the Forest Service in Juneau (see p.143) and can visit for a maximum of three days. Outside these dates no permit is needed, but then there are no fish and no bears. Permits are offered from March 1, and you'll need to get in early to get specific dates, though four permits for each day only become available three days prior to that date. It is often more effective to reserve early with one of the float-plane operators who drop off then pick up later in the day, charging around $150 round-trip: Try Wings of Alaska (Ⓣ789-0790, Ⓦwww.wingsofalaska.com). For permit application write to USFS, 8461 Old Dairy Rd (Ⓣ586-8790, downloadable at Ⓦwww.fs.fed.us/r10/tongass/districts/admiralty/packweb/applcatn.htm).

One of the best approaches is on one of the kayaking trips run by Alaska Discovery (see Basics, p.11). On their one-day trip ($495), you fly in by float plane, then kayak to Pack Creek for bear viewing and maybe hike a mile-and-a-half inland to the bear-viewing tower on Upper Pack Creek. The two-and-a-half-day trip ($985) follows the same pattern but includes two nights camped out near Pack Creek. Trips only run on certain dates and fill fast.

If you have your own boat or want to rent a kayak and paddle to Pack Creek, you'll need one of the permits described above. Kayakers need to be moderately experienced, particularly for the potentially rough crossing of Stephens Passage to Admiralty Island. Before setting off, ask for details of the tramway, which aids your portage at Oliver Inlet and saves you having to paddle right around the Glass Peninsula. Once here, you can hang around for a few days by camping half a mile away, on the east side of Windfall Island, or by staying at the Alaska State Parks' *Seymour Canal Cabin* ($35; Ⓣ465-4563) at the south end of the portage.

Pack Creek falls within the Kootznoowoo Wilderness, a section of the **Admiralty Island National Monument**, which covers most of the island. If you miss out on a Pack Creek permit, there are several other areas where bears congregate, and the adventure of going somewhere less populated can make your visit that much more appealing. The Forest Service in Juneau can provide details of likely destinations.

Glacier Bay National Park

When Captain George Vancouver sailed through Icy Strait in 1794, he didn't name Glacier Bay, largely because it didn't exist. Two hundred years ago this 65-mile-long branched fjord sixty miles west of Juneau was entirely taken up by the **Grand Pacific Glacier**, which was calving prodigious quantities of icebergs from its twenty-mile-wide 4000-foot-high face, almost choking the strait. Today, the seaward end of Glacier Bay seldom sees bergs because the Grand Pacific has reeled back 65 miles, its retreat creating Glacier Bay in the process. Nowhere in the world have glaciers retreated so fast, a phenomenon noted by John Muir when he came up by canoe in 1879, finding it an "icy wilderness unspeakably pure and sublime." In the 85 years between Vancouver's and Muir's visits, the Grand Pacific had already receded 48 miles. In 1925 Calvin Coolidge designated it a National Monument; Congress upgraded its status to **GLACIER BAY NATIONAL PARK** in 1980; and twelve years later the United Nations declared it a World Heritage Site.

All this receding ice has left behind a tranquil land of deep fjords lined by rock walls and encircled by towering mountains, in particular the 15,000-foot **Fairweather Range**, the tallest coastal mountains in the world. The various arms of Glacier Bay are fed by sixteen tidewater glaciers, a dozen of them calving on a regular basis. Huge sections of these intimidating walls of ice periodically come crashing down, captured by hundreds of video cameras onboard the cruise ships that make regular visits. In fact, if you've ever seen an image of a cruise ship dwarfed by the pure white face of a huge glacier, chances are that it will have been taken here in front of the **Margerie Glacier**, which flows down the slopes of Mount Fairweather. It travels so swiftly it has little time to

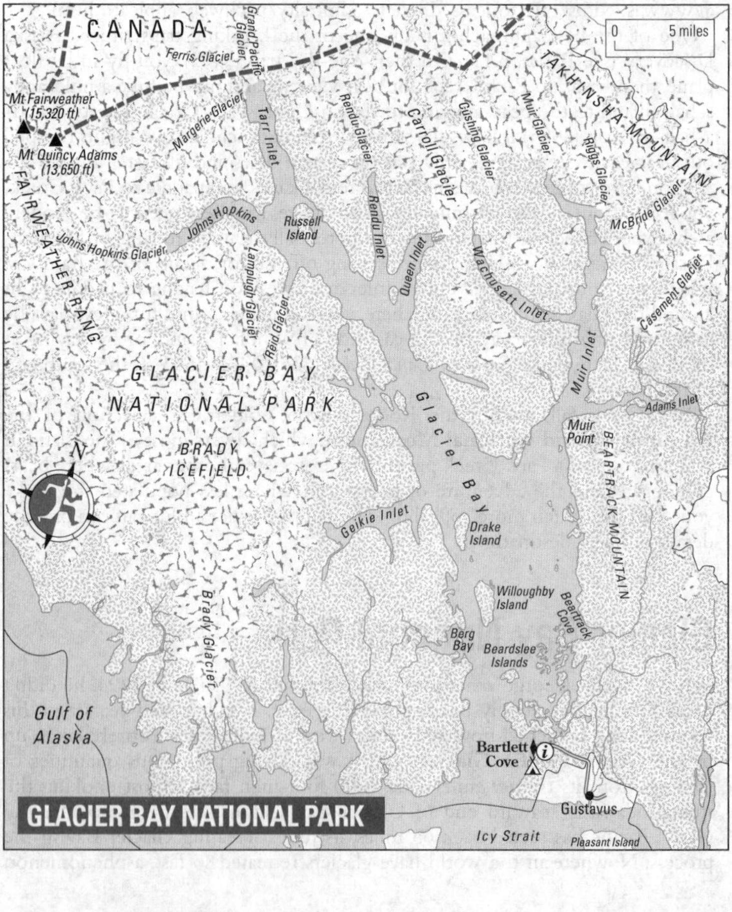

GLACIER BAY NATIONAL PARK

Glaciers for beginners

The existence of a glacier is always a balancing act between snow accumulation and melt rate. Snowfall dozens of feet thick at the **névé**, high in the mountains, gradually compacts to form clear blue ice, which feeds the glacier and flows downhill under its own weight. Meanwhile, ice is rapidly melting at the **terminal** of the glacier lower down the valley – the victor between these two processes determines whether the glacier will advance or retreat.

As the glacier moves down the valley, friction against the walls slows its sides, while its center charges headlong down the valley, creating the characteristic scalloped effect on the surface. Where a riverbed steepens, it forms a rapid; under similar conditions glaciers break up into an **icefall**, full of towering blocks of ice known as seracs, separated by crevasses.

In interior Alaska the long, slow-moving glaciers are often discolored because rock debris from the valley walls has accumulated on the surface – it's sometimes so thick that small forests can grow there. This material is deposited at the lowest point of the glacier, forming a **terminal moraine**.

But in much of Southeast and Southcentral Alaska the snowfall is so great that glaciers are still a thick tongue of ice when they reach the sea. These **tidewater glaciers** are perhaps the most spectacular of all, with a face sometimes three miles wide, rising 300ft or more above the water and stretching hundreds more below sea level. As the glacier creeps forward, the buoyancy of the seawater becomes insufficient to support the enormous weight of ice and chunks are calved off, littering the bay with bobbing white hunks. Anything rising more than 15ft above the water is classed as a fully fledged **iceberg**; smaller pieces are known as bergy bits; those between 3ft and 7ft high are growlers; and anything less is just brash ice. Another term you'll hear bandied around on ferries and glacier cruises is a shooter, which breaks off from the underside of the glacier and bobs up to the surface.

pick up the surface rubble typical of Alaskan glaciers, making this the most pristine. It shares the barren West Arm of Glacier Bay with two other glaciers: the **Johns Hopkins Glacier**, which calves so much ice that boats can seldom approach within two miles of its ice cliffs; and the still-majestic remains of the Grand Pacific Glacier, which in the 1920s receded to the point where boats viewing the face from close quarters were technically in Canada. It has since advanced back into the US, but shows signs of receding again.

The glaciers' recession hasn't just left a strikingly beautiful landscape, it has created a living classroom for the mechanics of plant succession and glacial rebound. As the earth sheds the immense weight of the glaciers, it breathes a sigh of relief, and measurements reveal that the land is rising at a rate of an inch and a half per year. At the same time the newly uncovered land acts as a blank canvas for progressive colonization by plant species. Near Bartlett Cove the earth was uncovered two centuries back and has a full cover of near-mature spruce forest, though the hemlocks seen elsewhere in Southeast are yet to establish themselves in any numbers.

You can see the succession process in reverse as you cruise up the bay, the spruce initially giving way to alder and cottonwoods, then stunted willows and finally the mosses and lichens that are the first to begin the colonization process. Animals have also been quick to populate the new habitat. In the water humpback whales, porpoise, seals, and sea otters can often be seen, while the banks occasionally reveal glimpses of brown and black bears, moose, mountain goats, and the colorful array of birds that have quickly made the area their home.

Over eighty percent of the park's visitors drift through on the limited number of mainstream cruise ships, while smaller numbers visit on a day cruise from Bartlett Cove and a few hardy souls make the effort of getting out there by kayak. But the action isn't just limited to the park, with worthwhile **whale-watching trips** leaving Bartlett Cove for Point Adolphus, on the south shore of Icy Strait.

Getting there, arrival, and information

A trip to Glacier Bay may well be one of the most memorable parts of your time in Alaska, but immaculate environments with almost complete solitude don't come cheap. Even a brief visit to Glacier Bay – spending perhaps one night in the settlements of either Gustavus or Bartlett Cove and one day exploring the bay either on the day cruise or by kayak – will be a minimum of $300, more likely $450. If money is tight, you might get a better return for your dollar by visiting Tracy Arm (see p.157), spending time around Prince William Sound, or viewing the glaciers on a flightseeing trip from Juneau, Haines, or Skagway.

The main access into Glacier Bay is from **BARTLETT COVE**, which consists of *Glacier Bay Lodge*, a campground, a Park Service visitor center, and a dock for small cruise boats. Everything else happens ten miles away at **GUSTAVUS** (Gust-AY-vus), a thinly scattered former homesteading settlement that is now home to an airport, ferry dock, and a host of luxury inns. There is **no entrance fee** for the park.

As AMHS ferries don't go to Gustavus, the cheapest way of **getting there** is by **flying** with Alaska Airlines, which has one thirty-minute flight from Juneau each afternoon in summer (June to mid-Sept) for around $120 round-trip. Smaller operators, such as LAB (Ⓣ766-2222 or 1-800/427-5966, Ⓦwww.labflying.com), charge around $65 each way between Gustavus and Juneau but have more flights.

Perhaps the best way to go is to fly one way and travel back on the **Gustavus Ferry** (late May–Aug Mon, Wed, Fri & Sun; $69 each way, kayaks $40, bikes $10; contact Goldbelt, see box below), a fast passenger-only catamaran which makes the three-hour run from Juneau (outside the Goldbelt Tours office downtown; 9am) to Bartlett Cove (noon), departs for a wildlife cruise in Icy Strait (see p.164), then calls at Gustavus (5pm) before retuning to Juneau (8.30pm).

Arrival

Whether arriving by boat or plane, you'll be met by someone who will take you straight to your lodge or B&B. Campers arriving by boat should either get off at Bartlett Cove or alight at Gustavus from where you can catch the free *Glacier Bay Lodge* bus to Bartlett Cove. If you get stuck, hitching usually works, or call TLC Taxi (Ⓣ697-2239, Ⓔtlctaxi@glacierbaytravel.com). Gustavus lodges usually run their guests to Bartlett Cove for the Glacier Bay cruise, kayaking companies pick up around Gustavus, and many lodges have free bicycles, but if you need a little more flexibility you can rent a car from Bud's Rent-a-Car (around $60 a day; Ⓣ697-2403).

> Commercial activities in the park – including the *Glacier Bay Lodge*, the Gustavus ferry and the Glacier Bay cruise – are run by a single park concessionaire, **Goldbelt Tours** (Ⓣ586-8687 or 1-800/820-2628, Ⓦwww.goldbelttours.com). The concession is being re-awarded for the 2004 and subsequent seasons, so details may change. Consult the park's website (see opposite) for the latest information.

With the limited scope for independent travel it makes sense to consider the **inclusive packages** offered by lodges and kayak companies. The most popular are those run by *Glacier Bay Lodge,* which has a three-day tour with two nights at the lodge ($480) and a three-night variation ($570) – both include the Glacier Bay day cruise.

Information

Gustavus has no visitor center, though it is worth checking out the community website (ⓦwww.gustavus.com). At Bartlett Cove there's a **National Park visitor center**, upstairs in the *Glacier Bay Lodge* (late May–Aug daily noon–8.45pm; ⓣ697-2661, ⓦwww.nps.gov/glba), which is a mine of general information and has some interesting natural history displays. Rangers lead daily hikes around Bartlett Cove and present several excellent **films** in the afternoon and evening (all free).

Anyone kayaking independently or staying at the campground must visit the **visitor information station**, by the dock in Bartlett Cove (mid-May to mid-Sept daily 7am–9pm; ⓣ697-2627), where you'll be put through a short orientation program.

Although there is a **post office** in Gustavus, there are **no banks** or ATMs anywhere around here.

Accommodation

The only indoor accommodation in the park is *Glacier Bay Lodge* (mid-May to mid-Sept; rooms ❼; contact Goldbelt, see box opposite) at Bartlett Cove. It's easily the largest of the lodges hereabouts and boasts a big, cozy lounge with a large stone fireplace and a suitably stately restaurant with a great deck overlooking the cove. The rooms are comfortable, if a little uninspired, although some have views of Bartlett Cove. The alternative is the free waterside first-come, first-served **campground**, 400yd from the dock, with wheelbarrows to transport your gear, a warming hut, firewood, and bear-resistant food caches. Showers ($1.25) are available at *Glacier Bay Lodge*, which also has bag storage ($5 a day) for campers.

Many more people stay at one of two dozen or more **lodges and B&Bs** in Gustavus, most of which cost at least $85 a night for two and range up to swanky places that charge $600 per person for a two-night all-inclusive package. One of the best deals is *Bear's Nest B&B* (ⓣ697-2440, ⓦwww.gustavus.com/bearsnest), which has a self-contained, fully furnished circular cabin (❹) with a double bed upstairs, a single futon down, and breakfast ingredients provided. (You'll have to bring everything else from Juneau or wander next door to the *Bear's Nest Café*.) There's a small A-frame cabin (❸), too, that also comes with a kitchen and all you need to cook, but no breakfast. If you are kayaking with Alaska Discovery, you'll probably be staying nearby at the *Alaska Discovery Inn* (ⓣ697-2411 or 1-800/586-1911; private bath ❺, shared bath ❹), a welcoming lodge with comfortable rooms, a hearty breakfast, free use of bikes, and transport to the ferry and Bartlett Cove.

Good River B&B (ⓣ697-2241, ⓦwww.goodriver.com; ❹) is also at the cheaper end of the range, with four rooms in the lodge, a rustic cabin nearby, a wholesome continental breakfast, and free use of bikes. Another good bet is the *Annie Mae Lodge* (ⓣ697-2346 or 1-800/478-2346, ⓦwww.anniemae.com; ❽), a large house close to the Good River with attractive wood-paneled rooms, superb meals, free use of bikes, and free local transportation for $215–260 a night for two ($135–155 single). At the top end, the pick is *Glacier Bay Country Inn* (ⓣ697-2288 or 1-800/628-0912, ⓦwww.glacierbayalaska.com; ❾), which has its own airstrip and concentrates on saltwater and fly fishing. Accommodation is either in very comfortable guestrooms in the main lodge or in one of the luxury cabins nearby; rates are around $400 a double including three wonderful meals a day.

Exploring the park

It would be perverse to come out this way and not explore Glacier Bay National Park, most easily done on the day-cruise run from Bartlett Cove, which visits several of the most spectacular glaciers. Sitting on a boat all day and viewing from a distance is a little limited, so there's a lot to be said for going kayaking, poking around little bays, investigating narrow fjords and camping out on rocky beaches. After a few days of that you'll welcome a return to the comforts and easy pace of Gustavus.

Cruises

The principal way of experiencing the park's wonders is the **Glacier Bay day cruise** (8hr; $159; contact Goldbelt, see box on p.162), a large launch that leaves Bartlett Cove at 7.30am and makes its way through miles of bergs to the faces of the Margerie and Grand Pacific glaciers. There's an NPS ranger on board, lunch is provided, and they'll get you back in time to catch the Gustavus Ferry or Alaska Airlines plane back to Juneau that afternoon.

Gustavus is also well placed for whale- and **wildlife-watching cruises** in Icy Strait ($195 from Juneau, $79 from Gustavus), a three-hour afternoon adventure that is effectively an extension of the Gustavus Ferry run. If you're coming on the Gustavus Ferry from Juneau, stay on board and you'll get three hours out in Icy Strait, around Point Adolphus, with almost guaranteed humpback whale watching and a fair chance of seeing Steller's sea lions, sea otters, and orcas. Wolf Track Expeditions (half-day $100, full day $180; ⓣ697-2326, ⓦwww.wolftrackexpeditions.com) runs more personal and in-depth trips in much the same area.

Kayaking

Everyone else goes kayaking which, if you're up for it, has to be the finest way to see Glacier Bay. **Guided day trips** don't get anywhere near the glaciers, instead sticking close to Bartlett Cove or Gustavus, perhaps venturing into the **Beardslee Islands**, a small archipelago immediately north of Bartlett Cove. Six-hour tours usually involve instruction for the small group followed by gentle paddling, learning something of the flora, fauna, and tidal patterns while hoping to catch sight of moose, black bears, deer, sea otters, and more. The main kayak companies (see below) also do multiday trips further up the bay into glacier-calving territory: five days with float-plane access is likely to cost around $2000.

If you are confident about camping for several days in potentially inclement weather, you may want to **go it alone** with rental kayaks. No prior kayaking experience is needed, but you will need to attend one of the park rangers' orientation programs at the visitor information station at Bartlett Cove (see p.163). You'll also want to bring all your food supplies from Juneau.

Again, the Beardslee Islands make a good and easily accessible destination with excellent beach camping, plenty of wildlife for the patient, and gentle, sheltered paddling with only the tidal currents (which need constant attention) to contend with. More ambitious paddlers will prefer to be dropped off close to the more distant sections of Glacier Bay where motorized traffic is banned. To avoid potentially hazardous open-water crossings, organize transport with the Glacier Bay day cruise, which sets kayakers down at several designated locations in the upper reaches of Glacier Bay – exact locations are frequently changed to avoid overly impacting particular sites. The charge for kayaker drop-off or pickup is $95, perfect if you want to do a one-way drop-off and then paddle back to Bartlett Cove over a week or so.

Alaska Discovery (☎780-6226 or 1-800/586-1911, ⓦwww.akdiscovery .com) has permits to go into Glacier Bay and run a six-hour day paddle ($125), a two-night trip ($800) specifically aimed at humpback whale watching around Point Adolphus, and a couple of longer expeditions (five nights is $2000, seven nights $2450).

Spirit Walker (☎697-2266 or 1-800/529-2537, ⓦwww.seakayakalaska.com) conducts very worthwhile trips elsewhere in the area, mostly to Pleasant Island from the Gustavus Dock. Half a day costs $70, a full day $120, overnight $487, and two nights $681.

To go at your own pace, **rent kayaks** from Glacier Bay Sea Kayaks (☎697-2257, ⓦwww.glacierbayseakayaks.com) at Bartlett Cove; fiberglass kayaks cost $60 a day for a double and $40 a day for a single, reducing to $45/$25 for three- to nine-day rentals. Sea Otter Kayak (☎697-3007, ⓦwww.he.net /~seaotter) also does rentals ($45 double, $35 single) and delivers to both Gustavus beach and Bartlett Cove.

Gustavus

Glacier Bay is very much the area's trump card, but **GUSTAVUS** can be a wonderfully peaceful spot with none of the frenetic activity engendered by cruise-ship and major ferry arrivals. Unusually for Southeast Alaska, the area has a very spacious feel, with plenty of flat ground on an alluvial fan, cut by a couple of meandering tidal rivers. There's very little specific to see, but it is a great place to simply hang out at your lodge, perhaps borrowing a bike or going for a stroll in the evening. You might wander down to the small boat harbor by the Salmon River or past the **Gustavus Dray**, a modern gas station beautifully fashioned in 1930s style.

Aside from the Glacier Bay cruises and kayaking, there are also a few Gustavus-based activities to tempt those with more time on their hands. Almost everyone you talk to seems to do fishing trips of some description and, if **mountain biking** is your thing, you might seek out Wolf Track Expeditions (see p.164), which runs full-day trips ($150) on old logging roads a short boat ride away. They also rent mountain bikes for $35 a day.

Even those who seldom play **golf** might fancy a round at Gustavus' nine-hole Mount Fairweather Golf Course, on State Dock Road, where you just stick your $15 in the honesty box, plus another $3 if you need to borrow one of the bags of clubs leaning up against the shed. You can tee

GUSTAVUS

Bartlett Cove (9 miles)

TONG ROAD

MOUNTAIN VIEW

WILSON ROAD

Gustavus Airport

Library

GUSTAVUS ROAD

Bear's Nest Café ■ ⒷⒸ

Ⓐ

Ⓓ

GOOD RIVER ROAD

Ⓔ

Gustavus Dray

Bear Track Mercantile

STATE DOCK ROAD

Ferry Dock

ACCOMMODATION
Alaska Discovery Inn	B
Annie Mae Lodge	E
Bear's Nest B&B	C
Glacier Bay Country Inn	A
Good River B&B	D

Icy Passage

Juneau (3hr)

0 400 yds

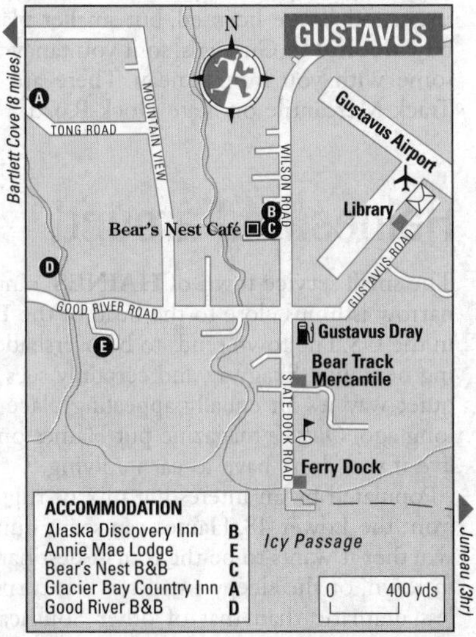

Hiking around Bartlett Cove

In the entire 3.3 million acres of Glacier Bay National Park, the only formed trails are three gentle affairs around *Glacier Bay Lodge* at Bartlett Cove.

Bartlett Lake Trail (8 miles round-trip; 3–5hr; 100ft ascent). A half- to full-day hike through temperate rainforest, gradually climbing moraine to reach the solitude of Bartlett Lake.

Bartlett River Trail (4 miles round-trip; 1hr 30min to 3hr; negligible ascent). Lovely, popular hike along the inter-tidal lagoon, where you might see shorebirds, waterfowl, and even bears.

Forest Loop Trail (1-mile loop; 30min–1hr; negligible ascent). A delightful stroll through hemlock forest, past several small ponds and the campground, much of it on a boardwalk.

off with the setting sun glinting off the distant snowcap of Mount Fairweather, but remember that respecting the wildlife is one of the course rules, even if a moose blocks the fairway or a raven steals your ball.

Eating and drinking

The *Glacier Bay Lodge* offers the only **eating** in Bartlett Cove, with buffet breakfasts ($12), burgers and sandwiches all day ($9), and nicely prepared dinners strong on Alaskan seafood (mains $13–25).

In Gustavus dining mainly centers on the lodge restaurants (usually open to non-guests, if booked in advance), which try to outdo each other and offer some of the best eating in Southeast. *Annie Mae Lodge* (see p.163) does superb three-course home-style dinners for around $30; meals at *Glacier Bay Country Inn* are possibly even more outstanding for a similar price. The only stand-alone **café** worth its salt is the *Bear's Nest Café* (call to make sure they are open ⓣ679-2440), good for coffee, cakes, and home-baked bread. They also prepare a limited range of delicious meals from chicken burgers ($8) to Dungeness crab ($22), using organic ingredients and vegetables from the garden. Several of the larger lodges are licensed, but smaller places aren't, and there are no stores to buy **alcohol** in Gustavus, so if you fancy a glass of wine with your meal, bring some with you from Juneau. There are very limited **groceries** at the Bear Track Mercantile on State Dock Road.

Haines and around

The small service town of **HAINES**, ninety miles north of Juneau, occupies a narrow isthmus close to the head of the **Lynn Canal**, the longest and deepest in the US. The town tends to be overshadowed by its more immediately arresting neighbor, Skagway, and certainly sees far fewer cruise ships, but in its own quiet way it's an equally appealing place to spend a few days. Indeed, not so long ago, *Outside* magazine put Haines on its list of top ten outdoors towns to live if you don't have to earn a living.

Populated by an interesting mix of rugged individualists and urban escapees from the Lower 48, Haines can seem quite schizophrenic. It never seems sure whether it wants to be the tourist destination it becomes when cruise ships are in town, or the sleepy small town it turns into when they leave. Its history is less dramatic than that of other Southeast communities, and its only major

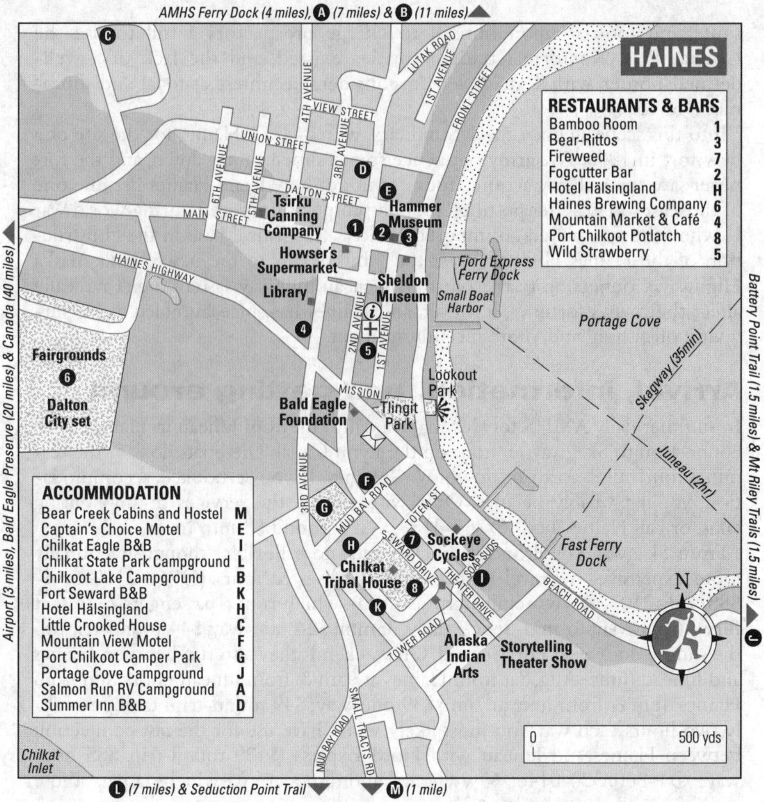

attraction, the mind-boggling congregation of up to four thousand bald eagles in the **Chilkat Bald Eagle Preserve** each November, happens well outside of the tourist season, giving the place an unspoilt authenticity.

With the waters of Lynn Canal lapping its shores and glaciers spilling out of the Chilkoot and Chilkat mountains on both sides, its location is nothing short of spectacular, particularly on a clear day when some of the town's hiking trails reveal wonderfully long views.

History hasn't completely passed Haines by either: its days as a military fort protecting the US border from marauding Canadians left **Fort William H Seward**, with its row of green-trimmed white mansions lending a certain weight to what would otherwise be a typically ragged Alaskan townscape.

Some history

Before the arrival of Europeans, this site at the mouth of the Chilkat River protected access to the Chilkat Valley, one of the very few glacier-free corridors to the interior. Chilkat Tlingit fiercely guarded their trading rights along the route, setting themselves up as middlemen between the Russian, American, and British traders along the coast and the Athabascans of the interior. This relationship continued after the arrival of the first traders and missionaries in the early 1880s, but as the Klondike gold rush got into full swing one Jack Dalton decided to ignore traditional trading rights along the route and took it upon himself to charge prospectors a toll to use the Chilkat Pass. No formal trading treaties existed, and the lack of a well-defined border with Canada led to considerable unrest at local and diplomatic levels.

Into this scene stepped the US military, which chose Haines for the site of a new fort in 1903. The army's presence soon calmed things down, and the fort never saw any military action. Troops soon got bored, and Haines became one of the least sought-after postings, though prospects improved during World War II when the fort played an important role as a logistical base in the construction of the Haines Highway over the Chilkat Pass to the newly built Alaska Highway. Connection to the North American highway system didn't radically affect the town's fortunes, however, and Haines has since bumbled along surviving off fishing and, more recently, tourism.

Arrival, information, and getting around

In summer daily AMHS **ferries** make a daily run from Juneau to Haines, with connection to Skagway, an hour up the Lynn Canal. The boats dock at the terminal four miles north of downtown Haines. If you've booked accommodation, you'll probably be met. Otherwise engage the services of any waiting taxis, or call Haines Taxi (T766-3188) – it's around $8 into town.

From Skagway you'll find it quicker and more flexible (though fractionally more expensive) to travel with Chilkat Cruises & Tours (T766-2100 or 1-888/766-2103, Wwww.chilkatcruises.com), which runs a passengers-only **fast ferry** (mid-May to mid-Sept 3 daily, 35min; $24 one-way, $44 round-trip) to the shuttle dock near Fort Seward. On weekends they also run between Haines and Juneau (June–Aug, Sat from Haines at 9am & from Juneau noon, Sun from Haines 4pm & from Juneau 7pm; $39 one-way; $49 round-trip) taking roughly two hours each way. You most likely won't have use for the fast connection between Haines and Juneau with Fjord Express ($129 round-trip, $85 one-way; T1-800/320-0146, Wwww.alaskafjordlines.com), which targets those wanting a full-day round-trip to Juneau with a city tour.

Drivers can reach Haines along the 151-mile Haines Highway, which runs south from Haines Junction, Yukon, on the Alaska Highway, and crosses from Canada into the US (for immigration details see "Crossing the border" box, p.174). The same route is followed by Alaska Direct **buses** (mid-May to Sept; T1-800/770-6652, Ealaskadirect@msn.com), which run to Haines three days a week from Tok ($100), Anchorage ($195), and Fairbanks ($185). RC Shuttles (May to late Sept; T479-0079 or 1-877/479-0079, Wwww.rcshuttles.com) runs more like a taxi service, coming here from Fairbanks pretty much whenever two seats can be sold ($150 each).

Although Alaska Airlines doesn't fly to Haines' tiny **airport** (T766-3609), three miles north on Haines Highway, regional carriers fly from Skagway, Juneau, and Gustavus. Skagway Air Service, 211 Willard St (T766-3233, Wwww.skagwayair.com), flies from Skagway ($45 one-way, $75 round-trip), Juneau ($80/$140), and Gustavus ($85/$160); LAB Flying Service, 390 Main St (T766-2222 or 1-800/427-5966, Wwww.labflying.com), charges a little more for the same routes.

Information

The **visitor center**, 122 2nd Ave (June to mid-Sept Mon–Fri 8am–7pm, Sat & Sun 9am–6pm; mid-Sept to May Mon–Fri 8am–5pm; T766-2234 or 1-800/458-3579, Wwww.haines.ak.us), has material on everything you need to know about the district, including campgrounds and Forest Service cabins and trails. They also stock the free *Haines Vacation Planner* booklet, the *Haines Visitor's Guide* newspaper, and the *History and Walking Tour* leaflet for Fort Seward.

If you are planning to visit all four of Haines' museums – Tsirku, Sheldon, Hammer and Bald Eagle – save yourself $3 by purchasing the museum pass ($15) at the first museum you visit.

Getting around and tours

If you are staying close to town, you can walk to most of the places you're likely to be interested in, though having your own transport opens up the fabulous road-accessible wilderness that's close at hand and provides access to the Chilkat Bald Eagle Preserve. **Bikes** can be rented from Sockeye Cycle Co, 24 Portage St (Ⓣ766-2869, Ⓦwww.cyclealaska.com), which charges $12 for two hours, $20 per half-day, and $30 per eight-hour day, with discounts offered for two- and three-day rentals. **Cars** can be rented from Eagle's Nest Rental Car (Ⓣ766-2891 or 1-800/354-6009, Ⓦwww.eaglenest.wytbear.com), which charges $45 a day, plus 35¢ a mile after the first hundred. The *Captain's Choice Motel* (see below) has unlimited-mileage vehicles for around $70 a day. Note that Canadian citizens are not allowed to drive vehicles rented outside Canada into Canada; all others should have no trouble driving rental vehicles through the Yukon.

When there's a cruise ship in town, Haines explodes with a couple of dozen companies keen to take you on **tours** of some description, most of which are entertaining and educational enough, but overpriced and a bit staged. Alaska Nature Tours (Ⓣ766-2876, Ⓦkcd.com/aknature) offers two good alternatives: a nature tour (several daily; 3hr; $50), which goes either to Chilkoot Lake or the Chilkat Bald Eagle Preserve, and the Chilkat Rainforest Nature Hike (4hr; $60), which takes you to the Battery Point trailhead for an educational walk with naturalists.

Sockeye Cycle Co runs a number of easy to moderate **bicycle tours**: the Chilkoot Lake Bicycle Adventure (3hr; $90) dawdles for eight miles around some flat dirt roads that are good for wildlife viewing; Chilkat Bicycle Adventure (1hr 30min; $42) is a little more strenuous, with the emphasis on local history; Glory Hole Bicycle Adventure (3hr 30min; $90) is tougher again and visits the Chilkat Bald Eagle Preserve; and there's the Chilkat Pass Bicycle Adventure (8hr; $120) heading up into the Yukon's Tatshenshini/Alsek Provincial Park, with an overnight camping option ($320).

Accommodation

Though Haines has no real luxury hotels, there is a reasonable selection of mid-range **places to stay** as well as a welcoming hostel. For some reason, many of the hotels and B&Bs have an overly casual feel, but the hosts manage to carry the day either by going out of their way to help, or just by being entertaining characters. As an incentive to visit, during the bald-eagle-watching season (mid-Oct to Jan) prices drop by a third and the *Captain's Choice Motel* does a room and rental-car deal. There is also an abundance of excellent campgrounds, the best of which we've listed below.

Hotels, motels, and B&Bs

Captain's Choice Motel 108 2nd Ave Ⓣ766-3111 or 1-800/478-2345, Ⓦwww.capchoice.com. The nicest and most modern of Haines' motels – although not the cheapest – with forty comfortable rooms and suites, featuring fridge, coffeemaker, and cable TV, and a great view across the fjord from the sun deck. Jacuzzi suite ❼, standard suites ❻, rooms ❺

Chilkat Eagle B&B 67 Soap Suds Alley, Fort Seward ⓣ766-2763, ⓦwww.eagle-bb.com. Central B&B in an old Fort Seward building with comfortable rooms and an entertaining and enthusiastic host, who'll tell you all you ever wanted to know about Haines and more. ❸

Fort Seward B&B 1 Officer's Row ⓣ766-2856 or 1-800/615-6676, ⓦwww.fortsewardbnb.com. Engaging B&B in what used to be the Chief Surgeon's house in Fort Seward, a three-story clapboard affair with a great veranda out front. There's courtesy ferry transfers, free use of basic bikes, a hearty breakfast, and a range of rooms. Rooms ❺, shared bath ❹

Hotel Hälsingland 13 Fort Seward Drive ⓣ766-2000 or 1-800/542-6363, ⓦwww.hotelhalsingland.com. Though no longer the grande dame of Haines' accommodation scene, this recently renovated hotel in converted Fort Seward houses is once again a fine place to stay. Modernized rooms come with TV and phone and some still have original features: ask for one with a clawfoot bath, an original fireplace, or just a good view (though none has all three). Private bath ❺, shared bath ❸

Little Crooked House 61 Helms Loop ⓣ766-3933 or 1-866/298-6287, ⓦwww.alaskafloattrips.com. Small, low-key homestay with three shared-bath rooms, free ferry pickups, and good breakfasts. The owners also run rafting trips. ❷

Mountain View Motel 57 Mud Bay Rd ⓣ766-2900 or 1-800/478-2902, ⓔbudget@mtnviewmotel.com. Nine comfortable rooms with cable TV and free coffee; most also feature functional kitchenettes. ❹

Summer Inn B&B 117 2nd Ave ⓣ766-2970, ⓦwww.summerinn.wytbear.com. Immaculately kept and nicely decorated downtown B&B with shared-bath rooms, some with sea views and all including a good cooked breakfast. It has a very homey feel with clawfoot baths, quilts, and fresh flowers. ❹

Camping and hostels

Bear Creek Cabins and Hostel just over a mile south of Fort Seward on Small Tract Rd ⓣ766-2259, ⓦwww.kcd.com/hostel. This small collection of cabins – a couple of which function as single-sex dorms – makes up for its inconvenient location with a coin-op laundry, free bikes, a well-equipped kitchen, no lockout or curfew, and $3 rides from the ferry terminal. Rates in the two dorms are $16, cabins cost $42 for two, and there's camping ($10 for one, $14 for two), which includes use of the hostel facilities. May–Sept. ❶

Chilkat State Park 8 miles south of Haines on Mud Bay Rd. Thirty spaces for tents and RVs, with three beachside tent sites, pump water, toilets, and a summertime campground host, in a beautiful setting near the south end of the Haines Peninsula, looking west towards the Takhinsha Mountains and the Davidson and Rainbow glaciers. $10.

Chilkoot Lake State Recreation Site off Lutak Rd, 11 miles north of downtown. Fairly large site for RVs and tents, with a location beside the Dolly Varden-rich Chilkoot Lake, pump water, toilets, and a boat ramp. $10.

Port Chilkoot Camper Park Mud Bay Rd beside Fort Seward ⓣ766-2000 or 1-800/542-6363, ⓦwww.hotelhalsingland.com. The best of the full-hookup sites ($23), right in the heart of things but still peacefully located among the spruce trees. Also suitable for dry RV camping ($16) and tents ($8).Pay-showers and a laundromat on site.

Portage Cove State Recreation Site Beach Rd, half a mile southeast of Fort Seward. A small first-come, first-served tent-only site designed for backpackers and cyclists only. It's right by the beach and has great views and potable water. No overnight parking. $5.

Salmon Run RV Campground Lutak Rd, 7 miles north of downtown ⓣ723-4229, ⓦwww.salmonrunadventures.com. Wooded RV park two miles north of the AMHS ferry dock, with dry camping ($13.50), camping cabins ($45–65), and showers ($2), but no hookups.

The town and around

Much of the early prosperity of Haines was founded on the half-dozen canneries that sprouted along the coast nearby. The only way you can get a sense of what went on is to visit the **Tsirku Canning Company**, 422 Main St at 5th Ave (roughly daily, times vary according to cruise-ship schedule; $10; ⓣ766-3474, ⓦcannerytour.com), an authentic canning line briefly operated to illustrate the process. Recently rescued from an abandoned cannery in Kodiak, the line is now fired up producing empty cans. The demonstration is followed by a ten-minute video.

Just down the street is Haines' one essential indoor sight, the **Sheldon Museum & Cultural Center**, 11 Main St (mid-May to mid-Sept Mon–Fri

11am–6pm, Sat & Sun 2–6pm, extended when cruise ships are in port; mid-Sept to mid-May daily except Sat 1–4pm; $3; ⓣ766-2366, ⓦsheldonmuseum.org), which does a great job of showing how Haines fits into its Chilkat environment, and the wider Tlingit world. In few other places (if any) can you see such fine examples of the distinctive yellow-and-black Chilkat blanket in wolf, raven, and killer-whale designs, as well as an intriguing example trimmed with pearl buttons and small "coppers." There are also bentwood boxes superbly carved from a single cedar plank made pliable by steaming with seaweed and hot rocks. Look, too, for the Tlingit armor, comprised of a moose-hide shirt with wooden slatted breastplate plus a thick wooden collar and wooden hat, the two combining to leave just a narrow slit. When threatened by some projectile the natural reaction is for the warrior to duck his head down between his shoulders, thereby closing the gap. For ceremonial headgear it is hard to beat the Murrelet Hat, which is loosely dated to 1740 but may be as much as a hundred years older. The hat-top murrelet figure moves to the rhythm when "danced," as happened when the hat was repatriated from a Lower 48 private collection a few years back. Also worth a look is the small Tsimshian box made from porcupine quills as well as the excellent artworks for sale in the store. Downstairs, there is less diverting coverage of Fort Seward and town life.

Across the street the **Hammer Museum**, 108 Main St (Mon–Fri 10am–5pm; $2; ⓣ766-2374, ⓔpahlfam@aptalaska.net), spins a surprisingly interesting tale of the development of this most basic of tools, with some 1200 hammers from the American colonial era to the present.

A stroll along the typically bustling Beach Road and up through Tlingit Park brings you to the home of the **American Bald Eagle Foundation**, 113 Haines Hwy at 2nd Ave (May–Sept Mon–Fri 10am–5pm, Sat 1–5pm; Oct–April call for hours; $3; ⓣ766-3094, ⓦwww.baldeagles.org), a nonprofit organization dedicated to maintaining the sanctity of the Chilkat Bald Eagle Preserve. Their public face is this wildlife museum, essentially just one large room with specimens of over 180 species, all found in the immediate vicinity – bears, moose, seals, sea lions, mountain goats, even lynx. It's not particularly exciting but some enjoy seeing such creatures up close and danger-free.

A couple of hundred yards south is **Fort William H Seward** (ⓦwww.fortwilliamhseward.com), less a fort than a large sloping grassy rectangle commonly known as the Parade Ground, which is surrounded by a dozen grand houses. It was established in 1903 in response to the general lawlessness of the gold-rush era and territorial disputes with Canada. With the limited resources at their disposal, the army fashioned a formal military outpost that seems more California than Alaska – rows of huge white clapboard houses with shingle roofs and broad verandas. The Canadian threat receded, and by the end of World War II the fort had outlived its usefulness. Fortunately, five war veterans and their families bought all 85 surplus buildings and proceeded to renovate them. Most are now put to good use as B&Bs, hotels, and condominiums, but you can wander around outside, equipped with the free *History and Walking Tour* leaflet from the visitor center.

At the far southeast corner of the Parade Ground, a former cannery and warehouse now operates as **Alaska Indian Arts** (Mon–Fri 9am–5pm and for cruise ships; free; ⓣ766-2160), with a gallery for locally produced sculpture, photos, and carving, and a back room where you can watch and chat with carvers as they work on huge totem poles. The center of the Parade Ground is dominated by the replica **Chilkat Tribal House**, scene of the summer salmon bake, Port Chilkoot Potlatch (see p.173).

In 1989 Haines was chosen as the location for the filming of Jack London's *White Fang*. A set of Dalton City – really just one short section of street – was created and later moved to the fairgrounds where it remains, partly put to use with a couple of shops and a microbrewery.

Haines doesn't just brew beer: Great Land Wines (Ⓣ766-2698, Ⓦwww.greatlandwines.com) makes its own wines from just about anything that will grow – rhubarb, strawberries, blueberries, rose petals, dandelions, even fireweed – and sells the product around town; call for a tour and free tasting.

Chilkat Bald Eagle Preserve

Local promotional material touts the annual congregation of bald eagles at the so-called Council Grounds in the **Chilkat Bald Eagle Preserve** around twenty miles north along the Haines Highway. Visit between late October and January (and especially Nov) and you'll see the world's largest gathering of bald eagles, perhaps four thousand, and up to two dozen in a single cottonwood tree, all here to feed on the extremely late run of chum salmon. By this time of year, most salmon rivers in Alaska are frozen and the fish long gone, but here water collects in alluvial gravels forming an underwater reservoir during the summer and, over time, percolates back into the river to keep it from freezing. The fish come to breed, the eagles come to eat them, and the people come armed with cameras and binoculars. The only problem is that, if you come at any other time of year, there really isn't a great deal to see. You might spot a few resident eagles, but you can see a handful of bald eagles any day of the week in coastal Alaska – so there is little point in making a special journey.

Hikes around Haines

Haines is blessed with several good trails right on its doorstep. The following hikes are all discussed more fully in the free *Haines is for Hikers* leaflet available from the visitor center.

Battery Point Trail (4 miles round-trip; 2hr; negligible ascent). Shoreline walk from the end of Beach Road, just south of Fort Seward, to Kelgaya Point. It initially parallels the beach through spruce, then traverses meadows to headland where you are free to camp for up to two weeks.

Mount Riley Trails (8 miles round-trip; 4–5hr; 1760ft ascent). A forest and muskeg walk to the summit of Mount Riley, starting about two-thirds of the way along the Battery Point Trail. By using one of several different routes down you can turn it into a long and varied day out, walking all the way from town.

Mount Ripinski Trail (10 miles round-trip; 5–7hr; 3650ft ascent). An exhausting but very worthwhile all-day undertaking, following the distinctive skyline ridge to the north of town. Pick a clear day to get the best views, and if you want to avoid hiking through patches of snow, don't even consider it until late July. Experienced hikers can avoid having to retrace their steps by continuing beyond the North Peak of Mount Ripinski and following the exposed ridgetop Skyline Trail to Peak 3920, from where you can descend to 7 Mile Saddle and the Haines Highway. This extended hike takes ten hours; you'll finish about ten miles from town, so either arrange for a lift, or get down early enough to hitch.

Seduction Point Trail (13.6 miles round-trip; 8–10hr; negligible ascent). Long but relatively easy beach and forest walk from Chilkat State Park (see "Camping," p.170) to Seduction Point, occasionally walking below the high-tide line (consult tide tables before starting). Camping is permitted along the route so you can make it an overnighter, and the mountain and forest scenery is gorgeous.

Around the second weekend in November, the American Bald Eagle Foundation promotes the five-day **Bald Eagle Festival** (Ⓣ766-3094), a series of photographic workshops, naturalist-guided excursions, and the like that takes place during the greatest gathering of eagles.

The preserve starts nine miles north of Haines and runs for thirty miles along the highway, but the main interpretive exhibits and the best viewing are around 21 miles north of Haines. During the summer, several of the city tours visit the Bald Eagle Preserve, but many people prefer to see the area from the water on a raft. There's no whitewater, so these are very much **float trips** specializing in a pleasant morning or afternoon looking for a few bald eagles and other wildlife along the shore. The very professional Chilkat Guides (Ⓣ766-2491, Ⓦwww.raftalaska.com), which runs half-day trips (early May to late Sept; $79), is the main operator. You can also go with Eco Orca Tours (Ⓣ766-3933 or 1-866/298-6287, Ⓦwww.alaskafloattrips.com) for $74, often in smaller groups.

Chilkat Guides also runs major multiday expeditions on the Alsek and Tatshenshini rivers to the north (see Basics, p.64).

Eating, drinking, and entertainment

Considering its diminutive size, Haines has a decent offering of restaurants and cafés (at least in summer, anyway), with a number of good places both downtown and around Fort Seward. **Groceries** are best sought at Howser's Supermarket at 211 Main St.

Bars tend to be straightforward drinking joints with little sophistication, though for something cultural you could attend the Chilkat Dancers' **Storytelling Theater Show** (generally when cruise ships are in; $10; Ⓣ766-2160), with dances and tales based on Chilkat life and legends. It takes place in the Tribal House in the Fort Seward's Parade Ground.

While here you should try to sample some birch syrup, a poor relation to its maple-sourced cousin, that's tapped from local trees and is available in many town gift shops.

Bamboo Room 11 2nd Ave near Main Ⓣ766-2800. Standard diner always popular for its well-prepared meals (especially the locally caught halibut and chip dinner, $18) and fresh-baked pies.

Bear-Rittos 12 Main St Ⓣ766-2117, Ⓦwww.alaskabearden.com. Chimichangas, burritos, and enchiladas with a choice of veggie, chicken, beef, salmon, and halibut for $5–11 to eat at booths or to take out.

Fireweed Restaurant Building 37, Blacksmith Rd Ⓣ766-3838. The pick of Haines' restaurants; a convivial, wood-floored place that's great for a coffee and one of their fresh pastries on the sunny deck, but equally good for more substantial dishes, often using organic ingredients. Eggs Benedict comes in half a dozen variations ($11–13), and there's great pizza ($10 for a personal one), sandwiches, gyros, falafel, daily soups, and things like mushroom ravioli ($16) and grilled mahi mahi ($19). Closed Sun.

Fogcutter Bar 122 Main St. Favorite late-night drinking hole for locals and visitors, with pool tables and sports on TV.

Haines Brewing Company Southeast Alaska Fairgrounds Ⓣ766-3823. Local microbrewery producing four mostly English-style ales for sale here in bottles for $8 a half-gallon or on draft at the *Fogcutter Bar*.

Mountain Market & Café 151 3rd Ave at Haines Hwy Ⓣ766-3340. Combined natural-food grocery and espresso bar that's one of the best places in town for a $5.50 bagel breakfast, a $7 tortilla wrap (the falafel is especially good), or just a muffin with your mocha.

Port Chilkoot Potlatch Parade Ground, Fort Seward Ⓣ766-2000. All-you-can-eat salmon bake (5–9pm; $23) on summer evenings, dates being defined by the presence of cruise ships.

Restaurant at the Hotel Hälsingland 13 Fort Seward Drive Ⓣ766-2000. Haines' finest dining in convivial surroundings with the chance to sample the likes of blackened tiger prawns with cilantro pita bread ($12) followed by braised lamb shank ($20) or duck breast marinated in cilantro and soy ($19).

Wild Strawberry 138 2nd Ave Ⓣ766-3608. Good café and deli, with espresso, fine chocolates, and

...t is less successful as a licensed ...izing in seafood but does decent salmon chowder ($8), blackened halibut tacos ($15), and Cajun king salmon ($20).

...al Bank, cnr 1st Ave and Main

Bookshop The Babbling Book, 225 Main St, is the best in town.

Festivals The Alaska Craft Beer and Homebrew Festival takes place in the third week of May (☎766-2476); cyclists racing in the 160-mile Kluane to Chilkat International Bicycle Relay descend on Haines on the Sat nearest the summer solstice in late June; there are the usual parades and fireworks for the Fourth of July; and the cookouts, crafts, and log-rolling of the Southeast State Fair take place in the second week of Aug along with the Bald Eagle Music Festival which draws blues and bluegrass players from all over the state. The annual highlight is November's Bald Eagle Festival (see p.173).

Internet access Free at the library (see below) and roughly $8 an hour at *Mountain Market* (see p.173).

Laundry and showers The Fort Chilkoot Camper Park has public showers by the quarter and a laundromat (7am–9pm).

Library The excellent, new Haines Public Library, 103 3rd Ave (Mon, Tues & Thurs 10am–9pm, Wed noon–9pm, Fri 10am–4.30pm, Sat & Sun 12.30–4.30pm), has free Internet access.

Medical assistance Haines Medical Center, 131 1st Ave ☎766-3121.

Post office cnr Haines Hwy opposite Tlingit Park (Mon–Fri 9am–5pm, Sat 1–3pm). The **General Delivery** zip code is 99827.

Taxes Haines imposes a 5.5 percent sales tax and an additional 4 percent bed tax. Both have been included in our accommodation prices.

Travel agency The Travel Connection, 115 2nd Ave near Main St ☎766-2681 or 1-800/572-8006, ⓦwww.alaska4you.com.

Skagway and around

The northernmost Inside Passage stop on the AMHS ferries, **SKAGWAY** ranks as one of the best-preserved gold-rush towns in the US, a tiny kernel of century-old buildings that has a history to match. Throw in the superb **White Pass & Yukon Route** mountain train trip, a relatively dry climate, and the opportunity to emulate the Klondike gold prospectors hiking the challenging **Chilkoot Trail** (see box, pp.186–187) and you've the makings of an enormously popular tourist destination.

But even when suitably forewarned, most people arrive unprepared for a place where, on a normal summer day, four or five huge boats will be moored at the foot of Broadway disgorging up to eight thousand passengers into a town with a year-round population of only eight hundred. In fact, there are

Crossing the border

Those traveling on into Canada, or continuing to northern Alaska through the Yukon, need to be aware that Canadian border controls are no less strict just because you are in transit. Everyone should carry a passport, though North Americans can get by with their birth certificate – a driver's license won't do. You are also supposed to carry sufficient funds to cover your expenses while in Canada and, although $150 a day is recommended, they'll let you in with a lot less than this (a credit card will often do the trick). As long as you look reasonably tidy, you probably won't even be asked. The Klondike Highway border between Skagway and Fraser, BC, is open around the clock: if in doubt call US customs (☎983-2325) or Canadian customs in Fraser (☎867/821-4111). The Haines Highway crossing is open around the clock when Alaska-bound, but only 7am–11pm (Alaska time) when Canada-bound.

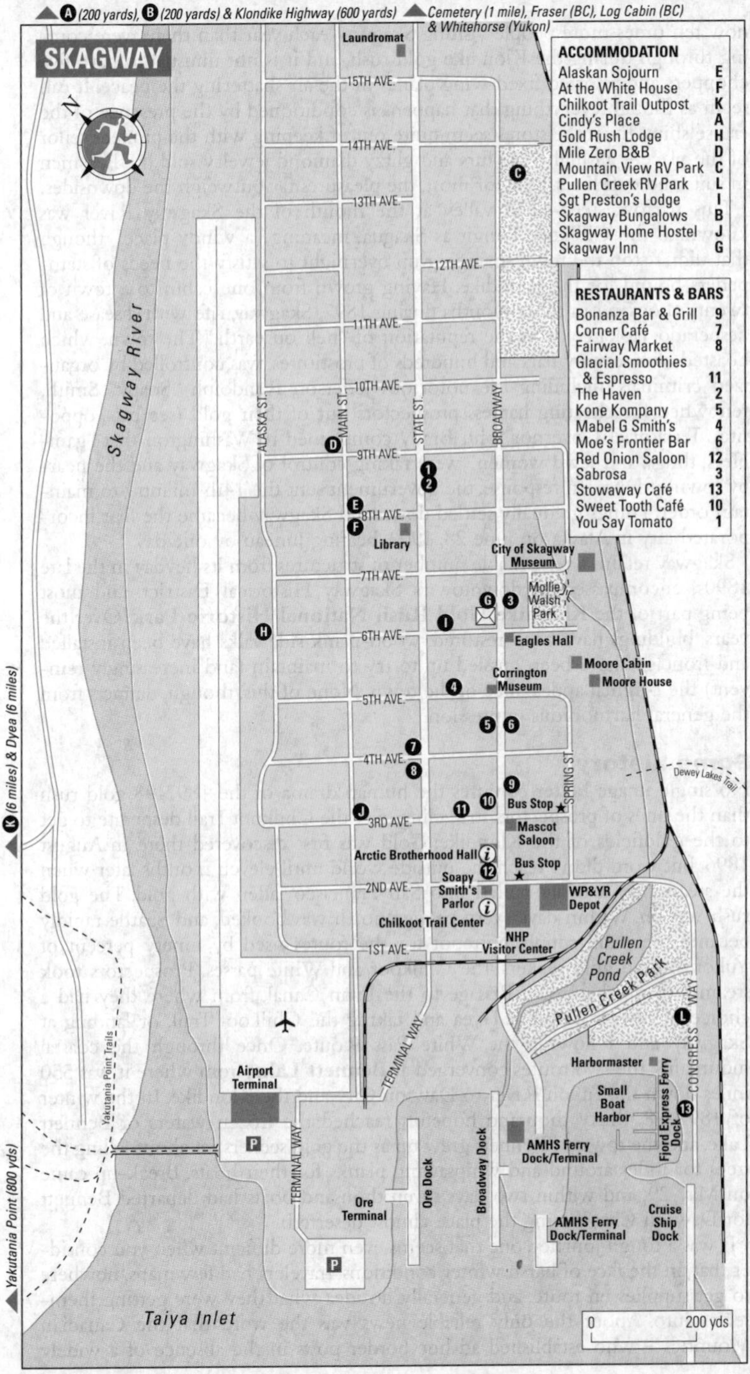
A (200 yards), B (200 yards) & Klondike Highway (600 yards)
Cemetery (1 mile), Fraser (BC), Log Cabin (BC) & Whitehorse (Yukon)
SKAGWAY
N
ACCOMMODATION
Alaskan Sojourn E
At the White House F
Chilkoot Trail Outpost K
Cindy's Place A
Gold Rush Lodge H
Mile Zero B&B D
Mountain View RV Park C
Pullen Creek RV Park L
Sgt Preston's Lodge I
Skagway Bungalows B
Skagway Home Hostel J
Skagway Inn G
RESTAURANTS & BARS
Bonanza Bar & Grill 9
Corner Café 7
Fairway Market 8
Glacial Smoothies & Espresso 11
The Haven 2
Kone Kompany 5
Mabel G Smith's 4
Moe's Frontier Bar 6
Red Onion Saloon 12
Sabrosa 3
Stowaway Café 13
Sweet Tooth Café 10
You Say Tomato 1
Laundromat
15TH AVE.
14TH AVE.
13TH AVE.
12TH AVE.
11TH AVE.
10TH AVE.
9TH AVE.
8TH AVE.
7TH AVE.
6TH AVE.
5TH AVE.
4TH AVE.
3RD AVE.
2ND AVE.
1ST AVE.
ALASKA ST.
MAIN ST.
STATE ST.
BROADWAY
SPRING ST
Skagway River
Library
City of Skagway Museum
Mollie Walsh Park
Eagles Hall
Moore Cabin
Moore House
Corrington Museum
Dewey Lakes Trail
Bus Stop
Mascot Saloon
Arctic Brotherhood Hall
Bus Stop
Soapy Smith's Parlor
WP&YR Depot
Chilkoot Trail Center
NHP Visitor Center
Pullen Creek Pond
Pullen Creek Park
TERMINAL WAY
CONGRESS WAY
Harbormaster
Small Boat Harbor
Fjord Express Ferry Dock
Airport Terminal
Yakutania Point Trails
AMHS Ferry Dock/Terminal
Ore Terminal
Ore Dock
Broadway Dock
AMHS Ferry Dock/Terminal
Cruise Ship Dock
K (6 miles) & Dyea (6 miles)
Yakutania Point (800 yds)
Taiya Inlet
0 200 yds

now ten times more people visiting Skagway each year than there were coming through during the Klondike gold rush, and it is not unusual to have five choppers and assorted fixed-wing planes in the air shattering the peace. It can seem as though everything that happens is conditioned by the presence of the cruise ships. Even the stores seem quite out of keeping with the pioneer tenor of the place – all high-class furs and glitzy diamond jewelry sold by slick men in suits and cuff links. Still, for most, the pleasures far outweigh the downsides.

This narrow, steep-sided valley at the mouth of the Skagway River was known to the Chilkoot Tlingit as Skagua, meaning "a windy place," though that didn't stop the town springing up overnight to satisfy the needs of stampeders bound for the Klondike. Having grown from one cabin to a town of twenty thousand in three months during 1897, Skagway, rife with disease and desperado violence, won the reputation of "hell on earth." The town, which boasted over seventy bars and hundreds of prostitutes, was controlled by organized criminals, including the notorious Jefferson Randolph "Soapy" Smith, renowned for cheating hapless prospectors out of their gold (see box, opposite). Territorial Governor John Brady complained to Washington that "gamblers, thugs, and lewd women" were taking control of Skagway and the nearby town of Dyea. In response, the government sent the 14th Infantry to maintain order. Things gradually settled down and Skagway became the first incorporated city in Alaska on June 28, 1900, beating Juneau by one day.

Skagway retains a remarkable number of structures from its heyday in the late 1890s, encompassed in downtown's Skagway Historical District, and most being part of the **Klondike Gold Rush National Historic Park**. Over the years, buildings have been restored, wood-plank sidewalks have been installed and frontages have been gussied up to try to maintain (and increasingly reinvent) the original appearance of the town. None of this, though, detracts from the general harmonious impression.

Some history

No single image better conjures the human drama of the 1897-98 gold rush than the lines of prospectors struggling over the Chilkoot Trail desperate to get to the goldfields of the Klondike. Gold was first discovered there in August 1896, but word didn't reach the outside world until eleven months later when the steamship *Excelsior* pulled into San Francisco laden with gold. The gold rush was on. Within days every passage north was booked, and Seattle rapidly became the main supply entrepôt for the routes used by ninety percent of Yukon-bound gold seekers, the Chilkoot and White passes. Prospectors took steamships up the Inside Passage to the Lynn Canal, from where they had a choice of disembarking at Dyea and taking the Chilkoot Trail, or landing at Skagway and following the White Pass Route. Once through the coastal mountains, the two routes converged at **Bennett Lake**, from where it was 550 miles down the Yukon River to Dawson City and the Klondike. In the winter of 1897–98, thirty thousand hopefuls reached the frozen waters of Bennett Lake, and the town of Bennett grew up as the gold seekers set about felling the trees for miles around and whipsawing planks for their boats. Break-up came on May 29, and within two days seven thousand boats had departed Bennett for Dawson City, leaving the place almost deserted.

It was a tough journey, one that seems even more difficult when you consider that, in the face of harsh winter conditions, travelers had few maps, nowhere to get supplies en route, and generally no idea what they were getting themselves into. About the only reliable news was the word that the Canadian Mounties – who established ad hoc border posts in the absence of a widely accepted frontier – were enforcing a rule that required all stampeders entering Canada to carry a year's supplies, roughly a "**ton of goods**." Introduced because of chronic shortages in the goldfields, the ruling probably saved many lives in the long run, but it laid enormous hardship on the backs of the stampeders. Altogether 22,000 prospectors made it over the Chilkoot Pass, many carrying their ton of supplies on their backs, sometimes making as many as fifty journeys through temperatures of –60°F and 80ft of snowfall.

Before the rush, Skagway (then known as Mooresville) was just one hut owned by William Moore, who helped the Canadian Government pioneer a new route from the coast to the interior from Skagway, up and over the White Pass to Bennett Lake. It was ten miles longer than the Chilkoot, but the pass was 600ft lower and had a gentler gradient, so it became the route of choice for prospectors wealthy enough to buy horses. Overuse, along with sharp rocks, boulder fields, and muskeg, made it very heavy going and over three thousand horses died on what soon became known as the "Dead Horse Trail." Neither trail was the slightest bit appealing, and as one experienced stampeder put it, "It didn't matter which one you took, you'd wished you'd taken the other."

Everything changed with the July 1900 completion of the White Pass & Yukon Route railway, which broadly followed the White Pass Trail. As one local newspaper noted, "What was formerly an all-winter's job for the gold seeker

The reign of Soapy Smith

Jefferson Randolph "Soapy" Smith and his gang of con men and cutthroats had a short but lucrative career preying on gullible gold stampeders until Soapy got his comeuppance nine months after his arrival in Skagway. Soapy came by his name after a con trick he'd pulled years before in Colorado where he sold $5 bars of soap, some containing large denomination bills. From the skeptical crowd, Soapy's accomplices emerged to buy the first few bars which, miraculously, contained a $20 or even $50 bill. The ensuing buying frenzy revealed that few of the remaining bars contained even a $1 bill.

In Skagway Soapy established a saloon from which he ran his empire of up to a hundred henchmen, who posed as newspaper reporters, priests, or savvy sourdoughs to ensnare greenhorns arriving at the docks. Victims would soon be swindled at one of Soapy's businesses: crooked gambling halls, bogus freight companies that simply commandeered your consignment, and an army enlistment tent where they'd steal your clothes and possessions while you visited the "doctor." There was also a telegraph office that received requests for money from loved ones back home but, in fact, had no telegraph link at all. Soapy could, of course, arrange to have the money wired for you.

Soapy got his cronies to do the dirty work and established himself as a solid, philanthropic citizen, funding Skagway's first church and starting an adopt-a-dog program at a time when Skagway was full of discarded, pull-nothing pooches. Many saw through the veneer, but he had the support of much of the business community, and he even stood next to the governor of Alaska during the 1898 Independence Day parade.

Things came to a head four days later when the vigilante "Committee of 101" gathered to discuss the situation at the Juneau Company wharf, led by one Frank Reid. Fearful of mob rule, Soapy went to address the meeting only to find himself in a gun battle with Reid. Soapy was shot in the heart and died immediately; Frank Reid died twelve agonizing days later from a gunshot wound to the groin. Both are buried in the Gold Rush Cemetery and, though Reid was no saint, it is obvious from the relative size of the monuments where the town's allegiances lay.

can now be achieved in four hours, for less than one tenth the financial outlay." By the time of its completion, however, the gold rush had subsided, but Skagway survived by maintaining the railroad and supporting the tourists who came to see this gold-rush town – the first tour boat arrived in 1900. Skagway got a new lease of life as a supply route for the construction of the Alaska Highway during World War II and continued as the main port for Yukon mineral-ore exports. Low returns for metals eventually closed the railroad in 1982 but the rising influence of tourism saw it revived in 1986.

Arrival, information, and getting around

The daily AMHS **ferry** (☎983-2229) from Juneau and Haines arrives 200yd from the main thoroughfare, Broadway. This is marginally the cheapest way to get here from Haines, though the Native-owned Chilkat Cruises and Tours (☎766-2100 or 1-888/766-2103, Ⓦwww.chilkatcruises.com) are a bit quicker (35min between ports) and charge $24 one-way and $44 round-trip on their three daily trips.

You probably won't have use for the fast connection between Skagway, Haines and Juneau with Fjord Express ($129 round-trip, $85 one-way; ☎1-800/320-0146, Ⓦwww.alaskafjordlines.com). It is aimed at those wanting a full-day round-trip to Juneau with a city tour included and is priced to discourage one-way traffic.

Bus routes to Skagway all come through Whitehorse in the Yukon. The cheapest to Whitehorse is Yukon Alaska Tourist Tours (☎983-2115), which charges $40 each way and runs twice daily: buy tickets from Sgt Preston's Trading Post, 2nd Avenue between Broadway and Spring, close to where the bus leaves. Alaska Direct (☎1-800/770-6652) runs once a week in summer from Whitehorse to Skagway and back ($50 each way); Alaskon Express, based at the *Westmark Inn* on 3rd Avenue (☎983-2241 or 1-800/544-2206), runs daily from Skagway to Whitehorse and back for $45 each way.

Though the superb White Pass & Yukon Route is primarily a tourist **train** service, it can be combined with Alaskon Express so that you travel from Whitehorse by bus to Log Cabin, BC, from where you ride the train into Skagway at a cost of $95.

The best source of general information is the **visitor center**, Broadway at 2nd Avenue (daily: May–Sept 8am–6pm; Oct–April 8am–5pm; ☎983-2854 or 1-888/762-1898, Ⓦwww.skagway.org), though there is also the Klondike Gold Rush National Historic Park visitor center, Broadway at 2nd Avenue (see p.180), and the Trail Center (see box, p.187).

The downtown area is eminently manageable on foot, but the SMART **bus** (May–Sept; ☎983-2743) tours downtown ($1.50 per journey; correct change needed) and is useful for a run up to 23rd Street ($2.50), a ten-minute walk from the cemetery.

Accommodation

Growth in tourism has meant a rise in standards for Skagway's accommodation. Prices tend to be quite high, but they generally offer good value. It is pretty much essential to reserve in advance in July and August and advisable a month on either side.

As well as the **campgrounds** listed here, you can camp on the trails out of town, though if you are still within city limits (such as at Lower Dewey Lake) you are required to alert the Skagway police (see p.183) of your presence. There are also two Forest Service **cabins** on the trails hereabouts (see box, p.183).

Hotels, motels, B&Bs, and cabins

Alaskan Sojourn Main St at 8th Ave ⓣ983-2030, ⓦwww.alaskansojourn.com. Well set-up hostel partly in an annex where there are spacious, single-sex, eight-bunk dorms ($20), each with its own bathroom. A good kitchen, cozy lounge area, sun room and free Internet access are all in the main house, which also has a private room ($50). There's no daytime lockout or curfew, and free ferry pickups are provided. ❶

At the White House 475 8th Ave at Main St ⓣ983-9000, ⓦwww.atthewhitehouse.com. High-standard B&B in one of Skagway's original homes, restored from its fire-damaged state and now with fully modernized rooms, some particularly spacious. All have phone, cable TV, ceiling fans, and super-comfy beds. A continental breakfast buffet is served and there's always tea, coffee, and home-baked cookies on hand. Large rooms ❻, otherwise ❺

Chilkoot Trail Outpost Dyea ⓣ983-3799, ⓦwww.chilkoottrailoutpost.com, ⓔinfo@chilkoottrailoutpost.com. Comfortable modern log cabins in the woods cluster around a fire pit and mosquito-free gazebo at this welcoming B&B, located almost 9 miles from Skagway and a quarter-mile from the start of the Chilkoot Trail. Hikers' cabins come with a double-plus-single bunk, private bathroom, satellite TV/VCR and buffet breakfast, but you'll need a sleeping bag. The larger cabins sleep up to four and come with bedding, microwave, and coffeemaker. Large cabins ❻, hikers ❸

Cindy's Place Mile 0.2 Dyea Rd, two miles from downtown Skagway ⓣ983-2674 or 1-800/831-8095, ⓦwww.alaska.net/~croland. Three cabins set in a beautiful spot in the woods, two of which are more luxurious, log-built cabins – with private bathrooms (one with a wood-burning stove), phone, and cooking equipment – while the budget third cabin is small but good value, with an indoor toilet, sink, microwave, fridge, kettle, and toaster, but no shower. It sleeps two ($53), but is perfect for one ($38); save $5 per person by using your own bedding and towels. All guests have free use of the hot tub and mountain bikes. Thoughtful little touches like fresh baking in the afternoon, a dozen varieties of tea and coffee in the cabins, and homemade jams and jellies for breakfast make this place special. Slight reductions for stays of two nights or more. May–Sept. Deluxe ❹, budget ❶–❷

Gold Rush Lodge 6th Ave at Alaska St ⓣ983-2831, ⓦwww.goldrushlodge.com. Immaculately kept and tastefully decorated motel, the smallness of the rooms compensated by appointments that extend to cable TV with VCR, phone, fridge, microwave, and coffeepot. Courtesy transfers available. ❹

Mile Zero B&B Main St and 9th Ave ⓣ983-3045, ⓦwww.mile-zero.com. Modern, purpose-built B&B with large rooms, each with a private entrance. A continental buffet breakfast is served in the communal lounge area, which is where you'll find the TV. ❺

Sgt Preston's Lodge 6th Ave at State St ⓣ983-2521, ⓔsgt-prestons@usa.net. Decent downtown motel with standard, and much nicer deluxe, rooms, all with cable TV and pickups by courtesy van. Deluxe ❹, standard ❸

Skagway Bungalows Mile 0.2 Dyea Rd ⓣ1-877/983-2986, ⓦwww.aptalaska.net/~saldi. A couple of large cabins in the woods next to *Cindy's Place*, each with king or queen bed, futon couch, an inside bathroom, and a big deck out front. March–Nov. ❹

Skagway Inn Broadway at 7th Ave ⓣ983-2289 or 1-888/752-4929, ⓦwww.skagwayinn.com. Turn-of-the-century former bordello now operating as a boutique B&B hotel with comfortable shared-bath rooms, each decorated with old furniture and bearing the name of an erstwhile occupant. Rooms vary considerably, so ask to see a few or simply go for one of the larger rooms, particularly the spacious, street-front "Alice." Fresh-baked breakfasts (included) are served in the restaurant downstairs. Large rooms ❻, otherwise ❺

Hostels and campgrounds

NPS Dyea Campground at Dyea, 9 miles northeast of Skagway. Simple and attractive first-come, first-served Park Service campground (not recommended for RVs) beside the Taiya River, with fire rings, picnic tables, pit toilets, and water that should be treated. $5 per site.

Pullen Creek RV Park Congress Way ⓣ983-2768 or 1-800/936-3731, ⓦwww.pullencreekrv.com. RV and tent park right by the harbor, with a dozen waterside RV sites. Showers are $1.25 extra. Mid-April to mid-Sept. Tent $14, tent and car $18, water, electricity and dump $25.

Skagway Home Hostel 3rd Ave at Main St ⓣ983-2131, ⓦwww.skagwayhostel.com. Traditionally run hostel in a century-old building, with bunks in fairly spacious single-sex dorms ($15 per night) and one private room ($40). Meals are shared, with an honesty box for your contribution for breakfast ($3) or a (typically) vegetarian dinner ($5), plus there's often fresh bread and fruit for a small contribution. Free bikes, basic supplies for cooking, a spacious yard, and no daytime lockout, but office hours are 5.30–10.30pm, and there is an 11pm curfew. Sheets are included in rates. Book using a credit card (particularly in July and Aug, and essential in winter) through the website, or try to catch them on the phone, though they are often unavailable. ❶

Skagway Mountain View RV Park Broadway at 12th Ave ⓣ983-3333 or 1-888/778-7700, ⓦwww.alaskarv.com. Large RV-dominated spot with all the expected facilities, water and electricity hookup ($25) and dry ($18) sites, and a few wooded tent sites ($14) that are in high demand.

The town and around

Almost everything in **downtown Skagway** happens on, or just off, Broadway, a half-mile-long strip lined with hotels, restaurants, a few bars, old buildings restored as museums, and a lot of swanky shops. It is a slightly unsettling blend, though you can come to terms with it all using the free and widely available *Skagway Walking Tour* leaflet. This is where you'll spend your time between forays on the White Pass & Yukon Route railway, out to the **Gold Rush Cemetery** and further afield to the scant remains of Dyea, the starting point for the multiday Chilkoot Trail hiking path.

Downtown Skagway

Most people arrive by boat and find themselves at the foot of Broadway, an area typically dominated by passengers disgorging from the White Pass & Yukon Route railway. A small park by the tracks contains an old snow-blowing locomotive once used on the line, as well as a statue of a Tlingit guide and prospector built to commemorate the town's centennial in 1998.

Many of Skagway's important historic buildings come under the auspices of the Klondike Gold Rush National Historic Park, including the **visitor center**, Broadway at 2nd Avenue (May–Sept daily 8am–6pm; ⓣ983-2921, ⓦwww.nps.gov/klgo), in what was the original WP&YR depot. Here you'll find plenty of information panels and park rangers ready to answer any questions, but it is best to time your visit to coincide with the excellent thirty-minute *Days of Adventure, Dreams of Gold* video (8am, 9am, 11am, noon, 1pm, 2pm, 4pm & 5pm; free), which tells the tale of the gold-rush prospectors' struggles over the passes to the Klondike. The center also runs ranger presentations (10am & 3pm; free) and walking tours of the downtown historic district (9am, 10am, 11am, 2pm & 3pm; free, but obtain tickets early in the day to be sure of a place). In a separate room there are great photos of those heady days a century back, along with a sample "ton of goods" – a lot more than you'd fancy hauling over the Chilkoot Trail.

Opposite the visitor center, a small building contains the **Chilkoot Trail Center** (see box, p.187), the first stop for all modern-day Chilkoot Trail aspirants, but otherwise of little interest. Around the corner stands **Soapy Smith's Parlor**, from where he ran his short-lived empire. The building is an 1890s original, though it was moved to this site in 1964 and is not currently open to the public. Across 2nd Avenue, the **Red Onion Saloon** is another transported building, though it is very much open for business (see p.188). Liquor was only one of the commodities formerly sold here, and you can now join the fifteen- to thirty-minute **Brothel Tour** (May–Sept daily roughly hourly 11am–4pm; $5), a tongue-in-cheek but historically accurate walk through what is left of the upstairs rooms (one of them restored) guided by "girls," suitably dressed in push-up bodices and feather boas, who stay in character throughout and tell a stack of entertaining tales. If this inspires you, consider the two-hour Haunted Red Light walking tour ($26, including a glass of bubbly), also done in costume with more amusing anecdotes delivered as you stroll around sixteen ghostly locations in the historic district. Ask at the saloon when the next tour is going.

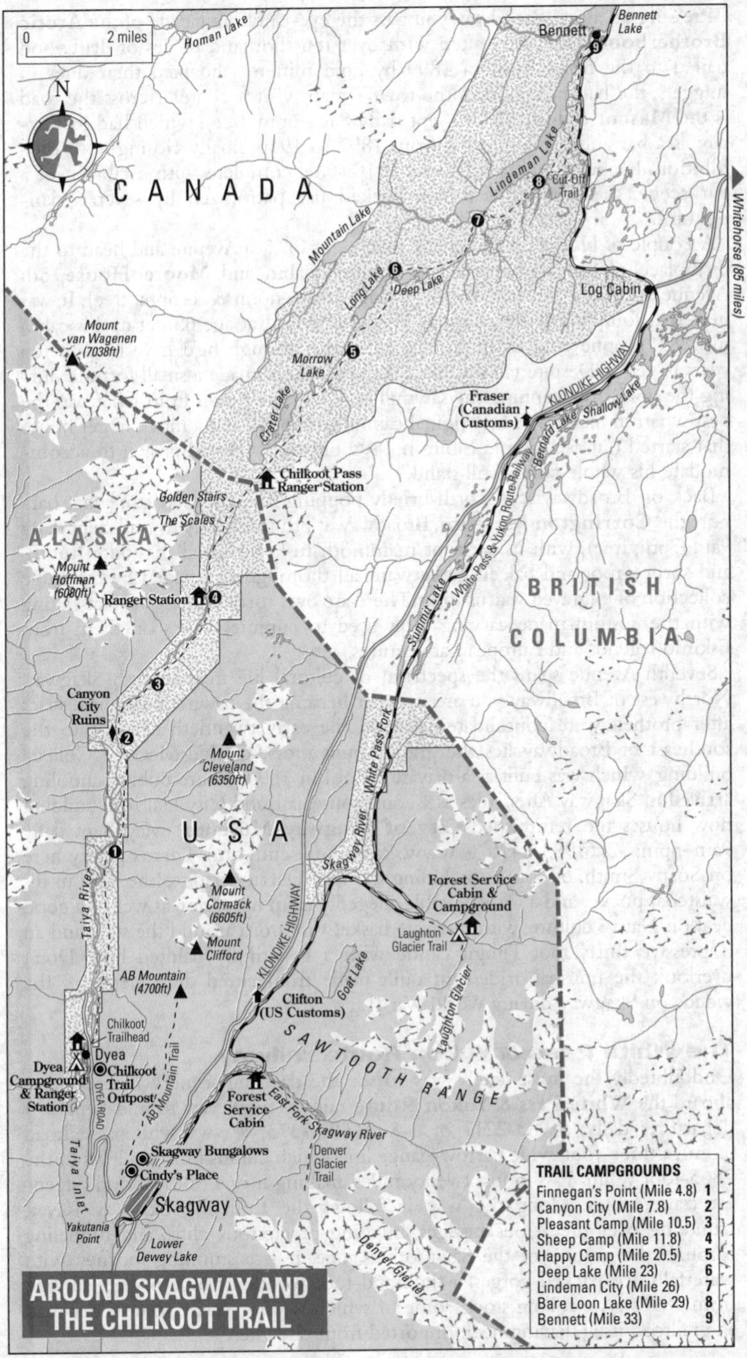
0 2 miles
N
CANADA
ALASKA
USA
BRITISH COLUMBIA
Homan Lake
Bennett
Bennett Lake
Lindeman Lake
Cut-Off Trail
Mountain Lake
Long Lake
Deep Lake
Log Cabin
Whitehorse (85 miles)
Mount van Wagenen (7038ft)
Morrow Lake
Crater Lake
KLONDIKE HIGHWAY
Fraser (Canadian Customs)
Bernard Lake
Shallow Lake
White Pass & Yukon Route Railway
Chilkoot Pass Ranger Station
Golden Stairs
The Scales
Mount Hoffman (6080ft)
Ranger Station
Summit Lake
Canyon City Ruins
Mount Cleveland (6350ft)
White Pass Fork
Skagway River
Taiya River
Mount Cormack (6605ft)
Mount Clifford
Forest Service Cabin & Campground
Laughton Glacier Trail
Goat Lake
Laughton Glacier
AB Mountain (4700ft)
Clifton (US Customs)
SAWTOOTH RANGE
Chilkoot Trailhead
Dyea
Dyea Campground & Ranger Station
Chilkoot Trail Outpost
DYEA ROAD
AB Mountain Trail
Forest Service Cabin
East Fork Skagway River
Taiya Inlet
Skagway Bungalows
Cindy's Place
Denver Glacier Trail
Skagway
Yakutania Point
Lower Dewey Lake
Denver Glacier
TRAIL CAMPGROUNDS
Finnegan's Point (Mile 4.8) 1
Canyon City (Mile 7.8) 2
Pleasant Camp (Mile 10.5) 3
Sheep Camp (Mile 11.8) 4
Happy Camp (Mile 20.5) 5
Deep Lake (Mile 23) 6
Lindeman City (Mile 26) 7
Bare Loon Lake (Mile 29) 8
Bennett (Mile 33) 9
AROUND SKAGWAY AND THE CHILKOOT TRAIL

Pressing on along Broadway you pass the eye-catching facade of the **Arctic Brotherhood Hall**, decorated with over ten thousand pieces of driftwood nailed to the front. Built in 1899 by gold miners who paid their dues in nuggets, the hall now houses the town's main visitor center. Across the road is the **Mascot Saloon** (May–Sept daily 8am–6pm; free), which had its heyday as a bar and gambling den from 1897 to 1916, finally closing with prohibition. It's been renovated to its 1910 state, complete with a tableau of a bar scene, the marvelous mirror-backed bar patronized by several mannequins.

A couple of blocks up Broadway, turn right on 5th Avenue and head to the birthplace of Skagway, marked by Moore Cabin and **Moore House**, 5th Avenue at Spring Street (May–Sept daily 10am–noon & 1–5pm; free). It was here that founding settler, Captain William Moore, at age 65, set up his cabin in 1887, prophesying an imminent gold rush, though he'd have to wait ten years to see it. Despite tales to the contrary, Moore made a small fortune during the gold rush, running the sawmill and collecting dues from what was the best wharf in Skagway. The original cabin (not open), and a much larger house that started out as a simple cabin in 1899 but by 1904 had grown to accommodate his whole family, still stand.

Back on Broadway, it is worth briefly popping into the craft store that harbors the **Corrington Museum**, Broadway at 5th (mid-May to mid-Sept daily 9am–7pm; free), with its six-foot mammoth tusk, fossilized mastodon tooth, and spruce-root and baleen basketware, all thoroughly upstaged by the huge collection of engraved walrus tusks. There are over forty of these artifacts, along with the custom-made carving tools used to conjure scenes on them from Eskimo legends and European adventures.

Seventh Avenue spans the spectrum of cultural life in gold-rush Skagway. Northwest of Broadway you are in what became the town's red-light district after brothels were consolidated here in the early twentieth century; to the southeast of Broadway lies the granite-built mock-Gothic McCabe College building, which was built as a private school in 1899, before public schooling arrived in Skagway. After roles as a courthouse, jail, and City Hall, the building now houses the refurbished **City of Skagway Museum** (May–Sept daily 9am–5pm; $2; ⓣ983-2420, ⓦwww.skagwaymuseum.org). There's plenty here on Soapy Smith, of course, including the tiny Derringer pistol he kept in his waistcoat pocket and a roulette table allegedly from his parlor, as well as a good deal on Native culture, with intricate basketware from around the state and an impressive thirty-foot Tlingit canoe with a beautifully painted bow. Don't overlook the unusual, iridescent quilt made from cured duck necks or the videos on Skagway during World War II.

The White Pass & Yukon Route railway

Undoubtedly the most stately way to see the dazzling scenery hereabouts is aboard the **White Pass & Yukon Route** railway (mid-May to mid-Sept; 2–3 departures daily; ⓣ983-2217 or 1-800/343-7373, ⓦwww.whitepassrailroad.com), a three-foot-wide narrow-gauge line which climbs from sea level to the 2865-foot White Pass in just twenty miles, making it one of the world's steepest train routes. Along the way it follows the tumbling Skagway River, trundling over precarious bridges, hugging precipitous cliffs, and tunneling through the granite of the Sawtooth Range. It is a stunning journey with waterfalls, ice-packed gorges, a thousand-foot wooden trestle bridge, all seen from 1890s-style rolling stock, some of which is very recent, some older than the railroad itself, having been imported from elsewhere.

Hikes around Skagway

To enjoy the good hiking available around Skagway, equip yourself with the u *Skagway Trail Map*, available free from the visitor center, with detailed descrip of a dozen walks in the area, the best of which are described below. Some of the trails are within an easy walk of downtown, while others can be reached via the WP&YR railway's summer hiker flag-stop service (June to early Sept). These trails can all be tackled in a day, though you could make use of the two Forest Service cabins in the area. Note that the Forest Service doesn't have an office in Skagway, so you'll need to book through their reservation service (ⓣ1-877/444-6777, ⓦwww.reserveUSA.com). Camping along the local trails is also possible, though you need to be fully self-sufficient and must register in person at the local police station, State Street at 1st Avenue (ⓣ983-2232).

AB Mountain Trail (9.5 miles round-trip from downtown; 6–8hr; 4700ft ascent). Strenuous hike up the southwest ridge of the prominent mountain immediately north of town which provides panoramic views from the alpine meadows near the summit. The trailhead on Dyea Road is most easily reached by the Yakutania Point Trail (see below). Some claim the mountain's name comes from the Arctic Brotherhood, while others contend it is for the letters A and B, which were once picked out in the melting snow: you can see them on old photos, such as one on a postcard in the *Mascot Saloon* on Broadway. Recent tree growth means you'll need a lot of imagination to see them these days, your best chance being in May and early June.

Denver Glacier Trail (6 miles round-trip; 4–6hr; 1200ft ascent). Moderate hike in the shadow of the magnificent Sawtooth Range to the scrubby terminal moraine of the Denver Glacier. The trailhead is six miles north of downtown Skagway and is accessed by the WP&YR railway's summer flag-stop service ($27 round-trip) departing from Skagway daily at 8am and 12.30pm, with Skagway-bound services passing the trailhead at 11.45am and 3.55pm. By the trailhead there is an old railroad caboose, which operates as a Forest Service cabin ($35).

Dewey Lakes Trails (1–8 miles round-trip; 40min–6hr; 500–3600ft ascent). A varied system of trails that starts near the end of 3rd Avenue and straggles up the hills to the south of Skagway to pretty, subalpine lakes and tumbling waterfalls. A steep ten-minute walk gets you to a great viewpoint over town, though it is worth continuing to Lower Dewey Lake (0.7 miles). If you're fairly fit, press on to the muskeg meadows around Upper Dewey Lake (3 miles), where there's a primitive free-use cabin, or even on to Devil's Punchbowl (4.2 miles), where there's a small alpine lake.

Laughton Glacier Trail (3 miles round-trip; 1hr to 1hr 30min; 200ft ascent). Easy stroll following the Skagway River ending in a wonderful rocky amphitheater surrounded by hanging glaciers. It is a short walk, but consider staying overnight, either camping or in the Forest Service cabin ($35) about half a mile from the trailhead and a mile from the glacier. The trailhead is fourteen miles north of Skagway and is accessed by the WP&YR railway's summer flag-stop service ($54 round-trip), departing from Skagway daily at 8am and 12.30pm, with Skagway-bound services passing the trailhead at 11.10am and 3.15pm.

Yakutania Point Trails (1.5 miles; 30–40min round-trip; negligible ascent). Gentle stroll to the pleasant picnic area at Yakutania Point or to another at Smuggler's Cove, a few minutes further. Start by following the path and footbridge by the airport buildings at the southwestern corner of town.

As with almost everything else around here, the railroad's construction was driven by gold. The relatively easy gradient of the White Pass made it amenable to the construction of a train line, and as thousands slogged their way to the goldfield over the Chilkoot and White passes, private interests were at work on Alaska's first railroad. In the two months from May 1898, four miles of track were laid. Things slowed considerably as workers had to be slung from ropes on the steep terrain to place blasting charges, and enormous bridges had to be built. Nonetheless, the entire 110 miles to Whitehorse was completed in just 26 months. Altogether 35,000 workers were employed building the railroad, but never more than 2000 at once, ample evidence of just how transient the population was at this time. It had cost its backers $10 million, but despite being completed after the great Yukon stampede was over, the railroad soon recouped the capital as prospectors abandoned both the Chilkoot and White Pass trails in favor of the railroad.

As the flood of gold seekers abated, the WP&YR settled into a more staid existence shipping metal ores from mines around Whitehorse to the sea at Skagway and acting as a supply route during the wartime construction of the Alaska Highway. Service along the route was suspended in 1982, only to be revived six years later with a view to tapping the cruise-ship market. Since then services have been progressively expanded, with trains now running as far as Bennett Lake, forty miles from Skagway. Unfortunately, this unmissable trip doesn't come cheap, and with heavy bookings from the cruise ships you seldom have the luxury of waiting for a fine day and travelling on the spur of the moment. The most popular run – and the one that most cruise passengers are funneled onto – is the three-hour White Pass Summit Excursion (mid-May to mid-Sept 2–3 daily; $89 round-trip), which runs from the **train station** at the junction of Broadway and 2nd Avenue to the Canadian border at the top of White Pass and back: sit on the left going up. All services are diesel-hauled except for the eight-hour Bennett Lake Excursion (mid-June to late Aug Fri & Sat only), which on Friday is diesel-hauled ($135) but on Saturday ($160) is drawn by a steam engine. The Excursion continues beyond the pass to Bennett Lake, British Columbia (the end of the Chilkoot Trail hiking route), where stampeders built boats before launching them five hundred miles down the Yukon to Dawson City. You get a couple of hours by the lake to eat your box lunch (included) and be shown around the evidence of those frenetic two years. In addition, there is the Skagway–Whitehorse Train+Bus service (mid-May to mid-Sept daily; $95 one-way to Whitehorse) on which you ride the train as far as Fraser (the Canadian border), then transfer to a bus for the run past Carcross to Whitehorse.

Gold Rush Cemetery and Dyea

No exploration of Skagway's gold-rush heritage would be complete without a visit to the **Gold Rush Cemetery**, the final resting place of many of the stampeders. Among them are Skagway's most famous outlaw, Soapy Smith, and his nemesis, Frank Reid, who according to his gravestone "gave his life for the honor of Skagway." Local prostitute Ella Wilson is also interred here, though her cheeky epitaph – "she gave her honor for the life of Skagway" – has now been removed. Still, it fitted nicely in a cemetery full of gentle conceits: most of the signs marking graves are modern additions put here when the cemetery was revamped for the benefit of tourists. It is a pleasant enough place to idle away half an hour; while there, be sure to take the short stroll to the 300-foot-high **Reid Falls**, which cascade down the hills behind the graveyard. The cemetery is about two miles from downtown: follow Alaska Street and keep going.

Those prospectors who weren't in Skagway trying to cheat death on the White Pass route to the Klondike were chancing their luck at the start of the Chilkoot Trail (see box, pp.186–187), nine miles away at the mouth of the Taiya River in **DYEA** (Dy-EE). At the height of the rush this was a bustling town of over five thousand where gold seekers stopped off just long enough to prepare for the three-month journey ahead, ferrying goods over the Chilkoot Pass. Initially favored by prospectors over Skagway, Dyea once ranked as the largest town in Alaska, but it went into rapid decline after the opening of the WP&YR railway. Most of the town's buildings have long since been torn down, but a few foundations remain, along with rotting stumps from the two-mile-long wharf and the **slide cemetery**, a mass burial place for the victims of a Chilkoot Trail avalanche that took sixty-odd lives at the former tent city of "the Scales" in April 1898. There's little else to show for the place, but it is a lovely spot to wander around, admiring the wildflowers and spotting birds, guided by interpretive panels and paths constructed by the Park Service. There's also a simple campground here and a sporadically attended ranger station, which runs free, **guided walks**, including a Dyea townsite tour (June–Aug daily 2pm; 1hr 30min) and a Chilkoot Nature Hike (twice a week; 1hr 30min to 2hr) along the first couple of miles of the Chilkoot Trail. Call the Park Service (Ⓣ983-2921) to confirm times.

Local tours and outdoor activities

Although it's easy enough to stroll around the downtown area and even hike out to the Gold Rush Cemetery, for more extensive exploration you might want to join one of the dozen or so cruise-passenger-oriented **local tours**. They come and go rapidly and change their itineraries seemingly annually, and so visit M&M Tour Brokers, 5th Avenue and Broadway (Ⓣ983-3900), for the latest. Frontier Excursions, Broadway at 7th Avenue (Ⓣ983-2512 or 1-877/983-2512, Ⓦwww.frontierexcursions.com), does a White Pass Summit and City Tour (2hr 30min; $35), which also visits the cemetery, a Dyea tour (3hr; $65), and a drive into the Yukon as far as Carcross (6hr; $85).

Sockeye Cycle Co, 5th Avenue at Broadway Street (Ⓣ983-2851, Ⓦwww.cyclealaska.com), offers a couple of guided **cycling tours**, neither requiring much effort: the Klondike Bicycle Tour (2hr 30min; $72) involves a narrated van ride up to the 3300-foot Klondike Pass and then a fairly steep descent back to Skagway with negligible pedaling; the Dyea Bicycle Adventure (2hr 30min; $72) also starts with a van ride, this time to the start of the Chilkoot Trail, followed by ninety minutes of gentle riding on the dirt roads around Dyea.

To get on the water contact Skagway Float Tours (Ⓣ983-3688, Ⓦwww.skagwayfloat.com), which runs **rafting trips**. Their staples are the Scenic Float Tour (3hr; $70) and the Hike & Float (4hr; $80), both involving about 45 minutes floating down the Taiya River at Dyea, plus plenty of natural history, and in the latter case a two-mile nature walk. For something more adventurous, go for a wild trip down the Class IV Tutshi River (6hr; $95) up at White Pass. Water levels dictate that the trip only runs from mid-June to mid-Aug and there is usually only about a trip a week, so call ahead to check their schedule.

Flightseeing trips from Skagway are understandably popular: the glacial scenery immediately around town is certainly impressive, and you're only a few minutes' flight from the majestic wonder of Glacier Bay. Some of the most popular local trips are with Temsco Helicopters (Ⓣ983-2900, Ⓦwww.temscoair.com), which does a flightseeing circuit with 25 minutes stopped on a flat section at the foot of one of the local glaciers (55min; $189). They will also whisk you up onto the Denver Glacier (2hr; $349), where they've installed several dog teams that will take you on a half-hour sled ride.

Planes lack the agility of choppers, but because they are cheaper to run and have a longer range, you tend to get a longer trip for your money. Planes are also able to fly over Glacier Bay. Three companies operate tours, including Skagway Air Service, 420 Broadway (Ⓣ983-2218, Ⓦwww.skagwayair.com),

Hiking the Chilkoot Trail

Alaska's most famous and popular hike, the 33-mile **Chilkoot Trail** (ⓦwww.nps.gov/klgo/chilkoot.htm and ⓦwww.parkscanada.gc.ca/lhn-nhs/yt/chilkoot/) is a three- or four-day journey through a giant wilderness museum, tracing the footsteps of Klondike-bound prospectors from the coast at **Dyea** through temperate rainforest, alpine tundra and the bare rocks of the Chilkoot Pass to **Bennett Lake** in British Columbia. The entire route is littered with haunting reminders of the past: ancient boilers that once drove aerial tramways, twisted metal fittings, collapsed huts, glass bottles, old boots, wooden tramway pylons, and even a stash of canvas and wood boats that were never used. Leave everything as you found it and try not to step on fragile relics.

The trail has an iconic status in the north and is consequently used by over three thousand hikers a year, many of whom would never consider any other multiday hike. Keen hikers shouldn't find it too challenging, though the less fit find it tough going, especially the much-hyped 45-degree scramble from the former tent city of "the Scales" to the top of the pass – 2500ft of ascent in one nine-mile day – which some people struggle to finish in twelve or fourteen hours. All this is made considerably more intimidating if the weather turns inclement, as it can do in any month of the year.

You need to be entirely self-sufficient and must camp in one of the nine approved **campgrounds**, each equipped with demarcated sites (sometimes on wooden platforms), pit toilets, and a central eating area overlooked by twenty-foot poles for hanging food out of bears' reach. With the exception of the one long day mentioned above, most campgrounds are spaced less than four hours apart, so you can take the whole trail at a leisurely pace.

The route

Most people hike from Dyea to Bennett, which keeps the strong prevailing winds at your back and makes for an easier scramble up the slippery rocks to the pass. From the trailhead you hike through temperate rainforest following the Taiya River past campgrounds at Finnegan's Point (Mile 4.8), Canyon City (Mile 7.8), and Pleasant Camp (Mile 10.5) before reaching **Sheep Camp** (Mile 11.8), the last before the big day over the pass. Get an early start from Dyea and it is easy enough to hike to Sheep Camp in one day: late risers should aim to cover the distance in two days. Leaving Sheep Camp at 4am or 5am ensures that you get over the pass and past an avalanche danger zone early in the day when it is safest. You initially climb through forest and tundra to "the Scales", where prospectors marshaled their gear before the arduous ascent of "Golden Stairs," a five-hundred-foot, hands-and-feet clamber over rocks to the top. At the pass there's an occasionally manned **Canadian border post** and a warming hut where you can brew up and gather your strength for the long hike down to **Happy Camp** (Mile 20.5). In June you'll have to cross extensive snowfields, but the stunning alpine scenery easily compensates. If you've got the strength you might want to continue on to the campground at Deep Lake (Mile 23), beautifully set beside some rapids, or even on to the lakeside campground at Lindeman City (Mile 26), where some prospectors built their boats. An early start from here takes you along a ridge parallel to Lindeman Lake and gets you to Bennett (Mile 33) in time for the train back to Skagway, though it is worth spending an extra day here exploring what is left of Bennett, basically a wooden church and a lot of junk the prospectors left behind.

From Bennett it is a seven-mile hike along the railroad tracks to the highway at Log Cabin, but you can take a **Cut-Off Trail** by Bare Loon Lake, where there's also a campground at Mile 29, midway between Lindeman City and Bennett, which saves about four miles but means you never see Bennett.

Reservations and permits

The trail is open all year, though most visit during the **hiking season** (early June to early Sept) when rangers patrol the trail, warming huts are open, and poles mark the route.

SOUTHEAST ALASKA | 186

You can still expect to encounter snow, however, up until the first or second week of July. Throughout the hiking season Parks Canada limits the number of hikers crossing the Chilkoot Pass into Canada to 50 per day. Of these spots 42 places can be booked in advance, while the remainder are offered on a first-come, first-served basis after 1pm on the day before you plan to start the trail from the Skagway **Trail Center**, Broadway at 1st Avenue (early June to early Sept daily 8.30am–4.30pm; ⓣ983-3655). **Reservations** (Can$10) are advised and are virtually essential during the peak season (July to mid-Aug). In the off-season call the reservation system (ⓣ867/667-3910 or 1-800/661-0486 between 8.30am and 4pm Pacific Standard Time, which is one hour ahead of Alaska time); from early June to early September reserve through the Trail Center. Be sure to have your desired hiking itinerary handy and an alternative schedule (including a list of the nights you intend to spend in each campground).

All hikers (either with or without reservations) need to go to the Trail Center to buy a **permit** (Can$50), sign a register (for customs purposes), and consult the weather forecast. You'll need to carry **identification**, which means a birth certificate or passport for North Americans (a driver's license is not acceptable) and a passport for everyone else. You may be required to deal with Canadian customs at the Chilkoot Pass ranger station but more likely you'll do it after your hike at the Alaska–Canada border post at Fraser or in Whitehorse.

Though it isn't really necessary, you may want to buy the Canadian Parks Service's *Chilkoot Trail* **map** ($4.50 from the Trail Center), which is about the best available.

Transport and supplies

To get to the start of the trail, nine miles northwest of Skagway at Dyea, you could arrange a lift or walk. As road walks go it is a very pleasant hike, and you might be able to thumb a lift if you get bored. Otherwise you'll have to engage the services of one of the **shuttle buses** ($10): Dyea Dave (ⓣ983-2731 or mobile ⓣ209-5031) or Frontier Excursions (ⓣ983-2512 or 1-877/983-2512, ⓦwww.frontierexcursions.com).

The trail finishes at Bennett from where you can **return to Skagway** on the WP&YR railway's Chilkoot Trail Hikers Service (June to early Sept Mon–Sat at 1pm Alaska time; generally $35 one-way to Fraser, $65 to Skagway, but on Saturday $65/$80), which is either a railcar or one carriage of the Lake Bennett Excursion that's specially designated for smelly hikers. Remember to buy your **tickets** at the WP&YR office in Skagway before you set off on the trail otherwise you'll have a $15 fee added to the ticket price for the convenience of buying your ticket on the train; and note that for customs reasons the train doesn't stop at Log Cabin. Riding the rails is the perfect complement to the hike, giving a sense of how important the train was to the prospectors.

Alternatively, hike from Bennett the eight miles along the tracks to the highway at Log Cabin and meet up with one of the shuttle buses ($25–30 for a combined drop-off and pickup). It isn't much fun walking along the tracks, so consider the shortcut off the trail, which avoids Bennett.

Continuing on to Whitehorse involves getting yourself to Log Cabin (by train or on foot), then picking up Yukon Alaska Tourist Tours (9.40am & 2.10pm Alaska time; $25; ⓣ983-2115).

When setting out from Skagway be sure to take wet-weather gear, matches, some method of water treatment, sunscreen, sunglasses, a flashlight, and **30ft of rope** so that you can sling your food, toothpaste, and any scented items over the bear poles at each campground. Rope is available from Skagway Hardware Co, Broadway and 4th Avenue. Early in the season when there's plenty of snow about, consider **gaiters** and **hiking poles**, which can be rented from the Mountain Shop in Skagway (see "Listings," p.190).

Almost all accommodations in Skagway offer free **gear storage** for their guests.

which has a Gold Rush Tour (45min; $70) around the White and Chilkoot passes, Bennett Lake, and the Juneau Ice Field, as well as an excellent Glacier Bay Tour (1hr 30min; $130), with views down to the main glaciers and sometimes straying as far as the Fairweather Range. They also fly to Skagway from Juneau (direct 45min, $85; with a Glacier Bay overflight 1hr 30min, $170), and from Gustavus ($95).

Eating, drinking, and entertainment

Most of Skagway's **bars** and **restaurants** lie in the touristy part of Broadway, where a five-minute stroll will reveal almost everything the town has to offer. As befits such a heavily visited town, the range is pretty decent, though the fast-food franchises haven't moved in yet. For **groceries** and trail supplies head to the Fairway Market, State Street at 4th Avenue, or for more exotic (and healthy) goods, visit You Say Tomato, State Street at 9th Avenue (Ⓣ983-2784).

Evening **entertainment** mainly revolves around the bars (all on Broadway), though you may want to catch some Robert Service poetry in the Eagle Hall at the *Days of '98 Show*, Broadway at 6th Avenue (May–Sept daily at 10.30am, 2.30pm & 8pm; $14, evening show $16; Ⓣ983-2545), where the story of Soapy and Frank is acted out in a gold-rush saloon atmosphere (only without the drinking). The evening show is preceded by an hour of fake gambling.

Bonanza Bar & Grill Broadway at 3rd Ave Ⓣ983-6214. Bustling sports bar with a range of microbrews and a select menu of burgers, sandwiches, and salads (all $8–11).

Corner Café State St at 4th Ave Ⓣ983-2155. Often smoky daytime diner that's much favored by Skagway's outdoor set and a good break from the press of people on Broadway just a couple of blocks away. Stuffed croissants with salad or soup for $7, or salmon burger for $9.

Glacial Smoothies & Espresso 3rd Ave at Broadway Ⓣ983-3074. A good spot where the name says it all.

The Haven State St at 9th Ave Ⓣ983-3553. Relaxed coffeeshop with sofas and stacks of magazines, serving good espresso, egg or granola breakfasts, mouthwatering panini and fresh salads – Santa Fe, Greek, Caesar – all available with added chicken ($7–9).

Kone Kompany 485 Broadway Ⓣ1-800/664-2370. Ever-popular little store selling homemade fudge, ice cream, yogurt, and excellent shakes.

Mabel G Smith's 342 5th Ave at Broadway Ⓣ983-2609. Low-key espresso bar with the best coffee in town, glazed pumpkin cookies with a reputation throughout the north, and a relaxed vibe.

Moe's Frontier Bar Broadway at 4th Ave Ⓣ983-2238. The place for straightforward drinking.

Red Onion Saloon Broadway at 2nd Ave Ⓣ983-2222. An 1898 wood-floored bar and former bordello where the bar staff don period dress and engage in role play that would be horribly cheesy if it wasn't done with such enthusiasm. It is an approach much loved by cruise-ship passengers, who flock in during the day, often with the ship's band in tow, ready to strike up a few jazz tunes. The girls who once plied their trade upstairs have unwittingly given their names to the excellent pizza, a theme followed with the named sandwiches washed down with the town's best selection of draft beers. Evenings bring out the locals, with bands several nights a week in summer.

Sabrosa Broadway at 6th Ave Ⓣ983-2469. Daytime café and bakery, tucked in behind the gift shops, that's great for breakfast (from $4) and lunches of burritos ($7), vegetarian chili (cup $3, bowl $6), and tarragon, pecan, and chicken salad ($8). Shaded outdoor seating for those hot days.

Stowaway Café 205 Congress Way Ⓣ983-3463. Stop by during the day for a top-quality lunch, perhaps of a halibut sandwich ($11) or a blackened-chicken Caesar ($9), and again in the evening for the likes of coconut prawns ($20), sweet and sour vegetables ($15), and pecan pie ($6), all served in a congenial atmosphere with views of the small boat harbor.

Sweet Tooth Café Broadway at 3rd Ave Ⓣ983-2405. Popular traditional American-style café, serving breakfast along with lunches featuring Reuben sandwiches ($7.50), halibut burgers ($8), and ice cream.

Robert Service: poet of the gold rush

With the possible exception of Jack London, no literary figure is more closely associated with the sub-Arctic North than English-born poet **Robert Service** (1874–1958), whose lilting, well-crafted rhymes captured the essence of the Klondike gold rushes. This "Bard of the Yukon" had only tenuous contact with Alaska – he traveled through Skagway and on the WP&YR railway to Whitehorse – but the material he dealt with, and the spirit with which he imbued his poetry, rings just as true in Alaska as it does in the Yukon. Accordingly, Service has been wholly adopted by the Alaskan tourist machine. All over the state you'll find crowds of visitors flocking to hear performers reciting Service's more crowd-pleasing Klondike works: *The Shooting of Dan McGrew*, *The Cremation of Sam McGee*, and *The Spell of the Yukon*.

Service's work is often derided by the literary establishment, who barely consider him a "real" poet let alone a "great" one, but, despite the unfamiliarity of his subject matter, he spoke to the average reader in language understood by all, his vibrant imagery delivered with a dramatic, almost metronomic intensity. Undoubtedly a people's poet, he once claimed, "The only society I like, is that which is rough and tough – and the tougher the better. That's where you get down to bedrock and meet human people." His sympathies certainly rested with the common people, but he was never the archetypal starving poet, and after the publication of his Yukon poems he quickly became very wealthy, some claiming that *The Shooting of Dan McGrew* alone brought in half a million dollars.

His three most famous poems were written in Whitehorse during a prolific few months at the end of 1906, eight years after the Klondike rush, a phenomenon that Service had missed entirely as he drifted around the southwestern US and Mexico. By 1904 he had returned to his original profession as a bank clerk and been transferred to Whitehorse, a town in decline as prospectors had moved on to richer Alaskan strikes, leaving the old claims to be worked over by mechanical dredges. Still, there were enough sourdoughs left to tell the tale, and when the local paper, which knew of his poetic leanings, asked for "something about our own bit of earth," he quickly tapped into a rich vein. Overheard yarns, shaggy-dog stories, and snippets gleaned from every source were woven together and soon became his first and most celebrated book, *Songs of a Sourdough*.

Numerous other books followed, some even being turned into films, but none of his later work captured the zeitgeist to the same degree, nor have any had the same enduring popularity. Service spent the rest of his long life pursuing all manner of interests and doing pretty much as he pleased, freed by the nest egg he had created in those few months in Whitehorse. He traveled the world, worked as a war correspondent, settled in Paris with a Frenchwoman, flirted with Marxism, narrowly escaped the German army after mocking Hitler in a poem he wrote for a newspaper, and died of a heart attack at his retreat in Lancieux, France, at the age of 84.

Listings

Banks Wells Fargo, Broadway at 6th Ave (Mon–Fri 9.30am–5pm) has 24hr ATMs.

Bicycle rental Sourdough Car Rentals (see below) rents basic runabouts for $10 a day; Sockeye Cycle Co, 381 5th Ave at Broadway (Ⓣ983-2851, Ⓦwww.cyclealaska.com), charges $12 for 2hr, $20 a half-day, and $30 an eight-hour day, with discounts offered for two- and three-day rentals.

Bookshop Skagway News Depot, Broadway at 3rd Ave (Ⓣ983-3354, Ⓦwww.skagwaybooks.com), has lots of Alaskana, a small selection of other books and magazines, and out-of-state newspapers.

Car rental The cheapest cars are offered by Sourdough Car Rentals, 6th Ave at Broadway (Ⓣ983-2523 or 1-800/478-2529, Ⓔsourdoughrentals@yahoo.com), which has compacts for $50 with unlimited mileage. PB Cruisers, 326 3rd Ave at Broadway (Ⓣ983-3385), rents vehicles from $60 a day but they don't allow their cars to go beyond Whitehorse. Avis, inside the *Westmark Hotel* at 2nd Ave and Spring St (Ⓣ983-2247), charges around $65 a day in high summer with unlimited mileage.

Festivals and events Klondike Trail of '98 International Road Relay (first weekend in Sept; Ⓣ1-867/668-4236, Ⓦwww.sportyukon.com) during which almost 200 teams of runners leave Skagway for Whitehorse, running through the night.

Internet access Free for half an hour at the library (see below); commercially at Alaska Cruiseship Services, 2nd Ave at State St, and *Glacial Smoothies & Espresso*, 3rd Ave at Broadway, which both have plenty of fast machines at reasonable rates.

Laundry and showers Pay-by-the-quarter showers next to the Harbormaster's office on Congress Way. Laundry at Services Unlimited, cnr State and 2nd (daily 7am–9pm), and at *Garden City RV Park*, State St at 16th St.

Left luggage Nothing formal, so when hiking the Chilkoot you'll have to rely on your hotel or hostel: most are amenable but it pays to ask.

Library Skagway Public Library, State St at 8th Ave (Mon–Fri noon–9pm, Sat 1–5pm).

Medical assistance Klondike Clinic, Main St at 15th Ave Ⓣ983-3311.

Outdoor gear The Mountain Shop, 355 4th Ave (Ⓣ983-2544), sells major brands and rents tents (first night $20, subsequent nights $10), sleeping bags ($16/$8), cooking stoves ($6/$3), packs ($14/$7), sleeping pads ($6/$3), trekking poles ($5/$3), snowshoes ($5), sea kayaks ($25 a day), and more.

Post office Broadway at 6th Ave (Mon–Fri 8.30am–5pm). The **General Delivery** zip code is 99840.

Taxes There's a four percent sales tax in Skagway; the tax on hotels amounts to eight percent, which we've included within our price codes.

Travel details

With the exception of the 372-mile loop between near neighbors Haines and Skagway, none of the towns in Southeast is connected by road, so ferries and planes take the load. The following ferry frequencies only apply from late May to early September (though there are limited services throughout the winter) – but **new ferries** scheduled to be introduced in the near future will provide more frequent trips and improve journey times. (For more on this, see Basics, p.37.)

Alaska Airlines links most of the main Southeast towns using Juneau as the main hub. It runs several frequent-stop "milk runs" daily, such as Juneau–Petersburg–Wrangell–Ketchikan–Seattle, Anchorage–Juneau–Sitka–Seattle, and Anchorage–Cordova–Yakutat–Juneau–Seattle.

Buses

Haines to: Anchorage (3 weekly; 18hr); Fairbanks (3 weekly; 15hr); Tok (3 weekly; 10hr).

Skagway to: Whitehorse (3 weekly; 3hr).

Ferries

Angoon to: Juneau (2 weekly; 11hr); Kake (2–3 weekly; 4hr); Sitka (2 weekly; 4hr); Tenakee Springs (2–3 weekly; 2hr 30min).

Bellingham, WA to: Juneau (1 weekly; 60hr); Ketchikan (weekly; 37hr).

Haines to: Juneau (1–2 daily; 4hr 30min); Skagway (1–2 daily; 1hr).

Hollis to: Ketchikan (2 daily; 3hr).

Hoonah to: Juneau (3–4 weekly; 3hr 15min); Tenakee Springs (1–3 weekly; 3hr 15min).

Juneau to: Angoon (3 weekly; 9–10hr); Bellingham, WA (weekly; 74hr); Haines (1–2 daily; 4hr 30min); Hoonah (3–4 weekly; 3hr 15min); Kake (1–3 weekly; 13hr 30min); Ketchikan (roughly daily; 21hr); Pelican (every 2 weeks; 6hr 30min); Petersburg (roughly daily; 8hr); Prince Rupert, BC (4–5 weekly; 24–30hr); Seward (1–2 monthly; 50hr); Sitka (daily; 4–5hr); Skagway (1–2 daily; 7hr); Tenakee Springs (2 weekly; 7–9hr); Valdez (1–2 monthly; 36hr); Wrangell (5–7 weekly; 12hr).

Kake to: Angoon (2–3 weekly; 4hr); Juneau (1 weekly; 15hr); Sitka (1–2 weekly; 8hr).

Ketchikan to: Bellingham, WA (weekly; 37hr); Hollis (2 daily; 3hr); Metlakatla (6 weekly; 1hr 30min); Petersburg (roughly daily; 10hr); Prince Rupert, BC (4–6 weekly; 6hr); Wrangell (4–6 weekly; 6hr).

Metlakatla to: Ketchikan (6 weekly; 1hr 30min).
Pelican to: Juneau (every 2 weeks; 6hr 30min).
Petersburg to: Juneau (roughly daily; 8hr); Kake (2–3 weekly; 4hr); Sitka (2–4 weekly; 11hr); Wrangell (4–6 weekly; 3hr).
Prince Rupert, BC to: Juneau (3–4 weekly; 24hr); Ketchikan (4–6 weekly; 6hr).
Sitka to: Angoon (2 weekly; 4hr); Juneau (daily; 4–5hr); Petersburg (2–4 weekly; 11hr); Tenakee Springs (2 weekly; 9hr).
Skagway to: Haines (1–2 daily; 1hr); Juneau (1–2 daily; 7hr).
Tenakee Springs to: Angoon (2–3 weekly; 2hr 30min); Hoonah (1–3 weekly; 3hr 15min); Juneau (1–2 weekly; 6hr).
Wrangell to: Juneau (5–7 weekly; 12hr); Ketchikan (4–6 weekly; 6hr); Petersburg (4–6 weekly; 3hr).

Flights

Glacier Bay/Gustavus to: Juneau (1 daily; 25min).
Juneau to: Anchorage (4 daily; 1hr 40min); Cordova (1 daily; 2hr); Fairbanks (2 daily; 3hr–3hr 30min); Gustavus (1 daily; 25min); Ketchikan (2 daily; 1–2hr); Pelican (2 a month; 6hr); Petersburg (1 daily; 40min); Seattle (6–9 daily; 3hr 20min–4hr 30min); Sitka (3 daily; 40min); Wrangell (1 daily; 1hr 30min); Yakutat (1 daily; 45min).
Ketchikan to: Anchorage (1–2 daily; 3–5hr); Craig (3 daily; 45min); Juneau (2 daily; 1–2hr); Metlakatla (15 daily; 10min); Petersburg (1 daily; 1hr 30min); Seattle (5 daily; 1hr 40min); Sitka (1 daily; 50min); Wrangell (1 daily; 40min).
Petersburg to: Anchorage (1 daily; 3hr); Juneau (1 daily; 40min); Ketchikan (1 daily; 1hr 30min); Seattle (1 daily; 4hr 50min); Wrangell (1 daily; 20min).
Seattle to: Juneau (6–9 daily; 3hr 20min–4hr 30min); Ketchikan (5 daily; 1hr 40min); Petersburg (1daily; 4hr 50min); Sitka (4 daily; 4–5hr); Wrangell (1 daily; 2hr 20min); Yakutat (1 daily; 5hr).
Sitka to: Anchorage (1 daily; 3hr); Juneau (3 daily; 40min); Ketchikan (1 daily; 50min); Seattle (4 daily; 4–5hr).
Wrangell to: Anchorage (1 daily; 3hr 40min); Juneau (1 daily; 1hr 30min); Ketchikan (1 daily; 40min); Petersburg (1 daily; 20min); Seattle (1 daily; 2hr 20min).
Yakutat to: Anchorage (1 daily; 2hr); Cordova (1 daily; 45min); Juneau (1 daily; 45min); Seattle (1 daily; 4hr 40min).

2

Anchorage

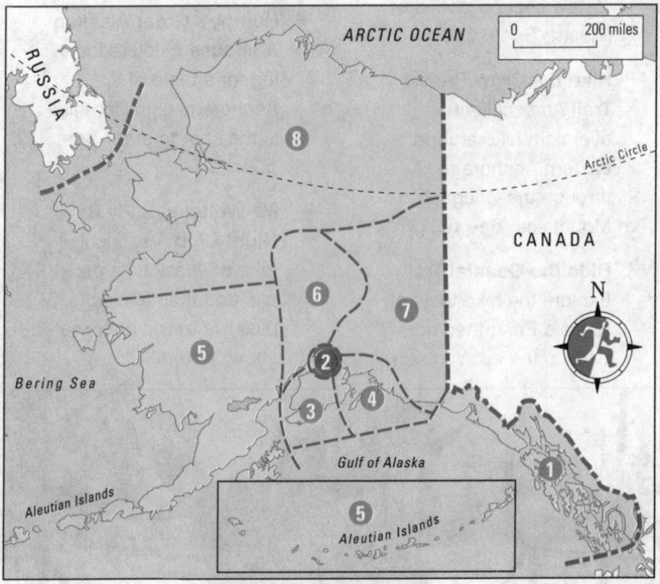
ARCTIC OCEAN
0
200 miles
RUSSIA
Arctic Circle
8
CANADA
6
7
N
5
2
Bering Sea
3
4
Gulf of Alaska
1
Aleutian Islands
5
Aleutian Islands

CHAPTER 2

Highlights

* **Hooking kings downtown** Fish for king and silver salmon in Ship Creek, virtually in the shadow of downtown skyscrapers. See p.208
* **Museum of History & Art** A first-class exploration of Alaska's culture and history, plus the state's best collection of fine art. See p.209
* **Hike the Crow Pass Trail** An excellent overnight hike around eastern Anchorage through the Chugach Mountains. See p.215
* **Ride the Coastal Trail** Explore the bike trails of Kincaid Park, then ride back in the evening sun along the Tony Knowles Coastal Trail. See p.212
* **Alaska Native Heritage Center** A pricey but welcome introduction to Alaska's Native peoples. Especially worth it if you're not going to visit their tribal homelands. See p.216
* **Humpy's Great Alaskan Alehouse** If you're looking for a taste of Anchorage nightlife, this is the spot to start. See p.221
* **Mr Whitekey's Fly By Night Club** A satirical take on Alaska, its people, and their foibles, plus live music after the show. See p.221

△ An unexpected visitor

2

Anchorage

A quarter of a million strong, **ANCHORAGE** is Alaska's only true city. It is home to 42 percent of Alaskans, is five times the size of its nearest challenger, Fairbanks, and is the state capital in all but name. Alaska's lifeblood, oil, plays a big part. Black gold is neither tapped, shipped, nor pumped anywhere near the city, but oil companies have established offices here, and oil-generated wealth has a tangible presence. In many ways it is the very antithesis of all things archetypally Alaskan, with gleaming cars, designer labels, and gourmet goodies present in a way you won't find anywhere else in the state. On these grounds alone Anchorage is loathed, or at least resented, by just about everyone who doesn't live in the big city. Whenever talk turns to moving the state capital away from Juneau to somewhere more central and accessible, Anchorage is the obvious choice, but for fear of concentrating even more power here, the rest of the state will never let that happen.

Flying into the **Anchorage Bowl** – the region encompassing the city and its immediate surroundings – you're instantly struck by the majesty of the setting, seated at the foot of the snowcapped Chugach Mountains on the edge of a great wilderness and girt by the shimmering water of Cook Inlet. Trouble is, the civic planners seem to have turned their backs on the location and managed to produce a replica of just about any American city west of the Great Plains: a couple of clusters of glass office blocks set in a fabric of shopping malls, all cemented together by fast food and family restaurants. "Condensed, instant Albuquerque," John McPhee called it in his 1977 classic *Coming into the Country*, and that's probably truer today than it was then. Some seventy percent of current residents were not here in 1980. Indeed, until very recently, Anchorage was always considered a stepping-stone to somewhere better (usually more remote, or warmer). Even today, it's likely you won't be in Anchorage long before some wag tells you that the great thing about the city is that Alaska is only half an hour away. It is certainly true that you have to travel only a short distance to experience glaciers, precipitous mountains, and wild bush country, but Anchorage itself has its charms. What other city has moose grazing alongside the highways and chomping through suburban flower gardens, Beluga whales breaching within yards of the coastal bike trail, twenty hours of midsummer sunlight, and magnificent hiking trails just a couple of miles from downtown?

Thanks to the warming effect of the Japan Current and the rain-shadowing beneficence of the Kenai and Chugach mountains, you can spend the summer days in shorts and a T-shirt cycling the coastal bike trail, hiking to hilltops with fabulous views of the Alaska Range, or even swimming in one of the city's small lakes. There are more urban attractions, too, not least the state's most

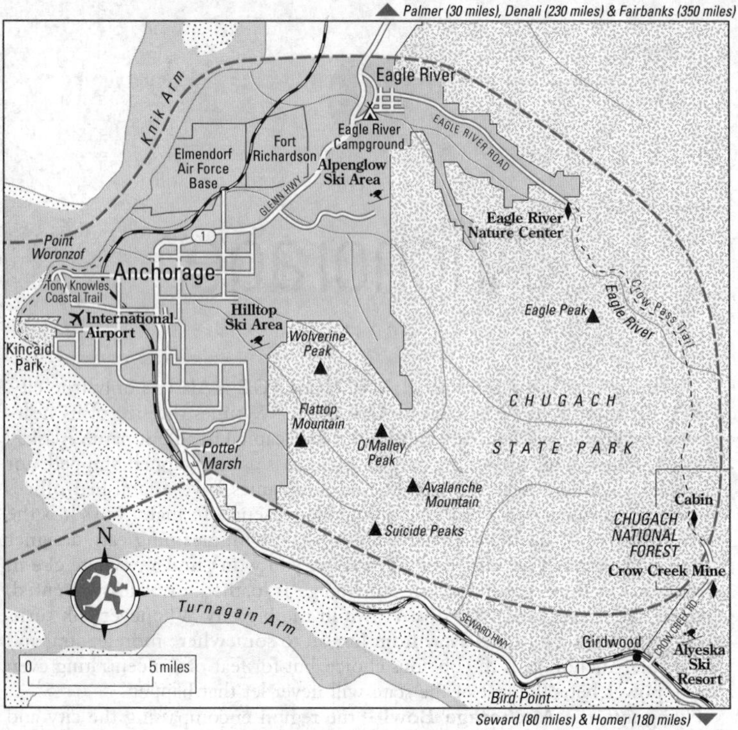

cosmopolitan, and tolerably affordable, dining and drinking scene, and a coffee culture as strong as that of any West Coast city. That alone is enough to justify stopping for a couple of nights, but there are also a couple of excellent museums – the Anchorage Museum of History & Art and the Heritage Museum – and the groundbreaking Alaska Native Heritage Center.

Some history

The banks of Cook Inlet were first discovered around five thousand years ago when proto-Eskimos occupied sites along Turnagain Arm. Dena'ina Athabascans took their place by the time early Russian explorers came to exchange copper and iron for fish and furs, and in 1778 traded with British captain **James Cook** who was here in search of the Northwest Passage. This waterway is now known as Cook Inlet in his honor, though he himself dubbed one branch **Turnagain Arm** as he about-faced and tacked off to search further west.

By Cook's time, the **Russians** were well established in the region, particularly in Eklutna, twenty miles north of Anchorage, where a Russian Orthodox church still stands. It wasn't until 1912 that Congress sensed the need for greater access to strategic inland coalfields and sanctioned the construction of a railroad linking the port of Seward and the navigable rivers of the Interior. Construction was centered on the ice-free shores of Cook Inlet, a flat and barren spot that soon sprouted the fledgling tent city of Anchorage. Within weeks Anchorage was home to two thousand construction hopefuls. Five months later the surrounding land was auctioned off in gridded lots, leaving the creekside site of the tent city as home to rail yards and docks. Some 650 lots were sold with the stipulation that any lots used for gambling, prostitution, or liquor production would be forfeited. The US post office used a literal description of the site and called the place Anchorage, a name which the residents failed to dislodge despite holding a referendum and picking Alaska City as the name for their new home. Since then Anchorage has been characterized by rapid but sporadic growth. By the beginning of the 1940s, the city still had only 3500 residents, but it was soon to see the effect of a developing infrastructure and a spin-off from the influx of New Deal settlers in the Mat-Su Valley. With the arrival of the military during World War II, Anchorage was firmly established as Alaska's dominant city, and statewide developments – such as the construction of the Alaska Highway – only served to reinforce this position. The population had jumped to 47,000 by the completion of the road link to Seward in the early 1950s – just in time for the discovery of oil on the Kenai Peninsula. This, statehood in 1959, and the establishment of Anchorage's international airport – which, being equidistant from New York and Tokyo, soon became a kind of subpolar crossroads for long-distance flights – set an optimistic tone for the new decade. Confidence was soon rocked by the 1964 **Good Friday Earthquake** (see box, p.207), which destroyed an entire suburb, wrecked the city, and imprinted itself on the memories of a generation.

During the 1950s, a small oil-drilling operation had been established on the Kenai Peninsula, so when enormous quantities of the commodity were

The Permanent Fund Dividend

Alaskans pay no state income tax, and on top of that they reap the benefits of the **Permanent Fund Dividend** (@www.pfd.state.ak.us), paid out in the first week in October each year to every man, woman, and child who has spent ten months of the previous calendar year in Alaska. Even a vagrant can claim it, if he can come up with a viable address. In recent years it has consistently topped $1500 (it peaked at $1963 in 2000), so for a family of five it might form a quarter of their annual income and provide an opportunity to stash some away for the kids' education or just get frivolous. By mid-September Alaskan companies start tapping into the mini-boom, luring customers with attractive offers: airlines offer multiflight trips in return for the dividend check, and with winter approaching snowmachine dealers do a roaring trade discounting their latest models. For people eking out a hand-to-mouth existence in the woods from hunting, trapping, and a little gold panning, the PFD is even more important. For them it is the only time in the year they have enough cash to stock up on spare parts, fishing lures, ammunition, fuel, and basic groceries.

Alaska took a smart approach to its oil revenues by instituting a state constitutional amendment in 1976 that set aside a quarter of all oil royalties as a kind of nest egg to be used as oil revenues declined. Very quickly the account reached embarrassing proportions, and in 1982 the state made its first payment to residents, distributing ten percent of the interest gained (averaged over the last five years) among those who qualified. The payment has become a staple of the Alaskan year – a strange situation in a state where anything that has the faintest whiff of socialism is widely reviled and ridiculed. It was long considered political suicide to drop or substantially cut the PFD, but recent state budget shortfalls mean that even this icon of the north is under threat.

With the bear markets of recent years the Permanent Fund has dropped in value from $28 billion to around $22 billion (and dividends have dropped accordingly: $1107 in 2003), but the interest still generates more income than the state receives from its oil revenue.

discovered at Prudhoe Bay in Alaska's Arctic north, it made sense for oil companies to consolidate their operations in Anchorage. Fairbanks was the base for the construction of the Trans-Alaska Pipeline (see box, p.488), but Anchorage continued to benefit from the new pool of skilled workers, both fueling the demand and providing the wherewithal for continued development. When the state's oil revenues started pouring in so fast they couldn't be spent, the benefits were divided proportionally to population, so it was Anchorage that got a slew of new and grandiose buildings downtown – library, sports arena, civic center, and more. But much of the money was diverted into the Permanent (see box, p.197), which helped ease the hardships brought on by low oil prices in the late 1980s. Today, Anchorage continues to grow, gradually shaking off its boom-and-bust persona and gaining a level of maturity as it copes with the economic difficulties thrown up by the decline in oil revenues.

Arrival, information, and city transportation

As Alaska's major gateway city, Anchorage sees a sizeable portion of the state's international arrivals. If you're not driving the Alaska Highway or cruising up through the Inside Passage you'll almost certainly arrive here. Most domestic **flights** arrive from Seattle: get a right-side window seat for views of the Inside Passage, fjords, and glaciers prior to the magnificent descent into Anchorage airport – renamed the Ted Stevens Anchorage International Airport (ANC) a few years back, for Alaska's senior senator (see box, p.533)

Direct flights from outside North America and all Delta flights arrive at the North (international) Terminal, which only has a small visitor desk (open for flight arrivals); to get to the main terminal board the Airport Shuttle that runs every ten to fifteen minutes around the clock. All other flights arrive at the main South (domestic) Terminal which, along with the usual restaurants and shops, has a **visitor information** desk (daily 9am–4pm) in the baggage claim area, ATMs (but no foreign exchange facilities), courtesy phones to some hotels, and luggage storage (see "Listings," p.226).

The airport is only five miles southwest of central Anchorage, so **getting downtown** is quick and fairly painless. Taxis cost about $18 and line up outside the terminal; the city's **People Mover bus** route #7 runs downtown every hour (Mon–Fri 7am–11pm, Sat 9am–9pm, Sun 10am–7pm; $1.25) from both terminals; and Downtown Connection (Ⓣ344-6667, Ⓔinfo@akdowntownconnection.com) have on-demand transportation from the airport to downtown hotels and the train station for $6 per person.

There's also a new train line for cruise-ship transfers, but there are currently no plans to start a passenger service downtown.

For your first night's accommodation (or last night before departure), it is also worth considering staying at one of the places closest to the airport (see "Midtown and the airport" accommodation, p.204), which offer a courtesy airport pickup and drop-off.

Drivers picking up **rental cars** will find desks for the major car rental agencies – Alamo, Avis, Budget, Dollar, Hertz, National, Payless, and Thrifty – in the South Terminal (see p.226), while the smaller companies will meet you at the airport if you have a confirmed reservation – always a good idea in the summer when vehicles are in demand, and booking ahead will usually get you

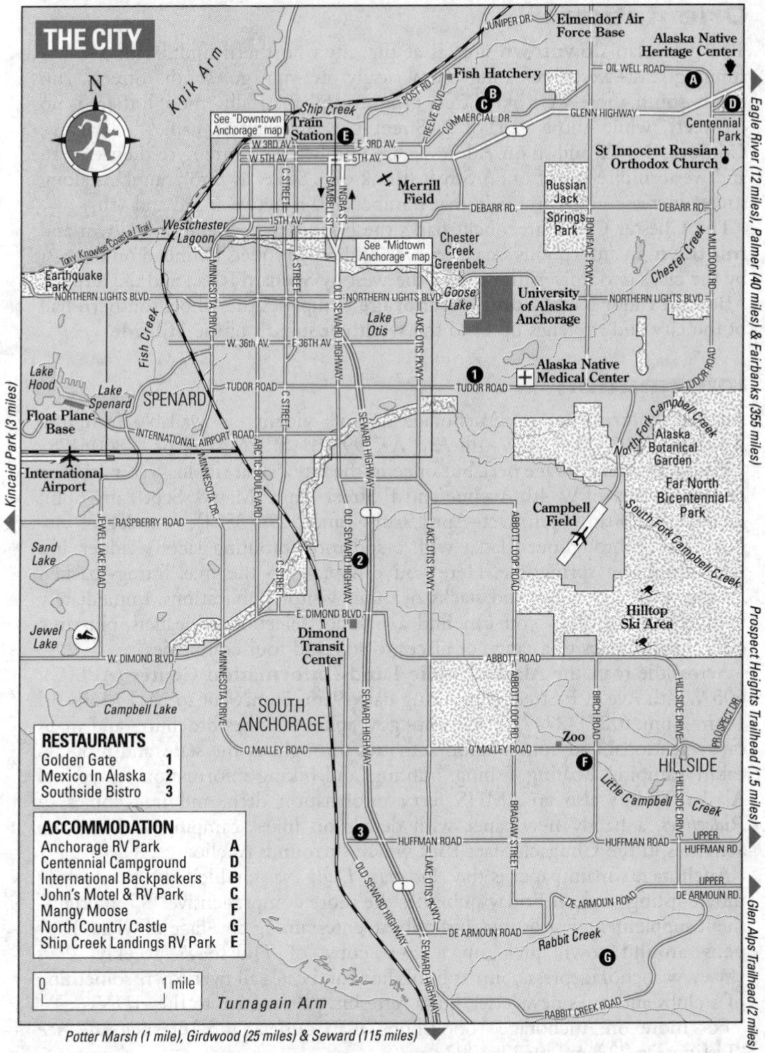

lower rates. Also note that these smaller companies frequently offer much lower rates in return for slightly older cars and that off-airport agencies can charge slightly lower rates by avoiding a tax imposed by the airport authorities.

The **train station** is downtown on 1st Street, a fairly easy walk from downtown hotels. Taxis meet all trains. Services are limited to a couple of trains a day (and are fully detailed in Basics, p.38); the ticket office (mid-May to mid-Sept daily 5.30am–5pm; mid-Sept to mid-May Mon–Fri 9am–4pm) fields inquiries and sells tickets for departures to Seward, Denali, and Fairbanks.

Various **long-distance buses** serve Anchorage and pick up around town (for more details see "Buses" on pp.201 and 226).

Orientation

The grid-plan **downtown** area is at the city's northern limit, with avenues running east–west increasing numerically as you go south. Streets run north–south, those west of A Street progress alphabetically (though there is no J Street), while those east of A Street get alphabetical names – Barrow, Cordova, Denali, and so on. Addresses are numbered according to their eastern and western direction from A Street (think of A Street as zero); numbers along streets increase going south so that number 320 is between 3rd and 4th.

The Chester Creek greenbelt marks the boundary between downtown and **midtown**, an amorphous smear of malls and broad streets bounded on the east by the city's two universities and to the west by Spenard Road and the airport.

Beyond Tudor Road, **South Anchorage** comprises the whole southern half of the city, and stretches up onto the wealthier suburb of the **Hillside**.

Information

Advance information on Anchorage and its vicinity is available from the **Anchorage CVB**, 524 W 4th Ave, AK 99501 (ⓣ276-4118 or 1-800/478-1255, ⓦwww.anchorage.net), but once in the city call at the log-cabin **visitor center**, corner of W 4th Avenue and F Street (daily: May & Sept 8am–6pm; June–Aug 7.30am–7pm, Oct–April 9am–4pm; ⓣ274-3531), a model for visitor centers throughout Alaska with a sod roof sprouting Jacob's ladder and wild onions in springtime. Here you can pick up the free, listings-packed *Anchorage Visitors Guide* and stacks of other visitor publications. Immediately behind the log cabin you can find a broader selection of leaflets, plus free direct-dial phones to a range of places to stay and tour companies.

Across the road, the **Alaska Public Lands Information Center** (APLIC), 605 W 4th Ave at F Street (June–Aug daily 9am–5pm; Sept to May Mon–Fri 10am–5pm; ⓣ271-2737, ⓦwww.nps.gov/aplic), supplies brochures and maps on recreational and conservation activities throughout the state, and provides cabin, camping, boating, fishing, hunting, and hiking information for central Alaska. There's also an AMHS ferry information desk, and free copies of *Ridgelines*, a handy newspaper with details on hikes, camping, and day-use activities in the Chugach State Park which surrounds Anchorage.

Anchorage's main paper is the *Anchorage Daily News*, which also prints daily movie listings and on Friday publishes the more comprehensive "8" entertainment supplement. For listings and offbeat, entertaining coverage of what's happens around town pick up a free copy of Thursday's weekly *Press* (ⓦwww.anchoragepress.com) at bookshops and cafés all over town; something of a clubs and cafés newsletter, but a refreshing alternative to the *ADN*.

For more on Anchorage's bookshops, map outlets, and Internet café, see "Listings," p.222 and pp.226–227.

City transportation

Anchorage is a city designed for cars, but you can see the major sights, eat in good restaurants, and get back to your accommodation using no more than your own feet and the city bus system. Try to do anything in a hurry, though, and you're out of luck – possibly the best argument for **renting a car** in Alaska. Once equipped with a vehicle, getting used to Anchorage's traffic is rarely a problem. **Parking** is easy; every mall has a huge parking lot, and even downtown you'll find low-cost parking meters within a couple of blocks of where you need to be.

Cycling is also viable and can be the most pleasant way to get around, especially using some of the city's excellent bike trails (see box, below).

Buses

For such a spread-out and thinly populated city, Anchorage's "People Mover" (ⓦwww.peoplemover.org) **bus system** does a remarkably good job of covering a lot of ground, though the limited hours of operation (Mon–Fri 6am–10pm, Sat 8am–8pm, Sun 9.30am–6.30pm) can be frustrating, with some less popular routes shutting down as early as 7pm. Drivers sell tickets ($1.25, correct change only, bills accepted) and all-day passes ($2.50).

Routes generally start at the **Transit Center**, 6th Avenue and G Street (the 24hr automated Rideline on ⓣ343-6543 has operator assistance Mon–Fri 8am–5pm), where you can obtain *The Ride Guide* ($1) with a route map and timetables for all services. South Anchorage is further served by the **Dimond Transit Center**, behind the Dimond Center Mall, five miles south of downtown. People Mover also runs the Ship Creek Shuttle (also $1.25), which loops through the downtown area, past the train station and to Ship Creek – though unless you're carrying heavy bags you may find it quicker and easier to walk.

You might also find some use for the **4th Avenue Trolley Tours**, 630 W 4th Ave (mid-May to mid-Sept 9am–5.30pm every 30min; one tour $10, all-day

Cycling and mountain biking around Anchorage

Anchorage's main roads are four-lane drag strips hogged by drivers whose lack of bike-awareness threatens cyclists' very existence: wear a helmet. Fortunately, green "Bike Route" signs herd riders onto the sidewalk – it's not exactly a bike path but the total absence of pedestrians makes it safer than the road. All People Mover buses are equipped with bike racks, and bikes ride free.

Cycling in Anchorage is best following one of the **bike trails** – smooth, paved affairs also open to walkers, rollerbladers, and rollerskiers – though they're seldom the shortest route between two points. Foremost among them is the **Tony Knowles Coastal Trail** (see p.212), which runs eleven miles from the western end of 2nd Avenue downtown to Kincaid Park, itself laced with more than forty miles of trails. On any fine day you'll have plenty of company, with everyone making the best of the long views over tidal flats to **Mount Susitna**, locally known as The Sleeping Lady (it takes some imagination, but apparently she has her arms crossed over her chest).

At Westchester Lagoon, a mile south of downtown, the **Lanie Fleischer Chester Creek Trail** cuts inland through the Chester Creek Greenbelt, a streamside meander through midtown verdure towards the university campuses.

Mountain bikers are also well served, with scope for exploring the Chugach Mountains (see box, pp.214–215) and a heap of cross-country ski trails, which make excellent bike routes from mid-May to mid-October. Pick up the *Anchorage Cross Country Ski Trails Map* ($5 from the visitor center) for details on miles of trails (for skiing in winter, biking in summer) primarily in the moose-infested **Kincaid Park**, through the undulating landscape, beaver pools, and mud of **Far North Bicentennial Park**, or in the more limited terrain of **Russian Jack Springs Park**.

There are several **bike rental** places around town, most offering fairly high-quality machines for $25–30 a day, including helmet, lock, and a map of good routes. The most convenient outlet downtown is Downtown Bicycle Rental, 333 W 4th Ave (mid-May to mid-Sept daily 9am–7pm, sporadically in winter; ⓣ279-5293, ⓦalaska-bike-rentals.com), which rents bikes on a first-come, first-served basis and requires a major credit card: rates are $15 for three hours and $29 for 24 hours; tandems go for $43 a day. In midtown the Bicycle Shop, 1035 Northern Lights Blvd (ⓣ272-5219), sells and repairs bikes and also offers bargain rental with mid-range mountain bikes for $20 for the first 24 hours then $15 a day thereafter.

Bike tours from Anchorage are run by Alaska Backcountry Bike Tours (ⓣ746-5018 or 1-866/354-2453, ⓦwww.mountainbikealaska.com), who have a number of day and multiday trips.

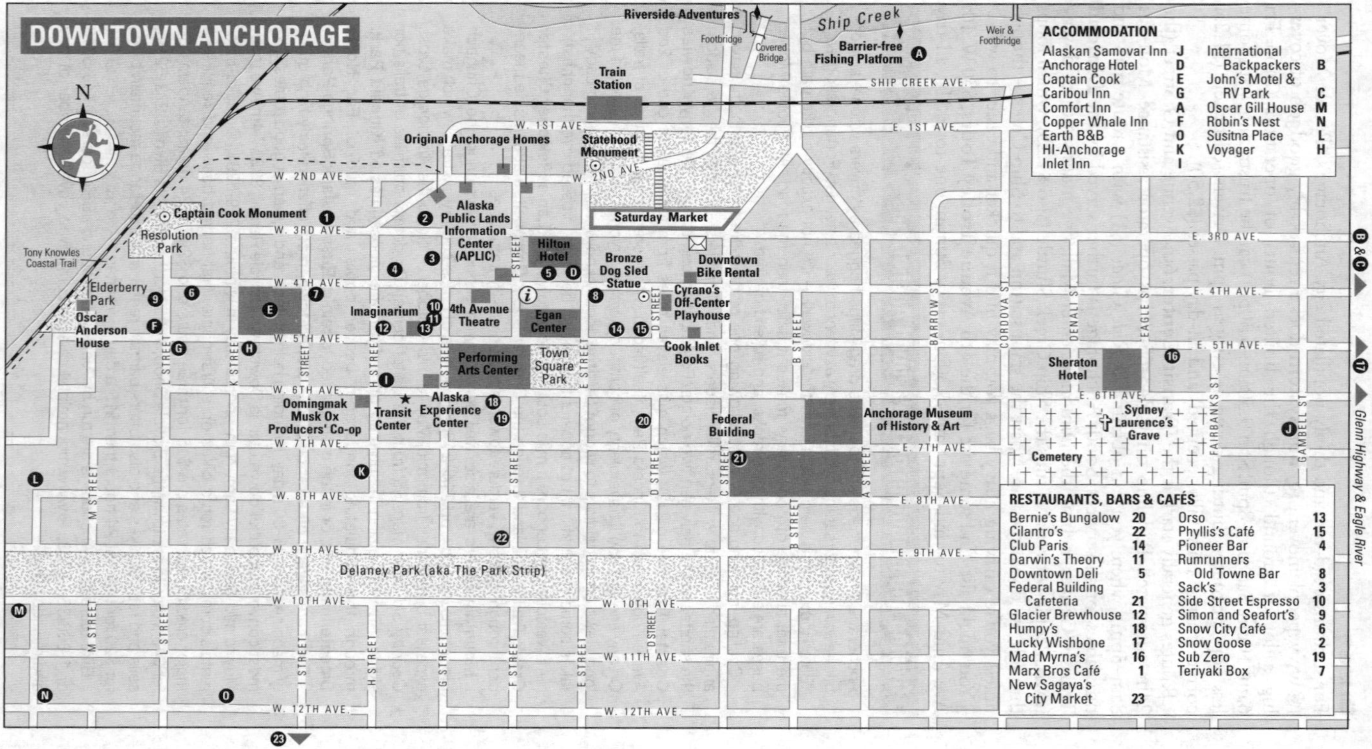
DOWNTOWN ANCHORAGE
ACCOMMODATION
Alaskan Samovar Inn J
Anchorage Hotel D
Captain Cook E
Caribou Inn G
Comfort Inn A
Copper Whale Inn F
Earth B&B O
HI-Anchorage K
Inlet Inn I
International Backpackers B
John's Motel & RV Park C
Oscar Gill House M
Robin's Nest N
Susitna Place L
Voyager H
RESTAURANTS, BARS & CAFÉS
Bernie's Bungalow 20
Cilantro's 22
Club Paris 14
Darwin's Theory 11
Downtown Deli 5
Federal Building Cafeteria 21
Glacier Brewhouse 12
Humpy's 18
Lucky Wishbone 17
Mad Myrna's 16
Marx Bros Café 1
New Sagaya's City Market 23
Orso 13
Phyllis's Café 15
Pioneer Bar 4
Rumrunners Old Towne Bar 8
Sack's 3
Side Street Espresso 10
Simon and Seafort's 9
Snow City Café 6
Snow Goose 2
Sub Zero 19
Teriyaki Box 7
Riverside Adventures
Footbridge
Covered Bridge
Ship Creek
Barrier-free Fishing Platform
Weir & Footbridge
Train Station
Original Anchorage Homes
Statehood Monument
Saturday Market
Captain Cook Monument
Resolution Park
Tony Knowles Coastal Trail
Alaska Public Lands Information Center (APLIC)
Hilton Hotel
Bronze Dog Sled Statue
Downtown Bike Rental
Cyrano's Off-Center Playhouse
Elderberry Park
Oscar Anderson House
Imaginarium
4th Avenue Theatre
Egan Center
Cook Inlet Books
Performing Arts Center
Town Square Park
Sheraton Hotel
Oomingmak Musk Ox Producers' Co-op
Transit Center
Alaska Experience Center
Federal Building
Anchorage Museum of History & Art
Sydney Laurence's Grave
Cemetery
Delaney Park (aka The Park Strip)
Glenn Highway & Eagle River
SHIP CREEK AVE.
W. 1ST AVE.
E. 1ST AVE.
W. 2ND AVE.
W. 3RD AVE.
E. 3RD AVE.
W. 4TH AVE.
E. 4TH AVE.
W. 5TH AVE.
E. 5TH AVE.
W. 6TH AVE.
E. 6TH AVE.
W. 7TH AVE.
E. 7TH AVE.
W. 8TH AVE.
E. 8TH AVE.
W. 9TH AVE.
E. 9TH AVE.
W. 10TH AVE.
W. 11TH AVE.
W. 12TH AVE.
M STREET
L STREET
K STREET
I STREET
H STREET
G STREET
F STREET
E STREET
D STREET
C STREET
B STREET
A STREET
BARROW ST
CORDOVA ST
DENALI ST
EAGLE ST
FAIRBANKS ST
GAMBELL ST
N

pass $16; ⓣ257-5609), which leave from outside the 4th Avenue Theatre and offer highly orchestrated bus tours which at least provide transport to a few places ill served by the city buses: Lake Hood, Alaskan Aviation Heritage Museum, Earthquake Park, and Westchester Lagoon.

Accommodation

Anchorage must have more **places to stay** than the rest of Alaska put together, but since most visitors to the state spend at least a couple of nights here places fill up fast. From the beginning of June until the end of August it is critical to have something booked a few days (or even weeks) in advance. Late May can be busy too, but by mid-September things quiet down considerably.

Campers and RV drivers will find sites scattered all around the city, but everyone else ends up **downtown**, or in **Spenard** close to the airport, or on the **Hillside**, Anchorage's swanky suburb and home to some of the best B&Bs.

Prices strictly follow demand. In summer, hotels can pretty much charge what they like, and they do. Even quite modest motels go for over $100 a night, while the big hotels let their most basic room for upwards of $200, the same price you'd pay for the presidential suite in winter. B&Bs vary their prices less, but they play to the same rules: expect thirty to forty percent reductions on summer rates once winter rolls around. Visitors in early May, late September, and October can expect shoulder-season prices somewhere between these extremes. Hostels and campgrounds tend to hold their prices year-round making them less competitive in the off-season, especially if you are traveling in a small group: in winter four people can stay at the *Sheraton* for little more than the cost of a dorm bed each at a hostel.

Hostels

Anchorage has Alaska's best range of hostels, from the basic-but-cheap to something approaching B&B luxury. Only the HI hostel is downtown.

Anchorage Guesthouse 2001 Hillcrest Drive ⓣ274-0408, ⓦwww.akhouse.com. This upscale backpacker-style hostel, just over a mile from downtown, is handy for midtown and the Coastal Trail (bikes available for $10 a half-day). Other perks include sheets, towels, breakfast, use of kitchen, free gear storage, free local calls, and reasonably priced Internet access. They offer dorms with bunks and single beds ($28) as well as private rooms with double or king-sized beds. ❷

HI-Anchorage 700 H St ⓣ276-3635, ⓦwww.alaska.net/~hianch. A functional hostel in a great downtown location – a block from the Transit Center – though the daytime lockout (10am–5pm), and 1am curfew are less than appealing. Kitchen, laundry, luggage storage ($1 a day per bag), and shuttle services (drop-off and pickup) are available. There's a five-night maximum stay in summer. Reserve well in advance for dorm beds (members $20, non-members $23) and private rooms. ❶

International Backpackers Hostel/Inn 3601 Peterkin Ave ⓣ274-3870. The cheapest beds in Anchorage are at this hostel which doubles as long-term accommodation. A couple of miles east of downtown in a less than salubrious neighborhood, there's no lockout or curfew. Take the #45 bus (every 40min, hourly at weekends) to Bragaw and Peterkin, and walk west three blocks. Camping on the grounds costs $10, dorm beds are $15 (max three per room) and there's a private room for $45. ❶

Spenard Hostel International 2845 W 42nd Place ⓣ248-5036, ⓦwww.alaskahostel.org. Friendly hostel about 1.5 miles from the airport and four from downtown with bikes for rent ($10 a day). Most dorms are single-sex, there are no private rooms, and you'll be expected to do a small chore, but at $16 a bunk it's great value. Also features a garden with barbecue, spacious communal areas, low-cost baggage storage, Internet access, and no lockout. You may even be able to do three hours' work in return for your night's stay.

Hotels and motels

There are two major concentrations of hotels and motels. In the heart of the **downtown** area business hotels predominate, some all-out five-star affairs, some more modest but still attractive. A few blocks to the east, as the high-rises melt away to the low-rent and semi-industrial areas around Merrill Field, you'll find a concentration of cheaper motels, the best of which we've listed below.

Many of the rest of the places – a couple of large hotels and lots of smaller motels – are in the **Spenard** neighborhood, close to much of the city's nightlife and the airport; all places offer airport pickups.

Downtown and north

Alaskan Samovar Inn 720 Gambell St at 6th Ave ⓣ277-1511 or 1-800/478-1511, ⓦwww.motel.ci.st. A reasonably priced motel within an easy walk of downtown, with large rooms, cable TV, and spa baths. Better still, they've got suites with a jacuzzi in the room, a bottle of champagne, and breakfast supplied. Suites ❻, rooms ❹

Anchorage Hotel 330 E St at 4th Ave ⓣ272-4553 or 1-800/544-0988, ⓦwww.historicanchoragehotel.com. This small hotel (once frequented by renowned Alaskan painter Sydney Laurence) has been around since the birth of Anchorage and acts as a counterpoint to the over-the-top business hotels surrounding it. The decor is understated and the overall feel is personal and relaxed but with all the business facilities, plus complimentary newspaper and continental breakfast. Suites and rooms ❽

Captain Cook 4th Ave at K St ⓣ276-6000 or 1-800/843-1950, ⓦwww.captaincook.com. The oilman's hotel of choice, the *Captain Cook* boasts every luxury imaginable – five restaurants with well-stocked bars, fabulous views (the best goes for $1500 in the penthouse suite), and a health club with pool. Suites $30–50 above normal room rates of $260. ❾

Caribou Inn 501 L St at 5th Ave ⓣ272-0444 or 1-800/272-5878, ⓔcaribou@alaska.net. It is worth stepping up from the cheapest hotels to these small and ageing but reasonably comfortable rooms, which come with complimentary airport and train station shuttle, HBO, off-street parking, and breakfast. Private and shared bath both ❹

Comfort Inn 111 W Ship Creek Ave ⓣ277-6887 or 1-800/424-6423, ⓦwww.choicehotels.com. Modern, corporate-style hotel with spacious, comfortable rooms (all with fridge, microwave, and cable TV) and abundant amenities including indoor pool, hot tub, free Internet access, plenty of parking, and a substantial continental breakfast. It is only ten minutes' walk from downtown but they run a 24hr free shuttle, and another to the airport. ❼

Inlet Inn 539 H St at 6th Ave ⓣ277-5541, ⓔinletinn@alaska.com. Undoubtedly the cheapest hotel rooms downtown, and the complimentary airport and train station shuttle, cable TV, and free local calls make it a bargain, though it can be noisy. The public areas and some of the decor leave a fair bit to be desired, and the presence of long-term guests doesn't help matters, but all rooms have private bath. ❸

Voyager 501 K St at 5th Ave ⓣ277-9501 or 1-800/247-9070, ⓕ274-0333, ⓦwww.voyagerhotel.com. The best of the mid- to upper-range hotels, featuring spacious rooms (with kitchenette) plus most of the amenities of the business hotels without the stuffiness. Entirely non-smoking and with a light breakfast included. Reserve well in advance in summer. ❼

Midtown and the airport

Arctic Inn Motel 842 W International Airport Rd at Arctic Blvd ⓣ561-1328, ⓕ562-8701. Good-value motel that's close to the airport (about $8 by cab) and local restaurants. The spacious and clean (if plain) rooms come with HBO, a microwave, and fridge, although those near the front can be a little noisy. ❸

Puffin Inn 4400 Spenard Rd at Turnagain Blvd ⓣ243-4044 or 1-800/478-3346, ⓦwww.puffininn.net. The most appealing of the mid-priced motels close to the airport. Well maintained with simple but attractive economy rooms and a new deluxe wing. Free local calls, cable TV, complimentary newspaper, coffee and muffins, and free airport transfers. Deluxe ❼, economy ❺

Qupqugiac Inn 640 W 36th Ave at Arctic Blvd ⓣ562-5633, ⓦwww.qupq.com. Excellent small hotel that offers simply furnished but attractively decorated rooms (some with private shower and toilet) each with satellite TV and phones with voice mail. Unusually, there's also a common room equipped with a full kitchen, free tea and coffee, and Internet access. Roadside rooms can be a little noisy. Private ❸, shared bath ❷

B&Bs

Anchorage's B&B market is booming, with new places opening all the time to cater to the massive summer influx. They range from modest houses to palaces where the attention to detail borders on fanatical. The two main concentrations of B&Bs are **downtown**, within easy walking distance of just about everywhere (including the bus station for ventures further afield), and in the **Hillside** area, over five miles southeast of the center on the flanks of the Chugach Mountains and close to the hiking trailheads. You really need a car to stay out here, but if you have one this is the place to be – scenic and quiet. It is worth bearing in mind that city ordinances limit the size and location of B&Bs signs, so you may need to look hard to find your bed for the night. Also, there is an increasing tendency to charge a premium (around $20) for one-night stays: ask when you book.

Downtown and north

Copper Whale Inn 440 L St ⓣ258-7999, ⓦwww.copperwhale.com. Large and welcoming B&B ideally situated in the center of downtown. Rooms are comfortably furnished and have fitted blackout shades – a boon on the long summer evenings – but (intentionally) come without phones or TVs. An extensive buffet-style breakfast is served in the lounge, which overlooks Cook Inlet. Private bath ❼, shared bath ❺

Earth B&B 1001 W 12th Ave ⓣ279-9907, ⓦwww.alaskaone.com/earthbb. Enthusiastically and liberally run, this is home away from home for Denali-bound climbers. It's fairly basic but very accommodating, with a garage for drying and sorting gear, bikes to use, a barbecue out back, and flexible deals for groups (particularly anyone doing anything adventurous). Continental breakfast included, and owner Margriet runs her own tour business (see website). Bus #3, #36 or #60 from downtown. Private bath ❺, shared bath ❹

Oscar Gill House 1344 W 10th Ave, ⓣ279-1344, ⓦwww.oscargill.com. Lovely B&B in a 1913 house, comprehensively restored while maintaining character and understated elegance. Two rooms share a bath while the largest has its own, and there's also an apartment for longer stays, all tastefully done and looked after by very welcoming hosts, Mark and Susan Lutz. Private bath ❺, shared bath ❹

The Robin's Nest 1225 W 12th Ave ⓣ279-0052, ⓦtherobinsnestbandb.com. Attractive, well-priced B&B close to downtown with just two rooms – one a spacious suite that's good for families – and a generous continental breakfast. Suite ❺, room ❹

Susitna Place 727 N St ⓣ274-3344, ⓦwww.susitnaplace.com. Central lodge with a comfortable communal area overlooking Cook Inlet and Mount Susitna. Rooms range from smallish shared-bath affairs to larger rooms with private baths, some with sundeck and water views, to the huge, and always popular, Susitna Suite with magnificent views, whirlpool tub and a private deck with views of Denali. Suite ❼, sea view ❺, rooms ❹

The Hillside and around

Mangy Moose 5560 E 112th St ⓣ346-8052, ⓦwww.alaskamangymoose. Neither the prominent moose's head in the lounge nor the rest of the house is the slightest bit mangy; in fact, this is one of the nicest B&Bs around. Attractive wood-paneled rooms either share bathrooms or have private facilities and everyone meets in the communal lounge with TV, VCR, and a self-serve kitchenette. Good breakfasts, too. ❻

North Country Castle 14600 Joanne Court ⓣ345-7296, ⓦwww.customcpu.com/commercial/nccbnb. Excellent value, if a little distant from the sights, this modern, informal home (as little like a castle as you could imagine) is tucked in among the white spruce at the southern limit of Anchorage. The smaller rooms share a bathroom and views of Flattop Mountain; the suite sports a wonderful view over Turnagain Arm from its private deck and has its own fireplace. Suite ❼, rooms ❻

Camping and RV parks

Campers are not well catered for in Anchorage: the nearest place that is at all pleasant to pitch a tent is *Centennial Campground*. With your own vehicle you might find it more pleasant commuting into the city from *Eagle River Campground* or at the wooded sites 27 miles south at Bird Creek. **RV drivers** are better served with several full-service (and pricey) places close to town.

Anchorage RV Park 1200 N Muldoon Rd ⓣ338-7275 or 1-800/400-7275, ⓦwww.anchrvpark.com. Very large, well-organized, and well-appointed RV park with wooded landscaping and pull-through sites with cable TV. No tents. Mid-May to mid-Sept. $31.

Centennial Campground 8300 Glenn Hwy off Boundary Ave ⓣ343-6986. Leafy first-come, first-served RV and tent site five miles east of downtown with sites for $15 and free showers. #3 and #4 buses from downtown stop within half a mile or so.

Eagle River Campground Glenn Hwy, Eagle River. An Alaska State Parks campground twelve miles north of Anchorage with fire pits, water, and outhouses, plus fishing, whitewater rafting, and short hiking trails right on the doorstep. First-come, first-served. $15. Take the Hiland Rd exit off the expressway.

John's Motel & RV Park 3543 Mountain View Drive ⓣ277-4332 or 1-800/478-4332, ⓦwww.johnsmotel.com. Although it's mostly a gravel lot next to a busy road, *John's* offers good value with a laundromat and free showers. Full hookup. $25.

Ship Creek Landings RV Park 150 N Ingra ⓣ227-0877 or 1-888/778-7700, ⓦwww.alaskarv.com. Very central RV and campground that's quite secluded despite being close to the train tracks. Tent sites on specially constructed sand pads ($14) and RV sites from dry ($18) to full hookup pull-through ($34).

The City

In their eagerness to hightail it into the "real" Alaska, visitors tend to overlook Anchorage, but it's well worth spending some time here experiencing the only big-city taste that the state has to offer. Those who do will find that there are plenty of things to occupy two or three days – even a week isn't unreasonable, if you fancy using the city as a base for day trips and local hikes. For the best introduction to the city, simply wander around **downtown**, getting a flavor of a city grown too fast, whose blend of old and new, urban blight and rural parks can still conjure something of a shantytown feel. You can't miss the evidence of Anchorage's boom-and-bust development, with prefabricated clapboard houses and abandoned lots lying in the shadow of the glitzy high-rise ConocoPhillips oil building, which critics half-jokingly refer to as the city's Capitol. The impact of oil revenue is equally visible in the Performing Arts Center and the **Anchorage Museum of History & Art**. Other key sights to take in while walking around the downtown area include the salmon waters of **Ship Creek**, along the shores of which the original tent city sprang up, and the cemetery full of the headstones of prominent sourdoughs.

Just south of the central business district is the **Park Strip** (also known as Delaney Park), a former airfield and golf course as well as the site of the fifty-ton statehood bonfire in 1959. Today, it mainly supports summer evening softball and soccer games. Head further south, and you're into the malls of **midtown**. You'll most likely find yourself here during the day buying books, renting outdoor equipment, eating, and visiting the **Heritage Museum**, and again at night for the bars of the Spenard district.

Immediately north of downtown, the city butts up against Elmendorf Air Force Base and Fort Richardson Military Reservation, both flanked by the Glenn Highway on its way north to the celebrated **Alaska Native Heritage Center**.

One of the best things about the city is the opportunity to be outdoors. On a fine day it's hard to beat a late afternoon stroll (or cycle) along the waterside **Tony Knowles Coastal Trail** or, more adventurously, a stiff hike up Flattop Mountain or Wolverine Peak in the encircling Chugach Mountains. Hidden in the wilder country beyond is the city's hiking gem, the two-day **Crow Pass Trail,** which ends by the delightful Eagle River Nature Center. There's plenty more to do in and around the city, including rock climbing and swimming (see "Listings," p.227) as well as salmon fishing (see box, p.208).

Good Friday earthquake

In the evening of March 27, 1964, Alaska was dealt a devastating blow when the most powerful earthquake ever recorded in North America rocked the new state's Southcentral region. Rating an astonishing 8.6 on the Richter scale – San Francisco's 1906 quake measured 8.3 – and lasting close to five minutes, the **Good Friday earthquake** flattened entire blocks of buildings, twisted railroad lines and roads, and pitched cars into shop windows, their tail fins pointing skyward.

Centered below Miners Lake on the northern edge of Prince William Sound, roughly eighty miles east of Anchorage, the quake and its numerous aftershocks were felt across Southcentral. An underwater landslide in Prince William Sound produced huge waves, which swept over Cordova, Valdez, Whittier, Seward, and Kodiak Island, accounting for 119 of the 131 deaths attributed to the quake. **Valdez** was devastated to the point that the site was abandoned and the town had to be completely rebuilt four miles away on more stable ground. Further along the coast **Kodiak** lost its boat harbor, and a fishing boat was pitched over waterfront buildings to be left high and dry two streets back. In Anchorage the twelve-foot drop between 3rd and 4th avenues hints at the devastation, and **Earthquake Park** now stands on land which liquefied – virtually swallowing the suburb of Turnagain Heights. All the houses have long since been cleared away, but explanatory panels and a rucked-up landscape tell the tale.

The big city peters out beyond the limits of the Anchorage Bowl, but there are a few places you might consider as **day trips from Anchorage**: to the south, Girdwood (p.235) and Portage Glacier (p.238) lie within an hour's drive along Turnagain Arm; and to the north Eklutna (p.351), Palmer (p.353), and the Independence Mine at Hatcher Pass (p.362) are also all easily accessible by car.

Downtown Anchorage

Immediately west of the visitor center is Anchorage's major Art Deco building, the classic pastel-toned **4th Avenue Theatre**, 630 W 4th Ave. Already architecturally dated when it was built in the early 1940s, it remains a fine example of the style, all mahogany and Italian marble, ziggurats and chevron friezes, and a proscenium flanked by floor-to-ceiling relief panels depicting Old and New Alaska scenes – uplifting and positive in true Deco fashion. It spent much of its life as Anchorage's premier cinema and, though now used for an evening dinner theater show, it is often open during the day so you can wander in and take a peek.

On the corner of 4th Avenue and D Street is the striking **Wendler Building**, Anchorage's only corner turret structure, which overlooks a bronze sculpture of a sled dog – the ceremonial kickoff point of the Iditarod (see box, p.360) and the real start for numerous races. Taking E Street north, the road slopes down a dozen feet – a consequence of the 1964 quake – to 3rd where a parking lot between here and C Street transforms itself into the **Saturday market** (mid-May to mid-Sept 10am–6pm; Ⓦ www.anchoragemarkets.com), selling everything from oversized Mat-Su vegetables to arts and crafts, some of it really good, some just cheap souvenirs. A block north is the **Statehood Monument**, a bronze statue depicting Eisenhower's head being attacked by a bald eagle – or so it seems from some angles. Below, the hillside drops away to the site of the original tent city, now occupied by rail yards and the restrained Art Deco form of the **train station**, and Ship Creek.

Second Avenue runs west from the Statehood Monument past a handful of Anchorage's original homes – nos. 542, 605, 610, and 618 (none open to the

Downtown fishing

Visitors to Alaska often spend thousands of dollars to fly to a remote lodge and hire a guide to help them catch a trophy specimen, but all the while there are kings and silvers five minutes' walk from downtown Anchorage just waiting to be hooked. Some city office workers even cast away their lunch hour at **Ship Creek**, where for under $50 a day you can obtain the appropriate license (for details see Basics, p.63) and rent rod, reel and waders from a creekside shack run by Riverside Adventures (☎258-7773).

The creek no longer supports a natural run, but fishery-raised salmon returning to the Elmendorf Hatchery provide ample sport. There's no guarantee of a good catch but it isn't unreasonable to expect to catch **king salmon** weighing 45lb (though 15–25lb is more common; season mid-May to mid-July), and **silver salmon** topping 20lb (7–12lb is typical; July–Sept). Two hours either side of high tide is generally regarded as the best time.

Through the summer, Ship Creek hosts two **salmon derbies** (Ⓦwww.anchoragederbies.com): a king salmon derby (second week of June; tickets $7 for one day, $30 for the duration) with a first prize of $5000 plus a tagged fish worth $10,000; and a silver salmon derby (second week of August; $7 for one day, $30 for the duration) with a $3000 top prize.

public) – to the start of the Tony Knowles Coastal Trail (see box, p.212). There's more to be seen at the corner of 3rd Avenue and L Street, where a nest of steps and viewing platforms known as **Resolution Park** is crowned by the **Captain Cook Monument**, a regal statue of the great navigator. The waters that once bore his ship, the *Resolution*, now bear his name and stretch away to Mount Susitna and the Alaska Range. On a clear day the dominant peaks of Mount Foraker and Denali can be seen presiding over the city in the distance.

Below the monument is the 1915 **Oscar Anderson House Museum**, 420 M St (June to mid-Sept Mon–Fri noon–5pm; $3), a lovely two-story, which was once the home of Oscar Anderson, a Swedish butcher who was the eighteenth resident of early Anchorage. Guides lead you through period-furnished rooms of what was the city's first privately built wood-frame residence, completed soon after the town's lots were auctioned off.

Back in the center of town, the **Alaska Experience Center**, 705 W 6th Ave at G St (daily: mid-May to mid-Sept 9am–10pm; mid-Sept to mid-May noon–6pm; ☎276-3730, Ⓦwww.alaskaexperiencetheatre.com), projects an eminently missable movie on the state and its wonders onto a 180-degree wraparound screen ($8). There's also a considerably more diverting earthquake exhibit ($6, joint entry $12), with displays on the 1964 quake (see box, p.207), and a fifteen-minute film (and jolting quake simulation) featuring a wonderfully Germanic-sounding professor expounding the geophysics of it all and poignant tales from Anchorage residents. Kids will be better off at the nearby **Imaginarium Science Discovery Center**, 737 W 5th Ave at G St (Mon–Sat 10am–6pm, Sun noon–5pm; $5; ☎276-3179, Ⓦwww.imaginarium.org), packed with hands-on experiments using prisms, pendulums, gears, and a contraption which makes giant soap bubbles around you, along with a tide pool full of local marine life and instructional material on earthquakes and the northern lights.

Big shows that make it to Alaska often play the acoustically impressive **Alaska Center for the Performing Arts**, 6th Avenue between F and G streets (aka PAC; tickets ☎1-800/478-7328 or 263-ARTS, Ⓦwww.tickets.com), where you might consider seeing one or more of the three 40- to 45-minute **audio-**

visual shows (all late May–early Sept; one show $8.75, two $15.50, three $22.75) which alternate throughout the day and start at the top of each hour. *Sky Song* is a northern lights and wildlife slide show put to classical music, but you may be more tempted by one of two IMAX films: *Alaska Spirit of the Wild*, with some impressive footage of breaching whales, bears catching salmon, polar bears reclining in the snow, and glaciers calving at something close to actual size; or *Bears*, with browns and blacks filmed mostly in Alaska, the polar variety mostly in Churchill, Canada.

Out front is the **Town Square Park**, a riot of blooms in summer, overlooked by a whales-in-the-Arctic mural by renowned environmental artist Wyland.

Heading east past the Anchorage Museum of History & Art (see below) you come to the **Anchorage Memorial Park Cemetery** (open daily), where Alaskans of note wish to be buried. Respected pioneers ended up along the north perimeter together with artist Sydney Laurence, who is marked with a palette-shaped headstone. Elsewhere the upright whalebone ribs marking Iñupiat graves mix with propeller blades of pioneer aviators and triple-bar Russian Orthodox crosses. It would be a peaceful place to idle away half an hour were it not for the constant drone of small planes from nearby **Merrill Field**, one of the nation's busiest airfields – only a mile from downtown – with more than 230,000 takeoffs and landings annually.

Anchorage Museum of History & Art

Even if you're only spending a night or two in Anchorage, be sure to drop by the **Anchorage Museum of History & Art**, 121 W 7th Ave at A St (mid-May to mid-Sept daily 9am–6pm & until 9pm on Thurs; mid-Sept to mid-May Tues–Sat 10am–6pm, Sun 1–5pm; $6.50; Ⓦ www.anchoragemuseum.org), a visit best timed to coincide with one of the free **museum tours** (hourly 10am–2pm) or one of the free **films** showing in the auditorium. It's easy to devote several hours to the collection and, if you find yourself lingering, you might want to take a break in the excellent atrium restaurant, an offshoot of downtown's *Marx Bros Café* (see p.218).

Upper floor

The legacy of the 1970s oil windfall is immediately apparent in the museum's opulent atrium with its fine-grained wood, preserved totem pole, and arresting sculptures, mainly by Native Alaskan artists. Museum displays occupy the upper floor moving chronologically through the state's history, beginning with exquisite dioramas of village life. These lead to full-size re-creations of Native houses along with an 1830 Russian blockhouse, relocated from where it once defended St Michael near the Yukon delta, and mock-ups of a gold-miner's hut, a 1920s Anchorage home, and a wartime Quonset hut. All this is given some context in well-laid-out displays that, though light on artifacts, illustrate the changes Alaska has undergone during the past two centuries. Here you'll also find gorgeous examples of carved walrus ivory, including cribbage boards, candleholders, and even an engraved map of the Yukon. Alongside there's a small but instructive collection of Native **basketware**: exemplary pieces illustrate the open-weave Yup'ik coiled-grass style, Tlingit spruce-root weaves, and Kobuk River woven birch-bark designs, plus super-fine Aleut baskets with up to 1000 stitches per square inch, and Iñupiat vessels constructed from whale baleen, a material that is traditionally worked only by men. Note the presence of Russian, and later American, influence as European patterns get worked into the designs.

The upper floor catches up to the present with thorough exhibits on the role of telecommunications in modern Alaska, the pivotal part played by air travel, logging displays with a rather camp-looking timber worker, and, inevitably, paeans to the oil industry with scale models of petrochemical installations and a short section of the pipeline.

Lower floor

The **lower floor** is given over to **Alaskan art**, mostly works by Alaskan (or adoptive Alaskan) artists, but also paintings of an Aleut man and woman from the late eighteenth century done by John Webber, ship's artist on James Cook's third voyage. Art-loving Alaskans all but genuflect at mention of **Sydney Laurence**, widely regarded as the most accomplished historical painter of the Alaskan landscape. He remains largely unknown outside the Pacific Northwest, but his masterwork, *Mount McKinley*, is given pride of place, the ice-white peak of Denali shining back at you through the alpenglow. Born in Brooklyn in 1865, Laurence spent time developing his style in Europe, then came to Alaska in 1904 to prospect for gold. Limited success gradually forced him into photography, his Anchorage studio supporting frequent painting forays into the wilds. By the mid-1920s his reputation, built on a lifelong passion for painting Mount McKinley, effectively gave him a monopoly on the mountain's depiction in oil. He died in 1940 and is buried in the Anchorage Memorial Park Cemetery (see p.209). There are more than two dozen Laurence works on display, along with his portable painting kit.

The museum has very little by his Detroit-born near-contemporary, **Eustace Ziegler** (or "Zieg" as he was usually known). His landscapes are less the subject than the frame in which to set his subjects – trappers, fishermen, Native Alaskans – who are often shown outside the stereotypical roles common in Alaskan art of the time. His vibrant *Alaska Fishermen* is a fine example.

Fred Machetanz, probably the most popular Alaskan artist of recent times, owed his ascendancy during the 1970s, at least in part, to purchases of his work by large corporations who found his anodyne canvases – with their recurrent motifs of polar bears, blue water and sky, and alpenglow – perfect for large public spaces and company boardrooms. *Serenity*, *Where Men and Dogs Seem Small* and others can seem little more than adult painting-by-numbers, but it is helpful when viewing them to look at some of his earlier works to see how his painting developed from early oils of sourdoughs and Native life.

Modern painters to look out for in the gallery include **Spence Guerin**, represented by his luminous cloudscape *Moon over Matanuska*, and **Rosemary Redmond**, whose abstract landscape *Somewhere East of the Sun and West of the Moon* stands in stark contrast to Laurence's *Mount McKinley* just along the wall. Look, too, for paintings and sculpture by Native Alaskans, particularly Lawrence Beck's humorous *Punk Walrus Spirit* and Lawrence Ullaq Ahvaliana's more sensitive *Waiting for the Wolf Dance*.

Midtown and the Coastal Trail

The Chester Creek Greenbelt runs east–west across the city a mile or so south of downtown, demarcating the northern limit of midtown Anchorage. Much of midtown is made up of sprawling malls, but the western shoreline is traced by the excellent **Coastal Trail**, which runs down to Kincaid Park, the airport, and **Lake Hood**, the focus for the city's float-plane activity. The nearby district of **Spenard** is short on sights in the usual sense, but you may find yourself gravitating here to get stuff done. The junction of Northern Light Boulevard and Spenard Road is especially handy in this respect, with loads of places to buy or rent outdoor gear, one of the city's best bookshops, some excellent restaurants, bars and clubs, and a post office and travel agent.

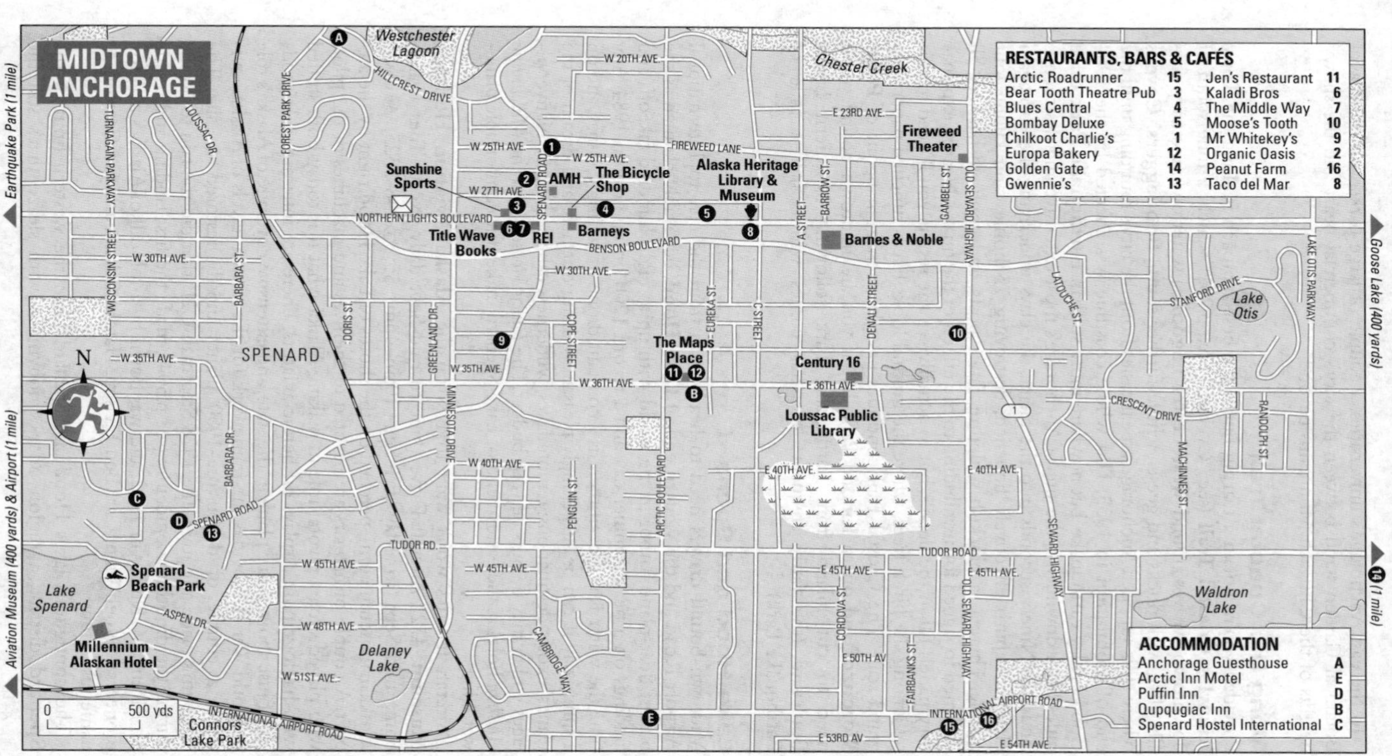

MIDTOWN ANCHORAGE
RESTAURANTS, BARS & CAFÉS
Arctic Roadrunner 15
Bear Tooth Theatre Pub 3
Blues Central 4
Bombay Deluxe 5
Chilkoot Charlie's 1
Europa Bakery 12
Golden Gate 14
Gwennie's 13
Jen's Restaurant 11
Kaladi Bros 6
The Middle Way 7
Moose's Tooth 10
Mr Whitekey's 9
Organic Oasis 2
Peanut Farm 16
Taco del Mar 8
ACCOMMODATION
Anchorage Guesthouse A
Arctic Inn Motel E
Puffin Inn D
Qupqugiac Inn B
Spenard Hostel International C
Earthquake Park (1 mile)
Aviation Museum (400 yards) & Airport (1 mile)
Goose Lake (400 yards)
14 (1 mile)
Westchester Lagoon
Chester Creek
Fireweed Theater
Sunshine Sports
AMH
The Bicycle Shop
Alaska Heritage Library & Museum
Title Wave Books
REI
Barneys
Barnes & Noble
The Maps Place
Century 16
Loussac Public Library
SPENARD
Spenard Beach Park
Lake Spenard
Millennium Alaskan Hotel
Delaney Lake
Connors Lake Park
Lake Otis
Waldron Lake
HILLCREST DRIVE
W 20TH AVE.
E 23RD AVE.
W 25TH AVE.
FIREWEED LANE
W 27TH AVE.
NORTHERN LIGHTS BOULEVARD
BENSON BOULEVARD
W 30TH AVE.
W 35TH AVE.
W 36TH AVE.
E 36TH AVE.
W 40TH AVE.
E 40TH AVE.
TUDOR RD.
TUDOR ROAD
W 45TH AVE.
E 45TH AVE.
W 48TH AVE.
E 50TH AV
W 51ST AVE.
E 53RD AV
E 54TH AVE.
INTERNATIONAL AIRPORT ROAD
TURNAGAIN PARKWAY
LOUSSAC DR.
FOREST PARK DRIVE
WISCONSIN STREET
BARBARA ST.
BARBARA DR.
DORIS ST.
GREENLAND DR.
MINNESOTA DRIVE
SPENARD ROAD
COPE STREET
PENGUIN ST.
CAMBRIDGE WAY
ASPEN DR
ARCTIC BOULEVARD
EUREKA ST.
C STREET
A STREET
BARROW ST.
DENALI STREET
CORDOVA ST.
FAIRBANKS ST
GAMBELL ST.
OLD SEWARD HIGHWAY
SEWARD HIGHWAY
LATOUCHE ST.
CRESCENT DRIVE
STANFORD DRIVE
MACHINNES ST.
RANDOLPH ST.
LAKE OTIS PARKWAY
N
0 500 yds

To the east Anchorage's universities, a couple of large parks, and the Alaska Botanical Garden stand between the city's commercial heart and the snowy heights of the Chugach Mountains beyond.

Along the Coastal Trail

Provided you're not in a tearing hurry, the best approach is along the **Tony Knowles Coastal Trail** (see "Cycling" box, p.201) which, a mile south of downtown, weaves around **Westchester Lagoon**, a waterfowl sanctuary usually alive with ducks and geese. A little further south, **Bootleggers' Cove** is where stills supplied Anchorage's speakeasies from the city's founding until the end of prohibition in 1933. This whole coastline was affected by the 1964 Good Friday earthquake, but nowhere more so than **Earthquake Park**, three miles from downtown, the site of Anchorage's most extensive and destructive landslide. Ninety seconds into the quake the clays underlying the Turnagain Heights suburb effectively liquefied, destroying 75 homes and killing four people. There is a blockish sculpture, fence posts, and concrete barriers, all designed in jagged forms, alluding to the effects of the quake. Nearby, explanatory panels fill in the details, but to actually see the results you'll need to ferret among the birch trees, where the ground looks like scrunched paper on a grand scale. The Coastal Trail continues past the teenage hangout of **Point Woronzof** and on to Kincaid Park, but if you are midtown-bound you'll need to cut inland from Earthquake Park following Northern Lights Boulevard (the fairly frequent #36 bus comes within half a mile of Earthquake Park).

Lake Hood and Spenard

Midtown-bound drivers need to head south from the city to International Airport Road and the western end of **Lake Hood**, believably claimed as the busiest float-plane harbor in the world with up to eight hundred takeoffs and landings on a peak summer day, and a record 1200 on one day in 1984. Any time the water isn't frozen there is a constant drone of taxiing Cessnas, and on a sunny day it can be surprisingly pleasant to hang out here and dream of the planes' exotic destinations: remote lakes, wilderness cabins and tiny Native villages which may be outside your budget. The *Fancy Moose* bar in the *Millennium Alaskan* hotel at the eastern end of Lake Spenard makes for comfortable plane-watching.

Aircraft fanatics won't want to pass up the **Alaska Aviation Heritage Museum**, 4721 Aircraft Drive (June to mid-Sept daily except Tues 10am–6pm; mid-Sept to May Fri–Sun 10am–4pm; $5; Ⓣ248-5325, Ⓦwww.alaskaairmuseum.com), perched on the shores of Lake Hood right by the airport. A couple of hangars are devoted to the lives and machines of the pilots who played such a pivotal role in making Alaska what it is today, both stuffed with hagiographic displays on heroic aviators. There are intricate scale models of just about every plane in the state, and extensive coverage of Alaska's role in World War II provides the framework for the crown jewels of Alaskan aviation, a couple of dozen pre-1950 planes mostly restored on site. The museum's pride and joy is the 1928 Stearman C2B that did the run to Nome during the diphtheria epidemic (see p.504), made the first landing and rescue on Mount McKinley in 1932, and was flown by a roll call of Alaska's aviation pioneers – Noel Wien, Carl Ben Eielson, Harold Gillam, and Joe Crosson, to name just a few.

The contiguous lakes Hood and Spenard form the western limit of the **Spenard** district, a region once synonymous with sleaze that's still the raunchiest part of town. The only sight in the traditional sense found here is the **Alaska Heritage Library & Museum**, 1st floor Wells Fargo Bank building, corner of C Street and Northern Lights Boulevard (Mon–Fri noon–4pm; free), a compact room of Native Alaskan artwork and artifacts that perfectly complements the contextual slant of downtown's Museum of History & Art. The emphasis here is on the pieces themselves, almost without exception beautiful works. Don't miss the bird parka made from the skins of over fifty murres, or the fragile-looking kayak and bleached seal-gut parka trimmed with auklet feathers and beaks. Though brittle when dry, seal gut becomes soggy and clingy in the sea yet remains breathable – Eskimo Gore-tex, and only three ounces are needed. Blankets sold to Tlingit people by the Hudson's Bay Company were also turned into clothing, here fashioned into a ceremonial coat used for potlatches with the owner's crest picked out in buttons. Basketware is also well represented, along with matchless ivory carving – from simple, stylized seals to whaling scenes depicted along the length of a walrus tusk. Look, too, for the ivory scale model of the *Bear*, a locally famous revenue cutter (effectively the Alaskan coast guard in the late nineteenth century) that patrolled Alaskan waters for forty years and first brought reindeer to the territory in 1885. Elsewhere there's a small collection of Russian icons as well as oils by leading Alaskan artists such as Laurence, Ziegler, and Machetanz.

Eastern midtown

Northern Lights Boulevard continues east until it meets the Chester Creek Greenbelt near **Goose Lake** on the northern flank of Anchorage's two universities – the University of Alaska Anchorage and Alaska Pacific University – neither of special interest to visitors. North of the universities lie the urban hiking and biking trails of **Russian Jack Springs Park**, which also contains the municipal greenhouse known as the Mann Leiser Memorial Greenhouses, 5200 DeBarr Rd (daily 8am–3pm; free; ⓣ343-4717). Keen horticulturists, however, are better off south of the universities at the **Alaska Botanical Garden**, Campbell Airstrip Road (June–Aug daily 9am–9pm; free; ⓦwww.alaskabg.org), boasting pleasant paths around perennial gardens, wildflower trails, herb gardens, and trails into the nearby woods.

The Botanical Garden lies within the **Far North Bicentennial Park**, a vast forested area butting up against the Chugach State Park, and an ideal spot for mountain bikers.

South Anchorage

It's not that hard to see Alaskan animals in the wild, but if you're not feeling too adventurous you can always check out the **Alaska Zoo**, 4731 O'Malley Rd (daily: May–Sept 9am–6pm; Oct–April 10am–5pm; $9; ⓦwww.alaskazoo.org), which specializes in Alaskan fauna but also has a few camels and Siberian tigers. Beyond the zoo, O'Malley Road continues to climb through the plush houses of the Hillside to the open flanks of the Chugach Mountains. The **Prospect Heights and Glen Alps trailheads** (see box, overleaf) give access to the widest range of hikes, and the latter offers expansive city and sea views from a viewing platform.

Twelve miles south of downtown, the New Seward Highway (Mile 115) arcs away from the Chugach foothills, effectively creating a seawall between Turnagain Arm and the 564 acres of **Potter Marsh** (unrestricted entry). Since 1971 it has been part of the **Anchorage Coastal Wildlife Refuge**, which (particularly late May to early June and late Aug to early Sept) acts as a stopover

Hiking and biking in the Chugach Mountains

Contrary to expectations, Alaska is not overly endowed with good, maintained hiking trails. Much of the state is too remote, too steep, or too boggy, but the **Chugach Mountains**, rising immediately behind Anchorage, are one major exception. Their western end forms part of the Chugach State Park which, at half a million acres, is the third largest state park in the country. The **major hikes** – all with fabulous views over the city, Cook Inlet, and north to the Alaska Range – all start from trailheads within half an hour's drive of Anchorage. Most can be tackled in a day and some can be combined into multiday affairs. The best source of information is the *Ridgelines* newspaper (free from APLIC; see p.200), which contains the latest trail information; for more details consult *55 Ways to the Wilderness of Southcentral Alaska* (The Mountaineers), which covers all walks in the Chugach State Park, including some south of Anchorage along Turnagain Arm.

Hiking season begins in May, but most trails aren't free of snow until early June. They stay clear until around the end of September. Without a car or bicycle, your access to the hills is limited: ride a bus to the Dimond Transit Centre in south Anchorage (routes #2, #7 & #9 from downtown) and take a taxi from there.

Bikes are not generally allowed along these trails with the exception of the run from the Glen Alps parking lot to the Powerline Trail, and the 13 miles along the Powerline Trail from Prospect Heights to Indian; hikers always have right of way.

From the Eagle River Nature Center

The nature center is the base for a couple of gentle nature trails (see p.217), and the finishing point for the Crow Pass Trail (see opposite). Sections of the Crow Pass Trail can be walked from this end, for example the relatively easy **Heritage Falls Trail** (9 miles round-trip; 4–5hrs; 100ft ascent) and the stiffer **Twin Falls Trail** (18 miles round-trip; 8–10hrs; 300ft ascent), which involves some stream crossings but rewards with beaver ponds and the Twin Falls themselves. To reach the center follow the Glenn Highway twelve miles north of Anchorage, turn onto Eagle River Loop Road, then follow Eagle River Road ten miles east. There is a parking fee of $5 for every twelve hours.

From Prospect Heights Trailhead

The Prospect Heights Trailhead (1050ft) is a 25-minute drive south of downtown Anchorage, reached by following O'Malley Road east until it becomes Upper O'Malley Road, then turning left into Prospect Drive and following it 1.3 miles to the parking lot, which has a $5 per day parking fee.

Middle Fork Trail (13 miles round-trip; 8–10hr; 1600ft ascent). Easy to moderate trail which starts on the Near Point Trail, then cuts right after 1.3 miles. It can get muddy underfoot as you gently climb through mountain hemlock and spruce towards beautiful alpine lakes set amid the open tundra under the precipitous face of Mount Williwaw. Anyone not needing to return to their vehicle can vary the return journey by descending via a different path to the Glen Alps Trailhead. Gets the early sun but is in shadow later in the day.

Wolverine Peak Trail (10.5 miles round-trip; 8–10hr; 3400ft ascent). Moderately strenuous trail which initially follows the Near Point Trail for two miles, then spurs up towards the bush line. The way up to the triangular, 4450-foot summit of Wolverine Peak is clear enough but you need to be sure where the path re-enters the bush on the way down. Besides the fabulous views and possible animal sightings – moose,

for more than two hundred species of migratory birds: Canada geese, mallards, pintails, green-winged teal, widgeons, canvasbacks, shovelers, and scaup are common, definitely more so than the trumpeter swans, bald eagles, northern

sheep, and arctic ground squirrel – you can spot parts of a wrecked plane near the summit.

From the Glen Alps Trailhead

The Glen Alps Trailhead (2250ft) is located near the tree line above Anchorage's swanky Hillside suburb, twenty minutes' drive south of downtown Anchorage: turn off Hillside Drive and follow Upper Huffman Road for 2.6 miles to the parking lot. There is a $5 per day parking fee.

Flattop Mountain (3.5 miles round-trip; 2–3hrs; 1300ft ascent). Good views over Anchorage and to the Alaska Range from Alaska's most hiked peak. It's a fairly steep haul through mountain hemlocks and out onto the tundra and requires some attention as hikers higher up can dislodge rocks.

Powerline Trail to Indian (11 miles one-way; 5–6hr; 1300ft ascent). Easy to moderate walking gradually gaining open tundra that's good for berry picking in fall. Start early in the day as it goes into shadow in the afternoon.

Williwaw Lakes (12 miles round-trip; 6–8hr; 740ft ascent). Easy to moderate walk that's best started early in the day to catch the sun. It climbs through spruce woods and mountain hemlock, joining the Middle Fork Trail (see opposite) for the climb above the tree line to Williwaw Lakes.

The Crow Pass Trail

The single best hike in the Anchorage area, the **Crow Pass Trail** (26 miles one-way; 2–3 days; 2500ft ascent, 3500ft descent) is a dramatic grind up a steep pass overhung by glaciers, then down a narrow wildlife-rich wooded valley strung with waterfalls. Along the way the trail passes the magnificent Raven Gorge where the fledgling Raven Creek plunges into a chasm sculpted into channels, chutes, and cauldrons. The Crow Pass Trail is also called the Historic Iditarod Trail in recognition of the days prior to the completion of the railroad in 1918 when miners used it as a winter track to get from the north side of Turnagain Arm to Knik. The hike is best done in summer and fall when avalanche danger is negligible.

The trail starts forty miles southeast of Anchorage and five miles inland from Girdwood at the end of Crow Creek Road, finishing at Eagle River Nature Center 22 miles north of Anchorage. Unless you can arrange for people to drop you off and pick you up at the other end, it makes sense to use the limited public transportation. Take one of the Kenai-bound buses to Girdwood, then either walk or hitch the five miles to the trailhead. At the other end hitch from the nature center to Eagle River and pick up bus #74, #76, or #102 back to Anchorage.

Despite the trail's length it isn't an especially arduous hike, though bad weather can turn it into a nightmare for the ill-prepared. The one objective difficulty is crossing the glacial Eagle River – a simple but cold calf-deep wade that can turn into a wide and impassable waist-high torrent, especially after a series of warm days when glacial run-off is greatest. Call the nature center (Ⓣ694-2108) for the latest information. Memorize the route before you leave and you're unlikely to get lost, but if you've any doubts at all, obtain the inch-to-a-mile Anchorage A6 and A7 quad maps.

For maximum flexibility (and the pick of the campsites) carry a stove, although there are numerous primitive **campsites** where campfires are allowed, as well as a six-berth **cabin** atop Crow Pass at Mile 3 (June–Sept; $35 for the cabin; book up to six months in advance Ⓣ1-877/444-6777, Ⓦwww.ReserveUSA.com).

harrier, snow geese, and short-eared owls also occasionally present. A boardwalk with interpretive displays provides a vantage point for viewing king salmon running below, but is too close to the highway to be really relaxing.

For details on the drive south along Turnagain Arm see the Kenai Peninsula chapter (p.231).

North Anchorage: the Alaska Native Heritage Center and Eagle River

The city's northern boundary is marked by the original townsite on Ship Creek, which, during the salmon runs, is lined with anglers eager to land the fish returning to the **Elmendorf State Fish Hatchery**, Post Road at Reeve Boulevard (unrestricted access). Every year over a million king salmon are raised here for sportfishing around the state and, while there's not a lot to see, there are spawning salmon aplenty visible from the adjacent **Salmon Viewing Area** (late May–Sept daily 8am–10pm).

Because downtown is perched on the extreme northern edge of Anchorage, heading out of town along the Glenn Highway gives the odd sensation of being in the countryside just a few blocks from the central business district. But before leaving the city completely, there's one essential – if expensive – sight, the **Alaska Native Heritage Center**, 8800 Heritage Center Drive (mid-May to late Sept daily 9am–6pm; closed winter; $21, Alaskans $9; infoline Ⓣ330-8000, Ⓦwww.alaskanative.net). The center, which opened in 1999, celebrates the traditions of Alaska's five main Native groups (for more on this, see the Contexts section of this book). Although the center takes a fairly broad, almost simplistic, approach and some key issues in modern tribal life are barely addressed, as an introduction to the people and their lives it is hard to beat – not least because it is staffed almost entirely by Native Alaskans.

Kick off your visit with the excellent twenty-minute film, *Stories Given, Stories Shared*, which gives a sense of peoples whose cultures are finally starting to be accorded the respect they deserve. After the film explore the center's small museum, a sparse display of lovely artifacts – ivory work, spirit masks, beadwork – interpreted by case studies and images that evoke what it is like to be a Native in modern Alaska. Outside, you'll find the main body of the center, five outdoor compounds arranged around a small lake, each representing a major tribal group – Athabascan, Yup'ik, Iñupiat, Aleut, and Tlingit/Haida/Tsimshian. The focus of each area is a house, built in the style appropriate for that particular group from traditional materials and surrounded by plantings typical of that region. Guides interpret the lifestyles of their people, though this sometimes has an artificial tone as much of the knowledge has been specially learned, rather than passed down as it once was. Look out, too, for the themes being pursued each summer, each chosen to study a particular aspect of Alaskan Native culture. During your visit try to catch one of the cultural performances – Native dance, storytelling, music – held in the main auditorium.

The center is seven miles northwest of the city: from downtown, head north along the Glenn Highway and take the Muldoon exit. Alternatively, ride city bus #4, which takes almost an hour to get out there from downtown.

Eagle River

The Glenn Highway expressway, twelve miles north of Anchorage, hurtles straight through **EAGLE RIVER**, a strip-mall suburb mainly of interest for the **Eagle River Nature Center** (June–Aug Mon–Thurs & Sun 10am–5pm

For details on the drive north past Eklutna to Palmer, see Chapter Six (p.347).

Fri & Sat 10am–7pm; May & Sept Tues–Sun 10am–5pm; Oct–Dec & Feb–April Fri, Sat & Sun 10am–5pm; parking $5 for each 12hr period; ⓣ694-2108, ⓦwww.ernc.org), twelve miles east of Eagle River at the end of Eagle River Road. It is in a gorgeous setting, nestled below 7000-foot peaks and surrounded by forest. Extensive outdoor decking and a cozy telescope-equipped lounge to let you view Dall sheep, eagles, coyote, and occasionally bears – moose come so close there's no need for magnification. The nature center sells coffee and a very limited supply of snacks and also offers bountiful information on surrounding **walks**. Easiest of these is the gentle **Rodak Nature Trail** (half-mile loop; 15–30min; 50ft ascent), which slopes down to an attractive salmon-viewing deck on stilts over a small lake. For something a little more strenuous, try the **Albert Loop Trail** (3-mile loop; 1–2hr; 100ft ascent) through the forest and across gravel bars of the glacial Eagle River, or the **Crow Pass Trail** (see box, p.215).

If you want to spend a night or two out here you've got a few possibilities. There is plenty of **free camping** at very basic sites (really just wide patches in the trail) along the Crow Pass Trail, and the nature center manages a modern eight-berth **cabin** and two **yurts** (one four-berth, one six-berth), deep in the woods just over a mile from the center, with sleeping platforms, wood stoves, firewood, and a lake for water. They each cost $55 a night and are often booked well in advance, especially on weekends and school vacations; check availability through the website.

Eating

Nowhere in Alaska will you find a more diverse range of places to eat than Anchorage. That's not to say you'd make a special journey for its culinary wonders, but after a week or two in the Interior it can seem like heaven. As the

Winter in Anchorage

Once the tourists have gone, the days start getting shorter, and the bike trails begin to grow thick with rollerski enthusiasts, you know that winter is approaching. When people talk skiing in Anchorage, they mean cross-country – and for good reason. **Cross-country skiers** are spoilt for choice, with backcountry skiing trails in and around the city. The eleven-mile-long Tony Knowles Coastal Trail is flat and groomed, with excellent views of Cook Inlet and the city, all the way to **Kincaid Park**, where over forty miles of well-maintained trails await. In less busy areas – east Anchorage's Bicentennial Park, for example – you'll find people **ski-joring**, a variation on cross-country skiing in which a dog, harnessed to your chest, takes the strain. There are also two **downhill skiing** venues in town – Hilltop, in south Anchorage, and Alpenglow, just north of downtown – but neither is particularly challenging. Instead, most head to Alyeska Resort (see p.236) 35 miles south.

Lakes freeze to produce eight outdoor **ice-skating** rinks and occasionally paths are cleared across the ice of Westchester Lagoon. **Snowmachine** riders head for the five areas of Chugach State Park set aside for their noisy activities; more retiring types huddle over holes in local lakes **ice fishing**.

Spectator-oriented events focus on the citywide Anchorage Fur Rendezvous (also known as **Fur Rondy** ⓦwww.furrondy.net), which runs two weeks from the third weekend in February and stems from the city's early days when trappers made one of their rare appearances out of the bush to sell their furs. But the highlight of the winter calendar is the ceremonial start of the 1100-mile **Iditarod** (see box, p.360) at 10am on the first Saturday in March.

state's population (and sophistication) has increased, so has the enthusiasm of food importers, to the point where the stock in exotic supermarket-cum-delis (such as New Sagaya's City Market) ranks with the best in the Northwest. Add to that the bounty of Alaska's seas and rivers, and you've got the basis for some pretty wonderful eating. And competition means that prices here are some of the lowest in the state, though newcomers to Alaska will still get a shock.

There are superb places to eat all over the city, which is liberally dotted with cafés, diners, ethnic restaurants, brewpubs, and fine-dining establishments. You'll find the largest overall concentration of restaurants in the **downtown** area, which has seen a burst of activity in recent years with new places popping up every few months. Midtown has a good stock, too, and there are a few places worth seeking out in the south of the city.

Buying **groceries** is easy enough with your own wheels, but without a car you're a bit stuck. There is nowhere to buy ordinary groceries downtown, only the gourmet New Sagaya's City Market. For lower prices head to Carr's at the junction of Northern Lights Boulevard and Minnesota Drive (bus #3, #4, or #36).

Downtown

Cilantro's 611 W 9th Ave ⓣ279-8226. Budget, authentic Mexican with a wide range of traditional favorites, and great ceviche. Closed Sun.

Club Paris 417 W 5th Ave between D and E sts ⓣ277-6332. Anchorage institution that survived the 1964 earthquake and flourished during the oil-boom years, specializing in what are undoubtedly Alaska's finest steaks ($19 "mini" sirloin to the $33 four-inch-thick filet mignon), served in the dim recesses of leather booths. Alaskan seafood is top-notch, too, lunches (Mon–Sat only) come in at modest prices and you can follow with key lime pie or crème caramel.

Downtown Deli 525 W 4th Ave ⓣ276-7116. The city's premier diner, owned by former governor Tony Knowles (seldom seen serving these days), and a long-standing Anchorage favorite for bagels, sandwiches, and the full range of breakfasts. Reasonable prices, and in summer there are seats outside.

The Federal Building Cafeteria 222 W 7th Ave at C St ⓣ277-6736. Breakfast and lunch cafeteria that's about the best budget eating downtown, and certainly a cut above the fast-food joints around. A large bowl of clam chowder or one of their entrées from a daily-changing menu will only set you back $5 or so.

Glacier Brewhouse 737 W 5th Ave ⓣ274-2739; ⓦwww.glacierbrewhouse.com. Typically rowdy, hectic, and hugely popular restaurant, bar, and microbrewery that serves wonderful food and drink. There are always at least half a dozen toothsome house-brewed beers on tap (a shot-glass sampler of five of them costs about $5), and the brewing grains go on to *Europa Bakery* (see opposite), returning as scrumptious bread served with an olive oil dip. Try the alder-wood-baked gourmet pizza ($11), the spit-grilled three-peppercorn prime rib ($23), or the steamed Alaskan king crab legs ($37), but leave room for outstanding bread pudding and something from their selection of ports.

Humpy's Great Alaskan Alehouse 610 W 6th Ave ⓣ276-2337. Though it functions primarily as a bar (see p.221) *Humpy's* also turns out some of the best-value meals in town. Charbroiled salmon, burgers, soups, and salads are all much better than you'd expect from a bar – and the halibut burger with a small Caesar salad is only about $10.

Lucky Wishbone 1033 E 5th Ave ⓣ272-3454. Anchorageites have been coming to "the Bone" since 1955 for its classic diner decor and a menu chiefly noted for its lightly battered panfried chicken (dishes mostly around $8). For the real enthusiast, they often serve gizzards, livers, and giblets.

The Marx Bros Café 627 W 3rd Ave ⓣ278-2133, ⓦwww.marxcafe.com. The best all-round fine dining downtown; gourmet cuisine served up in a historic house with views of the water. Start with the likes of Kachemak bay oysters with pepper vodka and ginger sorbet ($12) or Neapolitan seafood mousse ($12), and follow it up with yellow-fin tuna in a black-bean ginger *beurre blanc* with stir-fried baby *bok choy* ($26), or their signature dish, baked halibut rolled in a macadamia-nut crust and curry sauce and chutney ($27). Dinner only.

New Sagaya's City Market 900 W 13th Ave at I St. *The* place to get your groceries and deli take-outs – with prices to match its trendiness. But the choice is great – varied organic selection, unusual vegetables, great cheeses, on-site bakery – and it is about the only place to buy such things anywhere near downtown. There's also a café for eat-in meals (around $8) with Thai dishes, sushi and sashimi, pizza, wraps, sandwiches, and good coffee. Mon–Sat 6am–10pm, Sun 8am–9pm.

Orso 737 W 5th Ave ⓣ222-3232. Fine dining in a grand baronial setting where smartly dressed staff serve tempting Northern Italian dishes. *Crostini di funghi* is done well, as is the wild mushroom ravioli and the chocolate torte with sambuca syrup. Expect to pay $40–50 plus wine, which starts around $20 a bottle.

Phyllis's Café and Salmon Bake cnr 436 D St ⓣ274-6576. Outdoor seating and bustling atmosphere make this an essential summer stop for mounds of salmon, halibut, and ribs for under $20.

Sack's 328 G St ⓣ274-4022, ⓦwww.sackscafe.com. An appealing and modestly priced favorite. Everything is made with care from the crab and scallop cakes ($11) to the Caesar salad ($7.50). Entrées might include butternut squash ravioli ($19) or rack of NZ lamb ($28), and they do Saturday and Sunday brunches (11am–3pm) with a south-of-the-border variation on eggs Benedict.

Side Street Espresso 412 G St. Coffee is pretty much all they do, and they attract a loyal following for doing it right. Have your caffeine and browse the magazines and community notice board. Occasional live music. Mon–Fri 7am–5.30pm, Sat 7am–5pm, Sun 9am–5pm.

Simon and Seafort's 420 L St ⓣ274-3502. Consistently one of Anchorage's better restaurants, serving meals such as beer-battered fish and chips ($11) in the bar (see p.221) and beautifully prepared American favorites – steaks, ribs, salmon, and such – in a *c*.1900 saloon with wonderful views of Cook Inlet. Expect to pay $40–50 for three courses. Closed for weekend lunches.

Snow City Café 1034 W 4th Ave ⓣ272-6338, ⓦwww.snowcitycafe.com. Probably the city's best breakfast spot – eggs Florentine for $9, fruit & granola for $5 – and great for relaxing over a pot of Earl Grey and a slice of cake. Soups and salads pad out a lunchtime menu that might include pesto chicken pasta ($9) and tofu stir-fry ($9). Not open for dinner except for soup and sandwiches on Wednesday when there's an Irish music session and Sunday when it's open mic.

Teriyaki Box 401 I St ⓣ248-4011. Great little eat-in and takeout place that speedily serves tasty dishes such as wonton noodle soup ($6), shrimp yakisoba noodles ($8), and teriyaki halibut with rice and stir-fry veggies ($8.50), plus espresso coffees.

Midtown

Arctic Roadrunner 5300 Old Seward Hwy at International Airport Rd ⓣ561-1245. Few fancy trimmings, just good no-nonsense food, including a burger regularly voted the best in town. An eat-in and takeout Anchorage staple since 1964. Closed Sun.

Bear Tooth Theatre Pub 1230 W 27th Ave ⓣ276-4200, ⓦwww.beartooththeatre.net. Top-notch combination restaurant, bar, and cinema, where for $3 on top of your meal price you can dine while watching a movie (see "Listings," p.226). The menu has a wide range – Caesar salads ($6), burritos and tacos ($5–8), and gourmet pizzas ($15 for a 16-inch pie) – and the microbrews are excellent.

Bombay Deluxe 555 W Northern Lights Blvd ⓣ277-1200. The best of Anchorage's limited range of curry houses, reliably dishing up the standard range of biryanis, vindaloos and tikka masalas.

Europa Bakery 601 W 36th Ave ⓣ563-5704. Superb bakery where the utmost care is taken in producing all manner of loaves, including a spent-grain variety using the leftovers from the *Glacier Brewhouse*'s beer brewing. Excellent sandwiches ($7) to take out or eat in as well as fine pastries and cakes. It's also a popular place for an omelet breakfast on weekends.

Golden Gate 3471 E Tudor Rd ⓣ561-4274. Basic Chinese joint that's inconveniently located but well worth seeking out for heaving plates at bargain prices. The Mongolian beef ($6.50) is excellent, and they do combination dinners for one from $10.

Gwennie's Old Alaska Restaurant 4333 Spenard Rd at Forest Rd ⓣ243-2090. Something of an Anchorage institution, with two busy floors decorated with Alaskan memorabilia and old photos providing a family setting for all-day breakfasts – the sourdough pancakes are outstanding – as well as the usual range of burgers and sandwiches.

Jen's Restaurant 701 W 36th Ave at Arctic Blvd ⓣ561-5367, ⓦwww.jensrestaurant.com. Highly fashionable fine-dining restaurant and wine bar with a well-heeled crowd and a convivial atmosphere. The menu, which reflects the chef's Danish heritage, varies daily but you might expect to start with king salmon and king-crab pâté ($12) followed by panfried medallions of marlin on mango, jalapeño and citrus *beurre blanc* ($20). The wine list is equally impressive. Closed Sat lunch, Mon evening and all day Sun.

Kaladi Bros 1360 W Northern Lights Blvd ⓣ344-5483. Excellent coffee and a relaxed environment in a café attached to Title Wave Books. There's Internet access on Macs for $7/hr, plus wireless access for $4 a day.

The Middle Way 1200 W Northern Lights Blvd ⓣ272-6433. Low-key café specializing in low-fat, healthy and mostly vegetarian food, particularly soups, sandwiches, wraps and salads (mostly under $7), plus espresso, organic juices and smoothies including one offering "inner balance." Breakfast daily, lunch Mon–Sat.

Moose's Tooth 3300 Old Seward Hwy at 33rd Ave ⓣ258-2537, ⓦwww.moosestooth.net. A perennial favorite, always alive with diners tucking into some of the town's best gourmet pizza (in 42 variations) or imbibing one of a dozen or so house-brewed beers at the bar. On the first Thursday of the month they celebrate First Tap Thursday (9pm–1am), offering a band, a party, and an opportunity to meet the brewer over a glass of that month's new creation.

Organic Oasis 2610 Spenard Rd ⓣ277-7882. Earthy and reasonably priced lunch spot that's great for soups and organic dishes that are mostly vegetarian or vegan (though not exclusively). Try their wraps, sandwiches and mini pizzas (mostly $9–11) washed down with a shot of wheatgrass, fruit smoothie or (if you must) an espresso. From Tues to Sat there's usually some form of civilized live music. Closed Sun.

Taco del Mar 343 W Benson Blvd ⓣ563-9097. Northern outpost of this small Seattle-based chain serving enormous burritos, great Baja fish tacos, and other Mexican staples at low prices. Several vegetarian and vegan choices.

South Anchorage

Mexico in Alaska 7305 Old Seward Hwy at 73rd Ave ⓣ349-1528. Anchorage's most authentic Mexican restaurant. Although the food is slightly sanitized for northern tastes, you won't find better dishes than the *camarones Veracruzana* ($20) or the *chaquiles* done in a savory mole sauce for $12. For the budget-conscious, the $10 weekday lunch buffet is worth considering, and there are always bottles of the excellent Bohemia beer.

Southside Bistro 1320 Huffman Park Drive ⓣ348-0088, ⓦwww.southsidebistro.com. Some of the finest dining in the south of the city, particularly noted for its seafood and fresh pasta on the restaurant side (mains $20–25). The adjacent bistro has excellent hardwood-baked flat-bread pizza. Closed Sun & Mon.

Drinking and entertainment

Good bars abound in downtown Anchorage, and the atmosphere varies as much as the clientele. You don't need to dig far to find dark, block-built hide-away lounges left over from the oil-boom Seventies when they were meeting places for shady deals, and late at night the main drag of **4th Avenue** can seem like a surreal slalom course as you swerve to avoid the terminally drunk. But the downtown area also harbors half a dozen or more genuinely appealing places to drink, and even a little **live music**, most reliably at *Humpy's*.

The other lively area is **Spenard** – along Spenard Road between Northern Lights Boulevard and International Airport Road – which has long since shaken its reputation for sleazy excess, earned during the freewheeling oil days of the late 1970s, but still retains an edge. It can be a lot of fun as long as you are sensible, though women travelers may not find the wilder side of macho Anchorage quite as endearing as many locals seem to think it is, evident in some innocent-looking bars turning out to be strip joints. Here, too, you'll find live music, either at *Blues Central* and *Chilkoot Charlie's*, or after the main show, at *Mr Whitekey's*.

Beer drinkers should be very happy in Anchorage, which must have more top-quality microbreweries than any city of comparable size in the US. Breweries worth trying are the *Moose's Tooth*, *Bear Tooth*, *Glacier Brewhouse*, *Snow Goose,* and even *Humpy's*, which doesn't brew its own, but has a vast range on tap.

There isn't a great deal of live **theater** in Anchorage, particularly during the summer when it takes something really special to lure Alaskans indoors. For the rest of the year, the Alaska Center for the Performing Arts (aka PAC; ⓣ263-2900) puts its exemplary acoustics to the test with a variety of shows, plays, and concerts, and hosts both the Anchorage Opera (ⓣ279-2557, ⓦwww.anchorageopera.org) and the Anchorage Symphony Orchestra

(Ⓣ274-8668, Ⓦwww.anchoragesymphony.org). Look out, too, for the Anchorage Festival of Music (Ⓣ272-1471, Ⓦwww.anchorageconcerts.org), which takes place in mid-June.

It's a major step down in formality, though not ambition or invention, to the quirky Cyrano's Off Center Playhouse, 413 D St at 4th Ave (Ⓣ274-2499, Ⓦwww.cyranos.org), a theater that puts on a lively range of material from locally penned plays to the more edgy classics and frequently stages works performed by their resident troupe, the Eccentric Theater Company.

To find out what's on at any of the places listed below, consult the *Anchorage Daily News* – particularly Friday's comprehensive "8" entertainment supplement – or Thursday's free weekly *Press*, a kind of cafés and bars newsletter found all over town. Both also give a rundown of the first-run movies and occasional art-house flicks at the profusion of multiscreen **cinemas** in suburban malls (see "Listings," p.226).

Tickets for almost any major show can be bought from the CarrsTix office in the foyer of the Center for the Performing Arts (Mon–Sat noon–4pm; Ⓣ1-800/478-7328, Ⓦwww.tickets.com), and in any Carrs supermarket.

Downtown

Bernie's Bungalow 626 D St at 7th Ave Ⓦwww.berniesbungalowlounge.com. Very un-Alaskan chic martini bar fashioned from an old wooden house that shimmies to cool Latin and jazz grooves. They have an ever-expanding deck for the long summer evenings, but indoor seating is in short supply so come early and dress up.

Darwin's Theory 426 G St at 4th Ave. Straightforward bar for moderately priced boozing and beery encounters with colorful local characters.

Humpy's Great Alaskan Alehouse 610 W 6th Ave at F St Ⓣ276-2337; see p.218. An ever-popular watering hole with a college bar feel and what must be Alaska's widest selection of Pacific Northwest microbrews (over 30) as well as some expensive English and Belgian bottled beers. Whisky drinkers are also well catered for with more than thirty single malts, and there is live music nightly (free), often acoustic or Irish.

Mad Myrna's 530 E 5th Ave Ⓣ276-9762, Ⓦwww.alaska.net/~madmyrna. Anchorage's main gay dance club, usually open Wed–Sun from 9pm, with regular drag acts and karaoke. Small cover charge at weekends and when there's someone special performing.

Pioneer Bar 739 W 4th Ave Ⓣ276-7996. Traditional, dark downtown bar that has swapped its seedy reputation in favor of boisterous youthful drinking.

Rumrunners Old Towne Bar and Grill cnr 4th Ave & E St Ⓣ278-4493. Hugely popular bar attracting a young crowd with DJ-led dance most nights and showy cocktail mixing.

Simon and Seafort's 420 L St Ⓣ274-3502. Mainly an upmarket restaurant (see p.219), but the saloon bar is a great spot for cocktails or scotches and bourbons (over 100 varieties), especially if you can steal a seat close to the picture windows, which boast unsurpassed views of Cook Inlet and Mount Susitna.

Snow Goose 717 W 3rd Ave Ⓣ277-7727. Good restaurant and microbrewery chiefly noted for its wonderfully spacious deck that's perfect for those long summer evenings.

Sub Zero 612 F St. Currently the place to be seen, all steel and ice-blue lighting, and non-smoking to boot.

Midtown

Blues Central 825 W Northern Lights Blvd at Arctic Ave Ⓣ272-1341, Ⓦwww.bluescentral.net. A restaurant mainly notable as Anchorage's premier venue for blues (plus a little soul), operating every night until 2am, with a very popular jam session on Sunday night. $3–5 cover charge.

Chilkoot Charlie's 2435 Spenard Rd Ⓣ272-1010; Ⓦwww.koots.com. OK, so it's not everyone's idea of a good night out, and can be a cattle market, but "Koots" is Alaskan through and through. Every night this sawdust-strewn barn of a place packs them in for a wide range of pricey drinks (10 bars in total), pool, foosball, multiple floors of DJ-led dance and a band from 9.30pm. "We screw the other guy and pass the savings on to you!" they claim, but still have a cover charge, usually $2–6.

Mr Whitekey's Fly By Night Club 3300 Spenard Rd at 33rd St Ⓣ279-7726, Ⓦwww.flybynightclub.com. Zany cabaret and live music venue which, throughout summer, hosts *The Whale Fat Follies* (June to mid-Sept Tues–Sat 8pm; $13–20; 16 and over only), a satirical and occasionally bawdy slant on Alaska and its people which you'll understand and appreciate all the more at the end of your time in the state. There's usually live music after the show on weekends (around 10.30pm; free) and there's food, too, featuring Spam in ways you never thought possible. Smokefree shows on Tues & Thurs.

Peanut Farm 5227 Old Seward Hwy at International Airport Rd ⓣ563-3283. Straightforward sports bar, always lively and open very late. Their "burgers as big as your head" are best consumed on their big deck beside Campbell Creek on a warm evening.

Shopping

For Alaskans, Anchorage offers the best shopping this side of Seattle, and is often the only place you can get your hands on the goods. As a visitor, shopping is likely to be fairly low on your list of priorities, though with no state sales tax to pay, it can be a good place to buy **books** and **outdoor equipment**. Consider putting some cash aside for **Native craftwork**, such as spirit masks, ivory carving, and etched baleen (though see our comments on transporting restricted goods in the box on p.224). Some of what's available can be tasteless souvenir junk, but much of it is beautiful and superbly made with prices to match. Some judicious shopping around, however, can turn up affordable pieces.

Books

Wherever you are in Alaska you'll have no problem finding books about the state or by Alaskan authors, but if you've got specific needs Anchorage is by far your best bet. Also see the "Books" section of Contexts for specific recommendations.

Barnes & Noble 200 Et Northern Lights Blvd ⓣ279-7323. The chain bookshop has its usual solid selection of new books and newspapers. Daily 9am–11pm.

C & M Used Books 215 E 4th Ave ⓣ278-9394. Downtown secondhand bookshop where, amid the apparent chaos, they've got some good books available at half the cover price (or quarter price with a similarly priced trade). Mon–Sat 9am–5pm, closed Sun.

Cook Inlet Book Co 415 W 5th Ave at D St ⓣ258-4544, ⓦwww.cookinlet.com. Anchorage's handiest source for new and used books, magazines and newspapers, that's particularly strong on Alaskan titles. Daily 9am–10pm in summer.

Cyrano's 413 D St ⓣ274-2599. Specialist bookshop with a good line in the arts, literary fiction, the classics, and Alaskan titles. Mon–Sat 9am–5.30pm.

Title Wave 1360 W Northern Lights Blvd ⓣ278-9283 or 1-888/598-9283, ⓦwww.wavebooks.com. Wondrous midtown emporium with the widest selection of used books in the city and a large and well-chosen selection of remaindered and new titles plus new and used CDs. Kaladi Bros Internet café (see p.219) on site. Mon–Thurs 9am–9pm, Fri & Sat 9am–10pm, Sun 11am–7pm.

Camping and outdoor equipment

If you're planning to spend a fair bit of time in the Alaskan outdoors, you'll need the right gear. Your best bet is to head to Anchorage's outdoor supply ghetto – at the junction of Spenard Road and Northern Lights Boulevard, in midtown – where you'll find pretty much everything you need: canoes, tents, climbing tackle, fishing gear, and bicycles, some of it also available for renting (see "Listings," p.226).

Alaska Kayak 2605 Barrow St 3, between Northern Lights & Fireweed blvds ⓣ522-7710. Anchorage's specialist canoe and kayak store, which rents canoes and whitewater kayaks from $60 for 2 days.

Alaska Mountaineering & Hiking 2633 Spenard Rd ⓣ272-1811, ⓦwww.alaskan.com/amh. Rock climbers and mountaineers are best served here at AMH, which also covers hiking needs, rents mountaineering and ski equipment at competitive rates, and has a used-equipment board. Mon–Fri 9am–7pm, Sat 9am–6pm, Sun noon–5pm.

Barney's Sport Chalet 906 W Northern Lights Blvd ⓣ561-5242. A little more personal than the bigger REI, strong on top-quality tents, backpacking equipment and, in winter, cross-country ski equipment. Mon–Fri 10am–7pm, Sat 10am–5pm.

Great Outdoor Clothing Co 1200 W Northern Lights Blvd ⓣ277-6664. The best spot for low-cost fleeces, hats, and thermal underwear. Daily 10am–6pm.

REI 1200 W Northern Lights Blvd ⓣ272-4565, ⓦwww.rei.com. This one-stop specialist store stocks Alaska's widest selection of camping, hiking, canoeing, climbing, and skiing gear plus clothing, footwear, and freeze-dried foods. They also do an extensive range of rentals. A single lifetime family payment of $15 gives you membership in the co-op and substantial discounts on retail and rental gear. Mon–Fri 9am–9pm, Sat & Sun 9am–6pm.

Crafts

Most of the tourist-oriented shops in Anchorage stock the usual array of garish T-shirts and overpriced rubbish, not much of it even kitschy enough to be enticing. Amongst the dross you will find some excellent **Native crafts** – Anchorage has the best selection in the state since craftspeople visiting the big city from outlying villages tend to bring in their work for sale. When buying here you lose some of the satisfaction of dealing directly with the artisan and will probably pay more than you would at source. Before buying anything containing parts of endangered animals, read the box on taking your purchases out of the state (see overleaf).

Alaska hasn't quite shaken its Russian influence and accordingly there are several shops downtown stocking **Russian-made goods**. Look for porcelain tea sets from Lomonosov in St Petersburg and nested *matryoshka* dolls – the wooden ones that fit into each other – in traditional designs and modern variations: American football teams, *South Park* characters, and political genealogies from Lenin to Putin.

Alaska Native Medical Center 4315 Diplomacy Drive, off Tudor Rd ⓣ729-1122. Serious buyers should definitely make for the craft shop on the ground floor of this hospital. Items are brought in by folk from Native villages when they come to visit recuperating friends and relatives. Good range and fair (though not cheap) prices. Mon–Fri 10am–2pm and first and third Saturday of the month 11am–2pm.

Alaskan Ivory Exchange 700 W 4th Ave ⓣ272-3662. A small shop chock-full of carved walrus ivory and fossilized whalebone products; some simple and fairly cheap, others more intricate and pricey.

Aleksandr Baranov 321 W 5th Ave ⓣ274-9090. Russian-run emporium full of icons, nested dolls and other imported goodies.

Anchorage Museum of History & Art 121 W 7th Ave at A St ⓣ343-4326. The museum shop in the foyer (no entrance fee) stocks a wide selection of quality Native crafts along with Russian lacquerwork and Alaska books.

Antique Gallery 1001 W 4th Ave, Suite B ⓣ276-8986, ⓦwww.theantiquegallery.com. A real treasure trove, packed to the rafters with pre-twentieth-century artifacts you'd normally only see in museums; and everything's for sale. Avoid sticking your foot through the thousand-dollar canvases that line the aisles and browse through $1500 baskets woven from whale baleen, Tiffany lamps, suits of armor, ormolu clocks, stacks of shotguns and pistols, Russian icons, and even the occasional $40,000 oil by Laurence, Ziegler, or Machetanz.

Aurora 713 W 5th Ave ⓣ274-0234. Colorful store with a wide range of Native arts and crafts, much of it quite expensive but top quality.

Kobuk Coffee Company 504 W 5th Ave ⓣ272-3626, ⓦwww.kobukcoffee.com. Mainly a coffee and tea emporium, but it also sells beautiful Russian tea services and offers free samples of samovar tea.

Oomingmak Musk Ox Producers' Co-operative 604 H St ⓣ272-9225, ⓦwww.qiviut.com. Small shop selling garments knitted from qiviut, the under-fur of the musk ox, by natives of western Alaska, where each village has its own distinctive design. Most products are fawn, with a scarf going for $250–350, a hat for $125–175. (For more on this organization and these ancient beasts, see p.355.)

Buying Native crafts and taking them back home

There's always something satisfying about **buying** direct from the artist, and there's often a financial benefit, too, though with Native crafts this is offset by the cost of flying out to remote villages where most of the artists live. If you can't buy from the artist you'll want to be sure of what you are buying and its authenticity. Ask questions: a reputable dealer should know the artist's cultural background, the materials used and maybe even have some sort of biography of the artist. Look, too, for signatures and consider the feel of the piece; for example, genuine ivory will feel a lot heavier than any plastic imitation. If something is cheap, it's probably fake. Carved ivory usually costs at least $100 an inch.

Also keep an eye out for the **Silver Hand** logo, which indicates traditional artwork made in Alaska by an Alaskan Native currently resident in the state. Many genuine artists don't participate in the scheme, however. Silver Hand stickers bear a permit so you can call for verification (Ⓣ269-6610 in Anchorage or 1-888/278-7424). A "Made in Alaska" sticker only means that it is made in the state.

Taking stuff home

In an attempt to preserve traditional lifestyles, particularly in remote villages, Native Alaskans are allowed to trade in raw materials otherwise proscribed by the Convention on International Trade in Endangered Species (CITES). Although it is perfectly legal to buy Native artifacts such as walrus-tusk cribbage boards, spirit masks, whalebone sculpture, etched pieces of baleen, and the pelts of wolves, otters, walruses, seals, and bears, the customs people back home may take a dim view of any attempt to bring such things with you.

Strictly speaking, it is illegal to export from the US products containing parts of bears (black and brown), cormorants, eagles, loons, puffins, ravens, sea lions, snowy owls, waterfowl, and whales of any kind, though you are unlikely to be stopped leaving the country. Canada, the United Kingdom, Australia, New Zealand, and many other countries ban the import of such products, along with those made from lynx, otters, walruses, wolves, and wolverines. It is possible to import some items into some countries with the appropriate paperwork, and any reputable shop will provide a US Department of the Interior CITES Personal Property Exemption form and preferably documentation of who made the item and where. If you think you are likely to buy Native crafts, the best bet is to check import restrictions before you leave home. One publication worth checking out is *A Customs Guide to Alaska Native Arts*, which includes a country-by-country list of which species are legal, permissible with paperwork, or illegal.

Export and import restrictions are irrelevant for **US residents**, though they can't take banned goods into Canada, even in transit. Many people manage to carry stuff through customs without any problem, but it is worth being aware that your souvenirs may be confiscated and you could be fined.

Listings

Airport Ted Stevens International Airport Ⓣ266-2526, Ⓦwww.dot.state.ak.us/anc. For details of airlines and flights, see Basics p.34.

American Express American Express Travel Service, Suite 104, 5011 Spenard Rd, near the airport (Mon–Fri 9am–6pm; Ⓣ266-6600, Ⓕ266-6689), operates as a travel agency, exchanges foreign currency, and handles client mail.

Banks and currency exchange Banks are located all over town, many of them drive-thru. ATMs are even more abundant, some located in bars. Downtown there's a First National Bank branch at 646 W 4th Ave between F and G sts and a Wells Fargo outpost in the Fifth Avenue Mall at D St (Mon–Sat 10am–6pm), which handles foreign exchange.

△ A view of Anchorage

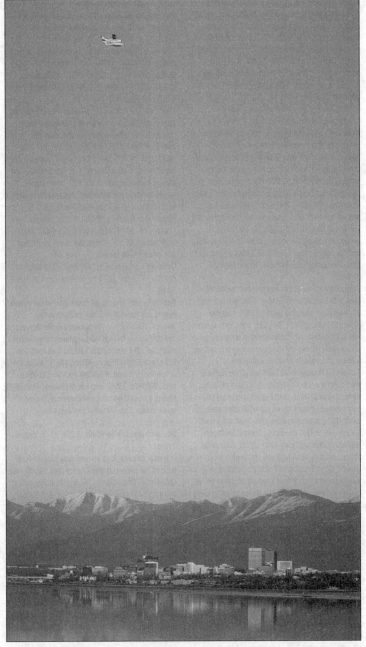

Buses (long-distance) The following services operate roughly from mid-May to mid-Sept, though it pays to book ahead at the end of the season when services may not run if there are too few customers. (See Basics on p.41 for route details.) Alaska Direct Bus Line (ⓣ1-800/770-6652; in Anchorage ⓣ227-6652) departs from *Days Inn*, 321 5th Ave, and the *HI-Anchorage* hostel for Whitehorse, Yukon (Wed, Fri, and Sun only) via Palmer, Glennallen, and Tok; Alaska Park Connection (ⓣ245-0200 or 1-800/266-8625) picks up outside the Egan Convention Center on 5th Ave for the morning run to Talkeetna and Denali, outside the *Bear Best Western* for the afternoon run north, and for runs to Seward; Alaska Trails & Tours (ⓣ1-888/600-6001) picks up at the *HI-Anchorage* hostel and goes to Fairbanks; Homer Stage Line (ⓣ868-3914) runs to Soldotna, Kenai and Homer from *HI-Anchorage* and *Spenard Hostel*; The Magic Bus (ⓣ441-8420) does a run to Girdwood leaving the visitor center at 4.30pm daily; and the Seward Bus Line (ⓣ563-0800) picks up at 3335 Fairbanks St in midtown for the run to Seward.

Camping and outdoor equipment rental REI (see p.223) rents tents from $15 for the first day, $7 thereafter; sleeping bags $15/$7; cooking stoves $10/$5; canoes $45/$15 and more. In summer a lot of this stuff is reserved in advance, so phone early. These are member prices but savings quickly offset the $15 membership fee.

Car rental Renting a car from one of the desks at the airport operated by Alamo, Avis, Budget, Dollar, Hertz, National, Thrifty, and Payless incurs an additional eleven percent tax on top of all other taxes, so for anything other than a very brief rental it works out cheaper to rent off-airport. Budget, Thrifty, and numerous local agencies have depots close to the airport, but they can't pick you up, so grab a cab (around $8; refundable with some agencies), or go to your hotel and they'll drop a vehicle off when you're ready for it free of charge. The cheapest (and oldest) vehicles are from Denali Car Rental, 1209 Gambell St (ⓣ276-1230 or 1-800/757-1230, ⓔdcr1@alaska.net), which has compacts from $40 a day with 150 free miles a day (15¢ a mile thereafter). CDW is only $12 a day with $1000 deductible. They're based far from the airport so go to your lodging and they'll deliver. For one- or two-year-old vehicles starting at around $50 a day try: Advantage, 421 Spenard Rd (ⓣ243-8806 or 1-888/877-3585, ⓦwww.ineedacarrental.com); Affordable New Car Rentals, 4707 Spenard Rd at Breezewood (ⓣ243-3370 or 1-800/248-3765, ⓦwww.ancr.com); Airport Car Rental, 502 W Northern Lights Blvd (ⓣ562-0897, ⓕ561-1437, ⓦwww.alaskan.com/airportcarrental); Alaska Car & Van Rentals, 3934 Spenard Rd (ⓣ243-4444 or 1-800/243-4832, ⓦwww.alaskacarandvan.com); or Arctic, 1130 W International Airport Rd (ⓣ561-2990, ⓦwwwarcticrentacar.com). Local numbers for the majors are: Alamo ⓣ248-0017; Avis ⓣ277-4567; Budget ⓣ243-0150; Dollar ⓣ248-5338; Hertz ⓣ243-3308; National ⓣ265-7553; Thrifty ⓣ276-2855; and Payless ⓣ243-3616.

Cinemas The Anchorage Museum of History & Art (see p.209) has a program of classic and less mainstream contemporary movies (mid-May to mid-Sept Sat & Sun 3pm & 6pm; $6); the *Bear Tooth Theatre Pub* (see p.219) plays movies a couple of months old and often has film festivals and classic-movie nights, all for $3. The remaining movie theaters are suburban multiplexes: closest to downtown is the Fireweed Theater, 661 E Fireweed at Gambell (ⓣ566-3328); otherwise try Century 16, 301 E 36th Ave (ⓣ929-FILM; $8.50, early shows $5.50). Check the *Press* for listings and other movie houses.

Consulates Canada, 3512 Campbell Airstrip Rd ⓣ333-1400; UK, 3211 Providence Drive ⓣ786-4848.

Festivals and events All major (and many minor) events are listed at ⓦwww.anchorage.net/events. The pick are: Anchorage Fur Rendezvous, a ten-day winter festival held in March (ⓦwww.furrondy.net); the start of the Iditarod Trail Sled Dog Race (see p.360) in early March; the Blues on the Green Festival held in Kincaid Park in mid-June (ⓣ1-800/478-7328); and the Anchorage Festival of Music, a classical music celebration held over a week in late June (ⓦwww.festivalmusic.org).

Gay and lesbian helpline ⓣ258-4777; daily 6–11pm.

Internet access Sign up and wait for your free hour at the main Loussac Library (see below). Also Café Fonte, Dover St off C St and 36th Ave, where there's free access and good coffee; and Kaladi Bros (see p.219).

Laundry K-Speed Wash, 600 E 6th Ave (open Mon–Sat 7am–10pm; ⓣ279-0731).

Left luggage There is luggage storage (daily 5am–2am) at the airport's main domestic (South) terminal. For up to 24 hours storage they charge $6 for a suitcase or backpack and $14 for a set of antlers.

Library ZJ Loussac Library, 3600 Denali St at 36th St (Mon–Thurs 10am–8pm, Fri & Sat 10am–6pm, Sun 1–5pm; closed Sun in summer), has a huge selection of books with plenty on Alaska as well as free Internet access (see above). Buses #2 and #60 are most convenient from downtown.

Maps The Maps Place, 601 W 36th Ave (ⓣ563-6277) stocks a wide selection of topo and other maps. Topographical and geotechnical maps are also available from USGS Earth Science Information Center, 4230 University Drive, in Grace Hall at Alaska Pacific University (ⓣ786-7011, ⓕ786-7050), but are probably more detailed than you need.
Medical assistance Alaska Health Care Clinic, 3600 Minnesota Drive at 36th Ave (Mon–Fri 8am–7pm, Sat 10am–4pm; ⓣ279-3500); Anchorage Medical & Surgical Clinic, 718 K St (Mon–Fri 8am–5.30pm; ⓣ272-2571); and Providence Alaska Medical Center (ⓣ562-2211, ⓦwww.providence.org/Alaska/default.htm).
Newspapers The *Anchorage Daily News* and the weekly *Press* are available all over town. For papers from the Lower 48, your best bet downtown is Cook Inlet Book Co (see p.222).
Pharmacy There's a 24-hour pharmacy in Carr's, cnr Minnesota Drive and Northern Lights Blvd (ⓣ297-0560); Fred Meyer's, 1000 E Northern Lights Blvd (ⓣ264-9633), has a pharmacy open daily 8am–11pm.
Photographic supplies Stewart's Photo Shop, 531 W 4th Ave between E and F sts (Mon–Sat 8.30am–6pm; ⓣ272-8581), caters to pretty much all film and camera needs.
Post office The most central post office (Mon–Fri 10am–5.30pm) is located downstairs in the Ship Creek mall on W 4th Ave between C and D sts and is the best place to use as **General Delivery** (zip code 99510).
Rock climbing The nearest rock climbing to the city is the quarried embankment alongside the Seward Highway and train line between fifteen and thirty miles south of the city. It is close enough for locals to pop out after work – if you want to join them just drive along and look for likely spots or purchase the local guidebook *The Scar* (see "Books," p.222). Indoors, there's the Alaska Rock Gym, 4840 Fairbanks St (daily noon–10pm or thereabouts; ⓣ562-7265, ⓦwww.alaskarockgym.com), which charges $14 a visit.
RV rental See our general comments about RV rentals in Basics (p.44).
Swimming Cook Inlet isn't suitable for swimming but a couple of lakes are: Spenard Beach Park, at the eastern end of Lake Spenard (bus #7 or #36) has a roped-off area patrolled by lifeguards and a beach with picnic tables and volleyball; Jewel Lake, where Jewel Lake Rd meets Dimond Blvd, has similar facilities (bus #7). To swim indoors, try any high school pool (typically $3.50). Numbers are listed in the white pages under Schools – Senior High and the pool usually has a separate number. There's also H2Oasis Indoor Waterpark, 1520 O'Malley Rd (daily 10am–10pm; $20, kids $15; ⓣ344-8610, ⓦwww.h2oasiswaterpark.com), with wave pool, lazy river, hot tubs, pirate ship lagoon, and water-coaster, among other aquatic delights.
Taxes There is no sales tax in Anchorage, but the city does impose an eight percent bed tax, which is already included in our accommodation prices.
Taxis Alaska Cab ⓣ563-5353; Checker Cab ⓣ276-1234; Yellow Cab ⓣ272-2422. Expect $6 for a journey downtown, $8–10 between downtown and midtown and $16–18 from downtown to the airport.
Travel agency New World Travel, 1200 W Northern Lights Blvd ⓣ276-7071.

Travel details

As Anchorage is the heart of Alaska's land and air transport networks, you'll almost certainly find yourself passing through, even if you're not interested in the city. The following journey frequencies all apply to the summer season and are greatly reduced in winter.

Trains make one round-trip a day each to Seward and Whittier, and there's one service a day in each direction between Anchorage and Fairbanks, via Talkeetna and Denali. **Bus routes** are more extensive, with individual lines fanning out to Seward, Homer, Tok, and Denali, with one service continuing to Fairbanks. Most **planes** follow simple there-and-back flight schedules, though the strung-out nature of Southeast Alaska and the importance of Seattle make long multistop runs more suitable. Major towns – especially Juneau, Ketchikan, and Seattle – have direct nonstop services, while smaller places are reached on multistop routes such as: Anchorage–Juneau–Sitka–Ketchikan–Seattle; Anchorage–Cordova–Yakutat–Juneau–Seattle; and Anchorage–Juneau–Petersburg–Wrangell–Ketchikan–Seattle.

Trains

Anchorage to: Denali Park (daily; 7hr 30min); Fairbanks (daily; 12hr); Seward (daily; 4hr 20min); Talkeetna (daily; 3hr 10min); Wasilla (daily; 1hr 30min); Whittier (daily; 2hr 20min).

Buses

Anchorage to: Denali Park (4 daily; 5–6hr); Fairbanks (1 daily; 9–10hr); Girdwood (3 daily; 1hr 15min); Glennallen (3 weekly; 4hr 30min); Homer (1 daily; 5–6hr); Nenana (1 daily; 7hr); Ninilchik (1 daily; 4hr); Palmer (3 weekly; 1hr); Seward (2 daily; 3–4hr); Soldotna (1 daily; 3hr 30min); Talkeetna (2–3 daily; 3hr); Talkeetna Junction (4 daily; 3hr); Tok (3 weekly; 8–9hr); Wasilla (4 daily; 1hr 15min); Whitehorse (3 weekly; 18hr).

Flights

Anchorage to: Barrow (2 daily; 3hr); Cordova (2–3 daily; 50min); Dutch Harbor (2–3 daily; 2hr–2hr 50min); Fairbanks (10–12 daily; 1hr); Homer (4–6 daily; 50min); Iliamna (1–2 daily; 1hr); Juneau (4 daily; 1hr 40min); Kenai (14–18 daily; 25min); Ketchikan (1–2 daily; 3–5hr); King Salmon (5–8 daily; 1hr–1hr 20min); Kodiak (6–8 daily; 50min–1hr 10min); Kotzebue (3 daily; 1hr 30min); Nome (3 daily; 1hr 30min–3hr); Petersburg (1 daily; 3hr); Prudhoe Bay/Deadhorse (1 daily; 1hr 40min); Seattle, WA (16 daily; 3hr 20min); Seldovia (4 weekly; 1hr 15min); Sitka (1 daily; 3hr); Valdez (2–3 daily; 40min); Wrangell (1 daily; 3hr 40min); Yakutat (1 daily; 2hr).

3

Kenai Peninsula

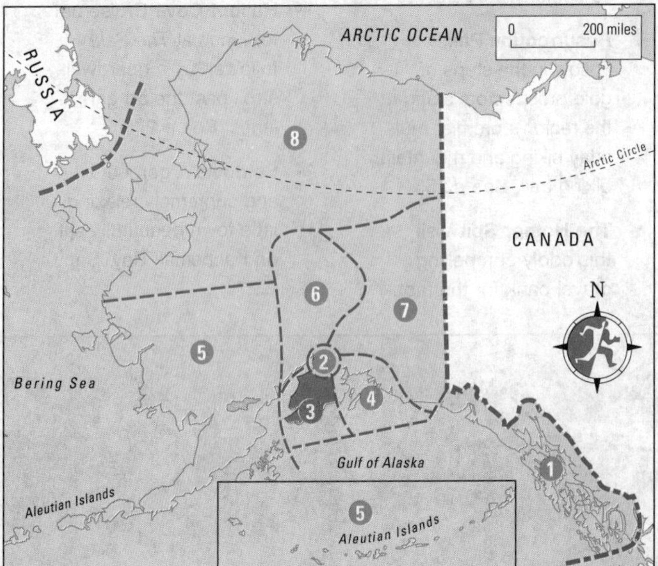

CHAPTER 3

Highlights

* **Sixmile Creek** Brace yourself for rafting some of the wildest whitewater in the state. See p.240
* **Kenai Fjords National Park** Seeing whales seems like a bonus on cruises past calving glaciers and a Steller sea lion colony. See p.242
* **Resurrection Pass** Follow in the steps of gold prospectors along the region's premier multiday hiking and mountain biking trail. See p.255
* **The Homer Spit** Visit this oddly compelling gravel bank for the fabulous sea views, sparkling light, and opportunities to go halibut fishing and kayaking. See p.268
* **Kenai River kings** Visit Soldotna and try to land a bigger salmon than you ever thought possible. See p.258
* **Halibut Cove** Cruise out for lunch at *The Saltry* followed by a boardwalk stroll past the art galleries. See p.275
* **Seldovia** A gorgeous and supremely relaxing little town beautifully set on Kachemak Bay. See p.276

△ Fishing at Homer Spit

3

The Kenai Peninsula

The **KENAI PENINSULA**, a 150-by-120-mile hunk of land immediately south of Anchorage, is sometimes lauded as Alaska in a nutshell. It is certainly true that a lot of what is great in the state can be found here shoehorned into what, by Alaskan standards, is a tiny area. You miss out on the extreme conditions of the Interior, the towering mountains of the Alaska Range, the full span of the state's cultural mix, and a lot more besides, but the Kenai (KEEN-eye) packs in a little of almost everything Alaska has to offer: tidewater glaciers, whale watching, outstanding halibut and salmon fishing, entertaining small towns, accessible hiking, and much more. In short, if you can only spend time in one part of Alaska, then this is probably your best bet.

Proximity to Anchorage has helped make the Kenai one of the most populated rural areas of the state, as well as one of the best connected, with a train line, a relatively dense network of roads, and good ferry services. These factors combine to make this one of the most popular parts of Alaska, and the pressure on accommodation can be a problem in summer. But having a lot of people around can be a benefit as the increased demand for all kinds of trips – flightseeing, cruises, kayaking, and the like – means you'll find more companies running a wider range of trips to more unusual destinations.

Before the arrival of Europeans, most of the Kenai Peninsula was Dena'ina country, populated by the Kenaitze sub-tribe. Whatever balance they had achieved with surrounding peoples was turned upside down by the arrival of Russians, who established a small town on the Kenai Peninsula in 1791. Once under US control the area was virtually ignored until gold was found along **Turnagain Arm** in 1897. After the gold played out, Seward became an important port at the southern end of the Alaska Railroad, but much of the peninsula was ignored until 1957, when oil and gas deposits were discovered along the northwestern coast. That small find was soon overshadowed by far greater finds elsewhere, but Kenai retains its gas-production platforms and oil refinery.

Leaving Anchorage, the **Seward Highway** follows Turnagain Arm, a broad finger off Cook Inlet that provided access for late nineteenth-century prospectors. The only town that has seen much activity in recent times is **Girdwood**, an easygoing place that is home to Alaska's premier downhill **ski resort** and the best-preserved of the old gold mines. Continuing south you've a choice: take Portage Road past **Portage Glacier** and head for Whittier or continue around the head of Turnagain Arm onto the Kenai Peninsula proper.

The old gold town of **Hope** makes a good base for hiking the wonderful Resurrection Trail and whitewater rafting down the thunderous Sixmile Creek. Crossing through the heart of the mountains, the Seward Highway continues to the south-coast port of **Seward**, where you can stand next to a

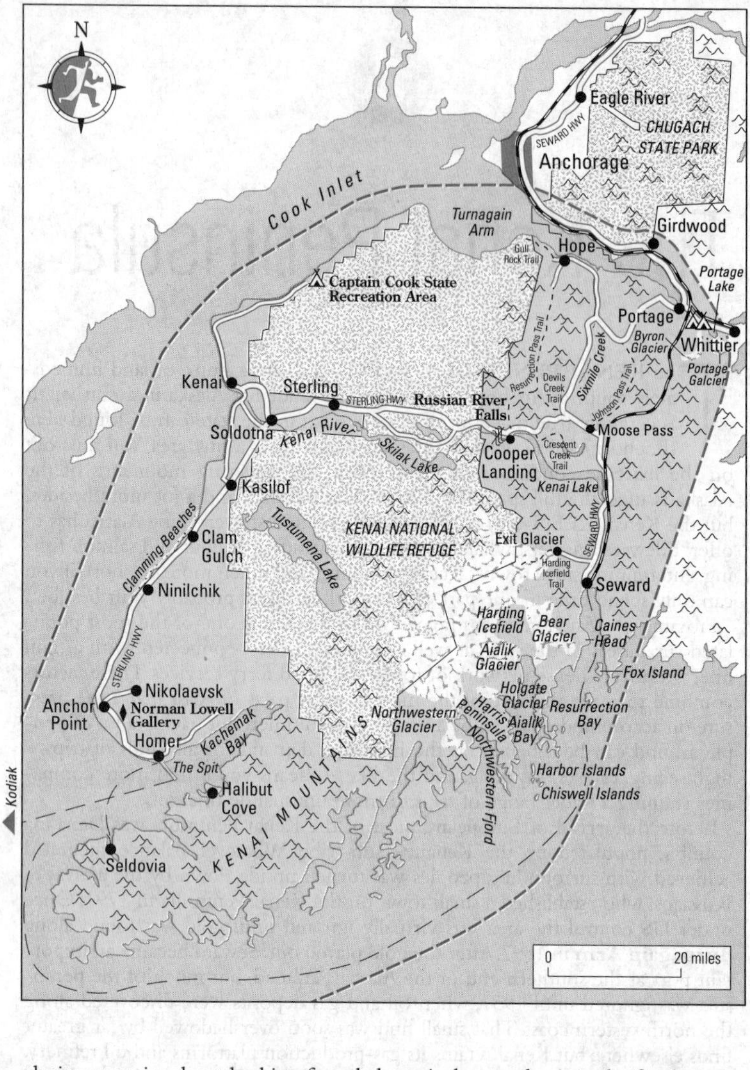

glacier or cruise about looking for whales as icebergs calve into the fjord nearby. The aquatic world will even come to you at the classy SeaLife Center. Stay in the mountains and there are hundreds of miles of first-class **hiking trails** just waiting for you to strap on your boots, and peaceful campgrounds where you can while away a warm afternoon. Follow the Sterling Highway south, and you enter serious **salmon-fishing** territory where some of the world's largest and most combative salmon are caught, particularly around the towns of **Soldotna** and **Kenai**. The whole peninsula is alive with moose, bears, mountain goats, and other large game, but few places boast greater concentrations than the **Kenai National Wildlife Refuge**, good canoeing and hunting territory. Further south, the **razor-clamming** beaches of Clam Gulch and

Ninilchik are marginal distractions from the main goal, easy-paced **Homer**, with its bohemian air and great halibut-fishing trips. It sits beside Kachemak Bay, a beautiful mountain-backed sound where water taxis and short cruises provide access to great hiking and the gorgeous village of **Seldovia**.

All of this is within five hours' drive of the big city, and therein lies a problem. With so much to do and such ease of access, everyone gets the same idea, and you can sit on the highway for two hours behind a line of RVs only to end up at a packed campground. As ever, it only takes a little imagination to beat the crowds, but forewarned is forearmed.

Turnagain Arm, Girdwood, and Portage Glacier

Drive twelve miles south of downtown Anchorage, and you are already a world away from the city, hemmed in between the Chugach Mountains and **Turnagain Arm**, a 45-mile-long tendril of Cook Inlet that separates the Chugach range from the Kenai Peninsula. Road and train line run parallel along the shore, a superb run between snow-capped mountains and glistening, opaque waters. The tidal range here is the second greatest in North America (after Nova Scotia's Bay of Fundy), something that helps create a **tidal bore** that sweeps up the arm on extremely low tides. The bore is best seen from roadside pull-outs also used as vantage points for spotting the white **Beluga whales** that can occasionally be seen chasing salmon. At low tide the broad expanse might look enticing, but the **mudflats** are dangerous, and you should steer well clear of them. The glacial silt here is so fine that once you break the surface crust your leg sinks in and is almost impossible to remove; then the tide comes in, quickly.

Turnagain Arm first saw white men in the 1890s when a small gold rush erupted, with bursts of activity at Independence Mine, Sunrise City, Resurrection Creek, and Hope City. By the summer of 1901 the strike in Nome had lured miners elsewhere, but a couple of small mines remain as testaments to the dreams of prospectors in an unmapped and untamed land. The best of these is just outside **Girdwood**, a growing dormitory community for Anchorage with its own downhill **ski resort** – Alyeska – and enough rat-race refugees to give it a bohemian character.

Turnagain Arm finally narrows to a point at the old town of Portage, now abandoned after the land around here dropped by six to eleven feet as a result of the 1964 earthquake. From here a road runs inland to the relatively unspectacular but always popular **Portage Glacier**, and continues through a combined road and rail tunnel to Whittier (see Chapter Four, p.288).

Tide tables

If you want to fish, spot Turnagain Arm's bore tide, go clamming along the Kenai's western shore, or simply stroll along the shore at low water, you'll need to know the state of the region's thirty-plus-foot tides. The free annual **Southcentral Alaska Tide Tables** booklet is available from fishing tackle shops, visitor centers, grocery stores, and many banks. Along with details of tide times around the region, tide heights, and good fishing days, they handily include sunrise and sunset times, expected salmon run dates, notes on clam digging techniques, fishing knots, and a guide to gauging a halibut's weight from its length.

The Seward Highway

From Potter Marsh wildlife refuge, twelve miles south of Anchorage, the **Seward Highway** runs for nearly forty miles along the shore of Turnagain Arm to Portage and the junction for Portage Glacier and Whittier. Just as you leave the Potter Marsh wetlands behind, an ancient snow-clearing locomotive marks the Potter Section House Historic Site, where the 1929 section house, once a maintenance depot for a stretch of the railroad, now serves as the **Chugach State Park Headquarters** (Mon–Fri 10am–noon & 1–4.30pm; ⓣ345-5014, ⓦwww.dnr.state.ak.us/parks/units/chugach). A couple of wagons attached to the engine contain the **Kenai Peninsula visitor center** (May–Sept daily 9am–4.30pm; ⓣ336-3300, ⓦwww.kenaipeninsula.info), which stocks leaflets on the whole peninsula and gives access to the interior of the snow plow.

All along the highway there are great views across the water to the snow-capped Kenai Mountains, but none better than from **McHugh Creek Wayside**, Mile 112, some four miles south of Potter Marsh (daily 9am–9pm), where a refreshing waterfall cascades past the start of several hiking trails (see box, opposite) and some barbecue areas.

In recent years, the numbers of Beluga whales in Cook Inlet has rapidly decreased, perhaps as part of a natural cycle, though some blame overzealous Native hunting. The frequency of sightings has dropped accordingly, but your best chance of spotting them as they chase salmon up the inlet from May to August is at the **Beluga Point Interpretive Site**, Mile 110. This is also a prime location for viewing Turnagain Arm's tidal bore (see box, below).

Anchorage rock climbers hone their skills on the roadside cliffs on the way to the tiny settlement of **Indian**, Mile 104, the turnoff for the Indian Valley Trail (see box, opposite), and the site of the **Indian Valley Mine** (mid-May to mid-Sept daily 9am–9pm; $1; ⓦwww.indianvalleymine.com), which captures the area's mining history from 1920 to 1939 through a small collection of artifacts found at the site and displayed (along with a gift shop) in the original assay office. You can pan for gold (from $3) and see the old underground mine entrances, but little else.

A mile further south, the trailhead for the Bird Ridge Trail heralds **Bird Creek**, scene of frenetic summer "combat fishing" where anglers are shoulder to shoulder along the riverbank casting for silver and pink salmon (mid-July to Aug, though closed for highway construction in 2004). The *Bird Creek Campground*, Mile 101, just east of the Bird Creek bridge ($10; pump water),

Turnagain's tidal bore

When low tides are extremely low, it is possible to see Turnagain Arm's tidal bore, a broken wave of foaming whitewater up to 6ft high that sweeps up the arm towards Portage once every tide. It is a rare phenomenon that only occurs at perhaps sixty places around the world, two of them in Alaska – a smaller one is found on Knik Arm, just to the north of Anchorage. Bores are caused by a combination of extreme tidal variation (almost 39ft in Turnagain Arm) and the local marine geography, here accentuated by the arm's funneling effect. It is at its most impressive a day or so either side of full moon, when the tidal variation is at its greatest. Under less auspicious conditions, however, the bore is barely noticeable. At Beluga Point the best time for viewing – and possibly seeing keen board-riders surf the bore – is an hour and a quarter after low tide in Anchorage (2hr 15min at Bird Point, 3hr at Girdwood): check tide times in the *Anchorage Daily News* (ⓦwww.adn.com/weather) and look for a low tide of minus 4.5ft or lower.

Hikes from Turnagain Arm

With the Kenai Peninsula drawing you on it is tempting to skip the hikes beside the Seward Highway, but the sparkling views from sea level, and steep slopes rising straight from the road, do make these a worthwhile venture. Hikes are listed in order of distance from Anchorage.

Turnagain Arm Trail (9.4 miles one-way; 5–6hr; negligible ascent). Easy coastal trail following a path forged by Dena'ina Natives and consolidated by gold-miners. The views of Turnagain Arm are tremendous, and you might see spring wildflowers or Dall sheep among the crags. It runs from the Potter Section House to Windy Corner, passing numerous access points that make it easy to do in shorter stretches. Since this trail runs along the highway, you can easily make this a one-way hike, arranging for someone to pick you up or hitching a ride back to the trailhead.

McHugh Lake Trail (14 miles round-trip; 6–8hr; 2750ft ascent). Moderately stiff hike that leads from the McHugh Creek Wayside up McHugh Creek to the tundra-girt McHugh Lake and the larger Rabbit Lake below the rugged form of Suicide Mountain.

McHugh Scenic Overlook (2 miles round-trip; 1hr; negligible ascent). Wheelchair-accessible paved path with handrails and seating, offering views of Turnagain Arm and wind-sculpted trees.

Indian Valley Trail (12 miles round-trip; 5–7hr; 2100ft ascent). An easy to moderate trail on a well-graded path climbing out of the tall coastal woods to a pass among alpine tundra and back. Hardy hikers can continue beyond the pass and link up with the Ship Creek Trail behind Anchorage (in winter this becomes a cross-country ski trail). The trailhead is just over a mile off the Seward Highway (Mile 103.1) at the end of a gravel road.

Bird Ridge Trail (8 miles round-trip; 4–6hr; 2500ft ascent). A steep trail following Bird Ridge from a trailhead parking lot (Mile 102.1) up onto the alpine tundra. Once again, the views are wonderful, the chances of spotting Dall sheep are high, and wildflowers carpet the ground in early spring, replaced by berries in the fall. Note that it is exposed above the tree line and can be windy.

has tent sites away from the RV parking, but you'll need to arrive early to get a site away from the highway. The excellent *Bird Ridge Café and Bakery*, Mile 101, renowned for its burgers, espresso, and fruit pies, is handily less than a mile further on.

From here, the highway continues to hug the coast four miles to the **Bird Point Scenic Overlook**, an elaborate series of viewpoints and walkways with information panels telling you when to expect the tidal bore to sweep past. The overlook also marks the start of a coastal **bike trail**, which follows the old undulating road the remaining six miles to Girdwood. It can be windy along here in the afternoons, so ride early if you can.

Girdwood and Alyeska Resort

Almost forty miles southeast of Anchorage, Turnagain Arm and the Chugach Mountains briefly release their grip on the Seward Highway, which now runs across broad wetlands. The wetlands were the original site of Girdwood, abandoned after it sank six to eight feet during the 1964 earthquake. In the process the roots of hundreds of black spruce were immersed in the brackish waters of Turnagain Arm. They soon died, but remain standing in a semi-petrified state and are now afforded some degree of legal protection.

GIRDWOOD relocated a couple of miles inland and has developed into a modest and active woodland community populated by neo-hippies, outdoor

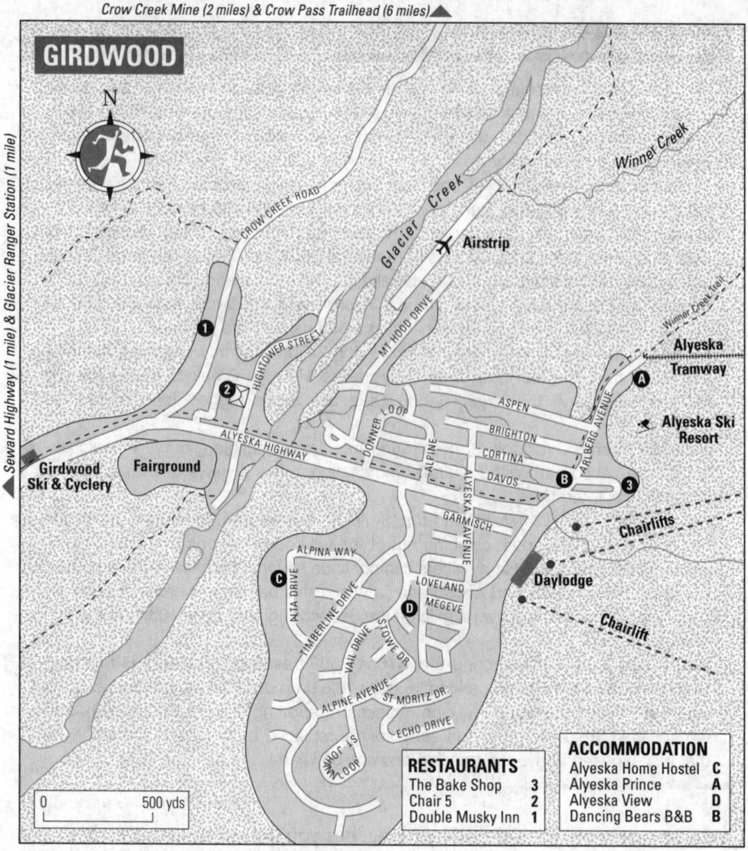

enthusiasts, and escapees from Anchorage. It sits among the spruce below the 3939-foot summit of Mount Alyeska, the low-rise sprawl given some focus by the presence of the **Alyeska Resort** (ⓣ754-2285, snow report ⓣ754-7669, ⓦwww.alyeskaresort.com), Alaska's premier downhill ski complex. This is the lowest-elevation ski resort in the world, with tows that start just 250ft above sea level, and yet it manages a six-month season (Nov to mid-April, and weekends through to the first weekend in June) courtesy of an average annual snowfall of nearly 50ft. Factor in a healthy range of runs (including half a dozen perilously steep double black diamond descents), stupendous views, relatively mild temperatures (usually in the twenties), plus the chance to see the aurora borealis, and an Alaskan skiing holiday here takes on considerable appeal. Until 1993 Alyeska resembled one of the small municipal resorts in the Rockies, but a huge influx of cash has given it many new downhill runs, a first-class hotel, and an extensive night-skiing operation (Christmas to New Year and weekends Jan–March, until 9.30pm). Lift **tickets** cost $46 a day ($19 at night) and you can rent basic downhill equipment for $28 a day; quality ski gear or snowboard and boots cost $38.

From around mid-June to September the relatively snow-free slopes make decent hiking country, notably along the ridge-crest Alyeska Glacier View Trail, which can be followed as far as your fitness allows. To get to the trail, head to the *Alyeska Prince* resort and take the **Alyeska Tramway** gondola (late May to mid-Sept daily 10.30am–9.30pm; $16), which swoops you up to the *Seven Glaciers* and *Glacier Express* restaurants perched high on the mountain. If you are also planning to dine up here, expensive menus can be offset to some degree by buying a Tram & Lunch Combo ($20), which includes a bite to eat in the *Glacier Express*. Should you choose to hike up, the ride down is free. The top of the tramway also serves as a launch pad for rides with Chugach Tandem **Paragliding** (June–Sept; $150; ⓣ754-2400, ⓦwww.alyeskaadventure.com).

Low-level hiking is best done along the **Winner Creek Trail** (7 miles round-trip; 3hr; 100ft ascent), which heads east from the base of the tramway and weaves through moss-carpeted hemlock and spruce to a plunging gorge. You eventually come to a primitive hand-hauled high-wire tram across Winner Creek Gorge. Go across just for the fun of it, but it is best to then turn back the way you came. Alternatively, continue half a mile beyond the tram to visit the Crow Creek Mine.

Girdwood is also home to Class V Whitewater, which runs **rafting** trips on Sixmile Creek (see box, p.240), as well as float trips on the Portage River (3hr; $50).

A mile back towards the Seward Highway from Alyeska, the unimproved Crow Creek Road penetrates five miles further into the heart of the Chugach Mountains. After 300yd you pass the *Double Musky Inn*, an excellent restaurant, and press on three miles to **Crow Creek Mine** (mid-May to mid-Sept daily 9am–6pm; $3, gold panning $5; ⓣ278-8060; ⓦwww.crowcreekgoldmine.com). The mine was established here in 1898 and soon became the most productive of the Turnagain Arm gold strikes. The so-called Crow Creek Boys instituted hydraulic mining operations to scour away the gold-bearing gravels and left in their wake all manner of detritus, which today litters the valley. It is still worked on a small scale but is mostly set up for tourists, with eight of the mine buildings still on their original foundations and prettied up with planters, moose racks, and ageing artifacts.

The trailhead for the **Crow Pass Trail** lies four miles beyond the mine up Crow Creek Road (for more on the trail, see p.215).

If you're in the vicinity around the Fourth of July weekend, head to the Girdwood Fairgrounds, Alyeska Highway Mile 2.2, for the **Girdwood Forest Fair** (ⓦwww.girdwoodforestfair.com; free), originally an arts and crafts fair but now as much a music festival, which seems to draw out every artist and neo-hippy in Southcentral Alaska.

Practicalities

Trains between Anchorage and Seward make a request stop on Brudine Road a couple of miles from Girdwood where the Alyeska Highway to Girdwood spurs off the Seward Highway. If you need to get here by public transportation, it makes more sense to come by bus: Homer Stage Line (ⓣ868-3914) and the Magic Bus (ⓣ441-8420) both drop off in town on request.

The closest thing to a visitor center in these parts is the Forest Service's **Glacier Ranger Station** (Mon–Fri 8am–5pm; ⓣ783-3242), at the start of Alyeska Highway, which concentrates on hiking and outdoor activities in the region. Alternatively, log on to ⓦwww.girdwoodalaska.com. Since there is no public transportation, anyone without a car should visit Girdwood Ski and Cyclery, Mile 1.5 (ⓣ783-2453; closed Mon & Tues), which rents city **bikes**

($5/hr, $25/day) that are adequate for the immediate surroundings and the six-mile ride along the new bike path to Bird Point. In winter and spring they rent telemark and backcountry equipment for $25 a day.

Rack rates at the eight-story *Alyeska Prince* resort (ⓣ754-2111 or 1-800/880-3880, ⓦwww.alyeskaresort.com; ❽) are outside most budgets, but throughout the summer there are deals offering two nights plus a tramway ride for $329 per room. Even if you can't afford a room, you may want to treat yourself to a meal in one of the restaurants or check out the health spa ($5) complete with pool, hot tub, and views up to Mount Alyeska.

More affordable **accommodation** starts with $12.50 bunks at the tiny *Alyeska Home Hostel*, Alta Drive (ⓣ783-2222; ⓦwww.alyeskahostel.com, ❶), which is open year-round and has mountain views, cooking facilities, and a relaxed atmosphere. There are no motels or hotels, but several people have turned their hand to **B&Bs**. The Austrian-run *Alyeska View B&B*, Vail Drive, off Timberline Drive (ⓣ783-2747, ⓦwww.alyeskaview.com; ❸–❹), is good and cheap; while *Dancing Bears B&B*, Cortina Road at Arlberg Avenue (ⓣ783-2481, ⓦwww.dancingbearsbb.com; en suite ❺, private bath ❹), offers comfortable, art-adorned rooms and a cooked breakfast in a house owned by a young artist and a massage therapist. There is also good, basic **camping** up by the Crow Creek Mine ($5).

Skiers, mountain bikers, in fact just about anyone with a hunger for tasty low-cost **food** should make for *The Bake Shop* (ⓣ783-2831) on Olympic Circle at the base of the ski tows. The soup and sourdough bread are legendary, and they serve great breakfasts until 1pm. *Chair 5*, Lindblad Avenue (ⓣ783-2500), is good for moderately priced gourmet pizza, burgers, fresh seafood, and microbrews, but the restaurant that really draws the Anchorage foodies is the *Double Musky Inn*, Crow Creek Road (closed Mon, no reservations). It has been an institution since 1962, and its dark bar and airy conservatory are always bustling with diners eager to get their lips around the Louisiana Cajun cuisine and tender steaks. Expect halibut ceviche, scallop-stuffed mushroom Rockefeller, rack of lamb, and salmon in green peppercorns and brandy, and set aside $40 apiece.

Portage Glacier

The five-mile-long, mile-wide **Portage Glacier** is the single most visited sight in the state. The impressive calving which earned its reputation is a thing of the past, but proximity to Anchorage – just fifty miles to the northwest – and assiduous promotion by Gray Line Tours ensure that it remains *the* destination for day trips from the city. Not so many years ago visitors could see the glacier from the access road, but its retreat has been so profound that it can now only be seen by taking an hour-long **cruise** across the lake its retreat has created. Throughout the summer, tour buses decant their passengers onto the *Ptarmigan* (mid-May to mid-Sept 10.30am–4.30pm every 1hr 30min; $25; day trip from Anchorage with Gray Line $59; ⓣ277-5581), which shoulders its way through small icebergs and spends half an hour patrolling the face of the glacier as everyone hopes for a display of calving. A measure of how much it has retreated can be gauged by the location of the **Begich, Boggs Visitor Center**, Mile 5.5 (June–Aug daily 9am–6pm; Sept–May Sat & Sun 10am–5pm; ⓣ783-2326), built on the moraine which marks the furthest extent of glacial advance a century ago, now three and a half miles from the face. Even when the visitor center was built in the mid-1980s you could spot the glacier from the huge picture windows, something no longer true. Though the center still screens its glacier-oriented *Voices from the Ice* video (hourly; $1), it has been revamped to spread its coverage to include the ecology of the whole Portage and Whittier

The road to Whittier and Prince William Sound

Until summer 2000 Portage Glacier was the end of the road, but a single-lane road and rail tunnel (see box, p.289) now continues to Whittier; delays mean that you will have to wait in the staging area a mile on from the Begich, Boggs Visitor Center.

region, with interactive displays offering plenty to see, touch and listen to.

Still, the center is a sheltered spot from which to admire the surrounding glaciers, mostly bearing the names of British poets – Burns, Shakespeare, and Byron. For closer inspection, strike out along the trail to the base of **Byron Glacier** (0.7 miles one-way) where you can sometimes see slender, black **ice worms** living on the surface of the glacier. To learn more about this intriguing wee beastie – which many believe only exists in a poem by Robert Service – you can join the free, two-hour **Iceworm Safari** (July & Aug usually on Sat and one weekday; call in advance) from the visitor center.

Without joining the cruise, the best views of Portage Glacier are now from the approach road to the Whittier tunnel: drive through the first short tunnel (free) to a large viewing area about half a mile on.

Practicalities

Portage Glacier lies six miles off the Seward Highway (Mile 79) and is reached from a junction marked by a copse of salt-damaged trees, which make an especially picturesque backdrop for a couple of dilapidated buildings slowly sinking into the mire, both victims of the 1964 earthquake. From here, Portage Road runs up the Portage Valley passing two **campgrounds** – *Black Bear*, Mile 3.7 ($9; pump water) and the very pleasant *Williwaw*, Mile 4.2 ($12; pump water). Next to the latter reds and chums come up to spawn from mid- to late summer below a platform at the **Williwaw Salmon Viewing Area** (Mile 4.3).

Alongside Portage Lake there's the visitor center and boat dock (roughly a mile apart) and the *Portage Glacier Lodge* (mid-May to mid-Sept daily 9am–7pm), a gift shop and decent **café** with hearty soup, sandwich, and drink lunch specials for under $8. Just behind, the 400-yard **Moraine Nature Trail** is an easy way to get away from the tour-bus crowds and has a viewpoint fine for a picnic. In spring and fall it might also be a good place for **bird watching**, since the forested and steeply sided valley is used as a flyway for birds spending the summer in western Alaska.

Northeastern Kenai Peninsula

The northeastern third of the Kenai Peninsula is mostly mountainous country with the Chugach and Kenai mountains meeting around the head of Turnagain Arm. Numerous peaks top 4000ft and a few soar up over 5000ft, creating a near-impenetrable barrier to the lusher flatlands to the south. Only the Seward Highway finds a passage by climbing Turnagain Pass and continuing to Seward, while the Sterling Highway peels off west through the Central Kenai to Homer. In summer the high country beside the highway is used by hikers and bikers here to tackle some of the excellent trails, and nearby **Sixmile Creek** gets crowded with rafters, risking some superb whitewater.

The only real destination is **Hope**, a former gold town on the shores of Turnagain Arm that's great for just kicking back for a couple of days, perhaps doing a little **gold panning** in Resurrection Creek.

Turnagain Pass and Sixmile Creek

Where the road to Portage Glacier and Whittier spurs off from the Seward Highway, a copse of salt-ravaged trees marks **Big Game Alaska**, Mile 79 Seward Hwy (daily: summer 9am–7pm, winter 10am–4pm; $5; ⓣ783-2025, ⓦwww.biggamealaska.com), a 140-acre wildlife center where injured and orphaned animals are brought for rehabilitation. Most can't be returned to the wild and are kept here in fairly naturalistic grassland enclosures which can be toured either by car or on foot. This may be the easiest place in Alaska to see moose, bison, elk, musk ox, caribou, deer, and bears all in under an hour.

Continuing on, the Seward Highway loops around the head of Turnagain Arm and hugs the water for a few more miles before turning inland for the steady five-mile climb up to the 1000-foot **Turnagain Pass** (Mile 68). The altitude and shadowing effect of the surrounding 4000-foot peaks means that spring comes late up here. Even into mid-June you may see Anchorage weekenders cross-country skiing and snowmachining: motorized on the west side of the road, human-powered on the east.

It is a broad and fast road right through here with nothing in the way of services, so it is tempting to hurry on straight to Hope, Seward (about 60 miles away), or Homer (around 170 miles). Still, the scenery is striking with highwayside alpine meadows threaded by glacial streams, so you might want to stop a night or two in one of the campgrounds and consider tackling some of the long hikes (see box, p.235). Summer wildflowers abound. You may well see false

Rafting the Sixmile

Just off the Seward Highway, a mile along the road to Hope, rafters amass for the wildest stretch of commercially rafted whitewater in Alaska that doesn't require expedition logistics. With a maximum descent of 50ft per mile the **Sixmile Creek** is thrilling stuff, and justly popular. The river's three canyons – all beautiful with crisp, clear, and very cold water – progressively increase in difficulty, and rafting companies accommodate all comers, tailoring trips to suit. The **rafting season** runs from May to September but peaks from mid-June to August. Sometimes in July high water levels mean trips have to be canceled.

The **first canyon** (Class III; 1hr 30min on the water) is suitable for beginners and families, but still has one section that kicks up to Class IV in high flows. This bit can be avoided by a short walk. Trips often combine the first with the **second canyon** (Class III–IV; 1hr on the water), which ups the ante a little with four major drops in succession. Most companies have a higher minimum age limit (usually 16) and require some kind of swimming ability test before letting customers down the exciting **third canyon** (Class IV–V; 1hr on the water) with its long sequences of tough rapids. Companies generally use paddle rafts, which means you'll be expected to paddle – hard.

Girdwood-based Class V Whitewater (ⓣ783-2004, ⓦwww.alaskanrafting.com) runs excellent trips on the first canyon ($75), first two canyons ($95), and all three ($130), and you often have the option of adding on the third canyon, if you're still feeling confident after the first two. Trips leave Girdwood at 9am and 3pm, or you can arrange to meet them at the river an hour later.

You can also go with a couple of other operators. Chugach Outdoor Center (ⓣ277-7238 or 1-866/277-7238, ⓦwww.chugachoutdoorcenter.com) offers the upper and middle canyons (9am & 2pm; $85), and all three (9am & 2pm; $135): meet at their base at Mile 7.5 on Hope Highway. Nova (ⓣ1-800/746-5753, ⓦwww.novalaska.com) meets near the junction of the Seward and Hope highways for either the top two canyons (9am & 2pm; $85) or all three (9am & 2pm; $125).

hellebore, valerian, wild geranium, chocolate lily, and shooting stars, all occasionally visited by a hoary marmot.

Descending from Turnagain Pass, milepost numbers continue to decrease towards Seward, the highway passing a couple of first-come, first-served Forest Service campgrounds in the next five miles – *Bertha Creek*, Mile 65 ($10), and *Granite Creek*, Mile 63 ($10) – both handy for one-day forays up part of the **Johnson Pass Trail**, which leaves the highway between the two.

At Mile 57 the Seward Highway sweeps high across the whitewater-rafting waters of **Sixmile Creek**, and then the Hope Highway branches right to run sixteen miles to the small town of Hope, passing the negligible remains of the gold-rush town of Sunrise at Mile 8.

Hope

At the end of a sixteen-mile asphalt spur off the Seward Highway, the small former gold-rush town of **HOPE** sits quietly beside the south shore of Turnagain Arm. It is mostly populated by loners and rat-race refugees but is close enough to Anchorage to draw in hikers, anglers after salmon (particularly pinks from mid-July to mid-August), and even gold seekers. There may be less than 200 residents now, but in the last five years of the nineteenth century the whole of this area was alive with gold prospectors. The town survived long after the gold did, leaving a dusty collection of picturesque, weather-worn log buildings. To get a sense of what it was like at its peak, visit the small **Hope and Sunrise Historical Museum**, in the old town (late May to early Sept Mon & Fri–Sun noon–4pm; free), full of old-time photos and gold-mining paraphernalia. There's still **gold** in the creeks, too, and you're free to make use of the Forest Service's claim close to the start of the Resurrection Pass Trail (see box, p.255). Pans can be rented from *Resurrection Trail Resort*, half a mile further along, for $10 for four hours.

Hikers who aren't up for something as taxing as the Resurrection Pass Trail (see "Hiking and biking in northern Kenai" box, p.255) should drive to the *Porcupine Campground* (see below), at the end of the Hope Highway, which marks the beginning of the gentle and heavily used **Gull Rock Trail** (10 miles round-trip; 4–6hr; constantly undulating). This trail follows a narrow old wagon road along Turnagain Arm through spruce, birch, and aspen woods, and past the scant remains of an old sawmill to a viewpoint atop Gull Rock where there are some primitive camping spots. The trail can be tackled any time from May to October, though late summer is good for low-bush cranberry picking. From the beginning of July, the trail is also open to **mountain bikes**. Moderately skilled riders should be able to handle the first three miles and last mile without too much difficulty, but abundant rocks and tree roots in the middle section dictate more pushing and carrying than riding.

Practicalities

At the first road junction as you drive into town along the Hope Highway, a left turn leads five miles up Resurrection Road to the start of the Resurrection Trail. Straight on at the junction, the new *Discovery Café* marks the start of the old town, reached down the road on the right. This eventually rejoins the Hope Highway for the final mile to the road-end *Porcupine Campground*.

The best all-around place to **stay and eat** is the *Seaview Café*, Main Street in the old town (ⓣ782-3300, ⓦwww.home.gci.net/~hopeak; ❶; May–Sept), in a cluster of 1896 buildings, nicely sited close to Turnagain Arm. There are rustic cabins without running water but sleeping up to four, a rather exposed place to camp ($15 for power hookup, $10 for tents), a great restaurant noted for its baked goods, especially the apple pie, and a bar that stays open to midnight. They even have a sunny deck outside. **Campers** have other options: just over a mile beyond Hope the *Porcupine Campground* ($10; pump water; no fees or water in winter) has neatly tended sites among the woods with fire rings, picnic tables, and even some Turnagain Arm views, but it is often full; budget tenters who don't mind being over four miles up Resurrection Road can camp beside the river for nothing near the start of the Resurrection Pass Trail. This area has been set aside for recreational **gold panning**, and you are free to try your hand, though you'll need your own pan.

There's also a very comfortable fully equipped cabin sleeping five at *Hope Gold Rush B&B* (ⓣ782-3436, ⓔfayrene@alaska.net; ❹), where a hearty breakfast is included; and simple but comfortable and appealing streamside cabins with access to a hot tub at *Discovery Cabins* (ⓣ782-3730, ⓦwww.adventurealaskatours.com/cabins.htm; ❸).

Apart from the *Seaview*, eating is best at the *Bear Creek Lodge*, Mile 15.7 Hope Hwy (ⓣ782-3141, ⓦwww.bearcreeklodgencafe.com), or at *Tito's Discovery Café*, Mile 16 Hope Hwy (ⓣ782-3274), with great breakfasts and a tasty halibut and chips ($12).

The Seward Highway: south from Turnagain Pass

South of Hope, the Seward Highway continues past the first-come, first-served *Tenderfoot Creek Campground*, Mile 46 ($10), which has creekside sites and pump water, then reaches **Tern Lake**, Mile 37, an important migration stop for waterfowl, including arctic terns, for which the lake is named. From the waterside viewing platform you might also spot common loons, pintails, bald eagles and even a beaver. Here, two highways part company: the Sterling Highway turns right and runs 143 miles through the central Kenai Peninsula to Homer, while the Seward Highway carries straight on towards Seward, 37 miles distant.

Around five miles on from Tern Lake, the Seward Highway passes the trailhead for the Johnson Pass Trail (see p.254), then runs a couple of miles to the scattered community of **MOOSE PASS** (ⓦwww.moosepassalaska.com), originally established along the original Iditarod Trail in a spot littered with moose. It comprises little more than a few cabins in the woods and a post office, all beautifully set beside Upper Trail Lake. A few of the cabins operate as B&Bs, and there's even a grocery, a couple of places to eat, a lodge, and an RV park, but there's not much action except at summer solstice when the town holds the Moose Pass Summer Festival, with cookouts, craft stalls, and all sorts of kids' games. If you fancy staying, try *Spruce Moose B&B* (ⓣ288-3667, ⓦseward.net/sprucemoose; ❻), where you get a whole self-contained chalet complete with satellite TV, hot tub, sauna, and full kitchen.

Along the last half-hour of the drive into Seward, you'll pass *Snow River Hostel* (see p.246), a few more fine campgrounds, and the trailheads for a couple of hikes listed in the box on p.247.

Seward and the Kenai Fjords National Park

There's a beguiling charm to **SEWARD** (SOO-erd), nestled between the shores of Resurrection Bay and the icy wastes of the Kenai Fjords National

Park, 130 miles south of Anchorage. It is a small town, with a good deal less bustle than Homer and yet a perfect balance of distractions. It is also a strategic spot as the southern terminus of the Alaska Railroad and a major port (at least by Alaska's modest standards) with cruise ships coming and going on a fairly regular basis, though seldom intruding on the slow pace of life.

With a couple of minor exceptions, it is Seward's proximity to the **KENAI FJORDS NATIONAL PARK** that makes it so appealing. Only created in 1978, it remains a little-known park almost entirely covered in ice, much of its western portion composed of the **Harding Icefield**, a vast icy tableland thought to be up to 4000ft thick in places and spreading over almost 300 square miles. The ice at the edges spills over the mountains as steep glaciers – 32 of them in all – which forge down U-shaped valleys. **Exit Glacier** comes so close to Seward that they've built a road to its terminus. Spectacular though it is, few can resist joining one of the **cruises** that visit some of the eight tidewater glaciers that regularly calve icebergs into the fjords along the park's southeast flank. Cruising the waterways and fjords only nibbles at the fecund edges of the park and to really get a sense of its barren, icy immensity you need to fly over it (see "Listings," p.253), or hike up beside Exit Glacier for a glimpse of this sheet of white punctuated by bare pyramidal mountains known as nunataks, an Eskimo word meaning "lonely peaks."

The park's marine environment is readily on view in Seward in the form of the **SeaLife Center**. This sits close to the spot where, in 1903, John Ballaine established his railroad to serve a new port on the shores of Resurrection Bay. Ballaine called the place Seward, in honor of the man who was responsible for the US purchase of Alaska from Russia. Although there were already two towns called Seward in Alaska, Ballaine's petitioning prevailed, and this became the true Seward. Around the same time Seward was the gold-shipping port at the end of the Iditarod Trail, with huge quantities arriving by sled from Nome and the Interior. The railroad went through several incarnations before being incorporated into the construction of the Alaska Railroad, in 1915, after which Seward continued to prosper as a railhead and port for both goods and commercial fishing. Everything looked set to change when the 1964 earthquake caused whole chunks of the waterfront to slide into the bay and set the town ablaze, but Seward was rebuilt, and the town continues, building on its fishing and tourism industries.

Arrival, information, and getting around

Seward is remarkably well connected, with ferries, buses, trains, a good highway, and even a network of long-distance hiking trails ending not far from town. The four-hour **train** journey from Anchorage (see Basics, p.40) pulls in at Seward's desolate platform, a couple of hundred yards north of the small boat harbor.

It is considerably cheaper and quicker to travel by **bus**, and two companies run daily from Anchorage in summer: Seward Bus Line, 1915 Seward Hwy (Ⓣ224-3608, Ⓦwww.sewardbuslines.com; $40 one-way, $75 round-trip), and the slightly more expensive Park Connection (Ⓣ245-0200 or 1-800/266-8625, Ⓦwww.alaskacoach.com), which also has service from Denali and drops off around town. Homer Stage Line makes a weekday run from Homer in summer (Ⓣ224-3608, Ⓦwww.homerstageline.com; $45 one-way, $80 round-trip) and arrives at the Seward Bus Line depot.

AMHS **ferries** (Ⓣ224-5485) stop at the dock near the train station twice a week, once westbound to Valdez, and once on the return run to Kodiak. There's also a cross-gulf service from Juneau twice a month in summer (see Basics, p.36).

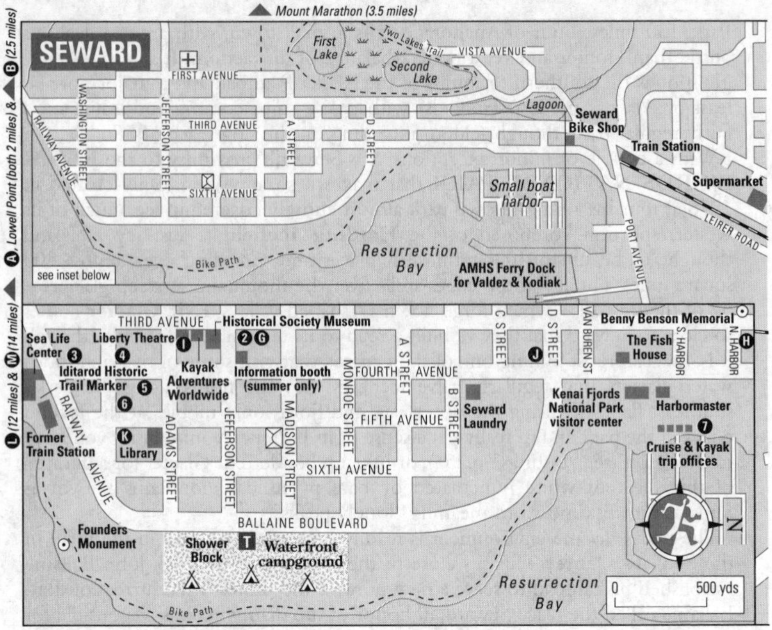

City transportation

Once in Seward, **getting around** the central sights is easy on foot, but you might want to make use of **Seward's Trolley** (late May to early Sept daily 10am–7pm every 30min; $2 one-way, $5 all day), which makes a loop from the SeaLife Center past the small boat harbor, the ferry dock, and the visitor center. For further explorations (to Exit Glacier, for example) **rent a bike** (see "Listings," p.253).

Information

The **visitor center** (mid-May to mid-Sept daily 8am–6pm; mid-Sept to mid-May Mon–Fri 8am–5pm; ⓣ224-8051, ⓦwww.sewardak.org), on the approach to town at Mile 2 on the Seward Highway, holds a broad range of general information, and there's also an **information booth** in an old railcar at 401 3rd Ave (June–Aug daily 9am–5pm). For outdoor-oriented information visit the **Kenai Fjords National Park visitor center**, 1212 4th Ave, in Seward's small boat harbor (late May to early Sept daily 9am–6pm; early Sept to late May Mon–Fri 8am–5pm; ⓣ224-3175, ⓦwww.nps.gov/kefj), which provides maps, shows a couple of worthwhile videos and slide shows, and has details on regional hikes.

Accommodation

Seward has **accommodation** to suit most tastes. There are three **hostels** (one in town, one more rural, and a third on the highway 16 miles north along the road to Anchorage), a wide selection of **campgrounds** (one conveniently right in the center beside Resurrection Bay), motels, and several good B&Bs, some downtown, though many of the best places are inconveniently sited for those without a car.

A bit further out, Resurrection Bay and the shores of Kenai Fjords National Park have **cabins** and even a couple of more formal lodges accessible by kayak, water taxi, or cruise.

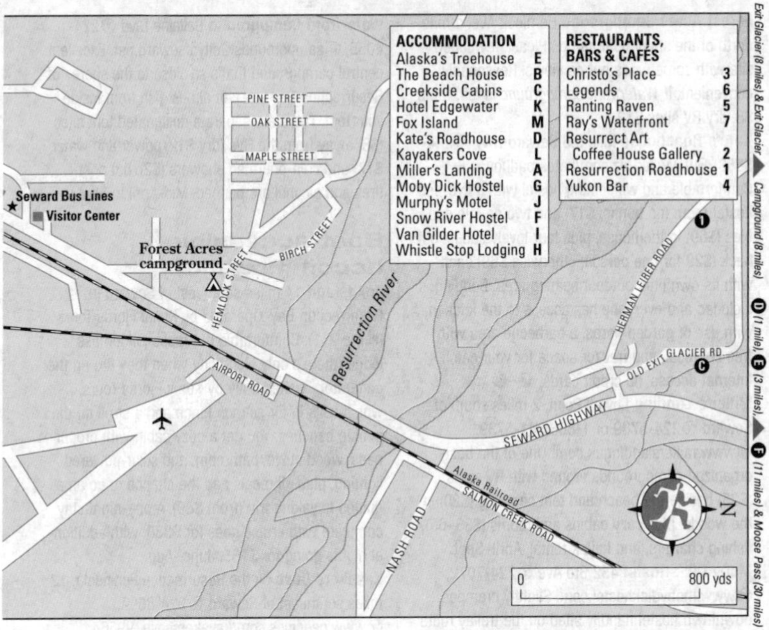

Hotels, motels, and B&Bs

Alaska's Treehouse Forest Rd ⓣ224-3867, ⓦwww.seward.net/treehouse. Very attractive and welcoming B&B in a large timber house seven miles out along the Seward Highway (turn into Timber Lane Drive then Forest Rd). There's one room with a private (but separate) bathroom and a suite which sleeps up to five. Everyone gets a full sourdough pancake breakfast and access to a hot tub out on the deck among the spruce trees. Suite ❺, room ❹

The Beach House Lowell Point, 2.5 miles south of Seward ⓣ224-7000, ⓦwww.beachhousealaska.biz. Two self-catering apartments with space for up to seven, though compact enough to be comfortable for two. Good bay views, peaceful location, and good walking to Caines Head nearby. ❻

Creekside Cabins Old Exit Glacier Rd, 3.5 miles from town ⓣ224-1996, ⓔcreekside@seward.net. Four attractively set log cabins in the woods, each with heating, refrigerator, coffeemaker (coffee and juice provided), and outdoor fire pit, as well as access to a streamside sauna. There are also a couple of walk-in campsites for $20. ❷–❹

Hotel Edgewater 200 5th Ave ⓣ224-2700 or 1-888/793-6800, ⓦwww.hoteledgewater.com. Modern hotel with a range of comfortable rooms with in-room dataports, cable, and VCR. Other amenities include hot tub, sauna, and mini-gym room, plus free shuttle to railroad and harbor. View rooms ❽, queen rooms ❻, atrium rooms ❺

Murphy's Motel 911 4th Ave ⓣ224-8090 or 1-800/886-8191, ⓦwww.murphysmotel.com. Well-kept motel close to the small boat harbor with great bay and mountain views from many rooms, especially those in the new block. All come with microwave, fridge, dataport, and cable TV, though older rooms are smaller. New rooms ❻, older ❺

Van Gilder Hotel 308 Adams St ⓣ224-3079 or 1-800/204-6835, ⓦwww.vangilderhotel.com. Original 1916 hotel right in the heart of town that's been fully restored. The small but modernized rooms are mostly decorated in Victorian style and have cable TV and dataports – those with a full bath are better value than the budget rooms. Suites ❼, rooms with bath ❻, shared bath ❺

Whistle Stop Lodging 411 Port Ave ⓣ224-5050, ⓦwww.sewardak.net/ws/. Just two rooms unusually sited in a reconstructed World War II railcar close to the small boat harbor. The rooms, which have great views of the fjord, aren't luxurious but are comfortable and come with private bath. A kitchenette costs $10 extra. ❺

Hostels and campgrounds

Exit Glacier Campground at Exit Glacier, 13 miles northwest of Seward. Attractively set first-come, first-served walk-in tent sites with outhouse, pump water, fire rings, and bear-resistant food storage. Free.

Forest Acres Campground Hemlock Ave, a mile north of the small boat harbor. Pleasant wooded site with some grass but no views. Reasonably convenient, if *Waterfront Campground* is full. Tents $8, dry RV sites $12.
Kate's Roadhouse Mile 5.5 Seward Hwy ⓣ224-5888, ⓦwww.ak-biz.com/katesroadhouse. Comfortable and welcoming hostel with a five-bed hostel room (no bunks; $17) and two private doubles ($69) in the house, plus four lovely cabins out back ($29 for one person, otherwise $69) each with its own little outdoor seating area. Bedding is included and everyone has access to the kitchen with use of garden herbs, a barbecue area with free charcoal, and freezer space for your catch. Internet access, no credit cards. ❶–❸
Miller's Landing Lowell Point, 2 miles south of Seward ⓣ224-5739 or 1-866/541-5739, ⓦwww.millerslandingak.com. One of the best-organized campgrounds around with RV spots ($25) beside the beach and tent camping ($20) in the woods, plus cozy cabins and rooms ($35–65), fishing charters, and kayak rental. April–Sept.
Moby Dick Hostel 432 3rd Ave ⓣ224-7072, ⓦwww.mobydickhostel.com. Slightly cramped downtown hostel handily sited on the trolley route with bunks ($18), limited kitchen facilities, and small private rooms ($49; some with kitchenettes, $65). April–Oct. ❶–❷
Snow River Hostel 22634 Seward Hwy, 15.7 miles out from Seward ⓣ440-1907. Fairly rustic but attractive and welcoming hostel with men's and women's dorms ($15), a private room, and a separate, quaint cabin, all supplied with bedding. All have access to a well-stocked kitchen and there are several nearby trails to keep you entertained. Cabin & room ❶
Waterfront Campground Ballaine Blvd ⓣ224-4055, ⓔcampgrounds@cityofseward.net. Excellent central campground that's so close to the shores of Resurrection Bay you can almost fish from inside your tent. There are separate designated tent sites ($8) away from the RVs (dry $12, power and water $17) and coin-operated showers ($2), but open fires and alcohol are banned. Mid-April to Sept.

Boat-accessible accommodation

Fox Island 14 miles southeast of Seward in Resurrection Bay. Operated by Kenai Fjords Tours (see p.251). Comfortable but rustic wilderness lodge (there's only electricity when they fire up the generator), visited daily by Kenai Fjords Tours, which calls in for salmon lunch and a stroll on the pebble beaches. You get a cozy cabin with proper beds, wood stove, bathroom, and solar-powered lighting, plus all meals and the chance to go on a guided kayaking trip (from $89). A one-night stay complete with cruise goes for $330, with additional nights going for $165. June–Aug.
Kayakers Cove on the Resurrection Peninsula, 12 miles southeast of Seward ⓣ224-8662, ⓦwww.geocities.com/kayakerscove_99664, ⓔkayakerscove@alaska.com. A lovely rustic lodge (no electricity) that makes a great retreat for a couple of days' hiking, paddling, fishing, and reading. Accommodation is in either a 12-bunk dorm (bring a sleeping bag or rent bedding) or a private cabin, and there's a full kitchen along with dining and sitting areas in the main lodge. You can paddle out there, but most arrive by water taxi ($45 round-trip with *Miller's Landing*), then rent kayaks at the lodge (singles $20 a day; doubles $30). Mid-May to mid-Sept. Cabin $60, bunks $20.

The town and around

The center of town is small and short on sights except for the superb **SeaLife Center**; from there it's a stroll down to the small boat harbor, site of most of the companies running cruises and kayaking trips out onto Resurrection Bay and into the glacier-fed waters of the **Kenai Fjords National Park**, a prime spot for **whale watching**. At some point, everyone finds their way to **Exit Glacier**, one of the few glaciers in Alaska that you can walk right up to. Fewer people make it out to the World War II gun emplacements at Caines Head State Recreation Area, partly because of the long walk and need to monitor the tide times.

One activity not normally associated with Seward is **dog sledding**, but Godwin Glacier Dog Sled Tours (June–Aug; $380; ⓣ224-8239; ⓦwww.alaskadogsled.com) will gladly whisk you by helicopter up to the Godwin Glacier, where you'll spend about ninety minutes with the dogs, part of it being towed around on a sled. It is great fun, but cost may force you to opt for the snow-free equivalent with IditaRide Sled Dog Tours (June–Aug; $39; ⓣ1-800/478-3139, ⓦwww.iditaride.com) involving a look around the kennels

Mount Marathon and other hikes around Seward

The event of the year in Seward is the Fourth of July race up **Mount Marathon**, the big chunk of rock that looms more than 3022ft above Seward. Over ten thousand visitors pack the town center for the race, for which up to eight hundred competitors from all over the state and beyond train to tackle the steep, taxing, and frequently dusty conditions. The winner usually features on the front page of the next day's *Anchorage Daily News*.

The event allegedly started with a barroom wager in 1909 (or maybe 1911), when a couple of sourdoughs speculated as to whether it was possible to climb the mountain and return in under an hour. They just failed, but the event soon became an annual fixture with times rapidly dropping to under 53 minutes by 1928. Eight-time winner Bill Spencer set the current record of 43 minutes 23 seconds in 1981. The women's record holder is Nancy Pease, who took 50 minutes 30 seconds in 1990, and in 2003 Nina Kemppel became the first competitor to win nine titles, eight of these consecutive.

The race route starts and finishes at the junction of Fourth and Adams and follows Jefferson Street before beginning the climb up the steep ridge, averaging 38 degrees. The route returns down an obvious line of loose rock and scree. A gentler and more **scenic route** up Mount Marathon (3.5 miles round-trip; 3–4hr; 3000ft ascent) starts by a gate at the western end of Monroe Street and follows a Jeep track up to the town's former reservoir, then skirts north around the flank of the mountain to Scheffler Creek waterfall, where you gain a skyline ridge to "Race Point," where competitors turn back. You'll probably want to follow their example, but it is possible to hike higher to the true 4603-foot summit of Mount Marathon.

Other hikes

There are a few interesting trails in Seward's immediate vicinity, ranging from the short and gentle Two Lakes Trail right in town to the stiff Harding Icefield Trail. As well as those listed below, there is a coastal trail from Lowell Point to Caines Head (see p.249) and a stack more a few miles back up the Seward Highway around Moose Pass and Cooper Landing (see box, p.254).

Harding Icefield Trail (7.8 miles round-trip; 5–8hr; 3000ft ascent). A taxing but superbly gratifying hike up a steep and occasionally slippery trail on the north side of Exit Glacier, providing wonderful views of the glacier and, once you get high enough, of the Harding Icefield itself. The trail can usually be hiked from late June to mid-October, but upper sections have snow until late July. The trail starts near the base of Exit Glacier at the beginning of the Lower Loop Trail and finishes at an excellent viewpoint half a mile past the Harding Icefield emergency shelter. Take water and be prepared for all kinds of weather.

Lost Lake Trail (7 miles one-way; 3hr; 1800ft ascent). Moderately difficult and very scenic trail starting in Lost Lake subdivision at Mile 5.3 of the Seward Highway and winding through spruce forest. Four miles along there is a 1.5-mile side path to *Clemens Memorial Cabin* ($35), though day-hikers should continue up above the tree line at Mile 5 to Lost Lake. From here you can either return the way you came, or follow the **Primrose Trail** (8 miles one-way; 3–4hr; 1500ft descent) north, mostly following an old mining road to *Primrose Campground*, beside Kenai Lake, rejoining the Seward Highway at Mile 17. This makes a good loop but leaves you twelve miles along the Seward Highway from where you started; hitch back or plan your hike to coincide with the bus schedule.

Two Lakes Trail (1-mile loop; 20–30min; 100ft ascent). Easy and enjoyable downtown trail encircling two small lakes and passing a salmon-spawning creek. Starts at the back of a parking lot near the junction of 2nd Avenue and B Street.

and a short ride on a wheeled sled out in the forest by the *Resurrection Roadhouse*.

Alaska SeaLife Center

Before taking a cruise to the Kenai Fjords National Park, consider spending a couple of hours on Seward's waterfront at the **Alaska SeaLife Center**, 301 Railway Ave (daily: May to early Sept 8am–8pm; April & rest of Sept 9am–6pm; Oct–March 10am–5pm; $12.50, children $10; ⓣ1-800/224-2525; ⓦwww.alaskasealife.org), a unique attempt to integrate research, rehabilitation, and public education under one roof. It owes its genesis to the *Exxon Valdez* oil spill (see box, p.296), which highlighted the need for a coldwater marine research facility in the western hemisphere. When marine mammals and seabird populations were severely harmed by the spill, the lack of baseline information hampered attempts to measure just how severely. Altogether some $37 million was diverted from the various civil and criminal settlements against Exxon and funneled into this nonprofit facility.

The SeaLife Center opened in 1998 and, despite years of funding difficulties, has since firmly established itself on the tourist circuit, not as some bells-and-whistles marine circus, or even an aquarium in the traditional sense, but as a genuine educational and research facility. It can sometimes feel too earnest, but generally balances its priorities well. Certainly, there are nicely displayed tanks of fish, but all the marine specimens are native to this part of Alaska and displayed in context, usually to illustrate some facet of the local marine environment. The impact of the oil spill is covered, along with the conflict between commercial fishing and the well-being of marine mammals, and the need for habitat protection in old-growth forests to protect the purity of salmon-spawning streams. As you stroll around you'll pass windows overlooking wet labs and outdoor compounds where you might see sea lions recovering from illness or measurements being taken from coho salmon, which swim up a fish ladder from Resurrection Bay. There's also child-friendly coverage of the Bering Sea, which in addition to providing half the seafood consumed in the US also supports a severely declining population of Steller sea lions now being studied by the center.

The main concession to entertainment is a series of tanks with underwater viewing windows: one containing Steller sea lions, another harbor seals, and a third captive-bred pigeon guillemots, cute "underwater swimming" tufted puffins, and common murres. There are no shows as such, but aquarium habits die hard, and everyone flocks to the appropriate tank or window when feeding is announced. If closer views of a working research facility seem enticing, call in when you first hit town to book a spot on the **Behind the Scenes Tour** (daily in summer, usually 2.30pm; $5).

The rest of downtown and the small boat harbor

From the waterfront, follow 3rd Avenue a couple of blocks north to the Resurrection Bay **Historical Society Museum**, 336 3rd Ave (mid-May to mid-Sept daily 9am–5pm; $3), which is full of moderately interesting displays on Seward's early days, including its role as a Russian shipyard in the early nineteenth century, treatment of its rail heyday, and coverage of the devastating effects of the 1964 earthquake. More detail can be gleaned a few blocks away at the **library**, 238 5th Ave, where slides of the 1964 earthquake are shown (Mon–Sat 2pm; $3). Returning to the SeaLife Center, notice a small marker indicating the start of the **Iditarod Trail**, a route now mostly associated with the Anchorage to Nome sled dog race, though at the beginning of the twentieth century it was the overland trail to the goldfields of the Interior. The distinctive green 1917 building nearby was the train station until the 1964 earthquake, and now languishes unused.

From here, follow the bike path along the shore, past a concrete obelisk to Seward's founders, taking in the bay views all the way to the small boat harbor,

Eight stars of gold on a field of blue

Near the small boat harbor, at the corner of 3rd Avenue and N Harbor Street, the **Benny Benson Memorial** remembers the orphaned Alutiiq 13-year-old boy who designed the state flag in 1927 while he was studying here. From 142 competition submissions, a panel immediately selected his simple design of a deep-blue background adorned with golden stars – the Pole Star and the seven stars of the Big Dipper, its Latin name, Ursa Major (the great bear), a further allusion to iconic Alaska.

often a more lively place than downtown. The only sight at the small boat harbor is the **Benny Benson Memorial** (see box opposite), but this is where you'll come to organize trips out onto the Resurrection Bay and to the tidewater glaciers (see p.251). You'll also find a few places to eat, and it can be a pleasant place to spend an afternoon planning the rest of your stay and watching the day's catch come in.

If you want to catch something yourself, call at the Fish House, on Fourth Avenue (Ⓣ224-7108 or 1-800/257-7760, Ⓦwww.thefishhouse.net), where you can rent a pole, reel, and line for salmon fishing ($10/day) and for halibut fishing ($15/day), though you'll need to buy your own lures. Full-day charter rates are around $180 for one species, $240 for both halibut and salmon.

Exit Glacier

One of the most popular activities in Seward is to drive thirteen miles to **Exit Glacier** (never closed; fee charged late May to early Sept $5 per car, $3 per hiker or biker, both valid 7 days), a four-mile-long tongue of ice poking out from the Harding Icefield that is one of the few glaciers in the state you can approach by car. During early explorations of the Harding Icefield in the 1960s, the glacier was found to be convenient as an "exit" route from the icy wastes above.

To get there, follow the Seward Highway four miles north, then turn onto the nine-mile Herman Leirer Road (snow-free mid-May to mid-Oct) beside the Resurrection River. Along the final mile, date markers beside the road indicate the location of the glacier's terminus as it has retreated at an average of 50ft a year: the 1790 marker is two miles from the current face of the glacier. Though the ice moves forward at roughly 2ft per day, it melts back slightly more, leaving a broad outwash plain of gravel in its wake.

The road ends at the *Exit Glacier Campground* (see p.245) and a brand-new **nature center** (late May to early Sept daily 9am–7pm) with interpretive displays on the glacier, Harding Icefield, and local ecosystems. From here an easy half-mile trail leads to the glacier. Compared to the calving glaciers out in the fjords it is not especially impressive, but there are wildlife-viewing opportunities – moose, bears, and mountain goats especially – and a couple of other short loop trails giving a more elevated view into deep-blue crevasses. Rangers lead free nature walks (late May to early Sept daily at 11am, 3pm & other times at busy periods) around the base of the glacier, and occasionally (usually July & Aug Sat 9am, but call Ⓣ224-3175 to check) guide all-day treks up the Harding Icefield Trail (see box, p.247).

Those without a car may want to cycle (see p.253 for rentals), walk, or call one of the local taxi companies (see p.253).

Lowell Point and Caines Head State Recreation Area

South of downtown, Lowell Point Road runs a couple of miles south along the fjord to **Lowell Point**, a small scattered community with the *Miller's Landing Campground*, some B&Bs, and a couple of kayak-rental places. Just as you enter Lowell Point, the Lowell Point State Recreation Area marks the start of a 4.5-mile tide-dependent hiking trail following old army roads to

Caines Head State Recreation Area, a site occupied by **Fort McGilvray** during World War II. On a strategic headland 650ft above the tide with mountains and alpine meadows all about, the fort still has the remains of gun emplacements and ammunition magazines used to defend the southern terminus of the Alaska Railroad. *Miller's Landing* will water-taxi you there ($30 one-way, $40 round-trip), and it is possible to kayak there in a couple of

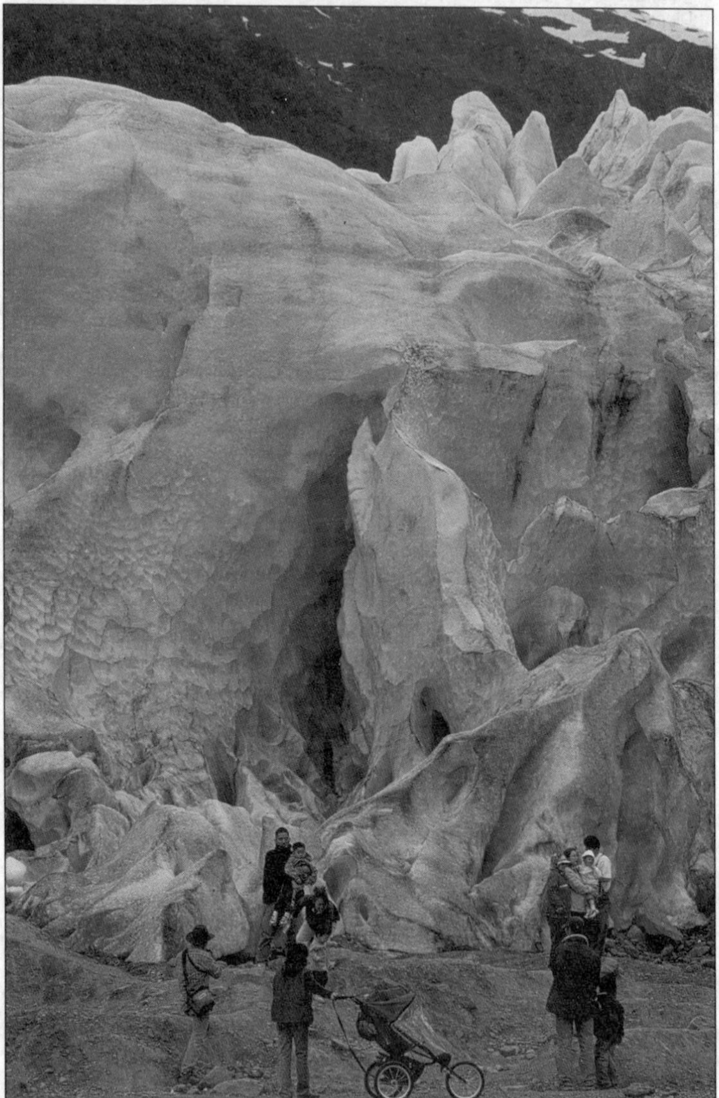

△ Exit Glacier

hours. If you choose to **hike** (4.5 miles one-way; 2–3hr; 700ft ascent), you'll need to take into account the tide, which must be at its lowest ebb on the middle section of the hike: set off (and head back) two hours before low tide. Unless low tides fall in the early morning and late evening, you'll have to stay overnight, either at one of several free campsites, or at one of the two **cabins** ($50 each; reservations ⓣ262-5581, ⓦwww.dnr.state.ak.us/parks), Derby Cove or Callisto Canyon, both at the northern end of the recreation area around four miles from the trailhead.

Resurrection Bay and Kenai Fjords cruises

A visit to Seward wouldn't be complete without time spent on the water. Several companies offer cruises, between them running four basic circuits.

The shorter and generally cheaper **cruises** travel around **Resurrection Bay**, where you might expect to see Dall's and harbor porpoises, sea lions, sea otters, mountain goats on the hillsides, and large numbers of birds – bald eagles, puffins, black-legged kittiwakes, murres, and more. It is definitely worth the extra expense and time to go beyond the limit of the bay into the **Kenai Fjords National Park**, where the larger open bodies of water improve your chances of seeing humpback and gray whales, orcas, and maybe the huge fin whales. These trips also visit the **Chiswell Islands Wildlife Refuge**, at the mouth of Aialik Bay, a major summer nesting site for fifty thousand birds from eighteen species, such as tufted and horned puffins, storm petrels, common murres, and auklets. The refuge is also the only Steller sea lion pupping area in Alaska that you can legally approach and observe. This is particularly special since, for reasons as yet undetermined, the number of Steller sea lions has dropped rapidly in recent years and they are now protected under the Endangered Species Act.

Slightly longer trips venture into Aialik Bay for a close encounter with the Holgate Glacier, an impressive example of a calving **tidewater glacier**, with the chance to see towers of ice crashing into the water. The longest cruises go further into the park into **Northwestern Fjord**, where three glaciers all calve into the same bay.

The biggest and most popular of the cruise companies is Kenai Fjords Tours (ⓣ276-6249 or 1-800/478-8068, ⓦwww.kenaifjords.com), which offers a huge array of trips from the basic Resurrection Bay (3hr; $56) up to the mighty Northwestern Fjord (9hr; $149). Several cruises call at their simple wilderness lodge on **Fox Island** (see "Accommodation," p.246) for lunch or dinner, adding around $20 to the cost. Trips run from late May to early September, with a couple of them extending a week or two at either end of the season. Early-season visitors can enjoy the Gray Whale Watch Cruise (late March to early May; 5hr; $69), which hopes to catch some of the twenty thousand California gray whales as they pass on their spring migration to the Arctic.

Under the guise of Mariah Tours, Kenai Fjords Tours also runs **small-boat cruises**, trading some boat stability and speed for more personal attention and slightly lower cost. Their main trip is to Northwestern Fjord (10hr; $135).

The main competition is Major Marine Tours (ⓣ224-8030 or 1-800/764-7300, ⓦwww.majormarine.com), which has national park rangers on board their cruises to Resurrection Bay (4hr; $69) and Holgate Glacier (8hr; $109), the latter with a worthwhile option of a salmon and chicken lunch buffet ($12). Renown Charters & Tours (ⓣ224-3806 or 1-800/655-3806, ⓦrenowncharters.com) offers a budget Resurrection Bay taster (2hr 30min; $39) and a Holgate Glacier trip (7hr; $89) and specializes in early-season whale-watching trips (mid-Feb to mid-May; 4hr; $59).

Resurrection Bay and Kenai Fjords kayaking

Resurrection Bay offers wonderful **sea-kayaking** territory, often with far less cruise-boat traffic than you would expect. Further afield there's even more spectacular paddling around the fjord-indented coast of Kenai Fjords National Park, particularly around Aialik Bay. The more remote Northwestern Fjord is less visited, though possibly less varied unless you are skilled enough to venture out onto more open waters at the fjord's mouth. The best approach is to get a charter boat to deliver you and your kayak: typical fares are $300 per person round-trip for Aialik Bay, and more like $400 for Harris Bay or Northwestern Fjord. You can then spend several days either hopping from one campsite to another or basing yourself at one of several water-accessible **cabins** ($35; reserve through APLIC in Anchorage ⓣ271-2737). The Kenai Fjords visitor center (see p.244) has a stack of good advice to help your trip planning.

Lowell Point's Sunny Cove Sea Kayaking Co (ⓣ224-8810 or 1-800/770-9119, ⓦwww.sunnycove.com), offers a wide range of tours direct from their base, with guided paddles on Resurrection Bay (3hr for $59; 8hr for $125 including lunch) and a three-hour evening paddle at 7pm. They also team up with Kenai Fjord Tours to offer a cruise, a meal at Fox Island, and three to four hours of kayaking ($149–169). To paddle among icebergs you'll need the cruise-and-paddle trip to Aialik Bay (10hr; $289), or you can join one of their many overnight trips: paddling to Caines Head and spending the night there ($289); two nights in Aialik Bay ($850); or four nights in Northwestern Fjord ($1300).

There's a more personal and flexible feel paddling with Kayak Adventures Worldwide, 328 3rd Ave (ⓣ224-3960 or 1-800/288-3134, ⓦwww.kayakak.com), which also has guided trips around Resurrection Bay (4hr for $55; 7hr for $99). Utilizing water taxis to extend range, they run day trips to the Resurrection Peninsula ($225) and Aialik Peninsula ($230), and even do fly-in paddling trips to Bear Glacier ($495), with its huge icebergs. Those suitably experienced can **rent kayaks** from them (single $35/day; double/$45) and explore at will. Relatively close destinations include Caines Head State Recreation Area, which has two cabins, and *Kayakers Cove* (see "Accommodation," p.246).

Eating, drinking, and entertainment

The presence of a significant number of tourists raises Seward's culinary scene a notch above the Alaskan small-town norm, with several worthwhile **restaurants** spanning the spectrum. Most are downtown, though there are a few around the small boat harbor worth seeking out. The majority of the restaurants listed below are licensed, but a handful of good **bars** also exist around the waterfront end of 4th Avenue. Entertainment is limited to second-run **movies**, nightly at the Liberty Theatre, 304 Adams St, though most people are content to eat and then spend the long evenings wandering along the waterfront or paying a late visit to Exit Glacier.

For **groceries**, there's virtually nothing downtown, but the Eagle Quality Center at Mile 2 on the Seward Highway has a good selection.

Christo's Place 113 4th Ave ⓣ224-5255. Reliable, cover-all-the-bases Alaskan-style dining, where you can get pizza, pasta, Mexican, and gyros ($16–19), as well as salmon and halibut steaks ($19–22). There's a good wine list, too, with everything available by the glass.

Legends cnr 5th Ave & Washington St. Family restaurant with hearty breakfasts and, for later on, a good range of soups, pastas, and fajitas ($11–15), plus $20 steaks, trout, locally caught halibut, and scallops.

Ranting Raven 238 4th Ave ⓣ224-2228. Gift

shop with attached bakery and café serving tasty and good-value quiches, pastries, croissants, bagels, and espresso in a sunny wooden-floored room.

Ray's Waterfront 1316 4th Ave ⓣ224-5606, ⓦwww.alaskaone.com/waterfront. Fine dining by the small boat harbor in a building distinctively topped by a fake lighthouse. Take in the great mountain views as you tuck into the likes of roasted elephant garlic ($9), crab cakes ($13), pan-seared Thai scallops ($24), and prime rib ($27), all beautifully cooked using herbs grown in the small greenhouse alongside. April–Oct.

Resurrect Art 320 3rd Ave ⓣ224-7161. Seward's best café inhabits a former church, with seating on the main floor, surrounded by quality local arts and crafts, and up in the choir, where there are sofas, books, and board games. Good coffee and cakes at agreeable prices, plus occasional acoustic music and book readings in the evening. Open daily to 6pm or later.

Resurrection Roadhouse Mile 0.7 Exit Glacier Rd ⓣ224-7116. Large, modern log-built restaurant and bar offering daylong smart-casual dining for a dollar or two more than you'd pay downtown. It is worth the drive for daytime burgers and sandwiches, gourmet pizza ($13), moussaka ($16), and more substantial mains, such as reindeer ragout ($20) and king crabs ($26), plus a decent range of microbrews and wines, all available by the glass.

Yukon Bar 201 4th Ave at Washington St ⓣ224-3063. Lively bar with a good range of beers and live music throughout the summer – jam session (Mon), karaoke (Wed), live bands (Thurs–Sat), and usually a set or two from Kenai Peninsula legend Hobo Jim on Sunday.

Listings

Banks There are several around town with 24hr ATMs, including First National Bank, 303 4th Ave.

Bike rental Kayak Adventures Worldwide offers basic town bikes for $6 a half-day; Seward Bike Shop (ⓣ224-2448) in the railcars at Fourth and Port has cruisers ($12/half-day; $19/day) and full-suspension mountain bikes ($18/32).

Car rental Hertz, 604 Port Ave ⓣ224-4378.

Flightseeing Scenic Mountain Air (ⓣ288-3646, ⓦwww.scenicmountainair.com) runs flightseeing trips from Seward airport out over Kenai Fjords and the Harding Icefield (30min; $79, min 2).

Internet access The free thirty-minute sessions at the library are in high demand, so you might find it easier to visit Grant Electronics, 222 4th Ave (Mon–Thurs & Sat 10am–6pm; ⓣ224-7015), where rates are reasonable, or one of several other places that spring up each summer.

Laundry Seward Laundry and Dry Cleaning, 804 4th Ave (Mon–Sat 8am–8pm; ⓣ224-5727) has coin-op and service laundry.

Library Seward Community Library, 238 5th Ave (Mon–Fri 11am–8pm, Sat 11am–6pm; ⓣ224-3646) has free Internet access.

Medical assistance Providence Seward Medical Center, 417 1st Ave at Jefferson St ⓣ224-5205.

Post office 507 Madison St at 6th Ave. The **General Delivery** zip code is 99664.

Showers The Harbormaster's office by the small boat harbor has coin-op showers for $2, and Seward Laundry (see above) has showers with towel and soap for $4.

Taxes The six percent city tax is charged in all purchases. With an additional four percent bed tax, ten percent is added to hotel prices and has been factored into our price codes.

Water taxi *Miller's Landing* at Lowell Point ⓣ224-5739, ⓦwww.millerslandingak.com.

Western Kenai Peninsula

Few places in Alaska exhibit a more dramatic change of scenery than the transition from the tight-bound, almost claustrophobic, mountains of the northeast to the flatlands of the **western Kenai Peninsula** just twenty-odd miles away. Almost the entire western half of the peninsula is low and swampy country studded with shallow lakes ringed by spruce trees. In fact, this area is one of the largest areas of flat, useable land in Alaska; only the Mat-Su Valley and the region around Fairbanks have comparable acreages. This has its benefits with numerous interconnected lakes and level portages forming superb canoe routes, but it has also left the region open to unfettered development. Much of the area around the towns of Kenai and Soldotna was developed with no thought of town planning. The coast north of Kenai is also one of Alaska's most industrialized on account of the oil and natural gas sucked out of the ground underneath Cook Inlet.

Depressing though that may sound, it mars only a small area, and the vast majority of the region is wonderfully pristine, much of it falling under the control of the **Kenai National Wildlife Refuge**. A tranche running through the center of the peninsula from the far northern tip to Kachemak Bay was originally set aside by Franklin D Roosevelt in 1941 as a moose-hunting preserve, and then expanded into the Kenai National Wildlife Refuge in 1980. Very little has highway access, making its trails and lakes some of the least-visited in the region, though it does get busy in the campgrounds along the Skilak Lake Loop Road. Much the best source of detailed information is the park visitor center in Soldotna.

In summer **Soldotna** is overrun by Alaskans and outsiders seeking some of the world's best king salmon **fishing**. Nearby **Kenai** is popular for its fish, but it has some history, too, best seen in its beautiful Russian Orthodox church. Get anywhere near the coast on a fine day and it is hard to be unimpressed by the sight of the two conical volcanoes – Redoubt and Iliamna – across the

Hiking and biking in northern Kenai

The mountains of the northern Kenai Peninsula are laced with the most extensive network of multiday hiking trails in Alaska, over two hundred miles in total. All are fairly long, and none finish close to where they start, but it is quite possible for experienced hikers to spend a week or ten days piecing together a circular loop, or hiking across the peninsula from Hope, on the shores of Turnagain Arm, to Seward on Resurrection Bay.

The whole region falls within the bounds of the Chugach National Forest, which manages over a dozen first-come, first-served forest campgrounds in the region, along with sixteen public-use cabins ($35–45; reserve on ⓣ1-877/444-6777, ⓦwww.ReserveUSA.com), the more popular being available for three-day stays, while you can stay in others for a week.

It is worth remembering that the Kenai mountains typically receive a lot of snow, so don't expect the upland sections of any of these trails to be snow-free until early June, or later. The main **hiking season** is from mid-June until the first significant snowfall, usually in late September.

Mountain biking is also a possibility on the smoother trails, though many are closed to bikers from April to June and will be under snow from October to April. The months to go are July, August, and September.

Trails

Crescent Creek Trail (6.4 miles one-way; 3–4hr; 860ft ascent). Well-maintained trail with great mountain views, climbing up through birch and alder forests and wildflower meadows, and finishing beside Crescent Lake where there's a primitive campground and the *Crescent Lake Cabin* ($45; by reservation only). The trailhead is at Mile 3.5 on Quartz Creek Road, which turns off the Sterling Highway at Mile 45. Also one of the best **mountain biking** trails in the region.

Johnson Pass Trail (23 miles one-way; 2–3 days; 1000ft ascent). Fairly easy and particularly beautiful trail with a predominance of treeless subalpine country with wondrous long views. From the north trailhead at Mile 64 on the Seward Highway (close to the *Granite Creek Campground*), it climbs steeply through hemlock, willow, and alder, and then, as the trail levels out, there are more wildflowers and shrubs as well as great camping spots. At the highest point of the trail around Johnson Pass the terrain is open enough for you to explore away from the trail pretty much as you

water, though the best views are south of Soldotna where the highway runs close to the clifftops past the state's finest razor-clam beaches.

Cooper Landing and around

Tern Lake Junction marks the point where the Sterling Highway splits off from the Seward Highway. Mileposts for Homer-bound traffic confusingly start at Mile 37, reflecting the distance from Seward in the days before these roads were connected to Anchorage. With the exception of a couple of campgrounds, there is very little in the way of facilities along the Sterling Highway until **COOPER LANDING**, another of those strung-out Alaskan highway towns where you're never quite sure if you've arrived or not, until you've passed through. It was named for Joseph Cooper, who sought gold here in 1884 and set up a trading post, though the place never really got off the ground until **salmon-fishing** enthusiasts began to congregate here for the red-salmon run on the Russian River (mid-June to late Aug), and various runs on the Kenai River.

You might prefer to hike the first few miles of some of the region's trails (see box, below), or try some fairly gentle **rafting** on the Kenai River, with great opportunities for spotting eagles and moose. Alaska Rivers Co, Mile 50 (Ⓣ595-

please. The trail finishes just west of Moose Pass at Mile 32.5 on the Seward Highway. This is a very popular mountain-biking trail.

Resurrection Pass Trail (39 miles one-way; 2–4 days; 2100ft ascent). Superb and justly popular trail following the long valley of Resurrection Creek up to Resurrection Pass, then down to the Sterling Highway near Cooper Landing. It was the scene of frenetic activity in 1888, when this was the site of a brief but intense gold rush, during which the prospectors forged the trail now used by hikers. The trail is mostly fairly easy going with a gradual grade and is well maintained, though it can be boggy with June snowmelt. Apart from the superb mountain scenery – about a third of the distance is above the tree line – there's abundant wildlife and good fishing in three lakes towards the southern end of the trail; take a rod and a license. You can camp in the many designated camping spots (usually just off the trail), though there are also eight **cabins**, evenly distributed along the route.

Without an amenable driver, you'll have to hitch from the Seward Highway fourteen miles into Hope and then hitch (or more likely, walk) the four miles up Resurrection Road to the trailhead. The southern trailhead is at Mile 52 on the Sterling Highway near Cooper Landing, from where you can pick up passing buses to your next destination, hitch back to Hope if your car is there, or continue hiking along the Russian Lakes Trail. **Mountain bikers** can also tackle the Resurrection Pass Trail in around ten to twelve hours making it possible to do it in a day, leaving your gear with someone who can meet you at the other end. Bikes are banned from April to June, making July, August and September the only feasible months.

Russian Lakes Trail (21 miles one-way; 2–4 days; 1100ft ascent). A less arduous alternative to the Resurrection Pass Trail that's fairly gently graded and well maintained, most of it through spruce forests well below the timberline. It may not be as dramatic as some of the other hikes, but it's good for spotting moose, bears, Dall sheep, and even wolves. Fishing is rewarding, especially for rainbow trout in Upper and Lower Russian lakes. Without transport, access is a problem as the best starting point is twelve miles off the Sterling Highway (Mile 48) at Cooper Lake, where there's the *Cooper Lake Campground* ($13 camping, $6 trailhead parking). The trail finishes at Mile 52 of the Sterling Highway close to Cooper Landing.

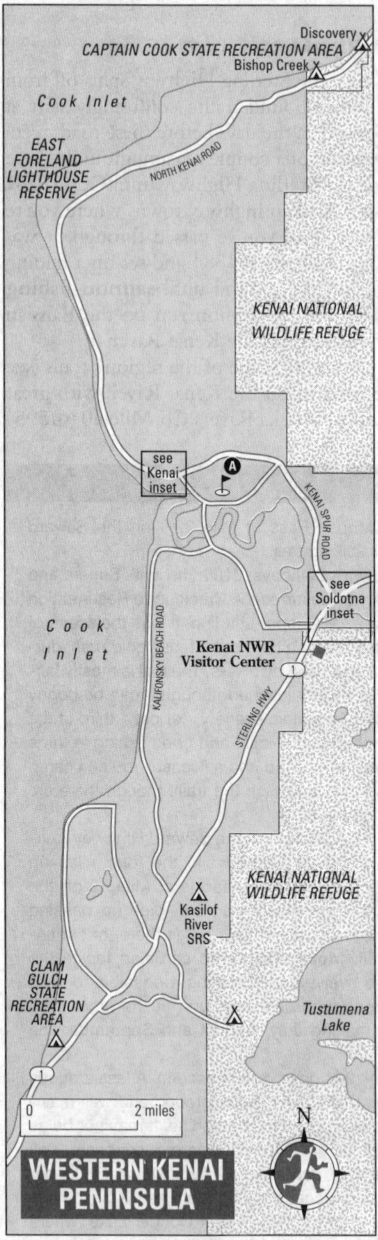

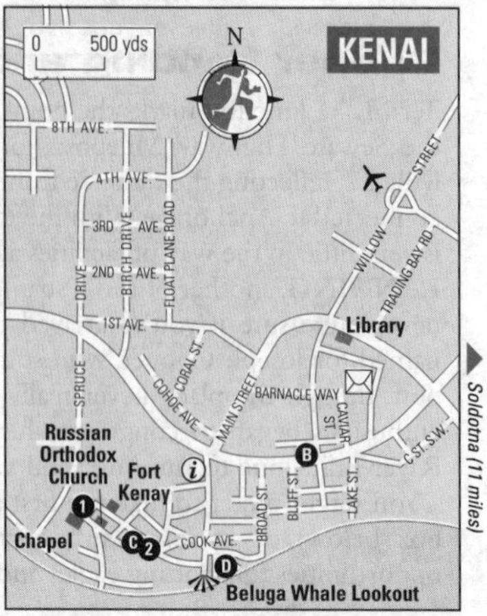

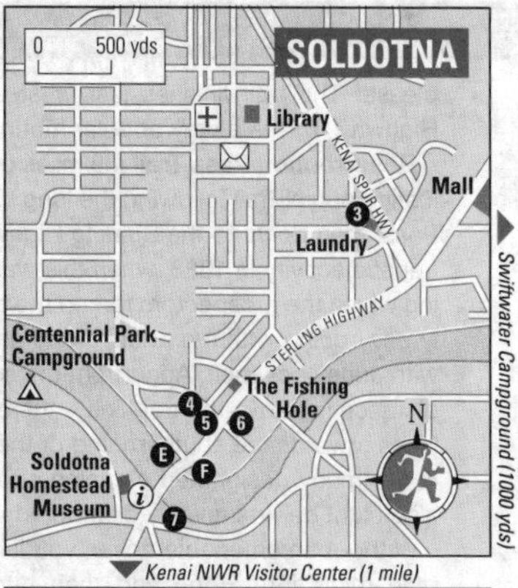

ACCOMMODATION

Beluga Lookout RV Park	C
Best Ball B&B	A
Harborside Cottages	D
Hooligans Lodge	F
Kenai Merit Inn	B
Kenai River Lodge	E

RESTAURANTS, BARS & CAFÉS

BJ's	5
Kaladi Brothers Coffee Co	4
Mykel's	3
Old Town Village Restaurant	2
Sal's Klondike Diner	6
Tides Inn	7
Veronica's Coffee House	1

1226, Ⓦwww.alaskariverscompany.com), runs raft-fishing trips on the Kenai River (half-day $90, full day $150) and pure rafting trips, with a two-hour trip (Class II; $42) or a seven-hour run through the Kenai River Canyon and across Skilak Lake (Class III; $95). They also run $35 guided hikes along the Russian Lakes Trail (see box, p.255) and rent rustic but comfortable cabins (❸), one by the river. There's nothing shoddy about Alaska Rivers' trips, but there's an altogether slicker approach to those run by Alaska Wildland Adventures, Mile 50 (Ⓣ595-1279 or 1-800/478-4100, Ⓦwww.alaskarivertrips.com). Most of their business comes from all-inclusive packages, such as three nights staying in their comfortable lodge and two days spent fishing for salmon and trout ($1350), although they also do rafting (2hr float, $45; 7hr canyon, $110) and day-fishing trips on the upper Kenai (9hr; $195).

Fishing trips are also available from *Gwin's Lodge*, Mile 52 (Ⓣ595-1266, Ⓦwww.gwinslodge.com), a classic roadhouse that has been serving diner meals for over fifty years, around the clock during the red-salmon run. Their drift-boat fishing trips are either half-day ($125–155) or full-day ($165–225) and they also do fly-in trout fishing at remote streams from as little as $110. *Gwin's* has **accommodation** in the form of salubrious cabins with plumbing and proper beds (❹–❻).

Meanwhile, **campers** are well served with campgrounds beside red-salmon spawning grounds: *Cooper Creek*, Mile 50.7 ($10), which has riverside sites, and the larger and enormously popular *Russian River*, Mile 52.6 ($13; RVs $20; day parking $6).

Russian River marks the start of the handicap-accessible **Russian River Falls Trail** (5 miles round-trip; 2–3hr; 200ft ascent), which winds through the forest to a viewing platform that's perfect for watching salmon leaping a series of falls. They aren't exactly high, but are fast-flowing enough to make you wonder how the sockeye can get up it.

Frugal types not wanting to pay for parking can leave their vehicle 1.5 miles down the road at the trailhead for the **Resurrection Pass Trail** (see box, p.255). Even if you're not up for the whole thing, consider hiking the first four miles to sixty-foot Juneau Falls, and perhaps a couple of hundred yards beyond to a bridge over the creek and a nice little primitive camping spot.

A little further on you enter the **Kenai National Wildlife Refuge** and pass the campground at *Kenai-Russian River Access Area*, Mile 55, typically full of RVs and anglers, who use a small passenger **ferry** ($8 round-trip) to get to favored spots on the far bank. A couple of miles on, the trailhead for the **Fuller Lakes Trail**, Mile 57 (8 miles round-trip; 5–6hr; 1700ft ascent), heralds the Kenai National Wildlife Refuge **contact station** (mid-May to mid-Sept daily 10am–4pm), where you can pick up information on Skilak Lake Loop Road (see below).

Skilak Lake Loop Road

From Russian River Falls the Sterling Highway barrels west through forested lake country; rather than sticking with the highway, consider taking **Skilak Lake Loop Road**, a 19-mile diversion past Skilak Lake and several lakeside campgrounds. Leaving the Sterling Highway at Mile 58, stop after half a mile and follow the easy, signposted **Kenai River Trail** for about fifteen minutes to a nice little viewpoint high above the swirling waters of the Kenai River Canyon.

Most people come to Skilak Lake to hang out at one of the five **campgrounds**, maybe do a little swimming in the shallows, and mess about in boats on the lake. Although there are no formal facilities – bring everything with you – it is worth the detour, even for just a night camped beside a lake. *Hidden Lake* and *Upper Skilak* campgrounds ($5–10) are the most popular, leaving *Lower Skilak, Lower Ohmer* and *Engineer Lake* (all free) for those after more seclusion.

Skilak Lake Loop Road rejoins the Sterling Highway at Mile 75. The highway then runs through dull **Sterling**, which sprawls for eight miles along the highway with no focus and little of interest. Best push on to Soldotna, or beyond.

Soldotna

There is hardly anywhere in Alaska where fishing isn't a big deal, but nowhere is it quite so all-consuming as in **SOLDOTNA**, 47 miles west of Cooper Landing. The town sits on the banks of the Kenai River which, in summer, is the single busiest salmon river in Alaska, and for good reason: it regularly produces some of the largest **king salmon** ever caught. The current record, caught in 1985, is a 97-pound monster now mounted and on display in the visitor center. Fish over 80 pounds are not uncommon. Elsewhere a 50-pound king would be considered a trophy, but here you'll have to land something over 75 pounds.

Fishing aside, Soldotna is a dull place characterized by a strip-mall sprawl of supermarkets and fast-food restaurants, having grown up since being homesteaded by returning World War II soldiers in the late 1940s. Veterans were given first preference, and they flocked here despite the lack of roads and the need to either fly in or make the difficult hike from the coast at Kenai.

It is this homesteading connection that provides Soldotna's only tangible sight, the **Soldotna Homestead Museum** (mid-May to mid-Sept Tues–Sat 10am–4pm, Sun noon–4pm; donations appreciated), around the corner from the visitor center, a classic example of showcasing Alaskan "history," which mostly happened less than half a century back. It occupies six original log cabins that have been moved to the site, their interiors arranged to illustrate homesteading life with everything from beds and stoves to oil lamps and preserving jars. One cabin was the former schoolhouse, built by the teacher and pupils' parents.

Though the Kenai National Wildlife Refuge is scattered over the peninsula's western lowlands, Soldotna is home to the main KNWR **visitor center** (June to early Sept Mon–Fri 8am–5pm, Sat & Sun 9am–6pm; early Sept to May Mon–Fri 8am–4.30pm, Sat & Sun 10am–5pm; ⓣ262-7021, ⓦkenai.fws.gov), a mile off the Sterling Highway at Mile 96, near the Soldotna visitor center. Pop in for the extensive displays about the region, wildlife videos in the theater, and the opportunity to stroll along a couple of easy **woodland trails**.

There are further wildlife-watching opportunities across Cook Inlet in the form of **bear-viewing** trips. Most go from Homer, but there are sometimes bargain flights from here.

Fishing the Kenai

Salmon fishing is king in Soldotna, but it may not be the wilderness experience you might expect. With kings, reds silvers, pinks (in significant numbers only in even-numbered years), rainbow trout, and Dolly Varden all spawning in the river, it is busy throughout most of the summer. The peak is from mid-May to early July, when the first run of kings come in. A combination of the deep and wide Kenai River, and the sheer size of the fish means that they keep to the middle, so successful anglers fish from boats, and the river can be thick with people zipping back and forth in their outboard skiffs. On average, it takes 31 hours of fishing to get a king, though odds can be improved threefold with a guide. Not only do they know the best spots and techniques, they're also up with the byzantine regulations (which differ from the rules on other rivers).

For a recorded fishing report (and the latest regs) call ⓣ262-6737.

The visitor center can put you in touch with fishing guides and boat-rental places, but if this all sounds too complicated and expensive you could always just wet a line from the wheelchair-accessible boardwalk just in front of the visitor center, or fish the Kasilof River, fifteen miles south, where the fish are a little smaller but can be caught from the bank.

Fishing guides can be found using links from the chamber of commerce website (ⓦwww.soldotnachamber.com), but before committing in advance, be sure to ask lots of pertinent questions – hours of fishing, tackle supplied, fish-cleaning services and so forth – to be sure you're getting what you want. Generally, the more experience the guide has on the Kenai the better your chances will be. For further advice as well as tackle, contact the Fishing Hole, 139b Warehouse St (ⓣ262-2290, ⓦwww.thefishinghole.com).

Timing is everything, and you want to be sure you're here for the **season** for your target species: kings (first run mid-May to July, second run last two weeks of July); reds (first run late May to early June, second run mid-July to early Aug); silvers (late July to late Aug); pinks (late July to late Aug in even years only); rainbow trout (mid-June to Oct); and Dolly Varden and lake trout (all year). For a bit of spectacle, arrive during the **Kenai River Classic** (two days at the start of July), an invitational fishing tournament with 180 participants that's dedicated to raising funds for the preservation of the local fishery – past tournaments have raised over $1 million.

Practicalities

Homer Stage Line (ⓣ262-4584 in Soldotna) passes through Soldotna (daily in summer) and will drop off at the **visitor center**, 47900 Sterling Hwy (May–Sept daily 9am–7pm; Oct–April Mon–Fri 9am–5pm, Sat noon–5pm; ⓣ262-1337, ⓦwww.soldotnachamber.com), beside the Kenai River at Mile 69. They have all you need to know about fishing in the area and hold brochures for dozens of B&Bs scattered around. For **accommodation** try *Kenai River Lodge*, 393 Riverside Drive (ⓣ262-4292, ⓦwww.kenairiverlodge.com; ❺), directly across the river from the visitor center, which has deluxe motel rooms all with river views and fishing from the hotel grounds. *Hooligans Lodge*, 44715 Sterling Hwy (ⓣ262-9951, ⓦwww.hooliganslodge.com; ❹), across the highway, is less salubrious but cheaper. There is no budget accommodation, but **campers** can stay close to the river at the wooded *Centennial Park Campground* (ⓣ262-5299; $10), which is large but still manages to fill up early in the day from around mid-May to mid-July, or the similarly busy *Swiftwater Park Campground* on E Redoubt Avenue ($10).

There's a good selection of **places to eat** in Soldotna, with almost everything visible along the highway. The major fast-food chains are represented, but everyone seems to end up visiting *Sal's Klondike Diner*, 44619 Sterling Hwy (ⓣ262-2220), which serves home-style dishes like biscuits, gravy, and two eggs ($4.50), veggie skillet ($7), and ridiculously large and sticky cinnamon rolls ($3.50). On a sunny day try the riverside deck of the *Tides Inn*, 44789 Sterling Hwy (ⓣ262-1906), where you can get a burger and brew for as little as $8, or go slightly upscale to *Mykel's*, 35041 Kenai Spur Rd (ⓣ262-4305), for great steaks and shrimp. *Kaladi Brothers Coffee Co*, 315 S Kobuk St (ⓣ262-5980), has good espresso, and *BJ's*, 44695 Sterling Hwy (ⓣ262-1882), has beer and live bands including Soldotna's resident troubadour, Hobo Jim (Thurs to Sat).

You'll find **banks** along the highway, laundry and showers at Soldotna Wash & Dry, 121 S Frontage Rd (daily 8am–10pm, and 24hr in peak summer), and a **library** at 235 Binkley St with free **email**.

Kenai and around

On initial acquaintance, **KENAI**, eleven miles northwest of Soldotna, is little better than its southern sibling, suffering from the same unplanned development – in fact both have spread so far they almost join. That said, it can be a pretty place, especially on clear days when there are wonderful views of Iliamna and Redoubt volcanoes across Cook Inlet. There is also a tangible sense of history, though perhaps less than you would expect in what is the second oldest permanent European settlement in the state.

The Russians arrived in 1791 looking to obtain sea-otter pelts and built Redoubt Nikolaevsk (Fort St Nicholas) to protect their interests. Despite a battle over fur trading with the local Dena'ina Athabascans in which a hundred people were killed, the Russians stuck around, building a productive brickworks in 1841 and a school in 1864, just three years before they sold Alaska to the United States.

Apart from a few homesteaders and fishermen, no one took much notice of the place until 1957 when oil was discovered along the Swanson River. Subsequently, natural gas was found under Cook Inlet, and today over a dozen production platforms send oil and gas to the refinery north of town.

Stop first at the **Kenai Visitors and Cultural Center**, corner of Kenai Spur Highway and Main Street (June–Aug Mon–Fri 9am–8pm, Sat & Sun 11am–7pm; Sept–May Mon–Fri 9am–5pm, Sat 10am–4pm; ⓣ283-1991, ⓦwww.visitkenai.com), where the cultural center ($3) usually has some top-quality exhibition to bolster an already fascinating section on local history, with good examples of baleen and ivory baskets and an Athabascan necklace fashioned from shells and Russian trade beads. You can also pick up the free *Old Town Kenai Walking Tour* leaflet, and then walk a quarter of a mile to the historic part of town, on a bluff overlooking Cook Inlet and the mouth of the Kenai River. This is the remains of the Russian settlement built around the striking Holy Assumption of the Virgin Mary Orthodox Church, Mission Street (June–Aug Mon–Sat 11am–3pm; $1 donation appreciated; ⓣ283-4122 at other times), with its three, blue onion domes representing the Father, Son, and Holy Spirit. The beautiful interior is dominated by a huge chandelier that came from Irkutsk in 1875 and contains an ancient Bible brought here by Father Nicolai, much loved locally for his dedication in administering the smallpox vaccine, while Natives in other communities were dying by the hundreds. Icons and religious images, some dating back two hundred years, cover the walls: look particularly for the image of Russian patriot and hero Alexandr Nefsky (on the doorway to the left of the altar).

Nearby, you'll find the bare-wood **Chapel of Saint Nicholas**, built in 1906 over the grave of Father Nicolai, who apparently presided over such a wide area that it would take a year to complete his "circuit" of baptisms.

Across the road from the church is the site of the US army barracks of **Fort Kenay**, Mission Avenue, though the buildings (closed to the public) are reconstructions built in 1967 for the Alaska Centennial. Continuing southeast along Mission Avenue you come to Eric Hansen Scout Park, corner of Mission Avenue and Main Street, a clifftop viewing platform ideal for **Beluga whale watching**, though the sight of them chasing salmon is increasingly rare these days.

Practicalities

Homer Stage Line **buses** (ⓣ262-4584 in Soldotna) stop in Kenai once in each direction on their run between Seward and Homer. With Homer (or Seward, or even Anchorage) beckoning, there is really not much reason to **stay** in Kenai, although RV drivers at the end of a long day might want to hook up at *Beluga Lookout RV Park*, 929 Mission Ave (ⓣ283-5999, ⓔbelugarv@ptialaska.net; $18) right by the church. Almost equally handy are the *Kenai Merit Inn*, 260 S Willow St (ⓣ283-6131 or 1-800/227-6131; ④), which has comfortable rooms, complimentary breakfast and a restaurant, and *Harborside Cottages*, 813 Riverview Drive (ⓣ283-6162 or 1-888/283-6162, ⓦwww.harborsidecottages.com; ⑥), where you stay in individual cottages with great views of the Kenai River mouth. You might also try *Best Ball B&B*, 101 Highbush Lane (ⓣ283-2265, ⓦwww.bestballak.com; ④), near the golf course with a self-contained suite separate from the host with TV, VCR and continental breakfast supplied. **Campers** are better served at the Captain Cook State Recreation Area (see below).

For something to **eat**, *Veronica's Coffee House*, 604 Peterson St (ⓣ283-2725), is well placed opposite the church and has outdoor seating as well as places inside where you can read magazines over a good coffee or tuck into soups, sandwiches, and quiches. On occasional weekend evenings there's live acoustic music, too. Nearby, the *Old Town Village Restaurant*, 1000 Mission St (ⓣ283-4515), has a standard Alaskan menu of burgers, pasta dishes, and halibut and chips, plus an all-you-can-eat Sunday brunch for $10.

For other practical needs, you'll find **banks** across the road from the visitor center, and **Internet** access at the Kenai Public Library, 163 Main St Loop (Mon–Thurs 10am–8pm, Fri & Sat 10am–5pm, Sun noon–5pm; ⓣ283-4378).

Captain Cook State Recreation Area

North of Kenai the suburban sprawl bleeds easily into **Nikiski**, which in turn fades out as the highway briefly brushes the coast. Take a quick look at the volcanoes across Cook Inlet before your view is blocked by the oil refinery and the fertilizer plant, which uses natural gas from the rigs dotted out to sea. The road then weaves inland through trees until, 25 miles north of Kenai, it hits the **Captain Cook State Recreation Area**, a peaceful area with road access to lake swimming, camping, and some wonderful canoeing. Although they're approached from here, the multiday Swanson River and Swan Lake canoe routes fall within the Kenai National Wildlife Refuge: for details call at their visitor center in Soldotna (see p.259).

You first come across the small *Bishop Creek Campground* ($10), which has walk-in tent sites, paths down to the beach, and potable water, and is an easy walk from the **swimming** beach on **Story Lake**. Three miles on the larger *Discovery Campground* ($10) has the best Cook Inlet views and spacious drive-in campsites among the trees. Limited supplies are available at the *Bishop Creek Bar* and liquor store, a couple of miles back down the highway, but it is best to stock up with supplies in Soldotna or Kenai.

South of Soldotna

The Sterling Highway makes its final 84-mile run to Homer mostly following the western coast of the Kenai Peninsula along the shores of Cook Inlet, a wonderful drive on a clear day when the snowcapped volcanic peaks of Iliamna and Redoubt dominate the views. There are a handful of small settlements along the way – the most interesting being **Ninilchik** with its Russian Orthodox church – but the coast is really known for its **clamming beaches**.

Clamming on the Kenai

At almost any low tide along the western shores of the Kenai Peninsula, you'll see dozens of people up to their knees in mud digging out **razor clams** (*Siliqua patula*). These sharp-edged bivalves, which burrow a foot or two under the sand, make especially good eating, if you can catch them. As they're typically around three to four inches long (though sometimes up to seven), you only need a dozen or so each for a good meal, served up either lightly panfried or in clam chowder. The best source of information about the rules and necessary skills for clamming is the free *Kenai Peninsula Razor Clams* leaflet, available widely but specifically from the Soldotna office of Fish and Game at 34828 Kalifonsky Beach Rd. Essentially, you need to equip yourself with a state sportfishing license (see Basics, p.63), knee-high rubber boots, rubber gloves, a narrow-bladed shovel, and a bucket, all available to buy or rent locally. Once you're kitted out, wait for a low tide (the lower the better), look for a dimple in the sand and quickly dig just on the seaward side of it to avoid breaking its fragile shell. After two or three shovels, dig around with your hand and grab the clam before it scuttles away. Dump them in salt water, and they'll naturally clear themselves of sand, saving you a lot of trouble.

Clams can be harvested the entire year, but the most succulent are found during the early summer before spawning season. The best digging is usually an hour before and two hours after a low tide. Generally, the daily limit is 60, though on the most popular beaches you can only take the first 45 dug: no throwing back those with broken shells. You should also be aware of paralytic shellfish poisoning (PSP), a buildup of natural toxins, which sometimes happens towards the end of summer: if it occurs, there will be warnings posted widely advising you not to eat.

For more information on clamming visit ⓦwww.dnr.state.ak.us/parks/units/clamglch.htm.

Kasilof and Clam Gulch

The Sterling Highway and Kalifonsky Beach Road converge at **KASILOF**, fourteen miles south of Soldotna, a small fishing community mainly of interest for its collection of simple **campgrounds**, beside lakes or fishing streams, the best being the small *Kasilof River State Recreation Site*, Mile 109 ($10).

Ten minutes further south, **CLAM GULCH**, Mile 117, is really just a post office, and a few cabins beside the most northerly of the major clamming beaches. With its broad, gently shelving strand, Clam Gulch is widely regarded as one of the best hunting grounds, and has the double convenience of the *Clam Gulch State Recreation Area* (day-use $5, camping $10) right by the beach, and *Clam Shell Lodge*, Mile 118 (ⓣ262-4211), where they'll rent you a shovel for $5 and sell you tasty bowls of clam chowder.

Ninilchik

Down the coast another seventeen miles you reach **NINILCHIK**, a loosely defined community spreading a couple of miles along the highway and centered on the mouths of two rivers, the Ninilchik River to the north, and Deep Creek a mile to the south. Most visitors come for the exemplary **clamming**, but there is interest, too, in the picturesque **Russian Orthodox church** (usually closed) and cemetery superbly set atop the hill overlooking town. The church was built in 1901, some eighty years after employees of the Russian-American Company first established a town here. Unlike many Russian communities, Ninilchik wasn't deserted when the Russians sold Alaska to the US, and the descendants still live hereabouts.

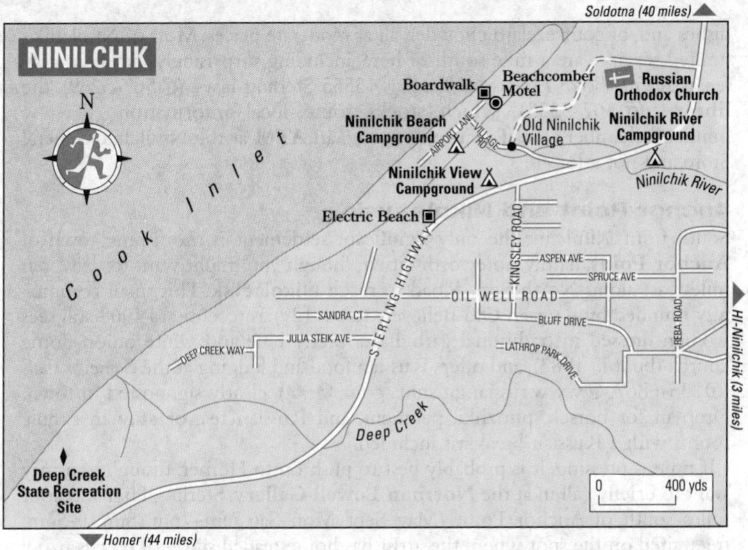

After admiring the exterior of the church, head down the highway to **Old Ninilchik Village**, a collection of cabins and engagingly dilapidated shacks bounded on three sides by a bend in the Ninilchik River where old fishing boats rest on the shore. Much of the village was lost when the ground sank 3ft during the 1964 earthquake, but you can still visit the restored nineteenth-century cabin known as the **Village Cache**, a quality craft shop where you can pick up the free *Tour of Ninilchik Village* leaflet. Spend a few minutes here before walking round to the main beach where the best of the clamming happens.

Practicalities

When the weather is good, Ninilchik is certainly appealing enough to make you want to stay the night, and if you're here for the clamming it seems in the spirit of the enterprise to **camp** by the beach. This is easily done either on gravel sites at the exposed *Ninilchik Beach Campground* ($5) or a mile south at the larger Deep Creek State Recreation Site ($10), which is heavily used by clammers (day-use $5). There are also more sheltered and secluded $10 sites inland and close to the highway at *Ninilchik River* and also at the small *Ninilchik View Campground*, high up and with great volcano views from some sites.

Right on the beach, there are simple **rooms** at the *Beachcomber Motel* (Ⓣ567-3417; ❸), and about three miles inland there's the *HI-Ninilchik* **hostel** (also known as the *Eagle Watch*), Mile 3 Oilwell Rd (mid-May to mid-Sept; office 8–10am & 5–10pm; Ⓣ567-3905; members $10, non-members $13), sited on a high bluff above a meandering creek where moose often graze. It is a spotless and well-organized hostel in a family home with separate men's and women's dorms, and a communal kitchen, downstairs. Tea, coffee, and some kitchen necessities are supplied, they'll pick up from the highway with prior warning and they run clamming sessions ($5 if you stay at the hostel the night before) when the tides are low enough and four people can be rounded up.

There isn't much choice for **eating**, but about the best place is the *Boardwalk* (no phone), almost opposite the *Beachcomber*, where you can sit inside or out admiring the view as you dine on build-your-own subs, burgers, halibut dishes and, of course, clam chowder, all at moderate prices. Most of Ninilchik's limited services are a mile south of here, including surprisingly excellent coffee at *Electric Beach Espresso & Tanning*, 15555 Sterling Hwy (ⓣ567-3269), the **library** (ⓣ567-3333), which stocks some local information (ⓦwww.ninilchikchamber.com if you want more), an **ATM** at the Ninilchik General Store and not a lot else.

Anchor Point and Nikolaevsk

South from Ninilchik the only significant settlement is the fishing town of **Anchor Point**, hardly noteworthy itself, though you might want to drive ten miles east along North Fork Road to reach **Nikolaevsk**. This small community founded by Russian Old Believers (see p.129) as recently as 1968 still sees women dressed in traditional garb, has a pretty blue and white onion-dome church (built in 1983), and offers Russian food and lodging at the *Samovar Café* (ⓣ235-6867, ⓦwww.russiangiftsnina.com; ❶–❷), clearly signposted in town. Drop in for borsch, pirozhki, pel'meni, and Russian tea, or **stay** in simple rooms with a Russian breakfast included.

If time is pressing, it is probably best to push on to Homer, though you may want to briefly call in at the **Norman Lowell Gallery**, Sterling Highway, four miles south of Anchor Point (May–Sept Mon–Sat 7am–7pm, Sun 1–5pm; free), sited on the spot where the artist has homesteaded since 1959. His pastel canvases of archetypal Alaskan scenes won't be to everyone's taste, so you may want to pass straight through the shop (unframed prints $250–750) and head for Homer, twelve miles south.

Homer and around

HOMER, 44 miles south of Ninilchik, exerts a strong pull on Alaskans and visitors alike. Its combination of superb location, fairly mild climate, and proximity to **Kachemak Bay** have long drawn a mix of people, from 1960s dropouts to the so-called **Old Believers**, who rejected reforms of the Russian Orthodox Church and came seeking religious freedom. Artists, in particular, have taken to the town's relative isolation and slow-paced charms, adding a creative element to the community that seems at the same time more varied and more integrated than you find elsewhere in Alaska.

Arriving on a cloudy day, the town's beauty can seem over-hyped, but you can easily fall under its relaxed spell, hanging out on the **Spit**, a distinctive four-mile gravel bank where everyone comes to fish for salmon, charter halibut boats, or simply admire the backdrop of snowcapped mountains.

The area across the bay provides a welcome retreat in places like **Seldovia** and **Halibut Cove**, and a water taxi ride gives access to a wondrous array of hikes on the south side of Kachemak Bay.

The first whites to come to Kachemak Bay were Russians who arrived in search of sea otters. They found plenty and nearly wiped them out, but the otters have rebounded in such numbers that you'll likely see several on any bay cruise. No significant settlements were established until the end of the nineteenth century when an English company developed a mine to exploit coal seams on the north shore of the bay.

Homer was founded in 1898 at the tip of the Spit by Homer Pennock, something of a con man who had convinced a fifty-strong party of men to come here to look for gold. Little was discovered, but they stayed on and set up an isolated community based on herring fishing and coal. As the herring-salting industry took off in the early years of the twentieth century, communities sprang up around Kachemak Bay, notably Seldovia, which soon became the main town of the region. After 1951, when new gravel roads connected Homer to the rest of the state highway system, Homer began to take over that mantle, a position consolidated by the effects of the 1964 earthquake, which virtually destroyed Seldovia. The Homer Spit sank 6ft, swamping a stand of spruce and the fields where cows once grazed, and making the end of the Spit an island at high tide. It has since taken considerable effort to restore and maintain road access along its length, something justified by the thriving commercial port and tourism based around the small boat harbor.

Arrival, information, and getting around

You'll most likely arrive in Homer by car or on one of the **buses** run by Homer Stage Line (☎235-2252), which through the summer has a daily service from Anchorage and a weekday run from Seward. It is an impressive approach with sweeping views of Kachemak Bay, the Spit, and Homer itself from high on a bluff just before you enter town. The highway continues almost five miles out to the end of the Spit, the western limit of the continuous US highway system. The terminal here (☎235-8449) is where the **AMHS ferry** *Tustumena* docks on its thrice-weekly run to Kodiak and weekly service to Seward. Visitors in a hurry might want to **fly** from Anchorage to Homer's airport on FAA Drive with ERA Aviation (☎235-5205 or 1-800/866-8394), which charges around $100 one-way and around $150 for an advance-purchase round-trip.

Once here it is quite possible to walk around downtown and around the Spit, but to span the four miles between the two you'll need to hitch, call a taxi (see p.271), or **rent a bike** from Homer Saw and Cycle, 1532 Ocean Drive, at the

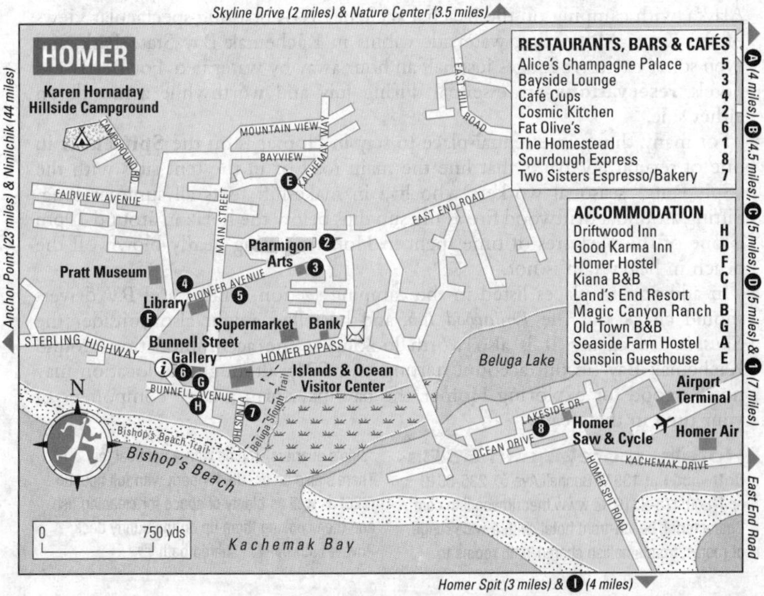

head of the Spit road (ⓣ235-8406, ⓔhomersaw@xyz.net), which charges $15 for half a day ($25/day) for quality off-road machines. There's a handy bike path beside the road along the Spit.

Car rental is available at the airport from Hertz of Homer (ⓣ235-0734, ⓦwww.hertzofhomer.com), with rates from $63 with a hundred miles included, or from Polar Car Rental (ⓣ235-5998 or 1-800/876-6417), whose rates are fractionally cheaper.

Information

The town's **visitor center**, 201 Sterling Hwy (late May to early Sept Mon–Fri 9am–8pm, Sat & Sun 10am–6pm, early Sept to late May Mon–Fri 9am–5pm; ⓣ235-7740, ⓦwww.homeralaska.org), is the place to pick up free advertising-laden magazines, consult with the knowledgeable staff, and make reservations on their free-phone service. Homer is also the headquarters for the Alaska Maritime National Wildlife Refuge, a vast tract of Alaska covering large sections of the Alaska Peninsula, the Aleutian Islands, and the Pribilof Islands, that was set up mainly to protect seabirds – all 40 million of them. Although none of the refuge is particularly close to Homer, the refuge runs the brand-new **Islands & Ocean Visitor Center**, 95 Sterling Hwy (late May to early Sept daily 9am–6pm, plus limited winter hours; ⓣ235-6961, ⓦwww.islandsandocean.org), designed to showcase various facets of the refuge through interactive exhibits, replica seabird cliffs, and displays on the work of biologists in remote locations, all approached through a foyer designed to resemble an intertidal zone. Throughout the summer they also run free hour-long guided **birding walks** (late May to early Sept variable days) and free tide-pooling beach walks along Bishop's Beach on days which have the lowest tides: dates are posted at the visitor center.

Accommodation

Accommodation in and around Homer is about as diverse as you'll find in Alaska, with camping on the beach, excellent B&Bs boasting spectacular views of the Kenai Mountains, waterside cabins in Kachemak Bay State Park, and even some exclusive lodges just half an hour away by water taxi. For B&Bs and hotels, **reservations** are essential during July and worthwhile a month on either side.

For many, the quintessential place to stay in Homer is on the **Spit**, either in one of several RV parks that line the main road or in the tent sites with the "Spit Rats," seasonal workers who live in makeshift tents all summer long. Sitting around a driftwood fire as the sun dips below the horizon around 10pm is one of the pleasures of time spent in Homer; getting nearly blown off the beach in heavy rain is not.

In addition to places listed in the camping section, tenters and RV drivers should check out the *Driftwood Inn*, and hostellers might also consider the *Sunspin Guesthouse*. It is also worth looking at the accommodation around Kachemak Bay (in our account starting on p.271): although the location may not be good for exploring Homer, the bay may form a large component of your time in the area.

Hotels, motels, and B&Bs

Driftwood Inn 135 W Bunnell Ave ⓣ 235-8019 or 1-800/478-8019, ⓦwww.thedriftwoodinn.com. Characterful, beach-front hotel, with a wide range of rooms, from smallish shared-bath rooms to "ship's quarters" rooms with a nautical feel. There's also an on-site RV park with full hookup ($26) as well as plenty of space for cleaning fish and then cooking them up on the sunny deck. Private bath ❹–❺, shared bath ❸

Good Karma Inn 57480 Clover Ave, 5 miles east ⓣ1-866/435-2762, ⓦwww.goodkarmainn.com. Modern Scandinavian-style log-house with fabulous glacier views and comfortable, tastefully furnished en-suite rooms, all with TV, VCR and local artwork adorning the walls. A hearty, self-serve continental breakfast sets you up for the day, and there's a barbecue to cook your catch and freezer space for what's left. ❻

Kiana B&B Mile 5 East End Rd ⓣ235-8824, ⓦwww.akms.com/kiana. Very hospitable B&B occupying the upper floor of a modern house with great views from the guest lounge and some rooms. There's also a great little cabin out the back, a hot tub under the stars, and a full continental breakfast. En suite ❺, private bath ❹

Land's End Resort 4786 Homer Spit Rd ⓣ235-0400 or 1-800/478-0400, ⓦwww.lands-end-resort.com. It is all about location here at the end of Homer Spit, an incomparable spot that means there's little point going for a landside room. Opt for the comfortable bayside rooms, which all have a small deck, full bath, and TV. Guests have access to a lap pool, small gym, and beachside hot tub, plus there's a restaurant and bar. Sea-view suites ❽, sea-view rooms ❻, land-view rooms ❺

Magic Canyon Ranch Mile 5.5 East End Rd ⓣ235-6077, ⓦwww.magiccanyonranch.com. Welcoming B&B surrounded by peaceful countryside (with llamas) and great Kachemak Bay views. Rooms are quite comfortable and tastefully decorated, all having en-suite or semi-private bathrooms. The Glacier View Suite, with its antique four-poster, clawfoot bath and good view of Grewingk Glacier, is the best of the lot. Breakfasts to remember. Suite ❺, rooms ❹

Old Town B&B 106 W Bunnell Ave ⓣ235-7558, ⓦwww.xyz.net/~oldtown. Beautiful, three-room B&B in a 1936 building in the oldest part of Homer. The rooms have wooden floors and a restrained decor of antiques, quilted bed covers, and old-fashioned bathroom fittings; two have tremendous sea views (one with a private bathroom; ❹). All are reached by a seriously crooked staircase. Breakfast is at the *Two Sisters* bakery down the street. ❸

Sunspin Guesthouse 358 E Lee Drive ⓣ235-6677 or 1-800/391-6677, ⓦwww.sunspin.com. Large B&B in a spacious hillside house offering a shared bunkroom ($35 per person), shared-bath private rooms (❸), and considerably more appealing rooms with private bath (❹). There's a large deck with a barbecue for guest use, and rates include airport or ferry pickup, plus a large breakfast.

Hostels and camping

Homer Hostel 304 Pioneer Ave ⓣ235-1463, ⓦwww.homerhostel.com. Convenient, centrally located hostel in a converted home where you sleep in comfy doubles or made-up beds and bunks ($22) in 4- to 6-bed dorms and relax in a big TV lounge with a great view of the mountains. There's no curfew or lockout, and bikes and fishing rods can be rented for $10 and $5 a day respectively. Rooms ❷

Homer Spit Camping ⓣ235-1583. Several locations, mostly along the western shore of the Spit with spots on the beach (mostly tents) and round the fishing hole (mostly RVs). Within a short walk of each site, you'll find drinking water, toilets, and fish-cleaning tables – dump stations are also nearby. Fees of $6 for tents and $10 for RVs are payable at the office by the fishing hole. Rules forbid late-night rowdiness, generator use, and homemade tents – though "Spit Rats" add extensions of driftwood and blue-plastic tarps all the same.

Karen Hornaday Hillside Campground Campground Rd ⓣ235-1583. Wooded sites (some with views) on the slopes above Homer and away from the bustle of the Spit. The campground has potable water, toilets, picnic tables, and fire rings on hand, but no hookups or showers. Tents $6, RVs $10.

Seaside Farm Hostel Mile 5 East End Rd ⓣ235-7850, ⓦwww.xyz.net/~seaside. One of the best hostels in Alaska, set on a small farm that runs down to the shores of Kachemak Bay. Dorms (bunks $15) are in the main house, which makes the best of the long summer days by having a large outdoor cooking and lounge area. There are rooms in a farmhouse ($40) and several cabins ($55), including the cozy, almost waterside Sea Shell Cabin, which has a small deck. There's even camping ($6 per tent plus $3 per shower), with the use of an outside kitchen area. May–Sept. ❶

The Town

Apart from the new **Islands & Ocean Visitor Center** (see opposite), the only real sight in town is the **Pratt Museum of Homer**, 3779 Bartlett St (mid-May to mid-Sept daily 10am–6pm; mid-Sept to mid-May Tues–Sun noon–5pm; $6; ⓦwww.prattmuseum.org), a highly informative and well-presented trawl through local and natural history – mounted examples of sea mammals, tide pools, the handiwork of the peninsula's Native peoples – with special attention to major issues of recent years. For example, one room is devoted to the *Exxon Valdez* oil spill, where you can hear the deadpan communication between Captain Hazelwood and the US Coast Guard immediately after the ship struck the Bligh Reef and listen to the reaction of members of the region's Native communities to the mess. Elsewhere there's material on the **spruce bark beetle**, which has ravaged the Kenai Peninsula's forests in recent years, and discussion of the economically devastating crash in king crab and shrimp stocks since the late 1980s. One of the best sections covers Kachemak birdlife, particularly that of **Gull Island** (see p.273), which is equipped with a remote-controlled camera giving unsurpassable close-ups of nesting glaucous-winged gulls, murres, puffins, and cormorants. Buttons allow you to pan and zoom in on whichever birds attract your attention. Outside, a **homesteaders' cabin** hosts old-timers telling tales of bygone days. The museum also runs hour-long **walking tours** of the Spit (June–Sept Thurs–Sat 3pm; $5) starting by the *Salty Dawg Saloon*.

Elsewhere, the work of Homer's community of artists, potters, sculptors, and craftspeople fills numerous **galleries**. Pick up the free *Downtown Homer Art Galleries* leaflet and choose from such long-standing favorites as the non-profit Bunnell Street Gallery, 106 W Bunnell St (Ⓣ235-2662, Ⓦwww.xyz.net/~bunnell/), which exhibits work by a changing roster of cutting-edge artists, and Ptarmigan Arts, 471 Pioneer Ave (Ⓣ235-5345, Ⓦwww.ptarmiganarts.com), which takes a more commercial and craft-oriented approach, often with artists in residence.

With your own transport, it is also worth taking a drive five miles from downtown up E Hill Road to Skyline Drive, which runs along the top of a series of bluffs a thousand feet above town. The views across the glistening waters of the bay to the glaciers and mountains beyond can be tremendous, but even when clouds are low it is worth calling in at the **Carl E Wynn Nature Center**, E Skyline Drive (mid-June to early Sept daily 10am–6pm; $5; Ⓦwww.akcoastalstudies.org). Here, the Center for Alaskan Coastal Studies has gone to considerable lengths to interpret the local flora and fauna, both through displays in their small visitor center and outside along gentle and well-formed trails, wildflower meadows, and spruce forests. To appreciate more of the mushrooms, lichens, and mosses, or learn to identify the animal tracks you come across, join one of the naturalist-led **tours** (10am, noon, 2pm & 4pm).

Further afield, you might fancy a slice of pie at the board-floored **Fritz Creek General Store**, Mile 8, E End Rd, a great little piece of living Alaskana. It is a general store in the truest sense of the word, complete with post office with ancient private boxes, video rental joint, liquor store, gas station, general community meeting place, and a café, which serves pizza slices and espresso, in addition to their excellent fresh fruit pie.

Homer Spit

Homer's defining feature is the **Spit**, a narrow bank of gravel that runs for over four miles out into Kachemak Bay almost cutting off the inner bay from Cook Inlet. For a place that is one of Alaska's most powerful tourist magnets, it is oddly ugly: the shimmer of the water is often outdone by the sheet-metal glare of hundreds of RVs, the snowy mountains have to compete with the rusting machinery of a working port, and large gravel areas are likely to be stacked high with logs, felled after falling victim to the spruce bark beetle.

Nonetheless, it has become activity-central for Kachemak Bay: this is where you'll come to catch ferries to Seldovia or Halibut Cove, and to organize day cruises, halibut-fishing trips, and kayak rentals (all covered in our Kachemak Bay

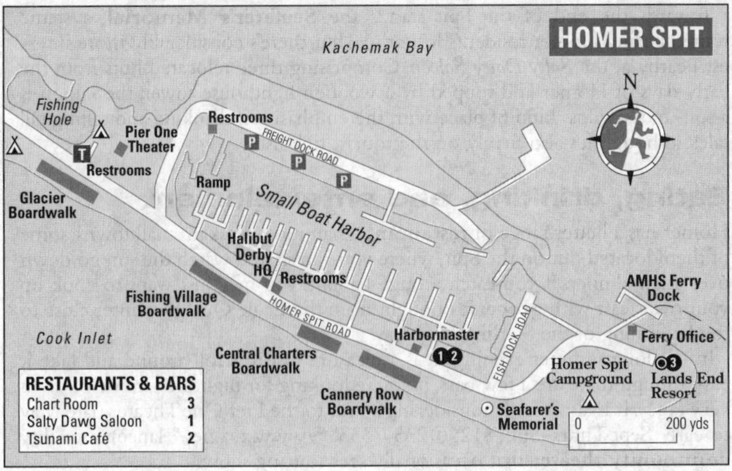

account starting on p.271). Charter-company offices, fishing-tackle shops, espresso bars, restaurants, and small fish-processing operations are arranged in a series of short rows raised off the beach on pilings and linked by boardwalks. You can spend a good part of the day wandering around here, though there are no real sights. Perhaps the biggest lure is the **Fishing Hole** (mid-May to mid-Sept), a small man-made harbor stocked with hatchery-raised salmon, which return here to spawn and find nowhere to go. Visitors stand cheek by jowl hoping to land one of the late-run kings (late July to early Aug), known to have topped sixty pounds (but average half that), or smaller pinks and silvers. Fish the incoming tide as if it were a river, or relax on the beach and try a bobber and bait.

Hiking and biking around Homer

The most exalted hikes hereabouts are those in the Kachemak Bay State Park on the south side of Kachemak Bay, but if you just want a good walk and don't fancy paying $50 just to get to the trailhead, there are a couple of moderately interesting hikes right on the doorstep. Starting at the eastern end of Bunnell Avenue the **Beluga Slough Trail** (200yd) runs along a boardwalk beside some wetlands, then continues with the **Bishop Beach Trail** (as long as you want to make it), which heads north along the beach and is best done at low tide when hiking is easier and tide pools more numerous. The beach is passable for around eleven miles, with good sea views all the way, a popular spot for sea otters to raft up offshore after three miles, and highway access at seven miles.

The visitor center has free leaflets detailing how to access the **Homestead Trail** (6.7 miles one-way; 3hr), a route mostly on car-free dirt roads that link Roger's Loop Road to Skyline Drive near the Bridge Creek Reservoir. You gain height quickly and get great views to the west and south, but it is a fairly long walk and you may have to do it twice unless you can talk someone into driving your car to the end trailhead.

A **bicycle** is an ideal way to get around Homer, and you can challenge those thigh muscles riding up to the bluff-crest Skyline Drive, which is relatively flat once you get up there. There is no biking in the Kachemak Bay State Park, but you can take your machine over to Seldovia or Jakolof Bay and ride to Red Mountain Valley (15 miles round-trip; 3hr; 1200ft ascent), an old mining area.

Towards the end of the Spit stands the **Seafarer's Memorial**, a statue remembering Homer residents lost at sea, but there's considerably more interest nearby at the *Salty Dawg Saloon*. Comprising three relocated huts from the early days of Homer and topped by a wooden lighthouse tower, the saloon is a spit-and-sawdust kind of place with the emphasis on drinking and telling tall tales, although it's also firmly on the tourist tick list.

Eating, drinking, and entertainment

Homer has a better range of **restaurants** than most Alaskan small towns, some of them located out on the Spit, where you can sit and watch the sun go down over a late dinner. If you catch a huge halibut, you may just want to cook up your own feast with **groceries** bought from the Eagle Quality Center close to the beginning of the Sterling Highway.

In the long summer evenings it is a pleasure just to stroll around and take it easy, though there are a few bars, if you're looking for nightlife – none of them very fancy. It is also worth considering a visit to the Pier One Theater (late May to early Sept Thurs–Sun; $12; ⓣ235-7333, ⓦwww.xyz.net/~lance), a quality **community theater** that occasionally sees touring shows.

Downtown and around

Alice's Champagne Palace 195 Pioneer Ave ⓣ235-0630. Neither a palace, nor known for its bubbles, except in the form of good beer served in a fun, dark bar, where bands frequently play between nights of DJs and karaoke.

Bayside Lounge 453 Pioneer Ave ⓣ235-9921. Straightforward boozing bar with a pool table and good jukebox.

Café Cups 162 Pioneer Ave ⓣ235-8330. Justly popular licensed restaurant, unmissable with its huge sculpted cups above the door, good for lunch or dinner inside or on the small deck. Come during the day for their Cosmic Halibut sandwich ($8.50), and later for a tofu coconut curry ($16), or perhaps breaded prawns with a honey habanero dip ($18).

Cosmic Kitchen 510 Pioneer Ave ⓣ235-6355. Budget eat-in and takeout joint specializing in Mexican dishes (burritos $5–9), burgers ($5–7), and breakfasts. Try the fajita omelet ($7.50) and an espresso.

Fat Olive's 276 Olsen Lane ⓣ235-3448. Chic modern Italian-ish restaurant in a former bus garage, suitably funked up with corrugated iron sheeting and a lively color scheme. Kick off with roasted sweet garlic ($8) or a beef tenderloin salad ($12) and follow with an excellent gourmet pizza ($14–20; also sold to take away under the name *Fat Rack Pizza*). There's also a good selection of microbrews and a convivial atmosphere.

The Homestead Mile 8.2 East Rd ⓣ235-8723. One of Homer's top restaurants, open nightly for dinner, which might be crab-and-shrimp cakes ($13) followed by Mediterranean pasta ($20), half a pound of king crab ($23), sautéed scallops ($21), or something from the extensive specials board.

Sourdough Express 1316 Ocean Drive ⓣ235-7571. Excellent on-site bakery and restaurant justly noted for its down-home breakfasts ($5–7), buffalo and falafel burgers ($9), and salmon and halibut dinners ($18). Probably the best place to have lunch made up for your day out on the water.

Two Sisters Espresso/Bakery 233 E Bunnell Ave ⓣ235-2280. Great little spot for that morning coffee, either inside the bakery or at tables out on the small deck. Good, too, for pizza, soups, and quiches at moderate prices.

The Spit

Chart Room *Land's End Resort*, 4786 Homer Spit Rd ⓣ235-0400. Tasty, well-presented meals at reasonable prices come with great views of Kachemak Bay from the end of the Spit. Good-value breakfasts (eggs Ben for $8.50), sandwiches and salad lunches, and dinners which might start with a seafood quesadilla ($11) and feature grilled halibut ($19) or rack of ribs ($20).

Salty Dawg Saloon Homer Spit Rd. No self-respecting drinker should pass up a few jars in the *Dawg*, with its dark interior, life-preserver vests pinned to the wall, and what is reliably claimed to be the only surveyors' benchmark located in a bar in the US.

Tsunami Café 4460 Homer Spit Rd. Diminutive restaurant with tables outside by the small boat harbor serving delicious dishes at modest prices. Closed Wed.

Listings

Banks Branches of the Wells Fargo at 203 Pioneer Ave and 4014 Lake St; and First National Bank on the Homer Bypass at Heath St: all with 24hr ATMs.
Bookshop Homer Bookstore, 332 Pioneer Ave (Mon–Sat 10am–7pm, Sun noon–5pm). A good selection of books, plus espresso.
Festivals The Kachemak Bay Shorebird Festival (Ⓣ235-7337), over the first weekend of May, coincides with the Wooden Boat Festival, but they are really only worth the journey if you're a keen birder. The last week of May sees the Kachemak Kayak Fest (Ⓣ235-7740, Ⓦwww.kachemakkayakfest.com), with workshops, demos, instruction, and guided trips.
Horseback Riding Trails End Horse Adventures, Mile 11.2 E End Rd (Ⓣ235-6393), has horseback rides ($20/hour, $65/4hr and $110/day) along the river flats and the shores of Kachemak Bay.
Internet access There's free email at the library in half-hour blocks; for pay access go to Tech Connect, 432 Pioneer Ave (Ⓣ235-5298).
Laundry Washboard Laundromat, 1204 Ocean Drive (Ⓣ235-8586), has laundry and showers.
Library The Homer Public Library, 141 Pioneer Ave (Tues & Thurs 10am–8pm, Wed, Fri & Sat 10am–6pm; Ⓣ235-3180, Ⓦlibrary.ci.homer.ak.us).
Medical assistance South Peninsula Hospital, 4300 Bartlett St Ⓣ235-8101.
Post office on Sterling Hwy at Lake St. The **General Delivery** zip code is 99603.
Taxi Kache Cab Ⓣ235-1950.

Around Homer: Kachemak Bay

Even tourists on a busy schedule often spend a week around Homer, not so much for what the town offers, but for its access to wonderful country nearby. Most people's focus is **Kachemak Bay**, a forty-mile-long and eight-mile-wide tongue of water with a southern shore that has been carved by the glaciers that still peel off the Kenai Mountains behind.

Kachemak Bay is almost divided in two by the Homer Spit, its central position and deep harbor making it the nerve center for activities around the bay and a staging point for day cruises, ferries, and water taxis. Boats crossing the bay almost always spend a few minutes bobbing around in the waters off **Gull Island**, a guano-encrusted rock three miles off the tip of the Spit that is typically alive with up to sixteen thousand squawking, screeching seabirds: glaucous-winged gulls, black-legged kittiwakes, tufted puffins, and pelagic and red-faced cormorants, and perhaps common murres rafting up offshore ready to wing in and lay their eggs among the rocks. The boats get right up close to the steep cliffs, so you get a great view, aided by the binoculars many boats make available. The birds almost certainly appreciate the super-rich waters of the bay, something which is also dear to the hearts of anglers who have made Homer something of a **halibut-fishing** mecca.

The surrounding mountains give Kachemak Bay a relatively mild and dry climate with conditions further enhanced by the Homer Spit, which provides some protection from swells. Nonetheless, **kayakers** largely stick to the even more sheltered fjords of the **Kachemak Bay State Park**, which encompasses most of the southern shoreline and the hill country inland. Easy multiday trips are possible by making use of several free campsites along the shore and kayak-accessible cabins, which are also used by **hikers** (see box, p.273).

Just outside the state park lie the two most popular and highly picturesque destinations around Homer: **Halibut Cove**, with its tiny boardwalk community, art galleries, and *The Saltry* restaurant; and the larger **Seldovia**, a peaceful former herring-canning town where there is not a great deal to do, and that's just perfect.

Beyond the confines of Kachemak Bay, there's great bear watching over on the Katmai Coast: in fact, Homer is the closest road-accessible base for the state park, and bear viewing from here can be better value than visiting Katmai National Park (see p.332) via King Salmon.

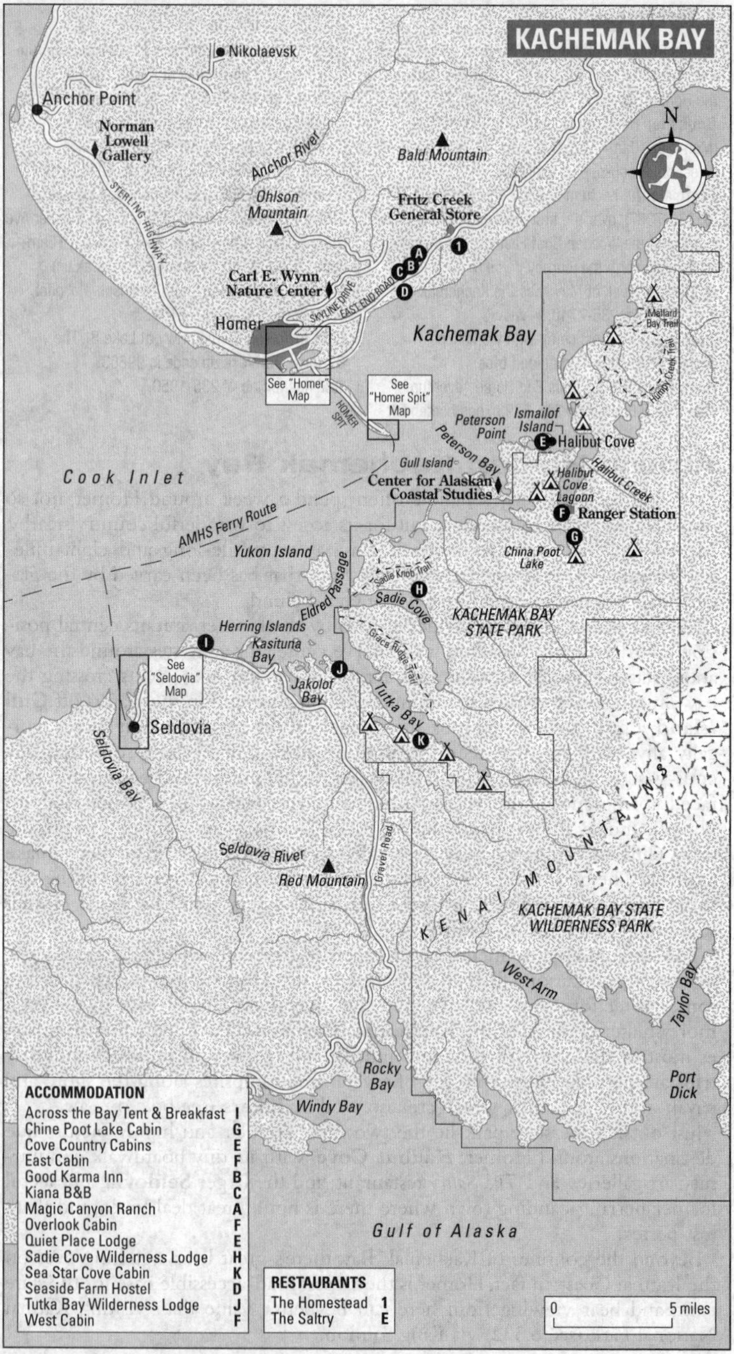
KACHEMAK BAY
Nikolaevsk
Anchor Point
Norman Lowell Gallery
Anchor River
Bald Mountain
STERLING HIGHWAY
Ohlson Mountain
Fritz Creek General Store
Carl E. Wynn Nature Center
SKYLINE DRIVE
EAST END ROAD
Homer
See "Homer" Map
See "Homer Spit" Map
HOMER SPIT
Kachemak Bay
Mallard Bay Trail
Humpy Creek Trail
Peterson Point
Ismailof Island
Halibut Cove
Peterson Bay
Gull Island
Center for Alaskan Coastal Studies
Halibut Cove Lagoon
Halibut Creek
Ranger Station
Cook Inlet
AMHS Ferry Route
Kodiak & Seward
Yukon Island
China Poot Lake
Sadie Knob Trail
Eldred Passage
Sadie Cove
KACHEMAK BAY STATE PARK
Herring Islands
Kasitsna Bay
Grace Ridge Trail
See "Seldovia" Map
Jakolof Bay
Tutka Bay
Seldovia
Seldovia Bay
KENAI MOUNTAINS
Seldovia River
Red Mountain
Gravel Road
KACHEMAK BAY STATE WILDERNESS PARK
West Arm
Taylor Bay
Rocky Bay
Port Dick
Windy Bay
Gulf of Alaska
N
0 5 miles
ACCOMMODATION
Across the Bay Tent & Breakfast I
Chine Poot Lake Cabin G
Cove Country Cabins E
East Cabin F
Good Karma Inn B
Kiana B&B C
Magic Canyon Ranch A
Overlook Cabin F
Quiet Place Lodge E
Sadie Cove Wilderness Lodge H
Sea Star Cove Cabin K
Seaside Farm Hostel D
Tutka Bay Wilderness Lodge J
West Cabin F
RESTAURANTS
The Homestead 1
The Saltry E

Hiking in Kachemak Bay State Park

The south side of Kachemak Bay has some wonderful hiking along a forty-mile series of interlinked trails, none penetrating far into the interior of the Kenai Mountains, but most providing access to shoreline walks, fishing streams, small lakes, seasonal berry picking, and the Grewingk Glacier. Those listed here are just a taster of the sixteen trails currently included on the *Kachemak Bay State Park Hiking Trails* leaflet ($2.50), which also pinpoints a dozen simple, trail-accessible **campsites** (first-come, first-served; no permits required; free) and five **cabins** ($50; sleeping 6–8), bookable through the website or the state park office (ⓣ269-8400, ⓦwww.alaskastateparks.org). There are three cabins at the head of Halibut Cove Lagoon (*Lagoon Overlook*, *Lagoon East*, and *Lagoon West*), the *China Poot Lake Cabin* is next to China Poot Lake, and the *Sea Star Cove Cabin* sits on the western shore of Tutka Bay.

Access is by water taxi (see below) and costs $45–60, depending on the distance between the Homer Spit and your destination.

Glacier Lake Trail (2.2 miles one-way; 1hr to 1hr 30min; negligible ascent). A very easy trail with good Grewingk Glacier views that links the Glacier Spit and Saddle trailheads and has a number of potential (longer) variations. The *Rusty's Lagoon Campsite* is close to the Glacier Spit trailhead.

Grewingk Glacier Trail (13 miles round-trip; 4–6hr; 500ft ascent). Easy and relatively flat trail with superb views of the glacier and surrounding area. Makes a good day trip from Homer – get dropped at Glacier Spit with an evening pickup at the Saddle Trailhead – though there are good campsites along the way.

Wosnesenski River Trail (11 miles one-way; 8–10hr; 300ft ascent). One of the longest hikes in the park and one of the most scenic, starting from the Haystack Trailhead in China Poot Bay and following a broad river valley through cottonwoods before climbing over a low ridge to a series of three lakes. It finishes at China Poot Lake, where there is a cabin and a choice of trails to reach Halibut Cove Lagoon.

Cruises and kayaking

The Homer Spit is packed with companies keen to get you out on the water. We've covered halibut fishing (p.274), transport to Halibut Cove (p.275), and Seldovia (p.276) separately, but there are also several cruises, some operated by companies that double as water taxis, as well as a handful of companies running guided paddling trips and renting kayaks. Most of the people offering trips operate through one of the small number of agencies along the boardwalks at the end of the Spit: the biggest is Central Charters (ⓣ235-7847 or 1-800/478-7847, ⓦwww.centralcharter.com).

The most visited spot in Kachemak Bay is **Gull Island**, which can be seen inexpensively on boat trips to Seldovia or Halibut Cove, or more thoroughly on a cruise run by St Augustine's Charters (2hr; $45; ⓣ235-6126).

Commit the whole day on the excellent-value Low Tide Tour and Coastal Forest Hike (7–8hr; $90) run by the nonprofit **Center for Alaskan Coastal Studies** (ⓣ235-6667, reservations through Jakolof Ferry Service ⓣ235-2376, ⓦwww.jakolofferryservice.com). The organization promotes appreciation and conservation of Kachemak Bay by broadening people's understanding of the marine and forest ecosystems with a visit to their field station in Peterson Bay. Here, you can explore the beaches and intertidal life, walk through the forest, or learn something of the local flora, fauna, and first peoples. You can even stay over in their dorm-style yurts for $15 a night.

There's greater intimacy with the surroundings when **kayaking**, best done with True North Kayak Adventures (ⓣ235-0708, ⓦwww.truenorthkayak.com),

Water taxis and bookings

Whether you are just going hiking for the day, spending time kayaking, or staying in one of the luxury lodges, you'll need to get from the Spit across to the southern shore of Kachemak Bay. For this you'll need a **water taxi**. Competition keeps the prices steady at around $50 per person round-trip to the closest bits of the Kachemak Bay State Park and roughly $60 for the more distant corners. Several companies can be booked through Central Charters, 4241 Homer Spit Rd (Ⓣ235-7847 or 1-800/478-7847, Ⓦwww.centralcharter.com), but two of the most active and reliable are Mako's Water Taxi (Ⓣ235-9055, Ⓦwww.makoswatertaxi.com) and Jakolof Ferry Service (Ⓣ235-2376, Ⓦwww.jakolofferryservice.com).

which makes a point of being ecologically sensitive. Their basic trip ($125) involves a water-taxi ride to their base across the bay on Yukon Island, followed by around six hours, paddling, including a break for a tasty lunch. For something more ambitious, go for the two-day Eldred Passage Overnight ($290) with extended paddling around Tutka Bay, Sadie Cove, and Eldred Passage (see p.276) and camping somewhere on a beach (save $40, if you have your own camping and cooking gear). Custom multiday wilderness expeditions cost around $325 for three days and $125 for each extra day. Experienced paddlers can **rent kayaks** (doubles $65, singles $45); those less sure of their abilities can join a one-day trip and head off solo afterwards. Similarly priced kayaking trips can be booked through Central Charters (see box above) and Seaside Adventures Ecotours (Ⓣ235-6672), both of which use water taxis to get you across the exposed Kachemak Bay and into the sheltered waters of the far shore.

Halibut fishing

The waters around Homer have become inextricably tied to halibut fishing. The very biggest ones aren't caught here, but a combination of good halibut waters close to town and the lucrative summer-long halibut derby have created enough of a buzz that it seems every RV driver wants an ice chest full of the succulent white flesh. Wander along the Spit in the late afternoon, and you'll see small groups of people lined up for photos behind the boat's catch of the day. Two-hundred-pound fish are relatively common, and three-hundred-pounders get landed each summer, but something in the twenty- to forty-pound range is more common. Even at this size it can be quite a strain reeling the thing in.

Every year there are sob stories about people who bagged a huge halibut that would have claimed a $50,000 jackpot prize in the annual **Halibut Derby** (May 1 to Labor Day; Ⓦwww.homerhalibutderby.com), but had failed to buy a derby ticket. With prizes for landing various tagged fish, as well as monthly prizes and an overall biggest-fish jackpot, you really should buy a $10 ticket from the Derby Headquarters (daily 5.30–8am & 3–7pm), a log cabin by Ramp 4 at the small boat harbor on the Spit.

Trips are typically all-day affairs with boats powering an hour or two out into the bay, then bobbing around for about six hours, with some anglers using herring to land their two-fish limit and (on rougher days) others hanging over the back laying down ground bait. The going rate is $150–175 depending on the season (mid-June to mid-Aug being the most expensive); add $25–30 if you also want to go after saltwater king salmon as they make their way towards the spawning streams. With all the charter companies located close to each other on the Spit it is worth spending a few minutes wandering around to get the best deals, asking about the size and speed of the boat, comfort, number of other customers, amount of fish cleaning and filleting they'll do, lunch, and so on.

There is really no need to book anything in advance, but you could try Homer Ocean Charters (Ⓣ235-6212 or 1-800/426-6212, Ⓦwww.homerocean.com), or Rainbow Tours (Ⓣ235-7272, Ⓦwww.rainbowtours.net), which does a half-day trip for $85.

Bear viewing

Homer makes a convenient starting point for bear-viewing trips to Katmai National Park (see p.332) and McNeil River State Game Sanctuary (see box, p.334), both on the Alaska Peninsula, around sixty to ninety minutes' floatplane flight away. From mid-May to September, there are always bears to be found somewhere, either clamming and grazing on sedge in the early season, or gorging themselves on salmon swimming up their spawning streams from July onwards. The air-charter companies always know the best spots. Trips typically cost $500–600 per person for a round-trip flight and around six hours on the ground viewing, and there's usually a two- or three-person minimum. Try Bald Mountain Air Service (Ⓣ235-7969 or 1-800/478-7969, Ⓦwww.baldmountainair.com), which charges upwards of $525, or the comparably priced trips run by Emerald Air Service (Ⓣ235-6993, Ⓦwww.emeraldairservice.com). For a cut-price deal, consider backtracking to Soldotna, home of Talon Air (Ⓣ262-8899, Ⓦwww.talonair.com), which sometimes has trips for under $300.

It is also possible to view bears from dedicated boat trips that give less bear-viewing time but combine the possibility of seeing sea mammals. If this tempts you, get in touch with Sea Bear Charters (Ⓣ235-0123, Ⓦwww.xyz.net/~seabear), which runs full-day trips in June and July for around $300 per person.

Halibut Cove

One of the most popular day trips from Homer is to the small private community of **HALIBUT COVE**, a gorgeous enclave of boardwalks, art galleries, a restaurant, and some accommodation (but no roads), on Ismailof Island, eight miles east of the tip of the Homer Spit on the southern shore of Kachemak Bay. The island was once the site of a herring industry, which peaked in the 1920s when there were over a thousand people here working 36 salteries. The community petered out to the point where there were just a few old bachelors left when, in the late 1940s, fisherman Clem Tillion and his artistic wife Diana were spellbound by the isolation and beauty and decided to stay. Their presence encouraged others to remain, and the community revived. By the late 1970s other artists began to arrive, and today with a hundred-strong population a creative tenor prevails.

It is hard not to be enchanted as you stroll the boardwalks, follow the paths through Sitka spruce forests, or just mooch around the three high-quality **art galleries**. Those who aren't buying tend to spend time at the only **restaurant**, *The Saltry* (late May to early Sept; reservations recommended Ⓣ296-2223), where you can sit on the deck on pilings over the water and dine on a bowl of clam chowder ($8.50), caramelized goat cheese salad ($10), or pesto halibut ($19), all washed down with wine or microbrews.

Almost everyone arrives direct from Homer on the *Danny J* (book through Central Charters, see opposite), a quaint old fishing boat that leaves from behind the *Salty Dawg Saloon* twice a day. One sailing leaves at noon (returns 5pm; $45 round-trip) and takes in Gull Island en route to Halibut Cove, where you get two and a half hours to have lunch and wander the boardwalks. The second, more direct, sailing is at 5pm (returns 10pm; $22), and you must have a dinner reservation or a room booked, but the savings on the price of this later boat journey just about pay for your dinner (typically $15–25). During the middle of summer, the press of visitors during the day can rob the place of some of its tranquility, something circumvented by **staying at Halibut Cove**. The cheapest option is the self-catering *Cove Country Cabins* (ⓣ296-2257, ⓦwww.xyz.net/~ctjones; ❹), which has no running water or indoor plumbing, though the cabins are perfectly decent. If you've got the budget, go for the *Quiet Place Lodge* (ⓣ235-1800, ⓦwww.quietplace.com; ❽), where you get a luxurious cabin, a sumptuous breakfast, and free use of their rowboats. They cook dinner four nights a week (around $30) or they'll take you across to *The Saltry*.

Ismailof Island sits in a body of water somewhat confusingly also known as Halibut Cove. The head of the cove is Halibut Cove Lagoon, part of Kachemak Bay State Park and a popular spot for the hiking trails that surround it and the three state park cabins – *West*, *East*, and *Overlook* – on its southern shore. Water taxis aren't allowed to run you to *The Saltry*, but they can bring you here (around $50 round-trip), dropping you at the trailhead close to the **Halibut Cove Lagoon Ranger Station**, which is staffed full time from late May to early September.

Sadie Cove, Tutka Bay, and Eldred Passage

Moving further southwest along the southern shores of Kachemak Bay, you'll pass **Peterson Bay** with its Center for Alaskan Coastal Studies field station, accessible on day cruises (see p.273). The wide mouth of the bay opens onto Gull Island, visited on just about every local cruise, and provides access to **China Poot Bay**, a sheltered spot for paddling and the starting point of some good hiking trails (see box, p.273). To get around to **Sadie Cove** and **Tutka Bay**, you have to pass through **Eldred Passage**, a broad channel with the mainland on one side and Cohen Island, Yukon Island, and Hesketh Island on the other. This is some of the most gorgeous paddling and cruising territory in Alaska with plenty of wildlife (especially sea otters, seals, and sea lions), steep beaches for camping, and even some caves around the high-tide line on the north shore of Yukon Island.

Exploring the region doesn't necessarily mean camping out. The state park maintains *Sea Star Cove Cabin* ($50) on the western shore of Tutka Bay, and there are a couple of **luxury lodges** only accessible by sea or float plane. The slightly cheaper of the two is the elegant yet rustic *Sadie Cove Wilderness Lodge* (ⓣ235-2350 or 1-888/283-7234, ⓦwww.sadiecove.com; ❾), where the nightly fee of $275 includes all meals, lodging in a private cabin, and use of fishing tackle and a kayak, but you'll have to pay for the water taxi to get here ($60 round-trip). You'll pay the same access cost and be required to stay a minimum of two nights at the *Tutka Bay Wilderness Lodge* (ⓣ235-3905 or 1-800/606-3909, ⓦwww.tutkabaylodge.com; ❾), which ranks as one of the finest wilderness lodges in Alaska, with comfortable cabins linked by a series of boardwalks in a beautiful setting. Plenty of beach walking, tide pooling, and fishing and sightseeing excursions are also available, all for $580 per person for a two-night stay, including all meals and assorted activities.

Just around the point from Tutka Bay is **Jakolof Bay**, which is linked by the only road on the south side of Kachemak Bay to Seldovia.

Seldovia

Although it's just fifteen miles across Kachemak Bay, **SELDOVIA** seems a world away from the bustle of Homer. This maze of peninsulas, waterways, lakes, and steeply raked beaches manages to balance seclusion and sophistication, with superb B&Bs and a couple of good places to eat ensuring that you're not deprived of civilization as you slow to the pace of the place. It is a tremendously picturesque spot, draped around its small boat harbor with snow-clad mountains behind, a view of Redoubt and Iliamna volcanoes across the bay and a few vestiges of the boardwalks that once made the place famous. In the quaintest section, brightly painted houses are artistically perched on pilings over the slough and when the weather plays ball there's nothing better to do than sit on the boardwalk trying to spot sea otters, or lean over the rails of the bridge coaxing a salmon onto your hook.

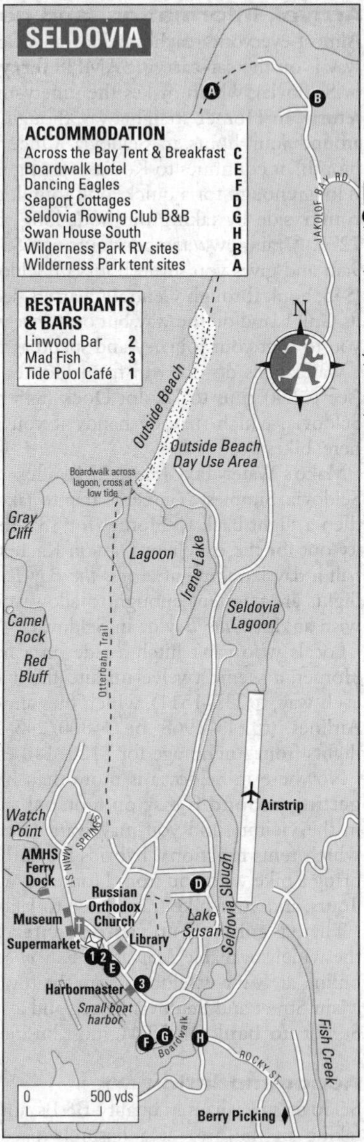

This is the oldest port on Kachemak Bay, and was named Zaliv Seldovoy, or Herring Bay, by a Russian captain in 1852. Initially, the trade was in sea-otter pelts, but the eponymous herrings soon had their day and several canneries sprang up during the 1920s when many Scandinavians came here, staying on to fish for salmon, halibut, and crab over the next forty years. Wooden boardwalks along the waterfront were built during this time to facilitate travel between the dozens of buildings built on pilings. With the closure of most of the canneries, Seldovia went into decline, something hastened by the 1964 earthquake, which dropped the land around here by 4ft and destroyed much of the town. A new town was created on landfill, and although only short sections of the boardwalk survived, much of the character was retained.

If you're in the vicinity around June 21, consider making it here for the **Seldovia Summer Solstice Music Festival** (Ⓣ234-7614), an intimate affair costing $15 a day, $25 for both days.

Arrival, information, and getting around

Almost everyone reaches Seldovia by boat or plane from Homer. The cheapest way is on the car-carrying AMHS **ferry** *Tustumena* ($27 each way; ⓣ234-7868 in Seldovia), which makes the ninety-minute crossing twice a week. It usually returns to Homer straightaway, though in summer the Tuesday run gives you around four hours in Seldovia. Once a month (usually second Tues of the month), it continues to Kodiak, staying in Seldovia for a couple of hours, which is long enough for a quick look round. You'll see a lot more of the surrounding countryside by taking the hour-long shuttle run by Rainbow Tours (ⓣ235-7272, ⓔrainbow@rainbowtours.net; $35 round-trip), which leaves Homer at 9am and gives you seven hours in Seldovia. Alternatively, go with the *Discovery* ($45; book through Central Charters, see p.274), which leaves at 11am and visits Gull Island on the way, but only gives you three hours in Seldovia. Both allow you to split your journey and spend as many nights as you wish in Seldovia.

Water taxis do not run from Homer to Seldovia, but Jakolof Ferry Service (see p.274) runs to Jakolof Dock ($45 round-trip), twelve miles by road from Seldovia, which may be handy if you are planning to do some cycling over here: bikes go free.

Mako's Water Taxi (see p.274) offers a couple of ways to see something of Seldovia. Simplest is a scenic trip to Jakolof Bay, a taxi to Seldovia, lunch there, then a flight back to Homer for $85, though if you fancy some aquatic activity opt for the excellent Day on Kachemak Bay combo ($165), which adds in half a day kayaking at *Across the Bay Tent & Breakfast* (see opposite). Boats and flights are frequent enough to allow you to tailor your stay for as long as you wish at *Across the Bay* or in Seldovia.

Locals who can't hitch a ride on a neighbor's fishing boat usually **fly** from Homer, a scenic twelve-minute flight best done with Smokey Bay Air ($28 each way; ⓣ235-1511), which flies almost hourly in summer. Great Northern Airlines (ⓣ243-1968 or 1-800/243-1968, ⓦwww.gnair.com) runs direct flights from Anchorage for $120–140 each way.

Nowhere in Seldovia is more than half a mile from the dock or airstrip, so **getting around** is easy on foot, but there are dozens of miles of gravel roads in the vicinity, and you may want to **rent a bike** from Main Street Market, which rents functional hybrids for $10 an hour ($40 overnight). Alternatively, bring a bike with you from Homer: it will cost you $5 each way with Rainbow Tours, and your bike travels free to Jakolof Bay with Jakolof Ferry Service.

There is currently no **visitor center**, but everything you need to know is on the widely available *Map of the City of Seldovia* leaflet, and you can check it out online at ⓦwww.seldovia.com. In town you'll find a **post office**, corner of Main Street and Seldovia Street, and a sporadically open **library**, 260 Seldovia St, but **no bank or ATM**: most businesses accept credit cards.

Accommodation

Seldovia specializes in quality B&Bs, and staying at one sets the perfect tone for taking in the area at a leisurely pace. There's great **camping**, too, at the *Wilderness Park*, Mile 1.5 Jakolof Bay Rd, where RVs get sites ($8) among the trees. Tent campers are better off at tent sites ($5) scattered along the foreshore a quarter-mile from the RV sites. You'll find pump water and outhouses near the RV sites, and the nearest **showers** are at Sweet-n-Clean Laundry, 226 Main St (daily 11am–8pm; $5 including towel and soap). Before heading out to camp, register and pay at the City Office, 346 Dock St (ⓣ234-7643) by the state ferry dock. The 6.5 percent local tax has been included in our price codes.

Across the Bay Tent & Breakfast Kasitsna Bay, Mile 8 Jakolof Bay Rd May–Sept ⓣ235-3633, Oct–April ⓣ345-2571, ⓦwww.tentandbreakfastalaska.com. A collection of canvas-walled platform tents (with fresh flowers, hot showers, pit toilets, and a wood-fired sauna) beside the beach eight miles east of Seldovia that is a great place to hang out for a while, perhaps taking a guided sea-kayaking trip ($95), or doing a little bike riding (rentals $25 a day). Get a water taxi from Homer to Jakolof Dock (roughly $45 round-trip) or a boat to Seldovia. They charge $63 per person for tent and breakfast, or $95 if you also want them to provide their excellent seafood-based meals. Everyone chips in with the evening entertainment. Bring a sleeping bag. ❺

Boardwalk Hotel Main St ⓣ234-7816 or 1-800/238-7862, ⓦwww.alaskaone.com/boardwalkhotel. Seldovia's main hotel has only fourteen rooms, many with great harbor views. There are savings to be made by taking either the One-Night Package (from $129), which includes a cruise over and a scenic flight back to Homer, or the Two-Night Kayak Special (from $279), adding a day of kayaking and an extra night at the hotel. Deluxe ❻, sea view ❺, town view ❹

Dancing Eagles ⓣ234-7627, ⓦwww.dancingeagles.com. Superbly sited B&B, perched on rocks right above the water. The rooms (shared-bath) in the lodge are great value, but the real star is the fully self-contained "cabin" with fabulous views and enough room for six ($50 extra per person). A breakfast basket is provided to either take to your room or eat on the secluded deck. Cabin ❼, rooms ❺

Seaport Cottages 313 Shoreline Drive ⓣ234-7483, ⓦwww.xyz.net/~chap. A little cluster of ageing, but attractive and well-priced, fully self-contained cottages that are perfect for longer stays, plus one that's great for families. Although there are no sea views, it's a short walk to the harbor, and you can explore using the free bikes. Suite sleeping five ❺, cottages ❸

Seldovia Rowing Club B&B The Boardwalk ⓣ234-7614, ⓦwww.ptialaska.net/~rowing. Floral rooms in a friendly boardwalk B&B, built on stilts and overlooking the slough. Just two suites, each with sitting room, deck, and private bath, plus a huge gourmet breakfast. ❺

Swan House South ⓣ234-8888 or 1-800/921-1900, ⓦwww.alaskaswanhouse.com. Large and spacious B&B featuring a beautiful deck with great views of the slough and Mount Iliamna. The interior is light and airy, rooms come with all the comforts, and a substantial breakfast is served up on cue. Luxury is taken to the next level in the suites, which also get a VCR and free use of mountain bikes. Suites ❽, rooms ❼

The Town

Seldovia is ideally suited for hanging out: strolling around the harbor, stopping somewhere for coffee, and browsing some of the better-than-average craft shops. Easily the most scenic section is along what's left of the **original boardwalks** at the southern end of Main Street, where you can walk the plank streets high above the water past wonderfully picturesque, brightly painted houses perched on stilts over the slough.

Late July to mid-September is berry-picking time, and the best hunting ground for the abundant salmonberries and blueberries, as well as cranberries, mossberries, and lowbush cranberries, is along Rocky Road to the south of town. Labor Day weekend marks the **Blueberry Festival** when everyone scours the hills and fills their baskets with rich fruit. Either pick on Jakolof Road or get a permit from the Seldovia Native Association.

Saint Nicholas Russian Orthodox Church is Seldovia's only traditional sight, idyllically set on a knoll above the harbor. It was built in 1891, and restored ninety years later, but is usually closed. At the foot of the knoll, there's the **Alaska Tribal Cache Museum**, Main Street (June–Aug Mon–Sat 10am–6pm, Sun 11am–5pm; free), which contains a tiny assortment of ivory, a whalebone bowl, and a samovar, but most of all is a good spot to buy homemade berry jam.

If you're looking to do some light exercise, follow Main Street and duck up Spring Street to the start of the **Otterbahn Trail** (1.5 miles one-way; 1hr; 100ft ascent), a track through the coastal forest and over lagoon boardwalks diligently carved out by local high school students. It reaches Kachemak Bay at a steeply shelving, diminutive beach, then rounds a headland to **Outside**

Beach, reached by crossing a tidal slough which may be impassable at high tide (or require some wading). Check the tide tables at the Harbormaster office or on a board by the trailhead. Outside Beach has a day-use area and can also be easily reached by road (see map, p.277). For something more vigorous, try the **Rocky Ridge Trail** (2.5-mile loop; 2–3hr; 800ft ascent), which is steep in places and slick underfoot but rewards with great views over the town and across Cook Inlet to Mount Iliamna. The trailhead is half a mile east of town along Rocky Street.

Outdoor activities

With miles of protected bays, coves, and islands to explore, especially around Eldred Passage, Sadie Cove, and Tutka Bay, **kayaking** from Seldovia is something not to be missed. Kayak'atak (Ⓣ234-7425, Ⓦwww.alaska.net/~kayaks) runs guided day trips (3hr for $80, 5hr for $120), as well as overnight outings ($180 each, discounts for three or more) for which you'll need your own sleeping bag and rain gear. Departures are designed with the ferry schedules in mind. More confident paddlers can rent kayaks at $50 for a single and $75 for a double ($30 and $50 respectively for second and subsequent days).

With several miles of former logging roads, **mountain biking** is great, either with a bike rented here or one brought over from Homer. The road to Jakolof continues south to the Gulf of Alaska coast via **Red Mountain**, a huge lump of chromium ore that was once mined and is now cloaked in stunted vegetation – rather than the huge trees found elsewhere. It is about 35 miles to the end of the road, and while it can be done in a long Alaskan day an overnight trip is better. Before you go, ask about local conditions and obtain a permit ($1 a day; $10 per season) from the SNA office at 328 Main St (Ⓣ234-7625).

For a little **fishing**, consider a full-day halibut trip with Mad Viking Charters ($175; Ⓣ234-7838), or just hang off the bridge over the slough where there is always something running after mid-May: consult the sport fishing regulations posted at the head of the gangway to the boat harbor.

Eating and drinking

With all the day trippers (and a fair number of overnight visitors) Seldovia's **eating** scene has boomed in recent years. The pick for good espresso, breakfast, and lunch is *The Tide Pool Café*, 267 Main St (Ⓣ234-7502), which does an excellent Santa Fe chicken salad ($10), plus a marinated steak with chilies wrap ($11), and fish and chips ($11) – all served on a deck that's almost overhanging the harbor, or inside among sea fans, starfish, and shells. Moving upscale, the *Mad Fish Restaurant* (Ⓣ234-7676; closed Mon) is a great place to watch harbor life go by while savoring roasted garlic, white bean, and sun-dried tomato dip ($7) or Szechwan seafood noodle salad ($14.50), followed perhaps by local salmon in a delicate ginger orange sauce ($18). They make great desserts, too. For **groceries**, head along Main Street to *Main Street Market*, which has fairly limited supplies.

Long sunny evenings in Seldovia can be beautiful, and when you tire of fabulous scenery there's always the dark interior of the *Linwood* **bar**, 257 Main St.

Travel details

Trains

Seward to: Anchorage (daily; 4hr 20min).

Buses

Girdwood to: Anchorage (3 daily; 1hr 15min); Seward (2 daily; 2hr).
Homer to: Anchorage (1 daily; 5–6hr); Ninilchik (1–2 daily; 1hr); Seward (1 Mon–Fri; 4–5hr); Soldotna (6–9 weekly; 1hr 30min).
Ninilchik to: Anchorage (1 daily; 4hr); Homer (1–2 daily; 1hr).
Seward to: Anchorage (2 daily; 3–4hr); Girdwood (2 daily; 2hr); Homer (1 Mon–Fri; 4–5hr).
Soldotna to: Anchorage (1 daily; 3hr 30min); Homer (3–6 weekly; 1hr 30min).

Ferries

Homer to: Kodiak (2–3 weekly; 9hr 30min); Port Lions (weekly; 10hr); Seldovia (2 weekly; 1hr 30min); Seward (1 weekly; 9–10hr).
Seldovia to: Homer (2 weekly; 1hr 30min).
Seward to: Juneau (1–2 monthly; 50hr); Kodiak (weekly; 13hr 15min); Valdez (weekly; 11hr).

Flights

Homer to: Anchorage (4–6 daily; 50min); Seldovia (several daily; 12min).
Kenai to: Anchorage (14–18 daily; 25min).
Seldovia to: Anchorage (4 weekly; 1hr 15min); Homer (several daily; 12min).

4

Prince William Sound

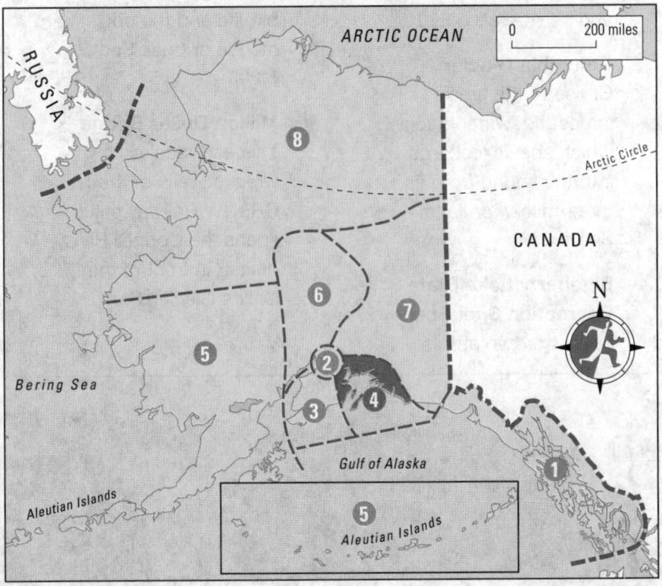

CHAPTER 4

Highlights

* **Whittier** More a curiosity than a highlight, this long-isolated town provides an excellent base for kayaking. See p.289

* **Kayaking the sound** Paddle in front of calving glaciers, camping on remote beaches and staying alert for whales and seals. See p.290

* **Columbia Glacier** Cruise to the area's largest tidewater glacier, which spews icebergs into the sound from its three-mile-wide face. See p.298

* **Blueberry Lake State Recreation Site.** Spend a night or two at this ridgeline campground, amid the jagged, snowy peaks of the Chugach Mountains. See p.302

* **Copper River Delta** Drive the Copper River Highway through this gorgeous network of ponds, sloughs, and wetlands, alive with birdlife and the odd moose or bear. See p.308

* **Million Dollar Bridge** This earthquake-wrecked relic of the CR&NW Railway still spans the Copper River, defiant in front of the Childs Glacier. See p.309

△ Whales in Frederick Sound

4

Prince William Sound

If you've come to Alaska hoping to see huge chunks of ice crashing into deep fjords where harbor seals loll on icebergs and mountain goats dot the hillsides, then **PRINCE WILLIAM SOUND** is the place for you. It's the perfect place for sea kayaking: bobbing around the face of tidewater glaciers while scanning the horizon for breaching whales, you'll quickly understand why it's hard to surpass these sheltered waters, with their three thousand miles of convoluted coastline and myriad uninhabited islands. The sound itself is a ragged bite out of the northern reaches of the Gulf of Alaska, ninety miles long and 15,000 square miles in area – roughly the size of Switzerland or twice that of Massachusetts. This expanse provides plenty of elbow room for the sound's rich **wildlife**, which includes seven pods of orca, several fifty-ton humpback whales, numerous Dall's porpoises, ten thousand sea otters and over two hundred species of birds.

Many compare the sound favorably with Southeast's Glacier Bay, citing a larger number of glaciers and ease of access, though that same accessibility robs Prince William Sound of some of the isolated qualities possessed by Glacier Bay. This is also where the *Exxon Valdez* went aground on Bligh Reef in 1989, spilling millions of gallons of oil and killing thousands of birds and sea mammals. Many species have yet to fully recover, but there are no longer any visual reminders of those appalling times, just sparkling blue water and abundant animal life.

You'll likely approach the sound from one of the three towns on its shores: **Whittier**, a strange former military port connected by road and rail to Anchorage; the port of **Valdez**, with its massive oil terminal, extreme skiing, and superb kayaking opportunities; or isolated **Cordova**, which stands as a gateway to the **Copper River Delta**, with its vast wetlands, glaciers feeding icebergs into the Copper River, and the famed Million Dollar Bridge.

It hardly matters which town you choose as your base, but each town's cruises and kayak trips tend to focus on a particular area of the sound. Around Whittier the prize destinations are **College Fjord**, with its collegiate tidewater glaciers, Harvard and Yale, and the nearby **Harriman Fjord**, almost entirely encircled by glacier-white mountains. King of all the Prince William Sound glaciers is the **Columbia Glacier**, the largest tidewater glacier in Southcentral Alaska, named for New York's Columbia University and best accessed from Valdez. It is an astonishing sight, protruding forty miles from the peaks of the snowbound Chugach Mountains out into the sound, where its three-mile-wide face is forever calving off huge bergs. Actually, icy chunks are falling off faster than they are being replaced, and the glacier's terminus has retreated almost ten miles over the past twenty years, leaving behind a huge bay choked

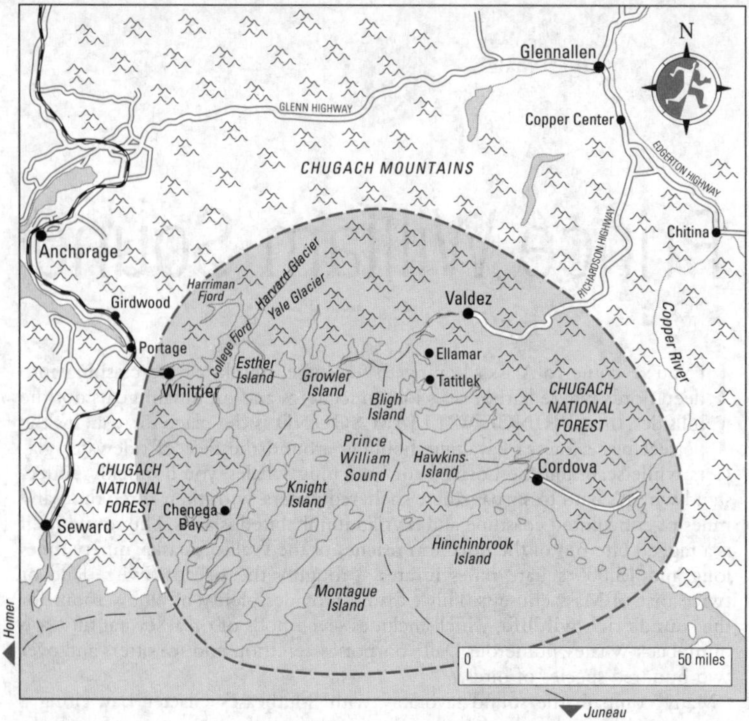

with bobbing hunks of ice. Although it's usually impossible to get close enough to see any impressive calving, this is a brilliant place to spend time listening to the popping of melting ice. Around Cordova much of the interest focuses on the Copper River Delta, though glaciers also feature here with the Childs Glacier looming large above the Million Dollar Bridge.

Money, time, and your taste for adventure will determine how you explore the sound. Even an experience as brief as a ferry trip between Whittier and Valdez gives a sense of the region's beauty, affords distant views of glaciers, and may offer a few sightings of seals and perhaps whales. If you have the time, go **kayaking**, which can be as easy-going as you wish and gives a much more realistic sense of the scale of everything than you would get from a big cruise boat.

Some history

In pre-European times, the Prince William Sound area was primarily occupied by the Chugach people, who settled around its shores, and the Eyak, who lived further east around the Copper River Delta and traded inland with the Ahtna. Russians were the first whites to arrive: Vitus Bering and his crew set foot on Alaskan soil in 1741, on Kayak Island near present-day Cordova.

One of the first Europeans to gain a sense of what lay behind the sheltering band of islands here was **James Cook**, who sailed through in 1778 when searching for the Northwest Passage. He named it Sandwich Sound in honor of his patron, the Earl of Sandwich, but on Cook's return to England the earl was out of favor and the House of Lords changed the name to recognize the king's son, William Henry, who later became King William IV. Spanish explorer **Don Salvador Fidalgo** arrived in 1790 also looking for the Northwest Passage. He took longer to decide he hadn't found it, and in the process named Galena Bay, Puerto Fidalgo and Puerto Valdes, renamed Valdez during the Spanish-American War at the end of the nineteenth century. He approached Columbia Glacier but turned away, as he thought the loud roar and spray of calving icebergs was the action of a live volcano.

Portuguese and French sailors followed, but it was Americans who brought the first real changes to the area, flocking to Valdez during the Klondike gold rush in the late nineteenth century. The discovery of copper inland at Kennicott drove the development of Cordova, and World War II effectively created Whittier, as the US needed a deep-water port safe from Japanese bombers.

A very different instinct was at work in 1907 when President Theodore Roosevelt established one of the country's first national forests, the **Chugach National Forest**, which cloaks much of Southcentral Alaska and completely encircles Prince William Sound. After Southeast's Tongass National Forest, it is America's largest and, like the Tongass, the issue of logging is highly controversial. Clear-cutting does take place, but in most of the places you're likely to visit, all you'll see is untouched forest running down to the steep gravel beaches.

Getting around the sound

Two of Prince William Sound's three main towns – Whittier and Valdez – are accessible by road, but the way to travel is by boat. Not only is it quicker than driving, it's also the easiest way to get a true flavor of the area.

The cheapest passage between the three towns, and the only option if you have a vehicle, is one of the AMHS **ferries** that visit the Prince William Sound ports. Much the most frequent is the *Bartlett*, which plies a seemingly random pattern between Whittier, Valdez, and Cordova that ensures a ferry at least every

The Harriman Expedition

At the end of the nineteenth century, the Klondike gold rush sparked interest in the previously ignored territory of Alaska. Railroad magnate Edward H Harriman was more proactive than most, and with the support of the US Biological Survey he financed the **Harriman Expedition**, a grand scientific tour along the Alaskan coast. Resources were quickly marshaled, and within weeks the *SS George W Elder* was refitted, a route up the panhandle to the Bering Strait laid out, and leading scientists recruited. The group included **John Muir**, already a recognized expert on Alaska from his two previous visits in 1879–1880 and 1890. Their departure in May 1899 was front-page news all over the world.

Though only two months long, the expedition was deemed a great success, vastly increasing knowledge of Alaskan flora and fauna and yielding surveys of long sections of coastline. Perhaps its most evident legacy is Prince William Sound's **College Fjord**, where the glaciers ranged along each side are named after Eastern US colleges. Along the south side were the Seven Sisters women's colleges – including Wellesley, Bryn Mawr, and Smith – while those along the northern side were men's schools – Dartmouth, Amherst, and Williams among them – with Yale and Harvard at the head of the fjord. Naturally, Harvard was the biggest, its face a mile and a half wide and 400ft high. Around the corner from College Fjord, the trip leader is honored with **Harriman Fjord**, the sound's most popular multiday kayaking destination, with plenty of opportunities for camping on beaches, with short paddles between interesting glaciers, particularly Harriman Glacier and Surprise Glacier, usually the most active calving glacier hereabouts.

couple of days to each destination. This is due to be replaced in 2005 by the *Chenega*, a much faster boat that will have a more frequent schedule.

Valdez also gets visits from the *Tustumena*, with almost weekly connections out of Prince William Sound to Seward, Kodiak, and Homer. Finally, the *Kennicott* runs once or twice a month between Juneau and Valdez – the so-called "Cross-Gulf" trip. If you are not planning to take one of the dedicated glacier cruises, you should at least do the ferry run between Whittier and Valdez, which passes within sight of the Columbia Glacier. It is a popular run and, while foot passengers seldom have trouble getting a space, drivers should **reserve in advance**. Ferry fares are roughly half the cruise fares and are listed in Basics (see pp.38–39).

Whittier

The tiny port of **WHITTIER**, sixty miles southeast of Anchorage, is a bizarre place, effectively a sprawling rail depot hemmed in by heavily glaciated mountains. Almost all of the town's three hundred residents live either in the single apartment tower or the scruffy low-rise Whittier Manor. Until June 2000 the town had only been reachable by sea or by train, an isolating state of affairs shattered by the conversion of the rail tunnel for combined road use: at two and a half miles it is the longest highway tunnel in the US.

Many of the townsfolk opposed road access fearing a flood of tourists once access was eased, but three years after the tunnel first opened to vehicular traffic their fears seem to have been unfounded. Still, visitor numbers are slowly increasing, and the town has even won a contract with one of the major cruise lines – Princess Cruises – so large passenger ships will again be coming up the fjord after a lapse of over ten years.

Adapting to these changes, wasteland has been assigned for vehicle parking, new businesses are springing up along the waterfront, and the Forest Service is putting some effort into creating a network of hiking trails so that people have some reason to be here other than to get on a cruise. The new road may yet signal Whittier's renaissance, though as one tourist put it, "I went through the longest tunnel in North America and all I got was Whittier."

Some history

Whittier was founded as an alternative ice-free port during World War II when the profusion of boats waiting to unload cargo onto the Alaska Railroad at Seward was seen as an easy target for Japanese bombers pressing eastward from the Aleutians. Whittier's location at the head of Passage Canal Fjord and almost permanent cloud cover made it an ideal location for a secret base. A sequence of two tunnels was bored through the surrounding mountains, and by 1943 a rail link was established to Portage and Anchorage. Soon after the end of the war, the army began consolidating their position by building the six-level **Buckner Building**, now a hollow shell, but once known as the "city under one roof" with living quarters, shops, rifle range, hospital, cinema, bowling alley, and swimming pool. The all-in-one design dramatically reduced snow removal problems in an area notorious for heavy dumps. The same principle was applied when they built the fourteen-story, flesh-toned **Begich Tower**, which is now home to more than half the town's residents. The army pulled out in 1960, and the town ticked over serving the railroad, the AMHS ferries to Valdez and Cordova, and a few tourists looking to take glacier cruises.

The Whittier tunnel

To drive in or out of Whittier you have to negotiate the single-lane Whittier Tunnel (officially, the Anton Anderson Memorial Tunnel; toll only charged when Whittier-bound: cars and motorbikes $12, RVs under 28ft $20, RVs over 28ft $35), a rail-only passage that's been converted to also accommodate road traffic. The tunnel is **open daily 6am–11pm** and only handles traffic in one direction at a time. Typically, it's open in fifteen-minute blocks once an hour each way, but breaks in the schedule to accommodate passenger trains mean that if you turn up at a bad time you may have to wait two hours to get through. Therefore be sure to check schedules, locally, or online (Ⓦwww.dot.state.ak.us/creg/whittiertunnel/index.htm), or by tuning to AM530 in Whittier and AM1610 in Portage.

The town, cruises, and kayaking

Whittier's mountains, glaciers, and glistening fjord make a dramatic first impression, but there isn't a great deal to do in town. It is worth setting aside an hour or two to enjoy some of the local hikes (see box, p.291), but otherwise you'll want to get out on the water. Almost all of the cruises and kayak trips initially head across Passage Canal to **Kittiwake Rock**, where ten thousand black-legged kittiwakes nest beside several waterfalls cascading right into the fjord.

Cruises

Biggest and slickest of the local cruises is waterfront-based Phillips' Cruises & Tours' five-hour 26 Glacier Cruise (mid-May to late Sept; $129; Ⓣ276-8023 or 1-800/544-0529, Ⓦwww.26glaciers.com), which makes a 135-mile tour of all 26 of the glaciers in Harriman and College fjords on a remarkably speedy and stable catamaran. Stops are necessarily brief, but you see a lot and have a fair chance of spotting plenty of wildlife.

Slightly less pressured big-boat cruises include Prince William Sound Cruises

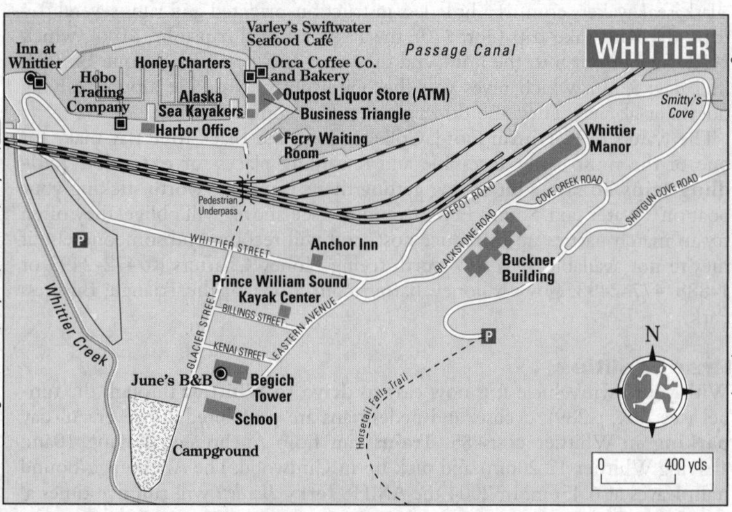

& Tours (mid-May to mid-Sept; 6hr; $109; ⓣ277-2131 or 1-800/992-1297, ⓦwww.princewilliamsound.com), also on the waterfront, which calls at the world's second largest salmon hatchery, winds through the hairline Esther Passage, and spends time around the tidewater glaciers in Barry Arm; and the excellent-value and more leisurely Glacier Lovers Cruise (late May to early Sept; 5hr; $103; ⓣ274-7300 or 1-800/764-7300, ⓦwww.majormarine.com), which travels slower and can include a worthwhile all-you-can-eat buffet ($12 extra) as you visit Blackstone and Beloit glaciers.

Whereas the above tours all tend to be fairly crowded and cursory, marine wildlife biologist Gerry Sanger of Sound Eco Adventures (ⓣ472-2312 or 1-888/471-2312, ⓦwww.soundecoadventure.com) offers much more intimate contact with the aquatic environment (and more time on the water). Using a small boat able to get close in and make beach landings, he covers the main calving-glacier territory on trips into College Fjord (8hr; $165), Barry Arm (5–6hr; $145), and Blackstone Bay (5–6hr; $145), and also ranges into more peaceful waters for whale watching (10hr; $195), viewing seabirds on remote islands (8hr; $165), or catching fjord wildlife at its most active in the early morning (over 4hr; $117). Best to book in advance, especially for multiday trips (from around $750 a day).

Kayaking

In the calm waters of Prince William Sound, you really need no prior experience to go on guided sea-kayaking trips such as those run by Prince William Sound Kayak Center (ⓣ472-2452 or 1-877/472-2452, ⓦwww.pwskayakcenter.com), which runs a number of guided day trips with the emphasis on teaching skills and preparing customers for future unguided trips. Take the trip across the bay to the Kittiwake Rookery (3hr; $65–85 depending on numbers), and for just a few dollars more you can add in instruction and the opportunity to spend the rest of the day exploring the coastline. The full-day Blackstone Bay trip ($210 each for four people) involves a water-taxi ride, lunch and plenty of paddling through berg-filled waters. Those suitably skilled can **rent kayaks** for the day (single $45, double $70), two days ($90/$140), three days ($130/$185) or more.

Alaska Sea Kayakers (ⓣ472-2534 or 1-877/472-2534, ⓦwww.alaskaseakayakers.com) is a little less instruction-oriented and runs several day trips: the Kittiwake trip (3hr; $70); the Passage Canal trip (6hr; $100), which heads further out into the fjord; and the water-taxi-based Blackstone Bay trip (full day; $250), which gives you the opportunity to paddle around calving tidewater glaciers. They also do kayak rentals at comparable rates.

The waters of Harriman Fjord, College Fjord, and Blackstone Bay make for one of the most easily accessible and rewarding places for **extended paddling trips**. To save a bit of slog getting there, it may be worth sticking your boat on a water taxi. Sound Eco Adventures (see above) will oblige: they often try to match parties up to reduce costs and will recommend someone else if they're not available. It is also worth trying Honey Charters (ⓣ472-2493 or 1-888/477-2493, ⓦwww.honeycharters.com) down at the Triangle Business Park.

Practicalities

With your own vehicle it is now easy to **drive to Whittier** through the tunnel (see box, p.289); cyclists and pedestrians are prohibited, however. All-day **parking** in Whittier costs $5. **Trains** run from Anchorage (leaving 10am, arriving Whittier 12.20pm) and pick up in Girdwood. The Anchorage-bound train leaves at 6.45pm. In 2004 the AMHS **ferry** *Bartlett* will run five times a

Hiking around Whittier

It is worth planning your schedule to leave a couple of hours spare to explore Whittier's developing range of trails. Ten minutes past any trailhead you won't believe Whittier is just half a mile away.

Horsetail Fall Trail (2 miles round-trip; 1hr to 1hr 30min; 700ft accent). Beautiful trail climbing into an alpine bowl up behind Whittier, mostly on boardwalks and steps. At the treeline you've got great views over the town and across the fjord to Billings Glacier. The trailhead is up behind the Buckner Building, reached by following Shotgun Cove Road and turning right.

Portage Pass Trail (3 miles round-trip; 2hr; 750ft ascent). A trailhead close to the entrance of the tunnel marks the start of a fairly steep route that was once followed by gold prospectors, who would climb to the pass and descend across Portage Glacier (a route no longer feasible as the glacier has receded to form Portage Lake). Hike up to Divide Lake and a little further to the top of the pass, from where there are great views back down the fjord, only superseded by those down to the Portage Glacier.

Shotgun Cove Trail (go as far as you want; gently undulating). The first mile along Salmon Run Road east of Whittier is gravel but vehicle-accessible and takes you to the **First Salmon Run** picnic area (1 mile from Whittier), a lovely spot with glacier and fjord views. Beyond there the road becomes impassable, so you'll need to strike out on foot along a narrow gravel road to the trailhead proper (3 miles from Whittier). From here the trail sticks more or less to the shoreline with occasional access to the water, with one good spot only fifteen minutes from the trailhead. That's far enough for many people, although the trail just goes on and on, enabling you to make a full day of it if you wish.

week to Valdez and once direct to Cordova, though from summer 2005 the new fast ferry *Chenega* should be making daily runs from Cordova to Valdez and Whittier and back the same day.

Most cruise and kayak trip departures are timed to coincide with the train schedule, so it is unlikely you'll have to spend more than a couple of hours in Whittier. If you find you need **to stay**, the best bets are: the **campground** ($10 per site; showers at the Harbor Office for $4; early June to Sept), tucked in behind the Begich Tower; *June's B&B* (Ⓣ472-2396 or 1-888/472-2396, Ⓦwww.breadnbuttercharters.com; ❺), spread over several condos inside the Begich Tower; and, on the waterfront, the brand-new and very flash *Inn At Whittier* (Ⓣ472-7000 or 1-866/472-5757, Ⓦwww.innatwhittier.com; ocean-view rooms ❾, mountain-view ❽).

Most businesses and **restaurants** cluster along the waterfront, either at the Triangle Business Park or behind the small boat harbor. *Orca Coffee Co and Bakery* has great views up the fjord and a deck for enjoying salmon chowder ($5), burgers ($7–9) and espresso drinks. Nearby, *Varley's Swiftwater Seafood Café* (Ⓣ472-2550) serves super-fresh halibut and chips ($9) along with bottled microbrews and good coffee. Local renegade and political activist Babs serves burgers, sandwiches, pies, and ice cream (among other things) from a glassed-in cabin overlooking the small boat harbor known as the *Hobo Trading Company* (Ⓣ472-2374; mid-May to mid-Sept, closed Tues). The *Inn At Whittier* has a swanky restaurant with great fjord views and serves up smoked salmon mousse, Dungeness crab salad, and Dijon crusted lamb.

There is a sporadically open **post office** on the first floor of the Begich Tower, a grocery store at the *Anchor Inn* on Whittier Street, and an **ATM** in the Outpost Liquor Store at the Triangle. Whittier does not have a bank.

Valdez and around

VALDEZ possesses one of the most remarkably picturesque settings in Alaska, nestled under some of the world's tallest coastal mountains on the shores of Valdez Arm, a curving tentacle threading twelve miles north off Prince William Sound. A small town without a great deal to actually see, Valdez easily makes up for its nondescript nature by its proximity to some wonderful cruising and sea-kayaking waters and the stupendous **Columbia Glacier**.

There are fewer than five thousand residents in Valdez (Val-DEEZ), but its status as North America's northernmost ice-free port has brought it considerable prosperity, largely as the southern terminus for the trans-Alaska oil pipeline. Tankers seem almost perpetually moored across the water at the Alyeska Marine Terminal, a constant reminder that the **Exxon Valdez disaster** (see box, p.296–297) happened just a few miles away.

But the oil spill was only the latest chapter in a catalog of grim events to have befallen Valdez over the years. The first was in 1897, when the Klondike gold rush inspired thousands of ill-prepared prospectors to set off north from Valdez Arm, an arduous journey that rewarded precious few (see box, opposite). Soon after, a potential boost came with the 1900 discovery of huge deposits of copper at Kennicott (see p.415), a hundred miles to the northeast. When a railroad was proposed to transport the copper to a port, Cordova and Valdez battled over the privilege, with a gunfight even taking place in Keystone Canyon between rival rail companies. Valdez eventually lost the battle and life passed by quietly until 1964, when the area was struck by the **Good Friday earthquake**, the most powerful on record in North America (see box, p.207). The ensuing tsunami claimed 33 lives and destroyed the town, which was subsequently rebuilt on more stable ground four miles to the west.

Although a few old buildings were relocated, the overall effect of the move is the modern, characterless town you see today. The layout comes with dead-end streets, a devilish design for snow plows struggling to cope with some of the heaviest snowfalls in the state: the 7000-foot barrier of the Chugach Mountains encourages storms to dump an average of 27ft of snow – and a record 46ft in the winter of 1989-90 – on the town each winter, a joyous thing for skiers, boarders and the like.

Valdez's fortunes improved when it was selected as the southern terminus of the trans-Alaska pipeline. Construction of the pipeline and the huge oil terminal brought boom times to the town, but everything was about to change. On Good Friday 1989 the *Exxon Valdez* catapulted the town into world headlines, when the fully laden tanker struck Bligh Reef at the entrance to Valdez Arm, exactly 25 years after the 1964 earthquake. Since then, Valdez has settled back into a fairly sleepy existence, trying to lure visitors as a hedge against the day when the oil stops flowing.

Although the main attraction for visitors is the Columbia Glacier and the surrounding islands and bays of Prince William Sound, there is interest on land with a couple of diverting museums and a few spots for salmon viewing. Inland the Richardson Highway heads through the rafting waters of Keystone Canyon towards the glacial heights of Thompson Pass. The scattered nature of these land-based sights means you really need your own vehicle to get around.

Arrival and information

AMHS **ferries** from Valdez and Cordova cruise right up Valdez Arm and dock at the ferry terminal (Ⓣ834-4800), a quarter of a mile west of downtown

Valdez's first ice climbers

During the Klondike gold rush of 1897, American gold seekers quickly became wary of Canadian regulations and taxes on the White Pass and Chilkoot trails from Skagway to the Yukon. So there was a ready audience when the *Seattle Post-Intelligencer* reported that the **All-American Route** from Valdez Arm to the Interior was not only two hundred miles shorter than other routes but "altogether in American territory . . . and said to be not difficult." No one mentioned that Valdez was just a handful of tents set on mudflats, or the need to cross the Valdez and Klutina glaciers, a twenty-mile route riddled with killer crevasses. Roughly 3500 prospectors set off from Valdez, and as one gold seeker put it, "It was a wonderful sight to stand on the summit of that glacier five thousand feet above the sea and look back eighteen miles to the coast and see the black serpent of humanity winding its way over the snow and ice like a huge snake." Gold fever outweighed prudence, and most set off entirely unprepared, with hundreds dying of starvation and scurvy. Those who tried to hike during the day struggled desperately through the soft snow or succumbed to snow blindness and groped unseeing into gaping crevasses. Most were forced to travel at night with minimal protection from the terrible cold. Few prospectors reached the Klondike in time to stake a paying claim.

Valdez. Arriving **by road** from Glennallen is equally spectacular on the most dramatic section of the Richardson Highway, where it negotiates the towering Chugach Mountains: our account starts on p.424.The demise of a once-regular **bus service** means that the only public transportation by road is Alaska Trails & Tours (ⓣ1-888/600-6001), which runs here from Fairbanks, Delta Junction, and Glennallen when numbers make the journey viable.

The only scheduled **flights** into Valdez are with ERA Aviation (ⓣ1-800/866-8394), which flies direct from Anchorage ($100–125 each way) three times daily to Valdez airport, four miles east of town along Airport Road. A **taxi** into town with Valdez Yellow Cab (ⓣ835-2500) will cost around $10. For more flexibility visit the airport **rental car** office of Valdez-U-Drive (ⓣ835-4402 or 1-800/478-4402 in Alaska, ⓦwww.valdezudrive.com), which charges around $50 a day for a compact.

Once in town, everywhere is accessible on foot from the central **visitor center**, 200 Fairbanks St (mid-June to mid-Sept Mon–Fri 8am–7pm, Sat 9am–6pm, Sun 10am–5pm; ⓣ835-4636 or 1-800/770-5954, ⓦwww.valdezalaska.org), which has a free map of town. Outside there's a free-call phone linked to some of the town's B&Bs. In winter information is available from the **CVB** (Mon–Fri 8am–5pm) in the same building.

Accommodation

Traditional **accommodation** is fairly expensive in Valdez, though you'll find more satisfying and cheaper rooms at the assortment of downtown and neighborhood **B&Bs**, the descendants of the city's first crop, which sprang up during the *Exxon Valdez* clean-up when there weren't enough beds to go round. In high summer downtown is swamped with RVs occupying soulless, if well-placed, gravel lots. The nearest leafy **campground** is five miles away; signs downtown discourage free camping, but for one-night stays creative campers should find a quiet spot a mile or so west of the center along Mineral Creek. If the recommendations below prove fruitless, try contacting the handy Independent Network of B&Bs (ⓦwww.valdezbnbnetwork.com).

Hotels and B&Bs

Blueberry Mary's B&B 810 Salmonberry Way ⓣ835-5015, ⓦwww.alaska.net/~bmary. Secluded B&B a mile from town with stupendous views of Valdez Arm, comfortable rooms, a sauna, and a breakfast of pancakes with blueberries from the local hillside. ❹

Downtown B&B Inn 113 Galena Drive ⓣ835-2791 or 1-800/478-2791, ⓦwww.alaskaone.com/downinn. Good-value small hotel with a handy downtown location and a substantial continental breakfast. A little shabby in places, but some of the newer rooms have private bath. Private bath ❺, shared ❹

In the Woods B&B 5380 Snowflake Circle ⓣ835-3758 ⓦhome.gci.net/~inthewoods. Excellent-value B& (maybe) B ten miles east of Valdez with just two rooms, both with private bathroom, pond-side setting, and access to a kitchenette and the Internet. One has a double bed, the other twin beds and a sauna. With breakfast ❸, without ❷

Keystone Hotel 401 W Egan Drive ⓣ835-3851 or 1-888/835-0665, ⓦwww.alaskan.com/keystonehotel. Modern hotel with steel-clad exterior and well-appointed but small rooms, all of which come with private bathrooms and a complimentary continental breakfast. ❹

L&L's B&B 533 W Hanagita St ⓣ835-4447, ⓦwww.lnlalaska.com. Comfortable five-room B&B with shared bathrooms in a modern home a ten-minute walk from the center. There are bikes for getting around and a good self-serve breakfast. ❸

Lake House Mile 6 Richardson Hwy ⓣ835-4752, ⓦwww.geocities.com/lakehousevaldez. Lovely and very welcoming B&B about ten miles east of Valdez, run by John, who was mayor of Valdez when the *Exxon Valdez* went aground. The comfortably furnished rooms are all en suite, and most have balconies overlooking Robe Lake. There's also a good help-yourself continental breakfast. ❺

Valdez Harbor Inn 100 Fidalgo St ⓣ835-4391 or 1-888/222-3440, ⓦwww.valdezharborinn.com. Valdez's top hotel (a *Best Western*) has recently renovated rooms, all the expected facilities, and a great waterside location. The best views are reserved for the restaurant/bar. ❻

Hostels and campgrounds

Allison Point Ocean Front Campground Mile 5 Dayville Rd ⓣ835-2282. Gravel RV sites ($10) with water and outhouses, and most sites wedged between Dayville Rd and the waters of the bay. Oil terminal traffic makes it less than peaceful, but the view is great. Late May to early Sept.

Bear Paw Camper Park 101 N Harbor Drive ⓣ835-2530, ⓦwww.bearpawrvpark.com. Not the cheapest of the downtown RV parks ($19 dry, $25 full hookup), but it's in a great location and has a heated sitting area with modem jacks. There's also an adult-only area (full hookup $30), plus a tent section ($19) in the alders away from the RVs.

Valdez Glacier Campground Mile 2.3 Airport Rd ⓣ835-2282. Spacious and leafy, Valdez's only rural campground is located five miles east of town, by the airport. Sites ($10) are well spaced with picnic tables and fire rings. Mid-May to mid-Sept.

The town and around Valdez Arm

With its mountain-girt setting perched beside a deep fjord, Valdez can be a great place just to walk around, perhaps along the Overlook Trail or the Dock Point Trail (see box, p.299) to gain a better vantage or heading for the small boat harbor later in the day when huge halibut are landed and strung up.

About the only distraction in town is the **Valdez Museum**, 217 Egan Drive (late May to mid-Sept Mon–Sat 9am–6pm, Sun 8am–5pm; mid-Sept to late May Mon–Sat noon–4pm; $3; ⓦwww.alaska.net/~vldzmuse), an eclectic regional collection with the old Fresnel lens from the Hinchinbrook Lighthouse at the entrance to Prince William Sound, a field gun from Fort Liscum, which closed in 1922 and is now the oil terminal, and the superb mirror-backed Pinzon Bar from pre-quake Valdez. Notice the copper panel covering the holes in the bar that were cut for soda siphons during prohibition. Photos of yesteryear show the effect of the earthquake, while others from the big-snow year of 1989–90 illustrate just how much of a problem snow clearance can be. There's even a three-quarters-of-an-inch-thick piece of the hull from the *Exxon Valdez*, which sounds rugged enough, until you consider that it was the only thing between 53 million gallons of crude and a pristine marine environment.

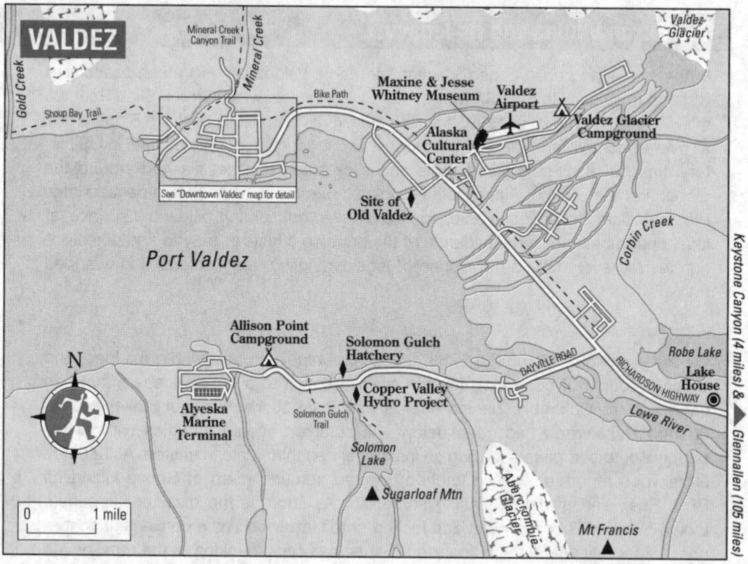

The associated **Valdez Museum Annex**, 436 S Hazelet Ave (June–Aug daily 9am–4pm; $1.50), is more focused than the Valdez Museum, with much of the floor space taken up by a huge and historically accurate model of Valdez as it was in 1963, before the earthquake. Impressive as it is, the earthquake displays demand more of your time, particularly if you have patience to watch the whole of the 45-minute *Though the Earth Moved* video. It is worth it, if only to see the 8mm footage shot from aboard the *Chena*, which was moored at Valdez dock. Despite being buffeted by huge waves, then having the sea sucked out from under them, two crew members somehow managed to keep filming throughout. Elsewhere there are interactive displays and a working seismograph with its sensor in College Fjord, epicenter of the 1964 quake.

Once upon a time you could tour the Alyeska Marine Terminal across the bay, but due to security concerns you now have to make do with the Video Tour of Alaska's Petroleum Industry & Pipeline Exhibit (mid-May to mid-Sept daily 9.30am, 11.30am & 1.30pm; $5, or $7 in combination with the Whitney Museum; Ⓣ834-1600) at the Community College. Along with coverage of the pipeline and oil terminal, there is material on the tankers and on the wildlife of Prince William Sound.

On a warm afternoon it's a pleasant wander half a mile out along E Egan Drive to the **Crooked Creek Salmon Viewing Platform** (unrestricted access). Located on the site of a former hatchery, it's still a good place to spot pink and chum salmon, especially during spawning season from mid-July to early September. There's an underwater camera, so you can watch the spawning inside the adjacent Crooked Creek Information Site (June–Aug daily 9am–6pm), which, outside the spawning season, shows a video of last year's performance.

Around Valdez Arm

From Valdez waterside roads run along both sides of Valdez Arm providing access to a few minor sights and plenty of great views. Drive along E Egan

The Exxon Valdez and its legacy

In the American public consciousness the name Valdez isn't so much associated with the town as with the 987-foot tanker *Exxon Valdez*, which struck Bligh Reef, 25 miles to the southwest in 1989. It spilled eleven million gallons of North Slope crude all over Prince William Sound – the biggest and most catastrophic **oil spill** in US history. Images of oil-smothered birds and slick black beaches flashed around the globe, and the State of Alaska looked on as if paralyzed. More than a decade later, Prince William Sound looks as unspoiled as ever, but scratch below the surface (at least on the beaches) and evidence of the ongoing effects is easy to find, a realization revived every time a new round of legal wrangling over settlement is wrapped up.

The spill

On the evening of March 23, 1989, the *Exxon Valdez* left port with a full load, and within a couple of hours had to take evasive action to avoid an iceberg that had calved off the Columbia Glacier. After issuing instructions, hot-shot tanker captain **Joseph Hazelwood** had gone below – a common enough practice with all the paperwork to complete – leaving an inexperienced third mate in charge. At 12.04am Hazelwood reported, "We've fetched up hard aground north of Goose Island off Bligh Reef, and evidently leaking some oil." As soon as the disaster happened, Exxon hired a PR company, which locked onto Hazelwood as a convenient scapegoat, especially when it was reported that he had been drinking at the *Pipeline Inn* immediately before taking command. Remedial action would have been more useful, but the sole response barge was under 14ft of snow, delaying the clean-up team for three days. A tenth-anniversary report on the incident stated that "11 million gallons of oil spread slowly over open water during three days of flat calm seas. Despite the opportunity to skim the oil before it hit the shorelines, almost none was scooped up . . . Even if [the response barge] had responded, there were not enough skimmers and booms available to do an effective job. Dispersants were applied, but were determined to be ineffective because of prevailing conditions. Even if dispersants had been effective, however, there was not enough dispersant on hand to make a dent in the spreading oil slick." The State of Alaska's 1993 report described it as "a botched response."

The effects

Altogether 1500 miles of coastline were befouled – 200 miles badly – and some slicks found their way to shore almost 500 miles from Bligh Reef. Animal population studies estimate that as a direct result of the spill almost 3000 sea otters perished along with 300 harbor seals, up to 22 orcas and a quarter of a million seabirds, including 250 bald eagles. Salmon streams as far away as Kenai and Kodiak were

Drive four miles to Mile Zero of the Richardson Hwy, where Alaska Avenue runs 400yd down to the **Old Townsite**, little more than a couple of building foundations and a memorial plaque. On the other side of the Richardson Highway, Airport Road runs a mile to the airport, where you'll find the **Maxine & Jesse Whitney Museum** (May to mid-Sept daily 9am–8pm, winter by appointment; $5; ⓣ834-1615), which contains one of the finest collections of sculpted ivory and Eskimo artifacts in the state. The enormous stuffed bull moose, caribou, bison, and polar bear loom over beautifully made mukluks, a parka made from ground-squirrel pelts, another made from murre skins, and a large umiak which uses whale baleen for its ribs. Two moose hides with mountain scenes are hung next to each other to illustrate the changing Alaskan landscape. The images are thought to be of the same place:

affected. Of the 28 species impacted by the oil spill, only two are considered to have fully recovered: bald eagles and river otters. The rest are all still affected in some way, with one study showing that hydrocarbons present in crude oil at concentrations as low as one part per billion can harm herring and salmon eggs.

Ten thousand people were involved in the clean-up at a cost to Exxon of around $2 billion. Only eleven percent of the oil was recovered. The futility of the process was highlighted by Alutiiq village chief Walter Meganack, who described spending "all day cleaning one huge rock, and the tide comes in and covers it with oil again. Spend a week wiping and spraying the surface, but pick up a rock and there's four inches of oil underneath."

Commercial fishermen were badly hit. The 1989 fishing season never began, and fish stocks were hurt for years. Although some say stocks are still suffering, with the passage of time and widespread over-fishing, among other factors, it is increasingly difficult to blame the oil spill for the woes of the local fishing industry. In Native villages subsistence hunting for seals and the harvest of herring eggs from kelp were ruined for years, and many residents fled to Valdez, some getting jobs on oil-spill response crews.

The current situation

Change has been forced by federal and state laws and newly created monitoring organizations, such as the Prince William Sound Regional Citizens' Advisory Council (ⓦwww.pwsrcac.org), a permanent industry-funded citizens' group which struggles to maintain its independence from industry lobbyists. Today Prince William Sound has more weather buoys than any similar body of water in the world, the coast guard monitors a much wider area, and the oil companies, under the eye of the advisory council, are testing an innovative iceberg detection system. Other changes include the introduction of a powerful and highly maneuverable escort tug to guide boats from as far as the entrance to Prince William Sound, drug and alcohol tests for tanker captains before sailing, improved oil skimming and storage capability, and regular response drills.

Meanwhile, Exxon has wrestled in the courts over restitution. In 1991 Exxon, the federal government, and the State of Alaska reached an out-of-court settlement requiring Exxon to pay the other two parties $100 million in criminal restitution for fish, wildlife, and lands; and $900 million as a **civil settlement** with payments spread over ten years. Forty thousand commercial fishers and other parties who suffered as a result of the spill then joined forces in a class-action suit against Exxon. In 1994 a jury awarded them $5.2 billion. Exxon immediately appealed and, though this money has been put in escrow and is gaining interest, the fishers have seen little of it. In December 2002 the appeal judge reduced the award to $4 billion, but still the fishermen wait.

the first (undated) with a cabin in the newly tamed wilderness and the second a few years later (1913) with the cabin in disrepair and moose reclaiming the territory. The ivory room is crammed with pieces veering well away from the typical walrus-tusk cribbage boards, ranging from grotesque figures traditionally used to ward off evil spirits, to a model of a Pan-Am 747 carved in the 1970s.

Some seven miles out of town along the Richardson Highway (Mile 2.9), Dayville Road cuts around the head of the bay and, four miles on, reaches the **Solomon Gulch Hatchery** (unrestricted entry), where you can pick up a leaflet and follow a free self-guided tour along waterside boardwalks passing tanks of salmon in various states of growth. It is hoped that the salmon will be here in large enough numbers to support this commercial fishery once the oil

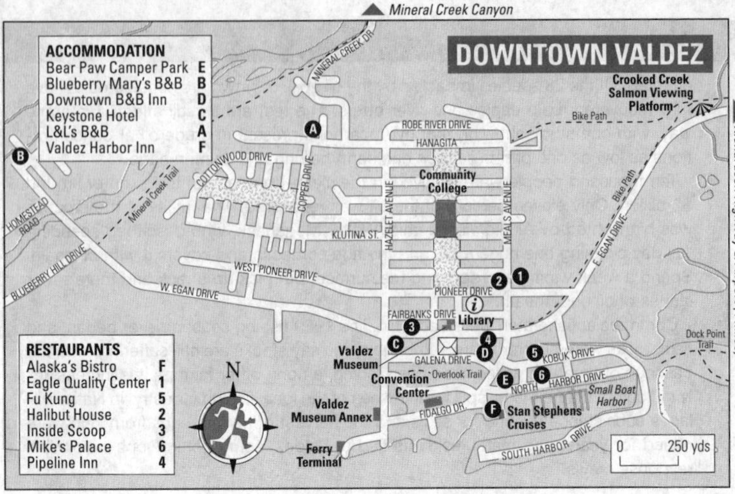

stops flowing. Across Dayville Road a similarly forward-looking policy helped create the diminutive **Copper Valley Hydro Project**, which channels water from high-country lakes through turbines, providing power to Valdez and Glennallen. The penstocks above the power station can be seen on the **Solomon Gulch Trail** (see box, below), which starts a mile further on by the *Allison Point* RV park. The road finishes at the Alyeska Marine Terminal (no access), built on the site of the former Fort Liscum, the terminus of the WAMCATS telegraph wire to Eagle (see box, p.440) from 1900 to 1923.

Cruises and outdoor activities

You really haven't experienced the best of Valdez until you've been out on the water, either on a cruise to Prince William Sound and the Columbia Glacier or on a kayak trip around Valdez Arm and beyond. Fishing and whitewater rafting round out the aquatic activities, or you could just take a helicopter flight over the whole lot. On land there are some pleasant, short-ish hikes (see box opposite), and if you come in winter, the extreme skiing and boarding is second to none (see box, p.300).

Cruises

Valdez is superbly placed for cruises out to Prince William Sound. The most popular are those with Stan Stephens Glacier & Wildlife Cruises (Ⓣ835-4731 or 1-866/867-1297, Ⓦwww.stanstephenscruises.com), which runs three Valdez-based cruises. The Columbia Glacier Cruise (mid-May to mid-Sept daily; 6hr; $85) mainly visits the glacier, but there's usually plenty of time for watching whales or whatever else makes an appearance; the Columbia and Meares Glacier Cruise (June to Aug, 4 weekly; 9hr; $119) also takes in the advancing Meares Glacier; and – if you're prepared for a 7am start – the Columbia Glacier Express (late June to mid-Aug, 4 weekly; $80), which whips out and back before lunch.

For a small boat, a more leisurely approach, and plenty of whale watching, try a five-hour cruise with Glacier Wildlife Cruises aboard the *Lu-Lu Belle*

Hiking and biking around Valdez

Much of the best hiking around Valdez requires a vehicle for access, but there are a couple of good hikes which start right in town. These should be largely snow free from early June to late September. **Mountain bikers** can explore the first mile of the Shoup Bay Trail, but are better off on the approach to Mineral Creek Canyon.

Dock Point Trail (1 mile loop; 30min; 100ft ascent). A peaceful nature walk on gravel trails and boardwalks with interpretive signs. It leads from the east end of the small boat harbor to a knoll and a couple of viewpoints looking across the bay.

Mineral Creek Canyon Trail (2 miles round-trip; 1hr; 100ft ascent). Pretty decent trail leading up to the abandoned gold stamp mill of Hercules Mine near the base of the Johnson Glacier. Drive the rough six-mile road up to the trailhead, if you have a high-clearance vehicle, or bike up there.

Overlook Trail (100 yards; 5min; mostly steps). A flight of steps running off South Harbor Drive leads up to a shelter with great views over town and Valdez Arm.

Shoup Bay Trail (24 miles round-trip; 1-2 days; mostly flat). Beautiful, easy (but long) hike along the shores of Port Valdez to Shoup Bay, where there are three beautifully sited six-bunk state park **cabins** looking at the face of Shoup Glacier ($50; book through APLIC in Anchorage ⓣ269-8400, check availability on ⓦwww.dnr.state.ak.us/parks/cabins/pws.cfm) The hike is particularly good for keen birders, although direct access to the shores of the fjord is limited.

Solomon Gulch Trail (3.8 miles round-trip; 1hr 30min to 2hr 30min; 620ft ascent). Starting thirteen miles from Valdez on the road to the pipeline terminal, the trail initially follows the gravel road laid atop the penultimate mile of the oil pipeline as far as Solomon Gulch. Surplus tubing from the pipeline was used for hydro station penstocks, which are followed to the glacial waters behind the Solomon Gulch Dam, overlooked by Sugarloaf Mountain (3484ft) and a distant glacier at the end of the lake.

($75; ⓣ835-5141 or 1-800/411-0090, ⓦwww.lulubelletours.com), which also visits the Columbia. There's even an opportunity to attend the Chapel of the Sea, a one-hour cruise (Sun 8am) for a nondenominational service at sea (free, but a collection is taken).

Kayaking

Although the cruises in the area are excellent, there's an undeniably more intimate feel aboard a kayak. One of the most popular destinations is **Shoup Glacier**, which drains out into Valdez Arm eight miles west of Valdez. Like most Alaskan glaciers, this is currently retreating, but over the centuries it has made two significant advance-and-retreat cycles, leaving two terminal moraines, which have created Shoup Bay. At high tide you can paddle up from Shoup Bay to the lake immediately below the glacier and paddle close (but not too close) to the face of the glacier. As you bob around on the opaque gray-green water thick with brash ice, it feels like you're paddling in a giant frozen margarita. Through most of the summer, one prominent rock is completely covered by some twenty thousand black-legged **kittiwakes** which nest here. It is even possible to stay in one of the three Alaska State Parks cabins nearby (see box above).

Two companies, both with offices along N Harbor Drive, offer nearly identical **kayaking** trips: Anadyr Adventures (ⓣ835-2814 or 1-800/865-2925, ⓦwww.anadyradventures.com) and Pangaea Adventures (ⓣ835-8442 or 1-800/660-9637, ⓦwww.alaskasummer.com). Shop around to see which company has the best deals and a schedule that fits your timetable.

Anyone after a gentle paddle with opportunities for spotting seals, sea lions,

Winter in Valdez

Valdez likes to promote itself as "**Snow Capital of Alaska**," and with good reason: with 27ft of snowfall per year, it gets more snow than any other seaside town in the world. A few miles inland in the Chugach Mountains that average almost triples, and the dense, wet nature of coastal snow makes this perfect territory for extreme skiing in ludicrously steep chutes. There's also some wonderful heli-skiing on more forgiving slopes. No one has built any permanent downhill skiing facilities, but there is plenty of scope for snowmachining, backcountry skiing, and dog mushing around Valdez, or ice climbing on the waterfalls of Keystone Canyon. For a full list of operators, obtain the free annual *Valdez Vacation Guide* from the Valdez visitor center (or visit Ⓦwww.valdezalaska.org).

A good way to organize a winter visit to Valdez is to coincide your trip with one of the town's **winter festivals**, which start in early March with the Valdez Ice Climbing Festival (Ⓦalaskagold.com/ice), continue in late March with the Alaskan Local Snowboarding Championships, and conclude with the Mountain Master Extreme Snowboard Competition during the first two weeks of April. Although it's nearly impossible to see any of the extreme skiing or snowboarding up close, just being in town for the associated activities and partying is excuse enough for a visit. Snowmachine fans will want to check out some of the regular events run by the Valdez Snowmachine Club (Ⓦwww.valdezsnow.com) from January to April, especially the Mountain Man Hill Climb at Thompson Pass in early April.

and shorebirds should opt for the Duck Flats trip (3–4hr; $55), or the more ambitious coastal paddle to Gold Creek (6hr; $75–80). It is really worth dedicating the time and money to reach distant paddling destinations, accessed by water taxi: principally Shoup Glacier (8hr; $145) and Columbia Glacier (10hr; $185–190).

Both companies also offer **kayak rentals** (single $45, double $65, triple $80), the rates for which reduce by $5–10 a day after the first or second day. In addition, Anadyr offers a diversion in the form of **WindRiders** ($49 a half-day, $85 a day), which are like three kayaks lashed together and equipped with a sail: easy to learn and lots of fun.

Anadyr and Pangaea also have multiday guided trips, either camping out, based at a remote lodge, or using a mother ship for sleeping and getting between paddling spots: for more details see the company websites and Basics (p.64).

Fishing, rafting, and helicopter flightseeing

During summer Valdez holds two **fishing derbies** – one for halibut (mid-May to Aug), the other for silver salmon (Aug) – both with prizes of $15,000 for the biggest fish caught during the derby period. To participate, you'll need a ticket ($10 a day or $50 a season per species), available from several stores and campgrounds around town. The small boat harbor is full of boats ready to take you out to catch that winner; try Northern Comfort Charters (Ⓣ835-3070 or 1-800/478-9884, Ⓦwww.northerncomfortcharter.com), which charges a competitive $115 for a half-day of salmon fishing and $195 for the full day necessary to get out to good halibut waters.

Keystone Raft & Kayak Adventures (Ⓣ835-2606 or 1-800/328-8460, Ⓦwww.alaskawhitewater.com) runs whitewater-**rafting** trips on the Lowe River through Keystone Canyon (June–Aug; $35) with an hour on the water tackling predominantly Class II–III rapids and floating under dramatic waterfalls, and longer trips in Class IV rivers including the Tsaina (3hr; $70), the

Tonsina (all day; $85), and the Tana, in the Wrangell Mountains (4 days; $995).

For **flightseeing**, go with ERA Helicopters (ⓣ835-2595 or 1-800/843-1947, ⓦwww.era-aviation.com), whose Prince William Sound Safari (1hr; $229) heads out over the Columbia Glacier and lands briefly beside Shoup Bay.

Eating and drinking

There's little special about dining in Valdez, but there are several perfectly adequate places, some with harbor views, and a couple of dark bars to keep you entertained in the evening. **Groceries**, along with deli selections, baked goods, and espressos are available from the two supermarkets, the best being the Eagle Quality Center, at the corner of Pioneer Drive and Meals Avenue.

Alaska's Bistro in the *Valdez Harbor Inn* ⓣ835-5688. Tasty, well-presented food in a range of styles, and a wonderful harbor-view setting make this the pick of Valdez's restaurants. Loosely Mediterranean in style, the menu ranges from deluxe burgers and bar snacks to crab-stuffed halibut ($25) and shrimp, scallops, and artichokes over linguini ($25). There's an extensive wine list, too.

Fu Kung 207 Kobuk St ⓣ835-5255. Korean-run restaurant serving mainstream Mandarin, Szechwan, Cantonese, and Japanese dishes, plus several banquet dinners for $14–19 per person.

Halibut House 208 Meals Ave ⓣ835-2788. Budget halibut sandwiches, salmon wedges, chicken nuggets, and assorted fried goodies, mostly for under $6 and served in spartan surroundings.

The Inside Scoop 321 W Egan Drive ⓣ835-9000. Great ice cream, espresso drinks, and Internet access for $8/hr.

Mike's Palace 201 N Harbor Drive ⓣ835-2365. Good Italian-oriented restaurant on the waterfront, though in true Alaskan fashion they also do burgers, Mexican dishes, Greek salads and baklava. Their lasagna ($12) is super-tasty, the pizzas (from $10 for a 12in) are reliable, and a couple of enchiladas can be had for $9.

The Pipeline Inn & Club 112 W Egan Drive ⓣ835-4332. Dim booths in a room off the main bar create a suitable ambience for this oil-boom survivor. It's still a favorite of the tanker crews, who come for the menu of top-quality steak and seafood that features a 12oz filet mignon dinner ($28), a salmon, shrimp, halibut, and scallop combo ($22), and the Pipeline Pu Pu house special – sliced steak sautéed with onion, bell pepper, tomatoes, and soy sauce on a bed of rice that's a bargain at $16. Burgers and sandwiches can be had at the bar, which is the most likely place to find live music and dancing.

Listings

Banks and exchange Valdez has only two banks: Wells Fargo, 337 Egan Drive (ⓣ835-4745), and First National Bank, 101 Egan Drive (ⓣ834-4800). Both have 24hr ATMs.

Bike rental Anadyr Adventures on N Harbor Drive (ⓣ835-2814) offers bikes for $8/hr or $30 a day.

Camping equipment Beaver Sports, 316 Galena Drive (ⓣ835-4727), sells high-quality hiking, camping, and general outdoors gear. The Prospector, 141 Galena Drive (ⓣ835-3858), targets the hunting and fishing set but also stocks good standard gear that can be a bargain.

Festivals Most of the major annual events happen in winter (see box, opposite), but in late June there's the **Last Frontier Theater Conference** (ⓣ834-1615), which is earning a reputation beyond the state border, especially for its long-standing association with noted playwright Edward Albee, who usually attends. New plays by Alaskan writers are read and performed along with an Albee piece or two.

Internet access Free access at the library (below) and for a fee at *The Inside Scoop* (see above)

Laundry and showers Like Home Laundromat, Valdez Mall, 121 Egan Drive (daily 8am–9pm; ⓣ835-2913), has washers and dryers; the Habormaster's office on N Harbor Drive offers ten-minute showers for $4.

Library Valdez Library, 200 Fairbanks Drive (Mon & Fri 10am–6pm, Tues–Thurs 10am–8pm, Sat noon–5pm; ⓦwww.ci.valdez.ak.us/library), has a good selection of books and free Internet access bookable by the hour.

Medical assistance Valdez Medical Clinic, 100 Meals Ave (ⓣ835-4811), for walk-in care; and Valdez Regional Health Authority, 911 Meals Ave (ⓣ835-2249), for more serious attention.

Pharmacy Village Pharmacy, cnr Pioneer Drive

and Meals Ave (Mon–Thurs 9am–6pm, Fri 9am–7pm, Sat 10am–noon).
Post office cnr Galena Drive and Tatitlek St (Mon–Fri 9am–5pm, Sat 10am–noon; ⓣ835-4449). The **General Delivery** zip code is 99686.
Taxes There is no sales tax in Valdez; a hotel tax of six percent has been included in our prices.

North along the Richardson: Keystone Canyon and Thompson Pass

The site of old Valdez marks the beginning of the **Richardson Highway** (for more on the origins of this important artery, see box, p.427), sections of which constitute some of the finest road in the state, particularly the southern forty miles or so where it winds from Valdez through the steep rock walls of Keystone Canyon and up over Thompson Pass through the seemingly impenetrable rock-and-ice barrier presented by the Chugach Mountains.

Keystone Canyon

The Richardson Highway initially traces the right bank of the Lowe River, a wide expanse of water, heavily braided at first and then, thirteen miles outside Valdez, constrained by **Keystone Canyon**, a narrow four-mile-long passage cutting through angled bedrock. During the gold rush, the canyon proved one of the most difficult obstacles faced by prospectors on the route into the Interior, with many preferring the hazardous journey across the Valdez Glacier. All this changed in 1899 when the army cut the **Goat Trail** high on the cliffs, 200–300ft above the north bank, a path just wide enough for two horses to pass. Today most drive straight through, pausing only long enough to photograph **Horsetail Falls** (Mile 13.5) and the five-leap 400-foot **Bridal Veil Falls** (Mile 13.8). If you feel like stretching your legs, you can follow part of the Goat Trail from a turnout opposite Bridal Veil Falls. The best section is the short climb up to the Bridal Veil Falls overlook (400yd each way), but the trail then contours along for a couple of miles high above the canyon floor. Though pleasant enough, it is less exciting than it might be, with restricted views, no relics of the gold days, and no convenient way to turn it into a loop. After the successful completion of the Goat Trail, several companies tried to push a train line along the bottom of the canyon. None was ever completed, but the remains of a hand-cut tunnel can still be seen at Mile 15.

Thompson Pass

As you emerge from Keystone Canyon the country opens out again, this time into broad river flats hemmed in by mountains spilling glaciers down their flanks towards the road. The highway then begins its steep climb towards **Thompson Pass**, a 2771-foot alpine saddle between 6000-foot craggy peaks. Midway up, a mile-long access road leads to *Blueberry Lake State Recreation Site*, Mile 24 ($12; pump water), one of the finest campgrounds in the state, with ten popular sites high on a ridge with 360-degree views of sawtooth mountains and creaking crystalline glaciers – though many sites remain snow-covered well into June. From here it is only a couple of miles to the crest of the pass where grayling and rainbow trout fill a number of small lakes. The low tundra around the lakes is spotted with stunted willow and makes inviting territory for a half-hour **hike**, which should see you up

Our account of places further north along the Richardson Highway begins on p.424.
Wrangell-St Elias National Park coverage starts on p.408.

at the snow line even in late summer. The majestic grandeur of the area is only spoilt by maintenance sheds for the pipeline, which crosses the mountains here, and road-clearing equipment needed to keep the Richardson open in winter, when it sees some of the heaviest snowfall in the state (a record 81ft in the winter of 1952–53), though the road is largely safe from avalanches. For southbound travelers the pass will give you your first glimpse of the mountains to the south, but little indication that Valdez and the sea are only twenty miles away.

The descent through the northern foothills of the Chugach Mountains is more gradual, initially passing the three-pronged **Worthington Glacier**, Mile 28.7, which threatens to envelop the highway. It is part of a day-use-only state recreation site where you can drive within 200yd of the glacier, then follow a short trail along the lateral moraine almost to its face.

Cordova and around

CORDOVA can feel like a town displaced. It is on the eastern shores of Prince William Sound, and yet seems a world apart from the day-cruise bustle of Whittier and Valdez. The town is tentatively linked to the Interior by an old railroad up the Copper River Valley, but you can only get here by boat or plane. Even its waterfront canneries and large fishing fleet seem out of place, more like something out of Southeast Alaska, four hundred miles away.

Cordova's 2500 residents (a number that doubles in summer) go quietly about their business, balancing the day-to-day needs of a small town with the demands of a busy port and fledgling tourist industry. With less than one cruise-ship visit a week in summer, and a ferry schedule that is infrequent enough to discourage many visitors, Cordova has remained off the main tourist circuit. There's a definite charm to wandering the streets (some still with wooden boardwalks), which straggle up the hillside, or strolling past the waterside canneries perched on rows of forty-foot stilts, their sides all rusted corrugated iron spot-painted in half-hearted patch jobs. Much of the time all of this is blanketed in low cloud and damp mist, giving a suitably ethereal atmosphere to the surrounding spruce-specked islands.

Much of downtown dates back to 1909 when Irish railroad engineer, Michael J Heney, selected this cannery site as the place to export copper from the mines at Kennicott and began forging a railroad between the two outposts. Cordova, which Heney named after his favorite Spanish city, prospered thanks to its docks, railroad, and canneries until 1939, when the mines and railroad closed for good. In recent years the biggest threat to the town's livelihood came when a big slick from the *Exxon Valdez* destroyed most of the fishery.

Long after the railroad closed down, the route was turned into the Copper River Highway, which provides access to the immense birding wetlands of the **Copper River Delta**, the partly destroyed **Million Dollar Bridge** over the Copper River, and the **Childs Glacier** right by it.

Arrival and information

Arriving by **ferry** (Ⓣ424-7333 in Cordova) from Valdez or Whittier, you'll be dropped an easy fifteen-minute walk north of the town center. If you can't be bothered, call Wild Hare **taxi** service (Ⓣ424-3939) or Cordova Taxi service (Ⓣ424-5151). Usually, the *Bartlett* is only here for an hour or so on Monday and Wednesday, but on Friday the ferry stays in port for nearly six hours before returning to Valdez, making it possible to visit on a long day trip. This will change in 2005 when the new Cordova-based fast ferry, *Chenega*, starts doing daily runs to Valdez and Whittier.

Alaska Airlines (Ⓣ1-800/225-2752), Jim Air (Ⓣ243-5161), and ERA Aviation (Ⓣ1-800/426-0333) all run daily scheduled **flights** from Anchorage, and also arrive from Seattle via the Southeast towns of Yakutat and Juneau. They land at the Merle K "Mudhole" Smith International Airport (Ⓣ424-7151), named for an early bush pilot, located thirteen miles east of town along the Copper River Highway. The airport shuttle (Ⓣ424-3272; $12 each way) meets each plane and runs into town.

Those looking to fully explore the Copper River Highway will want to **rent a car**, either from JB Transportation (Ⓣ424-3272 or 1-800/770-3272), Copper Coast Car Rentals (Ⓣ424-5356), or from Cordova Car Rental (Ⓣ424-5982, Ⓦwww.ptialaska.net/~cars), which has slightly older cars. **Bikes** are also a viable option, even for exploring the Copper River Highway: rent from Cordova Coastal Outfitters (see p.306; $15 a day).

The main **visitor center** is the Chamber of Commerce, 404 1st St (May to early Sept Mon & Sat 10am–2pm, Tues–Fri 10am–5pm; early Sept–April Mon–Fri 11am–3pm; Ⓣ424-7260, Ⓦwww.cordovachamber.com). If they're not open, check out the booth at the museum. Information on hikes, cabins, and wildlife is best sought at the Forest Service's **Cordova Ranger District Office**, 610 2nd St (Mon–Fri 8am–5pm; Ⓣ424-7661), which has a few mildly interesting displays on the local natural history.

Accommodation

Cordova's accommodation is fairly varied, and most people should find somewhere that suits. There is no hostel, however, and **camping** close to town is limited – although there are plenty of good places along the Copper River Highway for those with transport.

Alaskan Hotel 600 1st St Ⓣ424-3299, Ⓔhotleak@ctcak.net. Old and fairly low-standard hotel in one of the town's original buildings. The price is right, however, with shared-bath rooms at around $40 and ones with private bath for about $60. Go for the rooms on the right to minimize noise and smoke from the bar below. ❶

Cannery Row 1 Cannery Row Ⓣ424-7119, Ⓔcanneryrow@alaska.com. Former cannery manager's home right on the old dock, with wood floors and a 1920s feel. It has been converted to a gorgeous self-catering apartment, which sleeps up to six but is still good value for two. ❻

Cordova Lighthouse Inn Nicholoff Way Ⓣ424-7080, Ⓦwww.cordovalighthouseinn.com. Small, modern inn right by the small boat harbor with four well-appointed rooms, some with great views, plus morning coffee and pastries in the café downstairs (see p.306). ❹

Cordova Rose Lodge 1315 Whitshed Rd Ⓣ424-7673, Ⓦwww.cordovarose.com. Unusual B&B a mile south of downtown that's been imaginatively converted from a barge landlocked by the shores of Odiak Slough. They've kept the nautical theme throughout, the rooms feeling somewhat like cabins, each with its own character and all sharing a communal lounge with library, TV/VCR, and a great view. There's also a separate three-room, self-contained annex with a fishing theme. Hearty breakfast and dinner can be arranged. With breakfast ❺, without ❹

Northern Nights Inn 500 3rd Ave Ⓣ424-5356, Ⓔnorthernnightsinn@hotmail.com. Spacious and attractively decorated rooms in one of Cordova's original homes, all with private bathroom, cable TV, and phone, and most with kitchenettes and harbor views. The owners don't provide breakfast, though you can prepare your own. Great value, and they do low-cost airport pickups for guests. ❷–❸

Odiak Camper Park Whitshed Rd Ⓣ424-6200. Just a gravel lot next to the town dump with token-operated showers and a view of town. It's fine for RVs ($18) but not especially pleasant or good value for campers ($18).

Prince William Motel 501 2nd St Ⓣ424-3201 or 1-888/796-6835, Ⓦwww.ak-biz.com/princewilliammotel. Modern, spacious motel, some rooms with kitchenettes (❹) and all with cable TV and phones with free local calls. ❸

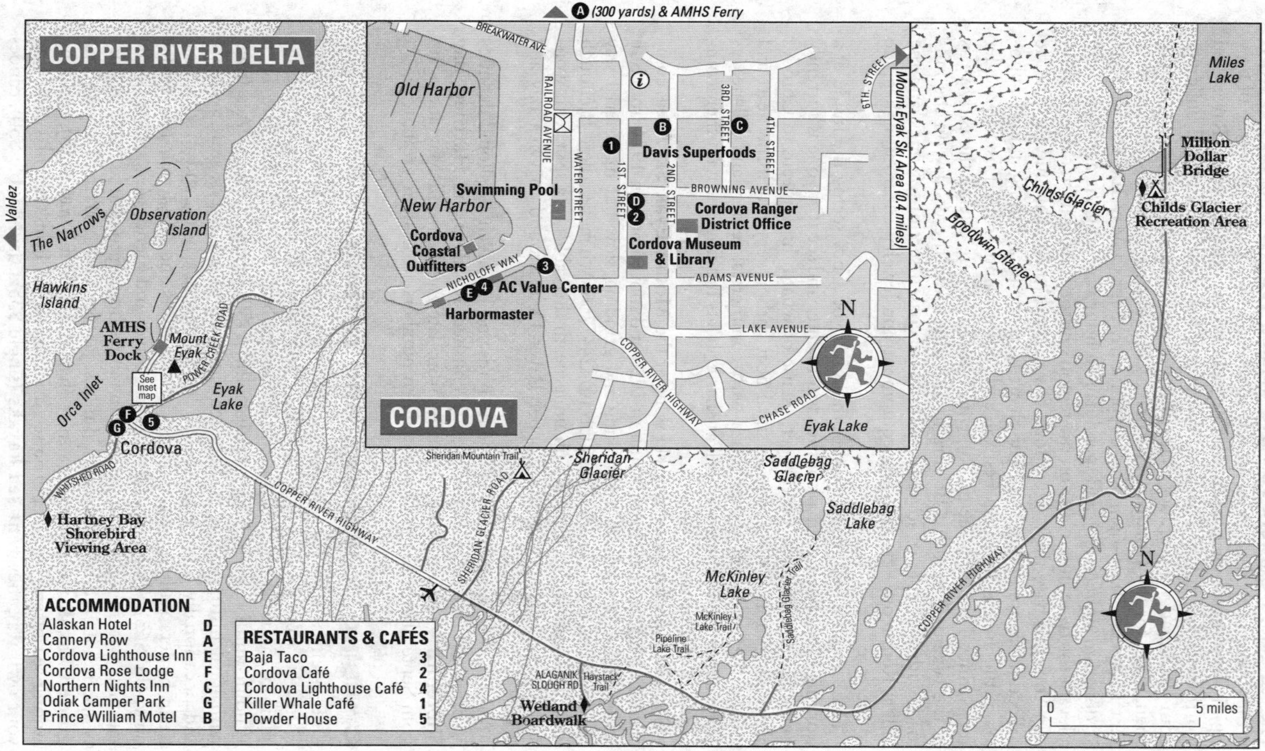

COPPER RIVER DELTA
CORDOVA
A (300 yards) & AMHS Ferry
Mount Eyak Ski Area (0.4 miles)
Valdez
Old Harbor
New Harbor
Swimming Pool
Cordova Coastal Outfitters
Harbormaster
AC Value Center
Davis Superfoods
Cordova Ranger District Office
Cordova Museum & Library
BREAKWATER AVE.
RAILROAD AVENUE
WATER STREET
1ST. STREET
2ND. STREET
3RD. STREET
4TH. STREET
6TH. STREET
BROWNING AVENUE
ADAMS AVENUE
LAKE AVENUE
NICHOLOFF WAY
COPPER RIVER HIGHWAY
CHASE ROAD
Eyak Lake
N
The Narrows
Observation Island
Hawkins Island
AMHS Ferry Dock
Mount Eyak
POWER CREEK ROAD
See inset map
Orca Inlet
Cordova
WHITSHED ROAD
Hartney Bay Shorebird Viewing Area
Sheridan Mountain Trail
SHERIDAN GLACIER ROAD
Sheridan Glacier
Saddlebag Glacier
Saddlebag Lake
Saddlebag Glacier Trail
McKinley Lake
McKinley Lake Trail
Pipeline Lake Trail
ALAGANIK SLOUGH RD
Haystack Trail
Wetland Boardwalk
Childs Glacier
Goodwin Glacier
Million Dollar Bridge
Childs Glacier Recreation Area
Miles Lake
0 5 miles
ACCOMMODATION
Alaskan Hotel D
Cannery Row A
Cordova Lighthouse Inn E
Cordova Rose Lodge F
Northern Nights Inn C
Odiak Camper Park G
Prince William Motel B
RESTAURANTS & CAFÉS
Baja Taco 3
Cordova Café 2
Cordova Lighthouse Café 4
Killer Whale Café 1
Powder House 5

The town and around

The self-guided **Cordova Historic Walking Tour** (pick up the free leaflet at the visitor center) is a pleasant way to spend an hour, getting a sense of how rapidly the town developed as the railhead for the Copper River and Northwestern Railway. The town center still has plenty of original buildings from 1908 that give Cordova a fairly harmonious townscape. When the clouds open, make for the **Cordova Historical Museum**, 620 1st St (June to early Sept Mon–Sat 10am–6pm, Sun 2–4pm; early Sept to May Tues–Sat 1–5pm; $1 donation appreciated), and spend half an hour watching the ageing but still relevant thirty-minute video on the region's history (ask if it isn't already playing). You then have the context for a few minutes' poking around the eclectic collection spanning Aleut and Tlingit artifacts, the local fishing industry, photos of the annual Iceworm Festival, and minor paintings by Eustace Ziegler and Sydney Laurence (see p.210), who both lived here during the early years of the twentieth century. Be sure to also check out the display on the railroad, with a couple of lovely aquatints – a coastal section of track and the mill at Kennicott – track-laying equipment, and jewelry cut from high-grade copper ore.

That's about it for genuine sights, though if you fancy seeing the inside of a working cannery, you can ask at the visitor center and see if anyone is currently running tours. Equally, you can get a sense of what fishing means to Cordova by strolling around the extensive small boat harbor, very much the heart and soul of the town and always abuzz with commercial seiners and gill-netters going about their business as well as charter boats heading out with their complement of tourists.

Cordova even has a downhill ski slope at the **Mount Eyak Ski Area**, complete with an antique chairlift built in 1936 and moved here in 1974 from Sun Valley, Idaho. It works in a chunking and grinding, slow but magisterial way and is operated by the local ski club (Ⓣ424-7766) whenever there is enough snow. In summer you can hike up underneath the cables to a spot with wonderful views right across the Copper River Delta around to Orca Bay and Prince William Sound.

Anyone who is interested in wading birds and has a vehicle should definitely drive the seven miles out along Whitshed Road to the **Hartney Bay Shorebird Viewing Area**, especially from late April to mid-May and again from September through October, when numbers are at their greatest.

Cruising, kayaking, and rafting

One essential stop for any active visitor to Cordova is Cordova Coastal Outfitters (Ⓣ424-7424 or 1-800/357-5145, Ⓦwww.cdvcoastal.com), located in a cabin floating in the small boat harbor off Nicholoff Way. Their Wildlife and Natural History **cruise** (4hr; $150) heads out into Orca Inlet, with local history filling in between sightings of sea otters, seals, seabirds, and occasionally Sitka black-tailed deer, Steller sea lions, and maybe orca. Keen birders will be better served by the Birds and Mud tour (early May only; 4hr; $65), which floats down Eyak River and spends time sitting by the mudflats within sight of the mountain ranges hoping to spot as many as thirty species, including sandpipers, dunlins, jaegers, and harriers. They also do **guided kayak tours** on Orca Inlet (half-day $75; full day $115), paddling among sea otters, harbor porpoises, and maybe sea lions. If you'd rather go your own way, they **rent sea kayaks** (single $35 a day; double $50), canoes

($30), 30hp outboard-equipped skiffs ($115, $90 for second and subsequent days), and fishing and camping gear.

An excellent way to see something of the Copper River Delta and get in a little **rafting** is to join one of the trips run by Alaska River Rafters (Ⓣ424-7238 or 1-800/776-1864, Ⓦwww.alaskarafters.com), based at the Cordova airport. There's immediate appeal in the half-day Sheridan Glacier Adventure (late May–Aug; $75), paddling among icebergs in the moraine lake and then rafting the Class II–III water, but the company also does multiday trips on the Copper River (5 days $1350, and 10 days all the way from McCarthy for $2150).

Eating and drinking

If you are cooking your own meals or surviving on snacks, make use of the large AC Value Center **supermarket** on Nicholoff Way, which has the best selection as well as a good deli counter and bakery, and is open to 9pm or later nightly; Davis Superfoods at 512 1st Ave is more convenient but stocks less. For more substantial **meals** there's a reasonable selection of places in town, and the *Powder House* a mile "out the road," but nothing beyond that.

Baja Taco Nicholoff Way Ⓣ424-5599. Order your taco ($2.75), huevos rancheros ($7.50) or chicken mole ($9.50) from the bright-red school bus and wander across the street to watch the fishers return to the small boat harbor, or hang out on the sunny deck, or retreat to the Mexicana-filled dining room and eat off old metal Corona tables. Mon–Thurs 8am–4pm, Fri–Sun 8am–8pm.

Cordova Café 604 1st St inside *Cordova Hotel* Ⓣ424-5543. Windowless greasy spoon that looks closed most of the time but is usually full of fishermen tucking into $4 stacks of sourdough pancakes and other diner favorites.

Cordova Lighthouse Café Nicholoff Way Ⓣ424-7080. Superb breakfasts, lunches, salads, and sandwiches, plus freshly baked artisan breads, gourmet pizzas (mainly weekends; $17–22), and rich cakes – all homemade and served in convivial surroundings. Closed Mon.

Killer Whale Café 507 1st St Ⓣ424-7733. Tables and benches on a couple of mezzanines inside Orca Books where you will find three-egg omelet breakfasts ($8.50), sandwiches on a choice of French stick, whole wheat, or croissant ($9), imaginative salads ($7–9), and good coffee. A favorite with Cordova's slackers. Open to 4pm, closed Sun.

Powder House Mile 2 Copper River Hwy Ⓣ424-3529. Restaurant and bar built in a former gunpowder storage shed from the CR&NW Railway days, now with a deck overlooking Eyak Lake.

Listings

Banks Wells Fargo, 510 1st St (Ⓣ424-3258) has an ATM, as does the AC Value Center supermarket.

Bookshop Orca Books and Sound, 507 1st St Ⓣ424-5305.

Festivals The Cordova Iceworm Festival (Ⓦwww.iceworm.org) takes place in mid-Feb with the annual march of the ice worm (a 100ft-long costume with dozens of feet sticking out) down the main street; the Copper River Delta Shorebird Festival (Ⓦwww.ptialaska.net/~midtown) attracts birders from all over on the first weekend of May.

Internet access See Library.

Laundry Prince William Laundromat, down alley beside Davis Superfoods (daily 8am–8pm; Ⓣ424-3201).

Library Cordova Public Library, 620 1st St (Tues–Fri 10am–8pm, Sat 1–5pm; Ⓣ424-6667), has free Internet access.

Medical assistance Cordova Community Medical Center, Chase Rd Ⓣ424-8000.

Post office Railroad Ave and Council Ave (Mon–Fri 10am–5.30pm, Sat 10am–1pm). The **General Delivery** zip code is 99574.

Showers Harbormaster Office ($4 for 10min, token available, Mon–Fri 8am–5pm); the Bob Korn Memorial Pool on Railroad Ave is only a dollar or two more, and you get a swim as well.

Taxes Cordova imposes a six percent sales tax, plus a six percent bed tax, which has been included within our price codes.

Hiking and biking from the Copper River Highway

Don't just drive the highway to the Million Dollar Bridge, take time out to explore some varied trails. Most are best done from June to September and all can be muddy after rain. **Mountain bikers** are poorly served by the usually soggy terrain, but the Saddlebag Glacier Trial is usually a good bet. (Trails are listed in order of their distance from Cordova.)

Sheridan Mountain Trail (6 miles round-trip; 4–5hr; 2000ft ascent). A frequently wet trail which climbs gradually up through the forest to open country for tremendous views of Sheridan and Sherman glaciers. Go late in the season, preferably after a dry spell. The trailhead is three miles north of the highway at Mile 13.

Haystack Trail (1.6 miles round-trip; 1hr; 50ft ascent). Easy hike mostly over boardwalks, taking you to a small knoll from where the whole delta and parts of the coast spread out before you. The trailhead is at Mile 18.8.

McKinley Lake/Pipeline Lake trails (5 miles round-trip; 2–3hr; negligible ascent). Gentle forest hike to McKinley Lake and the *McKinley Lake Cabin* (see opposite), where a rough trail leads to the remains of the 1920s Lucky Strike Mine. About halfway back, turn right onto the Pipeline Lakes Trail, which follows the line of an abandoned pipeline used to supply locomotive water for the Copper River and Northwestern Railway. It reaches the highway at Mile 21.4, 0.2 miles from the McKinley Lake Trailhead at Mile 21.6.

Saddlebag Glacier Trail (6 miles round-trip; 2–3hr; 100ft ascent). A pleasant and easy walk through moss-hung spruce forest and cottonwoods to Saddlebag Lake, where the glacier is visible among steep cliffs. Watch for mountain goats. The trailhead is a mile north of the highway at Mile 25.

The Copper River Delta and the Million Dollar Bridge

You should really spend at least one of your days in Cordova driving the fifty-mile-long **Copper River Highway**, and if you are equipped for camping then two or three days would be better: pick up the Chugach National Forest's free *Copper River Delta* and *Take A Hike!* leaflets from the visitor center. There's plenty to explore, not least the **Copper River Delta**, the largest intact wetland on the Pacific coast, stretching for sixty miles east of Cordova. It is a wonderfully rich area of marshes, ponds, and sloughs fed by the outwash from half a dozen glaciers, myriad channels of the mighty Copper River, and more than 160 inches of rainfall. Almost every stream offers opportunities for patient **fishers**, with Dolly Varden and cutthroat trout biting throughout the summer (cutthroat from mid-June only), and more seasonal runs of red (late May to mid-July), and silver salmon (Aug to mid-Sept). **Bird watchers** are even more richly rewarded, especially in spring (late April to late May) during the massive migration of around twenty million waterfowl and shorebirds, including almost the entire world population of western sandpipers.

The highway is laid on the old bed of the **Copper River and Northwestern Railway** (see box, p.412), which linked the ice-free port of Cordova with the copper mines at Kennicott by way of the Copper River Valley. When the mines closed in 1938, the railroad was pulled up, and Cordova boosters have since promoted the idea of using the trackbed to connect their town with the outside world. Congress appropriated funds to lay a road on the old trackbed in 1954, but ten years later, before work really started, the Good Friday earthquake partially destroyed the crucial Million Dollar Bridge. Despite numerous attempts to revive the plan, proponents are still waiting.

For maximum freedom you really need a car, though it is also rewarding (if often wet) to explore by bike, which can be rented in Cordova (see p.303). Allow at least a day in each direction to the end of the Copper River Highway, or use Cordova Coastal Outfitters' shuttle service to drop you off and ride back ($100 to the road end for up to three people). Alternatively, organize your trip to be in Cordova on Wednesday afternoon when Copper River and Northwest Tours (late May to early Sept; $45; ⓣ424-5356) runs a five-hour sightseeing and wildlife-spotting outing by minibus, complete with a box lunch at road's end.

The road is always kept open to the airport and will usually be **snow-free** to the Copper River by late April, though the last mile or two to the Million Dollar Bridge may not be cleared until mid-May or later.

Along the Copper River Highway

The Copper River Highway leaves Cordova past the *Powder House* restaurant, then bursts out of the mountains which hem in the town. From here on there are broad views on all sides as you drive across outwash fans from the Scott, Sheridan, and Sherman glaciers, all visible off to the left. With streams and ponds all about, you seldom seem to be on firm ground for long, except around Cordova's airport (Mile 12). Here, the asphalt gives out, though it remains a good, fast road all the way. A couple of miles on, Sheridan Glacier Road runs four miles inland to the trailhead for the **Sheridan Mountain Trail**, where there's an attractive little streamside **campground** (officially one-night stays only; free) with fire rings, picnic tables, and stream water.

Back on the highway you'll soon come to Alaganik Slough Road (Mile 16.8), a three-mile access road through lily ponds to a picnic area and a 300-yard-long **wetland boardwalk**, which leads to a raised platform that's perfect for viewing waterfowl. Between miles 18 and 25 you are again on firm ground, and a couple of side roads provide access to interesting hiking trails. There are also a couple of rare foot-accessible public-use **cabins**: *McKinley Trail Cabin*, 100yd along the trail, and *McKinley Lake Cabin*, right by the lake almost three miles from the trailhead. Both sleep six and cost $35; book on ⓣ1-877/444-6777, ⓦwww.reserveUSA.com.

Soon the highway hits the Copper River and begins eleven miles of island hopping to get across the river's multiple, broad, gray channels. The final few miles run along the eastern bank of the river and end at a point unnervingly close to two glaciers – the Miles and the Childs – both of which feed icebergs into the river. This is where railroad maestro Michael Heney chose to build his huge, four-span, steel and concrete **Million Dollar Bridge**, one of the biggest engineering headaches during the construction of the CR&NW Railway between 1908 and 1910. Heney was undaunted, boasting "give me enough dynamite and snoose and I'll build a road to hell." He did manage to build a railroad to Kennicott, though only just, and died of exhaustion just months before its completion. As his workers battled temperatures of –60°F, winds reaching 95mph, and 34ft of snow a year, the Childs Glacier unexpectedly began advancing at around 35ft per day, threatening to destroy the bridge. By feverish hacking away at the ice and a fortuitous halt in the glacier's advance, the bridge was saved, only to succumb to the 1964 earthquake. The northern-most span was dislodged so that the trackbed now drags in the river, though a ramp has been rigged up so that pedestrians, bikes, and even high-clearance vehicles can cross the downed span and explore the half-mile of unmaintained road on the other side. Recently, there has been a proposal to repair the bridge to provide access to a planned lodge on the far side, but don't hold your breath.

The highway ends at the south side of the bridge at the **Childs Glacier Recreation Area**, separated from the three-mile-wide face of the Childs Glacier only by the quarter-mile-wide river. Enormous snowfalls in the Chugach Mountains feed the twelve-mile-long glacier, which bulldozes its way east, kept in check only by the undercutting currents of the Copper River. In mid-summer (mid-June to mid-July) stay alert as you wait for ice to calve into the river, as large chunks periodically break off, creating powerful ten-, twenty-, or even forty-foot-high waves which have been known to wash small icebergs into the day-use area and salmon into the trees. People have been injured, so you might feel safer on the viewing platform – on high ground away from the river's edge – from where you may also see harbor seals, which chase salmon up the river. Wherever you stand, this is about as close as you are going to get to a large calving glacier: it is a magnificent and underrated sight. Nearby, in a more protected spot, there's a good **campground** (late May or early June to Sept; $5; water and outhouses).

Travel details

Trains

Whittier to: Anchorage (1 daily; 2hr 20min).

Buses

Valdez to: Delta Junction (on demand; 5hr 30min); Fairbanks (on demand; 7–8hr); Glennallen (on demand; 3hr 15min).

Ferries

Cordova to: Valdez (3–7 weekly; 3–5hr); Whittier (2–7 weekly; 4–7hr).

Valdez to: Cordova (3–7 weekly; 3–6hr); Juneau (1–2 month; 36hr); Seward (weekly; 11hr); Whittier (4–7 weekly; 3–6hr).

Whittier to: Cordova (2–7 weekly; 4–7hr); Valdez (4–7 weekly; 3–6hr).

Flights

Cordova to: Anchorage (2–3 daily; 50min); Juneau (1 daily; 2hr); Seattle (1 daily; 6hr); Yakutat (1 daily; 45min).

Valdez to: Anchorage (2–3 daily; 40min).

5

Southwest Alaska

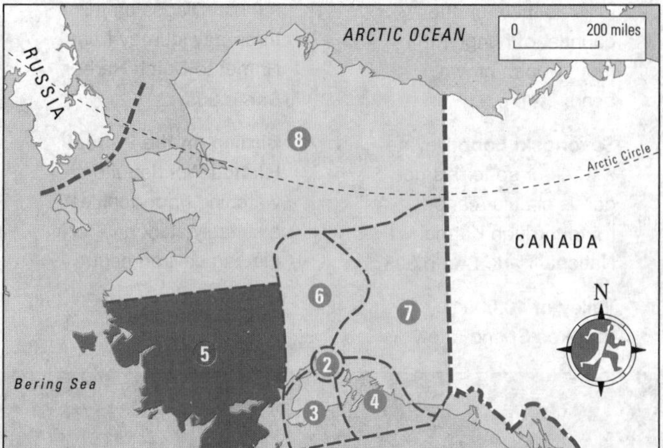

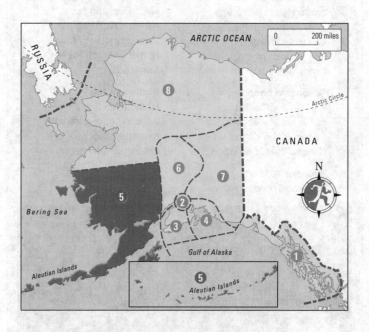

CHAPTER 5

Highlights

* **Kodiak Island** Fascinating Russian and Native history, plus the chance to explore the only real road system in the Southwest. See p.315

* **Bear viewing** Watch salmon leap up Brooks Falls as they run the gauntlet of hungry, mouth-open brown bears. See p.332

* **Savonoski Loop** Devote a week or so to this gorgeous circular canoe route through Katmai National Park. See p.333

* **Valley of 10,000 Smokes** Spend a few days hiking in this desolate landscape of sculpted volcanic ash within Katmai National Park. See p.333

* **Aleutians ferry trip** See whales, dolphins, a string of snowcapped volcanoes, and tiny remote villages on this three-day journey from Homer to Dutch Harbor. See p.335

* **Birding on the Pribilof Islands** Wonderful bird-watching opportunities in a suitably stark and forbidding environment. See p.345

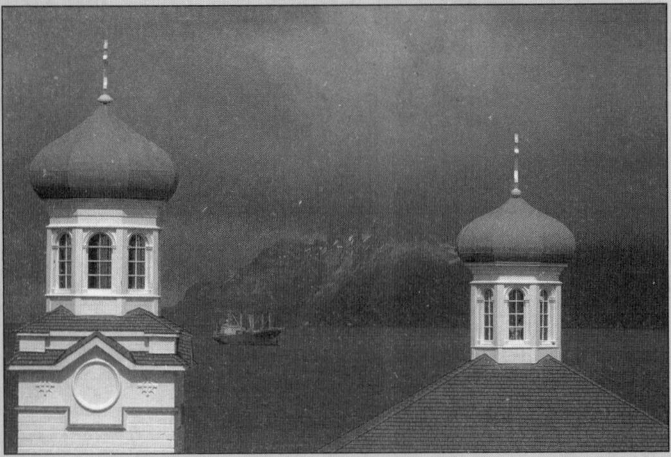

△ Church rooftops, Dutch Harbor

5

Southwest Alaska

Even by Alaska's standards, few places are as isolated as the Southwest, a vast region that stretches 1600 miles from Anchorage, along the Alaska Peninsula and out to the tip of the Aleutian Chain. From its southern shore, the Alaska Peninsula rises steeply to its snowy backbone, the Aleutian Range, and then drops away to the north towards the swampy lowlands of the Lake Clark and Katmai national parks. Further west the peninsula tapers off until breaking up into the string of Aleutian Islands, each the top of a volcano rising from the sea bottom – the area contains 27 of the US's 47 active volcanoes. Altogether less than 25,000 people call this region home.

The weather bears much of the blame for its inhospitable reputation, as arctic winds whip up ferocious seas and warm currents from Japan generate dense fogs that can hang around for days. Yet those who can stick it out are often rewarded – fishermen working two short seasons in these rich waters can haul in over $100,000 a year – a temptation that's hard to resist.

With these quick returns, there's a sizable group of transient workers who fly into Kodiak or Dutch Harbor from the Lower 48, stay six weeks, then head somewhere warm until the next seasonal opening. Visitors come, too, but the high cost of transportation keeps numbers low. Only the truly dedicated and those with an adventurous spirit bother to make the effort to experience Southwest Alaska, something that adds to the region's appeal.

For those who do visit, there are substantial rewards, not least the striking topography of almost fifty **volcanoes**, many of them classic snowcapped cones: Spurr, on Anchorage's doorstep; Redoubt and Iliamna in Lake Clark National Park; Augustine, an island at the mouth of Cook Inlet; Novorupta in Katmai National Park; Shishaldin, at the end of the Alaska Peninsula, which erupted as recently as 1999; Makushin on Unalaska Island; and many more.

At more than 10,000ft, Redoubt and Iliamna are two of the tallest, overlooking **Lake Clark National Park**, where exclusive fishing lodges allow keen anglers to hook salmon on their way upstream from Bristol Bay. The salmon-rich rivers are used by rafters and experienced canoeists who tackle one of the three designated National Wild Rivers within the park's bounds. People also come to fish for salmon in **Katmai National Park**, but most folks prefer to see the fish eaten by the hungry brown bears congregating around Brooks Falls. If you can score a position on the platform, there's a chance of getting the ultimate in Alaskan wildlife photography: a snap of an open-jawed bear about to snag a leaping salmon.

Both parks can only be reached by expensive flights; the rest of the Southwest, however, is accessible by ferry, with frequent services visiting **Kodiak Island**, with its concentration of enormous Kodiak bears. This is

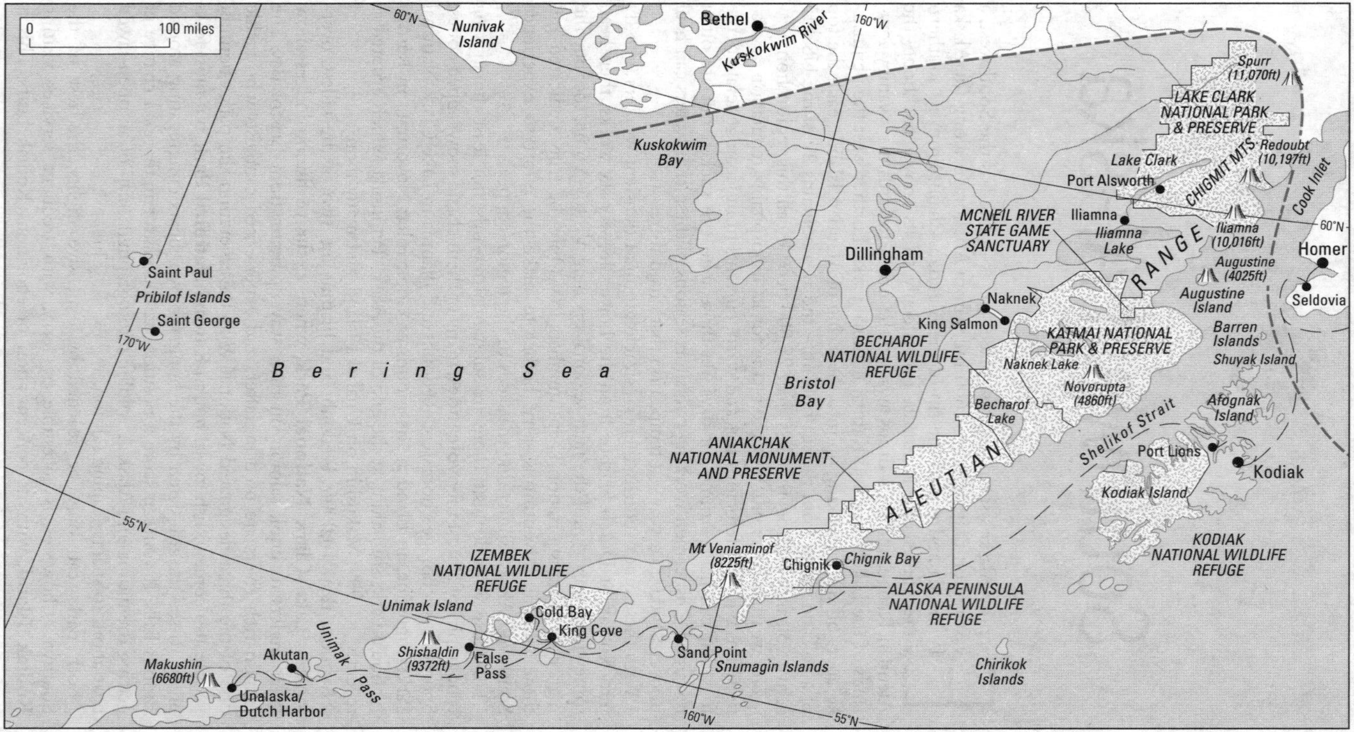
0
100 miles
Bethel
Kuskokwim River
Nunivak Island
60°N
160°W
Kuskokwim Bay
Spurr (11,070ft)
LAKE CLARK NATIONAL PARK & PRESERVE
Redoubt (10,197ft)
CHIGMIT MTS
Lake Clark
Port Alsworth
Cook Inlet
Iliamna
Iliamna (10,016ft)
Iliamna Lake
MCNEIL RIVER STATE GAME SANCTUARY
RANGE
Homer
Seldovia
Augustine (4025ft)
Augustine Island
Barren Islands
Shuyak Island
Dillingham
Naknek
King Salmon
KATMAI NATIONAL PARK & PRESERVE
Naknek Lake
Novorupta (4860ft)
BECHAROF NATIONAL WILDLIFE REFUGE
Becharof Lake
Bristol Bay
Saint Paul
Pribilof Islands
Saint George
170°W
Bering Sea
Afognak Island
Shelikof Strait
Port Lions
Kodiak
Kodiak Island
KODIAK NATIONAL WILDLIFE REFUGE
ANIAKCHAK NATIONAL MONUMENT AND PRESERVE
ALEUTIAN
Mt Veniaminof (8225ft)
Chignik
Chignik Bay
ALASKA PENINSULA NATIONAL WILDLIFE REFUGE
55°N
IZEMBEK NATIONAL WILDLIFE REFUGE
Unimak Island
Cold Bay
King Cove
Sand Point
Snumagin Islands
Chirikok Islands
Shishaldin (9372ft)
False Pass
Unimak Pass
Akutan
Makushin (6680ft)
Unalaska/ Dutch Harbor

where the Russians set up their first capital, while enslaving the Native Aleut people to ensure a profitable supply of sea-otter pelts. The ferry continues further southwest calling at tiny fishing ports en route to **Unalaska/Dutch Harbor**, at the start of the Aleutian Chain; California gray whales can sometimes be seen migrating, heading north in April to the Bering Sea and Mexico-bound in September. The rest of the long Aleutian Chain, strung out beyond Dutch Harbor, is barely inhabited, expensive to get to (Alaska Airlines charges $1100 round-trip to Adak from King Salmon) and usually well off the tourist itinerary, though specialist bird-watching trips occasionally venture out here.

To the north, the **Pribilof Islands** stand apart from the Aleutian Chain, their treeless tops covered with lush grass and wildflowers in spring. There's a windswept beauty to the place, but the few visitors who make it here come specifically to admire the sea cliffs, alive with thousands of nesting birds, and the rocks and beaches below, usually packed with basking seals.

Kodiak Island and the archipelago

On most days an ethereal mist wreaths the green hummocky hills of **KODIAK ISLAND**, a ragged, once-glaciated slice of the state adrift in the Gulf of Alaska. At a hundred miles long and sixty wide, it ranks as the largest island in the US.

Most of the residents are tucked into the top-right corner, around the town of Kodiak, leaving the rest of the island to some three thousand of the biggest brown bears in the world. Weighing in at anywhere from 800 to 1500 pounds, they are so large they even get a separate name, **Kodiak bears**. Their size is a product of their rich diet; in fact, so abundant are the salmon here that bears often only bother with the fattiest, most nutritious parts (the skin and the roe) and discard the rest. With such a comfortable lifestyle, it is hardly surprising that the island supports as many bears as there are grizzlies in the whole of the Lower 48. Most of the bears are deep within the **Kodiak National Wildlife Refuge**, which encompasses the entire western two-thirds of Kodiak, all of neighboring Uganik Island, and parts of Afognak Island to the north. The refuge is also home to Sitka black-tailed deer, mountain goat, red fox, Roosevelt elk, and plenty of bald eagles, but not a single moose. Come during the salmon runs between mid-June and early September for the best chance of seeing bears, and set aside a good wad of cash for the flights required.

Human settlement began with the Alutiiq people who have occupied sites around here for upwards of seven thousand years, gradually developing a sophisticated culture based on fishing and hunting. That all changed in the middle of the eighteenth century when **Russian fur traders** arrived and, by forcefully separating families, kidnapping, and even burning villages, forced the Natives to hunt sea otters for sale rather than for their own needs. So profitable was the trade that by 1784 the enterprising Siberian merchant **Gregorii Shelikov**, along with his wife and over a hundred Russian men, established Alaska's first white settlement at Three Saints Bay, halfway down the east coast of Kodiak Island. After a couple of years, word of his ruthless methods got out and he was recalled to Russia, only to be replaced in 1790 by **Alexandr Baranov**. After a tsunami nearly destroyed the Three Saints Bay settlement, Baranov set up Pavlovsk at St Paul Harbor, the current site of Kodiak, as the new Russian-American Company headquarters. Pavlovsk's golden period only lasted a decade, and as the region's sea otters were killed off the focus of

Russian interest shifted towards Sitka, where Baranov moved his capital of Russian Alaska in 1808. (For more on Alaska's Russian period, see p.524.)

Today Kodiak Island has some wonderful kayaking and good hiking, all within easy reach of the historic and attractively set town of Kodiak. Add in a busy fishing fleet, a few good festivals, plus the possibility of surfing at road-accessible beaches, and you can easily fill a few enjoyable days, possibly supplemented by more remote kayaking around **Shuyak Island** further north. Be warned, though, that the **weather** throughout the archipelago is cool and wet most of the summer, with low clouds covering the island.

Kodiak

The town of **KODIAK** was transformed on March 27, 1964, when the huge earthquake that rocked Southcentral and parts of Southwest Alaska caused a thirty-foot tsunami to sweep over the town. The wave was so powerful that fishing boats were washed onto dry land, one fisherman reporting to a state trooper, "It looks as though I'm behind the Kodiak schoolhouse, about six blocks from the waterfront"; a plaque on Lower Mill Bay Road still marks the spot. Much of the town was destroyed in the process, but land uplifted in the quake created a new flat surface that turned out to be perfect for the reconstruction of downtown, a largely modern place with a couple of Russian-era buildings contributing the only architectural interest.

As the big wave drew out, it sucked the water from the channel between Kodiak and the offshore Near Island, but the fishing harbor survived and is as busy as ever, with almost eight hundred boats calling Kodiak home. King crab

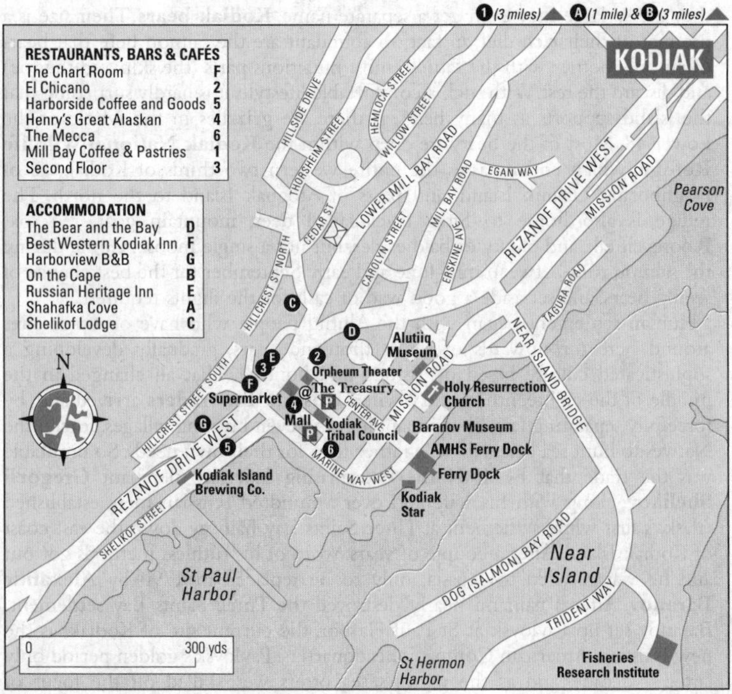

used to be the big-money catch, but they have been mostly fished out, and today the boats go out for salmon, halibut, Dungeness and Tanner crab, and bottom fish, such as gray cod, pollock, and sole. The day's catch is brought to channel-side canneries, such as the one built around the *Star of Kodiak*, a World War II ship brought here after the tsunami as emergency accommodation and subsequently converted for fish processing.

After its days as the capital of Russian Alaska, Kodiak ticked by quietly until World War II when the US **navy** moved in, setting up a huge base south of town and constructing a decoy Kodiak topped with lights to draw enemy fire away from the blacked-out town. During the war 25,000 people lived here, but the population has now dropped to around 10,000, with most living off fishing and fish processing. In the past twenty-odd years, high wages have attracted immigrants from the Philippines, Laos, Vietnam, Mexico, Hawaii, Samoa, and elsewhere, and Kodiak has taken on a fairly cosmopolitan tenor.

Although quite easy to reach from Homer, Kodiak sees relatively few tourists, and it can be refreshing to wander the streets stopping into the excellent Baranov and Alutiiq **museums**, checking out Near Island's Fisheries Research Institute, and visiting the moody clifftop forest of **Fort Abercrombie State Historic Park**.

Getting there and arrival

The *Tustumena* **ferry** from Homer ties up at the dock right in the heart of town beside the AMHS office (Mon–Fri 8am–5pm, Sat 8am–4pm; ⓣ486-3800 or 1-800/526-6731). Through most of the summer there are three ferries a week: on Sunday and Monday the ferry is in town for only a couple of hours before heading back to Homer, but on Wednesday you have the full day (from 9am to 4.30pm) to explore, making a round-trip from Homer a great short cruise, especially if you see whales and the other marine mammals that frequently show themselves around the Barren Islands north of Kodiak. About every fourth Wednesday sailing continues west along the Alaska Peninsula to Unalaska/Dutch Harbor (see p.337), after first spending the day in Kodiak.

ERA Aviation (ⓣ487-4363) and Alaska Airlines (ⓣ487-4361) jointly dispatch seven **flights** a day from Anchorage to Kodiak airport. Fares vary a fair bit, but they can often be as low as $250 round-trip with Alaska Airlines; both airlines often have excellent web specials on weekends. Flight delays due to bad weather are not uncommon. The airport is five miles southwest of Kodiak town, and with only a very infrequent local bus service (see below) you'll probably want to catch one of the waiting taxis, or call A & B Taxi (ⓣ486-4343), and pay around $8 into town.

Information and getting around

The main **visitor center**, 100 Marine Way (mid-June to mid-Sept Mon–Fri 8am–5pm, Sat & Sun dependent on ferries; mid-Sept to mid-June Mon–Fri 8am–noon & 1–5pm; ⓣ486-4782, ⓦwww.kodiak.org), is downtown right by the ferry dock. For information on the **Kodiak National Wildlife Refuge** call at their visitor center, 1390 Buskin River Rd (June–Aug Mon–Fri 8am–7pm, Sat & Sun noon–4pm; Sept–May Mon–Fri 8am–4.30pm; ⓣ487-2600, ⓦwww.r7.fws.gov/nwr/kodiak), close to the airport, four miles south of town. It is an essential stop before any trip into the refuge and worth a call anyway for the mounted animals and seventeen-minute video about the island and its wildlife.

The downtown sights can all be seen on foot, without recourse to the KATS **bus** system ($2; ⓣ486-8308), which operates just two weekday services

(Mon–Fri 6.30–7.45am & 5–6.20pm) on a route from the big Safeway three miles northeast of town through the main shopping and residential areas to the airport and back. So to explore outside the center you really need to either **rent a car** or a **bike** (for both see "Listings," p.322), or consider joining Kodiak Tours (Ⓣ486-3920 evenings) for a **bus tour** of the town and surrounds (half-day $50, full day $85).

Accommodation

As in most of Alaska you'll need to book in advance to secure a room during the peak three months of summer. Kodiak has no hostel, and the eleven percent local tax hikes up the already high room rates, so those on a tight budget will want to make use of the two local **campgrounds**.

Along the roads **outside town**, accommodation is fairly limited, though there is plenty of freelance short-term camping beside beaches, and one more formal spot at Pasagshak (see opposite).

Chartering a float plane opens up access to seven public-use **cabins** ($30) inside the Kodiak National Wildlife Refuge. Each comes with a kerosene heater, a pit toilet, and sleeping platforms for at least four people: you'll need to carry everything else including a cooking stove. In practice, it can be hard to get a place as the cabins are made available by lottery several months in advance. If there are spaces after the lottery is drawn, the cabins are let on a first-come, first-served basis: for details contact the refuge visitor center. In addition, there are a couple of state-run cabins on Afognak Island (Ⓣ486-6339, Ⓦwww.alaskastateparks.org; $35).

There are also some forty **wilderness lodges** dotted around the archipelago, almost all in gorgeous remote locations, with canoes and kayaks. Many are pitched towards the rod-and-gun set, but will also cater to birders, wildlife photographers, and those who just want a few days' complete relaxation. All require float-plane access and most charge $300–400 per person a day: the Kodiak visitor center has a full list, and you can check out many of their websites through the "Wilderness Lodges" section of Ⓦwww.kodiak.org.

Hotels, motels, and B&Bs

The Bear and the Bay 216 Rezanof Drive East Ⓣ486-6154, Ⓦwww.bearandthebay.com. Central B&B in a modern home with harbor views, comfortable rooms, and a really good continental breakfast. Two-night (or longer) stays preferred. Private bath ❹, shared bath ❸

Harborview B&B 310 Rezanof Drive West Ⓣ486-2464 or 1-888/283-2464; Ⓦwww.kodiakfishkonnection.com. Comfortable and centrally located B&B with good sea views, cable TV, home-cooked breakfast, and one room with a wonderful view of the harbor. ❺

Kodiak Inn 236 Rezanof Drive West Ⓣ486-5712 or 1-888/563-4254, Ⓦwww.kodiakinn.com. The closest Kodiak gets to an upscale hotel, a Best Western with eighty pleasant and well-equipped rooms plus a restaurant and bar. ❻

On the Cape 3476 Spruce Cape Rd Ⓣ486-4185, Ⓦwww.onthecape.net. Attractive B&B three miles north of downtown Kodiak, with ocean-view rooms, a large deck, hot tub, and a buffet breakfast. ❺

Pasagshak River Accommodations Mile 8 Pasagshak Rd Ⓣ486-6702, Ⓦwww.pasagshakriver.com. Fully self-contained two- and three-bedroom homes 45 miles from Kodiak town and close to the beach. Always popular with salmon fishers, this is one of the few places in this area to get a roof over your head. Charged at $90 a night per person. ❼

Russian Heritage Inn 119 Yukon St Ⓣ486-5657, Ⓦwww.ak-biz.com/russianheritage. Decent enough motel-style rooms with private bath, cable TV, and microwave and refrigerator, plus some rooms with full kitchen. Kitchen room ❹, standard room ❸

Shahafka Cove 1812 Mission Rd Ⓣ486-2409, Ⓦwww.ptialaska.net/~rwoitel. Over a mile north of town, but with a huge waterside deck, views over the channel, and a full breakfast. ❷–❹

Shelikof Lodge 211 Thorsheim Ave Ⓣ486-4141, Ⓦwww.shelikoflodge.com. Kodiak's cheapest hotel rooms, and pretty decent ones, too, with TV and on-site bar and restaurant. ❸

Camping

Buskin River State Recreation Site 4.5 miles southwest of town. Close to the airport, this campground lies adjacent to the Kodiak National Wildlife Refuge Visitor Center and its associated nature trail. Fire rings, picnic tables, and potable water. $8.

Fort Abercrombie State Historical Park 4 miles north of town. The best of the local campgrounds with sites dotted among the Sitka spruce and World War II fort remnants all around, fire rings, picnic tables, and potable water. $8.

Pasagshak State Recreation Site 45 miles south of town. Casual beachside camping spots close to a fishing stream. There's an outhouse and hand pump, but no other facilities. Free.

The Town

The *Explore Kodiak* magazine (free from the visitor center) contains a detailed walking tour around town, but you miss little by limiting yourself to a few highlights. Opposite the visitor center stand Kodiak's two most architecturally harmonious buildings, both Russian in design and execution. Straight ahead is **Erskine House**, a white-weatherboard building with green trim, built as a fur warehouse and office for the Russian-American Company around 1808, making it not only the oldest building in Alaska but the oldest extant structure on the West Coast of North America. It houses the **Baranov Museum**, 101 Marine Way (late May to early Sept Mon–Sat 10am–4pm, Sun noon–4pm; early Sept to late May Tues–Sat 10am–3pm; $2), a small but intriguing collection of Native and Russian pieces, including intricate woven grass baskets, a kopek note printed on sealskin, and a three-place *baidarka* made from sea-lion hides. One room is filled with high-quality furniture from the Russian era, illustrating just how much money was being made from the sea-otter pelts. Elsewhere, there's a corner devoted to local Alutiiq boy Benny Benson, who designed the Alaska state flag (see p.249).

Behind Erskine House is the **Holy Resurrection Russian Orthodox Church** (free tours late May to early Sept daily 1–2pm; services all year Thurs 6.30pm, Sat 6.30pm, and Sun 9am), another weatherboard structure, prim and white but for two flamboyant blue onion-dome cupolas. Sadly, it isn't authentic, the original having burnt down in 1943, but does contain some interesting artifacts: a 1790s icon brought from Russia, ornate candle stands, and the reliquary of St Herman, a Russian missionary to Alaska who became the first canonized Orthodox saint in North America. You can see his monk's hat and thirty-pound chains, and if you're here around the second week in August, join the 300-strong annual boat pilgrimage to Monk's Lagoon, on nearby Spruce Island where he spent his later years. To the right of the main church entrance lie some of the original bells, cast here between 1794 and 1796, the first on the West Coast, and there's a small gift shop (daily 11am–5pm) packed with Russian icons, nested dolls, porcelain and the like.

Across the street, the **Alutiiq Museum**, 215 Mission Rd (June–Aug Mon–Fri 9am–5pm, Sat 10am–5pm; Sept–May Tues–Fri 9am–5pm, Sat 10.30am–4.30pm; $2; Ⓦ www.alutiiqmuseum.com), plays a crucial role in preserving the history of Kodiak's Native people by facilitating interaction between the local Native community, anthropologists, and archeologists. When the Russians arrived in Alaska they assumed the Alutiiq people were the same as the Aleut they'd encountered further west, but the Alutiiq actually have far greater cultural and linguistic associations with the Yup'ik further north. Some confusion is perhaps excusable since Kodiak has long been something of a cultural crossroads, as evident from sites unearthed by archeologists that date back 7500 years. Some of these sites have come under threat since the *Exxon Valdez* disaster; hose spraying during the beach cleanup washed away precious evidence, and newly uncovered sites were vandalized.

One positive outcome of the oil spill was funding for the establishment of the Alutiiq Museum. Though the entire collection is huge, there are only ever a few artifacts on display – but all are beautiful. Cases separate pieces into those associated with men's work, principally hunting and skin sewing, and those with women's work, such as food preparation and making clothing. There's also a lovely example of a skin kayak, plus the obligatory stuffed Kodiak brown bear. If all this sparks some interest, and you can spare a few days, consider joining the museum's community **volunteer archeology program**, working at a dig somewhere out on the road system during the day, then returning to Kodiak in the evening.

Near Island and Pillar Mountain

A narrow channel separates Kodiak from **Near Island**, reached over the modern Fred Zharoff Memorial Bridge (aka "The Bridge to Nowhere"), renamed for an Alaska state senator and Native leader who died a few years back. Until then it was known as the Hoser Bridge, for the Kodiak fire department's Dalmatian which, shortly after the bridge's completion, took a suicide leap off the middle span.

Near Island is now home to Kodiak's second commercial fishing harbor, St Herman's, the float-plane dock, and the Kodiak Fisheries Research Center, 301 Research Court (Mon–Fri 8am–4.30pm; free), easily reached from town in twenty minutes on foot. There isn't a lot to see, but the building is beautifully sited by the ocean, and what's on display is well presented, particularly the cylindrical aquarium stocked with several species of crab, assorted starfish, colorful anemones, mussels, and more. Behind is the touch tank, a riot of purples, reds, blues, and oranges: dip your hand in to feel the silky-smooth sea cucumbers and inspect at close quarters the scarlet blood star. Notice, too, the panel showing where various species of salmon spend their lives before returning to Alaskan rivers to spawn.

With wheels you might fancy driving up the anonymous gravel road to the top of **Pillar Mountain** (1270ft) immediately behind town. The wide selection of radar and communications towers on top aren't especially pretty, but turn your back on them and you can see down to the town and harbor and inland across the lumpy interior.

Fort Abercrombie State Park

By far the best short outing from town is to **Fort Abercrombie State Historic Park**, four miles northeast of downtown. The prominent headland of Miller Point is now shrouded in towering, moss-draped Sitka spruce, but this was once an important defense position developed following the Japanese attack on Pearl Harbor in 1941. Stroll through the woods, and you will come across moldering, but neatly labeled, World War II remains: ammunition magazines, searchlight bunkers, observation platforms, and the shattered mounts for a couple of eight-inch guns. It is a great place to idle away some time, with orchids and wildflowers blooming in spring, and an opportunity to view bald eagles, puffins, and humpback whales (mid-May to mid-Aug) migrating past at the **Miller Point headland**. Here you'll also find the largest of the ammunition bunkers, at the **Kodiak Military History Museum** (late May to early Sept Mon, Wed, Sat & Sun 1–4pm and by appointment; $3; ⓣ486-9781), which concentrates on World War II history, especially communications in this remote outpost. There's also a small visitor center (Mon–Fri 8.30am–5pm; ⓣ486-6339) and walking tracks which lead around **Gertrude Lake**, good for tidepooling and even swimming for the very keen.

Kayaking and fishing

The Kodiak archipelago has some of the finest **sea kayaking** around. Near Island and its acolytes, just across the channel from the town, have all sorts of narrow straits and shallow coves where you can bob around looking down through crystal-clear water at brilliantly colored starfish and anemones. Alaskan Wilderness Adventures (Ⓣ486-2397, Ⓔakwild@ptialaska.net) runs morning, afternoon, and evening trips around the area for $60 (minimum 2). Longer trips can be customized to suit and are charged at $100 a day plus $75 per night for overnights. Kodiak Kayak Tours (Ⓣ486-2722) also runs four-hour local trips (9am & 2pm) for $60.

There are so many people prepared to take you **fishing** it is hard to know where to start, but Kodiak Fish Konnection (late May to late Sept; Ⓣ486-2464, kodiakfk@ptialaska.net) will take you out for a full day of salmon or halibut fishing for $175, including processing (gutting, filleting, freezing, and packing) what you catch. If they don't do the sort of thing you're after, they'll put you in touch with someone who does.

Kodiak is also said to have some of the best roadside salmon fishing in the state: the Alaska Department of Fish and Game, 211 Mission Rd (Ⓣ486-1880, Ⓦwww.adfg.state.ak.us), has a list of guides, knows the regulations, and can sell you a license. Cy's Sporting Goods, 117 Lower Mill Bay Rd (Ⓣ486-3900, Ⓦwww.kodiak-outfitters.com), will sell all the gear you need, have locally made flies, and all the latest on where fish are biting; they also organize fly-ins.

Eating, drinking, and entertainment

The range of restaurants in Kodiak is adequate for a few days, and **grocery** prices from Food For Less downtown are only around ten percent higher than in Anchorage. About the only regular entertainment is seeing a **movie** at the Orpheum Theatre, 102 Center St (Ⓣ486-5449), or watching the **Kodiak Alutiiq Dancers** (June–Aug Mon, Wed & Fri 2pm; $12; Ⓣ486-4449), who perform an hour-long celebration of traditional dance in the Kodiak Tribal Council hall downtown at 312 W Marine Way. Look out for the **microbrews** of the island's own Kodiak Island Brewing Co, which sells on tap around town and by the bottle from their brewery at 338 Shelikof St (Ⓣ486-2537). If you're keen, stop by for a brief free tour (daily 2–7pm). To combine sightseeing and eating head out on the characterful old *Sea Breeze* launch (Ⓣ486-5079, Ⓔmarion@ptialaska.net) for a gourmet **dinner cruise** based around local seafood (3–4hr; $100).

The Chart Room 236 Rezanof Drive West, inside the *Best Western* Ⓣ486-8807. Kodiak's most formal dining, with good harbor views as you enjoy $30 king crab legs or $17 halibut steaks. Don't miss the photos of the 1964 tsunami aftermath in the hallway.

El Chicano 103 Center Ave Ⓣ486-6116, Ⓦwww.elchicano.com. Reliable Mexican meals are dished up either inside or on the sunny deck. The menu is filled with the usual suspects – enchiladas, burritos, and the like – for $10–12, but they also do plates of chorizo, eggs, rice, and beans ($11) and for the brave, menudo, a kind of tripe soup.

Harborside Coffee and Goods 216 Shelikov St Ⓣ486-5862. Just the spot for hanging out over an espresso, soup, or cinnamon roll to watch the harbor activity out the window.

Henry's Great Alaskan 512 Marine Way Ⓣ486-8844. A combined sports bar and restaurant with microbrewed beer and a good range of salads, sandwiches, burgers, and dinners, such as halibut and fries, all around $10–12.

The Mecca 302 Marine Way Ⓣ486-3364. Typically lively bar often with live music and even the occasional touring band.

Mill Bay Coffee & Pastries 3833 Rezanof Drive East Ⓣ486-4411, Ⓦwww.millbaycoffee.com. The best café-style eating on the island, with sofas and mismatched furniture for sipping good espresso coffees or tucking into the likes of chicken Caesar salad ($9), quiches, and a sumptuous array of

French pastries. There's even outside seating for those rare sunny days.

Second Floor 116 Rezanof Drive West ⓣ 486-8555. An unlikely find, this Japanese restaurant does sushi well. Try the Kodiak Roll – sushi made from local seafood – one of the tempura dishes, and a Japanese beer, and expect to pay at least $25 a head.

Listings

Air-charter companies Andrew Airways ⓣ 487-2566, ⓦ www.andrewairways.com; Highline Air Service ⓣ 486-5155, ⓔ highline@ptialaska.net; Island Air Service ⓣ 486-6196, ⓦ kodiakislandair.com; Kodiak Air Service ⓣ 486-4446, ⓔ willie@kodiakair.com; Sea Hawk ⓣ 486-8282 or 1-800/770-4295, ⓦ www.seahawkair.com.

Banks There are several around town, including Key Bank, 422 E Marine Way, in The Mall. All banks and the supermarkets have ATMs.

Bike rental Fairly basic bikes are available downtown from the *Russian Heritage Inn* ($25 a day), but better hardtail machines can be had a mile north at either 58°North, 1231 Mill Bay Rd (ⓣ 486-6294, ⓔ thowland@ptialaska.net), which charges $25 for a full 24 hours, or next door at Orion's Mountain Sports, 1247 Mill Bay Rd (ⓣ 486-8380), which does an identical deal.

Books Several places around town have free book swaps, including the *Harborside Coffee and Goods* (see p.321). For new books visit The Treasury, 104 Central St (ⓣ 486-0373).

Car rental The best deals are Rent-a-Heap, inside Port of Kodiak Gifts in The Mall, 508 Marine Way (ⓣ 486-8550, ⓔ carrent@ptialaska.net), which charges $37 a day plus 37¢ a mile for a compact, and Budget, same address and at the airport (ⓣ 487-2220, ⓔ budget@eagle.ptialaska.net), which rents unlimited-mileage compacts for $60.

Festivals In late March or early April, there's the Pillar Mountain Golf Classic (ⓣ 486-2931, ⓦ chiniak.net/pillar), a one-hole par-70 course in which you have to hit 1400ft up Pillar Mountain in the depths of winter snow, with ball-spotters

Hiking on Kodiak Island

Hiking on Kodiak is limited to forest walks and a few trails up hills close to Kodiak town. Those smooth green hills might look tempting for off-trail exploration, but foot-tangling grasses, and thickets of willow and alder make it very heavy going once you leave a defined path. Pick up the free *Hiking on Kodiak* leaflet from either visitor center.

Out in the **Kodiak National Wildlife Refuge** hiking trails are few, and you'll be pretty much making it up as you go along. If you fancy engaging the services of a guide, you'll find a list of operators at the refuge visitor center.

Remember that Kodiak weather is fickle even by Alaskan standards, so you'll need to be well prepared. If you need to rent gear (or extra gear), contact Kodiak Kamps (ⓣ 486-5333).

Barometer Mountain (5 miles round-trip; 3–4hr; 2500ft ascent). The most popular hike on the island climbs to the summit of this 2452-foot peak by the steep east ridge with views improving all the way up. The trail starts almost opposite the end of the airport runway a hundred yards south of a sharp bend in the road. After heading into the brush, it switchbacks up to a fork where you branch right along a gravel road for 500yd until the path up the ridge heads off on your left.

North End Park (half a mile; 20min; 100ft ascent). Easy shoreline trails starting beside the Zharoff Bridge on Near Island, ideal for an evening stroll and for salmonberry picking in July and August.

Pillar Mountain (2.5 miles round-trip; 1–2hr; 800ft ascent). A moderate hike to the summit, beginning at Pillar Mountain Road on the left just past the quarry a third of the way up the mountain. From the summit a second trail leads three miles southwest towards the Tie substation, where a gravel road leads down to the highway a mile or so north of the airport.

Pyramid Mountain (4 miles round-trip; 3–4hr; 2200ft ascent). This hike starts at the ski area on Anton Larsen Bay Road, a couple of miles past the golf course. From the parking lot it climbs steeply through brush to a broad shoulder on alpine tundra. The views are great from here, but the more adventurous will want to press on to the top.

allowed but no radio communication or dogs; Memorial Day weekend draws enthusiasts from Anchorage and elsewhere for the Kodiak Crab Festival (☎486-5557), with all manner of races, a blessing of the fishing fleet, crab eating, and music; mid-July's Bear Country Music Festival (☎486-8766) has over fifty bluegrass, folk, jazz, and country bands from around the state playing at the Kodiak State Fairground ($10–15 a day); and on Labor Day Weekend there's the Kodiak State Fair.

Internet access Free for an hour at the library (see below), and also for reasonable rates at The Treasury (see "Books" above).

Laundry Dillard's, 218 Shelikof St, has laundry and shower facilities.

Library 319 Rezanof Drive West (Mon–Fri 10am–9pm, Sat 10am–5pm, Sun 1–5pm).

Medical assistance Kodiak Island Medical Center, 1915 Rezanof Drive East ☎486-3281.

Post office The main post office is at 419 Lower Mill Bay Rd (Mon–Fri 9am–5.30pm), but the Food For Less supermarket has a handier branch inside (Mon–Sat 10am–6pm). The **General Delivery** zip code is 99615.

Taxes Kodiak has a six percent sales tax and an additional five percent bed tax, all included in accommodation price codes.

Travel agency US Travel, 340 Mission Rd ☎486-3232.

Around the island and the archipelago

Outside the main town, Kodiak Island gets pretty quiet. There are a few small communities dotted throughout the indented coastline, but most are only accessible by boat or float plane. Kodiak's **road system** barely tops a hundred miles (mostly gravel) and doesn't really contain any essential sights, but if you've come this far it is worth renting a car and exploring, especially if you strike clear, sunny weather. To see more than just the roads you'll need to go **flightseeing**, and most flights set off with the express aim of seeing some of the island's huge **bears**, observed from riverbank platforms erected for the purpose.

Kodiak Island is the largest in an archipelago, but several more warrant attention for the superlative kayaking all about. **Afognak and Shuyak islands** are the most obvious and accessible destinations.

Along the road system

You can easily explore the island's road system in a day, though the rocky coastlines, accessible beaches, and fossil-hunting opportunities may tempt you to venture out for longer. Bear in mind that there are few places to stay and even fewer to eat, so come prepared, especially if you fancy **camping** out for a few days. There is only one semi-formal campground, but you can pitch a tent or park an RV in numerous spots along the road provided you respect people's private property. Pick up the CVB's *Kodiak Guide,* which contains a mile-by-mile rundown on these "Backcountry Byways."

Five miles south of town, the airport marks the main junction of the island's road system. Here, **Anton Larsen Bay Road** branches northwest and winds twelve miles over a low mountain pass to Anton Larsen Bay, where there's a small dock used by residents of **Port Lions**, a village just across the water but hidden behind a headland. It is a pretty drive, but there's not a great deal to see, except for Kodiak's golf course a couple of miles along, an odd vision of verdure in this untamed land.

At the airport junction, **Chiniak Road** runs south past the entrance to the former military base at Women's Bay, now the nation's largest **coast guard base** with over two thousand personnel patrolling the fishing grounds and providing search and rescue for the whole of Southwest Alaska. About ten miles south of town, you'll pass the *Rendezvous* bar and see the last of the Sitka spruce trees that blanket the eastern third of the archipelago. The road now breaks into more open country past Bell's Flat (once the island's dairy farm)

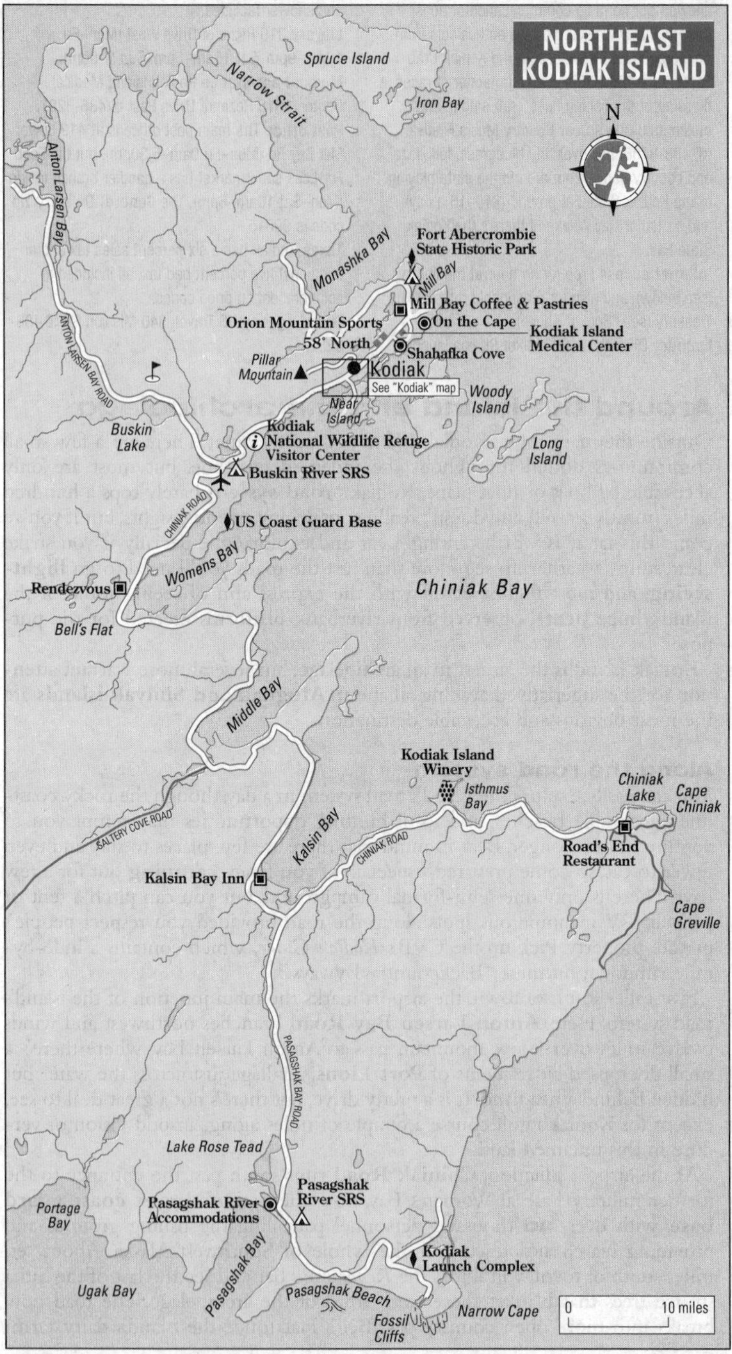
NORTHEAST
KODIAK ISLAND
N
Spruce Island
Narrow Strait
Iron Bay
Anton Larsen Bay
Monashka Bay
Fort Abercrombie
State Historic Park
Mill Bay
Mill Bay Coffee & Pastries
On the Cape
Orion Mountain Sports
Kodiak Island
Medical Center
58° North
Shahafka Cove
Pillar
Mountain
Kodiak
See "Kodiak" map
Woody
Island
Near
Island
ANTON LARSEN BAY ROAD
Buskin
Lake
Kodiak
National Wildlife Refuge
Visitor Center
Long
Island
Buskin River SRS
CHINIAK ROAD
US Coast Guard Base
Womens Bay
Rendezvous
Chiniak Bay
Bell's Flat
Middle Bay
Kodiak Island
Winery
Isthmus
Bay
Chiniak
Lake
Cape
Chiniak
SALTERY COVE ROAD
Kalsin Bay
CHINIAK ROAD
Road's End
Restaurant
Kalsin Bay Inn
Cape
Greville
PASAGSHAK BAY ROAD
Lake Rose Tead
Pasagshak
River SRS
Pasagshak River
Accommodations
Portage
Bay
Pasagshak Bay
Kodiak
Launch Complex
Ugak Bay
Pasagshak Beach
Narrow Cape
Fossil
Cliffs
0
10 miles

and hugs the coast, where there's occasional beach access and bald eagles nesting in cottonwood trees. *Halsin Bay Inn* at Mile 28 is mostly a bar but also serves reasonable diner meals. A patch of farmland at the head of Halsin Bay heralds the Pasagshak Road junction (Mile 30). Chiniak Road continues along the coast through a scattered residential area where you'll find Kodiak Island Winery, Mile 36.2 (Ⓣ486-4848, Ⓦwww.kodiakwines.com), one of the very few wineries in the state that's open to the public. Their tasting room (June–Aug daily 1–6pm) gives you a chance to sample wines made from the likes of salmonberries, rhubarb, blackberries, and whatever can be collected from the wild. The road ends at Mile 42 where there's the *Road's End Restaurant* (Ⓣ486-2885), another bar that does a great halibut sandwich, and the Chiniak airstrip, in service from World War II until 1967 and surrounded by abandoned bunkers and gun emplacements.

Pasagshak Road runs eight miles south from the Pasagshak Road junction to **Lake Rose Tead**, filled with red salmon in August and home to a variety of birds, especially swans, throughout the year. Nearby, **Pasagshak State Recreation Site** is good for beach walking and has free beachside camping with an outhouse and hand pump close by. For greater comfort, seek out *Pasagshak River Accommodations* (see p.318). The road then continues three miles to Pasagshak beach, where Kodiak's **surfers** come for the best waves and there's beachside camping (no facilities). Three miles on the road enters the **Kodiak Launch Complex**, a private site for launching low-orbit polar satellites. It saw its first launch in 1998 and has recently been pressed into use launching dummy targets for the latest version of the missile defense system. The road ends a mile on at Narrow Cape where fossil-filled cliffs are accessible at low tide to the left.

Bear viewing and flightseeing

For many, the reason to come to Kodiak is to view some of the island's three thousand Kodiak bears as they fish the salmon streams. Highway sightings are rare, so you'll need an expensive flight into the **Kodiak National Wildlife Refuge**. From June to August (and sometimes Sept and even Oct), **flightseeing tours** go out on four-hour runs, allowing you to spend a fair bit of time on the ground at several locations viewing at reasonably close quarters. Common destinations are **Frazer Lake**, where there is a fish ladder a mile down the Dog Salmon River, and **Karluk Lake**, both in the south of the island. There are several companies (see "Listings," p.322) to choose from. Flights typically cost around $400, and from late June to August you've got at least a ninety percent chance of seeing bears.

Any of the companies will also do charter flightseeing trips – possibly offering distant views of the bears – but if you can't get a planeload together considering joining Island Air Service on one of their mail-runs around the archipelago, briefly landing at Native villages, old canneries, and remote wilderness lodges. Some flights run all year, but from mid-May to mid-September there's a Kodiak Island loop (3 weekly; 3hr; $300) calling at Alitak, Moser Bay, and Olga Bay; and an Afognak Island loop (twice weekly; 2hr; $190) around Kitoi Bay and Port Williams.

Shuyak Island

Shuyak, the northernmost island in the archipelago, lies forty minutes by float plane northwest of Kodiak. Cloaked in virgin Sitka spruce, it is entrusted to the Shuyak Island State Park, which protects a deeply incised network of passages and islands encompassed by Big Bay, Western Inlet, Carry Inlet, and

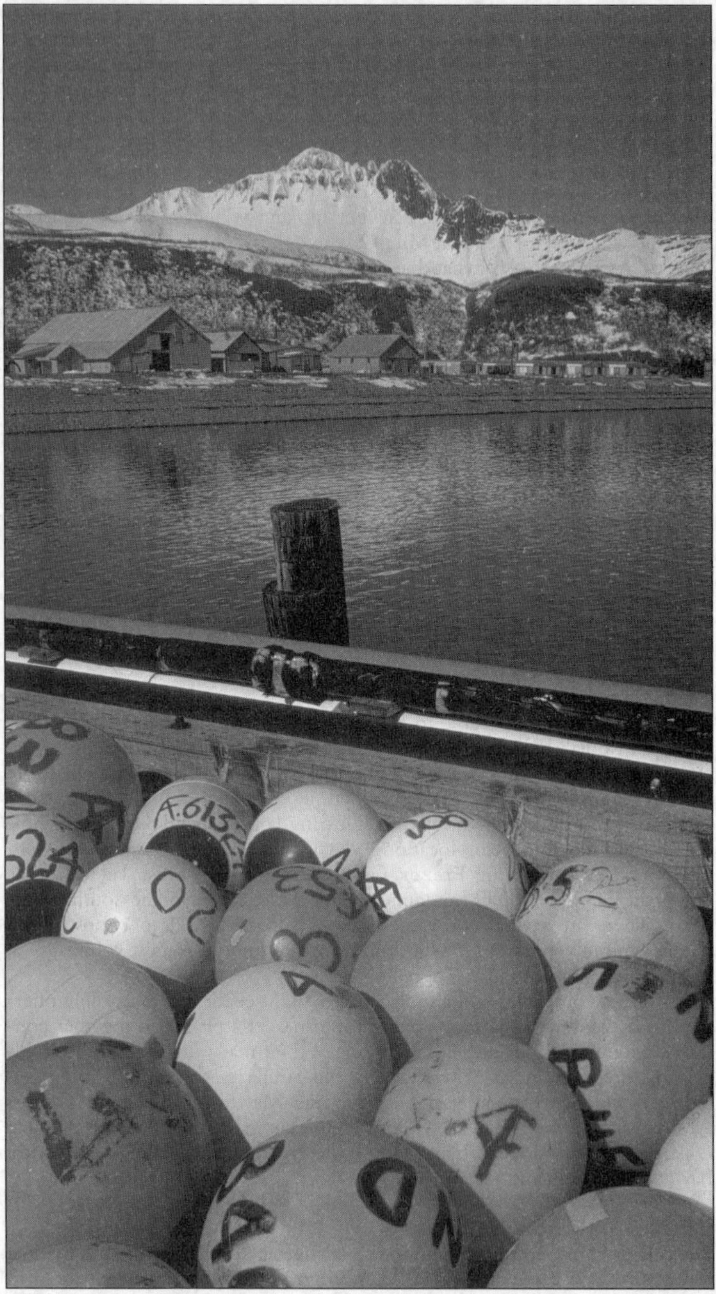

△ Fishing buoys, Chignik

Shanigan Bay. This is ideal territory for intermediate and experienced **kayakers**; pick up the sea-kayaking leaflet detailing several loop paddles from one of the visitor centers on Kodiak. This region has four well-equipped shoreline **cabins** sleeping eight (contact Alaska State Parks ⓣ486-6339, check availability at ⓦwww.dnr.state.ak.us/parks/cabins/kodiak.cfm; $65), which are accessible by kayak. Some of them are linked by short trails.

Access to Shuyak is usually by air charter, the smallest planes costing $200–250 for drop-off, the same for pickup. Kayaks are expensive to transport, so consider bringing a folding model, or better yet rent from Mythos Expeditions (ⓣ486-5536, ⓦwww.thewildcoast.com), which has multiday rentals at Shuyak Island (doubles $171 for 3 days, singles $141 for 3 days) and runs guided trips.

Lake Clark National Park

Considering that **LAKE CLARK NATIONAL PARK** (ⓦwww.nps.gov/lacl) is only a hundred miles west of Anchorage and has scenery to match any in the rest of Alaska, it is surprisingly little visited. With no dense congregations of bears or calving glaciers, it is left off many itineraries, and yet this is quintessential Alaska. Modest numbers of anglers come to remote lodges to fish for the abundant sockeye salmon in what is one of the most important spawning grounds for the Bristol Bay fishery, but apart from that only a few hardy hikers and teams of rafters taking on the three federally designated National Wild Rivers seem to get up this way.

The park gets its name from the 42-mile-long **Lake Clark** in its southwest and features two conical snowcapped volcanoes – **Redoubt** (10,197ft) and **Iliamna** (10,016ft) – both visible from Anchorage and dominating the western horizon along the Kenai Peninsula's Cook Inlet coast. They form part of the Pacific Ring of Fire and are sporadically active, Redoubt as recently as 1990, when it spewed clouds of ash that briefly closed Anchorage airport. The volcanoes lie between Cook Inlet and the **Chigmit Mountains**, a jagged and glacially sculpted geological jumble where the Alaska Range meets the Aleutian Range. Glaciers still peel off the slopes feeding rivers which either cut into the wild interior of the park, or tumble steeply through Sitka and white spruce to the coastal cliffs.

It is a spectacularly diverse park with a remarkable range of plant communities from coastal rainforest to boreal forest typical of Interior Alaska and alpine tundra. Fauna is equally varied, from the seabird rookeries on the Cook Inlet sea cliffs to the moose, black and brown bears, Dall sheep, and caribou of the park's interior.

Hiking and rafting

The only community inside the park is **PORT ALSWORTH**, on the southern shores of Lake Clark, which is where the park's one well-formed trail leads to the **Tanalian Falls** (2.5 miles one-way) and on to **Kontrashibuna Lake** (3.5 miles one-way). After that you're on your own. Keen hikers prepared to follow an unmarked route over rugged terrain can tackle the **Telaquana Trail** (50 miles one-way), which follows an old Dena'ina route later used by trappers and miners during the early 1900s. It runs north from Lake Clark through boreal forest and across alpine tundra and requires fording glacial rivers that can at times be impassable.

Lake Clark National Park is perhaps most visited for its multiday **rafting trips** on three National Wild Rivers. Most of the time spent on these rivers will be occupied watching the scenery, with patches of Class III and IV whitewater in between. All rivers are raftable from June to September (with the highest water being in July and early Aug), and all require float-plane access and egress. The *Lake Clark Inn* in Port Alsworth (see below) rents rafts for $85 a day.

The easiest is the **Mulchatna River** (Class II–III), usually run from Turquoise Lake (about thirty miles north of Lake Clark), from where it descends into a shallow and rocky bed through the Bonanza Hills for a couple of days, then eases to a gentle float down to its confluence with the Chilikadrotna River, taking perhaps five days in all. The **Chilikadrotna River** (Class III) is a slightly tougher four- to five-day proposition running sixty miles down from Twin Lakes on the western flanks of the Alaska Range.

The put-in for the **Tlikakila River** (Class III–IV) is Summit Lake, a good hiking area on the eastern edge of the park that is easily reached direct from Kenai or Anchorage. From there it is 51 miles down to Lake Clark through a densely forested valley with occasional sections of Class III and one section of potentially Class IV (depending on water levels), though this can be portaged.

The weather in the park is cool, rainy, and unpredictable, so come prepared for anything, including bugs, which tend to be less brutal in August and September, the best months for hiking and rafting – if there's enough water.

Practicalities

Before traveling to Lake Clark, get detailed information and advice in advance by contacting the Port Alsworth **field headquarters** (May–Oct daily 8am–4.30pm; ⓣ781-2218). Call in once you reach Port Alsworth for interesting natural history displays, plus video programs and nature walks and hikes conducted on request.

Almost everyone **flies** into the park, either direct to one of the expensive lodges, or by air taxi from either Port Alsworth or Iliamna, thirty miles to the southwest. Both of these small towns have frequent flights from Anchorage: Iliamna is served by PenAir (ⓣ1-800/448-4226), which flies daily for around $350 (booked 14 days in advance); Port Alsworth is reached by Lake Clark Air (ⓣ781-2208 or 1-888/440-2281) for $315 round-trip.

It is best to organize an air charter to your desired destination and not hang around either town, though there are appealing **places to stay** in Port Alsworth: *Wilder House B&B* (ⓣ781-2228 or 1-888/741-2228; ❹), which offers a self-contained cabin that sleeps five, with access to a hot tub and exercise room, and the *Lake Clark Inn* (ⓣ781-2224, ⓦwww.lakeclark.com; ❻).

Katmai National Park

Although there are several places in Alaska where bears congregate in large numbers, only **KATMAI NATIONAL PARK** (ⓦwww.nps.gov/katm), more than two hundred miles southwest of Anchorage, combines the bear viewing with wonderful scenery, relatively easy access, convenient accommodation, and a stock of other activities in case viewing bears begins to pale. None of this comes cheap, but it is hard to put a value on standing twenty yards from a large brown bear as it stands atop the five-foot Brooks Falls ready to chomp on any sockeye salmon that is foolish enough to leap within striking

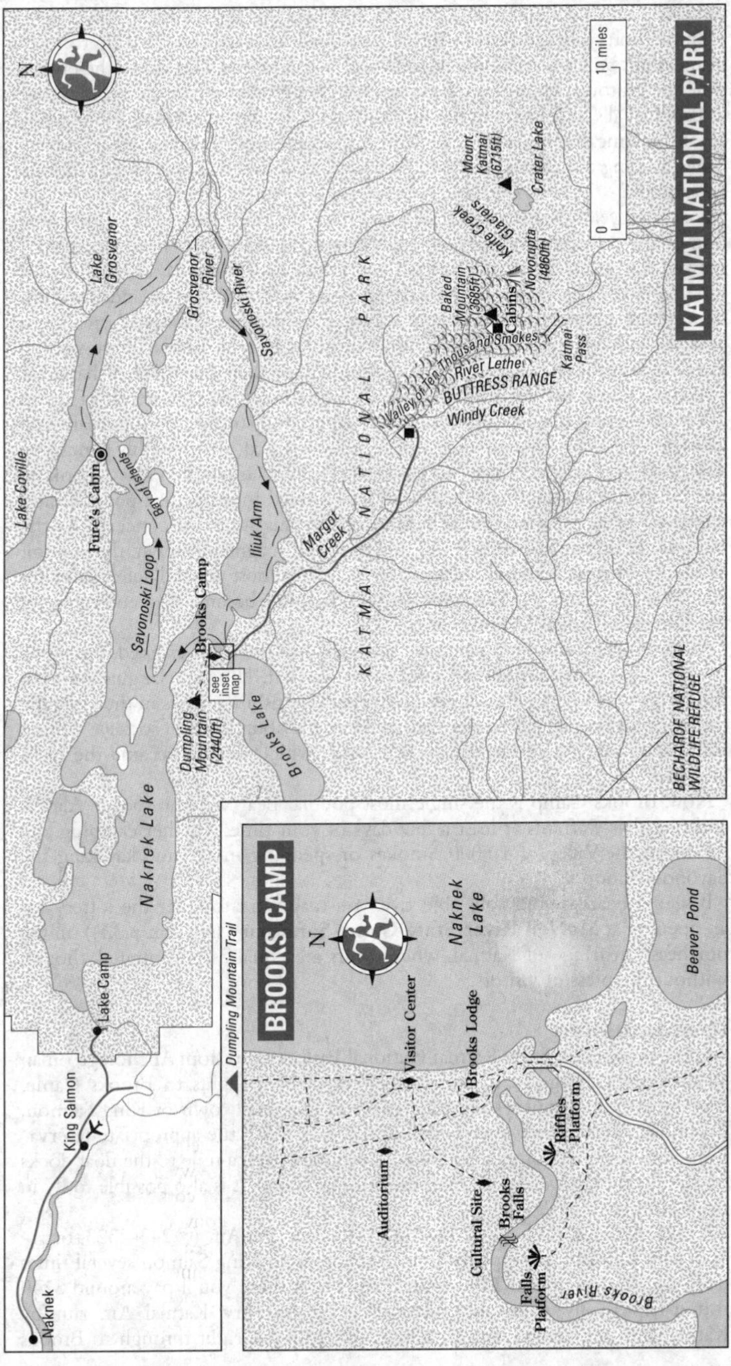

KATMAI NATIONAL PARK
0
10 miles
N
Lake Coville
Lake Grosvenor
Fure's Cabin
Bay of Islands
Savonoski Loop
Grosvenor River
Savonoski River
Iliuk Arm
Brooks Camp
see inset map
Dumpling Mountain (2440ft)
Brooks Lake
Naknek Lake
Lake Camp
King Salmon
Naknek
Margot Creek
KATMAI NATIONAL PARK
Valley of Ten Thousand Smokes
River Lethe
BUTTRESS RANGE
Windy Creek
Baked Mountain (3685ft)
Cabins
Novorupta (4860ft)
Knife Creek Glaciers
Mount Katmai (6715ft)
Crater Lake
Katmai Pass
BECHAROF NATIONAL WILDLIFE REFUGE
BROOKS CAMP
N
Naknek Lake
Beaver Pond
Dumpling Mountain Trail
Visitor Center
Brooks Lodge
Auditorium
Cultural Site
Brooks Falls
Riffles Platform
Falls Platform
Brooks River
Valley of Ten Thousand Smokes (25 miles)

distance.

Throughout July the Brooks River is so thick with sockeyes that up to forty bears might be scattered along its mile-and-a-half length. This is also the busiest time for visitors, coming to a head again in September when the bears gather at Brooks Falls to feast on dying fish. You won't see bears catching fish in mid-air at this time, but you will see enormous bears fattened up for winter, sometimes topping a thousand pounds. Bear activity is low or non-existent in June and August.

For many years, Katmai was only known for the most violent volcanic eruption of the twentieth century, when **Novorupta** (Latin for "newly erupted") spewed out seven cubic miles of ash and pumice for three days beginning on June 6, 1912. The cloud of ash drifted as far as North Africa, and northern hemisphere temperatures dropped a couple of degrees effectively creating a year without a summer. People a hundred miles away in Kodiak were wading knee-deep through volcanic ash and couldn't see their outstretched hand for two days. Close to Novorupta, intensely hot ash settled to a depth of up to 700ft blanketing the volcanic gases and vaporizing streams. As the steam and gases forced their way to the surface, they created an unearthly landscape described by *National Geographic* geologist Robert Griggs, in 1916, as looking like "all the steam engines in the world, assembled together, had popped their safety valves at once and were letting off surplus steam in concert." As the Novorupta fireworks emptied the underground magma chamber, the summit of nearby **Mount Katmai** collapsed to form an almost perfectly circular crater lake. Two years later the **Valley of 10,000 Smokes** became the centerpiece of the Katmai National Monument.

As the underground temperatures subsided and the gases escaped, the number of active vents diminished until none was left. The park languished until the 1940s when Ray Petersen set up five remote fishing camps in the park, the most popular being at **Brooks Camp**. Here the abundance of sockeye salmon was just as much of a lure for brown bears, which rapidly became the main attraction.

Now, Brooks Camp is the single most popular bear-viewing spot in Alaska, and one that warrants at least a few days of your time, whether camping and hiking in the Valley of 10,000 Smokes or spending more time kayaking the Savonoski Loop.

If seeing bears is your sole objective, you may want to enter the lottery for an opening at **McNeil River State Game Sanctuary** (see box, p.334) on the northeastern fringe of Katmai, where bears are equally concentrated, though without the press of visitors.

Practicalities

Almost everyone visiting Katmai National Park does so from Anchorage on an all-inclusive package or a connecting sequence of flights to Brooks Camp, thereby avoiding unnecessary time spent in the small town of King Salmon, five miles outside the western edge of the park. With the appropriate reservations you'll be met at the King Salmon airport, driven a mile to the float docks on the Naknek River, and flown into Brooks Camp. It is also possible to fly in from Homer (see p.264).

Alaska Airlines (Ⓣ1-800/252-7522) jets and PenAir (Ⓣ243-2323 or 1-800/448-4226) twin-props **fly** from Anchorage to King Salmon several times daily, usually for around $380 round-trip. From there you'll pay around $140 round-trip to fly to Brooks Camp by air taxi: try Katmai Air, run by Katmailand (see below). PenAir allows you to book right through to Brooks

Camp from Anchorage for $532 round-trip (14-day APEX).

Alternatively, you can get between King Salmon and Brooks Camp using a **bus/boat combination** (mid-June to mid-Sept; 1hr; $154 round-trip). A shuttle bus leaves the *Quinnat Landing Hotel* (see below) at 7am for Lake Camp where you pick up the *Katmai Lady* to take you to Brooks Camp. You get around five hours in Brooks (though your return ticket is still valid if you want to return on a later date), and there's a boat/fly combo for $150.

The park concessionaire, Katmailand (Ⓣ243-5448 or 1-800/544-0551, Ⓦwww.katmailand.com), operates *Brooks Lodge*, rentals, and trips at Brooks Camp, as well as Katmai Air. They sell competitive inclusive packages with round-trip flights from Anchorage, accommodation at *Brooks Lodge*, and park fees (but not meals): day trip ($489), one night ($736), two nights ($1083), three nights ($1252), three-night off-peak special (June 1–20 & Aug 10–25; $994), and others. If you don't mind staying in King Salmon at the *Quinnat Landing* and commuting into the park, consider Alaska Airlines Vacations (mid-June to mid-Sept; Ⓣ1-800/468-2248) packages: the two-day affair ($683 double occupancy) and a more leisurely three-day trip ($805) both include bear viewing at Brooks Camp.

King Salmon and Naknek

The small bush community of **KING SALMON**, scattered between its airport and the broad tidal Naknek River 250 miles southwest of Anchorage, was once a Cold War military base and is now the main service town for the region. There's no reason to be here except as a staging point for Katmai or as access to some remote fishing. If you get stranded or have an hour to spare, call in at the King Salmon **visitor center**, right by the airport terminal (June to mid-Sept daily 8am–5pm; mid-Sept to May Mon–Fri 9am–5pm; Ⓣ246-4250), with interesting and informative displays, or wander a hundred yards along the street to the King Salmon Mall where, upstairs, you'll find the **NPS visitor center** (Mon–Fri 8am–4.30pm; Ⓣ246-3305), which has specific information on Katmai and Lake Clark national parks. The mall also has a **bank** (Mon–Thurs 10am–5pm, Fri 10am–6pm) with an ATM and *Mel's Diner* (Ⓣ246-7629), which serves lunch, good espresso, and has **Internet access**.

Accommodation in King Salmon is expensive, although if you have a sturdy, bug-proof tent you can easily find a quiet spot to **camp**. The cheapest rooms are at *Antlers Inn*, just behind the mall (Ⓣ246-8525 or 1-888/735-8525, Ⓔantlers@bristolbay.com; suite ❼, rooms ❻), which has self-contained apartments as well as smaller rooms that share bathrooms and a small communal kitchenette. They also have a camping area (free) with shower facilities ($8) and use of barbecue area.

The only other possibilities are the *King Ko Inn* (Ⓣ246-3377 locally, 562-0648 in Anchorage or 1-866/234-3474, Ⓦwww.kingko.com; $209), which has fairly new and comfortable cabins, and the *Quinnat Landing Hotel* (Ⓣ246-3000 or 1-800/770-3474, Ⓦwww.quinnat.com; ❾), with international-quality hotel rooms for around $260.

King Salmon is pricey and **eating** options are limited to the two hotels, which serve similar menus with salads ($13), pasta dishes ($20), and steaks, salmon, and halibut ($20–30). There's a lively bar at the *King Ko*, though the view over the Naknek River from the restaurant/bar at the *Quinnat* is better.

If you are self-catering and haven't brought everything you need from Anchorage (as you should), pick up **groceries** from the limited supply at the City Market supermarket/deli/liquor store beside the mall.

Fourteen miles downstream, the Bristol Bay fishing village of **NAKNEK** is the scene of the world's largest sockeye run, with some twenty million fish passing between mid-June and the end of July (peaking in the first two weeks of July). Around seventy percent of all the world's red salmon are caught in Bristol Bay and three-quarters of those are caught in and around Naknek. Once the fishing season opens in late June, commercial fishing boats are gunwhale-to-gunwhale trying to be first to get their nets in the water, and both King Salmon and Naknek are alive with fishermen.

To get there, contact Redline Taxi (ⓣ246-8294), which charges around $15 for the ride from King Salmon, **rent a truck** from the *Antlers Inn* ($65 a day), or join Tim Cook of Bristol Bay Tours (mid-June to mid-Sept; $45; ⓣ246-4218, ⓦwww.bristolbaytours.com), a two-hour-plus minibus tour that picks up in King Salmon and visits Naknek, accompanied by loads of history and local anecdotes, and maybe a visit to a commercial cannery in action.

Brooks Camp and around

Bears are all over Katmai National Park, but your best chance of seeing them in any number is at **Brooks Camp** ($10 per day user fee), 47 miles east of King Salmon. It is essentially just a lodge, campground, and ranger station on the north side of the Brooks River, plus a couple of bear-viewing platforms – one by Brooks Falls on the south bank. The whole place is compact enough to walk everywhere.

Your first day is likely to be spent hanging around **Brooks Falls** watching and photographing up to a dozen bears, though you'll have to be patient since only forty people are allowed on the main platform, and rangers have to limit the time people can stay there so that everyone gets a chance. Even on the platform there's considerable jockeying for position as video cameras are poked between ranks of professional photographers and their tripods.

Things tend to be quieter early and late in the day when day-trippers are absent. The middle of the day can be spent tackling the **Dumpling Mountain Hike** (8 miles round-trip; 4–5hr; 2400ft ascent), which follows the only formed trail hereabouts and climbs to the mountain's summit, passing an overlook about halfway. The Park Service also runs a daily guided hike (free) going part the way up.

Kayaking and **canoeing** are superb ways to see more of the area, either on the Savonoski Loop (see box, opposite) or on shorter trips using boats rented (and booked in advance) from *Brooks Lodge*: double kayaks $16 an hour, $60 a day; canoes $12, $40. There's plenty of interest within a couple of hours' paddle, but if you are equipped for camping you could head twenty miles to the Bay of Islands (see box opposite), one to two days' paddle away, or ten miles to the islands around the mouth of Margot Creek, an area with a reputation for its bears. Either camp on the islands or turn it into one very long paddling day.

Fishing is also stupendous around here, and many visitors are happy to spend their day doing guided trolling for lake trout, and arctic char ($165 a half-day); taking a boat on Naknek Lake ($250 a day per boat); or employing a river guide for rainbow fishing ($50 an hour, $150 a day).

Activity at Brooks Camp revolves entirely around the presence of bears, so it is only open to the public from June 1 to September 17. On arrival, rangers will put you through a twenty-minute **orientation program**, partly to help you avoid having to deal with bears and partly to instill some common-sense rules so that up to three hundred sightseers and photographers can go about their business in relative harmony.

Savonoski Loop

Anyone with experience in backcountry camping and with moderate kayaking or canoeing skills shouldn't have too much trouble completing the **Savonoski Loop**, an 86-mile lake and river paddle which can be done in as little as three days by fit kayakers, although most people take seven to ten days. That said, it is a true wilderness experience and help may be days away, so you'll need to be able to handle braided rivers with sweepers and whitewater up to Class II. There's also one strenuous portage, and high winds can whip up across the lakes, so you need to be prepared to pitch camp and wait for bad weather to pass.

Almost everyone follows a clockwise course from Brooks Camp into the north arm of Naknek Lake and the **Bay of Islands**, myriad small islands with great camping spots, separated by crystal-clear water with good pike and trout fishing. Accommodation is available at **Fure's Cabin** (reservations through NPS visitor center in King Salmon; free), which is located at the start of the two-mile portage to **Lake Grosvenor**. At the southern end of the lake, you enter the Class I **Grosvenor River**, which typically has excellent wildlife viewing. Along the Class I–II **Savonoski River** the wildlife is most likely to be bears: you're advised to press through this section in one day to avoid camping among them. To complete the loop back to Brooks Camp you've then only got to cross **Iliuk Arm**, which is exposed and best traversed along its south shore. Pick a campsite away from the mouth of Margot Creek, which also has a reputation for bears.

If going alone sounds too difficult or intimidating, consider joining one of the Anchorage-based seven-day **kayak tours** with Lifetime Adventures (ⓣ746-4644 or 1-800/952-8624, ⓦwww.lifetimeadventures.net), which uses folding sea kayaks and charges $1500 a head including everything but food.

The only **rooms** at Brooks Camp are those available on package deals (see p.331) at *Brooks Lodge*, which fills up almost a year in advance for the prime viewing month of July. Everyone else stays at the **campground** ($8 per person), which has fire rings and bear-resistant food caches and also fills up early: book online or by phone (ⓣ1-800/365-2267 6am–6pm, ⓦreservations.nps.gov).

If you are **cooking** your own meals, you'll need to bring a camp stove and an empty fuel bottle: white gas (but not propane) is available in Brooks at the Katmai Trading Post, which also stocks a few snacks, film, and fishing gear, but little else. **Meals** are only available at *Brooks Lodge*, where they lay on all-you-can-eat buffet affairs (breakfast $12; lunch $18; dinner $26) open to all.

The Valley of 10,000 Smokes

Having forked out the cash to get to Brooks Camp it seems penny-pinching not to also visit the **Valley of 10,000 Smokes**, a virtually plant-free expanse of red, yellow, and tan wasteland some three miles wide and twelve long, deeply incised by river-carved gorges a hundred feet deep. It is reached along a 23-mile dirt road by Katmailand's Natural History Tour (8.30am–4.30pm; $81 round-trip, $48 one-way for hikers), which uses a 4WD bus for the ninety-minute run to Three Forks Overlook, where there's a wonderful view over the desolate landscape and a shelter to protect you from the wind and the volcanic ash it carries. The on-board ranger then leads an instructive three-mile round-trip hike (700ft ascent) down the **Ukak Falls Trail** to the confluence of Knife, Lethe, and Windy creeks, and the spectacular falls themselves. The tour is often full throughout the summer, so it pays to sign up at *Brooks Lodge* when you arrive.

You can also see the valley on an hour-long **flightseeing** trip from Brooks Camp ($130 per person, minimum two), cycle the road on **mountain bikes** rented from *Brooks Lodge* for $35 a day, or even walk the road, although you must be at least five miles from the lodge before camping.

To really explore the area, spend a few days **hiking**, best done in late August and early September when the weather is relatively benign, most snow cover has melted, and bugs are at their least menacing. Most hikers spend their first day heading southeast through the Valley of 10,000 Smokes to reach some abandoned US Geological Survey **cabins** (free) on the flanks of Baked Mountain. There are nicer campsites further to the southeast, but the cabins have the advantage of providing shelter from the wind, though there's no water source. By setting up a base camp you are then free to explore the half-mile-wide crater of **Novorupta**, **Mount Griggs** with its nested craters from successive eruptions, the 2600-foot **Katmai Pass**, which was used as a mail route during the Nome gold rush, and the turquoise, ice-encrusted crater lake of **Mount Katmai**. The latter requires crampons, ice ax, and glacier travel skills, and if you have these you may also want to play around on **Knife Creek Glaciers**, now stagnant and slowly melting since the 1912 collapse of Mount Katmai robbed them of the ice fields which fed them.

With the rapid erosion in the area, conditions change quickly, so you'll need to get the latest information and route guides from the NPS visitor center in King Salmon. They'll issue free backcountry and fire permits and sell you the Trails Illustrated *Katmai National Park and Preserve* topo map ($10). The NPS will also tell you where you can get water and warn you about hazardous river crossings, since very deep narrow gorges can often fill up and appear to be shallow pools, the bottom invisible through the silty water. Ferocious ash-laden winds occur quite frequently, so, along with a strong tent, you'll want protective goggles or wraparound sunglasses and perhaps a bandana to breathe through. Bear-resistant food canisters can be obtained free of charge from the NPS visitor centers in Brooks Camp and King Salmon.

McNeil River State Game Sanctuary

If you want to see a lot of bears without the crowds, try to visit **McNeil River State Game Sanctuary**, 110 miles west of Homer, an enclave in the northeastern corner of Katmai National Park. From early July to mid-August, brown bears come to feast on chum salmon struggling up **McNeil River Falls**, a mess of rocks and whitewater a mile inland from Cook Inlet. Here you might easily see twenty or thirty bears at one time and perhaps a hundred over the course of a day. In June slightly smaller numbers (say 15–20 individuals) congregate for the sockeye run at **Mikfik Creek** a few miles away.

The trouble is, you are unlikely to experience this, because only ten people are allowed to come here on any one day (between June 7 and Aug 25), with places given only to winners of an annual lottery. What's more, each place is valid for four days, so the turnover is low. If that is not deterrent enough, you have to pay $25 simply to enter the lottery (where your chances are around one in ten), then a further $350 ($150 for Alaska residents) for the permit if your name is drawn, plus around $350 round-trip for the flight from Homer. If you are staying overnight you'll have to be self-sufficient for camping at McNeil River, and should bring hip waders. There are also three standby places (again distributed by lottery: $25 for the application; $175 for the standby permit, $75 for Alaskans) so that there are people on hand if someone fails to show or doesn't take their full quota of four days. On a more hopeful note, Kachemak Air Service (Ⓣ235-8924; Ⓦwww.alaskaseaplanes.com), which flies float planes to McNeil River from Homer, usually hears about any places that do come free: call them and you might be able to grab a spur-of-the-moment opportunity.

Enter the lottery before March 1 either online or by mail sent to ATTN: McNeil River Application, Alaska Department of Fish & Game, Division of Wildlife Conservation, PO Box 228080, Anchorage, Alaska 99522-8080. A full set of lottery rules and an application form can be found at Ⓦwww.wc.adfg.state.ak.us/mcneil.

The Alaska Peninsula and the Aleutian ferry trip

Beyond the vast national parks of Lake Clark and Katmai, and west of Kodiak, lies the **Alaska Peninsula**, a slender arm reaching out to Asia and separating the Bering Sea from the north Pacific Ocean. It ends eight hundred miles southwest of Anchorage, but the mountainous spine effectively continues as the **Aleutian Islands** (*al-OO-shun*), an 1100-mile-long necklace of volcanic islands along the seam of the American and Pacific plates that stretches to within five hundred miles of Russia's Kamchatka Peninsula. The whole arc of the peninsula and islands is an isolated, windswept, and almost treeless place where fierce gales, earthquakes, and vulcanism add a spectacular component to a region as often as not cloaked in silent mist.

Few people live out this way. The Native Aleut (*AL-ee-oot*) wrested a living from the sea around small villages throughout the region, then Russian fur traders began more substantial towns as bases for their operations. Ultimately, it was the Japanese occupation of the two westernmost islands – Attu and Kiska – during World War II and the subsequent military buildup that brought the first modern development to the region, something consolidated by the fishing industry. Now almost every community lives off the sea, with subsistence fishing and hunting in the remaining Native villages and commercial fishing from **Dutch Harbor** – the US's most productive fishing port – and smaller ports along the peninsula.

There are only two realistic ways to visit this area. You can fly direct from Anchorage to Dutch Harbor, where you could easily spend a week, though two or three days is more likely; or take the **three-day ferry journey** to Unalaska/Dutch Harbor aboard the *Tustumena* from either Homer or Kodiak. It briefly calls at all the isolated fishing communities along the southern shore of the Alaska Peninsula giving a real sense of just how isolated these places are. Unless you've a highly developed sense of adventure, and a fat wallet, you probably won't see any of the Aleutians beyond Unalaska, though birding fanatics occasionally take specialist cruises out to the more distant islands to add Asiatic accidentals to their life list.

The Aleutian ferry trip

Any trip to Alaska should have at least one real adventure, and the best value has to be riding the AMHS ferry *Tustumena* along the southern coast of the Alaska Peninsula to the beginning of the Aleutian Chain. Once a month from April to October the ferry leaves Homer for Kodiak, then continues west (typically leaving Kodiak on the second Wed) for the two-and-a-half-day trip to Unalaska/Dutch Harbor, arriving early Saturday morning. The town warrants more of your time than the five or six hours' turnaround time, but the only solution is to stay for a while and then fly back to Anchorage: it'll cost you more, but it may be preferable to spending another three days on the boat getting back to Homer or Kodiak (especially if the weather forecast is foul).

Along the journey the ferry sails parallel to the treeless grassy lowlands of the Alaska Peninsula, which periodically rise up to lofty volcanoes, some of which let out small eruptions from time to time. Catch it all through a fine patch with calm seas and blue skies and it can be glorious, but the "Trusty Tusty," as the ferry is often called, has to regularly weather rough waters and can spend the whole journey easing its way through dense fog with the coastline barely discernible: bring a good book just in case. There's no guarantee of good weather, but the

June, July, and August sailings are probably the best bets. At this time, there's also a naturalist on board helping interpret the things you might encounter along the way: sea otters, assorted birds, and probably dolphins and whales.

The *Tustumena* is no cruise ship, but a working ferry with a mission to call in at the half-dozen fishing ports along the way to drop off vehicles, people, and supplies. All the villages have airfields, but the ferry remains the lifeline, and half the pleasure is in chatting to those on board as you sail through the night to get to the next godforsaken fishing community. The ferry seldom stops for long, but the hour or two you spend in port is enough to make a brief inspection and be on your way.

The ferry passenger **fare** from Homer to Unalaska is currently $285 each way ($237 from Kodiak), with Alaska Airlines charging around $370 (14-day advance purchase) for the one-way fare back to Anchorage. If you live outside the US and buy your ticket in advance, you can take advantage of the "Best of the West Airpass" (see p.35) and fly back to Anchorage for $109.

The *Tustumena* is one of the smaller ferries in the AMHS fleet, but it's still big enough to have a car deck, restaurant with meals at fair prices, and cabins (a two-berth from Homer to Unalaska costs $245, plus your individual passenger fares). There is no solarium or reclining chairs, but you can save money on a cabin – if you don't mind the discomfort – by sleeping on the floor and taking full advantage of free showers and free hot water for tea, noodles, or whatever you bring with you.

Chignik and Sand Point

From Kodiak the ferry heads northwest between Kodiak and Afognak islands, threading through Whale Pass to reach the **Shelikof Strait**, which separates Kodiak from the Alaskan Peninsula. From there it swings southwest, conveniently making the only open-water passage through the night. By morning you're hugging the coast, jagged white mountains stretching as far as you can see on the starboard side. Towards noon the ferry enters Chignik Bay, surrounded on three sides by snowcapped mountains and approached past the soaring spires and plateau rock of Castle Cape. The hour-long stop in **CHIGNIK** (pop. under 200) is all you need to go ashore and briefly inspect the outside of the fish-processing plants and the few dozen houses strung along the shore.

It is another nine hours to **SAND POINT**, reached at about 10pm. It sits on Popof Island, where the Russians first established a community in the nineteenth century, and now has a permanent population of around a thousand, giving it the feel of a real town. There are even two bars, and since you should have a couple of hours in port there is time enough to hike into town, look at the bald eagles that are almost always in the trees, and join the locals for a game of pool in the *Sand Point Tavern*.

King Cove and Cold Bay

An overnight passage brings you to **KING COVE**, yet another small community entirely dependent on fishing and fish processing. Use your two-hour layover to walk into town, where (as in many remote communities) the school is by far the biggest and best-kept building. Nearby there is a Russian Orthodox church, modern in execution but equipped with icons and exterior bells moved here in the 1980s from the now abandoned town of Belkofski, twelve miles to the southeast.

The shortest hop on the whole trip passes through a narrow channel surrounded by beautiful mountains and the conical form of Morzhovoi Volcano to **COLD BAY**, a tiny settlement with a level of importance that outweighs its hundred-strong population. In 1941 this became Fort Randall, a major base from which the war in the Aleutians was orchestrated. During the army's occupation as many as twenty thousand troops were stationed here in Quonset huts, some contributing to the construction of the third longest airport runway in the state. Cold Bay is now an air hub for the Aleutian and Pribilof islands, an alternative airport when Anchorage is socked-in, and even, it is said, a last-ditch alternative landing zone for the space shuttle. This ability to handle big planes has brought controversy to the region: residents of King Cove have demanded the construction of a thirty-something-mile road to Cold Bay so that in poor weather, when their own small airport is closed, they can still fly out from the larger airport. Medical emergency is cited as the reason, though cynics suggest that easy access to good hunting is a stronger driving force. None of this would be contentious except that the proposed road would cross critical wetlands within the **Izembek National Wildlife Refuge**. King Cove has already been granted millions for a new airport and ferry service on condition that the road wouldn't be built, but they continue to push for its construction.

The refuge attracts 142 species of birds, but was originally set aside for brant geese, the entire North American population of 100,000 feeding on the world's largest eelgrass beds during the spring and fall migrations. Catch one of the fall ferry sailings and you may also see some of the 70,000 Canada geese that migrate through here. Unless you are an enthusiastic birder, you'll probably only stop at Cold Bay for a few minutes, enough to hike the half-mile length of the jetty from ferry to land and back, should you wish.

False Pass and Akutan

Later that afternoon you'll hit tiny **FALSE PASS**, which marks the entrance to the 150-foot-wide channel between the end of the Alaska Peninsula and the easternmost of the Aleutian Islands, **Unimak**. For centuries Aleut had used the channel to travel between the Bering Sea and the Gulf of Alaska, and the Russians followed suit, but large American ships found the strait too perilous and named it False Pass to encourage shipping to go around the western end of Unimak Island. The community that built up around the early twentieth-century cannery took on the name of the pass and now supports under a hundred people.

Outbound ferries chug through the night straight to Unalaska, but the eastbound service stops very briefly at **AKUTAN**, three hours after leaving Unalaska. Akutan hunkers below the 4275-foot Akutan Volcano, which last erupted in 1978. It was established in 1878 as a fur-storage and trading port, though cod fishing soon took precedence. The residents here were evacuated to Ketchikan during World War II and few returned, but those who did have recently been nursing their dying language, which looks to be on the cusp of recovery. Hop off to see the historic **Alexandr Nevsky Chapel**, a Russian Orthodox structure built in 1918 to replace an 1878 original. The ferry only spends 45 minutes here, then skips False Pass but calls at all the other ports on its way back to Kodiak.

Unalaska and Dutch Harbor

In a state full of remote spots, it is hard to outdo **UNALASKA/DUTCH HARBOR**, located on a foggy, windswept, and treeless Aleutian island rising out of the North Pacific, eight hundred miles southwest of Anchorage.

The nearest town of any size is Kodiak, nearly six hundred miles away, and yet here you'll find the eleventh most populous locale in Alaska, as big as Homer and bigger than heavyweight names such as Seward, Cordova, and Skagway. The reason is simple: this has been the United States' most productive fishing port for the past decade or so, both in terms of weight and dollar value. The 4000-strong town almost doubles in size for the winter fishing and crabbing season when storm-tossed trawlers and 600-foot-long factory ships periodically call in to offload their catch. From August to November, and again from January to March, the season is open on some of the world's richest fishing grounds – salmon, crab, cod, pollock, yellowfin, mackerel – and the town is alive with Mexicans, Filipinos, Russians, Vietnamese, Americans up from the Lower 48, in fact just about anyone who's after a quick buck.

Short-stay profiteering and the eternally erratic nature of the fishing industry do little to foster a developed community, and there's a certain frontier spirit to the place, but less than you might imagine. Taxes on fishing-boat catches have made Unalaska a wealthy town, so most of the roads are paved, health and public services are maintained to a high standard, and you can sleep in a top-class hotel. Even the fish-processing factories are conveniently tucked away from view (many in Captains Bay), and only the container port gives any kind of an industrial tenor to the place.

In summer, when most visitors arrive, the commercial fishery gives way to lively bouts of **sportfishing**, primarily for huge halibut. In the past few years, the world mark has twice been broken around Dutch Harbor, and the record now stands at a whopping, barn-door-sized 459 pounds. There's plenty of hiking, mountain biking, and kayaking to take advantage of, and wildlife fans will appreciate the whales passing by each spring and fall, the sea mammals that amass in huge numbers hereabouts, and the unusual seabirds that turn up. Birders come especially to see the **crested auklet**, which is seldom found anywhere else.

There's interest, too, in the legacy of three nations – Aleut, Russian, and American – which have combined to leave a fascinating history, though not a great deal of tangible evidence. The Aleut have been here for close on nine thousand years, but Russian fur traders suppressed much of their culture. The US military helped complete the near-genocide during World War II (see box, p.340) and left behind hilltop bunkers and the shells of Quonset huts still visible in the hills. Fortunately, something of Aleut culture has been preserved in the **Museum of the Aleutians**, and local language and culture is again being taught at the town's schools.

History

Evidence from archeological digs around Unalaska indicates that the Unangan people (see box, p.340) have lived here for around nine thousand years, but recorded history doesn't begin until Stephan Glotov led a crew of fur buyers

Unalaska or Dutch Harbor?

The airport is designated Dutch Harbor, but ferries officially dock at Unalaska. In truth, no one much cares whether you call the contiguous settlement **Unalaska or Dutch Harbor**, and the terms are used pretty much interchangeably. To locals, the settlement on the island of Amaknak is Dutch Harbor, now linked by the "Bridge to the Other Side" to Unalaska Island and the town of Unalaska, which is where mail gets sent.

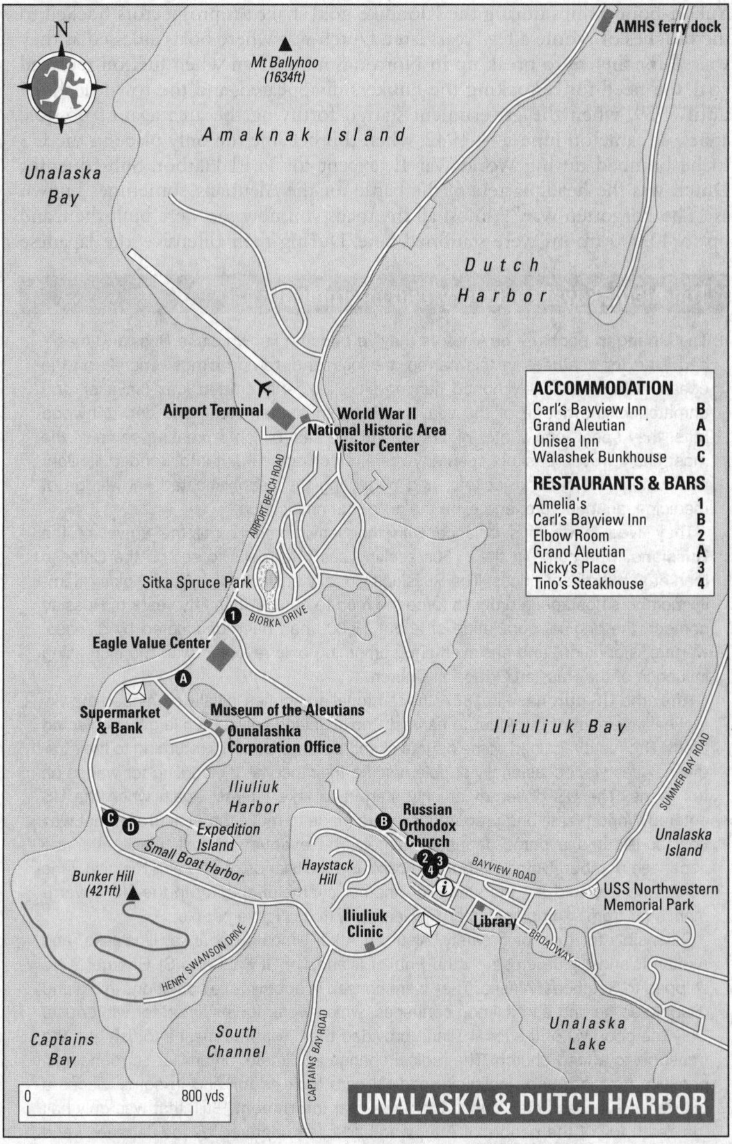

here in August 1759. They stayed for three years and laid the groundwork for what became a key link in the chain of Russian settlements along the American coast as far down as northern California. Ultimately, their main legacy was the Russian Orthodox Church, which remains the most important religion among the Aleut.

Under the US government, Dutch (as it is often known) became the base for seal harvesting in the Pribilof Islands and subsequently a coal-supply depot for

Yukon-bound ships during the Klondike gold strike. As prospectors flocked to the beaches of Nome a few years later, Dutch was where boats amassed as they waited for the ice to break up in Norton Sound. Then when fuel oil replaced coal, the need for restocking the bunkers disappeared, and the town declined until 1939, when the government started fortifying the area against possible attack. It came on June 3–4, 1942, when this became the only place in the US to be bombed during World War II, except for Pearl Harbor. Subsequently, Dutch was the headquarters of the battle for the Aleutians, sometimes known as "The Forgotten War." Almost all the roads you now see were built then, and up to 40,000 troops were stationed here. During their offensive, the Japanese

The Aleut: kayaks, slavery, and internment

The **Unangan** people – or Aleut as they've become known since Russian times – had lived for centuries in this barren, treeless land, relying almost entirely on the ocean, using their finely honed hunting skills, expertly crafted iqax (kayaks), and unmatched knowledge of the sea. In their semi-subterranean sod-and-driftwood huts, they spent long winter nights around the seal-oil lamp creating some of the most finely woven baskets seen anywhere, stitching seal gut into wonderfully light and waterproof hunting jackets, and perfecting their sophisticated knowledge of medicine, acupuncture, and even the art of mummification.

They lived in tenuous balance with their environment until the arrival of the **Russians**, who came in the 1750s seeking sea-otter pelts to sell on the Chinese market at exorbitant prices. The Russians virtually enslaved the Aleut, holding family members hostage in order to force the men to hunt. Within fifty years of Russian contact, the original population of about 15,000 had been decimated by disease, warfare, starvation, and enslavement, something only reversed with the increasing influence of the Russian Orthodox Church.

After the US purchase in 1867, the territorial authorities initially continued the virtual enslavement of the Aleut to harvest Pribilof Island seals, then largely neglected them. The Aleut regained some degree of self-determination by returning to their traditional lifestyle, occasionally supplementing their income by working for wages on fox farms. The US government only started to take interest again when the US entered World War II, and preparations were made to move the Aleut from what was now considered a prime Japanese target. The **evacuation** took place after the Japanese bombed Dutch Harbor and captured the islands of Attu and Kiska in June 1942, and it would set the stage for another shameful chapter in the US government's far from exemplary history in dealing with its Native people.

Ostensibly for their own safety, Aleut on Atka, Umnak, Sedanka, Unalaska, and Akutan islands, plus those on the Pribilof Islands of St Paul and St George, were shipped to Southeast Alaska. They were housed in abominable conditions in old and dilapidated herring and salmon canneries, which were not insulated for winter use. Only the goodwill of the local Tlingit provided them with the means to fish and the transport to attend church. The radical change in climate, unfamiliar surroundings, primitive housing, and negligible medical care took its toll and in some places a quarter of evacuees died during the three-year **internment.** Still, that was only half the death toll of the people of Attu, who had been captured by the Japanese and spent the rest of the war on Hokkaido.

In 1943 some men were allowed to return and were put to work harvesting fur seals, but most waited in the camps until 1945. On their return they discovered their homes looted and destroyed and whole villages burned. Many villages were never rebuilt, and some islands remained under military control, principally Adak, about halfway along the chain. The military base on Adak was still in operation until 1995 when it was finally handed over to the local Native corporation, a small but significant step in the restitution of the Aleut people.

seized the westernmost Aleutian Islands of Attu and Kiska. Although they intended it as a diversion from the real battle at Midway, the Japanese found that the Americans became so intent on regaining their territory that they dug in and were only ousted eleven months later in an intensely bloody, and largely pointless, battle.

Military involvement aside, Unalaska/Dutch Harbor was still a small town until the 1970s when super-lucrative crab fishing, and the get-rich-quick attitude that it engendered, turned it into the most productive seafood port in the nation. As successive fisheries declined, different species were targeted, and the boom and bust cycle has been repeated several times. A quota system has now been introduced in the hopes of stabilizing the situation.

Arrival and tours

There's no better way to reach Dutch Harbor than on the AMHS **ferry** *Tustumena* (see p.335), which arrives around the middle of each month (April–Oct only) early Saturday morning. It stays in port a little over five hours, so if you are heading back on the boat the best bet is to join a two-hour **tour** with Extra Mile Tours (mid-May to mid-Sept daily; Ⓣ581-6171, Ⓦwww.unalaskadutchharbortour.com), which visits the main sections of town and heads out along some of the rougher roads into the surrounding countryside ($50); there's also an extended four-hour trip for $90.

Alaska Airlines and PenAir (both Ⓣ1-800/448-4226) jointly run daily **flights** direct from Anchorage with $900–1000 spur-of-the-moment prices; two-week advance purchases come down to $760 round-trip ($380 one-way). There are occasional low-priced specials: shop around, especially if your dates are flexible. Foreigners who book before leaving home can get excellent use out of the "Best of the West Airpass" (see p.336), flying for $109 each way.

Getting around and information

The twin towns are spread out, but fairly flat, so it is quite possible to **get around** on foot. If arriving with luggage, you may want to engage the services of one of the many taxis, which charge almost $20 to get into town from the ferry: try Blue Checker Taxi (Ⓣ581-2186). Rental cars are available from Northport Rental (Ⓣ581-3880) and BC Vehicle Rentals (Ⓣ581-6777, Ⓔchecker@arctic.net), both at the airport, for $55 a day with unlimited mileage for a compact and $85 for a pickup or Explorer.

The **visitor center** (Mon–Fri 9am–5pm, Sat noon–5pm; Ⓣ581-2612 or 1-877/581-2612, Ⓦwww.unalaska.info) is in the Burma Road chapel in Unalaska. Many visitor facilities are congregated nearby, including the two supermarkets, each with a bank and ATM, and the main **post office** (Mon–Fri 9am–5pm, Sat 1–5pm). There's another post office branch downtown, on Airport Beach Road, a few steps away from the **Iliuliuk Clinic**, 34 LaVelle Court (Ⓣ581-1202), plus a **laundromat** at 111 Blue Fox Alley, and the **library** (Mon–Fri 10am–9pm, Sat & Sun noon–6pm), which has free **Internet access**.

Accommodation

High- and moderate-standard **accommodation** is available in Unalaska, but nowhere comes cheap, and there are no campgrounds, though camping is possible in the hills all around (see p.343). There is no hostel as such, but fish-factory **bunkhouses** cater to the cheaper end of the market, none demanding the kind of communal sleeping arrangements the name might imply. Handiest and best value is the *Walashek Bunkhouse*, 116 Gilman St (Ⓣ581-4357, Ⓔwalashek@arctic.net), which is often full with fishermen and construction crews, but has singles for $55. The modern and slightly chintzy *Carl's Bayview Inn*, 606 Bayview (Ⓣ581-1230 or 1-800/581-1230; suites ❼, rooms ❻), is conveniently sited downtown and has comfortable studio rooms with kitchenettes and some bay-view suites, and all with cable TV and free airport transfer.

You'll save a little by staying at the decidedly faded *Unisea Inn* on Gilman Street (Ⓣ581-3844 or 1-866/581-3844, Ⓦwww.grandaleutian.com; ❺), but it's a major step up to its younger sister, the *Grand Aleutian*, 498 Salmon Way (same contacts; ❼), an imposing three-story four-star hotel that's the acme of luxury in the these parts and is so out of keeping with the general tone of the area it is sometimes referred to as the "Grand Delusion."

The Town

Easily the most imposing building in Unalaska is the **Russian Orthodox Cathedral of the Holy Ascension**, its green onion-dome tower endlessly reproduced on postcards and tourist brochures, usually with one of the town's abundant **bald eagles** regally perched on top of the triple-bar cross. It ranks as the oldest existing Russian Orthodox church in the state, built on the site of a church constructed in 1808, and a later model jointly built by Father Ivan Veniaminov and the local Aleut in 1826. The current structure was built in the mid-1890s and survived considerable neglect to rise gloriously restored in 1996. You can normally only go inside for services (Sat 6.30pm & Sun 10am), but you can make the effort to see one of the finest collections of **religious art** in Alaska: call Father Peter Bourdukofsky (Ⓣ581-6404) and offer a contribution towards the restoration program (say $5 or so). There are almost seven hundred icons and relics, amassed over the years as the other half-dozen village churches on Unalaska Island closed when the villages were abandoned. Adjacent is the small **Bishop's House**, which was originally built in San Francisco in 1882 and subsequently reassembled here. It is currently being restored and is not open to the public.

The cathedral looms over Unalaska's sweeping arc of gravel beach, which is backed by the heart of downtown. Stroll to the far eastern end of the beach where there's a memorial to the **USS Northwestern**, a retired freighter pressed into use during World War II as civilian accommodation, but bombed by the Japanese. After burning for five days the boat was later scuttled, and its steel prow can still be seen rising above the waters at the head of Captains Bay. The propeller was recovered for the fiftieth anniversary and now forms the centerpiece of the memorial. Beyond here, Summer Bay Road leads three miles to Summer Bay, where there's good beach walking, a small lake, and a hike across an isthmus to Agamgik Bay (see p.344).

West of downtown Unalaska, the "Bridge to the Other Side" crosses South Channel onto Amaknak Island, once five separate islands now joined by landfill. Immediately over the bridge, a dirt road runs left around the base of Quonset huts (long semicircular sheet-metal huts used in military World War II installations), then up to the summit of **Bunker Hill** (aka Hill 400; 421ft), the commanding site of a World War II gun emplacement. It only takes about fifteen minutes to hike up the road past the remains of the huts, ammunition stores, and tunnel entrances to reach the summit, with its concrete bunkers and circular turntable for directing the 155mm guns at anything approaching.

Back on the main Airport Beach Road, turn right onto Gilman Road to reach the recently opened **Museum of the Aleutians**, 314 Salmon Way

(June–Sept Mon–Sat 10am–5pm, Sun noon–5pm, Oct–May Wed–Sat 11am–4pm, Sun noon–4pm; $4; Ⓦwww.aleutians.org), built on the existing foundations of a World War II warehouse, which provides the terrazzo flooring of the entrance area. Inside, temporary displays augment the permanent collection, which aims to interpret the history and culture of Unalaska Island and the Aleutian region. There's coverage, too, of the Russian involvement in the area, the herring salteries that flourished in the 1920s, and the World War II military buildup, represented here by the lower two-thirds of a Tlingit-style totem pole carved by bored servicemen stationed on Kiska. Artifacts include a 4000-year-old pumice mask unearthed from Margaret Bay, a seal-gut wallet handmade in the 1930s, and seal-bone harpoon points dating back two thousand years.

Sitka Spruce Park, a short walk to the north, contains three trees which remain from the Sitka Spruce Plantation, laid out by Russian settlers around 1805. Nearby, and around the flanks of Mount Ballyhoo, you'll see all manner of remnants of military activity during World War II, mostly abandoned but in some cases incorporated into modern functions: for instance, an old torpedo-production facility is now a six-lane bowling alley. This all forms part of the **World War II National Historic Area**, which maintains a **visitor center** (May–Oct Tues, Thurs, Sat & Sun noon–6pm, Wed & Fri 3–9pm; Nov–April Tues, Thurs & Sat noon–6pm, Wed & Fri 3–9pm; $4; Ⓣ581-1276) in the Aerology Building a short walk from the airport, with a stack of info on the area, the battle for the Aleutians, and the removal of Aleut to Southeast Alaska.

Hiking, biking, and kayaking

With miles of treeless terrain right on the town's doorstep there is plenty of scope for hiking, either along the small number of accessible trails, or heading off wherever you please. There's also an extensive network of old World War II roads that make wonderful mountain-biking territory. Bring a sturdy tent, and you increase the scope of your explorations immeasurably, but all the land hereabouts is private and you need to obtain **permits** either from the Ounalashka Corporation, 400 Salmon Way, Margaret Bay Subdivision (Mon–Fri 8am–5pm; Ⓣ581-1276, Ⓦwww.ounalashka.com), or from the WWII NHA visitor center (see above). One permit covers you for hiking, biking, and camping and currently costs $6 a day per person or $15 a week (families cost $10 & $20 respectively).

Camping is possible close to town, although it is hard to find anywhere that is flat, dry, protected from the wind, and relatively inconspicuous on these bald hills. You also need to take account of the weather, which can whip up winds of 70mph in no time: locals even suggest taking a packet of balloons so you can ensure the fly and inner stay separated.

June is a good month for **hiking**. You will still encounter snow on the tops, the 120 varieties of wildflower are magnificent, and the summer grass is not yet too tall. July and August are likely to have better weather (and juicy salmonberries and blueberries), although you still need to keep to the ridge if you want relatively dry feet. You should also carry a compass since the fog comes in quick and thick. Also note that, despite an extensive cleanup in recent years, there is still a slim possibility you may come across **unexploded ordnance** left over from World War II; don't disturb any rusted-up bits of metal. After all these warnings, it is comforting that there are no bears, and the bugs aren't too bad.

The easiest of the local hikes is up **Mount Ballyhoo** (4 miles round-trip; 3hr; 1600ft ascent), which rises behind the airport and offers views to Makushin Volcano and the rest of Unalaska Island. The hike can be extended by continuing north along the ridge to Ulakta Head. The **Agamgik Bay Trail** (8 miles round-trip; 3–5hr; 500ft ascent) is also worthwhile though it starts an inconvenient four miles from town at Summer Bay, reached along Summer Bay Road.

The twin towns have 38 miles of regular roads, and many more miles of disused tracks from World War II, challenging terrain that is perfect for **mountain biking** using hardtail machines rented from Aleutian Adventure Sports (Ⓣ581-4489, Ⓦwww.aleutianadventure.com) for $25 a half-day and $35 for the full day. The same company also rents kayaks (double $85 a day, single $65) and leads a wide range of excellent **guided kayak trips**, including the Harbor and Captains Bay tours (3–4hr; $55 and $65 respectively), which are open to complete novices, the more demanding paddle northwest to Wide Bay (10–12hr; $145), and four- to six-day extended trips ($550–1100). **Guided hiking** and mountaineering trips take place through the summer months, with a visit to Akutan Volcano and the nearby hot springs (4 days; $1100), and one to the snowcapped 6680-foot summit of Makushin Volcano on Unalaska Island.

Halibut fishing and birding

Keen birders and halibut fishers usually fly in on Anchorage-based packages, a couple of the best offered in conjunction with the *Grand Aleutian Hotel* (see p.342), which provides accommodation and meals. Their Whiskered Auklet tour comes in three variations, each a day charter out to see these rare birds, along with tufted and horned puffins, petrels, jaegers, and all sorts of marine mammals: two nights for $505, three nights for $838, and four nights for $1408.

The hotel's Halibut Heaven (June–Aug) is a two-night sportfishing package for $803, with one-night increments up to seven nights for $2954 with charters each day. If you are here and just fancy a day **halibut fishing**, expect to pay around $170 (minimum two people) and go with Shuregood Adventures (Ⓣ581-2378 or 1-877/374-4386, Ⓦwww.arctic.net/~shurgood) or F/V *Lucille* (Ⓣ581-5949, Ⓦwww.unalaskahalibutfishing.com). Between mid-May and mid-September you can also enter the **halibut derby** ($10 a day, $50 a week) and hope to land one of the weekly, monthly, or overall prizes (max $5000), or perhaps break that 459-pound world record.

Eating, drinking, and entertainment

Unalaska is reputed to have a cost of living almost thirty percent higher than Anchorage, so you can expect **eating** to be pricey. The best way around this is to prepare your own food with groceries from the huge Eagle Value Center near the *Grand Aleutian*, which has good deli and bakery sections and sells espresso.

Nearby, *Amelia's*, corner of E Point Road and Airport Beach Road (Ⓣ581-2800), has a diverse menu and specializes in hearty breakfasts from 6am and Mexican dishes. The *Grand Aleutian* undoubtedly has the finest food around and is as expensive as you'd expect, though the $25 Sunday brunch is good value.

In downtown Unalaska, *Nicky's Place*, at the junction of 2nd and Bayview (Mon–Sat 10am–6pm, Sun 1–5pm; Ⓣ581-1570), is good for espresso while browsing new and secondhand books and maps. *Tino's Steakhouse*, 11 N 2nd St (Ⓣ581-4288), does good steaks and much more, including fairly authentic Mexican dishes – chicken fajitas for $18, *camarones a la diabla* for $20, and a whopping *carne asada* burrito meal for $20 – as well as excellent breakfasts from waffles to omelets and reindeer sausages and eggs.

There was a time when a survey declared that the *Elbow Room* (☎581-1271) was the second roughest **bar** in the US, with tales of near-constant fights and people left bleeding out in the snow. It is considerably toned down now (at least in summer when most visitors arrive and most fishermen are away) and makes a good place for a lively evening, though there's often more action down the road in the large dark bar at *Carl's Bayview Inn*.

The Pribilof Islands

Nature enthusiasts salivate over visiting the **PRIBILOF ISLANDS**, an archipelago of two inhabited volcanic crests – St Paul Island and St George Island – and assorted islets rising from the bed of the Bering Sea nine hundred miles west of Anchorage and two hundred miles north of Dutch Harbor. A bleak place of treeless, tundra-covered hills, the Pribilofs are saddled with the wet and misty weather typical of the Aleutians and an average summer temperature below fifty degrees. Unappealing as this may sound, the islands have two major draws: an incredibly rich gathering of honking seals and some of the most densely packed **seabird cliffs** found anywhere.

The islands were uninhabited when Russian Gerassim Pribylov discovered the fur-clad bounty he was looking for in 1786. It wasn't long before Aleutian Islands Natives were virtually enslaved and shipped to the Pribilofs to harvest the seals, in time reducing seal numbers to the brink of extinction. Nonetheless, pickings were still healthy enough for the United States to look to the islands to recoup some of their costs after the 1867 purchase from Russia. The US initially continued the harsh treatment of the Aleut, manipulating virtually every aspect of their lives, and during World War II forced the Pribilof Aleut to evacuate to Southeast Alaska (see box, p.340). Since their return to the islands, the Aleut have managed to gain some degree of self-governance.

By 1910 seal numbers were down to around 125,000 and stayed low until 1957, when the United States, Japan, Canada, and the Soviet Union created the North Pacific Fur Seal Commission to control indiscriminate killing. Seal harvesting finally stopped in 1986 and now every summer some 800,000 northern fur seals (three-quarters of the world population) vie for space at the breeding rookeries on the rocky beaches, accompanied by harbor seals, Steller sea lions, walruses, and sea otters. Camouflaged viewing hides have been set up along the beaches, and if your attention should waver, you can always wander along the hiking trails to other positions with a better angle on the nesting seabirds that cram onto every available ledge and squeeze into impossible crevices. The islands attract around two million birds from over two hundred species: mostly murres, puffins, fulmars, kittiwakes, cormorants, and auklets, but also small numbers of Asiatic vagrants which turn up mostly in May. Come a little later in the season and the endless summer days bring out blankets of wildflowers. Only the most curmudgeonly of city types could fail to be impressed by this spectacular convergence of birds, seals, and flowers, but the cost of getting and staying here puts many off.

Most visitors end up on **ST PAUL**, which at fourteen miles by eight is the larger of the two inhabited islands, supporting a population of eight hundred Aleut, the world's largest such community. Their spiritual center is the **SS Peter and Paul Church**, its plain exterior giving little hint of the rich Russian Orthodox interior, all icons and fuschia-colored carpet. Basic roads and hiking trails ring the island and provide access to half a dozen bird cliffs and seal-viewing areas.

ST GEORGE only has a couple of hundred Aleut residents, its own impressive church, **St George the Martyr**, and a few seals. It excels, however, when it comes to seabird cliffs, some of which rise a thousand feet from the crashing waves. It's small enough to hike around and find your favorite viewing spot.

Practicalities

The Pribilofs can be reached independently on scheduled flights from Anchorage with PenAir (Ⓣ243-2323), which has four or five flights a week to both islands in summer. With fares at least $800 and the limited scope for independent travel, it usually works out better to join an organized tour. The most frequently run (and easiest to squeeze into a tight schedule) are those operated by Alaska Birding & Wildlife Tours (Ⓣ1-877/424-5637, Ⓦwww.alaskabirding.com), who from mid-May to late August have trips including flights from Anchorage to St Paul, accommodation at the *King Eider*, and a naturalist guide: stay durations range from two nights ($1361) to seven nights ($2375) including everything except meals. The Pribilof weather frequently disrupts flight schedules for days at a time, so be sure to allow some flexibility in your schedule and have some cash spare for those extra nights at the *King Eider*.

Once on the islands, choices are few and neither island allows camping. On St Paul Island the only **place to stay** is the plain but comfortable *King Eider* (Ⓣ546-2477; ❺). Meals are available from the cafeteria of the local fish-processing plant and will set you back around $40 a day. On **St George Island** you can sleep at the historic *St George Tanaq* (Ⓣ272-9886; ❼), which has shared bathrooms and a kitchen where you can prepare food, best brought over from Anchorage but available locally at a price. There are **no restaurants** on St George.

Travel details

With the exception of a fourteen-mile road from King Salmon to Naknek, no Southwest towns are linked by road. Transport is predominantly by air, although the *Tustumena* sails to Kodiak from Homer three times a week and continues along the Alaska Peninsula to Unalaska/Dutch Harbor once a month in summer.

Ferries

Chignik to: Kodiak (one a month; 18hr 30min); Sand Point (one a month; 9hr 15min).
Cold Bay to: False Pass (one a month; 4hr 15min); King Cove (one a month; 2hr).
Dutch Harbor to: Akutan (one a month; 15hr); Chignik (one a month; 37hr); Cold Bay (one a month; 17hr); King Cove (one a month; 19hr); Kodiak (one a month; 61hr); Sand Point (one a month; 27hr).
False Pass to: Cold Bay (one a month; 4hr 15min); Dutch Harbor (one a month; 13hr).
King Cove to: Cold Bay (one a month; 2hr); Sand Point (one a month; 6hr 30min).
Kodiak to: Chignik (one a month; 18hr 30min); Cold Bay (one a month; 42hr); Dutch Harbor (one a month; 61hr); False Pass (one a month; 48hr); Homer (2–3 weekly; 9hr 30min); King Cove (one a month; 39hr); Port Lions (weekly; 2hr 30min); Sand Point (one a month; 30hr); Seward (weekly; 13hr 15min).
Port Lions to: Homer (weekly; 10hr); Kodiak (weekly; 2hr 30min).
Sand Point to: Chignik (one a month; 9hr 15min); King Cove (one a month; 6hr 30min).

Flights

Anchorage to: Iliamna (1–2 daily; 1hr); King Salmon (5–8 daily; 1hr–1hr 20min); St George (4 weekly; 4hr); St Paul (4 weekly; 3hr).
Dutch Harbor to: Anchorage (2–3 daily; 2hr–2hr 50min).
King Salmon to: Anchorage (5–8 daily; 1hr–1hr 20min); Brooks Camp (4–8 daily; 20min).
Kodiak to: Anchorage (6–8 daily; 50min–1hr 10min).

6

Denali and the western interior

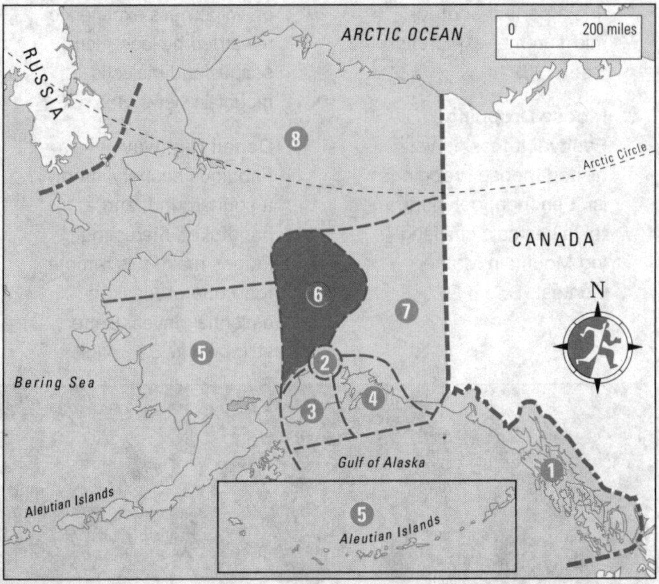

CHAPTER 6

Highlights

* **Eklutna Historical Park** Wander amid the colorful "spirit house" graves that surround a striking onion-domed Russian Orthodox church. See p.351

* **Independence Mine** Beautifully preserved mine workings set in an alpine bowl high above the Mat-Su Valley make this a perfect spot for mid-summer exploration. See p.362

* **Moose Dropping Festival** If tossing varnished moose droppings isn't enough, get along to Talkeetna's challenging Mountain Mother Contest. See p.367

* **Mount McKinley flightseeing** A flying visit to North America's tallest peak is an essential part of any trip to the Interior and is enhanced by a glacier landing. See p.373

* **Hiking in Denali's backcountry** Exploring Denali National Park's backcountry on foot is a full-on wilderness experience rewarded by lonely landscapes and majestic mountain views. See p.393

* **Denali Highway** Fabulous scenery, hardly a soul around, and a handful of interesting lodges make this remote road one of Alaska's essential drives. Better still, bike it. See p.399

△ Nenana Ice Classic tripod and warehouse

6

Denali and the western Interior

Interior Alaska is the Alaska of popular imagination – a land of wild and untamed beauty spreading west from the Canadian border. For the most part, it is a low plateau of permafrost swampland only feebly drained by small streams. Wherever you go, you'll feel the presence of the mountains, either as a barrier to where you're trying to get to or as an icy backdrop to broad river valleys. Nowhere is this more true than around **Denali and the western Interior**, where the Alaska Range arcs in a great crescent with its crown, Mount McKinley, forming the centerpiece of **Denali National Park**.

Originally, this was **Athabascan** country, populated by Native Americans who share their heritage with the Navajos and Apaches of the American Southwest. Their presence is still strong in the area, though they mainly keep to themselves in villages off the beaten track: you're more likely to run into the somewhat sanitized vignettes of their lifestyle occasionally presented for tourists. Over the past century the region has been settled by miners, hunters, and trappers, and though towns have grown up to serve the scattered communities, the pioneer spirit shows itself in the modern-day sourdoughs who chose it as their home. Most of the significant communities lie along the **Alaska Railroad**, which first linked Anchorage and Fairbanks in 1913, although since 1973 it has been the almost parallel **George Parks Highway** that has driven development.

In the lowland **Mat-Su Valley**, there's considerable interest in the depression-era farming colony that kick-started Alaska's limited arable tradition, but it is the hills that draw you on, principally to **Hatcher Pass** and the magnificently sited ruin of **Independence Mine**. But this is small cheese compared with what's to come, the 20,000-foot **Mount McKinley**. Screaming up from the tundra at just 2000ft above sea level, Mount McKinley boasts the greatest vertical rise of any mountain anywhere. It is known to many as Denali, probably a Dena'ina word for "the Great One," and to say that it dominates the Alaska Range is an understatement. There are few other ranges in the world where the highest peak is fifty percent higher than the peaks all around it, and none where that peak is the highest on a continent. The giant mountain dictates local weather patterns, with moisture-laden coastal air forced above it, dumping thousands of tons of snow – the raw material for a dozen glaciers – into the area. In the summer Denali is obscured by clouds

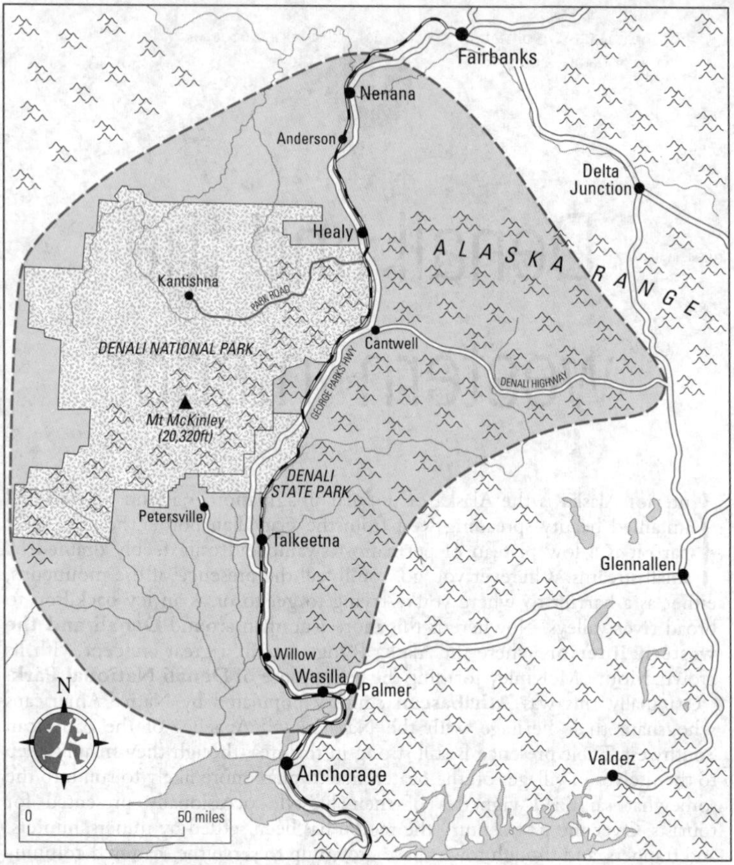

two days out of three, and your best chances of a good view are from the wonderfully oddball village of **Talkeetna**, home of the famed Moose Dropping Festival, base for flightseeing and, in spring, alive with Denali summit aspirants. North of the Alaska Range is the heartland of **Denali National Park**, where the unparalleled wildlife viewing constitutes Alaska's single greatest draw – though you only need a pinch of determination to leave the crowds behind for a wilderness hiking experience that is little short of spiritual. Before the creation of the George Parks Highway, the only road access to Denali was the **Denali Highway**, now a scenic dirt road hemming the southern skirts of the Alaska Range. With very little habitation, few visitors, and a refreshing lack of rules and restrictions, it is a wonderful place to spend a day or two exploring.

Uniquely for Alaska, the Anchorage–Fairbanks corridor is fairly easy to get around, with a fast highway, a train line, and several bus companies operating along sections of the Parks Highway. That said, services are skeletal; having your own transport is definitely a bonus, giving the freedom to travel at your own pace and explore whatever backroads you find.

For up-to-date information on Interior road conditions contact ⓣ456-7623, ⓦwww.dot.state.ak.us.

Eklutna and around

Heading north out of Anchorage, it would be easy to race past the hamlet of **EKLUTNA**, 25 miles to the north, but this would be a mistake. Long before Anchorage existed, this Native settlement had become the most important village in Cook Inlet through trade with the Russians. Athabascan and Russian influences combine intriguingly at the Eklutna Historical Park, while across the Glenn Highway the impressive **Thunderbird Falls** mark the access road to the boating, biking, and hiking nexus of **Eklutna Lake**.

Eklutna Historical Park

In 1830 Russian settlers constructed **St Nicholas Russian Orthodox Church**, a low-built, log-shaped structure with a shingle roof sporting three triple-barred crosses that ranks as the oldest extant building in the Anchorage area. Filled with rare icons brought here before Alaska was sold to the United States, the church now forms the centerpiece of **Eklutna Historical Park** (mid-May to mid-Sept Mon–Sat 10am–6pm, last tour 5.15pm; $6; ⓣ688-6026; ⓦwww.eklutna.com), a fascinating blend of Russian and Athabascan culture, with a cemetery which is densely packed with the state's finest collection of **spirit houses**. There are more than eighty of these mostly waist-high huts, their yellow, red, blue, green, or even candy-striped pitched roofs topped with a crenellated crest in technicolor. In place of the familiar headstone, tradition requires that when an Orthodox Russian Athabascan dies a new blanket is placed over the grave and a three-bar Orthodox cross is planted at the foot. Forty days after burial, the deceased's family builds a spirit house over the grave using the family's traditional colors to denote who is interred. Other clues to look for are a small house within a larger one, thought to indicate joint burial of a mother and her child, and a house surrounded by a picket fence indicating that the dead person was neither Tanaina or Russian Orthodox.

Thunderbird Falls and Eklutna Lake

The same exit from the Glenn Highway accesses **Thunderbird Falls**, a pretty 200-foot, two-leap cataract (an icefall in winter) at the end of a mile-long trail through birch forest. Wilder scenery is on hand nearby at the end of the ten-mile Eklutna Lake Road, which ends at **Eklutna Lake**, a bush-girt mountain reservoir in the heart of the Chugach Mountains that provides tap water to half of Anchorage. It is bordered by the sizable *Eklutna Lake Campground* ($10 includes parking fee; pump water; fire rings), a summer-only ranger station, and the **Eklutna Lake Recreation Area** (parking $5 a day), where Lifetime Adventures (mid-May to mid-Sept Mon–Fri 11am–7pm, Sat & Sun 10am–8pm; ⓣ746-4644, ⓦwww.lifetimeadventures.net) rents kayaks (single $25/half-day, double $30/half-day) and bikes ($15–20/half-day, $25–30/day). A "peddle and paddle" combo ($70) allows you to kayak to the end of the lake and bike back.

Most activity happens along the gentle **Eklutna Lakeside Trail** (12.7 miles one-way; 4-5hr; 300ft ascent), which is open to ATVs from Sunday to Wednesday, but on Thursdays, Fridays, and Saturdays bikers and hikers have it to themselves. The "trail" follows a roadbed once used by the military to access the Eklutna Glacier for winter training, and runs for seven miles to the head of the lake (often ducking off the road along a narrowed cycle track), then beyond to the calming Serenity Falls (Mile 12). Beyond the end of the abandoned roadbed hikers can continue along **Eklutna Glacier Trail**, which turns rockier and tougher as you approach the snout of the Eklutna Glacier across glacial gravel bars which were under hundreds of feet of ice as little as fifty years ago. Here, the Mitre and Benign Peak rise over 6000ft above you, and views of steep canyon walls and waterfalls surround. The Lakeside Trail provides access to two further trails: five miles along Eklutna Lake you can strike off north up the arduous **Bold Ridge Trail** (7 miles round-trip; 4–6hr; 2500ft ascent), which climbs up to open tundra inviting further exploration for the committed; and at the 10.5-mile mark the narrow **East Fork Trail** (13 miles round-trip; 6–8hr; 700ft ascent) spurs off along, unsurprisingly, the East Fork of the Eklutna River fording numerous streams. In addition, the steep and rugged **Twin Peaks Trail** (6.5 miles round-trip; 4–5hr; 1500ft ascent) climbs up the mountainside to the north of the campground to great lake views from above the tree line and fall berry picking.

The whole area is perhaps best explored by spending a night in one of the simple **backcountry camping** areas, such as the *Eklutna Alex Campground* at Mile 9 of the Lakeside Trail, equipped with fire rings and nearby stream water. Alternatives include the *Eklutna Lake Cabin* ($40; reserve through APLIC in Anchorage) at Mile 3 and the lovely *Serenity Falls Cabin*, Mile 12 (reserve in person through DNR Public Information Center, Suite 1260, 550 W 7th Ave, Anchorage ⓣ269-8400), where you can rent individual bunks (single $10, double $15).

The Mat-Su Valley

Somewhat criminally overlooked by tourists speeding north from Anchorage to Denali, the glacially contorted **Mat-Su Valley** is in fact made up of two valleys, shaped by the erosive powers of the Matanuska and Susitna rivers and spotted with lakes, open plateaux, and towering mountains. It is a huge area divided by the rugged granite forms of the **Talkeetna Mountains** which, despite only just topping 7000ft, are an impressive sight, particularly with fall's first dusting of snow.

This vast catchment contains just two substantial towns. **Palmer** is the more appealing of the two, the result of a grand experiment in co-operative farming. Its prim town center is surrounded by dairy farms dotted with Midwest-style colony barns, scenically framed by the snowcapped ridges of Pioneer Peak. **Wasilla** is less inviting, the embodiment of a regional boom which during the 1990s saw the population increase by thirty percent. If time is strictly limited, take a quick whirl through the Palmer backroads checking out the colony barns, then follow one of the loveliest alpine drives in the state to **Hatcher Pass** and the dramatic remains of the **Independence Mine**.

Both Palmer and Wasilla have small visitor centers, but the main **Matanuska-Susitna CVB** (mid-May to mid-Sept daily 8.30am–6.30pm; closed in winter; ⓣ746-5000, ⓦwww.alaskavisit.com) is located at Mile 35.5 of the Parks Highway, just north of the "Y" where the Parks and Glenn highways part company.

Palmer

For thousands of years, glacial silt was carried by the Matanuska River and deposited in the Matanuska Valley, creating the most fertile land in Alaska, upon which sprung up the small farming community of **PALMER**, 42 miles north of Anchorage. Though the soil's fertility was recognized early, and the Alaska Railroad linked Palmer to Anchorage in the 1920s, the city's great leap forward only came in 1935 when, as part of his New Deal, President Franklin D Roosevelt drew up the unusual Matanuska **Colony Program**. The plan involved bringing some two hundred families from the drought-stricken Midwest states of Minnesota, Wisconsin, and Michigan to resettle here on forty-acre tracts. The government gave $3000 loans to help the settlers build homes, clear land, and eat until their first crop came in. In return the government received $5 an acre for the land and ran a highly un-Alaskan co-operative system whereby the crops grown became the property of the group who shared the profits. Though glad to escape their dusty farms back home, many felt the disapproval of the original homesteaders, who believed the newcomers were getting something for nothing.

The settlers eschewed the Alaskan log-cabin customs and constructed frame houses and gambrel-roofed barns of their home states, each with jutting eaves supporting winch jibs. These **colony barns** and their associated grain silos remain a feature of the region today, but improved transportation made goods shipped in from Seattle and elsewhere increasingly competitive and farms were steadily sold off and subdivided. Much of the best farmland in the state is now prime real estate: although Alaskan supermarkets stock local dairy products, most of their ingredients now come from the Lower 48.

There is one agricultural enterprise that is still economically viable, though not particularly visible to the casual observer. The region is renowned throughout Alaska for its **Matanuska Thunderfuck**, reputedly some of the strongest marijuana anywhere.

Mat-Su's mega-veggies and the Alaska State Fair

The happy convergence of twenty hours of summer sunlight and a deep, rockless bed of loess (a type of glacial soil) allows the Mat-Su Valley to produce **gargantuan vegetables**, notably freak cabbages weighing in at close to a hundred pounds, as well as six-pound onions, eight-pound carrots, and once a single pea pod weighing a quarter of a pound. Astoundingly, the record pumpkin for the area is almost 350 pounds.

In late summer and fall, produce that is merely huge can be bought from pick-your-own farms all round the district – peaches, apples, and other fruit work out at bargain prices – but to see record-breakers you'll need to go to Palmer's **Alaska State Fair** (day tickets $8; ⓣ745-4827 or 1-800/850-3247, ⓦwww.alaskastatefair.org), held at the State Fairground two miles south along the Glenn Highway, on the ten days leading up to Labor Day. Though it is really just Palmer's annual fair, it fights off all contenders to the "state" title by being by far the biggest around, with just about every sector of the Alaskan economy and arts scene represented; in fact it is hard to find a band playing anywhere else in the state when the fair is on. Expect everything from staples like monster-truck displays, rodeo, and lumberjacking competitions to Native dance and blanket tossing, and oddball events like the Husband Holler, the potato-stacking contest and a competition in which the organizers grow a potato patch, then contestants dig as fast as they can striving to fill their two-gallon bucket first. Some kind of historical authenticity is lent by the homesteading events like wood splitting and water hauling, but the highlight for the valley growers is the giant vegetable weigh-off.

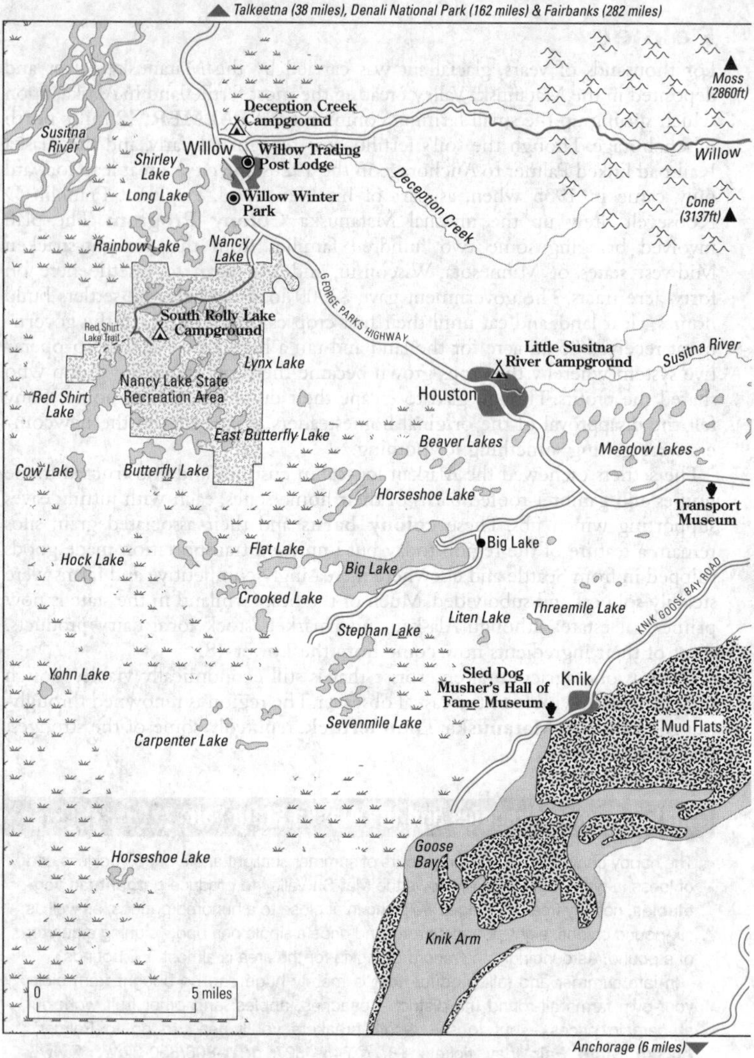

The town and around

In keeping with its origins, Palmer could still pass for a small Midwestern town with its gleaming water tower, its neatly maintained train station (though there are no passenger services), and a grid of small streets with shops and a steady trickle of pedestrians. Almost everything worth seeing lies outside town, but you can pass a pleasant few minutes in the small, free pioneer **museum** downstairs in the visitor center (see p.357), then follow a self-guided walking tour through the town. Outside the visitor center, there's a demonstration patch of oversized vegetables (see box, p.353), though they don't reach Brobdingnagian proportions until late August. Following E Elmwood Avenue you pass the **Colony Memorial**, a sculpture dedicated to the 202 families who first settled

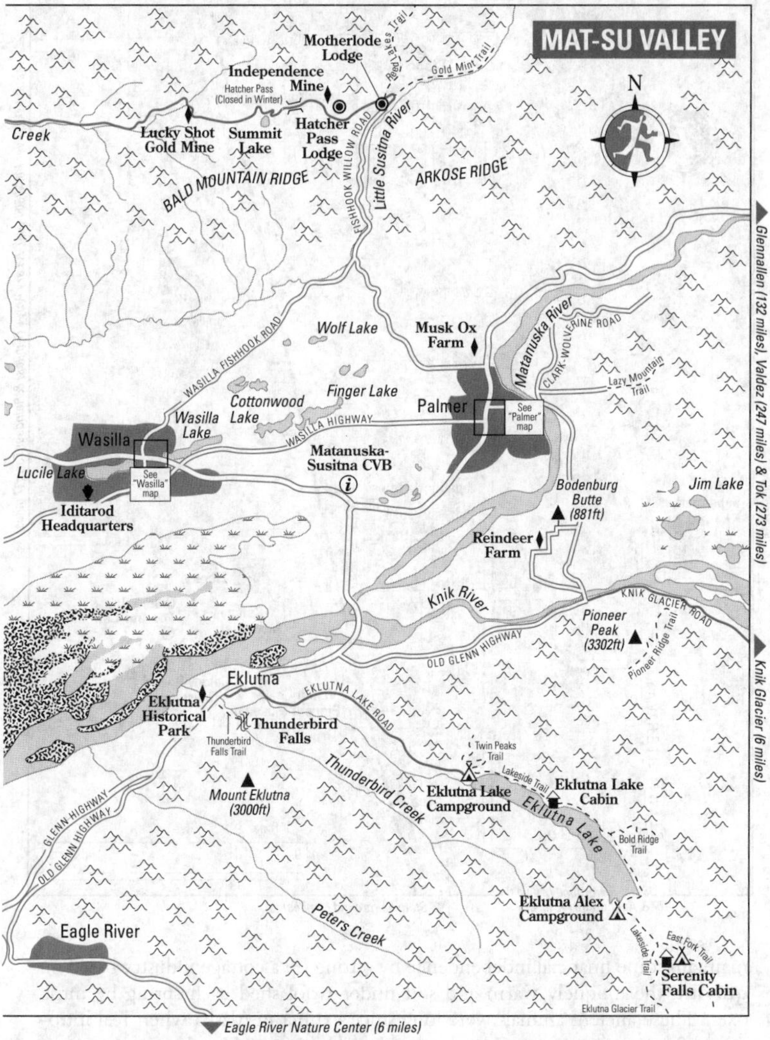

here, and the **Colony House Museum**, 316 E Elmwood Ave (mid-May to mid-Sept Mon–Sat 10am–4pm; $2), a nicely restored and furnished example of the type of houses built here in 1935.

The place that really draws visitors to these parts is the **Musk Ox Farm**, Mile 50 Glenn Hwy, seven miles north of town (mid-May to late Sept daily 10am–6pm; tours every half-hour; $8.50; Ⓦ www.muskoxfarm.org), where you are guided past a few dozen of these ancient straggly beasts grazing on the lush pasture. They're often pretty inactive in the warmth of a Mat-Su summer day – early morning is best to see them move about – but they manage to look cute enough in a dopey sort of way. They aren't just here for tourists to pet though. In 1930 anthropologist John Teal envisaged helping the people of the Arctic to

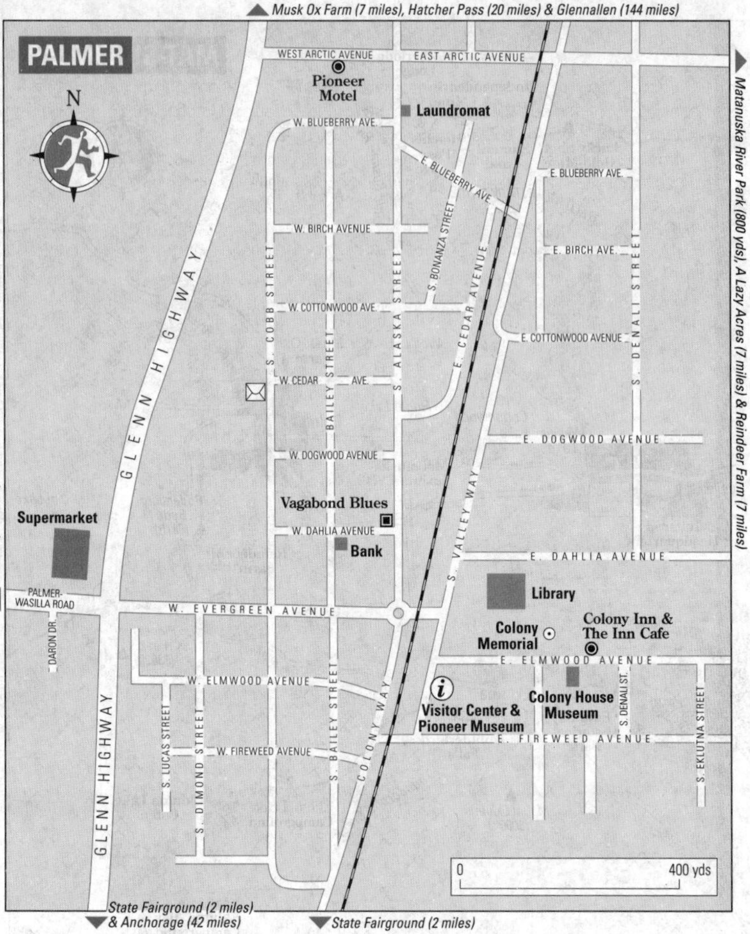

maintain some financial independence by setting up a cottage industry based on **quiviut**, the uniquely warm and soft under-wool shed each spring by musk oxen. These ancient animals were long since extinct in Alaska when Teal introduced 34 specimens from Greenland and set about breeding them and reintroducing them into the wild: three thousand of their descendants now roam the Arctic tundra. Gathered quiviut is spun into fine yarn and sent, undyed, to scattered western Alaskan villages, where knitted garments are produced using patterns individual to that village and based on motifs once common on clothing and baskets made there. The garments are sold through the shop here at the Musk Ox Farm and at Oomingmak Musk Ox Producers Cooperative in Anchorage (see "Shopping," p.223). They often sell out, but you might not find yourself too disappointed at missing out on that $300 fawny-brown shawl.

Domesticated wild animals are also on display some seven miles south of Palmer on one of the original Colony farms now operating as the **Reindeer Farm**, Bodenburg Butte Road, off the Old Glenn Highway (June–Aug daily

Hikes around Palmer

The proximity to towns and farms makes Palmer an unusual hiking area in the Alaskan context, but the trails listed here (and those in Hatcher Pass; see box, p.364) easily justify an extra day or so in the area.

Bodenburg Butte (2 miles round-trip; 1hr to 1hr 30min; 800ft ascent). The shortest of the local hikes. The steep ascent is eroded and not that inspiring, but you soon rise out of the aspens for great views of farmland, the Knik Glacier, and the surrounding mountains. The trailhead is right by the Reindeer Farm (see p.356). Parking $3 per car.

Lazy Mountain Trail (5 miles round-trip; 3–5hr; 3600ft ascent). The best and most convenient hike near Palmer offers outstanding views of the valley and farmland. Parts can be pretty steep, but it is worth it. The trail can be turned into a full day of hiking by combining it with other trails described in the free *Lazy Mountain & Morgan Horse Trails* leaflet available from the Palmer visitor center. To reach the trailhead take Arctic Avenue east across the Matanuska River, then a mile along Clark–Wolverine Road and right onto Huntley Road. The trailhead is at the end, a mile or so along.

Pioneer Ridge Trail (12 miles round-trip; 6–8hr; 5100ft ascent). A fairly tough day-long hike requiring reasonable fitness to slog up through steep underbrush, though it eases as it reaches alder thicket and becomes almost gentle on the subalpine tundra approaching the high point of 5300 feet on the ridge below Pioneer Peaks. Progress beyond here requires rock-climbing skills and tackle, but it is still a rewarding hike with long views to the north and west, and the chance to see Dall sheep, moose, and black bears. The trailhead is four miles along Knik Glacier Road.

10am–6pm; $5), where hand-feeding and photo-taking is very much the order of the day. The journey out here is made considerably more worthwhile by the short hike up **Bodenburg Butte** (see box, above), which starts along Bodenburg Butte Road, almost opposite.

A further three miles south, the Old Glenn Highway crosses the Knik River, and the unpaved eleven-mile Knik Glacier Road runs up beside the river past the **Pioneer Ridge** Trailhead (see box, above) towards Knik Glacier, which can be visited on four-hour airboat tours run by Knik Glacier Adventures (Ⓣ746-5133; Ⓦwww.knikglacieradventures.com; $65; minimum 3).

Practicalities

Alaska Direct **buses** running between Anchorage and Tok (Wed, Fri & Sun in both directions; Ⓣ1-800/770-6652) will drop off on request, and you can use the local weekday-only Mascot bus service (Ⓣ376-5000, Ⓦwww.matsutransit.com; $2) to get here from Wasilla. Both call outside the **visitor center**, 723 S Valley Way at Fireweed Ave (mid-May to mid-Sept daily 9am–6pm; mid-Sept to mid-May Mon–Fri 10am–4pm; Ⓣ745-2880, Ⓦwww.palmerchamber.org), which is close to some good central **accommodation**. The basic but clean and cable-equipped *Pioneer Motel*, 124 W Arctic Ave (Ⓣ745-3425; ❷), is easily outdone by the *Colony Inn*, 325 E Elmwood Ave (Ⓣ745-3330 or 1-800/478-7666; ❹), a lovingly restored teachers' dormitory from the Colony days, with attractive rooms dressed in unfussy period decor. There are several good B&Bs hereabouts, not least the very friendly and welcoming *A Lazy Acres*, Helmaur Place (Ⓣ745-6340; ❹), seven miles northeast of town up on Lazy Mountain; consider, too, staying at *Hatcher Pass Lodge*, up by the Independence Mine (see p.363). **Campers** should make for *Matanuska River Park*, 350 E Arctic Ave ($10, RVs $15) with wooded sites, showers for $2 and a day-use area all located half a mile east of town on the Old Glenn Highway.

There are several reasonable **places to eat** in the vicinity, but few really worth seeking out. The big surprise is *Vagabond Blues Café*, 642 S Alaska St (☎745-2233), a cool, bohemian kind of place with a huddle of old worktables (one dedicated to chess playing) for sipping good coffee or tucking into great salads and soups, several of them vegetarian. On weekends this is the place to come for live music, usually acoustic and sometimes with a small cover charge. *The Inn Café*, 325 E Elmwood Ave (☎746-6118), in the *Colony Inn* building, is prim by comparison, but they bake their own pies and pastries, and serve good-value lunch and dinner specials ($9 and $11 respectively); entrées such as New York steak or Cajun shrimp stir-fry go for $18–23.

Downtown Palmer has a **laundry** with showers at 127 S Alaska St; a **library** with free **Internet access** at 655 S Valley Way; a **post office** at the corner of S Cobb Street and W Cedar Avenue; and levies a three percent sales **tax** plus a five percent bed tax. You'll find a Wells Fargo **bank** at 705 S Bailey St.

Wasilla, Knik, and around

At first glance **WASILLA** (Wa-SILL-a), forty miles north of Anchorage, embodies all that is wrong with the kind of urban sprawl so prevalent in America today: countless strip malls line almost eight miles of the Parks Highway north of the "Y" junction, and the only indication it has any center at all is the presence of a train station. The blight, though, is only skin-deep, with some beautiful lakes just off the highway and a couple of good museums nearby. Provided you've got wheels it can make an agreeable place from which to explore the Mat-Su Valley: after all, you are only ten miles west of Palmer and Hatcher Pass is close at hand.

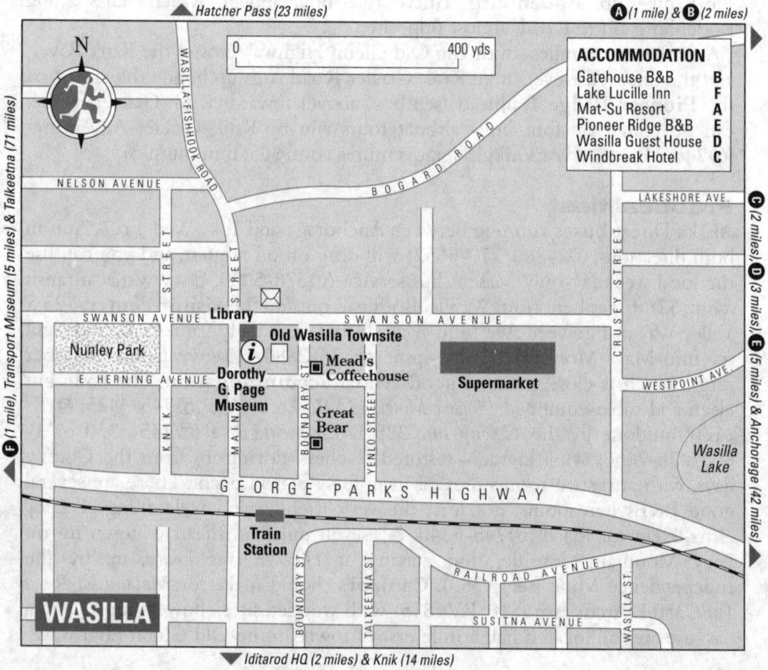

Wasilla started out in the late nineteenth century as a way station and service center on the Carle Wagon Road between Knik – then a significant tidal port – and the gold mines at Hatcher Pass. With the advent of Anchorage and the construction of the railroad, Knik's *raison d'être* disappeared, and Wasilla became just a minor stop on the Anchorage to Fairbanks line. Everything changed with the construction of the George Parks Highway in the early 1970s and the threat of the capital moving to Willow (see p.365). All of a sudden this moribund village became hot property, and Wasilla began its rampant growth fueled by overspill from Anchorage.

The blue-ribbon event on Wasilla's calendar is the **Iditarod Restart**, held the day after the first Saturday in March, when dogs, sleds, and mushers all get bundled off the trucks that have brought them from the previous day's ceremonial run to Eagle River and kick off the race proper (see p.360–361).

Dorothy Page and Alaska Transportation museums

The **Dorothy G Page Museum**, 323 Main St (April–Sept Tues–Sat 9am–5pm; $3; ⓣ373-9071), does a good job of capturing and presenting historic Wasilla. The main body of the museum comprises an eclectic assortment of everything from a Native sealskin coat with patchwork trim to a translucent white raincoat made from walrus intestines, to simple dogsleds and material on Balto, the dog famed for his role in the epidemic-busting Serum Run (see p.504). In the basement there's all manner of gold paraphernalia including a mock hard-rock mine akin to those up at Hatcher Pass and an assay office where the quality of the gold was measured. The most diverting stuff is out the back in the **Old Wasilla Townsite**, a corral of half a dozen mostly log-built structures relocated here from around the region. Alongside Wasilla's first one-room schoolhouse and huge sauna and community bathhouse is the Capital Site Cabin prematurely built for Governor Jay Hammond at Willow when it was thought the state capital was going to move there.

Five miles north of town, the privately run **Museum of Alaska Transportation & Industry**, Mile 47 Parks Hwy (May–Sept daily except Mon 10am–5pm; Oct–April Sat 10am–5pm; $8; ⓦwww.alaska.net/~rmorris/mati1.htm), hoards just about everything imaginable to do with transport in the state: a Native umiak, homesteading sleds, the first motorized pump fire engine to work in Anchorage, the first hang glider to be launched off the summit of Denali, and a line of restored railroad carriages. It can all be a bit overwhelming, unless you can engage the deeply passionate and knowledgeable owner in some contextualizing conversation.

Knik

Back by the train station in Wasilla, Knik Goose Bay Road runs fourteen miles southwest to the tiny settlement of **KNIK** (ka-NICK), a former Russian mission site and onetime transport and supply hub for the gold towns of the Interior. Stop along the way at the **Iditarod Headquarters**, Mile 2.2 Knik Goose Bay Rd (mid-May to mid-Sept daily 8am–7pm; mid-Sept to mid-May Mon–Fri 8am–5pm; donation appreciated), the state's foremost shrine to the Iditarod Sled Dog Race (see box, overleaf). One wall is like a giant scrapbook of newspaper clippings reporting on the 1925 Serum Run and the early years of the Iditarod; there's also a sled with the traces that attach to the dog team and the large bag for carrying gear, myriad trophies – including the winner's trophy, which is always kept here – and the 23-minute video *Beyond Courage*, which successfully captures the spirit of the race. Look, too, for the immortalized Togo, stuffed and displayed nearby, who led the final sprint across the ice into Nome during the Serum Run. Outside, a bronze statue remembers the "Father of the Iditarod," Joe Redington, Sr, who died in 1999. Nearby, beside a cabin decked out like an Iditarod checkpoint, you can board a wheeled sled ($5) and get towed around a set course through the woods.

If the Iditarod Headquarters has whetted your appetite for more, continue twelve miles to Knik itself and the **Knik Museum and Mushers' Hall of**

The Iditarod

On the first Saturday in March, the world's press descends on downtown Anchorage for the ceremonial start of the **Iditarod**, the highlight of Alaska's winter calendar and the world's longest dog-sled race, across the barren wastes of the Interior to Nome on the Bering Sea. Every year since its inception in 1973, mushers from the US – mostly from Alaska but also from many of the northern Lower 48 states – and from countries as far afield as Scotland, Spain, and Australia have raced behind their teams of up to sixteen dogs. The "official" length is 1049 miles – a round thousand plus a reminder that this is the 49th state – but it is actually considerably longer: the shorter northern route through Ruby, followed in even-numbered years is around 1150 miles, while the 1180-mile southern route traced in odd-numbered years passes through the gold-rush ghost town of Iditarod – a mispronunciation of "Hidedhod," Ingalik for "a distant place."

For mushers it is the culmination of weeks of logistical preparation on top of several years spent learning how to handle and care for their dogs. Breeding plays a major part; only the perfect team will do for negotiating this winter-only route over two mountain ranges, across muskeg, along 150 miles of the frozen Yukon River and across the iced-in Norton Sound. Temperatures well below freezing are often exacerbated by gale-force winds reducing the visibility on days already short of daylight, but competitors are rewarded by wonderful scenery and the overwhelming sense of accomplishment. Certainly, the financial rewards are not the motivation for most, though the first prize is about $60,000 and a shiny new truck. Only a handful of mushers make a viable living from their kennels and winnings, and despite a purse distributed between the first twenty teams only a few might hope to recoup their costs for running the race. The cost of maintaining a support crew and supplying dog food along the route typically exceeds $15,000.

Getting it all started

The Iditarod had its genesis around the beginning of the twentieth century when fledgling gold towns were linked by a winter mail and supply route – mail and food in, gold out – from the ice-free port of Seward through the Interior mining camps to Nome. By the late 1960s, four decades of reliable air transport had done away with the need for regular dog-sled routes to remote communities, and the advent of affordable snowmachines was threatening to hammer the final nail in the dog-sledding coffin. Then in 1967 historian **Dorothy Page** sought to enliven the Wasilla-Knik Centennial commemoration by running a dog-sled race: a 56-mile sprint was run for a purse of $25,000. She soon joined forces with local musher, **Joe Redington, Sr** – the "Father of the Iditarod" – and together they began promoting their idea of retracing the old mail route and capturing the spirit of the Serum Run (see box, p.504), on which an influenza vaccine was whisked across the Interior to Nome by a relay of dog teams during an epidemic in 1925.

Finally, in March 1973 the first full-blown Iditarod set off along more or less the modern route from Knik to Nome. Twenty-two mushers (around half the field) astounded doubters by completing the course that year. Though they were most definitely races, in the early years they were also endurance events; just completing the course was regarded as an honorable achievement. Today, everything has

Fame (June–Aug Fri–Sun 2–6pm; $2; to visit off-season call ⊕745-4751), its lower floor packed with pioneer artifacts that seem little different from what your grandmother might have used, illustrating just how young Alaska is. The more interesting material is upstairs in the Iditarod Hall of Fame, an homage to the race, which comes right past the door of the museum each year. Trophies, cups, and medals abound along with maps of the two main routes, some excellent photos of mushers in action, charcoal drawings of the winners up to 1984,

become much more professional, the degree of organization taking away from the true musher spirit (at least in the eyes of some critics) and turning it into a carefully managed series of short sprints. The criticism is overly harsh, but some purists prefer the rigors of the Yukon Quest (see "Winter in Fairbanks" box, p.457), or other long races such as the Kuskokwim 300.

Racing today

Since 1983 the race has had a **Ceremonial Start** in Anchorage, something of a circus with truckloads of snow being dumped along 4th Avenue for the teams, which set off at two-minute intervals. The public even bid to ride briefly in a sled's "basket" as an "Iditarider." One enthusiast recently paid $7500 to ride on the sled of three-time winner Jeff King.

The absence of a suitable route north of Eagle River means that teams are then trucked 35 miles to Wasilla for the staggered restart the following morning. The last checkpoint accessible on the road system is Knik, fourteen miles southwest of Wasilla, but there is more than just wilderness up ahead. The trail is broken by enthusiastic snowmachiners, and checkpoints are attended by volunteers supported by a fleet of bush planes ferrying race organizers and veterinary staff. Far fewer women compete than men, but from 1985 to 1990 all but one race was won by a woman, four of them by Susan Butcher, a record only beaten by Rick Swenson, who has won five times, with victories in three separate decades. In 2003, Norwegian Robert Sørlie became the first non-American to win the Iditarod.

The **race record** of 8 days, 22hr, 46min was set by Swiss-born Big Lake resident Martin Buser in 2002. But **prizes** aren't only awarded at the finish line. There's one for the first to Unalakleet, the first to the Yukon River gets an eight-course meal from the chef of a top Anchorage hotel, and there's another prize for the first to the halfway point, considered the halfway jinx – only five of its recipients have subsequently gone on to win at Nome. In recognition of one of the great mushers of the Serum Run, the Leonhard Seppala Humanitarian Award is presented to the musher who exhibits the most concern for his animals, according to the votes of fellow mushers. In fact, **animal care** is a sensitive issue. For the vast majority of mushers, the dogs are their lives, but the occasional death has led to usually unfounded accusations of mistreatment. Consequently, regulations require mushers to always have a supply of booties for the dogs' feet and enforce compulsory layovers – two of eight hours and one of 24. Race rules also insist that the sleds carry a heavy sleeping bag, an ax, snowshoes, a cooking stove, a pot, a veterinarian notebook, and dog food at all times – the last remaining nod to self-sufficiency.

Over the years the Iditarod has developed its own lore. As the mushers leave Anchorage the "Widow's Lamp" is lit in Nome and attached to the official finish line, the Burl Arch. To honor all who complete the course, it remains lit until the last musher – known as the "red lantern" – arrives, a link to the days when dog teams were the only means of transport and a guiding light was hung in the window of roadhouses.

The official Iditarod website, loaded with information on the race's history, the course, and past winners is at ⓦwww.iditarod.com.

and the winning sled from the first full-blown Iditarod in 1973, a lightweight sporty-looking affair.

Practicalities

Trains and Park Connection **buses** stop at, or close to, the train station, and you can even reach Wasilla on a combination of city buses: Anchorage's People Mover to Eagle River, then the weekday Mascot (Ⓣ376-5000, Ⓦwww.matsutransit.com; $2.50) to Wasilla. The trouble is, unless you have your own vehicle you'll find yourself stranded a fair distance from anywhere you want to be, though you could walk to the Dorothy Page Museum and visit the simple **visitor center** inside (same hours). **Accommodation** is reasonably priced, and often nicely sited beside the lakes off the highway. There's the low-cost and welcoming *Wasilla Guest House*, 3950 Carefree Drive (Ⓣ357-3699, Ⓦwww.wasillaguesthouse.com; beds $23, private room ❷, B&B ❸), a combined hostel and B&B in a spacious home surrounded by birch trees about fifty yards off the Parks Highway at Mile 39. It is clean, relaxed, and the dorms have beds rather than bunks. There's also Internet access and bike rental. The lakeside *Mat-Su Resort*, 1850 Bogard Rd (Ⓣ376-3228, Ⓦwww.alaskan.com/matsuresort; ❹), offers comfortable rooms along with pedal-boat and jet-ski rental. Further along the same road, about a mile and a half from the train station, nestles the equally appealing *Gatehouse B&B*, 2500 Bogard Rd (Ⓣ376-5960 or 1-888/866-9326, Ⓦwww.gatehousealaska.com; ❹), where the best spot to rest your head is the lakefront cabin. Fairview Loop Road, which leaves the Parks Highway further east at Mile 38, leads after a mile and a half to *Pioneer Ridge B&B*, 2221 Yukon Drive (Ⓣ376-7472 or 1-800/478-7472, Ⓦwww.pioneerridge.com; suites ❻, shared bath ❹), one of Alaska's best-known B&Bs, set in a converted milk barn with a couple of lovely large suites, four themed shared-bath rooms (go for the Iditarod one), a cozy cabin, and a spacious lounge with panoramic views of the surrounding valleys and mountains. The cheapest hotel rooms are just east of town at the *Windbreak Hotel*, Mile 40.5 Parks Hwy (Ⓣ376-4484, Ⓦwww.windbreakalaska.com; ❸), which has ten clean, simple rooms and a café renowned for sating serious appetites with low-cost specials.

Elsewhere, **eating** is largely a matter of choosing your favorite franchise, though there are a few alternatives. For coffee, cakes, soups, sandwiches, and Internet access visit *Mead's Coffeehouse*, 405 E Herning Ave (Ⓣ357-5633), just behind the Dorothy Page Museum; try the *Great Bear*, 238 N Boundary St (Ⓣ373-4782), just nearby, for burgers, salads, substantial entrées ($15–18), and tasty made-on-site microbrews; or drive out to *Lake Lucille Inn*, Mile 43.5 Parks Hwy (Ⓣ373-1776), a Best Western hotel with a lovely deck overlooking the water, for a relaxing meal; choices include beef teriyaki, stir-fried scallops, sandwiches, and burgers. For **entertainment**, *Mead's* occasionally has live music.

Hatcher Pass and Independence Mine

Even if you don't plan to stop in the Mat-Su area, set aside half a day to drive to Hatcher Pass and the Independence Mine, high above the tree line among the shattered granite peaks of the Talkeetna Mountains. An asphalt road leads up to the Independence Mine and is kept open all year as far as *Hatcher Pass Lodge*, just a mile short of the mine. To the west of here the Hatcher Pass Road

Though there are ATMs further north, Wasilla's malls have the last banks before Fairbanks.

(mid-June to Sept) twists and turns for 31 mostly unpaved miles, climbing through the high tundra of the 3886-foot pass (Alaska's second highest after Atigun Pass, north of Fairbanks), then dropping down through a picturesque valley with a burbling stream and numerous beaver-dammed pools. The rugged road over the pass can make it slow going, but it is an excellent drive, and great **cycling** route.

The Mine and around

The roads up here were built for wagons serving hard-rock gold mines now preserved in the **Independence Mine State Historic Park** (always open but generally accessible without skis from early June to early Sept; $5 per vehicle; Ⓦwww.dnr.state.ak.us/parks/units/indmine.htm), a cluster of semi-dilapidated houses and mine workings spread 3500ft up in a beautiful alpine bowl twenty miles north of Palmer. It is a spectacular place: the fragile timbers and winding gear cast long shadows in the late afternoon sun while the silver-and-red paintwork of the old bunkhouses stands in dramatic contrast to the blue of the sky and the snowcapped peaks. Prospectors in the Susitna Valley found gold-bearing quartz in 1897 and surmised its source lay high in the mountains. By 1906 the first shafts were being sunk and miners were ferreting along tunnels in search of thick quartz veins. Large-scale investment soon put the grubstake miner out of business, and before long the whole area was riddled with holes and humming with activity.

It all came to a halt in 1942 when the government decreed that gold mining was not essential to the war effort, and pretty much overnight the place was abandoned, leaving everything where it stood. Over the decades much was allowed to artfully rot away, but since the 1980s various bunkhouses and workshops have been restored. The former manager's house is now the **visitor center** (early June to early Sept daily 11am–7pm; Ⓣ745-2827) and the place to head for some history and fascinating photographs. Call the visitor center for the exact times of guided tours (early June to early Sept, 2–3 each afternoon; $5), which start here and give you a chance to explore inside three of the buildings that are otherwise out of bounds. If you choose to wander around unescorted you can go inside the **Assay Office**, complete with a wrecked furnace and rusted-out old safe, and stand in the entrance to an old **Water Tunnel** and feel the underground air, naturally kept at a chilly 38°F.

Palmer–Fishhook Road and Wasilla–Fishhook Road head north from their respective towns and join to become Fishhook–Willow Road at the Little Susitna River. For the next six miles it passes through some gorgeous country, with the tumbling waters of the river framed by rocky spires poking up through aspen and cottonwood. The *Motherlode Lodge*, Mile 14 Palmer–Fishhook Rd (Ⓣ745-61714 or 1-888/745-6171, Ⓦwww.motherlodelodge.com; ❺), offers a comfortable bed and continental breakfast, as well as fine dining at weekends, and marks the start of **Gold Mint Trail** (see box, overleaf).

A mile before the mine lies *Hatcher Pass Lodge*, Mile 18 Fishhook–Willow Rd (Ⓣ745-5879, Ⓦwww.hatcherpasslodge.com; cabins ❺, rooms ❹), a group of modern and spacious cabins with limited facilities (but with a separate sauna building) clustered around an A-frame restaurant (open all day, all year) fabulously sited on the rim of the valley looking down to Palmer far below. The rooms are very popular with folk up here for the **Nordic trail skiing** in winter, as is the restaurant, where the stupendous view easily justifies the slightly inflated price of coffee, gourmet pizza, soup, and assorted sandwiches and burgers (some vegetarian).

Hatcher Pass and the Lucky Shot Gold Mine

To continue over Hatcher Pass (typically open late June to mid-Sept but sometimes longer) to **Willow** take the road opposite *Hatcher Pass Lodge*, which climbs steeply a couple of miles up to the pass and then drops down to **Summit Lake**, a beautiful high-country tarn at the heart of the Summit Lake State Recreation Site. This is the region's prime spot for paragliding, and there's usually someone out flying on breezy summer weekends.

From here the road descends four miles to the **Lucky Shot Gold Mine** (Ⓣ746-0511, Ⓦwww.luckyshotgoldmine.com), which was worked from 1918 until 1950. Unlike at Independence Mine, here you get to go underground on one-hour tours (June–Aug Thurs–Sun 11am–7pm; $10).

Descending further you join the cascading Willow Creek through beautiful open mountain scenery and past beaver ponds before eventually reaching the George Parks Highway.

Along the George Parks Highway: Big Lake, Nancy Lake, and Willow

There's not a lot between Wasilla and Fairbanks, some three hundred miles north, save the Alaska Range, Denali National Park, a lot of spruce forest, and some beautiful lakes. The most popular of these is **BIG LAKE**, on a side road fifteen miles west of Wasilla (at Mile 52.3), a large sheet of water lined by log houses and vacation homes typically with a float plane or boat tethered alongside. It's big with weekenders from Anchorage, but unless you've specifically come to motor about on the water (in which case you'll need your own gear) then there isn't a lot of reason to leave the highway: there are prettier and quieter lakes not far ahead.

Campers may want to rest up at the large, wooded, and peaceful *Little Susitna River Campground*, Mile 57.3 Parks Hwy ($10; tap water), at the hamlet of **Houston**, or press on to **Nancy Lake State Recreation Area**, accessed by a

Hiking and biking around Hatcher Pass

Hatcher Pass, and the area around the Independence Mine in particular, invites freelance exploration: equip yourself with food, drink, sunscreen, and a camera and head for the hills. Dangerous old mine workings and loose rocks are hazards, but if you keep your eyes open and act sensibly, you can have a fabulous afternoon up here. Lower down there are a couple more formal trails accessed from Fishhook–Willow Road: all are best done from mid-June to September when there is unlikely to be snow.

This area is open for free **camping** wherever you can find an appropriate spot: take a cooking stove as you don't find much firewood.

Gold Mint Trail (18 miles round-trip; 6–8hr; 500ft ascent). An easy and delightful trail which follows the Little Susitna River – keep it on your right heading up – through a gently sloping valley past the ruined remains of the Lonesome Mine and on to the river's source at Mint Glacier. The first four miles are good for biking, but it gets too brushy after that. The trailhead is opposite *Motherlode Lodge*.

Reed Lakes Trail (7 miles round-trip; 3–5hr; 1800ft ascent). Another fairly easy hike, though one section is steep and involves some boulder hopping. It starts along a broad track (good for biking for the first 1.5 miles), then climbs to the head of the valley and Lower Reed Lake. Upper Reed Lake is another mile on beyond a waterfall. The trailhead is just over a mile up Archangel Road, which leads up Archangel Valley half a mile uphill from *Motherlode Lodge*.

good gravel road off the Parks Highway at Mile 67.2. Rolling hillsides make up the landscape, with the low ridges and hummocks providing glimpses through the trees of an almost unfathomable network of small lakes and sloughs linked by small creeks. If you are equipped with camping gear and mosquito repellent, this makes perfect canoeing country and is good, too, for a little fishing or easy hiking. The large and beautifully sited *South Rolly Lake Campground*, six miles off the highway (well water; outhouse; fire rings), is the place to base yourselves either for the day (late May to early Sept; parking $5) or overnight ($10 camping fee includes day-parking). **Hikers** should find the nearby trailhead for **Red Shirt Lake Trail** (6 miles round-trip; 3–4hr; negligible ascent), the pick of several well-signposted local trails, which sticks to higher ground and ends up at a primitive campsite by Red Shirt Lake. Here you can continue using **canoes** secured at the lakeside and rented from Tippecanoe ($20–26 for 8hr, $27–33 per 24hr day, $72–78 for up to 7 days; Ⓣ495-6688, Ⓦwww.paddlealaska.com), which has a hut by the *South Rolly Lake Campground*. Canoeing on Red Shirt Lake opens up access to four highly popular, six-berth backcountry **cabins** ($35 a night; reserve through APLIC in Anchorage Ⓣ269-8400, Ⓦnutmeg.state.ak.us/ixpress/dnr/parks/matsu.dml), each with a wood stove but little else: bring everything but your tent.

There are enough waterways here to keep you entertained for a week or more, but most will be satisfied with the popular two-day loop of the **Lynx Lake Canoe Route**, which pieces together fourteen lakes by means of short well-marked portages and starts at the Tanaina Lake Canoe Trailhead 4.6 miles off the Parks Highway. Primitive campsites and backcountry cabins (including an especially beautiful one beside James Lake) dot the route, which can be extended almost infinitely.

Willow and north to Talkeetna Junction

Periodically, pretty much everyone except Juneau residents raises the issue of moving the state capital to somewhere more accessible. Every few years a referendum gets defeated, but in the mid 1970s – when the state was flushed with the promise of untold oil riches – this process went further than usual, and **WILLOW**, at Mile 69 on the Parks Highway, was selected as the preferred site for the new state capital. Its location between Anchorage and Fairbanks, and the proximity to the rail line and the newly completed highway, swung the decision away from other contenders. Opponents distorted the projected costs into the billions, however, and the electorate soundly defeated the funding referendum in 1982. Read John McPhee's book *Coming into the Country* for extensive coverage of the issue.

Despite Willow's ambitions, you'll barely notice the town as you drive through, and on a clear day you are much more likely to gaze out at Denali, visible here for the first time. Nonetheless, Willow refers to itself as "Alaska's State Capital – of recreation," a half-joking promotion of its boundless opportunities for fishing and winter activities. Though shared by several other towns, its claim to be "Alaska's dog mushing capital" is a justified one, with numerous successful kennels hereabouts, including that of DeeDee Jonrowe, currently the state's top female musher.

Willow strings along the highway, where you'll find a grocery, an ATM, gas, and a post office – the very definition of small town. As the town is close to the western approach to Hatcher Pass, you might want to spend the night here, and about the best **place to stay** is *Willow Winter Park*, Mile 68.1 Winter Park Rd (Ⓣ495-7547, Ⓦwww.alaskan.com/willowwinterpark; ④), a pleasant B&B that has a beautiful deck (with hot tub) overlooking the calm Winter Park Lake. The last bit of Willow to remain by the tracks is the lakeside *Willow Trading Post Lodge*, Mile 69.5 Parks Hwy (Ⓣ495-6457 or 1-888/239-6679, Ⓔwillowtradingpostlodge @gci.net; rooms ❷, cabins $38, RVs $18, tents $9), a traditional roadhouse with simple cabins, very spacious rooms, space for RVs and tents, sauna, laundry, and a bar. The restaurant sells reasonably priced and filling meals, though food gourmands are better served at the *Pioneer Lodge*, Mile 71.4 Parks Hwy (Ⓣ495-1000), an RV park, bar, and restaurant that produces surprisingly excellent food. Steaks, halibut, and salmon are still the staples but they're served with wild rice and fresh, *al dente* vegetables; the chicken masala is especially good, and they have a selection of gourmet pizzas all for very reasonable prices.

North of Willow and the turnoff for Hatcher Pass (at Mile 71), it all gets pretty quiet for a while, though you could stop at Lucky Husky, Mile 80 (Ⓣ495-6470, Ⓦwww.luckyhusky.com), to see if they have restarted their wheeled-sled rides. Alternatively, your kennel tour is included when staying at *Susitna Dog Tours B&B*, Mile 91.5 (Ⓣ495-6324, Ⓦwww.susitnadogtours.com, ❹), a good spot for wintertime dog mushing (Dec to mid-March; $95). Otherwise just continue on to Mile 98.7, where a side road leads you to one of Alaska's most inviting towns, Talkeetna.

Talkeetna

With dirt roads, log cabins, and an international flavor lent by the world's mountaineers congregating to take on Denali, **TALKEETNA** makes for an unusual and essential stop. The intimate downtown area, two blocks long and one wide, is the social center for the town's six hundred residents, some of whom can often be seen playing their fiddles and guitars with ever-present dogs in attendance. In short, it makes it the perfect place to kick back for a day or two and stroll through the woods or along the sandy river banks.

Rumor has it that this eclectic hamlet was the model for Cicely in the early 1990s TV series *Northern Exposure* and residents claim they can identify the source of every character – except for the retired astronaut. To its credit, Talkeetna doesn't use this as tour-bus bait, but that's not to say the tourists aren't coming. Several years as a hot destination on the travelers' grapevine have had an impact on the tourism mainstream, spawning a head-in-a-moose photo opportunity and an abundance of tacky souvenir shops. Some years back, the big tour-company lobbyists got a new bus-accessible train station built on the edge of town, and since then there's been a minor boom in new lodges and adventure tour operators. The road into town is even being widened and improved, but the backlash keeps buses barred from the main street.

Poking around town or walking out to some of the local lakes during the day and then returning for a good chinwag in the bar that night is a great way to get a feel for the area. But to get a real taste of what Talkeetna has to offer, you're going to have to get out of town, either by boat or plane, and there is no shortage of people ready to advise you and provide the logistics. The biggest attraction is **flightseeing around Mount McKinley**, though if you can time it right, drop by for the Moose Dropping Festival (see box, opposite).

Some history

Talkeetna – rivers of plenty in Dena'ina – lies at the confluence of the Talkeetna, Chulitna, and Susitna rivers, where the search for gold brought early prospectors in 1896. By 1910, Talkeetna had established itself as a riverboat station supplying

Mountain Mothers, Wilderness Women, and Moose Droppings

Talkeetna's festivals are better than most – and certainly weirder. Topping the bill is the summer's biggest celebration, the **Moose Dropping Festival** (Ⓣ733-2487), on the second weekend in July. The very mention of the event allegedly caused one outraged Florida resident, who apparently mistook a noun for a verb, to reach for the phone and demand that the Chamber of Commerce tell him how far they actually drop the poor moose. The festival, in fact, focuses on the brown droppings that are revealed in their millions with the spring snowmelt and are then sold throughout the town (complete with a heavy coat of varnish) for use as earrings, necklaces, and brooches. Leave space in your luggage for these essential items, especially Talkeetna's iconic moose-dropping-on-a-stick, the "lollipoop." (Several on the same stick is known as a "shish kapoop.") In addition to these prized lumps of Alaskana, the festival features craft stalls, dancing, drinking, and a **moose dropping toss**, which is somewhat akin to penny toss, played on a moose-shaped board with those shellacked ovoid excreta.

The festival wouldn't be complete, though, without the **Mountain Mother Contest** (on the Sunday), in which contesting mothers sling a ten-pound "baby" on their back, don hip waders, and set off on a course involving a simulated river crossing using a log and stepping stones while carrying groceries, archery, carpentry, fly casting, diaper changing and cream-pie making. Fast mothers have completed the course in under four minutes.

The town comes together again on the first weekend in December when the Talkeetna Bachelor Society hosts the **Wilderness Woman Competition** (Ⓣ733-3939), designed to "select the lady who best exemplifies the traits most desired by a Wilderness Man." Competing "bachelorettes" struggle to complete a series of wintertime tasks – chopping wood, driving a snowmachine through an obstacle course – to reach the kitchen where she then prepares a sandwich and delivers it (along with a beer) to her bachelor, who sits watching football on TV. The event culminates in the Bachelor Auction and a Bachelor Ball at the *Fairview Inn*.

The more traditional **Talkeetna Bluegrass Festival** (four days in mid-Aug; Ⓦwww.talkeetnabluegrass.com; $35) has become too large for the town that bears its name and now takes place at Mile 102 on the Parks Highway.

miners and beaver trappers and would have slipped into river-port obscurity were it not for its selection in 1915 as the local headquarters for the construction of the new Seward-to-Fairbanks railroad. With the completion of the line, **President Warren Harding** visited Nenana to drive in the golden spike, then stopped by Talkeetna on his way south. He died a few days later apparently from complications of the flu, but Talkeetna residents take a perverse pride in variously claiming that he was supplied with poisoned tobacco, was fed a dodgy stew at the *Fairview Inn*, or that the conviviality of the place induced him to indulge in one too many drinks. For the next few decades all Talkeetna had was this manufactured claim to infamy; the population steadily declined, a process only reversed by road access from 1964.

Arrival and information

The daily northbound **train** from Anchorage and a southbound one from Fairbanks and Denali stop at the station, half a mile south, where Talkeetna Taxi & Tours (Ⓣ733-8294) can run you into town for a small fee. Northbound travelers who can't afford the full train fare from Anchorage to Fairbanks should catch a bus to Talkeetna, then ride the train on to Denali from here – the most spectacular section of the journey.

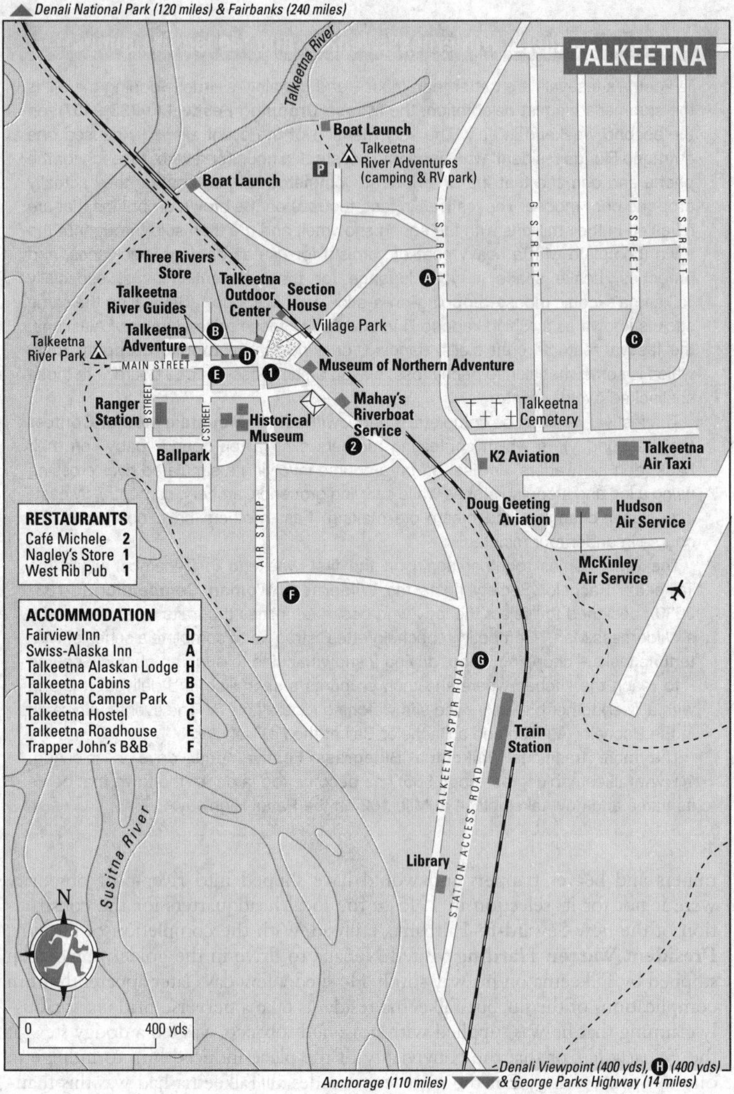

Arriving by road you turn off the Parks Highway at Talkeetna Junction (Mile 98.7), then drive fourteen miles into town. Most shuttle buses shoot straight along the Parks Highway, dropping off at Talkeetna Junction, from where it is usually easy to hitch into Talkeetna. The only daily **direct bus** to Talkeetna in the summer is the Park Connection (daily from Anchorage; $41; ⓣ1-800/266-8625), though during the climbing season (mid-April to mid-July) you can ride with Talkeetna Shuttle Service ($55 one-way, $100 round-trip; ⓣ733-1725 or 1-888/288-6008; ⓦwww.denalicentral.com), which picks up once or twice daily from Anchorage's airport, hostels and hotels.

A couple of gift shops in town provide information, but pretty much everything you need is right in front of your eyes. Mountaineers and those gripped by the climbing lore of the Alaska Range should drop by the **Talkeetna Ranger Station** (late April to early Sept daily 8am–6pm; early Sept to late April Mon–Fri 8am–4.30pm; ⓣ733-2231, ⓦwww.nps.gov/dena/mountaineering), staffed by well-informed mountain enthusiasts and a comfortable spot for browsing the mountaineering magazines and planning your days ahead in Denali.

Accommodation

Talkeetna has never been the sort of place where visitors expect to be pampered. The rustic charms of the *Talkeetna Roadhouse* are more in keeping with the spirit of the place, but a recent clutch of new **hotels** and luxury cabins is resetting the tone. Still, there is plenty of reasonably priced and welcoming accommodation as well as several **campgrounds**, though some campers choose to pitch illegally on the river flats beyond the western end of Main Street.

During the season, **climbers** can often find space to doss down in the hangar of the people they're flying with: ask in advance.

Hotels and B&Bs

Fairview Inn Main St ⓣ733-2423. This old inn, built in 1923 as an overnight resting point on the railroad, is perfectly halfway between Fairbanks and Seward. It has only been minimally modernized since then, with seven smallish rooms all with shared bathrooms. Nice as these are, be warned that the bar swings most nights until the early hours, so it can get loud; but once it closes you don't have far to stagger. ②

Swiss-Alaska Inn F St ⓣ733-2424, ⓦwww.swissalaska.com. Large inn with modern, comfortable rooms, handily sited close to town with its own restaurant (see p.374). ⑤

Talkeetna Alaskan Lodge Mile 12.5 Talkeetna Spur Rd ⓣ733-9500 or 1-888/959-9590, ⓦwww.talkeetnalodge.com. New hotel built of raw logs and river stones high on a ridge behind town with wonderful views of the Alaska Range. Even if you're not staying, it is worth popping up for a drink or a bit of relaxation beside the central fireplace. The attractive rooms are to international standards with satellite TV, dataports, and coffeemakers, but you'll have to reserve well in advance to get one of the $350-plus Denali-view rooms in the main lodge. ⑧

Talkeetna Cabins C St ⓣ733-2227 or 1-888/733-9933, ⓦwww.talkeetnacabins.org. Spacious four-berth cabins right downtown with a full kitchen, lounge, and satellite TV. ⑥

Talkeetna Roadhouse Main St ⓣ733-1351, ⓦwww.talkeetnaroadhouse.com. Talkeetna's other old inn dates to 1917, with simple, but tidy, rooms sharing baths. With no bar, it doesn't have the robust atmosphere of the *Fairview*, but easily makes up for it with very hospitable staff and a cozy lounge, which in spring and early summer is full of climbers planning their summit strategy. They have single rooms, doubles, and a couple of larger, deluxe rooms, which share a bathroom with a clawfoot tub. Closed on weekdays from mid-Sept to mid-April. Deluxe ④, doubles ③, singles and bunks ①

Trapper John's B&B ⓣ733-2353, ⓦwww.alaska.net/~trapperj. A wonderfully rustic cabin near the Susitna River, with full kitchen and rustic outhouse, an easy walk from downtown. It sleeps up to four, but can be taken by two, and breakfast at the roadhouse is included in the price. ⑤

Hostels and camping

Talkeetna Camper Park Talkeetna Spur Rd ⓣ733-2693, ⓦwww.talkeetnacamper.com. The most convenient RV parking, located on the road into town and offering electrical ($21) or full ($26) hookup.

Talkeetna Hostel International I St ⓣ733-4678, ⓦwww.talkeetnahostel.com. Welcoming house in the woods about a ten-minute walk from downtown, with clean, comfortable dorm bunks for $25, a private double room, a small but well-equipped kitchen, and free Internet access. Late May–Sept. Room ③, bunks ①

Talkeetna River Adventures ⓣ733-2604. Large campground and RV park in the woods a short walk from town, with showers and laundry facilities. $12 per site.

Talkeetna River Park This tent-only campground at the western end of Main Street costs $12 per site, paid to the summertime host.

Talkeetna Roadhouse (see above). This characterful old inn maintains a four-berth bunk room ($21), with sheets and towels provided. ①

Tackling Denali

Of the great mountains of the world, Denali (North America's highest peak at 20,320ft) is not particularly high: dozens of Andean peaks are higher, and if it were moved to the Himalayas Denali would barely rate a mention. Nonetheless, its subarctic location makes it one of the world's coldest mountains, and its extreme and unpredictable weather conditions raise its profile to the point where Denali is regarded as one of the world's most difficult mountains to climb. That very difficulty, and the sheer lonesome majesty that makes it one of the most sought-after peaks, has engendered a long and fascinating history of summit attempts and heroic conquests.

Some history

No one, certainly no European, had ever stepped on the slopes of Denali until the twentieth century, but interest in conquering the mountain quickly reached fever pitch. In 1903, Alaska district judge and future congressman **James Wickersham** rounded up four local lads, equipped them with primitive climbing gear and led them up to 8000ft on the north side, where what is now known as the Wickersham Wall halted their progress. A couple of months later the explorer **Frederick Cook** led an exhausted party overland up to 11,300ft. He later claimed to have reached the summit on his second expedition, in 1906; however, few believed it then or do so now. In 1906 he telegrammed to the world that he had successfully summited Denali, backing it up with a photo of himself on the summit and a detailed summit diary. The speed of his ascent immediately alerted the mountaineering community to possible deception, but he became the toast of American society, which was even more enthusiastic about his equally dubious claims to have beaten Robert Peary to the North Pole in 1909. Pertinent questions were soon being asked, and Cook's reputation was already in tatters when, in 1910, Belmore Brown settled the matter by replicating the "summit" photograph on an 8000-foot peak twenty miles from Denali.

As Brown took his photo he little realized that Denali's North Peak – 850ft lower than the South Peak – had already been scaled by a group of Kantishna-based gold miners now known as the **Sourdough Expedition**. In what is still regarded as one of the most extraordinary mountaineering feats ever, four prospectors – led by an overweight 50-year-old Welshman, **Tom Lloyd** – with no technical mountaineering experience and only the most rudimentary gear, succeeded in proving not only that Cook's claim was false, but that locals could outclimb anyone from "Outside." According to the *Fairbanks Daily News-Miner*, they carried "less 'junk' with them than an Eastern US excursion party would take along for a one-day's outing in the hills"; certainly they wore only normal winter clothes and ate little but bacon, beans, and caribou meat. Nonetheless, they reached the North Peak without major incident and planted a fourteen-foot spruce trunk which they had hauled up to use as a flagpole. The Stars and Stripes they had hoped would be visible from Fairbanks wasn't, and in the light of the Cook farce their claim was widely disbelieved.

All speculation was laid to rest in 1913 when respected Episcopal missionary Archdeacon **Hudson Stuck** led a shoestring expedition that not only vouched for the Sourdoughs' success – the spruce pole was still upright three years on – but also entered the record books as the first to reach the true summit. Doubters were satisfied and interest in the mountain waned to the point that it was nearly twenty years before anyone summited again, and almost forty before anyone thought of climbing it any other way than via the Muldrow Glacier route from the north, which had been used by all successful early expeditions.

In 1947, **Bradford Washburn** entered the scene and succeeded in climbing Denali along with his wife Barbara – the first woman to summit. But Washburn's real contribution was his detailed surveying work, which identified the West Buttress Route, first climbed by a party led by Washburn in 1951. What made this route possible was the novel practice of glacier landings, allowing climbers and equipment to be deposited at 7,200ft on the Kahiltna Glacier, on Denali's southwest side. Washburn's initial attempt was followed up by numerous other successes, and the West Buttress Route became firmly established as the preferred line of attack. The next twenty years perfected the approach and coincided with mountaineering's transformation into a mainstream sport: by the mid-1970s, every weather window from mid-April through to the end of July saw parties setting off for the mountain.

Since then new routes have been pioneered and increasingly contrived "firsts" have been attempted: the first winter expedition in 1967, the first solo ascent in 1970, the first hang-glider descent in 1976, and the first sled-team ascent in 1979. Meanwhile, even people who would barely class themselves as mountaineers were attempting Denali by engaging **guides**. One of the first guides was **Ray 'the Pirate' Genet** – a veteran of the first winter ascent on which he earned his nickname for the skull and crossbones with which he used to mark his clothing – who, together with **Don Sheldon**, bush pilot *par excellence*, helped scores of climbers reach the top. Genet died while guiding on Everest in 1979; in 1991 his son, Taras, at the age of 12 became the youngest climber to summit Denali. Ten years later this record was broken by the 11-year-old Galen Johnston. The oldest climber summited at 71.

Climbing Denali today

Over the years the level of mortality, the high public profile of the mountain, and its administration by the Denali National Park have caused considerable controversy, and it has taken the efforts of numerous working groups to finally settle on a system of administration that provides a tolerable level of safety without sacrificing the sense of adventure.

Today all climbers must register their intentions at least sixty days in advance of their climb and pay $150: details are available online (Ⓦwww.nps.gov/dena/home/mountaineering/home.html) and in *Mountaineering: Denali National Park and Preserve*, a free booklet in eight languages available from the Talkeetna Ranger Station (see p.369). Almost all summit attempts now start with a flight – roughly $280 for the round-trip with gear – from Talkeetna to the Kahiltna Glacier at 7200ft where the Park Service maintains a ranger station throughout the climbing season. Radio contact with Talkeetna improves safety on the mountain and allows climbers to call for a flight out once they're finished. Of the twelve hundred or so climbers who make the attempt annually, around fifty percent are successful, and over eighty percent of those use the West Buttress Route, typically making a series of gear shuttles to establish progressively higher camps over three weeks. The emphasis is very much on self-reliance, but emergency assistance is available at a medical camp at 14,200ft, where staff actually spend much of their day picking up trash left by expeditions – typically over 1000 pounds a season. The presence of rangers on the mountain and scores of others scrabbling for position at regular campsites could lead to overconfidence, but as veteran climber Jonathan Waterman writes, "The fact that the West Buttress Route is not technically difficult should not obscure the need to plan for extreme survival situations . . . the West Buttress route is a terribly underestimated climb."

If you fancy giving it a go, half a dozen authorized guiding services are listed on the Denali National Park website (see above); expect to pay a little over $4000 for an attempt at the West Buttress Route.

The Town

As you walk around town you'll notice plaques on over a dozen historic buildings, all detailed on the *Talkeetna Historical Society Walking Tour* leaflet (free). These are available from the **Talkeetna Historical Society Museum**, one block south of Main Street (May–Sept daily 10.30am–6.30pm; March, April & Oct–Dec Fri–Sun 10.30am–6.30pm; $3), a cluster of four buildings including **Ole Dahl Cabin**, the oldest building in town. Inside you'll find the usual collection of pioneer artifacts, photos of Talkeetna old-timers, coverage of the antics of local bush pilots, and plenty on the construction of the railroad. The highlight is the topographically accurate twelve-foot-square scale **model of McKinley**, based on years of detailed aerial photography done by Bradford Washburn, who is an authority on just about anything to do with the mountain (see box, pp.370–371). Excellent examples of the work, which earned him the title of the "Ansel Adams of the North," are arranged around the walls, and there are more up at the *Talkeetna Alaskan Lodge* (see "Accommodation," above). Look, too, for the biographies of Denali heroes, press clippings, and letters, such as one from the widow of Frederick Cook (see box, pp.370–371) asking for the opinion of rumbustious mountaineer and longtime Denali guide Ray Genet on her husband's summit claim. His reply is instructive. Throughout the summer the free ranger program features hour-long talks on the mountain's conquerors using the McKinley model as a prop.

Climbers die almost every season on the mountain – approaching a hundred in total – adding more and more names to the memorial in the **Talkeetna Cemetery**, a salutary reminder that despite the climbing traffic, the presence of two ranger stations on the West Buttress route, and specialist rescue helicopters permanently on call, the mountain always has the last say. The cemetery contains the grave of "the climber's pilot," Don Sheldon, and is the spiritual resting place of Genet, whose body remains on Mount Everest.

On the road into town, there's the **Museum of Northern Adventure** (May to mid-Sept daily 10am–6pm; $2), displaying two dozen waxwork dioramas depicting archetypal Alaskan lifestyles; note the letter to the Presley estate for permission (refused) to display a moose-dropping Elvis.

On a clear day – perhaps one in three in summer, more in winter – don't miss the hike (or drive) to the **viewpoint**, a mile south along Talkeetna Spur Road, from where the Alaska Range, even sixty miles away, looks simply magnificent.

Outdoor activities

As more and more people come to Talkeetna, entrepreneurs are busy devising ways to keep visitors entertained. The well-established flightseeing, jetboating, rafting and fishing trips are now being supplemented by horseback riding and even sled-dog rides.

The **Alaska Railroad** even runs the Talkeetna–Hurricane flag-stop service (mid-May to mid-Sept Thurs–Sun at 12.15pm; $66), a diesel railcar that makes a five-hour jaunt north to Hurricane and back. Though primarily run for local residents heading off to their cabins in the woods, it makes for an entertaining and scenic day out of town. There are no reservations and no food is available, so pack what you need.

If you just want to go your own way, but need to buy **camping and mountaineering supplies** or pick up some USGS topo maps, visit Talkeetna Outdoor Center (see "Rafting," opposite).

Flightseeing

You might have to wait around for a couple of days until the weather plays ball, but an essential part of any visit to Talkeetna is a flightseeing trip to Mount McKinley. Don't delay until you get to Denali: you are closer to the mountain here, and the weather tends to offer better viewing from the south side of the range. Half a dozen air-taxi companies (see "Listings," p.375) all run similar four- to five-passenger bush planes and offer similar packages at competitive prices: shop around and see who will offer you the best deal. Planes book up rapidly in summer, can be hard to fill after mid-September, and in May are mostly reserved by climbers who fly to the mountain from here.

There's a choice of three different circuits, all flying over the confluence of the Susitna, Chulitna, and Talkeetna rivers, then across the Peters and Dutch hills in Denali State Park to the Alaska Range itself. The most **basic package** (1hr; $120–125) links the Tokositna and Ruth glaciers on the southeast side of the mountain, and flies up Great Gorge, a deep vertical-walled canyon filled with ice to a depth of 4000ft. The mid-priced flight (1hr 15min; $145–160) includes all the above but also loops around the back of the 14,573-foot Mount Hunter to the 7200-foot base camp on the Kahiltna Glacier – the fifty-mile-long tongue of ice that slices through the Alaska Range separating Mount McKinley from the second highest peak in the range, Mount Foraker. If you can afford it, go for the grand tour (1hr 30min; $175–180), which climbs higher up the Kahiltna and then makes a complete mountain circuit with views of the 14,000-foot Wickersham Wall and the main body of Denali National Park on the north side of the range. When snow conditions permit, you can add a **glacier landing** (additional $50–60) either on the Kahiltna Glacier (typically April to early July) or at the Don Sheldon Amphitheater (April–July, and occasionally into Aug), a glacial cirque at the head of the Ruth Glacier.

Some operators are now offering a **summit overflight** (1hr 20min; $205), which includes all of the above (though no glacier landings) plus a bird's eye view of the tops of Denali, Foraker and Hunter.

Jetboat trips and fishing

For a little gentle adventure, sign up with Mahay's Riverboat Service (mid-May to Sept; Ⓣ733-2223 or 1-800/736-2210, Ⓦwww.mahaysriverboat.com), which runs a fifty-seat jetboat on some of the area's shallow, braided rivers, almost scraping gravel bars and hoping to catch sight of moose and bald eagles. The Jetboat Safari (2hr; $50) leaves several times a day and includes a fifteen-minute guided nature walk, while the Wilderness Safari (4hr; $95) heads further upstream to the former townsite of Curry. The more committed can opt for either the Talkeetna Canyon (4hr; $125) or the Devil's Canyon (6hr; $175) trip, both in the smaller jetboats needed to negotiate the Class III whitewater.

Mahay's also runs **fishing trips**, either guided (5hr for $135, 8hr for $185) or unguided, where they rent you some gear ($25 a day) and drop you seven miles upstream ($45), returning later for you and your salmon and trout.

Rafting

A more peaceful alternative to the jetboats is rafting with Talkeetna River Guides, Main Street (Ⓣ733-2677 or 1-800/353-2677, Ⓦwww.talkeetnariverguides.com), which offers the gentle two-hour natural-history float trip (mid-May to mid-Sept daily 11am, 2pm & 5pm; $54), and a four-hour run on the Chulitna River ($89) which includes a little gold panning. Rafters after a little more adventure can try fly-in overnight trips such as three days on the Talkeetna River ($1250), taking in the Talkeetna

Canyon, fourteen miles of Class III and IV water – claimed to be the longest such whitewater stretch in the world. The Talkeetna Outdoor Center, behind the *Fairview Inn* (ⓣ733-4444 or 1-800/349-0064, ⓦwww.alaskajourneys.com), runs a similar trip for $875 and may even have better deals on a space-available basis.

Other activities

Should the bucolic nature of the surroundings inspire you to see more, join D&S Alaskan Trail Rides (ⓣ745-2207, ⓦwww.alaskantrailrides.net) for guided **horseback riding** (1hr for $57, 2hr for $87) through the woods to good Denali viewpoints. Prefer dogs? Talkeetna Sundog Kennels (ⓣ733-3355 or 1-800/318-2534, ⓦwww.sundogkennel.com) will drive you from their office on Main Street to the nearby kennels where you get to meet the dogs and enjoy a four-mile **sled-dog ride**, either in a wheeled buggy in summer ($45) or a proper sled in winter ($50).

Beyond their bread-and-butter McKinley flights, the air-taxi companies will turn their hands to just about anything that involves flying. Talkeetna Air Taxi, in particular, specializes in tailored one- and two-day **glacier treks**, snowshoeing, and high-country skiing with all equipment provided. Backcountry trips can also be organized, flying you to a base camp for a few days. Prices depend greatly on numbers, the need for guides, and flying time, but $1000 for three days' snowshoeing, trekking, and glacier skiing is typical.

Eating and drinking

There isn't a very broad selection of places to go in Talkeetna, and many spots close quite early, so the pickings are often slim. As for evening entertainment, it tends to revolve around the **bars** at the *Fairview Inn* and the *West Rib*.

Café Michele Talkeetna Spur Rd ⓣ733–5300, ⓦwww.cafemichele.com. Downtown's finest dining in an airy room with a tempting menu of organic dishes. Lunches are modestly priced (gringo chili, $13), though you'll pay more for dinner entrées ($19–20), which might be soy-ginger king salmon ($25), roasted half-chicken ($22) or basil walnut chicken pasta ($19).

Fairview Inn Main St ⓣ733-2423. A classic, small-town Alaskan bar, with rough-wood floors and sepia-toned walls hung with beaver pelts, that's very much the place to be. Portraits of former bar-proppers line the walls while a broad cross-section of tall-talking Talkeetna characters entertain visitors to the *Fairview*. Most weekends and some weeknights there's top-flight Alaskan live music (usually $5); if not, there is always the bar piano and guitar.

Nagley's Store Main St. Basically a grocery store but one which sells good cheap espresso, deli sandwiches, and ice cream along with fishing gear and animal furs. It also must be one of the last places in America still selling cigarettes individually. Upstairs there's an ATM.

Swiss-Alaska Inn F St ⓣ733-2424. The *Inn*'s restaurant serves hearty breakfasts (their omelets are particularly good), steak, and seafood dinners ($14–20), with specialties such as Wiener schnitzel and German sausage salad ($9).

Talkeetna Roadhouse Main St ⓣ733-1351. The *Roadhouse* features Talkeetna's best bakery and a great daytime café, which pleases guests with breakfasts (until 1pm) of sourdough hotcakes served with real maple syrup or eggs, bacon, home-fried potatoes, and toast – the $7 half-plate is plenty for hearty eaters, the $10 full plate is for McKinley returnees. For lunch build your own sandwiches or try the cheese pinto beans on a grilled corn muffin with salsa ($6). Closes at 3pm but reopens in the evening (5–10pm) for light snacks, dessert, and coffee.

West Rib Pub & Grill Main St ⓣ733-3354. Good diner food with a pleasant deck for warm days where an outdoor grill is put to use preparing burgers and sandwiches ($7–9 with nightly burger and beer specials). The bar inside has the town's finest selection of craft beers, including Guinness on tap and top Alaskan microbrews.

Listings

Air-taxi companies Doug Geeting Aviation ⓣ733-2366 or 1-800/770-2366, ⓦwww.alaskaairtours.com; Fly Denali ⓣ733-7768 or 1-866/733-7768, ⓦwww.flydenali.net; Hudson Air Service ⓣ733-2321 or 1-800/478-2321, ⓦwww.alaskan.com/hudsonair; K2 Aviation ⓣ733-2291 or 1-800/764-2291, ⓦwww.flyk2.com; McKinley Air Service ⓣ733-1765 or 1-800/564-1765, ⓦwww.McKinleyairservice.com; Talkeetna Aero Services ⓣ733-2899 or 1-800/660-2688, ⓦwww.talkeetnaaero.com; Talkeetna Air Taxi ⓣ733-2218 or 1-800/533-2219, ⓦwww.talkeetnaair.com.

Banks The nearest bank is in Wasilla, over an hour away, but there's an ATM at Three Rivers store on Main St.

Bike rental Talkeetna Outdoor Center, behind the *Fairview Inn* (ⓣ733-4444 or 1-800/349-0064, ⓦwww.alaskajourneys.com), has mountain bikes for $15 a day, $25 for 24hr.

Gas Three Rivers store, Main St, has reasonably priced gas.

Internet access Free at the library (see below) but faster at Talkeetna Travel (ⓣ733-8728) beside *Café Michele.*

Laundry and showers Three Rivers store, Main St, has a coin-op laundry (daily 8am–9pm) and showers ($2).

Library The library (Mon–Fri 11am–6pm, Sat noon–5pm; ⓣ733-2359) is a mile south along the spur road and has free Internet access.

Post office Mon–Fri 9am–5pm; the **General Delivery** zip code is 99676.

Taxes The town imposes a two percent sales tax and a five percent bed tax, already included in accommodation prices.

Denali State Park

From Talkeetna Junction the Parks Highway continues north, and from Mile 132 to Mile 169 – still two hours' drive short of the entrance to Denali National Park – you're in **Denali State Park**. It is a land of braided rivers, a thousand lakes, and tundra-capped hills rising above the spruce forests. There's none of the rigid organization of the national park (which shares a similar name but remains a completely separate entity), far fewer people, and yet sports many of the same attributes – great McKinley views and abundant moose, grizzlies, and black bears. There is little infrastructure here (and nowhere local to get information), so unless you come prepared for hiking and camping you may find it all a little too much trouble. With the national park beckoning, you could easily pass through.

If you choose to stop, there are a few hikes worth leaving time for and a couple of campgrounds to use as bases; but stock up on groceries and any hiking maps and information you might need before you arrive. The key geographical feature for most park users is the 4500-foot Kesugi Ridge, which parallels the highway to the east and is followed by a sequence of hiking trails.

In the southern reaches of the park the highway passes *Mary's McKinley View Lodge*, Mile 134.4 (ⓣ733-1555; ❷), with decent diner-style meals and very reasonable rooms, some with Denali views. Half a mile on, **Denali Viewpoint South** has a huge turnout where boards point out the high points – Mount McKinley, Mount Hunter, and Moose's Tooth – and the glacial highlights – the Ruth, Buckskin, and Eldridge glaciers. The *Lower Troublesome Creek Campground*, Mile 137.2 ($5 per vehicle; pump water), marks the southern trailhead for the **Troublesome Creek Trail**, which finishes at the large *Byers Lake Campground*, Mile 147.1 ($10; pump water), the most organized around with a camp host in summer, a public-use cabin ($35; reservations ⓦnutmeg.state.ak.us/ixpress/dnr/parks/matsu.dml), and excellent swimming as well as grayling and trout fishing. For the best McKinley views you need to

Hikes in Denali State Park

Hikers hoping to tackle the park's longer trails must bring all camping gear (including a stove and fuel as no backcountry fires are allowed) and be competent with a map. Topo maps are available from the Alaska Public Lands Information office in Anchorage where you can also get the free, schematic *Denali State Park* leaflet. Note that the two longer hikes described below are both one-way hikes, though hitching back along the Parks Highway is seldom a problem, or you could even organize for one of the Anchorage–Denali buses to pick you up.

Byers Lake Loop Trail (4.8-mile loop; 2–3hr; negligible ascent). Gentle and scenic stroll around the lake starting and finishing at the *Byers Lake Campground*. Late May to Sept.

Kesugi Ridge Trail (27.4 miles one-way; 2–3 days; 4000ft ascent). A magnificent trail starting at the *Byers Lake Campground* and climbing rapidly above the tree line, where you stay right until the descent to the Little Coal Creek Trailhead. If all that isn't enough, you can add 1000ft of climbing to take in the summit of Indian Peak, close to the northern end of the trail. Mid-June to Sept.

Troublesome Creek Trail (15.2 miles one-way; 7–9hr; 2000ft ascent). Black bears gorging on salmon in July and August earned the name for this creek, which is followed from the *Troublesome Creek Campground* before the moderate climb up onto open tundra that's pocked with small lakes. The views are spectacular, though you'll need to keep your eyes down to follow the rock cairns which lead back into the forest and down to the *Byers Lake Campground.* This can be combined with the Kesugi Ridge Trail to make a 36-mile expedition. June–Sept.

get to the superb *Lakeshore Campground* (free; lake water), accessible by either walking 1.8 miles along the **Byers Lake Loop Trail** or paddling across the lake.

Yet more mountain views reveal themselves from **Denali View North**, Mile 162.7, a large parking lot where you can overnight ($10 per vehicle) either in your RV or in a tent pitched at some nice walk-in sites. Before leaving the park you pass the Little Coal Creek Trailhead, Mile 163.8, the northern terminus of the **Kesugi Ridge Trail**.

Cantwell and Broad Pass

The Parks Highway has been gradually climbing ever since Wasilla, but five miles after leaving Denali State Park it crosses Hurricane Gulch, Mile 174, on a single-span bridge 260ft above the stream, then begins a more rapid ascent to Broad Pass, Mile 201, where both the train line and the highway squeeze through a rent in the Alaska Range. From here on everything flows north into the Yukon River and then west to the Bering Sea, including the fledgling Nenana River, which gently eases down into **Cantwell**, Mile 210. Here, the Parks Highway meets the **Denali Highway** (see account starting on p.399), which heads off 135 miles east to Paxson through remote country with limited services. If you're headed that way, fill your tank, and your stomach at one of the two roadside diners.

The Parks Highway continues 27 miles north to the Denali National Park entrance, passing through a narrow defile which opens out onto long views of Mount Fellows with its ridgeline rocks said to look like a musher and her sled dogs. Thirteen miles before the park entrance you pass **Carlo Creek**, then six miles later reach **McKinley Village**. Both are really just clusters of places to stay but make feasible bases for forays into the park: accommodation and restaurants in both settlements are listed in the following account.

Denali National Park

The six million acres of **DENALI NATIONAL PARK**, 240 miles north of Anchorage, hold a special, almost holy, place in the minds of Alaska's visitors – a vast wilderness carved out of the Alaskan heartland preserving an entire ecosystem. This is where everyone comes to see big game: bears browsing in the low brush, moose chomping on aquatic weed at Wonder Lake, a lone wolf loping along a river bar, or a herd of caribou disappearing into the infinity of the Teklanika Valley. It is scenes like these that bring home the sheer scale of the place; the park is about the same size as Massachusetts, or half the size of Wales, and a round-trip along the road from the park entrance to Wonder Lake, right in the heart of the park, takes a full twelve hours.

For most, Denali's grail is the sight of the 20,320-foot **Mount McKinley**, equally known by its Athabascan name, **Denali**, "the Great One." And great it is, rising 18,000ft from tundra to tip, ranking as North America's highest mountain and boasting the greatest vertical rise of any mountain on the globe. It simply towers over its neighbors, most barely rising above 12,000ft, and even its 17,400-foot neighbor, Mount Foraker, is dwarfed firmly in second place. These are the king and queen of the **Alaska Range**, a 600-mile crescent of jagged snowcapped peaks, which arcs through the Alaskan Interior to form the backbone of Denali National Park, a mountain fastness still locked in the last ice age, spewing glaciers left and right. To the south the Ruth and Kahiltna glaciers have gouged out deep canyons on their fifty-mile passage out to the vegetated lowlands, while to the north the Muldrow crooks its arm around 7000-foot foothills and melts away to become the McKinley River, one of the dominant features of the central wilderness area of the park.

Denali's scenic grandeur is made wonderfully accessible by the **Park Road**, ninety miles of gravel which winds from lowland **taiga** to alpine **tundra** on

Getting the best from Denali National Park

Visiting Alaska without seeing Denali is unthinkable to most people, and therein lies the park's major problem. The place has become such an icon that few question why they are going and what they expect when they get there. Inevitably, some visitors come away disappointed after spending hours on a bumpy, dusty bus ride only to catch distant glimpses of caribou and moose, or upon discovering that Mount McKinley isn't even visible from the park entrance, remains shrouded in cloud for two days out of three in summer, and is often better viewed from Talkeetna.

Spectacular as the scenery is, it is no more stunning than that along the Denali Highway, which spurs off the George Parks Highway 27 miles to the south, where the access is a lot simpler and the crowds incomparably thinner. Indeed, although Denali affords a chance to roam across trackless tundra, if it's backcountry hiking you want, then pretty much all of Alaska is out there waiting for you.

If you set expectations properly and carefully plan your visit, however, a visit to Denali can be supremely rewarding. If you only have a few hours, then just drive the first fifteen miles of the Park Road, stopping to observe any wildlife you may come across. At Savage River there's a two-mile walk so you can say you've hiked in Denali. On a longer visit, it really pays to reserve campsites and shuttle buses in advance (see p.381). Doing so, you can avoid much of the lining up and waiting around in the visitor access center and can progress smoothly out into the park. With a night spent in a park campground you'll get a real feel for the place, but the full rewards are only gained through spending several days out there hiking and camping in the backcountry.

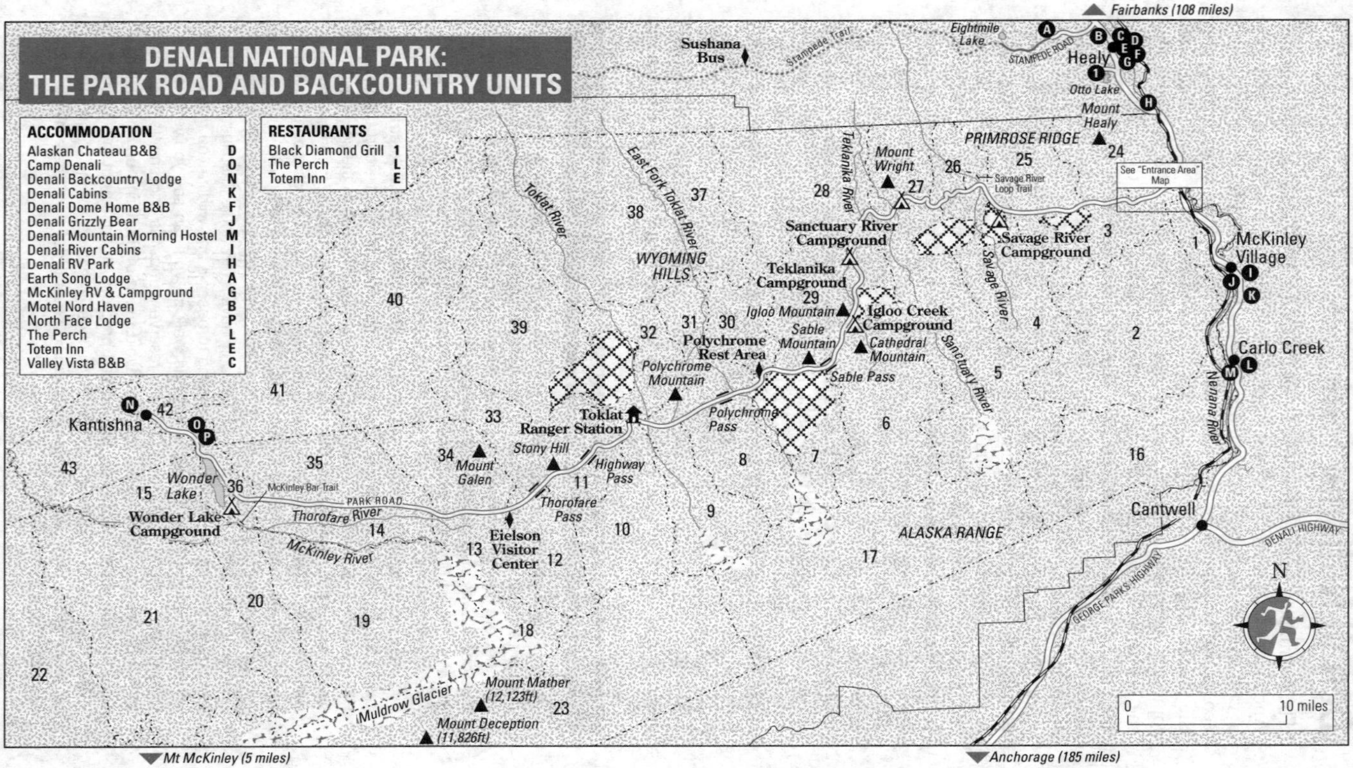
DENALI NATIONAL PARK:
THE PARK ROAD AND BACKCOUNTRY UNITS
ACCOMMODATION
Alaskan Chateau B&B D
Camp Denali O
Denali Backcountry Lodge N
Denali Cabins K
Denali Dome Home B&B F
Denali Grizzly Bear J
Denali Mountain Morning Hostel M
Denali River Cabins I
Denali RV Park H
Earth Song Lodge A
McKinley RV & Campground G
Motel Nord Haven B
North Face Lodge P
The Perch L
Totem Inn E
Valley Vista B&B C
RESTAURANTS
Black Diamond Grill 1
The Perch L
Totem Inn E
Fairbanks (108 miles)
Mt McKinley (5 miles)
Anchorage (185 miles)
Sushana Bus
Stampede Trail
Eightmile Lake
STAMPEDE ROAD
Healy
Otto Lake
Mount Healy
PRIMROSE RIDGE
See "Entrance Area" Map
Savage River Loop Trail
Mount Wright
Teklanika River
East Fork Toklat River
Toklat River
WYOMING HILLS
Sanctuary River Campground
Savage River Campground
Savage River
Teklanika Campground
Igloo Mountain
Igloo Creek Campground
Sable Mountain
Cathedral Mountain
Sanctuary River
Polychrome Rest Area
Polychrome Mountain
Sable Pass
Polychrome Pass
Toklat Ranger Station
Stony Hill
Highway Pass
Thorofare Pass
Mount Galen
Eielson Visitor Center
Kantishna
Wonder Lake
Wonder Lake Campground
McKinley Bar Trail
PARK ROAD
Thorofare River
McKinley River
Muldrow Glacier
Mount Mather (12,123ft)
Mount Deception (11,826ft)
ALASKA RANGE
McKinley Village
Carlo Creek
Nenana River
Cantwell
DENALI HIGHWAY
GEORGE PARKS HIGHWAY
N
0 10 miles

its passage through half a dozen river catchments and over as many high passes. Private vehicles are banned and visitors must board a system of shuttle buses, which grind along offering a wonderful vantage for spotting, and photographing, wildlife almost undisturbed by human presence. The limited number of shuttle buses creates a bottleneck around the park entrance, but it is this that preserves the sanctity of the park itself and makes the wilderness so appealing once you get into it. For both human safety and animal protection, bus etiquette demands that you stay in the bus when animals are about, but otherwise you can, and should, get off sometime and explore away from the road.

Some history

The caribou, Dall sheep, and moose so prized by photographers were once quarry to Athabascan Indians. Hunters followed the herds through the Alaska Range foothills in the summer months, picking berries, and gathering plants along the way, then descended to the river valleys in the colder months. Towards the end of the nineteenth century, long before there were roads, railroads, or even bush planes anywhere near Denali, gold prospectors entered the area. One Princeton-educated hopeful, William Dickey, spent time in the area reporting the existence of a huge mountain to the New York *Sun* (estimating it to be over 20,000ft high); he named it after William McKinley, Republican nominee for the presidency. By 1905 prospectors found their El Dorado in Kantishna and a full-blown stampede ensued, sprouting a tent city and then a boom town. Like so many gold towns it barely lasted out the winter, but the area did catch the attention of one **Charles Sheldon**, an East Coast naturalist intent on studying Dall sheep. Deploring the wreckage and unfettered hunting around Kantishna, as well as recognizing the unique nature of an almost intact ecosystem north of the Alaska Range, he lobbied Washington for the creation of a national park. In 1917 this central area between the ranges and stretching from Kantishna to the Nenana River was designated as McKinley National Park, the first in Alaska. Access was provided in 1923 by the railroad, and in 1957 by the Denali Highway from Paxson, but it was the completion of the George Parks Highway in 1973 that really sealed the park's future as Alaska's premier tourist destination.

In recognition of the mountain's Athabascan moniker the park was renamed Denali National Park, but despite petitions and thousands of newspaper column inches the mountain officially remains Mount McKinley.

Arrival, orientation, and information

Undoubtedly the finest way to arrive at Denali is by rail. **Trains** pull into Denali Park station and are met by a phalanx of courtesy buses run by individual hotels. If you're not being met by a bus to your accommodation, you'll need to unravel the complexities of the shuttle bus system (see box, pp.382–383): the Riley Creek Loop bus stops at the rear of the train station parking lot close to the new interpretive center.

All **long-distance buses** pick up and dropoff at the visitor access center, and most will let you down at any of the local hotels. If you alight at the visitor access center you'll again have to master the shuttle buses to get any further.

If you are planning to travel beyond Mile 15 of the Park Road, you should call at the visitor center to pay the park **entrance fee** of $5 per person ($10 per family; valid 7 days).

Orientation

Getting into Denali National Park involves spending at least some time on the eastern fringe, in and around the nameless huddle of buildings known variously

Denali's seasons

Mount McKinley so dominates its surroundings that it creates its own distinct **weather**, turning the moist drafts coming off the Gulf of Alaska into rain and, at higher elevations, snow. This affects the weather along the Park Road, but north of the Alaska Range precipitation is low – around fifteen inches a year – limiting the amount of snowfall. Nonetheless, it can snow in any month of the year along the Park Road. June, July, and August are liable to have the best weather, but also the most bugs. May generally avoids the worst of the mosquito season and basks in long days, though snow cover may limit your movements. In September it is getting colder and darker, but the fall colors and berry picking easily compensate.

From early June to early September, Denali is at full tilt, then everything just shuts down for the rest of the year. Unless we've told you otherwise you can assume that all trips, tours, hotels, and restaurants mentioned in and around Denali are only guaranteed to be open through this summer season. The **shoulder seasons** (essentially the last two weeks of May and middle two weeks of Sept) are grayer; some things are operating and others not. As the winter snows melt in the early weeks of May, the Park Road becomes accessible to cyclists, and eventually the Park Service opens it to private vehicles as far as Teklanika (Mile 30). Hotels and restaurants start to open, then on about May 20 the season starts: the visitor center is fully operational, shuttle buses start shuttling, private vehicles are limited to the first fifteen miles of the Park Road, and everything moves into top gear (though the Park Road won't open all the way to Wonder Lake until mid-June). Frenetic activity continues until mid-September, when shuttle buses stop and many hotels and restaurants close or reduce their menus. Then, for a four-day period, the road is open to those who have won the **road lottery** (see p.382). If the snow holds off after September 18 this can be a good time to visit as private vehicles are again allowed to drive as far as Teklanika.

In winter Denali is hard but beautiful. The moose are still about, the aurora is often on display, and both the mosquitoes and the bears are sleeping. The only way in, however, is by snowshoe, ski, or dog team. Snowmachines are not permitted, and there are no services except for the *Riley Creek Campground*. One excellent (if pricey) way to explore the park in winter is on multiday **dog-sled tours** with Denali Dog Sled Expeditions (see Basics, p.65) based at *Earth Song Lodge* (see p.384).

Before heading into the park in winter, make sure you call during the week at the **Park Headquarters**, Mile 3.5 Park Rd (Mon–Fri 8am–4.30pm; ⊕683-2294), to let them know your itinerary and when you are likely to return.

as Denali Park, Nenana Canyon, or **Glitter Gulch**. This is where you'll come to dine, visit offices of rafting and flightseeing operators, and perhaps stay.

About a mile south of Glitter Gulch (Mile 237.3) the Park Road cuts west and winds ninety miles right through the heart of the park to the former gold mines of Kantishna. Most of your time in the park will be spent close to this road, initially along the first two miles, an amorphous region known as the **entrance area**. Here you'll find the visitor access center, a campground, a post office, grocery store, the train station, and the new interpretive center.

The demand for accommodation close to the entrance of the park is so great in summer that a couple of other clusters of hotels have popped up along the George Parks Highway: **McKinley Village**, seven miles south of the entrance area, and **Healy**, a still functional coal-mining town twelve miles north which has some of the best accommodation options.

Information

Park formalities all revolve around the **visitor access center** (VAC: early to late May daily 10am–4pm; late May to late Sept daily 7am–8pm; closed in winter; ⓣ683-2294, ⓦwww.nps.gov/dena), where you'll need to go to book campsites and shuttle buses, and access the backcountry. Here you can also pick up free copies of the schematic *Denali Park Map* and *Alpenglow*, a seasonal visitor guide with comprehensive coverage of park facilities and ranger programs, as well as a guide to the various shuttle buses, campgrounds, and so forth. For more detailed maps you'll need to duck into the **bookshop** section of the visitor center, just next door to the **cinema**, which puts on a free orientation slide show every half-hour.

From the start of the 2005 summer season, the park will also have a new **interpretive center** close to the train station. With loads of exhibition space, a bookshop, and a food court, it is designed to relieve the load on the visitor access center, which will continue to be the place to organize campgrounds, shuttle buses, and backcountry passes.

Getting around

To relieve congestion and preserve the natural qualities of the park, the majority of the park is only open to official shuttle buses, bicycles, and foot traffic. If you aren't traveling by car but decide to stay around Healy for a day or two, you might find it handy to **rent a car** locally or just use taxis to get back and forth between the park and Healy (for both see "Listings," p.396).

Grappling with the various **shuttle buses** can be intimidating at first but with the aid of our box (pp.382–383) you should quickly grasp the basic points: the green buses are run by the Park Service and are designed to link the campgrounds, train station, visitor access center, and interpretive center; while various courtesy buses link Glitter Gulch or McKinley Village to the visitor center. Shuttle buses that run into Denali along the Park Road must be booked either at the VAC or in advance (see box, below).

Driving Denali

Drivers can explore the first fifteen paved miles of the Park Road, as far as Savage River (see p.389). For further exploration, you'll have to abandon your vehicle in the *Riley Creek Campground* overspill parking area (not the visitor access center lot) and make use of the shuttle buses. **RV drivers** can get special dispensation to drive to the *Teklanika River Campground* (see p.387).

Reserving in advance

By planning in advance and making reservations you can save a lot of time at the visitor center and unnecessary nights spent in the entrance area. Various tours, as well as **campgrounds** – *Riley Creek*, *Savage River*, *Teklanika River*, and *Wonder Lake* – and the **shuttle buses** used to reach them, can all be reserved in advance. By **phone**: bookings up to a day in advance of your arrival can be made by phone (in US ⓣ1-800/622-7275; international ⓣ272-7275) between 7am and 5pm (Alaska time) from mid-February to mid-September. Pay by Visa, MasterCard, AmEx, or Discover.

By **fax** and **mail**: any time after December 1 the previous year, but at least a month before your travel date (two days for fax on ⓕ264-4684), you can send your requests to Doyon ARAMARK Joint Venture, 241 W Ship Creek Ave, Anchorage, AK 99501. A form can be downloaded from the Denali NP website (see above) detailing the information required: number of adults and children, desired dates and alternatives, credit card numbers and their expiry dates. The entrance fee ($5 for individuals, $10 for a family) should be included in any payments (check or money order).

Depending on snow conditions, the road is often open to drivers as far as Teklanika River (Mile 30) for a couple of weeks in early May and again after mid-September. Better still, you could enter the **road lottery**, which allows four hundred vehicles to drive the entire length of the Park Road to Kantishna on each of four days in mid-September. There are usually around 12,000 applicants for the 1600 places, but if you feel lucky, then write (during July) to Road Lottery, Denali National Park, PO Box 9, Denali NP, AK 99755, enclosing a stamped self-addressed envelope along with your preferred dates.

Cycling in Denali

One of the best ways of getting around is by **mountain bike**. You don't entirely avoid the tyranny of the visitor access center as you'll still need to book campsites, but making your way along the Park Road at your own pace has obvious advantages. Certain rules restrict your movements, so you won't be allowed to stray off designated roadways and can only leave your machine overnight in the bike racks at the *Sanctuary River*, *Igloo*, and *Teklanika River* campgrounds (and possibly at the *Eielson Campground*). On the plus side, you can hoist your bike onto a camper bus (see box below) at no extra charge, get off where you want, then ride from there, even using a sequence of buses and campsites to explore the whole road. Bikes can be left in campgrounds while you head off for a few days into the wilderness (with the appropriate permit, of course). Some riders make full use of the long

Denali's shuttles and tours

Shuttle buses operate from the third week in May to the middle of September. The tour buses tend to operate for an extra week at either end of the season when they drop their rates slightly. Park Road shuttles are listed in order of importance to most readers.

Entrance area

Courtesy Shuttle (free). Several hotels run frequent courtesy shuttles, which are free to all. Circuits all visit Glitter Gulch and the visitor access center, and one also goes to McKinley Village. No reservations.

Riley Creek Loop (green; free). Makes a continuous run between the *Riley Creek Campground*, the visitor center, Horseshoe Lake Trailhead, and the train station. Schedules are posted at bus stops. No reservations.

Sled Dog Demo (green; free). Runs two miles from *Riley Creek Campground* and the visitor center to the Park Headquarters in time for the daily sled-dog demos at 10am, 2pm and 4pm. Note that there is no vehicle parking at the Park Headquarters. No reservations.

Shuttles along the Park Road

Park Shuttle (green; Savage River free, Eielson $23 round-trip, Wonder Lake $31.75, Kantishna $34.50). Often known simply as "the Shuttle," this is the primary means of entering the backcountry. It leaves the visitor center every half-hour for Eielson (3hr one-way) and every hour for Wonder Lake (5hr), with a few continuing to Kantishna (6hr). Schedules are well organized – even providing late train arrivees with a service to Polychrome Pass and back in the evening. To maximize your time in the park and your chance of seeing early-bird wildlife, try to get on one of the early buses (they start at 5am) and return on a late one (the last leaves Toklat at 6.30pm and arrives back at the visitor center at 9pm). **Reservations are essential** when outbound but coming back it is first-come, first-served (guaranteed seat on the bus you went out on); campers will sometimes be picked up, if they're not full. Apart from

evenings by riding the Park Road at night, after the last shuttle bus has stopped around 10.30pm.

During the spring and fall when there are no buses running and road closures are in effect, cyclists are still permitted to ride beyond closed gates, though you must still use designated campgrounds and are not allowed to camp beyond Mile 30.

Bike rental is available from Denali Outdoor Center, Mile 238.5 George Parks Hwy (Ⓣ683-1925 or 1-888/303-1925), which charges $7 an hour or $40 for the first day and $35 for subsequent days.

Accommodation

The greatest concentration of places to stay is a mile north of the park entrance in **Glitter Gulch**, conveniently located among the restaurants and shops along the George Parks Highway and easily accessible by frequent shuttle buses. The trouble is that in Glitter Gulch you have to decide between camping (see box, p.386) and paying at least $150 a double (more likely $200), though *McKinley Denali Cabins* offers some middle ground.

With your own wheels you'll do better price-wise heading twelve miles north to the small town of **Healy**, where there's a number of competitively priced B&Bs and motels, all much better value than places closer to the park. Consider, too, the small cluster of places near *McKinley Village Lodge*, seven

the day-trip fees there are several passes, notably the **Three-for-Two Pass** (Eielson $46, Wonder Lake $63.50, Kantishna $69), which allows three days' travel as far as your chosen destination for the price of two.

Savage River Shuttle (green; free). A subspecies of the Park Shuttle, leaving from the *Riley Creek Campground* and the visitor center but only going as far as Savage River (Mile 15; 1hr). No reservations.

Camper Bus (green; $23). Buses with extra backpack and bike space designed to get both backcountry hikers and those using the campgrounds into the park from *Riley Creek* and the visitor center. These run five times a day, are only available to those with campground reservations or backcountry permits, and usually have a less comprehensive commentary than the shuttle buses. They won't usually pick up non-campers as they have an obligation to campers encountered along the way. Each camper bus can carry two bicycles, at no extra cost, and your fee is valid for any number of trips during your entire stay west of Savage River. A reservation is required for your first trip into the park; after that they'll pick you up if they have room.

Tours

Kantishna Wilderness Trails (red and white; early June to early Sept; $115; Ⓣ1-800/230-7275, Ⓦwww.seedenali.com). A marathon day driving the entire 95 miles to Kantishna and back (13 hours in all) with lunch, gold panning, and dog-sled demo at the *Kantishna Roadhouse*. Sadly, there is limited time for wildlife stops.

Natural History Tour (tan; $41; Ⓣ1-800/276-7234). Three-hour guided bus ride as far as Primrose Ridge (Mile 17) with a natural history angle. Park entrance fee included. Runs three times daily. Try for the Grand Slam: all the state's large furry animals – bears, wolves, caribou, moose, Dall sheep – in their natural habitat.

Tundra Wilderness Tour (tan; $77.25; Ⓣ1-800/276-7234). Full-day (6–8hr) drive along the Park Road as far as Toklat River (Mile 53) stopping frequently to observe wildlife. Box lunch and park entrance fee included. Runs twice daily.

miles **south of the park entrance**; although shuttle buses are too irregular and infrequent to encourage much to-ing and fro-ing, you can get by. We've listed a couple of places even further south along the George Parks Highway around Carlo Creek, including the region's only **budget hostel**.

Other than camping, the only accommodation **inside the park** is at **Kantishna**, ninety miles west of the park entrance at the end of the Park Road. It is not an especially attractive area by Denali standards, but access to genuine wilderness is second to none. There are four resorts, all expensive and all offering comfortable accommodation, gourmet breakfast and dinner, a wide range of activities, and complimentary bus travel from the park entrance (fly-ins extra), which bypasses the visitor center bottleneck. One-night visits are discouraged so you may need some flexibility to fit in with fixed schedules, and will probably need to book several weeks in advance.

The Park Service allows **RVs** into three of their Denali sites – *Riley Creek*, *Savage River*, and *Teklanika River* (see box, p.386) – and you should really do everything you can to secure a place in one of these. Failing that, you're left with the commercial sites that line the George Parks Highway, almost all of them little more than gravel parking lots with hookups but few concessions to aesthetics. The best are several miles south of the park or in Healy, twelve miles north.

Glitter Gulch

Denali Rainbow Village RV Park Mile 238.6 ⓣ683-7777, ⓦwww.denalirvrvpark.com. Gravel parking lot right in the middle of Glitter Gulch. $18 dry, $28 with electricity and water. Showers are $2 extra.

Denali Riverview Inn Mile 238.4 ⓣ683-2663 or 1-866/683-2663, ⓦwww.denaliriverviewinn.com. Plain modern rooms with a double and a queen bed, private bath, and satellite TV, all featuring a small deck with river views. Rates drop forty percent in the first and last two weeks of the season. ❻

Denali Sourdough Cabins Mile 238.8 ⓣ683-2773 or 1-800/544-0970, ⓦwww.westmarkhotels.com. Individual cabins with a queen bed, well separated by spruce trees and without TV or phone. ❺

McKinley Denali Cabins Mile 238.5 ⓣ683-2733. Some very basic "hostel" cabins – just a canvas and wood frame and a mattress with no heat or electricity – charged at $32 for one up to $48 for four; plus "tent" cabins with heat, electricity, and bedding, and private cabins with TV, refrigerator and bathroom. Private cabins ❺, tent cabins ❷, hostel cabins ❶

Healy and north of the park entrance

Alaskan Chateau B&B Sulphide Rd ⓣ683-1377, ⓦwww.alaskanchateau.com. Very comfortable and nicely decorated log cabins open year-round, all with private bathroom, fridge, microwave, coffeemaker, and toaster, and some with full kitchen and a separate living area (❼). The ones in the A-frame above the garage are especially appealing. Turn off the George Parks Highway at Mile 248.8 onto E Healy Spur, then right after 0.9miles. ❺

Denali Dome Home B&B 137 E Healy Spur Rd ⓣ683-1239 or 1-800/683-1239, ⓦwww.denalidomehome.com. Large geodesic dome with huge lounge areas and great views of the Alaska Range. The six rooms all have private bath (one has a sauna), and the breakfast is fantastic. Turn off the George Parks Highway at Mile 248.8. Year-round. ❺

Denali RV Park Mile 245.1 ⓣ1-800/478-1501 or 683-1500. Desolate RV park located six miles north of Glitter Gulch offering "dry" sites for $15 and full hookup for $28. There is no provision for tents, but they do have pay showers, family units (❺), and simple motel rooms with private bath (❸).

Earth Song Lodge Mile 4, Stampede Rd, Healy ⓣ683-2863, ⓦwww.earthsonglodge.com. A beautifully-sited cluster of charming, comfortable cabins (all with bathroom and coffeemaker) with mountain views and access to a communal lodge with its own library. There's a good chance of spotting wildlife out your window, and you can even tour the on-site sled-dog kennel. All meals are available at the adjacent *Henry's Coffeehouse*, where a nightly slideshow takes place. Stampede Road runs west from the George Parks Highway at Mile 251.1. Two-bedroom cabins ❻, standard cabins ❺

McKinley RV & Campground Mile 248.5 ⓣ683-2379 or 1-800/478-2562, ⓔrvcampak@mtaonline.net. The best RV park hereabouts and good for campers, too, though access to the park is difficult. Sites are all in the trees and there is a coin-op laundry and showers ($2.50). Tent sites $17.50, power and water $26.50.

Motel Nord Haven Mile 249.5 ⓣ683-4500 or 1-800/683-4501, ⓦwww.motelnordhaven.com. High-standard motel just north of Healy, with large rooms the match of any twelve miles further south. Each is equipped with queen bed, phone, dataport and TV, and there's free newspapers, tea and coffee, and a continental breakfast. Year-round. ❻

Valley Vista B&B Mile 0.6 E Healy Spur Rd, ⓣ683-2842 or 1-877/683-2841, ⓦwww.valleyvistabb.com. Attractive half-basement B&B decorated in minimalist style with three rooms, each with private bathroom and spa bath, satellite TV, self-serve continental breakfast, and a separate guest entrance. ❺

South of the park entrance: McKinley Village and Carlo Creek

Denali Cabins Mile 229, eight miles south ⓣ644-9980 or 1-888/560-2489, ⓦwww.denali-cabins.com. Spacious cabins in a nice grassy area with a couple of hot tubs, just far enough away from the park to see the prices drop a little. Courtesy van available. Suite ❽, full cabin ❼, duplex cabin ❹

Denali Grizzly Bear Cabins & Campground Mile 231.1, six miles south ⓣ683-2696, ⓦwww.denaligrizzlybear.com. The most appealing commercial campground anywhere near Denali, set in the trees close to the Nenana River and with a range of attractive cabins all around. There are central cooking shelters (though no pans or crockery), coin-op showers, a store, and a courtesy shuttle leaves from across the road at *McKinley Village Lodge*. Lowest rates are for campsites ($17.50 for up to four; water and electrical hookup $6 extra), then there are tent cabins ($26), and a range of more substantial walled cabins, some with cookstoves and showers, some of them quite luxurious. ❶–❻

Denali Mountain Morning Hostel and Lodge Mile 224, thirteen miles south ⓣ683-7503, ⓦwww.hostelalaska.com. One of the best hostels in the state, in wooded seclusion a little distant from the park entrance but with a bargain shuttle service ($3 a day). Accommodation is in spacious dorms or separate cabins, there's an efficient kitchen, all manner of games and the hosts will do everything to facilitate your Denali visit. They even rent full kits for camping in the park. Private cabins ❹, private rooms ❷, semi-private rooms $50, bunks $23

Denali River Cabins Mile 231.1, six miles south ⓣ683-8000 or 1-800/230-7275, ⓦwww.denalirivercabins.com. Some of the best full-price rooms in the immediate area: all new cedar cabins, with showers, linked by wooden walkways that drop down to the riverside deck and sauna. There's a hot tub and big lounge area, too, but dining options are limited, with only a choice between the restaurant at *McKinley Lodge* and the *Denali Roadhouse* restaurant and bar. Otherwise you'll need to catch the shuttle into Glitter Gulch. Rates drop thirty percent in May and September. Riverside ❼, others ❻

The Perch Mile 224, thirteen miles south ⓣ683-2523 or 1-888/322-2523, ⓦwww.denaliperchresort.com. A tight cluster of relatively low-cost cabins, located at Carlo Creek, made all the more appealing by their proximity to *The Perch* restaurant (see p.395). Cabins without bathroom (❸) sleep four and come furnished with raw-log furniture and sofa with linen provided. Those with bathroom (❹) are larger with an extra bed in a loft. ❸–❹

Inside the park: Kantishna

Camp Denali ⓣ683-2290, ⓦwww.campdenali.com. *Camp Denali* is undoubtedly the place to stay inside the park bounds and is the only place with views of McKinley. It was the first lodge here in 1951, founded by pioneering conservationists Celia Hunter and Ginny Hill Wood. The camp's ecological ethos extends to all aspects of the place, from homegrown vegetables in the restaurant to naturalist tours often guided by visiting experts. *Camp Denali* comprises seventeen cabins strewn over a ridge, each with separate outhouse, and lovely communal lounge areas. Not licensed, but you can drink your own wine anywhere but the restaurant. They also run *North Face Lodge*, a traditional hotel with a block of fully plumbed rooms without Denali views. Both lodges are open early June to early September and with fixed departure dates that dictate minimum stays of three nights (Fri–Sun) or four (Mon–Thurs). $400 per person per night all-inclusive. ❾

Denali Backcountry Lodge ⓣ1-800/841-0692, ⓦwww.denalilodge.com. Without the fabulous views of *Camp Denali*, but with similarly immediate access to wonderful surroundings. Accommodation is in cedar cabins with private facilities, arranged around a spacious lodge, and there's a stack of self-guided walks and structured activities such as hikes, gold panning, naturalist presentations, and so on. Rates for double occupancy are $365 per person. ❾

Campgrounds in Denali

The difficulty with camping in Denali is getting a place in one of the campgrounds through a booking system (see box, p.381) that is as infuriating as it is effective at controlling access to sites in the park. All the sites at *Riley Creek*, *Savage River*, *Teklanika River*, and *Wonder Lake* campgrounds can be reserved in advance, with any remaining sites available from the visitor access center up to two days in advance. Once you have booked your first night in any Denali campground you can then book up to fourteen consecutive nights at any of the sites where there is space. When you go into the visitor access center you'll see a board with all the campgrounds listed along with the number of sites available for the next two nights (ie tonight and tomorrow night): in mid-summer your preferred sites may not be available, and you will either have to resign yourself to staying in a less popular campground for a night or two, or spend your first night in a hotel or commercial campground. Line up at the VAC very early the next morning as it is common for there to be dozens of people waiting for campsite reservations. Staying at campgrounds can also be combined with backcountry camping (see p.393).

Once you're booked in for your first night you should find it pretty easy to reserve subsequent nights at that or any other campground, even the much sought-after *Wonder Lake*, because you will have priority to do so. Hikers without vehicles often have an easier time than drivers since they can self-register at the walk-in section of the *Riley Creek Campground* (that key first night), then trot down to the VAC to reserve the remainder of their stay.

Whichever way you do it you'll have to pay the campsite **registration fee** ($4), which covers your entire stay at any one campground: changing sites means another $4 registration fee at each place. You are limited to a total stay of fourteen nights in campsites and in the backcountry.

Of the six campgrounds, all except *Sanctuary River* and *Igloo Creek* have potable tap water and all are equipped with either flush or pit toilets. They are open from May to September, though *Wonder Lake* only opens sometime in June (depending on snow cover) and *Riley Creek* is open all year. Vehicles are only permitted at *Riley Creek, Savage River*, and *Teklanika*. *Riley Creek, Teklanika*, and *Wonder Lake* have a free program of **ranger talks**, which varies each night.

Activities in and around the park entrance

With a vast proportion of Alaska's visitors making their way to Denali at some point, it is hardly surprising that a considerable industry has built up to tap this rich vein. Except for the very organized travelers who have everything booked in advance, in high season almost everyone spends half a day around the entrance area sorting out plans or simply waiting for a campsite or backcountry unit to become available. There are a few walks (see box, p.388) to keep you entertained, but you'll soon find yourselves kicking your heels. Daytime relief comes in the form of **rafting** the Nenana River, **flightseeing** along the Park Road, **horseback riding** (see "Listings," p.396) or attending the forty-minute **sled-dog demonstration** (daily at 10am, 2pm & 4pm; free). The Park Service still maintains kennels and patrols the park in winter with dog teams, so hop on the free shuttle from the visitor center to see dogs put through their paces hauling a wheeled sled. It is a well-orchestrated show, and you can't help but smile at the dogs' huge enthusiasm at the prospect of a run.

In the evening the **Cabin Nite**, at *McKinley Chalet* in Glitter Gulch (nightly 5.30pm & 8.30pm; $46), draws quite a crowd to its "dinner theater," which features a cabaret-style performance and the waitstaff dishing up heaps of ribs and salmon while in character. Leave your critical faculties at home, and it can

The following campsites are listed in order of distance from the George Parks Highway.

Riley Creek Mile 0.5 (146 sites; May–Sept walk-in $12, drive-in $18; Oct–April free). Large, vehicle-accessible family campground among the woods at the eastern extremity of the park that's often full of RVs. It is far superior to the commercial RV parks along the highway and comes equipped with a sewage dump station. Reserve in advance or pop by the nearby visitor center (p.380), and you'll be assigned a site. No water in winter.

Savage River Mile 13 (33 sites; May–Sept $18). Drive-in tent and RV site accessible without going through the backcountry access system, and offering distant views of Mount McKinley from its position high and dry above the river. Good hiking hereabouts up onto Primrose Ridge. Reserve in advance or at the visitor center.

Sanctuary River Mile 23 (7 sites; May–Sept $9). Primitive, wooded, tent-only site overlooking the river that makes a good hiking base. It is the first campground that requires use of the camper bus for access, only has river water (which needs treating), and open fires are not permitted. Reserve at visitor center.

Teklanika River Mile 29 (53 sites; May–Sept $16). Large site open only to vehicle campers, who are given a pass to drive here but must then leave their vehicle here for a minimum of three nights before driving out. They can explore further using the Teklanika Pass ($22.50), which allows one reserved seat on either the camper bus or Park Shuttle, then unlimited use of those buses on a space-available basis.

Igloo Creek Mile 34 (7 sites; May–Sept $9). Small, secluded, and quiet site requiring use of the camper bus for access. No piped water and no open fires. Has been closed in recent summers due to wolf activity.

Wonder Lake Mile 85 (28 sites; June–Sept $16). The jewel in Denali's crown. A beautiful campground with well-distributed campsites laid out across the sparse taiga, almost all of which have sweeping views of the Alaska Range with McKinley's 14,000-foot Wickersham Wall right in front of you. Arrive early in the day to avoid being relegated to the less fashionable sites without the grand view. Access by camper bus. Reserve in advance or at the visitor center.

be quite fun. If something scuppers your wildlife-viewing plans in the park, there's some compensation in visiting the **Northern Lights Theater** (daily at 9am, 1pm, 5pm, 6pm, 7pm & 8pm; $6.50), for a 35-minute showing of a DVD on the aurora projected onto a 34-foot screen and put to symphonic music.

Rafting

Half a dozen rafting companies (all but one based in Glitter Gulch) cover two stretches of the Nenana River several times a day. Upstream from Glitter Gulch, the seven-mile "**Wilderness**" section (Class I and II; 1hr 30min to 2 hours on the water) makes a pleasant drift on a sunny day, but is unlikely to reveal much remarkable wildlife. The lower "**Canyon**" section (Class III, and sometimes IV in high water), downstream from Glitter Gulch, is altogether more thrilling – definitely a whitewater run. Oared rafts and more maneuverable paddle rafts (see Basics, p.60) are used for the two-hour run through the Nenana Canyon to Healy. You will get wet, and the river is always very cold – around 38° in June – so all companies kit you out in a **dry suit**; in addition, bring thermal underwear and a fleece if you have them.

Typically, you can expect to pay $60–65 for the Wilderness run, a similar amount for the Canyon run, and around $85 for the four-hour combination.

One reputable and fun local company catering predominantly to independent travelers and small groups is Denali Outdoor Center (Ⓣ683-1925 or 1-888/303-1925, Ⓦwww.denalioutdoorcenter.com), or try the Healy-based Nenana Raft Adventures, Mile 248.5 George Parks Hwy (Ⓣ683-7238 or 1-800/789-7238, Ⓦwww.raftdenali.com). Most companies take anyone over 5 years of age on the Wilderness run, 12 for the Canyon.

In addition, Denali Outdoor Center runs a whitewater kayak school and operates **inflatable-kayak tours** (daily 8am & 1.30pm; $75) in self-bailing, blow-up boats on the Wilderness section. Having to control your own vessel is a much more challenging proposition than riding in a raft, but anyone with reasonable physical fitness can participate.

Flightseeing

The shortest and most competitively priced flights to Mount McKinley leave from Talkeetna, south of the Alaska Range, but a couple of local companies fly from Glitter Gulch and give the Talkeetna set a good run for their money. Denali Air (Ⓣ683-2261, Ⓦwww.denaliair.com) charges around $220 for a fixed-wing trip of just over an hour, overflying the Park Road, turning up the Muldrow Glacier and heading for the Wickersham Wall. ERA (Ⓣ1-800/478-1947) runs fifty-minute helicopter trips covering less ground for $245.

Exploring the park

After booking in advance or lining up in the Visitor Access Center to obtain shuttle bus tickets, campground reservations, and maybe even a backcountry allocation, you're finally ready to explore the park. This could be as simple as driving the first fifteen miles of the Park Road to Savage River or hopping a shuttle bus to Wonder Lake, or it may be a complex combination of bus journeys, campground visits, and days spent exploring the park's wilder areas.

Entrance area hikes

There are essentially two types of hiking in Denali: arduous backcountry hiking (see p.393), and the relatively gentle strolls along smooth well-managed paths around the entrance area. The latter suffer to some degree from proximity to Glitter Gulch, but otherwise make for good hikes with a fair chance of seeing some wildlife. Some of these feature as part of free **ranger-led hikes** (consult the *Alpenglow* visitor guide), and all make good fillers while you are waiting to get access to the park proper.

Horseshoe Lake Trail (1.5 miles round-trip; 1hr; 200ft ascent). The most popular of the entrance-area walks is a jaunt through taiga forest to a placid beaver-dammed oxbow lake, best done in the early morning or late evening when wildlife takes over. Park just as you cross the train tracks, follow the line north for 100yd then follow the signs on the right.

Taiga Trail (1 mile one-way; 30min; 150ft ascent). Links the parking area to the start of the Mount Healy and Rock Creek trails.

Mount Healy Overlook Trail (4.5 miles round-trip; 2–4hr; 1700ft ascent). Although the most strenuous of the entrance-area hikes, this one is easy at first as you gradually pull out of the trees to a scenic overlook (500ft ascent). The second half follows unimproved trail getting progressively tougher to the finish, just below a rocky bluff from where it is possible to see the whole of the Riley Creek catchment, and McKinley on a clear day.

Rock Creek Trail (2 miles one-way; 1hr 30min; 400ft ascent). A pleasant trail away from the road, best done on your return from the sled-dog demo at Park Headquarters.

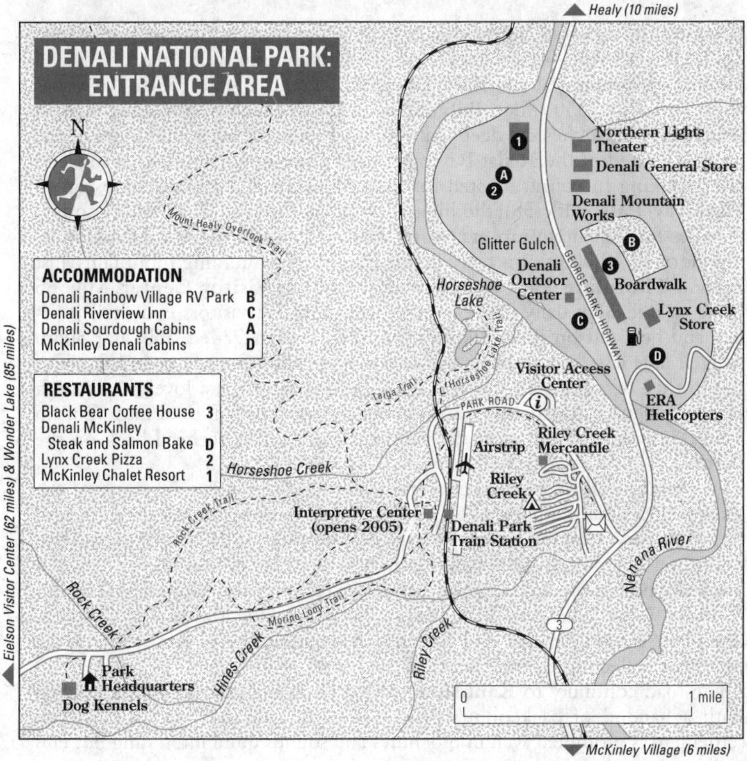

The Park Road

Almost everyone who visits Denali National Park uses the shuttle buses that ply the **Park Road**, a ninety-mile strip which winds its way into the heart of the park, providing access to the backcountry. The road – asphalt to Mile 15 and gravel thereafter – runs at right angles to the rivers, twisting and climbing from one watershed to another over six passes, each topping 3000ft. That might sound a modest elevation, but even in July and August it is not unknown for these to be temporarily blocked by fresh snow.

The Park Road leaves the George Parks Highway and climbs from the Nenana River, passing the visitor access center, train station, and new interpretive center in the first two miles. Spruce forest gives way to willow around Mile 7 – good territory for spotting moose – and between miles 9 and 12 you get a brief glimpse of Denali, the last you'll see of it until just before Eielson. Private vehicles can only go as far as the **Savage River checkpoint**, Mile 15, where there is a two-mile loop trail for hikers along the river. Shuttle buses continue past the popular hiking territory of Primrose Ridge and descend to the Sanctuary River and campsite. Across a low pass you reach the Teklanika River, where there is a huge rest area used by all shuttles (Mile 30) and a campsite. Again, this is good hiking territory. The small *Igloo Creek Campground* nestles between Igloo and Cathedral mountains, both impressive lumps of rock which make challenging destinations for those so inclined.

Beyond the 3800-foot **Sable Pass**, a long bridge crosses the East Fork of the Toklat River (Mile 44) and finishes at the Polychrome Rest Area, often used for hikes beginning at the river. The main channel of the Toklat River lies ahead over the 3500-foot **Polychrome Pass**, which seems aptly named when late sun catches the deep maroons, rust reds, and even faint blues of the rocks. The bed of the Toklat River provides more opportunities for lowland river-walking in country noted for its caribou, then the road climbs up to **Highway Pass** (Mile 58), the highest point on the road at 4100ft. A couple of miles further on you round **Stony Hill** to a superb view of Denali in its full glory, all 18,000ft of it truly dominating the surrounding mountains. Just beyond **Thorofare Pass** you descend to **Eielson Visitor Center**, Mile 66 (June to mid-Sept daily 9am–7pm), where most day-visitors end their journey and head off on short hikes or join the easy ranger-led walk at 1.30pm daily. It lasts less than an hour and covers everything from flora and fauna to the history of mining in the area. The visitor center has a lovely deck with views of Denali, informative panels about the area, a small bookshop (but no food of any kind), and a standby list for those wanting to head back on the shuttle.

In a region full of spectacular scenery, the next few miles are some of the most scenic, with the heart of the Alaska Range framing the vegetated face of the **Muldrow Glacier**, which comes within a mile of the road. You traverse rolling terrain dotted with beaver ponds favored by moose as you descend gradually beside the broad, gravel-bedded expanse of the McKinley River to **Wonder Lake** (Mile 86). Without some serious hiking, this is as close to the mountain as you can get and presents the ubiquitous postcard shot of the mountain reflecting alpenglow across the waters of the lake.

The road continues to **Kantishna** (Mile 91), an old gold-mining inholding with a handful of backcountry lodges (see "Accommodation," p.385). The settlement is promoted well in brochures and sounds quite interesting but fails to live up to its promise. "No Trespassing" signs are everywhere, generators run much of the time, and though the lodges are undoubtedly luxurious, this may not be the Denali you were after.

Day trips into the park

If time is tight, or you just want to supplement your other park escapades, then **drive to Savage River**, fifteen miles along the Park Road (there's no need for permits, tickets, or even park entrance fees). There are a number of pull-outs where you can park (but not overnight) and trudge off across the tundra, and on a clear day you can get a distant view of Mount McKinley near Mile 12. Even with this limited penetration you're still likely to see moose, especially in the late afternoon; bears, caribou, and Dall sheep tend to stay deeper in the park. Those without cars can achieve much the same by riding the **Savage River Shuttle** (see box, p.383), which goes as far as the *Savage River Campground*.

It is definitely worth taking at least one bus ride along the Park Road, if you've made it this far. The cheapest option is the **Park Shuttle** (see p.382), which runs right out to Wonder Lake at the far end of the road. It is a wonderful trip but at eleven hours for the full there-and-back journey you may find that going as far as Eielson (7hr round-trip) is enough.

Leave early enough, and you can engage in a little shuttle-bus surfing, hopping off when something strikes your fancy, hiking up a ridge or across the tundra for a few hours, then leaping on the next one that has room – although in the height of summer there isn't much space available, and you may well find yourself stranded for an hour or so. Strictly speaking, you must pay for west-

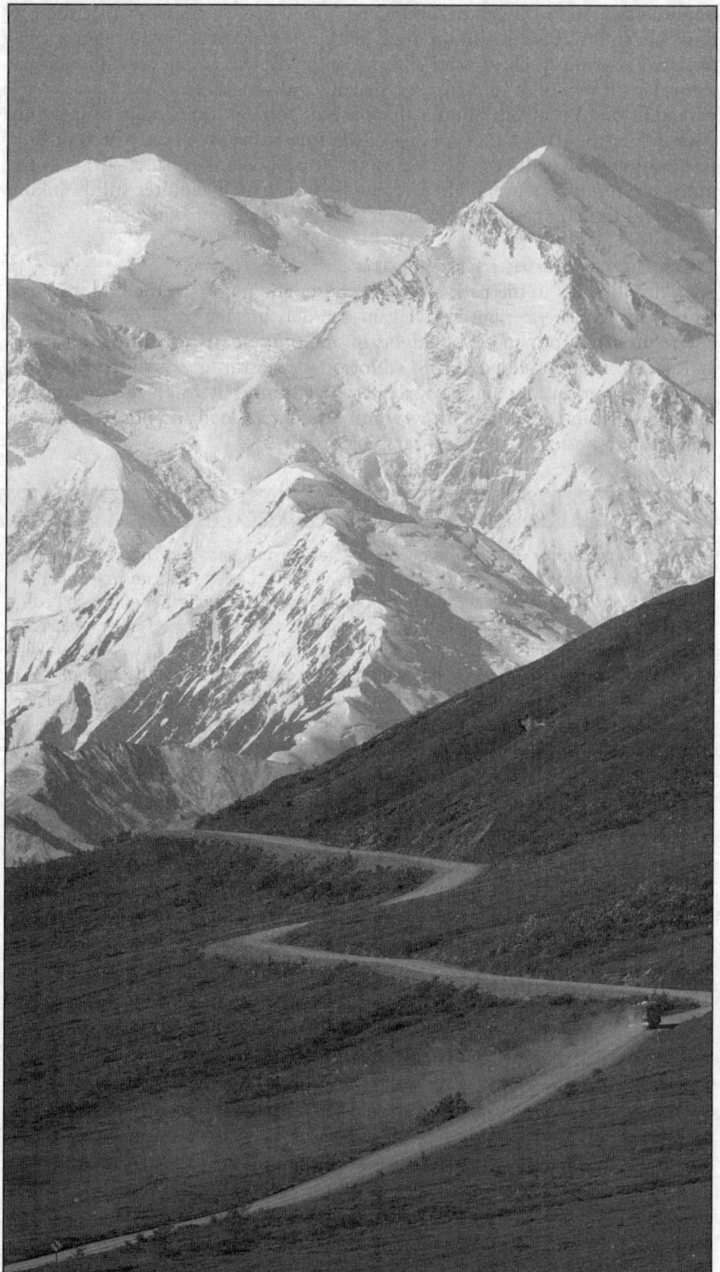
Gravel road over Tharofare Pass, Denali National Park

bound travel and you get eastbound bus rides free. Remember that there is nowhere to buy anything in the park (except for books at Eielson visitor center): take a good stock of food and drink for the day, along with binoculars, camera with plenty of film, insect repellent, and sunglasses.

In addition to the Park Shuttle, there are a couple of other ways of spending your day in the park, either on one of the **bus tours** (see box, p.383) or on a free **ranger-led walk**, the best being to Horseshoe Lake (daily; 2hr), and the more strenuous Discovery Hike (daily; 3–4hr), which requires sturdy hiking boots and the purchase of a bus ticket ($22.50) to get into the park.

Overnight stays in the park

Spending the day in the park riding the buses and going for the odd stroll is a wonderful experience, but you'll gain a much greater sense of the place if you're prepared to spend a few nights in one of the **campgrounds** (for reservation information see box, p.381). Not only does this give you the opportunity to get out on foot and do some serious hiking, but you'll also see animals in a more natural environment, away from the Park Road and not trying to get away from a busload of shutter-snapping visitors.

Backcountry units

Every **backcountry unit** has its own character, advantages, and limitations, all of which can take some time to work out, especially under pressure from others packed into the visitor center trying to do the same. What we've set out to do here is lay down a few general points to guide you in the right direction. Units are marked on our park map (see p.378), but for more detail, consult *The Backcountry Companion* (available for viewing in the visitor center), which has descriptions of each unit, and Trails Illustrated's 1:200,000 *Denali National Park and Preserve* map ($10), the best general map showing terrain and unit boundaries.

When planning your trip, first make a note of regions permanently or temporarily closed to protect animal breeding habitats: maps at the backcountry desk in the visitor center make this clear. For your first night you will need to look at the 29 units (of the park's total of 43) that border the Park Road; the slow pace of travel in Denali and the sheer size of each unit dictates that your first and last backcountry night will be in one of these. For extended trips, carrying all your food can become a chore, one fortunately eased by provision of food caches at Toklat, Eielson, and Wonder Lake where you can stash extra supplies.

The order of the following descriptions follows the road westbound.

Units 1, 2, 3, 24 & 25: the five units closest to the visitor center are just about accessible without using the camper bus but a little noisy with air traffic. This area was less recently glaciated and is therefore more richly vegetated than the rest of the units, making the ridges and river valleys the best passage. Great fall berrying, and wonderful colors, possible sightings of black bears and moose.

Units 16 & 17: south of the Alaska Range and wetter than the rest of the units. Normally accessed from outside the park near Cantwell through Unit 16 but can be reached through Unit 2.

Units 4 & 5: gradually narrowing river valleys with some thick brush and possible high crossings into neighboring units.

Units 26 & 27: plenty of good, dry, high-country hiking (Mount Wright and Primrose Ridge), good wildflowers, and sheep plus walks along Savage River Canyon. Drinking water can be scarce in parts.

Units 6, 7, 8, 29, 30 & 31: mixed area of broad rivers, accessible high country (Igloo, Sable, and Cathedral mountains) and rolling hills of varying colors and textures that

Drivers can use their own vehicles to get to *Riley Creek*, *Savage River*, and *Teklanika River*, but for all other sites you'll need a place on the **camper bus**, usually less packed than the Park Shuttle. **Cyclists** can use their bikes, but for the more distant sites it might be better (or at least a lot easier) to use the camper buses as well. Those without gear can **rent equipment** from Denali Mountain Works (see "Listings," p.396).

There is no reason why you have to stick exclusively to campgrounds: one of the best ways to stay in the park is to combine campgrounds with backcountry camping. In fact, spending a few days in the backcountry (see below) can be a very good way to bide your time while you wait for a particular campground to come free. The possession of a reservation for a backcountry unit gives you the freedom to then book a sequence of nights both at campgrounds and in backcountry units (up to a maximum of fourteen nights).

Hiking and camping in the backcountry

The ease of access, availability of piped water, and the presence of park rangers make the campgrounds appealing, but the essence of Denali only

offer very rewarding hiking. Some dry tundra and great views of the Alaska and Outer ranges. Large areas closed for habitat protection.

Units 28, 37, 38 & 39: multiday-hiking territory only accessible from neighboring units. A vast and little-visited region of large rivers and spruce forests harboring black bears.

Units 9, 10 & 32: wide, braided valleys with spectacular glaciers at the headwaters but sometimes difficult river crossings. Steep slopes limit crossings between valleys.

Units 11 & 33: be prepared to get your feet wet in interesting little canyons or stick to the rolling and rugged hills with loose, exposed rock. Tough going but good views.

Unit 23: the backbone of the Alaska Range (including McKinley), all rock and ice and only for serious mountaineers.

Units 12, 13 & 18: easy hiking close to Eielson visitor center and good views of nearby glaciers but quickly getting tougher, especially crossing the Muldrow Glacier or heading across the Thorofare River up into the steep mountains, glaciers, and scree of Unit 18.

Units 34, 35 & 36: plenty of rolling wet and dry tundra with some heavy brush and beaver pools making for hard going in the low country. Follow ridges and knolls or aim for the summit of Mount Galen. Wonderful views of the whole Alaska Range and Mount McKinley.

Units 14 & 15: swampy and mosquito-ridden with heavy brush making hiking difficult but great views of the Alaska Range. Access to units 19, 20 & 21 across the river is difficult. No camping in the day-use area around Wonder Lake.

Units 19, 20, 21 & 22: these are all south of the McKinley River making access very difficult. You need either glacier-travel skills to cross the Muldrow Glacier or to be prepared for a complex and often dangerous waist-deep crossing of the McKinley River. All are rugged with glaciers coming down to the lowlands and rigorous hiking. Unit 22 requires expedition logistics and consequently has no quota.

Units 40, 41, 42 & 43: lowland tundra with taiga high up and some thick brush to contend with, but great Alaska Range views, if you're on the right side of the hills. Some difficult river crossings and some private property around old gold claims.

truly reveals itself if you go **backcountry camping**. You'll have to show a fair bit of determination and flexibility, but it's worth the extra effort and there is no charge.

The original Mount McKinley National Park, which covered a thirty-mile-wide strip northwest of the central Alaska Range, is now designated as Denali National Park's **wilderness area**, and has been divided into 43 **backcountry units**, large chunks of land each with a daily quota of overnight stays. If you want to stay inside the park but outside the designated campgrounds, you'll have to get yourself on this quota, something done in person at the visitor center. There are no advance reservations for backcountry units.

Anyone intending to spend the night in the backcountry must first view the backcountry simulator video (25min), which teaches you about dealing with bears, or, more to the point, how to avoid having to deal with them. Next, consult the Quota Board, which lists the number of free spaces in each backcountry unit. You can only make **reservations** for your first night two days in advance (for example, reserve Fri for Sun night), and even though there may be nights available three days hence, you can't book them unless you already have a booking for the night after tomorrow. Once you've secured the first night, you can go ahead and reserve up to fourteen continuous nights, so arrive at the visitor center early, accept what you can get for the first night or two, then home in on your desired area after that. Smaller groups have a better chance, and lone campers (a discouraged breed) can often get something at short notice. The backcountry desk at the visitor center has information on the backcountry units and topo maps, and we've given a few pointers below.

Once in the backcountry, you can keep returning to the road and using the camper buses to access the next unit you have booked, but too much chopping and changing can easily wreck the continuity of your wilderness experience and it is usually preferable to concentrate on one area, hiking well away from the Park Road. It is probably asking too much, but it is better if you can arrive without too many preconceptions of where you want to hike, and just make the best of what you can get.

With your backcountry reservations made you'll be handed a free **bear-resistant food container** (see Basics, p.56), which is yours for the duration of your backcountry stay. Tuck it under your arm and amble over to the shuttle-bus desk to book onto a camper bus that will get you to within striking distance of your unit.

Hiking and camping practicalities

Chances are that hiking in Denali will be unlike anything you've experienced before. Forget the usual advice about sticking to the trail and avoiding cutting switchbacks: there are **no managed trails** in the main body of the park, so no switchbacks to cut. It is a guesstimation of which line might afford easiest passage, then constant reappraisal while negotiating **tundra** – likened by some to hiking on foam-rubber basketballs on a waterbed. It is a continual process and (the physical difficulties aside) a much more tiring one than following a trail. Take heed: if twenty-mile treks across moors or along sierra trails are your norm, you'll need to revise your daily estimates down to five or six miles, at least until you learn the rhythm of the land.

This is a land where **following ridgelines** often provides the easiest passage. But if you don't want to go up – and you can quite quickly reach the snow line even in the height of summer – then your best bet is to follow one of the many rivers; and that means getting your feet wet. With few exceptions it is hard going, but the rewards can be great: miles of barely touched wilderness deserted by man, with only the animals to keep you company; slopes drenched in wildflowers in the spring; or a larder of berries in fall.

A consequence of all this is that we have intentionally avoided suggesting any routes to follow. The rangers won't suggest any either; after all, the whole point of hiking in Denali – and its most inviting feature – is that you can make it up as you go along. This seems alien at first. You'll occasionally come across what are known as "social trails" where others have gone before you and worn a passage, and it takes a force of will not to follow them. You should find your own route (and this goes for each person in your party) to avoid creating "social trails." For the same reason, when it comes to camping, select an apparently unused spot and never stay for more than two nights.

Aside from all the usual considerations of bear safety and backcountry travel (for both, see Basics, p.56), it goes without saying that any party going into the backcountry needs at least one person who is a competent **map reader**. Backcountry rules dictate that you **must camp more than half a mile from the Park Road** and out of sight of it. Without some competence with topographical maps, you may find a huge mountain or impassable river between you and your planned camping spot.

Eating and drinking

Eating is expensive in and around Denali, but there is quite a range of options. Campers, and those taking long day rides into the park on the shuttle buses will need **groceries**. If you're prepared to lug them from Anchorage or Fairbanks, then you'll open up your culinary options considerably (particularly with fresh fruit and vegetables, which are almost unheard of in Denali's shops) and save yourself some money, but you can buy some food here. Riley Creek Mercantile, Mile 0.5 Park Rd (which has an espresso bar), and two stores in Glitter Gulch, all sell more or less the same limited range at similar prices; and Denali Mountain Works sells freeze-dried camping meals.

Most of the places listed below are in Glitter Gulch, though we've also listed the best in Healy and points south of the park entrance.

Black Bear Coffee House Mile 238.6, Glitter Gulch ☎683-1656. A tiny log cabin with a sunny deck (and an attached cyber-lounge) serving good coffee and cakes, plus soup, bagels, and build-your-own sandwiches for $7.

Black Diamond Grill Mile 1 Otto Lake Rd, Healy ☎683-4653. A relaxed licensed restaurant at Healy's golf course that's worth the journey out from Glitter Gulch for beautifully prepared and presented food at reasonable prices. Lunch on their herb-crusted prime rib sandwich ($9) or come in the evening for prosciutto-wrapped prawns on seasonal greens ($11) followed by chicken in pesto cream on parmesan risotto ($18). Otto Lake Road runs west off the George Parks Highway at Mile 247.

Denali McKinley Steak and Salmon Bake Mile 238.5, Glitter Gulch ☎683-2733. A favorite on the tour-bus schedule so it fairly churns them through, but still provides a good salmon-bake dinner ($13), halibut dinner ($14), and salmon, halibut and ribs combo ($16).

Lynx Creek Pizza Mile 238.7, Glitter Gulch ☎683-2547. Good pizza (from $13) competes for your attention with a gut-busting nachos grandissimo ($10 for veggie, $12.50 for chicken). Wash it all down with draft microbrews, then stick around for more until midnight.

McKinley Chalet Resort Mile 239.1, Glitter Gulch ☎683-8200. Eating at all levels in this large hotel complex, from a good espresso bar (daily 5am–11pm); the *Courtyard Café* with burgers, sandwiches and a salad bar; and the upscale *Nenana View Grille* with its open kitchen dishing up the likes of King crab fondue ($9) followed by halibut with fried polenta, braised spinach and wild mushrooms ($17).

The Perch Mile 224, 11 miles south at Carlo Creek ☎683-2523. Two restaurants in one. There's a daytime bakery serving bagels, coffee, desserts, and pizza right by the highway; and an excellent restaurant perched on a bluff with views down to Carlo Creek from the picture windows and large deck. It is open year-round serving a full menu throughout the day: eggs Benedict for $9, pasta dishes from $16, steak and crab legs ($25–28). They even do packed picnic lunches for park visitors ($9).

Totem Inn Mile 248.7 Parks Hwy, Healy ⓣ683-2420. Lively bar with live music through summer (generally Wed–Sun; $3–5) and an hourly free shuttle from Glitter Gulch whenever there's a band on.

Listings

Banks Wasilla and Fairbanks have the closest banks to Denali, but the Lynx Creek store has an ATM, and there are several more in Healy, 11 miles north of the park entrance.
Camping gear Denali Mountain Works, Mile 239 in Glitter Gulch (ⓣ683-1542), sells camping gear at reasonable prices and rents two-person tents ($18 for first day, then $9 a day, or $60 a week), sleeping bags ($12/$6/$42), and binoculars ($9/$5/$25), and fills your bottles with white gas. Bring a credit card for a deposit. Riley Creek Mercantile also fills your bottles with bulk white gas at good prices.
Car rental Denali Car Rental (ⓣ683-1377) rent late-model cars for $75 a day, and they'll meet you at the train station, though drivers without their own insurance may not be allowed to rent: check first.
Gas There's a summer-only gas station in Glitter Gulch, and slightly cheaper stuff year-round in both Healy and Cantwell.
Horseback riding To give your feet a rest, let the horses at Denali Saddle Safaris, Mile 4 Stampede Rd (ⓣ683-1200, ⓦwww.denalisaddlesafaris.com), take you through the northern reaches of the park, charging $65 for an hour-long taster or $140 for a half-day ride with views of Denali.
Internet access at the *Black Bear Coffee House* (see p.395) for $2.50–3 for each 15min.
Laundry *McKinley Campground* in Healy, 12 miles north of the park entrance, has laundry facilities (tokens available 8am–10pm).
Left luggage Lockers behind the visitor access center cost only 50¢ for as long as you care to leave stuff, but at busy times you may have to wait a while for one to become free.
Long-distance buses The Park Connection (ⓣ1-800/266-8625) and Alaska Trails & Tours (ⓣ1-888/600-6001) both pick up at the visitor access center.
Maps The visitor center stocks maps. Most quad maps ($7 each) cover three or four backcountry sectors at one inch to the mile (1:63,360).
Medical assistance The Healy Clinic, E Healy Spur Rd (Mon–Fri 9am–5pm; ⓣ683-2211), is located in the Tri-Valley Community Center, 13 miles north of the park entrance.
Post office Next to *Riley Creek Campground* in the entrance area. The **General Delivery** zip code is 99755.
Showers Riley Creek Mercantile (daily 6am–8pm) offers $4 unlimited-time showers.
Taxes Denali and Healy both impose a seven per-cent bed tax, which we've included in our price codes.
Taxis Healy's taxi companies run to the park entrance area for around $25 for two people. Try Ask Alaska Tours (ⓣ277-4676), Caribou Cabs (ⓣ683-5000), Denali Taxi Service (ⓣ683-2504), or Vantastic (ⓣ683-7433).

North of Denali

From Denali it is 120 miles to Fairbanks, a journey which largely follows the course of the Nenana River to the town of the same name and then cuts across the hills flanking the Tanana River. For the first few miles the Parks Highway jostles for position with the railroad as they squirm through the Nenana Gorge hugging the cliffs high above the rapids. The valley widens out at **HEALY**, a coal-mining town since 1918 and now home to the Usibelli power station, fed by open-cast mines artfully disguised behind a few rows of spruce. It is mainly of interest to Denali visitors as a provider of accommodation (see p.384) and food (see p.395), so unless you plan to stay you might as well continue on through.

The Stampede Trail

One point of passing interest on the road north is the start of the **Stampede Trail**, a rugged track that heads west through the northern reaches of Denali

National Park. It is mainly a winter trail to Kantishna in the heart of Denali National Park, but can be followed some of the distance in summer. The trail was built in the 1930s to access an antimony mine, but in recent times has gained a certain notoriety as the refuge and final resting place of Chris McCandless, the subject of John Krakauer's 1997 biography *Into the Wild* (see Contexts, p.545). After drifting across the States searching for some kind of inner peace in the wilderness, McCandless wound up, in the spring of 1992, at what is now known as the **Sushana bus**, a former Fairbanks City Transit System bus which was towed here by bulldozer in the 1950s. With few survival skills and no map he seemed to want to live by force of will . . . and failed. He expired four months after his arrival, probably from ingesting poisonous berries combined with simple starvation.

The tale evidently strikes a chord, because the bus has become something of a point of pilgrimage, though not one you'd want to undertake without suitable consideration and preparation. Stampede Road spurs west off the Parks Highway (Mile 251.1) and runs eight miles (four of them dirt) to a trailhead. From here the bus is nineteen miles and two river crossings away. If you have a rugged, high-clearance 4WD you can get a few more miles, but otherwise it is bike or foot. The same snowmelt-swollen Teklanika River that prevented McCandless' escape may well halt progress about ten miles from the trailhead. Indeed, your intrepid author only made it that far and thus can't confirm the rumored existence of a kind of shrine comprising a cache of survival gear – sleeping bags, first aid kit, food supplies – along with Krakauer's book and a copy of the original *Outside* magazine article it was based on.

If you want to go, ask locally for advice, aim to go late summer, and be prepared for a lot of bog walking. Better still, go in winter on a **dog-sled tour** with Denali Dog Sled Expeditions (see Basics, p.65).

North towards Nenana

At Mile 276, the Parks Highway crosses to the right bank of the Nenana River and, eight miles on, passes a side road to the ballistic-missile early-warning station at **Clear**, first established at the height of the Cold War in 1958. There is no public access to the site. On the last weekend in July or first in August you might want to continue to **Anderson**, six miles west of the Parks Highway, for the **Anderson Bluegrass Country Music Festival** (Ⓣ582-2500, Ⓦwww.americanbluegrass.com), a country and bluegrass extravaganza with regular acts from all over the state alongside Lower 48 headliners. You can stay at the spacious *Riverside Park RV & Camping* ($12 dry, $15 with electricity; dump station available), and eat and drink at the nearby *Dew Drop Inn*.

Nenana

Alaskan winters are long and break-up – the symbol of summer's imminent arrival, when icebound rivers finally thaw allowing vast sheets of jagged ice to crash and flip their way to the ocean – is the most anticipated event of spring. Nowhere celebrates this better than the small town of **NENANA**, at the confluence of the Nenana and Tanana rivers, 67 miles north of Denali National Park (Mile 305). Every year from the beginning of February to the first week in April local citizens begin compiling entries for the **Nenana Ice Classic**, a huge statewide lottery in which people chance $2.50 on their estimate of the time and date that the ice will break up. The festivities begin during the first week in March when a thirty-foot-high four-legged "tripod" is hauled 100yd out onto the four-foot-thick ice of the Tanana River and firmly embedded

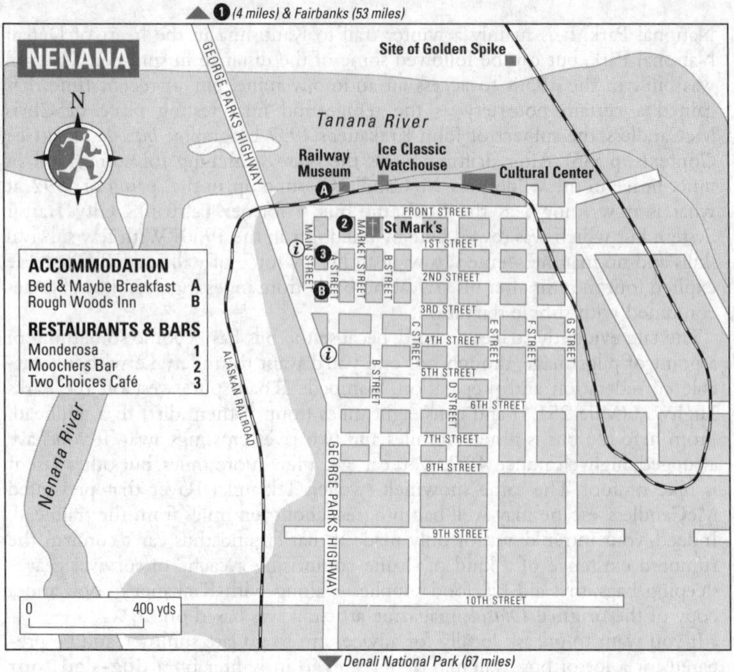

there. A trip wire is then attached to a clock which stops the moment the ice moves a hundred feet downstream. Back in 1917, railroad engineers wagered a total of $800 on the first such event: the pool now usually tops $600,000, half going to the organizers (for taxes, salaries, and promotion), and half split between those who guess the right time. The earliest the clock has stopped was 3.27pm on April 20 in 1940, the latest was 11.41am on May 20 in 1964. It almost always happens between 9am and 9pm. During the summer the only place you can buy a ticket for next year's event is in Nenana (the visitor center sells them among other places), otherwise drop your entry into one of the red boxes found everywhere from early February to early April. For more information visit their website at Ⓦ www.nenanaakiceclassic.com.

For most of the year, the **tripod** stands next to the **watchhouse**, with its window theatrically set up with the clock frozen at the trip time of the last break-up, and to the book of entries open at the winners' page. Standing beside what is the fastest navigable river in Alaska it is hard to imagine that these broad rolling waters would ever freeze up, but freeze they do, and the subsequent break-up proved to be the major obstacle to engineers trying to complete the Seward to Fairbanks railroad. Every year tumbling ice would wipe out the trestles of earlier bridges until they constructed the 700-foot Tanana River Bridge, then the longest single-span bridge in the country. In 1923 President Warren Harding came to drive in the **golden spike** on the north side of the river.

Being at the junction of two rivers, Nenana was important long before the railroad came through, and from 1866 through to the mid-1950s wooden steamboats used to ply the thousand miles of navigable waterways throughout the Interior. Nenana still serves as a goods entrepôt with trains offloading onto barges which, through the 120 ice-free days of summer, supply remote villages with fuel, building materials, and vehicles. Recently the waterfront has been cleaned up a little and you can stroll along learning some of the history and looking across the water at fishwheels (see "Glossary," p.551) going about their automatic harvest. While you're in the vicinity it is worth briefly dropping into the **Alfred Starr Nenana Cultural Center**, on the waterfront (late May to early Sept daily 9am–6pm; free), which concentrates on Athabascan lifestyle and artifacts with a little on historical Nenana and dog mushing for good measure. **St Mark's Episcopal Church**, just across the road is usually open during the summer and is worth a few minutes of your time for the altar dressings made of bleached moosehide by local Athabascan women.

A block west, the baggage room of the former train station is now given over to the **Railway Museum** (mid-May to Sept daily 8.30am–6pm; donation appreciated), easy to dismiss as a miscellaneous collection of bear traps, telegraph insulators, and railroad ephemera, but actually quite interesting for its material on the Ice Classic, including old entry books several inches thick.

Practicalities

Trains stop on request, but even without getting off you can still get a brief look at the town's main sites. As you wind through you go right past the Ice Classic watchhouse and tripod, catch a good view of town as you cross the bridge, then get a close-up of the plaque marking the spot where Harding drove in the golden spike, something you can't see from the road. For a more thorough investigation you'll need to drive, or arrive on the Alaska Trails **bus**, which runs between Anchorage, Denali, and Fairbanks. The **visitor center** (late May to early Sept daily 8am–6pm; ⓣ832-5239) is located where the Parks Highway meets A Street, the town's main drag, which runs the gauntlet of trinket shops to the former train station. Should you decide **to stay**, try: *Rough Woods Inn*, corner of A and 2nd streets (ⓣ832-5299, ⓔroughwoods1@juno.com; ❷), with spacious but ageing rooms, and even larger suites with kitchen (❸); or *Bed & Maybe Breakfast* (ⓣ832-5556; ❷) with four comfortable shared-bath rooms fashioned from the former station master's apartment inside the train station.

The **best burgers** for miles around are served at *The Monderosa*, Mile 309 Parks Hwy, four miles north of town. In Nenana you'll find all you need along A Street: the *Two Choices Café* does good-value **meals** in the Alaskan tradition, and *Moochers Bar* is a convivial place with an extensive liquor selection.

If none of this takes your fancy, press on twenty-odd miles towards Fairbanks (now only 53 miles to the north) to *Skinny Dick's Halfway Inn*, Mile 328, a bar and diner famed throughout the Interior for its extensive range of puerile T-shirts and souvenirs playing on the inn's name.

The Denali Highway

The 135-mile-long **Denali Highway** (typically open mid-May to Sept) runs through some fine Alaska scenery along the south side of the Alaska Range. The land either side is administered by the Bureau of Land Management (BLM), which allows a great deal more freedom than the national park authorities, giving easy access to great views and wildlife viewing without the formal procedures. The road was originally built in 1957 (long before the George Parks Highway was even mooted) to provide road access into Denali National Park from the Richardson Highway, but with the 1972 completion of the Parks

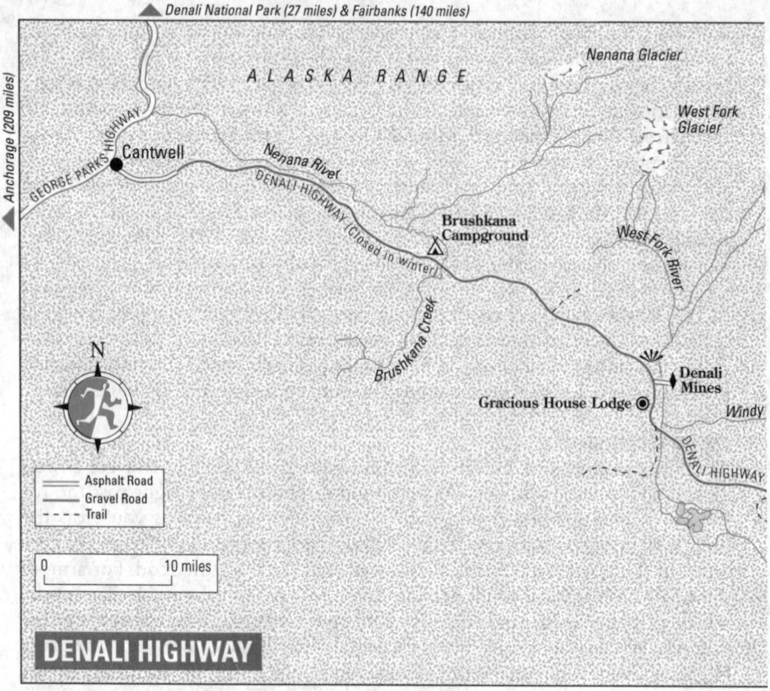

Highway the Denali Highway was left mainly for recreation. If you're headed up the Parks Highway and not desperately eager to get to Fairbanks it is well worth nipping up to Denali National Park and then doubling back to drive the Denali Highway to the eastern Interior.

There are no towns along the way – just a handful of roadhouses – and all but 21 miles are gravel. This is a sizable deterrent to RV drivers and those who obey their car-rental agency's demands to stick to hard-surfaced roads, leaving the road wonderfully free of traffic for everyone else. In particular, this is excellent **mountain-biking** territory: wonderful scenery, little traffic, and the freedom to camp where you want.

The road is broad and firm but bumpy in places, though this doesn't seem to stop locals hurtling along at a fair lick. The full 135 miles can certainly be traversed in a day, but it is rewarding to spend a night or two out here either in one of the roadhouses or at one of the great campgrounds. You can even sleep beside the road, though all too often it is easy to tell where less considerate souls have done so before you: leave your spot cleaner than when you arrived. On the intervening days, stop a while to seek out trumpeter swans, moose, bald eagles, beavers, bears, and perhaps some of the 45,000-strong Nelchina caribou herd; or dip a line into one of the numerous lakes for grayling, char, and lake trout. **Hikers** mostly have to compete with ATVs on designated trails, but for a wilderness experience you can just make it up as you go along: pick a direction and go, but be prepared for wet conditions underfoot. Late season is best when the willow flats and arctic birch shrubs are ablaze with yellows, reds, and oranges.

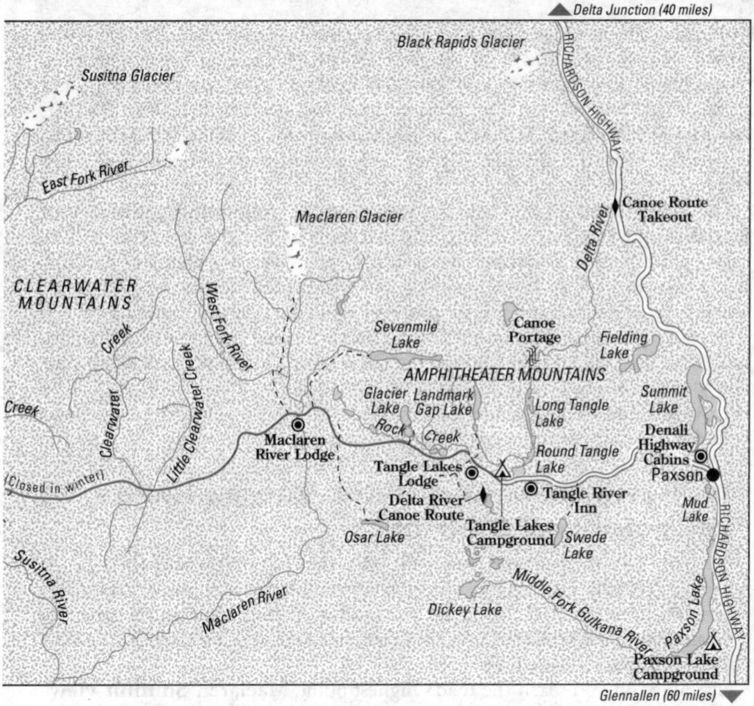

The one season when the Denali Highway is less than quiet is during the first three weeks of September, when it becomes "boys with toys" territory. This is **hunting season**, and everyone is out for moose or caribou: RVs lumber along towing trailers loaded mainly with four-wheeler ATVs, but also eight-wheeler amphibious vehicles, and even Everglades-style airboats, in fact just about anything to get to their quarry across this tough terrain. You'll see them parked up peering into their spotting scopes until something turns up, then they'll hop on their rig and hurtle off across the tundra hoping to beat the next guy to the kill. Presumably they get bored; the road signs here are more bullet-ridden than anywhere in the state – some achievement.

Remember that there is very little out here and you'll need to **come prepared**. Bring all the groceries you need and make sure your spare is good: expensive towing is available from Paxson, Gracious House, and Cantwell, and there is tire repair at *Maclaren River Lodge*, but little else. **In winter** the road is impassable for ordinary traffic but becomes a popular route for snowmachiners, dog teams, and cross-country skiers.

Cantwell to the Maclaren River

Turning off the Parks Highway at **Cantwell** (Parks Hwy Mile 210; Denali Hwy Mile 135), the first reason to stop is at a viewpoint at Mile 124, from where Mount McKinley is visible on a clear day. Every few miles along this stretch there are good spots to roll out your sleeping bag in hopes of a crystalline dawn, but the first formal campground is the well-sited *Brushkana Campground*, Mile 104.5 ($6; pump water). For a roof over your head, press on to *Gracious House Lodge*, Mile 82.5 (ⓣ333-3148 or 1-877/822-7307, ⓦwww.alaskaone.com/gracious; ❹, private bath ❺; late May to mid-Sept), which has rooms with or without private bath, RV parking ($16), camping ($8), and showers ($6). You can eat a good **meal** here, too, drink at the *Sluice Box* bar, buy gas, get tires fixed, and even go **flightseeing** for an hour ($280 for up to 3 people) over the Susitna Glacier and past Mount Deborah and Hess Mountain.

The lodge makes a good base for exploring the **gold-mining district of Denali**, located up a six-mile dirt road that spurs off the highway at Mile 79.5, right by the Susitna River, the largest in these parts. There is plenty of day hiking in here; make it up as you go along, but remember that existing gold claims are fiercely protected, and private property signs shouldn't be treated idly.

For the next forty miles you follow moraine-formed hummocks and ridgelines with long views south, though the Clearwater Mountains now block your views of the Alaska Range to the north. Along the way, small hills are cut by narrow streams feeding kettle lakes, where you might spy trumpeter swans drifting gracefully or moose grazing on aquatic weed.

Maclaren Summit and the Tangle Lakes Archeological District

Where the Denali Highway crosses the Maclaren River, *Maclaren River Lodge*, Mile 42 (ⓣ822-7105, ⓦwww.akpub.com/akbbrv/macrl.html; cabins ❹, rooms ❸, bunkhouse ❶; open all year), offers decent food and a range of accommodation from bunks in an old miners' cabin sleeping six ($30) to basic rooms and much nicer cabins.

Five miles on you reach the road's highest point, **Maclaren Summit viewpoint** (Mile 37), from where the entire Maclaren River watershed is spread out before you, the Maclaren Glacier tucked into the mountains on the right disgorging its milky waters south and west through a broad landscape dotted with kettle lakes that could easily pass for a subarctic Wyoming.

You now enter the **Tangle Lakes Archeological District**, which flanks the highway for the next twenty miles (Miles 37–16). Here, the acidic soils of the subarctic tundra have preserved a dense cluster of five hundred sites collectively recording ten thousand years of human occupation, much of it spent hunting bison. There are no real sites to visit, and ATVs are also entitled to tear up the trails, but if you are still keen on hiking, try to get hold of the free *Trail Map and Guide* to the area from local visitor centers and inns and look for trailheads at Mileposts 37, 24.6, and 16.

Tangle Lakes to Paxson

Dropping down from Maclaren Summit there are magnificent views north through **Landmark Gap**, a glacial cut through the mountains used as a migration route by the Nelchina caribou herd. At Mile 22, the large and modern *Tangle Lakes Lodge* (ⓣ822-4202, ⓦwww.tanglelakeslodge.com; cabins ❸) has nice lakeside cabins and one larger affair ($200) sleeping up to twelve, ideal for birding groups who flock here in June to spot arctic warbler, Smith's longspur, gyrfalcon, and long-tailed jeager. Here you'll find a year-round restaurant serving breakfast, burgers, sandwiches, salads, and steak and seafood evening meals; rental canoes ($30 a day); and plenty of good short hikes nearby – ask locally.

Virtually across the road is the *Tangle Lakes Campground*, Mile 21.5 (free; pump water), which sits in open country with wonderful mountain views, and acts as the starting point for running the Delta River and the Middle Fork of the Gulkana River **canoe routes** (see box, below). To explore the beautiful subalpine **Tangle Lakes** themselves, rent canoes ($3/hr, $24/24hr) from *Tangle River Inn*, Mile 20 (ⓣ822-3970, ⓦwww.tangleriverinn.com; cabins ❸–❹, rooms ❷–❸; mid-April to Sept), which offers simple but comfy cabins and rooms, plus a deluxe bunkhouse with two beds per room for $30 per person, showers ($5), gas, and reliable, tasty diner fare.

The final 21 miles of the highway are nice smooth asphalt, dropping down into the Gulkana River Valley, leaving behind your final glimpse of the Alaska Range and the small Gulkana and Gakona glaciers. The views to the south are no less impressive, the dominant peaks of the Wrangell Mountains – Sanford, Drum, and Wrangell – easily visible from the viewpoint at Mile 13. The highway ends at **Paxson** (Richardson Hwy Mile 185), where you'll find little more than *Denali Highway Cabins* (see p.428), an excellent base for the eastern end of the road.

Canoeing the Delta and Gulkana rivers

Keen paddlers with a sense of adventure and an appreciation of the Alaskan wilderness should seriously consider tackling either the **Delta River** or one of the two main routes on the **Gulkana River** system. They run through outstanding scenery, the low rolling tundra framed by the peaks of the Alaska Range, and all require some knowledge of topographic maps, wilderness camping ability, and enough paddling skill to negotiate sweepers and Class II rapids. The remote nature of these trips and the difficulty of some of the rapids makes carrying some kind of patching kit essential. Alaska Public Lands Information Centers in Anchorage, Fairbanks, and Tok (and visitor centers locally) supply detailed leaflets on all three canoe routes, which can usually be run from early or mid-June to mid-September.

Most rental places don't allow their canoes on rivers such as these, but you can **rent canoes** from Paxson Alpine Tours (see p.428) who can also arrange for drop-off and pickup.

Delta River (29 miles; 2–3 days; Class I and II). The route starts at *Tangle Lakes Campground*, Mile 21.5 Denali Hwy, and follows a series of small interconnected waterways through rolling tundra nine miles north to Lower Tangle Lake. Edging into the Amphitheater Mountains, a mile or so of Class II water is followed by a 15-foot waterfall which must be portaged using a half-mile marked trail. A little more Class II–III and twelve miles of Class I–II follow until a tributary makes the river glacial and braided to the pull-out at Mile 212.5 on the Richardson Highway. It is possible to continue to Black Rapids (an additional 17 miles; 1–2 days; Class III) but is only recommended for kayaks and rafts.

Main Branch Gulkana River (47 miles; 3–4 days; Class I, II and III). From *Paxson Lake Campground*, Mile 175 Richardson Hwy (see p.428), cross three miles of the lake to enter demanding Class II and III rapids before joining the Middle Fork for several miles of easy floating. After twenty miles you hit the Class III–IV Canyon Rapids (easily portaged on a quarter-mile trail), which are followed by nine miles of shallow and potentially damaging Class II and III water, then eighteen miles of Class I to the finish at the *Sourdough Campground*, Richardson Mile 147.5.

Middle Fork Gulkana River (76 miles; 6–7 days; mostly Class I and II). The boat launch at Mile 21.5 on the Denali Highway gives access to the southern sequence of Upper Tangle Lakes, negotiated with three short, unmarked but easy to determine portages. A fourth (1.2 miles) brings you to Dickey Lake (possible float-plane access; subtract 1–2 days) and the start of the Middle Fork, which descends through three miles of shallow water to a steep and rocky canyon (Class III–IV) requiring careful lining or a portage. After the canyon the river eases and joins the main stem of the Gulkana River (see above) down to the *Sourdough Campground* pull-out.

Travel details

The most pleasurable way to get between Anchorage, Talkeetna, Denali, and Fairbanks is by train, which takes in the best of the scenery in comfort, at a price. Buses (listed along with route descriptions in Basics, p.41) are more frequent and broader in their coverage. Again, the Anchorage–Denali–Fairbanks corridor is the busiest, with three companies doing a daily run in summer.

With the exception of occasional trains (see Basics, p.38), nothing runs after the middle of September or before the middle of May.

Trains

Denali Park to: Anchorage (1 daily; 7hr 30min); Fairbanks (1 daily; 3hr 45min); Talkeetna (daily; 4hr 40min); Wasilla (1 daily; 6hr 20min).

Talkeetna to: Anchorage (1 daily; 3hr 10min); Denali Park (1 daily; 4hr 40min); Fairbanks (daily; 9hr); Wasilla (1 daily; 1hr 40min).

Wasilla to: Anchorage (1 daily; 2hr); Denali Park (1 daily; 4hr); Fairbanks (1 daily; 10hr 30min); Talkeetna (daily; 1hr 40min).

Buses

Denali to: Anchorage (4 daily; 5–6hr); Fairbanks (1 daily; 3hr 30min); Talkeetna (1 daily; 3hr); Talkeetna Junction (4 daily; 3hr).

Nenana to: Anchorage (1 daily; 7hr); Fairbanks (1 daily; 2hr).

Palmer to: Anchorage (3 weekly; 1hr); Glennallen (3 weekly; 2hr 30min); Whitehorse, Yukon (3 weekly; 17hr).

Talkeetna to: Anchorage (2–3 daily; 3hr); Denali (1 daily; 3hr).

Talkeetna Junction to: Anchorage (4 daily; 3hr); Denali (4 daily; 3hr); Fairbanks (1 daily; 7hr).

Wasilla to: Anchorage (4 daily; 1hr 15min); Denali (4 daily; 4–5hr); Talkeetna Junction (4 daily; 1hr 15min).

7

Wrangell–St Elias and the eastern Interior

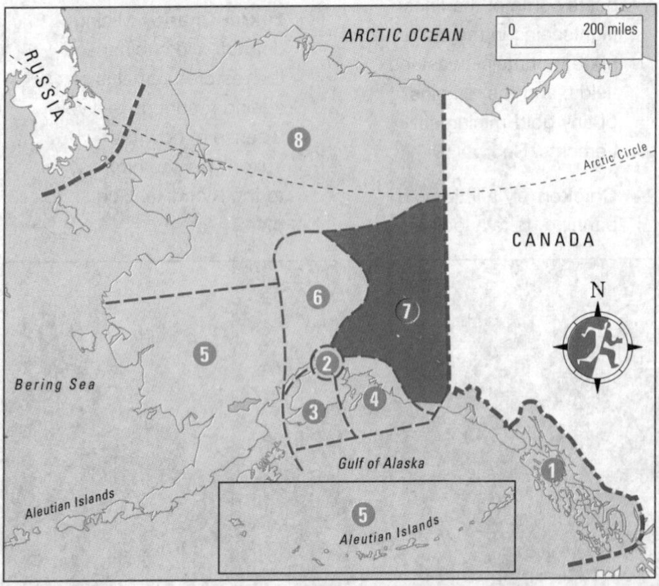

CHAPTER 7

Highlights

* **McCarthy and Kennicott** Twin settlements in the heart of the Wrangell–St Elias National Park with great scenery, wonderful old mill buildings, and bags of character. See p.415

* **Wrangell–St Elias flightseeing** McCarthy hosts some of the finest flightseeing in the state: huge mountains, vast ice fields, and the remains of tiny gold-mining settlements. See p.419

* **Chicken** Try a little gold panning, take a look at an old gold dredge, but most of all stick around for an evening in the *Chicken Creek Saloon*. See p.436

* **Eagle** Delightfully ordered former garrison town on the banks of the Yukon River. See p.439

* **Float through the Yukon-Charley** Mining detritus, old cabins, and the restored remains of ageing roadhouses give a sense of how the Yukon was the highway to the Klondike. See p.442

△ McCarthy Lodge

7

Wrangell–St Elias and the eastern Interior

Alaska's densest crush of mountains, the largest of its ice fields, and some of the vastest swathes of forest coexist around **Wrangell–St Elias and the eastern Interior**. Outside Alaska it is Denali that gets all the attention, but to those in the know the Wrangell-St Elias National Park is the real jewel, a trackless glacial wonderland where major mountain ranges ruck up against each other to create an almost impenetrable wilderness that stretches over the border into Canada. Here you'll find the beautifully complementary twin towns of Kennicott and McCarthy, the former the decaying wreck of a copper mine and stifling mill town, the latter a rumbustious place that still buzzes with life. Plan on a few days to ease into the pace of the place, and several more if you want to get out into the stupendous backcountry. So remote is the park that only two minor roads penetrate its interior and none of the region's major highways comes close. It is this that makes your journey so much more worthwhile once you finally make it to your destination.

Along the park's western fringe the **Richardson Highway** forms the backbone of the eastern Interior's road system, running from Valdez to Fairbanks. This was the first of the Interior highways and was also the course chosen for the **Alaska Pipeline**, which slices through the center of the state. Access into the region from Anchorage courses along the Glenn Highway, which meets the Richardson at workaday Glennallen, the hub of the central roads. From there the Tok Cutoff connects to the Alaska Highway at the crossroads town of **Tok**, which is a springboard for trips along the **Taylor Highway** into the Fortymile River region. Star attractions here are the oddball hamlet of **Chicken** and the Yukon riverbank town of **Eagle**, the Interior's first city, now a fascinating historical remnant.

People are hugely outnumbered by animals: moose, Dall sheep, grizzly bears, and herds of caribou sweep over seemingly endless swaths of taiga and tundra. Day-to-day weather can vary enormously with even more severe seasonal variations: in winter temperatures can drop to –50°F for days at a time, while summer days reach a sweltering 90°F. The major problem during the warmer months, however, is large quantities of huge mosquitoes; don't set off without insect repellent.

The eastern Interior is a region that's easy to get around, though public transportation is infrequent, so you'll do well to get hold of a car. With your own

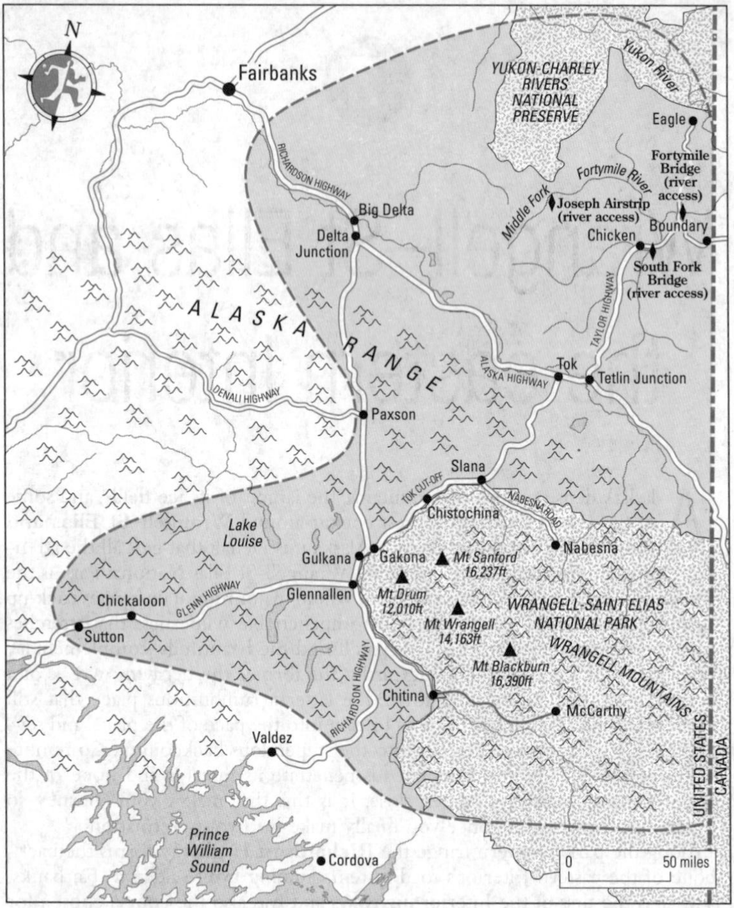

transport you'll have the freedom to travel at your own pace and, if you are camping, it will allow much better access to roadside campgrounds.

The Wrangell–St Elias National Park

The **Wrangell–St Elias National Park** fills out the extreme southeast corner of the Alaskan Interior, on the point where four of the continent's great mountain ranges – the Wrangell, St Elias, Chugach, and Alaskan – cramp up against each other. At 13.2 million acres, it is bigger than Death Valley,

For up-to-date information on Interior road conditions, contact ⓣ456-7623 or click your way to Traveler Info/Road Conditions at ⓦwww.dot.state.ak.us.

Yellowstone, Grand Canyon, and Everglades national parks put together, and larger than Switzerland. It is a place that defies superlatives. Even the usually unsensationalist US National Park Service literature breaks out in a rash of (justifiable) hyperbole by saying, "Incredible. You have to see Wrangell–St Elias . . . to believe it." Everything in Wrangell–St Elias is writ large: peak after peak (including nine of the sixteen highest in the US, each over 14,000ft, and fourteen over 10,000ft), glacier after enormous glacier (some the size of small states), canyon after dizzying canyon – all laced together by braided rivers, massive moraines, and icy-cold lakes, with the volcanic 14,163-foot monster of Mount Wrangell still steaming in the background.

As if all this weren't enough, it forms part of a contiguous cross-border wilderness with Canada's Kluane National Park Reserve and Tatshenshini-Alsek Park, and the Southeast's Glacier Bay National Park, together forming the largest protected area on the planet that is recognized as a **World Heritage Site**.

Vegetation struggles to take hold in the higher reaches of the park, though it tenaciously hangs on enough to support mountain goats and Dall sheep. Lower down the diversity goes wild: riparian fringes and wooded, silty lowlands are home to bears, moose, and three sizable herds of caribou.

The park was created in 1980 and remains – in terms of access and development – in its infancy, with private landowners still holding large chunks of its putative territory. It sees less than a tenth of the visitors Denali gets, and though bush-plane landing sites stud the territory, only two roads penetrate the park. The **Nabesna Road** cuts into the northern fringes, but most visitors approach the park along the **McCarthy Road**, a sixty-mile epic along the Copper and Chitina rivers to freewheeling **McCarthy** and the copper-mining ghost town of **Kennicott**, with its thirty big, disused buildings now preserved as a National Historic Landmark. It is a fascinating place, dramatically sited and wonderfully photogenic, but the appeal of the area is as much its access to stiff **hikes**, several easily accessible and others requiring a bush plane.

Some history

In July 1900 two prospectors, "**Tarantula Jack**" Smith and **Clarence Warner**, started poking around the tributaries of the Chitina River in search of gold. They found none, but didn't go away empty-handed. Legend has it that they spotted what looked to be a promising patch of grazing well above the snow line close to the crest of a sawtooth ridge. As experienced prospectors with little interest in sheep pasture, it seems likely they knew full well that the green patch was something much more valuable than grass. Whatever the truth, they hightailed it up the slope and unearthed what became the **Bonanza Mine**, one of the continent's richest copper deposits, predominantly chalcocite, a phenomenally rich copper ore, which sometimes assayed at almost eighty percent and averaged thirteen percent, at a time when commercial mines in Utah and Arizona were getting two percent.

Mining engineer Stephen Birch bought their claim (and others nearby), and with the backing of financier JP Morgan and the Guggenheim brothers, formed what was to become the Kennecott Copper Corporation. The mines were worthless without some means of getting the ore to smelters in the Lower 48, and the company set about the gargantuan task of building the Copper River & Northwestern Railway (see box, p.412). Work also began on what was to become the dedicated 600-strong company town of **Kennicott**. Everything had to be hauled in – mostly on sleds during the winter when the rivers froze – so that processed ore would be ready to ship out to Cordova when the first train arrived in 1911. Overnight, the Kennecott mines became the richest in the world.

Meanwhile, five miles down the tracks, business-minded John Barrett had leased his homestead land to the CR&NW for turntable and switching operations. With a flood of prospectors making for Skolai Pass and **Chisana** (pronounced SHU-shan-na), for what turned out to be Alaska's last gold rush in 1914, Barrett was able to sell off more land, setting the stage for the development of **McCarthy**.

The Great Depression of the 1930s sent copper prices spiraling down, and when the Chitina Bridge washed out in 1932 the mines closed. They reopened in 1935, but thirty years of frantic production came to an end in 1938: the last train arrived in Kennecott on November 11 apparently with instructions for the station agent to collect his papers and belongings in ninety minutes and climb on board the return service.

Once the railroad bed was turned into a road a few years later, it became open season on looting anything not nailed down, and a fair bit that was. In the 1960s the Kennecott land was turned over to a faceless corporation that sold the managers' cabins to whichever hippies and recluses were interested. With the formation of the national park in 1980 and the Park Service's purchase of the whole site (except for the private inholdings) in 1998, the steady decay has been arrested, and visitors have begun to come in increasing numbers.

Information

Anyone planning to spend any time in the mountains to the east should call in

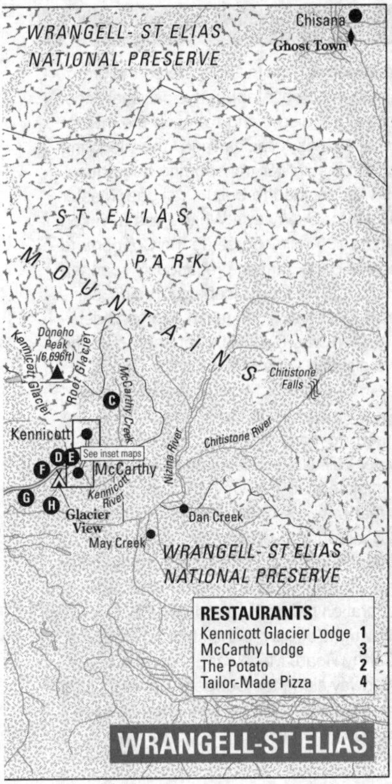

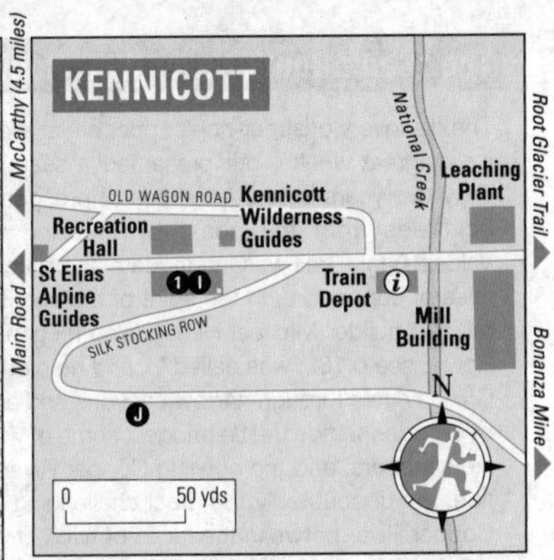

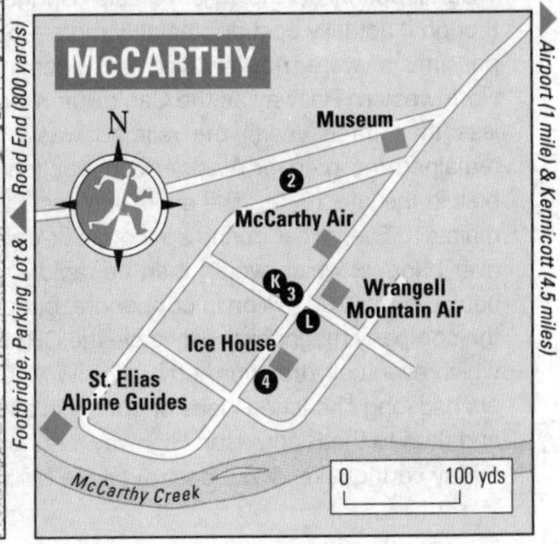

at the Wrangell–St Elias National Park Headquarters **visitor center** (late May to early Sept daily 8am–6pm; early Sept to late May Mon–Fri 8am–4.30pm; ⓣ822-7440, ⓦwww.nps.gov/wrst) at Mile 106.8 on the Richardson Highway. Here rangers help plan hikes, sell books and topo maps, and generally offer advice on the area. While you're here, pick up the useful and free *K'elt'aeni* newspaper, which has all the latest on the park and activities within it. The center is spectacularly sited with great views of Mount Drum, offers diverting interpretive material, and shows some excellent footage of the park on the 22-minute *Crown of the Continent* (every hour on the hour; free) presentation.

There's also a visitor center in Chitina (p.413) and another in the original train depot at **Kennicott** (see p.415).

Before leaving Glennallen or Valdez, you should fill your tank and stock up with any groceries you may need. Chitina generally has limited groceries and gas; you won't find either in McCarthy and Kennicott, or a **bank** or a **post office** for that matter.

Getting into the park: the Edgerton Highway and the McCarthy Road

Getting into the Wrangell–St Elias National Park is half the fun. It is an at times rugged backcountry drive that follows the smooth Edgerton Highway 33 miles

The "Can't Run & Never Will" Railway

The discovery of super-rich copper ore at the Bonanza Mine in 1900 offered the promise of great wealth, but presented a seemingly insurmountable physical challenge. Only two years before hundreds of prospectors had died trying to reach the Interior goldfields from the coast by crossing the Valdez Glacier, and the fledgling Valdez–Eagle Trail was inadequate and much too distant for transporting huge quantities of copper ore. In the spirit of the age, it was decided to build a railroad. Master railroad builder Michael Heney (also responsible for Skagway's White Pass & Yukon Route, see p.182) was called in, and he plotted a 196-mile course up the Copper and Chitina rivers through narrow canyons and across deep gorges, precariously spanned by wooden-lattice trestle bridges, some of which survive today. Icebergs, rapids, shifting sandbars, and the howling Copper River wind all had to be taken into consideration, but undoubtedly the most challenging section was the 1550-foot span over the Copper River between the faces of two active glaciers – the Miles and the Childs.

Construction on the Miles Glacier Bridge – dubbed the "**Million Dollar Bridge**," though it actually cost appreciably more – began in earnest in the spring of 1908, but pessimists were not swayed and continued to refer to the Copper River & Northwestern Railway as the Can't Run & Never Will. Nonetheless, by March 1911 (in less than three years) the railroad was completed all the way to Kennicott and remained the premier Alaskan construction feat until the Trans-Alaska Pipeline was built in the late 1970s. The entire line cost $23 million to build and almost as much to maintain. Every year during spring break-up careering ice would wipe out many of the river bridges, which would then be rapidly rebuilt. During its 27-year life the railroad hauled over $200 million in copper ore, but operation halted for good in 1938. In 1941 the company magnanimously gave the CR&NW right-of-way to the state government, which eventually transformed it into the McCarthy Road. Meanwhile, Cordova boosters had long cherished ideas of putting in a highway along the Copper River to Chitina and then to the Richardson Highway, but hopes were dashed in 1964 when the Good Friday earthquake all but destroyed the Million Dollar Bridge.

to the village of Chitina, then the rough-dirt McCarthy Road to McCarthy and Kennicott. For nearly sixty bone-shaking miles, it twists along the former trackbed of the Copper River & Northwestern Railway, which throws up sharp rocks: beware of punctures and make sure your spare (preferably, not the space-saving variety) is functional. Conditions vary with the frequency of grading, but at best it is slow going and can be an exacting drive.

Transport is a limiting factor. In general, rental agencies won't insure their vehicles for the journey, not that that seems to stop many people. Hitching can be a hit-or-miss affair, so you may need the services of Backcountry Connections (mid-May to mid-Sept Mon–Sat; Ⓣ822-5292 or 1-866/582-5292 in Alaska, Ⓦwww.alaska-backcountry-tours.com). They pick up in the morning from hotels and campgrounds around Glennallen and charge $99 for a same-day round-trip, $115 to spread it over several days; from Chitina the round-trip to McCarthy is $80 or $100. An excellent alternative is to **fly to McCarthy**, perhaps with a bit of aerial tour thrown in, obviating the need for a flightseeing trip once in McCarthy. In summer Wrangell Mountain Air (see p.419) runs two daily flights into McCarthy from Chitina ($140 round-trip) and hooks up with Backcountry Connections to offer a fly/drive round-trip (also $140).

The Edgerton Highway to Chitina

The all-weather **Edgerton Highway** cuts off the Richardson Highway 36 miles south of Glennallen (Mile 82.6), and apart from the wonderful mountain scenery, there's little to distract you – though you may fancy the **Copper River Trail**, Mile 12.6 (7 miles round-trip; 3hr; mostly flat), which runs to the Copper River through excellent bird-watching territory. The small but beautifully formed *Liberty Falls State Recreation Site*, Mile 23.6 ($10; pump water), huddles by a cascading stream adjacent to the **Liberty Falls Creek Trail** (1 mile round-trip; 15–25min; 300ft ascent), which leads up through the spruce forest to a small ridge-end plateau with views of the cascading Liberty Creek and across the Copper River to the Wrangell Mountains.

The Copper and Chitina rivers join forces at **CHITINA** (CHIT-na), Mile 33, a hamlet locked in an aspen- and spruce-cloaked fold with an ancient, dilapidated appearance that belies its relatively recent genesis. It sprang to life in 1910 as a way station for the CR&NW Railway and a transit point for rail passengers from Cordova taking the stage to Fairbanks and points inland. In the early 1940s the rails were pulled up and buildings removed to the extent that Chitina became virtually a ghost town, a point illustrated by one of the few local residents, who painted phantoms on the walls of the remaining buildings. The red and king salmon runs on the silt-laden waters of the Copper River still drew dipnetters every July and August, but it wasn't until the creation of the national park in 1980 and the upsurge in tourism that Chitina started to revive. One short row of shopfronts has been tastefully preserved, notably Spirit Mountain Artworks, which is worth a few minutes of your time for locally produced paintings and photography, plus quality Alaskan crafts. If it is open, call in at the national park **visitor center** (generally late May to early Sept daily 10am–5pm; ⓣ823-2205) in the former home of a stagecoach-company manager, bedecked with fascinating photos of old-timers working the riverboats that carried supplies during the railroad construction. Eating options have been narrowed in recent years, but *Chitina Trading Post and Café* serves breakfast, sandwiches, homemade pizza, and fruit pie, and you can drink at the *Chitina Bar & Grill* (ⓣ823-2201). Nice **cabins** with electricity and an outhouse are available at *Chitina Guest Cabins*, Mile 32 Edgerton Hwy (ⓣ823-2266, ⓦwww.pawandfeathers.com; ❸), where you also get a continental breakfast.

Bikers should consider detouring south along O'Brien Road (which is navigable for a few miles in dry conditions by ordinary vehicles) and onto the **Copper River Trail** (see box, overleaf) – not to be confused with the identically named one above – but for everyone else the McCarthy Road beckons.

The McCarthy Road

The **McCarthy Road** (typically open May to mid-Oct) has a speed limit of 35mph, but if you've any respect for your rig you won't be troubling the state troopers. The sixty miles from Chitina to McCarthy are likely to take you at least two, maybe three, hours as you climb from 500ft to 1500ft through spruce, cottonwood, and aspen.

The scenery is ruggedly mountainous, but you occasionally come across incongruous patches of private property where a roadside airstrip provides access to a cluster of cabins, often with smooth lawns and brilliant flower beds. Soon after leaving Chitina the road crosses the Copper River on the concrete bridge that replaced the old railroad trestle, which washed out every year at spring break-up and was rebuilt annually until 1938. Silt from glaciers on the

Wrangell-St Elias National Park can also be accessed along the Nabesna Road, about eighty miles further north. Our account is on p.420.

southern flank of the Wrangell Mountains makes ordinary fishing impossible; this is one of only four Alaskan rivers where dipnetting and **fishwheels** are permitted: you may well see them in the river, if they're not obscured by the dust storms that howl up the Copper River. On the east bank a free but often windswept **campground** offers little temptation with the knowledge that you are now within the Wrangell–St Elias National Park and can informally camp beside the road (though not on any private property). There is slightly more formal accommodation at the commercial *Silver Lake Campground*, Mile 10.9, which has tent sites and "dry" RV camping (both $10), does tire repair, and rents canoes and rowboats for lake trout fishing ($5/hr), and the *Strelna Zephyr Bunkhouse*, two miles north up Nugget Creek Road at Mile 14.5 (Ⓣ240-3055; ❸), a log cabin with just four bunks, a wood stove, and a sauna nearby: bring a sleeping bag. Nugget Creek Road also leads to the **trailhead** for the Dixie Pass and Nugget Creek trails (for both see box, below).

At Mile 17 the road teeters precariously over the **Kuskulana Bridge**, 238ft above the Kuskulana River. It must have been a nerve-wracking crossing before the metal guardrails were added in 1988. In the late 1990s the bridge

Hiking and biking off the McCarthy Road

With McCarthy and Kennicott drawing you onward, it is tempting to charge headlong to the end of the McCarthy Road. Off-road cyclists, however, should consider turning off at Chitina and following the Copper River Trail, while hikers should leave the road at Mile 14.5 and follow Nugget Creek Road to the **trailheads** for the challenging Dixie Pass Trail and the appreciably easier Nugget Creek Trail. Consult the staff at the park headquarters (p.411) for appropriate maps and more detailed trailhead information.

Copper River Trail (3.5 to 20 miles one-way; 1hr to 2 days; mainly flat). Though access has been much curtailed by recent landslides, it is still possible to explore the first 3.5 miles of the old CR&NW trackbed south from Chitina. The remainder of the road is officially closed, though remains in use by locals. The track flanks the surging gray water of the Copper River past some spectacularly crumbling old trestle bridges – now bypassed by the track – as well as a couple of places where the narrowness of Wood Canyon forces the route into two short tunnels. Mostly it is too flat to be an exciting walk, but makes great cycling country, with numerous places where you can throw down a tent for the night.

Dixie Pass Trail (24 miles round-trip; 2–4 days; 3300ft ascent). A fairly tough, but popular, there-and-back hike which offers one of the few backcountry experiences in the park that doesn't require a fly-in. The trail initially follows a well-defined streamside track, then requires a bit more route-finding to approach the 5100-foot Dixie Pass. The ascent of the pass is strenuous, and some make it a day hike from their camp at the base, but committed types are rewarded by the chance to camp high on the alpine tundra with stupendous vistas all around. You can either retrace your steps to the trailhead, or make a long loop (45 miles in all; 5–7 days) by continuing north over Dixie Pass and down Rock Creek to join the **Kotsina Trail** which follows the Kotsina River as it loops around the western end of Hubbard Peak to the trailhead.

Nugget Creek Trail (29 miles round-trip; 2–4 days; 1700ft ascent). An easy-to-follow hike (or bike ride), gradually climbing through the forest along an old mining road up the Kuskulana valley, eventually offering great views of the Kuskulana Glacier. It isn't that hard, though at the wrong time of year the bugs can be awful, and there are several boggy stream crossings. At the end is a poorly maintained NPS hut with bunks and a wood stove, which can be used as a base for further explorations up the valley and around old mine buildings. Return the same way.

was briefly the scene of a bungy-jumping operation, which offered free goes to Alaskans jumping naked. The offer was stopped when it proved too popular, and the Department of Transportation finally closed the operation down.

There's a pleasant, wooded camping spot (donations) at Mile 27, with a couple of picnic tables and an outhouse, and beyond that an excellent example of an old wooden trestle bridge. The tumbledown form of the **Gilahina Bridge** (Mile 29) has tempted many a photographer: it is far from safe, so stay well clear. The only reason to stop before the end of the road is the crafty *Fireweed Mountain Arts*, Mile 56.5 (Ⓣ554-4420), which sells USGS maps, fixes tires, and offers a rental cabin. From here it is just a couple of miles to the road end and the cluster of places to stay on the west of the Kennicott River.

McCarthy, Kennicott, and around

In their heyday Kennicott and McCarthy perfectly complemented each other, with McCarthy the licentious safety valve for the stiff-collared company town up the hill. Kennicott had all the amenities – hospital with dental office, grade school, recreation hall, ballpark, skating rink, and even a dairy – but McCarthy had the restaurants, pool halls, hotels, saloons, and brothels. The arrangement suited everyone: labor was short in the district, and the company knew that few disgruntled workers quitting Kennecott would make it past McCarthy with their pockets full and so would soon return to work. Kennicott was always "dry," but even during prohibition McCarthy flaunted the Feds' rules and stills were commonplace.

In some respects the distinction remains; **MCCARTHY** is still very much the social center of the district; the restaurants, and especially the bar, always seem packed with the residents of this scattered hamlet. All around, ancient log cabins, frame houses pieced together from whatever was available, and assorted rusting hulks give the town a kind of junkyard beauty. Cars can only get across the Kennicott River in the frozen depths of winter, so traffic is negligible, and you can spend a couple of happy hours just ambling about, at some point directing yourself to the original CR&NW depot now transformed into the **McCarthy–Kennicott Historical Museum** (late May to early Sept daily 11am–6pm; free), with a model of boomtown McCarthy and material on life in the two towns, mining, and the coming of the railroad. While you're there, pick up the *McCarthy Self-guided Tour* brochure ($1) and use it to identify some of the town's more interesting buildings. McCarthy is expertly characterized in a poignant chapter in Pete McCarthy's book *The Road to McCarthy* (Hodder & Stoughton), essential reading for an advance flavor of the place.

At some point, almost everyone spends at least half a day five miles up the main road at **KENNICOTT**, reached by shuttle bus along the road once traced by train tracks or on foot along the parallel Old Wagon Road. Kennecott's distinctive industrial buildings – all red with white trim – hug the mountainside on the moraine-strewn flanks of the Kennicott Glacier, and now all fall under the auspices of the **Kennecott National Historic Landmark**. Back in the 1920s when three hundred people worked here, the glacier was 500ft higher and completely obscured Fireweed Mountain across the valley, but the diminished hunk of ice now reveals magnificent mountain views as you hike up the tracks through town.

Since it took over in 1998, the National Park Service has been replacing roofs and generally stabilizing the rotting structures, but the work is far from complete and most of the buildings are off-limits. The old train depot is being turned into a new **visitor center** (late May to early Sept daily 9am–6pm), and the old Recreation Hall will hold educational programs and concerts, but to

Kennicott or Kennecott?

Although explorer Robert Kennicott, part of the Abercrombie expedition in the 1860s, never came up this valley, he lent his name to the glacier that creaks off Mount Blackburn and the river it spawns. A slip of the quill, however, forever destined the mines and the mining company to the name Kennecott. Although the train station was known as Kennicott, the former post office was Kennecott, and the National Park Service has followed suit, naming the whole area Kennecott National Historic Landmark. In practice, both names are widely used, but we've stuck with Kennicott for everything except the company, the mill, and the mines.

really get inside the mill buildings you need to take one of the **excellent tours** (see "Kennecott Tours," opposite). Outside, you can still wander the hillside paths looking for that photogenic angle of the fourteen-story ore mill, the power plant, workers' bunkhouses, and numerous dilapidated cabins.

Arrival and getting around

Almost at the end of the McCarthy Road (Mile 58.8) a national park **information board** offers some local background, but you might as well continue three-quarters of a mile to the Road End, a bleak and unsightly gravel parking lot ($8 a day). From there visitors must cross the Kennicott River using a footbridge and proceed to McCarthy on foot: it is only half a mile to McCarthy, and a further four and a half miles to Kennicott. If you don't fancy the short walk into town, you may strike it lucky and find one of the **shuttle buses** ready to transport you to either town. A couple of companies ply the route between McCarthy and Kennicott ($5 each way), together providing around one bus an hour throughout the day. The most convenient bus stop is the museum. Anyone with reservations in Kennicott can expect to be picked up from the bridge end: just use the free phone by the bridge.

One of the best ways to make the most of your time here is to **rent a bike** from *Glacier View Campground* ($25 a day, see opposite), though more leisurely explorations can be conducted on **horseback** or on a **wagon ride**. The Pilgrim family (see box, p.418) drive their horse-drawn wagon along the old wagon road between McCarthy and Kennicott, charging around $35 per person; they will also take you for a ten- to fifteen-minute jaunt around McCarthy for $10–15 or horseback riding from $35 an hour. You'll see them around town and may find them waiting by the footbridge as you enter McCarthy.

Accommodation

McCarthy and Kennicott are both sufficiently remote to keep prices high. Following their roots, Kennicott goes for the more refined approach, while McCarthy offers something altogether more rustic (though not lacking in comfort). If you've got the cash and don't mind lugging your gear over the footbridge, you'll want to stay in McCarthy or Kennicott, but there is a growing cluster of accommodation west of the Kennicott River, along the final mile of the McCarthy Road. All accommodation is marked on the map on p.411.

Those on a tight budget will want to **camp**, either at the *Glacier View Campground* or at a new Park Service walk-in campground that is planned for McCarthy. It should be located off the Old Wagon Road between McCarthy and Kennicott, near the base of the Kennicott Glacier and close to the airstrip. Expect a cooking pavilion, bear-proof food storage, vault toilets and water, and a small fee. Informal camping exists beside the Root Glacier Trail a mile or so from the Kennecott Mill Building.

West of the Kennicott River

Fireweed Mountain Arts Mile 56.5 ⓣ554-4420, ⓔfireweedmtnarts@starband.net. A small cabin a short walk into the woods with a wood stove, propane cooking, and a light breakfast all for $50 a couple. Bring your sleeping bag. ❶

Glacier View Campground Mile 59 ⓣ554-4490, ⓔglacierview@gci.net. Commercial campground on a gravel lot with space for tents ($12) and dry camping for RVs ($12). Showers ($5) are open to all, and there is mountain-bike rental for $25 a day. June to mid-Sept.

Kennicott River Lodge and Hostel Mile 59.4 ⓣ554-4441, ⓦwww.ptialaska.net/~grosswlr. A modern log-built house with large common kitchen, a lounge with good mountain views, and a series of comfortable cabins, some fitted with four bunks and a sleeping loft for two and charged at $28 per bed; bring a sleeping bag (or rent for $2). Showers are free to guests and $10 for non-guests. Cabins ❹, bunks ❶

Swift Creek Cabins Mile 57 ⓣ554-1234, ⓦwww.swiftcreekalaska.com. A couple of cabins in the woods, sited on a bluff with great views, and each equipped with a small kitchen and relaxing porch. There's an outhouse and a semi-outdoor shower, plus a barbecue grill. ❹

West McCarthy Wayside Park Mile 59.6, right at the end of the road ⓣ746-0606, ⓔsyren@mtaonline.net. Essentially a parking lot with camping in the woods and beside the glacier moraine. Tent or RV $15. A water supply is planned, but it is best to bring your own.

WSEN B&B Mile 58.6 ⓣ554-4454, ⓦwww.mccarthy-kennicott.com. Appealing B&B a couple of miles down a side road from the Road End, with two cozy cabins and a caravan, plus a common bathhouse with flush toilet and shower. One cabin and the caravan have full kitchens, and a slightly cheaper cabin has only electricity and a coffeepot (but no running water). All have breakfast goodies supplied. ❸

McCarthy

Hillbilly Heaven at the Motherlode Lodge ⓣ554-4473. An unusual opportunity to spend time out in the backcountry, but still with some of the comforts of home. Located at the abandoned Motherlode copper mine thirteen miles northeast of McCarthy, accommodation is either in the lodge or in one of several fairly rustic but comfortable guest cabins. The real attraction is to stay with the Pilgrim family (see box, p.418), who seem like throwbacks to a gentler time that never really existed. Explore a bit of the old mine, ride horses, hike the mountains, or just relax with the family, who will try to organize whatever you want to do. You could ride in, though most fly (around $80 round-trip), and family-style meals are extra. ❹

Lancaster's Backpacking Hotel ⓣ554-4402, ⓦwww.mccarthylodge.com. The budget arm of *Ma Johnson's*, this recent conversion of a 1920s building offers simple shared-bath rooms fitted with bunks and going for $40 for one, $60 for two. Showers are an extra $6. ❶

Ma Johnson's Hotel ⓣ554-4402, ⓦwww.mccarthylodge.com. The place to stay in McCarthy, built in 1923 and evoking an appropriate atmosphere with small, but pleasant, shared-bath rooms, and a full breakfast over the road at *McCarthy Lodge*. ❻

Kennicott

Historic Kennicott B&B 14 Silk Stocking Row ⓣ554-4469. Comfortable B&B in a former mine manager's house. ❺

Kennicott Glacier Lodge ⓣ554-4477 or 1-800/582-5128, ⓦwww.kennicottlodge.com. Easily the largest hotel around, offering comfortable, modern shared-facility rooms, the best of which have balconies and glacier views. Rooms with private bath are planned for 2004, and rates include a transfer from McCarthy and a Kennicott town tour. Check the website for good-value multinight vacation packages including meals. Private bath ❽, shared bath ❼

Kennecott Tours

If you have the slightest interest in Alaska's industrial heritage, be sure to join one of the two-hour **Kennecott Tours** (late May to early Sept; $25) run by St Elias Alpine Guides (ⓣ554-4445 or 1-888/933-5427, ⓦwww.steliasguides.com). This is the only way you can get into any of the major buildings. You'll be guided through the nicely preserved post office, the general store with its empty shelves which were still fully stocked until plundered in the 1970s, and the powerhouse which powered the mill and provided underground steam heating to prevent the town's walkways from freezing up. A highlight of the tour is catching all fourteen floors of the mill itself, including the steps along the high-grade ore chute on which John Denver sang during a

The Pilgrims, the Feds, and the Motherlode

In Alaska there's a constant tension between the pro-development majority, the environmental preservationists, and the hermit set that wants to live simple lives in the backwoods. The state is full of people who have come from elsewhere for the wide open spaces and heaps of opportunity. For some it is the opportunity to savor one of the world's largest virtually untouched landscapes; for others it is the opportunity to exploit its resources unfettered by rules and regulations.

The "smaller government" mantra rings loud here, though some sort of local authority is usually encouraged if it means people are going to get schools and emergency services. State government is grudgingly accepted as a necessary evil, and one that provides for its people from oil revenues. But the federal government is always perceived as the heavy: it taxes your income, meddles in your life, and "locks up" land in national parks and preserves.

Nowhere does the conflict between such divergent views come into sharper focus than McCarthy, which has traditionally attracted people who don't want much to do with authority. Even so, there is heated debate about the state's role in development. Should the state pave the McCarthy Road? It would make access easier for residents but also encourage more tourists. Should vehicular access to the town from the road end be improved? The sort of tourists who make it to McCarthy generally appreciate the need to walk into town, but some residents want to get their four-wheelers across the footbridge (which the authorities continually try to prevent), and others want a proper road bridge.

The community has lived with these sorts of arguments for decades, and since 1980 it has also had to cope with being in the heart of the federally administered Wrangell–St Elias National Park. That has only been a problem since 1998, when the National Park Service purchased most of the Kennecott Mill and associated buildings and began to lay a heavier hand on its management of the area.

And then, in 2002, came the **Pilgrim family**, a bluegrass-playing, highly devout, hillbilly Christian family with sixteen kids – with names such as Bethlehem, Lamb, Hosanna, and Psalm – who moved onto private land within the national park (an inholding) thirteen miles northeast of McCarthy, thereby virtually doubling the region's year-round population. To get from McCarthy to their home beside the old Motherlode Mine they must travel along an old miners' route through the national park, where the use of motorized transport is banned. Since the Pilgrims favor horse travel that's fine, but when they decided to drive a bulldozer down the old track to improve access to their home the Park Service put its foot down. Pilgrim supporters argue that an arcane, century-old state law makes the miners' route a legal road and therefore exempt from park regulations, but even if that is the case, clearing it by bulldozer seems to be illegal. Some conservation groups sided with the Park Service, not wanting this to set a precedent for inholdings across the state.

To protect its patch, the Park Service began surveying the route of the newly (re)formed road and assessing whether land clearance up at the Motherlode property has strayed into the national park itself. Despite taking issue with local park rangers on the issue, the Pilgrim family can't bury their good nature and have been helping haul survey equipment and providing lunch. No matter what the legal rights and wrongs of the situation, it is hard to begrudge them the right to drive their horse and trap to their home.

1970s TV special – droll guides have dubbed the stairs the "John Denver Memorial Staircase."

Glacier hiking and ice climbing

From their office in Kennicott, St Elias Alpine Guides also run a highly professional mountain-guide service that runs unroped **glacier hikes** (half-day

$50), hikes up to Bonanza, Jumbo, and Erie mines ($95 a day), **ice climbing** ($100 a day), and customized **backcountry expeditions** ($125 a day). Serious commitment is required for their longer adventures: ten days hiking the Chitistone Canyon ($2000) with one guide to two customers, or a fourteen-day attempt on an unclimbed peak in the Wrangell Mountains ($3800–5300 depending on numbers). There's a slightly more intimate and personal feel to the trips run by Kennicott Wilderness Guides (Ⓣ554-4444 or 1-800/664-4537, Ⓦwww.kennicottguides.com), which also works out of an office in Kennicott and offers a more limited range of trips, from the half-day glacier trek ($50) to the full-day ice climbing ($100).

Flightseeing

Several companies operate flightseeing trips from McCarthy's airport, from where fabulous scenery is visible straight away. It only gets better with wave upon wave of snowy peaks harboring vast ice fields. For spectacle alone, flights over Wrangell–St Elias match those around Denali from Talkeetna, and may just surpass them. For personal service, a relaxed atmosphere, and a very knowledgeable pilot, fly with McCarthy-based McCarthy Air (Ⓣ554-4440 or 1-888/989-9891, Ⓦwww.mccarthyair.com), which runs a thirty-minute taster ($60), although you should really fork out for an hour ($100), which gives you a pretty good look around Mount Blackburn, glaciers, waterfalls, and old mine sites. To also see Canada's Mount Logan and the Bagley Icefield, you'll need the full ninety minutes ($140).

Also based in McCarthy, Wrangell Mountain Air (Ⓣ554-4411 or 1-800/478-1160, Ⓦwww.wrangellmountainair.com), quotes good prices starting with the underpowered "Glacier Tour" (35min; $60), and going up to the much more satisfying "Backcountry Tour" (50min; $85) and the mammoth "Grand Tour" (90min; $140) over the Bagley Icefield and right around the Wrangell Mountains. Both companies will also drop you off for hikes in the vast backcountry (see box overleaf) and advise an itinerary to suit.

Rafting

If the chilly glacial waters don't put you off, go rafting with Copper Oar, at the Road End parking lot (Ⓣ554-4453 or 1-800/523-4453, Ⓦwww.copperoar.com), which runs the Nizina Canyon trip (daily; 5–8hr; $245–265 depending on numbers), with five miles on a Class II–III stretch of the Kennicott River followed by the spectacular scenery of the Nizina Canyon and a return scenic flight. For more of a wilderness experience (with small portions of whitewater), you'll need to book ahead on trips like Chitina to Cordova (6 days; $1890) and the Source to the Sea Expedition (15 days; $3900).

St Elias Guides (see above) also does rafting trips offering Nizina Canyon (1 day; $245), the relatively gentle Chitina River (3 days; $1200), and the mammoth trip down to the mouth of the Copper River (11 days; $2800–3600 depending on numbers).

Eating and drinking

Where you eat will largely be dictated by where you are staying, as the range of places is fairly limited – though the standard is surprisingly high. In Kennicott the restaurant at the *Kennicott Glacier Lodge* is your only option, but down the hill the choice is wider and improving all the time.

Glacier View Campground Barbecue stand serving burgers ($8), hot dogs, and bratwurst, plus rib or pork chop specials on holidays like July 4 and Labor Day.

Kennicott Glacier Lodge Kennicott Ⓣ554-4477. The only place to eat in Kennicott, serving breakfast ($8–12), lunch, snacks throughout the day, and a table d'hôte evening meal for $25–30. The restaurant is not licensed. Reserve for dinner.

McCarthy Lodge McCarthy ☎554-4477. Casual but excellent restaurant where gourmet concoctions are served throughout the day in a dining room festooned with mining paraphernalia. Soups and sandwiches are the norm for lunch (under $10), but they turn it on for their fixed-price three-course evening meals ($28). The selection is limited and changes nightly, but it is always good. The lodge also has a lively bar, open year-round, with occasional bands in summer.

The Potato McCarthy. Essentially a takeout burger joint, but everything is cooked fresh each morning, and they do a good espresso. Opt for the popular Potatohead burrito or the Spudnik.

Tailor-Made Pizza McCarthy. Serves superb gourmet concoctions (starting around $15) on a mosquito-netted deck or around a wood-burning stove.

The Nabesna Road

Despite the mind-boggling immensity of the Wrangell–St Elias National Park, the only road access into the park aside from the McCarthy Road is the 42-mile-long **Nabesna Road**. This threads its way east between the Mentasta and

Hikes around Kennicott and into the backcountry

Wonderful though it may be to simply wander around McCarthy and Kennicott, **hiking** is where the area truly comes to life. The views are breathtaking, especially if you choose, as many do, to take a short flight into the wilderness and begin hiking from there. Since there aren't any maintained trails, some mental preparation is required: read our comments in the Denali account (p.394). No backcountry permits are required, but you should complete an itinerary at a park office and leave it with someone trustworthy. No one will come looking for you unless someone requests a search – discussing emergency contingencies with your pilot is essential. You'll almost certainly be camping in the wilderness, though the Park Service people at the park headquarters will help you locate the eight free first-come, first-served fly-in **cabins** in this part of the park. Below, we've listed a couple of local trails – one easy, one less so – along with one backcountry suggestion, though there are dozens of others. Again, ask your pilot for ideas.

Root Glacier Trail (4–8 miles round-trip; 2–4hr; 200ft ascent). From Kennicott the track leads north through the main mill buildings and out onto the lateral moraine, giving excellent views of the surrounding mountains and the gleaming-white Kennicott Glacier, which is accessible in places: don't stray far. There are some marginal **campgrounds** up here with an outhouse, bear-resistant food lockers, and untreated water from Jumbo Stream. Eventually, the trail turns east to the Stairway Icefall and the remains of the Erie Mine bunkhouse.

Bonanza Mine (13–16 miles round-trip; 4–7hr; 3500ft ascent). A wonderful hike initially following a 4WD road and soon rising high above Kennicott as you approach the substantial ruins of Bonanza Mine. The road to the tree line is only passable by the fittest and most determined **mountain bikers**, but if you're motivated to ride up there it is a superb, and fast, ride down (though keep an eye out for ascending hikers). Start by following the Root Glacier Trail and turn uphill as you leave the last of the houses, then continue past the end of the road (roughly halfway) on a rough track past a fretwork of gantries and wooden pylons perched on rocky bluffs still carrying cables strung as they were when everyone left town. **Carry water**, especially if you are planning to camp out up there.

Goat Trail (25 miles one-way; 3–8 days; 3000ft net descent). The park's most popular fly-in multiday hike, which follows the Chisana prospectors' route through the narrow Chitistone Canyon, twenty miles east of McCarthy, and past the 400-foot Chitistone Falls, the highest continuously flowing falls in Alaska. It is a strenuous venture with several deep river crossings between the airstrips at each end. Expect to pay $200 for drop-off and pickup.

Wrangell mountains into the northwestern corner of the park, ending at Nabesna, a privately owned (and therefore off-limits) former gold mine which was worked from 1923 to 1942.

The Nabesna region is a far less developed corner of the park than the area around McCarthy, and there is considerable scenic pleasure in simply driving the road, camping out a night or two, and maybe taking off on some remote hikes. In many ways **hiking** here is more accessible than from McCarthy, where you really need to fly in. The trouble is, most routes are also used by off-road vehicles and can be boggy underfoot: ask at the visitor center (see p.413) for recommendations.

The road is mostly gravel, but it is generally in better condition than the McCarthy Road. Glacial stream crossings at miles 29.4, 31.2, and 35.5, sometimes make the road impassable to ordinary vehicles in hot weather and after heavy rain.

Slana and along the Nabesna Road

The Nabesna Road runs east from the Tok Cutoff at tiny **SLANA** (Mile 60), little more than a post office and the **Nabesna District Visitor Center** (late May to early Sept daily 8am–6pm; early Sept to late May Mon–Fri 8am–4.30pm; ⓣ822-5238), the place to call for advice on road conditions, park-related information, and the free *Nabesna Road Guide*. There's comfortable B&B accommodation at *Hart D Ranch*, Mile 0.7 Nabesna Rd (ⓣ822-3970, ⓦwww.hartd.com; ❹), and at *Nabesna House*, Mile 0.8 (ⓣ822-4284, ⓦwww nabesnahouse.com; ❷), but it is more entertaining staying at the lovely, rustic *Huck Hobbit's Homestead Retreat & Campground* (ⓣ822-3196; cabins $20 per person, camping $5 per person), which has cozy log cabins with wood stoves, campsites each with picnic table and fire ring, canoes for rent ($35 a day), and bargain meals. It is four miles east of Slana, then up a four-mile side road: the last mile can only be negotiated on foot or by ATV, so be sure to call ahead.

Beyond the end of the paved road, four miles from Slana, there are very few places offering any sort of facilities. Primitive **campgrounds** at *Twin Lakes*, Mile 27.8, and *Jack Creek*, Mile 35.3, have outhouses and some sort of water supply, but come equipped and you can pitch pretty much anywhere you can find some flat ground. One especially scenic spot is at Mile 16.6 with views across a lake to Mount Sanford and dozens of its neighbors.

At Mile 24.7 you cross the watershed divide from the headwaters of the Copper River (which flows into the North Pacific) to the headwaters of rivers flowing into the Yukon and the Bering Sea. Locals and the occasional visitor converge on *Sportsman's Paradise Lodge*, Mile 29 (ⓣ822-7313, ⓔdfrederick@starband.net; ❷), more for the convivial bar than the basic cabin accommodation or the very limited food. You can press on to the end of the maintained road where there's a rough airstrip and the rustic *Devil's Mountain Lodge*, but you are still four miles from the Nabesna Mine site itself.

The Glenn Highway to Glennallen

The **Glenn Highway** – and its logical and geographical continuation, the **Tok Cutoff** (see p.427) – is the shortest road route from Anchorage to the Lower 48, meeting the Alaska Highway at Tok, 328 miles to the northeast. The highway gets its name from Captain Edwin Glenn, who explored the area prior to

World War II when an old system of tracks was upgraded to connect Anchorage to the Alaska Highway, then under construction.

The entire road runs through sparsely populated country that, even on good asphalt, still feels very remote as you climb from one watershed to another over a series of low passes. Initially, you ascend beside the Matanuska River, which drains west to Cook Inlet, but you eventually end up beside the Tazlina Valley, which spills down the Copper River into Prince William Sound. There's some very fine scenery, too, with the Talkeetna, Alaska, and Chugach ranges soaring up on either side and immense glaciers poking out of the mountains.

The presence of a fast highway seems to encourage people to drive straight through in a few hours, and while there are few specific attractions there is a fair bit to see, with some perseverance. Wildlife may be more elusive than in Denali, but the animals are out there: the Dall sheep usually far up the roadside crags, bears in the woods, moose in and around the small lakes, and caribou roaming the glacial river bars.

Sutton, Chickaloon, and the Matanuska Glacier

Leaving Anchorage the Glenn Highway runs past Eagle River and Eklutna (see p.351) and into Palmer in the Matanuska Valley (see p.353) before swinging east. Pulling out of Palmer (Mile 42) on the Glenn Highway you first pass the junction with Fishhook–Willow Road (for Hatcher Pass and Independence Mine; Mile 49.5) and continue a dozen miles to **SUTTON**, a small community which flourished in the 1920s around a rail siding from the days when this was coal country. The only reason to pause is the **Alpine Historical Park**, Mile 61.5 (mid-May to mid-Sept daily 9am–7pm; donation appreciated), a selection of relocated buildings on the former site of the Sutton Coal Washery, including the Chickaloon Bunkhouse and a coal museum in the old Sutton post office with material on the construction of the Glenn Highway and the local Athabascans.

From Sutton the highway winds along the Matanuska Valley, gradually climbing as you penetrate deeper into the mountains that tower on both sides. After fifteen miles a wide spot in the road with a post office, small store, and gas station constitutes **CHICKALOON** (Mile 76.5), home to Nova (Ⓣ1-800/746-5753, Ⓦwww.novalaska.com), which runs the most popular **rafting** trip in Alaska – the four-hour Class III–IV **Lion Head** (June–Aug 9am & 2pm; $75 & $80 respectively) along the upper reaches of the Matanuska River, for which there is a minimum age of 12. Highly scenic and with a stop to explore the foot of the Matanuska Glacier, it is a wonderful trip made all the better by taking the evening run (mid-June to mid-July 7pm; $95) when the day's meltwater is at its peak – they even stop for a mid-trip burger. Downstream from Chickaloon township the river relents to Class II, run on the gentle family-oriented Matanuska trip (June–Aug; 2hr 30min; $70, kids aged 5–11 $35). Across the road from the Nova office sits *King Mountain Lodge* (Ⓣ745-4280), which has been serving down-home Alaskan meals for over fifty years, has a bar full of wise-cracking signs, and a small stage for weekend bands. You can camp at the adjacent *King Mountain State Recreation Site* ($10; pump water) among the white spruce, some sites with river and King Mountain views.

The scenery just keeps getting better further up the valley and is made more inviting by the presence of the diminutive **Lower Bonnie Lake**, a day-use area two miles off the highway at Mile 83.2, which has good grayling fishing throughout the summer.

Around Mile 100 you catch your first glimpse of the **Matanuska Glacier**, a 24-mile-long tongue of ice poking out of the Chugach Mountains. During the last ice age it stretched as far as Palmer, and though it has been chipped back considerably, it's still almost four miles wide at its terminus. Close contact can only be achieved by parting with $10 to drive to within 300yd of the foot of the glacier through *Glacier Park Campground*, Mile 102 (ⓣ745-2534 or 1-800/253-4480; mid-May to mid-Oct). From the end of the road, you can hike onto the glacier and visit the office of MICA Guides (ⓣ1-800/956-6422, ⓦwww.micaguides.com), which runs guided **glacier treks** (1hr 30min for $30, minimum 4; 3hr for $60, minimum 2) and beginner **ice-climbing** trips (6hr for $120, minimum 2). There's dry camping nearby for $10 per site.

More distant, but still impressive, views of the glacier can be had from the short hiking trails that thread along a bluff from *Matanuska Glacier State Recreation Site*, Mile 101.1 ($15 per vehicle; pump water), or from the magnificent picture windows at the hunting-lodge-style *Long Rifle Lodge*, Mile 102.2 (ⓣ745-5151 or 1-800/770-5151; ❸). They serve excellent homemade meals and have functional but pleasant rooms.

Tahetna Pass to Lake Louise

Excellent views of the Matanuska Glacier continue as you climb steadily east past Lion Head, a small mountain right in the middle of the valley named for its appearance from the east. Beyond Lion Head the valley opens out into country that's great for hiking or just sitting back with binoculars spotting wildlife. There are a couple of good **places to stay** in these parts. The lovely *Tundra Rose B&B*, Mile 109.5 (ⓣ745-5865 or 1-800/315-5865, ⓦwww.alaska.net/~tundrose/; suite ❺, cottage ❹), with its fabulous glacier views, is based around a log-built home with adjacent self-catering cottage and two-bedroom suite. Just below a hill renowned for its population of Dall sheep stands *Sheep Mountain Lodge*, Mile 113.5 (ⓣ745-5121 or 1-877/645-5121, ⓦwww.sheepmountain.com; cabins ❻, bunkhouse ❶), with ten spacious, fully fixtured cabins, plus a bunkhouse rented at $15 per person or for groups ($60 for the first 4 people and $5 for each extra up to a total of 10). There's also a hot tub and sauna (free to cabin guests, bunkhouse users $10) and a modestly priced **restaurant** that is a substantial cut above the average roadside diner, serving classy homemade meals and drinks from a well-stocked bar.

Glance back for a view of Lion Head, then press on past the **Squaw Creek** viewpoint and trailhead (Mile 118.4) to the 3000-foot **Tahetna Pass** at Mile 121, the site of a couple of lodges and a gas station, and a good spot to look back at **Gunsight Mountain**, visible for miles approaching from the east, and distinguished by the missing-tooth serration on its summit ridgeline. The road passes the 1937 *Eureka Roadhouse*, the oldest on this highway, to the 3321-foot Eureka Summit (Mile 129), the highest point on the Glenn Highway. Views now expand south to the ice-capped Chugach Mountains and north across flatter country pocked by myriad small lakes and threaded by small creeks. The road stays high for a time, until you reach the Little Nelchina River and the small, waterside *Little Nelchina River Campground*, Mile 137.7 (free; river water).

Lake Louise

At Mile 159.8 a scenic gravel road spurs nineteen miles north to the shores of **LAKE LOUISE**, a popular spot with vacationing Alaskans, chiefly for chilly swimming and lake trout fishing, the latter best done in spring and early summer. Campers can stay right by the lake at the *Lake Louise State Recreation Area*, Mile 17 ($10; pump water), the less hardy at *The Point Lodge*, Mile 17 (ⓣ822-

5566 or 1-800/808-2018, ⓦthepointlodge.com; ⑤), which has its own family-style restaurant and a bar, and caters for those wanting to fish, boat, hike, and go flightseeing.

Glennallen and the central highways

Glennallen is effectively the hub of the central highway system, from which the major roads spoke out to just about everywhere of interest, including Wrangell–St Elias National Park to the southeast. Coming from Anchorage you arrive on the Glenn Highway, which continues to Tok as the Tok Cutoff, a road built in the early 1940s to connect the Alaska Highway to the rest of the Interior. Crossing the Glenn Highway is the Richardson, the original Interior road from Valdez, on the coast, to the heart of the state at Fairbanks.

Glennallen

GLENNALLEN, 145 miles east of Palmer (Glenn Hwy, Mile 187), is far enough away from everywhere else that almost everyone stops here, if only for gas and a bite to eat. Apart from wonderful views of mounts Sanford (16,237ft), Drum (12,010ft), Wrangell (14,163ft), and Blackburn (16,390ft) to the east, there's little reason to stay, though the town, being at the hub of the Interior highway system, has adequate lodging for long-haul drivers. Those needing transport into the Wrangell–St Elias National Park may also find themselves stranded here for the night. The town straggles along the highway for a couple of miles east of the intersection of the Glenn and Richardson highways at **Glennallen Junction**, where you'll find the Copper River Valley **visitor center** (summer daily 8am–7pm; ⓣ822-5555, ⓦwww.traveltoalaska.com).

Bus travelers using Alaska Direct buses will be dropped in Glennallen outside the *Caribou Hotel* (see below); Alaska Trails passengers are dropped at Glennallen Junction and may have to walk or thumb into Glennallen.

For **buses into the Wrangell–St Elias National Park** along the McCarthy Road, contact Backcountry Connections (see p.412), which picks up in Glennallen and around the region. Alternatively, you can **rent a vehicle** to drive the McCarthy Road from Northwind Rentals at *Carol's B&B* (see below) for around $80 a day.

Crack-of-dawn departures mean that those without their own vehicles will probably have to spend the night here **camping**, either at the *Northern Nights Campground and RV Park*, Mile 188.2, close to the visitor center (ⓣ822-3199, ⓔnnites@yahoo.com; tent $12, full hookup $20), or just dossing down in any quiet spot you can find. The *Dry Creek State Recreation Site*, Mile 118, three miles north of Glennallen Junction ($10 per vehicle; pump water), is better-suited to drivers and comes with some quiet walk-in tent sites but lots of mosquitoes.

For a roof over your head you've the choice of **cabins and rooms** at *Brown Bear Rhodehouse*, three miles west along Glenn Highway at Mile 183.6 (ⓣ822-3663; rooms ④, cabins ③), smarter rooms at the *Caribou Hotel*, Mile 186.6 (ⓣ822-3302 or 1-800/478-3302 in Alaska, ⓔchotel@alaska.net; ⑥), or a B&B such as *Carol's*, Birch Road at Mile 186.9 (ⓣ822-3594, ⓔneeley@alaska.net; ④), which has shared-bath rooms. **Meals** are no great shakes in Glennallen, but there are summertime espresso stalls beside the highway. You can fill your stomach adequately on diner meals at the *Caribou Café*, part of the hotel complex, and the *Hitchin' Post*, Mile 187.3 (ⓣ822-3338), which is noted for its $4 break-

△ Gilahina trestle bridge, McCarthy Road

fast specials, but is otherwise less good. Further afield there is better dining at Gulkana and at Copper Center (below).

If you've got to get a few things sorted, you'll find everything you need along the highway: a **BLM office** (Mon–Fri 8am–4.30pm; ⓣ822-3217) at Mile 186.4; the **library** (Mile 186); the **pharmacy** and 24hr emergency clinic of Cross Road Medical Center (ⓣ822-3203) at Mile 186.5; the **post office** (Mile 186.9); a **bank** (Mile 187); and a **laundry** plus **groceries** (Mile 187.5).

South of Glennallen: The Richardson Highway

South of Glennallen, the Richardson Highway (see box, opposite) runs 120 miles to Valdez on the shores of Prince William Sound (see p.302). Much of it crosses open country studded with permafrost-stunted spruce, often with stupendous views east to the snow-shrouded Wrangell Mountains. It is a good year-round paved road, occasionally dotted with roadhouses, some with cabins, plus primitive RV and campsites, food, and usually fuel. That said, it is best to fill the tank and stock up with food, if you're planning to make use of some lovely **campgrounds** along the way.

This is also the primary access route for the Wrangell–St Elias National Park (our account starts on p.408), which maintains its headquarters **visitor center** at Mile 106.8 (see p.411). Stop for a great view of the mountains and a look at the film even if you're not headed into the park.

Copper Center

Briefly divert off the Richardson Highway at Mile 106 along the Old Richardson Highway to visit the Athabascan hamlet of **COPPER CENTER**, which boomed in 1898 when three hundred stampeders who made it over the Valdez and Klutina glaciers stopped here at the ferry crossing for the Copper River. They came to recuperate, but there was little comfort through the harsh winter and many died, their headstones still evident in the **Stampeders Cemetery** in town. The heart of town beats around the *Copper Center Lodge*, Mile 101 (ⓣ822-3245, ⓦwww.coppercenterlodge.com; ❺; mid-May to mid-Sept), an authentic descendant of the original roadhouse with smallish, fairly ordinary rooms let on a bed-and-breakfast basis, plus there's a good restaurant. Two log bunkhouses formerly part of the lodge are now operated as the **George Ashby Memorial Museum** (June–Aug Mon–Sat 1–5pm; donations appreciated), packed to the rafters with memorabilia from the stampede and the copper years along with Russian icons and Athabascan basketwork.

Through the Chugach Mountains

The Wrangell-St Elias region has long been ignored by the mainstream tourist industry, but that all changed in 2002 when Princess Cruises opened the *Copper River Princess Wilderness Lodge*, Mile 102 Richardson Hwy (ⓣ822-4000 or 1-800/426-0500, ⓦwww.princessalaskalodges.com; ❽; mid-May to mid-Sept), a large hotel high on a bluff. Even if you're not staying, call in for lunch or a drink and soak up the fabulous mountain views from the lounge.

Twenty miles south of the lodge (Mile 83), McCarthy-bound drivers turn east along the Edgerton Highway (see p.412), which leads to the McCarthy Road, while those continuing south towards Valdez pass the forest-girt *Squirrel Creek State Recreation Site*, Mile 80.3 ($10; pump water), with some nice waterside sites. Although the pipeline runs parallel to the road for much of the way,

Thompson Pass, Keystone Canyon, and the run into Valdez are covered on p.302.

it is most evident fifteen miles on around **Pump Station No. 12**, Mile 64.7, which forces the oil over the Chugach Mountains ahead.

As you start to climb up towards **Thompson Pass**, you'll pass a couple of handy roadhouses: *Tiekel River Lodge*, Mile 56 (Ⓣ822-3259; cabins ❶, with private bath ❹; March–Oct), which has dry RV and tent camping ($10) plus cabins, and *Tsaina Lodge*, Mile 34.7 (Ⓣ835-3500, Ⓦwww.alaska.net/~tsaina/; cabins ❼; March to early Sept), set amid majestic sawtooth ridges and offering a restaurant, bar, cabins, and a bunkhouse.

Northeast of Glennallen: the Tok Cutoff

A single road runs fourteen miles north from Glennallen to **Gakona Junction**, where you can continue straight on along the Richardson Highway bound for Delta Junction (see p.429) or turn right to travel along a section of the Glenn Highway known as the **Tok Cutoff**. The latter route runs along the Copper River, then sneaks over a low pass in the Mentasta Mountains into the spruce forests around Tok, 125 miles away. There's not a lot to stop for along the way, and you can do the run in a little over two hours, though you may consider exploring the **Nabesna Road** into the northern reaches of the Wrangell–St Elias National Park (see p.420).

Like all such Alaskan roads, it is thinly peopled, with only the occasional roadhouse and gas station. The busiest section of the highway is the first five miles, where you'll pass through **GAKONA**, centered on the *Gakona Lodge*, Mile 2 Tok Cutoff, a 1929 roadhouse, on the site of a 1905 ranch, that still plays the role, now with a gas station, natural food store, and the *Carriage House* restaurant next to the Gakona River. It is a mile on to River Wrangellers (Ⓣ822-3967 or 1-888/822-3967, Ⓦwww.alaskariverwrangellers.com), which operates **rafting trips**, pretty much to order, on at least half a dozen rivers in the Wrangell Mountains and Copper River Valley, such as the full-day Class III–IV

The Richardson Highway

The **Richardson Highway** is the oldest road in the Interior, yet in its full 368-mile journey from Valdez to Fairbanks it never passes through anything more than a small town. Its original construction was prompted by the abominable suffering of those who tried the Valdez Glacier route to the Yukon goldfields in the winter of 1898 (see p.526). The following year, Congress approved funds for the US Army to build a military road linking Fort Liscum in Valdez with Fort Egbert in Eagle, and Captain Abercrombie began surveying the route on April 21. Using sleds, packhorses, and mules in trying conditions made worse by harsh weather and mosquitoes, he soon had the Goat Trail cut through Keystone Canyon, bypassing the Valdez Glacier. In the few short months of summer, 93 miles of wagon road were forged and a further 114 miles were cleared and the streams bridged. The road was completed in 1900, but the gold-rush focus soon shifted to Fairbanks, and so did the main trail. The full journey from Valdez to Fairbanks could take up to two weeks, with travelers spending nights in roadhouses spaced a day's travel apart, which was particularly important during the winter when they had to journey in open carriages (the roads were so rough that closed carriages induced motion sickness) with only wolf robes and a charcoal brazier for warmth. General Wilds Richardson had the road upgraded to a wagon road in 1907, the Alaska Roads Commission improved it for automobile use in the 1920s, and the road was finally paved in 1957.

Tonsina River ($85). If you need to stay here, there's *Gakona RV Park*, Mile 4.2 (Ⓣ822-3550), with tent sites for $12 and full hookup for $22.

A few years ago the roadhouse in the hamlet of **Chistochina**, Mile 33, burnt down and hasn't been rebuilt, so you barely notice the place as you drive by, though there are a couple of B&Bs in the area, if you need to stop.

The **Nabesna Road**, which cuts off at the hamlet of Slana (Mile 60), provides the only distraction on the road north, which passes a couple of **campgrounds**: the scenic streamside *Porcupine Creek State Recreation Site*, Mile 64.2 ($12; pump water), and *Eagle Trail State Recreation Site*, Mile 109.3 ($12; pump water). The latter has a mile-long nature trail and a 2.5-mile hiking trail to an overview of the Tok Valley with evidence of the old Valdez–Eagle Trail and the telegraph line that followed it. There is even scope to hike up Clearwater Creek for around eight hours to get into Dall sheep country. From here it is sixteen miles to the crossroads town of Tok (see p.432).

North of Glennallen: the Richardson Highway

North of Glennallen, the Richardson Highway runs fourteen miles to **Gakona Junction** (see p.427) and continues 137 miles to Delta Junction, initially traveling through open, rolling country peppered with small lakes feeding tiny streams. **Campers** should consider stopping twenty miles north of Gakona Junction at the BLM's large *Sourdough Creek Campground*, Mile 147.5 ($6; pump water), right where the Trans-Alaska Pipeline crosses the Gulkana River, with sites dotted among the sparse black spruce. It comes equipped with a fishing deck, observation platform, and boat ramp where canoeists paddling the Gulkana (see box, p.403) pull out. If you are not kitted out for cooking, you can still stop here and stroll a couple of hundred yards north to eat at the friendly *Sourdough Roadhouse*.

The Richardson then begins to climb into the foothills of the Alaska Range, imperceptibly at first, then more forthright as it rounds the 2641-foot Hogan Hill on the way to Meiers (3363ft), which overlooks *Meier's Lake Roadhouse*, Mile 170 (Ⓣ822-3151), offering gas, groceries, a mediocre restaurant, and boat rental for use on the nearby lake.

At Mile 175 a side road leads a mile and a half down to the extensive, partly lakeshore *Paxson Lake Campground* ($6; pump water), with a dump station, walk-in sites for $3, and a boat launch for the Gulkana River canoe trip to *Sourdough Campground* (see box, p.403).

Ten miles on **PAXSON**, Mile 185, marks the eastern terminus of the Denali Highway (see p.399), but comprises little more than the gas, basic food, and unappealing lodging at the *Paxson Inn & Lodge*. If you are looking for a place to stay, there's *Denali Highway Cabins* (Ⓣ822-5972, Ⓦwww.denalihwy.com; ❺), with some superb modern log cabins, each with private bath, TV, a small deck looking out towards Paxson Mountain, and the sound of the Gulkana River right outside. The owner is an avid birder, ecologist, and guide for Paxson Alpine Tours, which runs three-hour Evening Wildlife Float Trips ($45) in a raft through the Paxson Wildlife Reserve, with the emphasis firmly on spotting nesting waterfowl and eagles, spawning sockeye salmon, moose, and whatever else might turn up.

From midsummer well into September, **red salmon** can be seen spawning right by the highway from a turnout at Mile 190. The road then skirts Summit Lake, which is appropriately named, though with the mass of the Alaska Range stretching to the horizon in both directions you barely realize you are anywhere near a summit. In fact, the 3000-foot **Isabel Pass** lies just ahead with the **Gulkana Glacier** bearing down on it from the northeast. A 1.5-mile access road off Mile 200.4 of the Richardson runs to Fielding Lake, where there's an appealing lakeside **campground** (free; lake water), with a boat ramp heavily used by fishers after lake trout, burbot, and grayling. The highway then follows the Delta River through a gap in the Alaska Range, where red and gray scree slopes cascade down the mountainsides, and continues to **Black Rapids Glacier**, Mile 225.4. It is now a retreating shadow of what it was in the winter of 1936–37 when this "Galloping Glacier" surged three miles, almost overrunning the road: mounds of terminal moraine can be seen half a mile from the highway. A 500-yard hike on the east side of the road leads to Black Rapids Lake.

The Delta Valley now broadens out past another appealing campground, the *Donnelly Creek State Recreation Site*, Mile 238 ($10; pump water), and on to a couple of spectacular viewpoints: at Mile 241.3, where panels explain the genesis of the **Delta buffalo herd** (see below), which can often be seen in the distance across the river; and at Mile 244, where there are stupendous views south to the dominant peaks of the Alaska Range – Deborah, Hess, and Hayes. Four miles on a short gravel road leads to a trailhead for a well-worn but unmarked path leading up the north ridge of the 3910-foot **Donnelly Dome** (1900ft ascent), the alder and willow eventually thinning to reveal a great view of the Delta and Tanana rivers and the Alaska Range. Delta Junction is another eighteen miles on, beyond **Pump Station No. 9**, and through the Fort Greely military base, once a way station for planes taking part in the wartime Lend-Lease program with Russia and now part of the new national missile defense program, which is supposed to be operational by late 2004.

Delta Junction and the road to Fairbanks

DELTA JUNCTION (Alaska Hwy, Mile 1422; Richardson Hwy, Mile 266) proclaims itself to be the end of the Alaska Highway, which starts 1422 miles to the southeast in British Columbia. Technically, this is accurate, as the remaining 98 miles of road to Fairbanks (the Richardson Highway) already existed when the Alaska Highway was completed in 1942. The Delta Junction CVB does a nice line in selling "I completed the Alaska Highway" certificates; however, most people choose to celebrate their endeavors when they get to Fairbanks, a real city and a more fitting end to such an epic trip.

Still, Delta Junction makes a better spot to recuperate than Tok, attractively set with farmland homesteads stretching all the way east to the Clearwater River system. To the south the Granite Mountains rise up majestically, and if you are lucky in spring and fall, the skies can be filled with skeins of migrating geese.

Though close to the old Valdez–Fairbanks Trail, Delta Junction didn't really come into being until the 1920s, when it was known as Buffalo Center, the site chosen for the government's **buffalo importation program**, designed to establish a sporting herd in Alaska five hundred years after the species had died out here. In 1928, 23 Minnesota plains bison were released and immediately developed a taste for the local barley crop. They still occasionally wander onto farmland around harvest time, but since its creation in 1979, they mostly confine themselves to the Bison Range, a 90,000-acre preserve some twenty miles to the south. Today the herd is around five hundred strong and can withstand a winter hunting season during which 15,000 hunters pay $10 just to apply for one of the 100–130 permits.

With the founding of Fort Greely on the outskirts of town during World War II, Delta Junction has long had military influence. This waned in the 1990s with the ending of the Cold War, and Fort Greely looked set to close, though it is now being revived for the new Ground-Based Midcourse Defense system (that's Star Wars II to you and me). **Missile silos** are being built through 2004, making accommodation in the area hard to come by: reserve in advance.

If you are in the vicinity around the last weekend of August, call ahead and check dates for the three-day **Deltana Fair**, a small-town agricultural fair with events such as the Cow Drop, in which a ten-by-ten checkerboard of two-foot squares is laid out and folk lay bets on where a cow will place its mark.

The town and around

Delta Junction lines the three main roads that make up the town, spreading out from the central "Y" and dominated by the visitor center (see below). Behind it sits the **Sullivan Roadhouse** (late May to early Sept Mon–Sat 9am–5pm; free), which was built a few miles from Delta Junction in 1905 on what was then a winter-only shortcut off the Valdez–Fairbanks route. With the improvements made to the Richardson Highway, the shortcut became little used and the roadhouse lay abandoned from 1922 until it was designated a historic landmark and moved to its current location in 1996. It has now been outfitted with period items, many of them originals – the double bed and stove in particular – donated by those who at some point lifted them in the first place (or their descendants). There's good material, too, on the roadhouse tradition, all brought to life with excerpts from the diary of early roadhouse worker James Geoghegan, who also turned his hand to photography.

Roadhouses continue to be the main attraction nine miles north on the Richardson Highway at the **Big Delta State Historic Park** (mid-May to mid-Sept daily 8am–8pm; free), a compact and manicured riverside park full of neatly tended c.1900 log buildings. They've missed a great opportunity with the two-story centerpiece, **Rika's Roadhouse** (daily 9am–5pm; Ⓦwww.rikas.com), an original from the early days of the Valdez–Fairbanks Trail, which should at least have been turned into a museum, rather than a large gift shop. The Swede who ran the place until 1947, Rika Wallen, would be horrified, but it remains a fine log-built building, erected beside an important ferry crossing over the Tanana River. Outside, things improve with assorted outbuildings, such as a Swedish-style barn, a spring house used as a cool store in summer, and a workshop now fitted out as a small **museum**, with artifacts from pioneer life. Here, too, is a WAMCATS telegraph station (see box, p.440) and a reasonable café/restaurant.

A couple of hundred yards north (Mile 275.4) the Alaska pipeline spans the Tanana River on a graceful 1200-foot suspension structure, the longest of its kind along the route.

Practicalities

That precious "I've driven the Alaska Highway" certificate can be obtained for a dollar at the **visitor center** (late May to early Sept daily 8am–8pm; Ⓣ895-5068 or 1-877/895-5068, Ⓦwww.deltajunctionalaska.com) at the junction of the Richardson and Alaska highways. **Campers** are spoilt for choice here. Right in town you've got the wooded and convenient *Delta State Recreation*

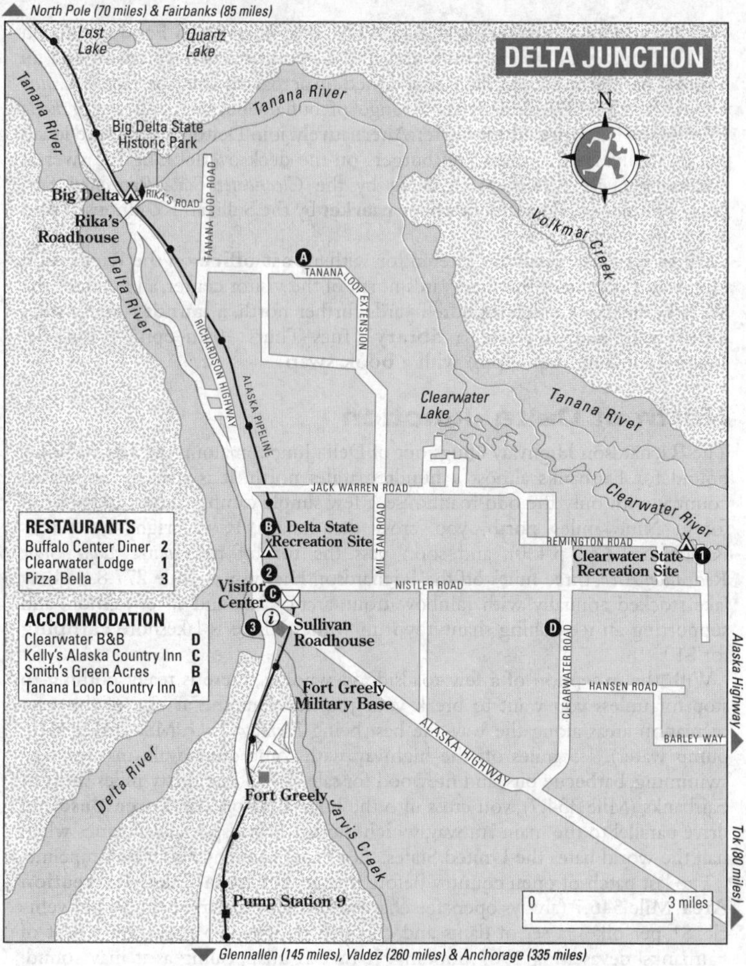

Site, Mile 267 ($10; pump water), and the better-equipped, RV-oriented *Smith's Green Acres RV Park and Campground*, Mile 268 (Ⓣ895-4369 or 1-800/895-4369, Ⓦwww.greenacresrvpark.com), one of the most highly rated in the state, with full hookups for $22.50 and tent sites for $15, including showers. *Clearwater State Recreation Site*, eight miles north of Mile 1415 on the Alaska Highway ($10; pump water), is even more appealing, beautifully tranquil as well as on the spring and fall migration routes of sandhill cranes and geese; and there's $5 parking space at *Big Delta*, beside Rika's Roadhouse.

For **rooms** try the spacious and central *Kelly's Alaska Country Inn*, in the center of town (Ⓣ895-4667, Ⓦwww.kellysalaskacountryinn.com; ④); the *Clearwater B&B*, 3170 Clearwater Rd (Ⓣ895-4842, Ⓔjay@davejay.org; ③); or *Tanana Loop Country Inn*, Tanana Loop Extension (Ⓣ895-4890; ④), a log-built home on a commune six miles from town, with full kitchen access, plus Internet access and satellite TV.

If all you need is **groceries** and an **ATM**, drop in at Delta Food Cache, on the Fairbanks road, where you'll also find a decent bakery, ice cream and an espresso bar. More substantial fare is dished up across the street at *Buffalo Center Diner* (ⓣ895-5989), which has a range of buffalo burgers, and *Pizza Bella* (ⓣ895-4841), by the visitor center. Alternatively, join Deltoids – as some locals call themselves – for steaks and burgers on the deck overlooking the river at *Clearwater Lodge* (ⓣ895-5152), right by the *Clearwater State Recreation Site*. Local produce is sold at the **farmers market** by the Sullivan Roadhouse (Wed & Sat 10am–6pm).

Other everyday needs are catered for with a **post office** on the Richardson Highway a couple of hundred yards north of the visitor center, a branch of the Wells Fargo Bank a few hundred yards further north, a **laundry** a few steps north again and, opposite, a **library** (Tues–Thurs 10am–6pm, Fri & Sat 10am–4pm, Sun noon–4pm) with a **book swap**.

North of Delta Junction

The Richardson Highway chugs out of Delta Junction along the Tanana Valley bound for Fairbanks almost a hundred miles north. It is sparsely populated country with only the odd roadhouse, a few simple campgrounds, and a lot of forest. Nine miles north, you cross the Tanana River, right by Rika's Roadhouse (see p.430), and soon pass the turnoff to *Quartz Lake State Recreation Area*, three miles off the Richardson Highway at Mile 277.8, a glassy lake stocked annually with rainbow trout, arctic char, and silver salmon, and supporting an ice-fishing shantytown in winter. There is lakeshore **camping** for $10.

With the exception of a few roadside viewpoints, there is really nothing to stop for unless you want to break your journey camping at one of the state recreation areas along the way, the best being *Harding Lake*, Mile 321.5 ($10; pump water), 1.5 miles off the highway with some quiet walk-in sites, lake swimming, barbecue pits, and firewood for sale ($5). Some thirty miles short of Fairbanks (Mile 334.7), you cross into the huge **Eielson Air Force Base** and drive parallel to the main runway, which is often busy, especially at times when half the world hates the United States: they're very touchy about that pipeline.

The last patch of open country before the city is **Chena Lakes Recreation Area**, Mile 346.7 (always open; fee charged late May to early Sept; $4 per vehicle, $1 per bike), a set of dams and channels designed to prevent a repeat of Fairbanks' devastating 1967 flooding. It isn't as unappealing as it may sound, with a lovely 2.5-mile nature trail, boating on Chena Lake (canoe, $6 an hour or $24 a day; rowboat, $8/$32), biking along the levees, and wooded **camping** ($10; pump water).

Tok and around

For most people, there is little reason to stop in **TOK** (pronounced Toke), Mile 1314 Alaska Highway, a scattered collection of RV parks, gas stations, motels, and diners at the junction of two major highways. But for drivers arriving from Canada along the Alaska Highway this is the first town of consequence and a thoroughly welcome opportunity to rest up, wash down the rig, fill up with Alaska-priced gas, and plan your next move. That said, there's certainly nothing to detain you more than one night, and you may fancy pressing straight on to Delta Junction (an easy two-hour drive to the west), cutting south along the

Tok Cutoff (see p.427) towards Glennallen and the Wrangell Mountains, or following the Taylor Highway north to Chicken and Eagle.

The settlement began life as Tokyo Camp, which provided workers' accommodation during the construction of the Alaska and Glenn highways in the early 1940s, and shortened its name during World War II. Although maintained as a way station on the highways, it got a boost in 1954, when the US Army built the now-defunct, eight-inch fuel supply pipeline from Haines through Tok to Fairbanks, and again in 1976, when four prominent 700-foot masts were built as a long-range aid to navigation.

Tok now acts as a service town for numerous Athabascan villages scattered around the vicinity, but it thrives on passing visitors lured in by offers of a free car wash with a tank of gas and the like. Attractions don't rise much above the gift shops full of Alaska T-shirts and **Mukluk Land**, three miles west along the Alaska Highway at Mile 1317 (June–Aug daily 1–9pm; $5), where the minigolf, bouncy igloo, and gold panning will keep the kids happy.

Practicalities

The Alaska Highway and Tok Cutoff meet at the town's main intersection, a stopping point for Alaska Direct and Alaska Trails **buses** (see p.41 for details). Here you'll find the **Tok visitor center**, Mile 1314 (early May to mid-Sept daily 8am–7pm; ⓣ883-5775, ⓦwww.tokalaskainfo.com), in what is reputed to be the largest log-built structure in the state. It's simply packed with information on the whole state and a selection of displays – stuffed animals and material on the 1990 fire, which nearly engulfed the town. Next door is the **Alaska Public Lands Information Center** (June–Aug daily 8am–7pm; Sept–May Mon–Fri 8am–4.30pm; ⓣ883-5667, ⓦwww.nps.gov/aplic), which is stocked with specific material on wildlife and wilderness matters as well as material on the Tetlin National Wildlife Refuge.

If you just need food and cash, then Three Bears, almost opposite the Tok visitor center, has a reasonable selection of **groceries**, a branch of the Denali State Bank (Mon–Fri 10am–6pm), and an **ATM**. The **post office** (Mon–Fri 8.30am–5pm, Sat 11am–4pm) is just along the Alaska Highway towards Fairbanks. The **library**, behind the visitor center (Tues–Thurs 10am–6pm, Fri & Sat 10am–4pm), has thirty-minute free Internet access.

RV parks abound in Tok, and all are trying to outdo each other – most charge $20–25 for full hookup. The *Golden Bear Motel and RV Park*, Mile 124.3 Tok Cutoff (ⓣ883-2561 or 1-866/883-2561, ⓔgoldenbear@aptalaska.net; ❹), is consistently reliable, right in town, and has full hookup for $20, dry camping for $10, $3 showers, modern motel rooms, and a good **espresso bar**. Dry campers can also **stay free** at the site behind the *Gateway Salmon Bake* (see overleaf) in return for the purchase of a meal. **Campers** wanting a little more tranquility can head eighteen miles west to *Moon Lake State Recreation Site*, Mile 1332 ($10; pump water), with a boat launch, picnic area, good swimming, and even access for float planes, which can often be seen tethered to the bank. Alternatively, head five miles east to the extensive *Tok River State Recreation Site*, Mile 1309.3 ($10; pump water), on the east bank of the Tok River.

If you aren't camping, the cheapest **place to stay** is the *Tok Hostel* (ⓣ883-3745; ❶; mid-May to mid-Sept), a rustic place in an ex-army tent with electricity, good hot showers (unless you're third in line), and two dorms ($10). It's neither in town nor well signposted – to find it head eight miles west along the Alaska Highway (Mile 1322.5), then 0.7 miles down Pringle Drive. For something more convenient, try *Tok Bed, Breakfast & Hostel*, Mile 1313.5 Alaska Hwy (ⓣ883-3602; cabins ❷, bunks ❶), less than a mile east of the intersection

Moving on from Tok

Drivers headed west towards Fairbanks should continue with our account of Delta Junction (p.429); and those headed southwest to Glennallen, Anchorage, and the Wrangell–St Elias National Park should follow our account of the Tok Cutoff (p.427) in reverse order. The Alaska Highway to the Canadian border, and the Taylor and Top of the World highways to Eagle and Dawson City, are covered on the following pages.

Hitchhikers might expect that, as an important junction, it would be easy to thumb a lift from Tok, but for some reason it isn't. People have been known to wait days, and those bound for Canada can be turned back at the border. This may be a good time to engage one of the **bus services** (for the lowdown on routes, see "Travel details," p.444). All stop close to the junction of the Alaska Highway and Tok Cutoff: Alaskon Express picks up at the *Westmark Inn*; Alaska Direct stops by the Village Gas, opposite *Tok RV Park*; and Alaska Trails pulls up by the visitor center.

and offering pleasant log cabins and dorm bunks in a trailer with a big breakfast and free "wholesome" movies for $25 (plus $5 if you don't have a sleeping bag). For a little more, *Winter Cabin B&B*, Mile 1316.5 Alaska Hwy (Ⓣ883-5655, Ⓦwww.alaska-wintercabin.com; ❸), is a far better bet with cozy and well-equipped wild-animal-themed log cabins in the forest 2.5 miles west of town.

Good all-you-can-eat **meals** of salmon, halibut, and reindeer are served all day at the *Gateway Salmon Bake*, Mile 1313.1 Alaska Hwy, for around $19; the nearby *Fast Eddy's* serves a broad selection of diner fare along with gourmet pizzas ($20 is enough to two) and groaning plates of nachos ($8).

Towards the Canadian border: the Tetlin National Wildlife Refuge

Heading southeast from Tok, the Alaska Highway runs towards the **Canadian border**, 92 miles away at Mile 1222. The initial arrow-straight twelve miles takes you past the *Tok River State Recreation Site*, Mile 1309.3 (see p.433), to **Tetlin Junction**, Mile 1301.7, where the Taylor Highway heads north to Chicken, Eagle, and Dawson City in the Yukon.

Along most of the rest of the journey to the border, the Alaska Highway forms the northern boundary of the **Tetlin National Wildlife Refuge** (Ⓦtetlin.fws.gov/index.htm), broad marshy flatlands spotted with hundreds of miniature lakes. Here the glacial waters of the Nabesna and Chisana rivers, flowing south from the Alaska Range foothills, make up the headwaters of the Tanana River, one of Alaska's major fluvial arteries. These wetlands are right on the migration flightpath and provide a perfect habitat for one of the highest densities of waterfowl in the state – 114 nesting species and 68 migrants – as well as large numbers of black and grizzly bears, moose, caribou, wolves, and beavers. The Alaska Highway provides access to the northern reaches, along with various pullouts: interpretive panels at Mile 1228; Desper Creek (Mile 1226), with a canoe launch spot; and Highway Lake (Mile 1225), with its beaver lodge at the east end. You can **hike** and camp pretty much anywhere in the refuge, although Native corporations manage some areas and permission is required. A couple of the best **camping** spots, both on lakes and with great mountain views and wildlife viewing, are: *Lakeview Campground*, Mile 1256.7 (free; untreated water only); and *Deadman Lake Campground*, Mile 1249.3 (free; untreated water only), with its thousand-yard nature trail.

The Alaska Highway and the Canadian border

About the best way to earn a true appreciation of what Alaska is all about is to drive there through northern Canada along the epic **Alaska Highway** – formerly the ALCAN and still sometimes known by that name. It will only give you the vaguest sense of what early prospectors and trappers were up against, but you'll at least realize just how far Alaska is from everywhere else: once you hit the Yukon Territory, you're still almost nine hundred miles from Fairbanks.

The 1422-mile Alaska Highway (85 percent of it in Canada) was built in response to the United States' entry into World War II. A route was selected to link a series of pre-existing air bases through the Canadian north and construction began on March 9, 1942 with co-opted US soldiers working from both ends in atrocious conditions: mosquitoes, mountains, swamps, frigid rivers, and astonishingly bad weather even for these latitudes. Incredibly, the two teams met less than seven months after starting, a magnificent effort costing $140 million. Travelers driving the Alaska Highway right through British Columbia and the Yukon should obtain a copy of the *Rough Guide to Canada*, though there's limited coverage in this book in Basics (see p.41). Once **on Alaskan turf** it is two hundred miles to the "official" end of the Alaska Highway at Delta Junction, where the road meets the Richardson Highway for the final 98 miles to Fairbanks.

Crossing the Canadian border

Alaska and the Canadian Yukon share two border crossings: the important **Alaska Highway crossing** (open 24 hours all year), 92 miles east of Tok, and the summer-only **Top of the World Highway crossing** (late May to mid-Sept daily 8am–8pm Alaska time, 9am–9pm Yukon time), 122 miles northeast of Tok. And remember you'll have to **set your watch** back an hour heading to Alaska, forward an hour if Yukon-bound.

For those Canada-bound, a Yukon **road-condition** report can be found at ⓦwww.gov.yk.ca/roadreport or by calling ⓣ867/456-7623 or toll-free in Yukon 1-877/456-7623.

Eastbound travelers should call at APLIC in Tok (see p.433); coming from the Canadian border, call at the Tetlin Wildlife Refuge **visitor center**, Mile 1229 (late May to early Sept daily 8am–5pm), where you'll find free copies of the *Tetlin Passage* newspaper, heaps of detailed hiking and camping information, and a welter of interpretive talks, books, and displays.

The Fortymile and the Taylor Highway

The **Fortymile gold district** butts up against Canada's Yukon Territory between the Yukon River (once the main access to the Klondike and the catalyst for development) and the Alaska Highway (now the main road artery through the region). This was the grandfather of all Alaskan goldfields, experiencing its rush in 1886 when the town of Eagle became the supply hub, connected to the Gulf of Alaska by the Valdez–Eagle Trail. As fortunes shifted elsewhere the trail fell into disrepair and the region languished until the completion of the Alaska Highway in the early 1940s prompted the construction of the **Taylor Highway**, a new road into an old area, at least by Alaskan standards.

Mining still continues across the region, which is scattered with the detritus of pioneering attempts to make a living from the earth: sagging old cabins,

Saving the caribou

As recently as 1920 the **Fortymile caribou herd** numbered half a million beasts, the largest herd in the north, its domains spreading from Alaska over into the Yukon. For years numbers had been dwindling, mainly from loss of habitat from wildfires and human encroachment. The construction of the Taylor Highway further pressured a fragile population as hunters could now gain easy access and exploit lax hunting regulations. By the early 1990s numbers were down to around 6000 and, despite stricter hunting laws, wolf predation was preventing caribou numbers from rebounding. From 1996 to 2001 a controversial program of wolf sterilization and relocation gave the caribou a chance to grow and expand their territory. The herd now numbers close to 50,000, and it is hoped that this is enough to naturally withstand the attentions of the wolves and sustain a substantial enough hunting quota to keep the locals happy.

dilapidated sluices, even rusting hulks of dredges. Look, but don't get too close and stick to recognized highways – these people are fiercely protective of their claims (and have guns).

If you're headed out this way, you'll need to resupply in **Tok**, a dull crossroads town that will be the first real opportunity to fill up your belly and find a soft Alaskan bed, if you've just driven up through Canada. Heading into the Fortymile you enter caribou country (see box above), a sparsely populated land with only a couple of places that deserve to be called towns: the likeable **Chicken**, with its welcoming bar and frontier spirit, and **Eagle**, one of Alaska's best-preserved historic towns, neatly perched beside the roiling Yukon River.

The Taylor and Top of the World highways

As soon as you reach Tetlin Junction, twelve miles east of Tok, and turn off the Alaska Highway onto the **Taylor Highway** (generally open mid-April to mid-Oct), it immediately feels more remote. There's no human habitation whatsoever until you reach the quirky settlement of **Chicken**, sixty miles down the line, then only the rusting hulks of gold dredges to remind you of what this area once meant to prospectors. Press on along narrow and lumpy roads, and you can choose between the ordered former garrison town of **Eagle** and the Top of the World Highway into Canada and Dawson City, the final destination of the Klondike gold rush.

The asphalt surface currently reaches Chicken, though there are promises of running the blacktop to the Canadian border starting in 2006. Since most rental cars are banned on gravel roads, you may have to use Alaska Trails buses (see "Travel details," p.443), which go through Chicken to Boundary and Dawson City. Hitching can be a dispiriting experience, though it is not impossible.

The **Taylor Highway** – detailed in a free BLM leaflet found locally – follows a tortuous course from one drainage to the next, climbing above 3500ft three times – Mount Fairplay, Polly Summit, and American Summit – on its 160-mile journey to Eagle. The road to **Mount Fairplay Summit** (Mile 33) gives long views over mixed forests and myriad tributaries of the Fortymile River before descending across tannin-rich rivers the color of strong tea. The only **camping** place before Chicken is the fairly pleasant *West Fork Campground* ($8; pump water) at Mile 49.

Chicken

Having unearthed gold, early prospectors founded a tent city and decided to name it for the plump, poorly flighted, and tasty birds found in profusion hereabouts; but ptarmigan was too much for their collective lexicon, and they settled on **CHICKEN**, now a tiny settlement 66 miles along the Taylor Highway. There's not much to the place now, with fewer than twenty permanent residents, but it divides neatly into three sections. Apart from fairly pricey gas and a post office on the highway, there's little in the way of facilities. There isn't even a payphone in town, nor any roofed accommodation, but RVers are well catered for, and there's a great bar.

Downtown Chicken, on Airport Road (Ⓦwww.chickenalaska.com), may just be the Alaska you're looking for, a classic piece of Alaskana comprising no more than a Western-style wooden sidewalk linking a gift shop, the *Chicken Creek Café*, and, best of all, the wonderfully battered old *Chicken Creek Saloon*, with a free pool table, a kick-it-to-make-it-go jukebox and draft Silver Gulch beer. You never know who you might meet in the bar – gold panners, hunters, curious tourists, geologists – but somehow everyone gets on, oiled by beer and the congenial Susan, who runs the whole show.

There is nowhere formal **to stay** here, but you can stagger out to your RV parked overnight on the dirt lot or throw up a tent on the grassy verge. Periodically, make for the *Chicken Creek Café* for chicken soup ($4), huge tooth-rotting cinnamon rolls ($3.50), or the nightly salmon bake ($16), with homemade dill tartar sauce: they usually close around 7pm, so come early.

A few steps down Airport Road, **Chicken Gold Camp** (Ⓣ235-6396, Ⓦwww.chickengold.com) is built around the Pedro Dredge, moved here in the late 1990s from its final working claim a mile up the river. There are plans to open it up for tours inside, but currently you can only walk around the outside and past a still worked gold claim. There's a tank where you can pan for gold ($5 all day), RV parking (dry $8), and an espresso bar also doing panini and soups and providing Internet access.

The now abandoned township of **Old Chicken** lies just across the highway from Downtown Chicken and is liberally festooned with private property signs. The track through it is actually public, but since all the interesting buildings are private you might as well troop a couple of hundred yards along the highway to *The Goldpanner*, a creekside gas station, gift shop, and RV park (dry parking $10, water & electricity $15) which runs the **Historical Town of Chicken Tour** (June–Aug daily 9am & 1.30pm; $5). It is a fascinating hour-long stroll around dilapidated buildings now being colonized by willow, made all the more poignant if you've read Robert Specht's *Tisha*, the true story of Anne Purdy (née Hobbs), who taught at the schoolhouse here in 1927. Like all the other buildings, the **schoolhouse** was later put to an alternative use by the FE gold company, which mined the area until the late 1960s. As the winter of 1967 set in, they hauled out as usual, leaving all their gear ready for the next spring, but never returned. Everything remains in a state of partially arrested decay, scattered with enamel plates, incomplete record books, a *Glamour* magazine, and a wonderfully dated Sears catalog. The best-preserved building is the **hay barn**, later used as the dredge maintenance store and still sweetly smelling of hay and grease. Inside, copper gaskets hang on the wall, the repair schedule lies open on the bench, a working lathe sits in the corner, and all the pulleys still spin smoothly.

The Top of the World Highway and the road to Eagle

Beyond Chicken the highway starts to deteriorate noticeably, passing the BLM's Chicken Field Station, Mile 68, which marks the start of a trail to a lovely overlook of the **Cowden Dredge** in Mosquito Fork (2 miles round-trip; 1hr 30min). The highway continues wending its way from one Fortymile tributary to another, at Mile 75.3 reaching the **South Fork Bridge**, main access point for the Fortymile Canoe Route (see box, below). You can **camp** seven miles up the road at *Walker Fork Campground*, Mile 82 ($8; pump water), or continue past the rusting carcass of Jack Wade Dredge, Mile 86.

At Mile 95.7 you reach **Jack Wade Junction**, where the Taylor Highway continues north to Eagle and the **Top of the World Highway** spurs east towards Canada, appropriately running high along a broad subalpine ridge with expansive views down into the Fortymile mining district. **BOUNDARY** lies nine miles along and consists solely of *Boundary Lodge* (no phone; ❶), a one-family operation with a cozy café, gas that's expensive but usually slightly cheaper than in Dawson, and a couple of simple cabins with beds and a wood stove, which sleep three – and as many as you can fit on the floor – for $40. From there it is four miles to the 141st meridian, which defines the US–Canadian frontier (for border formalities, see p.115), then 65 miles on to Dawson City.

Paddling the Fortymile

Driving the Taylor Highway through Chicken to Eagle only gives you a small taste of a prospector's lot in the time when all travel was done by river. Organized visitors can still sample something of this life by undertaking one of the multiday canoe journeys on the wild and scenic **Fortymile River**, a totally absorbing experience requiring considerable confidence in your abilities. You'll be spending at least one night (possibly a whole week) camping beside the river, seeing few people, and having no one to help you if you swamp your boat or lose your supplies. It is important that you recognize which rapids should be portaged: misjudgments can have grave consequences, though the river's popularity in summer means that someone will eventually happen along.

First step is to obtain detailed route **information** from the BLM's Tok Field Office (Ⓣ883-5121), which is located next to the APLIC outpost. One free leaflet simply states the access points and float times, another adds more information on facilities and hazards along the way and a list of the appropriate inch-to-the-mile maps. If you haven't got your own gear, you'll need to look at **renting a raft or canoe** from Eagle Canoe Rentals in Eagle (mid-May to mid-Sept; Ⓣ547-2203, Ⓦwww.aptalaska.net/~paddleak/), which charges $160 per two-berth canoe and $350 per six-berth raft for four days. Alternatively, contact Tok-based Canoe Alaska (Ⓣ883-2628, Ⓦwww.canoealaska.net), which rents canoes from Tok and does customized guided rafting trips on the Fortymile and the Yukon.

The most commonly run section of the river is from the put-in point at South Fork Bridge (for access points, see the map on p.408) down **to Fortymile Bridge** (38 miles; 10–16 hours' paddling time) passing the few standing structures remaining from **Franklin**, a gold town which flourished in the late 1920s. A couple of miles above the pullout you'll probably have to line your boats through the Falls, a Class III–IV rapid portaged on the right. Keen boaters may wish to continue from **Fortymile Bridge to Eagle** (101 miles; typically 4–5 days) past the abandoned Steele Creek townsite, negotiating Deadman's Riffle and Canyon Rapids (both Class II–III), paddling into Canada and then joining the Yukon River at the Fortymile townsite (deserted but being preserved) for the final fifty miles northwest to Eagle. Even more adventurous types can fly into the remote Joseph airstrip on the Middle Fork of the Fortymile River and paddle from there down to Fortymile Bridge (88 miles; 4–5 days) and then continue to the Yukon River and Eagle. Contact Tok-based 40-Mile Air (Ⓣ883-5191, Ⓔfortymi@aptalaska.net) for fly-ins.

You should also be aware that if you are planning to paddle below the Fortymile Bridge take-out on down to the Yukon River and Eagle, you'll be crossing into Canadian territory and will need to **contact US and Canadian customs** (see p.115).

Eagle

From Jack Wade Junction, the **Taylor Highway** becomes increasingly narrow and winding, passing the Fortymile Canoe Route access point of **Fortymile Bridge**, Mile 112.6, on its 64-mile run to the Yukon River. **EAGLE**, 94 miles north of Chicken on the south bank of the Yukon River, spent the middle years of the twentieth century neglected, but in the past twenty years has reinvented itself as the best-preserved town in the Interior. This is no museum, however; although small and isolated, it is very much alive, catering to prospectors and a few tourists in summer, and trappers in winter. Hugging an outside bend of the Yukon River only twelve miles downstream from the Canadian border, it is flanked by the pyramidal 1400-foot Eagle Bluff, where the birds that gave the town its name formerly nested.

Eagle's core is little changed since 1905, the result of sixty years of neglect and forty years of preservation at the hands of the Eagle Historical Society, which was formed in the mid-1960s. They've done a wonderful job: all over town there are clapboard buildings restored and painted a fetching (but not original) white with green trim. The buildings are all brought marvelously to life on the society's tours, which have undoubtedly contributed to the group's worldwide membership, which at three hundred members is around twice the population of Eagle.

As the largest river town between Dawson and the Arctic Circle community of Fort Yukon, Eagle supports an extensive bush community sequestered in the forests beside tributaries of the Yukon. Most now only use mining and trapping to supplement other sources of income, but in essence their lives aren't much different from those of the people so vividly described in John McPhee's *Coming into the Country* (see "Books" in Contexts, p.545).

Some history

Eagle started life as a trading post on Belle Isle in the middle of the Yukon in 1880 and subsequently moved to the south bank when the townsite was surveyed in 1898. Unscrupulous land agents tried to talk up their price with exaggerated reports of gold-rich streams hereabouts, even trying in vain to flog off

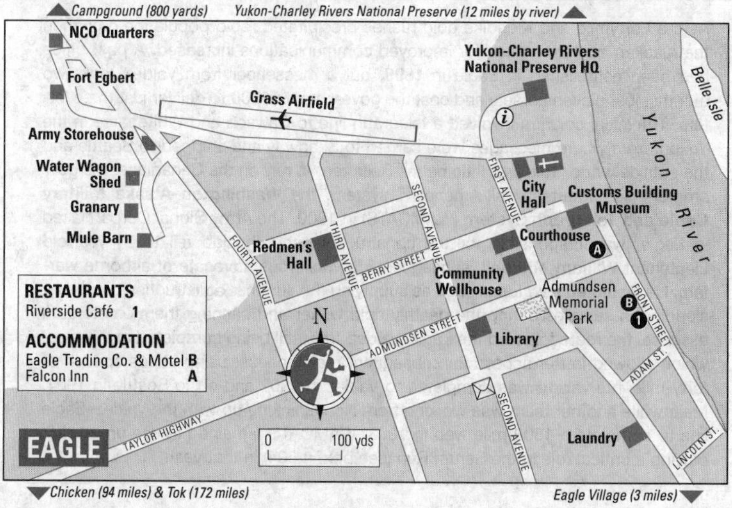

a corner lot to Jack London, who passed through in June 1898. Nonetheless, eager prospectors came in numbers, and the town soon had a population of 1700. Lawlessness and a desire to control the Interior induced the US government to blaze the Valdez–Eagle Trail using soldiers stationed at Eagle's Fort Egbert.

From outside, Alaska was gradually seen in civilian rather than military terms, and in 1900 Congress passed legislation for taxation, licensing, and the establishment of three judicial districts, one being in Eagle. From here James Wickersham presided as US District Judge over almost half of Alaska, and a year later Eagle was incorporated as a city – the first in Interior Alaska. Anchorage wouldn't even be thought of for another sixteen years, and Fairbanks was just a mudbank in the Chena River.

Eagle played another major role in the civilization of the north as a critical node in the Washington–Alaska Military Cable and Telegraph System (see box, below). Though geographically remote, it was no longer isolated. In fact, in December 1905 this was the best-connected community in the Interior, a unique feature that lured explorer **Roald Amundsen** across four hundred miles of frozen rivers and mountain ranges by dog team. He came to announce to the world that, in the thirty months since he left his native Norway, he had successfully negotiated the Northwest Passage – the mariner's grail for much of the previous two centuries – and to beg his backers for more funds to continue the journey. It seems he liked Eagle (it had to be better than his sloop, locked in the polar ice of the Beaufort Sea for the nine-month winter), so he stayed a couple of months in a cabin off 1st Avenue on what is now Amundsen Street.

With the departure of Wickersham to burgeoning Fairbanks in 1904 and the closure of Fort Egbert in 1911 (though the telegraph and wireless operators stayed until 1925), Eagle began its steady decline in population: from around two hundred when the fort closed, to sixty-odd when the last sternwheeler paddled off in 1947 and a low point of only nine in 1953, when the completion of the Taylor Highway reversed the trend. The population now hovers around 160.

WAMCATS

As the Fortymile and Klondike gold rushes precipitated rapid population growth in the Alaskan bush, the need for improved communications increased. A post office had been established in Eagle in 1899, but a messenger from Valdez took two months, lost eleven horses, and cost the government $3000 to deliver just three letters. The initial solution involved a telegraph line to Dawson and Whitehorse in the Yukon, from where messages were carried to Skagway and shipped to Seattle and the outside world. This was little better. Reluctant to rely on the Canadians, the government set about an "all-American" system, the **Washington–Alaska Military Cable and Telegraph System** (WAMCATS) in 1900. The Army Signal Corps, based in Eagle, was responsible for the construction, and the job fell to 21-year-old Lieutenant **William Mitchell**, subsequently a vociferous advocate of airborne warfare. He instituted new ideas such as supplying the summer construction camps by sledding in supplies during the deathly cold winter and banning thermometers. In essence, the route followed the Eagle–Valdez Trail, still being completed at the time, which allowed better access for subsequent maintenance, using sheds spaced at forty-mile intervals. It was completed to Valdez in 1902 and on to Seattle in 1904. Meanwhile another team was working from Nome, linking up with the Valdez–Eagle line to complete a 1500-mile web in 1903. WAMCATS remained in use until 1925, playing a critical role in the Serum Run (see box, p.504) in that year.

The Town

Eagle's waterfront is no longer the hotbed of activity it was in the town's sternwheeler heyday, but it is still a place to which you are inexorably drawn. Stand on the rough promenade of Front Street and it feels as though the swirling silt-laden waters below are waiting to suck you all the way to the sea. You'll have to retreat a few steps to reach the geographical and social center of town, the **community well house**, an unmissable pagoda-roofed frame structure topped with a cupola housing a bell which can still summon the townsfolk to fight a fire. The windmill hasn't worked for years so, on a daily basis, it is a pump which provides water for the large proportion of residents who live without running water: you'll often see folk in trucks pulling up to fill drums from the gas-pump nozzle.

Next door stands **Wickersham's Courthouse**, corner of 1st Avenue and Berry Street, built in 1901 and with an upper floor still laid out much as it would have been in those early days. The desk Wickersham last used in 1904 still contained his papers in 1975 when the historical society began its restoration. Nowadays local guides from the society convene here for the absorbing three-hour **Historical Society Tour** (late May to early Sept daily at 9am; $5; or by appointment Ⓣ547-2325, Ⓦwww.eagleak.org), the only way you can get into the historic buildings. The tour continues downstairs in a small museum devoted to Wickersham's tenure, Amundsen's visit, and operations at Fort Egbert, which, together with efforts to supply fuel for the riverboats, succeeded in completely denuding the surroundings. Eagle is still a border port, but it no longer has a permanent customs officer, obviating the need for the 1918 customs house, now turned into the **US Customs house museum** (visited on the tour), with period furniture arranged among beautifully hand-drawn pilots' charts of the Upper Yukon. The tour continues to **Fort Egbert**, a collection of wooden buildings dotted on the grass at the end of the airstrip. The granary contains a Model T Ford and a Model B dump truck, still both used for the annual Fourth of July parade through town, and the adjacent mule barn is much as it was left, with four dozen stalls each marked with the name of its last occupant.

The tour varies a little depending on who is guiding that day, but might also include the plain, wooden hall of the Improved Order of Red Men, an

McQuesten's thermometer

Trader Leroy Napoleon "Jack" McQuesten left a huge legacy in the North. He never found much gold, but when scouting around the Tron-diuck River in the Canadian Yukon he decided he'd seen enough color to justify widespread interest and sent word south that there was gold to be found, thereby kick-starting the gold rush in the "Klondike" (his bastardized version of Tron-diuck). He set up trading posts as a representative of the Alaska Commercial Company, including one at Fort Reliance on the Yukon, where he once tried his hand at plowing his land with two young moose. Here he financed prospectors and, to aid newcomers in judging their outdoor plans, instituted **McQuesten's Thermometer** (aka the Sourdough Thermometer). It comprised a series of four vials – mercury (freezing point -40°F), coal oil (-50°F), Jamaica ginger (-60°F), and Perry Davis' painkiller (-75°F) – in a rack outside along with a note instructing people to shake each bottle in turn. If the mercury was frozen it was too cold to be out on the trail at night, and even the daytime was dangerous if the coal oil was solid. When the ginger froze folks should stay in their cabin, and when the painkiller wouldn't budge you shouldn't stray from your stove.

Yukon-Charley Rivers National Preserve and paddling the Yukon

You'll need a fair degree of commitment to see anything of the **Yukon-Charley Rivers National Preserve**, a whopping 2.5 million-acre chunk of unglaciated Alaskan Interior flanking the Yukon River – and its major tributary, the Charley River – for 130 river miles from just below Eagle, almost to Circle (see p.481). It is remote country almost devoid of human impact, though it was appreciably busier fifty to eighty years ago when sternwheelers forged their way up past Eagle to Dawson, and prospectors worked the area for paydirt. A few of their spiritual descendants remain, hardy types (only 30 in the whole park year-round, but more in summer) spinning out a subsistence lifestyle along the river or up the small tributaries. Most are reclusive enough that you won't see them, but you'll spot their nets, fish camps, and maybe a cabin or two, with the regular slap of Han Athabascan fishwheels as accompaniment.

In winter the river flows clear under 6ft of ice, its surface used by snowmobiles and dog teams – the Yukon Quest dog-sled race comes right through here – but in summer the way to travel is by canoe. Paddling through the park, and along the Yukon River in general, is the only way to gain a sense of the region's interconnectedness; an appreciation of how much Dawson, Fortymile, Eagle, and Circle were part of a riverine continuum that's impossible to achieve using the highways. The pleasure in traveling this country is the sheer sense of isolation, but you can fish while you drift, stop to hike up small streams, and pause to root around the few relics of the gold-rush era that remain: abandoned townsites, disused roadhouses, and the detritus of commercial gold dredging, including the preserved Coal Creek Dredge in the heart of the park.

Practicalities

There are no roads or maintained trails in the Yukon-Charley, nor even any publicly maintained airstrips, so unless you can get a bush pilot to fly you into the upper Charley River, your only access is by boat. In Eagle, the Yukon-Charley Rivers

organization dedicated to "friendship, brotherly helpfulness, fraternal love, and good fellowship," though this didn't extend to the "red" men who lived in the district – it was strictly whites only.

If you want to get out on the river, consider a **cruise** on Gray Line's *Yukon Queen II* (mid-May to early Sept; in Dawson ⓣ867/993-5599 or 1-800/544-2206, ⓦwww.graylinealaska.com), which runs day trips from Dawson to Eagle and back, leaving Dawson City at 9am (Yukon time) and departing Eagle at 2pm (Alaska time). Unfortunately, the trip is four hours each way, most spaces are filled by tours, and from this end the schedule only suits those who want to overnight in Dawson, but places (US$87 each way) are usually available and can be purchased at *Eagle Trading Company* (see below). Bicycles usually travel free, but call to check if there's space.

Practicalities

Most of the town's commercial activity revolves around the *Eagle Trading Company*, Front Street (ⓣ547-2220, ⓦwww.eagletrading.com; ❸), a well-stocked grocery selling **gas** at inflated prices, operating a **motel** with comfortable spruce-paneled rooms, and letting functional **RV sites** by the river for $16, including showers. You'll need to book as far in advance as you can manage to stay at *Falcon Inn B&B*, 220 Front St (ⓣ547-2254, ⓦaptalaska.com/~falconin/; ❸), a modern log house with spectacular river views and tasteful decor that makes it one of the most appealing B&Bs in the Interior. The guests'

National Preserve **visitor center** (mid-May to mid-Sept daily 8am–5pm; mid-Sept to mid-May call at the adjacent park headquarters Mon–Fri 8am–5pm; ⓣ547-2233, ⓦwww.nps.gov/yuch) provides information and sells maps. You can **rent a canoe** in Eagle from Eagle Canoe Rentals (mid-May to mid-Sept; ⓣ547-2203, ⓦwww.aptalaska.net/~paddleak/) for the float down to Circle (165 miles; 5 days; $175 per canoe). Alternatively, head to Dawson and hire a canoe at *Dawson City River Hostel* (ⓣ867/993-6823; ⓦwww.yukonhostels.com) for the float down to Eagle (105 miles; 3–4 days; $110 rental per canoe). Both trips can be undertaken at a steadier pace (canoes at an additional $25 a day), or you can take an epic combination from Dawson to Circle (270 miles; 9–10 days; $275). Canoes can be dropped in Circle, but you'll need to fly back to your starting point: this is best arranged beforehand with Circle Air (ⓣ520-5223 or 1-866/520-5223, ⓦwww.circleair.com), which charges around $300 an hour for charters and also does fly-ins.

A convenient alternative is to organize your trip from Fairbanks through GoNorth (see box, p.468), which runs Fairbanks-based trips flying into Eagle, letting you canoe down to Circle, and then flying you back to Fairbanks for $345.

June to September is the time to travel, avoiding freeze-up (typically three weeks in mid-Oct) and break-up (usually two weeks in early May), when huge chunks of tumbling ice make river travel extremely perilous or impossible. Once on the river self-sufficiency is paramount. Obviously, you'll need to be competent paddlers – a midstream spill in such a broad, cold river can be lethal – and carry everything you need. You'll be **camping** on open beaches and river bars, where insects are kept at bay by the breeze, except for at five free public-use **cabins** (let on a first-come, first-served basis), including one at the two-story, log-built *Slaven's Roadhouse*, long deserted, but now converted for visitors' use. Through the summer *Slaven's* has a resident ranger, who conducts free hikes of the Cold Creek Dredge.

Remember to leave a float plan at the park headquarters in Eagle (and let them know you're safe at journey's end), take along your fishing tackle, and stay bear-aware.

lounge even has a wonderful turret and deck perfect for watching Eagle's daily routine or, with luck, the aurora. The town's peaceful **campground** ($8; untreated river water) lies half a mile northwest of Fort Egbert on the route of a water-supply line which once supplied Fort Egbert from American Creek. Ferret around in the trees, and you'll come across the remains of structures where fires once heated the pipe to prevent it freezing. Eagle's only **restaurant** is the *Riverside Café*, Front Street, a good diner that is ideal for just sitting and watching the river roll by. Eagle is "damp," which means that there are **no alcohol sales** in town, but no one is going to stop you bringing a bottle or two in.

Travel details

With no train lines, Alaska's eastern Interior is most easily explored along the web of highways that link the region to Anchorage, Prince William Sound, Fairbanks, and Canada. Your own vehicle gives the most flexibility, but limited bus services do exist in the summer. Alaska Trails and Alaska Direct (for details of both, see Basics, p.41) are the only two companies running between major towns, though Backcountry Connections (see p.412) does a daily run from Glennallen to McCarthy.

Buses

Chicken to: Dawson City, Yukon (3 weekly; 4hr); Fairbanks (3 weekly; 7hr 30min); Tok (3 weekly; 2hr).
Delta Junction to: Dawson City, Yukon (3 weekly; 9hr 30min); Fairbanks (3 weekly; 2hr 45min); Glennallen (on demand; 3hr); Tok (3 weekly; 2hr); Valdez (on demand; 5hr 30min).
Glennallen to: Anchorage (3 weekly; 4hr 30min); Chitina (1 daily; 1hr 30min); Delta Junction (on demand; 3hr); Fairbanks (on demand; 4hr 30min); McCarthy (1 daily; 4hr); Tok (3 weekly; 3–4hr); Valdez (on demand; 3hr 15min).
Tok to: Anchorage (3 weekly; 8–9hr); Chicken (3 weekly; 2hr); Dawson City, Yukon (3 weekly; 7hr); Delta Junction (3 weekly; 2hr); Fairbanks (3 weekly; 5hr); Glennallen (3 weekly; 3–4hr); Whitehorse, Yukon (3 weekly; 9hr 30min).

8

Fairbanks and the Arctic North

CHAPTER 8

Highlights

* **Winter in Fairbanks** Come in late February and early March to catch the Yukon Quest sled-dog race, the ice-carving competition, and the aurora at its best. See p.457

* **Aurora borealis** Make a special trip in March or hang around until mid-September (or later) to see the northern lights in all their glory. See p.460

* **University of Alaska Museum** One of the state's best museums is getting better as it expands. See p.463

* **Nome** Camp on the near-Arctic beach with the gold dredgers and rent a car to explore the gorgeous roads round about. See p.500

* **Chena Hot Springs** Hike the trails, then relax in the outdoor pool at Alaska's most developed thermal resort. See p.475

* **Pinnell Mountain Trail** Excellent two-day ridgetop trail experiencing midsummer midnight sun and early fall aurora displays. See p.482

* **Floating in the Brooks Range** Set time and money aside for a rafting trip on one of the rivers draining the remote Brooks Range. See p.486

* **Dalton Highway** Alaska's biggest driving adventure, 500 miles from Fairbanks north to Arctic Deadhorse, and gravel most of the way. See p.487

△ Sign on Dalton Highway

8

Fairbanks and the Arctic North

A journey to Alaska seems incomplete without time spent in the **Far North**, a region comprising the Alaskan Arctic and Fairbanks, the state's second largest city and the hub of the north. It is stunningly dramatic, with long winter nights lit by the shimmering strands of the **aurora borealis**, extreme temperatures that demand extraordinary measures just so that people can live here, and settlements which all seem to claim some superlative: lowest temperature, most isolated cabin, or furthest north something or other. The area is also where the legendary pipeline-building days of the mid-1970s were played out, with construction crews earning big money and then coming to town to squander fistfuls of cash nightly.

Today the North is actually wilder than it was a century ago. Abandoned cabins remain where gold rushes once bustled with activity, and sternwheel steamers have been replaced by bush planes as the transportation mode of choice. The heart of the region is **Fairbanks**, a flat, sprawling place that does a good job of balancing urban life with the needs of the cabin dwellers on its doorstep. If you've just spent some time in the Interior, city luxuries will be welcome, and it's easy to spend a few days here making forays out to assorted gold-rush relics and soaking up the late evening sun as it glows off the Alaska Range. Before long you'll want to stray further, and the road system lends itself to easy trips to the resort at **Chena Hot Springs** and increasingly more challenging journeys to the modest **Circle Hot Springs**, the near-primitive **Manley Hot Springs**, or even on to the daunting 500-mile **Dalton Highway**, which runs along the route of the pipeline to **Deadhorse**, almost on the Arctic Ocean.

Fairbanks' roads will also take you to a few manageable hikes and easy canoe routes, but for the really challenging stuff – weeklong treks and float trips – you'll need to get out to the **Gates of the Arctic National Park** or the **Arctic National Wildlife Refuge**, which jointly encompass much of the **Brooks Range**. Beyond the Brooks Range, the 4000-strong Iñupiat town of **Barrow** clings to the edge of the land with only the ten-month-frozen sea between it and the North Pole. As a large Eskimo community, Barrow has a lot in common with **Kotzebue**, a springboard for the inland **sand dunes** beside the Kobuk River. Kotzebue is often visited jointly with its near neighbor

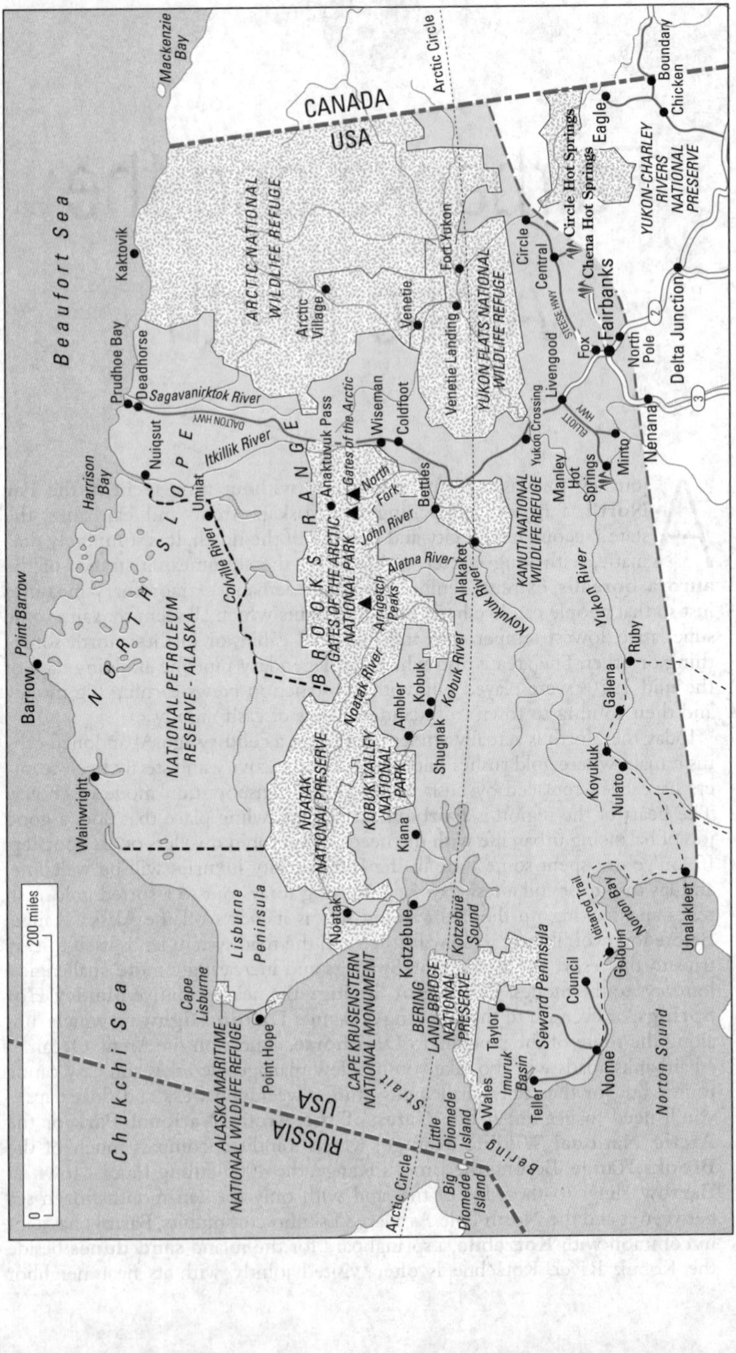
Beaufort Sea
Mackenzie Bay
CANADA
USA
Arctic Circle
Boundary
Chicken
Eagle
YUKON-CHARLEY RIVERS NATIONAL PRESERVE
Circle Hot Springs
Chena Hot Springs
Circle
Central
STEESE HWY
Fairbanks
Fox
North Pole
Delta Junction
2
3
Nenana
Livengood
ELLIOTT HWY
Minto
Manley Hot Springs
Yukon Crossing
YUKON FLATS NATIONAL WILDLIFE REFUGE
Fort Yukon
Venetie Landing
Venetie
ARCTIC NATIONAL WILDLIFE REFUGE
Arctic Village
Kaktovik
Prudhoe Bay
Deadhorse
Sagavanirktok River
DALTON HWY
Wiseman
Coldfoot
Anaktuvuk Pass
Gates of the Arctic
North Fork
Bettles
John River
KANUTI NATIONAL WILDLIFE REFUGE
Allakaket
Koyukuk River
Alatna River
Arrigetch Peaks
GATES OF THE ARCTIC NATIONAL PARK
BROOKS RANGE
Itkillik River
Nuiqsut
Harrison Bay
Umiat
Colville River
NORTH SLOPE
NATIONAL PETROLEUM RESERVE - ALASKA
Point Barrow
Barrow
Wainwright
Noatak River
Kobuk River
Kobuk
Ambler
Shugnak
Yukon River
Ruby
Galena
Koyukuk
Nulato
NOATAK NATIONAL PRESERVE
KOBUK VALLEY NATIONAL PARK
Kiana
Noatak
Kotzebue
Kotzebue Sound
Lisburne Peninsula
Cape Lisburne
ALASKA MARITIME NATIONAL WILDLIFE REFUGE
Point Hope
CAPE KRUSENSTERN NATIONAL MONUMENT
BERING LAND BRIDGE NATIONAL PRESERVE
Seward Peninsula
Council
Iditarod Trail
Norton Bay
Golouin
Unalakleet
Taylor
Imuruk Basin
Nome
Teller
Wales
Norton Sound
Chukchi Sea
RUSSIA
USA
Bering Strait
Little Diomede Island
Big Diomede Island
0
200 miles

Nome, a former gold town where miners flocked to sift the precious metal from its sands before eventually following the gold rush east to found Fairbanks.

Fairbanks is generally **snow-free** from sometime in May to late September or beyond, but to get the most out of the northern parks the best weeks are those of June and the first half of July.

Fairbanks

FAIRBANKS, 358 miles north of Anchorage, is the end of the road for most tourists and marks the ultimate conclusion of the **Alaska Highway** from Canada. If you've just driven the full 1500 miles from Dawson Creek in British Columbia, then some kind of celebration is in order. Catch it right and you can conduct your revelry under the ethereal glow of the **northern lights**, for this is aurora central, with sightings on some 240 nights a year.

Most visitors arrive in summer when nights aren't dark enough for aurora viewing, but residents play midnight baseball games in the 21 hours of natural light. At this time, it can be disconcerting stumbling out of a bar at 2am into bright sunshine, but it is better than the dead of winter when Fairbanks receives only three hours of direct sunlight daily and residents suffer from a high rate of depression.

Fairbanks lies just 188 miles south of the Arctic Circle and far from the moderating effects of the sea, a combination resulting in one of the most extreme temperature ranges found anywhere. The thermometer can rise to over 90°F in summer, but temperatures of –40°F are not uncommon in winter. Car (and truck) use in the winter is a problem: strategically placed electrical sockets enable engines to be plugged in and kept from freezing up, but some people leave their engines on when running errands resulting in exhaust fumes freezing into a disgusting photochemical smog known as **ice fog**, which blots out the weak winter light. This has forced Fairbanksans – as they call themselves – to relocate from the city center into the surrounding wilderness, producing one of the most thinly populated cities imaginable and further encouraging vehicle use. Indeed, Fairbanks has more vehicles per capita than LA, and a network of four-lane freeways that could hardly be less friendly to pedestrians.

Fairbanks bills itself as Alaska's "**Golden Heart**," a moniker reflecting its geographical position and the sense of community that has managed to outlast the rapid urbanization. Of course, it also alludes to the city's history as a gold town, a status that draws busloads to **Gold Dredge No. 8**, the state's only publicly accessible gold dredge, **El Dorado Gold Camp**, and a couple of entertaining burlesque shows recalling those heady days. For more intellectual pursuits, the **University Museum** is among the best in the state, with entertaining shows on the aurora borealis and Alaskan Native sports. To learn more about Alaskan sports, you can enjoy the traditional games to their fullest each July during the **World Eskimo–Indian Olympics**.

Some history

Fairbanks was founded accidentally in 1901 by former Washington State miner **ET Barnette**. After serving five years in a Washington prison for stealing his partner's gold, Barnette headed for Alaska and eventually found himself on the *La Velle Young,* steaming up the Tanana River, bound for the Valdez–Eagle Trail where he hoped to set up a trading post. The river level was low, and Barnette talked the boat's captain into trying a "short cut" up the equally shallow Chena River (pronounced "CHEE-na"). Grounded, the frustrated captain dumped Barnette's 130 tons of mining equipment and supplies on the bank where 1st Avenue now meets Cushman Street, and left him and his wife alone in the wilderness two hundred miles short of their destination.

Meanwhile, hapless Italian émigré, **Felix Pedro** – who had earlier discovered a wondrously rich stream and then lost it – was stumbling around the Tanana Valley almost out of food when he spotted smoke from the *La Velle Young* and headed towards it, eventually settling in with Barnette and company. Pedro continued his prospecting, and the following summer unearthed a small find. Barnette saw his chance to make a buck off eager gold seekers and dispatched his cook to Dawson City to spread "the Great Lie" about a rich strike, managing to convince three hundred prospectors to make the journey. Fortuitously, more gold was eventually found, and in 1904 thousands joined the **gold rush**, flocking to the new city of Fairbanks, named for the Indiana senator Charles Fairbanks, who later became vice-president under Theodore Roosevelt.

Within five years Fairbanks was the largest and busiest city in Alaska, its 18,000 inhabitants enjoying electric lights, a sewerage system, fire and police departments, and a federal jail established in 1904. In this climate, Barnette was able to make a fortune, largely by embezzling a million dollars from the Washington-Alaska Bank, hastening his 1911 departure from the town he had originally founded.

The early surface gold strike turned out to be a freak occurrence. Most of the gold was deep below yards of frozen gravel – a mixed blessing because slow gold recovery sustained Fairbanks well beyond the two-year boom-and-bust cycle typical elsewhere. By the 1920s professional mining engineers came to exploit the deeper deposits using modern dredges that worked the rivers, scooping gold-bearing gravel with giant buckets, then spewing the spent "tailings" out the rear. Their heyday lasted only thirty years, but the evidence – vast piles of gravel and the occasional rusting hulk of a dredge – is hard to miss around neighboring Fox and Ester, and along the Chatanika River.

World War II bolstered the region's fluctuating population, as huge **military bases** were built to thwart possible Japanese attacks and provide a stepping-stone for American planes on their way from Montana to Russia and the European battlefields as part of the **Lend-Lease program**. Fairbanks then sputtered along until the city was chosen as the logistical headquarters for the construction of the **trans-Alaska oil pipeline** (see box, p.488). For four years in the mid-1970s, more than 20,000 oil workers were based here. Generous wage packages, sometimes topping $1500 a week (not much less than the price of a small sedan at the time), fueled rapid expansion and generated a free-wheeling atmosphere. Fairbanks became a byword for excess, infamous for its riotous bars and well-patronized brothels. Then the pipeline was finished, and so it seemed was Fairbanks: unemployment hit twenty percent, property prices crashed, and the city's economy collapsed. Things have since stabilized, but the scars remain, especially downtown, where empty parking lots have replaced blocks once solid with bars and bulging wallets.

Arrival, information, and city transportation

The once-daily Alaska Railroad **train** (once-weekly in winter) offers the most relaxing way to get here from Anchorage or Denali. It creeps through the suburbs of Fairbanks and currently pulls up at the **train station** on Driveway Street (ticket office Mon–Fri 7am–3pm, Sat & Sun 7–11am), five minutes' walk north of downtown, at around 8pm each summer evening. A new station is due for completion for the summer of 2005, inconveniently sited at the junction of the Johansen Expressway and Danby Road over a mile northwest of downtown. Hopefully, the MACS buses will meet trains, but there will certainly be taxis. **Long-distance buses** (see "Listings," p.474 and "Travel details," p.520) mostly drop off downtown outside the visitor center, some also calling at hostels and the main hotels.

You are most likely to use **Fairbanks International Airport**, four miles southwest of downtown, for bush- and float-plane flights into the Arctic, and if you're flying in via Anchorage. The MACS **bus** Yellow Line (Mon–Sat, not Sun; $1.50) only takes half an hour to get from the airport to downtown, but the long wait between services makes it worth grabbing a **taxi** (around $12 to downtown).

Information

Buses and trains arrive a few steps from the **visitor center**, 550 1st Ave (June to mid-Sept daily 8am–8pm; mid-Sept to May Mon–Fri 8am–5pm; ⓣ456-5774 or 1-800/327-5774, ⓦwww.explorefairbanks.com), which is well equipped to handle general inquiries about Fairbanks and points north. For anything outdoorsy it is better to head to the nearby **Alaska Public Lands Information Center** (APLIC), lower level, 250 Cushman St (June to early Sept daily 9am–6pm; early Sept to May Tues–Sat 10am–6pm; ⓣ456-0527), which covers everything to do with recreational use of public lands in the northern third of the state. Excellent displays and free videos detail wildlife, land use, survival techniques, river rescue, and canoe-trip planning, and the helpful staff are good at helping channel your hiking and canoeing ambitions. They've also got stacks of relevant books for sale and the most popular topographical maps; for all other maps, visit the Map Office on the UAF campus (see "Listings," p.474).

City transportation and tours

Even if you've made it this far without a vehicle, when you reach Fairbanks you should think seriously about **renting a car** (for local agencies, see "Listings," p.473). For a city of only 60,000 souls, Fairbanks is incredibly spread out and designed around the needs of drivers. By using buses and maybe renting a bike, it is possible to see most of Fairbanks, but services are painfully infrequent, and two or three people traveling together will soon find a car a very good investment, particularly once you start straying outside the city limits. Most rental agencies won't insure their ordinary vehicles on gravel-surfaced roads (though your own insurance may cover you; check before leaving home), so if you are planning to visit Manley Hot Springs or drive the Steese Highway to Circle Hot Springs, consider renting from Affordable, Northern Alaska, or GoNorth.

If money is tight, or you're traveling alone, you may find yourself drawn to the MACS **bus** system, with its hub at the **transit center**, corner of Cushman Street and 5th Avenue (Mon–Fri 6.15am–7.45pm, Sat 9am–6.15pm; transit hotline ⓣ459-1011). There are five routes, most running every hour or so from around 7am to 7pm on weekdays, with restricted services on Saturday and none at all on Sunday. The most useful lines are: Yellow, from downtown past Pioneer Park and along Airport Way to the airport; Red, along College Road to the university campus; and Blue, past Pioneer Park and several shopping centers to the university. **Fares** are $1.50 per ride; $3 day-passes and $5 five-ride concessions are available from the driver. Alternatively, you could simply get around by **taxi** (for numbers see "Listings," p.474).

Another option is to **rent a bicycle** (see "Listings," p.473), although it is worth considering that even sights within the immediate vicinity of Fairbanks are widely scattered: Fox is eleven miles north, North Pole is fifteen miles southeast, and Ester is six miles northwest. Dedicated cycle trails are rare, but the invaluable *BikeWays* map (available free from the visitor center) details multiuse paths, quiet roads with broad shoulders, and the expressways where bikes are not permitted, along with the location of hills. Bike-rental places will be able to point you in the direction of **mountain-bike** trails, mostly in the cross-country ski area behind the university known as Skarland Trails (maps from the UAF Wood Center) and in Birch Hill Recreation Area just north of downtown (display near entrance).

Accommodation

Fairbanks' accommodation is broadly distributed over an already spread-out city. With a few exceptions, non-drivers will want to stay **downtown** (roughly within twenty minutes' walk of the visitor center), where you'll have the best access to the bus system. **Hotels and motels** here are generally either pricey or drab, but fortunately there are a couple of good hostels and some excellent **B&Bs** at reasonable prices.

Having your own wheels opens up **suburban Fairbanks**, the domain of better-value motels, more good B&Bs, hostels, and some surprisingly sylvan campgrounds. Some of the best B&Bs and campgrounds lie beyond the city limits, often giving better access to the sights around Fairbanks without the hassle of the big city.

Reservations are pretty much essential from June to August when **prices** are correspondingly high, especially during the Golden Days festival in mid-July (see box, p.465). With the exception of major festivals, such as the Ice Art competition (see box, p.457), the city is free from visitors through much of the **winter**, and hotel rates are about half those of summer.

Hostels

Fairbanks is not especially well supplied with hostels. Although there are a couple of decent places, neither is downtown.

Billie's Backpackers Hostel 2895 Mack Rd ⓣ479-2034, ⓦwww.alaskahostel.com. Handily sited place that always seems to be packed, partly because Alaska Trails buses finish various runs here. Comfortable and relaxing, with mountain bikes for rent and free Internet access. Dorms ($22) each have their own bathroom and kitchen, there is a barbecue area outside, and laundry and bag-storage facilities are available. Tent spaces $12 per person. Close to the MACS Red bus route. ❶

Boyle's Hostel 310 18th Ave ⓣ456-4944. Bargain-basement hostel with dorms ($17) and budget rooms on a suburban street (near the MACS Red bus route) that will be unacceptably cluttered and too dark and dingy for many, though Mr Boyle is friendly and helpful. Low-cost laundry, some cooking facilities, and rattling bikes for rent. ❶ **GoNorth Base Camp** 3500 Davis Rd ⓣ479-7272, ⓦwww.gonorthalaska.com. Based around a series of large fixed tents each with five beds ($20; bring a sleeping bag), this forest-girt place has a real outdoors feel with an open-sided (but with protection from bugs) kitchen and lounge that's great in good weather and OK when it's wet. There's camping, too ($8), rental bikes ($20 a day), and handy access to all the trips and equipment offered by GoNorth (see p.468). May to mid-Oct.

Hotels and motels

In summer almost all the hotels are packed with tour groups being paraded around the state after their cruise up the Inside Passage. Tour companies often

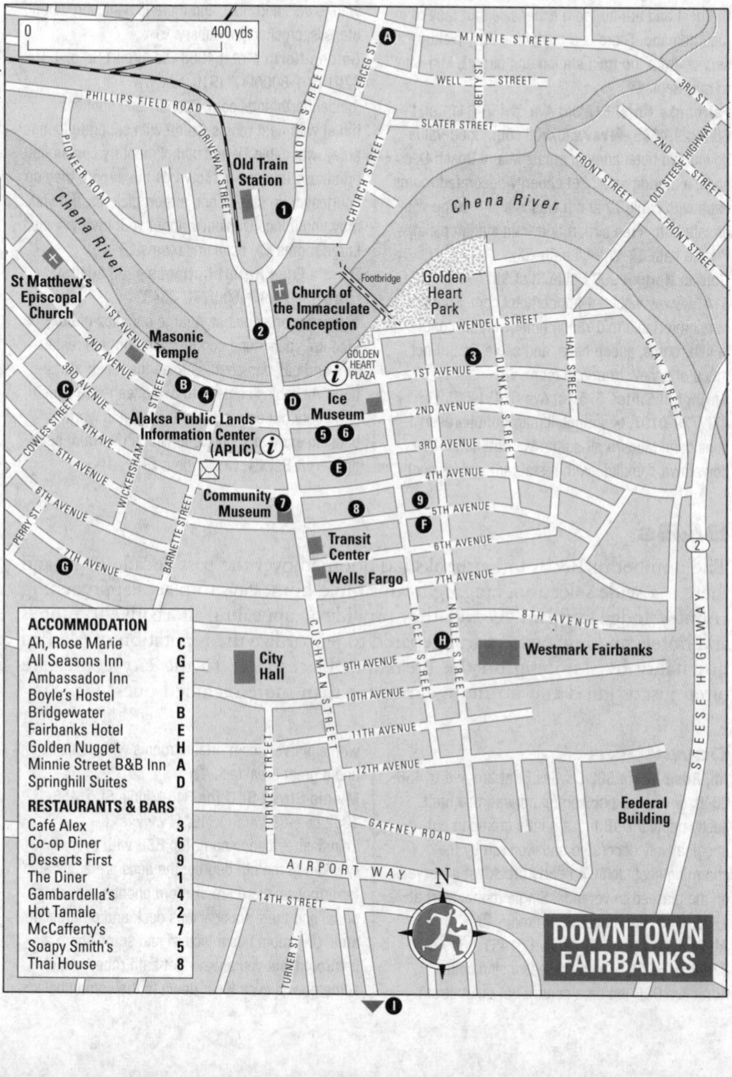

book a handful of large, lackluster places scattered around town, none of which really warrants a mention. We've listed a few smaller, more personal places along with a range of the city's best motels.

Downtown

Ambassador Inn 415 5th Ave ⓣ451-9555. Family-run hotel with quite a few long-term residents and some fairly scruffy public areas, but the rooms, with cable TV and a full kitchen, are central and pretty good value. ❹

Bridgewater 723 1st Ave ⓣ452-6661 or 1-800/528-4916, ⓦwww.fountainheadhotels.com. Slightly dated but quality tourist hotel with comfortable rooms, a restaurant, and a nice lounge area. The larger corner rooms with river views are the best and are no more expensive, but they're in high demand. There is a complimentary pickup service from the train station and airport. Mid-May to mid-Sept. ❺

Fairbanks Hotel 517 3rd Ave ⓣ456-6411 or 1-888/329-4685, ⓦwww.fbxhotl.com. Good-value downtown hotel done in ersatz Miami Beach Deco style, featuring small but cheerily decorated rooms each with cable TV and a washstand – some with private bath. Free airport and train station pickups. Private bath ❹, shared bath ❸

Golden Nugget 900 Noble St at 9th Ave ⓣ452-5141, ⓦwww.golden-nuggethotel.com. Spartan but comfortable mid-range hotel with air-conditioned rooms, queen beds, and cable TV, but not much of a view from any room. ❹

Springhill Suites 575 1st Ave ⓣ451-6552 or 1-877/729-0197, ⓦspringhill.marriotthotelreservations.com. Modern all-suites Marriott hotel right downtown complete with restaurant, indoor pool, exercise room, and free breakfast buffet. Rooms are spacious with fridge, microwave, cable TV and dataport. ❼

Suburban Fairbanks

College Inn 700 Fairbanks St ⓣ474-3666, ⓔmyoung@mosquitonet.com. Long-term residents and the ageing infrastructure make this a fairly dispiriting and characterless place to stay, but it is cheap, handy for the university, and on the MACS Blue and Red bus routes. Shared-bath rooms come with towels and HBO, and there is a kitchen, but no utensils, crockery, or cutlery. ❷

Golden North Motel 4888 Old Airport Rd ⓣ479-6201 or 1-800/447-1910, ⓦwww.goldennorthmotel.com. Friendly and spotless motel with neat rooms (some with separate lounge area) with cable TV and complimentary continental breakfast. Located out towards the airport, they do courtesy train station and airport pickups, but you may find it inconvenient without your own wheels. Large rooms ❹, economy rooms ❸

River's Edge Resort Cottages 4200 Boat St ⓣ474-3601 or 1-800/770-3343, ⓦwww.riversedge.net. A large complex of boxy, modern, year-round cottages with on-site restaurant and bar, and shuttles to all the major attractions. All cabins come with two queen-size beds and doors out onto a patio, though it is worth booking early to secure one with a riverfront setting. Fri & Sat ❼, weeknights ❻

B&Bs

The number of B&Bs in Fairbanks has boomed over the past decade or so, and there is a wide selection, ranging from simple homestays to places approaching country-lodge standard. As ever, they provide an appealing alternative to motels and hotels, and few owners are prepared to jeopardize the reputation of Alaskan hospitality by skimping on the breakfasts. Places close to the city center are often just as good and no more expensive than more secluded ones.

Downtown

Ah, Rose Marie 302 Cowles St at 3rd Ave ⓣ456-2040, ⓦwww.akpub.com/akbbrv/ahrose.html. Justly popular B&B that's a little cramped but imaginatively decorated and well run by the charming host, John. A hearty breakfast is served on the glassed-in veranda. Single rooms start at ❷, shared- and private-bath room ❸

All Seasons Inn 763 7th Ave ⓣ451-6649 or 1-888/451-6649, ⓦwww.allseasonsinn.com. Attractive B&B inn on a central but quiet street with eight very comfortable rooms with cable TV and a great breakfast. ❹

Minnie Street B&B Inn 345 Minnie St ⓣ456-1802 or 1-888/456-1849, ⓦwww.minniestreetbandb.com. Top B&B with every luxury taken to the nth degree: the beds are adjustable for firmness, there are in-room phones with dataports, and there's a spacious deck and a barbecue area. One room has a jacuzzi and some share a bathroom, but you always get bath robes, which some guests even wear down to the communally served full breakfast. There's also a business center with fax, copier, and Internet access. Room with jacuzzi ❼, private bath ❻, shared bath ❺

Suburban Fairbanks

7 Gables Inn 4312 Birch Lane ⓣ479-0751, ⓦwww.7gablesinn.com. Popular and ever-expanding upscale B&B that is large enough to qualify as a small hotel; large rooms all with cable and VCR (and most with spa bath) and flashy suites with a small kitchen. Suites ❻, rooms ❺

Forget Me Not Lodge – Aurora Express 1540 Chena Ridge Rd, about 8 miles west of downtown ⓣ1-800/221-0073, ⓦwww.aurora-express.com. A fun B&B partly in a lodge and partly in a set of old train carriages, with great views over Fairbanks towards the Alaska Range. Suites and carriage rooms ❺–❻, lodge rooms ❸

Midge's Birch Lane 4335 Birch Lane ⓣ388-8084 or 1-800/479-4895, ⓦwww.alaskaone.com/midgebb. One of the best-value B&Bs in the city. It's neat, clean, and friendly, with access to a large lounge with fireplace, a piano, and stacks of Alaska books and videos. All rooms are comfortable and one has a large queen bed, a walk-in wardrobe, private bath, and a deck that gets the afternoon sun. Breakfasts are excellent and may include blintzes or salmon quiche. A twenty-minute walk from the university. Private- and shared-bath rooms ❸

Out of town

Cloudberry Lookout 351 Cloudberry Lane, Mile 2.6 Goldhill Rd ⓣ479-7334, ⓦwww.mosquitonet.com/~cloudberry. Welcoming B&B in a kind of log castle set in woodland with its own "aurorium" tower accessed by an impressive spiral staircase. Spacious rooms all have private bath, big windows, and ancient furniture. A tasty continental breakfast is served. March–Oct. ❹

Fox Creek B&B Mile 1.1 Elliot Hwy, Fox ⓣ457-5494, ⓦwww.foxcreekalaska.com. Just two rooms in a secluded house twelve miles north of downtown and close to the *Howling Dog Saloon*. Quiet and comfortable, with big, cooked breakfasts. No credit cards. Private bath ❹, shared ❸

A Taste of Alaska Lodge 551 Eberhardt Rd, Mile 5.3 Chena Hot Springs Rd ⓣ488-7855, ⓦwww.atasteofalaska.com. Somewhere in between a B&B and a small country lodge, located on 280 acres on a ridge with wonderful views south over the city to the Alaska Range. Comfortable rooms have cable TV and all the expected appointments, plus there's a hot tub for guests' use and panning on their gold claim. Two-bedroom log house ❽, suites ❼, rooms ❻

Trailhead Cabins Middle Fork ⓣ374-0717, ⓦwww.trailheadcabins.com. A real Alaskan experience is waiting here in these cabins, tucked just below the tree line on Haystack Mountain. It's a little inconvenient for Fairbanks (5 miles off the Elliott Hwy and 35 minutes' drive north of town), but makes a great base for exploring the North. The single-room cabins ($65) have a double and a single bunk and come with cooking facilities, breakfast requisites, an outhouse, and supply of water, but no shower or running water. The website has a map to the cabins and a local trail map. ❷

Campgrounds and RV parks

Fairbanks is well served with places to park an RV, and many sites are pleasant places to pitch a tent, though none is entirely RV-free. Campgrounds within the city limits are right on bus routes, though drivers can save a few dollars by staying a short drive out of town.

Suburban Fairbanks

Chena River Recreation Site University Ave at Airport Way ⓣ451-2695. A state parks campground by the Chena River that is surprisingly wooded and quiet for what is essentially a city campground. There are toilets, tables, a dump station, volleyball courts, and even a boat launch. Walk-in sites for $10, vehicle slots for $15. On the MACS Blue bus route.

Former K-Mart parking lot Airport Way between Peger Rd and University Ave. It really is just a parking lot, but good enough for parking up your RV at no charge. No facilities.

Pioneer Park Airport Way at Peger Rd ⓣ459-1087. Park your RV in the Pioneer Park parking lot and use their toilets, water, and dump station; no showers. $10 a night (four nights maximum). Reached by the MACS Blue and Yellow buses. Mid-May to mid-Sept.

River's Edge RV Park 4200 Boat St ⓣ474-0286 or 1-800/770-3343, ⓦwww.riversedge.net. Fairbanks' largest RV park, adjacent to the *River's Edge Resort Cottages* (see p.454). Full hookup sites go for $28, tent sites are $16. The Yellow MACS bus passes outside. Mid-May to mid-Sept.

Tanana Valley Campground 1800 College Rd at Aurora Drive ⓣ456-7956, ⓦwww.tananavalleyfair.org/campground. Peaceful, spruce-shrouded campground that's best for tenters and RVers who only want electrical hookups. Sites all come with tables and fire pits (wood sold), showers are free ($3 for non-guests), and there's a laundry, free Internet access, and a camp kitchen serving good meals throughout the day. Best of all, it is located midway between downtown and the university area on the MACS Red bus line (hourly or better). They also have free bikes for guests. Electrical hookups $16, dry RV sites $13, tent sites $9. Reserve a day or two in advance. Mid-May to mid-Sept.

Out of town

Chena Lakes Recreation Area Mile 346 Richardson Hwy. Wooded camping and RV sites with no hookups located in an attractive recreation area seventeen miles southeast of Fairbanks. $10.

Ester Gold Camp Old Nenana Hwy, Ester ⓣ479-2500 or 1-800/676-6925, ⓦwww.alaskasbest.com/ester. Basic RV park without hookups, but with a dump station, showers, and a free coffee-and-muffin breakfast. Located at Ester (see p.467), six miles northwest of town. Late May to early Sept. $15.

The city and around

Downtown Fairbanks is on the up, with a rash of new building and a bit of civic pride finally taking hold. It's about time, too, as the double whammy of mall mania and the absence of oil cash, which kept downtown buoyant in the 1970s, had turned once vibrant blocks into a depressing collection of neglected truck showrooms and parking lots with weeds pushing through the cracks. The streets are still partly populated by residents without the financial wherewithal to buy their own cars, and the exodus of business to the strip malls of Airport Way or the slightly more bohemian enclave of College Road seems to have halted. Some of the old miners' cottages have been co-opted by small businesses – hairdressers, accountants, and graphic-arts companies. Still, downtown shouldn't take up much of your time: besides the visitor center, APLIC, and a couple of small museums, there isn't a great deal to divert your attention.

The most concentrated area of genuine interest for visitors is on the city's northern flank along College Road towards the university. Outside of the school's first-class museum, sights tend to revolve around animals and nature: you can visit a waterfowl refuge, walk around the pleasant confines of the **Georgeson Botanical Gardens**, or drive north to view the musk oxen and caribou at the **Large Animal Research Station**.

There's an appreciably more kitschy approach at the forty-acre **Pioneer Park** complex, which showcases early Fairbanks buildings and the restored SS *Nenana* sternwheeler along with assorted kids' entertainments; it can be quite fun and most of it is free. In contrast, rides along the Chena River on the replica sternwheeler, **Riverboat Discovery**, represent mass tourism in its most packaged form and are far from cheap.

The sights in Fairbanks might only keep you entertained for a day or so, but the city makes the best base for attractions in the immediate vicinity. No one with kids will be able to keep them from visiting Santa at **North Pole**, fifteen miles to the southeast; fans of gold-rush poet Robert Service will want to spend an evening in **Ester**, six miles west; and the district's mining heritage can be experienced at one of three extensive sites in **Fox**, eleven miles to the north.

Downtown

Unless you've developed a deep interest in the machinations of Fairbanks' early civic leaders, skip the detailed self-guided downtown tour ($1 booklet from the visitor center) and concentrate on a few key sights. The visitor center lies on the south bank of the languid Chena River where logs were once floated along for the construction of the town. It is now flanked by small patches of parkland, some long neglected, others overly tended. Foremost among the latter is **Golden Heart Plaza**, an open riverside area focusing on Malcolm Alexander's

Winter in Fairbanks: ice art and the Yukon Quest

Fairbanks' winter temperatures stay below 0°F for months on end, metal-snapping freezes below –40°F are expected and –60°F is not unknown, so it is no surprise that most visitors stay away from the end of September (when the temperatures are already getting nippy) until the end of April, when the last of the snow melts away. Still, a few hardy visitors do venture up this way, notably Japanese honeymooners, who put great store in consummating their marriage under the **northern lights** (see box, pp.460–461), and those making pilgrimages to Fairbanks' two major winter events. Intending winter visitors should obtain the *Winter Guide* from the visitor center (also available at Ⓦwww.explorefairbanks.com).

The Yukon Quest

The first of these events is the **Yukon Quest** International Sled Dog Race (Ⓦwww.yukonquest.com), a thousand-mile classic between Fairbanks and Whitehorse, Yukon, over some of the wildest and most sparsely populated country anywhere. By most estimations it ranks second to the Iditarod in the sled-racing hierarchy (and is around a hundred miles shorter), but many mushers cite its infrequent checkpoints to support their claim that it is the tougher of the two races. It is less a series of sprints between checkpoints than a grueling endurance test requiring heavier loads and more sleeping rough on the trail, rigorously testing the self-sufficiency, determination, and dog-driving ability of the competitor. The race has been run in the second week of February (when river ice is at its thickest) since 1984 and alternates direction each year, starting in Fairbanks in even-numbered years. It largely follows the route of the Steese Highway from Fairbanks to Circle so, unlike the Iditarod, spectators can watch at various points. From Circle it then heads up the Yukon River through the Yukon-Charley National Preserve past Eagle to Dawson City, where there is a compulsory 36-hour layover before the final run into Whitehorse. Most competitors use a team of fourteen dogs and take ten to fourteen days, hoping to take home the first prize of around $30,000.

Fairbanks also hosts a number of shorter races, notably the **North American Sled Dog Races** (Ⓦwww.sleddog.org), twenty-mile "sprints" which take place in March, starting and finishing downtown.

Ice art

Though the Yukon Quest is spectator-friendly, far more visitors come during the first two weeks in March for the **World Ice Art Championships** in the Ice Park on Phillips Field Road. It is virtually the Olympiad of ice carving, with sculptors from around the world (Morocco, Australia, and Brazil among others) striving to produce larger-than-life sculptures from blemish-free blocks of ice. The chunks are fashioned using saws, picks, chainsaws, chisels, sanders, angle grinders, even electric irons into sculptures up to 35ft high. Along with prosaic natural subjects – polar bears, caribou, Natives ice fishing – fantasy themes are popular, with images of medieval castles and jousting contests.

The event starts with the Single Block Classic, in which teams of two spend two and a half days shaping a single 8000-pound block measuring 5ft x 8ft by 3ft thick. This is followed (after a couple of days' rest) by the Multi-Block Classic, where teams of four have five and a half days to transform twelve 3000-pound blocks measuring 4ft x 4ft by 3ft. Competitors work through the day and night, with colorful lighting illuminating the works as they take shape. The work remains on display during the Winter Carnival throughout the remainder of March. The whole process, along with details of next year's contest, can be found at Ⓦwww.icealaska.com.

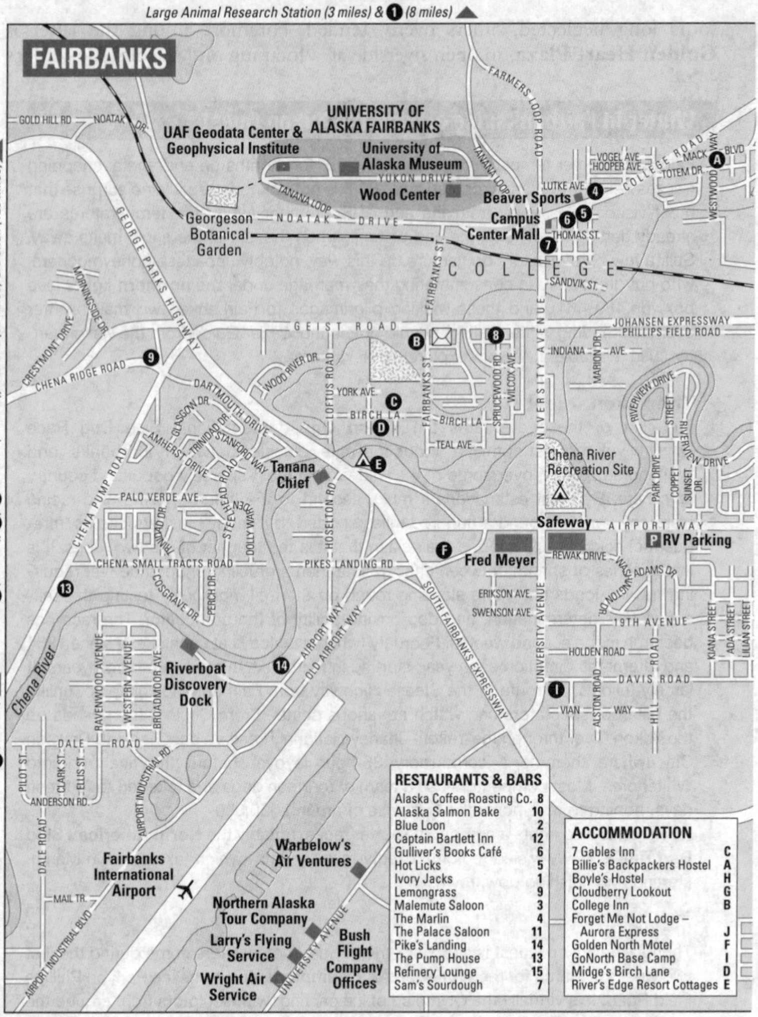

statue *Unknown First Family*, dedicated to the "indomitable spirit of the people of Alaska's Interior." Immediately west, a plaque marks the spot where Fairbanks' founder, ET Barnette, was left stranded with his supplies in 1901.

Cross the Chena River on the Cushman Street bridge to the prim **Church of the Immaculate Conception** (Mon–Fri 8am–4pm), which wouldn't look out of place in New England and contains an ornate pressed-tin ceiling and a beatific Madonna. The church was built south of the river in 1904 and moved to its current site during the winter of 1911. Back on the south bank, a walk west along 1st Avenue takes you past the 1906 **Masonic Temple**, originally built for ET Barnette, then adapted with the addition of a second story for the Masons in 1913 and later used by President Warren Harding when he addressed the populace in 1923. Continuing along 1st Avenue, you find a string

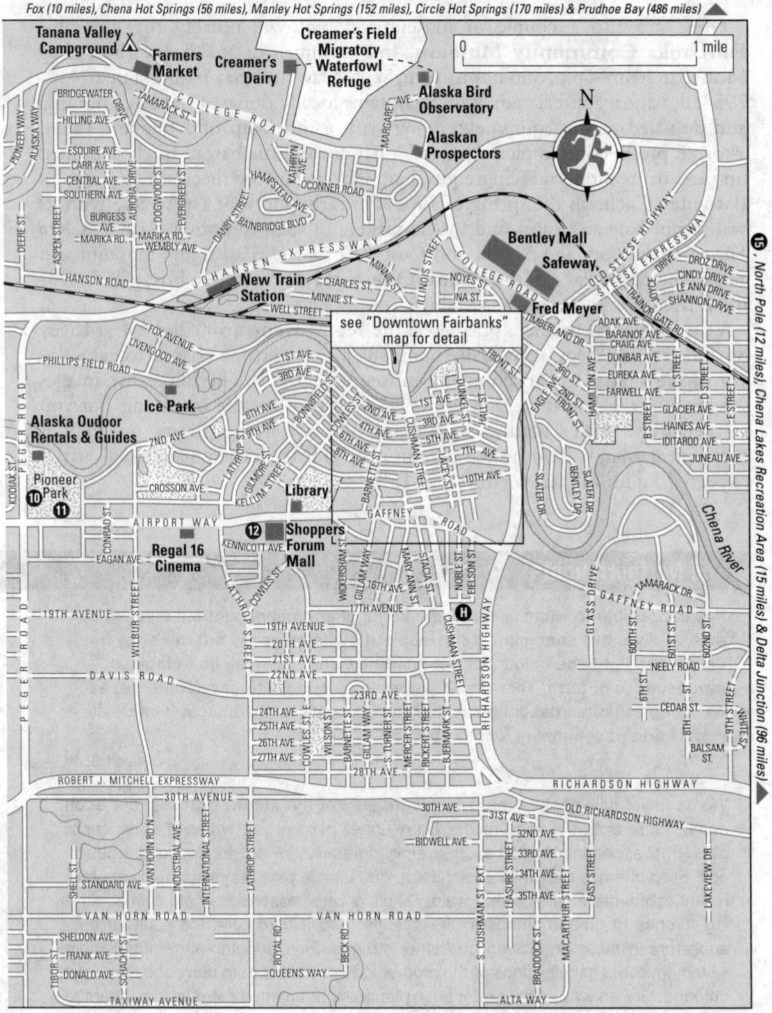

of historic log cabins gone to seed – structures that would have been restored into residences or craft shops anywhere else in America.

It isn't often you see a stained-glass depiction of an Alaskan sled dog or an Iñupiat on his way to church in the snow, but you can inside the 1947 **St Matthew's Episcopal Church**, 1029 1st Ave. It replaced the 1905 original built for Hudson Stuck, archdeacon of the Episcopal Church in Alaska from 1903 to 1920, a man noted primarily for being the first to reach Mount McKinley's summit (see box, p.370). Another glass shows him leaving for the mountain complete with a huge cross around his neck, which was later placed at the summit. A couple of blocks further on there's a classic example of a "**grow-house**" at 1323 1st Ave, a basic log cabin that was extended out back with each new addition to the family, in this case four times.

There are also a couple of museums downtown, notably the enjoyable **Fairbanks Community Museum**, 450 Cushman St at 5th Ave (June–Aug Mon–Sat 10am–6pm, Sun noon–4pm; Sept–May Tues–Sat 10am–6pm; ⓣ452-7954; donation appreciated), which contains locally donated trapping, mining, and dog-sled-racing equipment, along with a mock-up of a trapper's cabin, assorted prospecting implements, and a handmade Athabascan birch sled lined up next to its modern racing equivalent. Check out the nice little diorama of Barnette's Cache in the spring of 1902, the early photo of 1st Avenue with its waterfront bars and cafés, and movie posters of such forgotten classics as *Red Snow*, *Alaska Seas,* and Abbott and Costello's *Lost in Alaska*. The museum also acts as the public face of the **Yukon Quest** sled dog race (see box, p.457), selling related books, videos, and T-shirts.

A similar winter theme is pursued at the **Ice Museum**, 500 2nd Ave at Lacey St (June to mid-Sept daily 10am–6pm; $8), a summertime chance to get a flavor of the annual Ice Art competition (see box, p.457). The impressive images screened in the half-hour slide show fall well short of the real thing, but you can see a few small sculptures by walking into two freezer rooms, one kept at the typical March daytime temperature of 20°F, the other maintained at the expected nighttime temperature of –15°F.

The Northern lights

It is impossible to witness such a beautiful phenomenon without a sense of awe, and yet this sentiment is not inspired by its brilliancy but rather by its delicacy in light and colour, its transparency, and above all its tremulous evanescence of form. There is no glittering splendour to dazzle the eye, as has been too often described; rather the appeal is to the imagination by the suggestion of something wholly spiritual...

Robert Scott

Words never fully capture the dynamic majesty of the **aurora borealis**, but Scott comes close and, in *Arctic Dreams*, Barry Lopez perceptively writes of a "banner of pale light" appearing like "a t'ai chi exercise: graceful, inward-turning, and protracted." Everyone has their own explanation: one Inuit legend suggests the lights represent spirits playing ball with a walrus skull; another asserts they are spirits carrying torches to guide nomads to the afterlife; and a third sees the souls of their ancestors in these undulating gossamer strands. Ever hopeful, early prospectors saw them either as reflections of the mother lode or vapors from rich deposits as yet unfound. Galileo was loath to offer an explanation, but named them Aurora, after the Roman goddess of the dawn.

As you gaze at these celestial pyrotechnics you feel no need or desire to explain them. It is enough just to marvel as silken curtains of light miraculously materialize, then just as soon curl up and disappear, or hang around for hours on end folding back on themselves, delicately changing hue from rose pink to pale green and on to white, fading with the early light of dawn. The curtain effect isn't illusory; the band of light may hang from an altitude of three hundred miles down to forty miles above the earth and stretch for hundreds of miles, and yet be only a hundred yards wide.

The University of Alaska Fairbanks is at the forefront of scientific research into the northern lights (and their southern hemisphere counterparts the aurora australis). Both are caused by an interaction between the earth's magnetic field and the **solar wind**, an invisible stream of charged electrons and protons continually blown out into space by the innate violence of the sun. The earth deflects the solar wind like a rock in a stream, the magnetic field channeling the charged particles down towards

Along College Road and around the university

From the downtown area College Road arcs out along the northern flank of the city (followed by Blue and Red MACS buses), and buildings become scarce after a mile or so, revealing the open fields of **Creamer's Field Migratory Waterfowl Refuge**, 1300 College Rd (unrestricted entry), on the site of Creamer's Dairy. It was established in 1903 with three cows brought from Nome by the brother-in-law of Charles Creamer, who operated it until 1965. Four years later, the state bought it and decided to continue the dairy's rotation-planting program of oats, barley, and peas to further foster the attention of migratory wildfowl. The grasslands now provide a temporary resting place for several large species, including thousands of **sandhill cranes**, which leave their wintering grounds in Texas and New Mexico and pause here to recuperate in the spring, some sticking around through the summer, others flying on to Siberia. Many return in fall to fatten up for the return flight south. **Canada geese** make a slightly shorter passage from the Pacific Northwest – the first V-shaped skeins heralding the arrival of spring – and you might also expect to see predatory peregrine falcons and bald eagles, along with pintails, golden plovers, and mallards. Visitors and locals park up beside College Road, training binocu-

the earth's magnetic poles. Here the protons and electrons release some of their energy as visible light – much like a neon sign – the common yellowish green produced by oxygen atoms, while the purples and rare deep reds are caused by nitrogen.

While their manifestations may seem gentle, the forces involved are immense, occasionally blocking out radio communications and inducing magnetic fields in pipes, making them more susceptible to corrosion; even the oil pipeline is affected. The aurora's electrical charge can also cause power blackouts: on March 13, 1989 much of eastern Canada and the northeastern US was dark for six hours as a result of unusually powerful aurora activity.

The northern lights are a circumpolar phenomenon, and it is only at times of extreme solar activity that they are seen at lower latitudes; in Fairbanks, however, they are almost continual. In summer there is too much daylight to see them clearly, but as the nights grow longer your chances of a good showing increase. The **best viewing** is when the sky is clear and the air chilly, preferably at the vernal equinox around March 20. At this time the worst of the winter temperatures have passed, and Fairbanks hotels do a roaring trade, some specializing in aurora packages aimed mostly at the Japanese, who have a particular passion for the lights, some believing that children conceived under the aurora will be successful in business.

For more information, consult the *Aurora Watcher's Handbook* by Neil Davis (University of Alaska Press) or UAF's aurora website (Ⓦwww.gi.alaska.edu/predict.php3), which has a weekly aurora forecast with map, and a stack of other material pertaining to the phenomenon.

Photographing the aurora isn't easy: expect to be disappointed with your results. If you're still keen, load up with a 200 or 400 ASA film, pick a time when the aurora is fairly stable, use a wide-angle lens, and go for exposures from one to thirty seconds using a tripod. Short exposures are usually better, but take notes and experiment on subsequent nights. You should also protect your camera from the cold, ground it to a large metal object so that static electricity doesn't cause streaks on the film, and wrap the camera in a plastic bag when you return inside to prevent damage from condensation.

lars and telephoto lenses at the fields, but you may as well head to the pleasant **trails** in the woods beside the original dairy buildings, which now house an instructive **visitor center** (June–Aug daily 10am–5pm; Sept–May Sat noon–4pm). From there you can pick up one of two trails through the woods: the educational Boreal Forest Trail (2 miles) follows a packed-earth path and boardwalks through birch bog and out through grasslands regenerating after a fire; the seasonal Wetland Trail (1 mile) is best early summer but worthwhile later to visit the bird-banding station where from August to mid-September you're likely to encounter songbird research in practice. If you can time it right, try to join one of the two-hour **nature walks** led by volunteer naturalists (June–Aug Mon & Wed 9am, Tues & Thurs 7pm; free; for subject matter call ⓣ452-7307).

A further trail leads east across the refuge to the **Alaska Bird Observatory**, 418 Wedgewood Drive (mid-May to Sept Mon–Fri 10am–6pm, Sat 10am–5pm; Oct to mid-May Mon–Fri 10am–4pm; ⓣ451-0505, ⓦwww.alaskabird.org), which conducts the refuge's banding operation, has a small display of mounted bird specimens and some active feeding stations, and is a must for keen birders.

Half a mile west is the site of the **Farmers Market** (May–Sept Wed 11am–4pm, Sat 9am–4pm, ⓦwww.tvfmarket.com), a forum for local growers to sell their produce along with crafts, freshly baked sourdough bread, and more. As much as anything, it is a local meeting place, drawing a typically oddball cross-section of Alaskans: bush-dwellers, students, neo-hippies, and suburbanites.

A couple of miles further along College Road there is a small knot of restaurants, cafés, bars, and shops that constitutes the suburb of **College**, at the foot of the ridge from which the **University of Alaska Fairbanks** commands great views of the distant Alaska Range. This is the state's original campus, and it still considers itself the most prestigious, though Anchorage now has a larger enrollment. The main reason to venture up here is to visit the University of Alaska Museum (see opposite), though during the school year you might want to wander into the **Woods Center** and see what's happening around campus. You'll find a library (open to all), campus cafés and bars, and a handy rides board.

The **UAF Geophysical Institute**, Elvey Bldg, 903 Koyukuk Drive, presents a free educational program (June–Aug Wed 2.30pm; ⓣ474-7558), with slide show, aurora video, and a visit to the Alaskan earthquake information center. This is immediately followed by a walk through the adjacent **International Arctic Research Center** (same dates 3.30pm), a headquarters for scientists studying Arctic and global climates.

Nearby, at the western end of the campus, a narrow track leads 400yd down through the fields to the **Georgeson Botanical Gardens**, W Tanana Drive (May–Sept daily 8am–8pm; $2; ⓣ474-1944). In spring and early summer, the gardens are filled with colorful flowers and lush leafy greens, and as the summer wears on, you'll see huge vegetables almost as large as those produced in the Mat-Su Valley. It is perfect for a sunny afternoon or evening, full of seats and shady bowers where you can breathe in the fragrant air and gaze at the Alaska Range. There's a small visitor center (daily 10am–6pm), and free guided tours take place in summer (June–Aug Fri 2pm).

Unless you join one of the city tours, you'll need your own transport to get to the **Large Animal Research Station**, north of the university on Yankovich Road, off Farmers Loop Road. A roadside parking lot with viewing platforms gives you the chance to see herds of caribou and musk oxen, all part of the university's research program into their nutrition, physiology, and behavior. For a true sense of the ongoing work, hook up with one of the $10 guided tours (mid- to late May and early to mid-Sept Tues & Sat 1.30pm;

June–Aug daily 1.30pm; late Sept Sat 1.30pm; reservations not needed except for large groups; ⓣ474-7202, ⓦwww.uaf.edu/lars) that meet outside the main gate.

University of Alaska Museum

Most people agree that the **University of Alaska Museum**, 907 Yukon Drive (mid-May to mid-Sept daily 9am–7pm; mid-Sept to mid-May Mon–Fri 9am–5pm, Sat & Sun noon–5pm; $5, combination package with the two shows $13.50; 24hr infoline ⓣ474-7505, ⓦwww.uaf.edu/museum), is one of the finest in the state, and it is about to make its bid for outright honors. Come the summer of 2005 it will open its dramatically designed new wing with increased display space and a new gallery to show the museum's huge collection of Alaskan art.

Dramatic sculptures – including a couple of fine, modern totem poles – point the way to the existing displays, which are shoehorned into one large room, divided thematically. Stuffed examples of just about every Alaskan animal herald a section on extinct animals from dinosaur fossils and a huge-tusked mammoth skull to a reconstruction of **Blue Babe**, a steppe bison found in the permafrost in a local placer mine during the summer of 1979. It died 36,000 years ago and, over time, the phosphorus in the tissue reacted with the iron-rich soil to produce an all-over blueish tinge. Nevertheless, the bone, marrow, and skin were so well preserved that the cause of death – at the claws of the now extinct American lion – could be determined.

Other sections are devoted to major geographic regions of the state, the Arctic partly represented by a replica of the **Boulder Patch**, an undersea garden of soft corals and sponges found in the Beaufort Sea, which is frozen over for much of the year. The kelp manages to store photosynthesized energy in the summer, then goes through its growing period while frozen over from November to April when the required nutrients are present. Elsewhere, there's a two-ton lump of solid copper from the Wrangell Mountains; assorted ephemera of early Fairbanks life; engaging, if gruesome, footage of traditional whale and seal hunting alongside wooden snow goggles and a seal-gut parka with auklet-feather detail; and the *Forced to Leave* video on the appalling conditions suffered by the Aleut during their internment in Southeast Alaska in World War II: a powerful and moving indictment of US policy towards a group of its own people.

For those with a scientific bent, there is lengthy coverage of various strange aspects of permafrost (see box, p.495), along with a weighty discussion of the aurora. If interested, check out **Dynamic Aurora** ($4), a slightly nerdy physics lecture that doesn't convey the poetry of the northern lights, but is enlivened by some excellent slides and the chance to wear prismatic glasses. Check with the museum for location and times during the museum expansion.

There is perhaps a broader appeal to the **Northern Inua Show** ($6.50), a fast-paced 45-minute celebration of traditional Alaskan games. All major tribal groups are represented, though you are left without much of an impression of the distinction between the tribes. Many of the games are highly athletic, harking back to necessary honing of traditional hunting and survival skills: the stick pull is said to represent hauling hunted seals from the water and involves competitors sitting on the floor facing each other, the soles of their feet touching, with both holding onto a stick. The one who gets pulled up or lets go loses. These are included in the World Eskimo-Indian Olympics (see box, p.465), while others are simply for entertainment through the long winter nights – one, for example, is based on a competitor making faces while others have to refrain from laughing as long as possible.

Pioneer Park

Somehow almost everyone winds up at **Pioneer Park**, Airport Way at Peger Road (park grounds always open, shops open late May to early Sept daily 11am–9pm; free), a kind of low-key theme park reached using the Blue and Yellow MACS buses. The place seems unsure of what it wants to be, though acquits itself well enough in fine weather, especially if you've got kids, who will undoubtedly enjoy the play areas, miniature golf, and toy train. Otherwise it is better to come in the late afternoon, take a quick tour of the buildings, and stick around for the **Alaska Salmon Bake** (see p.471) and perhaps the nightly show at the *Palace Saloon* (see p.472).

Pioneer Park was set up in 1967 as part of the state's centennial of the Alaska purchase and as a way to save some of Fairbanks' original log buildings. Some thirty historic structures have been preserved and lined up to form a pioneer street, though almost all the architectural and historical merit is camouflaged by the shelves of the trinket stores that now occupy the houses. It is still worth strolling along, pausing to duck into the period-furnished **Kitty Hensley House** (late May to early Sept daily 11am–9pm; free) and the **Wickersham House Museum** (late May to early Sept daily 11am–9pm; donations appreciated) in the onetime residence of Judge James Wickersham; the restored **Harding Car** that the president used when visiting Nenana in 1923 to drive the railroad's golden spike; and the **Pioneer Museum** (late May to early Sept daily 11am–9pm; free), with its material on early telegraph systems during the gold rush, a small collection of foot warmers used in open stages and sleighs, and an 1897 Rand McNally map showing trails to the Yukon and Klondike goldfields, including winter river routes. The adjacent forty-minute **Big Stampede Show** (6 times daily; $4) has the audience seated on a large turntable which revolves as fifteen scenes from the gold rush that have been painted on the walls are spotlighted in turn.

Though beached and in need of a lick of paint, the **SS Nenana** sternwheeler (late May to early Sept guided tours on demand daily 11am–9pm; $3, diorama only $2) lends the park a dramatic focus. It was launched in 1933, the last and one of the most luxurious of the great wooden-hulled sternwheeler steamers, coming at the end of the era when the Interior waterways were the easiest (if not the only) way to get around in summer. But she was really a workhorse, carrying three hundred tons of cargo and pushing up to six barges, making the 770-mile run from Nenana to the mouth of the Yukon and back ten times in the five-month season. Until its conversion to oil in 1948, lumberjacks often worked with dog sleds through the winter to supply wood stockpiles. By 1955 air transport had rendered the steamers uneconomic, and the *Nenana* languished until rescued in 1967 for Pioneer Park. For a deeper insight into how the *Nenana* and her sisters influenced the development of the Interior, look around the detailed 300-foot-long Tanana/Yukon Rivers Historical Diorama, which shows a couple of dozen villages along the two rivers.

The riverboats

Unlike Pioneer Park's static *Nenana*, you and seven hundred others can actually ride on the **Riverboat Discovery**, Discovery Road, near the airport (mid-May to mid-Sept daily 8.45am & 2pm; $45; ⓣ1-866/479-6673), a replica sternwheeler that packs in the tour groups for its slick and not overly thrilling three-and-a-half-hour cruises. The Binkley family takes pride in now having their fourth generation of riverboat captains at the helm for this narrated trip on which you'll call at a replica Athabascan fishing village, watch salmon being

Fairbanks festivals

In early February the Yukon Quest sled-dog race is in town, and the World Ice Art Championships take place over the first two weeks in March (see box, p.457), immediately followed by the revelry of the Fairbanks Winter Carnival. Summer gets into full swing at the summer solstice (June 20 and 21) with the Midnight Sun Fun Run, the 30,000-strong Midnight Sun street fair, and the **Midnight Sun Baseball Game**, a long-standing tradition from the gold days (first played around 1905) in which Fairbanks' semi-pro team, the Goldpanners, plays without artificial lights from dusk (around 10.30pm) until sunrise some two or three hours later. Around the middle of July the **World Eskimo-Indian Olympics** (Ⓦwww.weio.org) pits Native athletes against 25 grueling tests of skill, strength, and cunning, such as the Ear Pull, in which a loop of string is passed around an ear of each contestant in a tug of war and the first to let the loop slip off or slacken loses; the Knuckle Hop, a race in which competitors hop along on knuckles and toes; the One-Foot High Kick, where the contestant hops, kicks a foot up to touch a sealskin ball and lands on the same foot without falling over.

At much the same time, the town comes alive for **Golden Days**, a festival with all manner of games, parades, and events all ostensibly celebrating Felix Pedro's discovery of gold in the area (held the week between the second and third weekends in July). The last major event of the summer is the **Tanana Valley State Fair**, a traditional selection of rides, demonstrations, and giant-produce competitions held on the State Fairgrounds on College Road during the first week of August. Up-to-date details of events can be found on the CVB's website, Ⓦwww.explorefairbanks.com.

prepared for air-drying, be entertained by a bush pilot doing a short takeoff and landing beside the river, and see four-time Iditarod winner Susan Butcher demonstrate dog sledding. If you can't be bothered getting out of your seat, you can watch it all on closed-circuit TV.

In recent years the **Tanana Chief** (mid-May to mid-Sept; Ⓣ452-8687, Ⓦwww.greatlandrivertours.com) has set up in competition using a 1984 replica sternwheeler, which plied the Mississippi until being brought north in 2000. With a far smaller boat it is a much more intimate experience, taking a couple of hours to head downstream to the confluence with the Tanana River and back. Their dinner cruise (6.45pm; $50) runs nightly, there's a Sunday brunch special (noon; $37), and you can skip the meals and take either cruise for pure sightseeing ($25).

Fox

The only major route north of Fairbanks – and the access to most of the area's hot springs, canoe routes, and hiking trails – is the Steese Highway. Following this a couple of miles north from downtown, you reach the junction for **Birch Hill Recreation Area**, a cross-country skiing area in winter and the venue for summer Shakespeare plays (see p.472). Just beyond, the road to Chena Hot Springs diverts east. The Steese Highway continues north to the **Hagelbarger Road viewpoint**, with views of the Alaska Range, and the **trans-Alaska pipeline viewpoint**, Mile 8, where you can stand next to the pipeline, examine a section of the pipe and an old-style cleansing pig (see box, p.488) and glean information from the visitor center (late May to early Sept Mon–Sat 8.30am–5.30pm).

FOX, eleven miles north of Fairbanks, appears to be an inconsequential road junction, with little of interest except for the *Howling Dog Saloon*, *Silver Gulch Brewery*, and the *Turtle Club* restaurant (listed on p.472–73). Fox, however, has long been the center of the Fairbanks mining district – over the years the most lucrative of all of Alaska's goldfields – so far yielding some seven million ounces of the metal. All around, the stripped hillsides, mounds of tailings, and abandoned heavy machinery betray the decades spent unearthing gold, while the "Keep Out" signs underline the continued search.

Felix Pedro first struck gold on what is now Pedro Creek, five miles northeast of Fox, setting in motion the establishment of Fairbanks and sparking the last of the major gold rushes. Loose flakes relatively easily teased from streambed gravels were soon gone, and miners had to turn to increasingly more troublesome and labor-intensive methods of extraction. In some cases, up to 100ft of frozen low-grade gravel had to be cleared away to reach ore-bearing layers. Several techniques were used, all requiring huge quantities of water, which grubstake miners couldn't obtain. They were then supplanted by large mining companies that funded the construction of the **Davidson Ditch,** which from 1928 until 1959 brought water from the Chatanika River using six miles of pipe and 83 miles of ditch, parts of it still visible along the Steese Highway.

Three local tours provide different perspectives on the eternal quest. **Gold Dredge No. 8**, Mile 9 Old Steese Hwy (mid-May to mid-Sept daily 9.30am–5pm last tour 3.30pm; $23; ⓣ457-6058, ⓦwww.golddredgeno8.com), is the only place in Alaska where you can safely walk around the inside of an authentic gold dredge, in this case a steel-hulled affair operated from 1928 to 1959, devouring cubic yard after cubic yard of gold-bearing gravel from Goldstream and Engineer creeks. Operations finally came to a halt after statehood when taxes increased and legal changes imposed by the federal government meant that workers could no longer be exploited to the same degree. The ensuing neglect also scuppered the dredge, which now rests on the bottom of its pond, but looks no less impressive. An hour-long tour around the dredge's workings – sieves, separation tables, and gold-collection riffles – comes sandwiched between a video on Alaska's dredging history and an opportunity to try your hand with a poke (small bag) of gold-bearing gravel ($5). Additional pokes are available, and you can stay all day panning poorer gravel from a nearby heap if you wish; just don't expect to make a fortune. The workers' mess has now been converted into a dining room, where a basic, all-you-can-eat stew is served daily between 11am and 3pm ($9.50).

A more venerable method of obtaining gold from dirt is illustrated a couple of miles north at **El Dorado Gold Mine**, Mile 1.5 Elliott Hwy (mid-May to mid-Sept two-hour tours Tues–Fri & Sun 9.45am & 3pm, Mon & Sat 3pm; $28; ⓣ479-7613 or 1-866/479-6673, ⓦwww.eldoradogoldmine.com), reached by riding a replica of the Tanana Valley Railroad train that once ran through the main street of Fox. It now passes through a tunnel hewn from permafrost ground to reach the mining area, where time-honored sluicing and separating techniques still used in small mines all over Alaska are demonstrated. It is all pretty light-hearted but quite informative, and there is, again, the opportunity to walk away with some gold at the end of the day. A free shuttle bus runs here from Fairbanks picking up around an hour before the start of each tour at various hotels and the visitor center.

To link the early twentieth-century experience to the modern day, visit the **Fort Knox Mine** (ⓣ488-GOLD ext 2800, ⓦwww.fortknoxalaska.com), some eight miles to the northeast along the Steese Highway. This is the largest gold mine in Alaska, an open-cast affair where banks of gravel are blasted daily to feed massive mills that process 40,000 tons of ore a day. Two-hour **tours** (June–Aug, 2 daily; Sept–May, 2–3 weekly; $21) begin at a parking lot on Twin

Creek Road just off the Steese Highway at Mile 20 and require donning hard hat and safety glasses before wandering around the crusher building, mill, and control room and peering into the vast pit from an overlook. The tour ends with the opportunity to lift a gold bar worth $90,000.

Ester

During the day there is no reason to drive the six miles west of Fairbanks to the former gold town of **ESTER**. All you'll find are a few houses scattered in the woods and the remains of large-scale mechanized mining equipment from the town's boom time from the late 1930s until the 1950s. In the evenings tour buses arrive for shows centered around the **Ester Gold Camp**, Old Nenana Road (everything open late May to early Sept; ⓣ479-2500 or 1-800/676-6925, ⓦwww.akvisit.com), a reconstruction of the original town which incorporates a couple of authentic early miners' cabins but has had so many false fronts and Western-style boardwalks added that everything you see is fake. The camp puts on "Service with a Smile" (nightly 9pm, additionally at 7pm on Wed–Sat in July; $15), a cheesy ninety-minute cabaret packed with gold-rush songs and poetry by Alaska's adopted son **Robert Service** (see box, p.189). The Bard of the North's best-known work is *The Shooting of Dan McGrew*, in which the action happens in the **Malemute Saloon**, a name revived for the rough-wood-and-sawdust bar where this nightly revue takes place. The saloon is actually quite modern, but incorporates part of the bar once installed in the *Royal Alexandra Bar* in Dawson City on which Service reputedly jotted down some of his lines.

To make a night of it you could start off by dining at the *Bunkhouse Restaurant,* which offers an all-you-can-eat **crab buffet** (daily 5–9pm; $30, $18 without crab), then amble over to the Firehouse Theatre for the 45-minute "Crown of Light" **photosymphony** (daily 6.45pm & 7.45pm; $8), LeRoy Zimmerman's medley of aurora and nature photos set to ponderous classical music – a poor substitute for the real thing.

If you feel liable to indulge in one too many Dan McGrew or Lady Lou cocktails, then make use of the **complimentary bus** service (pickups from most major Fairbanks hotels in time for the Malemute shows; reservations required), or arrange to stay either in the on-site RV park (see p.456) or the comfortable, if somewhat institutional, rooms at the *Gold Camp Hotel* ($70).

North Pole

For those who don't mind tourist-trap kitsch, **NORTH POLE**, just fifteen miles southeast of Fairbanks, is an essential stop. The town was incorporated and named in 1953 by local boosters who tried to entice toy manufacturers with the prospect of labeling their products "Made in the North Pole." The idea didn't quite work out as planned, but one trader moved here, opened up **Santa Claus House** – easily identified by the 22-foot Santa outside – and established the town as the self-appointed home of Santa Claus (mid-May to mid-Sept 8am–8pm, mid-Sept to mid-May 10am–6pm; ⓣ488-2200 or 1-800/588-4078, ⓦwww.santaclaushouse.com). If a child addresses a letter to "Santa Claus, North Pole," it ends up here, and the kids' letters pinned up on a wall inside the gift shop are the most charming thing about the place. Inquiries about the spirits of the elves, the health of the reindeer, and the temperature up at the North Pole are commonplace.

You can arrange for a North Pole franked letter from Santa to be sent in December for $7.50, the smaller kids can sit on Santa's knee, and there are cute reindeer in the compound out the back. To add to the entertainment value, they stuck to the theme when naming streets around here: to see Santa, take the Santa Claus Lane exit from the Richardson Highway into St Nicholas Avenue; or call for a free shuttle pickup at Fairbanks hotels and RV parks.

Outdoor activities

Fairbanks presents an unparalleled opportunity to get out into the wilderness; a number of activities are firmly associated with Fairbanks itself, but the proliferation of local bush-plane companies throws the **Arctic north** wide open to Fairbanks visitors. In general, we have covered the remoter canoe and backpacking trips in the appropriate sections of the chapter – in particular, see our accounts of the Gates of the Arctic National Park (p.496) and Arctic National Wildlife Refuge (p.499) – but to give a sense of the scope available, consult "Exploring the north," below.

Hiking and biking

Roaming along the banks of the Chena River or through Creamer's Field can be pleasant enough, but for more robust **hiking** you'll need to get out of town,

Exploring the north: tour and bush-plane companies

We've discussed various trips throughout the text, but several companies operate a string of tours worth knowing about. We've listed the better ones below along with their most enticing trips.

Cape Smythe Air ⓣ852-8333 in Barrow, ⓣ442-3020 in Kotzebue, ⓣ443-2414 in Nome, ⓦwww.capesmythe.com. Useful for Arctic adventurers with deep pockets keen to string a sequence of coastal town visits together. If you want to visit Prudhoe Bay, Barrow, and Kotzebue (and perhaps some smaller villages), you could travel to Prudhoe Bay by bus or Alaska Airlines, then catch daily flights from there to Barrow, on to Point Lay, Point Hope, and then Kotzebue, where you can pick up Alaska Airlines to travel on to Nome or Anchorage. At around $600 all up, it works out cheaper than separate trips based in Anchorage or Fairbanks and is a good deal more interesting.

Frontier Flying Service 5245 Airport Industrial Rd ⓣ474-0014 or 1-800/478-6779, ⓦwww.frontierflying.com. Important bush operators with regular services to small communities all over the north and west of Alaska – Anaktuvuk Pass, Barrow, Deadhorse, Fort Yukon, and others.

GoNorth 3500 Davis Rd ⓣ479-7272 or 1-866/236-7272, ⓦwww.gonorthalaska.com. Professional year-round operation running guided tours of all types throughout the Brooks Range and around Fairbanks, and helping organize a wide range of unguided trips. Whether you want a simple float down the Chena River or a major hiking expedition into Arrigetch Peaks in the Gates of the Arctic National Park, they'll help organize it from their base camp (see "Hostels," p.453). Standard trips include rafting the Middle Fork of the Koyukuk River (5 days; $1200), canoeing the Yukon River from Eagle to Circle (8 days; $1450), hiking in the Gates of the Arctic (6 days; $1800), winter back-country skiing trips into Tolovana Hot Springs (5 days; $550), and much more. They also have campers for trips up the Dalton Highway (see "Listings," p.474) and rent gear such as canoes ($35/day, $190/week), whitewater canoes ($40/$200), road bikes ($22/$90), mountain bikes ($27/$115), and all manner of camping gear.

Northern Alaska Tour Company PO Box 82991, Fairbanks, AK 99708 ⓣ474-8600 or 1-800/474-1986, ⓦwww.northernalaska.com. Well-organized operation running a slew of flightseeing trips, some with remote landings, others using road transport for

preferably along either the Chena Hot Springs Road for the Granite Tors Trail, Angel Rocks Trail, and Chena Dome Trail (for all see box, p.477), or still further away along the Steese Highway for the Pinnell Mountain Trail (see box, p.482). APLIC (see p.451) is the place to go for the latest information and brochures, and you can rent gear from Beaver Sports (see p.473).

Fairbanks is surprisingly poorly served for **mountain-biking** trails. The hiking trails are either unsuitable or biking is banned, leaving only bike paths through town. Further afield, try the fairly tough biking around the Angel Rocks Trail (see p.477) out along Chena Hot Springs Road.

Paddling

There is little whitewater around Fairbanks, so most of the paddling activity is canoeing along gentle rivers, perhaps dangling a line in the hope of hooking a fish, or even doing a mini bar crawl through Fairbanks. The handiest rental location is Alaska Outdoor Rentals & Guides (ⓣ457-2453, ⓦwww.akbike.com) on Peger Road right beside the Chena River at the back of Pioneer Park, from where you can rent a single kayak (half-day $21, full $32), double ($24/$36) or a canoe ($29/$41). With a couple of hours to spare, simply rent a canoe, paddle downstream past *The Pump House* and *Pike's Landing* restaurants (see p.472), and get picked up and brought back to base ($15 first boat, $5 extra boats). For

part of the journey. They do several trips to the Arctic Circle and Prudhoe Bay (covered in detail on p.487) as well as: Native Culture Adventure (8hr; $399), a drive up to the Arctic Circle followed by a flight to Anaktuvuk Pass for a village tour escorted by a Nunamiut Eskimo, then a flight back to Fairbanks; Arctic Circle Air Adventure (4hr; $249), overflying the Arctic Circle and Gates of the Arctic National Park and spending a short time in Bettles; Barrow Adventure (8hr; $399), a round-trip flight to Barrow with a village tour; the Brooks Range Adventure ($349), flying to Coldfoot Camp, visiting Wiseman, returning to Coldfoot to sleep, and then driving back to Fairbanks; and Prudhoe Bay Adventure (3 days; $749), flying up to Deadhorse, taking a tour of the oil fields, then driving the Dalton back to Fairbanks. Extensions to take in Barrow, Nome, and Kotzebue are possible.

Trans Arctic Circle Treks 4825 Glasgow Drive ⓣ479-5451 or 1-800/336-8735, ⓦwww.arctictreks.com. This outfit runs several excursions north including a minivan tour to the Arctic Circle (12hr; $129); a three-day Prudhoe-and-back road trip with an Arctic Ocean tour and evenings in Prudhoe and Coldfoot, camping both nights in the Brooks Range ($599, with all meals and lodging); and a four-day "Arctic Blast" ($1299), which includes a two-day run up to Prudhoe, Arctic Ocean tour, flight to Barrow, an overnight there, a tour to Point Barrow and flight back.

Warbelow's Air Ventures 3758 University Ave South, E Ramp, Fairbanks Airport ⓣ474-0518 or 1-800/478-0812, ⓦwww.warbelows.com. These folks run a culturally sensitive evening visit to Fort Yukon with escorted village tour (4hr; $259), and another to Anaktuvuk Pass (8hr; $499), plus several bush-mail flights (3–4hr; $228) briefly visiting a few villages, some over the Arctic Circle. Also low-cost flights between Fairbanks, Eagle, and Circle – useful if you are floating the Yukon downstream from Eagle.

Wright Air Service 3842 University Ave South ⓣ474-0502, ⓔwrightas@ptialaska.net. Reliable and flexible company running charters and scheduled flights to villages mostly over the Arctic Circle. Stay-on-board village circuits vary depending on demand but the morning trip to Arctic Village ($290 round-trip) usually stops in Fort Yukon and Venetai. Bettles is $270 round-trip.

a longer paddle, get dropped upstream and drift through downtown Fairbanks back to base, or paddle the eighteen-mile middle section of the Chena River from Nordale Road ($35 drop-off). Further commitment is required to paddle some of the upper sections of the Chena River (see p.476), or down the Tanana to Nenana (see p.397), a sixty-mile trip covered in one long stint or two more relaxed days with a night camped on the riverbank. More distant possibilities include the Chatanika and Birch Creek canoe routes (consult APLIC for details).

Flightseeing

No matter how tight your budget, you really shouldn't miss out on a little **flightseeing**. If you feel you need to justify the expense, then visit one of the remote communities such as Bettles or Arctic Village, or take a whirlwind tour of a few of them on one of the **mail flights** that makes a circuit of three or four settlements, dropping off essential supplies and picking up the post. Another favorite approach is to take one of the **Arctic Circle overflights**, usually tracing the silver thread of the pipeline and issuing a certificate to verify the fact you entered Arctic airspace. The best of both these trips are listed in "Exploring the north" on p.468–469.

Other activities

If all the talk of gold around Fairbanks has fired your imagination, you can try your hand at **gold panning** on the local streams with equipment and advice from Alaskan Prospectors, 504 College Rd at Blanch Ave (Wed–Sat 10.30am–5pm; ⓣ452-7398), a treasure trove of minerals and gems that caters to just about all gold-digging needs. They sell a starter kit ($20) that includes a pan, magnet, collection vial, a sample bag of gold-bearing gravel, and instructions. Alternatively, they'll set you up for the real thing for about $15 and point you in the right direction.

You might also want to try learning something of **dog mushing** at Alaskan Tails of the Trail ($25; ⓣ457-1117, ⓦwww.maryshields.com) with Iditarod veteran Mary Shields, the first woman to complete the course back in 1974. Over a couple of hours she'll show you the ropes and let you meet the dogs at her place off Goldstream Road, five miles north of town.

Eating

Fairbanks is one of the few places in northern Alaska where you can escape from the culinary tyranny of salmon, halibut, and burgers. As long as your tastes aren't too exotic and you are prepared to drive around, you should be able to find pretty much anything you want here. And for no apparent reason, Thai seems to have become a Fairbanks specialty: there's even a Thai takeaway wagon, *Bahn Thai,* on 2nd Avenue. Broadly, the cheaper places congregate around the western end of College Road towards the university, and the pricier places are further out, with the gaps being plugged by mid-range places and all the franchise joints you could ask for – especially along Airport Way. If you are thinking of bringing a jacket and tie, forget it. As long as your hiking boots are clean you'll not be turned away.

You'll find **grocery stores** in just about all the major malls: the most convenient are the Fred Meyer and Safeway stores, paired at the eastern end of College Road close to downtown, and also next to each other around the intersection of Airport Way and University Avenue (all 24hr). For the freshest vegetables head to the Farmers Market (see p.462).

Downtown

Café Alex 310 1st Ave ⓣ452-2539. Fairbanks' first and only tapas bar, where the trick is to go with a group and sample widely from stuffed artichokes, mini pizzas, *queso fundido*, nutty wild rice salad, and more. They're $8–9 a plate and are served at the bar, in the main dining area, or in a cluster of intimate side rooms. Good wine by the glass, too.

Co-op Diner Co-op Plaza, 535 2nd Ave ⓣ451-9128. The best bet for all-day diner food ($7–10) downtown, served either in booths or at the counter.

Desserts First 412 5th Ave ⓣ451-5537. Desserts aren't all they do, but go easy on the likes of the spicy veggie melt ($7.50) and chicken and bacon salad ($8) to leave room for their sumptuous cakes ($4), which vary daily. Open for breakfast, lunch, and weekend dinners.

The Diner 244 Illinois St ⓣ451-0613. Reliable diner in the best old-fashioned tradition (though with a dedicated non-smoking area) serving straightforward diner fare cooked to perfection and served with fried okra or half a dozen other sides. A full breakfast ($7–9) will set you up for the day, and even the single giant pancake ($2) is enough for most appetites.

Gambardella's 706 2nd Ave ⓣ457-4992. Fairbanks' best Italian restaurant is surprisingly well priced, especially considering that this is one of the city's finest spots. Weather permitting, diners spill out onto the terrace for lasagna, eggplant parmesan, and gourmet pizza, all helped down with good Italian and American wines. They also have an extensive takeout menu. Closed for Sun lunch.

Hot Tamale 112 N Turner Rd ⓣ457-8350. Authentic Mexican decorated in a kind of "cantina kitsch" style, with a full Mexican menu, though particularly noted for their all-you-can-eat $10 buffet lunch and dinner.

McCafferty's 408 Cushman St ⓣ456-6853. Relaxing and cheerfully decorated daytime coffeehouse serving good espressos, soups, and cakes often to lunchtime musical accompaniment. Also open Friday and Saturday evenings for live music. Mon–Thurs 7am–6pm, Fri 7am–11pm, Sat 10am–11pm, Sun 10am–4pm.

Soapy Smith's 543 2nd Ave ⓣ451-8380. Photos of the Klondike and an ancient kayak strung from the ceiling hardly make a convincing theme, but the food is pretty decent: barbecue ribs come in under $8, and they do a delicious California burger with shrimp, avocado, and Swiss cheese ($8), also available in vegetarian form.

Thai House 526 5th Ave ⓣ452-6123. A small but justly popular eatery serving the usual range of Thai dishes, all beautifully prepared and at modest prices around the $10 mark. The green and red curries with zucchini, peas, and peppers are especially good. Closed Sun.

Near the university

Alaska Coffee Roasting Co W Valley Plaza, 4001 Geist Rd ⓣ457-5282. Fairbanks' best coffee, roasted daily on the premises and served (in real cups if you want) in a cozy café hung with carpets and wood carvings from the owner's native Ethiopia. There's a good selection of wraps, cakes, and muffins, too.

Gulliver's Books Café 3525 College Rd ⓣ474-9574. Pleasant café, tucked above an excellent bookshop, serving chicken tarragon wraps, pesto turkey melts, bagels, biscotti, and coffee all at reasonable prices, plus free Internet access to boot. A rear deck catches the summer sun nicely.

Hot Licks 3453 College Rd, near University Ave ⓣ479-7813. A roadside shack with some outdoor seating selling shakes, espresso, and excellent ice cream made from local cream and natural flavors. May–Aug.

Sam's Sourdough 3702 Cameron St at University Ave ⓣ479-0532. About the best greasy spoon in town, with the usual diner menu as well as reindeer sausage and eggs ($8.25) and Sharon's Sourdough Omelet ($8.25) – complete with ham, mushrooms, onions, olives, and sour cream.

Suburban Fairbanks

Alaska Salmon Bake at Pioneer Park on Airport Way ⓣ452-7274 or 1-800/354-7274. Really hungry? Here's a stuff-in-as-much-salmon-ribs-and-halibut-as-you-can-for-$23 affair set on the flanks of Pioneer Park out among relic mining machinery (and mosquitoes in high summer). It is open for dinner (mid-May to mid-Sept daily 5–9pm), and there are shuttle buses ($2) from the bigger hotels.

Captain Bartlett Inn 1411 Airport Way ⓣ452-1888. A good and reasonably priced spot for a breakfast of, say, eggs Benedict ($8) or a lunch of burgers and wraps, inside or out on the sunny deck.

Ivory Jacks 2581 Goldstream Rd, four miles northeast of the university ⓣ455-6666. Being a little out of town doesn't seem to stop this place being inordinately popular, as much for its late-night bar scene and frequent live bands as for the dining. Food ranges from crab-stuffed mushroom appetizers ($7) to half-pound cheeseburgers ($9), 12-inch pizzas ($17–20), and a halibut dinner ($18).

Lemongrass Chena Pump Plaza, cnr Parks Hwy and Chena Pump Rd ⓣ456-2200. Another low-cost quality Thai restaurant that challenges *Thai House*. Sparsely furnished with Thai musical instruments around the walls and very well-prepared dishes for $8–11, plus *Hot Licks* ice cream desserts.

Pike's Landing Mile 4.5 Airport Way ⓣ479-6500. A popular riverside complex with sports bar, Alaska's largest deck beside the Chena River, and some of Fairbanks' finest dining with the likes of jumbo black-tiger prawns ($27), crab-stuffed filet béarnaise ($30), or pecan crusted chicken ($25). Lunchtime salads and sandwiches cost around $10, and there's a standout Sunday brunch ($19) with a huge well-prepared spread and as many glasses of champagne as you could reasonably expect to drink.

The Pump House Mile 1.3 Chena Pump Rd ⓣ479-8452, ⓦwww.pumphouse.com. A local favorite and rightly so, this historic pump house by the Chena River comes stuffed with gold-mining paraphernalia and serves great food. The deck is the place to watch river life go by while tucking into burgers and halibut nuggets (both around $9), mostly charged at half-price during happy hours (Sept–May 4–6pm & 10–11pm). The dining room is more formal, serving hearty portions of reindeer stew ($19), crab cakes ($21), or grilled salmon ($22); you may not have space for one of the wonderful desserts.

Out of town

Turtle Club Mile 10 Old Steese Hwy, Fox ⓣ457-3883. The *Turtle Club*'s reputation for the quality and quantity of its prime rib – $22 for the 16oz Turtle Cut, $29 for the 24oz Miners Cut – extends throughout the North, but they also do delicious jumbo prawns weighing in at five to the pound. Evenings only. Reservations recommended.

Two Rivers Lodge Mile 16 Chena Hot Springs Rd ⓣ488-6815, ⓦwww.tworiverslodge.com. Although it is a bit out of town, this restaurant, with its stunning glassed-in dining area and lakeside deck, promises to reward you for your trouble. Appetizers of king crab bisque ($11) or spicy Louisiana alligator tail ($11) are followed by halibut, shrimp, and scallop pasta ($26) or blackened salmon salad ($18). There's also an extensive, mostly Californian, wine list. Open evenings, and from 3pm on weekends.

Drinking and entertainment

You'll be disappointed if you arrive in Fairbanks expecting high fashion and up-to-the-minute music, but the city can provide a rollicking good time. Many visitors find themselves at one of the nightly cabaret revues at some stage, but there is usually a bar or two with a band thrashing away in the corner of a dark room. Perhaps more than any other large town this is a place where Alaska's famed predominance of men is most apparent, and you'll never be short of a drinking partner in any of the numerous traditional Alaskan bars.

Check the Fairbanks *Daily News-Miner* for listings (especially on Thurs). Look out, too, for Fairbanks Shakespeare Theatre plays held in the Birch Hill Recreation Area on the last three weekends of July (Thurs–Sun 8pm; tickets $16; ⓣ457-7638, ⓦwww.fairbanks-shakespeare.org).

In Fairbanks

Captain Bartlett Inn 1411 Airport Way. The inn's *Dog Sled Saloon* offers straightforward peanut-shells-on-the-floor drinking with a log-cabin interior and sports on big screens.

The Marlin 3412 College Rd ⓣ479-4646. Poky, wood-paneled cellar bar that supports the cutting edge of Fairbanks' music scene with live bands – blues, jazz, and rock – playing most evenings from around 9pm; small cover charge, if any.

The Palace Saloon at Pioneer Park on Airport Way ⓣ456-5960 for reservations. Mock-up of a gold-rush-era music hall that plays host to the entertaining, if slightly cheesy, cabaret-style Golden Heart Review (mid-May to mid-Sept nightly 8.15pm with occasional extra shows at 6.30pm; $15). The show pokes fun at historic Alaskan life (specifically Fairbanks) through songs and stories, including a dog-mushing interpretation of the old Abbott and Costello "Who's on

First?" routine. On weekends the review is usually followed by their considerably more risqué and topical Late Night Cabaret (typically mid-May to mid-Sept Fri & Sat 10.30pm; $10), which is limited to adults only.

The Pump House (see "Eating," opposite). The preferred watering hole for Fairbanks' smarter young set, who come to shoot pool or more likely hang out on the deck with a cocktail or two.

Near Fairbanks

Blue Loon Mile 353.5 Parks Hwy, Ester ⓣ457-5666, ⓦwww.theblueloon.com. A cavernous late-closing hot spot five miles west of Fairbanks which hosts local and touring bands (or maybe a DJ) several nights a week; $5 cover unless a top name is in town. They also screen cult and mainstream movies that don't make it to the local multiplex (typically Tues–Sat 7pm; $5–6). Closed Mon.

Howling Dog Saloon Mile 11 Old Steese Hwy, Fox ⓣ457-8780. The wildest watering hole in the district and a local legend promoted as the farthest north rock and roll bar in the world. It actually goes one better by having the bands perform (every Fri & Sat, plus Wed & Thurs in mid-summer; usually no cover) on what is fondly referred to as the "Pope and the Dope" carpet, the red pile on which John Paul II met Ronald Reagan in 1984 when they both happened to be making pit-stops on the tarmac in Fairbanks – the first time that an American president and the pope met on American soil. If you're hungry, they'll dish up fine pizzas, but most come to drink in the wood-floored bar with pinball, flags of every nation, and knickers and bras hung from the moose rack. May–Oct.

Malemute Saloon Ester Gold Camp, Old Nenana Rd, Ester. Nightly cabaret entertainment (see p.467) six miles west of Fairbanks, not far from the *Blue Loon*.

Refinery Lounge Old Richardson Hwy, North Pole ⓣ488-0335. Typical dark bar with a large military clientele. It's a friendly spot with an entertaining weekend band (Thurs–Sat) playing Top 40 tunes and "No Country." No cover.

Silver Gulch Brewery Mile 11 Old Steese Hwy, Fox ⓣ452-2739. Not really a bar, but worth a mention for the Friday evening tasting session (5–7pm), which is something of a local meeting point with the chance to sample the product of the US's northernmost brewery.

Listings

Airlines Alaska ⓣ1-800/252-7522; Northwest ⓣ1-800/225-2525; United ⓣ1-800/241-6522. See box on p.468–469 for a roundup of bush-plane services.

Banks and exchange Banks are located all over town (many of them drive-thru), all with ATMs, which also crop up in supermarkets and convenience stores. Downtown there's a Key Bank branch at 100 Cushman St; Wells Fargo at 613 Cushman St exchanges foreign bills.

Bicycle and canoe rental If you're not at one of the hostels that has bikes, rent mountain bikes from Alaska Outdoor Rentals & Guides (ⓣ457-2453, ⓦwww.akbike.com), which rents from several outlets around town, including the *Fairbanks Hotel* (see p.454) and their base on Peger Road, at the back of Pioneer Park. Rates are $6 an hour or $27 a day, and they even have bikes set up for winter use (at increased rates) and suggest riding along the frozen Chena River. Also try 7 Bridges Boats and Bikes at the *7 Gables B&B*, 4312 Birch Lane (ⓣ479-0751), which rents town and mountain bikes for $20 a day. Canoe rental is best from Alaska Outdoor Rentals & Guides or 7 Bridges. Beaver Sports, 3480 College Rd (ⓣ479-2494, ⓦwww.beaversports.com), also rents bikes and canoes and has biking and canoeing gear for sale.

Bookshop Gulliver's Books, 3525 College Rd (ⓣ474-9574, ⓦwww.gullivers-books.com), offers the city's best selection of new and used books. They're also at Shopper's Forum Mall, 1255 Airport Way (ⓣ456-3657).

Buses (long distance) Fairbanks has just two long-distance bus services, both operating roughly mid-May to mid-Sept, but call to check at the ends of the season, which may run longer or be cut short. Alaska Direct (ⓣ1-800/770-6652) runs to Delta Junction, Tok, and Whitehorse departing Sunday, Wednesday, and Friday; and Alaska Trails (ⓣ1-888/600-6001) has a daily run to Denali and Anchorage, a thrice-weekly service between Fairbanks and Dawson City, Yukon via Tok and Chicken, and a reservation-only service from Fairbanks through Delta Junction and Glennallen to Valdez, all picking up at the visitor center and *Billie's Backpackers*.

Camping equipment Beaver Sports, carries the best selection of camping and general outdoor gear, along with various guidebooks and maps.

Car rental International agencies all have desks at the airport; smaller local agencies frequently offer more competitive rates in return for slightly older vehicles and a poorer backup network. To get unlimited mileage and a courtesy pickup from your hotel expect to pay around $50 a day in July and Aug; phone around. Agencies include: Airport (ⓣ456-2023, ⓦwww.alaskan.com/airportcarrental); Arctic (ⓣ561-2990, ⓦwww.arcticrentacar.com); and U-Save (ⓣ479-7060 or 1-877/979-7060). Only a few companies allow you to drive off paved roads. Affordable, 3101 S Cushman St (ⓣ452-7341 or 1-800/471-3101), has cars from $45 with unlimited mileage and allows you to go everywhere except on the Dalton Highway. Arctic Outfitters (contact Northern Alaska Tour Company on ⓣ1-800/474-1986) will rent you a Ford Taurus for the run up the Dalton for $79 a day, including 250 miles a day and then 35¢ a mile, but you'll need your own insurance. GoNorth (ⓣ479-7272 or 1-866/236-7272, ⓦwww.gonorthalaska.com) offers a range of camper trucks ideal for exploring the Dalton and charges from $62 a day plus 35¢ a mile ($97 a day unlimited mileage) up to $105/$170 for a more luxurious and spacious model. There's an additional $50 preparation fee on top and liability damage waiver will cost $16 a day.

Cinema The Regal 16, 1855 Airport Way (ⓣ456-5113, ⓦwww.regalcinemas.com), screens mainstream releases, offering $3 off tickets on shows starting before 6pm; the *Blue Loon* in Ester (see p.473) shows more alternative and cult movies.

Emergencies Police, fire, and ambulance ⓣ911; Crisis Line ⓣ452-4357.

Gold prospecting Alaskan Prospectors, 504 College Rd at Blanch Ave (ⓣ452-7398), caters to just about all gold-digging needs. They'll sell you a starter kit ($20) or set you up for the real thing for about $15 and point you in the right direction. Wed–Sat 10.30am–5pm.

Hitchhiking As with any city it pays to get beyond the city limits before trying to thumb a ride: for the Richardson Highway the Green bus will take you to North Pole, and the Blue bus works best for the Parks Highway. A sensible alternative is to try to get a lift by consulting the rides board inside the Wood Center at the university.

Internet access *Gulliver's Books* (see p.473) offers 30min free use with a café purchase; the Noel Wien Library (see below) has free access bookable by the hour; and *College Coffeehouse*, 3677 College Rd (ⓣ374-0468), has 15min free access with a purchase, then $2 for every subsequent 15min.

Laundry and showers B&C Laundromat, 3677 College Rd (daily 8am–9.30pm; ⓣ479-2696), and Cushman Plaza Laundry, 2301 S Cushman St (7am–midnight; ⓣ452-4430), both have competitively priced washing machines and showers for $3. A dip at Hamme Swimming Pool, 931 Airport Way (Mon–Fri 6am–9pm, Sat 9am–5pm; ⓣ459-1086, ⓦwww.co.fairbanks.ak.us), costs under $4.

Library The Noel Wien Library, 126 Cowles St at Airport Way (Mon–Thurs 10am–9pm, Fri 10am–6pm, Sat 10am–5pm; ⓣ459-1020). The MACS Blue bus passes close by.

Maps The Alaska Public Lands Information Center (see p.451) handles most needs, and the Map Office, Room 204, International Arctic Research Center, N Koyukuk Drive, on the university campus (Mon–Fri 8am–5pm; ⓣ474-6960, ⓦwww.gi.alaska.edu/services/MapOffice), sells topographic maps for the whole state at 1:250,000 ($7) and 1:63,360 scales. ($6).

Medical assistance Fairbanks Memorial Hospital, 1650 Cowles St ⓣ452-8181.

Money transfer Western Union has outlets at Fred Mayer and Safeway supermarkets (see map p.453).

Pharmacy Fred Meyer and Safeway supermarkets all have pharmacies (see map, p.458–459). The best is probably Fred Meyer, 3755 Airport Way (ⓣ474-1433).

Photographic supplies Fairbanks Fast Foto, Shoppers' Forum Mall, 1255 Airport Way (ⓣ456-8896), is a good camera shop selling all the usual stuff as well as slide and pro film.

Post office 315 Barnett St (Mon–Fri 9am–6pm). For **General Delivery** use the 99707 zip code.

Road conditions Interior roads ⓣ456-7623; state highways ⓣ1-800/478-7675.

Taxes A hotel tax of eight percent is charged and has already been incorporated into our price codes.

Taxis Alaska Cab ⓣ456-3355; Diamond ⓣ455-7777; Eagle Cab ⓣ455-5555; Fairbanks ⓣ452-3535.

Travel agency US Travel, 1211 Cushman St (ⓣ452-8992), is open Mon–Fri 8am–6pm.

Around Fairbanks

Fairbanks' importance stems less from the appeal of the city itself than from its location at the hub of the only four significant roads to penetrate the Alaskan north, three of which end at **hot springs**. One is smooth blacktop all the way; the rest are dirt roads twisting and bucking their way through the white- and black-spruce forests that cloak the surrounding rolling hills. Since public transportation is not an option, you'll need a car to get around, or be prepared for some slow hitching.

Beyond the immediate environs of Fairbanks there is very little sign of human activity. Small communities occasionally throw up a roadhouse, and riverbeds have obviously been turned over by gold dredges, but after a very short time both seem like blots on the pristine landscape. Predominantly, this is country to go **hiking**, **canoeing**, fishing, and, in winter, cross-country skiing and snowmachining – all followed by a well-earned soak in a hot tub.

Easily the most accessible of these arterial spokes, and the only one you can explore in depth with the blessing of rental-car agencies (see our comments under "City transportation and tours" on p.451), is **Chena Hot Springs Road**, which follows the Chena River – a gentle canoe and raft route – past trailheads for three excellent hikes to the most developed of the region's hot springs.

The **Steese Highway** is longer and feels appreciably more remote as it threads its way northeast past the arduous but immensely satisfying two-day Pinnell Mountain Trail to the Yukon River. The only westbound road is the **Elliott Highway** across 160 miles of ridgetop forest to the charming community of **Manley Hot Springs**, with its ancient roadhouse and primitive tanks filled by a naturally heated stream. The first few miles of the Elliott provide access to the start of the last of the North's four roads, the Dalton Highway, which runs five hundred miles to Prudhoe Bay on the Arctic Ocean.

There are no visitor centers of any consequence out here, so find out all you need in Fairbanks at the Alaska Public Lands Information Center, which publishes a handy free leaflet detailing the points of interest along the Steese and Elliott highways. Fairbanks is also the place to stock up on any supplies you might need, rent your outdoor gear and fill up with gas.

Chena Hot Springs and around

Of the spas around Fairbanks, **Chena Hot Springs**, sixty miles to the northeast, is the easiest to reach and the most developed. It is also the largest after considerable redevelopment in recent years. Weary miners and Fairbanksans have been coming out this way to ease their bones since 1905, when the Swan brothers discovered the rumored springs after a month-long slog up the Chena River. Travel wasn't much easier for early devotees who regularly took two weeks to get there, but the situation improved, and by 1912 the route was even passable by bicycles, and is now asphalt. It is easy enough to zip there in an hour or so, but the **Chena River State Recreation Area**, with some attractive campgrounds, three excellent hikes (see box, overleaf), and a gentle canoe trip (see box, below) make this an appealing area to spend a day or two. And, of course, you can soak away your aches at the springs.

Paddling the Chena River

The clear and very cold waters of the **Chena River** flow west through gently rolling wooded country, eventually joining the Tanana River near Fairbanks. The narrower and more overhung upper sections are Class II and require some skill, but below the *Rosehip Campground* access point it is a gentle float trip for canoes, kayaks, and rafts, ranging from a couple of hours up to several days. The rapids may not be too challenging, but trees frequently fall into the river creating dangerous "sweepers" and log-jams that you need to be aware of: ask locally. You'll also need to scout ahead when the river braids confusingly, but it is mostly pretty easy going and wonderfully relaxing: fishing and looking for moose, brown bears, beavers, and river otters while lazing in the sun. With frequent access points you can do as much or as little as you want, even staying on the river to **camp**, either in established campgrounds or on river bars where the breeze keeps bugs at bay (though keep an eye on water levels if it has been raining).

Unless you've got your own gear, you'll want to **rent a canoe** in Fairbanks (see "Bicycle and canoe rental" on p.473) and either avail yourself of the agency's delivery service or (perhaps more cheaply) rent a car and be prepared to hitch back to your vehicle.

If you have some experience with Class II rivers and water levels are adequate (usually early to mid summer), use the highest access point at the **Angel Rocks Trailhead**, Mile 48.9, and be prepared to line your canoe around log-jams and obstacles. Over the next 22 miles down to **Rosehip Campground**, Mile 27 (8–13hr in all), there are five access points spaced thirty minutes to three hours apart. In general, the river gets progressively easier as you go, but if you're in any doubt, put in at *Rosehip* for the easy float to Grange Hall Road, Mile 20.8 (2–4hr). It is even possible to paddle into Fairbanks (8hr beyond Nordale Rd).

For more **information**, visit APLIC in Fairbanks, discuss your plans with the staff, and pick up the free leaflets put out by Alaska State Parks and the US Army Corps of Engineers, both detailing access points, levels of difficulty, and expected float times.

There is no public transportation out this way, but given three days' notice *Chena Hot Springs Resort* (see below) can offer a **shuttle** (first person $80 round-trip, additional passengers $40). Hitching is feasible.

Along Chena Hot Springs Road

Twenty-six miles northeast of Fairbanks, you enter the Chena River State Recreation Area and soon find yourself repeatedly crossing bridges, the main access points for paddling the Chena River. Along here, hikers should keep their eyes open for trailheads for the **walks** listed in the box opposite.

There is very little **accommodation** along the road, except for a road-accessible cabin, *North Fork*, Mile 47.7 (Ⓣ451-2695; ❶), and **camping** at the excellent *Rosehip Campground*, Mile 27 ($10; pump water), the slightly less inviting *Tors Trail Campground*, Mile 39.5 ($10; pump water), or the lakeside *Red Squirrel Campground*, Mile 42.8 ($5; pump water); all are spacious and equipped with picnic tables and fire rings.

Chena Hot Springs

Only an hour from Fairbanks, Chena Hot Springs has become the getaway of choice from Fairbanks with locals and visitors seeking a sybaritic day's relaxation. If you've experienced the more rustic hot springs elsewhere in Alaska, *Chena Hot Springs Resort*, Mile 56.5 (Ⓣ451-8104 or 1-800/478-4681, Ⓦwww

.chenahotsprings.com; suites ❼, rooms ❺, cabins and yurts ❸), may come as something of a surprise, with numerous buildings containing hotel rooms, scattered around a clearing in the forest. There's all manner of activities to keep you occupied, but the real stars are the hot pools themselves. The indoor chlorinated pool and an assortment of hot tubs have now been outclassed by the large outdoor Rock Pool (no under-18s), a chest-deep sandy-bottomed lake of hot water with a massaging jet of spring water and a cooling fountain in the center.

The hotel's facilities and activities are all open to the public, as are **the pools** (daily 7am–midnight; $10 for a day-pass), which are free to hotel guests though not those staying at the campground and RV park. Rooms are comfortable and bland, but there are substantially more characterful, rustic cabins without

Hikes in the Chena River State Recreation Area

The **Chena River State Recreation Area** flanks thirty miles of Chena Hot Springs Road, encompassing the bald, spruce-flanked mountains on either side. Periodically, you'll see **granite tors**, gnarled rock pinnacles poking up from the ridges and providing the focus for a couple of lovely hikes. These were formed millions of years ago when molten rock forced its way through fissures, cooling into hard rock which has weathered better than the softer material that surrounded it.

APLIC in Fairbanks stocks free Alaska State Parks **information leaflets** on all these trails, which are restricted to foot traffic except for Chena Dome Trail, on which **mountain biking** is permitted (though it is very challenging). Hikes are listed in order of their distance from Fairbanks.

Granite Tors Trail (15-mile loop; 5–8hr, 2700ft ascent). An excellent hike of moderate difficulty starting along boardwalks over muskeg, then climbing through thick woods and out onto alpine tundra past ancient granite outcrops rising up to 60ft from the ground. You can do the hike in a day, camp out overnight, or sleep in the small free-use shelter at the midpoint; bring everything except a tent and expect to share it with others. It is a popular and highly scenic rock-climbing venue when dry; but if wet, misty weather brings out the best in the area, and the ghostly tors are wreathed in swirling clouds of fog, exaggerating the already dramatic landscape. The trailhead is at Mile 39.5.

Angel Rocks Trail (3.5-mile loop; 2–3hr; 900ft ascent). The easiest of the local trails, it follows a beaver-dammed creek, then climbs moderately to granite outcrops commanding a great view down the Chena River Valley. It is especially striking in July when wildflowers are in full bloom. There are two alternative routes back to the trailhead (at Mile 48.9), and more ambitious hikers can continue from Angel Rocks to Chena Hot Springs (8.7 miles total; 3–4hr; 2000ft ascent in total), a route which passes a free-use cabin.

Chena Dome Trail (29-mile loop; 2–4 days; 6000ft ascent). An arduous expedition (with a good viewpoint after one mile for the less committed) entirely encircling the Angel Creek drainage by means of a series of subalpine ridges separated by steep valleys and saddles. There are some wondrous views from the high points (Chena Dome reaches 4421ft), and there is always a chance of coming across a bear or wolverine, though July wildflowers and August blueberries are more likely. You can rent the *Angel Creek Cabin* by reserving in advance through the Division of Parks & Outdoor Recreation in Fairbanks (☎451-2695; $25 a night; sleeps 5), but it is inconveniently sited in a valley 2000ft below the trail near Mile 22.5 – it is far better to **camp**. Keep in mind that there is little (or no) **water** along the trail: carry as much as you can and be prepared to treat whatever you can find. The trailhead is at Mile 50.5, and you've got a 1.4-mile road walk back to the trailhead at the end of the hike.

plumbing, and simple yurts with three beds but no bedding, RV parking ($20), and **camping** by the river ($20). It is always worth asking for discounts in spring and fall, and small groups can often land a large room at a very reasonable rate. When you've soaked enough you can have a massage ($65/hr), rent bikes ($6/hr, $27/day), go horseback riding ($85 for 2hr 30min), and eat and drink in the restaurant/bar, which does sandwiches and salads along with well-prepared mains ($20–25).

Winter is peak season here. Room rates go up by one price code reflecting the demand for viewing the aurora borealis. Dog-sled mushing, rides on a snowmachine, and cross-country skiing take over, and there are advanced plans to construct a Gothic-style **ice hotel** (mid-Nov to March) in the grounds, complete with gargoyles and jousting knights. There'll be a bar and six rooms where for the privilege of kipping in sleeping bags on reindeer hides you pay at least $400 a room.

Circle Hot Springs and around

Until recently, **Circle Hot Springs**, 135 miles northeast of Fairbanks, managed to achieve an agreeable balance between the overdevelopment of Chena Hot Springs and the simplicity of Manley Hot Springs. Through the summer of 2003 the *Arctic Circle Hot Springs* Resort was closed down, but hopes remain high that it will be sold and reopen in 2004 – fingers crossed. Even if it does, you'll need to weigh your desire for a steamy soak against a 270-mile round-trip that will definitely make you earn your dip. Unless you've shopped around you may find that your rental car isn't insured off blacktop roads and, even if it is, the trip is probably only worthwhile when combined with other activities: hiking the **Pinnell Mountain Trail**, canoeing Birch Creek (consult APLIC in Fairbanks for details) or undertaking a little **gold panning** along the Chatanika River. If you are keen on gold panning, visit Alaskan Prospectors in Fairbanks (see p.474) for details and equipment – a legacy of the times when the area was heavily mined. Around the turn of the twentieth century, sourdoughs on the Yukon headed to fresh prospecting grounds inland, blazing the Circle–Fairbanks summer trail along a sequence of ridge tops south of the Chatanika River. Today a section of this is followed by the Circle–Fairbanks Historic Trail, a loosely defined 58-mile hiking and horse trail. This winter trail, mostly using frozen watercourses, is now traced by the annual Yukon Quest International Sled Dog Race (see box, p.457).

Along the Steese Highway: Fox to Central

North from Fairbanks the Steese Highway passes through **FOX**, from where it works its way northeast towards the Yukon River. At Mile 16.5, it passes the **Felix Pedro Historic Monument**, which marks the spot where, in July 1902, Felix Pedro discovered gold in the region. The creek across the road is open for recreational panning; there is a nostalgic quality to dipping your pan in here, even if it has been worked over so often that you'll never find anything worthwhile. There is still gold around, though, most of it being pulled out of **Fort Knox Mine** (see p.466) a few miles further on.

The highway then climbs steeply to **Cleary Summit**, Mile 20, a small-scale downhill ski area from where there are great views of the White Mountains to the north and Mount McKinley to the south. A steep descent drops you into a land only just beginning to recover from the ravages of intensive gold mining. Historically one of the most active centers of gold extraction was the township of **CHATANIKA**, Mile 28, once the terminus of the narrow-gauge Tanana Valley Railroad, which supplied the region from Fairbanks. There's little left of Chatanika now, but something of the glory days can be found in the artifacts strewn around *Chatanika Gold Camp*, Mile 27.5 (ⓣ389-2414, ⓦwww.fegoldcamp.com; cabins ❸, rooms ❷), formerly a 200-man camp centered around a 1921 bunkhouse which now operates as a hotel, bar, and good restaurant serving American and Italian cuisine, as well as a $12 Sunday brunch. It is well worth stopping for a meal or a few drinks, which may induce you to stay the night, either in the characterful, well-kept shared-bath rooms upstairs or in the appealing modern log cabins.

A mile up the road, *Chatanika Lodge*, Mile 28.6 (ⓣ389-2164; ❷), also serves decent food and has functional rooms. Opposite, **Gold Dredge No. 3** looms from behind a heap of tailings like some beached galleon. The dredge is on private property, but no one is going to worry if you follow one of the short trails for a quick look.

A mile further on lies **Poker Flat Research Range**, the USAF's rocket-launch facility mainly used for aurora investigations; it can be visited on a two-hour **tour** (late May to late Aug roughly every second Thurs 1.30pm; free; ⓣ474-7558, ⓦwww.pfrr.alaska.edu), which starts at the gates.

In the thirty miles east of Chatanika there are two attractive **campgrounds**: the wooded, riverside *Upper Chatanika River State Recreation Site*, Mile 39 ($10; pump water), and *Cripple Creek Campground*, Mile 60 ($8; pump water), again by the river and with some walk-in sites. Both are access points for the Chatanika River Canoe Route (consult APLIC in Fairbanks for details), a Class I–II float down to Mile 11 on the Elliott Highway.

At Mile 57, a few miles beyond the end of the asphalt, **US Creek Road** spurs north towards Nome Creek Valley, which borders the southern reaches of the White Mountains National Recreation Area. A couple of hundred yards along US Creek Road are the remains of one of the pipeline sections of the **Davidson Ditch**, which supplied sluicing water to the Fox diggings (see p.466). The road then climbs over a thinly wooded ridge and drops down to

Nome Creek, seven miles off the Steese Highway. From here *Ophir Creek Campground* ($6; pump water) and *Mount Prindle Campground* ($6; pump water) make good bases for recreational gold panning, catch-and-release grayling fishing, or just hanging out. They are mostly gravel plots designed for RVs, but they're lovely spots.

As the Steese Highway climbs out of the Chatanika Valley, trees thin visibly until they virtually disappear at the watershed of **Twelvemile Summit**, Mile 85.5, the finishing point for the Pinnell Mountain Trail (see box, p.482). The road then continues to the Pinnell Mountain Trail starting trailhead at **Eagle Summit**, Mile 107.3. It is a bleak spot with a long row of L-shaped snow poles marking the road ahead. Eagle Summit has even been known to receive snow on the summer solstice, when the surrounding hilltops become favored spots for viewing the passage of the **midnight sun** as it brushes the horizon and begins its ascent for the new day.

From Eagle Summit the Steese descends for twenty miles to the small junction town of Central past Mammoth and Mastodon creeks, where wonderfully preserved examples of these ancient animals have been discovered embedded in the permafrost before being carted away to museums.

Rolling into **CENTRAL**, 127 miles northeast of Fairbanks, it is difficult to see just what it is central to, but back in the heady gold days this was the heart of the Circle Mining District, the place from which prospectors would disperse up the gulches to stake their claims. The region revived on the back of rocketing gold prices in the late 1970s and has since maintained a solid following of summertime miners pursuing the dream. An insight into the power of gold over the prospectors' psyche comes through from the **Central District Museum** (late May to early Sept daily noon–5pm; $1), where staggering statistics of the quantity of gold pulled out of the surrounding hills are backed up by large nuggets and fascinating artifacts from the tough early years.

Only a few dozen souls permanently occupy Central, but this small town may nonetheless provide the creature comforts – simple cabins, straightforward

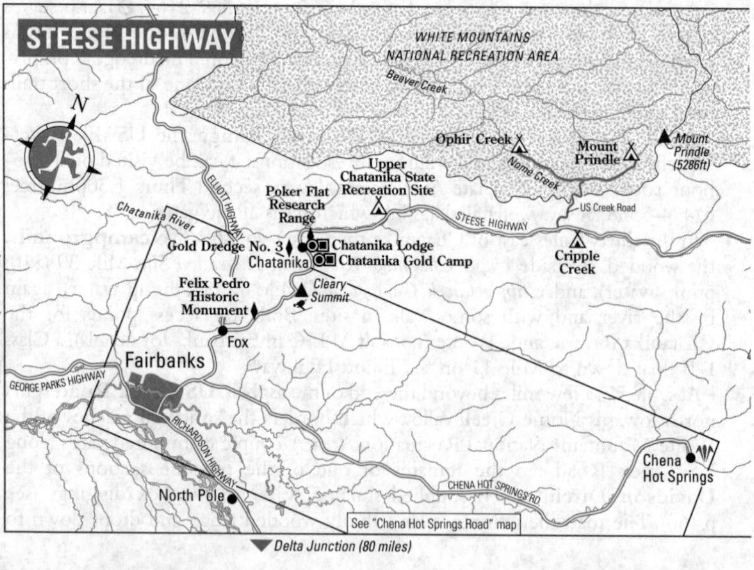

diner food, and showers – you've been hankering after if you've just spent a couple of nights out on the Pinnell Mountain Trail. Choose between the *Central Motor Inn* (☎520-5228; ❸), where camping costs $12, and showers cost $3, and the adjacent *Crabb's Corner* (☎520-5599; rooms ❸, cabins ❷), which has cabins with electricity (some with water) sleeping up to six, at a pinch, and free tent camping; showers are $3, laundry $2. Both have decent restaurants and sell gas, though it isn't cheap.

Circle Hot Springs

From Central, Circle Hot Springs Road spurs eight miles south to **CIRCLE HOT SPRINGS**, essentially just the *Arctic Circle Hot Springs Resort* (☎520-5113), which is **currently closed** but may reopen in 2004. If it does, you can expect vast quantities of hot spring water filling a large outdoor swimming pool (open 24hr; free to those with rooms and cabins, otherwise around $5 all day), which has traditionally been chlorinated because of heavy use. The tone of the place shies away from "health spa" and leans more towards having fun in the warm waters and simply getting away from it all, but there were various massage treatments available. The original 1930 building housed a restaurant, a bar, and a range of rooms, and there were cabins as well as space for RVs and camping.

Without your own vehicle, **access** is limited to $99 each-way flights from Fairbanks with Warbelow's Air Ventures (Mon–Sat only; ☎474-0518 or 1-800/478-0812).

Circle

Beyond Central, the progressively deteriorating Steese Highway runs 35 miles to the Yukon River. In the days before a road was constructed to the oil fields of Prudhoe Bay, this was the farthest north you could drive in the US, falling fifty miles short of the Arctic Circle; of course, that didn't stop geographically challenged miners from picking **CIRCLE** for the name of the first supply post

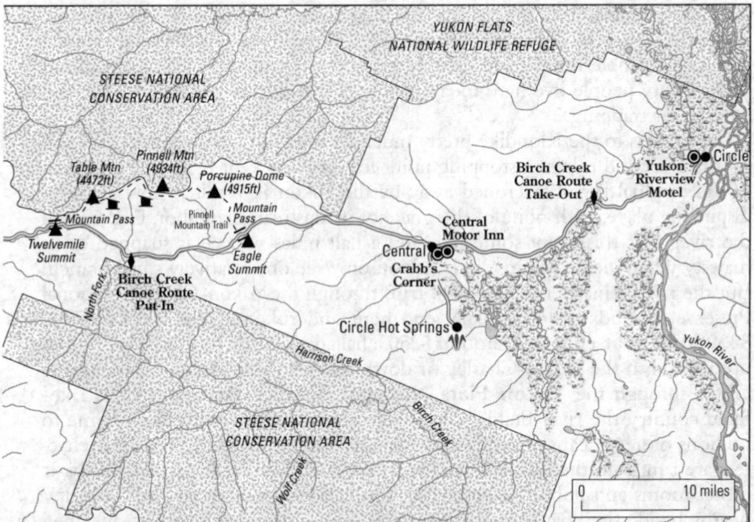

Pinnell Mountain Trail

As you thread your way along an exposed ridgeline between Pinnell Mountain and Porcupine Dome on the **Pinnell Mountain Trail** (27 miles one-way; 2–3 days; 3200ft ascent), the 5000-foot elevation combines with the proximity to the Arctic Circle – just seventy miles to the north – to make the midnight sun visible from June 18 to 24. Understandably, this is the busiest time to be up here – particularly the summer solstice on June 21 – but at any time from mid-June to mid-September you'll find great views of the Alaska and Brooks ranges. After an initial climb the trail follows a high, windswept and treeless ridge seldom dropping more than a few hundred feet before scaling the next low mountain. It can get a little monotonous, but long views and the occasional caribou maintain interest, and the threat of bear encounters adds zest. If this sounds too intense, just hike the first couple of miles from either of the two trailheads for great views and palpable solitude.

The hike is perhaps best done over two or three days, spending the night in one or both of the emergency shelters (Ptarmigan Creek at 10.1 miles and North Fork at 17.8 miles), which are small but fully weatherproof (though not mosquito-proof) and can just about sleep six. Roof **rainwater** collected in a barrel outside can be used for cooking and is likely to be all you'll find along the way – come prepared. The large number of posts and cairns marking the route attest to the sometimes **atrocious weather** up here, so it is a good idea to **bring a tent**, also advisable at popular times when the shelters may be full.

Leave your vehicle near the finish at **Twelvemile Summit** (3190ft), Mile 85.5, and hitch back to the start at the higher of the two trailheads, **Eagle Summit** (3685ft), Mile 107.3. The hitch can be a long and dispiriting experience and is best not left until you are tired and hungry (and possibly wet and cold) at the end of your hike.

APLIC in Fairbanks stocks the excellent *Pinnell Mountain Trail* leaflet, which includes a map detailed enough for hiking, though as a precaution you should always carry the appropriate topo maps.

to be built on the Yukon River, established here in 1893. Until the rise of Dawson City during the Klondike rush five years later, Circle was known as the largest log-cabin city in the world, with a population of more than a thousand and a waterfront a mile and a half long. It even had its own opera house, prompting some to dub it the "Paris of the North," though the long winters and hard-scrabble mining life quickly made that a laughable characterization. Only eighty people live here today, making a living from mining, fishing, and a bit of fur trapping.

The exodus to the Klondike pretty much cleaned out Circle, but its location on the river and role as a stopping point for steamers kept it alive. With much of the original townsite eroded away by the Yukon River, it is now a faintly dispiriting place, with none of the grace of its upstream neighbor, Eagle. Even the river – at this point some two and a half miles wide – is stripped of its majesty when viewed from Circle, as you only see one relatively small branch. But the river remains the lure: float trips through the Yukon-Charley National Preserve (see box, p.442) usually end here, and Yukon River Tours (ⓣ773-8439) runs **boat charters** (around $250 a half-day) for up to five people either upstream into the Yukon-Charley or downstream to Fort Yukon on the Arctic Circle through the **Yukon Flats National Wildlife Refuge**. In this lake-filled country, the river braids out to over a sixty-mile breadth that's home to millions of geese, canvasbacks, swans, teal, scaup, and widgeon. The boat charters are run from the *Yukon Riverview Motel* (ⓣ773-8439; ❸), which has basic motel rooms and public showers ($4). You can set up camp or park your RV nearby beside the boat launch, where there's an outhouse and tables, and then wander across to the Yukon Trading Post for expensive groceries, café food, and the bar.

Manley Hot Springs and around

Though recently straightened and improved, the **Elliott Highway** remains a fairly rough road, leading 160 miles north and west from Fairbanks through boreal forest into what seems like nowhere. The highway is now paved for the first seventy miles to where the Elliot and Dalton highways part company, but it remains a four-hour run. The road ends at the Tanana River, three miles beyond **Manley Hot Springs**, which is little more than a clearing in the woods with a classic roadhouse that claims to be Alaska's oldest continuously operated example of these archetypal hotel-cum-restaurant/bars. Nearby, a hot spring feeds tubs inside a greenhouse where grapes can be plucked off the vines trained above.

Along the Elliott Highway

The Steese Highway runs eleven miles north from Fairbanks to Fox, from where the **Elliott Highway** (officially open all year, but difficult after snow; contact Fairbanks Department of Transportation ⓣ451-5204) winds its way north then southwest. If taken at a reasonable pace the road shouldn't provide any difficulty for ordinary cars, though services are almost nonexistent: stock up with crisp, **fresh water** at the Fox Spring, Mile 0.3, and with **gas** either in Fairbanks or at the Hilltop Truck Stop, Mile 5 – there is no more until you reach Manley Hot Springs almost 150 miles on.

For most of the journey there is little reason to stop other than to linger over the gorgeous wilderness you're driving through. North of Fox, the Lower Chatanika River State Recreation Area harbors the waterside *Olnes Campground*, Mile 10.6 (free; lake water, which should be treated), with drive-up sites just over a mile off the highway. No longer state-maintained, it remains popular with Fairbanksans up here to fish the lake.

The highway then approaches the western end of the **White Mountains**, an eye-catching limestone range that stretches off to the northeast. Because much of the area is boggy, the majority of trails are only passable in winter. The one significant summer hiking trail is the arduous **Summit Trail** (44 miles round-trip; 4–5 days; 1000ft ascent, 2000ft descent), which starts at a trailhead at Mile 27.7 and initially crosses boardwalks and through dense forest before climbing up to tundra ridge tops. It ends at the lowland *Borealis–LeFevre* cabin (Fri & Sat $25, otherwise $20; reserve through the BLM ⓣ1-800/437-7021), but many prefer to turn back after camping in the high country, making it a two- or three-day hike. If you are intent on getting to the cabin, ask locally about high water levels in Beaver Creek (during spring snowmelt or high rainfall) that make cabin access difficult.

The highway continues north to the tiny homesteading community of **JOY**, which comprises little more than the Wildwood General Store (also known by its old name, Arctic Circle Trading Post), Mile 49.3, good for grabbing a muffin and coffee or something from their huge stock of souvenir T-shirts. At Mile 62.5 you'll find the rustic **Fred Blixt Cabin** (Fri & Sat $25, otherwise $20; reservations up to 30 days in advance; call the BLM on ⓣ1-800/437-7021), the only drive-in cabin in the area, which sleeps five comfortably and has an outhouse nearby. Spring water, which should be treated, is readily available, but you'll need to bring white gas for the cooking stove and firewood for heating.

Ten miles on (Mile 73) the Dalton Highway continues north to Prudhoe Bay and the Elliott Highway turns left to Manley Hot Springs, passing the trailhead (Mile 92) for a fairly tough eleven-mile hiking trail leading south to **Tolovana Hot Spring**, where two wooden tubs huddle next to a gurgling stream. There are a couple of privately owned rental cabins nearby with gas cooking stoves and lights but nothing else: one sleeps four, while the other sleeps eight (Fri & Sat $150, otherwise $100). Use of the hot springs and adjacent cabins is by reservation (Ⓣ445-6706, Ⓦwww.mosquitonet.com/~tolovana), and once booked you have the whole place to yourselves.

Around Mile 95 there are impressive views over **Minto Flats**, a state game refuge which spreads south of the predominantly Athabascan village of Minto, reached by a side road at Mile 110.

Manley Hot Springs

MANLEY HOT SPRINGS, 160 miles northwest of Fairbanks, seems hacked out of the bush and consists of an airstrip, a post office-cum-general store, gas station, and a few houses clustered beside the placid tree-hung Hot Springs Slough. When gold was discovered at the nearby Tofly and Eureka goldfields in the early 1900s, miners came to clean up in freely available hot water and relished the fresh vegetables that could be grown in the warmer ground, a rare boon in Alaska. In 1902, JF "Daddy" Karshner set up a 320-acre market-gardening homestead around the springs – then known simply as **Hot Springs**. Four years later he was bought out by a man going by the alias of **Frank Manley**, who turned up with several hundred thousand dollars and a shady reputation from his Texan past. He was later forcibly returned there, but was eventually acquitted of horse thievery. Manley established the first resort, a log-built four-story affair with electricity, a dance hall, billiard table, steam heating, and a "natatorium" for taking a dip at any time of year. It was an immediate hit with Fairbanks residents. The resort waned with Fairbanks' fortunes and finally burned down in 1913, but Manley's name lived on, and in 1957 it was attached to the name of the town. Don't go calling the place Manley, though, or you'll raise the hackles of older residents. As river traffic came to a halt in the early 1950s, Manley Hot Springs' fate looked bleak, but the completion of a gravel road in 1959 has allowed for a trickle of tourist traffic.

The local population barely touches a hundred, and on a good Saturday night it seems they're all around the pool table and horseshoe bar inside the 1906 *Manley Roadhouse* (Ⓣ672-3161; rooms ❶, with private bath ❹, cabins ❹; mid-May to Oct), a wonderful chunk of Alaska's living heritage with good diner meals, beat-up chairs huddled around the oil-barrel stove and pianola, and rooms upstairs. The older rooms are small and share facilities, but they have more character; cabins sleep five. The patch of grass across the road makes a good **campground** ($5 per site; pay at the roadhouse).

For the **hot springs**, head to the Bath House (open 24hr, 365 days; $5 per person paid to the amiable owners, Chuck and Gladys, at the nearby house; Ⓣ672-3231), a verdant, heated greenhouse containing three simple concrete tubs supplied with cooled but untreated spring water. Grapes and Asian pears flourish here, and you are welcome to sample whatever is ripe as you loll back for a few hours. Essentially, once your group pays up the whole place is yours for an hour, though at busy times you might want to welcome others in. To reach the Bath House from the roadhouse, cross the bridge over the slough and take the third road on the left, about 300yd towards Fairbanks.

△ Gold mining operation, Fairbanks

Arctic Alaska

Exactly what constitutes **Arctic Alaska** is hard to pin down, but it does encompass some of America's finest wilderness, fierce and shockingly desolate and yet shot through with an intricate, fragile beauty. To geographers it is anywhere north of the **Arctic Circle**, an imaginary line at 66° 33' above which the sun fails to set at the summer solstice (June 21), or rise on the winter solstice (December 21). For botanists the true Arctic begins at the tree line, where spruce give way to willows which creep along the ground, often for tens of yards, but never get off it. Meanwhile, ethnologists might argue that the Arctic is the preserve of the Iñupiat and Yup'ik peoples.

Whichever way you define the Arctic, it covers pretty much everywhere north of Fairbanks. This is the land of the midnight sun, where summer days are endless and intense low-angled rays warm the air almost to 100°F. For three brief months the thin covering of snow melts, and the near-flat tundra thaws to a soggy, peaty landscape studded with myriad tiny lakes. Rainfall here is minimal, often less than in some parts of the deserts of the American Southwest, but much of the North is underlain by **permafrost** (see box, p.495), which impedes drainage enough to sustain the lakes. Bears, caribou, moose, and arctic foxes go through accelerated reproductive cycles in time for the arrival of the savage nine-month winter (spring and fall hardly exist), when snow blows across the tundra and the northern lights glow overhead.

Arctic Alaska is split by the **Brooks Range**, which extends almost the width of Alaska. It is the tail end of the continental dividing range that starts at the southern tip of the Andes and stretches right up through the Mexican cordilleras and the US and Canadian Rockies. To the south the Alatna, Chandalar, John, Koyukuk, and Sheenjek rivers drain through the Interior forests into the Yukon and out to the Bering Sea; to the north the Anaktuvuk, Colville, and Sagavanirktok rivers flow across the barren flatlands of the **North Slope** into the Beaufort Sea.

Despite the protection offered by a confusing patchwork of national parks, preserves, and wildlife refuges, much of the wilderness is under threat. Many of the more individualistic Alaskans object to the very idea of "tying up" land in this way, but the greatest danger is from the **oil lobbyists**. The face of the far north has already changed with the exploitation of the Prudhoe Bay field and its satellites, as well as the construction of the pipeline. As reserves dwindle, oil companies are campaigning for access to other areas. The National Petroleum Reserve – Alaska (NPR-A) – west of Prudhoe Bay was set aside for the navy in 1923 and has already been explored, though in recent years environmentalists have argued that it should remain free from development. They have a stronger hand in protecting the Arctic National Wildlife Refuge (ANWR) to the east, although with the high oil prices of recent times there is considerable political pressure being applied to allow exploration in the refuge's northern coastal strip. The Bush administration was very keen to get ANWR exploration on a major energy bill in 2003, but there was enough opposition that the government backed down . . . for the moment.

Exploring the region

The only road access into the Alaskan Arctic is along the 500-mile Dalton Highway to **Prudhoe Bay**, which runs parallel to the trans-Alaska oil pipeline.

Unless you are up for a heroic (and potentially epic) road trip in your own vehicle, it is best done as part of an organized tour taking in the Arctic Circle monument, the oil installation, the Arctic Ocean, and a lot of grand scenery. As it crosses the Brooks Range, the Dalton divides two of Alaska's largest and most remarkable protected areas, both conveniently visited directly by air from Fairbanks. To the west lies the **Gates of the Arctic National Park**, wonderful remote hiking and canoeing country accessed through the tiny village of **Bettles**. To the east is the still more remote **Arctic National Wildlife Refuge**, again good for hiking and floating.

Much of the North is thinly populated, with only a few dozen tiny Native communities scattered across this vast area. The smaller hamlets are not really set up for visitors, so that really just leaves three towns to explore. There is an obvious draw to **Barrow**, the most northerly town on the continent; besides having the world's largest Eskimo population, it serves as the occasional stomping ground of polar bears. **Kotzebue** is smaller but has a higher percentage of Native Alaskans, lending it a more traditional feel. Located well inside the Arctic Circle, it is a good jumping-off point for trips out to the Kobuk Valley National Park. The onetime gold-rush town of **Nome** doesn't claim any superlatives, but it is perhaps the most immediately inviting of the three, with enough of a road system to encourage wider exploration. Nome also serves as the end of the annual 1100-mile Iditarod sled-dog race from Anchorage.

The Dalton Highway to Prudhoe Bay

The Arctic location and remote nature of the **Dalton Highway** exert an almost irresistible pull, all five hundred lonely, desolate miles of it from Fairbanks to the Arctic Ocean, three hundred miles beyond the **Arctic Circle**. It is certainly an adventurous journey, but all you get at the end of the road is Prudhoe Bay, miles of pipes, and the industrial camp of **Deadhorse**, which is nowhere near as exotic as it sounds. You can't even get to the Arctic Ocean except on a fairly perfunctory tour. For most of the year the Arctic packice butts right up against the shore and it is not uncommon to have polar bears roaming through Deadhorse. Things are different in summer, when you are likely to be there, as both the bears and the ice floes are away over the northern horizon.

Those who like their wilderness pristine will be disappointed to learn that the **pipeline** runs above ground most of the way to Prudhoe Bay, though it quickly becomes a faithful companion pointing the way north. Both road and pipeline run down the center of a ten-mile-wide corridor managed by the Bureau of Land Management (BLM) and equipped with a few basic campgrounds. Along the way there are small lakes and streams that, after the rivers have cleared of snowmelt turbidity (July to mid-Sept), offer good **fishing** for grayling, Dolly Varden, lake trout, and northern pike. Hiking is more problematic, with neither formal trails nor waymarked trailheads, though sections of the highway as it passes through the Brooks Range present opportunities for freelance exploration, and if you are prepared to hike across tundra you can go wherever you want.

All around is federally managed wilderness: the **Yukon Flats** and **Arctic** national wildlife refuges to the east; the **Kanuti National Wildlife Refuge** and **Gates of the Arctic National Park** to the west. With all this controlled land about, it is no surprise that there is plenty of **wildlife**. If you're lucky, the most impressive sight you'll see is the 30,000-strong Arctic caribou herd, which migrates in late April and early May through Prudhoe Bay to the Kuparuk oil fields where the cows calve, then returns to the Brooks Range in August for the abundant lichen. Grizzlies, Dall sheep, moose, and foxes are also present, and musk oxen sometimes congregate near the pipeline – binoculars are a boon.

Flights and tours to the Arctic Circle and Prudhoe Bay

Alaska Airlines flies large jets into Prudhoe Bay/Deadhorse airport once or twice daily from Anchorage. Unless you are entitled to use the "Best of the West Airpass" (see p.35), this will set you back about $620 if bought two weeks in advance – probably more than you want to pay to see an oil field. Frontier

Arctic oil and the trans-Alaska pipeline

It is hard to overstate the importance of **oil** to the 49th state. Some jokingly contend that Alaska should break from the union and become an independent OPEC state, an idea that is not so far fetched when you consider that Alaska produces seventeen percent of US oil and five percent of what the nation consumes. Alaskan taxes and royalties account for a third of the value of each barrel, an income that provides a whopping eighty percent of the state revenue. It is no surprise then that Alaska is virtually controlled by oil interests, and it is easy to get the impression that state politicians are little more than puppets for the oil companies.

Oil rises naturally to the surface along the North Slope, historically providing lamp oil for Native Iñupiat and alerting hopeful white newcomers to the presence of deeper deposits. In February 1968 years of exploration paid off when the Atlantic Richfield Company (now part of ConocoPhillips) discovered a 23-billion-barrel reserve 9000ft under **Prudhoe Bay**. This constituted one of the world's largest finds, but the bay's location on the Arctic Ocean, where tankers could only penetrate the pack-ice for two months of the year, posed a problem. The solution was to build a $900 million pipeline running across the middle of the state to the northernmost ice-free port at Valdez. There was an immediate reaction from Alaskan Natives: the route of the planned pipeline would cut across areas claimed by Native groups and not covered by any treaty. Consequently, the 1971 **Alaska Native Claims Settlement Act** (ANCSA) was rushed through, offering land and cash in return for Natives relinquishing their claim on the remaining territory. Environmental concerns over damage to the tundra, disruption of animal migration routes, and the very idea of having a steel tube running hundreds of miles through untouched wilderness almost put a stop to the whole project, but the Arab oil embargo of 1973–74 finally forced the federal government's hand.

Over the years oil production has declined, and in the late 1990s the rallying cry of "No decline in '99" rang around halls of the Alaskan legislature in an effort to convince the state government to allow further exploration on the North Slope, particularly along the coast of the Arctic National Wildlife Refuge. At a time when oil prices were low, a report stated that there are "no economically recoverable amounts of oil" under ANWR if the price stays below $15 a barrel. On cue, the price of crude oil shot up towards $30 a barrel; the oil companies continue to apply pressure for more drilling, backed by many Alaskans as well as the Iñupiat-owned Arctic Slope Regional Corporation, which stands to profit from royalties on any oil extracted.

Even without new development, production will continue until at least 2030, and with current high demand for natural gas, there is even talk of a parallel pipeline to exploit North Slope natural gas. After all, Alyeska, the pipeline-operating company, has an obligation to restore the pipeline corridor to its original state once production ceases – something they want to put off as long as possible.

Flying Service (Ⓣ474-0014, Ⓦwww.frontierflying.com) flies direct from Fairbanks almost daily, but you'll pay around $650.

There seems a lot more purpose to the whole venture when combined with a road trip up the Dalton Highway, and by joining a **bus/plane tour** you won't wreck your vehicle and will (generally) avoid doing the journey in both directions. Trips mostly involve driving up the Dalton in two days, taking the Arctic Ocean tour at Prudhoe Bay, and then flying back either to Anchorage or to Fairbanks. Some do the same in reverse, but go for the former if you can: two days on the road certainly heightens the drama of arrival.

Most companies run trips fairly infrequently, so it pays to inquire a week or two in advance (for contact addresses, see box on p.468). The widest range (and cheapest) of the all-inclusive packages – including road transport, flights, and accommodation but not food – is with Northern Alaska Tour Company, which runs a Prudhoe Bay Adventure (3 days; $749), with a flight to Prudhoe Bay,

The pipeline

The pipeline (Ⓦwww.alyeska-pipe.com) is 800 miles long and in places looks like a four-foot-wide silver anaconda draped across the land. Altogether only 380 miles are buried: where it encounters permafrost, the pipeline gracefully emerges from the ground, rising onto ten-foot-high support brackets, and then embarking on a zigzag passage across the skyline, the kinks designed to accommodate earthquake movement, as well as expansion and contraction in Alaska's extreme weather.

Pipeline construction began in November 1973, and employment peaked at over 21,000, with workers laboring away for wage packages of legendary proportions. With overtime and hardship bonuses, pipeline workers were pulling in up to $1500 a week (several times the national average at the time). Workers flocked up from the Lower 48 only to discover the work was long, hard, often lonely, and conducted in atrocious conditions, right through the Arctic winter.

The pipeline was finished in June 1977 at a cost of $8 billion, almost ten times the original budget, and the first oil was pumped from Prudhoe Bay on June 20, 1977. A Nenana Ice Classic-style lottery was conducted with $30,000 at stake for whoever could pick the exact time of the oil's arrival in Valdez – which turned out to be 38 days, 12 hours, and 56 minutes after it set off. Oil now makes the journey in 8–9 days (averaging 4mph), its passage through a complex series of pumping stations and valves managed from Valdez.

More than five hundred **animal crossings** had been incorporated into the pipeline, some just short runs of buried pipe, others achieved by raising sections of pipe more than usual above ground. The jury is still out on the success of these measures: caribou congregate in spring around the pipe, where the grass tends to green up earlier, but pregnant cows tend to avoid the pipeline altogether.

Twelve **pump stations** were designed to move the oil along, each equipped with Rolls-Royce jet engines. As production has declined, four pump stations – nos. 2, 6, 8 and 10 – have been mothballed. This leaves long sections without significant permanent staff, possibly compromising security. There have been small spills ever since the pipeline came on stream, but consequences of a major pipeline rupture were brought into sharp focus by the *Exxon Valdez* disaster (see box, p.296), and independent groups now monitor Alyeska's safety performance. They are continually highlighting weaknesses in the spill-response plan, leaking information on poor maintenance procedures, and generally driving home the idea that the pipeline is now approaching thirty years old and needs increased maintenance if a catastrophic environmental disaster is to be avoided.

then a minivan back down the Dalton with nights at Prudhoe Bay and Coldfoot. There's an optional overnight extension taking in Barrow (additional $449). If you want to rough it, try Dalton Highway Express (Ⓣ452-2031, Ⓦwww.daltonhighwayexpress.com), which effectively runs a bus service making the trip to Prudhoe Bay in a day (3 days a week; 16hr), then heads back down the next day. They charge $125 each way (bikes cost $60). Try Trans Arctic Circle Treks for an arduous three-day Prudhoe-and-back road trip with an Arctic Ocean tour and camping both nights in the Brooks Range ($599). Barrow and bush-flight extensions are available.

For those only wanting to visit the **Arctic Circle**, Northern Alaska offers a number of variations starting with the full-day Arctic Circle Adventure (16hr; $129), driving up to the Arctic Circle and back. The Arctic Circle Fly Drive (11–12hr; $249) speeds the whole thing up by taking a flight to Coldfoot. Arctic Circle Native Culture (15hr; $399) also flies one-way and includes a couple of hours in the Brooks Range village of Anaktuvuk Pass. Dalton Highway Express does a very basic one-day up-and-back road trip to the Arctic Circle ($79, bring your own lunch), and Trans Arctic Circle Treks takes minivans on a one-day trip to the Arctic Circle (12hrs; $129).

Driving the Dalton Highway

From Fairbanks the route north follows the Steese and Elliott highways 73 miles north to Livengood, where you'll find the start of the 414-mile **Dalton Highway** (open year-round but chains needed Sept–May), named for James Dalton, an Arctic engineer who played a major role in the early oil discovery and development of the North Slope. Old hands know it by its original working title, the North Slope **Haul Road**, named in honor of its fast, stop-at-nothing trucks and built in an astonishing five months in the summer of 1974 in preparation for the construction of the pipeline alongside.

For years the road was limited to pipeline traffic, but regulations were gradually relaxed until the whole road was finally opened to the general public in 1995. Nonetheless, there remains a distinct work-camp tenor along its length. There are no real villages or rest stops, just slightly remodeled work camps mostly comprising prefabricated accommodation blocks. Don't expect much in the way of supplies either, and remember that everything you buy will have an Arctic price tag.

Driving the Dalton Highway mustn't be undertaken lightly, and you should seriously consider joining one of the bus tours. That said, conditions are improving with miles of fresh blacktop being added each year. Two hundred miles are paved between Fairbanks and Deadhorse, but that still leaves three hundred miles of gravel. The word is that the entire road should be asphalt by 2008, but such dates have a habit of being continually put back.

The problem is less the driving itself (two hard days in each direction) than the consequences if something goes wrong. There are only three places to buy gas on the Dalton–Yukon Crossing, Coldfoot, and Deadhorse – and between Coldfoot and Deadhorse there is a 230-mile stretch with no services of any sort: towing fees can soon become astronomical. If you are determined, you'll either need your own vehicle or be prepared to shell out for an expensive **rental vehicle**. Most companies don't allow their cars on gravel roads, and though you might choose to take the risk on the Steese or Elliott highways, this would be foolhardy on the Dalton. Your best bets are with sedans from Arctic Outfitters and campers from GoNorth, both covered under Fairbanks listings on p.474.

Travelers' folklore has it that the Dalton is always in one of two states, muddy or dusty; worse still, the forty-odd eighteen-wheelers that ply the road each day supplying Prudhoe Bay have a nasty habit of hefting large rocks through windshields. For high-clearance trucks serving the oil community the road is passable **in winter**, but the cold (down to –50°F), darkness, and the general hostility of the environment pretty much rule it out for everyone else.

Whenever you go the rule is to **be prepared**. Allow for a couple of punctured tires (take two full-size spares with plenty of tread) and a cracked windshield, drive with your lights on and expect to wait a while for help if you need it. Some even carry a CB radio tuned to Channel 19 to pick up the conversations between truckers and tour-bus drivers but, in summer at least, there is a reasonable amount of traffic and it is enough to carry emergency supplies – food, water, sleeping bag, and perhaps a cooking stove. For more **information** visit APLIC in Fairbanks and pick up their free and comprehensive *The Dalton Highway* brochure, or check out the Coldfoot Interagency Visitor Center website (Ⓦaurora.ak.blm.gov/arcticinfo).

If you are thinking of **hitching** to Deadhorse, then persistence and patience will eventually pay off, usually with hunters, miners, and road crews but seldom with Prudhoe-bound truckers. Remember to take everything you'll need to camp out for several days. The occasional **cyclist** with a spoke loose also makes the journey, but it is tough, and mud and dust are a constant irritation. At least you can fix your own punctures, and once there you can get a ride back to Fairbanks with Dalton Highway Express (see opposite), which charges $60 for the bike.

Designated campgrounds turn out to be the best places you can **camp**. You are generally free to camp anywhere along the highway, though in practice the only places sufficiently off the road are gravel parking lots.

Mile 0 to Mile 175

Leaving Fairbanks you initially follow the Steese and Elliott highways 73 miles to Livengood, Mile 0 of the Dalton Highway. The Dalton now sets off across a rolling landscape dotted with white and black spruce and strung with the gleaming pipeline. There's little reason to stop before Mile 56, where the road crosses the broad, dirty swirl of the **Yukon River** on the sloping 2290-foot EL Patton Bridge, which has the pipeline strapped to its side. This is the only road crossing of the Yukon downstream of Whitehorse in Canada.

Just over the bridge the grandly titled **YUKON CROSSING** comprises a muddy (or dusty) expanse and the scruffy *Yukon River Camp* (Ⓣ655-9001; ④), with shared-bath work-camp rooms and a café (7am–9pm) serving a buffet to tour-bus passengers, as well as burgers ($9), salads ($11), and steak, fish or pasta dinners ($16–20) to all comers. Adjacent, Yukon River Tours (Ⓣ452-7162,) runs hour-long boat trips (June–Aug, 3 daily; $25) downstream past hand-built fishwheels, with an environmental and culturally oriented narrative.

On the other side of the highway, the **BLM contact station** (June–Aug daily 9am–6pm; no phone) provides information on the countryside flanking the Dalton. Four miles up the highway, the *Sixty-Mile Campground* (free; water) sits on the site of an old pipeline-construction camp, right by the *Hotspot Café* (June–Aug 10am–midnight; Ⓣ451-7543; ④), which produces great burgers served inside or out and has slightly dressed-up work-camp rooms at good prices.

North of the Yukon River the land begins to open out: trees become more sparse, and the pipeline views get better. At Mile 98 the ancient forty-foot granite tor of **Finger Rock** pokes up from the bleak tundra, crooked as if warning of the perils of the road ahead. The adjacent nature trail and viewpoint overlooks the shallow pools that form the headwaters of the Kanuti River, the

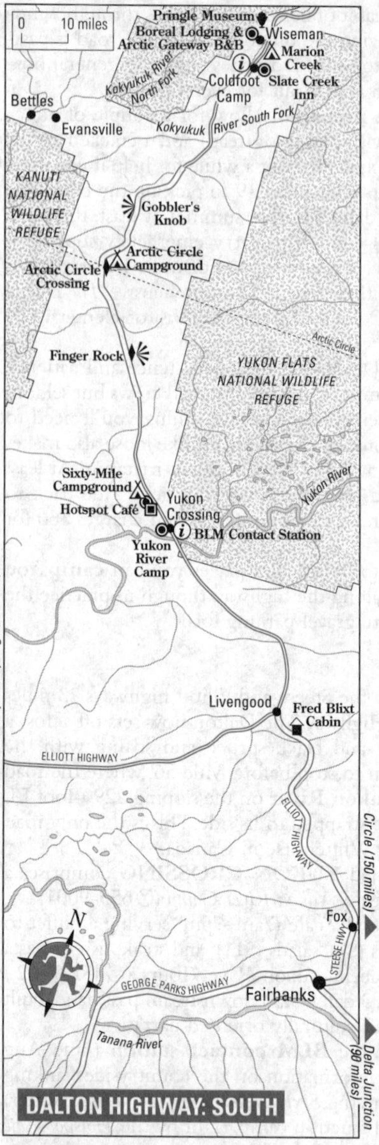

main watershed encompassed by the **Kanuti National Wildlife Refuge** to the west. With acres of relatively dry tundra, this makes a good spot for a couple of hours' hiking: pick a likely-looking destination and go.

The **Arctic Circle** is crossed at Mile 115 and marked by a series of explanatory panels, where everyone has their photo taken. There's a simple mosquito-ridden **campground** (free; water from Fish Creek a mile to the south) and picnic areas with barbecues among the aspen and black spruce, with a slightly breezier (and therefore less buggy) site a quarter-mile up the hill. Unfortunately, the hills to the north preclude seeing the midnight sun from here, even on the solstice, so if this is what you've come for you'll need to press on to **Gobbler's Knob**, Mile 132, where there are panoramic views. About four miles further north, the former pipeline-constructors' **Prospect Camp** holds the record for the lowest temperature recorded in Alaska: –80°F (–62°C) on January 23, 1971. There was once a campground here, and you can still find decent flat spots a mile off the road.

Coldfoot Camp

As the miles roll by, the open Arctic tundra gives way to the foothills of the Brooks Range, blunt, conical hills skirted with white birch rising above broad willow-studded glacial valleys. Gradually, the valleys deepen into the Middle Fork of the Koyukuk River, and you hit the former highway-construction base of **COLDFOOT CAMP**, Mile 175. It bills itself as "the world's northernmost truck stop," and except for a couple of B&Bs at Wiseman (see opposite) Coldfoot is indeed your last chance for accommodation, food, and gas (open 24hr) before Deadhorse 239 miles on. Nothing comes cheaply, but unless you are camping, there isn't much choice. Most tours spend the night here, too. Coldfoot supposedly gets its name from prospectors moving north for more golden pastures and getting metaphorical cold feet around this point, but a literal interpretation suits equally: in 1989 the mercury stayed below –60°F for seventeen days in a row. But it also gets hot here in summer: 1988 recorded a high of 97°F. Workers' **accommodation** has been transformed to create the *Slate Creek Inn* (in Fairbanks ⓣ474-3500, locally ⓣ678-5224, ⓦwww.coldfootcamp.com; ❻), with reasonably comfortable shared-bath twin rooms, a truckers' café (open year-round, 5am–midnight), and a parking lot where you can camp ($15) and hook up an RV ($30). Showers are $10 extra, and there's laundry for $3. You'll also find very limited groceries, a post office (Mon, Wed & Fri 1.30–6pm), and phones. There are even flightseeing trips over the Brooks Range (45min; $89) and a float trip from Wiseman to Coldfoot down the Middle Fork of the Koyukuk River (3–5hr; $79): contact Northern Alaska Tour Company on ⓣ1-800/474-1986.

You get an indication of Alaska's aspirations for making the Dalton Highway a tourist route by the presence of the **Coldfoot Interagency Visitor Center** (late May to early Sept daily 10am–10pm; ⓣ678-5209, ⓦaurora.ak.blm.gov/arcticinfo/), which opened across the highway from Coldfoot Camp in 2003. Attractively designed, beautifully landscaped, and fitted with flush toilets, it is very un-Dalton in character, but it provides a welcome spot to get off the road, sit around the wood-burning stove to read up on the journey ahead, buy books and topo maps, obtain bear-resistant food canisters for backcountry trips and attend nightly slide shows and talks (8pm; free). **Campers** are better served five miles north of Coldfoot Camp at *Marion Creek Campground* ($8; pump water and free firewood), where there are tables, fire pits, a summertime campground host, and great views of the Brooks Range.

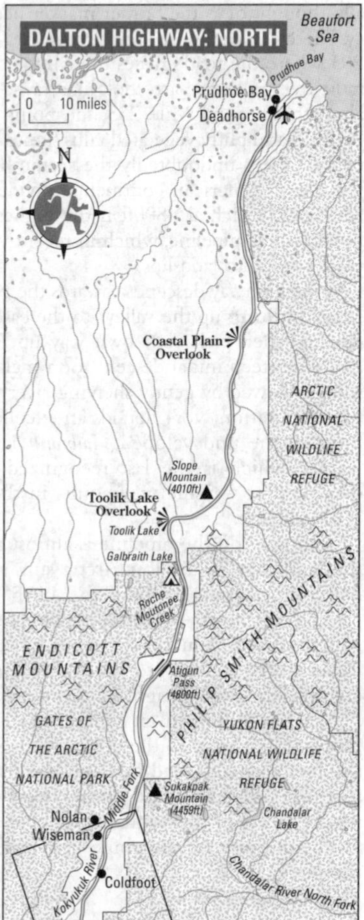

Wiseman to Mile 414

Miners prospecting in 1908 who weren't put off by the low temperatures of Coldfoot Camp chose to settle thirteen miles north at **WISEMAN**, a couple of miles off the highway on the Middle Fork of the Koyukuk River – the "willow river." It is now a small, thriving cluster of log cabins hacked out of the spruce, supporting a couple of dozen people year-round and a few dozen more who arrive for summer hunting, fishing, and gold extraction. Several original buildings have survived, one of which houses the **Pringle Roadhouse & Historical Museum** (June–Aug nominally daily 9am–1pm & 2–5pm but actually very sporadic; free), full of evocative old photos and assorted mining equipment. If you are not up for camping, Wiseman makes an appealing alternative to Coldfoot for **accommodation**: *Boreal Lodging* (Ⓣ678-4566, Ⓔboreallodge@juno.com; cabin ❺, rooms ❸) has comfortable work-camp rooms with access to a well-equipped, cozy kitchen-cum-day room and a more luxurious cabin; *Arctic Getaway B&B* (Ⓣ678-4456, Ⓦwww.arcticgetaway.com; ❹ & ❻) has one large log cabin sleeping four and a smaller two-berth affair.

Wiseman also makes for a good jumping-off point for hiking into the eastern fringes of the **Gates of the Arctic National Park**, the only way to experience the park without a costly flight. Consult APLIC in Fairbanks or the Coldfoot visitor center for details.

As you head north from Wiseman, views to the right are dominated by the great marble face of the 4459-foot **Sukakpak Mountain**, which is traditionally thought of as the border marker between Iñupiat and Athabascan territory. There's an outhouse and parking area adequate for ad hoc **camping** at Mile 205 where the road crosses the Middle Fork of the Koyukuk River. The sporadic trees in these parts look like frayed matchsticks, and they finally disappear altogether around Mile 235, the point where you start to climb the Brooks Range past lightly vegetated talus slopes cascading from snowcapped 7000-foot peaks. This is undoubtedly the scenic highlight of the journey as you breach the North American continental divide, cresting at the scenic **Atigun Pass**, Mile 245, which at 4800ft is the highest road in Alaska. It is also the highest point for the pipeline, which in recent years has been considerably rerouted in places prone to landslips.

As the highway descends towards the North Slope, there are opportunities for rugged **hiking** up the valleys to the east. There are no trails, so choose a good day and then pick your own way up Roche Moutonee Creek around Mile 266. The steep initial descent soon mellows as you enter a broad glacial landscape followed by gently shelving river valleys.

Pump Station No.4 heralds an excellent place to break the last leg of your journey, the undeveloped *Galbraith Lake Campground*, Mile 275 (free; lake water), which is the last recognized site in the North. People do park overnight at wayside viewpoints further on, but there is nowhere to camp at Deadhorse.

From now on the pipeline is almost always above ground, gleaming across the landscape in the low Arctic sun, especially around **Toolik Lake**, Mile 284 (no camping), where the UAF operates an Arctic biology research camp. Dall sheep are often in evidence on the flanks of **Slope Mountain**, Mile 301, which marks the point where the Dalton joins the Sagavanirktok River on its journey to the Arctic Ocean at Prudhoe Bay. You know you are onto the final straight when you hit the **Coastal Plain Overlook**, Mile 356, a low hilltop from where you can see the sixty miles of the North Slope fading away to the ocean while steadily losing 600ft of elevation. The sky seems endless, and the land begins to exhibit truly arctic phenomena – **pingos**, **polygons**, and **thaw lakes** (see box, opposite) – all caused by arcane facets of the annual thaw over hundreds of feet of permafrost. Most visible of these are the pingos, conical mounds rising as high as 200ft above the plain.

Pingos, polygons, and permafrost

One of the defining features of the Alaskan north goes almost entirely unseen, though its effects can be very evident, particularly on the North Slope. Year-round temperatures are so low that most of the ground remains frozen as **permafrost**, stretching from a foot or so below the surface to a depth of up to 2000ft. Nothing would be able to grow, except that the weak summer sun manages to warm enough of the surface to form an **active layer** in which plants can take root and burrowing insects can go about their business.

The permafrost shrinks slightly during the cold winter, forming small vertical cracks. In spring these fill with meltwater and refreeze, a cyclic process that, over the years, forms an **ice wedge**, broad near the surface and tapering to a point several feet underground. There's often a hump on the ground above an ice wedge, and when several form next to one another they create a surface pattern made up of **polygons**, typically ten to seventy feet across. If the top of the ice wedge becomes exposed it may melt to form a **thermokarst lake**, or just a very wet active layer. As the active layer begins to freeze, it pushes up the ground to form a **pingo**, a rounded hummock on the surface that can grow, over several hundred years, to more than 200ft high. Eventually, the pingo will break through the insulating active layer, and the ice will begin to melt, gradually destroying all trace of the formation.

Deadhorse and Prudhoe Bay

The end of the road comes at **DEADHORSE**, 640 miles north of Anchorage. You're still eight miles short of the Arctic Ocean and another 1200 miles from the North Pole – Alaska's southernmost town, Ketchikan, is closer. Deadhorse is a weird place, not really a town at all but an industrial area where venturing outdoors (and there is little reason to do this) risks stumbling onto restricted territory or getting bowled over by a fifty-ton truck. Nonetheless, the shallow lakes and flat tundra all around can be attractive enough on a warm evening: the median summertime temperature is only 40°F, but it feels warmer in the constant sun. Tucked in among the power plants, workshops, and aircraft hangars are a couple of sets of workers' rooms that have been converted into tolerably comfortable hotels.

The fence and checkpoint that mark the ultimate end of the Dalton Highway separate Deadhorse from **PRUDHOE BAY**, the production facility where North Slope oil begins its eight-day journey south to Valdez. There are few refinery-style flare stacks or sci-fi fractionation columns here, just a dendritic web of pipelines. But it's not just wasteland. In between lie acres of marshy grasslands and lakes seemingly undamaged by the industry all around. Quite likely it will appear as though nothing is happening: most of the activity is in the winter when ice roads, built to protect the tundra, make transport easier than it would be across boggy permafrost.

Practicalities

After such a long journey to get here, there is just one way to get a real sense of closure. The only way you can see anything of Prudhoe Bay is to take the **Arctic Ocean Shuttle**, an hour-long tour (June–Aug daily at 8am, 10am, 1.30pm, 3.30pm & 5.30pm; $37) offered by the *Arctic Caribou Inn*, which briefly drives past some of the oil operations, then visits a less than idyllic breakwater on Prudhoe Bay where you can dip your toe in the **Arctic Ocean**: full immersion is possible (and surprisingly common) from late July until early September when the pack ice melts away from the shore. For security reasons tours no longer visit Mile Zero of the pipeline and even for the "shuttle" you need to provide details of a your driver's license or passport at least 24 hours in advance: call, fax, or email the *Arctic Caribou Inn*.

Accommodation is either at the *Prudhoe Bay Hotel* (Ⓣ659-2449, Ⓦwww.prudhoebayhotel.com; private bath ❼, shared bath ❻), which includes three meals in its rates (otherwise $12 for breakfast, $15 for lunch, and $20 for dinner), or the *Arctic Caribou Inn* (Ⓣ659-2368 or 1-877/659-2368, Ⓦwww.arcticcaribouinn.com; room with private bath ❻). Neither spot is particularly salubrious, but they're decent by Haul Road standards. The *Arctic Caribou* also serves meals, but there are no other dining options in town.

RVs can park up beside the *Arctic Caribou* ($15 with electricity, showers $10), but there is no designated campground. Both Deadhorse and Prudhoe Bay are "damp" areas, so there are no liquor sales, though you can bring your own.

The lone Prudhoe Bay General Store (10.30am–9pm) contains the **post office** (1–3.30pm & 6.30–9pm) and stocks the *Anchorage Daily News*, a very modest supply of **groceries**, hardware, and the North Slope's finest selection of Arctic work wear. It also contains *Polar Brew Espresso*, serving a full range of coffees and fruit smoothies.

Gates of the Arctic National Park

In the great American tradition of naming vast tracts of wilderness after a single geographic feature the **Gates of the Arctic National Park** (no entry fee), two hundred miles northwest of Fairbanks, gets its name from Frigid Crags and Boreal Mountain, a pair of mountains in the far eastern reaches of the park. As **Robert Marshall** was forging his way up the North Fork of the Koyukuk River in the 1930s, the wilderness advocate encountered "a precipitous pair of mountains, one on each side" and was immediately struck by how these sentinels framed the way north, the veritable "Gates of the Arctic." His early interest in preserving the region eventually led to the creation of the national park in 1980.

These "Gates of the Arctic" now form part of the nation's second largest national park (after the Wrangell–St Elias), occupying an area four times the size of Yellowstone, the largest park in the Lower 48. The park straddles the central Brooks Range, a labyrinth of rugged mountains rising in waves up to 8000ft, deeply incised by plunging U-shaped valleys that give the whole place an uncanny openness. It all comes cloaked in boreal forest, alder thickets, and a thin mantle of energy-sapping Arctic muskeg, a result of the permafrost that underlies the whole of the park. Such conditions don't support a great variety of animals, though on a longish trip you might reasonably expect to see brown bears, wolves, moose, Dall sheep, caribou, and wolverines.

Kobuk Eskimos and Koyukon and Kutchin Athabascans have lived in harmony with the land for centuries, as they continue to do in the Native villages of Allakaket, Anaktuvuk Pass, Evansville, Shungnak, and Kobuk, using the land for subsistence hunting, fishing, trapping, and gathering. Their ancestors, back in 1885 and 1886, guided early white explorers and prospectors, who eventually turned up payable quantities of gold on the Koyukuk, sparking the rush of 1898. All of a sudden there were small paddle steamers and riverboats churning upstream from the Yukon River bound for trading posts at Bettles, Coldfoot, and Wiseman. For the next three decades miners scoured the southern flanks of the central Brooks Range with varying degrees of success, followed by the geological, geographic, and mineral-survey teams which brought Robert Marshall to the area.

Much of the land here was only surveyed while planning the park – the last place in the US to be fully mapped – and few landmarks are named, even on the largest-scale topo maps. It remains wholly remote. There is only one Native village – Anaktuvuk Pass – within the bounds of the park, and eight others dotted around the perimeter, none claiming over four hundred souls. Within the park itself there are no facilities and no roads, not even tracks apart from those left by Dall sheep, the migrations of the western Arctic caribou herd, and those made by subsistence hunters in pursuit.

Getting to the park

Wright Air Service (see box, p.469) has regular daily flights from Fairbanks to Bettles (see p.468), charging around $270 round-trip. Northern Alaska (see box, p.468) runs their excellent-value, evening-only **Arctic Circle Air Adventure** (4hr; $249), giving you a flight north from Fairbanks along the route of the pipeline, then among the southern peaks of the park, low through the John River Valley to Bettles, and back to Fairbanks. *Bettles Lodge* (see p.499) offers a similar **Arctic Circle Tour** ($420), which includes lunch at the lodge and their Koyukuk River Tour. By paying a bit more, you can also spend the night (around $500 in total, based on double occupancy).

The biggest **wilderness operator** in the Gates of the Arctic is Bettles-based Sourdough Outfitters (Ⓣ692-5252, Ⓦwww.sourdough.com), which offers a staggering array of guided, guide-assisted, and unguided trips for all seasons – hiking, paddling in inflatable canoes, rafting, wildlife viewing, and dog sledding. Prices are dependent on group size in the case of unguided trips and inclusive of flights from Fairbanks for the guided trips. Select from unguided backpacking to the Arrigetch Peaks (7 days; $430 per person assuming four passengers), unguided canoeing on the headwaters of the Noatak (7 days; $800), guided backpacking around the Arrigetch Peaks (7 days; $2000), and guided rafting on the John River (6 days; $2100). They also **rent gear** by the day with every fifth day free: rigid canoes ($25), small rafts ($35), canvas-wall tents ($15), sleeping bags ($5), and so on. Even if you are planning your own excursion, you might consider taking along a guide ($250 a day plus the guide's transport cost). Apart from providing peace of mind, the guide is usually bursting with information about the area's cultural significance, good fishing spots, or ways up apparently inaccessible peaks and saddles. Note that float trips are best in June and July when the water levels are high.

The folks at the *Bettles Lodge* (see p.499) also organize a smaller, but competitively priced, range of planned but unguided trips.

Exploring the park

To travel here you need to be completely self-sufficient, and since the scale and logistics are so mind-boggling, those who come tend to stay for a while. Only around four thousand recreational visitors make it into the park each year (about what Denali gets in a day), and they stay an average of eleven days. For those prepared to make the commitment of time, energy, and money, it is a hugely rewarding place to be. Most people come to either **hike** or take a multiday **float trip** on one of six designated **Wild Rivers** – the Alatna, John, Kobuk, Noatak, North Fork of the Koyukuk, and Tinayguk – all possible under your own steam, but a good deal easier with guided or guide-assisted trips, mostly operated from Bettles. These trips concentrate on only a few spots, so much of the rest of the park remains entirely untouched – one research biologist apparently spent five months each summer season here for eleven years and saw only six people the whole time.

Even more than most places in Alaska, your experience will be dictated by **the weather**. Most visitors arrive after mid-June when frozen rivers have completed their thaw and move on by early September. Mosquitoes can be so bad in June, July and early August that head nets are *de rigueur*, thus making late August and September particularly appealing, provided you're prepared for cooler temperatures and some rain. On average it snows eight or nine months of the year, and some years only July is snow-free. Throughout summer you'll seldom experience a completely dark night, and the park receives continuous sunlight for thirty days in June and July. Consequently, July basks in a relatively balmy average daily maximum of 70° (average daily minimum 46°F). Over the whole park rainfall is low, but most falls in late summer so you'll need to take proper protection for that time.

Access in summer is almost exclusively by float plane from Bettles (reached by scheduled bush flights from Fairbanks). Before entering the park you'll be required to work through a "backcountry simulator" program in Bettles or Anaktuvuk Pass to ensure you are fully competent in outdoor skills. Leave no trace is the ethic: such is the delicacy of the Arctic environment that even minimal impact takes a long time to recover, so special care is needed in the more heavily visited areas. Two of the most popular **float trips** are on the headwaters of the Noatak River (5–9 days; Class I–II), among wonderful angular peaks and with possible access from Kotzebue (see p.511); and the North Fork of the Koyukuk (5 days; Class I–III), with the entry point in the shadow of the Gates themselves, followed by a float down to Bettles. You are unlikely to be totally alone on these rivers, but adventure operators and bush pilots in Bettles can advise on more solitary rivers. **Hiking areas** are more widely distributed. Essentially, you can arrange to be flown in pretty much anywhere there is water or a gravel river bar to land on, and then either use that as a base or hike to some pre-arranged pickup point. Again, there are more popular areas, but it is probably best to ask about places less frequented, if only to reduce impact on busier areas.

Keen hikers and rock climbers should head a hundred miles northwest of Bettles to **Arrigetch Peaks**, the granite spires rising 3000ft from the surrounding land that grace numerous Gates of the Arctic publicity brochures. The name – loosely "fingers of an extended hand" – comes from a Nunamuit Eskimo legend of the Creator, who placed his glove on the land as a reminder of his presence.

Bettles

BETTLES, 185 miles northwest of Fairbanks and 35 miles above the Arctic Circle, is an object lesson in how planes have changed life in bush Alaska. When gold was being sifted from the Koyukuk River around the turn of the twentieth century, Bettles stood on its bank as the highest point accessible to sternwheelers. Here supplies bound for Wiseman and Coldfoot were transferred to flat-bottomed scows that could negotiate the riffles upstream. During World War II, planes were being ferried to Russia on the Lend-Lease scheme, and the military needed an airstrip midway between Fairbanks and Barrow. Bettles was the spot, but the best land lay on a gravel bar five miles upstream. An airstrip was built and over the years the whole town relocated, leaving **Old Bettles** moldering on its cut-bank, the willows, cottonwoods, and alders taking over the sagging remains of the cabins.

The population of Bettles and its contiguous Native twin, **Evansville**, only amounts to fifty-odd, and the airstrip is the center of town. There are no roads to the outside so everyone comes in or out by plane. Unless you arrive with immediate plans to fly off to the park you can suddenly feel stranded. A way out is to join *Bettles Lodge* for their two-hour **Koyukuk River Tour** ($65), which checks out former gold-prospecting sites and Old Bettles.

Summer is the busiest time in Bettles as the town fills with those bound for the Gates of the Arctic, but in March, viewing of the **northern lights viewing** is the attraction and Japanese becomes the town's lingua franca.

Information, accommodation, and food

Before heading into the park, you'll need to pop along to the Bettles Ranger Station and **visitor center** (mid-June to mid-Sept daily 8am–5pm; mid-Sept to mid-June Mon–Fri 8am–5pm; ⓣ692-5494), where you can participate in the required backcountry **orientation program**, discuss your trip plans, and obtain the essential bear-resistant food canister.

On the way to the visitor center, you pass the 1948 *Bettles Lodge* (ⓣ692-5111 or 1-800/770-5111, ⓦwww.alaska.net/~bttlodge; rooms ❼, bunks ❶), effectively a bush truck stop, with pilots dropping in for their morning coffee. It has a nice mosquito-proof veranda for knocking back a beer or two during the long evenings. **Accommodation** is either in the rustic lodge, where rooms share a central bathroom; in less characterful modern rooms, some with jacuzzi; in a very basic bunkhouse ($18); or outside, where there's free camping (showers $5). *Bettles Lodge* also runs a day trip ($420), with flights from Fairbanks and a boat ride on the river, and an overnight trip including meals at the lodge ($486, en suite $500). The only other accommodation in town is *Holly Hollow Cabins* (contact Sourdough Outfitters ⓣ692-5252, ⓦwww.sourdough.com; ❸, ❼ with breakfast and dinner), modern self-catering cabins sleeping up to four.

You'll almost certainly be **eating** at *Bettles Lodge*, where the meals are decent (book for dinner; around $20), and burgers come at tolerable prices. There are also a couple of espresso vendors in the peak season.

Arctic National Wildlife Refuge

The **Arctic National Wildlife Refuge** is something special, a profound wilderness where human impact is so slight that you will inevitably find yourself slowing to the pace of the land. It is the largest and northernmost of all America's wildlife refuges, encompassing the entire northeastern corner of Alaska. At roughly nineteen million acres, its enormous size enables it to present the full sweep of Arctic and subarctic ecosystems. Heavily wooded, serpentine river valleys dominate the south, notably those containing the Sheenjek, Ivishak, and Wind rivers, all three now designated National Wild Rivers. North of the Brooks Range (which bisects the refuge) lies the treeless expanse of the North Slope, threaded by braided river systems and innumerable lakes, laden with arctic char and winding across open tundra through caribou-calving areas.

It is one of the last true wildernesses, so thick with wildlife that it has been dubbed an Arctic Serengeti, with not a single introduced species. It is a critical calving area for the 180,000-strong **Porcupine caribou herd** and the most important polar-bear denning habitat in the US. Moreover, 140 bird species have been spotted, with ducks, loons, geese, and swans in astounding numbers. It was the protection of the Porcupine herd that drew the attention of some of Alaska's earliest and most effective conservationists, **Celia Hunter** and **Ginny**

Wood, who along with other like-minded souls met in Fairbanks in 1960 to establish the statewide Alaska Conservation Society. Ecologists Olaus and Margaret Murie lent weight to the campaign – Margaret later writing of their northern travels in *Two in the Far North* (see p.547) – and within months they had helped establish the Arctic Refuge. Unfortunately, such refuges have always had limited protection, and oil interests are now keen to offset declining reserves by surveying within the northern sectors of the Arctic Refuge. Public pressure has so far limited exploration.

If oil production ever goes ahead, it will be the first time the hand of man has ever fallen heavily on this land. The Native Gwich'in have traditionally relied upon the caribou migrations for their survival, and trappers and hunters have built the odd riverside shack over the decades, but there is really nothing but wilderness: no roads or visitor facilities of any kind. If you do set aside the time and the considerable chunk of money needed to get into the reserve, you'll be on your own, except for some of the thickest swarms of Alaska's most voracious mosquitoes. That said, the Kongakut River has a brief couple of months of relative popularity each summer as enthusiasts from both sides of the political fence come up to see just what it is they are fighting about.

Many of the companies operating trips into the Arctic Refuge do so through the small Gwich'in village of **FORT YUKON**, 140 miles northeast of Fairbanks and eight miles north of the Arctic Circle. It lies at the confluence of the Porcupine and Yukon rivers right on the southern edge of the Arctic Refuge and was one of the first Interior villages to find its way onto white men's maps when, in 1847, it was transformed into a Hudson's Bay Company trading post.

Getting there

Getting into the Arctic Refuge is neither easy nor particularly cheap, and staying means being totally self-sufficient. Most people who come here do so on a guided float trip with one of several companies (see p.468).

If you are heading into the refuge independently, you've got a choice of bush-plane companies (see box on p.468–469) that make regular flights to Fort Yukon from Fairbanks for around $88 each way and will advise on pilots for onward travel. If you just want a taster, join one of the trips run by Warbelow's Air Ventures: a regular bush-mail flight (3–4hr; $228), which briefly calls here and continues to other small villages, or the Native Village Tour (3–4hr; $259), which starts with the bush-mail flight and then includes a 45-minute tour of the village. Larry's Flying Service also runs a bush-mail flight and an equivalent to the Native Village Tour ($249).

Nome and around

Of all the towns in the Alaskan north, the former gold town of **NOME**, over five hundred miles northwest of Anchorage and a similar distance west of Fairbanks, has the greatest all-around appeal. The town's appearance may be unprepossessing, but it is a fascinating place with a diverting history and a slew of fun events throughout the year, not least the **Iditarod** sled-dog race, which finishes here in March. Though not connected to the Interior highways, Nome also lies at the hub of a relatively extensive road system which fans out across the **Seward Peninsula**, giving access to miles of bird-rich coastline, untold acres of undulating tundra periodically dotted with the detritus of gold mining, some secluded hot springs, and a couple of small towns, including the Iñupiat Eskimo village of Teller.

Locals say, "There's no place like Nome," and that is true enough. Once the greatest and most exuberant of Alaska's gold-rush towns, it is now down to around four thousand people – about half white, half Eskimo – but retains a kind of subarctic Wild West feel, particularly along the main Front Street, its seaward side lined with what seems like an endless row of initially intimidating dark bars. The streets are dusty, the restaurants scruffy, and drab buildings which may not be old look like they've seen many a hard winter. Houses sit on stubby poles to prevent them sinking into the mire of thawed permafrost and come surrounded by gardens where grass has been replaced by the odd dredge bucket, parts of a dismembered snowmachine and maybe an old freight container. Still, it is attractively set on **Norton Sound**, which remains frozen from around mid-November through late May, but thaws to reveal Nome's golden beach – famed not for the quality of its sand but for the **gold** contained in it which drew thousands at the end of the nineteenth century.

People still work the beach, and with no claims to stake, visitors are welcome to try their hand, though most of the twenty thousand annual visitors are content to watch the professionals and explore the surroundings, relishing the 24hr light that comes from being just a hundred miles shy of the Arctic Circle. Many hope to see animals, but despite the seasonally icy seas, you are very unlikely to see **polar bears** around Nome, though they sometimes make an appearance around the northern Seward Peninsula when the pack ice is firm. A much better bet are the **reindeer**, which have been grazed across the peninsula since they were introduced over a hundred years back as a meat source. **Musk oxen** were reintroduced here in the 1970s from a growing herd near Delta Junction and now number around 1800. The Seward Peninsula is considered prime **birding** territory with 180 species either resident or paying a flying visit from late May to July, when Asiatic transients can be found. As the sea ice melts, the birds congregate along shore margins and in newly opened ponds, making shorebird and waterfowl spotting particularly good from the road system. The visitor center keeps track of recent sightings.

Some history

Long before the town of Nome existed, British navigators plotted the coastline, almost arbitrarily giving headlands and inlets the names of their patrons or home towns. The story goes that on a particularly uninspired day in the 1850s one officer spied the eminence on the northern shore of Norton Sound and merely marked "? Name" on his chart. Back home, cartographers mistook his scribble for C. Nome, and Cape Nome it became.

At the time, there were only a few Iñupiat encampments along the coast, and it looked likely to stay that way after the Reverend Hudson Stuck visited in the 1890s and declared, "A savage forbidding country, this . . . Seward Peninsula, uninhabited and unfit for habitation; a country of naked rock and bare hillside and desolate, barren valley, without amenities of any kind and coursed with a perpetual icy blast." It remained almost uninhabited until 1898 when the "**Three Lucky Swedes**" – actually two Swedes and a Norwegian – found gold below a mountain with a tall rock in the shape of an anvil. They called it Anvil Creek and the waterside settlement that formed four miles to the south became Anvil City. This was easily confused with the nearby village of Anvik, so the US post office forced a change and **Nome** took the name of the nearby cape.

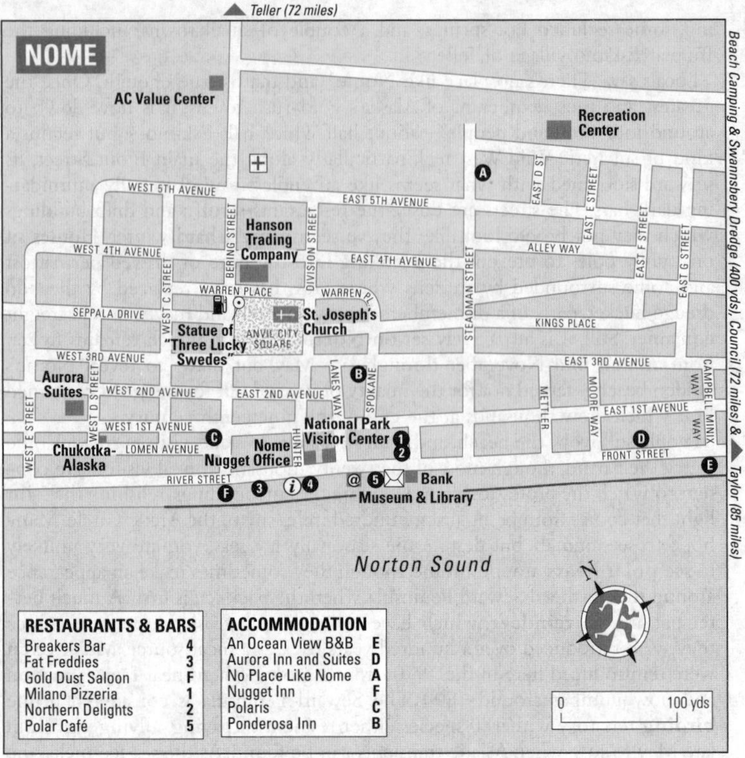

Initially, the rush to Nome was no different from the dozens of others across Alaska over the last few decades of the nineteenth century. There were only 250 people here when, in July 1899, John Hummel, a prospector from Idaho who was too sick to go to the rich creeks, realized that the ruby-colored sand at his feet was laced with gold. This beach made of gold soon became known as the "Poor Man's Paradise" since prospectors needed none of the usual miners' trappings – a bucket, a shovel, and a primitive rocker would suffice. There were no stakes to claim since the beach was open to all, and if another prospector left his diggings, you could move in. Better still, there was no desperate overland struggle as in Klondike, no icy passes to cross, and no frozen ground to thaw, just golden sands ready for sifting as soon as you stepped off the steamer. The pickings weren't especially rich, but three thousand prospectors arrived before winter ice halted the steamers, and many more arrived overland by any means possible, even cycling (see box, above).

By 1900 the beach was overrun with tents, some 25 miles of them with their owners standing shoulder to shoulder extracting paydirt – over $2 million worth in total. As you'd imagine, claim jumping was rife, some of the best of the stories retold by Rex Beach in *The Spoilers* (see Contexts, p.547). The US census in 1900 recorded that one-third of all non-Natives in Alaska were in Nome – a total of 12,488 people, though estimates put the real figure closer to 20,000, and some claim more like 40,000. Nome was briefly the biggest city in Alaska. So much for the thoughts of Hudson Stuck, though he returned fifteen years after the founding of Nome and his opinions hadn't changed. He wrote, "Nothing in the world could have caused the building of a city where Nome is built except the thing that caused it: the finding of gold . . . It has no harbor or roadstead, no shelter or protection of any kind; it is in as bleak and as exposed a position as a man would find if he should set out to hunt the earth over for ineligible sites."

Nome had the typical gold-town plethora of churches, bars, and brothels (not necessarily in that order), plus a French lingerie store and four piano movers, but by the end of 1900 the population was already beginning to decline. Still, it remained an important service town to mining communities around the Seward Peninsula and as the terminus for the **Iditarod Trail**, a winter route across the Alaskan Interior from Seward through the short-lived gold town of Iditarod. Life in Nome ticked by, beleaguered by storms and fires that destroyed the downtown area, until it hit the headlines again in 1925 with the diphtheria epidemic that would have killed hundreds but for the heroic exploits of those who took part in the **Serum Run** (see box, overleaf).

Arrival, getting around, and information

To get to Nome you have to fly, and with the high cost of tickets many choose to come on one of the Anchorage-based **package tours** run by Alaska Airline Vacations (late May to early Sept; ⓣ1-800/468-2248): either a day trip ($369), a two-day affair with a night at the *Nome Nugget Inn* ($399), or three days with overnights in both Nome and Kotzebue ($550). All overnights are based on double occupancy.

Flights with Alaska Airlines to Nome cost around $390 round-trip, if bought 21 days in advance (otherwise $635), although there are sometimes web specials for under $350. It is also worth considering an Anchorage–Kotzebue–Nome–Anchorage loop that will cost around $530, if booked three weeks in advance.

The airport is just over a mile west of town: walk, stick out your thumb, or call a cab (try Checker Cab ⓣ443-5211 or Louie's Cab ⓣ443-6000), which will cost about $5. Once in town you can walk everywhere, though to explore the road system you'll need either to **rent a car** (see "Listings," p.506) or to join the entertaining Richard Beneville of Nome Discovery Tours (ⓣ443-2814, ⓔdiscover@nome.net), who conducts half-day tours ($45) visiting the town, an Arctic gold mine, and the tundra, and full-day tours ($70) that see more of the road system.

The **visitor center**, 301 Front St (mid-May to mid-Sept daily 9am–9pm; mid-Sept to mid-May Mon–Fri 9am–6pm; ⓣ443-6624, ⓦwww.nomealaska.org), has everything you need to know about Nome and its environs, plus a selection of videos on the region and a stuffed musk ox. Anyone thinking of exploring the Bering Land Bridge National Preserve, or any of the national parks, preserves, and monuments further north, should call in at the **National Park Visitor Center**, 179 Front St (mid-May to mid-Sept Mon–Fri 8am–4.30pm, Sat 10–4.30pm; mid-Sept to mid-May Mon–Fri 8am–4.30pm; ⓣ443-2522 or 1-800/471-2352, ⓦwww.nps.gov/bela). They have a stack of wet-day videos including material on reindeer herding and traditional Native uses of Serpentine Hot Springs (see p.510).

Accommodation

Nome remains essentially a frontier town, and accommodation is both expensive and generally not to a very high standard. There are central and modestly priced **B&Bs** and smaller hotels, but unfortunately there's nowhere really

The Serum Run

As much as for gold, Nome is known for the **Serum Run**, a desperate attempt in the 1920s to save the lives of sick Nome residents by delivering an antitoxin. In January 1925 three Nome children were diagnosed with the highly infectious diphtheria, and memories of the influenza epidemic that killed 91 people seven years previously soon panicked the community. Immediate quarantine laws were enacted, but with only a meager stock of ageing half-spent antitoxin available a call for external help was tapped out on the telegraph. Adequate supplies were dispatched from Seattle, but that was over a month's sail away; fortunately, a decent stock of antitoxin turned up in an Anchorage warehouse, and thoughts turned to using one of Alaska's two planes. Aviation was primitive and winter conditions were atrocious, so it was decided to make use of an existing mail route and deliver the serum 674 miles by dog sled. The glass vials (suitably insulated) were immediately sent by train to Nenana, where they were transferred to the first of a special relay of dog teams designed to cover the route much faster than the normal thirty-day passage. Instead of being relieved every 100–125 miles, mushers were mostly staged twenty miles apart, though champion dog musher **Leonhard Seppala** was allotted a ninety-mile section – more than double that of any other musher. Naturally, he needed his best team and rejected one of his weaker dogs, **Balto**.

As time went on the need for the serum intensified, but bad weather brought down the telegraph wires and made communication impossible. Several teams were sent out from Nome to relieve Seppala along the final leg and it was **Gunnar Kaasen**, hauled by the rejected Balto, who brought the serum through a whiteout into Nome just five days and seven and a half hours after it left Nenana. The vials were frozen but still useable, the epidemic was stemmed, and the nation rejoiced.

All the mushers involved were rewarded with cash payouts and presented with a medal by President Calvin Coolidge, but, as the team that actually delivered the serum, Kaasen and Balto were feted with the greatest praise. This rankled Seppala, especially when Kaasen and Balto were taken on national lecture tours and offered film roles, Kaasen was given $1000 by the manufacturers of the serum, and Balto even had his statue erected in New York's Central Park, where it remains today.

In recent years, Seppala's name has become the better known. Every year during the Iditarod – a race founded on the spirit of the Serum Run but following a quite different route – the Leonhard Seppala Humanitarian Award is awarded to the musher who exhibits the most concern for his animals.

cheap: those on a budget will have to **camp** on the beach, an accepted (and often very pleasant) practice, around a mile east of the visitor center. It is free but the only facilities are a couple of outhouses: water can be obtained from a hose outside the visitor center, and there are **public showers** at the recreation center (see "Listings," p.507).

The main busy season is from late May to August, but if you are thinking of coming to see the end of the Iditarod, you'll want to plan your accommodation up to a year in advance. Places fill up fast and you definitely don't want to arrive with nothing arranged. The eight percent tax is included in our price codes.

An Ocean View B&B 209 E Front St ⓣ443-2133, ⓦwww.nomebb.com. Attractive B&B right beside the Bering Sea with a lovely communal lounge built around a stone fireplace. Shared- and private-bath rooms. ❹

Aurora Inn and Suites 302 E Front St ⓣ443-3838 or 1-800/354-4606, ⓦaurorainnome.com. Currently Nome's top-line hotel, opened in 1999 and featuring a sauna and large, comfortable rooms, some with kitchenettes and sea views. They also have an "executive wing" at West 2nd Ave & West D St with larger suites. Apartments and kitchen rooms ❼, suites and standard rooms ❻

No Place Like Nome 605 Steadman St ⓣ443-2451, ⓔbente@nook.net. About the cheapest B&B in town, but it's a pleasant spot with five rooms. ❹

Nugget Inn 315 Front St ⓣ443-4189 or 1-877/443-2323, ⓦwww.nomenuggetinn.com. Long-standing hotel, right by the Burl Arch (see below), that's patronized by tour groups despite the fairly basic, poky rooms with small private bathroom. Rooms do come, however, with cable TV, and some have sea views. ❺

Polaris Hotel 202 Bering St ⓣ443-2003. Although they do have private-bath doubles, this fairly scruffy and sometimes noisy hotel is only recommended for lone travelers not geared for camping: basic shared-bath singles, which don't really meet expected standards, go for $40. Private-bath doubles ❸

Ponderosa Inn 291 Spokane St at 3rd Ave ⓣ443-5737. Some of the nicest rooms in town, with fairly simple but tasteful decor, cable TV, and the option of a full kitchen. Suites ❻, rooms ❹

The Town

To get your bearings, follow the *Historical Walking Tour* brochure obtained free from the visitor center on Front Street. The tour starts outside by the finish line of the Iditarod, where the **Burl Arch** – usually stashed off to the side during summer – is wheeled into place in March to mark the end of the final sprint down Front Street.

Following Front Street and keeping the huge boulders of Nome's protective seawall on your right, you pass the offices of the **Nome Nugget** (ⓦwww.nomenugget.com), the town's newspaper, which claims to be the oldest in the state, though the *Wrangell Sentinel* challenges the claim. Always a good read, the weekly paper comes out each Thursday at a cost of 50¢ – the same as it was when it was founded in 1900 when the gold-rush economy inflated prices enormously. Diagonally opposite, below the library, sits the **Carrie M McLain Memorial Museum**, 223 Front St (June–Aug daily noon–8pm; Sept–May Tues–Sat noon–6pm; $1 donation appreciated; ⓣ443-6630), a small-town museum that packs in the history of the Serum Run, stacks of photos and artifacts from the gold rush, a large ivory collection and assorted changing exhibits.

Continuing in the same direction, you can **pan for gold** anywhere along the mile of beach between the end of the seawall and the *Fort Davis Roadhouse*. The nearby Country Store, 1008 E Front St (ⓣ1-800/478-3297), sells gold pans (around $7 for a decent-sized 14" model) so you can join the beach miners. They spend the summers with their sluice boxes and suction dredges working the beach and the shallow coastal waters while camped in a motley collection of faded tents and draped tarps. Don't expect to get rich: this area has been well panned already, though you'll probably get a few flakes.

A measure of how little gold is left lies further on (about a mile from the visitor center) where the rusting **Swanberg Dredge** has lain idle beside the road since the 1950s. It is now the centerpiece of Swanberg Rocker Gulch Park, where you'll find explanatory panels and assorted mining paraphernalia scattered about.

Back in town the distinctive focal point is the slender spire of **St Joseph's Church**, which thrusts upwards as if mocking the over-optimism of 1900, when there were perhaps twenty thousand souls to minister to. Blindingly white in the low subarctic sun, it casts its shadow over **Anvil City Square**, a wide expanse of grass with one corner graced by statues of the **Three Lucky Swedes**, none looking especially delighted with his good fortune.

Eating and drinking

Eating in Nome is more a function than a pleasure, although as the largest town for hundreds of miles there is a reasonable choice of places to dine, at a price. Those on a tight budget may prefer to patronize the AC Value Center, about a mile north of downtown on Bering Street, with its deli, bakery, and **groceries**, or the Hanson Trading Company, also on Bering Street but closer to town. Both have groceries costing around forty percent more than in Anchorage. It may also be worth checking out the *Fort Davis Roadhouse*, two miles east of town along Front Street, which is rumored to be reopening for the closest thing Nome gets to fine dining.

The approach to **drinking** may be unsophisticated, but locals from Nome and the surrounding "dry" villages bring the Front Street bars enthusiastic patronage.

Breakers Bar 243 Front St ⓣ443-2531. Ever-popular drinker's bar that vies with the *Anchor Bar*, just down the street, for top conviviality honors.

Fat Freddies 305 Front St ⓣ443-5899. Reliable family-style dining at fairly decent prices.

Gold Dust Saloon in the *Nugget Inn*, 315 Front St. Lively bar with a sea view that's a good deal more sophisticated than the frontier-style places along the street.

Milano Pizzeria 250 Front St ⓣ443-2924. The best restaurant in town, offering pretty decent pizzas ($12–16 for a 13-inch), pasta and Japanese dishes. There's also a good-value lunch special for $9.

Northern Delights 245 Front St ⓣ443-5200. The town's only espresso café, also serving bagels and muffins.

Polar Café 205 Front St ⓣ443-5191. The best value of the downtown restaurants, with great sea views and all-day breakfasts of reindeer sausage, eggs, and hash browns ($9). It's also good for burgers and sandwiches ($6–10) and dinners of liver and onions ($12) or a plate of battered halibut and trimmings ($17).

Listings

Airlines Alaska Airlines ⓣ443-2288; Bering Air ⓣ443-5464; Cape Smythe Air ⓣ443-2414, ⓦwww.capesmythe.com.

Banks Wells Fargo, 107 Front St (Mon–Thurs 10am–5pm, Fri 10am–6pm), has an ATM in the foyer.

Books Arctic Trading Post, 302 Front St (ⓣ443-2686), and Chukotka–Alaska Inc, 514 Lomen Ave (ⓣ443-4128), have the town's best selection of books on the region, the Iditarod, and more.

Car rental Stampede Ventures, at the *Aurora Inn* (ⓣ443-3838 or 1-800/354-4606, ⓔaurorainn@gci.net), rents 4WD pickups and SUVs for $95 a day with unlimited mileage and passenger vans for $115. Alaska Cab Garage (ⓣ443-2939) has competitive rates for similar vehicles.

Cycling Nome's road system is great for biking, and if you're thinking of bringing yours, get in touch with Keith Conger, who runs Bering C Bikes, 500 Spinning Rock Rd (ⓣ443-4994, ⓔcong06@gci.net), located in the suburb of Icy View, a mile or so north of Nome. As well as operating a bike repair shop and offering general logistical support for kayaking and wilderness trips, Keith offers van-supported bike tours of Nome's road system, providing meals, backup, and local knowledge. Rates depend on numbers (though expect $150–200 a day), and you'll need to bring a bike with you. June and July offer the best weather.

Festivals The Nome calendar abounds in festivals, kicking off with a bunch of events designed to coincide with the Iditarod Sled Dog Race around the second and third weeks in March, notably the Miners & Mushers Ball and the Bering Sea Ice Golf Classic (third Sat), a six-hole charity tournament with Astroturf greens, orange balls, huskies dressed up as caddies, arcane rules, and warming tots of vodka. At summer solstice, around June 21, Nome celebrates the longest day with the Midnight Sun street festival, which usually coincides with the Nome River Raft Race, using home-built rigs. With all this revelry you might be induced to enter the Polar Bear Swim in 35°F water with a certificate for full immersion. And in September (Labor Day), there's a Rubber Duck Race and a Bathtub Race along Front Street, with water, bubbles, and a bather, soap, and a bath mat in each tub.

Fishing Reasonable salmon, pike, and grayling fishing in the region's rivers. Nome Outfitters, 125 W 1st Ave (ⓣ443-2880 or 1-800/680-6663), is the best contact for gear and local knowledge.

Internet access See Library, below.

Laundry There is no public laundromat, so take your dirty smalls back to Anchorage.

Library The Kegoayah Kozga Library, 223 Front St (Mon–Thurs noon–8pm, Fri & Sat noon–6pm; ⓣ443-5133), has a free paperback swap and free Internet access booked by the half-hour.

Medical assistance Norton Sound Regional

Hospital, at Bering St & E 5th Ave (☎ 443-3311), is open 24hr.

Post office 113 E Front St. The **General Delivery** zip code is 99762.

Shopping Nome is a good place to buy Iñupiat and Yup'ik crafts, with a good range at fair prices, and the person selling may know (or be) the person who did the work. Try the Arctic Trading Post, 302 Front St (☎ 443-2686); Ivory Jim's, 213 Front St; and Chukotka–Alaska Inc, 514 Lomen Ave (☎ 443-4128), which along with superb local Eskimo crafts stocks a fabulous treasure trove of books, Russian watches, dolls, T-shirts, and Lomonosov porcelain.

Showers Recreation Center, 208 E 6th Ave (Mon–Fri 6am–10pm, Sat closed, Sun 2–10pm; ☎ 443-5543), where your $5 entry fee gets you all-day use of racquetball courts, gym, weight room, sauna, and bowling alley.

Swimming In the sea if you dare (it is typically 40–50F in summer), or at the high-school pool three miles northwest of town (☎ 443-5717), though it is usually closed in July and August.

Taxes Nome imposes a four percent sales tax, plus a four percent bed tax (which we've included in our prices).

Around Nome

Though Nome is interesting itself, the real pleasure in visiting the Seward Peninsula is getting out on the three fascinating roads in the vicinity – three hundred miles in total – which is something you can't really do from any other Alaska bush community. Along the way you'll see stacks of mining castoffs, abandoned buildings from dozens of old mining claims, the rusting hulks of earth movers, unidentified ironmongery, and ditches dug across the hills to divert essential sluicing water to the diggings. It is even said that there are 44 dilapidated **gold dredges** visible from the road system, though it will take eagle eyes to spot them all. There is also plenty of **wildlife** viewing, with musk oxen often

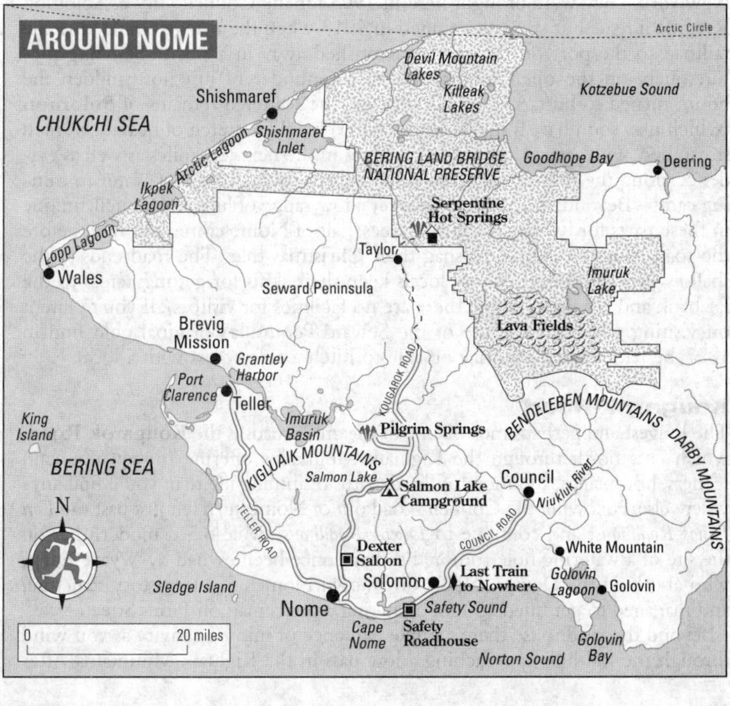

close to the road, a good chance of seeing some of the ten thousand semi-nomadic reindeer that roam the peninsula, bears, and rare birds blown over from Asia, including bristle-thighed curlew, bluethroat, and white and yellow wagtails.

Generally, the roads are open early to mid June depending on the thaw and close once the snows arrive around the end of September. Other than a couple of stores in Teller and one bar on the Council Road, there are no services anywhere outside Nome or any gas stations, so go prepared. Of course, there is no public **transport**, so either bring your own bicycle or rent a car from Nome (see "Listings," p.506).

To explore beyond the road system, you'll have to take to the air, either into the **Bering Land Bridge National Preserve**, or across the Bering Strait to the **Russian Far East** and the garrison town of Provideniya.

Council Road

At the turn of the twentieth century, there were small gold towns all around Nome, but most died away as quickly as they formed. **COUNCIL**, 72 miles northeast of Nome, is one of the few survivors, with a few dozen summer residents and just a handful of hardy year-rounders. It is reached along **Council Road** (usually snow-free June–Sept), which heads east from Nome along the coastline, which is littered with beach shacks where miners work the sands and fishers dry their catch on driftwood frames. The road continues past the expansive viewpoint of **Cape Nome** at Mile 13 and the prime **birding wetlands** of **Safety Sound** at Mile 20 to the nearby *Safety Roadhouse*, a characterful bar which acts as the last checkpoint on the Iditarod before Nome. At Mile 30 the road turns inland by the roadside "**Last Train to Nowhere**," at Mile 33, a rusting line of steam locomotives which originally pulled the elevated railway in New York. They were brought here in 1903 for the Council City & Solomon River Railroad, but were abandoned in 1913 when the bridge connecting the railroad to the port on the coast was washed away in a storm. Standing picturesquely on the open tundra, they're a reminder of just how sudden the boom turned to bust. A short distance on, the scattered remains of **Solomon** (which may soon have a small visitor center) herald a stretch of heavily worked streambed, with several abandoned dredges in the next few miles as well as evidence along the hillsides of where channels were dug to direct water to mining camps. Beyond, the road climbs over a low range of hills to Council, unique in these parts for its stand of spruce trees: half of Nome comes out here before the road closes in the fall to snag their Christmas trees. The road ends at the shallow Niukluk River, where locals keep their skiffs for getting across to the far bank and Council (where there are no facilities for visitors). If you're intent on visiting what was the site of the Seward Peninsula's original gold find in 1897, be patient and you may be able to hitch a ride across with a local.

Kougarok Road

The longest and perhaps most scenic of the area's roads is the **Kougarok Road**, which cuts north through the Kigluaik Mountains offering snowy mountain scenery, hot springs, and more of the detritus of mining life than you'll find anywhere else. Following the Council Road out of Nome, turn left just past the *Fort Davis Roadhouse* and continue to *Dexter Roadhouse*, Mile 8.5, a modern bar on the site of a watering hole rumored to have once been owned by **Wyatt Earp**, who also built the Dexter Saloon, downtown Nome's first two-story structure, and managed to get fined $50 for assaulting a policeman on Front Street.

Beyond the roadhouse there's ample evidence of mining activity as you wind through the foothills approaching a low pass in the Kigluaik Mountains. After

Mile 30 the scenery gets wilder as you near the picturesque Salmon Lake, where there's wonderful **free camping** at the BLM's beautiful, lakeside *Salmon Lake Campground*, Mile 40, with picnic tables, grills, an outhouse, and lake water which should be treated. As you pull out of the mountains, an unsigned side road at Mile 53.5 branches seven rough and gravelly miles left to the undeveloped **Pilgrim Hot Springs** (call Louie Green ⓣ443-5583 for permission to go there; it is almost always granted). At the end of the road, go through a gate, turn left, and follow the four-wheeler tracks for ten minutes or so to a simple wooden tank surrounded by wetlands and cottonwoods. Soak your cares away, but leave time to wander around the nearby locked clapboard Catholic church with its tiny steeple, the principal legacy of an orphanage which operated here from 1918 to 1941. Half a dozen ancillary buildings gently decay in its shadow.

Back on the Kougarok Road, you weave through fifteen miles of wetlands, occasionally climbing onto low hills crowned by craggy tors. Then, for the last fifteen miles, the tundra opens out giving long, long vistas and big-sky feeling. The road ends at the Kougarok bridge, from where it is possible to set out on foot twenty miles to **Taylor**, a private summer mining camp. Beyond Taylor an increasingly hard-to-follow trail leads a further twenty miles to Serpentine Hot Springs (see overleaf), altogether two to three days' walk from the road end.

Teller Road

The only substantial Native community accessible on the local road system is **TELLER**, a 150-strong Iñupiat reindeer-herding and subsistence village 73 miles northwest of Nome. It is picturesquely set, strung along a thin spit that separates Norton Sound from Grantley Harbor, but there really isn't a whole lot there. Unlike many Native communities, it is of fairly recent origin, founded as a trading center during the gold years around 1900. It was a barely viable community when, in 1926, bad weather forced Norwegian explorer **Roald Amundsen** to make an impromptu visit in his dirigible, *Norge*, after he completed the first transpolar flight, a seventy-hour 3500-mile journey from Spitzbergen.

The two-hour drive from Nome is a lovely one, out along the **Teller Road** (generally open early or mid May to mid-Oct), which runs past Nome's high school, where there is a sign marking the "Discovery Claim," close to Nome's original 1898 gold find in Anvil Creek. Beyond the marker you contour around the hills a couple of miles back from the coast, then head inland to open high country with spiky mountains. There is a fair chance of seeing **reindeer**, a species brought here to replace the native caribou which died out towards the end of the nineteenth century. As a way of trying to help the local Iñupiat regain some form of self-determination, the Reverend Sheldon Jackson (see p.130) imported a small herd from Russia and released them in 1892. After years of hunting them for meat, Native Alaskans were finally given formal ownership of all reindeer on the Peninsula in 1937, and since then have developed husbandry techniques to exploit the velvet for the Asian "medicinal" market. Of late, reindeer numbers have decreased as large numbers have run off with migrating caribou herds.

Around Mile 35 you drop down again to the coastal strip, and then pass an old wooden dredge (Mile 54) artfully decaying on the far bank of the adjacent river, before the final run into Teller. To get beyond Teller you'll have to engage the services of **Grantley Harbor Tours** (ⓣ1-800/478-3682, ⓦwww.grantleyharbor.com), which runs guided tours pretty much to order, along with a wildlife-viewing outing ($99) that also takes in a sample of Eskimo culture and

Trips to the Russian Far East

Even though Bering Air first broke through the "ice curtain" in 1988, and the nearest town is only an hour from Nome, tourist **visits to Russia** are still difficult. Officials, academics, and Natives with relatives on the other side make the trip frequently, but the nearest town of any size, the military port of **Provideniya**, remains a "closed" area. Throughout the 1990s it was gradually wound down, and few people now live there, but a Cold War mentality remains. Unless you have some special reason to visit, there are plenty of better ways to spend your time and money within Alaska, but if you are curious there are a couple of possibilities.

Should you still wish to go, contact Bering Air ($250 each way; ⓣ443-5620, ⓦwww.beringair.com). Note that you'll need to reserve several weeks in advance and will need to organize an invitation to visit the Chukotka region of Russia before applying for a visa ($235). Rules change frequently but Bering Air can put you in touch with the right people. They may also be able to arrange accommodation, usually in furnished apartments.

a trip to the spot where Amundsen put down. For something a good deal more ambitious, contact Iditarod veteran **Joe Garnie** (ⓣ642-2139), identifiable by the raucous kennel outside his house, who will teach you to run sled dogs while sharing the modern Iñupiat lifestyle of his home. Ideally, you'll want to devote ten days (at around $200 a day) so that you can learn the ropes for a few days in town before heading out to his cabin and sweatlodge sixty miles upriver, catching food for yourself and the dogs as you go. From mid-April to mid-May there's enough snow and 24hr light, but you'll need to fly into Teller as the road won't be open.

Watch where the locals are headed to locate the **store** (there are no signs), but don't expect any restaurants or accommodation.

Bering Land Bridge National Preserve

During the ice-bound Pleistocene era around 13,000 years ago, the sea level dropped so much that the 55 miles of sea between the Seward Peninsula and Russia was dry land and, it is thought, Asiatic peoples migrated into the unpeopled Americas. Evidence from Alaska's oldest known archeological site, the nine caves of Trail Creek (not open to the public), indicates that some of the first people to set foot on the North American continent strode across the low tundra that now forms the **Bering Land Bridge National Preserve** (ⓦwww.nps.gov/bela), seventy miles northeast of Nome.

There are no roads, no facilities of any kind, and hardly any people in this gently rolling and largely treeless landscape, so you'll need to come fully prepared. Access is by plane, though the lack of maintained airstrips limits your choices. The most popular destination is **Serpentine Hot Springs** (Iyat in Native parlance), a hundred miles north of Nome and forty miles beyond the end of the Kougarok Road. Here in the vast open country, water at 140–170°F wells up inside a bathhouse which is maintained by the Park Service along with the adjacent bunkhouse-style **cabin** (first-come, first-served; free), which sleeps at least fifteen and has a wood stove for heating and a propane stove for cooking; bring a sleeping bag and food. You can walk here from the end of the Kougarok Road (2–3 days each way) following an old ridgeline track also used by four-wheelers, or fly into the short, rough airstrip with Bering Air (see p.506) for around $350 for a planeload of four: or twice that if you also want them to pick you up. Remember that there are bears up here and no trees for food storage, so you'll need to bring bear-resistant food canisters.

If you want to join a very select group, you could try to bike in, though expect tough conditions and consult Keith Conger (see p.506) for advice and the latest conditions.

In winter, a moderately popular snowmachine destination is the otherworldly **lava fields** in the southern quarter of the park. There are no trails, so you can just make it up as you go along, though the staff at the visitor centers in Nome and Kotzebue will advise on likely itineraries.

Kotzebue and around

The town of **KOTZEBUE** perches on the outer edge of the slender Baldwin Peninsula some six hundred miles northwest of Anchorage. It is just 26 miles north of the Arctic Circle, but for that reason alone it has become a fairly popular destination for tourists lured by 24 hours of daylight (from mid-May to the end of July) and some 37 days around the solstice when the sun never goes down at all. The place was long known as Qikiqtagruk, but takes its current name from Russian navigator Otto von Kotzebue, who charted the area while searching for the Northwest Passage in 1816.

Kotzebue is second only to Barrow as the world's largest Eskimo community and is a predominantly Iñupiat town that exists on the cusp of mainstream Alaskan society. The comforts that people expect of town life are here, but there's also the tenor of a Native "village" that shares more in common with Barrow than it does with its (relatively) near neighbor Nome. Three-quarters of the three thousand residents are Iñupiat, and it is they who run the town, primarily through the Northwest Arctic Native Association (NANA), the regional corporation which represents the town and ten villages spread over much of northwest Alaska, half-owns the huge Red Dog zinc mine, ninety miles north of town, and manages a 6000-strong caribou herd. NANA, under the banner Tour Arctic, is also the public face of tourism here, operating package tours, the museum, and the main hotel. For this reason, **independent travelers** are poorly served: unless you are bound for the **wilderness rivers** to the northeast, or have friends here, you'll soon find yourself with little to do and facing the prospect of an expensive night in a hotel. Without a boat or a plane there is no way out of town, and even walking the streets you might find that people are not as interested in you as you may be in them. That said, NANA does a good job of presenting the local culture through the museum and "culture camp," and if you are prepared to take your time, contact with locals can be very rewarding.

Though the seascape is attractive, Kotzebue isn't a pretty town. Indeed, it gives the impression of being temporary: the streets are unpaved, telephone wires hang loosely, and the whole town can look like a graveyard for shipping containers with every second home having one as a storage shed. It can all seem very different, though, as you stroll along the beach in the golden light watching the **midnight sun** appear to roll along the tops of the hills across Kotzebue Sound.

Getting there and information

Like Nome, the only way to get to Kotzebue is to fly, and most people arrive on **packages** that are fairly inflexible but keep costs manageable. Reservations are handled by Alaska Airlines Vacations (Ⓣ1-800/468-2248) and Northern Alaska Tour Company (see box, p.468), which both run their tours jointly with NANA (Ⓣ1-800/523 7405, Ⓦwww.tour-arctic.com). The cheapest trip is the

Anchorage-based one-day tour ($415), which includes a village bus tour, a brief walk on the tundra, a visit to the museum and the culture camp. A choice of two-day trips ($515 based on double occupancy) combines Kotzebue with Nome, one spending the night at the *Nullagvik Hotel*, the other overnighting in Nome; and there's a three-dayer ($565) with nights in both towns.

Alaska Airlines **flights** from Anchorage to Kotzebue cost around $410 round-trip, if bought 21 days in advance, so it is worth considering an Anchorage–Kotzebue–Nome–Anchorage loop, which will cost around $535. Committed Arctic tourists could also get here directly from Barrow with Cape Smythe Air (ⓣ442-3020 or 1-800/478-3020; for details see box on p.468).

An alternative is to organize your travels through Anchorage-based Arctic Circle Educational Adventures (ⓣ276-0976, ⓦwww.fishcamp.org), which from mid-June to August runs *LaVonne's Fish Camp* (ⓣ442-6013) on the coast about five miles from Kotzebue. It is a peaceful spot, frequently visited by locals out hunting or gathering, and is great for birding or just lazing around in the 24hr light. Accommodation is in cozy cabins, family-style meals are served, and rates (typically $250–350 a day) depend on what you do since all trips are customized.

You'll probably walk wherever you want to go, but you can always call Polar Cab ⓣ442-2233.

The only source of tourist assistance in town is the **Western Arctic National Parklands Visitor Center**, 154a 2nd Ave (June–Aug daily 8am–6pm; Sept–May occasionally 3–5pm; ⓣ442-3760, ⓦwww.nps.gov/nwak), which manages Cape Krusenstern National Monument, Kobuk Valley National Park, and Noatak National Preserve, but will help with local queries. Free **Internet access** can be had at the Chukchi **library** on 3rd Avenue (Mon–Fri noon–8pm, Sat noon–6pm); a Wells Fargo **bank** with ATM resides at the corner of 2nd Avenue and Lagoon Street; and the **post office** is near the corner of Shore Avenue and Mission Street.

The Town

Visitors not taking the comprehensive local bus tour that comes as part of the Tour Arctic packages are left with little to do but wander the streets aiming for Shore Avenue (also known as Front St), where much of the town's activity takes place, and where, during the ice-free months of mid-June to mid-September, you'll see fuel oil and construction materials being unloaded from supply barges. Everything else (including cars) comes in by plane.

The showcase for the region's Iñupiat way of life, and a little of its history, is the **Museum of the Arctic**, corner of 2nd and 3rd avenues (mid-May to mid-Sept daily 10am–10pm), which does have some static displays – notably its room full of stuffed specimens of just about every Arctic animal – but focuses on its hour-long culture **demonstrations** (at 3pm & 6pm). These include a slide show, traditional dancing, storytelling, and a **blanket toss**, in which several people gather round a walrus-hide blanket and use it to toss one of their number into the air repeatedly, gaining height each time, somthing supposedly once practiced as an aid to spotting a potential meal. The museum and demonstration are run by NANA, which charges $25, but offers a joint $35 ticket that includes a visit to the adjacent **culture camp** (by itself $20). The aim of this forty-minute session is to show outdoor summer life as it is still practiced by the local Iñupiat. Driftwood racks are set up for drying salmon, smoky fires are started to keep the bugs off, ropes are made from walrus skin, and sewing and tanning procedures are demonstrated using alder bark for dye and sealskins to make waterproof pants.

Head along 3rd Avenue to the junction of Mission Street where a block is devoted to the town **cemetery**, complete with a few **spirit houses**. The large building nearby is the **Maniilaq Health Center**, an impressive new hospital with a lobby (Mon–Fri 9am–5pm) that is worth some attention for its excellent display of Native craftwork: a beautiful seal-gut parka, a soapstone and ivory Madonna, an ulu knife with a handle of mastodon ivory, an exquisite box made of Dall sheep horn and baleen, and much more.

Accommodation, eating, and drinking

Accommodation is scant, with most packages using the *Nullagvik Hotel*, 308 Shore Ave (ⓣ442-3331, ⓦwww.nullagvik.com; ⑦), which is comfortable enough though not great value for money. Almost next door you'll find the marginally cheaper but inferior *Bayside Inn*, Shore Avenue (ⓣ442-3600; ⑥), but you're better off at the friendly *Lagoon B&B*, 227 Lagoon St (ⓣ442-3723, ⓔmar8lwsw@otz.net; ④). There is no campground and free **camping** isn't particularly encouraged, nor is it a very appealing option, with the best spot being a narrow strip above the steeply shelving beach just south of the airport. If it is windy, tethering your tent can be a problem.

Eating options are as limited as accommodation and equally expensive. The *Nullagvik Hotel* has an **espresso bar** in its craft shop and the *Niggivik Restaurant* (literally "a place to eat"; summer only), has large picture windows overlook-

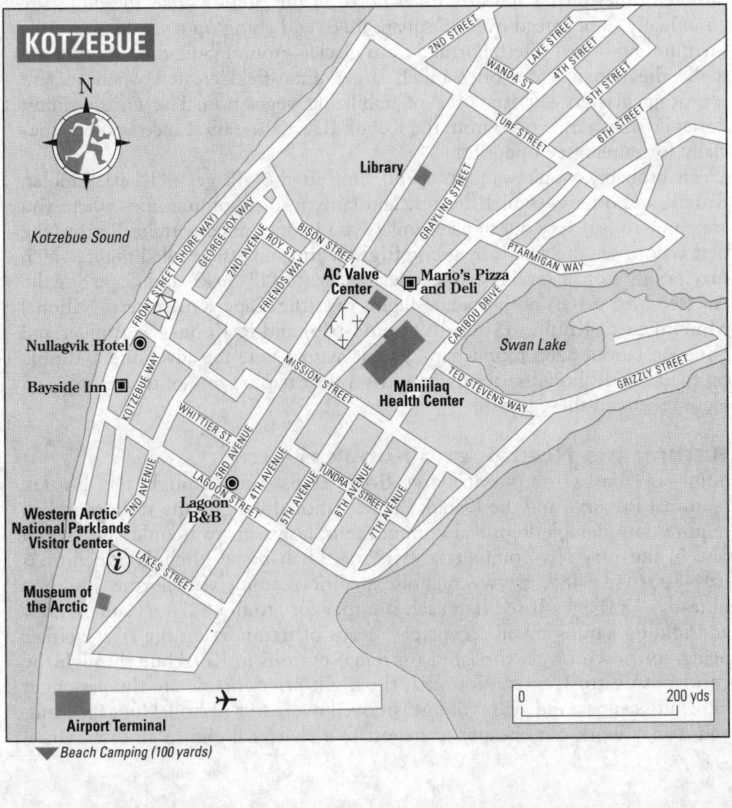

ing the sea and serves good meals from a standard Alaskan menu. The *Bayside* also has a restaurant, and you can eat in or take away at the spartan *Mario's Pizza & Deli*, 606 Bison St (ⓣ442-2666), which also does burgers and Japanese and Chinese dishes. **Groceries** are available from the AC Value Center. It is also worth remembering that Kotzebue has a six percent **sales tax**, plus another six percent hotel tax, though these have both been included within our accommodation price codes. Kotzebue is a damp community with no alcohol sales, though you can bring a bottle or two with you.

Around Kotzebue

Kotzebue may be a fairly limited destination in itself, but it does offer relatively easy access to some of the finest wilderness in the Alaskan Arctic, all encompassed by the Western Arctic National Parklands. Set aside $200 to see something of the **seabird oasis** of the Selawik National Wildlife Refuge, the Noatak National Preserve with its **superb rafting rivers**, and the massive sand dunes stranded miles from the sea in the Kobuk Valley National Park. Other worthy options include flying from Kotzebue to the Bering Land Bridge National Preserve (see p.510) and, for committed paddlers, **sea kayaking** along the bird- and sea-mammal-rich barrier islands of **Cape Krusenstern National Monument**.

The single most alluring sight around these parts is the **Great Kobuk Sand Dunes** in the southern reaches of the **Kobuk Valley National Park** – Alaska's smallest and one of the country's least-known national parks. Located over a hundred miles inland and fifty miles north of the Arctic Circle, the dunes are an unlikely sight spread over 25 square miles and rising up to 250ft above the surrounding boreal forest. Formed from glacier-ground sand, they are thought to be the remains of a once much larger dune-field created when ancient retreating glaciers left land free of stabilizing vegetation. The northernmost dunes lie only a mile or so from the Kobuk River, the easiest access point, especially for rafters (see opposite).

You probably won't want to spend time in the villages – Kiana, Ambler, Kobuk, and others – which are tiny and fairly insular communities where you are going to feel very out of place unless you know someone there. Perhaps the best way to see the area is by going **flightseeing** on a scheduled flight, which may briefly stop at several villages. Bering Air (ⓣ442-3943) and Cape Smythe Air (see box, p.468) both operate flights over the Cape Krusenstern National Monument to Kivalina ($140–160 round-trip) and to Kobuk via Ambler and Shugnak (about $280 round-trip). People with a taste for adventure and time on their hands should seriously consider a float trip on one of the remote and scenic rivers in these parts.

Rafting the Noatak and Kobuk rivers

Some of Alaska's most satisfying **float trips** run through the Noatak National Preserve and the Kobuk Valley National Park. None is short and all require considerable logistical commitment; however, you could always join one of the very few commercial trips: try Utah-based Nichols Expeditions (ⓣ1-800/648-8488, ⓦwww.nicholsexpeditions.com), which runs just one nine-day Fairbanks-based trip each summer for around $2700. Canoes, rafts, and folding kayaks are all acceptable means of transport on the rivers: either bring your own or get the latest on rental options in Kotzebue through the Parklands Visitor Center. Note that the flight prices below are the passenger fare; rafts, canoes, and gear will put you well over your personal luggage limit, and it may work out cheaper to negotiate a charter flight. In all cases, you'll need to be entirely self-sufficient on the river. There are no facilities except in the villages and you are unlikely to see many people, except during the fall hunting season when hunters drive noisy boats upstream to access prime caribou areas.

Access to the dunes is from the lower section of the **Kobuk River** (navigable June to late Sept; Class I) from Ambler to Kiana, a run of 85 miles usually taking 5–6 days. Flights into Ambler and out of Kiana with Bering Air cost a total of $250. To extend the trip by three or four days, start by flying into Kobuk, 45 miles further upstream. The truly committed can run the whole 260 navigable miles from Walker Lake in the Gates of the Arctic National Park (and accessed from Bettles) down to Kiana in fifteen to twenty days, although there are a few short upper sections where you'll need to portage or line your boats. The **Salmon River**, a tributary of the Kobuk with its confluence downstream of the dunes, is another popular float.

Like the Kobuk, there are several ways to approach the **Noatak River** (navigable June–Sept; Class I–II) with plenty of landing spots for float planes, allowing you to do as much or as little as you please. Again, Bettles is a good starting point for flying into the headwaters, from where you could take sixteen to eighteen days to float down to Noatak, and another couple of days to the mouth, which is just fifteen miles across Kotzebue Sound from Kotzebue. Kayaks and canoes (but not rafts, which are too susceptible to high winds) could then pick a calm morning and paddle across to Kotzebue. For more details on these and other rivers, consult Karen Jettmar's *The Alaska River Guide* (see "Books," p.549).

Barrow

Many people visit **BARROW**, five hundred miles north of Fairbanks, simply because it is the northernmost settlement on the North American continent, and just eleven miles from Point Barrow, the very tip of the United States. Though 330 miles north of the Arctic Circle, there are still eight hundred miles of ocean to the North Pole and for ten months of the year it is ice all the way. This far north the sun doesn't rise for two months in the middle of winter, but after the middle of May the sun doesn't set until the end of July – midnight sun for 82 days – and the ice gradually breaks up and melts away just over the horizon.

But the appeal isn't just geographic. This is the largest Eskimo community in Alaska with around 65 percent of the 4600 residents claiming Iñupiat heritage – you'll hear Iñupiaq spoken as much as English. It is also the administrative capital of **North Slope Borough**, a vast region of Arctic Alaska with another 4500 people distributed through eight widely scattered villages. The borough encompasses the North Slope oil fields, and the royalties from oil sales make this the richest Native region. Yet Barrow can look depressingly utilitarian, little more than a shantytown. They've got warm homes, well-stocked supermarkets, and a frequent jet service to Fairbanks and Anchorage, but no amount of money can combat the isolation, fierce weather, permafrost, and the ever-present threat of polar bears on the prowl.

Barrow is only slowly gearing itself towards tourism, and much of the people's daily life that makes the town special will be inaccessible to the casual visitor. A partial solution is to join one of the hotel-and-culture package **tours**, though this is still a somewhat mainstream experience. Fly here independently,

Whaling in the Arctic

Despite Barrow's wealth and modernity, whaling fundamentally defines the community. Whatever you may think about whaling elsewhere, it is hard to begrudge a people going about their life much as they have for thousands of years. During the spring or fall whale hunt, it is easy to get swept along by the buzz that goes around town when word comes in from the ice of a successful kill. There are no factory whaling ships here, just small skin boats and men with hand-held harpoons twenty or thirty miles out across the ice. They try to spear a thirty-foot bowhead as it passes – northbound in spring, southbound in the fall – along one of the narrow breaks in the sea ice known as "leads." Successful kills are hauled onto the ice by up to fifty people applying themselves to one end of a pulley system. Each village gets an annual quota based on the known population – Barrow is usually allotted about a dozen – but each strike is counted whether the whale is killed or not, so a poor season can be over pretty quickly.

and your moves are limited and fairly expensive, although there is an excellent museum, tours to Point Barrow with the hope of seeing polar bears, and plenty of good **birding** on the surrounding tundra.

The **timing** of your visit is all-important. In May, when the rest of the state is gearing up for summer, Barrow is still in the grip of winter: the sea ice doesn't usually break up and melt away until mid-July. May and early June is the spring whaling season, and it is white to the northern horizon. Mid to late June heralds the end of whaling and **Nalukataq**, a celebration of a successful hunt including a genuine blanket toss. Through May, June, and July, birders flock to Barrow for easy spotting on the treeless tundra, where birds nest on tufted mounds: eiders, snowy owls, jaegers, swans, and arctic terns are some of the feathery attractions. Winter begins to set in by the end of September, ice starts to form at the shore and spreads out to create an ice pack about 10ft thick. For most people winter is off-limits, though the fall whale hunt makes October a good time to visit if you want to see polar bears.

Arrival, information, and getting around

Most visitors arrive in Barrow on **package tours** jointly run by Tundra Tours, Northern Alaska Tour Company (see box, p.516) and Alaska Airlines Vacations (mid-May to mid-Sept daily; Ⓣ1-800/468-2248, Ⓦwww.alaskaair.com). These are hardly cheap but almost always work out to be the lowest-cost option, and include a town tour plus a "culture program" at the museum with storytelling, dances, and a blanket toss. The cheapest is the Day Tour ($404), though for the full midnight sun experience you'll want the Overnight Tour ($455), which gives you two full days in town and a night at the *Top of the World Hotel*. These are all from Fairbanks, but you can add one or more Anchorage legs for $85 each, a savings if you need to get back to Anchorage. There are also Fairbanks-based winter variations at similar prices with a tour to Point Barrow.

For more flexibility, take one of several **flights** a day with Alaska Airlines, which cost upwards of $410 round-trip from Fairbanks, and at least $470 from Anchorage.

Getting around is easy. The airport borders the south side of town, and you can walk anywhere you need to go in about ten or fifteen minutes. If you've got heavy bags, then pick up one of the Yellow Line **buses** (7am–10pm; $1 exact fare), which run every twenty minutes around the center from the transfer station on Ahkovak Street, a hundred yards to the left when you step out of the airport terminal. There's also the Red Line, which runs to **Browerville**, Barrow's eastern suburb about a mile away across Isatkoak Lagoon (also known as Middle Lagoon), and the Blue Line, which runs four miles out towards Point Barrow ($2). Alternatively, engage the services of one of the half-dozen **taxi** companies, which all charge around $5 anywhere within Barrow and Browerville: Barrow Taxi (Ⓣ852-2222) is as good as any. There are very few roads around here, but **rental cars** are available from UIC Construction Vehicle Rental (Ⓣ852-2700), just opposite the bus transfer station on Ahkovak Street, for around $85 a day.

There's free **Internet access** (though email is discouraged) at the Tuzzy Consortium Library (Mon–Thurs noon–9pm, Fri & Sat noon–5pm), right by the Iñupiat Heritage Center at the corner of Ahkovak Street and C Avenue. **Banking** needs are satisfied by Wells Fargo, 1780 Kiogak St (Mon–Thurs 10am–5pm, Fri 10am–6pm), and while there is an ATM, it can only be used during banking hours.

Accommodation

The town's biggest **hotel**, and the one where all the package tours stay is the *Top of the World*, 1200 Agvik St (Ⓣ852-3900, Ⓦwww.topoftheworldhotel.com; ❼), which has newish deluxe and noticeably ageing standard rooms (at opposite ends of the price code) with all the expected amenities. Cheaper and very pleasant rooms can be found at the *Barrow Airport Inn*, 1815 Momegana St (Ⓣ852-2525; ❹), which mainly caters to people up here on business and has some

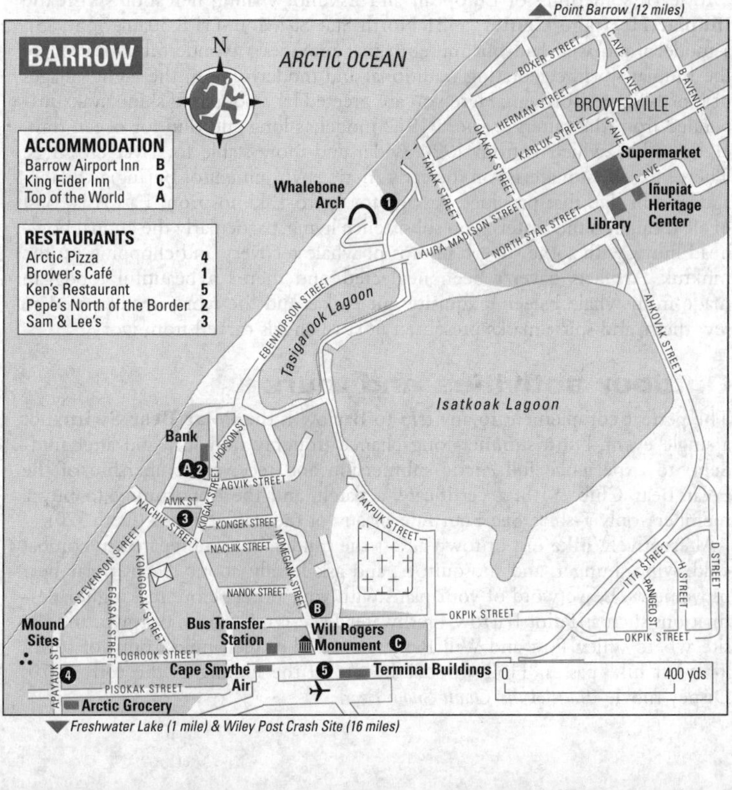

rooms with kitchenettes as well as cable TV and continental breakfast with fresh-baked bread. Barrow's newest hotel, the *King Eider Inn*, by the airport at 1752 Ahkovak St (Ⓣ852-4700, Ⓦwww.kingeider.net; ❼), has the nicest rooms in town (some with kitchenettes), a guest sauna, and free coffee and muffins.

There is no budget accommodation in Barrow and beach **camping** is discouraged, not least because, for much of the year, there are polar bears about. They seldom come into town, and when the sea ice has melted there are unlikely to be any around, but you can never be sure.

The Town

Barrow's airport goes by the grandiose title of the **Wiley Post/Will Rogers Memorial Airport**, in honor of pioneer aviator Wiley Post and entertainer, homespun philosopher, and all-round spokesman for rural America Will Rogers, who died in 1935 when their plane went down sixteen miles south of Barrow while they were searching for a new air route to Siberia. A concrete **monument** stands at the corner of Ahkovak and Momegana streets, just across from the terminal building.

Continue west along Ahkovak Street towards the sea, and overlooking the beach you'll find a series of low **mounds** that are nothing much to look at but represent an important archeological site with the remains of sod houses. Follow the beach to the northeast through what constitutes the center of town, and you'll eventually come to Barrow's original **whaling station**, now a restaurant, and beside it a **whalebone arch** that seems to feature on most postcards of Barrow.

To learn something of European and Eskimo whaling hereabouts visit the **Iñupiat Heritage Center**, 5421 North Star St (Mon–Fri 8.30am–5pm; $5), a modern and well-laid-out museum that provides a wonderful evocation of the Iñupiat spirit, celebrating traditional and modern life in the eight villages of North Slope Borough. Here you are greeted by a couple of skin kayaks suspended from the rafters – one, a 1912 model, is long and thin for ocean travel, the other, which is from 1920, wider and more stable for river crossings. There's excellent material on the early Arctic environment of Beringia, the ice-age land bridge that provided passage for proto-Eskimos from East Asia. Best of all, though, is the material on subsistence living, particularly the annual bowhead hunts with some superb photos of whale recovery and chopping up the muktuk. Artifacts haven't been neglected, and there's a beautiful toboggan made from whale baleen, exquisite gut parkas and the ivory needles used to sew them, and spirit masks presented next to angels carved from ivory.

Outdoor activities and tours

The perfect complement to any trip to Barrow is the **Polar Bear Swim**, not a single event, but a summer-long chance (roughly mid-July and after mid-Sept) to experience full Arctic submersion and receive membership of the Polar Bear Club ($10), a certificate, a patch, and the opportunity to buy a members-only T-shirt. See Fran Tate or any of the staff at *Pepe's* (see p.520).

Alternatively, **hike** out of town across the tundra, but go prepared to combat cold, wind, hunger, and mosquitoes, and ask locally about recent polar bear movements. Leave word of your plans with your hotel before making for destinations such as Point Barrow, Freshwater Lake, a mile south of town, and the site where Wiley Post and Will Rogers crashed sixteen miles south of town. This last hike passes "Hollywood," the site of the filming of the early 1970s Disney movie *Track of the Giant Snow Bear*.

The prime destination out of town is **Point Barrow**, twelve miles to the northeast and beyond the end of the road. To get there you really need to go on foot or on a tour. For some the attraction is just being at the **northernmost point in the US**, but when the sea ice is in, especially after a successful whale hunt when the waste is dumped there, this becomes prime **polar bear** territory. This wouldn't be a good time to walk, but John Tidwell of Alaskan Arctic Adventures (☎852-3800) leads customized tours out here, and elsewhere, in a caterpillar-tracked van or off-road vehicle, with the emphasis on viewing wildlife, such as arctic foxes, whales, seals, walruses, and loads of birds. The two-hour tour (Mon–Sat only) costs $130 for two people; get more together and costs go down.

From November to May, John's son, John, runs Arctic Mushing Tours ($85 for one, $150 for two; ☎852-6874), where you get a full two hours learning to run a **dog sled** and can even head off across the tundra viewing wildlife.

Eating and not drinking

Those on a tight budget should head for the AC Value Center, corner of Ahkovak Street and C Avenue in Browerville (daily 9am–10pm), the retail heart of Barrow, with everything from snowmachines, furniture, and clothing down to expensive **groceries** and even fresh flowers flown in daily from Anchorage. There's a **food court**, too, with a deli, pizzas, Mexican, subs, and cinnamon rolls. Groceries are also available more centrally from Arctic Grocery, corner of Pisokak and Apayauk streets in Barrow.

Dry Alaska

Most Native authorities recognize that excessive alcohol consumption is a major problem among their people, not just for its antisocial effects but as a serious health risk. Some estimate that approaching fifty percent of adult Natives have some form of alcohol problem, a state of affairs undoubtedly exacerbated by the erosion of traditional values.

After the American purchase in 1867, the sale of alcohol to Natives – who already had a reputation for drunkenness – was banned, a selective prohibition which continued until 1953, when federal laws overruled such discrimination. Drunkenness again became rampant, and in 1980 village councils were given the power to restrict sales within their own communities in an effort to contain the (self-)destructive behavior. Many communities decided that the route to redemption was through outlawing alcohol in the village altogether, and they became **dry**. Others chose to manage sales through stores owned or controlled in some way by the community, but remained **wet**. Some felt that problems could be dealt with more openly if they were **damp**, with drink sales proscribed, but importation of supplies allowed. Barrow and other villages chose to be **soggy**, periodically voting on their status. Whatever the moral benefits, dry towns appear to have lower instances of assault, homicide, and suicide.

Of course, any form of prohibition is of only minimal use. Alcohol does get in (or is made) and obtaining supplies can become more of an obsession than drinking the stuff ever was. Bootleggers can make huge profits on bottles of whisky, which can change hands for ten times the retail price. There is also an effect on "wet" airline-hub communities, particularly Fairbanks, which sell huge quantities of alcohol to those on a binge during infrequent town visits. The sight of the terminally drunk around the downtown bar quarter is a sad one, and it can only be hoped that, as Native communities regain their self-respect and revive their culture, the drive for binge drinking will subside and the necessity of managing alcohol availability will cease to exist.

There's a decent selection of **restaurants**, all as pricey as you'd expect for such a remote location and all serving burgers, sandwiches, and breakfasts as well as their specialty. *Pepe's North of the Border*, 1204 Agvik St (Ⓣ852-8200), serves genuine Mexican dishes under a ceiling strung with piñatas, with tacos starting from $4, a burrito plate for $18, Ortega burgers for $11, and steaks from $25 to $30. The best pizza is at *Arctic Pizza*, 125 Apayauk St (Ⓣ852-4222), which also has a huge range of salads, Mexican dishes, pasta dishes, even jambalaya, all served in an upstairs dining room with good sea views. *Sam & Lee's*, 1052 Kiogak St (Ⓣ852-5555), is good for Chinese, as is *Ken's Restaurant* on Ahkovak St (Ⓣ852-8888), which also has the best-value breakfasts in town ($8–12). If you find yourself over in Browerville, pop into the original whaling station, which now operates as *Brower's Café*, on Stevenson Street (Ⓣ852-5800), with views past the arched whale jawbones and out to sea as you dine or sip an espresso.

Barrow is currently a damp community, so there are **no alcohol** sales, but you can bring in a liter of spirits, a gallon of beer, or two liters of wine without a permit.

Travel details

As the only large town covered by this chapter, Fairbanks is understandably the hub of all transportation networks. Its only train line has daily service in summer (roughly mid-May to mid-Sept) running south to Denali National Park and Anchorage. Buses (again only mid-May to mid-Sept) run parallel to the train line to Denali and Anchorage and also run east towards the Canadian border and southeast to Valdez. Planes fan out to just about every tiny bush community imaginable, the most important of which we've listed below.

Trains

Fairbanks to: Anchorage (1 daily; 12hr); Denali Park (1 daily; 3hr 45min); Talkeetna (1 daily; 8hr 30min).

Buses

Fairbanks to: Anchorage (1 daily; 9–10hr); Chicken (3 weekly; 7hr 30min); Dawson City, Yukon (3 weekly; 12hr); Delta Junction (3 weekly; 2hr 45min); Denali (1 daily; 3hr 30min); Glennallen (on demand; 4hr 30min); Nenana (1 daily; 2hr); North Pole (8 daily, not Sun; 40min); Talkeetna Junction (1 daily; 7hr); Tok (3 weekly; 5hr); Valdez (on demand; 7–8hr).

Flights

Barrow to: Anchorage (2 daily; 3hr); Fairbanks (2 daily; 1hr 20min).
Bettles to: Fairbanks (2–3 daily; 1hr 20min).
Fairbanks to: Anaktuvuk Pass (1–4 daily; 1hr 30min); Anchorage (10–12 daily; 1hr); Arctic Village (1–3 daily; 1hr 30min); Barrow (2 daily; 1hr 20min); Bettles (2–3 daily; 1hr 20min); Juneau (2 daily; 3hr–3hr 30min); Prudhoe Bay/Deadhorse (1 daily; 1hr); Seattle (6–9 daily; 3hr 40min–6hr).
Kotzebue to: Anchorage (3 daily; 1hr 30min); Nome (2 daily; 45min).
Nome to: Anchorage (3 daily; 1hr 30min–3hr).
Prudhoe Bay/Deadhorse to: Anchorage (1 daily; 1hr 40min); Barrow (2 daily; 1hr 30min); Fairbanks (1 daily; 1hr).

Contexts

Contexts

History

Alaska's recorded history is both brief and frenetic, a tale of repeated exploitation to the point of exhaustion followed by stagnation until the next big boom. There is a parallel Alaska, however, populated by four main groups of Native people with a much longer oral history.

The first people

Alaska has been inhabited longer than anywhere else in the Americas. The recent discovery of skeletons exhibiting Caucasoid features points to early colonization of the "New World" from Europe, perhaps over a frozen North Atlantic. This conjecture is highly controversial, and there is greater agreement that Asiatic people arrived sometime after 15,000 years ago. One commentator on early Native American migrations describes the body of archeological evidence as "a confusing morass of conflicting data and opinions," but it is known that during the most recent ice age, from 25,000 to 12,000 BC, the sea level dropped enough to occasionally reveal the Arctic continent of **Beringia**, under what is now the northern half of the Bering Sea and the southern limit of the Chukchi Sea. This "**land bridge**" was, in fact, a flat, dry, intensely cold, windy, and generally inhospitable steppe-tundra several hundred miles wide. It existed for a geological blink of the eye, but long enough for many generations of proto-Aleut and Eskimos to make it their home as they followed herds of large herbivores such as bison and mammoths eastward. The romantic image of noble hunters crossing the land bridge and following deer through a sylvan corridor overhung with vast glaciers is almost certainly just that. The oldest confirmed archeological sites discovered so far – at Healy Lake near Fairbanks and the Mesa site on the North Slope – date back only around 11,000 years, so it seems that eastern Beringia (modern-day Alaska) probably wasn't populated until the land began to flood at the end of the last ice age, forcing the people to higher levels.

For millennia, that is where they stayed, their passage south to more temperate lands blocked by the great North American ice sheets. Some contend that there was just one major migration from which all Native Americans are descended, but linguistic and cultural evidence points to at least two separate and distinct groups arriving a significant period apart. From the earliest migration developed the forest-hunting culture that spreads throughout the Americas and gave us the Na-Dene language group which includes the **Tlingit** of the Alaskan Southeast, the **Athabascans** of the Alaskan Interior, and their close kin the Navajo and Apache of the American Southwest. A later migration – but still before the flooding of the land bridge – brought the Aleut-Eskimo groups, genetically the most Asiatic of all Native Americans, who pursued a culture based on sea mammals across the Arctic to Greenland. From this second migration evolved the **Aleut** and Alaska's two main Eskimo groups, the **Yup'ik** and **Iñupiat**. These groups occupied geographically and climatically distinct regions, forcing them to develop their own ways of shaping the land to their needs.

European exploration and occupation: 1640 to 1867

For the best part of 12,000 years, Native Alaskans forged their own destiny without interference from outside, though the Yearbooks of the Sung dynasty record that in 458 AD five Buddhist monks led by **Hwui Shan** sailed up the coast of the Kamchatka Peninsula, then east through the Aleutian Islands to mainland Alaska.

Significant impact on the affairs of Native Alaskans didn't come until late in the European "Age of Discovery," the high latitudes and short summers deterring all but the hardiest of explorers. Spaniard **Bartholeme de Fonte** made the first claim of discovery, having battled his way up from Spanish Mexico into the waters of the Inside Passage in 1640. He reported nothing of interest and almost a century passed before, in 1725, Russian Czar Peter the Great sent a party led by Danish explorer **Vitus Bering** to search for whatever lay to the east. After traveling for almost three years, he confirmed the suspicion that Siberia and the Americas were separate, and gave his name to the sea that divides the two landmasses, but fog prevented him spotting North America. It wasn't until his third journey, in 1741, that he finally set foot on the Alaskan mainland near what is now Cordova. Bering died of scurvy soon after, but his lieutenant, Alexis Chirikof, continued, making it as far as Sitka before returning to Russia with news of huge quantities of **sea otters**, their pelts then highly prized for fur hats. Over the next sixty years the Aleutian Islands were alive with Russian *promyshleniki* (traders and hunters) who found that the Aleut were far more efficient at killing otters than they were. They effectively enslaved the Aleut, forcing them to slaughter the otters to the brink of extinction. A revolt in 1743 was put down, and the Aleut resigned themselves to economic domination by the *promyshleniki* and cultural suffocation at the hands of the Russian Orthodox missionaries. Over the years the Aleut adopted the faith wholeheartedly and the Aleutian Chain remains an Orthodox stronghold, but they paid with their culture, their stories, and their way of life. It is only in the past few decades that the Aleut have begun to revive their traditions.

Soon the British, Spanish, and Americans were all after this sea-otter bounty, the Spanish (a waning but still major sea power) sending expeditions up the coast from their Mexican base at San Blas. But apart from adding a few Spanish names to the sea charts around Prince of Wales Island and carting off a few boatloads of furs, they failed to consolidate their claim to hegemony over the entire west coast of the Americas.

While the carnage continued, further exploration was driven by the search for the **Northwest Passage**, a long-sought trade route from the North Pacific into the North Atlantic. In 1778 **James Cook** sailed north from Vancouver Island, charting and naming features all the way to Turnagain Arm in Cook Inlet, near present-day Anchorage. He then continued west along the Aleutian Chain and up the coast to Icy Cape in the Arctic Ocean, 250 miles north of the Arctic Circle, where the pack ice drove him back. Cook's lieutenant, George Vancouver, returned in the 1790s and claimed the coast for Britain. With meticulous precision, he mapped the Inside Passage, leaving behind charts that were still in use at the turn of the twentieth century.

Despite Bering's earlier forays into Alaskan waters, it wasn't until 1784 that **Grigorii Shelikov** established the first non-Native settlement in Alaska at Three Saints Bay on Kodiak Island, and eight years later Catherine II granted him a monopoly on furs in Alaska as head of the **Russian-American Company**. In stepped the company's manager, **Alexander Baranov**, the self-styled "Lord of Alaska," to oversee the expansion of Russian interests. He moved the original Russian settlement up the coast to Kodiak in 1790, and within a decade his political guile and uncompromising business acumen extended Russian influence throughout southern Alaska, even as far as Fort Ross in northern California. As seal and otter populations plummeted he moved his operations to Southeast Alaska, establishing a fort in 1799. Three years later aggrieved Tlingits armed by the British and Americans destroyed the fort, but he returned in 1804, backed by a Russian navy warship, and re-established the Russian presence on the site, naming it New Archangel, later **Sitka**. Through savvy trading and pragmatic treaties with the Spanish, British, and Americans, they were able to develop a considerable mini-empire and fashioned Sitka as "an American Paris."

Russian influence spread quickly, even to areas where no Russians were seen. **Tlingit** traders adapted their existing trade patterns to obtain pelts from communities far from any foreign outpost; the *promyshleniki* then stayed in Alaska just long enough to load up the pelts and refresh their supplies. The more entrepreneurial Tlingit families turned good profits and raised the stakes at traditional **potlatches** (see p.84), holding them more frequently and giving away goods with impunity.

From the 1820s to the 1850s the sea otter and fur trade declined dramatically, and Russian energies were diverted to their troubles at home. This was still a largely unexplored land, only given some shape on world maps after an 1824 treaty between Russia, Britain, and the United States defined the boundaries of Alaska more or less along the current international frontier. It had become such a drain on resources that the Russian navy had to take control of the declining Russian-American Company. Mining engineer PP Doroshin subsequently uncovered a few flakes of gold in the Kenai River Valley, but this wasn't enough to revive interest, especially since Russia was now dogged by poor relations with Britain in the aftermath of the Crimean War of the 1850s. Meanwhile, expansionary pressure from Britain, through their Canadian territories, and from the United States, through the newly opened Pacific Northwest, made it increasingly obvious that Russia was liable to lose its Alaskan territory. They started looking around for a buyer.

Seward's Folly: American Alaska from 1867 to 1896

Russia had first tried to interest the United States in Alaska as early as 1859, but Congress' reluctance and the intervention of the American Civil War left the matter unresolved. Meanwhile, Russia's hold on its territory was being eroded by its own inability to finance armed forces so far from home and by the British Hudson's Bay Company, which had established trading posts in the Alaskan Interior. The Americans saw an opportunity, and on March 30, 1867, Andrew Johnson's secretary of state, **William Seward**, signed the **Treaty of Purchase** in Washington DC. On October 18, at a ceremony in the Russian Alaskan capital of Sitka, the Russian government formally signed over Alaska for a sum of $7.2 million, a paltry 2¢ an acre. Of course, the Russians didn't actually "own" the Alaska they were selling: no treaties had been entered into with the Natives, and none would be until ANCSA in 1971.

The Russian withdrawal was complete. After 120 years of contact, they left Alaska virtually unchanged except for a decimated sea-mammal population, a smattering of triple-bar crosses, a few picturesque Russian Orthodox churches, and the Aleut race almost wholly converted to the faith. The purchase price was undoubtedly low, but many Americans felt it was a waste of money and dubbed America's new land "**Seward's Folly**" or "Seward's Icebox." After all, the territory was largely uncharted, fur seals were all but wiped out, there was only the vaguest hint of the territory's gold wealth, and oil would have been considered of little value even if its presence had been known. The federal government now owned one of its territories outright, a unique state of affairs that has informed much of what has happened since. Alaskans might like to think they are masters of their own domain, but every significant stage of Alaskan development has been done with the approval of the federal government.

That is not to say that the Feds had immediate control over Alaska. Initially, there was very little to control: the Natives managed their own affairs, and no one else had much reason to go there. The United States took almost no notice of its new possession, keeping a loose rein and allowing the frontier ethic to prevail. Before they left, the Russians had managed to stabilize the fur-seal population on the Pribilof Islands in the Bering Sea, but in 1870 the American Commercial Company was given the monopoly in the region and resumed the slaughter. The company soon controlled much of Alaska's meager trade and still operates in bush Alaska today.

Meanwhile, naturalist **John Muir** visited the Southeast in 1879 and 1880 fired with enthusiasm for Alaska's glaciers, whose role in shaping the mountain landscape had only recently been unraveled. His *Travels in Alaska* catalogs his mainly fair dealings with the Natives, but he was less complimentary about the role of the American missionaries he often traveled with. By 1885 one of these missionaries, **Sheldon Jackson**, had whipped up the proselytizing zeal of as many denominations as possible, and they agreed to divide up Alaska into a number of ecclesiastical monopolies (see p.131). Each denomination got some easily accessible spots and some remote tracts and committed themselves to converting the Natives without treading on each other's patch.

The US Army was responsible for keeping the peace in Alaska and, fearing an Indian uprising, felt compelled to map as much of the territory as it could. Three **exploratory expeditions** were sent between 1883 and 1885: one up the Yukon River, one up the Copper River, and a third overland from the Copper River across the mountains to the Tanana River. The largely peaceful nature of the Indians they encountered allayed the government's fears and did little to encourage further investigation. Meanwhile, in 1884 the federal government passed the **Organic Act**, effectively providing local government for Alaska. Until this was extended in 1900, Alaska made do with just a judge, an attorney, and a marshal, all stationed in Sitka and with virtually no influence anywhere else. It wasn't a favored posting, and those who ended up there were often incompetent, if not wantonly unjust and self-serving. Alaska languished until the discovery of gold.

An Alaskan Eldorado

Alaska traces its modern development only as far back as the gold rushes that swept across the northwest of the continent mostly from 1880 to the early

1900s. They completely transformed the physical and social makeup, driving Alaska from neglected territory towards eventual statehood.

The first big Alaskan rush came in 1880 when **Joe Juneau** and **Richard Harris** discovered gold on the site of present-day Juneau. Hundreds flocked here and the town grew rapidly, though most of the benefit fell to big mining corporations who could exploit the hard-to-gain gold. More than two decades later Juneau would take over from Sitka as the capital of Alaska. Meanwhile, intrepid Interior prospectors had uncovered gold in the **Fortymile** district around Eagle, and together these sparked widespread interest in Alaska and the north. But everything up until now had just been a curtain-raiser for the big show that was about to unfold in the Canadian Yukon. In 1896 "Skookum" Jim Mason, "Dawson" Charlie and George Washington Carmack found gold on a tributary of the **Klondike** River and started a massive stampede to get to the fields through Alaska. In the twelve months from spring 1897 over sixty thousand hopefuls set off from Seattle and other Pacific ports, many struggling along the treacherous Chilkoot Trail over the Chilkoot Pass from Skagway, while others tried the All-American Route from Valdez, and the better-off rode sternwheelers up the Yukon River.

Initial gold strikes were wildly exaggerated, and few fortunes were made. Most prospectors gleaned modest sums and often returned to the Lower 48 after a season or two penniless, having blown their earnings in the bars and brothels that sprung up in the towns alongside the diggings. Typically, the initial tent city grew into a shambolic wooden town over the first year but lay almost abandoned by the second winter when the easiest pickings had been taken. Nonetheless, the Klondike gold rush opened up the Interior as never before. Few people had previously spent much time away from the coasts, but now sternwheelers were plying the Yukon and smaller rivers, the White Pass & Yukon Route railway was built from Skagway, telegraph lines were established, and all-weather roads eventually replaced the winter dog-sled routes.

Alaska had another gold rush in 1896, when gold was discovered around **Turnagain Arm**, close to present-day Anchorage. Hope, Girdwood, and Sunrise City sprung up, but by 1899 interest had been siphoned off north to the Seward Peninsula where the beaches of **Nome** produced as much gold as the Klondike, and then **Fairbanks**, the last of the major rushes, beginning in 1902. Mining has continued on a steadier scale ever since, occasionally buoyed by hikes in the price of gold, primarily in 1934 and again in the early 1970s. Wherever you go in rural Alaska, you'll find claims fiercely protected and meet eternally optimistic prospectors happy to tell you how much they're going to make next year.

To put all this in perspective, the Californian goldfields of the 1840s and 1850s gave up five times as much as all the Alaskan goldfields together, and South Africa produces more gold in a single year than Alaska has in a hundred.

The **effect on the Interior Natives** was profound. The newcomers failed to respect their "ownership" of the land, duped their hosts, and treated them inhumanely. They brought alcohol, destroyed the environment, and carried diseases that weren't cured by Native medicines but responded impressively to the white doctors' potions, thereby increasing dependence. And yet those with an entrepreneurial bent made the best of their circumstances, a case in point being the Chilkoot Indians who were aggressive businessmen and refused to let prospectors along their trail inland. Eventually, they opened it up, but monopolized the packing services along the trail, charging very respectable rates. Nonetheless, the events of the gold-rush years hastened the breakdown in Native society.

The federal government couldn't ignore Alaska any longer. Even if the rumors of lawlessness on the frontier were only half true, there had to be some form of local government. In response, a Civil Code was enacted in 1900 allowing for taxation, licensing, and the division of Alaska into three judicial districts, with judges at Sitka, Eagle, and St Michael. Communication between these three centers was so poor that Congress set the army to work building a network of telegraph cables known as the Washington–Alaska Military Cable and Telegraph System (WAMCATS; see box, p.440). Less than forty years after the purchase, Alaska was becoming well and truly American.

After the gold rushes

The changes initiated by the gold rushes were consolidated in the years immediately afterwards. By 1906 Alaska had a non-voting delegate in Congress, it attained territorial status in 1912, the first territorial legislature the following year gave women the vote (long before the federal government extended such a basic right), and in 1916 Judge James Wickersham introduced the first Statehood Bill. Alaska was getting aspirations. The infrastructure was improving too: WAMCATS was linked directly to Seattle by 1904, the first car drove the Richardson Highway between Valdez and Fairbanks in 1913, and in 1914 the federal government put its weight behind a new railroad between Seward and Fairbanks, in the process creating **Anchorage**.

While almost everyone's head was being turned by the gold, folk with a longer vision had begun to establish **salmon canneries**, the birth of an industry that was to become the mainstay of the Alaskan economy. The first cannery was built in 1878 at Klawock on Prince of Wales Island, and by 1900 there were fifty canneries operating between Ketchikan in Southeast and Bristol Bay on the Bering Sea.

With the easy pickings stripped from the goldfields, most people left, but others started to look around for a more settled life **homesteading**. The 1861 Homestead Act that paved the way for opening the American West was not applied to Alaska until 1898, and even when it was many found it impossible to make a living from their allocated 160 acres in Alaska's short growing season and had to supplement their income by hunting and trapping. It was a lonely life, as communities were reliant on slow river travel in the summer, hazardous sled-dog routes in the winter, and for four to six weeks each spring (break-up) and fall (freeze-up) were pretty much stuck. The situation began to change in the late 1920s with the advent of **bush planes**, which had more of an impact in Alaska than anywhere else in the US and remain an essential link in large sections of the state. All of a sudden a village a week's travel from Fairbanks could be reached in an hour, dog teams contracted to deliver the US mail started disappearing, and commercial sternwheeler services were reduced, though they didn't completely stop until the late 1950s.

For the next few decades, Alaska seldom featured in the national consciousness except for the **conquest of Mount McKinley** in 1913 and the Serum Run of 1925 (see box, p.504), when Nome was saved from an epidemic by a heroic delivery of antidote by a series of dog teams. Native Alaskans in particular had been ignored and denied voting rights, though a 1922 court case paved the way for Alaskan Natives (along with all other US Natives) to be granted citizenship. Despite this legal status, Alaska's first peoples remained marginalized with a crumbling social structure, weak leadership, and increasing problems with alcoholism. President Franklin Roosevelt took some notice in Alaska in 1935, when as part of his New Deal the **Matanuska Valley Colony** was established on some of Alaska's most fertile land around Palmer, just north of Anchorage. This was the only real attempt at organized settlement in Alaska, and though not wholly successful, Alaska could at last begin to partly feed itself. Until this point there was no large-scale agriculture, and everything that couldn't be obtained locally was imported from Seattle.

World War II and its aftermath

The United States' entry into World War II, after the Japanese bombing of Hawaii's Pearl Harbor in 1941, provided Alaska's next great leap forward. By 1940 war looked likely and Alaska's strategic importance and vulnerability were brought into sharp focus. The military machine swung into action – the first non-extractive industry to have an effect on the Alaskan economy – establishing military bases in Anchorage, Delta Junction, Dutch Harbor, Fairbanks, Kodiak, Nome, Sitka, and Whittier. The only way to get substantial quantities of materials and machinery up to Alaska was by sea, and the military wanted something safer and more easily protected. The answer was the **Alaska Highway** (also known as the ALCAN), a 1500-mile road punched through the wilds of northern British Columbia and the Yukon Territory to Fairbanks in Alaska. It was an immense and logistically difficult project, and yet it was completed (in a primitive but useable condition) in seven short months in 1942. It is now much improved and remains the only road link to the Lower 48. Military buildup continued apace, fueling a booming economy as the United States spent a total of a billion dollars to support up to 150,000 troops.

The tip of the Aleutian Islands is only around a thousand miles from northern Japan, and the US had no way of providing logistical support when, in 1942, the Japanese bombed Dutch Harbor and occupied the two remote Aleutian Islands of Attu and Kiska – the only successful invasion of US soil in the war (see "The Aleut" box, p.340). Apart from a brief postwar recession, the boom continued with increased military spending and construction during the Cold War. This, along with the civilian benefits of the Alaska Highway, brought tremendous population growth and economic expansion: the timber industry got under way, and both mining and fishing became more formalized. Alaska's carefree youth was coming to an end.

Statehood and the trans-Alaska pipeline

Alaska became a territory in 1912 (the same year as New Mexico and Arizona became the 47th and 48th states), but this had little appreciable effect on the land and its people. Renewed calls for statehood came in the early 1950s when the impotence of local representation in Congress started to rankle, and proponents claimed they needed statehood as protection from outside interests, particularly those engaged in over-fishing in the salmon industry. Counterclaims that Alaska would be a financial burden on federal resources won out for a time, but then in 1957 economically viable quantities of oil were discovered along the Swanson River on the Kenai Peninsula. All of a sudden Alaska looked more appealing, and in 1958 Congress approved the **Alaska Statehood Act**. President Dwight Eisenhower declared Alaska as the 49th state on January 3, 1959 (beating Hawaii to the title by eight months), and Alaskans could finally rid themselves of their perceived status as second-class citizens.

Until now, Alaskans had felt that a combination of limited funds and a small and thinly spread population had prevented them from truly taming this great land. Rural poverty was still the norm and though there was now a railroad linking the two biggest cities, the road system was still rudimentary and planes were beyond the means of most residents. Looking around the four-lane highways and shopping malls of Anchorage and Fairbanks today, it is hard to imagine just how different this was at the beginning of the 1960s. Statehood brought a spirit of optimism manifest in accelerated population and economic growth. This took a body blow five years later with the 1964 **Good Friday earthquake** (see box, p.207), which left a scar on the psyche of the Alaskan people, but came with the silver lining of the post-quake reconstruction.

Until statehood, the federal government had owned something like 99 percent of all the land in Alaska, the remaining one percent made up by land given up for homesteading. As part of the Statehood Act, and to help Alaska become self-sufficient, the US government promised to transfer control of over a quarter of the land, and the state of Alaska was given 25 years to make its choices. One of the earliest selections was large tracts of the North Slope, flanking the Arctic Ocean, where in 1968 the Atlantic Richfield company discovered huge **oil deposits beneath Prudhoe Bay**, thereby altering Alaska's financial destiny. The trouble was, the only feasible way to get the oil to market was by constructing an 800-mile pipeline right across the heart of the state. Environmentalists were immediately up in arms, but what worried the consortium of oil companies most was land ownership. The oil companies needed permission to cross land which was almost exclusively federally owned – and some of this territory was contested by newly resurgent Native groups who were demanding recognition of their first-people rights, a topic pointedly ignored at statehood. In the spirit of the late 1960s and early 1970s, Natives found a sympathetic ear in the federal courts and among the wider public. The government couldn't really approve pipeline construction until these Native claims were settled. There was also a desire to at least partially right the wrongs meted out to Native Alaskans over two centuries of white intervention, and with all that oil waiting to be tapped, whites were keen to settle. Understandably, Native leaders played it for all they could get. In 1971, Nixon signed the **Alaska Native Claims Settlement Act** (ANCSA) which extinguished Native land titles in return for almost $1 billion and 44 million acres – roughly a tenth of Alaska – spread between 60,000 people. At the time the settlement was widely regarded as the most generous and fair of any deal with aboriginal people, with every man, woman, and child getting $17,000. In hindsight, some believe the Natives were duped, their naive representatives sucked in by the machinations of international commerce and politics. Since ANCSA, oil companies have taken over $100 billion worth of oil off the North Slope, and the Alaska state government has received a third of that in taxes and royalties.

ANCSA drastically changed the economic status of Natives. The $1 billion was paid over a decade into twelve (later thirteen) regional corporations and over two hundred villages with the responsibility to invest half and distribute the rest to individuals and village corporations. Instead of being communal owners of the land, the people now became shareholders in their corporations, so the act effectively forced Native Alaskans into a capitalist world they neither wanted nor were prepared for. As John McPhee writes in *Coming into the Country*, "the bluntest requirement of the Alaska Native Claims Settlement Act was that the natives turn white." This came at a time when the Native way of life was under threat. Snowmachines were replacing sled dogs, homes were getting modern conveniences, and the men working on the trans-Alaska oil pipeline could send back weekly remittances large enough to supply the whole village with booze for a month. Binge drinking became the huge problem it still is today.

The regional corporations found themselves rich and immediately started buying up real estate, canneries, and businesses all over Alaska and beyond. A case in point is the Cook Inlet region's CIRI, which now owns sightseeing cruise companies in Prince William Sound and Kenai Fjords National Park, as well as hotels throughout Southcentral Alaska.

With Native opposition to the pipeline largely defused, the environmental challenge lost steam and eventually collapsed, and when oil prices went stratospheric as a consequence of the 1973 oil crisis, Congress gave the go-ahead. Construction of the **trans-Alaska oil pipeline** began in 1974, and as thousands of workers and hundreds of millions of dollars started flowing into the state, Alaskan aspirations went through the roof. Everyone was riding the oil wave, not least the workers with their huge pay packets: Fairbanks was the base for much of the construction and sprouted bars and brothels to cope with hordes of suddenly wealthy men; Anchorage boomed as the Alaskan headquarters of most of the oil companies; and Valdez tripled in size for the construction of the deep-water oil terminal.

This period also marked a shift in the sociopolitical makeup of the state. The heritage of gold prospecting, hunting, trapping, and commercial fishing left a strongly **libertarian** streak through the state, manifest in an almost paranoid mistrust of any form of authority and government. This point of view, however, had always been softened by a broadly liberal outlook: Alaskans even voted to legalize marijuana for home use in the 1970s (though this was later rescinded). With the discovery of oil and the construction of the pipeline, many of the newcomers were Southerners – from Texas, Oklahoma, and elsewhere in the Bible Belt – and Alaska shifted from being a mostly Democratic state to repeatedly returning Republican congressmen and senators.

Reaping the oily rewards

The pipeline was completed in 1977 at a cost of $8 billion, making it the largest private construction job in history. The crews went home (though many individuals stayed), and the state settled back to reap the proceeds of the oil. But there was unfinished business. The 1971 ANCSA agreement had established the size of the Native settlement, but not the details of how the lands would be divided up, something left for the 1980 **Alaska National Interest Lands Conservation Act** (ANILCA). In this, Congress set aside almost a third of the state in new or expanded parks. In a sense it marked the maturing of an Americanized Alaska: the old freedoms (however illusory) were perceived as being eroded as the land was "tied up." All of a sudden there were rules about where you could go, where you could hunt and how much fish and game you could take. As the Feds were perceived to be taking away, the state garnered popularity by abolishing all individual state taxes in 1980 and, two years later, by paying the first installment of the **Permanent Fund Dividend** (see box, p.197). More than $1000 has been paid annually to every resident.

Oil fueled massive growth in the mid-1980s with Alaskans enjoying the highest income of any state. The state's coffers were bulging and money was lavished on all manner of civic institutions, such as the museum and performing arts center in Anchorage. As a consequence of the 1976 **Molly Hooch Decree**, the state was obliged to provide secondary schooling in any community that had an elementary school, and though no other state would have had the money to comply, the timing was right and Alaska went ahead with the program. Now even tiny settlements have a swanky school; indeed, it's often the finest building in the district, and one that's usually put to multiple uses – community hall, sports hall, movie theater, and so on.

Despite widespread belief to the contrary, it couldn't last, and the bubble burst in 1986 when oil prices plummeted. Banks collapsed, thousands left the state, and property prices crashed. But recovery wasn't far behind, ironically riding on the back of the 1989 **Exxon Valdez disaster** (see box, p.296). When eleven million gallons of crude oil spilled from the *Exxon Valdez* tanker, a massive cleanup began, and many involved in the operation made a stack of cash, becoming known locally as the "spillionaires."

Present and future Alaska

Through the 1990s and into the new century, Alaska's traditional economic mainstays have been under threat. Oil remains the source of Alaskan wealth, and new fields are being tapped every couple of years, but these are small. As production declines from large fields like Prudhoe Bay, the net profits are waning. Oil companies are clamoring for new areas to be opened up for exploration, the most contentious being the coastal strip of the Arctic National Wildlife Refuge, which is thought to contain rich deposits currently inaccessible because of reserve status and public pressure. Moves to have the area designated a national monument failed to put the Arctic Refuge outside oil-company reach, leaving it open for George W Bush to push for exploitation. Oil still brings in eighty percent of Alaska's revenue, but the recent rise in world oil prices only serves to delay the inevitable need to diversify.

For the past few decades, **forestry** has been a big earner, with activities concentrated in the nation's two largest national forests, the Tongass, which encompasses almost the entire Southeast, and the Chugach, covering much of Southcentral and the southern Interior. Falling world prices for spruce pulp and timber have hit the industry hard, and pulp and saw mills have closed all over Southeast. Many lay the blame firmly at the feet of the federal government, which owns the forests and has cut back on the sale of timber-cutting rights. During the Clinton years, the government was seen as bowing to pressure from environmental groups seeking the preservation of some of the world's largest tracts of untouched temperate rainforest. Bush has tried to revive the industry with looser legislation, but so far without much success.

Alaska's fishery is the other big earner, particularly the super-rich **salmon fishing** industry, though annual catches are subject to wild swings. Over-fishing tends to get the blame for low returns, but poor years are often followed by bumper harvests. Still, supplies seem to be in ever greater demand, and the issue of international fish quotas came to a head in the summer of 1997 when

Canadian fishers sought to stop Alaskans "poaching" what they perceived to be Canadian fish. Fishing boats surrounded the tourist-laden Alaskan ferry *Malaspina* in the Canadian port of Prince Rupert and held it hostage for three days, eventually releasing it when the matter was resolved in an out-of-court settlement.

Over the years, other fish species, along with king crab and tanner crab, have been all but wiped out by over-fishing, and the industry now has a system of quotas aimed to prevent the recurrence of this cycle. More recently, foreign salmon farming has become the biggest threat, pushing down the price of Alaska's wild salmon.

Nepotism, favoritism, and the pork barrel

Most people have to wait until they're dead to get stuff named for them, but Alaska's senior US senator, **Ted Stevens**, has jumped the gun. In 1999, Anchorage's airport became the Ted Stevens Anchorage International Airport in recognition of the man's huge influence in bringing federal money to the 49th state. Stevens is one of the US's longest-serving senators, having been in the role since the late 1960s, and he heads the powerful Senate Appropriations Committee, which is responsible for allocating over half a trillion dollars in federal funds each year. He hasn't been shy about using his position to benefit Alaska. Indeed, he is the master of **pork-barrel politics**. When it comes time to push through a crucial bill that must pass, he'll regularly slip in a few dozen pet projects amounting to tens of millions of dollars. Wags in Washington have dubbed his chase for tax dollars, Alaska's second gold rush.

Despite being one of the country's least populous states, Alaska gets around $8 billion in federal funding each year, which equates to roughly $12,000 per resident, the highest per capita in the US. Of course, compared to the $200 billion California receives, it is small potatoes – Stevens even claims that Alaska has been shortchanged. Depending on who you ask, Stevens' activities are a source of either pride or acute embarrassment. Across the board, however, there's a grudging satisfaction in the good he does for the state and amusement in his barefaced favoring of all things Alaskan.

Things are no less murky back home, where Alaska runs a closed political shop. In 2002, Republican **Frank Murkowski**, who for years had been Alaska's second senator, became state governor and, with the right to appoint his successor as senator for the remainder of the elected term, chose his daughter **Lisa Murkowski** to fill his seat in Washington. If that sounds a little dodgy, read on. In the summer of 2002, Murkowski knew that he might win the gubernatorial race. He also knew of the governor's prerogative to appoint a senator to any vacant position and that, because he wouldn't take office until a month or so after the election, the privilege would fall on the incumbent, Democrat Tony Knowles. Knowing he would have the support of the Republican-dominated state legislature, our Frank pulled political strings to tease through a law that would delay the appointment of a replacement for fifty days, long enough for him to take office. Knowles vetoed the bill, but Frank had enough backing to get the veto overridden, and into law it went. Soon after taking office, Murkowski appointed his daughter to his vacated post.

In addition to its two senators, Alaska has one congressional representative, Republican **Don Young**, who has held the post continuously since 1973. Now one of the highest-ranking Republicans in the House of Representatives, he chairs the Transportation Committee and, like Stevens, is skilled at using his position to promote plum projects for his home state. Currently, he is championing a $200 million bridge from Ketchikan to its airport, and a $1 billion bridge from Anchorage across Knik Arm to Point MacKenzie. His efforts to sell taxpayers the Ketchikan "bridge to nowhere" recently earned him the Golden Fleece Award from Taxpayers for Common Sense, a government-spending watchdog. Young's response? "Very proud of that."

Ever since World War II, the **military** has been a big spender in the state, but with the end of the Cold War and progressive rounds of military belt-tightening things look bleak. So far Alaska has escaped the worst of the cuts, but no one is looking forward to a bright future.

Alaska has thrived on these boom-and-bust economies, but all currently look to be on a downward cycle. No one knows what the next boom will be, or if there will be one, so over the past decade or so Alaska has attempted – with limited success – to stabilize its economy. As elsewhere, the great hope is **tourism**, which has been expanding steadily over the past couple of decades and looks set to continue growing. Yet with such a short tourist season, and the prevalence of cruise-ship packages that see a lot of the profits leave the state, it seems unlikely that tourism can fill the void left by the decline of its extractive industries.

Alaska finds itself in a strange position. Speak to Alaskans and you'll hear a lot of libertarian rhetoric that borders on the survivalist. Anything that smacks of government interference is immediately jumped on hard, and yet Alaska has the highest per capita state spending in the country, pays an annual dividend of more than $1000 to every resident, runs the railroad and state ferry system, and owns almost a third of the state's entire surface area. Against these (whisper it) socialist tendencies there is the cherished lack of state income tax, though as oil revenues decline it seems only a matter of time until some form of taxation will have to be imposed. Already, intentions to dip into the Permanent Fund aren't dismissed completely out of hand, and the increased implementation of sales taxes is surely only delaying the inevitable.

Chronology

11,000 years ago ▸ earliest record of human presence in Alaska.

1725 ▸ Peter the Great sends Vitus Bering to explore the North Pacific.

1728 ▸ Vitus Bering sails through the Bering Strait naming St Lawrence Island.

1733 ▸ Georg Wilhelm Steller becomes the first naturalist to visit Alaska on Bering's second expedition.

1741 ▸ Bering sets foot on the Alaskan mainland on July 15 during his third expedition, but dies on the way home.

1745 ▸ Russian fur hunters overwinter in the Aleutian Islands; first European habitation.

1774 ▸ Spaniard Juan Perez sights southern end of Prince of Wales Island.

1778 ▸ English Captain James Cook charts Alaska coast and reaches Unalaska.

1784 ▸ Grigorii Shelikov establishes first white settlement at Three Saints Bay, Kodiak.

1792 ▸ Catherine II grants Alaskan fur monopoly to Grigorii Shelikov.

1795 ▸ The first Russian Orthodox church established in Kodiak.

1804 ▸ Russians establish settlement at modern-day Sitka.

1847 ▸ Hudson's Bay Company establishes Fort Yukon at the confluence of the Porcupine and Yukon rivers; Russian hegemony in Alaska challenged.

1849 ▸ Russian mining engineer discovers gold and coal on the Kenai Peninsula.

1857 ▸ Coal mining begins at Coal Harbor on the Kenai Peninsula.

1865 ▸ Extensive exploration of Alaska as Western Union Telegraph Company prepares to put telegraph line across Alaska and Siberia.

1867 ▸ US purchases Alaska from Russia.

1871 ▸ Gold discovered at Indian River near Sitka.

1880 ▸ Tlingit Kowee leads Richard Harris and Joseph Juneau to gold near Juneau; Juneau established.

1881 ▸ Presbyterians under Sheldon Jackson begin mission schools.

1884 ▸ Congress passes Organic Act providing a civil government for Alaska.

1890 ▸ Large corporate salmon canneries begin to appear.

1897–1900 ▸ Klondike gold rush.

1898 ▸ Gold discovered in Nome.

1900 ▸ Civil Code for Alaska enacted.

1902 ▸ Felix Pedro discovers gold near Fairbanks.

1906 ▸ Capital moved from Sitka to Juneau.

1910 ▸ The Sourdoughs make first ascent of North Peak of Mount McKinley.

1911 ▸ Sea otters given complete protection after international agreement between US, Great Britain, Canada, Russia, and Japan.

1912 ▸ Alaska given territorial status.

1915 ▸ Anchorage established as a construction camp for the Alaska Railroad.

1923 ▸ President Warren G Harding comes to Alaska to drive the last spike in Alaska Railroad.

1935 ▸ Matanuska Colony Project brings New Dealers to Alaska.

1940 ▸ Beginning of military expansion.

1942 ▸ Japan bombs Dutch Harbor, invades Aleutians. ALCAN Highway built.

1959 ▸ Alaska becomes 49th state.

1964 ▸ Good Friday earthquake strikes Southcentral and parts of Southwest Alaska.

1968 ▸ Oil discovered at Prudhoe Bay.

1971 ▸ Alaska Native Claims Settlement Act signed into law.

1976 ▸ Molly Hooch Decree requires secondary schooling throughout the state.

1977 ▸ Trans-Alaska pipeline completed from Prudhoe Bay to Valdez.

1980 ▸ Congress passes Alaska National Interest Lands Conservation Act.

1982 ▸ First Permanent Fund Dividend paid out.

1986 ▸ Oil price drops below $10 a barrel, initiating economic slump.

1989 ▸ The *Exxon Valdez* oil tanker spills eleven million gallons of crude into Prince William Sound.

1994 ▸ Federal trial awards $5 billion in restitution for the *Exxon Valdez* disaster.

1997 ▸ Canadian fishermen detain Alaskan ferry over fishing rights.

1999 ▸ SeaLife Center opens in Seward, partly funded by restitution from the *Exxon Valdez* disaster.

2000 ▸ The state supports George W Bush in the presidential election.

2002 ▸ Republican Frank Murkowski takes over from Democrat Tony Knowles as state governor.

2003 ▸ Drop in oil revenue causes budget blowout; imposition of a state income tax narrowly averted.

Permanent Fund Dividend drops to lowest level for decades.

Public pressure sees oil development in Arctic National Wildlife Refuge dropped from federal energy bill.

Landscapes and wildlife

A visit to any Alaskan bookshop will reveal racks of books on the state's impressive geology, flora, and fauna, and indeed there is much to be covered: mountain ranges, deep fjords, lakes, and wetlands, and all sorts of species occupying those environments. What follows is a general overview of animals, plants, and landscape you can expect to find along the way.

Glaciers, volcanoes, and earthquakes

Most people's expectations of the Alaskan landscape are based on the realities of Southeast Alaska, where ancient **glaciers** carved out deep **fjords** since filled in by the sea to create the narrow channels of the Inside Passage. Here, pine- and spruce-cloaked islands shelve steeply into deep water, and beaches are rare. In several places glaciers calve off icebergs directly into the fjords, but many glaciers have receded to the point where they no longer reach the water. The most rapidly shrinking glaciers are those in Glacier Bay, where they have receded seventy miles over the past two hundred years. Lichens only just manage a toehold on recently revealed rock near the glaciers; once land has been ice-free for around two hundred years it achieves the mix of mature spruce and hemlock found all over Southeast.

Large sections of Southcentral around Prince William Sound and on the Kenai Peninsula have a similar topography, although here there's no narrow network of channels. In Southcentral several tidewater glaciers are fed by large **ice fields** high in the Wrangell, Kenai, and Chugach mountains, where enormous quantities of snow accumulate.

Further north, the Interior is sliced through by the **Alaska Range**, a jagged chain of icy peaks topped by **Mount McKinley**, the highest mountain in North America. Glaciers exist here, too, but precipitation is much lower than on the coast, and with less weight driving them downhill they tend to move much more slowly. By the time the ice reaches the terminus (possibly hundreds of years later) most Interior glaciers have accumulated so much surface debris they appear an unappealing brown – a contrast to the clean and white glaciers of the coast.

Once winds reach northern Alaska most of their moisture has been lost as snow over the coastal mountains and the Alaska Range, leaving nothing for the **Brooks Range**, the ultimate northern extension of the Rockies. Though glacially sculpted, there is no longer the snowfall to support large glaciers, and most of the tops remain bare.

Most Alaskan mountain ranges are the result of the folding of the earth's crust, but in places this process is given a helping hand by **volcanoes**, around fifty of which form an orderly line from the highest, the 14,000-foot Mount Wrangell in the east, out along the Alaska Peninsula and right out to the western end of the Aleutian Islands. They add a certain grace to the skyline, particularly from the western shore of the Kenai Peninsula and from the ferry trip along the Alaska Peninsula to Dutch Harbor.

The volcanoes form part of the **Pacific Ring of Fire** where the North American and Pacific tectonic plates meet. It is the interaction of these two plates that is at the root of all Alaska's **earthquake** activity. It is said that in the twentieth century, a quarter of all the energy released worldwide by earthquakes was released in Alaska. Little wonder then that an earthquake of over seven on the Richter scale is expected on average every fifteen months, and three of the ten largest earthquakes ever recorded occurred in Alaska, the 1964 Good Friday quake (see box, p.207) coming in second.

Forests, taiga, and tundra

Alaska has four main vegetation zones: temperate forest, boreal forest, taiga, and tundra. Most of the southern coastal regions come cloaked in deep-green temperate **rainforests**, mainly comprising the huge **Sitka spruce** – the state tree – and **western hemlock**, with a little yellow and red cedar mixed in. With spruce commonly measuring up to eight feet in diameter, it is not surprising that the loggers have been hard at work. Some areas have been clear-cut, most noticeably on Prince of Wales Island, but for long stretches in Southeast rainforest covers every square inch of land up to the tree line. Closer inspection reveals an understory of low scrub made almost impenetrable by abundant **devil's club**, with its broad green leaves and five-foot stems covered in spines. Above the tree line, thickets of **alder** and **willow** predominate before giving way to alpine tundra.

In clearings and along roadsides you'll see tall stems of **fireweed**, which chart the progress of summer. The bottom of the stem flowers early in summer and the flowering zone moves progressively up the stem, finishing with a flourish as the uppermost section blooms in late August. When it has gone to seed, it is said to be only six weeks until the first snowfall.

Southcentral Alaska also has its share of rainforest, though cedar doesn't make it this far north, and only spruce makes it as far as Kodiak, the western limit of the rainforest. North of Anchorage, dense woods continue only to the Matanuska Valley, where **boreal forest** takes over. Characterized by scattered stands of white spruce, cottonwood, lodgepole pine, and paper birch, it lacks the grandeur of the rainforest, but makes up for it with spectacular seasonal changes, the buds of the deciduous trees producing fully opened leaves in what seems like hours, the leaves then turning to shades of gold in fall, which also goes by in a flash.

Further north, particularly beyond the Alaska Range, you're into **taiga**, a Russian word meaning "little land of sticks." It is an appropriate description for a sparse landscape only periodically dotted with short white and black spruce, the latter taking decades to grow by an inch in diameter. The trees are usually interspersed with dwarf willow and **muskeg**, a kind of swampy peat bog that in wetter areas develops into a network of ponds linked by small slow-moving streams.

Trees finally disappear altogether in the Brooks Range, where **moist tundra** takes over and runs all the way to the Arctic Ocean. Many of the taiga species are still in evidence, but are usually more stunted: nothing grows above knee height. As everywhere in the north, there are species of willow, which here might only be an inch high but spread for up to a hundred yards along the ground. On very flat ground the land becomes soggy **wet tundra**; the limited rainfall, unable to penetrate the underlying permafrost, collects on the surface, forming numerous lakes.

Anywhere in the state with hills high enough will allow you to climb out of the forest and into **alpine tundra**. Again the vegetation is very low on the ground, with heather and an abundance of wildflowers, including the state flower, the beautiful blue **forget-me-not**.

Wildlife

One of the most enticing things about a visit to Alaska is the opportunity to see the sort of **wildlife** rarely on view elsewhere. The highlights among the land dwellers – bears, moose, caribou, and wolves – can usually be seen with a

Wildlife watching

The single most popular outdoor activity in Alaska is looking for **wildlife**, sometimes on a dedicated cruise or nature tour, but as often as not from cars, trains, buses, and cruise ships.

Almost everyone who comes to Alaska wants to see whales, bald eagles, grizzly bears, black bears, caribou, and moose, and hopefully more elusive animals such as Dall sheep, mountain goats, wolves, and even polar bears. As long as you spend some time in the Interior and along the coast, you should at least see the back and tail flukes of whales, or the rear of a bear as it scuffles away into the undergrowth. It is unlikely to be as spectacular as you've seen on TV or in magazines, but unless you've set your expectations unreasonably high even that feels like a privilege – and sometimes animals come surprisingly close. Undoubtedly, the best investment you can make is in a pair of **binoculars**; boats running whale-watching trips and the like will supply several sets, but these have to be shared around, so having your own is a boon. A pocket-sized 7x20 pair is perfect for most people: larger models are more unwieldy for casual use, and higher magnifications can make it both difficult to find your subject and hard to keep the image steady when you do. Buy the best you can afford, as quality makes a big difference.

If you are on a bus in Denali National Park or a cruise boat in Prince William Sound, someone will spot something, the driver/captain will stop or slow down, and everyone will take photos and video footage until the animal gets bored, or spooked, and moves away. On foot, your approach is more important. Your biggest assets will be **patience** and the ability to keep quiet and blend in with your environment. A little prior knowledge about an animal's habits (and the shape of their tracks and scat) should help you choose the right area for viewing, and then you can stay in one place and let them come to you. Provided you are not upwind of them, animals may approach very close without even knowing you're there. When approaching an animal, don't try to get too close and watch for signs that the animal is getting edgy about your activities. Mammals tend to raise their head and look toward you with ears alert; get closer and they'll either run or get aggressive. Birds will keep their eye on you, cry out, or even pretend to have a broken wing when they feel threatened. In either case, back off before they flee, and if birds do fly (especially if they are on a nest) be sure to move on straight away.

Wildlife photography is a specialist undertaking, and people return from Alaska disappointed with their collection of brown smudges they claim are bears, and photos of wide open seas where whales were moments previously. If you've any aspiration of returning with quality images, you'll need a camera capable of taking lenses with focal lengths of at least 200mm (preferably 300mm or even 500mm), a tripod (or at least a monopod), and fast film (400ASA minimum) to capture animals in the low light of dawn and dusk when they tend to come out.

little patience anywhere that's not built-up, although chances are best in Denali National Park where the shuttle buses give direct access to wild country. Here we've just covered the large mammals that are the main attraction for most visitors. For tips on wildlife watching, see box (p.539).

Bears

With the exception of the city centers, the mountaintops, and a few islands, Alaska is **bear** country.

Most of the bear-viewing sites around the state focus on the **brown bear**, which goes by three names – **brown, grizzly, and Kodiak** – but is essentially the same species and is easily identified by its shoulder hump and broad, stubby face. Whatever the name, they've become something of an icon of all places wild. There are only around three hundred left in the Lower 48, but up here there are almost 40,000 of them.

In inland areas they're known as **grizzlies**, generally solitary animals each roaming over fifty square miles of territory to satisfy its mixed diet of berries, roots, willow shoots, ground squirrels, and occasionally something bigger, like a moose calf or caribou. Except during the mating season around July, you'll usually see solo males or mothers still being followed by cubs, which stay with them for two summers before being forced out on their own.

Large grizzly males can stand up to seven feet tall and weigh six hundred pounds, although this is small in comparison with their coastal kin, the **brown bears**. The presence of salmon-rich streams means that all a brown bear has to do is wait for the salmon run, stand by the stream, and pluck out fish until sated. Later in the season it is even easier as the salmon die and float downstream where the bears scavenge. Brown bears put on a huge amount of weight at this time, attaining something close to eight hundred pounds. The ready food also reduces the amount of territory needed for each bear, and so at places such as Brooks Camp in Katmai National Park and Pack Creek near Juneau you'll see several brought together by the rich pickings. The biggest of all brown bears are **Kodiak brown bears**, on Kodiak Island, which are the world's largest land carnivore, occasionally reaching eleven feet and 1400 pounds.

Alaska also has **black bears**, mostly around the coast where you'll see them foraging along the shore, but also inland where they prefer denser undergrowth, seldom venturing out onto open ground. They're usually much smaller than grizzlies but can't always be distinguished by their color, which can vary from black through cinnamon brown to a rare blue-gray known as a **glacier bear**. The lack of a shoulder hump and a much narrower pointy face than the grizzly makes them easy to identify.

Anyone with a little patience will see black and brown bears while they're in Alaska, but **polar bears** are a different matter. They inhabit the Arctic rim, roaming the pack ice for most of the year hunting seals and only heading south onto land when the ice forms along the coast in winter. They then return to the polar region in spring. At up to eleven feet and reaching 1400 pounds, they are an impressive sight, and people go to great expense to see them. The best bets are northern coastal settlements, such as Barrow and Kaktovik, during their spring and fall whaling seasons in May and September. The whale's entrails are usually left at a dump site where the bears come scavenging.

Moose

Lugubrious-looking **moose** are a much more visible part of the Alaskan landscape than bears, and are found everywhere except the islands of Southeast,

Kodiak, and the Aleutians. You'll see them (usually alone or with a calf) grazing in city parks in suburban Anchorage or standing belly-deep in roadside ponds chomping on aquatic vegetation and willow shoots. Alaskan moose are the largest of all moose, itself the largest member of the deer family. A bull (male) will weigh in at over 1200 pounds and stand five feet high at the shoulder. Size usually distinguishes bulls from cows (females), but a bull also grows an impressive set of antlers, usually known as a "rack" – up to 75 inches across, though 45 is more normal – which is shed annually and regrown through the summer. To see the bull moose in full-racked glory, you need to be here in fall, which is also hunting season. Throughout most of the year, cows have one or two calves in tow, only chasing them away in spring when they are about to give birth again.

Caribou and reindeer

Caribou are also members of the deer family but are less than half the size of moose and live socially in huge herds that are constantly on the move. They graze on open ground for a while and then, at the slightest hint of danger, flit off across the landscape at great speed. This is their first line of defense against their main predator, wolves. Alaska's million or so caribou are found in over a dozen main herds, mostly occupying areas far away from human habitation, especially north of the Brooks Range, though you've a fair chance of spotting them in Denali National Park and along the Denali Highway. In late fall there are also viewing possibilities in the Interior along the Taylor, Richardson, and Glenn highways. They migrate throughout the year, in winter searching out areas with little snow cover so that they can use their broad hooves to scrape away for the limited grazing below – caribou means "scraping hooves" in the Maine Algonquin dialect. Uniquely within the deer family, the females also grow antlers, both sexes shedding them every year.

Caribou are very closely related to **reindeer**, a northern European and Asian subspecies – shorter and stockier – that has been domesticated. A number of animals were imported from Siberia late in the nineteenth century and their dscendants are still found on the Seward Peninsula near Nome, though some have escaped and joined caribou herds.

Wolves

For centuries the **wolf** has been feared, despised, and hunted to extinction in many parts of the world, but extensive research over the past few decades – much of it in Alaska – is beginning to balance the prejudice with some respect for this complex animal. Wolves are found throughout Alaska, although their natural shyness and sensitivity to human development makes them hard to spot. Shaded from black to almost white, they tend to live in packs of six to twelve, and sometimes up to thirty, usually sticking to a home territory but ranging widely in search of caribou. It is this behavior that puts them in danger, since wolves are not protected in Alaska. Even those that normally live in protected areas, such as the wilderness sections of Denali National Park, often stray into unprotected areas and are shot. Of Alaska's roughly 8000-strong wolf population, around 1500 are shot or trapped each year, partly to manage caribou numbers, but also for sport.

Dall sheep

Dall sheep are the world's only wild white sheep. Although their color undoubtedly provides suitable camouflage in winter, it looks like a poor evolutionary move in summer when you can spot them high in the hills from miles away. Their agility on steep terrain and a tendency to stick to high ground gives them some protection, as do the rams' distinctive curled horns, which grow a little bit fiercer each year. Along the Seward Highway south of Anchorage, around the Copper River Delta near Cordova, and in Denali you'll see visitors training their binoculars on distant hills watching Dall sheep graze oblivious to the spectators.

Musk oxen

If you drive along the roads near Nome or slog your way up the Dalton Highway towards Prudhoe Bay, you've a reasonable chance of seeing wild **musk oxen**. Originally native to Alaska, they died out several millennia ago but were reintroduced in 1936, when 34 specimens were imported from Greenland and released on Nunivak Island in Southwest Alaska. Numbers grew and all other Alaska herds were populated from there. The Seward Peninsula around Nome was seeded with 71 beasts, and the area now has more than nine hundred animals.

Marine life

Alaska is surrounded by a rugged shoreline that offers sanctuary to enormous numbers of marine mammals. Migrating **whales** pass through northbound in spring to their summer feeding grounds in the Arctic Ocean, then return in fall to their subtropical breeding territory. Others stay year-round feeding on the abundant fish and crustaceans. And herein lies the conflict that is threatening sea mammal populations. Commercial fishing fleets are getting ever more efficient at emptying the sea of their target species, making it increasingly difficult for sea mammals to feed themselves. Quota systems attempt to strike a balance, but economic interests often prevail, especially in small communities where fishing is the sole livelihood.

A lot of Alaska's visitors spend a huge portion of their time standing beside rivers casting a line in the hope of hooking a prize **salmon**, but this isn't all the rivers have to offer. **Trout** are also prevalent in several varieties, probably the largest and most sought-after being the **steelhead**, which normally weighs around ten pounds, fights hard once on a line, and tastes good. Others go for the smaller **cutthroat**, **rainbow**, **brook**, and **lake trout**, or the oddly named **Dolly Varden**, which gets its moniker from its pink spots, said to resemble a dress worn by the Dickens character of the same name from *Barnaby Rudge*.

Rivers in the far north are often devoid of salmon and trout, but are full of **arctic grayling**, a small fish mostly weighing under a pound and distinguished by its sail-like dorsal fin.

Sea mammals

Kings of the sea are the whales, which can usually be seen on whale-watching trips throughout Southeast and Southcentral Alaska. **California gray whales** make their migration in April when tourists are generally absent, while **humpback whales** are more accommodating, usually passing through in May and September, with some hanging around for most of the summer. You may be lucky enough to see one **breaching**, rising completely out of the water before crashing back into the sea.

Probably the most common sightings are of **orca**, previously known as killer whales, though they are in fact the largest in the dolphin family. Usually around twenty feet long, they have a distinctive black and white patterning and a very pronounced dorsal fin. There are pure-white **Beluga whales** (sometimes known as belukha to distinguish the whale from the sturgeon) in Cook Inlet, though numbers are in decline and sightings less frequent.

Another marine mammal in decline is the **Steller's sea lion**, named by Georg Wilhelm Steller, a naturalist aboard Bering's second voyage in 1733. It is a huge beast, with bulls weighing over a ton, something achieved by eating a lot of pollock. This bottom-dwelling fish has been caught in huge quantities in the past few decades (primarily for use as imitation crab), roughly corresponding to the drop in Steller's sea lion numbers. Those that are left favor rookeries on remote islands, and sightings are rare unless you make a specific journey.

The **northern fur seal** is a slightly smaller member of the same family, and it spends much of its time out at sea before returning each summer to the cramped beaches of the Pribilof Islands, where up to a million fur seals breed. Hunting of fur seals has been banned by international treaty since 1911, when the same protection was afforded the **sea otter**. Because of its supremely soft and immensely valuable fur, the sea otter was hunted very close to extinction, but a few survived in remote spots and since 1911 numbers have increased dramatically. They can be seen all around the southern Alaskan coast, their expressive faces peering back at you inquisitively as they float on their back cracking open a mussel using a stone they've picked up from the bottom.

Salmon

If there is one creature that is discussed more than any other in Alaska, it is **salmon**, a fish that supports huge commercial operations and is the subject of the state's main pastime. There are five species of Pacific salmon, all prevalent in Alaska and all going by two names, which are used interchangeably. Wherever you go in Alaska, there is an enormous quantity of information about the different types, their characteristics, and the **unusual life cycle**, which sees them spending a few years at sea and then returning to the stream they were born in to breed and then die. Here, we've just provided the most basic information to get you started.

The largest of the species is the **king salmon** (or **chinook**), a deep-bodied fish which can grow up to 97 pounds, though 11–40 pounds is more common, except in the Kenai River which has a reputation for huge fish. They typically run fairly early in the season from mid-May to mid-July. **Silver salmon** (or **coho**) have a similar full-bodied shape, but are much smaller, averaging 6–12 pounds, and run late, mostly in September right through to mid-November. **Red salmon** (**sockeye**) are widely considered to be the best-tasting and have brilliant-red flesh. As they swim up the rivers in June and July their skin turns from a greenish-blue to a green head and deep-red body. They average around 10 pounds. The most abundant of the five species are **pink salmon** (or **humpback** or **humpies**), which grow to around 4–6 pounds and have a pronounced hump on their back. They run from mid-August to mid-September, though many get caught before they ever make it into the rivers and are canned. Lastly, there's **chum salmon** (or **dog**), the lowliest of the breed and the species traditionally caught for feeding to sled dogs. They weigh 10–20 pounds and typically run from mid-August to mid-September.

Birds

Alaska has exemplary birdlife. There have been some 440 species recorded here, and some come in countless quantities, completely covering vast areas of wetlands.

The one bird most (at least most Americans) want to see is the **bald eagle**, a national symbol that remains relatively rare in the Lower 48 but is so abundant in Alaska that after a while you'll almost cease to notice them. The white-feather hood that gives them their bald appearance certainly lends a noble countenance, something enhanced by their unruffled posture as they sit in the trees, but they often eschew the noble art of hunting in favor of some opportunistic scavenging. The familiar coloration – black body, yellow beak and talons, and a white head and tail feathers – doesn't appear until the birds are about five years old, but they can live to twenty years or more. **Golden eagles** are also in evidence, mostly in the Interior where they hunt for small mammals on the tundra.

Waterfowl and shorebirds make up a large portion of Alaska's summer bird population, and the numbers are staggering: over twenty million pass through the Copper River Delta each spring, including the world's entire population of **western sandpiper**; and some 24 million nest and feed on the delta of the Yukon and Kuskokwim rivers between May and September, including sandhill cranes, black brants, the entire North American populations of emperor geese and spectacled eider, and assorted loons and ducks. Worth special mention are the world's largest waterfowl, the **trumpeter swans**, with wingspans up to seven feet. They were once thought to be on the brink of extinction, until a large flock was discovered in the Copper River Delta, still the best place to see them.

Alaska's state bird is the **willow ptarmigan**, a poorly flighted game bird similar to a large quail. They live throughout inland Alaska, mostly in high country where they burrow into snowdrifts to protect themselves from the cold, and from hungry wolves. They're even blessed with feathers on their legs and feet to protect them, but otherwise their survival instinct is poor: early pioneers found them easy to catch and good eating.

Books

Many of the following books are widely distributed in Alaska but have limited availability outside the state. If you are keen to buy before you travel, the easiest solution is to check booksellers on the web such as ⓦwww.powells.com, ⓦwww.amazon.com or .uk, ⓦwww.barnesandnoble.com, and others. Alaskan booksellers with online retailing include: Alaska Natural History Association (ⓣ274-8440, ⓦwww.alaskanha.org); Cook Inlet Books (ⓣ1-800-240-4148, ⓦwww.cookinlet.com); and Title Wave (ⓣ278-9283, ⓦwww.wavebooks.com). Where two publishers are given, these refer to US and UK publishers respectively; wherever we've cited a single publisher, it's the same publisher in both countries. Books that are especially recommended are marked with a ★.

Travel and impressions

Jon Krakauer *Into the Wild* (Anchor/Pan). In 1992, in an abandoned bus just north of Denali National Park, idealistic young Chris McCandless died after repeatedly ingesting mildly toxic plant matter while pursuing high-minded but poorly thought-out dreams of self-sufficiency and aesthetic purity. Climber, author, and *Outside* magazine contributor Jon Krakauer reconstructs the peregrinations of Chris's last couple of years and weaves them in with tales of like-minded adventurers and his own youth. A fascinating and unashamedly self-indulgent tale.

Mark Lawson *The Battle for Room Service: Journeys to all the Safe Places* (o/p /Picador). Denali, Fairbanks, and Barrow make for an entertaining chapter on Lawson's world tour of "activity challenged" and "differently interesting" places. Astute observations of both the state and those drawn to it.

Barry Lopez *Arctic Dreams* (Vintage/The Harville Press). Lopez takes you forever deeper into the interstices of Arctic life and landscapes, weaving together philosophy, science, ethics, polar history, and ecology into a magisterial volume that is in turns poetic, pragmatic, and lyrical. It's essential reading for anyone visiting the Arctic north of Alaska or with even the faintest interest in Arctic ecosystems.

Joe McGinniss *Going to Extremes* (o/p /Pan). McGinniss ranks alongside John McPhee as a spot-on commentator on the turbulent mid-1970s oil-boom years but takes a different slant. Whereas McPhee writes about what he likes, McGinniss writes about what he doesn't; some cheap shots perhaps, but funny and often just as true today as when it was written.

★ **John McPhee** *Coming into the Country* (Noonday). The single most accurately observed and sharply written volume on modern Alaska, even if it is over a quarter of a century since McPhee traveled in the Brooks Range, along the Yukon River, and through the Interior. His evocation of Alaska and the Alaskan character is both matchless and timeless.

★ **John Muir** *Travels in Alaska* (Mariner). A powerful collection of reflections on his trips to the Alaskan Southeast between 1879 and 1890, a time when very few Americans had been there, and most of them were missionaries. There are tediously long descriptions of forests and glaciers (their land-sculpting actions barely understood at this time), which are offset by his tremendous enthusiasm for the landscape and indomitable spirit of exploration.

Gary Paulsen *Winterdance: The Fine Madness of Alaskan Dog Racing* (Harvest Books). Entertaining and harrowing autobiographical account of Paulsen's seventeen-day ordeal as an ignorant novice undertaking the Iditarod sled-dog race.

Alastair Scott *Tracks across Alaska: A Dog Sled Journey* (Atlantic Monthly/Abacus). Wilder-the-better travel writing which transcends the genre. Scott arrived in Alaska with almost no knowledge of dog sledding, but ended the winter making a month-long sled journey from Manley Hot Springs to Nome, a trip which he uses as the thread that links deep insights into the bush. Well worth seeking out.

History, society, and politics

Ernest S. Burch and Werner Forman *The Eskimos* (University of Oklahoma Press). Informative and well-written treatise on the traditional Eskimo way of life that is pan-Arctic in scope but with frequent reference to the Alaskan experience. Beautifully photographed, with an emphasis on some exquisite Eskimo crafts.

Brian M. Fagan *The Great Journey* (o/p /Thames & Hudson). Probably the best lay-reader's explanation of current anthropological and archeological theories about the origins of Native Americans. More information than most people need to know but a good read nonetheless.

Jay Hammond *Tales of Alaska's Bush Rat Governor* (o/p). Enjoyable and thoroughly readable autobiography of Alaska's Republican (but very independently minded) governor from 1974 to 1982 – the state's most formative oil-industry years. Outspoken, self-effacing, and seldom pulling punches, Hammond charts his life from bush pilot, trapper, and fishing guide on remote Bristol Bay to the chains of high office and the governor's mansion in Juneau.

Nick Jans *The Last Light Breaking: Living among Alaska's Iñupiat Indians* (Alaska Northwest Books). A rare Alaskan voice amid all the impressions of outsiders, beautifully written and with insightful discussion of the Alaskan bush and Iñupiat Eskimos.

Claus M. Naskee and Herman E. Slotnik *Alaska: A History of the 49th State* (University of Oklahoma Press). Probably the best all-around history of Alaska.

Don O'Neill *The Firecracker Boys* (St Martin's Press). Indictment of government action and arrogance over Project Chariot, a real-life plan to carve a new harbor out of the Alaskan coast, just north of Kotzebue, with six thermonuclear bombs.

Harry Ritte *Alaska's History* (Alaska Northwest Books). A handy, pocket history of the state, with plenty of photos and anecdotes, though a little superficial for history buffs.

John Strohmeyer *Extreme Conditions: Big Oil and the Transformation of Alaska* (Cascade Press). A damning 1993 study of how oil-inspired greed has altered the face of Alaska and still threatens to bring about the state's downfall. Too earnest at times, but an entertaining eye-opener.

Memoirs

Rex Beach *The Spoilers* (Indypublish.Com). Firsthand tales of the Nome gold rush written in 1919 and currently only available in expensive reprints, though second-hand copies can be found.

Art Davidson *Minus 148°* (The Mountaineers). Huddled in a tiny snow cave at Denali Pass with temperatures at –50° and wind speeds reaching 150mph, the team making the first successful ascent of Mount McKinley in winter (in 1967) experienced a wind chill off the bottom of the scale, below –148°. Drawing on the diaries and reminiscences of the others involved, Davidson has woven an Alaskan mountaineering classic, free of unnecessary jargon and with human frailty playing as important a part as selfless heroism.

Ray Hudson *Moments Rightly Placed: An Aleutian Memoir* (Epicenter Press). A kind of "Zen and the Art of Basket Weaving" title in which Washington State native Ray Hudson tells of his years in Unalaska during which he shocked the locals by taking up basket weaving – traditionally a woman's task. A sensitive and moving story of the assimilation from stranger to friend.

Beth Johnson *Yukon Wild* (Berkshire Traveler Press). The adventures of four Texas women who paddled 2000 miles through America's last frontier down the Yukon River. Sometimes wordy but always interesting.

Lael Morgan *Good Time Girls of the Alaska – Yukon Gold Rush* (Epicenter Press). Life and high times on the Alaskan goldfield as seen by the other kind of gold digger. An empathetically told series of true stories with a heap of fascinating detail and a good deal of humor.

Margaret Murie *Two in the Far North* (Alaska Northwest Books). A very readable memoir by one of Alaska's earliest conservationists that gives a real sense of how Alaska has changed over the decades, from her youth in Fairbanks in the 1910s, through trips into the Arctic in the 1920s and 1950s, to her involvement in the creation of national parks and wildlife refuges (especially ANWR) in the mid-1970s.

Jonathan Raban *Passage to Juneau* (Vintage/Picador). Raban continues his later-life maritime peregrinations up the Inside Passage from Seattle, haunted by the ghost of British explorer George Vancouver and the spirit of two temperamental underwater Native American gods. It is a fascinating journey through history, literature, art criticism, and his own rites of passage, even if only part of it is actually in Alaska.

Kim Rich *Johnny's Girl* (Alaska Northwest Books). Intriguing and well-written tale of growing up in 1960s and 1970s Anchorage as the daughter of one of the major players in the fledgling city's small-town gambling and prostitution gangland. An interesting insight into Alaska's underworld machinations and their impact on modern Anchorage.

Jonathan Waterman *In the Shadow of Denali* (Lyons Press). Well-written personal odyssey touching on all aspects of Denali as a mountaineer's quarry and lifelong focal point. Subject matter jumps around – brief life stories, tales of mountain guiding, and work as a park ranger – but the whole still manages to convey a vivid impression of what the mountain means to its devotees. A good read for anyone already drawn by Denali.

Literature

Susan B. Andrews and **John Creed** (eds) *Authentic Alaska: Voices of its Native Writers* (University of Nebraska). A rare chance to read Native Alaskan literature unfiltered by white eyes: forthright stories of life as it is lived today in rural Alaska.

Sue Henry *Murder on the Iditarod Trail* (Avon Mystery). The first and perhaps best-known novel by this popular Alaskan murder mystery writer. An easy and entertaining tale of intrigue on Alaska's 1100-mile dog race with much of the background material factually correct. *Termination Dust* and *Sleeping Lady* are also worth checking out.

★ **Jack London** *The Call of the Wild*; *White Fang* (Signet Classic/Wadsworth). Two classic tales describing London's view of the human condition portrayed through the life of a domestic dog progressively turning wild in the former, and pretty much the reverse process in the latter. Though mostly set in the Yukon during the Klondike rush, the scenes of hardship, camaraderie, and arduous dog sledding translate to the Alaskan experience at the same time.

★ **Wayne Mergler** (ed) *The Last New Land: Stories of Alaska Past and Present* (Alaska Northwest Books). Modern anthology with excerpts of everything from Native legends and early exploration to the oil years and climbing Denali. A great starting point.

James A. Michener *Alaska* (Crest/Random House). A lumbering brick of a book that's about what you'd expect from the master of rambling historic novels, partially redeemed by a guide to where fiction parts company from fact. Forget it and read John McPhee instead.

Robert Service *The Best of Robert Service* (Perigee). The best value for your money of all the Service poetry anthologies, including favorites such as *The Shooting of Dan McGrew* and *The Cremation of Sam McGee*.

★ **Robert Specht** *Tisha* (Bantam). One of Alaska's most popular reads, written as a romantic novel, but in fact a largely true story of Anne Hobbs, a 19-year-old white schoolteacher who, in 1927, lived in Chicken and courageously insisted on treating everyone as equals, in the process falling in love with a half-Athabascan.

John Straley *The Woman Who Married a Bear* (Signet/Orion). The best of Alaskan crime fiction by Sitka-based Straley, telling tales of ineffectual private investigator Cecil Younger, who has a habit of being in the right spot as convoluted stories solve themselves. *The Curious Eat Themselves*, *The Music of What Happens*, and *Death and the Language of Happiness* are also worth reading.

Barbara Vine *No Night is Too Long* (Penguin). Ruth Rendell takes on a *nom de plume* for this engaging psychological thriller mostly set in the Alaskan Southeast and Pacific Northwest. The denouement is as convoluted and unguessable as you'd expect from Rendell at her best.

★ **Velma Wallis** *Two Old Women: An Alaskan Legend of Betrayal, Courage and Survival*; *Bird Girl and the Man Who Followed the Sun: An Athabaskan Legend from Alaska* (Harper Perennial). Modern retelling of traditional Alaskan folk tales, simply told, but immediately engaging.

Reference and specialist guides

The Alaska Almanac (Alaska Northwest Books). Definitive, annually updated Alaska fact book chock-full of everything from air services to the Yukon Quest Sled Dog Race, and with irreverent quips from Anchorage oddball comic Mr Whitekeys (see p.221).

The Milepost (Vernon). Alaska's biggest-selling travel book, full of mind-numbing detail, including just about every stream crossing, pullout, and gas station on the entire Alaskan road system, mile by mile.

Wildlife

Robert H. Armstrong *Guide to the Birds of Alaska* (Alaska Northwest Books). The pick of the general bird books to Alaska, with a section on identification, clear photos, and detailed material on habitat.

Rita M. O'Clair, Robert H. Armstrong, and Richard Carstensen *The Nature of Southeast Alaska* (Alaska Northwest Books). Lively field guide to the plants, animals, and habitats of Southeast Alaska that eschews dry lists in favor of weaving together and interpreting the ecosystem. Highly readable and full of entertaining insights for the non-specialist.

Tom Walker *Alaska's Wildlife* (Graphic Arts Center Publishing Co). Beautifully presented coffee-table book with superb shots of the best of the state's fauna taken by Alaska's premier wildlife photographer. The text includes discussion of how the shots were taken.

Hiking, mountaineering, and backcountry travel

Dean Littlepage *Hiking in Alaska* (Falcon). A comprehensive guide to hiking throughout the whole state, with a hundred hikes spanning a range of abilities, each laid out with maps and elevation plans.

Jon Nierenberg *Backcountry Companion: Denali National Park and Preserve* (Alaska Natural History Association). A fairly brief but clear and understandable introduction to Denali's backcountry units, their flora, terrain, and wildlife. Helpful for planning your backcountry travels and rightly avoids suggesting hikes.

R.J. Secor *Denali Climbing Guide* (Stackpole Books). Accurate and detailed guide to most of the routes up Denali. Well researched and perfect for the summit aspirant, but intriguing also for those who just dream.

Kristian Sieling *The Scar: Southcentral Alaska Rock Climbing* (Global Motion). Definitive guide to the region's rock climbing, mostly covering Anchorage's after-work rock playground and the crags along the Seward Highway south of the city.

Canoeing, kayaking, and rafting

Andrew Embick *Fast & Cold: A Guide to Alaska Whitewater* (Falcon). The serious kayaker's guide to Alaska with all the big stuff – the Turnback Canyon of the Alsek, Devil's Canyon on the Talkeetna – included in detail and plenty of inspirational boating history and river-running accounts.

Karen Jettmar *The Alaska River Guide: Canoeing, Kayaking and Rafting in the Last Frontier* (Alaska Northwest

Books). A general guide for river runners with little in the way of inspiration, but plenty of relevant information –simple diagrams, pointers to more detailed maps, access to put-ins and takeouts, craft suitability – and a few black-and-white photos.

Jim and Nancy Lethcoe *Cruising Guide to Prince William Sound* (Prince William Sound Books). Detailed coverage of sea kayaking in Prince William Sound divided into two volumes covering the eastern and western areas.

CONTEXTS | Books

Glossary of Alaskan terms

Alaska Day Commemorates the formal transfer of Alaska from Russia to the US in Sitka on October 18, 1867.
Aleut (pronounced "AL-ee-oot") Native of the Aleutian Islands.
Alpenglow Rich pink hues around the mountains particularly in the low winter light.
Alutiiq (pronounced "a-LOO-tick") Academic but increasingly general term for Alaskan Natives living between the west end of the Alaskan Peninsula and Prince William Sound, including Kodiak Island.
AMHS Alaska Marine Highway System. The state-run ferries.
ANCSA Alaska Native Claims Settlement Act (see p.530).
ANILCA Alaska National Interest Lands Conservation Act (see p.531).
Athabascan (also Athapascan) Native of the Alaskan Interior.
Baleen Long, black, fibrous strips from the mouth of a baleen whale, used by Eskimos to make fine baskets and souvenirs.
Beluga (or more correctly belukha) Species of small, white whale.
Bidar, baidarka Russian terms for Eskimo skin vessels. A bidar is a large, open boat (see "Umiak"); the baidarka is a kayak with one, two, or three hatches.
Blanket toss Eskimo game using a walrus hide to toss an individual into the air. Originally used for spotting whales and other quarry over the horizon.
BLM Bureau of Land Management. A federal agency.
Bore tide A broken wave of foaming whitewater up to six feet high. A rare phenomenon that only occurs in perhaps sixty places around the world, two of them in Alaska.
Break-up Two-week period in April or May when warmer temperatures, longer days, and melting snows build up pressure below the ice, then burst through causing the resulting ice floes to thunder down the flooded Interior rivers. Signals the end of winter.
Bunny boots Thermal footwear made of double-skinned white rubber with an air layer in between, developed by the US Army in the Korean War and said to keep active feet warm down to –60°F.
Bush Rural Alaska away from the rail and highway systems.
Cabin fever Irritable and depressed state brought on by extended periods indoors during the long, dark Alaskan winter.
Cache A tiny food-storage cabin raised high above the ground by stilts out of reach of bears and other animals. By extension, any food store.
Cannery Any waterside fish-processing plant. The original salmon canneries are largely a thing of the past.
Cheechako Pejorative jargon for a newcomer or first-time visitor who has not wintered in Alaska or mastered Alaskan ways.
Damp community Town where alcohol sales are banned but imports for personal use are permitted.
Dena'ina (pronounced "DEH-na EE-na") Name of the Athabascan language and people of Southcentral Alaska around Cook Inlet.
DEW Line Array of Distant Early Warning sensors built across the North Slope in the mid-1950s to detect Soviet missiles.
Diamond dust Tiny ice crystals suspended in the winter air.
Dolly Varden Possibly the only fish named for a fictional character, in this case Dolly Varden from Dickens' *Barnaby Rudge*, who wore a pink-spotted dress, which the markings on this trout are said to resemble.
Eskimo General term for northern people; in Alaska this includes the Yup'ik and Iñupiat peoples, and in Canada the Inuvialuit and Inuit. Though the word is said to derive from an Algonquin word for "eater of raw flesh," it is not considered disparaging or offensive in Alaska.

Eskimo ice cream (aka *akutuq* in Iñupiaq and *akutak* in Yup'ik) Traditional dessert made from whipped seal oil, berries, and snow.
Fishwheel Mechanical fish harvester used in murky glacial rivers. Can catch up to a thousand salmon a day on a good run.
Flume Artificial channel for water, used in gold mining.
Freeze-up The opposite of break-up, usually in late October.
Frost heaves Undulations in the road surface or house foundations built on permafrost, caused by repeated annual freezing and thawing.
Grubstake mining Process whereby a banker or trader would supply a prospector with the means – food, tools, etc – to pursue his prospecting on the understanding that the advance would be repaid manyfold when he struck paydirt.
Haida (pronounced "HI-da") Coastal Natives of the Southeast.
Homesteading Now largely defunct practice of giving settlers land in return for building a house and making the land "useful" within a certain period.
Honey bucket Outhouse slops receptacle in places where it is not possible to dig a pit.
Igloo Iñupiat Eskimo word for house or dwelling. In Alaska traditional houses were often made of driftwood and sod, not the ice houses used by Canadian Eskimos when out hunting.
Inuit See "Eskimo," above.
Iñupiaq Language of the Iñupiat.
Iñupiat Alaskan Eskimos in northwest Alaska as far south as Unalakleet. Distinct from Yup'ik.
Kayak Yup'ik and Iñupiat word for the familiar one-person, skin-covered boat.
Lower 48 The contiguous United States, a term often used disparagingly.
Mukluks Knee-length boots, made of sealskin or moose hide and bound with thongs; lightweight, warm, and perfect for cold snow.
Muktuk Whale blubber and the associated skin layer (usually from bowhead or Beluga whales) eaten as an Eskimo delicacy raw, pickled, frozen, or boiled and fermented.
Muskeg Mossy peat bogs that cloak much of Interior Alaska, often covered with short plants such as blueberries or crowberries.
Native Alaskan Refers to anyone born in the state, except when the "N" is capitalized, when it refers only to those with indigenous heritage.
North Slope Gently shelving Arctic flatlands north of the Brooks Range.
Outhouse Outside toilet comprising a hole in the ground surrounded by anything from a poorly built hut to a sturdier more modern structure. The outhouse has been raised to both an art form (bookshops stock several outhouse picture books) and a sport with several summer festivals featuring outhouse-carrying races.
Outside Everywhere that's not Alaska, see "Lower 48."
Outsider Not an Alaskan.
Panhandle Nickname for Southeast Alaska, derived from the shape of the state.
Permafrost Soil that remains frozen throughout the year.
Permanent Fund The state's invested profits from oil royalties and taxes.
Poke A small bag containing gold dust, or sometimes just gold-bearing gravel.
Potlatch A massive feast thrown by Southeast coastal Natives.
Qiviut (pronounced "KIH-vee-yoot") Soft underhair of the musk ox that is knitted or woven into scarves and other garments.
Rack Set of antlers, generally used to refer to a moose rack.
RV Recreational vehicle or motorhome.
Ski-joring Cross-country skiing while being helped along by a dog in traces out front.
Skookum Native word for "strong", used favorably as a nickname particularly during the early gold rushes.
Sled dog Any dog used to pull a sled. Most sled dogs in Alaska are not huskies.
Slough (pronounced "sloo") Slow-moving backwater that loops off the main river.
Smolt Juvenile salmon large enough to enter and survive in salt water.
Sourdough Long-time Alaskan and what a cheechako becomes after about thirty years. Derived from the long-lasting yeasty mixture carried by pioneers to lighten breads and hotcakes.

Subsistence Living off the land (and sea). Controversially, all Alaskans (not just Natives) have rights to undertake subsistence hunting and fishing.
Taiga Marginal subarctic landscape sparsely populated by spruce and birch.
Termination dust The first snow that covers the top of the mountain in the fall. So called because this is a sign of the termination of summer in Alaska.
Tlingit (pronounced "thling-get") Major coastal Native peoples of Southeast Alaska.
Traces Reins used to attach a team of sled dogs to the sled.
Tsimshian (pronounced "SIM-shee-an") Southeast Alaskan Natives originally from British Columbia.
Tsunami A seismic wave often misnamed a tidal wave.
Tundra A treeless expanse covered with low-lying plants.
Ulu, Uluaq The Iñupiat and Yup'ik words for the broad semicircular-shaped knife, often also called a woman's knife.
Umiak Open sealskin boat about thirty feet long and fitted with a sail, often used as a support boat while men in kayaks hunted.
Williwaws Sudden gusts of wind caused by air building up on one side of a mountain, then bursting through into an otherwise sheltered area.
Yup'ik Eskimo people of central western Alaska.

Rough Guides

advertiser

...music & reference

Africa & Middle East
Cape Town
Egypt
The Gambia
Jerusalem
Jordan
Kenya
Morocco
South Africa, Lesotho & Swaziland
Syria
Tanzania
Tunisia
West Africa
Zanzibar
Zimbabwe

Travel Theme guides
First-Time Around the World
First-Time Asia
First-Time Europe
First-Time Latin America
Gay & Lesbian Australia
Skiing & Snowboarding in North America
Travel Online
Travel Health
Walks in London & SE England
Women Travel

Restaurant guides
French Hotels & Restaurants
London
New York
San Francisco

Maps
Algarve
Amsterdam
Andalucia & Costa del Sol
Argentina
Athens
Australia
Baja California
Barcelona
Boston
Brittany
Brussels
Chicago
Crete
Croatia
Cuba
Cyprus
Czech Republic
Dominican Republic
Dublin
Egypt
Florence & Siena
Frankfurt
Greece
Guatemala & Belize
Iceland
Ireland
Lisbon
London
Los Angeles
Mexico
Miami & Key West
Morocco
New York City
New Zealand
Northern Spain
Paris
Portugal
Prague
Rome
San Francisco
Sicily
South Africa
Sri Lanka
Tenerife
Thailand
Toronto
Trinidad & Tobago
Tuscany
Venice
Washington DC
Yucatán Peninsula

Dictionary Phrasebooks
Czech
Dutch
Egyptian Arabic
European
French
German
Greek
Hindi & Urdu
Hungarian
Indonesian
Italian
Japanese
Mandarin Chinese
Mexican Spanish
Polish
Portuguese
Russian
Spanish
Swahili
Thai
Turkish
Vietnamese

Music Guides
The Beatles
Cult Pop
Classical Music
Country Music
Cuban Music
Drum'n'bass
Elvis
House
Irish Music
Jazz
Music USA
Opera
Reggae
Rock
Techno
World Music (2 vols)

100 Essential CDs series
Country
Latin
Opera
Rock
Soul
World Music

History Guides
China
Egypt
England
France
Greece
India
Ireland
Islam
Italy
Spain
USA

Reference Guides
Books for Teenagers
Children's Books, 0–5
Children's Books, 5–11
Cult Football
Cult Movies
Cult TV
Digital Stuff
Formula 1
The Internet
Internet Radio
James Bond
Lord of the Rings
Man Utd
Personal Computers
Pregnancy & Birth
Shopping Online
Travel Health
Travel Online
Unexplained Phenomena
The Universe
Videogaming
Weather
Website Directory

Also! More than 120 Rough Guide music CDs are available from all good book and record stores. Listen in at www.worldmusic.net

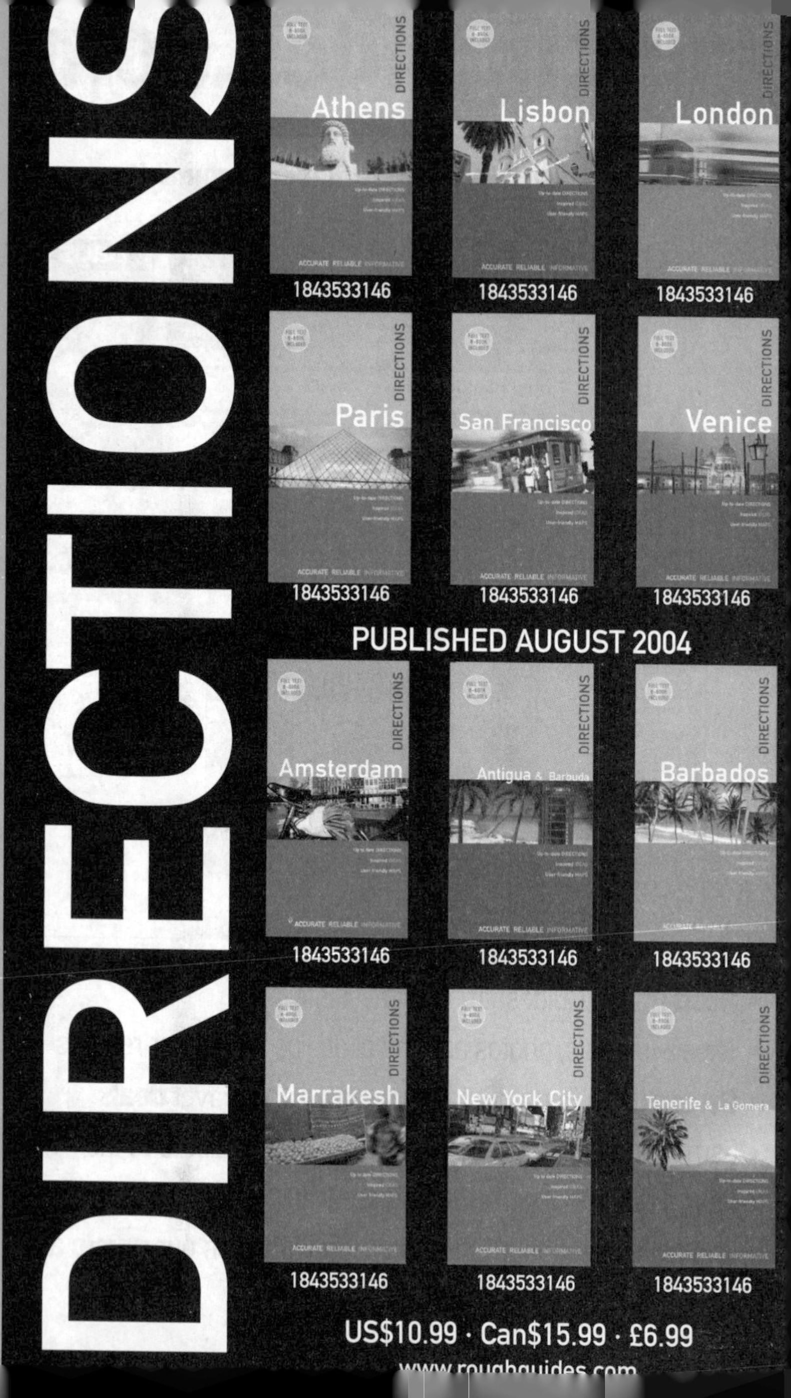
DIRECTIONS
Athens
DIRECTIONS
1843533146
Lisbon
DIRECTIONS
1843533146
London
DIRECTIONS
1843533146
Paris
DIRECTIONS
1843533146
San Francisco
DIRECTIONS
1843533146
Venice
DIRECTIONS
1843533146
PUBLISHED AUGUST 2004
Amsterdam
DIRECTIONS
1843533146
Antigua & Barbuda
DIRECTIONS
1843533146
Barbados
DIRECTIONS
1843533146
Marrakesh
DIRECTIONS
1843533146
New York City
DIRECTIONS
1843533146
Tenerife & La Gomera
DIRECTIONS
1843533146
US$10.99 · Can$15.99 · £6.99
www.roughguides.com

Index

and small print

A Rough Guide to Rough Guides

In the summer of 1981, Mark Ellingham, a recent graduate from Bristol University, was travelling round Greece and couldn't find a guidebook that really met his needs. On the one hand there were the student guides, insistent on saving every last cent, and on the other the heavyweight cultural tomes whose authors seemed to have spent more time in a research library than lounging away the afternoon at a taverna or on the beach.

In a bid to avoid getting a job, Mark and a small group of writers set about creating their own guidebook. It was a guide to Greece that aimed to combine a journalistic approach to description with a thoroughly practical approach to travelers' needs – a guide that would incorporate culture, history and contemporary insights with a critical edge, together with up-to-date, value-for-money listings. Back in London, Mark and the team finished their Rough Guide, as they called it, and talked Routledge into publishing the book.

That first *Rough Guide to Greece*, published in 1982, was a student scheme that became a publishing phenomenon. The immediate success of the book – with numerous reprints and a Thomas Cook prize shortlisting – spawned a series that rapidly covered dozens of destinations. Rough Guides had a ready market among low-budget backpackers, but soon also acquired a much broader and older readership that relished Rough Guides' wit and inquisitiveness as much as their enthusiastic, critical approach. Everyone wants value for money, but not at any price.

Rough Guides soon began supplementing the "rougher" information about hostels and low-budget listings with the kind of detail on restaurants and quality hotels that independent-minded visitors on any budget might expect, whether on business in New York or trekking in Thailand.

These days the guides – distributed worldwide by the Penguin group – offer recommendations from shoestring to luxury and cover more than 200 destinations around the globe, including almost every country in the Americas and Europe, more than half of Africa and most of Asia and Australasia. Our ever-growing team of authors and photographers is spread all over the world, particularly in Europe, the USA and Australia.

In 1994, we published the *Rough Guide to World Music* and *Rough Guide to Classical Music*; and a year later the *Rough Guide to the Internet*. All three books have become benchmark titles in their fields – which encouraged us to expand into other areas of publishing, mainly around popular culture. Rough Guides now publish:

- Travel guides to more than 200 worldwide destinations
- Dictionary phrasebooks to 22 major languages
- History guides ranging from Ireland to Islam
- Maps printed on rip-proof and waterproof Polyart™ paper
- Music guides running the gamut from Opera to Elvis
- Restaurant guides to London, New York and San Francisco
- Reference books on topics as diverse as the Weather and Shakespeare
- Sports guides from Formula 1 to Man Utd
- Pop culture books from *Lord of the Rings* to Cult TV
- World Music CDs in association with World Music Network

Visit **www.roughguides.com** to see our latest publications.

Rough Guide credits

Text editor: Jeff Cranmer
Layout: Dan May
Cartography: Miles Irving
Picture research: Veneta Bullen
Proofreader: Derek Wilde

Editorial: London Martin Dunford, Kate Berens, Helena Smith, Claire Saunders, Geoff Howard, Ruth Blackmore, Gavin Thomas, Polly Thomas, Richard Lim, Lucy Ratcliffe, Clifton Wilkinson, Alison Murchie, Fran Sandham, Sally Schafer, Alexander Mark Rogers, Karoline Densley, Andy Turner, Ella O'Donnell, Keith Drew, Andrew Lockett, Joe Staines, Duncan Clark, Peter Buckley, Matthew Milton; **New York** Andrew Rosenberg, Richard Koss, Yuki Takagaki, Hunter Slaton, Chris Barsanti, Thomas Kohnstamm, Steven Horak
Design & Layout: London Dan May, Diana Jarvis; **Delhi** Madhulita Mohapatra, Umesh Aggarwal, Ajay Verma
Production: Julia Bovis, John McKay, Sophie Hewat
Cartography: London Maxine Repath, Ed Wright, Katie Lloyd-Jones, Miles Irving; **Delhi** Manish Chandra, Rajesh Chhibber, Jai Prakesh Mishra, Ashutosh Bharti, Rajesh Mishra, Animesh Pathak
Cover art direction: Louise Boulton
Picture research: Mark Thomas, Jj Luck
Online: New York Jennifer Gold, Cree Lawson, Suzanne Welles, Benjamin Ross; **Delhi** Manik Chauhan, Amarjyoti Dutta, Narender Kumar
Marketing & Publicity: London Richard Trillo, Niki Smith, David Wearn, Chloë Roberts, Demelza Dallow, Kristina Pentland; **New York** Geoff Colquitt, David Wechsler, Megan Kennedy
Finance: Gary Singh
Manager India: Punita Singh
Series editor: Mark Ellingham
PA to Managing Director: Julie Sanderson
Managing Director: Kevin Fitzgerald

Publishing information

This second edition published May 2004 by
Rough Guides Ltd,
80 Strand, London WC2R 0RL.
345 Hudson St, 4th Floor,
New York, NY 10014, USA.
Distributed by the Penguin Group
Penguin Books Ltd,
80 Strand, London WC2R 0RL
Penguin Putnam, Inc.
375 Hudson Street, NY 10014, USA
Penguin Books Australia Ltd,
487 Maroondah Highway, PO Box 257,
Ringwood, Victoria 3134, Australia
Penguin Books Canada Ltd,
10 Alcorn Avenue, Toronto, Ontario,
Canada M4V 1E4
Penguin Books (NZ) Ltd,
182–190 Wairau Road, Auckland 10,
New Zealand
Typeset in Bembo and Helvetica to an original design by Henry Iles.

Printed in Italy by LegoPrint S.p.A

576pp includes index
A catalogue record for this book is available from the British Library

ISBN 1-84353-258-1

1 3 5 7 9 8 6 4 2

Help us update

We've gone to a lot of effort to ensure that the 2nd edition of **The Rough Guide to Alaska** is accurate and up to date. However, things change – places get "discovered," opening hours are notoriously fickle, restaurants and rooms raise prices or lower standards. If you feel we've got it wrong or left something out, we'd like to know, and if you can remember the address, the price, the time, the phone number, so much the better.

We'll credit all contributions, and send a copy of the next edition (or any other Rough Guide if you prefer) for the best letters. Everyone who writes to us and isn't already a subscriber will receive a copy of our full-color thrice-yearly newsletter. Please mark letters: "**Rough Guide Alaska Update**" and send to: Rough Guides, 80 Strand, London WC2R 0RL, or Rough Guides, 4th Floor, 345 Hudson St, New York, NY 10014. Or send an email to **mail@roughguides.com**

Have your questions answered and tell others about your trip at **www.roughguides.atinfopop.com**

Acknowledgments

The **author** would like to give special thanks to the staff of tourist offices all over the state, who have been unstintingly generous with their time, and to the operators of tour companies, hotels, hostels, museums, transport companies, and the good people of Alaska who have gone out of their way to help make sure this book is as accurate as possible.

Thanks and respect, too, to Jeff Cranmer for skilled and dedicated editing that has made the book far better than it would otherwise have been; and to Andrew Rosenberg and the Rough Guide crew in New York for helping in all aspects of the book.

In Alaska thanks go out to: Diane Sanzone in Fairbanks, Chris Barefoot at GoNorth, Grace Kirkwood and Karen Petersen on Prince of Wales Island, Milo and Paula Burcham, Len Laurance in Ketchikan, Doug and Neil in McCarthy, Cindy Roland in Skagway, Linda Mickle, Sharon Gaiptman and Barbara Fairbanks at AMHS, and Tim Burford in Anchorage for some fine suggestions.

For that home on the road, a huge debt is owed to Colleen Shannon in Anchorage who made long periods of research much more bearable. Also to Kristiann, Lois, Jessica and Nathan who helped make Anchorage fun. The long drive to and around the state were greatly enhanced by the company of Colin Megson, Mike Day and Sharon Alexander who all contributed in their own way. Also to Irene Gardiner for great patience, support, a sympathetic ear and forbearance in the face of long absences. And lastly a dedication to Roger, for admired keyboard and mouse skills to the end.

Readers' letters

Thanks to all the readers who took the trouble to write in with their comments and suggestions (and apologies to anyone whose name we've misspelt or omitted): J.C.E. van den Brandhof, Britaini Carroll, Dave and Yvonne Waldron-Kelly, and Andrew Young.

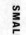

Photo credits

Cover credits
Main front: Wonder Lake, Mount McKinley © Getty
Front top: Hydaburg © Alamy
Front lower: Kayaking © Alamy
Back top: Northern Lights © Alamy
Back lower: Denali National Park © Robert Harding

Introduction
Graffiti on cabin wall, Sitka © Masterfile/Andrew Wenzel
Meadow, Independence Mine State Park © Art Directors/Trip
Portrait of racing husky © B & C Alexander Photography
Old snowshoes on cabin wall © Art Directors/Trip/Vince Steano & Carol Havens
A solitary kayaker at sunset, Lynn Canal © B & C Alexander Photography/John Hyde
Haida Totem pole, Ketchikan © B & C Alexander Photography
Thorofare Pass, Denali NP © Paul Whitfield
Panning for gold near Fairbanks © B & C Alexander Photography
Trans-Alaska Pipeline, Delta Junction © B & C Alexander Photography
Creek Street, Ketchikan © Art Directors/Trip/Warren Jacobs

Things not to miss
01 White Pass & Yukon Railroad, Skagway © Art Directors/Trip/J Greenberg
02 View of St Michaels, Russian Orthodox church, Sitka © B & C Alexander Photography
03 Downtown Chicken © Paul Whitfield
04 Tidewater view of Margerie Glacier, Tarr inlet © B & C Alexander Photography/John Hyde
05 Humpback whale breaching © Art Directors/Trip/Viesti Collection
Brown bear sow and cub, Denali NP © Alamy Images
Bald eagle on upended tree trunk, Homer © Paul Whitfield
Walruses huddled together © Heather Angel/Natural Visions
Caribou on tundra, Denali NP © B & C Alexander Photography/John Hyde
06 Denali Highway © Paul Whitfield
07 Halibut haul, Homer © Paul Whitfield
08 Sea plane takes off from Naknek Lake © Art Directors/Trip/Ask Images
09 Aurora Borealis, Denali NP © Alamy Images
10 Tlingit Button Blanket, Saxman Village © Art Directors/Trip/Streano/Havens
11 Bunkhouse in show, Independence Mine © Paul Whitfield
12 Fishing boats at sunset, Seldovia © Paul Whitfield
13 Afternoon light at Taiga, Denali NP © Paul Whitfield
14 Start point for the Sled dog team race © Corbis/Paul A Sonders
15 Log Walk at Mountain Mother contest, Talkeetna © Paul Whitfield
16 Arctic fish drying on the riverbank © Corbis/Joel W Rogers
17 Women kayakers, Tracey Arm fjord, Terror Wilderness © B & C Alexander Photography/John Hyde
18 Million Dollar Bridge © Paul Whitfield
19 Yukon River, Eagle © Paul Whitfield
20 Anglers on the beach in the Homer Spit Fishing Hole © Corbis/Steve Kaufman
21 Aleutians Ferry Trip at Dutch Harbor © Paul Whitfield
22 Hiking in Denali National Park © B & C Alexander Photography
23 Brown bear catching salmon in a stream © B & C Alexander Photography/John Hyde
24 Kennicott Mine, St Elias NP © Art Directors/Trip/Ask Images
25 The Train to Nowhere, near Nome © Paul Whitfield

Black and whites
Tourist walks past a mural © B & C Alexander Photography (p.76)
Sitka harbor & waterfront © B & C Alexander Photography/John Hyde (p.131)
Moose approaching a front porch © Corbis/Paul A Sonders (p.194)
View of Anchorage © Paul Whitfield (p.225)
Fishing at Homer Spit © Corbis/Morton Bebe (p.230)
People at base of Exit Glacier © Paul Whitfield (p.250)
Whale tails in Frederick Sound © B & C Alexander Photography/John Hyde (p.284)
Church roof tops, Dutch Harbor © Paul Whitfield (p.312)
Fishing buoys, Chignik © Paul Whitfield (p.326)
Nenana Ice Classic Tripod & watchouse © Paul Whitfield (p.348)
A gravel park road over Thorofare Pass © Corbis/Paul A Sonders (p.391)
Wooden cart, McCarthy Lodging © Art Directors/Trip/B Crawshaw (p.406)
Gilahina Tressel Bridge, McCarthy Road © Paul Whitfield (p.425)
Artic Circle sign, Dalton Highway © Paul Whitfield (p.446)
Gold mining operation, Fairbanks © Corbis/Nik Wheeler (p.485)

Index

Map entries are in color

C

D

T

U

V

W